ICPSR

(Inter-University Consortium
for Political & Social
Research) pg 26

PSU - Primary
Sampling
Units
(pg 58)

NSFH
(National Survey of
Families + Households)

accessible through
the BADGIR
utility

pg 51

APPLIED STATISTICS FOR THE SOCIAL AND HEALTH SCIENCES

This book provides graduate students in the social and health sciences with the basic skills that they need in order to estimate, interpret, present, and publish quantitative research studies using contemporary standards.

This book shares the following key features with *Regression Analysis for the Social Sciences* (also published by Routledge and authored by Professor Gordon):

- Interweaving the teaching of statistical concepts with examples developed for the book from publicly available social and health science data or drawn from the literature;
- Thorough integration of teaching statistical theory with teaching data processing and analysis;
- Teaching of both SAS and Stata "side-by-side" and use of chapter exercises in which students practice programming and interpretation on the same data set and of course exercises in which students can choose their own research questions and data set.

Applied Statistics for the Social and Health Sciences differs from *Regression Analysis for the Social Sciences* in five major ways:

1. Inclusion of new literature excerpts, with broader coverage of the public health and education literatures.
2. Use of the National Health Interview Survey for chapter exercises (rather than the National Organizations Survey).
3. Inclusion of sections in many chapters that show how to implement the analysis techniques for data sets based on complex survey designs.
4. Coverage of basic univariate and bivariate descriptive and inferential statistics.
5. Coverage of the generalized linear model and maximum likelihood techniques for dichotomous outcomes and for multi-category nominal and ordinal outcomes.

Rachel A. Gordon is an Associate Professor in the Department of Sociology and the Institute of Government and Public Affairs at the University of Illinois at Chicago. Professor Gordon has multidisciplinary substantive and statistical training and a passion for understanding and teaching applied statistics.

TITLES OF RELATED INTEREST

Social Theory Re-Wired: New Connections to Classical and Contemporary Perspectives by Wesley Langhofer and Daniel Winchester
GIS and Spatial Analysis for the Social Sciences by Robert Nash Parker and Emily K. Asencio
Regression Analysis for the Social Sciences by Rachel A. Gordon
Social Statistics by Thomas J. Linneman
Statistical Modelling for Social Researchers by Roger Tarling

APPLIED STATISTICS FOR THE SOCIAL AND HEALTH SCIENCES

Rachel A. Gordon
University of Illinois at Chicago

Routledge
Taylor & Francis Group

NEW YORK AND LONDON

First published 2012
by Routledge
711 Third Avenue, New York, NY 10017

Simultaneously published in the UK
by Routledge
2 Park Square, Milton Park, Abingdon, Oxon OX14 4RN

Routledge is an imprint of the Taylor & Francis Group, an informa business

© 2012 Taylor & Francis

Library of Congress Cataloging in Publication Data
Gordon, Rachel A.
 Applied statistics for the social and health sciences/Rachel A. Gordon.
  p. cm.
 Includes bibliographical references and index.
 1. Social sciences—Statistical methods. 2. Public health—Statistical methods. I. Title.
 HA29.G685 2011
 519.5--dc23   2011040016

List of Trademarks that feature in the text

Stata	Microsoft Word
SAS	WordPerfect
Microsoft Excel	Notepad
TextPad	DBMS/Copy
UltraEdit	SPSS
StatTransfer	R
LISREL	Minitab
AMOS	S-Plus
Mplus	Systat
EQS	

ISBN: 9780415875363 (hbk)
ISBN: 9780203135297 (ebk)

Typeset in Times New Roman
by RefineCatch Limited, Bungay, Suffolk

Go to **http://www.routledge.com/cw/gordon/** for an invaluable set of resources associated with *Applied Statistics for the Social and Health Sciences* by Rachel Gordon

TABLE OF CONTENTS IN BRIEF

TABLE OF CONTENTS IN DETAIL

APPLIED STATISTICS FOR THE SOCIAL AND HEALTH SCIENCES

PART 2: BASIC DESCRIPTIVE AND INFERENTIAL STATISTICS

PART 3: ORDINARY LEAST SQUARES REGRESSION

PART 4: THE GENERALIZED LINEAR MODEL

PART 5: WRAPPING UP

APPENDICES

PREFACE

This text is intended for year-long graduate statistics sequences in masters and doctoral programs in the social and health sciences.

We cover basic descriptive and inferential statistics, ordinary least squares (OLS) regression models for continuous outcomes, and the generalized linear model and maximum likelihood estimation for dichotomous outcomes and for multi-category nominal and ordinal outcomes.

Applied Statistics for the Social and Health Sciences shares several goals and strategies with the text *Regression Analysis for the Social Sciences*, the latter of which is intended for a semester-long course on ordinary least squares regression. In addition to coverage of additional topics, *Applied Statistics for the Social and Health Sciences* also has some unique features, outlined below.

Both books aim to fill a gap in the textbook market. Although statistics textbooks abound, relatively few aim specifically at basic graduate sequences in the social and health sciences. We target the social and health science branches such as education, human development, psychology, public health, social work, and sociology, to which students bring a wide range of mathematical skills and have a wide range of methodological affinities. For some of these students, a successful basic statistics sequence will not only offer statistical content but will also help them to overcome their anxiety about statistics and to develop an appreciation for how quantitative techniques might answer some of the research questions of interest to them. Other students are eager to gain a strong foundation in statistical theory and statistical analysis so they can take advanced courses, secure research assistantships, and begin their own quantitative projects.

To meet these objectives, both of our textbooks have three distinctive features:

1. Use of examples of interest to social scientists including both:
   a. Literature excerpts, drawn from a range of journals and a range of subfields;
   b. Examples from real data sets, including two data sets carried throughout the book;

2. Thorough integration of teaching statistical theory with teaching data processing and analysis;
3. Parallel teaching of SAS and Stata.

Applied Statistics for the Social and Health Sciences differs from *Regression Analysis for the Social Sciences* in five major ways:

1. Inclusion of new literature excerpts, with broader coverage of the public health and education literatures.
2. Use of the National Health Interview Survey for chapter exercises (rather than the National Organizations Survey).
3. Inclusion of sections in many chapters that show how to implement the analysis techniques for data sets based on complex survey designs.
4. Coverage of basic univariate and bivariate descriptive and inferential statistics.
5. Coverage of the generalized linear model and maximum likelihood techniques for dichotomous outcomes and for multi-category nominal and ordinal outcomes.

THE IMPETUS FOR THIS BOOK

Over the last few decades, the landscape of quantitative empirical work in the social and health sciences has changed dramatically, raising the bar on the basic skills that scholars need in order to produce and read quantitatively based publications. One impetus for these changes was the initiation and maturation of a number of large-scale studies of individuals, families, and organizations (for example, the National Longitudinal Survey of Youth began annual interviews in 1979, spawned the Children of the NLSY in 1986 when investigators began to follow the children of mothers from the original cohort, and required an acronym change, to NLSY79, when a new cohort, the NLSY97, was first interviewed). Another impetus for change was the expansion of computing power, allowing these data sets to be readily analyzed on the desktop, and the development of the Internet, which now puts many of these data sets only a click away.

Changing technology has also raised the bar on how the results of quantitative analyses are presented. Increasingly, multimedia is integrated into everyday lives. Succinct, clear presentations are required for results to stand out from a flood of information. Clearly organized and presented manuscripts have always been important, but this is increasingly true given demands on reviewers' and editors' time and attention, and pressures to conserve journal space. Strategies for presentation are also important for students and scholars who want to make their work accessible to practitioners, policymakers, and the public, something encouraged by current developments across fields (e.g., public sociology, applied developmental science).

Although many statistics texts exist, none completely meets the needs of core graduate training in the social and health sciences, instead typically being targeted at a different level, audience, or niche. For example, texts aimed at the undergraduate level often do not meet the goals and coverage of graduate sequences intended to prepare students to understand primary sources and conduct their own publishable research. These texts are sometimes used because they are at the right level for graduate students who are less mathematically inclined, but they do not fully satisfy the needs of graduate students and the faculty. Texts aimed at other disciplines are also problematic because they do not connect with students' substantive training and interests. For example, econometrics texts typically use economic examples and often assume more advanced mathematical understanding than is typical of other social science disciplines.

Like our semester-long text *Regression Analysis for the Social Sciences*, the year-long text *Applied Statistics for the Social and Health Sciences* aims to address this current landscape. The goal of the books is to provide graduate students with the basic skills that they need to estimate, interpret, present, and publish quantitative studies using contemporary standards. Key features include:

■ Interweaving the teaching of statistical concepts with examples developed for the book from publicly available social and health science data or drawn from the literature;
■ Thorough integration of teaching statistical theory with teaching data processing and analysis;
■ Teaching of both SAS and Stata "side-by-side" and use of chapter exercises in which students practice programming and interpretation on the same data set and of course exercises in which students can choose their own research questions and data set.

Applied Statistics for the Social and Health Sciences differs from *Regression Analysis for the Social Sciences* in several ways. *Applied Statistics for the Social and Health Sciences* is aimed at a two-semester graduate statistics sequence, and thus covers basic univariate and bivariate statistics and regression models for nominal and ordinal outcomes, in addition to covering ordinary least squares regression which is the focus of *Regression Analysis for the Social Sciences*. *Applied Statistics for the Social and Health Sciences* also incorporates new literature excerpts and a different data set for chapter exercises, aiming for expanded coverage of the literature in education and public health. Finally, *Applied Statistics for the Social and Health Sciences* includes sections in many chapters that show how to implement analytic techniques when data come from complex survey designs.

THE AUDIENCE FOR THE BOOK

Applied Statistics for the Social and Health Sciences is designed for year-long statistics' sequences in masters and doctoral social and health sciences programs. Such courses typically occur early in graduate programs, and the skills, motivations, and interests of students vary considerably.

For some students, anxiety is high, and this core sequence comprises the only statistics courses that they plan to take. These students will better engage in the sequence if the concepts and skills are taught in a way that recognizes their possible math anxiety, is embedded in substantive examples, connects with the students' research interests, and helps them to feel that they can "do quantitative research." Part of the challenge of connecting with students' research interests, though, is that they are typically just starting their graduate programs when they take their statistics sequence, so the sequence needs to explicitly make connections to students' budding interests.

Other students in the sequence are eager to gain a deep understanding of statistical concepts and sophisticated skills in data management and analysis so that they can quickly move on to and excel with advanced techniques. Many of these students will come into their programs believing that quantitative research would be a major part of their career. Some want to use the skills they learn in the basic statistics sequence to secure coveted research assistant positions. Many of these students enter the program with solid math skills, prior success in statistics courses, and at least some experience with data management and analysis. For these students, the sequence will be frustrating and unfulfilling if it doesn't challenge them, build on their existing knowledge and skills, and set them on a path to take advanced courses and learn sophisticated techniques.

Students also vary in their access to resources for learning statistics and statistical packages beyond the core statistics sequence. In some departments, strategies for locating data, organizing a research project, and presenting results in a manuscript are easily learned from mentors and research teams (including through research assistantships) and through informal conversations with fellow students. Some programs also have separate "capstone" courses that put statistics into practice, typically following the core sequence. For other students, there are few such formal and informal opportunities. These students will struggle with implementing the concepts learned in statistics courses without answers to practical questions such as "Where can I find data?" "How do I get the data into SAS (or Stata or SPSS) format?" "How do I interpret a codebook?" "How should I organize my files?" "How do I present my results in my manuscript?" Integrating this practical training within the core statistics sequence meets the needs of students (and faculty) in programs with few formal and informal learning opportunities for such practical skills. We also use this integrated approach in the book to help students practice the statistical concepts they are learning with real data, in order to help reinforce their learning, engage them in the sequence, and give them confidence in conducting quantitative research.

THE GOALS OF THE BOOK

The goals of the book are to prepare students to:

1. Conduct a research project from start to finish using basic descriptive analyses and using basic regression analyses appropriate for nominal, ordinal, or continuous outcomes;
2. Have the basic tools necessary to be a valuable beginning research assistant;
3. Have the basic knowledge and skills needed to take advanced courses that build on core concepts of descriptive and inferential statistics, of ordinary least squares regression, and of the generalized linear model and maximum likelihood estimation; and
4. Intelligently and critically read publications that utilize these techniques.

We focus especially on concepts and techniques that are needed either to publish basic regression analyses in journals in the relevant fields (for goals 1–3) or read publications using these models in those journals (for goal 4).

At every stage of the book, we attempt to look through the lens of the social scientist in training: Why do I need to know this? How is it useful to me? The book is applied in orientation, and frequently makes concepts concrete through examples based on social and health sciences data and excerpts from recent journal publications.

Although the book is applied, we introduce key mathematical concepts aiming to provide sufficient explanation in order to accommodate students with weaker math backgrounds. For example, students are taught to find meaning in equations. Throughout the text, students are shown how to manipulate equations in order to facilitate understanding, with detailed in-text explanations of each step. The goal is to help all students feel comfortable reading equations, rather than leaving some to skip over them. For more advanced students, or students returning to the book later in their careers, we provide references for additional details. We also attempt to present concepts and techniques deeply and slowly, using concrete examples for reinforcement. Our goal is for students to learn an idea or skill well enough that they remember it and how to apply it. This pace and approach allows sufficient time for students who struggle with learning statistics to "really get it" and allows sufficient time for students who learn statistics easily to achieve a more fundamental understanding (including references to more advanced topics/readings).

As part of this approach, we unpack ideas and look at them from multiple angles (again with a goal toward what is needed when preparing a manuscript for publication, or reading a published article). For example, we spend considerable time on understanding how to test and interpret interactions (e.g., plotting predicted values, testing differences between points on the lines, calculating conditional slopes).

We assume that students have had an introductory course (perhaps high school or undergraduate) in research methods and in descriptive and inferential statistics, although we review concepts typically covered in these courses when we first use them.

THE CHAPTERS OF THE BOOK

The first part of the book introduces quantitative social and health sciences research through a number of literature excerpts and teaches students how to locate data, use statistical software, and organize a quantitative research project. The second part covers basic univariate and bivariate descriptive and inferential statistics. The third part covers basic ordinary least squares (OLS) regression models in detail. The fourth part introduces the generalized linear model and maximum likelihood estimation and applies these techniques to basic nominal and ordinal outcomes. The final chapter pulls together the earlier material, including providing a roadmap of advanced topics and revisiting the examples used in earlier chapters.

Part 1: Getting Started

Part 1 of the book aims to get students excited about using regression analysis in their own research and to put students on common ground by exposing them to literature excerpts, data sets, statistical packages, and strategies for organizing a quantitative research project. As noted above, this leveling of the playing field is important because students will vary in the prior statistics courses that they have taken and their prior experience analyzing data as well as in opportunities in their program to learn how to put statistical concepts into practice.

- Chapter 1 introduces students to quantitative analyses using several literature excerpts. By using a range of substantive applications and a range of data sources, a major goal of the excerpts is to get students excited about using quantitative analyses to their own work. In this chapter, the examples were also selected because they were completed when the authors were graduate students and published in top journals, thus giving students attainable role models. The examples are also meant to begin to help students read and interpret published quantitative analyses (beyond their experiences reading articles that report quantitative analyses in substantive courses). And, the examples in this chapter were selected to preview some of the central topics to be covered in later chapters (e.g., controlling for confounds, examining mediation, testing for interactions) and others of which will be pointed to in the roadmap in the last chapter of the book (e.g., negative binomial models).

- Chapter 2 discusses strategies for organizing a research project. Especially with large secondary data sets with numerous variables, it is easy to get lost "playing with the data." We encourage students to keep theoretical ideas and a long-range perspective in mind throughout a project. This chapter directly addresses the variability in formal and informal opportunities for research experiences mentioned above, and attempts to pull together various "words of wisdom" about planning and documenting a project and locating data that some students might otherwise miss. The chapter also exposes students to a breadth of secondary data sets, which can provide the knowledge and comfort needed to access secondary data as their interests develop over the years of graduate study. The chapter teaches students basic skills in understanding documentation for secondary data sources and selecting data sets. The data set carried throughout the in-text examples, the National Survey of Families and Households (NSFH), is introduced in the chapter.

- Chapter 3 introduces the basic features of data documentation and statistical software. The chapter begins with basic concepts of how data sets are stored in the computer and read by statistical packages. The rationale for using both SAS and Stata is provided, along with the basic types of files used and created by each package. The chapter also covers how to organize files in a project and how to identify relevant variables from large existing data sets. The chapter example uses the data set carried throughout the in-text examples (NSFH). The chapter exercise introduces the data set used for the chapter exercises throughout the remainder of the book (National Health Interview Survey).

- Chapter 4 teaches students how to write basic statistical programs. To reach a broad audience of instructors, and to expose students to the flexibility of moving between software packages, SAS and Stata are presented side-by-side. The chapter begins with the basics of the Stata and SAS interfaces and syntax. We then cover how to create new variables and to keep a subset of cases. The chapter ends with recommendations for organizing files (including comments and spacing) and for debugging programs (identifying and fixing errors).

Part 2: Basic Descriptive and Inferential Statistics

■ Chapter 5 demonstrates how to calculate key statistics to describe the variables in an analytic dataset. We emphasize the importance of thinking about a variable's type when choosing statistics, covering the percentage distribution and mode for nominal variables, the percentiles (including the median) for ordinal variables, and the box plot (and interquartile range), the histogram, and the mean and standard deviation for interval variables.

■ Chapter 6 introduces the basic ideas of a sampling distribution, the standard error, and the central limit theorem. We review the basic features of a normal distribution, and discuss the empirical rule and standardized variables.

■ Chapter 7 introduces basic concepts of hypothesis testing of bivariate associations using the test statistic and confidence interval approaches. We cover in detail the chi-square test for two categorical variables, the two-sample t-test and analysis of variance for one categorical and one interval variable, and the Pearson correlation for two interval variables.

Part 3: Ordinary Least Squares Regression

■ Chapter 8 covers basic concepts of bivariate regression. Interpretation of the intercept and slope is emphasized through examining the regression line in detail, first generally with algebra and geometry and then concretely with examples drawn from the literature and developed for the book. We look at the formulas for the slope coefficient and its standard error in detail, emphasizing what factors affect the size of the standard error. We discuss hypothesis testing and confidence intervals for testing statistical significance and rescaling and effect sizes for evaluating substantive significance.

■ Chapter 9 covers basic concepts of multiple regression. We look in detail at a model with two predictors, using algebra, geometry, and concrete examples to offer insights into interpretation. We look at how the formulas for the slope coefficients and their standard errors differ from the single predictor variable context, emphasizing how correlations among the predictors affect the size of the standard error. We cover joint hypothesis testing and introduce the general linear F-test. We again use algebra, illustrations, and examples to reinforce a full understanding of the F-test, including its specific uses for an overall model F-test and a partial F-test. We re-emphasize statistical and substantive significance and introduce the concepts of R-squared and Information Criteria.

■ Chapter 10 covers dummy variable predictors in detail, starting with a model with a single dummy predictor and extending to (a) models with multiple dummies that represent one multicategory variable, and (b) models with multiple dummies that represent two multicategory variables. We look in detail at why dummy variables are needed, how they are constructed, and how they are interpreted. We present three approaches for testing differences among included categories.

■ Chapter 11 covers interactions in detail, including an interaction between two dummy variables, between a dummy and interval variable, and between two interval variables. We present the Chow test and fully interacted regression model. We look in detail at how to interpret and present results, building on the three approaches for testing among included categories presented in Chapter 10.

■ Chapter 12 covers nonlinear relationships between the predictor and outcome. We discuss how to specify several common forms of nonlinear relationships between an interval predictor and outcome variable using the quadratic function and logarithmic transformation. We discuss how these various forms might be expected by conceptual models and how to compare them empirically. We also show how to calculate and plot predictions to illustrate the estimated forms of the relationships. And, we also discuss how to use dummy variables to estimate a flexible relationship between a predictor and the outcome.

■ Chapter 13 examines how adding variables to a multiple regression model affects the coefficients and their standard errors. We cover basic concepts of path analysis, including total, direct, and indirect effects. We relate these ideas to the concept of omitted variable bias, and discuss how to contemplate the direction of bias from omitted variables. We discuss the challenge of distinguishing between mediators and confounds in cross-sectional data.

■ Chapter 14 encompasses outliers, heteroskedasticity, and multicollinearity. We cover numerical and graphical techniques for identifying outliers and influential observations. We also cover the detection of heteroskedasticity, implications of violations of the homoskedasticity assumption, and calculation of robust standard errors. Finally, we discuss three strategies for detecting multicollinearity: (a) variance inflation factors, (b) significant model F but no significant individual coefficients, and (c) rising standard errors in models with controls. And, we discuss strategies for addressing multicollinearity based on answers to two questions: Are the variables indicators of the same or different constructs? How strongly do we believe the two variables are correlated in the population versus our sample (and why)?

Part 4: The Generalized Linear Model

■ Chapter 15 introduces the basic concepts of the generalized linear model and maximum likelihood estimation in the context of a continuous outcome. We look in detail at maximum likelihood for estimating the mean and estimating the intercept and slope based on the normal distribution. We discuss various other distributions and links for the generalized linear model. Estimating a proportion based on the binomial distribution is used as an example. We cover basic ideas of iterative solutions and convergence problems.

■ Chapter 16 applies the basic maximum likelihood and generalized linear model concepts to models with dichotomous outcomes, specifically logit and probit models. We motivate how the models are derived and discuss how to estimate and test coefficients and how to interpret the results. We also cover basic concepts of percentage change and percentage points.

■ Chapter 17 applies the basic maximum likelihood and generalized linear model concepts to models with multi-category outcomes, specifically ordered logit and multinomial logit. We focus on how to estimate and test coefficients and interpret results, using several examples from the literature and developed for the book.

Part 5: Wrapping Up

The final chapter provides a roadmap of topics that students may want to pursue in the future to build on the foundation taught in this book. The chapter organizes a range of advanced topics and briefly mentions their key features and when they might be used (but does not teach how to use those techniques). Students are presented with ideas about how to learn these topics as well as gaining more skill with SAS and Stata (e.g., searching at their own or other local universities; using summer or other short course opportunities). The chapter also revisits the Literature Excerpts featured in the first chapter of the book.

SOME WAYS TO USE THE BOOK

The author has used the complete textbook in a two-semester sequence with two 75-minute lectures and a weekly lab session. Typically, chapters can be covered in a week, although extra time is often taken with the earliest chapters in Part 2 (two weeks each on the basics of bivariate regression, the basics of multiple regression, dummy variables, and interactions).

To meet the needs of a heterogeneous pool of instructors and students, we provide comparable SAS and Stata commands for the same task throughout the book. Depending on the local resources and the expertise of the instructor and teaching assistant, however, the book can be used to teach only SAS, only Stata, or both. We also hope that putting the commands side-by-side helps students to see the similarities (and differences) between the two languages and helps to prepare students for the varied and often unexpected directions their interests may take them. Even when instructors use one package, the side-by-side presentation allows the most motivated students to implement both (during the sequence or after the sequence is completed).

With a few exceptions, each chapter has a common set of materials at the end: key terms, review questions, review exercises, chapter exercises, and a course exercise.

- Key Terms are in bold within the chapter and defined in the glossary index.
- Review Questions allow students to demonstrate their broad understanding of the major concepts introduced in the chapter.
- Review Exercises allow students to practice the concepts introduced in the chapter by working through short, standalone problems.
- Chapter Exercises allow students to practice the applied skills of analyzing data and interpreting the results. The chapter exercises carry one example throughout the book (using the National Health Interview Survey) allowing students to ask questions easily of one another, the teaching assistant, and instructor as they all work with the same data set. The goal of the chapter exercises is to give students confidence in working with real data, which may encourage them to continue to do so to complement whatever other research approaches they use in the future.
- The Course Exercise allows students to select a data set to apply the concepts learned in each chapter to a research question of interest to them. The author has used this

option with students who have more prior experience than the average student, who ask for extra practice because they know that they want to go on to advanced courses, or who are retaking the sequence as they begin to work on a masters or dissertation. The course exercises help students to gain confidence in working independently with their own data.

Answers to the review questions, review exercises, and chapter exercises, including the batch programs and results for the chapter exercises, are available on the textbook web site (*http:// www.routledge.com/cw/gordon*). The data sets, programs, and results from the in-text examples are also available on the textbook web site.

ACKNOWLEDGMENTS

This book reflects many individuals' early nurturing and continued support of my own study of statistics, beginning at Penn State University, in the psychology, statistics, computer science and human development departments, and continuing at the University of Chicago, in the schools of public policy and business, in the departments of statistics, sociology, economics and education, and at the social sciences and public policy computing center. I benefited from exposure to numerous faculty and peers who shared my passion for statistics, and particularly its application to examining research questions in the social and health sciences.

UIC's sociology department, in the College of Liberal Arts and Sciences, was similarly flush with colleagues engaged in quantitative social science research when I joined the department in 1999 and has provided me with the opportunity to teach graduate statistics for more than a decade. This book grew out of my lecture notes for that course, and benefits from numerous interactions with students and colleagues over the years that I have taught it. Kathy Crittenden deserves special thanks, as she planted the idea of this book and connected me with my publisher. I also have benefitted from interacting with my colleagues at the University of Illinois' Institute of Government and Public Affairs, especially Matthew Hall and Robert Kaestner, as I continued to study statistics from multiple disciplinary vantage points.

My publisher, Steve Rutter, was instrumental in taking me over the final hurdle in deciding to write this book and has been immensely supportive throughout the process. He has ably provided advice and identified excellent reviewers for input as the book took shape. The reviewers' comments also importantly improved the book, including early reviews of the proposal by Peter Marsden at Harvard University, Timothy Hilton at North Michigan University, Robert Kaufman at Ohio State, Alan Acock at Oregon State, Sarah Mustillo at Purdue University, Evan Schofer at the University of California, Irvine, François Nielsen at the University of North Carolina, Chapel Hill, and Thomas Pullum at the University of Texas at Austin; first chapter reviews by Gretchen Cusick at the University of Chicago, Erin Leahey at the University of Arizona and Tom Linneman at William and Mary; and special thanks to John Allen Logan at the University of Wisconsin, Madison and Scott Long at the University of Indiana, who provided excellent comments on the first and revised draft of many chapters. I also want to express my appreciation to Stata for their Author Support Program, and especially thank Bill Rising for providing comments on some chapters of the book. I also want to thank all of the staff at Routledge who helped produce the book, especially Leah Babb-Rosenfeld and Mhairi Bennett. Any remaining errors or confusions in the book are my own.

I also dedicate this book to my husband, Kevin, and daughter, Ashley, celebrating 20 years of marriage as well as Kevin's 50th and Ashley's 10th year of life.

Every effort has been made to trace and contact copyright holders. The publishers would be pleased to hear from any copyright holders not acknowledged here, so that this acknowledgment page may be amended at the earliest opportunity.

Part 1

GETTING STARTED

Chapter 1

EXAMPLES OF QUANTITATIVE RESEARCH IN THE SOCIAL AND HEALTH SCIENCES

CHAPTER 1: EXAMPLES OF QUANTITATIVE RESEARCH IN THE SOCIAL AND HEALTH SCIENCES

"Statistics present us with a series of techniques that transform raw data into a form that is easier to understand and to communicate or, to put it differently, that make it easy for the data to tell their story."

Jan de Leeuw and Richard Berk (2004)
Introduction to the Series
Advanced Quantitative Techniques in the Social Sciences

Regression analysis,* a subfield of statistics, is a means to an end for most social scientists. Social scientists use regression analysis to explore new research questions and to test hypotheses. This statement may seem obvious, but it is easy to get sidetracked in the details of the theory and practice of the method, and lose sight of this bigger picture (especially in introductory statistics courses). To help keep the big picture in sight, this chapter provides excerpts from the social and health science literature.

These excerpts also help to focus attention on how regression analyses are used in journal articles, consistent with two of the major reasons graduate students learn about regression analysis: (a) to be able to read the literature, and (b) to be able to contribute to the literature. You have probably already read at least some articles and books that report the results of regression analyses (if not, you likely will be doing so in the coming weeks in your substantive courses). Examining such literature excerpts in the context of a course on regression analysis provides a new perspective, with an eye toward how the technique facilitates exploring the questions or testing the hypotheses at hand, what choices the researchers make in order to implement the model, and how the results are interpreted. At this point, you do not have the skills to understand fully the regression results presented in the excerpts (otherwise this book would not be needed!), so the purpose of this chapter is to present these features in such a way that they overview what later chapters will cover, and why. We will revisit these excerpts in the final chapter of the book, to help to reinforce what we have covered (and what advanced topics you might still want to pursue).

We have purposefully chosen excerpts in this chapter to hopefully appeal to you because they were written by young scholars who published work that they completed as graduate students (in later chapters, we use shorter excerpts, including some from more senior scholars). To appeal to a broad array of interests, we have also selected the examples from a range of subfields and with different levels of analysis (person, community, informal organization). Several of the articles use existing data, but they illustrate a wide variety of sources of such data (including ethnographies). Although using existing data presents some limitations (discussed for each excerpt), doing so can let you answer questions of interest to you in less time and cost, and with a larger and more representative sample, than you could have achieved with new data collection. Chapter 2 helps you to identify similar data sources for your own research.

* **Terms in color** in the text are defined in the glossary/index.

1.1: WHAT IS REGRESSION ANALYSIS?

Later chapters will develop the statistical details of regression analysis. But, in order to provide some guideposts to the features we will examine in the literature excerpts, it is helpful first to briefly consider what regression analysis is conceptually, and what are some of its key elements.

Why is it called regression, and why is it so widely used in the social sciences? The term regression is attributed to Francis Galton (Stigler 1986). Galton was interested in heredity and gathered data sets to understand better how traits are passed down across generations. The data he gathered ranged from measures of parents' and children's heights to assessments of sweet peas grown from seeds of varying size. His calculations showed that the height or size of the second generation was closer to the sample average than the height or size of the first generation (i.e., it reverted, or regressed, to the mean). His later insights identified how a certain constant factor (such as exposure to sunlight) might affect average size, with dispersion around that group average, even as the entire sample followed a normal distribution around the overall mean. Later scientists formalized these concepts mathematically and showed their wide applicability. Ultimately, regression analysis provided the breakthrough that social scientists needed in order to study social phenomena when randomized experiments were not possible. As Stephen Stigler puts it in his *History of Statistics* "beginning in the 1880s ... a series of remarkable men constructed an empirical and conceptual methodology that provided a surrogate for experimental control and in effect dissipated the fog that had impeded progress for a century" (Stigler 1986: 265).

Regression analysis allows scientists to quantify how the average of one variable systematically varies according to the levels of another variable. The former variable is often called a **dependent variable** or **outcome variable** and the latter an **independent variable, predictor variable, or explanatory variable.** For example, a social scientist might use regression analysis to estimate the size of the gender wage gap (how different are the mean wages between women and men?), where wage is the dependent variable and gender the independent variable. Or, a social scientist might test for an expected amount of returns to education in adults' incomes, looking for a regular increment in average income (outcome) with each additional year of schooling (predictor). When little prior research has addressed a topic, the regression analyses may be exploratory, but these variables are ideally identified through theories and concepts applied to particular phenomena. Indeed, throughout the text, we encourage forward thinking and conceptual grounding of your regression models. Not only is this most consistent with the statistical basis of hypothesis testing, but thinking ahead (especially based on theory) can facilitate timely completion of a project, easier interpretation of the output, and stronger contributions to the literature.

An important advantage of regression analysis over other techniques (such as bivariate *t*-tests or correlations) is that additional variables can be introduced into the model to help to determine if a relationship is genuine or spurious. If the relationship is spurious, then a third variable (a confounder, common cause, or extraneous variable) causes both the predictor and outcome; and, adjusting for the third variable in a regression model should reduce the association between the predictor and outcome to near zero. In some cases, the association may not be erased completely, and the predictor may still have an association with the outcome, but part of the initial association may be due to the third variable. For example, in initial models, teenage mothers may appear to attain fewer years of schooling than women who do not have a child until adulthood. If family socioeconomic status leads to both teenage motherhood and academic achievement, then adjusting for the family of origin's education, occupation, and income should substantially reduce the average difference in school attainment between teenage and adult mothers. In Chapters 9 and 13, we will discuss how these adjustments are accomplished, and their limitations.

Such statistical adjustments for confounding variables are needed in the social sciences when randomized experiments cannot be conducted due to ethical and cost concerns. For example, if we randomly assigned some teenagers to have a child and others not to, then we could be assured that the two groups were statistically equivalent except for their status as teenage mothers. But, of course, doing so is not ethical. Although used less often than in the physical sciences to test basic research questions, experiments are more frequently used in certain social science subfields (e.g., social psychology) and applications (e.g., evaluations of social programs). When experiments are not possible, social scientists rely on statistical adjustments to **observational data** (data in which people were not assigned experimentally to treatment and control groups, such as population surveys or program records). Each literature excerpt we show in this chapter provides examples of using control variables in observational studies in an attempt to adjust for such confounding variables.

Regression models also allow scientists to examine the **mechanisms** that their theories and ideas suggest explain the association between a particular predictor variable and an outcome (often referred to as mediation). For example, how much of the wage gap between men and women is due to discriminatory practices on the part of employers and how much is due to differences in family responsibilities of men and women (such as child-rearing responsibilities)? If the mediators—discriminatory practices and family responsibilities—are measured, regression models can be used to examine the extent to which they help to explain the association between the predictor of interest—in this case, gender—and the outcome—wages. In Chapter 13, we will discuss how these mechanisms can be identified in regression models and some of the challenges that arise in interpreting them. Some of the literature excerpts we discuss below illustrate the use of mediators.

Social scientists also use regression models to examine whether two predictors jointly associate with an outcome variable (often referred to as moderation or interaction). For example, is the gender wage gap larger for African Americans than for whites? Are the returns to education larger for workers who grew up in lower versus higher income families? In Chapter 11, we will discuss how such research questions can be examined with regression models, and below we illustrate their use in the literature.

Regression models rest on a number of assumptions, which we will discuss in detail in later chapters. It is important for social scientists to understand these assumptions so that they can test whether they are met in their own work and know how to recognize the signs that they are violated when reading others' work. Although the basic regression model is linear, it is possible to model nonlinear relationships (as we discuss in Chapter 12) and important to check for cases that have a great effect on the slope of the regression line, referred to as outliers and influential observations (as we discuss in Chapter 14). Other technical terms that you may have seen in reading about regression models in the past, and that we will unpack in Chapter 14, include the problems of heteroskedasticity and multicollinearity. Although these terms undoubtedly merely sound like foreign jargon now, we will spend considerable time discussing what these terms mean and how to test for and correct for them, such that they become familiar.

It is also helpful from the outset to recognize that this book will help you to understand a substantial fraction, but by no means all, of what you will later read (or potentially need to do) with regression models. Like all social scientists, you may need to take additional courses, engage in independent study, or seek out consultation when the research questions you pose require you to go beyond the content of this textbook. Important skills for a developing social scientist are being able to distinguish what you know from what you need to know and being able to find out how to learn what you still need to know. We use the literature excerpts in this chapter, and the excerpts in future chapters, to begin to help you to distinguish between the two. One of our goals is to provide a solid foundation that adequately prepares you for such advanced study and help seeking. Chapter 18 provides a roadmap of advanced topics and ideas about how to locate related courses and resources.

In the interest of space and to meet our objectives, we extract only certain details from each article in the extracts below. Reading the entire article is required for a full picture of the conceptual framework, method and measures, results and interpretations.

1.2: LITERATURE EXCERPT 1.1

Lyons, Christopher J. 2007. "Community (Dis)Organization and Racially Motivated Crime." *American Journal of Sociology*, 113(3): 815–63.

A paper by Christopher Lyons published in the *American Journal of Sociology* illustrates the innovative use of several existing data sources to examine the correlates of hate crimes. Lyons (2007, 816) summarizes his research questions this way: "Are racial hate crimes the product of socially disorganized communities low in economic and social capital? Or are racially motivated crimes more likely in communities with substantial resources to exclude outsiders?" Lyons creatively used multiple existing data sources to examine these questions. He took advantage of the Project on Human Development in Chicago Neighborhoods (PHDCN) which had gathered data that precisely measured concepts about social organization for the same time period in which he was able to obtain Chicago Police Department statistics on hate crimes for the same communities. The availability of these data provided a unique opportunity to go beyond other community measures that would be less close to the concept of social organization (e.g., measures of the poverty rate or mobility rate in the area from the US Census Bureau).

Bringing together these various data sources is an important innovation of the study. On the other hand, using existing data sources means the fit with the research questions is not as precise as it could be with newly gathered data (e.g., as Lyons discusses, the community areas might ideally be smaller in size than the 77 Chicago community areas, which average some 40,000 people, and the police districts and PHDCN data had to be aggregated to that level with some imprecision; pp. 829, 833–4). But, the creative combination of existing data sources allowed a novel set of research questions to be tested with moderate time and cost by a graduate student. Furthermore the results raise some questions that might be best answered with in-depth methods targeted at the problem at hand. Yet, the existing data provide an important first look at the questions, with the results suggesting a number of next steps that could productively be pursued by any scholar, including a post-doc or young assistant professor building a body of work.

Lyons identifies three specific hypotheses that are motivated by theory and are testable with regression analyses. Importantly, the third hypothesis produces expectations different from the first two, increasing intellectual interest in the results. If hate crimes are similar to general crime, then Lyons (p. 818) expects that two traditional models would apply:

1. *Social disorganization theory* predicts more crimes in disadvantaged areas with low levels of social capital.
2. *Resource competition theories* specify that crimes are most likely when competition between racial groups increases, especially during economic downturns when resources are scarce.

The third model is unique to hate crimes, and differs from the others in its predictions:

3. The *defended community perspective* implies that interracial antagonism is most likely in economically and socially *organized* communities that are able to use these resources to exclude racial outsiders.

Lyons also posed a subquestion that is an example of a statistical interaction (a situation in which the relationship between the predictor and outcome variables differs for certain subgroups). In particular, Lyons expected that the defended community result would be particularly likely in a subset of communities: "Social cohesion and social control may be leveraged for hate crime particularly (or perhaps exclusively) in racially homogenous communities that are threatened by racial invasion, perhaps in the form of recent in-migration of racial outgroups." (p. 825).

Lyons separately coded antiblack and antiwhite hate crimes because of theoretically different expectations for each and because antiwhite hate crimes have been understudied. Literature Excerpt 1.1a provides the results for the regression analyses of antiblack hate crime (Table 6 from the article).

The table may seem overwhelming at first glance, but as you learn regression analyses you will find that it follows a common pattern for reporting regression results. The key predictor variables from the research questions and other variables that adjust for possible confounders are listed in the leftmost column. The outcome variable is indicated in the title ("antiblack hate crimes"). Several models are run, and presented in different columns, to allow us to see how the results change when different variables are included or excluded. In the final chapter of the book, we

Literature Excerpt 1.1a

Table 6. Negative Binomial Regressions: Community Characteristics and "Bonafide" Antiblack Hate Crimes, 1997–2002

	Model 1	Model 2	Model 3	Model 4	Model 5	Model 6	Model 7	Model 8	Model 9	Model 10	Model 11
Constant	-4.01*	-6.36**	-6.29**	-6.38**	-5.64**	-14.78***	-11.15**	-10.11**	-11.10**	-10.18**	-12.67**
	(2.32)	(2.39)	(2.39)	(2.66)	(2.60)	(3.71)	(4.05)	(4.12)	(4.76)	(4.79)	(5.75)
Ln population 1990	.46**	.67**	.67**	.60**	.67**	.88**	.67**	.70**	.68**	.75**	.78**
	(.22)	(.23)	(.23)	(.25)	(.26)	(.25)	(.26)	(.26)	(.26)	(.26)	(.24)
Spatial proximity	.67**	.31	.30	.25	.26	.24	.20	.22	.19	.21	-.15
	(.34)	(.31)	(.31)	(.30)	(.30)	(.32)	(.29)	(.29)	(.29)	(.29)	(.28)
Disadvantage		-.65***	-.60**	-.22	-.05				.03	.19	.17
		(.18)	(.20)	(.34)	(.32)				(.37)	(.37)	(.35)
Stability		.11	.13	.17	.24				.03	.11	.16
		(.15)	(.15)	(.15)	(.16)				(.18)	(.18)	(.17)
White unemployment			-.02								
			(.02)								
%white 1990				.013			.01*		.013		
				(.01)			(.006)		(.01)		
%black 1990					-.018**			-.01**		-.018**	
					(.01)			(.006)		(.01)	
%Hispanic 1990				.01	-.007		.01	-.002	-.012	-.005	.02**
				(.01)	(.01)		(.01)	(.01)	(.01)	(.01)	(.01)
Informal social control						1.50**	1.34**	1.35**	1.31**	1.29**	1.48**
						(.60)	(.59)	(.58)	(.67)	(.66)	(.90)
Social cohesion						-.22	-.23	-.26	-.24	-.26	-.43
						(.47)	(.56)	(.53)	(.59)	(.57)	(.50)
%change in black population, 1990–2000											-.52
											(.44)

Table 6. Continued

	Model 1	Model 2	Model 3	Model 4	Model 5	Model 6	Model 7	Model 8	Model 9	Model 10	Model 11
Informal social control × %white											-.002 (.02)
Informal social control × %change in black population											.14 (.13)
%white 1990 × %change in black population											-.02* (.01)
Informal social control × %white × %change in black											.005** (.002)
Overdispersion	1.23 (31.00)	.87 (.25)	.87 (.25)	.80 (.24)	.76 (.23)	.84 (.25)	.71 (.23)	.70 (.22)	.71 (.23)	.67 (.22)	.31 (-.16)
Log likelihood	146.17	139.10	-138.87	137.73	-136.46	-139.27	-136.19	-135.21	-36.17	-134.90	-126.23

Note.—N = 77 Chicago community areas; unstandardized coefficients; SEs are in parentheses.
* P<.10.
** P<.05.
*** P<.001.

■ Literature Excerpt 1.1a—continued

Table 7. Predicted Antiblack Hate Crime, Chicago Communities, 1997–2002

	White Communities (85% White)		Nonwhite Communities (10% White)	
	Threat[a]	No Threat[b]	Threat[a]	No Threat[b]
High informal social control	34.7	3.9	3.1	2.1
Low informal social control	.1	.9	.1	.3

Note.—See table 6, model 11. Except for %white, informal social control, and change in %black, all variables held at mean values. High informal social control: 1 SD above mean; low informal social control: 1 SD below mean.
[a] Black in-migration 15%.
[b] Black in-migration 0%.

Source: Lyons, Christopher J. (2007). "Community (Dis)Organization and Racially Motivated Crime." *American Journal of Sociology*, 113(3): 815–63.

will return to this table to link all the pieces of the table to what we have learned (such as the term "unstandardized coefficients") or what is left to be learned, in our roadmap of advanced topics (such as the term "overdispersion"). For now, we will consider the major evidence related to Lyons' research questions based on the significance (indicated by asterisks) and sign (positive or negative) of the relationship of key predictor variables to the outcome.

In Lyons' Table 6, a green circle encloses the coefficient estimate of a three-way interaction between social control, percentage white in 1990, and percentage change in black between 1990 and 2000 which is relevant to the defended communities hypothesis. The asterisks indicate that the interaction is significant. It is difficult to interpret this interaction based only on the results in Lyons' Table 6. His Table 7 (also reproduced in Literature Excerpt 1.1a) provides additional results from the model that aid in interpretation of the interaction results (we will detail how to calculate such results in Part 2).

Each cell value in Lyons' Table 7 is the number of antiblack hate crimes that the model predicts for a cell with the listed row and column characteristics. The results show that when white communities are under threat (have experienced black in-migration of 15 percent or higher) and are high in social control, they have substantially more antiblack hate crimes (predicted number of 34.7, circled in green) than any other communities. This is consistent with the author's expectation about which communities would be most likely to conform to the defended communities perspective: racially homogeneous areas with recent in-migration of racial outgroups. Although less extreme, it is also the case that other communities conform to the defended communities perspective: within each column, communities with high social control have more predicted antiblack hate crimes than those low in social control (i.e., two to four versus fewer than one antiblack hate crime predicted by the model).

Literature Excerpt 1.1b shows the regression results for antiwhite crime, Table 8 in Lyons' article.

Literature Excerpt 1.1b

Table 8. Negative Binomial Regressions: Community Characteristics and "Bonafide" Antiwhite Hate Crime, 1997–2002

	All Chicago[a]		Excluding Outliers[b]								
	Model 1	Model 2	Model 2	Model 3	Model 4	Model 5	Model 6	Model 7	Model 8	Model 9	Model 10
Constant	−6.12** (1.84)	−5.34** (1.87)	−5.82** (1.83)	−5.85 (1.84)	−6.24** (1.89)	−5.97** (1.97)	−2.31 (2.68)	−3.95 (2.96)	−3.63 (3.17)	−7.83** (3.77)	−5.59* (3.13)
Ln population 1990	.64*** (.18)	.56** (.18)	.59** (.17)	.59 (.17)	.64** (.19)	.63** (.18)	.58** (.18)	.68*** (.19)	.66*** (.19)	.69** (.20)	.69** (.20)
Spatial proximity	.69** (.22)	.73** (.24)	.57** (.24)	.58 (.24)	.54** (.24)	.53** (.24)	.59** (.21)	.46** (.23)	.49* (.24)	.46* (.24)	.45* (.24)
Economic disadvantage		.13 (.12)	.30** (.12)	.29 (.14)	.26 (.21)	.20 (.21)				.33 (.25)	.28 (.25)
Residential stability		−.15 (.12)	−.26** (.12)	−.25 (.12)	−.26** (.13)	−.27** (.13)				−.28** (.13)	−.30** (.14)
Black unemployment 1910				.01 (.01)							
% black 1990					.001 (.01)					.004 (.01)	
% white 1990						−.003 (.005)		−.005 (.01)			−.01 (.01)
% Hispanic 1990					−.004 (.01)	−.005 (.01)		−.007 (.01)	−.005 (.01)	.000 (.01)	−.004 (.01)
Informal social control							−1.10* (.58)	−1.11* (.58)	−1.10* (.58)	−.54 (.61)	−.56 (.61)
Social cohesion							.18 (.40)	.44 (.50)	.30 (.30)	.77 (.51)	.85 (.52)
Overdispersion	.36 (.16)	.34 (.16)	.24 (.14)	.24 (.14)	.23 (.14)	.24 (.14)	.24 (.15)	.21 (.14)	.21 (.15)	.18 (.13)	.18 (.13)
Log likelihood	−130.39	−129.06	−116.68	−116.67	−116.31	−116.21	−118.32	−117.63	−117.91	−115.13	−114.80

Note.—Unstandardized coefficients, SEs are in parentheses.
[a] N = 77 Chicago community areas.
[b] N = 74 Chicago community areas.
* P < .10
** P < .05.
*** P < .001.

Source: Lyons, Christopher J. (2007). "Community (Dis)Organization and Racially Motivated Crime." *American Journal of Sociology,* 113(3): 815–63.

A key finding here is that the basic results differ substantially from those seen for antiblack crime (compare results enclosed by black circles in Literature Excerpts 1.1a and 1.1b). For antiwhite crime, the results are consistent with social disorganization theories: in Model 2, economic disadvantage associates with more antiwhite hate crimes (asterisks and positive sign) and residential stability associates with less antiwhite hate crimes (asterisks and negative sign; see again the black circle in Literature Excerpt 1.1b). In contrast, for antiblack crime, economic disadvantage is associated with less antiblack hate crime (asterisks and negative sign) and residential stability is not associated with antiblack hate crime (no asterisks; see again the black circle in Literature Excerpt 1.1a).

1.3: LITERATURE EXCERPT 1.2

Vaisey, Stephen. 2007. "Structure, Culture, and Community: The Search for Belonging in 50 Urban Communes." *American Sociological Review*, 72: 851–73.

Stephen Vaisey provides an example that applies regression techniques to a collection of ethnographies, illustrating one approach to combining quantitative and qualitative methods. In particular, Vaisey reanalyzed dozens of ethnographies of urban communes using regression analyses to test several research questions about how a sense of collective belonging develops in groups; his particular interest was in how structural and cultural mechanisms influence the development of collective belonging.

The data that Vaisey analyzes were originally gathered in the mid-1970s. As discussed further in Chapter 2, these data have been made publicly available, allowing researchers such as Vaisey to reanalyze them. In the original study, communes were drawn systematically from a known sampling frame (list of all members of the population) making the results more generalizable than they would be if the ethnographies were conducted with a convenience sample of communes. Specifically, fieldworkers developed lists of communes in six US metropolitan areas (Atlanta, Boston, Houston, Los Angeles, New York, and the Twin Cities). Ten communes were selected from the list in each of the six areas, with a goal of a good representation of communes associated with key constructs (ideology, size, longevity). To be listed, a group had to have at least five members and, so as to exclude monasteries and convents, the commune had to have at least one member of each sex (or resident children). Participant observers gathered data from each commune. They completed standardized forms based on their interactions and experiences in the commune, and they asked commune members to fill out surveys about their attitudes, beliefs and relationships.

Using existing data has disadvantages as well as advantages for Vaisey's research questions. For example, Vaisey notes that communes are not representative of all groups that develop collective belonging, his broader conceptual interest. The studied communes' members were "whiter, younger, and more educated" than the general population (p. 855). On the other hand, communes are "bounded" groups, making it easier to examine their social interactions than would be the case with larger groups with less clearly defined boundaries. And, because of the sampling frame, the included communes are more diverse than the stereotypical commune (e.g., the majority of studied communes are religious, political, or countercultural, although some more simply serve alternative family or cooperative living functions) and have considerable variation on the constructs of interest.

Vaisey drew on both reports from the participant observers and the ratings from the commune members to construct variables representing the concepts of interest to him. The outcome, referred to as *gemeinschaft*, captures a "sense of we-feeling, a sense of collective self, or the feeling of natural belonging" (p. 852). It is operationalized using a scale comprised of six measures, including the ethnographer's overall rating of the "feeling of community" in the commune and members' reports of whether they see the other members as their true family, as people who care about others in general and the respondent in particular, and whether they expect to be in the commune 10 years in the future and would leave if offered $10,000 to do so (reversed).

Other variables capture the major processes that Vaisey expects explain the outcome, including structural processes (properties of the organization) and substantive processes (cultural meaning of the group). The structural processes suggest that belongingness is a by-product of frequent interaction among group members, similarity (homophily) of group members, required investments from group members, and strict leadership (authority). The substantive theories suggest that structural factors are not sufficient to produce belongingness; rather, shared moral culture allows groups to "withstand centrifugal forces" (p. 854). The moral culture was assessed by the ethnographer's rating of the consensus among members on ideology, values, and beliefs and the importance of ideology, values, and beliefs in the commune's life as well as members' responses to questions about having clear beliefs of a "right" and "wrong" way to live. Vaisey also introduces variables to the model to adjust for confounders, which might be correlated with the predictors and outcome (e.g., group size—number of members, age—number of years the commune had been in existence, and origin of the commune—whether arose from a prior group).

Vaisey uses bivariate correlations and regression analyses (as well as a technique called "fuzzy set analysis" beyond the scope of this book). He sees the unique advantage of regression analyses as allowing him to identify the "proximate mechanism" leading to belongingness (*gemeinschaft*). Indeed, nearly all variables are correlated with belongingness in the expected direction (see Literature Excerpt 1.2a, which has asterisks on all of the theoretically motivated variables except the three measures of homogeneity and the measure of density—persons per room—circled in green). But, in the regression analysis shown in Literature Excerpt 1.2b, when all variables are entered together in the model, only three variables remain significantly associated with the outcome: authority, investment, and moral order having asterisks. Importantly, the sign for authority reverses when all variables are included together in the regression model. It was positive in the bivariate correlations and now is negative in the regression model (see black circles in Literature excerpts 1.2a and 1.2b; we will have more to say about why such sign reversals may be observed, and how to interpret them, in Chapter 13).

Vaisey interprets the regression results in Literature Excerpt 1.2b as indicating that, with the exception of investment, the structural constructs are not as important as the theory suggests;

■ **Literature Excerpt 1.2a**

Table 1. Correlations between *Gemeinschaft* Scale and All Predictor Variables

	ρ	s.e.		ρ	s.e.
SPATIOTEMPORAL	*.355*	*.155***	MORAL ORDER	*.713*	*.094****
Meetings	.352	.122**	Ideological unity	.707	.084***
Eating together	.456	.126***	Importance of ideology	.693	.069***
Density	.124	(.133)	Role certainty	.580	.116***
			"How to live"	.564	.119***
AUTHORITY	*.379*	*(.124**)*	TYPE OF GROUP	n/a	
Authoritarian governance	.337	.125**	Eastern religious	.330	.202
Extent of authority	.364	.145*	Christian	.688	.153***
Number of rules	.469	.112***	Political	.053	.208
			Counter cultural (hippie)	−.362	.155*
INVESTMENT	*.543*	*.122***	Alternative family	−.169	.225
Time spent	.301	.136*	Household	−.489	.157**
Communism	.630	.081***	Personal growth	−.256	.117*
Bar to entry	.441	.172*			
Assigned chores	.714	.111***	CONTROLS	n/a	
			Size of group	−.033	.134
HOMOGENEITY	n/a		Age of group	.123	.119
Age	.044	(.141	Evolved from previous	.538	.152***
Education	.178	.139			
Class	−.193	.139)			

Notes: Italicized statistics are for scale measurements. Categorical variables use polychoric correlations. Other variables use Pearson's *r*.
* $p < .05$;** $p < .01$;*** $p < .001$ (two-tailed).

Source: Vaisey, Stephen. 2007. "Structure, Culture, and Community: The Search for Belonging in 50 Urban Communes." *American Sociological Review*, 72: 851–73.

and, "in fact, there is evidence here that the direct effects of authority can be alienating." The latter interpretation reflects the negative sign of authority, with the other variables controlled. In contrast, the author tells us in a footnote that the association between moral order and belongingness increases with the other variables controlled (again a result we will discuss further in Chapter 13). The author concludes that, in contrast to prior theorizing, "*reciprocity and trustworthiness do* not *simply 'arise' from social networks, except, perhaps, as that interaction is either animated by or productive of shared moral understandings*" (p. 866, italics in original). In other words, structure alone does not produce collective belonging; moral order is essential.

■ **Literature Excerpt 1.2b**

Table 2. OLS Regression of *Gemeinschaft* Scale on Independent Variables

Mechanisms	b	β	t
Spatiotemporal Interaction	−.281	−.192	−1.300
Authority	−.665	−.595	−3.170**
Investment	.485	.374	2.460**
Strength of Moral Order	1.033	.936	4.360***
Group Types			
Eastern religious	(reference)		
Christian	.403	.153	1.470
Political	.315	.106	.780
Counter cultural	−.095	−.034	−.220
Alternative family	.655	.203	1.410
Household	−.050	−.018	−.110
Personal growth	.250	.061	.490
Controls			
Size of group	−.017	−.155	−1.310
Age of group	.118	.191	2.010
Evolved from previous	.457	.220	1.790
Constant	−.464		−1.630
N			50
R^2			.754
Adjusted R^2			.665

** $p < .01$; *** $p < .001$ (two-tailed).

Source: Vaisey, Stephen. 2007. "Structure, Culture, and Community: The Search for Belonging in 50 Urban Communes." *American Sociological Review*, 72: 851–73.

1.4: LITERATURE EXCERPT 1.3

Li-Grining, Christine P. 2007. "Effortful Control Among Low-Income Preschoolers in Three Cities: Stability, Change, and Individual Differences." *Developmental Psychology*, 43(1): 208–21.

As we discuss in Chapter 2, numerous large-scale data sets are now available that follow individuals over time. These data sets are particularly well-suited to regression analyses because they are drawn to represent a population (often with a stratified, clustered design; we will consider some of the implications of these complex sampling designs in later chapters). They often have large enough sample sizes to allow the estimation of complicated models with numerous conceptually important variables and control variables. And, more recent data sets are frequently designed to oversample subgroups of interest to social scientists, such as racial-ethnic groups or single-parent households.

Christine Li-Grining uses one of these data sets—Welfare, Children, and Families: A Three-City Study—to examine how preschoolers develop the ability to control impulses. This capacity, referred to by Li-Grining as *effortful control*, is an important predictor of children's later academic achievement (Duncan et al. 2007). Thus, understanding how this skill varies among low-income children, and what predicts better effortful control, is important.

Li-Grining's central research goals are:

■ describing typical patterns of stability and change over time in effortful control among low-income preschoolers;
■ examining to what degree characteristics of children and stressors associated with poverty explain variation in effortful control among low-income children;
■ testing whether results differ by race-ethnicity and gender.

The fact that the Three-City Study investigators took well-established methods typically used to measure effortful control in small psychology labs and adapted them for use in a large-scale study allowed Li-Grining to address these goals. Doing so was also facilitated by the large size of the study overall and within the African American and Latino subgroups. Of course, the data set also has limitations. For example, it was drawn to represent three cities (Boston, Chicago, and San Antonio) rather than the nation. And, it focused on low-income children, preventing comparisons with higher income children. However, the data provide an opportunity for her to begin to address her research questions and to contribute to the growing literature on effortful control.

Li-Grining considers two separate but interrelated aspects of effortful control: the ability for children to inhibit impulses (delayed gratification) and the ability of children to focus attention (executive control). Both are assessed with rigorous procedures, such as coding whether children peek at presents while they are being wrapped and whether they can stay in the lines while tracing a turtle's versus a rabbit's path home.

Literature Excerpt 1.3 shows the results of regression models examining her second goal: predicting each outcome based on child characteristics and poverty-related risk factors. Among the child factors, race was not significantly related to either type of effortful control (no asterisks), but gender was significantly related to delayed gratification (see asterisks in green circle). As we will learn in Chapter 10, the negative sign indicates that boys score lower than girls on this outcome, consistent with other literature that shows boys' poorer performance on behavioral than on cognitive control. Among the poverty risk factors, low birth weight is significantly related to less effortful control of both types (negative sign and asterisks circled in black). Tests for interactions reported in the text indicate that gender also moderates the association for delayed gratification: low birth weight is associated with delayed gratification only for boys. Several other poverty-related risks are related to only one type of effortful control (asterisks only in one, rather than both, columns).

■ **Literature Excerpt 1.3**

Table 3. Regressions: Child Characteristics, Risk Factors, and Child–Mother Interaction Predicting Delayed Gratification and Executive Control at Wave 2

Variable	Delayed Gratification					Executive Control				
	R^2	ΔR^2	B	$SE\ B$	β	R^2	ΔR^2	B	$SE\ B$	β
Child characteristics	.19					.42				
Age			.35***	.05	.42			.55***	.05	.62
Gender			−.27**	.08	−.19			−.04	.08	−.03
Negative emotionality			.00	.01	.00			−.01	.01	−.03
Race										
European American (omitted)										
African American			.08	.19	.06			.34	.25	.22
Latino			.00	.18	.00			.43†	.25	.28
Other			.27	.24	.07			.35	.29	.09
Risk factors and child–mother interaction		0.04**					0.07***			
Low birth weight			−.27*	0.13	−.09			−.48**	.17	−.16
Psychosocial risk			.02	0.04	.03			.04	.04	.05
Sociodemographic risk			−.01	0.03	−.01			−.08**	.03	−.15
Residential risk			−.01	0.05	−.01			−.16*	.07	−.16
Dyadic connectedness			.21**	0.06	.19			.07	.06	.06

*$p < .05$. **$p < .01$. ***$p < .001$. †$p < .10$.

Source: Li-Grining, Christine P. 2007. "Effortful Control Among Low-Income Preschoolers in Three Cities: Stability, Change, and Individual Differences." *Developmental Psychology*, 43(1): 208–21.

1.5: LITERATURE EXCERPT 1.4

Baker, Dian L., Michelle T. Dang, May Ying Ly, and Rafael Diaz. 2010. "Perception of Barriers to Immunization among Parents of Hmong Origin in California." *American Journal of Public Health,* 100: 839–845.

Dian Baker, Michelle Dang, May Ying Ly, and Rafael Diaz provide an example of a community-based participatory research study that implements regression analyses.

The project was initiated by Dr. Baker, when she was a doctoral candidate, in collaboration with the Hmong Women's Heritage Association (located in the Central Valley of California). The partners were interested in better understanding the low immunization rates among Hmong children, especially in relation to parents' perceived barriers to immunization. They framed the importance of this issue in the particularly high rates of cervical and liver cancer among the

Hmong, both cancers which can be prevented with immunization, although Hmong children are the least likely Asian group to obtain such immunizations. To inform this issue, they interviewed over 400 Hmong parents of young children (at least one child aged 9 or younger) who were recruited primarily from Hmong New Year events in Central Valley and San Joaquin Valley California.

The authors conducted a number of analyses, including the regression models presented in their Table 2 (reproduced in Literature Excerpt 1.4). They framed their study using the social determinants of health perspective, and the explanatory variables in their regression model include income, education, age of arrival to the U.S., years lived in the U.S., language, and type of provider used for nonemergency health care. Their outcomes were parents' responses to three subscales regarding their perceptions of barriers to immunization, including *Access* barriers (such as the clinic not being open at the time the parent could go), *Safety* concerns (such as worries about what is in shots), and lack of *Importance* (such as thinking children's shots aren't important).

The authors focused their interpretations on three sets of variables that significantly predicted barriers, consistent with their social determinants model: socioeconomic position, nativity, and traditional Hmong health care practices. Significance was identified by small values in the column labeled *P* in their Table 4. For example, the *P*-values are smaller than .10 in all three sets of columns in the *Income* row (and smaller than .02 in two cases). The negative signs on the values in the columns labeled *b* and *B* indicate that higher-income parents perceived more barriers to access, expressed more safety concerns, and thought immunization was less important than did lower-income parents.

Similarly, the *P*-values were all small (less than .04) for the *Language* variables. The sign of the *b* and *B* variables in the rows labeled *Hmong or mostly Hmong* and *Hmong and English equally* were all positive, indicating that parents who spoke Hmong most of the time or equally with English perceived more barriers to immunization than did parents who primarily spoke English. Likewise, the *P*-values are generally small, and the *b* and *B* values positive, for the use of traditional methods (on their own and in combination with Western practices) in comparison with Western doctors (in private practices or HMOs).

We will learn in Chapters 8 and 9 why the authors can draw conclusions about significance based on the *P*-values, why they can interpret the direction of associations based on the signs of the b and B values (and the difference between these two types of "b" values). We will also learn in Chapter 10 the meaning of the note on *Language* which reads "Reference group for language was English and mostly English" (as well as the similar note about the reference group for the type of nonemergency health care variables). Later chapters will also address additional details shown in the table (e.g., the R^2 values and *F*-values in the table notes; what it means to restrict the analysis to participants without missing values) and mentioned elsewhere in the article (e.g., tests for multicollinearity and heteroskedasticity presented on page 840 of the article).

■ **Literature Excerpt 1.4**

Table 2 Multiple Regression Analysis of Sociodemographic Variables and Perceptions of Barriers to Immunization Among Hmong Respondents, by SHOTS Subscale: California, 2008

	Subscale 1–Access[a] (n = 368)			Subscale 2–Safety[b] (n = 377)			Subscale 3–Importance[c] (n = 378)		
	b (SE)	B	P	b (SE)	B	P	b (SE)	B	P
Income	−0.83 (0.28)	−0.15	.003	−0.29 (0.17)	−0.09	.088	−0.33 (0.13)	−0.13	.015
Education	−0.30 (0.22)	−0.07	.184	0.02 (0.14)	0.01	.872	−0.05 (0.11)	−0.03	.650
Age of arrival in United States, y	−0.03 (0.07)	−0.03	.637	0.01 (0.04)	0.02	.778	−0.04 (0.03)	−0.09	.233
Years lived in the United States	0.02 (0.08)	0.01	.856	0.05 (0.05)	0.07	.334	0.08 (0.04)	0.15	.037
Language[d]									
Hmong or mostly Hmong	7.40 (1.77)	0.28	.000	2.64 (1.11)	0.17	.018	1.86 (0.87)	0.15	.032
Hmong and English equally	5.50 (1.87)	0.16	.003	4.08 (1.15)	0.20	.000	3.28 (0.90)	0.21	.000
Type of nonemergency health care[e]									
Western, community clinic	−2.27 (1.77)	−0.06	.200	−1.17 (1.06)	−0.06	.272	−1.40 (0.83)	−0.09	.095
Western and traditional	7.14 (1.91)	0.18	.000	4.36 (1.19)	0.18	.000	3.02 (0.93)	0.16	.001
Traditional only	7.13 (1.86)	0.18	.000	3.57 (1.18)	0.15	.003	1.25 (0.90)	0.07	.167
No health care provider	12.87 (4.50)	0.13	.005	7.24 (3.13)	0.11	.021	1.71 (2.21)	0.04	.440

Note. SHOTS = Search for Hardship and Obstacles to Shots. Analysis was restricted to participants without missing values.
[a] This subscale assessed barriers such as inconvenient clinic hours ($R^2 = 0.22$; $F_{10\,367} = 10.15$; $P < .001$).
[b] This subscale assessed concerns about vaccine safety ($R^2 = 0.13$; $F_{10\,376} = 5.51$; $P < .001$).
[c] This subscale assessed beliefs about the importance of immunization ($R^2 = 0.12$; $F_{10\,377} = 4.90$; $P < .001$).
[d] Reference group for language was English and mostly English.
[e] Western indicates health care from conventional American providers; traditional indicates care from Hmong shamans and herbalists. Reference group was Western health care providers in private practice and health maintenance organizations.

Source: Baker, Dian L., Michelle T. Dang, May Ying Ly, and Rafael Diaz. 2010. "Perception of Barriers to Immunization Among Parents of Hmong Origin in California." *American Journal of Public Health*, 100: 839–845.

SUMMARY
1

1.6: SUMMARY

The four literature excerpts in this chapter cover a diverse range of applications of regression analysis to examine interesting research questions. All represent research completed when the authors were graduate students with existing data sources.

Lyons' research on hate crimes shows that a seemingly positive aspect of community—social capital—can work to achieve ingroup goals at the cost of outgroup members. Socially organized areas are observed to have more antiblack hate crime. This is especially evident in primarily white communities that have experienced high levels of black in-migration. A different process applies for antiwhite hate crimes, which correlate with characteristics of neighborhoods as emphasized by general theories of crime, especially residential instability.

Vaisey's research shows that all communes are not the same. Frequent interactions among members and investments in the commune are not sufficient to produce a sense of collective belonging; rather, interactions and investments need to occur in the context of shared values and beliefs to produce belonging. Vaisey also unexpectedly finds that once these values, and aspects of structure, are adjusted, strict authority can alienate members.

Li-Grining's research contributes to the growing literature on young children's ability to control impulses, an important factor in later school success. She found that low-income boys are generally less able than low-income girls to delay behavioral impulses and this is particularly true for boys born with low birthweight. Her large data set allowed her better to test for differences by race than prior studies, and she found evidence of similarity in impulse control among low-income children from different racial backgrounds.

Baker and colleagues offer new insights into why Hmong children have such low immunization rates, finding parents who have less socio-economic status, speak less English, and use traditional medicine perceive more barriers. Their research is important, given the particularly high rates of cervical and liver cancer among the Hmong, cancers which can be prevented through better immunization.

In future chapters we will dig deeper to understand questions these excerpts may have raised for you. For example: how do we interpret the size (not just the significance and sign) of coefficients? Why do coefficients change when other variables are controlled? How exactly does the regression model test for an interaction? We hope that these excerpts spark enthusiasm for answering these questions and learning how to implement regression models in your own work.

KEY TERMS

KEY TERMS
1

Dependent Variable (or Outcome Variable)

Independent Variable (Predictor Variable or Explanatory Variable)

Mechanisms

Observational Data

Regression Analysis

CHAPTER EXERCISES

CHAPTER
EXERCISES
1

1.1. Locate a journal article using regression analyses, preferably on a topic of interest to you. You can use an article you already have or draw something from the syllabus of one of your substantive classes or search a bibliographic database. Read (or reread) the article, paying particular attention to the research questions or hypothesis statements and how these are examined in the regression models. Examine at least one table of regression results in detail, and pull out some of the features that were discussed in this chapter (e.g., significance and sign of coefficients relevant to the study's research questions and hypotheses). Write a short paragraph discussing what is easiest and most difficult to understand about the article's regression analysis. Keep a copy of this article to revisit in the chapter exercise in the final chapter of the book.

1.2. Answer the following questions to help your instructor get to know you better and help you think about your goals for the course. Some questions may be difficult to answer, especially if your research interests and empirical approach are still developing, so answer as best you can. In addition to helping your instructor tailor lectures and interactions, this exercise can also help you to think about how to get the most out of the course.

(a) Have you taken previous statistics courses? (If yes, what/when? How well do you feel you mastered the material?)

(b) Have you worked, or are you currently working, as a research assistant on any research projects (qualitative and/or quantitative)?

(c) Have you collected your own data or analyzed existing data for a prior paper, including for an undergraduate senior thesis or a graduate master's thesis (qualitative and/or quantitative)?

(d) What do you hope to get out of the current class?

(e) Do you see yourself more as a qualitative researcher, a quantitative researcher, both, neither, or are you unsure? Elaborate as desired.

(f) What is the substantive area of your research (or what major topics do you think you would like to study as a graduate student)?

(g) Provide an example of a regression-type relationship from your area of research; that is, list an "outcome" (dependent variable) with one or more "predictors" (independent variables).

COURSE EXERCISE

COURSE EXERCISE 1

Write three research questions in your area of interest. Be sure to identify clearly the outcome (dependent variable) and one or more predictors of interest (independent variables) for each question. Ideally, your outcome could be measured continuously for at least one research question so it will be appropriate for the techniques learned in Part 2 of the book. You can either modify this outcome for use in Part 4 of the book, as we show how to do with chapter exercises, or also select outcomes with two or more categories for at least one of your research questions.

If you are able to write your research question ("Do earnings differ by gender?") as a hypothesis statement (e.g., "Women earn less than men.") you should do so, but if prior research and theory do not offer enough insights for a directional hypothesis statement, a nondirectional research question is fine at this stage.

If your interests are still developing, you may want to get ideas by scanning a number of articles, chapters or books from one of your substantive classes, perusing the table of contents of recent top journals in your field, or by conducting a few bibliographic literature searches with key terms of broad interest to you.

The research questions should be of interest to you and something that you would like to examine as you move forward with the course. They could be already well studied in your field (i.e., you do not need to identify a dissertation-type question that makes a novel contribution to the literature). You may modify and refine them as you progress, especially so that you can apply the techniques learned in future chapters (e.g., modeling different types of variable, testing for mechanisms, etc.).

Chapter 2

PLANNING A QUANTITATIVE RESEARCH PROJECT WITH EXISTING DATA

CHAPTER 2: PLANNING A QUANTITATIVE RESEARCH PROJECT WITH EXISTING DATA

A primary goal of this chapter is to help you to plan for a quantitative research project. Whether you collect your own data, or use existing data, careful planning will produce a more efficient project. You will be able to complete it more quickly and to interpret the results more easily than you could otherwise. At the planning stage you should think through questions such as: what variables are needed to operationalize my concepts? Can I predict the direction of association between each predictor variable and the outcome? Do I anticipate that any predictor variables' associations with the outcome may change when confounding variables are included in the models? Do I anticipate that any predictor variables' associations with the outcome will differ for various subgroups? Doing so can help you to choose from among existing data sets (selecting the one that has the right variables and sample coverage). Forward thinking should save you time in the long run, because you will be less likely to have to backtrack to create additional variables or to rerun earlier analyses. Forward thinking will also help you to avoid being unable to examine particular research questions because subsamples are too small or constructs were not measured.

We focus on existing data in this book. We expose you to numerous data sets that are readily available on the Web. Knowing about these data sets should make it easier for you to engage in using regression analyses to examine research questions of interest to you. This chapter also contributes to our goal of leveling the playing field by offering information about where and how to look for such existing data, since not all students will have access to this information through mentors and peers.

Generally, existing data sources also have three distinct advantages over collecting new data:

1. They often provide designs and sample sizes that support more complex regression models and hypothesis tests.
2. They allow research questions to be addressed when resources for collecting new data are limited.
3. Their use provides a greater return on public investment in large-scale data collection.

There are instances where regression analysis might be used on non-random samples (Berk 2004). But, in order to support statistical tests based on regression analyses—and thus test hypotheses or answer research questions—a sample of adequate size (e.g., often 100 or more cases) should be drawn randomly from a known population. More complicated models, with more variables and interactions among variables, require even larger sample sizes, overall and within subgroups. Yet, gathering large-scale data sets drawn systematically from populations is expensive. If an existing data set has the relevant measures to answer a social scientist's research question, then the research can be conducted more quickly and with less cost than if the researcher attempted to gather new data. Turning first to existing data also best utilizes scarce resources for funding new studies. And, first testing a research question on existing data can provide the preliminary answers needed to modify the research questions and to demonstrate competence for seeking funding for new data collection.

That said, even though we focus on existing data in this chapter, the general strategies about planning for the analysis at the data-gathering stage also apply generally for your own data collection (e.g., being sure you ask all the questions needed to operationalize your constructs and oversample subgroups when needed). You should, of course, consult with mentors and, where needed, take advanced courses to prepare to implement your own data collection. We assume that you have taken, or will take, a basic research methods class, which covers a range of data collection methodologies.

2.1: SOURCES OF EXISTING DATA

Existing data come from a number of sources, including:

- multi-data set **archives**;
- single-data set archives;
- individual researchers.

Table 2.1 provides links to the resources we discuss below in each of these categories. Before turning to that discussion, we first want to emphasize the importance of checking with your local Institutional Review Board (IRB) regarding necessary IRB approval if you plan to use one of these sources for research purposes (versus for educational purposes only, such as course exercises). It may seem that IRB approval is not needed since some existing data sets are prepared for **public release**, for example with careful removal of all identifying information, and can be downloaded from the Web. Indeed, some local IRBs have determined that publicly available data sets accessed from preapproved data archives do not involve human subjects and thus do not require IRB review. But, current human subjects' policy requires researchers to verify this with their local IRB, rather than making such determinations independently (see Box 2.1 for an example). Some existing data sets also require special data use or data security agreements, for example that spell out special precautions for limiting access to the data. If you want to use these data for research, you should build in time for completing these agreements, which may require signatures from your adviser and administrators at your university, and for review by your local IRB. Some **restricted-use data sets** cannot be sent to you, but can be analyzed in special secure locations. These data sets require the greatest time lags for approvals, including local IRB review.

■ Box 2.1

The University of Chicago's Social and Behavioral Sciences Institutional Review Board provides a nice summary of its policies and procedures for four types of existing data sets: *http://humansubjects.uchicago.edu/sbsirb/publicpolicy.html*.

2.1.1: Multi-Data Set Archives

One of the oldest and largest multi-data set archives is the Inter-University Consortium for Political and Social Research (ICPSR; see Table 2.1). ICPSR began in 1962 to archive data from computer-based studies in political science. In the mid-1970s, the name "social" was added to the title to reflect the broader set of disciplines that were archiving data (Vavra 2002). The

Table 2.1 Examples of Data Archives

ICPS1A

General Multi-data Set Archives

Inter-University Consortium for Political and Social Research (ICPSR)	http://www.icpsr.org/
Henry A. Murray Research Archive at Harvard University	http://www.murray.harvard.edu/
Sociometrics	http://www.socio.com/

Government Multi-data Set Archives

US Census Bureau	
American FactFinder	http://factfinder2.census.gov/
Census Data Products	http://www.census.gov/mp/www/cat/
Integrated Public Use Microdata Series (IPUMS)	http://www.ipums.umn.edu/
NCHS Public Use Data	http://www.cdc.gov/nchs/surveys.htm
NCES Surveys and Programs	http://nces.ed.gov/pubsearch/surveylist.asp
NCHS Research Data Center	http://www.cdc.gov/rdc
Census Research Data Centers	http://www.census.gov/ces

Single-Data Set Archives

National Survey of Families and Households	http://www.ssc.wisc.edu/nsfh/
Urban Communes Data Set	http://sociology.rutgers.edu/ucds/ucds.htm
Three City Study	http://www.jhu.edu/welfare

Notes: NCHS = National Center for Health Statistics; NCES = National Center for Education Statistics.

founders recognized the need to store centrally the growing amounts of quantitative data being collected by political scientists across the country. This allowed other scientists not only to replicate the findings of the original scholar, but also to tap the data for additional purposes, beyond those within the interests and time limits of the original scholar (Vavra 2002; see Box 2.2). The archive is housed at the Institute for Social Research at the University of Michigan and over 600 universities from across the world are institutional members, giving their faculty and students access to tens of thousands of data sets.

Data sharing is common today in part because funders often require it. For example, the National Institutes of Health (NIH) now requires that all proposals requesting $500,000 or more in direct costs in any single year must include a plan for sharing the data (with appropriate removal of identifying information to protect confidentiality). In its policy, NIH notes the intention to give broader access to the data, once the original researchers have had a chance to pursue their main research objectives: "initial investigators may benefit from first and continuing use but not from prolonged exclusive use" (NIH 2003). Thus, archives have become important, as investigators deposit their data to meet such requirements.

Box 2.2

Today's new user of ICPSR is used to having a wealth of data at her fingertips over the Internet. The remarkable achievement underlying this ease of access to data sets spanning centuries is easy to overlook. Especially in recent decades, the speed with which hardware and software advanced made data sets vulnerable to being inaccessible, even if their files were stored. In other words, data sets stored in formats written for now obsolete operating systems or statistical packages are not directly readable on today's computers. Fortunately, the archives had the foresight to convert these data sets to more general formats, making them still usable to today's researchers (Vavra 2002).

ICPSR's coverage is the broadest among today's major data archives. At the time of this writing, ICPSR used 23 thematic collections covering broad topics including aging, criminal justice, demography, education, health and mental health, race and ethnicity, and terrorism. Data can also be browsed across 19 topics, including community and urban studies, education, health care and facilities, organizational behavior, and social institutions and behavior. The subtopic of family and gender, within social institutions and behavior, returns 160 results, ranging from one-time polls to multiyear surveys. A bibliography of publications using the archived data sets includes over 60,000 citations.

Two other data archives often used by social scientists are the Henry A. Murray Research Archive at Harvard University and the Sociometrics Archive (see again Table 2.1). The Murray Archive archives quantitative and qualitative data from the Institute for Quantitative Social Science (IQSS) and the IQSS DataVerse Network in areas including diversity, economic theory, demography, education, family, health, politics, and work. The Sociometrics archive focuses on nine topics: teen pregnancy, family, aging, disability, maternal drug abuse, HIV/AIDS STI, contextual data, child poverty, and complementary alternative medicine.

Federal government agencies also provide direct access to data that they gather. Census data, aggregated to geographic areas such as states, counties, and census tracts, are available freely from the Web or for purchase on DVD. Most students are familiar with the decennial census of population, but data are also available from the economic censuses, which survey business establishments every five years. Individual level data from the Decennial Census of Population are also available through the Integrated Public Use Microdata Series (IPUMS).[1] Similarly, the National Center for Health Statistics and the National Center for Education Statistics also make numerous data sets available, in public use and restricted formats.

The costs of accessing these data range from zero to several hundreds of dollars. Data in the ICPSR archive are free to faculty and students at ICPSR member institutions. In most cases, individual faculty and students can create an account using their institutional affiliation, and download data and documentation directly from the ICPSR web site.[2] Some of the other data resources are also freely available on the Web (e.g., Census American FactFinder, IPUMS); others have data set-specific use agreements and fees. Sometimes, multiple archives contain the same data set; at other times, a data set is available in only one archive, or is available in more detail in one archive. So, it is worth searching several archives when initially exploring data sets for a topic.

In addition to these resources, which allow a copy of the data to be analyzed at the researcher's place of work (sometimes with specific requirements to limit others' access to the data), the US Census Bureau and National Center for Health Statistics also make data available to researchers at several Research Data Centers across the country (the Web addresses listed in Table 2.1 include descriptions of the data sets available at the centers). Currently, there are Census Research Data Centers located in Berkeley, Los Angeles, and Stanford, CA; Chicago, IL; Ann Arbor, MI; Boston, MA; Ithaca and New York, NY; Washington DC; Durham, NC, and Minneapolis, MN. The NCHS has one Research Data Center, located in Hyattsville, MD, but the NCHS data sets and data from the Agency for Health Care Research are also available through the Census centers. At these sites researchers can access data that are not included in public releases. For example, researchers can identify individuals at small levels of geography and match the individuals to information about these contexts. In addition, firm-level data from the economic censuses can be linked across time to study the births and deaths of organizations. Although the time to get approval is longer for these restricted-use data than with publicly available data sets, and the fees for using the center can raise the cost of a project, these centers allow scholars to pursue unique and innovative projects.

2.1.2: Single-Data Set Archives

Some investigators archive their data individually. Sometimes these data sets are also available through multi-data archives. For example, the National Survey of Families and Households (NSFH), which we will use for examples throughout the book, maintains its own web site from which data and documentation can be freely downloaded. The first two waves of this data set are also available through the ICPSR and Sociometrics archives.

The data sets used in the literature excerpts in Chapter 1 also illustrate the range of access points for some data sets. The Project on Human Development in Chicago Neighborhoods, used in the first excerpt in Chapter 1, does not maintain its own public archive, but is available through ICPSR and the Murray Archive. The Urban Communes Data Set, which was used in the second excerpt highlighted in Chapter 1, is available freely on its own web site (once researchers establish a login and password) but is not available through any archives. The Three City Study, used in the third excerpt from Chapter 1, is documented on its own web site and the data are available from the Sociometrics and ICPSR archives. Table 2.1 provides links to each of the individual data set web sites.

2.1.3: Individual Researchers

It is also sometimes possible to access data through proximity to or a relationship with an individual researcher. Obvious cases are graduate students analyzing data collected by their advisers (or by other members of their department or university). Such data may not be generally publicly available, but accessible through local access or personal relationships. One example of reanalysis of locally available existing data is Robert Sampson and John Laub's use of data on juvenile delinquents originally gathered by Sheldon and Eleanor Glueck. As the authors write in their book *Crime in the Making* (1995: 1):

> Eight years ago we stumbled across . . . dusty cartons of data in the basement of the Harvard Law School Library . . . These data, along with the Gluecks' eighteen-year follow-up of the 1,000 subjects . . . were given to the Harvard Law School Library in 1972 . . . The papers and other items were sorted and fully cataloged as part of the Glueck archive. The cartons of data were simply stored in the sub-basement of the library.

The data had been gathered decades earlier, and were stored in boxes, rather than electronically. Thus, the first step Sampson and Laub took before analyzing these data involved extensive recoding and entering of the data. These investments paid off. Applying modern data analytic techniques to the data provided new insights into the correlates of juvenile crime and the factors that lead to stability and change in criminal behavior into adulthood (for example, the book won the annual book award from the American Society of Criminology). The data are now in the Murray Archive. You may similarly be able to access data through local depositories or personal networks.

2.2: THINKING FORWARD

Whether selecting an existing data set or planning for new data collection, thinking forward will improve the chances that your data can address your research interests and will reduce time spent on correcting course. Again, we focus on planning a project with existing data, because the details of planning and executing new data collection are beyond the scope of this textbook and are often taught in research methods courses.

Some key questions that can help to guide your selection of an existing data set include:

1. How was the sample identified?
2. What was the response rate?
3. How can I operationalize my key constructs with these data (including mechanisms through which a key variable associates with the outcome)?
4. Does the data set measure important confounding variables?
5. Do any of my research questions suggest that an association of a key predictor with the outcome differs by subgroups? If so, are the sample sizes large enough for these subgroups in the data set?

When multiple data sources exist that might address your research interests, the strengths and limitations of each data set across these questions can help you to choose among them (for example, all else equal, a data set with a higher response rate and larger sample would be preferred).

In choosing among data sets, it is also useful to consider constraints on time, money, and other resources, such as:

- What is your deadline?
- How much time and money can you devote to obtaining and analyzing the data by that deadline?
- How experienced are you already with statistical programming?

Clearly, planning for a course project differs from planning a thesis or dissertation. And, achieving goals by a deadline is easier if it covers a period with few other time demands (a summer semester funded by a fellowship versus a fall semester juggling other classes and teaching or research assistantships). In general, researchers tend to underestimate the time needed to complete a project using existing data. The time frame seems shorter because the data have already been gathered. Yet, time needs to be built in for locating the data set, understanding its design, extracting and coding variables from the raw data, running descriptive analyses, estimating regression models, and interpreting the results. Throughout, time is also needed to adequately double-check and document your work. More time is needed for each of these tasks when you are new to quantitative research and whenever using a new data set. When you have other concurrent demands and a short time frame (such as when writing a course paper), you may want to choose a data set with a simpler design (e.g., **cross-sectional** versus **longitudinal**) and to simplify your research questions where possible (e.g., replicate or modestly extend an existing study). For projects with longer timelines and higher expectations (such as theses or dissertations), you will likely want to take advantage of data sets with more complex designs and to address more nuanced questions.

As with other aspects of your research, you should draw on as much information as possible to identify the best existing data set for your particular research interests. This might include conversations with mentors and peers, looking at what data sets are used in published books and articles in your area, and searching archives on your topic. A review article on the topic of interest, for example in the *Annual Reviews*, may be a helpful starting point. Using the *Web of Science* to search forward and backward from the citations of key articles will likely be useful as well.[3] You may find it helpful to move back and forth among these strategies (talk to colleagues, read articles, search online) as you identify possible data sets and home in on those most relevant to your questions.

Because the ICPSR archive covers the largest number of data sets and broadest range of subjects, we will use it as an example. We will illustrate how to search for a data set relevant to a topic that we will then use as an example in the remainder of the book.

2.3: EXAMPLE RESEARCH QUESTIONS

Because we are using a research question for pedagogical purposes, we chose a fairly straightforward topic with a good body of literature. The data set we chose allows for more complicated analyses, but for instructional purposes we will focus on a small set of straightforward variables taken from one time point of the longitudinal study.

The research question involves the distance adults live from their mothers. The topic is important because at the same time that there may be benefits from moves away from family (such as access to new labor markets or a particular job) there may also be costs, both for an adult child who moves away (such as less access to help with childcare) and an adult parent who is left behind (such as less access to help during old age; Mulder 2007). Although some aspects of emotional and instrumental support can occur at a distance, direct instrumental support, such as assistance with childcare or household chores, require physical proximity. Prior studies have confirmed that such practical assistance is more likely when adult children live close to parents (Cooney and Uhlenberg 1992) and are less mobile (Magdol and Bessel 2003). There is also empirical support for a relationship between living close to family and frequency of contact (Lawton, Silverstein, and Bengtson 1994), and more frequent contact has in turn been associated with less loneliness (Pinquart 2003). One set of geographers argue that:

> Progress in understanding the nature and effects of kin proximity is of paramount importance if we are to be well prepared for the planning and policy decision that will accompany the arrival of the baby boom generation into its elderly years (Rogerson, Weng, and Lin 1993).

Prior literature has examined a number of correlates of geographic proximity, suggesting that characteristics of both the adult child and their parent will be relevant. For example, studies have found that higher education is associated with long-distance moves in general (Clark and Withers 2007) and distance from parents in particular (Rogerson, Weng, and Lin 1993). Having siblings, particularly sisters, has been found to reduce an individual's time spent on care for aging parents (Wolf, Freedman, and Soldo 1997), and the presence of siblings and sisters has been found to relate to greater distance from parents, although not always in expected ways (Michielin and Mulder 2007). Some research also suggests that women and minorities live closer to parents (Roan and Raley 1996). We will focus specifically on the following questions as we learn about the basic regression model in the remainder of the book:

■ Do higher education and earnings predict greater distance from the mother?
■ How do the number of brothers and sisters associate with distance from the mother?
■ How does proximity to the mother vary by the respondent's gender and race-ethnicity?

We will also adjust for the age of the respondent and mother in our models.

This example will raise a number of issues that we will resolve in later chapters. For example, what is the best approach to examining an outcome that is highly skewed (addressed in Chapter 12)? How can we best capture the effect of count and categorical predictor variables (such as number of siblings), especially when we anticipate that associations are not linear (addressed in Chapters 10 and 12)? In earlier chapters, we will look at simpler models that associate the continuous outcome (ignoring skewness) with continuous predictors. In later chapters, we will introduce other approaches for modeling these outcomes and predictors as well as strategies for thinking about which models are most conceptually appropriate and how to test between them empirically. In the remainder of this chapter, we illustrate how to locate a data set to examine these questions. We will identify, extract, and prepare the relevant variables in Chapters 3 and 4.

2.4: EXAMPLE OF LOCATING STUDIES IN ICPSR

Like most web sites, the ICPSR web site is regularly updated. Thus, the site's functionality may change after this book has been published. Here, we talk about three broad strategies that are likely to persist even in future releases:

(a) browsing the data holdings;
(b) searching the data holdings;
(c) searching the bibliography.

In most cases, using all three strategies will help you either to assure yourself that you have found the best data for your question (because it turns up through all three methods) or to help you to identify a data set (when two of the three come up empty). We used these three approaches to identify the data set used as an example throughout the book: the National Survey of Families and Households.

2.4.1: Browsing the Data Holdings

Browsing the ICPSR archives may take some time, but will give you the broadest overview of holdings in your area of interest. Such browsing may be especially helpful to stimulate and refine your research ideas, since it will expose you to a wide array of data sets available in the ICPSR archives.

Display C.2.1 shows the result after selecting the thematic area of "Social Institutions and Behavior" (found from the main page by choosing Find & Analyze Data) from the window, then selecting Browse By Topic, then choosing "H. Family and Gender", from within Social Institutions and Behavior, and then sorting by "Most Downloaded" and sorting by relevance. The results illustrate the broad array of studies available in the ICPSR archive, ranging from national surveys to studies of particular cities. The topics range from adolescent health to immigration to welfare to time use.

The number at the left of each study title is the ICPSR Study Number. It is helpful to take note of these numbers as you browse and identify studies of potential interest. You can use these easily to locate a study again in the archive (as discussed below).

Beyond its general archive, ICPSR also collaborates with other groups on special topic archives, such as on aging, childcare, crime, demography, education, health and medicine, and psychiatric epidemiology (found under Partners & Projects/Thematic Collections on the main page). For example, if your topic was on aging, you might go to the National Archive of Computerized Data on Aging and then use its thematic areas to narrow the studies for browsing.

The upper right corner of Display C.2.1 shows the main search utility on the ICPSR web site. This utility searches across multiple sources, including the descriptions of archived studies, the full text of the documentation, the variables (for about one-fifth of data sets), and the related citations. You can list multiple words in the search window, and results are returned that contain all of the entered words.

2.4.2: Searching the Data Holdings

Beyond the main search utility, the advanced variable search (shown in Display C.2.2) may be helpful for finding candidate data sets. This utility allows you to drill down to see which data sets hold individual questions that are needed for your analysis. The search covers the text of questions and response options, the name and label for the variable, and any notes associated with the variable. The search is limited, however, in that at the time of this writing just about one-fifth of studies had entries in the variables database.

Like the main search utility, you can list multiple words in the search windows for the variables database and results are returned that contain all of the entered words. For example, we entered "miles mother" to search for questions that might include "How many miles do you live from your mother?"

2.4.3: Searching the Bibliography

Searching the ICPSR bibliography is also a helpful strategy, allowing you to locate studies that have been published on topics similar to your own. This approach allows you to both identify candidate data sets and also to understand what has already been published based on those data sets (so that you can think about how to replicate and extend prior studies). Display C.2.3 provides an example of the results we obtained by typing the words "proximity mother" into the bibliography search screen (like the main search, the bibliography search returns results that contain all of the words that you type). The results we obtained identified a number of studies that look of interest, in relation to the distance parents live from adult children. The right hand side of the screen also offers filters that allow us to focus within the results on publications by specific authors, of certain types, and in specific years.

2.4.4: Complex Sampling Designs

Many of the studies in the ICPSR archive have complex sampling designs rather than simple random sampling designs (Heeringa 2010; Kalton 1983; Kish 1965; Lehtonen and Pahkinen 1994). When using secondary data (or analyzing data that you have collected directly) it is important to understand the features of the study's design and account for these features in your analyses. We will learn how to account for the design features in future chapters, but here we describe the basic types of samples and important features of their sampling designs.

Simple random samples are drawn such that each member of the population has the same chance of being selected into the study. All of the techniques discussed in this book are appropriate for simple random samples. Simple random samples can be difficult to implement, however. For example, it is often impractical and prohibitively expensive to obtain a list of every member of the population from which to draw a simple random sample (this list is referred to as the **sampling frame**). This is often true of samples meant to represent the population of the United States; drawing a simple random sample would require a list of every individual in the United States.

Complex sampling designs are an alternative. Complex sampling designs can be less expensive and more practical than a simple random sample when they use multiple stages to define the sampling frame. For example, a study of households in the U.S. might first randomly draw a sample of cities and then randomly draw neighborhoods within those cities and finally list each household in the selected neighborhoods so that households can be randomly chosen for the study. The units selected at the first stage are referred to as **primary sampling units (PSUs)**, the units selected at the second stage are referred to as **secondary sampling units**, and the units selected at the third stage are referred to as **tertiary sampling units**. In our example, cities are the PSUs, neighborhoods are the secondary sampling units, and households are the tertiary sampling units. The PSUs are critical for analyses, and should be included in your data files if the study used a multi-stage design. The selected PSUs are sometimes referred to as **clusters** (Kish 1965; see Box 2.3).

Complex sampling designs can have additional features that distinguish them from a simple random sample, beyond a multi-stage design. The most common are **stratification** and **oversampling**.

At first blush, stratification seems similar to the sampling units used in multi-stage designs, but the intent and implications of the two are quite different. With stratification, the population is divided into groups, which we call subpopulations or strata, and a separate sample is drawn within each of these groups, or stratum. One reason for using such stratification might be that separate analyses are planned within the subpopulations, and sampling within strata can ensure sufficient numbers of sample members within each subpopulation. For example, if most preschoolers in a population were in center-based child care and a study investigator wanted to compare preschoolers in center-based care to preschoolers in home-based care, then separate samples of equal size might be drawn from two strata: center-based and home-based child care. When these separate samples are combined, members from each stratum are found in the full sample. This is in contrast to what we described above for PSUs. PSUs are typically used to reduce cost by only listing the subpopulation within certain selected PSUs. Only some PSUs are selected into the sample. Members of the population from non-selected PSUs are not found in the full sample (Murphy 2008).

Another way that strata differ from PSUs is regarding whether there is an attempt to draw them such that subpopulation members are more similar to each other than to members of other subpopulations. Strata are often designed in this way (e.g., two strata might be large and small cities, for example, and we might expect that residents of large cities share something in common, as might residents of small cities). This within-strata similarity can be beneficial for analyses (as we shall see in later chapters). Members of PSUs may share similarities but this is less by design (e.g., it may simply result from the typical geographic nature of PSUs and the fact that people who live near each other often share something in common, like similar SES). Importantly, similarity of members of the same PSUs is disadvantageous for analysis (in contrast to similarity of members of the same strata which is advantageous). If strata are used in your survey, an indicator of the strata should be included in your data files.

Oversampling refers to the situation when different members of the population have different probabilities of being selected into the sample, with some members being over-represented in the sample relative to the population (thus they are "over" sampled). Oversampling may be used when one group is relatively small in the population, but a sufficient number of that group is desired in the sample to support subgroup analyses. For example, racial-ethnic minority groups are often oversampled. As we will discuss in more detail in later chapters, sampling weights are used to adjust for oversampling. These sampling weights are especially important when full sample descriptions are provided (as opposed to analyses specific to over- and under-sampled groups or, as we will discuss later, sometimes in regression models). Imagine, for example, that we have a data set drawn from a population of whites and African Americans in which African

Americans as a minority are oversampled. Suppose that in the population 90% of people are white and just 10% African American, but the oversampling results in a sample that is 50% white and 50% African American. Without adjustment, characteristics of the sample as a whole will reflect this oversampling. For example, if African American's earn less than whites, then the average earnings in the sample will be lower than the average earnings in the population. As we shall see in more detail in later chapters, sampling weights allow us to adjust for this oversampling, such that the average earnings in the sample, with the weights applied, will more closely approximate the average earnings in the population. Survey statisticians sometimes also use weights to adjust for the fact that some selected members of the population did not participate in the survey (known as **adjustments for non-response**) or to assure that the distribution of the sample on key demographic variables matches the population (known as **post-stratification adjustments**). If your secondary data included oversampling, you should include the sampling weights in your files (see Box 2.4).

■ Box 2.4

Some surveys will include multiple sampling weights, and you may need to carefully read the documentation and perhaps consult with colleagues or the survey staff to choose from among them. For example, longitudinal studies sometimes provide separate weights for cross-sectional and longitudinal analyses.

When selecting a secondary data set, it is also helpful to pay attention to how the survey population is defined. Often, some exclusions are made from the full population, for cost and practical reasons. For example, surveys of individuals in the U.S. often exclude those in institutions, such as hospitals and prisons, and sometimes exclude those on active duty in the armed forces. It is important to be familiar with such exclusions as you describe the study and when you write about your results. In general, you should be sure you have thoroughly and carefully read the study's documentation such that you have a solid understanding of its design before you begin analyses. We will provide an orientation to study documentation, using the NSFH as an example, in Chapter 3.

2.4.5: Putting It All Together

It is useful to use multiple strategies to identify possible data sets. Especially for a project that will result in a thesis, dissertation, or published work, once you have identified a set of candidate data sets, it is helpful to complete a broader search for publications on your topic, especially those that have used the identified data set(s). The ICPSR bibliography is a good starting point (you can use the search utility to search by ICPSR study number). You can use the Web of Science to move forward and backward to studies that are cited by or cite these references. And, you can use bibliographic databases from your library, such as JSTOR ("Journal Storage"), ERIC ("Educational Resources Information Center"), PsycINFO (the electronic version of the older "Psychological Abstracts"), and Sociological Abstracts, to search abstracts and/or full text for key terms for publications you may have missed (e.g., for our question, we searched for "NSFH" or "National Study of Families and Households" combined with "proximity," "distance," or "miles"). You can also talk to mentors and peers who work on related topics and may know about additional data sets.

With existing data, it is possible that other students or scholars have already used the data set to examine questions similar to yours. Don't get immediately discouraged, though, if you find work on your topic. Be sure to read the publications, and determine if and how you can make a contribution. And, as we have noted, replicating and modestly extending prior studies is often a good starting point, especially for a course paper.

2.5: SUMMARY

In this chapter, we introduced various strategies you can use to locate existing data relevant to your research interests. We covered archives that encompass a single data set or multiple data sets (summarized in Table 2.1) and strategies for locating data through your professional network and local resources. We introduced one set of research questions that we will use as examples in Part 2, and illustrated how to locate data sets in the ICPSR to address these research questions. We emphasized the importance of using multiple strategies to locate relevant data, and for choosing among identified data sets.

KEY TERMS

Adjustments for non-response

Archive

Cluster

Complex Sampling Design

Cross-Sectional

ICPSR

Longitudinal

NSFH

Oversampling

Poststratification adjustments

Primary Sampling Unit (PSU)

Public Release (Data Set)

Restricted-Use (Data Set)

Sampling Frame

Sampling Weights

Simple Random Sample

Secondary Sampling Unit

Stratification

Tertiary Sampling Unit

REVIEW EXERCISE

REVIEW EXERCISE 2

Use the ICPSR to search for a data set that might address a specific hypothesis or research question (either a topic assigned by your instructor or voted on by your class, or a research question of interest to you). Follow each of the three strategies discussed in the chapter (browsing and searching the data holdings; searching the bibliography) to locate data sets. Write a short paragraph discussing what you take away from this process (were you surprised by the number of data sets that you located? Which approach did you find most useful?).

CHAPTER EXERCISE

CHAPTER EXERCISE 2

Locate the NSFH data in ICPSR. Read the study description. Search the bibliography for publications using this data set. Search at least one other bibliographic database for publications using the NSFH. Write a short paragraph about what you found (for example, were you surprised by the number of publications? Would the NSFH be relevant to your research interests?).

COURSE EXERCISE

COURSE EXERCISE 2

Use the ICPSR to locate possible data sets for each of your hypotheses or research questions. Use the procedures discussed in the chapter to scan the documentation on key study features, including the sampling design, coverage of relevant subpopulations, measures of conceptual constructs, and historical timing of data collection. Use what you find to focus or refine your research interests. For example, are no data sets available for some research questions? Are several data sets available for others? When multiple data sets are available, what are the advantages and limitations of each (e.g., in terms of sampling design, coverage of relevant subpopulations, measures of conceptual constructs, recency of collection, etc.)? If possible, you can extend your search for relevant data by talking to mentors and peers, your instructor and classmates, and through general searches of the literature on your topic. Putting together the results from your search of the ICPSR archive with these additional sources will help you to identify the best data for your research interests (recognizing that for the course, you may want to choose a simple question or data set given the limited time frame and your newness to programming).

Chapter 3

BASIC FEATURES OF STATISTICAL PACKAGES AND DATA DOCUMENTATION

CHAPTER 3: BASIC FEATURES OF STATISTICAL PACKAGES AND DATA DOCUMENTATION

Once you have gathered your data or identified an existing data set, you have the raw material needed to examine your research questions. As a scientist, your job is to put those raw materials together in a creative way to make a novel product. To do this, you need to understand those raw materials in detail—what information do you have, exactly, and where are they stored? And you need a **statistical package** to serve as your tool for implementing your ideas about how to put together those raw materials. In this chapter, we offer the basic strategies you need to follow in order to understand what is contained in a raw data file and its documentation and what the advantages are of using various statistical packages. In the next chapter, we will learn how to use those statistical packages to access the data and create some of the variables we will need for our quantitative analyses.

Typically, at this stage, we want to jump forward to see the statistical answer to our research questions. Yet, once the raw data are identified, much work remains to understand it, prepare it, and analyze it. Doing so in a steady, systematic fashion avoids later backtracking to correct errors and allows the documentation needed for replication. Although it may seem tedious, seasoned researchers know that time spent at this stage of a project is essential and will pay off many times over in the long run.

3.1: HOW ARE OUR DATA STORED IN THE COMPUTER?

To students new to quantitative data analysis, a data file may seem mysterious at first. In reality, the file is a simple transcription of the data. Quantitative data are stored in a matrix of rows and columns, in which each cell represents a specific data point. A **data point** captures how a particular respondent answered a particular question. Typically, your project will begin with what is called a **raw data file**. The *raw data file* contains the participants' exact responses to the study's instruments. By convention, each row represents a study participant. The participants could be people, or they could be other entities such as organizations, schools, states, or countries (they are often more generally referred to as **cases**). Each column represents a variable.

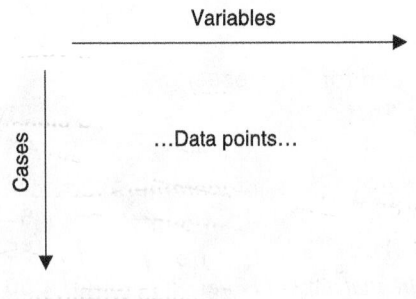

Typically, the first column contains a variable that identifies the participant (or case), often called a *caseid* for short. With public use data sets these **identifiers** are numbers and/or letters with no intrinsic meaning. The study investigators maintain a list that links the *caseid* to meaningful identifiers (the individual's first and last name or the name of the organization or geographic area). The process of removing all meaningful identifiers is called **de-identification**. This de-identification is a critical part of the process of preparing data for public release. It allows other researchers to analyze a data set while protecting the identity and preserving the confidentiality of the study participants (see Box 3.1). Although you will not use the *caseid* in basic statistical analysis, it is good practice to keep it in your data file. For example, you will need to if you ever need to link to other study information about participants (e.g., if the study's data are stored in multiple files or the study follows participants across multiple waves; See Box 3.2).

Table 3.1 illustrates how data might be arranged for some variables relevant to our example research questions, with the *caseid* in the first column and then the mother's education and age (in years) and distance from the respondent (in miles).

■ Table 3.1

caseid	momeduc	momage	mommiles	...
9332	13	73	4	...
8454	11	55	6	...
3743	15	42	1202	...
2581	2	65	13	...
5617	6	56	287	...
4668	4	57	348	...
1533	10	50	12	...
.	.	.	.	.
.	.	.	.	.
.	.	.	.	.

The first respondent in this hypothetical data set was given the *caseid* of 9332 by the study and reported that her mother had 13 years of schooling, was 73 years old, and lived 4 miles away. The seventh respondent in the datafile was given the *caseid* of 1533 and reported that his mother had 10 years of schooling, was 50 years old, and lived 12 miles away. Typically, the order of the variables follows the order of administration in the survey (the first variable in the first column, second in the second, and so on).

In the past, the raw data file was typically first stored in an *ascii* or **plain text file**, with just rows and columns of numbers. This plain text file could be viewed through any software program on any computer, including a text editor like Notepad. For example, the data from Table 3.1 above might have been represented as follows and saved as plain text:

■ Box 3.1

If you are analyzing data that you gathered, de-identification is still a good practice. When your project went through IRB approval, you were likely asked how you would protect the confidentiality of respondents. For example, you may keep a master list linking *caseids* to names in a locked file cabinet. Any data sets kept on your computer would include only the *caseid* as a variable.

■ Box 3.2

In more complicated designs, a data set may have more than one identifier. For example, your data set may have information about multiple members of a family. In this case, each family would have an identifier (perhaps called a *famid*). And, each member would have a unique identifier (perhaps called the *personid*). All members of the same family would have the same *famid*. But, each family member would have her own *personid*. Or, your data set might have information about multiple students in a classroom (in which case you would have separate identifiers for classes and for students). Or, your data set might have information about multiple families within neighborhoods, and separate identifiers for neighborhoods and families.

```
9332 13 73 4
8454 11 55 6
3743 15 42 1202
2581 2 65 13
5617 6 56 287
4668 4 57 348
1533 10 50 12
. . .
```

On its own, this data file is simply a series of numbers. To interpret these numbers requires information about what each value represents. The column labels in Table 3.1 gave us some information, but the information needed to interpret the numbers fully would more generally be found in the data's documentation. To prepare the data for analysis by a statistical package, we would need to instruct the software on what each value means. For example, we would tell the software which variables are located in which position (e.g., the case identifier, then the mother's education, then the mother's age, then the distance away the mother lives, separated by spaces). And, we would choose variable names for each variable (such as *caseid*, *momeduc*, *momage*, and *mommiles*). We might want to label the variables to remind ourselves about important details found in the documentation (e.g., that *momeduc* and *momage* are recorded in years and *mommiles* is recorded in miles). Our instructions would convert the numbers into a data file format that the statistical package recognizes. Once converted, the data would be ready for analysis by that statistical package, and could be saved in that package's format (see Box 3.3).

■ **Box 3.3**

You probably have experience with such software-specific files in word processing. A WordPerfect file is in a particular format. A Microsoft Word file is in another format. One format cannot be read directly by the other software, although nowadays the packages often have built-in conversion utilities (accessed by selecting the type of file from the File/Open menu). We will discuss some similar conversion utilities for statistical software below and in Chapter 4.

In the past, scientists received data in plain text format and needed to write instructions such as these to "read" the data. This process was time-consuming and error-prone. As we will see in our NSFH example, these days, the raw data file can often be obtained directly from an archive in a format ready to be directly understood by the statistical package. But, it still can be viewed in a row and column format, similar to Table 3.1.

3.2: WHY LEARN BOTH SAS AND STATA?

Many basic tools for working with the raw data—statistical packages—exist, and a first step in our project is to choose which tool to use. General purpose statistical software can accomplish a wide array of functions, ranging from **data management** (e.g., defining new variables) to **data analysis** (e.g., calculating statistics). You have likely heard of some of the most common statistical packages, such as SPSS, SAS, and Stata. Others exist as well (e.g., R, Minitab, S-Plus, Systat). Special purpose software typically has fewer data management utilities, and focuses on a particular statistical technique (often advanced techniques with names like "structural equation modeling" or "hierarchical linear modeling"). We include two general purpose packages—SAS and Stata—in this book. It is worth taking a moment to explain why, since some students in the social sciences find it tedious and frustrating to learn one statistical package, let alone two.

3.2.1: Social Scientists Commonly Use Multiple Statistical Packages

Many scholars today who regularly conduct quantitative research move back and forth among statistical packages. They are not "SAS users" or "SPSS users" or "Stata users." Rather, they choose one software package over another for a particular research project because one has a unique feature or capability needed for that project. Or, they may use a software package because another researcher or group of researchers in a collaboration uses that package. Some researchers use one package to manage the data and create variables (e.g., SAS) and another to run regression analyses (e.g., Stata). This is possible because data can now be easily moved between formats using file conversion software, such as StatTransfer and DBMS/Copy, which have been available since the mid-1990s (Hilbe 1996). With file conversion software, the researcher need only click a couple of buttons to tell the conversion software where the original file is located and its format and where to store the new file and in what new format (e.g., SAS, Stata, or SPSS). Depending on the size of the file, it typically takes only seconds to convert from one format to another. So, today, it is easy to use whichever software tool is best suited to the particular task at hand or particular collaborative project.

3.2.2: Different Packages Fit the Needs of Different Students and Instructors

Including both SAS and Stata in parallel fashion in the book also offers flexibility to the mixture of instructors and students teaching and taking graduate statistics courses in the social sciences. Your instructor may choose to focus on SAS or Stata because it fits her expertise or the local resources better (i.e., your access to SAS or Stata). Your instructor may also choose to focus on one, rather than teach both, because the majority of students in the class are apprehensive about learning statistics and are uncertain about using quantitative methods. In such cases, the book meets the needs of the subset of students who are eager to learn statistical computing. If you fit in that group, you can work through the examples using the second language on your own. Other students may realize after finishing the course that they need to know the other package in order to meet the needs of their thesis, dissertation, or research project. If you need to do so, you can easily go back and rework examples or revisit the parallel commands in the other package after completing the course.

Including both packages, and allowing students to learn the second package on their own during the course or afterward also meets the book's goal of preparing students for advanced courses and research assistantships. Sometimes, instructors in advanced courses require students to use a particular package, use multiple packages, or use a specialized package targeted at the technique being taught. Similarly, some faculty use a particular statistical package across projects or for a given project, and want research assistants to use that package. In either case, at least being exposed to (if not learning) both SAS and Stata offers you an advantage because:

(a) one or the other may be the package used in the course or by the faculty member, or (b) when you do not feel wedded to one package (you have seen the parallel language of another package), you will feel more comfortable and find it easier to learn an additional package (including others beyond SAS and Stata).

3.2.3: Each Package has Relative Strengths

As you prepare to learn SAS and Stata, it is also helpful to know something about their general comparative advantages, as well as those of SPSS (which is used within or alongside many introductory statistics textbooks).

Many researchers view SAS as having a comparative advantage in data management. As Alan Acock (2005: 1093) wrote in a review of SAS, Stata, and SPSS: "SAS is the first choice of many power users . . . The most complex data sets we use hardly tap the capability of SAS for data management." On the other hand, SAS is often seen as relatively difficult to learn. As Acock put it (2005: 1093–4): "SAS is a long way down the list on ease of use . . . Graduate instruction on methods gets bogged down on how to use SAS rather than on methodological and statistical issues." The documentation for SAS is extensive, with details that an advanced user will appreciate but that make it hard to find answers to the new user's common questions. We address these challenges of learning SAS by teaching selective aspects of its extensive capabilities and by doing so in small doses that are connected to the statistical techniques and substantive examples of each chapter of the book.

In contrast, SPSS's comparative advantage is ease of use, but with lesser capabilities for data management or statistical analysis. As Acock (2005: 1094) wrote:

> SPSS is the first choice for the occasional user who is doing basic data management and statistical analysis . . . [However] looking to the future, it is fair to say that it will be the weakest of the three packages in the scope of statistical procedures it offers. It can manage complex data sets, but often relies on brute force in the code required to do this.

Its Windows-based "point and click" interface makes it easy for users to open a data set and conduct analyses by choosing a procedure and variables from the menus. But, for social scientists, we argue that it is easier to organize and document a research project, even a seemingly small and simple project, using batch programming code. Although it is possible to write in SPSS code (or ask SPSS to generate the code written "behind the scenes" of the Windows interface), the actual code in SPSS is no easier to write and understand than the code in Stata or SAS. Finally, as Acock puts it "SPSS is the easiest of the three packages to grow out of" (Acock 2005: 1094). Because you cannot predict where your interests will take you, we see teaching in SAS and Stata as preferable to SPSS. We try to make this easier by using strategies that simplify teaching each language.

Stata is usually viewed as somewhere in between SAS and SPSS on these fronts, easier to learn and use than SAS but with stronger data management and statistical analysis capabilities than

SPSS. Stata also stays at the forefront of statistical analysis because it is easy for users to write code for things they would like to do but are not yet in the official release (Kolenikov 2001). Scholars regularly share such code, and user-written code is generally easy to install from the Internet. Not only does some such code allow users to conduct cutting-edge statistical analyses, but some code is also written explicitly to help users interpret and present results (e.g., code for interpreting regression models written by Long and Freese, see Long 2007; code for presenting results written by Ben Jann, see Jann 2007). As Acock wrote (2005: 1094–5) "Although Stata has the smallest development team, all their efforts are focused on the statistical needs of scholars. Looking to the future, Stata may have the strongest collection of advanced statistical features." Stata's code is also especially easy to pick up because it is very consistent across commands. Once you know how to write the command for one type of regression model in Stata, it is easy to write the command to run most types of regression models. Like SPSS's Windows-based interface, it is also easy to sit down and conduct analyses interactively with Stata's command line. This allows you to run a quick command or explore the data while staying within the straightforward and consistent Stata command language. Such interactive sessions can be tracked, and the code can be edited to the final desired results and saved for project documentation.

In short, we use both SAS and Stata because they are best suited to the needs of social scientists. Our goal is to present them in a parallel fashion so that it is easy for students to see the similarities (and differences) between the languages. And, we use a slow and steady building of knowledge and skills together in statistics and statistical programming. Let's get started!

3.3: GETTING STARTED WITH A QUANTITATIVE RESEARCH PROJECT

In the remainder of this chapter we will use the National Survey of Families and Households and the research questions presented in Chapter 2 as an example of getting started with a quantitative research project. We will cover the following topics:

- What are the basic SAS and Stata files?
- What are some good ways to organize these files?
- How do we identify the variables needed for our research question from a larger existing data set?

In Chapter 4, we will learn how to actually use the software to prepare the data for our regression models. To simplify what we need to teach at the outset, we save some basic data management tasks for later chapters (e.g., creating indicators for categorical variables), although in a real project you would implement them at this stage also.

3.3.1: What are the Basic SAS and Stata Files?

SAS and Stata are sometimes referred to as languages as well as statistical packages. Each has its own syntax which we use to tell the computer how to perform a particular task. Usually, both packages can achieve the same objective. Often, the syntax is similar in each language, but with slightly different conventions. There are some resulting benefits and costs of these similarities and differences, as with spoken languages: it is easier to learn a second language once you've learned one; but, when learning a second language, you can get confused, sometimes merging the two languages when you speak. Throughout the book, we set the syntax for the two packages side-by-side, making these similarities and differences very clear (and offering a ready reference to look up the details when forgotten).

The similarities and differences between the languages are also evident in the basic files used by each package. Display A.3 lists the three basic kinds of files used and created by each statistical package: data, batch programs, and results. Each has a standard extension, also listed in Display A.3. (As you probably know, an extension consists of the letters following the "." after a file name.)

It is best to stick with conventions, and use the file extensions listed in Display A.3. Even if, for example, using an extension like *.prg* would help you initially remember that a file contains a batch program, in the long run you will find it easier if you use the conventions *.sas* and *.do* for SAS and Stata batch programs, respectively, especially as you interact with others who use each package. Your computer also uses such extensions to determine which software to use to open a file, known as **file associations** (e.g., *.wpd* is usually associated with WordPerfect files; *.docx* is usually associated with Microsoft Word files). With a standard installation, your computer will associate the standard SAS and Stata extensions with the respective software, making it easy to launch the software by double-clicking an associated file. It is helpful to keep in mind, though, that there is nothing inherent in the extension that alters the content of the file (if you changed an extension from *.wpd* to *.docx* without converting the contents, the contents would remain in their original WordPerfect format). Some extensions will be assigned by default when SAS and Stata create files (e.g., when saving data files in the package's format). Some you will assign (e.g., when you write commands in batch programs).

Data Files

We already discussed above the contents of a raw data file. Display A.3 shows us that the typical extensions for raw data files are *.dat, .raw*, and *.txt* for the plain text versions and *.sas7bdat* and *.dta* for the SAS and Stata versions. The extensions *.sas7bdat* and *.dta* are also used for other data files that you create with the respective software. If your computer has SAS or Stata installed on it, and you (or your university's computer staff) allowed the default file associations with the installation, then the computer should recognize files with these extensions as SAS and Stata files, respectively (thus double clicking on the file will launch the associated software).

Below, we provide examples of two hypothetical data files in the folder *c:\data*. Notice in the Name column that each file has the extension relevant for each package (*.dta* for Stata; *.sas7bdat* for SAS). In the Type column we see that the computer recognizes the *.dta* file as a Stata dataset and the *.sas7bdat* file as a SAS data set. Thus, double clicking on either file would launch the appropriate software.

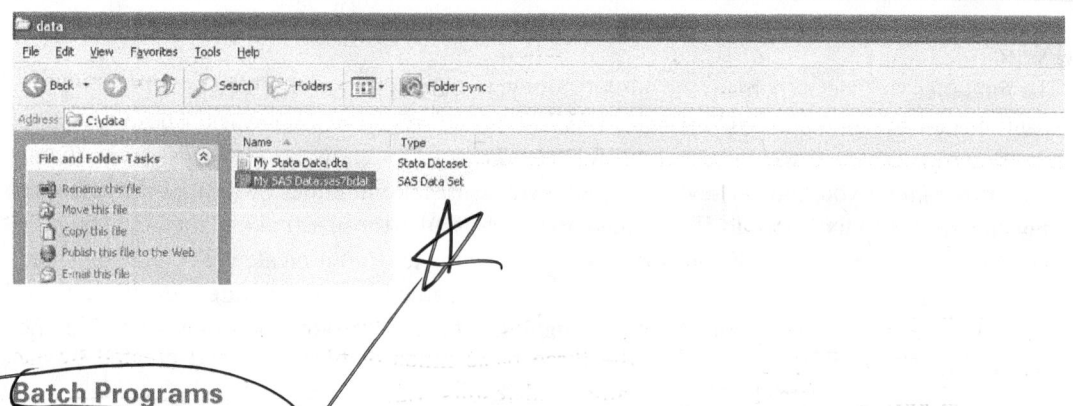

Batch Programs

A **batch program** is a list of instructions to modify or analyze your data, written with SAS or Stata syntax. We emphasize the use of such batch programs (rather than interactive variable creation and analysis). The word "batch" simply means that the series of instructions, in SAS or Stata syntax language, are gathered together so that the computer can run them one after another without prompting you for what to do next. When you gather your work together in such batch programs, you have a record of every step in your project, from raw data to final regression results. As we will emphasize in the next section, learning to organize your files is a critical piece of learning to conduct a quantitative data analysis project. Even the best and most insightful findings will be lost if you cannot find or recreate them. And, the ability of others to replicate your results will increase your credibility (to yourself and others; Freese 2007).

The extensions for these batch programs (*.sas* in SAS and *.do* in Stata) will also be associated with their respective software by the default installation, meaning that SAS or Stata will be launched when you double click on files with these extensions. When we discuss the interfaces used by SAS and Stata in Chapter 4, we will talk about what editors to use to create these files (they are always stored in plain text format).

For example, below we show two hypothetical batch programs with the appropriate extensions (*.do* for Stata and *.sas* for SAS). The computer recognizes these files as a Stata do-file and SAS program, and would launch the appropriate software if we double-clicked on the file. The word **"do-file"** reflects the fact that the extension *.do* is so commonly used for Stata batch programs that a Stata batch program is called a "do-file."

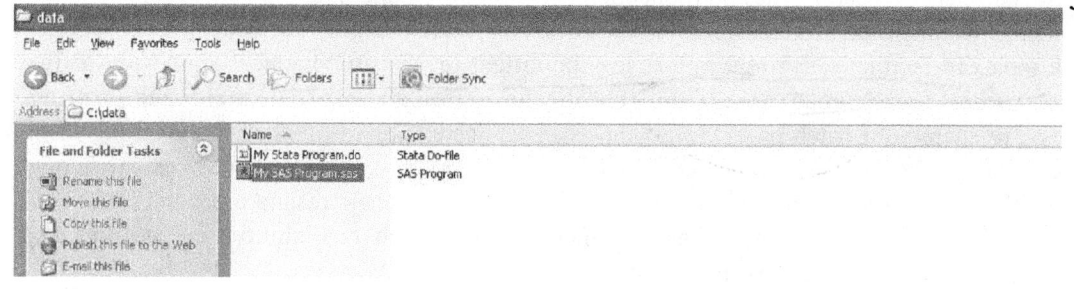

Results

The final files we discuss contain the output from your batch programs, which could range from basic means and tabulations of variables to sophisticated regression analyses. These files also contain error messages which are useful for "**debugging**"—removing the errors from—your batch program (if you make a severe enough syntax mistake in either language, the software may stop until you fix it, just as if you make too serious an error in a spoken language you may need to try again until the proficient speaker you are trying to communicate with can understand you). In SAS the output and the error messages are contained in two separate files (the *.rtf* and *.log* files, respectively, in Display A.3). In Stata, they are combined together in a single file (the *.log* or *.smcl* file in Display A.3).

Below are examples of the SAS and Stata files with the *.log* extension. Depending on the order and choices made during installation, *.log* files may be interpreted by the computer as being associated with SAS or Stata. On our computer, for example, they are associated with SAS.

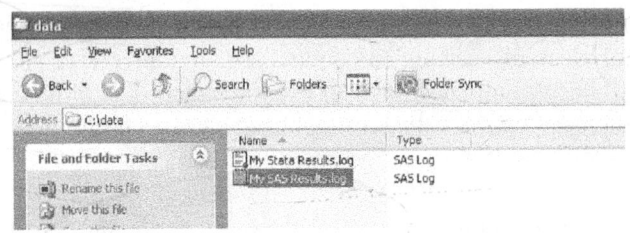

As noted above, this doesn't mean that the contents of the Stata *.log* file are now in SAS format; but we cannot double-click the *.log* file to open it in Stata. Because our computer has associated *.log* files with SAS, double-clicking will launch SAS. We would need to do something else (such as use the File/Open menu from within the software interface) to open the Stata results. We will have more to say about the other versions of the results files in Chapter 4 (*.rtf* in SAS and *.smcl* in Stata).

3.3.2: What are Some Good Ways to Organize these Files?

Social science research relies on replication (Freese 2007; Long 2009). By first replicating and then extending others' studies, new studies best contribute to a growing body of knowledge on a topic. To facilitate such replication, it is important for you to document your work so that others could repeat your steps. If you publish your results, another student or scholar may ask you to share your batch programs so they can replicate your results before extending them, especially when you use a publicly available data set. Some journals require researchers to make their data and batch programs available to others if their results are published in the journal. Being open to such sharing benefits the research community, and ensures that researchers take extra care with their own work.

Good organization is also important simply to be sure you can trace the steps of your project from start to finish, and can confirm that your calculations are correct. As we will see in Chapter 4, it is possible to analyze your data "interactively," especially in Stata; that is, you can type a command to create a new variable, examine that new variable's distribution, and then use that variable in an analysis, all typing commands one by one that simply scroll by on the computer screen (and aren't permanently saved).[1] You can also use menus to make it even easier to complete this kind of interactive variable creation and analysis (without remembering the syntax). Although most researchers do some of this sometimes, it is best to move quickly toward defining variables and analyzing them through batch programs, otherwise it is easy to forget exactly how a variable was defined (especially if you experiment with several coding decisions). Writing in batch programs and organizing these programs helps you to avoid these problems and allows you to document and check your work easily.

Project Folders

We recommend that when you start a new project you create a folder on your computer to store your data, batch program, and results files (see Box 3.4). It is useful to come up with a convention for naming your files (and variables) that makes it easy to remember their purpose and contents. The convention is up to you—it should be something that makes sense to you, making it easy for you to organize and locate your files. Two general suggestions for folder names are:

■ Use words and abbreviations that convey the meaning of the folder contents. For example, you might use *Chapter 4* as a folder name for the files created in the exercises of the next chapter. Or, you might put together a data set name (e.g., *nsfh*) and research topic (e.g., *distance*) to create a compound name such as *nsfhdistance*. Some researchers find it hard to distinguish these separate words, and use underscores or capitalization to make them stand out (*nsfh_distance* or *NsfhDistance*). Others find the underscores and capitals distracting or difficult to type, and stick with the original compound word.

■ Use words and abbreviations for the date that you create the folder or files (e.g., 2008jan15 or 20080115), again potentially with symbols or capitalization to increase readability (e.g., 2008_Jan15 or 2008_01_15). If you use this date strategy, it can be helpful to keep a separate log, on paper or electronically, to make notes about what you did on that date. In electronic form, such a log can be stored in the same project folder as the data set, batch programs, and results, so it is easy to find.

■ Box 3.4

Especially if you are using a restricted rather than public use data file, you may want to store the raw data file separately from your other files. Often, these data files can only be analyzed on a single computer with particular security safeguards (e.g., disconnected from the Internet). The data should not be removed from that computer, so often for these types of projects it is easier to store your programs and results separately from the data, so that you can copy the program/output files to a flash drive for backup, summarizing, and writing. Sometimes such policies also require that you delete your analytic data files at regular intervals, and in these cases you may also want to store your analytic files in a third, separate location to make it easy to locate them for such deletion (and leave untouched in other folders the raw data, programs, and results).

These strategies can be combined as well. We might create a folder called *nsfh_distance* for a larger project and then use dated folders within, such as *2008_Jan15*, to organize our work. For this course, think a little about which of these might suit your style, and try it (or try another strategy that you come up with). You can even experiment with different styles throughout the course to help choose one that works best for you (or realize that certain styles work better for certain tasks or projects; see Box 3.5).

▪ Box 3.5

In general it is a good idea to avoid spaces in names. If you do include spaces, then you will need to put them in quotes in your program (e.g., "nsfh distance"). The same holds for folder names on your computer. If you are working in a public lab, and the folder where your files are stored includes a space, then you need to enclose it in quotes (e.g., "c:\Documents and Settings\Rachel Gordon\My Documents").

Analytic Data Files

The public use version of a data file can be very large. The NSFH data set we will use as an example contains 4,355 variables from 13,007 participants. Data sets intended for public release, like the NSFH, typically cover a wide range of subjects so that they are of great utility to a broad research community, especially when funded by federal agencies. If you were conducting new data collection for your targeted research question, your data set would likely include fewer variables (and, you would likely not have the resources to achieve such a large sample size). For any project, but especially with such large public data sets, it is useful to create a smaller ***analytic data file*** which contains only the variables (and cases) needed for your particular project. Even though today's computing power often makes it possible to manipulate the large raw data file quickly, it will be easier to review the contents of a smaller file for completeness and accuracy. And, even today, software or computer memory limitations may prevent a very large raw data file from being read in its entirety.

For our example research question, we will focus on a subset of cases and a subset of variables from the NSFH. We will exclude adults whose mother is no longer living (since distance is irrelevant for these people). We will also exclude those who are coresiding with their mother (since decisions about whether to live in the same household may be explained by somewhat different constructs than the closeness of residences among those already living apart). And, we will exclude adults whose mothers live outside the USA. We also focused our research questions in Chapter 2 on a subset of constructs, including:

- distance between respondent and mother's residences;
- respondent gender, race-ethnicity, age, earnings, and number of brothers and sisters;
- mother's education and age.

In Chapter 4 we will show you how to create an analytic data file that contains just the relevant cases and variables.

You can, and should, use names that make sense to you for your analytic data files (we'll offer some suggestions in Chapter 4). But, do not under any circumstances make changes to the raw data file (such as keeping a subset of variables or a subset of cases) and "overwrite" missing data are captured with multiple codes, such as *refused, not applicable*, and *don't know*; sometimes these are already coded in a format that SAS or Stata will recognize as missing, although often they are stored with numbers in the raw data file and you must recode them so SAS and Stata recognize them as missing as we will show how to do in Chapter 4).

Using the NSFH Documentation

The NSFH data includes all of these kinds of documentation—measure lists, questionnaires, codebooks, and skip maps. We will illustrate each as we identify the variables relevant to our research questions. In the interest of space, we provide details for just a few questions to demonstrate the process you would follow in your own work.

The NSFH documentation is all accessible through the BADGIR utility. Usually, it takes several passes through a study's documentation to become familiar with it. Do not be surprised if you have to go back through materials a few times to understand the "big picture" and to locate the specific files you need. It is often helpful to approach learning a data set as you would detective work—as a process of iterative discovery.

Variable Lists

A helpful variable list is found in the first working paper written by the study investigators, titled *The Design and Content of the NSFH*, which is available within the *Metadata* section of BADGIR. This working paper provides relevant background about the data set, generally worth reading to help understand the data. For our current purposes, we will focus on *Section VIII*, beginning on p. 37, which provides an *Outline of the Content of the National Survey of Families and Households* with enough detail to allow us to pinpoint the location of relevant variables.

Display C.3.2 provides excerpts from this outline. Topics related to our research questions are found in two major sections of the outline: (1) Interview with Primary Respondent, and (2) Self-Administered Questionnaire: Primary Respondent. Within the Interview with Primary Respondent, the section of questions on Household Composition include age and sex of household members (including the respondent) and the section of questions on Social and Economic Characteristics include race and parent's education. Within the section on Parents, Relatives, and General Attitudes in the Self-Enumerated Questionnaire Number 13 "SE-13" we find the mother's age and current residence and the respondent's number of brothers and sisters.

Browsing the documentation also reveals that the study investigators created some variables based on the raw data, and include these in the data file. Such created variables can be useful for replicating prior studies and saving time and potential errors in recoding complicated questionnaire sections (e.g., with extensive skip patterns). We use one such variable which the study investigators created to capture the respondent's total earnings, from wages, salary, and self-employment. The details of their coding are found in Appendix I (*Instructions for creating income variables and poverty status*) of the "Other Documentation" on BADGIR.

Skip Maps and Questionnaires

Display C.3.3 shows where the relevant questionnaires and skip maps are found in BADGIR. Based on the sections that we identified in the variable lists, we check for the questions we needed in the primary respondent's main interview and self-administered questionnaires. In this section, we will look at the skip maps and questionnaires for the mother's age and distance as examples.

The NSFH skip maps provide an easy overview of the survey's questions. The skips among the questions about the respondent's mother are found in the file that opens when we click on *Skipmap: Wave 1 Self-Administered Questionnaire* in BADGIR (see again Display C.3.3). The relevant section of the skip map is duplicated in Display C.3.4. After reading through this section, we identify several items that will be relevant to our project. One question will help us to select the correct subgroup of adults whose mothers are still alive from the full data set: a skip from Question 1 directs subsets of respondents to relevant questions, depending on whether their mother is currently alive or deceased. Two items that we will want to include in our analyses are also found on this page. The second question captures the mother's age and the fifth question whether she lives from the respondent, if she is alive.

After identifying the relevant items in the skip map, we click on *Questionnaire: Primary Respondent Self-Enumerated Schedule* in BADGIR (see again Display C.3.3) to see the corresponding questions as completed by the respondent. The relevant section is reproduced in Display C.3.5. Notice that this page is laid out for self-administration. The questions to be answered by respondents whose mothers are living are in the left column. The questions to be answered by respondents whose mothers are deceased are in the right column. Thus, the skip pattern is clear in this relatively simple section of the questionnaire, with its straightforward layout. Our relevant questions about the mother's age (*2. How old is she? __ Years old*) and the mother's location (*5. About how far away does she live? ____ Miles ...*) should have been answered only by those respondents whose mother was living (although in paper and pencil format it is possible that some respondents may have incorrectly followed the instructions, so we would want to check for this possibility after downloading the data). The questionnaire also alerts us that we should expect to see in the data file that the mother's age is recorded in years and the distance in miles. The notes on Question 5 also clue us that respondents who coresided with their mother should skip to the next page, suggesting that there may be a code that will help us to select adults who do not coreside with their mothers. The particular wording of questions and associated notes are also important for understanding the data, even when not used directly in writing our batch programs (e.g., it appears that the study investigators calculated distances for respondents who did not know the distance, based on their report of the city and state where their mother lived).

Codebooks

Now that we understand the skip structure and questions for the items, we can use the codebook to see exactly how the responses were recorded in the data. We will rely on the BADGIR *Variable Description* section to access the codebook. The original codebooks are also available on the NSFH web site, but these tabulations reflect the data as they were released in the late 1980s, rather than the latest release. In contrast, BADGIR's codebook tabulations are based on the current version of the data set, which is the version we will download. (Like all researchers, investigators who gather data that is later made publicly available identify errors after its release; in fact, sometimes public users identify problems the initial investigators missed.)

Display C.3.6 provides an example of the codebook from BADGIR for Question 1 from the self-administered questionnaire regarding whether the mother is still living or deceased. Notice first that the name of this variable is E1301. This follows the study's naming convention. E13 represents the 13th self-administered questionnaire (see again top of Display C.3.4 with the title SE—13). And, 01 represents Question 1 in this section. This is the name we will use to refer to this variable in our batch program in Chapter 4. We will show below how to create new variables that we intend to use in our analysis, and we will use names that are meaningful to us for these new created variables. Like raw data files, we recommend not renaming or recoding the raw variables themselves (otherwise, later confusion will result!).

The *Values* column of the codebook shows us which values correspond to which categories (e.g., 1 = *Still Living* and 2 = *Deceased*). In the *N* column we see that over one third of respondents report that their mother is deceased, whereas close to two thirds report that she is alive. Even after excluding respondents whose mother is deceased, over 8,000 cases will remain. The tabulation in the codebook also shows us the values that the study investigators used to indicate types of missing data. As expected, based on the skip map, *Not Applicable* is not included as a type of missing data for this question, since all respondents should have answered Question 1 of this section (see note at top of Display C.3.4). But, over 250 cases are missing data because the respondent refused (one case), didn't know (13 cases), or didn't answer (252 cases).[2] These types of missing data are recorded with the values 7, 8, and 9, respectively.

The next example, in Display C.3.7, shows the codebook results for Question 2, on the age of the respondent's mother. Only the smallest and largest values are shown, since viewing all of the values requires scrolling across multiple screens online. Notice first that the file-naming convention is again followed for this variable, called E1302 (second question on the 13th self-administered questionnaire). The tabulation shows us that one respondent reported that her mother's age was 29, one reported 30, and three reported 33 and so on down to seven respondents reporting that she was 94 years old and seventeen respondents reporting that she was 95 years old. Notice also that *inapplicable* occurs as a missing value for this variable, recorded with the value of 96 for 4,466 respondents (who should be valid skips because their mother was not alive).[3] Ten cases are also recorded as *refusals*, 44 as *don't know*, and 305 as *no answer*, with the values 97, 98, and 99, respectively.

The third example, in Display C.3.8, shows the responses for Question 5, on the distance away from the respondent that the mother lives. Note again that the variable name follows the study's convention (E1305 for the fifth question on the 13th self-administered questionnaire). The distribution of values shows that a large number of respondents (1,020) reported that their mother lived just one mile away. In contrast, just a few report very large distances (two respondents report a distance of 7,000 miles, five report 8,000 miles, and three report 9,000 miles). In addition to the missing data codes we have seen already, this question has two specific codes that we can use for keeping the desired subset of cases: (1) 9995 indicates that the mother lived with the respondent (recall that these respondents were instructed to skip this question), and (2) 9994 indicates that the mother lived in a foreign country.[4] An additional 4,464 respondents are coded as *inapplicable* (9996), two respondents *refused* (9997), 22 said *don't know* (9998), and 321 provided *no answer* (9999).

Naming Conventions for Created Variables in Analytic Data Files

Just as with the naming of our analytic data files, we want to think forward to a naming convention for new variables that we create. Many programmers use names that signal the content of the variable (e.g., *miles* rather than E1305 for the distance the mother lives from the respondent). In the past, variable names were restricted to eight characters, forcing researchers to be quite creative in naming variables. These restrictions have been lifted in recent software releases, and currently, variable names in SAS and Stata can be up to 32 characters. However, most researchers still limit the length of variable names because shorter names are easier to read and better for display (some output will abbreviate long variable names). We recommend variable names of 12 characters or less because we have found that they display best in results output.

Let's plan ahead to think about what to name the variables we will create for our analytic data files. Display B.3.1 summarizes the variables that we will include in the analytic data file. We include the original variable name and description from the codebook. In addition, based on the frequency distribution in the codebook, we make notes about the codes used for missing data for each variable and relevant notes for recoding. We also include a name that we chose for each variable that we will create in the analytic data file (students are encouraged to think about other possible names that make sense to them, but if you use our naming conventions to follow along with the examples, it will be easiest to replicate our results). In our naming convention, we started the variable with either *g1* (to designate the Generation 1 mother) or *g2* (to designate the Generation 2 adult child respondent). We then chose a word or abbreviation to represent the content of the variable. We do not include variable names for variables that we will use only to subset the data (M497A, E1301), nor for categorical variables that we will learn how to recode in Chapter 10 (M2DP01, M484). And, we will keep the case identifier as named in the raw data file, MCASEID.

As a final step for preparing to write our SAS and Stata batch programs in Chapter 4, let's walk through the notes in Display B.3.1 for each variable so that we can anticipate how they will be used in the batch program.

- The variables M497A, E1301, and E1305 will be used to keep only a subset of cases. Distance is irrelevant unless the mother is known to be still alive, so we will only retain cases in which E1301 is coded as a "1" (still living). In addition, we treat coresidence and immigration as conceptually distinct events, and focus on distances when respondents live apart from their mother but both live in the USA. These are captured in the codes for E1305. Because the survey was completed in paper-and-pencil, some errors may have occurred (some distances are quite large, over 5,000 miles) and we use the respondent's country of birth (M497A) as an additional restriction to help exclude distances to foreign countries.

- For age (M2BP01 and E1302) and distance (E1305), we simply need to recode missing data values. If we left the numeric values of missing data, such as 96–99 for age or 9996–9999 for distance, our results would be inaccurate. Means would be drawn higher by the high value of these missing data codes. For example, nearly 100 cases are coded 96–99 on E1302, and would be treated erroneously as quite old rather than of unknown age if not recoded. Both SAS and Stata use the "." symbol to represent missing data (this can be read as "**dot missing**;" see Box 3.8). By default, SAS and Stata will exclude cases with such missing values from statistical calculations, which is preferable to including them in calculations with their arbitrary missing data values.[5]

- For the mother's years of schooling and respondent's number of siblings, we need to recode some valid responses, in addition to recoding missing values. For M502, a GED is represented by the value 25. We will treat GEDs as equivalent to 12 years of schooling, and recode any cases coded 25 on M502 to 12 on our new *glyrschl* variable. For E1332A and E1332B, respondents skipped the questions, and were coded *inapplicable* (96) if they said on an earlier question that they had no living siblings. Thus, cases with values of 96 on these original variables (E1332A and E1332B) will be coded as "0" on our new variables, *g2numbro* and *g2numsis*.

- For earnings, the respondents reported their wages, salaries, and self-employment income from 1986. Because of inflation, these levels of earnings will be difficult for contemporary readers to interpret substantively. Researchers commonly use the Consumer Price Index (CPI) to convert such values to more recent dollars, for which readers have ready benchmarks in mind. The conversion is the ratio of the annual CPI in the more recent year to the annual CPI in the earlier year. For 2007 to 1986, this ratio is 207.342/109.6 (U.S. Bureau of Labor Statistics 2008).

> **■ Box 3.8**
>
> As we will see in later chapters, SAS stores '.' missing as the lowest possible value and Stata stores '.' missing as the highest possible value. We will discuss in later chapters how this is important in appropriately accounting for missing data, especially when creating new variables. SAS and Stata both also allow for extended or special missing values. Both allow a letter to be placed after the . to designate different types of missing value (e.g., .a could designate not applicable, .b could designate refusal, and .c don't know). In Stata, excluding these extended missing values could be accomplished with <. and in SAS with >. in the if qualifiers discussed in Chapter 4. We focus on the . "system missing" for simplicity in the textbook, which can be addressed with -=. in the if qualifiers discussed in Chapter 4.

3.3.4: Complex Sampling Designs

The document *The Design and Content of the NSFH* which we discussed in the prior section is a helpful starting point for learning about the complex sampling features of the NSFH. Another document, also accessible from the *Metadata* page for *Wave I* of the study, provides additional technical details about the sampling design (The link to this document is called *NSFH Wave 1 Sample Design* and it is also referred to in the documentation as *Appendix L: The National Survey of Families and Households: A Sampling Report*).

As discussed in Chapter 2, we are particularly interested in learning whether the study used a multi-stage design with stratification and/or oversampling. If so, we want to identify the variables in the documentation that capture the primary sampling units (PSUs), strata and/or sampling weights. We also want to understand any exclusions from the study's target population, which are important for us to understand when we interpret our results.

The Design and Content of the NSFH describes the population covered by the study. The target population is defined as "persons ages 19 and older, living in households, and able to be interviewed in English or Spanish" (page 15 of *The Design and Content of the NSFH*). The section of the document on *Population Coverage* discusses the rationale—logistical and cost barriers—for excluding persons living in institutions or group quarters (especially nursing homes, college dorms, or military barracks).

A section on *Oversamples* in *The Design and Content of the NSFH* discusses the oversampling of certain groups, each of which was deemed important to the study goals but were projected to have been represented in insufficient numbers without oversampling. One oversampling category was race-ethnicity, and African Americans, Mexican Americans and Puerto Ricans were oversampled. Additional oversampling categories were certain types of households, including single-parent families, step-parent families, cohabiting families, recently-married couples, and households including a child with neither parent in residence.

A section on *The Sample* in *The Design and Content of the NSFH* describes the multi-stage design. The study's PSUs were counties or groups of adjacent counties. The study's design team identified a set of counties or county groups with the largest population sizes that were chosen with certainty to be in the study. The remaining counties and county groups were sorted into strata, meant to group similar counties/county groups together, and two counties/county groups were selected from each strata. Specifically, the strata were based on region and metropolitan status as well as one or more of the following: urbanization, economic growth, racial composition, and Hispanic composition. The first set of counties/county groups which were selected with certainty are referred to as self-representing PSUs. The second set of counties/country groups, two of which were selected within each strata, are referred to as non self-representing PSUs. In Chapter 4, we will show how to distinguish between these two types of PSUs in our analyses.

The study used additional stages before finally listing households from which individuals were selected. For a full understanding of the study, it is helpful to be familiar with these aspects of the design, although we will only identify the PSUs in our analyses. Specifically, within each PSU, the study selected small areas defined by the U.S. Census Bureau (referred to as block groups or enumeration districts) as secondary sampling units. Within these secondary sampling units, listing areas of 45 or more households were identified, and one listing area was selected from each secondary sampling unit. A study representative then went to the listing area to create an up-to-date list of all of the addresses in the area. About 20 houses were selected from each of these lists; only the selected households were visited by an interviewer for screening into the study.

The more detailed, technical document (mentioned above and referred to as *A Sampling Report*) describes how the study sampling weights were calculated. This report was written by the **sampling statistician** who led the design of the NSFH. A sampling statistician is an expert in complex sampling designs, and most large-scale surveys have a sampling statistician who advises the study investigators about selecting the best design and who prepares the indicators of the design features for the data release, including the sampling weights. These sampling weights are used in analyses to adjust for any oversampling.

In its most basic form, the weight is the reciprocal of the respondent's probability of selection into the study, which is referred to as the **base sampling weight**. Intuitively, it is helpful to imagine a situation in which members of one group have twice the chance of being selected into the study as members of another group. For simplicity, we will denote the probability of selection as 2 for members of the first group and 1 for members of the second group (i.e., twice as likely to be sampled in the first group as the second group). Then, the base weight is the inverse of these values, or $\frac{1}{2} = 0.5$ for the first group and $\frac{1}{1} = 1$ for the second group (see Box 3.9). Intuitively, these values make clear that the oversampled group is "downweighted" (with a weight less than one). We will examine how the weights affect analyses in detail in Chapter 5.

In most studies, additional adjustments are made to the base weight, so that the **final sampling weight** used in analyses reflects more than just the inverse of the probability of selection. In the NSFH, the base weight was adjusted in four ways. First, the weights were adjusted for non-response to the screening interview. Second, the weights were adjusted for non-response to the main survey interview. Third, the weights were adjusted so that the distribution of certain demographic characteristics in the NSFH sample (sex, age, race-ethnicity, and region) matched those of the U.S. as a whole, based on U.S. Census Bureau data (from the Current Population Survey for the month and year when the NSFH was fielded); as noted in Chapter 2, this type of adjustment is referred to as post-stratification. Fourth, the weights were scaled so that they summed to the NSFH sample size of 13,017. At times, for analysis, it can be important to further rescale the weights (Campbell and Berbaum 2010). We will show how to do this in Chapter 5.

> **■ Box 3.9**
>
> In reality, the probabilities of selection are usually decimals. For example, in the NSFH persons who were not oversampled had a probability of selection of: $\frac{1}{4,976}$ =.000200965; and, the oversampling was designed such that oversampled persons had double that probability of selection: $\frac{2}{4,976}$ =.000401929 (NSFH 1990b). So the base weight for a person who was not oversampled is: $\frac{1}{.000200965}$ =4,976. And, the base weight for a person who was oversampled is: $\frac{1}{.000401929}$ =2,488. The first person can be thought of as representing 4,976 members of the population and the second person can be thought of as representing half as many, or 2,488 members of the population. This process is described by the NSFH sampling statistician in the *A Sample Report* document (NSFH 1990b).

Now that we understand the sampling design, let's look for the identifiers of PSUs and strata and the variable containing the final weights in the documentation. We can identify the final weight variable by clicking on *Variable Description* under *Wave 1* in BADGIR and then selecting the section *Weights and Constructed Variables*. There are several weights listed, as well as other variables such as the non-response and post-stratification adjustments. Reading through descriptions of these variables, we identify the *Individual Case Weight* with the variable name *WEIGHT* as the weight of interest to us. It is described as:

> Case weight to be used when individuals are the unit of analysis. This weight takes into account the differential probability of selection depending on the whether the case is in the main or oversample; differential probability of selection depending on the number of adults in the household; differential response rates; and post stratification to replicate the distribution of the population by age, race, and sex in the Current Population Survey. (NSFH 1990a, p. R-2)

The PSU and strata take additional detective work to locate. They are not available in BADGIR, but instead must be downloaded from the NSFH support web page (*http://www.ssc.wisc.edu/nsfh/support.htm*). Looking at the document *sudaan.doc* we identify a variable named *PSU* and a variable named *Stratum*.

We list these three variables for the complex sampling design features (*WEIGHT, Stratum*, and *PSU*) in the final rows of Display B.3.1.[6]

3.4: SUMMARY

This chapter covered the process of planning for a quantitative research project once you have located an appropriate data set. We introduced the basic types of files used by software packages (data, batch programs, and results files) and helped you to think forward to how you can name and organize these files. We also introduced the basic types of files you will encounter in the documentation for most data sets (variable lists, skip maps, questionnaires, and codebooks). Using the NSFH as an example, we modeled the process of locating the variables needed for an analysis in such documentation. We discussed how to develop conventions for naming the new variables we will create based on these basic raw variables, again modeling the process of thinking forward to the next task (writing the commands to extract the variables, keeping the relevant subgroups from the full data, and creating the new variables needed for our analysis).

KEY TERMS

Analytic Data File

Base Sampling Weight

Batch Program

Codebook

Data Analysis

Data Management

Data Point

De-Identification

Debugging

"Do-File"

Dot Missing (System missing)

Extension

File Associations

File Conversion Software

Final Sampling Weight

Identifiers

Instruments

Measure/Variable Lists

Plain Text (Data File) (Ascii (Data File))

Project Folder

Questionnaire

Raw Data File

Sampling Statistician

Self-representing PSU

Skip Map

Statistical Package

REVIEW QUESTIONS

REVIEW
QUESTIONS
3

3.1. What are the conventional extensions for SAS and for Stata data files, batch program files, and results files?

3.2. What are some conventions you might use to name a project folder and to name your analytic data file, your batch program, and your results files?

3.3. What are some conventions you might use to name variables?

3.4. Why is a skip map useful?

REVIEW EXERCISE

Look in BADGIR for the documentation related to some of the variables listed in Display B.3.1, beyond E1301, E1302, and E1305 which we covered in the text. Locate the relevant sections in the variable lists and then find the corresponding sections in the skip maps, questionnaires, and codebooks.

CHAPTER EXERCISE

Throughout the book, we will use the National Health Interview Survey (NHIS) for end-of-chapter exercises.

The NHIS is an annual cross-sectional survey designed to track the health status, health care service use, and health behavior of individuals in the United States. Because the NHIS has been fielded since the mid-1950s and repeats many questions annually, the data can be used to document trends in health over time. Each annual survey also covers special topics, which provide estimates of health-related issues of particular interest in that year. The current set of core questions have been asked since the NHIS questionnaire was redesigned in 1997.

The NHIS uses a complex sampling design to survey the civilian non-institutionalized population residing in the United States. At the first stage, primary sampling units (PSUs) are selected; these PSUs either comprise a single county, a group of adjacent counties, or a metropolitan statistical area. The PSUs are stratified within states by size and (as needed) poverty (Botman et al. 2000, p. 6). At the second stage, geographically defined *area segments* of up to sixteen addresses or *permit segments* of housing units built after the 2000 Decennial Census of Population are used. The segments are stratified by the concentration of Hispanics, African Americans and Asians.

Households that contain Hispanic, African American and Asian individuals are also oversampled in two ways. First, area segments are oversampled if they have higher concentrations of these racial-ethnic groups. Second, within a random portion of each segment, households are screened out if they do not contain at least one member from these racial-ethnic groups. Within the households that remain in the study, some information is gathered about every member of the household. When a household contains multiple families, some data are also gathered at the family level. One adult and one child (if the family contains children) is sampled in each family and additional information is gathered about each S*ample Adult* and S*ample Child*. In a third type of oversampling, adults in the household who are 65 years old and older and are also Hispanic, African American or Asian are more likely to be selected as the Sample Adult than those who are younger or not of these racial-ethnic groups.

Information is gathered from household members through personal interviews. All adults (17 and over) who are present at the time of the survey respond for themselves. For children and adults not present at the time of the survey, another knowledgeable adult family member responds (usually a parent for children). Since 1997, responses have been recorded using computer assisted personal interviewing (CAPI). The data are gathered by the U.S. Census Bureau for the National Center for Health Statistics in the Centers for Disease Control and Prevention.

The NHIS maintains its own web site (*http://www.cdc.gov/nchs/nhis/*). Many of the NHIS surveys are also available through the ICPSR archive. We will use the data from ICPSR because we can download SAS and Stata data sets directly (the NHIS' own web site allows users to download ASCII data files and example programs to read the ASCII data files).

Specifically, for the chapter exercises throughout the book we will use the Sample Adult data from the NHIS 2009 (Study Number 28721; Persistent URL: *http://dx.doi. org/10.3886/ICPSR28721*) from ICPSR. Appendix E provides additional information about how to access the data files from the ICPSR archive. The Sample Adult data set is the 4th data set in the set of NHIS 2009 data sets. It is important to note that fully 80% of the adults selected for the Sample Adult interview responded to the questions. (Because 82.2% of eligible households and 99.3% of eligible families also participated, the total response rate for Sample Adults is 65.4% or 80.1*99.3*82.2; ICPSR 2010, p. 75). The final sampling weights released with the study adjust for non-response (as well as oversampling).

In our Chapter Exercises, we will examine various predictors of the respondent's *Body Mass Index*, including gender, race-ethnicity, age, and extent of exercise. We will also examine how body mass index and functional limitations predict missed days of work. For the purposes of the chapter exercises, we will examine fairly simple associations among these variables. Published sources offer more complex analyses of related associations (e.g., Cook and Daponte 2008; Cutler, Glaeser, and Shapiro 2003; Kumiko et al. 2008).

To examine these associations, we will extract variables that measure the following constructs from the Sample Adult data set. (*Note that each construct listed below may entail more than one variable*).[7]

1. Identifier for household, family, and person.

2. Information needed to adjust for complex sampling design (PSU, strata, and weight). *Note: The NHIS data file contains two weights; use the FINAL weight.*

3.   Sample adult's gender.

4.   Sample adult's race-ethnicity. (*Look for Hispanic origin and a constructed 6-category OMB race variable*).

5.   Sample adult's age.

6.   Sample adult's days of work missed last year due to illness or injury.

7.   Sample adult's limitation of functional activities. (*Look for 12 limitations*).

8.   Sample adult's times per week spent in vigorous, moderate, and strength-enhancing activity.

9.   Sample adult's body mass index.

To complete this Chapter Exercise, create a table similar to Display B.3.1 with the name of the original variable, its description, its missing data code(s), and any notes about the variables. Don't worry about coming up with created variable names yet. In the exercise for Chapter 4, we will think about how to create and name several variables.

Note that you may find that multiple variables measure similar constructs or that you need to look at several different documentation files in order to choose which variable to list in your table. There is always some such "detective work" that happens when working with data documentation. Learning the documentation is an iterative process, in which you may look back at different sources several times before deciding what to list. Going through this iterative process is part of the goal of this assignment, so don't become frustrated if you need to revisit the documentation several times. Remember that the table you are creating is your "crib sheet." If you were using the NHIS to write a paper, thesis or dissertation, such a table can serve as an essential quick reference, so that you can keep essential notes at your fingertips as you initially write and later revise your programs and papers.

COURSE EXERCISE

COURSE EXERCISE 3

Choose one of the data sets that you identified in Chapter 2 for one of your research questions or hypothesis statements. Use the data archive or study web site to access its documentation. Locate relevant lists of variables, questionnaires and skip maps, and codebooks. Use these to identify the variables you will need for your regression model, including at least the outcome variable (ideally a continuous variable) and at least two predictor variables (ideally a categorical and a continuous variable to use across later chapters). Also, identify the case identifier and any variables you will need to subset your data to the relevant subsample needed for your research questions.

Chapter 4

BASICS OF WRITING BATCH PROGRAMS WITH STATISTICAL PACKAGES

CHAPTER 4: BASICS OF WRITING BATCH PROGRAMS WITH STATISTICAL PACKAGES

We are now ready to "roll up our sleeves and get our hands dirty with the raw data." We know what variables we want to extract from the raw NSFH data file, what subset of the cases we want to keep, and how we want to create and name our new variables. We are poised to write our batch programs to accomplish these tasks, and in this chapter we will learn how to do so. We will start by illustrating the SAS and Stata interfaces and syntax with a few of the NSFH variables. We will write a small batch program to read these variables from the raw data set, verify that their values are what we expect based on the documentation, and save the results and an analytic data set. We will then learn how to create new variables, keep a subset of cases, add comments, check for errors, and some general finishing touches. Display A.4.2 provides a summary of the syntax we will learn throughout the chapter.

4.1: GETTING STARTED WITH SAS AND STATA

Like most people these days, you probably use lots of software, including for word processing, emailing, playing media, etc. The latest versions of SAS and Stata have windows and menu structures that should be generally familiar to you based on these experiences (see Box 4.1). As with most software, you can begin to use each statistical package and accomplish many needed

---

■ Box 4.1

Like most software, various versions of SAS and Stata are available. This book is written with Version 11 of Stata and Version 9.2 of SAS. Stata released Version 12 as this manuscript was being copy-edited. We show below how to assure your Stata code will run in future releases. Stata also comes in different formats, each with its own restrictions on the number of variables and number of observations it can analyze. We assume that you have access to at least the IC, SE, or MP formats (see StataCorp 2009a for more information about these formats). We also assume that you are using a Windows operating system, although both SAS and Stata are available for other operating systems. Your instructor will be able to guide you to local labs and resources to access the software, and your local computing support center should be able to help you to find out whether your university has licensing agreements that provide you with student discounts if you want to install the software on your own computer.

tasks by learning just some of its basic features. As you need to accomplish more complicated tasks, you may be motivated to learn some of the "bells and whistles" of the software. But, like most users, you will probably never need to learn all of the features of the software, similar to what is likely the case with software you use daily to read email or write papers.

Our goal in this book is to help you to feel as comfortable turning to SAS and Stata to accomplish *basic* data management tasks and estimate *basic* regression models as you feel turning to whichever word processing software you use. But, that means we set aside many of the sophisticated capabilities and nuances of each software, including approaches for accomplishing some tasks that are unique to that software package. Indeed, if you explore the menus and help files, you may feel overwhelmed by the possibilities. (We will show some examples of each software's help files in Appendix F.) If that happens, remember that you will be able to accomplish what you need for a basic regression analysis just with the syntax we introduce in each chapter of this book. When you are ready or desire to go beyond these basics, Chapter 18 provides numerous resources for learning more, including strategies for finding opportunities at your local university, on the Web, and across the country.

4.1.1: Locating Batch Program and Results Files

We will now take a look at the basic menus and windows in SAS and Stata, and see where our basic data, batch program, and results files are located. We will first connect each window to the types of file and organizational strategy that we discussed in Chapter 3. Then, we will show you more specifically how to enter the example batch program in your computer to duplicate our results.

To see the menus and windows, you first need to start the software. Like most software, you can accomplish this with SAS and Stata in multiple ways. You should be able to find SAS and/or Stata from the list of software programs in your computer's Start menu. There may be an icon for the software program on your desktop. And, as noted in Chapter 3, if your computer has a standard installation of SAS and Stata and you use standard extensions for your files (as shown in Appendix A.3), you can double-click on a file to launch its associated software (see Box 4.2).

> ■ **Box 4.2**
>
> You can change which software program is associated with an extension, even after installation. One easy way to do this is to "right click" on a file, choose "properties", and then click on the "change" button next to "opens with" on the "general" tab. However, if you are working on a computer in a public lab at your university you may not be allowed to use this function.

Once you start the software program, you are in a **session**. The session continues until you close the software. Keeping this in mind is important because, as we will discuss below, changes you make during a session are not always saved permanently. If you want changes to remain in the next session (the next time you start the software program), then you need to save them explicitly (as we will discuss below).

Let's now take a look at some of the basic features of the menus and windows that we see when we launch SAS and Stata.

Stata Menus and Windows

Display B.4.1 provides examples of the Stata windows for editing a batch program (panel a) and viewing the results on screen (panel b). When you first launch Stata, you will see something like the screenshot shown in Display B.4.1b. Notice that there are four main windows visible: (1) The large window which contains results and three smaller windows labeled, (2) Review, (3) Variables, and (4) Command (see Box 4.3).

■ **Box 4.3**

It is possible to change the background colors, and other features of the display (such as the size and color of text). From the Edit menu, choose Preferences (or right click on the large results window, and choose Preferences).

The small white box labeled Command is referred to as the **command window**. We can use the command window to work with our data interactively in Stata. We can type a command into this box, hit return, and view the results. Then, we can type another command, hit return, and view the results. And so on. Many users like to use Stata's command window to try out some commands easily before adding them to their batch programs.

The command window also offers us one way to open the window where we will write our batch program: by typing the word "doedit" in the command window, and hitting return (see Box 4.4). Doing so opens the **Do-File Editor**, Stata's built-in text editor (shown in Display B.4.1a). When it first opens, the main screen is blank (similar to any text editor or word processor). We can type text into this main white screen to write our batch program. Display B.4.1a shows the text we typed to create an example batch program based on the NSFH data (we'll have more to say about the contents of this batch program below). Once we have written our batch program, we want to save it so that we can ask Stata to run its contents (and so that we have a record of our work, which we can save and share with others). You can save the file in the same way as most windows software (File/Save, Ctrl-S, or the "save" button). We recommend saving your batch program frequently as you write, to avoid lost work. We saved our example batch program with the name *ReadAFewVariables.do* (shown in bold in Display B.4.1a). Stata will automatically give the extension *.do* when you save the batch programs you write in the Do-File Editor.

■ **Box 4.4**

Typically, there are several ways to accomplish a task in SAS and Stata software, like most software. To open the Do-File Editor, you can also click the icon circled in green in Display B.4.1b. You can also choose the Do-File Editor from the Window menu.

Once you have written a batch program, you are ready to ask Stata to run its commands, from beginning to end. One way to do this is to choose the icon circled in black in Display B.4.1a. We can also run the batch program by typing do ReadAFewVariables in the Stata command window (in Display B.4.1b). The word do is a Stata command that asks Stata to run all of the commands contained in the listed file (in our case, *ReadAFewVariables.do*). We do not need to put the extension *.do* explicitly at the end of the filename, because Stata assumes that we used that extension for our batch program.

We asked Stata to execute the *ReadAFewVariables* batch program by using the do command on the Command Window. The end result is what is shown in Display B.4.1b. Again, we'll examine the results more carefully below, but let's look for now at the Review and Variables windows. The Review window contains a list of the commands we have typed on the command window. Our Review window in Display B.4.1b lists just three things: (1) a command `cd c:\nsfh_distance\Stata` that we will discuss below, (2) the `doedit` command we used to open the Do-File Editor and, (3) the `do ReadAFewVariables` command we used to execute our batch program. A convenience of the Review window is that you can double-click on any item in the list to execute that command again. For example, if we double-clicked on `do ReadAFewVariables` in the list, it would run our batch program again. This feature is especially convenient as you write and debug a batch program (we will discuss how to do this in Section 4.6.2). The Variables window lists the four variables that our batch program read from the larger NSFH raw data file. You can double-click on variables in this list to include them in your command window, again a useful feature for interactive work.

SAS Menus and Windows

Display B.4.2 provides similar examples of the basic SAS windows and menus.

Display B.4.2a shows the windows that will be visible when you first open SAS. The window labeled "ReadAFewVariables.sas" contains our batch program. This window will be blank when we first open SAS, and here we can type the commands for our batch program. Again, we recommend saving frequently to avoid lost work (using File/Save, Ctrl-S, or the "save" icon). SAS will give the batch program the *.sas* extension by default, which is what we want to use.

When we are ready to run our batch program in SAS, we can choose the "run" icon (circled in green in Display B.4.2a) or choose Run/Submit from the menus. After SAS executes the commands, the Log window contains messages. As we will discuss in Section 4.6.2, the log window can be especially useful for debugging (locating and fixing errors). The Explorer window allows us to view our data (which we will do in the next section).

The Output window contains results, such as frequency distributions and regression estimates. Although this window is not visible initially, we can move to it by clicking the tabs at the bottom of the screen (see "Output—(Untitled)" the dotted circle in Display B.4.2a) or by choosing Window/Output from the menus. Again, we will discuss the results further below.

4.1.2 Viewing Data

Both SAS and Stata allow you to view the data in a spreadsheet format, similar to the layout we showed in Table 3.1. Although these spreadsheets can be used to modify the data, we do not recommend that you use them in that way as you work the exercises that go along with this textbook. But, the spreadsheet views can be useful for helping you get a "feel" for the data, and they can be a useful aid to verifying variable creation, as we will discuss in Section 4.3.2.

In Stata, the **Data Browser** can be used to view the data by typing "browse" in the command window (or by choosing Data/Data Browser from the menus or by clicking on the Data Browser icon, circled in black in Display B.4.1b). Doing so opens a spreadsheet view of the data, as shown in the Display B.4.3a. (The Data Editor in Stata allows the data to be edited as well as viewed).

In SAS, the **Table Editor** can be opened by double-clicking on the data set, located in one of the file drawers in the Explorer window. Our data set *ReadAFewVariables.sas7bdat* is located in the Library file drawer (circled in black in Display B.4.2a). Double-clicking the Library file drawer reveals a number of icons, such as this:

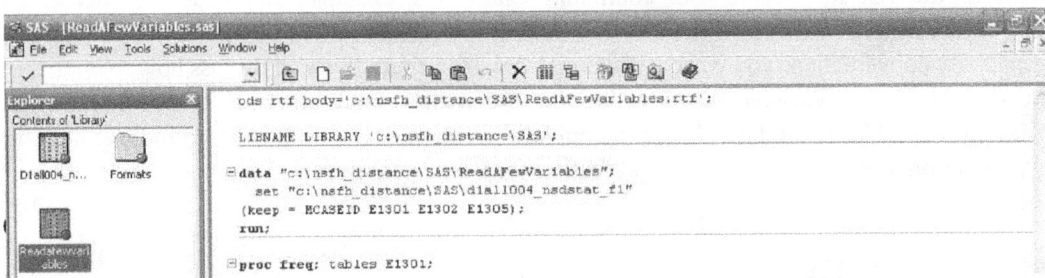

■ **Box 4.5**

The data are actually displayed with their formats by default. This means that each value is associated with a value label. For example a 1 for E1301 is displayed as "STILL LIVING." Such formats are useful because they allow you to link the meaning of values from the codebook to values in the data set. We will generally not rely on formats in this book, but mention them in Appendix D as we cover the process of reading the raw data.

■ **Box 4.6**

If you are using a computer in your school's computer lab, and cannot store to the *c* drive, you can choose the appropriate letter and folder name where you can store your personal files (e.g., *h:\rgordon\ nsfh_distance* if we have a personal folder called *h:\rgordon*).

Each of the two icons on the left represents a data set, the original raw NSFH data set begins with *D1all004_* and our small data set with four variables is called *ReadAFewVariables*. Double-clicking on *ReadAFewVariables* opens the spreadsheet view shown in Display B.4.3b. In both the SAS and Stata views, we show the first 15 cases in the data set in Display B.4.3. The values are the same in each view, as expected. For example, the first case has MCASEID of 3 with E1301 of 1, E1302 of 75, and E1305 of 2. We can look back to Display B.3.1 to remind ourselves that these data mean that the mother is still living (E1301 = 1), is age 75, and lives 2 miles away (see Box 4.5).

4.1.3 Organizing Files

In general, we find it easiest to keep our work organized if we use the same filename, but different extensions, for a batch program and the results and analytic data files that it creates. In our case, we used the same filename—ReadAFewVariables— with different extensions, for our batch program, results, and analytic data files so that it is easy to link them together. We chose the name using the convention of conveying the meaning of the task ("read a few variables") with capitalization to increase readability of the single word. We saved all of the files in our project folders (*c:\nsfh_distance\Stata* and *c:\nsfh_distance\SAS*; see Box 4.6).

We will take a look at screenshots of the files in these project folders, since it is often helpful for students to see these concretely as they start to work with the various files. For Stata, we have a set of four files in our project folder (*c:\nsfh_distance\ Stata*).

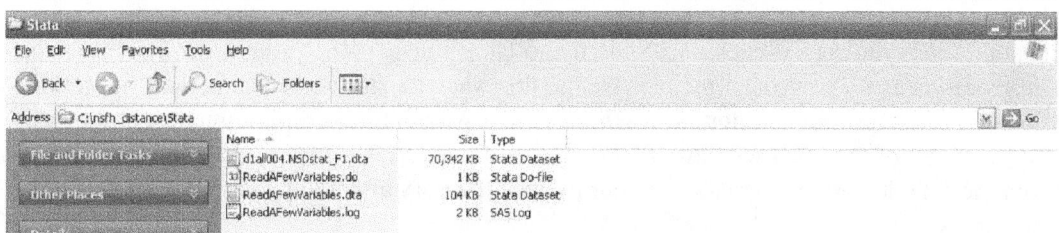

The first is the original raw data file (*d1all004.NSDstat_F1.dta*), which we discuss how to access in Appendix D. The remainder are the three Stata files: the Stata batch program (*ReadAFewVariables.do*), the analytic data set (*ReadAFewVariables.dta*), and the results file (*ReadAFewVariables.log*) that the batch program creates. Notice that the analytic data file is substantially smaller in size than the original raw data file (104 kbyte versus 70,342 kbyte), because our analytic data file keeps just four variables.

For SAS, we have five similar files in our project directory (*c:\nsfh_distance\SAS*).

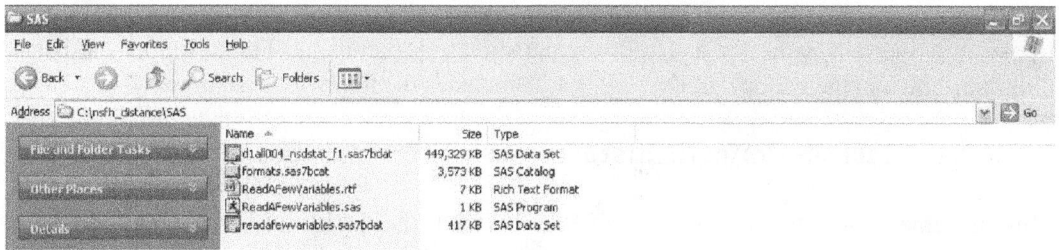

The project directory contains the original raw data file in SAS format (*d1all004_nsdstat_f1. sas7bdat*) and its associated formats file (*formats.sas7bdat*) as well as the SAS batch program (*ReadAFewVariables.sas*), the analytic data file (*ReadAFewVariables.sas7bdat*), and results file (*ReadAFewVariables.rtf*) that the batch program creates.

As we have noted, project directories such as these help us to keep our files organized, and doing so is important for checking our own work and sharing our work with others. The batch program provides a ready record of all of the steps from the raw data to the created analytic data file. Retaining this file allows you later to verify that the steps were correct, easily make modifications as needed, and readily share your work with others.

Your project directory is also important because you use it to tell SAS and Stata where to look for files and where to save files. When SAS and Stata were installed on the computer, default locations where they would look for and save information were defined. Some of the files that are created during a session are only saved temporarily to such default locations. They are erased when you exit the session (close the software). Both SAS and Stata provide ways to save changes permanently and shortcuts that allow you more easily to save files in your project directory.

Stata uses a concept called the **working directory**. The working directory is set by the default installation of Stata, usually as a file folder location, like *c:\data*. You can override the default location when you double-click on a Stata file to launch Stata. When you do so, Stata uses that file's location as the working directory. We did this when we started Stata and thus the working directory is our project directory, *c:\nsfh_distance\Stata*. This working directory is shown in the lower left of the Stata windows (the dotted circle in Display B.4.1b). You can also change from the default working directory to your project directory after launching Stata by typing:

```
cd c:\nsfh_distance\Stata
```

in the command window (`cd` stands for "change directory"). This can also be accomplished by selecting "File|Change Working Directory" from the menus, which allows browsing to the desired directory. Changing the working directory to your project directory is convenient because Stata will look for and store files in this location; thus, if we change our working directory to our project directory, we do not need to type the entire path when we want to refer to a file in our batch program (e.g., we can type *ReadAFewVariables* rather than *c:\nsfh_distance\Stata\ReadAFewVariables*).

SAS uses a concept called the **libname** ("library name") as a shortcut. You can use the libname to assign a shortcut name for a longer project directory pathname. For example, the batch program shown in the window in Display B.4.2a includes the following statement:

```
libname LIBRARY 'c:\nsfh_distance\SAS';
```

This libname associates the name LIBRARY with the path `c:\nsfh_distance\SAS`. It is because we had defined this libname that we were able to find our data files in the library file drawer icon (circled in black in Display B.4.2a) when we used the spreadsheet data view above.

We could use this *libname* more extensively in our batch program whenever we want to refer to files stored in our project directory, although we will generally not do this in this book because students sometimes find the necessary syntax too abstract. For example, to refer to the file:

```
c:\nsfh_distance\SAS\ReadAFewVariables
```

we would need to use the following syntax:

```
LIBRARY.ReadAFewVariables
```

Using *libnames* in this way provides a convenient shorthand especially if you move on to writing more complicated SAS batch programs in your future work; but, in this book, to keep our SAS batch programs less abstract, we will use full paths to refer to the location of files in SAS batch programs such as

```
c:\nsfh_distance\SAS\ReadAFewVariables
```

4.2: WRITING A SIMPLE BATCH PROGRAM

Display B.4.4 contains the contents of the *ReadAFewVariables* batch programs and a portion of the results. These simple batch programs contain the basic syntax we need to read a data file, save an analytic data file, obtain a variable's frequency distribution, and save the resulting frequency distribution. We will discuss each command in the text. They are also summarized in Display A.4.2. Appendix F provides information about using each software's help files to learn about more features for these commands (although what we provide in the text is sufficient for what we need to accomplish in this chapter).

4.2.1: Basic Syntax to Read and Save Data Files

In both SAS and Stata, we must first open a data file before we can analyze its contents, often referred to as "reading the data into memory" or "using the data file." If our batch program modifies a raw data set (for example, we read only a portion of its cases or variables into memory) we may also want to save this smaller analytic data set (so that we can share it with others or use it in future batch programs).

Reading a Stata Data File
The command we will use to read Stata data into memory is:

```
use <variable list> using <data filename>
```

Since this is the first command we will discuss in detail, we will comment on the conventions we will follow throughout the book. The commands will be shown in a `different font`. Items you will supply are in angle brackets < >. Optional items are shaded.

In our case, the <data filename> would be the raw NSFH data file `d1all004.NSDstat_F1.dta`. If your file name had spaces, you would need to put it within quotes `use "my file.dta"`. We also only want to use four of the 4,355 variables in the raw data file, so we will use the optional shaded portion of the command and write the names of the desired four variables, separating each name with a space, in place of <variable list>. This is the typical structure of a variable list (write the names of one or more variables, separated by spaces). The resulting command would be:

```
use MCASEID E1301 E1302 E1305 using d1all004.NSDstat_F1.dta
```

In Stata's language, this command asks Stata to read four variables (`use MCASEID E1301 E1302 E1305`) from the NSFH raw data file (`using d1all004.NSDstat_F1.dta`). If we wanted to read additional variables (as we will below) we can simply add them to the list. Notice that we do not include the path to the data filename because we assume you have changed the working directory to your project directory. Otherwise, we would need to type:

```
use MCASEID E1301 E1302 E1305 using c:\nsfh_distance\Stata\d1all004.NSDstat_F1
```

Since this is the first time we have written a Stata command, it is also helpful to point out that Stata is **case-sensitive**, meaning that if a variable name includes a capital letter, we must capitalize it and if a command name does not include a capital letter, then we must write it in lowercase. In other words, USE and Use are not equivalent to use, and, mcaseid and Mcaseid are not equivalent to MCASEID in Stata. The NSFH raw variable names were capitalized in the codebook and are capitalized in the raw data file, so we must capitalize them when we refer to them in our batch program.

Saving a Stata Data File

When we create a modified data file (e.g., reading just four of a data set's variables) that modified data file is available during the current session (until we close the software). We can always recreate the modified data file in a future session by re-running the batch program that created it; but if we want to save the modified data file, so that it is easier to use in the future or so that we can share it with others, we need to save it permanently. For example, when we expand our batch program below to define new variables, we will save an analytic data file with all the variables we need for analyses in future chapters.

Stata's command to save a data file is called **save**. The general syntax for this command is:

```
save <data filename>, replace
```

As emphasized in Chapter 3, we want to save such modified analytic data files with a different name from the original raw data file. We chose the name *ReadAFewVariables*. Stata automatically adds the *.dta* extension. So, our command would be:

```
save ReadAFewVariables, replace
```

The word **replace** after the comma is referred to as an **option**. (Generally, in Stata's syntax, words that follow commas are options.) We recommend using this option with the **save** command in your batch programs. You will often need to run a batch program multiple times. After the first run, when the data file already exists (e.g., once *ReadAFewVariables. dta* exists in the project directory), Stata would stop with an error message such as file ReadAFewVariables.dta already exists unless you use the option replace. Adding the option **replace** to the **save** command in your batch programs will avoid this error.

Reading and Saving a SAS Data File

In SAS, we use one set of commands, referred to as the **DATA Step**, to read and save data files (see Box 4.7). The basic syntax is:

```
data <path and data filename>;
  set <path and data filename>
  (keep= <variable list>);
run;
```

The <path and data filename> following the word `data` is the name of the file to be saved; in our case it will be *c:\nsfh_distance\ SAS\ReadAFewVariables* (see Box 4.8). The <path and data filename> following the word `set` is the name of the file we want to start with, in our case the raw NSFH data file *c:\nsfh_distance\ SAS\d1all004_nsdstat_f1.* Although students often find it counterintuitive that the original data file is listed on the second line of SAS's DATA step, we can think of it as starting with (*setting*) our original data (in this case the raw data file) and creating the new data file (in this case our analytic data file) listed in the first line.

The variable list is the same as we used in our Stata command above `MCASEID E1301 E1302 E1305`. Thus, substituting into the general syntax would give the following:

```
data "c:\nsfh_distance\SAS\ReadAFewVariables";
  set "c:\nsfh_distance\SAS\d1all004_nsdstat_f1"
    (keep = MCASEID E1301 E1302 E1305);
run;
```

Note that SAS assumes the extension *.sas7bdat* for our data files, so we do not need to list the extensions explicitly.

There are two general differences between SAS and Stata syntax that we will pause to point out. First, you may have noticed that each line of SAS syntax ends with a semi-colon. The semi-colon tells SAS where the command ends. Because SAS keeps reading until it reaches the semicolon, a command can extend over multiple lines. Breaking a command over multiple lines

---

■ Box 4.7

SAS separates its programs into two major sections, the DATA step and the PROC steps. The DATA step reads data into memory. Any data manipulation must occur in the DATA step, such as creating new variables, keeping variables, or keeping a portion of the data. The PROC steps calculate statistics. The programs we write in this book typically have one DATA step followed by one or more PROCs.

■ Box 4.8

If the path is omitted from the filename following the word data (e.g., data `ReadAFewVariables`) then the new data file is created temporarily. It is available during the current SAS session, but deleted when the session ends. In contrast, if a path is specified, the data set is saved in that location, and available in future SAS sessions. The advantage of the temporary file is to avoid cluttering the computer with data files (since the temporary file can always be recreated by re-executing the program). As we have noted, a permanent file is useful once you have finalized all of your data manipulation and are ready for analysis, especially if the raw data file is sizable, and when you need to share an analytic file with others. In Stata, we can similarly only create the analytic data file temporarily if we do not include a `save` command in our program.

can be useful in organizing your batch program (as we discuss in Section 4.6.1). In fact, above we put the keep portion of the set statement on a second line to make the command easier to read. We will learn later how to achieve this result in Stata, which by default requires commands to appear on only one line. Second, SAS (unlike Stata) is *not case-sensitive*. Your commands and your data file names and variable names are interpreted in the same way by SAS if written in lowercase, uppercase, or a mixture of both. In other words, Data and DATA are interpreted as the same command as data by SAS. In fact, the SAS documentation often capitalizes key command names when referring to them, as we will sometimes do in the text.

There is also one unique feature of SAS that we'll note here. The final line in our command is run; The RUN statement tells SAS to submit the DATA command for processing. We will see that most of the commands we use in SAS have a matching RUN statement at the end. Although technically there are many situations in which your batch program will successfully execute without these paired run; statements (and thus you may see that some peers or collaborators omit them from their batch programs) it is best to get into the habit of including the RUN statements (to avoid the problem of omitting them when they are essential).

4.2.2: Basic Syntax to Check Variables Against the Codebook

In the long run, it is worth spending the time to check that your downloaded variables are correct before moving forward. As an example of this process, we will check the frequency distribution of one of the NSFH variables, E1301, against the frequency distribution shown in the BADGIR codebook.

Checking a Variable's Distribution in Stata
In both SAS and Stata there are multiple ways to obtain a frequency distribution. We will use the following Stata command which provides useful information about the variable, including its frequency distribution:

```
codebook <variable list>, tabulate(400)
```

The option tabulate(400) is useful if some variables have many values (by default the frequency distribution is only shown for up to nine values; the tabulate option requests that it be shown for more values, for example we changed from the default to 400). As an example, we will just include a single variable, E1301, in the variable list:

```
codebook E1301, tabulate(400)
```

The results, shown in Display B.4.4, can be compared to the results from BADGIR, shown in Display C.3.6. Notice that the values and labels match BADGIR exactly, as does the number of cases listed for each value (column labeled *Freq* in Stata and labeled *N* in BADGIR). For example, both show that 8,307 respondents reported that their mothers were still living.

Checking a Variable's Distribution in SAS

We will use the SAS command statement PROC FREQ to similarly request a frequency distribution. The general syntax is:

```
proc freq; tables <variable list>; run;
```

Notice that like the DATA statement, the PROC FREQ statement has a matching RUN statement, which we recommend that you always include in your batch program. In our case, to request the frequency distribution for E1301 we would type:

```
proc freq; tables E1301; run;
```

As shown in Display B.4.4, the results match those seen for Stata and the original BADGIR codebook (Display C.3.6).

4.2.3 Basic Syntax to Save Results

By default, results appear only on the screen in the SAS Output Window and the Stata Results Window. Typically, we would like to save these to use when we write about our results in a paper (or when we answer homework questions for a class).

In Stata, we accomplish this with the command:

```
log using <filename>, replace text
```

Stata will add the *.log* extension to the saved results file. The option `replace` asks Stata to replace the file, even if it already exists, similar to the `replace` option on the `save` command. The option `text` asks Stata to store the results in plain text format. The default is a special format called `.smcl` which can only be read by Stata (whereas the plain text file can be read by any text editor or word processor). Our examples of Stata output in this book come from the plain text format. In our case, we want to use the same name for our log file as our batch program file, so we would type:

```
log using ReadAFewVariables, replace text
```

Each `log using` command should be paired with a `log close` command. We usually put the `log using` command near the start of our batch program, and put the `log close` command in the last line of our batch program. Then, all results between the two commands are saved in the *.log* file. Display B.4.4 provides an example of the full batch program.

Recent releases of SAS allow results to be saved in Rich Text Format (RTF). This format is convenient because it can be opened by any word processor, and retains special formatting, such as table gridlines. The command to create the *.rtf* file is

■ Box 4.9

SAS will prompt you to open the *.rtf* file with the program associated with *.rtf* extension on your computer (often Microsoft Word). If you open the file, be sure to close it before rerunning the program.

```
ods rtf body=<"path and filename.rtf">;
```

In our case, the command would be:

```
ods rtf body="c:\nsfh_distance\SAS\ReadAFewVariables.rtf";
```

This command should be paired with the `ods rtf close;` statement. As with Stata, we typically put these statements at the beginning and end of the batch program, respectively. Note that we placed the filename in quotes and explicitly put the *.rtf* extension in the filename used in the `ods` command. We have found that this improves performance (see Box 4.9).

4.3: EXPANDING THE BATCH PROGRAM TO CREATE NEW VARIABLES

The data file we created above included just four of the variables needed for our research questions (see again Display B.3.1). We now will expand the batch program to include the remaining variables and to create the new variables. We also kept all of the cases in the data file above, although we planned to make some exclusions for our research question (exclude respondents whose mothers are not alive, respondents who coreside with their mothers, and respondents whose mothers live outside the USA). We will add the command to keep only a subset of cases now as well. First, we will learn the use of expressions, a central part of all of these tasks.

4.3.1: Expressions

We use **expressions** to write with SAS and Stata syntax (using variable names, values, and mathematical symbols) how we would like to define a variable or subset the data. For example, to subset our data we might say in plain English "I would like to keep only respondents whose mothers are still living." Or, we could refer to the variable names and values, but still say this in English, "I would like to keep respondents who have the value 1 on the variable E1301." Similarly, we listed in Display B.3.1 a number of ways we would like to recode some of the values of some variables. We could again say this in plain English. For example, "I would like to treat respondents who completed a GED the same as those with a high school diploma." Or, referring to the variable names and values, we might say "If a respondent is coded a 25 on M502, I would like to replace her value with a 12." How do we communicate these requests to SAS and Stata? In each case, we use an expression—a combination of variable names, numbers, and mathematical symbols—to do so. The mathematical symbols are referred to as **operators** and common symbols used in expressions are listed in Display A.4.1.

The notes under Display A.4.1 tell us where on the keyboard to find some symbols that may be unfamiliar. SAS can use either the letter abbreviations or symbols. Although the letters may be easier for you to interpret at first, using the symbols will be more parallel to Stata and become easier to interpret over time. Most symbols are similar between SAS and Stata, with the exception of the highlighted cells in the top row. Stata uses the double equal symbol to denote equality in expressions, whereas SAS uses the single equal sign. For example, M502=25 in SAS means the same thing as M502==25 in Stata.

4.3.2: Creating and Modifying New Variables

It is worth reiterating here that we highly recommend not altering the variables in the raw data file. Instead, create a new variable for your analytic data file. Not only does this allow you to give your analytic variable a name that is meaningful to you, but it also preserves the original variables so that you can double-check your work and easily trace back to the raw data.

Stata Syntax for Creating and Modifying New Variables
The basic commands for creating and modifying variables in Stata are:

```
generate <variable name> =<expression> if <expression>
replace <variable name> =<expression> if <expression>
```

For example, referring to our summary in Display B.3.1 (in Chapter 3), for the respondent's age we might type:

```
generate g2age = M2BP01
```

Or, for earnings converted to 2007 from 1986 dollars, we might type

```
generate g2earn=IREARN*207.342/109.6
```

Importantly, this code has not yet addressed the missing data values. We can use Stata's optional if qualifier to do so. The if qualifier asks Stata only to run the command for the subset of cases that are consistent with its expression. For example, if E1301==1 would restrict a command only to cases in which the mother is living. The if qualifier can be used when creating new variables to ask that the command be processed only for cases that have valid values on the original variable. Any case that is not consistent with the if qualifier on the generate command will be coded a '.' missing on the new variable.

For example:

```
generate g2age = M2BP01                if M2BP01<97
generate g2earn= IREARN*207.342/109.6  if IREARN<9999997
```

will result in cases with missing value codes on each variable to be '.' missing on the new variable. We determined what value to use in the expression (97 versus 9999997) based on our notes in Display B.3.1.

Notice that we used the *less than* operator in the `if` qualifier. As with writing in English, programming syntax can be expressed in many different equivalent ways. Any that achieves the objective of conveying which cases to run the command for is fine, although some may be shorter than others. For example, based on Display B.3.1, we could write `if M2BP01<97` equivalently as `if M2BP01~=97 & M2BP01~=98`. Some students may find `if M2BP01~=97 & M2BP01~=98` easier to connect back to the two missing value codes for the variable M2BP01 summarized in Display B.3.1. You should feel free to use an expression that makes sense to you, as long as it conveys the right meaning (i.e., in this case the meaning in words is "if the respondent's age is not missing").

We can also use the `if` qualifier, along with the replace command, to address the other coding modifications in our notes to Display B.3.1. For example, in order to recode the GEDs when we create the *g1yrschl* variable, we could use the following syntax:

```
generate g1yrschl=M502 if M502<98
replace g1yrschl=12 if M502==25
```

The first command creates the new variable, `g1yrschl`, carrying over all the original values except missing data codes which are translated to '.' missing. The second command replaces the value of 25 with the value of 12 for respondents who report that their mother received a GED. Notice that in the expression of the `if` qualifier we use the double-equal sign to denote equality (see again Display A.4.1), but the equals sign is used in conjunction with the `replace` and `generate` commands (e.g., `replace g1yrschl=12`). In Stata, we use the double-equal sign within expressions, generally as part of an `if` qualifier, where the computer will check whether or not the expression is true (does M502 take on the value of 25 for this case?).

Checking Created Variables in Stata

Similar to our check that the frequency distributions of the downloaded data were consistent with the study's codebooks, it is important to check that newly created variables recode the original variable in the way that we intend. As you become more comfortable with programming, you may be tempted to skip this checking step, feeling you can look at the code to see that it is correct. We strongly recommend that you always check newly created variables. Identifying an error in a variable's creation early is much preferable to discovering it late (such as after a thesis has been submitted for defense or after a manuscript has been submitted for publication).

One concrete way to spot check created variables is to use the spreadsheet views we introduced in Section 4.1.2. After running a command that adds a new variable to the data set, that variable will appear as a new column in the spreadsheet view. This approach is particularly useful for variables that take on many values. For example, this approach might be helpful as a check of our *g2earn* variable. For variables that take on only a few values, we can get a more complete view of all of the cases by cross-tabulating the created variable against the original variable. This might be helpful for a variable such as the mother's education, in which we want to verify that the GED code of 25 on the original variables gets appropriately converted to a 12 on the new variable.

In Stata, the syntax for cross-tabulating two variables is:

```
tabulate <var1> <var2>, missing
```

We typically include the `missing` option. By default, Stata omits cases that are coded '.' missing on either variable from the cross-tabulation. But, we would like to verify that cases with missing value codes on the original variable are appropriately converted to '.' missing on the new variable, so we want to include them in the cross-tabulation.

In our case, for the education variable, we would type:

```
tabulate g1yrschl M502, missing
```

Display B.4.5 provides the commands and results for a short batch program that creates the new earnings and education variables. In the interest of space, we present just a portion of the cross-tabulated results between the created and original earnings variables. We also show a portion of the spreadsheet view of the new data.

In the cross-tabulation, we see that cases generally retain their value from the original variable to the new variable, as we expected based on the `generate g1yrschl=M502` portion of our command. For example, 290 cases were coded a *0* on the original variable and are coded a *0* on the new variable; and, 27 cases were coded a *1* on the original variable and are coded a *1* on the new variable. We can also see that our *if* qualifier, `if M502<98`, accomplished our goal of converting cases coded 98 or 99 on the original variable to '.' missing on the new variable (values in green circle in Display B.4.5). Finally, our `replace` command, `replace g1yrschl=12 if M502==25`, also worked as we desired. The value of 4 circled in black shows that four cases were originally coded a 25 on M502 and are now coded a 12 on *g1yrschl*.

The spreadsheet view also allows us to verify some values for the education variable (although no values of 25 on the original variable are visible in the cases shown in the screenshot, illustrating why the cross-tabulation is more helpful for this variable). The spreadsheet view is particularly useful for the earnings variable. The value of 1014.008 highlighted in the seventh row of the spreadsheet view allows us to spot check the results to see if `generate g2earn=IREARN*207.342/109.6` worked properly for this case. For the seventh case, we need to substitute the original value of IREARN into the formula `IREARN*207.342/109.6`. In the seventh row, IREARN is 536. Plugging into the formula gives us, 536*207.342/109.6=1014.0083 which matches the value of the new variable *g2earn* that is highlighted in the seventh row. Based on the spreadsheet, we can also see that the *if* qualifier, `if IREARN<9999997`, appropriately converted the visible cases larger than 9,999,997 on IREARN to '.' missing in the first and sixth rows.

SAS Syntax for Creating and Modifying New Variables

In SAS, there is not a command devoted to creating a new variable. We simply type:

```
<variable name>=expression;
```

For example,

```
g2age=M2BP01;
g2earn=IREARN*207.342/109.6;
```

Importantly, though, this command must occur within the DATA step (between the word DATA and the RUN statement). This means that we must anticipate all of the new variables that we will need in our batch program, and create them all in the DATA step or remember to put them between DATA and RUN when we later add them to the batch program. We cannot create a new variable outside of the DATA step, right before a PROC FREQ where we want to use it. (In contrast, Stata does allow variables to be created anywhere within a batch program, although we generally find it easier for proofing purposes to group variable creation together at the beginning of a Stata batch program.)

We can also use an `if` statement to address missing data in SAS, as in Stata. However, in SAS, the `if` qualifier comes at the *beginning* of the command and is paired with the word `then`. The general syntax is:

```
if <expression> then <variable name> = <expression>;
```

For example,

```
if M2BP01<97 then g2age = M2BP01;
if I REARN<9999997 then g2earn=I REARN*207.342/109.6;
```

Checking Created Variables in SAS

We can use both the spreadsheet view and the cross-tabulation to check our new variables in SAS, as we did in Stata. In SAS, we can use the PROC FREQ command to request cross-tabulations. The syntax is:

```
proc freq; tables <var1>*<var2> /missing; run;
```

The `/missing` portion of the command is a SAS option (in SAS, options follow a slash rather than a comma). As with Stata, the option requests that missing values be shown in the cross-tabulation.

For the education variable that we examined in Stata, we would type:

```
proc freq; tables g1yrschl*M502 /missing; run;
```

Display B.4.6 shows a short batch program in SAS that accomplishes the same tasks as the short Stata batch program shown in Display B.4.5. The SAS cross-tabulation and spreadsheet show the same results as did Stata (although in SAS, the '.' missing value is treated as the lowest rather than highest possible value, so it is listed in the first rather than the last row of the table; see Box 4.10).

4.4: EXPANDING THE BATCH PROGRAM TO KEEP A SUBSET OF CASES

We would like to restrict our entire analytic file using the variables capturing whether the mother is alive (E1301), whether the respondent was born in the USA (M497A), and whether the mother doesn't coreside with the respondent and doesn't live outside the USA (E1305). We can translate these plain English statements into SAS or Stata syntax expressions, similarly to what we did above in creating new variables, and then use `if` qualifiers to keep just a subset of the data.

> **■ Box 4.10**
>
> In the interest of space, we used additional options in SAS so that only the number in each cell was shown (rather than also row, column, and total percentages). So, our actual command was proc freq; tables g1yrsch1*M502 /nocum nocol norow nopercent missing; run;

Based on the documentation in Display B.3.1 and the operators in Display A.4.1, we can write the corresponding syntax expressions for these statements:

In Words	In Stata Syntax
Mother is alive	E1301==1
Respondent was born in the USA	M497A<=51 | M497A==990 | M497A==996
Mother doesn't coreside with the respondent and doesn't live outside the USA	E1305~=9994 & E1305~=9995

These three expressions can then be combined together with additional & operators to create an `if` qualifier:

```
if E1301==1 & (M497A<=51 | M497A==990 | M497A==996) & E1305~=9994 & E1305~=9995
```

Note that we put the second expression, which contains symbols for "or," in parentheses to help us proof it and assure that it is properly interpreted by SAS and Stata. In Stata, we can place this qualifier at the end of our `use` command. Then, Stata will only read into memory the subset of cases that meet the conditions of these expressions.[1] In SAS, we put a similar `if` statement in the DATA step (although the double equals must be changed to single equals for SAS; see again shaded text in Display A.4.1). We added these `if` qualifiers, and show in Display B.4.7 the full batch program, including all of the new variable creation listed in Display B.3.1. We also added some finishing touches to the batch program, which we will turn to in Section 4.6.

4.5: COMPLEX SAMPLING DESIGNS

We will create a separate version of the dataset for analyses that adjust for the study's complex sampling design. We do so for two reasons. First, most commands we will use to adjust for the study design expect us to include all cases (not just the subset kept in Section 4.4). Second, the PSU and Strata variables for the NSFH data require us to use two additional data management commands. Although we will not use these commands elsewhere in the book, they may be useful if you access other secondary data sets that require them.

Adding the *WEIGHT* variable is simple, because it is in the same file as the variables we have already kept, so we need only add it to our list of variables (see Display B.4.8). The other variables—PSU and Stratum—are in a different file. We must first read them into SAS and Stata format and then merge them together with our other variables. We will introduce some commands in this section to accomplish these tasks.

The *sudaan.dat* data file that we located in Chapter 3 from the NSFH documentation and which contains the PSU and Stratum variables is only available for download in *ascii* format. As we described in Section 3.1, this format is a plain text file of rows and columns of numbers. We must write a program in order to read *sudaan.dat* and then save it in SAS and Stata format. Display B.4.9 shows the program we wrote to read the *sudaan.dat* file. The new commands we used (infile, input, and lrecl in SAS and infix in Stata) are summarized in Display A.4.3. Before we began, we looked at the file *sudaan.doc* from the NSFH documentation which tells us which columns contain each variable in the *sudaan.dat* file:

```
1–5       Id
6–8       Stratum
9–11      PSU
12–13     NewLA
```

This tells us that in each row of the *sudaan.dat* plain text file, the person's id (which we will name *MCASEID* to match our other NSFH data file) will be in the first five columns (column 1–5), the *Stratum* variable will be in the next three columns (6–8), the *PSU* variable will be in the next three columns (9–11), and a variable called *NewLA* will be in the final two columns (12–13). *NewLA* indicates the listing areas that the NSFH used at the final stage of listing households.

We refer to these locations in our SAS and our Stata commands in Display B.4.9, listing each variable followed by its location:

```
MCASEID 1–5 Stratum 6–8 PSU 9–11 NewLA 12–13
```

In Stata, this list follows the command infix. In SAS this list follows the command input.

We tell Stata where to find the *sudaan.dat* file that contains these variables at the end of the infix command with the words using sudaan.dat. We tell SAS where to find the *sudaan.dat* file using the infile command; this commands ends with a command called lrecl that tells SAS how long each record is (13 columns total, through the last number for *NewLA*). Specifically, we wrote infile 'c:\nsfh_distance\sas\sudaan.dat' lrecl = 13; The rest of the SAS and Stata commands are parallel to those we used when creating our original analytic data file.

We asked SAS and Stata to save the data in their own formats with the name *sudaan* but the default extension *.dta* for Stata and *.sas7bdat* in SAS. If you replicate our code, you should see those new data files saved in your working directory. We also used `procfreq` in SAS and `codebook` in Stata to verify that the *Stratum, PSU* and *NewLA* variables were read correctly. If you replicate our code, you should find that the *Stratum* variable contains integers ranging from 1 to 199, that *PSU* contains integers ranging from 0 to 99, and that *NewLA* contains integers ranging from 1 to 27.

With these variables read and saved in SAS and Stata format, we next merge them together with the other variables in our analytic data file. To accomplish this task, we want SAS and Stata to find the *Stratum* and *PSU* values in our new files for each case (i.e., the stratum and PSU that correspond to each *MCASEID*) and match these values with the values of the other variables from our original files for each case (i.e., corresponding to each *MCASEID*). Display B.4.8 shows the syntax we used to accomplish this task; the new syntax is summarized in Display A.4.3. Comparing Display B.4.8 to Display B.4.7 notice that, for SAS, we use the command `merge` in Display B.4.8 where we had used the command `set` in Display B.4.7. After the `merge` command, rather than listing a single file we list the two files that we want to merge. We can keep just a subset of variables from one or both files within this merge command, as we do from the larger main NSFH file. We then have a new command directly after the merge command: `by` `MCASEID`. This asks SAS to merge the two datasets by *MCASEID*, so that the values for each case from one file are matched with the values for that same case in the other file. In Stata, we `use` the data as we had in Display B.4.7, although we have omitted the `if` expression at the end of the command (we will say more about that below). We have then added a new command `merge1:1` `MCASED` `using` `sudaan`.[2] This command asks Stata to merge the values for each case from the original main NSFH file with the values for each case in the new data file (`using` `sudaan`).[3]

There are three final sets of code that differ in Display B.4.8 versus Display B.4.7. First, as we noted above, we removed the `if` qualifier from the end of the `use` command in Stata. We also modified the related `if` expression in SAS. In both programs, we now want to keep all cases and create a new indicator variable that designates the cases we want to use in our analysis. We do this because this approach will allow us to obtain the correct results from complex survey commands in later chapters. Specifically, in both programs, we created a new variable called *DistanceSample* which is coded *1* if the case meets the conditions to be in our analytic sample (`E1301=1` `&` `(M497A<=51` `|` `M497A=990` `|` `M497A=996)` `&` `E1305~=9994` `&` `E1305~=9995`) and is coded *0* for all other cases (see again Display B.4.8).

Second, in both the SAS and Stata programs we added syntax to create an adjusted version of the weight variable. This adjusted variable accounts for the fact that the documentation indicates the variable should have five digits with four decimals (but the variable as we read it into the SAS and Stata files has five digits with no decimals). Thus, we created a variable *adjweight* which is the original *WEIGHT* variable divided by 10,000.

Third, in the SAS program, we created an adjusted version of the *Stratum* variable called *StratumC*. This variable recodes the certainty PSUs to all have the same value; the value is arbitrary, we use 999. We know from the NSFH documentation that the certainty PSUs all have PSU values above 100, so we use the statement `if Stratum>=100 then StratumC=999` to accomplish this recoding. This recoding is the first of two steps needed for SAS to appropriately adjust for the certainty PSUs. The second step is shown in Display B.4.10. The program in Display B.4.10 creates a data set called *rate.sas7bdat* which has one record for every Stratum and has a new variable called *rate* which is coded 1 for the certainty PSUs and coded 0 for the non-certainty PSUs. Although we will not need to use the syntax shown in Display B.4.10 again in the book, you could modify it if you use a secondary data set that has certainty PSUs. We will show how to use the *rate* data set in Chapter 5.

4.6: SOME FINISHING TOUCHES

We end the chapter by discussing some finishing touches for a batch program—adding comments and spacing to make the program easier to understand and proof, and checking the program for errors.

4.6.1: Comments and Spacing

Looking at Display B.4.7, you may realize that you have forgotten what some variables represent, what some code accomplishes, or why some decisions were made. Adding comments to your batch program helps you to remember such intents and decisions, especially when you come back to code that you wrote days, weeks, months, or even years earlier. These comments also help others, including your adviser, peers, or collaborators, to understand your batch program.

How can we add a comment? SAS and Stata cannot directly distinguish notes that we might type into our batch program from commands meant to manipulate or analyze the data. However, both packages provide special symbols that can be used to tell the software that what follows is not a command to be run.

■ In either SAS or Stata, comments may be added to batch programs using pairs of /* and */. These symbols can be used to "comment out" any section of the batch program. That is the software ignores whatever comes between the symbols. These comment symbols can be useful for lengthy comments as well as for excluding a subsection of the batch program from running (useful when debugging—locating and fixing errors).

■ Both SAS and Stata also allow single lines or commands to be "commented out" by placing an asterisk (*) at the beginning of the line or command.

■ Stata also allows the double slash // to be used to comment out anything from the double slash to the end of the line and the triple slash /// to be used to comment out the end-of-line delimiter allowing for commands to extend beyond one line.

Spacing can also be helpful to assist in understanding and debugging a batch program. You can add white space to your batch program simply by adding spaces, tabs, or lines. For example, commands do not have to begin in the first position of a line, but may be spaced or tabbed over.

We used such tabbing in our SAS code in the left column of Display B.4.7. We also added spacing within lines to make it easier to scan and check them (e.g., lining up the word `then`) cross multiple lines. We also added a comment to remind ourselves about the factor multiplied by `IREARN`. We included both what the factor did and where we obtained the CPI values online, so that it would be easy to return to the source if needed in the future.

Stata's default requirement that a command cannot extend over more than one line is sometimes limiting for adding spacing, and very long lines can be difficult to read. Stata does offer several ways around this default, though. The preferred method used by Stata programmers is to put three forward slashes (///) at the end of each continuing line (see Display B.4.7 for an example).[4]

4.6.2: Debugging

Students usually find it frustrating when their batch program ends with an error message, but even experienced programmers expect to spend some time finding and fixing errors—debugging—their batch program. Because the statistical software packages lack human intelligence, they cannot forgive our syntax mistakes as someone might if we were just learning a spoken language. Many typos will cause SAS and Stata to end abruptly and wait for us to fix the error and re-submit the batch program.

Common errors include misspelling commands, misspelling file or variable names, and (in SAS) forgetting the semicolon at the end of lines. SAS's **enhanced editor** is useful for finding many such errors. For example, it uses red font to show syntax it cannot understand as you type (even before you try running the syntax). Panel a in Display B.4.11 shows an example in which we misspelled `if` and `proc`. On your screen, these error messages would stand out in red font (circled in the Display). We also left the semicolon off of the end of one line. This error would not be displayed by SAS in red font, so it would not be quite as easy to see, but the `if` following the missing semicolon would be in black font rather than the blue font of the other `if` statements.

If you do not catch errors before submitting the batch program, then SAS will issue an error message in the Log window. Examples are shown in Display B.4.12. The errors again would stand out on your screen because they would be in red font. A message accompanies the ERROR note for each of our three errors. Some of these messages make it easy to diagnose the problem, while others do not. The middle message clearly tells us that we have forgotten a semicolon. But, the first simply says the statement is "out of order" and the last that there is "no default data file." In these cases, we have to scrutinize the syntax around the underlined code to look for errors (see Box 4.11).

> **■ Box 4.11**
>
> We like to use the shortcut keys F7, F6, F5 on your keyboard to move among the windows when we are debugging a SAS program. The key stroke Ctrl-E can also be used to erase the Log and Output windows before rerunning a program. Try typing F7, Ctrl-E, F6, Ctrl-E, F5, F8 (where F8 submits the program).

The use of color in Stata's editing window can also help you identify errors before running a program. Panel b in Display B.4.11 shows examples where we changed the first `generate` command to `genrate` and the `codebook` command to `codbook`. Both are now shown in black rather than blue font on the screen. However, Stata stops running the batch program when an error occurs, requiring you to fix the error before it moves forward in the code. In Display B.4.13 we show Stata's message when we create a spelling error in the command `generate`. Stata is also very careful about overwriting data and log files. As we noted above, unless we explicitly tell it to replace an existing data file, or log file, Stata will stop with an error message. Thus, it is useful to place the option `replace` at the end of `log` and `save` statements, as we suggested above.

Stata's caution about helping us to avoid losing our work can also result in errors when we rerun a batch program repeatedly, as we write it in stages or debug it. If a data set is already in memory or a log file is already open from the first run of the batch program, we will get an error message when we try to reopen the data or re-open the log in a second run of the batch program (e.g., `no; data in memory would be lost` or `log file already open`). We can avoid these problems by starting our batch program with the commands `capture drop _all` (which drops any data that may be in memory) and `capture log close` (which closes any logs that may be open). When we put these at the beginning of a batch program, they allow us to "start fresh" every time (knowing that our batch program will later use a data set and open a log).

It is also useful to start all of your Stata batch programs with two additional commands. The command `version 11` (or whichever version you are using) tells Stata what version to use when interpreting the batch program. This assures that your batch program will run, even if changes are made to future releases of Stata. We also like to type `set more off` at the beginning of a batch program, so that we don't have to press a key to move to the next screen as the results appear (instead, we will open the log file to view the entire set of results once the batch program has successfully run without errors).

Like naming files and variables, and writing expressions, there are many different ways to lay out and annotate a batch program. You should experiment with what works best for you, with the ultimate goal of making your batch programs easy for you (and others) to understand and proof.

4.7: SUMMARY

In this chapter, we learned the basics of writing batch programs in SAS and Stata. We learned how to work with each software package and where to write our batch programs, how to save and locate our results, and how to save and locate our analytic data files. We learned some basic syntax and wrote a short batch program to read data, check variables from the raw data file against the documentation, and check the creation of new variables for our analytic data file. In learning how to create new variables and to keep a subgroup of the full sample, we introduced how to use expressions in order to tell SAS and Stata what we want to accomplish. We also reinforced the importance of thoughtfully naming our files and storing them in project folders and of using comments and spacing to help us check and document our work.

KEY TERMS

Case-Sensitive

Command Window

DATA Step

Data Browser

Do-File Editor

Enhanced Editor

Expression

Libname

Operators

Option

Session

Table Editor

Working Directory

REVIEW QUESTIONS

4.1. Where in the batch program can you create new variables in SAS and Stata?

4.2. How do you tell SAS and Stata where a line ends, by default?

4.3. How can you add a comment to SAS and to Stata?

4.4. What are some instances in which we would need to use expressions?

4.5. What are key differences in operators between SAS and Stata?

REVIEW EXERCISES

4.1. Follow the steps in Appendix D to create the SAS and/or Stata raw data files for the NSFH data set.

4.2. Replicate the *ReadAFewVariables* example in SAS and/or Stata from Section 4.1.1; that is, launch the software, open the editor, and type the code to match the batch program shown in Display B.4.4. Be careful to check for typos (which can lead to error messages). Run the batch program and view the results. If necessary, use the suggestions from Section 4.5.2 to identify and fix errors.

4.3. Request the frequency distributions for E1302 and E1305 from SAS and/or Stata and compare them to the results in BADGIR (shown in Display C.3.7 and Display C.3.8) to confirm that these variables were correctly downloaded.

4.4. Write and run the *CreateData* example shown in Display B.4.7 in SAS and/or Stata. Use the techniques described in Section 4.3.2 to verify that the variables are created correctly.

CHAPTER
EXERCISE
4

CHAPTER EXERCISE

Download from ICPSR the NHIS 2009 Sample Adult data file in SAS and in Stata format (see Appendix E for suggestions).

Write a program to extract *all* of the raw variables that you identified in the chapter exercise to Chapter 3.

Create *three* new variables (We will create additional variables in future chapters).

Be careful to check that the new variables' values are as you expect using the methods discussed in the chapter (looking at the spreadsheet view of the data; using tabulations and cross-tabulations of original and created variables).

Save the analytic data file created by your program.

Created Variable Name	Variable Coding (In Words)
age	The NHIS documentation indicates that there are no missing data on AGE_P (be sure to verify that the AGE_P values all fall within the valid range of ages in your downloaded data). Our new variable *age* can thus be generated directly from AGE_P with no recoding needed.
bmiR	The NHIS documentation indicates that the variable BMI has two implied decimals, thus we need to divide BMI by 100 when we create our variable *bmiR*. We also need to translate the missing values, indicated by 9999, to '.' missing.

exfreqwR	We want *exfreqwR* to capture the number of times per week that the Sample Adult engages in physical activity, summing across vigorous (VIGFREQW), light/medium (MODFREQW) and strength-enhancing (STRFREQW) activities. Since each of these variables can range from 0 to 28 our new variable should range from 0 to 3*28=84 (be sure to check this after creating the variable). Each of the original variables has values that need to be recoded before calculating the sum (i.e., *95=never* should be recoded to zero, the missing value indicators of 97, 98, and 99 should be recoded to '.' missing, we will also treat *96=Unable to do* the type of exercise as '.' missing[5]). This can be easily achieved by first creating recoded versions of the three original variables (e.g., name them *vigfreqwR*, *modfreqwR*, and *strfreqwR*) and then summing the recoded variables.

Turn in: 1) your final *.sas* and *.do* programs and 2) a brief paragraph describing what you found most helpful and challenging in writing your programs.

COURSE EXERCISE

Choose one of the data sets that you identified in Chapter 2 for one of your research questions. Download the raw data. Create an analytic data set that contains at least three variables: the case identifier, a dependent variable, and an independent variable. Recode these variables as needed (e.g., to convert missing data codes to . missing).

If you identified multiple candidate data sets, you may want to focus on the simplest (e.g., a data set that can be downloaded directly in SAS or Stata format as a single file). Or, you can utilize one of the example data sets used in the textbook (NSFH or NOS).

Part 2

BASIC DESCRIPTIVE AND INFERENTIAL STATISTICS

Chapter 5

BASIC DESCRIPTIVE STATISTICS

CHAPTER 5: BASIC DESCRIPTIVE STATISTICS

With our analytic data file now ready, we are poised to begin to examine our research questions. We could open our analytic file in SAS or Stata and request basic statistics right now (possibly simply using the pull down menus). If we were thoughtful in examining the results, however, doing so would likely lead to many questions and considerable confusion. Indeed, much work lies ahead of us in learning how to appropriately estimate and interpret various statistics. We will begin in this part of the book with learning about basic descriptive and inferential statistics.

There are multiple reasons to calculate descriptive statistics. As we saw in Chapter 4, they help us verify our understanding of how a variable is measured and check for errors in data entry or data coding. In this chapter, we will focus on how we use descriptive statistics to help us become familiar with our data as we prepare for analyses. We will also begin to see how these descriptive statistics offer vital information to help us (and readers) interpret our regression results, something we will expand upon in future chapters.

We begin by reviewing various terminology often used to classify types of variables in the social sciences. We then present two excerpts from the social science literature that demonstrate how descriptive statistics for such different types of variables are presented in publications. This is followed by our use of the NSFH distance example to demonstrate the use of descriptive graphs and statistics to examine our own data. We focus on tools that are frequently used by social scientists, including histograms and box plots, calculation of percentages and identification of the mode, calculation of percentiles including the median and the related interquartile range, and calculation of the mean and standard deviation. You are probably already somewhat familiar with most of these terms from prior classes and general reading; We will define each more precisely in later sections of this chapter. You may read about or need to use additional descriptive tools, and many excellent reference books are available to learn more about them (Hoaglin, Mosteller, and Tukey 2000; Tukey 1977).

The statistics we will discuss can be usefully grouped into those that capture: 1) the "center" or "most common" of a variable's values and 2) the degree of variation across those values. These are two key features of a variable that help us to understand our data, summarize our data and interpret our analyses. For example, when studying individuals in the social sciences, we often want to know something about their demographic characteristics, such as the income distribution of study participants. We might interpret a study's results differently if we know that most participants have relatively low incomes (say typically $20,000) versus relatively high incomes (say typically $100,000). We might likewise interpret the results

differently if we knew that the study participants' incomes are concentrated around this typical value (say mostly varying within a few thousand dollars of it) versus being more widely dispersed around it (say varying by tens of thousands of dollars around it). Understanding these features of our data will also help us select appropriate models for our data and help us interpret those models in meaningful ways. As we shall see, the mode, median, and mean can all be used as measures of the central or most common value and the interquartile range and the standard deviation can both be used to measure variation. Such values are usually included in a table of descriptive statistics and summarized in the text of an article, to help the reader interpret a study's findings.

Graphs also help us visualize the most common value on a variable and the degree of variation around this most common value. Often, patterns that are somewhat difficult to discern in a table of numbers jump out immediately in a graph. And, some variables are distributed in ways that are not well summarized by just a single central value and related measure of variation (for example, distributions where most values are small but some are quite large or distributions which have two "peaks" representing two most likely values). When beginning a project, it is quite helpful to view each of the variables in our analytic data set graphically. These visual cues also help us understand our data better and allow us to make well-informed choices about our regression models. We typically cannot share all of these graphs with our readers, due to constraints on space and limits on the amount of information that readers can process. But, we might present some graphs of variables central to our research question or particularly unique to our data set (and we will learn how to use graphs to present regression results in future chapters).

5.1: TYPES OF VARIABLES

Social scientists use several ways of classifying variables into different types, each of which helps us understand our data and consider what types of statistical techniques are most informative for each variable. Table 5.1 summarizes several of these classifications, highlighting where they overlap.

The three variable types listed in the first column of Table 5.1 are likely already familiar to you, as they are widely used by social scientists.[1] The distinctions between them reflect whether the values on the variable capture order and/or magnitude. The values of a **nominal** variable allow us to classify groups that have no intrinsic order. Examples are gender, race-ethnicity, religion,

■ Table 5.1: Classifications of Types of Variables

Nominal	Qualitative		
		Categorical	Discrete
Ordinal			
Interval			
			Continuous/Quantitative

and region of the U.S. The values we use to designate the categories of such a nominal variable are completely arbitrary. For example, we could designate gender with a *1* for women and a *2* for men, or a *2* for women and a *1* for men, or even a *453* for women and *6554* for men, without any loss of information. There are simply two gender groups, men and women, and in our data set we need to designate each with some value.

ordinal

The values of **ordinal** variables reflect order but not magnitude. Cases with higher values on an ordinal variable have more of the construct captured by the variable than those with lower values, but the specific values of the numbers are arbitrary. For example, rating scales often use labels such as *strongly disagree, disagree, agree* and *strongly agree* to allow respondents to indicate their level of agreement with a statement. The values attached to these response categories should reflect the order of agreement, with *strongly agree > agree > disagree > strongly disagree*, but the distance between the values would be arbitrary. That is, 100, 40, 10, and 1 captures the four response categories as well as 4, 3, 2, and 1. Each set of values reflects the fact that people with a higher numeric value agree more than those with a lower numeric value, but how much more they agree is not known precisely.[2]

The values on **interval** variables reflect both order and magnitude. Any two values that are separated by the same numeric distance are separated by the same amount of the construct captured by the variable. Examples include earnings measured in dollars or distance measured in miles. Two people who earn $60,000 and $50,000 are separated by as much on their salaries as two people who earn $20,000 and $10,000. And, commuters who travel 35 versus 40 miles to work each day are separated by the same distance as those who travel 5 versus 10 miles to work each day.

The last two columns of Table 5.1 show another common way variables are classified, as discrete or continuous. **Discrete** variables can take on only a finite set of values, typically integers.

■ Box 5.2

SAS and Stata, like most statistical packages, allow users to define both numeric and string variables. String variables can store words rather than numbers. Such string variables could be used for nominal variables. For example, a string variable *gender* could use the word *male* to designate men and the word *female* to designate women. However, numeric variables must still be defined to capture the classes of nominal variables for some types of analyses (as we will see in Chapter 10). And, most secondary data sets store most variables with numeric values, even nominal variables (as the NSFH does for gender and race-ethnicity).

Continuous variables can take on an infinite set of values, typically with decimals representing any value between two integers. Nominal and ordinal variables are both discrete. The term **categorical** is also sometimes used for nominal and/or ordinal data (3rd column of Table 1), reflecting the various categories that the values of the variable represent. Interval variables can be either discrete or continuous. A **count** variable is a common example of a discrete interval variable, since a count takes on only integer values. Variables that record "numbers of" characteristics are all counts, such as a person's number of siblings or number of friends or the number of times a person has been married or been employed. In contrast, a continuous interval variable can be recorded with non-integer values such as earnings, income, or distance (although as discussed below variables which could be recorded continuously are sometimes recorded with integers, in order to reduce response burden—the time and mental effort required for a study participant to respond to a question).

The final set of terms from Table 5.1 that we have not yet discussed are qualitative and quantitative. **Qualitative** is synonymous with nominal. **Quantitative** is synonymous with continuous. Although you may sometimes see these terms used to refer to types of variables, we prefer to use the other terms in the table, because using qualitative and quantitative to refer to variable types can sometimes be confused with the distinction between qualitative and quantitative approaches to research (the latter encompassing statistical analyses of nominal as well as ordinal and interval variables).

Although the distinctions between the variables summarized in Table 5.1 can be precisely described in the abstract, the lines are often blurred with real data (Velleman & Wilkinson 1993). For example, real data are often collected such that variables which could be measured continuously are collected using discrete values, again often to reduce response burden. Such data collection strategies also reflect limits in the precision with which we can record and store numbers. For instance, age may be gathered in integer years rather than the difference between the moment of birth and moment of interview. Likewise, income is sometimes gathered in intervals (e.g., less than $5,000, $5,001–15,000, $15,001–$25,000) rather than exact values (and even when more exact income is gathered it is often recorded to the nearest dollar rather than, say, the nearest penny).

Even with such gray areas in real data, thinking about the characteristics of a variable in relation to the types summarized in Table 5.1 helps us choose appropriate statistical techniques and

---

■ Box 5.3

The concept of significant digits is helpful in thinking about how to record values with a comparable amount of precision, especially when the value can include decimals. Significant digits are the digits that carry meaning in a value. These include all non-zero digits, all zeros that appear between two non-zero digits, and trailing zeros. For example, 564.32 and 455.20 both have five significant digits. If we omitted the zero from 455.20 and instead wrote 455.2 it might be one of several values including 455.21, 455.22, and 455.23. The concept of significant digits is especially helpful when we need to choose how to round values for presentation in tables, and we will come back to it as we discuss rescaling in Chapter 8.

interpret their results correctly. We divide our discussion of descriptive statistics and graphs below into three sections, specific to nominal, ordinal, and interval variables. This helps us demonstrate that, generally, statistical computations for different types of measures are cumulative from nominal to ordinal to interval variables (Stevens 1946). We can define percentiles (including the median) for interval as well as ordinal variables. We can define percentages and the mode for interval and ordinal as well as nominal variables. But, the reverse is not true (the median is not appropriate for a nominal variable; the mean is not appropriate for nominal or ordinal variables).

Like with the often gray distinction between types of variables in real applications, the strict definition of certain types of analyses being appropriate for only certain types of variables is also sometimes hazy in practice. For example, ordinal variables are common in the social sciences and, not infrequently, means and standard deviations are calculated for them, sometimes informatively.

A similar situation arises with regression techniques, as we shall see later in the book. When our outcome or predictor variable in a regression model is ordinal, some regression techniques designed for interval variables are not strictly appropriate. However, social scientists sometimes use these regression techniques when their variables are ordinal. The extent to which such usage is problematic will vary from application to application (depending on the extent to which the ordinal variable is actually close to interval). As social scientists, we should at least understand our data well, recognize when we are applying techniques not strictly appropriate to a variable's type of measurement and, ideally, examine the assumptions (as we will demonstrate how to do in later chapters).

Thoughtfulness about type of measurement is especially important given that it is easy to ask statistical software to calculate statistics for all of the variables in a data set. In many instances, neither SAS nor Stata will stop with an error message when you ask it to do something strictly inappropriate for the type of variable, such as to compute the mean for a nominal variable. Even if we clearly understand that such calculations are not conceptually meaningful, we may end up inadvertently asking SAS and Stata to make such calculations (or worse yet include these results in a paper) unless we pay careful attention to our variables' type(s). Such extra attention will pay off in the long run as we select statistical procedures that are strictly appropriate for each of our variables (or recognize the assumptions that may be violated when we do not).

To achieve this goal, one strategy we find helpful is to think about whether each of our variables could be considered nominal, ordinal, and/or interval before beginning our analyses. As we do so, we often find that some of our variables fall in the gray area between two types. Looking back at the variables in Display B.3.1 that we extracted from the NSFH for our distance example, clearly the gender and race-ethnicity of the respondent are nominal variables. We can ask respondents to classify themselves into categories as we gather these variables, but there is no intrinsic order implicit in the values we assign in the data to designate these categories.

The remaining variables in our NSFH analytic data set, shown in Display B.3.1, are either ordinal or interval, although the distinction between ordinal and interval is not always clearcut. For example, we anticipate that most social scientists would designate the variables capturing distance from the mother, the respondent's and the mother's age, and total earnings as interval variables, since "one more" on these variables always represents the same amount (one more mile, one more year, one more dollar). Number of brothers and sisters and highest grade completed might be considered interval by many social scientists as well, since "one more" on these variables represents one more sibling (of each gender) and one more year of school completed. However, as we will see, the relatively few observed categories for number of brothers and sisters in our actual data may lead us to find statistics like percentage distributions more informative ways to describe these variables than means and standard deviations. And, education is sometimes gathered and at other times conceptualized in a way that leads us to treat it as ordinal rather than interval (e.g., if degrees are captured as well as—or instead of—number of years of schooling).

5.2: LITERATURE EXCERPTS 5.1 AND 5.2

In this section we provide two examples of the use of descriptive statistics to summarize a sample, a common use of descriptive statistics in social science publications. Not only are such values useful in helping the reader visualize the characteristics of the sample on which our analyses are based, but some of these descriptive statistics will also be used in interpreting regression results (as first discussed in Chapter 8).

■ Box 5.4

Before we turn to the examples, it is helpful to keep in mind that different disciplines and journals follow somewhat different style guidelines. To understand the style used in your field, you can consult style guides, such as the AMA Manual of Style (Iverson, Christiansen, Flanagin, et al. 2007), American Sociological Association Style Guide (American Sociological Association, 2007) and Publication Manual of the American Psychological Association (American Psychological Association 2009), and also refer to the submission guidelines for particular journals. Most offer guidance about how to construct tables and what symbols to use to designate various statistics. In general, style guidelines recommend that tables be self contained, so that readers can interpret much of a table's content without searching for details and definitions within the text.

5.2.1: Literature Excerpt 5.1

Our first literature excerpt comes from an article by Jay Teachman (2008) in the *Journal of Marriage and Family* which used the National Survey of Family Growth (Centers for Disease Control and Prevention 2010) to examine the dissolution of second marriages. Descriptive statistics for the study variables, including the percentage, mean and standard deviation, are shown in the article's Table 1 (reproduced as Literature Excerpt 5.1).

▪ **Literature Excerpt 5.1**

Table 1.   Descriptive Statistics for Covariates Used in the Analysis of Second Marital Dissolution: 2002 National Survey of Family Growth

Variable	M or %	SD
Age at second marriage	29.43	5.75
Race/ethnicity		
Hispanic	10.83	
Black	6.90	
White (baseline)	82.27	
Two parent childhood family until age 18	61.02	
Religion		
Catholic	35.77	
No religion	5.38	
Other religion (baseline)	58.85	
Mother's educational attainment	2.11	0.97
Respondent's educational attainment	12.88	2.32
Number of siblings	2.72	1.60
Wife at least two years older	0.64	
Husband at least five years older	20.61	
Husband married before	49.66	
Cohabitation history		
Cohabited with first husband only	11.35	
Cohabited with second husband only	36.83	
Cohabited with both husbands	23.35	
Cohabited with other than first husband	3.43	
Cohabited with other than second husband	8.62	
Never cohabited	16.42	
Husband's fertility		
Number of children from prior relationship	0.77	1.14
Husband's children lived with family	18.00	
Respondent's fertility		
Number of births from prior relationships	0.95	0.92
Intermarital birth while cohabiting with second husband	10.76	

Note: All values are weighted. $N = 655$ women.

Source: Teachman, Jay. 2008. "Complex Life Course Patterns and the Risk of Divorce in Second Marriages." *Journal of Marriage and Family,* 70: 294–305.

The variable names, and the levels of nominal variables, are shown in the first column of Teachman's table. The second column heading is M or %, standard abbreviations for the mean and percentage. The third column heading is SD, a common abbreviation for standard deviation. The notes at the end of the table often contain important information, and in this case they provide the sample size of 655 (abbreviated N) and keys us to the fact that the analysis is restricted to women. The notes also tell us that the values are weighted, a topic we will return to in Section 5.6.

Looking through the variables and values, we can deduce that the standard deviation is shown only in conjunction with the mean and only for apparently interval variables, including age, educational attainment, and numbers of siblings, children and births. The remaining variables appear to be nominal, and have percentages shown. Some of the nominal variables have more than two categories (Race/ethnicity, Religion, and Cohabitation history). For these, the percentage in each category is shown, and the total across all categories sums to 100%. Indentation helps us see which categories group together (e.g., the percentages in the Hispanic, Black, and White categories of Race/ethnicity of 10.83, 6.90, and 82.27 sum to 100%). The other nominal variables have two categories (family structure in childhood, wives' and husbands' relative ages,[3] husbands' prior marital status, husbands' coresident children, and birth while cohabiting). As is common for such two-category variables, the percentage in one category is shown, since the percentage in the other category can be easily deduced (e.g., $100 - 61.02 = 38.98\%$ of respondents did not live in a two parent family through age 18).

Teachman uses these data to describe the sample in the text (p. 300). For multi-category variables, he uses the category with the highest percentage (the mode) to typify the most common category.

> "The average age at second marriage in this sample is nearly 29 years. A majority of the women are White, grew up in two-parent families, express some religion other than Catholicism, have reasonably well-educated mothers (at least a high school degree), are high school graduates, come from moderate size families, and are approximately the same age as their husbands (although if there is an age difference, husbands are more likely to be older) . . ."

Such characterizations of the average characteristics of a sample are fairly common in publications that use regression analyses, and help readers paint a portrait of the sample in their minds.

A careful reading of the table and text illustrates the gray area often occupied by ordinal variables. The author described the sample as having "reasonably well-educated mothers (at least a high school degree)" although in Table 1, we see that the mean for "Mother's educational attainment" is 2.11. Looking back at the Method section of the article reveals that mother's education is actually better described as ordinal, being coded as "1 = *less than high school*, 2 = *high school graduate or GED*, 3 = *some college*, 4 = *bachelor's degree or higher*" (p. 298). An alternative way to present this variable would be to show the percentages in each of the four categories, similar to what was done for the multi-category nominal variables.

5.2.2: Literature Excerpt 5.2

Our second excerpt is taken from the *American Journal of Public Health* in which Gilbert Gee, Annie Ro, Amelia Gavin, and David Takeuchi (2008) used the National Latino and Asian American Study (Center for Multicultural Mental Health Research 2010) to examine how discrimination based on race and weight are associated with Asian American's measured body weight.

■ Literature Excerpt 5.2

Table 1. Sample Weighted Characteristics of Asian Respondents (n = 1956): National Latino and Asian American Study, 2002–2003

Characteristic	Value
BMI, kg/m², mean (SD)	24.2 (4.4)
Weight category,[a] %	
Underweight/normal	64.9
Overweight	26.9
Obese	9.3
Discrimination,[b] %	
None	25.4
Racial	41.7
Weight	0.8
Other	32.1
12-mo *DSM-IV* mental disorder, %	9.5
Self-rated physical health, %	
Excellent	17.2
Very good	32.5
Good	34.5
Fair	13.4
Poor	2.4
Social desirability bias,[c] mean (SD)	2.2 (2.1)
Age, mean (SD)	41.1 (15.6)
Gender, %	
Women	52.4
Men	47.6
Ethnicity, %	
Vietnamese	12.9
Filipino	21.6
Chinese	28.2
Other Asian or Pacific Islander	37.4
Employed, %	64.1
Immigrant status, %	
Respondent foreign born	76.6
Respondent born in US, at least 1 parent foreign born	14.1
Respondent and both parents born in US	9.4
Years in the US, mean (SD)	16.1 (15.5)
Marital status, %	
Married, living with partner	65.1
Never married, widowed, separated, divorced	34.9

Note. BMI–body mass index; *DSM-IV–Diagnostic and Statistical Manual of Mental Disorders, Fourth Edition*.[56]
[a] We classified BMI into the following categories: underweight (< 18.5 kg/m²), normal (18.5–24.9 kg/m²), overweight (2.50–29.9 kg/m²), and obese (≥ 30.0 kg/m²).
[b] Measures of discrimination were adapted from the Everday Discrimination Scale. In this scale, respondents are first asked to respond to 9 items on unfair treatment and then asked to state the main reason for this unfair treatment.
[c] The scale ranged from 0 (no social desirability bias) to 10 (highest social desirability bias).

Source: Gee, Gilbert, C., Ro, Annie, Gavin, Amelia, and David T. Takeuchi. 2008. "Disentangling the Effects of Racial and Weight Discrimination on Body Mass Index and Obesity Among Asian Americans." *American Journal of Public Health*, 98: 493–500.

Similar to the Teachman article, the values displayed in Table 1 of Gee and colleagues' article (shown in Literature Excerpt 5.2) are means, percentages, and standard deviations (although in the Gee et al. article the symbols designating the statistics are listed at the end of the variable names in the first column). Gee and colleagues also provide some details about abbreviations and measurement of some variables in the table notes, including the cutoffs used to classify study participants as underweight/normal, overweight, or obese.

Like the Teachman article, we see that means and standard deviations are provided for the apparently interval variables (BMI, which as noted in the Table footnote stands for body mass index, social desirability bias, age, and years in the U.S.). Percentages are provided for other variables, including categories of weight, type of discrimination, presence of a mental disorder, self-rated physical health, gender, ethnicity, employment status, immigrant status, and marital status.[4]

The grayness of how to classify and treat seemingly ordinal variables is again evident in Gee and colleagues' article, as we saw in Teachman's article. Unlike Teachman's treatment of mother's education, Gee and colleagues present percentages for most ordinal variables such as the weight categories and self-rated physical health. However, the authors show means and standard deviations for social-desirability, a scale which sums 10 true-false items, can range from 0 to 10, and has a mean of 2.2. Although it is common in the social sciences to treat such simple sums as interval variables, some argue that they should be viewed as ordinal (and item response theory approaches exist to convert the simple sums to interval values; de Ayala 2009; Embretson and Reise 2000; Frank and Kim 2004, a topic we will return to in Chapter 18).

We now turn to reviewing definitions of the descriptive statistics presented in these articles and showing how to request them for our own data in SAS and Stata.

5.3: NOMINAL VARIABLES

As we have seen, nominal variables are best described by their percentage distributions. The mode is often drawn from these distributions to describe the most common category.

5.3.1: Frequency Distribution

A frequency distribution is the count of the number of cases in each category of a variable. A relative frequency distribution divides these values by the total number of cases. A percentage distribution multiplies the relative frequencies by 100. Each of these types of distributions is sometimes used to describe nominal variables in social science publications, although as we saw in Literature Excerpts 5.1 and 5.2, percentage distributions are particularly common.

We already presented the basic SAS and Stata commands for obtaining such frequency distributions in Chapter 4, when we discussed how to check our downloaded data against a study's documentation. As summarized in Display A.4.2, in SAS, we used the proc freq command to request the frequency distribution for a single variable and the cross-tabulation between two variables; and, in Stata, we used the `codebook` command for a single variable's distribution and the `tabulate` command for the cross-tabulation. In this chapter, we focus on univariate statistics meaning that they are calculated for one variable at a time. In Chapter 7, we will discuss **bivariate** statistics (statistics calculated on two variables at a time, like the cross-tabulations requested in Chapter 4). In Stata, we can use `tabulate` not only for bivariate statistics but also for univariate statistics, but only for one variable at a time. If we want to request univariate frequency distributions for several variables at the same time, then we must switch to Stata's `tab1` command (where the 1 after tab can be thought of as requesting one-way distributions for each listed variable rather than cross-tabulations between the listed variables). The basic syntax is summarized in Display A.5.1.

Display B.5.1 shows our use of these commands to request the frequency distribution for the gender and race-ethnicity of the NSFH respondents using the analytic file that we created in Chapter 4 for our distance example (*CreateData*). As shown in Display B.3.1, the original variable name for the "Sex of Respondent" variable is *M2DP01*. And, the original variable name for the "Which Group Describes R (Race)" variable is *M484*. Thus, we use these names as the variable list in the general syntax for `proc freq` in SAS and `tab1` in Stata (see again Display A.5.1).

Both the SAS and the Stata output have columns that show the frequency of cases in each category (the column is labeled *Frequency* in SAS and *Freq.* in Stata). Both sets of output also have columns that show the percentage of cases in each category (the column labeled *Percent* in both sets of output). We will return to discuss the additional columns of numbers in Section 5.4.

Recall that we restricted the distance analytic data file to cases in which the respondent's mother was alive, lived in the U.S., and did not coreside with the respondent. Thus, the total sample size is 6,901. Of these 6,901 cases, Display B.5.1 shows that 2,785 are men (40.36%) and 4,116 are women (59.64%). Regarding race-ethnicity, most respondents are either Black (1,165 or 16.88%) or non-Hispanic white (5,384 or 78.02%). None of the remaining categories comprise over 3% of the sample and all but one of the remaining categories has fewer than 100 cases.

■ Box 5.5

You may have noticed that the first column of the output tables shows words rather than numbers. This is because the original NSFH variables have labels associated with the values that indicate each category (similar to what we saw in Display C.3.6 for *E1301* the variable indicating whether the mother was living or deceased). In Chapter 10 we will look in more detail at how to work with the numerical values associated with categorical variables in regression analyses (see Display C.10). For now, it is worth mentioning that the order in which the categories are shown in Display B.5.1 reflects the values attached to each category (e.g., men are coded a *1* and women are coded a *2* in the NSFH data, so the *MALE* category is shown before the *FEMALE* category). As we noted above, the values attached to the categories of a nominal variable are arbitrary, and this order has no intrinsic meaning. We will also point out that the last category shown for *M484* in Display B.5.1 is a missing data code (*No Answer* which has 3 cases or 0.04% of the sample). We will also return in Chapter 10 to discuss how to create variables for our regression analyses that appropriately recode these 3 cases to '.' missing.

5.3.2: Mode

The mode is simply the most frequent category. Clearly, the value with the highest number of cases will also have the highest proportion or percentage of cases, so any of the distributions (frequency, relative frequency, or proportion) can be used to identify the mode.

As illustrated with the sample summary quoted above in conjunction with Literature Excerpt 5.1, the mode can be particularly useful in describing the most common category of a nominal variable. In the NSFH, the modal category for gender is female (with 59.64% of the cases); and, the modal category for race-ethnicity is non-Hispanic white (with 78.02% of the cases; see again Display B.5.1). Although for both of these variables, the mode had a majority (over 50%) of the cases, this will not always be the case.

5.3.3: Literature Excerpt 5.3

Presentations like those shown in Literature Excerpts 5.1 and 5.2 are common ways of displaying frequency and percentage distributions in social science publications. As noted above, however, when space allows graphs often more effectively convey patterns to readers than tables of such frequencies of percentages. Literature Excerpt 5.3 provides an example of a figure based on the American Community Survey (U.S. Census Bureau 2010b) which was presented in a *Population Bulletin* written by Mark Mather (2009). The figure presents the distribution of country of origin for children of immigrant families in 2007. The modal category of Mexico is visually clear, with almost twice as many children as the next largest category (Asia). As national estimates, the actual values are also meaningful and salient, with over 6,700,000 immigrant children from Mexico in the U.S. in 2007.[5]

5.4: ORDINAL VARIABLES

Especially when an ordinal variable has only a few categories (such as Teachman's four-level variable for mothers' education) the percentage distribution and mode can be used effectively to describe the variable. When the categories of an ordinal variable are more numerous, percentiles—including the median—may be preferred. The median (and other percentiles) are also useful descriptive statistics for continuous variables, especially when the distribution of the variable is not symmetric (as we shall see in Section 5.5.6).

■ **Box 5.6**

Region of the U.S. provides an example in which the mode does not contain a majority of cases. The U.S. Census Bureau estimates that the regional distribution of the U.S. population in 2008 was 18% in the Northeast, 22% in the Midwest, 37% in the South, and 23% in the West (U.S. Census Bureau 2010a). In this case the modal region was the South although no region contained a majority of the population.

■ **Literature Excerpt 5.3**

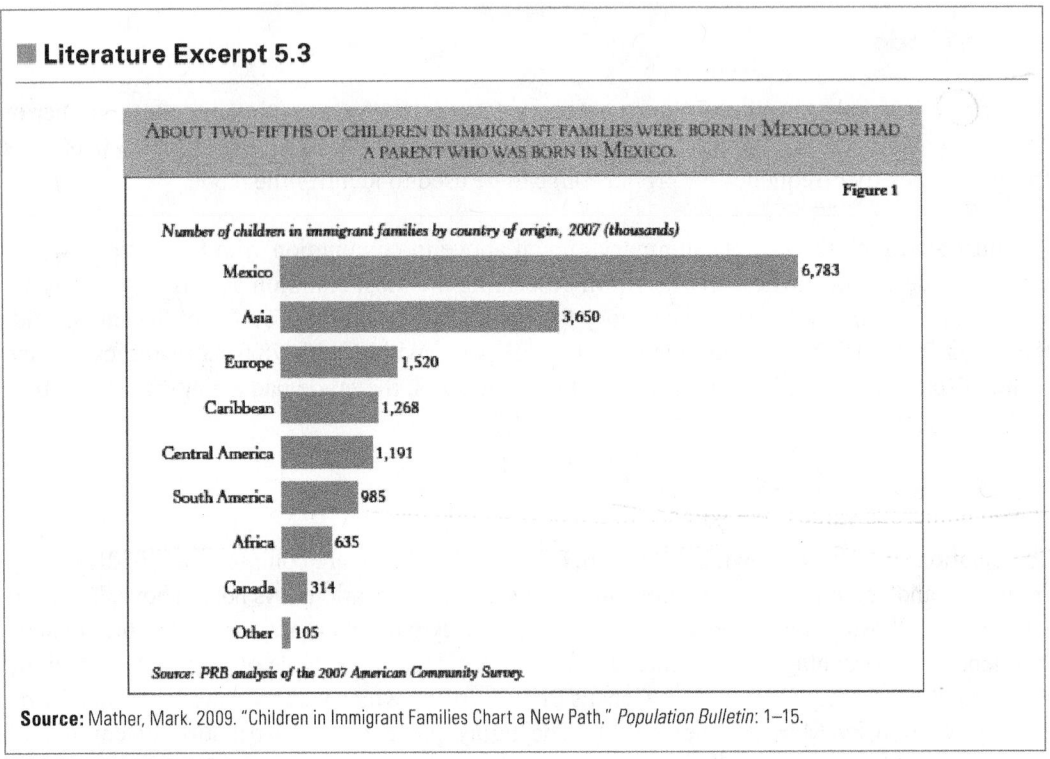

Source: Mather, Mark. 2009. "Children in Immigrant Families Chart a New Path." *Population Bulletin*: 1–15.

5.4.1: Percentiles

The **cumulative frequency** is the running total of the frequency distribution for all categories below and up to the current category. The **cumulative percentage** divides the cumulative frequency by the total sample size. A **percentile** is the category up to which a certain percentage of cases fall. Thus, it can be identified based on the cumulative percentage. Given the order implicit in these definitions, cumulative frequencies, cumulative percentages, and percentiles are not appropriate for nominal variables.

Quartiles and **deciles** are commonly used special cases of percentiles. Quartiles fall at every 25th percentile. The 1st quartile is the 25th percentile; the 2nd quartile is the 50th percentile; the 3rd quartile is the 75th percentile. Deciles fall at ever 10th percentile. The first decile is the 10th percentile. The ninth decile is the 90th percentile.

5.4.2: Median

The **median** is the 50th percentile (equivalently, the 2nd quartile and the 5th decile). It is the "middle" value that separates the data in two, with half of the cases having values that fall below it and half of the cases having values that fall above it. For categorical variables, the median is the category in which the cumulative percentage reaches 50%. For continuous variables, the median will also be the value for which the cumulative percentage reaches 50%, but in the continuous case the median can refer to a unique case whose value is above the value of half of the other cases and below the value of the remaining half of the cases. If we order the cases by their values on our variable of interest, this median case would fall in the $\frac{(n+1)}{2}$ position. If the sample size is even, the median value falls somewhere between the two middle cases (e.g., if $n = 12$ then $\frac{(12+1)}{2} = 6.5$ and the 6th and 7th cases are in the middle); in these cases, a specific value for the median is found by taking the average or the mid-point of the values of the two middle cases.

When ordinal variables take on just a few values, the percentage distribution and mode may be as or more useful than the percentiles and median in describing the variable. As noted above, percentiles including the median are particularly valuable descriptive statistics for variables that take on numerous values. We will see in the next section that they can be useful descriptors for interval variables, especially when such variables do not follow a symmetric distribution.

It can be tempting to refer to the median with the "most common" or "most typical" language used for the mode, although whether this characterization is accurate depends on the number of categories and the distribution of cases across the categories. Especially if there are relatively few categories, then the percentage of cases may jump sharply between categories. For example, the value below the median may have many fewer than 50% of the cases falling at or below it but the value at the median may have many more than 50% of the cases falling at or below it.

The distribution of self-rated heath from Literature Excerpt 5.2 provides a useful example. We redisplay the percentage distribution in the 2nd column of the table below and calculate the cumulative percentages in the third column. We have re-oriented the values to follow the convention of locating the lowest value in the top row and the highest value in the bottom row and having the cumulative percentage reach 100 in the bottom row.

Self-rated physical health	Percentage	Cumulative Percentage
Poor	2.4	2.4
Fair	13.4	15.8
Good	34.5	50.3
Very good	32.5	82.8
Excellent	17.2	100.0

Source: Literature Excerpt 5.2

In this case, "Good" is the median (since the cumulative percentage is 50.3% for the "Good" category). However, the percentages classified as "Good" and "Very good" are very similar and both contain about one-third of the respondents (32.5% and 34.5% respectively). The categories "Good" and "Very good" might thus together be described as the most common responses.

The next table adapts the literature excerpt, illustrating a case in which the median is also the mode.

Self-rated physical health	Percentage	Cumulative Percentage
Poor	8.0	8.0
Fair	19.0	27.1
Good	40.1	67.2
Very good	15.6	82.8
Excellent	17.2	100.0

Source: Adapted from Literature Excerpt 5.2

In this case, "Fair" falls well below the median, with just over one quarter of cases at or below it. But, "Good" falls far above the median, with over two-thirds of the cases at or below it. Here, the percentage distribution suggests that "Good" might be accurately described as the most common response, since about two-fifths (40%) of the cases fall in the category, and no other category contains even one-fifth (20%) of the cases.

5.4.3: NSFH Examples

Display B.5.2 shows the frequency and percentage distribution for the NSFH variable capturing the highest grade in school that the respondent's mother completed, *glyrschl*, based on the `proc freq` command in SAS and the `tab1` command in Stata. The cumulative percentage is shown in the last column of each set of output. The median is 12 since about one-third of the respondents' mothers have 11 or fewer years of schooling whereas over three-quarters of mothers have 12 or fewer years of schooling. In this case, the mode is also 12, with nearly half (44%) of mothers have exactly 12 years of schooling. Thus, 12 seems a good representation of the most common years of schooling attained by the respondents' mothers.

SAS and Stata both also have dedicated commands which allow us to request various percentiles, including the median.[6] In SAS, we can request a number of percentiles (the 1st, 5th, 10th, 25th, 50th, 75th, 90th, 95th, and 99th) by adding their keyword abbreviations (`p1`, `p5`, `p10`, `p25`, `p50`, `p75`, `p90`, `p95`, and p99 respectively) to the `proc means` statement (see Display A.5.1). In Stata, the `centile` command calculates percentiles. Any percentile may be requested by listing its value within the parentheses of the, `centile()` option (see again Display A.5.1). Display B.5.3 shows our use of these commands to request the quartiles for the *glyrschl* variable. As expected based on the results we already examined in Display B.5.2, the results list 12 as the median. The 3rd quartile (75th percentile) is listed as 12 as well in Display B.5.3, which is also consistent with the fact that we saw in Display B.5.2 that 78.37% of mothers have 12 or fewer years of schooling. Ten is listed as the 1st quartile (25th percentile) in Display B.5.3. Consistently, looking back at Display B.5.2 we see that 21.79% of mothers have 9 or fewer years of schooling whereas 28.17% have 10 or fewer years of schooling. (The final columns of the Stata output can be ignored; We will discuss confidence intervals in Chapter 7).

As noted above, some social scientists may consider number of brothers and sisters as interval variables (since one more on each variable means one more sibling of each gender). However, we may expect that these variables will take on relatively few values, and therefore the percentage distribution and percentiles may be a more informative way to describe them than the statistics and graphs that we will discuss in the next section. Display B.5.4 shows the frequency distribution for both of these variables in SAS and Stata. The distributions of the two variables are very similar; and, in each case, the cumulative percentages increase rapidly over the few smallest values. That is, one-third of respondents have zero siblings of each gender. Over 60% have one or fewer siblings of each gender. Over 80% have two or fewer and nearly 90% have three or fewer siblings of each gender. In each case, the mode and median differ (the modal category is zero for both, but the median is 1).

5.5: INTERVAL VARIABLES

Any of the statistics already discussed can be used to describe interval variables. However, unless interval variables are discrete and take on a fairly limited range of values (e.g., as we saw for number of brothers and number of sisters), frequency and percentage distributions will contain too many categories to be informative. Graphs like the box plot and histogram can better present continuous variables with numerous values (see Few 2004, 2009 and Tufte 2001 for additional guidance on creating effective graphs). Below we discuss how to request these graphs from SAS and Stata. We also review the formulas for the mean and standard deviation and show how to request these statistics. We end by reviewing the concept of skewness, and showing how each of these graphs and statistics can be helpful in identifying skewness.

5.5.1: Interquartile Range

Before presenting the box plot, we need to define our first measure of variation: the **interquartile range**. The interquartile range is the difference between the 3rd and 1st quartiles (the 75th and 25th percentiles). It should be intuitive that if this difference is small, then we can conclude that there is relatively little variation on the variable (because the values in the middle of the distribution fall close together). On the other hand, if this difference is large, then there is relatively much variation on the variable (because the values in the middle of the distribution fall far apart). Of course, what is small and large depends on the units of measure of the variable (i.e., how much of the construct does a one unit change encompass?). An interquartile range of four would be interpreted as much larger for a variable that captures years of schooling or hourly wages (where four years and four dollars per hour encompass relatively sizable amounts in the real world) than a variable which captures dollars of annual earnings or distance in miles between family members' residences (where four dollars per year and four miles encompass relatively small amounts in the real world).

We can utilize the results we already examined in Display B.5.3 to calculate the interquartile range of mothers' years of schooling. In this case, the 3rd quartile was 12 and the 1st quartile was 10, so the interquartile range was 12 − 10 = 2. Thus, the middle half of the distribution of mothers' educational attainment ranges over just two years.

5.5.2: Box Plot

The box plot was popularized by John Tukey (1977) and helps us visualize several key statistical features of a variable. Literature Excerpt 5.4 shows the basic features of the original box plot as laid out by Tukey (1977). As its name implies, a box is a key feature. When displayed vertically, as in Literature Excerpt 5.4, the box is drawn so that its upper and lower borders are the 3rd and 1st quartiles respectively (the 75th and 25th percentiles) and a horizontal line is drawn within the interior of the box at the median (50th percentile). In the standard box plot, lines are drawn from the box boundaries to the extreme values (the minimum and maximum) of the variable. Tukey (1977) conceived of this as a 5-number summary of the data (the two extremes, the median, and the 1st and 3rd quartiles).

■ **Literature Excerpt 5.4**

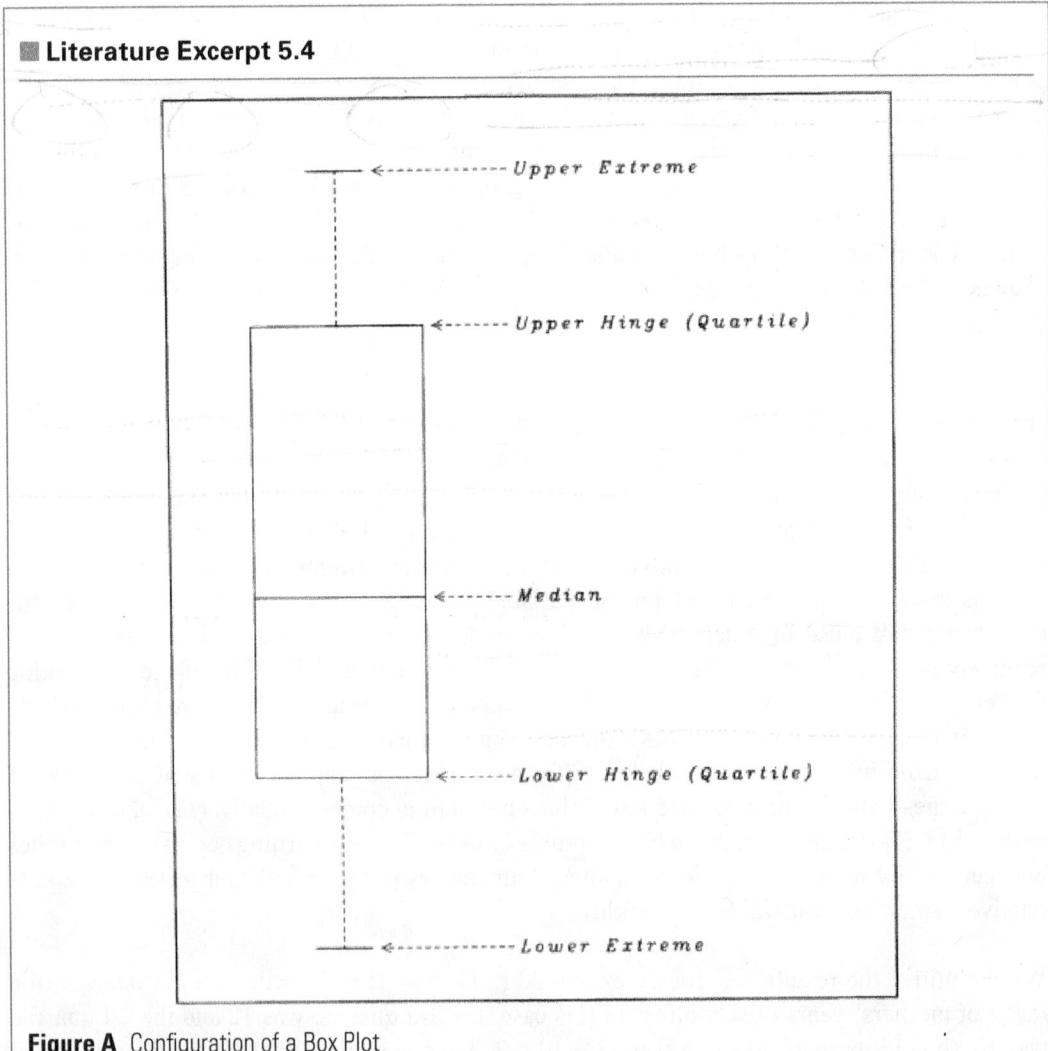

Figure A Configuration of a Box Plot

Source: McGill, Robert, Tukey, John W., and Larsen, Wayne A. 1978. "Variations of Box Plots." *American Statistician*, 32: 12–16.

The lines extending from the box are referred to as **whiskers**, and are used to help identify values that fall far from the rest of the data. Such values are often referred to as **outliers**. In the context of a box plot, an outlying value is defined based on the interquartile range. If a value falls more than 1.5 times the interquartile range above the 3rd quartile or more than 1.5 times the interquartile range below the 1st quartile then it is an outlying value. Typically, the whiskers are drawn to the closest value falling within these bounds. Then, outlying values are marked where they fall past these bounds. Sometimes different symbols are used to show values that fall very far from the other values, usually 3 or more times the interquartile range beyond the 1st and 3rd quartiles.

■ **Box 5.7**

Tukey (1977) used special terms to refer to many of the values in a box plot. For example, he referred to the 1st and 3rd quartiles as hinges. He referred to the locations 1.5 and 3 times the hinges as inner and outer fences respectively. And, values that fell beyond the inner and outer fences were called outside and far out values, respectively. You may see such terminology in some publications or documentation, although we will rely on more general terms for these values.

The latest versions of both SAS and Stata have powerful graphics capabilities, each of which includes box plots (Heath 2008; Mitchell 2008; Rodriguez, 2009).[7] In SAS, the command is `proc sgplot; vbox <var1>, run;` In Stata, it is `graph box <var1>`. SAS places the graph within the *.rtf* file with our other output. In Stata, we may easily export the graph in various formats using the `graph export` command. We find the Windows MetaFile and Windows Enhanced MetaFile formats easy to insert into word processors. Stata graphs can be easily saved in these format with the command `graph export <filename>.wmf, replace` where *.wmf* stands for Windows MetaFile or `graph export <filename>.emf, replace` where *.emf* stands for Windows Enhanced MetaFile (Note that an extension is required to indicate the format you would like Stata to use for saving the graph; in our case, .emf indicates the Windows Enhanced Meta File format).

Display B.5.5 shows our use of these commands to create boxplots of the *glage* variable (the respondent's mother's age). These plots reveal that the median line is around 60 and the quartiles (box boundaries) appear to be about 50 and 70. Thus, the interquartile range is about 20, and the whiskers extend 1.5 times this amount (or roughly 30 years). The circles at the top of each plot show us that there are a few outliers at the upper end of the distribution, but none at the lower end.[8]

5.5.3: Histogram

As noted, when a variable can take on many values, the values in a frequency or percentage distribution become too numerous to be informative. In these cases, it can be helpful to group values together before tallying the cases. **Histograms** plot the relative frequency of cases within such groups.

In histograms, we group categories into equal intervals (e.g., 5- or 10-year intervals for a variable capturing an adult respondent's age). Implementing this procedure is straightforward, but the immediate question that confronts us is: What interval should we use? SAS and Stata will choose a default interval, which can work well. We can revise the interval, if desired, aiming for intervals that are wide enough to reduce the values to a manageable number but not so few that too much variation is lost. Sometimes the top and/or bottom intervals are of different width than the rest. Using such unequal top and bottom bins can be helpful if few cases fall above or below some value, and thus the lower or upper interval is open (e.g., income greater than $250,000).

As for the box plot, SAS and Stata both have dedicated commands allowing us to request histograms. In SAS, the command is `proc sgplot; histogram <var1>, run;` In Stata, it is `histogram <var1>`. In Stata, we can also use the `width()` option, placing our desired bin width in the parentheses, to change the results.[9] As with the box plot, SAS places the histogram within the *.rtf* file with our other output. In Stata, we may again easily export the graph with `graph export <filename>.emf, replace`.

Display B.5.6 shows our use of these commands with the *glage* variable. Stata selects somewhat narrower bins than does SAS, making the distribution appear choppier. In Display B.5.7 we asked for a histogram with widths of 5 years, resulting in a much smoother distribution. You can experiment with the widths in this way in order to strike a balance of an accurate representation of the distribution without too much loss of information. If there are too many bins, the pattern may become quite choppy; but, if there are too few bins, the pattern may become too uniform. In either case, it may then be difficult to summarize an overall shape for the distribution.

5.5.4: Mean

The **mean** is the sum of a variable's values divided by the sample size.

$$\bar{Y} = \frac{\sum_{i=1}^{n} Y_i}{n} \tag{5.1}$$

In Equation 5.1, the subscript i stands for each "individual" case in the data set, n is the total sample size, and Y represents any of our interval variables. The summation symbol, $\sum_{i=1}^{n}$, offers us a succinct way to represent the process of summing the values of Y from the first ($i = 1$) person to the last ($i = n$) person.

A common analogy used to describe the mean is that of a balance. Consider measuring the distance from each case's value to the mean. We can define this difference as $Y_i - \bar{Y}$, where again i represents each case. The sum of all of these differences is zero, $\Sigma(Y_i - \bar{Y}) = 0$.[10] Thus, the

Box 5.8

The choppiness is also evident in the SAS histogram of Display B.5.6, although less pronounced than in Stata. Demographers often find that age distributions are lumpy when respondents do not know an exact age and round (such as to the nearest 5 or 10). This is likely in the NSFH where respondents were asked to report their mothers' age, which they may not know exactly (see again Display C.3.5).

■ **Box 5.9**

For the descriptive statistics used in Part 2 of the book, we use Roman letters to designate sample statistics. In Part 3 and Part 4 of the book, we use Greek letters with a hat symbol (also known as a caret) on top to represent estimates of population parameters. We do so because Roman letters are common in introductory statistics textbooks—such as those you may have taken as an undergraduate —and because they are commonly used for descriptive statistics in publication styles guides (e.g., American Psychological Association 2009: 119–123). In contrast, both Roman letters and Greek letters with a hat are used in regression textbooks to designate sample estimates of population parameters, and the latter is especially common in advanced statistics (thus using that notation provides a bridge to textbooks and literature that uses the approach).

distances to all values below the mean are offset by the distances to all values above the mean.

This concept of the mean has been understood for centuries, and earlier representations of it can help us visualize the balancing. For example, the Greek's understood this concept of balance around 500BC (Bakker and Gravemeijer 2006). They defined "the middle number b of a and c [as] the arithmetic mean if and only if $a - b = b - c$" (p. 152). As seen in Literature Excerpt 5.5, the Greeks represented magnitudes with lines, which help us visualize the way in which "the part of the longest bar that 'sticks out' (compared with the middle bar) compensates the corresponding part of the shortest bar" (p. 153).

■ **Box 5.10**

More precisely, Equation 5.1 is the arithmetic mean. Other means are relevant in some subfields (e.g., the geometric mean). However, the statistics we cover in this book rely on the arithmetic mean, and this mean is so common in most social sciences that the use of the word mean alone implies the arithmetic mean.

■ **Literature Excerpt 5.5**

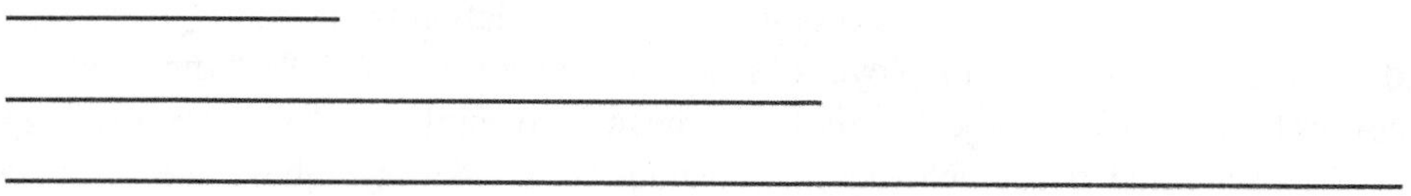

Figure 1 Greek representation of magnitudes as bars (2, 6, and 10)

Source: Bakker, Arthur and Gravemeijer, Koeno P.E. 2006. "The Historical Phenomenology of Mean and Media." *Educational Studies in Mathematics*, 62: 149–168.

Figure 5.1 provides a larger example of this balancing. Fourteen values are indicated by the x's in the figure. The fourteen values have a mean of 4. The lines represent the distance of each value from the mean. Most values are balanced off by a corresponding single value the same distance on the other side of the mean (e.g., a 1 and a 7; two 2s and two 6s; two 3s and two 5s). The three exceptions are shaded. Here the one positive value (7) has a deviation from the mean of +3 which is balanced by two values below the mean (a 3 and a 2 whose deviations from the mean of −1 and −2 add to −3).

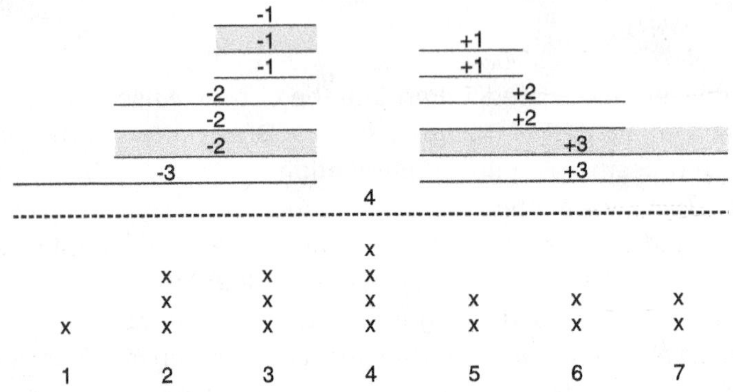

```
                      -1
                      -1                    +1
                      -1                    +1
                -2                              +2
                -2                              +2
                -2                                   +3
           -3                                        +3
                                4
----------------------------------------------------------------
                                x
            x       x           x
            x       x           x
       x    x       x           x       x       x
       1    2       3           4       5       6       7
```

Figure 5.1 Illustration of Mean

A Hypothetical Example

We will draw on a small hypothetical example throughout this chapter to show how to calculate the mean and standard deviation. You should verify that you can duplicate these hand calculations, for practice and to solidify your understanding of the concepts. The example is a dataset with 14 cases. We will imagine that they are 14 employees drawn using simple random sampling from all employees of a large firm. The variable of interest to us is the number of days that they were absent from work in the past month. In Table 5.2 we show two versions of this dataset that differ only in the number of days absent for one employee, which allows us to illustrate how the mean is sensitive to values that fall far from the rest of the data. We show the values themselves in each of these two versions of the dataset as well as the deviation of each value from the mean in that version of the dataset; examining the deviations provides us another concrete example of how the mean balances the distance to values above and below it.

Examining Table 5.2, we see that in the first version of the dataset—Example 5.1a–the mean number of days absent in the last month is 4 and that each employee who has a value below the mean is offset by an employee with a corresponding value above the mean. Four employees have days absent exactly equal to the mean of 4, thus their deviation from the mean (shown in the second column) is zero. Three employees have values of 3, one day below the mean, and three employees have values of 5, one day above the mean. Two employees have values of 2, two days below the mean, and two employees have values of 6, two days above the mean. As expected, the sum of these deviations from the mean is zero.

In the second version of the dataset—Example 5.1b—all employees have the same number of days absent except the last, who now has missed 20 days of work in the past month and thus her value falls much farther away from the others. The mean number of days absent in the second version of the dataset is larger than in the first version, 5 rather than 4. This is because of the large number of absences for the last employee: Her deviation from the mean, shown in the final column of the table, is $20 - 5 = 15$. To compensate for this large positive deviation, nine of the remaining employees now have days absent that fall below the mean: the four employees with 4 days absent now fall one day below the new mean of 5, the three employees with three days absent now fall two days below the mean, and the two employees with two days absent now fall three days below the mean. As expected, the deviations again sum to zero, because the sum of deviations for the nine

■ **Table 5.2: Two examples of the calculation of the mean:**

Hypothetical example of number of days absent from work in the past month for 14 employees selected with simple random sampling from a large firm

	Example 5.1a		Example 5.1b	
	Days Absent Y_i	Deviation from Mean $(Y_i - \bar{Y})$	Days Absent Y_i	Deviation from Mean $(Y_i - \bar{Y})$
Case 1	2	−2	2	−3
Case 2	2	−2	2	−3
Case 3	3	−1	3	−2
Case 4	3	−1	3	−2
Case 5	3	−1	3	−2
Case 6	4	0	4	−1
Case 7	4	0	4	−1
Case 8	4	0	4	−1
Case 9	4	0	4	−1
Case 10	5	1	5	0
Case 11	5	1	5	0
Case 12	5	1	5	0
Case 13	6	2	6	1
Case 14	6	2	20	15
Sum	$\sum_{i=1}^{n} Y_i = 56$	$\sum_{i=1}^{n}(Y_i - \bar{Y}) = 0$	$\sum_{i=1}^{n} Y_i = 70$	$\sum_{i=1}^{n}(Y_i - \bar{Y}) = 0$
Mean	$\dfrac{\sum_{i=1}^{n} Y_i}{n} = \dfrac{56}{14} = 4$		$\dfrac{\sum_{i=1}^{n} Y_i}{n} = \dfrac{70}{14} = 5$	

employees who fall below the mean $(-3 + -3 + -2 + -2 + -2 + -1 + -1 + -1 + -1 = -16)$ is balanced off by the sum of the deviations for the two employees who fall above the mean $(1 + 15 = 16)$.

NSFH Example

The SAS `proc means` command includes the mean in its default output, thus we can use the basic command `proc means; var <variable list>; run;` to request the mean for one or more variable (we can also explicitly ask only for the mean using the statistics keyword `mean` as in `proc means mean; var <variable list>; run;`). In Stata, the `summarize <variable list>` command includes the mean in its default output. In Display B.5.8, we used these commands to request the mean for the mother's age, which is 60.52.

5.5.5: Standard Deviation

The **standard deviation** provides a measure of variation of a variable in addition to the interquartile range. As we saw above, the sum of positive deviations from the mean are offset by the sum of negative deviations from the mean, such that $\Sigma(Y_i - \bar{Y}) = 0$. But, the squared deviations from the mean do not sum to zero, and this sum is the numerator in the formula for the standard deviation.

$$s_Y = \sqrt{\frac{\sum(Y_i - \bar{Y})^2}{n-1}} \qquad (5.2)$$

The denominator in this formula of $n-1$ is referred to as the degrees of freedom. Notice that if the denominator were n then the formula would be similar to the formula for the mean, but rather than capturing the average value it would capture the average squared deviation from the mean. In fact, if we had information for every member of the population, then we could calculate the population standard deviation as follows:

$$\sigma_Y = \sqrt{\frac{\sum(Y_i - \bar{Y})^2}{N}}$$

This is because for the population, the mean can be calculated exactly rather than being estimated by the sample. The loss of one degree of freedom in Equation 5.2 reflects the fact that we must first estimate the mean (based on our sample and Equation 5.1) in order to plug it into the formula for the standard deviation in Equation 5.2. Thus, the calculation is really based on just $n-1$ values of Y_i because if we know $n-1$ values of Y_i and $\bar{Y}$ we can figure out the *nth* value of Y_i (e.g., if we knew the mean of three values was 5 and two of the values were 4 and 5 we could figure out that the third value was 6).

 It is also important to keep in mind that because the standard deviation captures variation around the mean, it should be used only when the mean is appropriate (e.g., the standard deviation of a nominal variable is not meaningful). And, as we shall see below, both the mean and standard deviation are most meaningful for symmetric (as opposed to skewed) distributions.

A Hypothetical Example

Table 5.3 shows how to calculate the standard deviation using the hypothetical examples of days absent in the last month among fourteen employees of a small firm, which we used above to calculate the mean. Again it will be helpful for you to duplicate the calculations to solidify your understanding.

Table 5.3 repeats the first two columns shown in Table 5.2 for each version of the data set (the value of the number of days absent and the deviation of this value from the mean) and now adds a third column for each data set, the square of the deviation from the mean. The shaded value is the square of the deviation for the last employee in the second version of the data set, who had 20 days of missed work. We can see that the extremeness of this employee from the others is amplified when we square the deviation—this employee's squared deviation from the mean of 225 is much larger than the squared deviations for the other employees (which range from 0 to 9). As a consequence, the difference between the standard deviations in the two versions of the data set are even larger than the difference in means between the two versions of the data set:

■ **Table 5.3: Two examples of the calculation of the standard deviation:**
Hypothetical example of number of days absent from work in the past month for 14 employees selected with simple random sampling from a large firm

Example 5.2a

	Days Absent Y_i	Deviation from Mean $Y_i - \bar{Y}$	Deviation from Mean Squared $(Y_i - \bar{Y})^2$
Case 1	2	−2	4
Case 2	2	−2	4
Case 3	3	−1	1
Case 4	3	−1	1
Case 5	3	−1	1
Case 6	4	0	0
Case 7	4	0	0
Case 8	4	0	0
Case 9	4	0	0
Case 10	5	1	1
Case 11	5	1	1
Case 12	5	1	1
Case 13	6	2	4
Case 14	6	2	4
Sum	$\sum Y_i = 56$	$\sum (Y_i - \bar{Y}) = 0$	$\sum (Y_i - \bar{Y})^2 = 22$

Mean or St.Dev.

$$\frac{\sum Y_i}{n} = \frac{56}{14} = 4 \qquad \sqrt{\frac{\sum (Y_i - \bar{Y})^2}{n-1}} = \sqrt{\frac{22}{14-1}} = 1.30$$

Example 5.2b

	Days Absent Y_i	Deviation from Mean $Y_i - \bar{Y}$	Deviation from Mean Squared $(Y_i - \bar{Y})^2$
Case 1	2	−3	9
Case 2	2	−3	9
Case 3	3	−2	4
Case 4	3	−2	4
Case 5	3	−2	4
Case 6	4	−1	1
Case 7	4	−1	1
Case 8	4	−1	1
Case 9	4	−1	1
Case 10	5	0	0
Case 11	5	0	0
Case 12	5	0	0
Case 13	6	1	1
Case 14	20	15	225
Sum	$\sum Y_i = 70$	$\sum (Y_i - \bar{Y}) = 0$	$\sum (Y_i - \bar{Y})^2 = 260$

Mean or St.Dev.

$$\frac{\sum Y_i}{n} = \frac{70}{14} = 5 \qquad \sqrt{\frac{\sum (Y_i - \bar{Y})^2}{n-1}} = \sqrt{\frac{260}{14-1}} = 4.47$$

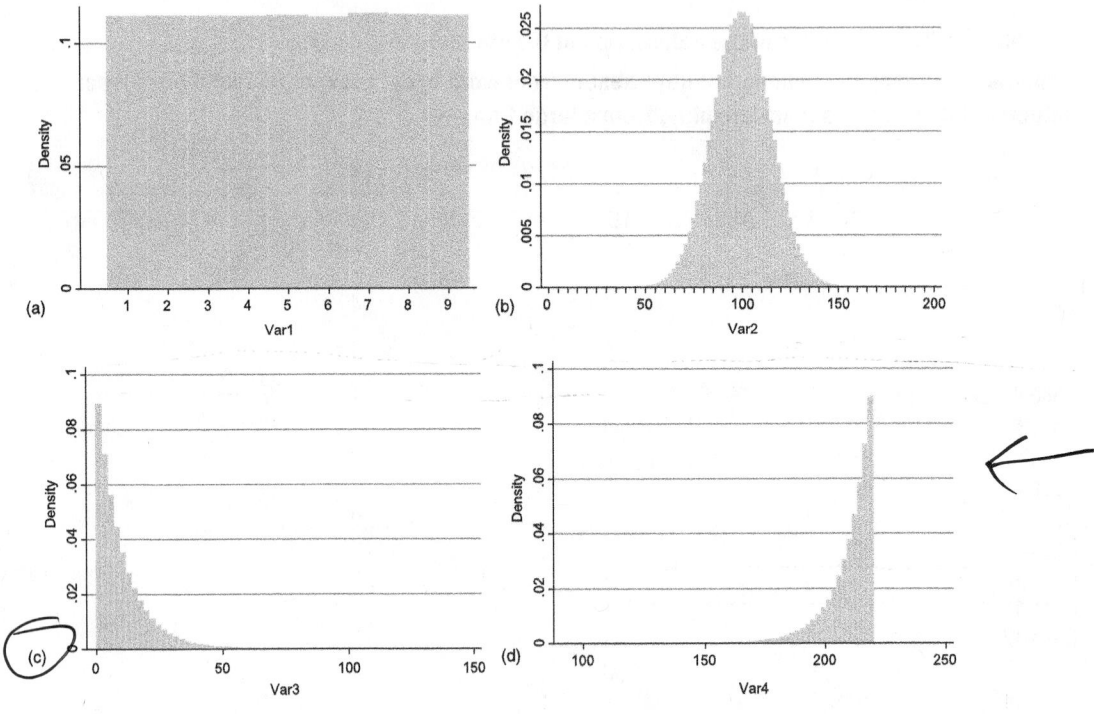

Figure 5.2 Hypothetical Examples of Histograms of Symmetric and Skewed Distributions

The standard deviation is 4.47 in the dataset with the employee who missed 20 days of work versus 1.30 in the dataset where that last employee missed 6 days of work.

NSFH Example

Although it is useful to practice a few hand calculations to understand the meaning behind the formulas, in practice, we needn't do so because the SAS `proc means` statement and Stata `summarize` command also include the standard deviation in their default output. Looking back at Display B.5.8 shows that the standard deviation for *glage* is 11.58. Beginning in Chapter 6 and continuing throughout the remaining chapters, we will learn about the usefulness of the standard deviation for interpreting our results.

5.5.6: Skewness

Figures 5.2 and 5.3 use histograms and box plots, respectively, to illustrate two symmetric and two skewed distributions. In a **symmetric distribution**, the left and right halves of the distribution look like mirror images of each other. Because as many cases fall above the mean as below the mean, the mean and median are equivalent in a symmetric distribution. This simplifies interpretation because the center of the distribution is unambiguous. Figures 5.2a and 5.2b shows histograms of two symmetric distributions. In Figure 5.2a, the mean and median are both 5. In Figure 5.2b, the mean and median are both 100. Consistently, the box plots of these variables, shown in Figures 5.3a and 5.3b, have the mid-line of the median drawn evenly between the upper and lower quartile lines of the box. The other measure of central tendency we discussed above, the mode, may be but need not be equivalent to the mean and median in a symmetric distribution. For example, in Figure 5.2a, all values are about equally probable (thus although 7 is the most probable value, the other values are almost as likely). In contrast, in Figure 5.2b, the distribution clearly peaks in the middle, and the mode is also 100.

In a **skewed distribution**, more cases fall on one side of the mean than the other; and, the mean and median differ. Specifically, the mean is pulled in the direction of the skew. If the distribution has a tail to the right (as in Figure 5.2c) then it is right skewed and the mean is larger than the median. If the distribution has a tail to the left (as in Figure 5.2d) then it is left-skewed and the mean is smaller than the median. Consistently, the box plots in Figures 5.3c and 5.3d show many outliers at the top and bottom, respectively. The median bar is also not in the center of the boxes in these figures. Rather, the median falls toward the bottom of the box in Figure 5.3c and toward the top of the box in Figure 5.3d. As expected, the mean for the right-skewed distribution in Figures 5.2c and 5.3c is larger than the median (about 10 versus 7);

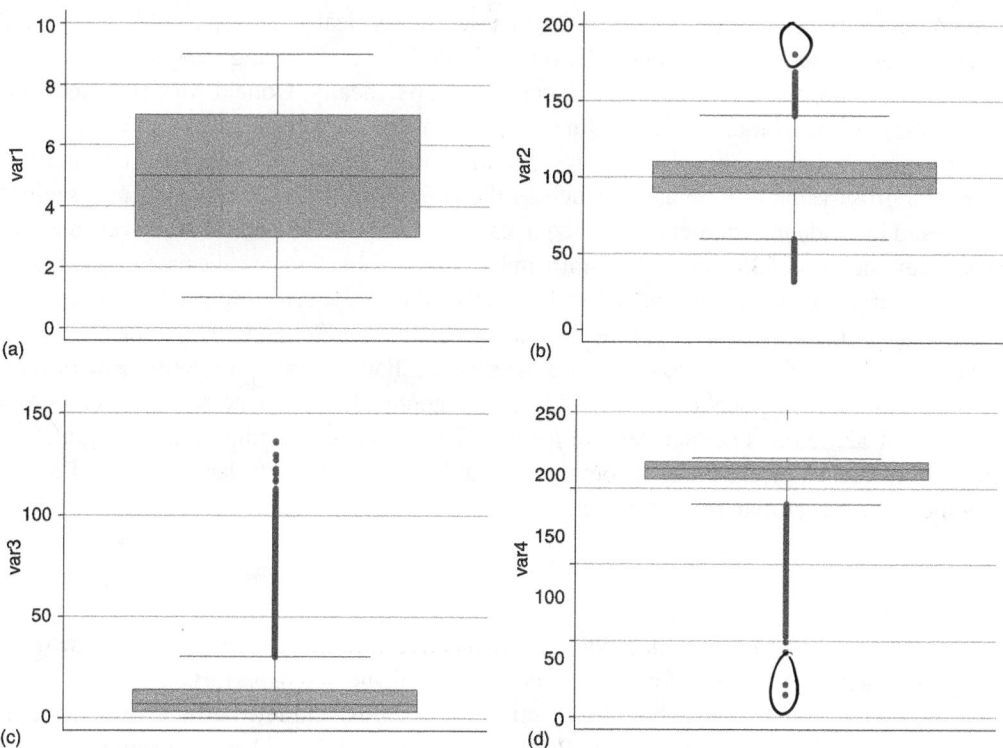

Figure 5.3 Hypothetical Examples of Box Plots of Symmetric and Skewed Distributions

and, the mean is smaller than the median in the left-skewed distribution shown in Figures 5.2d and 5.3d (210 and 213 respectively). Applying this same logic to Example 5.1b, in Table 5.2 the mean is larger than the median (5 versus 4), so the graph of this variable would be right skewed (whereas in Example 5.1a from Table 5.2 would have a symmetric distribution with the mean equal to the median, both being 4).

Skewed distributions make it difficult to unambiguously describe the center of the distribution: the middle value is different from the "balance" value (where differences to values below it are balanced by differences to values above it). Medians rather than means are often reported for skewed distributions since they are less affected by extreme values and are consequently more stable estimates of the center of a variable that is skewed (for example, if our sample happens to draw the only millionaire in a population, then the mean income will be considerably larger than it would be if our sample had all the same cases except the millionaire).

Variables that have a right skew are fairly common in the social sciences. Such right skew often occurs when a variable has a lower limit (like zero) but no upper limit, such as income, earnings, wealth, numbers of delinquent activities in a year, or number of shopping trips in a week.

Literature Excerpt 5.6

As just noted, measures of earnings, income and assets are typically skewed right in the United States, with most people having modest levels of each but some having very sizable values. Such right skew is evident in Literature Excerpt 5.6. Specifically, Donald McGrath and Lisa Keister (2008) use the National Longitudinal Study of Youth (U.S. Bureau of Labor Statistics, 2010) to examine how temporary employment influences asset accumulation. The authors measure the gross value of nine assets (such as the respondent's home, checking and savings accounts, and individual retirement accounts) in calendar year 2000 when the study respondents were between the ages of 35 and 43. McGrath and Keister's Table 2 shows the mean and median gross assets of all respondents and of respondents who had been employed in temporary positions two, four, and six years before the survey (in 1998, 1996, and 1994 respectively). In each case, the mean is about double or more the median. For example, in the first row of their table, the median gross assets of all respondents are about $120,000 whereas the mean gross assets is about $221,000. The fact that the mean is larger than the median reflects right skew common in measures of earnings, income and wealth, with some very large values of assets pulling the mean larger than the median.[11]

NSFH Example

We now return to our NSFH distance example to look at the degree of skewness in some of its interval variables. The boxplot for *glage* that we examined in Display B.5.5 looked fairly symmetric, with the median just about in the middle of the box, and few outliers. Similarly, the histograms for *glage* shown in Display B.5.6 and Display B.5.7 did not appear noticeably skewed. In contrast, the boxplots for the respondent's own age and especially for distance to the mother and own earnings have numerous outliers (see Display B.5.9) and the histograms for

■ Literature Excerpt 5.6

Table 2. Mean and Median Values for Gross Assets (2000)

	Gross Assets	
	Mean	Median
All respondents	$220,981 ($421,406)	$120,000
Temporary employees, 1994	$102,620 ($125,317)	$55,010
Temporary employees, 1996	$96,017 ($126,933)	$41,000
Temporary employees, 1998	$71,451 ($100,548)	$24,400

Note: Standard deviations are in parentheses.

Source: McGrath, Donald M. & Lisa A. Keister. 2008. "The Effect of Temporary Employment on Asset Accumulation Processes." *Work and Occupations,* 35: 196–222.

these variables each reveal some positive skew, again especially for distance and earnings (see Display B.5.10). Display B.5.11 lists the mean and median for these variables.[12] The mean and median are close for both age variables (about 61 and 60 respectively for *g1age*; about 35 and 33 respectively for *g2age*), reflecting the minimal skewness on these two variables. In contrast, the mean is much larger than the median for the distance and earnings variables (about 280 versus 15 for *g1miles*; about 29,614 versus 22,702 for earnings), reflecting the more substantial right skewness for these variables.

5.6: WEIGHTED STATISTICS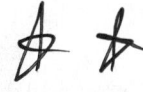

As discussed in Chapter 3, the NSFH used a complex survey design. One important feature of the NSFH design for the descriptive statistics that we covered in this chapter was the oversampling of blacks, Puerto Ricans, Mexican Americans, single-parent families, families with step-children, cohabiting couples and recently married persons (Sweet, Bumpass, and Call 1988). The base weights reflect this oversampling: The NSFH was designed so that each person who was not oversampled represented 4,926 people in the population (because their probability of selection was .000200965 and $\frac{1}{.000200965} = 4{,}926$); and, each person who was oversampled represented 2,488 people in the population (because their probability of selection was 000401929 and $\frac{1}{.000401929} = 2{,}488$). The NSFH sampling statisticians further modified the weights to adjust for the fact that only one adult was selected from each household as well as the fact that not all households agreed to be screened for study eligibility and that not all eligible respondents agreed to complete the survey. The weights were further adjusted to assure that the distribution of NSFH respondents' age, race-ethnicity, sex, and region of residence matched those based on the 1988 Current Population Survey (NSFH 1990). And, the final weights were rescaled to sum to the sample size. As we will discuss below, such rescaling can be critical for obtaining correct results for certain analyses with some software; and, we will show how to implement such rescaling later in the chapter.

Recall also that, in addition to weights, the other two important features of a complex sampling design are PSUs and strata. PSUs are the primary sampling units used to reduce costs. In the NSFH the PSUs are counties or county groups. And, the strata are the subgroups within which some of the PSUs were sampled. In the NSFH, strata were based on counties' region, urbanicity, economic vitality, and racial-ethnic composition.

SAS and Stata both have dedicated survey commands which calculate weighted means, weighted proportions, and (in Stata) weighted standard deviations (along with other weighted statistics). We implement these commands using the second version of the NSFH data set that we created in Chapter 4 which included the full sample along with a variable to indicate our desired subsample and which included variables that designated the complex sampling features (sampling weights, PSUs, and strata).

Adjusting for oversampling is essential so that the descriptive statistics covered in this chapter reflect the population from which the sample was drawn, and thus we will refer to the statistics as weighted means, weighted proportions, and weighted standard deviations. For completeness, we will also designate the cluster and strata in the SAS and Stata commands, although clustering and stratification will have more impact on the statistics that we discuss in later chapters than those in this chapter.

■ Box 5.11

SAS and Stata both also allow for weights to be applied when calculating many statistics, without accounting for the clustering and stratification aspects of the sampling design (SAS Institute 2009a: 41–45; StataCorp 2009d: 305–310). We will demonstrate how to use these options in Chapter 7, because they simplify the presentation in that chapter and because you may collaborate with others who use those commands. Using these weighting procedures will give the same results as those shown in Display A.5.2 for the weighted mean and weighted proportion (but not the weighted standard deviation). SAS's proc univariate command and Stata's summarize command with the det option can be used to obtain many weighted percentiles, including the median. In Stata, the weight syntax can also be used to obtain weighted boxplots and histograms. These commands, however, will not be appropriate when we move from descriptive statistics to statistical inference, if our complex sample also includes clustering and stratification. It is also important to be aware that weighting can be used for purposes beyond complex sampling designs (see SAS Institute 2009a: 41–45; StataCorp 2009d: 305–310). For example, in certain circumstances weights are not based on a complex sampling design but are used to indicate how many observations have the same pattern of responses across a number of variables. It is also important to pay attention to whether sampling weights have been rescaled to reflect the sample size rather than the population size (Lee and Forthofer 2006: 11–14). Generally, it is essential to understand how the weights have been scaled and how each SAS and Stata command treats the weight when using the weight options.

5.6.1: Weighted Mean

The **weighted mean** is defined as follows (Kish 1965; Lee & Forthofer 2006; SAS Institute, 2008a: 6487; StataCorp 2009d: 1024):[13]

$$\bar{Y}_w = \frac{1}{W} \sum_{i=1}^{n} w_i \times Y_i \tag{5.3}$$

where n is the sample size, i represents each individual case, Y_i are the values of one of our interval variables for each case, w_i are the individual weights for each case, and W is the sum of the weights over all cases ($W = \sum_{i=1}^{n} w_i$).

As we discussed in Chapter 4, weights can be scaled to sum to different amounts, such as to sum to the observed sample size or population size. The results for Equation 5.3 are not affected by such scaling. But, calculations of other statistics will be affected by scaling. Relative weights, which sum to the observed sample size, are preferred in these cases (Campbell and Berbaum 2010; Lee and Forthofer 2006: 11–14). Such relative weights are also intuitively appealing, because they can simplify Equation 5.3 above making it easier to compare to Equation 5.1. To show this, we will designate the relative weights as $w_i^* = \frac{w_i}{\bar{W}}$ where $\bar{W} = \frac{\sum_{i=1}^{n} w_i}{n}$, the average unadjusted weight. Since the relative weights sum to the sample size ($W^* = \sum_{i=1}^{n} w_i^* = n$) we can rewrite Equation 5.3 as:

$$\bar{Y}_w = \frac{1}{W^*} \sum_{i=1}^{n} w_i^* \times Y_i = \frac{1}{n} \sum_{i=1}^{n} w_i^* \times Y_i = \frac{\sum_{i=1}^{n} w_i^* \times Y_i}{n} \tag{5.4}$$

Thus, when the weights are re-scaled to sum to the sample size the difference between Equation 5.4 and Equation 5.1 is clear: Each value in the numerator is multiplied by its weight, thus the weights either adjust upward (if $w_i^* > 1$) or discount downward (if $w_i^* < 1$) that value's contribution to the sum.

A Hypothetical Example

To illustrate calculations based on these formulas, we will modify our first version of the hypothetical employee dataset—Example 5.1a from above—by incorporating weights. To do so, we will imagine that when we sampled the fourteen employees from the firm that we oversampled employees with low wages at double their representation in the population (the firm), so that their sampling weights are: $\frac{1}{2} = 0.50$.

In Table 5.4, we first show the calculation of the weighted mean based on the unadjusted (rather than relative) weights. This allows us to readily see in the first two columns of Table 5.4 that low-wage employees (Cases 5, 8, 9, 12, 13, and 14) were oversampled at double their representation in the firm, and thus have weights of: $\frac{1}{2} = 0.50$. The last column shows their days absent multiplied

■ Table 5.4: Example calculation of the weighted mean using the unadjusted weights: Hypothetical example of 14 employees selected with a complex sampling design from a large firm

	Group	Weight w_i	Days Absent Y_i	Weight×Days Absent $w_i \times Y_i$
Case 1	High Wage	1.00	2	2
Case 2	High Wage	1.00	2	2
Case 3	High Wage	1.00	3	3
Case 4	High Wage	1.00	3	3
Case 5	Low Wage	0.50	3	1.5
Case 6	High Wage	1.00	4	4
Case 7	High Wage	1.00	4	4
Case 8	Low Wage	0.50	4	2
Case 9	Low Wage	0.50	4	2
Case 10	High Wage	1.00	5	5
Case 11	High Wage	1.00	5	5
Case 12	Low Wage	0.50	5	2.5
Case 13	Low Wage	0.50	6	3
Case 14	Low Wage	0.50	6	3
Sum		$W = \sum_{i=1}^{n} w_i = 11$		$\sum_{i=1}^{n} w_i \times Y_i = 42$
Mean		$\bar{Y}_w = \dfrac{1}{W} \sum_{i=1}^{n} w_i \times Y_i = \dfrac{1}{11} \times 42 = \dfrac{42}{11} = 3.82$		

by their sampling weight. This makes explicit that for these oversampled cases only half of their value is added to the sum for the numerator of Equation 5.3. This makes intuitive sense, given that we oversampled members of this group at double their representation in the firm (there are twice as many low-wage employees in our sample as there would be in a simple random sample of employees from the firm). The weighted mean is slightly smaller than the unweighted mean (3.82 versus 4.00) reflecting the fact that the down-weighted values are more often larger than smaller values of days absent. The weighted sum of the Y values is 42 (versus the unweighted sum of 56 in Example 5.1a in Table 5.2). This weighted sum of the Y values is then divided by the sum of the unadjusted weights (W) rather than the total sample size (11 rather than 14).

In Table 5.5, we show this same example with relative weights. Doing so makes clear that the value of the weighted mean is the same whether the unadjusted or relative weights are used. But, it also shows the advantage of having the sum of the means be the observed sample size.

Specifically, we calculated the relative weights by dividing by the average of the unadjusted weights. The average of the 14 unadjusted weights from Table 5.4 is: $\dfrac{11}{14} = 0.785714$. Dividing by this value, the weights that were a 1 in Table 5.4 become $\dfrac{1}{0.785714} = 1.27$ in Table 5.5 and the weights that were a 0.5 in Table 5.4 become $\dfrac{0.5}{0.785714} = 0.63$ in Table 5.5.

■ Table 5.5: Example of calculation of the weighted mean, using relative weights: Hypothetical example of 14 employees selected with a complex sampling design from a large firm

	Group	Relative Weight w_i^*	Days Absent Y_i	Relative Weight × Days Absent $w_i^* \times Y_i$
Case 1	High Wage	1.27	2	2.55
Case 2	High Wage	1.27	2	2.55
Case 3	High Wage	1.27	3	3.82
Case 4	High Wage	1.27	3	3.82
Case 5	Low Wage	0.63	3	1.91
Case 6	High Wage	1.27	4	5.09
Case 7	High Wage	1.27	4	5.09
Case 8	Low Wage	0.63	4	2.55
Case 9	Low Wage	0.63	4	2.55
Case 10	High Wage	1.27	5	6.36
Case 11	High Wage	1.27	5	6.36
Case 12	Low Wage	0.63	5	3.18
Case 13	Low Wage	0.63	6	3.82
Case 14	Low Wage	0.63	6	3.82
Sum		$W^* = \sum_{i=1}^{n} w_i^* = 14$		$\sum_{i=1}^{n} w_i^* Y_i = 53.45$

Mean

$$\bar{Y}_w = \frac{\sum_{i=1}^{n} w_i^* Y_i}{n} = \frac{53.45}{14} = 3.82$$

To calculate the weighted mean based on the relative weights, we divide the sum of the weighted days absent (53.45) by the total sample size (14). As expected, the result is the same as in Table 5.4 (3.82). This is because the weights were rescaled by the average unadjusted weight in both the numerator and denominator of Equation 5.4.

NSFH Example

We do not need to calculate the weighted mean by hand, as both SAS and Stata have dedicated survey commands that will do so (see Display A.5.2). As noted, we will indicate the three key design features—strata, cluster, and weight—indicated by the variables *Stratum*, *PSU*, and *adjweight* respectively in our NSFH distance example. In SAS, statements included in each of our survey commands designate these design variables. In Stata, a separate command can be used to assign these design features for all future survey commands. We also draw on the variable *DistanceSample* which is coded '1' for the cases of interest for our analysis (respondents whose mother is alive and lives in the United States but not in their same residence) and '0' for the cases not of interest. As we discussed in Chapter 4, we need to retain the full sample and indicate the subgroup of interest in this way, rather than only keep the subgroup in the analytic data set, in order to obtain the correct results from the survey commands. We will use the survey commands in SAS and Stata to request the weighted means for the same variables for which we calculated unweighted means in Display B.5.11 (*g1age, g2age, g1miles*, and *g2earn*) so that we can compare the weighted to the unweighted results.

Specifically, in SAS, we use the following syntax (see again Display A.5.2).

```
proc surveymeans mean rate="c:\nsfh_distance\SAS\rate";
        var g1age g2age g1miles g2earn;
        domain DistanceSample;
        cluster PSU;
        strata Stratum;
        weight adjweight;
run;
```

The word `mean` in the first line tells SAS that we wish to calculate weighted means; and, the second line lists the variables for which we want to compute means. The words `rate="c:\nsfh_distance\SAS\rate"` in the first line tells SAS to use the *rate* data set we created in Chapter 4 to appropriately account for the certainty PSUs. The third line asks SAS to compute the means within the values of our *DistanceSample* variable. The final three lines provide the PSU, strata, and weight variables, respectively.

In Stata, we first store the design features with the `svyset` command:

```
svyset PSU [pw=adjweight], strata(Stratum) singleunit(certainty)
```

where the first word following `svyset` (in our case `PSU`) tells Stata which variable indicates the clusters. The final option `singleunit(certainty)` tells Stata to treat the strata with only one PSU as units drawn with certainty, reflecting the fact that (as discussed in Chapters 3 and 4) these large PSUs were selected without chance before the other PSUs were drawn randomly within strata.

These design features are then applied by Stata in later commands that begin with `svy:` such as the syntax below for `svy: mean`.

```
svy, subpop(DistanceSample): mean g1age
svy, subpop(DistanceSample): mean g2age
svy, subpop(DistanceSample): mean g1miles
svy, subpop(DistanceSample): mean g2earn
```

Notice that we listed each of our four variables in a separate `svy: mean` command. This is important if any of the variables have missing data, as is true in our case. If we list all of the variables in a single `svy: mean` command in Stata then they will be listwise deleted (as discussed further in Box 5.12 in the next section, this means that a case will be excluded from the calculation of the mean of every variable if it is missing for any of the listed variables).[14]

Display B.5.12 shows the results. Although the relationship between the weighted and unweighted means will differ in different applications, in our case the weighted means are all larger than the unweighted means (compare with Display B.5.11). The respondents average about 36 years of age based on the weighted mean and about 35 years of age based on the unweighted mean. Similarly, the respondents' mothers average about one more year of age with than without weights applied (about 62 versus 61 years). The respondents' mothers live an average of 311 miles away based on the weighted mean and an average of 280 miles away based on the unweighted mean. And, the respondents' earnings average about $32,000 with weights applied versus about $30,000 without weights. (The columns labeled "Std Error of Mean" in SAS and labeled "Linearized Std. Err." and "95% Conf. Interval" in Stata can be ignored. We will discuss these concepts in later chapters).

The degree and magnitude of difference between the weighted and unweighted means depends on the number of cases with large and small weights and how cases with larger and smaller weights differ on the analysis variables. For example, in our case, Blacks are the second largest group in the sample, next to non-Hispanic Whites (see again Display B.5.1). In subgroup analyses (not shown; we will learn such analyses in Chapter 7) we found that Blacks tend to have smaller weights than non-Hispanic Whites because Blacks were oversampled (the *adjweight* averages about 0.50 for Blacks but averages almost 1 for non-Hispanic Whites). When we similarly conducted separate analyses of the means on our analysis variables (*g1age, g2age, g1miles*, and *g2earn*) within race-ethnicity we also found that Blacks have lower average ages, live closer to their mothers, and earn less than do Whites. Thus, without adjusting for the oversampling of Blacks, the overall average age, distance, and earnings in the sample are lower than they would be had the NSFH drawn Blacks and non-Hispanic Whites in proportion to their representation in the population.

5.6.2: Weighted Proportion

The weighted proportion is defined similarly as the weighted mean (Kish 1965; Lee & Forthofer 2006; SAS Institute 2008a: 6492; StataCorp 2009b: 127). If we imagine a variable, C_i, that takes on two values: *'1'* if the case has a characteristic (e.g., the case is *male*) and *'0'* if the case does not have the characteristic (e.g., the case is *female*), then the sum of this variable over all cases ($\sum_{i=1}^{n} C_i$) would be the number of cases that have the characteristic (e.g., the number of men). If we multiply the value on this variable (C_i) for each case by the corresponding weight for each case, then the sum ($\sum_{i=1}^{n} w_i \times C_i$) is the weighted number of cases with the characteristic (say the weighted number of men). Dividing by the sum of the weights provides the weighted proportion. If we rely on relative weights, w_i^*, then we have:

$$weighted\ proportion = \frac{\sum_{i=1}^{n} w_i \times C_i}{n}$$

A Hypothetical Example

Table 5.6 provides a hypothetical example to make the calculation concrete. Here, we will imagine that our variable of interest, C_i, is a variable that captures whether a person cohabited with their partner before marriage. We further imagine that we examine the proportion who cohabited before marriage using a sample of 14 married people in which we oversampled people with below-poverty level incomes at twice their representation in the population.

Table 5.6 shows this data set. In the first column we see that there are 7 respondents with below-poverty level incomes ("Poor") and 7 respondents with above-poverty level incomes ("Non-Poor"). In the second column, the weight for the poor respondents is 0.5, since they were oversampled at twice their representation in the population. Because we have 7 such oversampled respondents, the average weight is: $\frac{10.5}{14} = 0.75$. Normalizing the weights by dividing by this average weight results in the weights of 1 becoming relative weights of $\frac{1}{0.75} = 1.33$ and the weights of 0.50 becoming relative weights of $\frac{0.50}{0.75} = 0.67$. These relative weights are shown in the third column of Table 5.6.

In the fourth column of the table, we see that 9 members of the sample cohabited before marriage (value of 1) and 5 members of the sample did not cohabit before marriage (value of 0). As discussed above, the unweighted proportion is the unweighted number of cases with the characteristic divided by the sample size. Thus, in our case this would be $proportion = \frac{\sum_{i=1}^{n} C_i}{n} = \frac{9}{14} = .64$. Multiplying by 100, 64% of the cases cohabited with a partner before marriage. The weighted proportion is

Table 5.6: An example of the calculation of the weighted proportion, with relative weights

	Group	Weight w_i	Relative Weight w_i^*	Value C_i	Relative Weight×Value $w_i^* \times C_i$
Case 1	Non-Poor	1.00	1.33	0	0
Case 2	Poor	0.50	0.67	0	0
Case 3	Poor	0.50	0.67	0	0
Case 4	Non-Poor	1.00	1.33	0	0
Case 5	Non-Poor	1.00	1.33	0	0
Case 6	Poor	0.50	0.67	1	0.67
Case 7	Poor	0.50	0.67	1	0.67
Case 8	Poor	0.50	0.67	1	0.67
Case 9	Non-Poor	1.00	1.33	1	1.33
Case 10	Non-Poor	1.00	1.33	1	1.33
Case 11	Non-Poor	1.00	1.33	1	1.33
Case 12	Poor	0.50	0.67	1	0.67
Case 13	Poor	0.50	0.67	1	0.67
Case 14	Non-Poor	1.00	1.33	1	1.33
Sum		$W = \sum_{i=1}^{n} w_i = 10.5$	$W^* = \sum_{i=1}^{n} w_i^* = 14$	$\sum_{i=1}^{n} C_i = 9$	$\sum_{i=1}^{n} w_i^* \times C_i = 8.67$

Proportion

calculated by summing the product of the relative weight and the indicator of cohabiting, and dividing by the sample size. That is, the contribution of each case to the sum in the numerator now depends on the weight ($\sum_{i=1}^{n} w_i^* \times C_i$). So, in the fifth column we see that the *poor* respondents who cohabited ($C_i = 1$) contribute less to this sum because the product with their relative weight is less than one (0.67) and thus $w_i^* C_i = 0.67 * 1 = 0.67$ for these cases. In contrast, the *non-poor* respondents who cohabited ($C_i = 1$) contribute more to this sum because their relative weight is larger than one (1.33) and thus $w_i^* C_i = 1.33 * 1 = 1.33$ for these cases. Since more poor than non-poor sample members cohabited (5 versus 4), the weighted percentage is somewhat lower, at 0.62*100 = 62%. In other words, the unweighted percentage is larger than it would be based on a simple random sample in our example for two main reasons: (1) poor respondents were over sampled and (2) poor respondents are more likely to have the characteristic (cohabiting with a partner before marriage).

NSFH Example

Again, in practice we do not need to calculate such proportions by hand because SAS and Stata will calculate them for us. Similar syntax is used in SAS to calculate the weighted proportion as the weighted mean, although in addition to listing the variables for which we want to calculate proportions in the `var` statement we also designate them in a `class` statement to indicate that the variables are classification (categorical) variables (see Display A.5.2). SAS then calculates proportions within each level of the categorical variable. In Stata, we use the `tabulate` rather than `mean` command (see again Display A.5.2), preceded by a `svyset` of the data. As was true with the `svy: mean` command, we request frequency distributions for each variable with a separate `svy: tabulate` command in Stata (due to cases with missing data).

Display B.5.13 shows our use of these commands to request the weighted proportions of the NSFH variables capturing gender and race-ethnicity. If we multiply these proportions by 100, we can then compare them to the unweighted percentages shown in Display B.5.1. Because Blacks were oversampled, we expect their percentage to be smaller when weights are applied, as it is (10.11% versus 16.88%). And, the weighted percentage of non-Hispanic Whites is larger than the unweighted percentage (85.45% versus 78.02%). Comparing Display B.5.13 and Display B.5.1 also reveals that the weighted percentage of women is smaller than the unweighted percentage (53.47% versus 59.64%) and likewise the weighted percentage of men is larger than the unweighted percentage (46.53% versus 40.36%).

5.6.3: Weighted Standard Deviation

Using the same logic as we used above for the weighted mean and weighted proportion, we can modify Equation 5.2 using relative weights to write the weighted standard deviation (Kish 1965; Lee & Forthofer 2006; StataCorp 2009b: 45):

$$s_{Y_w} = \sqrt{\frac{\sum w_i^* \times (Y_i - \bar{Y}_w)^2}{n-1}} \tag{5.5}$$

where w_i^* are the relative weights, scaled to sum to the sample size, n is the sample size, and $\bar{Y}_w$ is the weighted mean, as defined above.

A Hypothetical Example

Table 5.7 uses our hypothetical example from Table 5.5 of 14 employees sampled from a very large firm, with low-wage employees oversampled. Now we calculate the weighted standard deviation based on the relative weights.

As was the case with the weighted mean in Table 5.5, the weighted standard deviation is smaller than the unweighted standard deviation, reflecting the fact that the cases with weights less than one are more often employees with more than fewer days absent. But, the difference between the weighted and unweighted standard deviations is small (a standard deviation of 1.28 in Table 5.7 versus 1.30 in Example 5.2a of Table 5.3).

NSFH Example

We can ask both SAS and Stata to provide us with the weighted standard deviation defined in Equation 5.5, using their survey commands. Stata shows the standard error of the mean (but not

■ **Table 5.7: An example of the calculation of the weighted standard deviation, using relative weights**

	Relative Weight w_i^*	Days Absent Y_i	Deviation from Weighted Mean $(Y_i - \bar{Y}_w)$	Deviation from Mean Squared $(Y_i - \bar{Y}_w)^2$	Rel.Weight × Deviation from Mean Squared $w_i^* \times (Y_i - \bar{Y}_w)^2$
Case 1	1.27	2	−1.82	3.31	4.21
Case 2	1.27	2	−1.82	3.31	4.21
Case 3	1.27	3	−0.82	0.67	0.85
Case 4	1.27	3	−0.82	0.67	0.85
Case 5	0.63	3	−0.82	0.67	0.43
Case 6	1.27	4	0.18	0.033	0.042
Case 7	1.27	4	0.18	0.033	0.042
Case 8	0.63	4	0.18	0.033	0.021
Case 9	0.63	4	0.18	0.033	0.021
Case 10	1.27	5	1.18	1.40	1.78
Case 11	1.27	5	1.18	1.40	1.78
Case 12	0.63	5	1.18	1.40	0.89
Case 13	0.63	6	2.18	4.76	3.03
Case 14	0.63	6	2.18	4.76	3.03
Sum					21.17
St.Dev.			$s_{\bar{Y}_w} = \sqrt{\dfrac{\sum w_i^* \times (Y_i - \bar{Y}_w)^2}{n-1}} = \sqrt{\dfrac{21.17}{14-1}} = 1.28$		

■ **Box 5.12**

We use the `if` qualifier because Stata' `estat sd` command uses a different formula from Equation 5.5 to estimate the population standard deviation (Sribney 2009). It provides the same results as Equation 5.5 when we use the `if` qualifier to restrict the sample to our subpopulation – in our case our distance sample – but not within domains when we use the subpop option without an `if` qualifier. SAS also has a `std` option for the `proc surveymeans` command. However, the `std` option estimates the standard deviation of the total $\Sigma w_i^* \times Y_i$ (not an estimate of the population standard deviation of Y; SAS 2008a, p. 6478). In Chapter 7 we will see that it is also possible to use a weight option with Stata's summarize command to obtain an estimate of the population standard deviation based on Equation 5.5, similar to the weight option that we use for SAS's `proc means` command.

an estimate of the population standard deviation) in the default output for the `svy: mean` command. The `estat sd` command following `svy: mean` will calculate an estimate of the population standard deviation. In SAS, we add the `vardef = weight` and `weight` options to `proc means`. If we are analyzing a subgroup of the total sample (such as in our distance sample), we use an `if` qualifier to restrict the analysis to that subgroup in both SAS and Stata.

Display B.5.14 shows our use of these commands to estimate the weighted standard deviations for *g0age*, *g0age*, *g0miles*, and *g2earn*. Although the relationship between the weighted and unweighted standard deviations will vary in different applications, in our case, comparing to Display B.5.11 reveals that the standard deviations are consistently larger with weights applied than without weights. Specifically, whereas the unweighted standard deviation of mother's age was 11.58 the weighted standard deviation is 12.14. Similarly, the unweighted and weighted standard deviations of the respondent's age are 10.42 versus 11.12 respectively. In terms of distance from the mother, the unweighted standard deviation is 631.37 and the weighted version is 660.66. And, the respondent's earning has an unweighted standard deviation of $36,352 and weighted standard deviation of $39,500.

5.7: CREATING A DESCRIPTIVE TABLE

We now create a table similar to the tables shown in Literature Excerpt 5.1 and 5.2 based on the results we obtained above, to illustrate how such tables may be constructed in practice. As the differences between the tables in the two literature excerpts illustrate, there is no single way to construct such a table; some of the construction depends on personal preference, but style guides and existing publications can serve as examples (American Psychological Association 2009; American Sociological Association 2007; Iverson, Christiansen, Flanagin et al. 2007). It is good professionalization to start to practice how to create such tables (as you can do in the Chapter Exercise).

Our table summarizes the results from Displays 5.1, 5.11, 5.13, and 5.14. To help allow the table to "stand on its own" it also draws from our notes about the NSFH data (see again Display B.3.1)

Putting the statistics together in a table leads us to confront directly the issue of missing data. You may have noticed that the sample size differed somewhat for different variables in the displays based on our NSFH example. Such variation in missing data across variables (items) is called item-level missing data. There are many possible ways we could deal with such missing data (Allison 2001). A simple approach to this issue is called listwise deletion where we exclude cases that are missing from any of the variables to be used in our analysis. We will use this approach in some future chapters, where we will see that assuring we estimate various regression models using the same sample size is essential. We will also overview in Chapter 18 additional approaches to dealing with missing data.

and the restrictions we made and new variables we included when we created the data (see again Display B.4.7).

We can also write a short summary of the sample's descriptive characteristics, based on the table. There are again many different ways we might write this summary. It is helpful to begin to pay attention to how various authors do so in publications and to begin to practice doing so yourself. Although there is no single right or wrong way to do this, your summary will ideally be smooth and concise. For example, because the precise values are in the table, it is often helpful to round the values in the text description so that the description is easy to read (and not entirely duplicative of the table). It is also sometimes helpful to organize your text description somewhat differently from the order in which you list the variables in the table, to allow the text description to flow easily. Here is one example based on the weighted values in Table 5.8.

■ Table 5.8: Descriptive Statistics of Adult Respondents from Wave I of the National Survey of Families and Household (1987–1988)

Variable	Unweighted Values %	Weighted Values %	N
Gender			6,901
Male	40.36	46.53	
Female	59.64	53.47	
Race			6,901
White	78.02	85.45	
Black	16.88	10.11	
Other	5.10	4.44	
	Mean (SD)	Mean (SD)	
Respondent's Age (years)	34.84 (10.42)	36.04 (11.12)	6,900
Respondent's Earnings (2007 dollars)	29,614 (36,352)	32,332 (39,500)	6,433
Mother's Age (years)	60.52 (11.58)	61.87 (12.14)	6,801
Mother's Distance from Respondent (miles)	279.97 (631.4)	311.32 (660.66)	6,809

Note: Sample restricted to adults whose mother was alive, living in the United States, and not coresident with the respondent at the time of the survey.

After applying the sampling weights, we see that slightly over half of the respondents in the sample are women, their average age is about 36, and their mothers' average age is just over 60. Over eight-in-ten are of White race-ethnicity and just one-in-ten are of Black race-ethnicity. They average just over $30,000 in annual earnings (in 2007 dollars) and live over 300 miles from their mothers, on average.

5.8: SUMMARY

Table 5.9 summarizes the descriptive statistics and graphs covered in this chapter and what type of variable for which they are appropriately defined. We discussed how to request

■ Table 5.9: Summary of descriptive statistics and graphs

Central Tendency		Most Appropriate for:
Mode	The value which contains the highest percentage of cases.	Nominal Ordinal Interval
Median	The value that separates the variable's values in half. Fifty percent of the cases fall above the median and fifty percent of the cases fall below the median.	Ordinal Interval
Mean	The value that is the center of balance for the values. Positive differences from the mean are offset by negative differences from the mean, such that the sum of the difference between each case's value and the mean is zero.	Interval
Variation		
Interquartile Range	The range of values covered by the middle half of the data.	Ordinal Interval
Standard Deviation	The square root of the average squared deviation from the mean.	Interval
Graphs		
Frequency Distribution	Number of cases taking on each of a variable's values. Often converted to relative frequency (by dividing the frequency by the total number of cases) or percentage (by multiplying the relative frequency by 100). Most useful for variables with a relatively few number of values.	Nominal Ordinal Interval
Box Plot	Display of the minimum, maximum, and the quartiles of a distribution. Outliers may also be shown. Most useful for variables with a relatively large number of values. Helpful in identifying skewness.	Ordinal Interval
Histogram	Relative frequency distribution in which values are grouped into equal-spaced intervals before the frequency is calculated. Most useful for variables with a relatively large number of values. Helpful in visualizing skewness.	Interval

these statistics and graphs in SAS and Stata, using the basic commands that assume simple random sampling. For complex survey applications, we also showed how to request from SAS and Stata weighted means, weighted proportions and weighted standard deviations. When reporting descriptive statistics from data drawn based on a complex survey design, weighted values are preferred over unweighted values because the weighted values more closely approximate the values in the population from which the sample was drawn.

KEY TERMS
5

KEY TERMS

Bivariate

Box plot

Categorical Variable

Continuous Variable

Cumulative Frequency

Cumulative Percentage

Decile

Discrete Variable

Frequency Distribution

Histogram

Interquartile Range

Interval Variable

Mean

Median

Mode

Nominal Variable

Ordinal Variable

Outliers

Percentage Distribution

Percentile

Qualitative Variable

Quantitative Variable

Quartile

Relative Frequency Distribution

Skewed Distribution

Standard Deviation

Symmetric Distribution

Univariate

Weighted Mean

Weighted Proportion

Weighted Standard Deviation

Whiskers

REVIEW QUESTIONS

5.1. What are some basic types of variables commonly used in the social sciences? Provide examples of each (try to think of some examples that might be considered to fall in more than one type).

5.2. Which of the descriptive statistics introduced in this chapter are strictly appropriate for each type of variable?

5.3. What are frequency, relative frequency, and percentage distributions, respectively?

5.4. What are percentiles?

5.5. What is a histogram?

5.6. Define the mean, median and mode.

5.7. How do the mean and median relate to one another in symmetric, right skewed and left skewed distributions?

5.8. Define the two measures of variation discussed in the chapter.

5.9. What five values are shown in a standard box plot? How are outliers indicated?

5.10. Why is weighting needed for complex sampling designs?

5.11. How do the calculations of the weighted mean, proportion, and standard deviation differ from the calculation of the unweighted mean, proportion, and standard deviation?

REVIEW EXERCISES 5

REVIEW EXERCISES

5.1. Consider the three education variables whose survey questions and response categories are listed below. Discuss which of the types of variables listed in Table 5.1 are consistent with each variable (allowing each variable to have more than one type, where relevant). What do you see as some challenges to describing the distribution of each of these variables? Are there other ways you might gather education that might be more informative?

hidegree	yrschl	educ
"What is the highest degree you have completed?"	"How many years of school have you completed?"	"How far did you get in school?"
1=high school diploma	0 to 25 years	9=9th grade
2=GED		10=10th grade
3=associate's degree		11=11th grade
4=bachelor's degree		12=12th grade
5=master's degree		13=high school diploma or GED
6=PhD		14=some college
7=JD		15=associate's degree
8=MD		16=bachelor's degree
9=other (specify)		17=master's of professional degree
		18=doctoral degree

5.2. Suppose that you have gathered a sample of 22 people who live in the following regions of the U.S.

Case	Region	Case	Region	Case	Region
1	South	9	South	17	South
2	West	10	South	18	Midwest
3	Midwest	11	South	19	Northeast
4	South	12	Northeast	20	Northeast
5	South	13	Midwest	21	Midwest
6	Northeast	14	South	22	South
7	Northeast	15	South		
8	Northeast	16	South		

a. What is the frequency distribution of the *Region* variable?

b. What is the percentage distribution of the *Region* variable?

c. What is the mode of the *Region* variable?

5.3. Imagine you have a sample of 17 respondents who report that they have completed the following years of schooling.

id	yrschl	id	yrschl	id	yrschl
1	9	7	12	13	9
2	13	8	14	14	16
3	12	9	16	15	12
4	12	10	14	16	12
5	11	11	14	17	12
6	15	12	13		

a. What is the frequency distribution of the *yrschl* variable?

b. What is the percentage distribution of the *yrschl* variable?

c. What is the mode of the *yrschl* variable?

d. What is the cumulative percentage distribution of the *yrschl* variable?

e. What is the median of the *yrschl* variable?

5.4. Imagine you have three separate samples of eight respondents who report the following household incomes:

Sample #1		Sample #2		Sample #3	
caseid	income1	caseid	income2	caseid	income3
1	25,323	1	25,323	1	25,323
2	40,000	2	40,000	2	40,000
3	10,568	3	10,568	3	10,568
4	30,300	4	30,300	4	30,300
5	20,444	5	20,444	5	20,444
6	56,000	6	56,000	6	56,000
7	42,500	7	42,500	7	42,500
8		8	32,100	8	150,000

a. What is the mean of each variable (*income1*, *income2*, and *income3*)?

b. What is the standard deviation of each variable (*income1*, *income2*, and *income3*)?

c. What is the median of each variable (*income1*, *income2*, and *income3*)?

d. Discuss the relationship between the mean and median of each of the three variables.

5.5 If the 25th, 50th and 75th percentiles of household income in your data are $15,000, $32,000 and $48,000 respectively, then what is the interquartile range of income in your data?

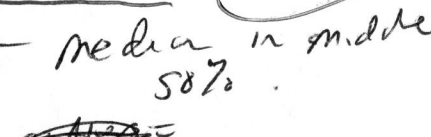

5.6. Discuss where you would expect the value of the mean to fall relative to the median and the mode in a symmetric, left skewed and right skewed distribution.

CHAPTER EXERCISES

In these Chapter Exercises, you will write a SAS and a Stata batch program to calculate some descriptive statistics ("SAS/Stata Tasks"). You will want to have Display A.5 handy as you write your batch programs. You will use the results to answer some questions related to the substance of what we learned in Chapter 5 ("Write-Up Tasks").

To begin, prepare the shell of a batch program, including the commands to save your output and helpful initial commands (e.g., In SAS, use the `libname` command to assign the SAS library where the formats can be found; In Stata, turn more off, drop any data in use, and close any open log; see Display A.4.2). Use the NHIS 2009 dataset that you created in Chapter 4. When you use/set the data, be sure to *exclude any cases with missing values on SEX, RACERPI2, vigfreqwR, bmiR, age, or exfreqwR.*

When answering the write-up tasks, be sure to provide the steps that lead you to your answer.

5.1 **Nominal Variables**

   a) SAS/Stata Tasks.

   i)   Calculate percentage distributions for the SEX and RACERPI2 variables.

   b) Write-Up Tasks.

   i)   What is the mode for SEX and for RACERPI2?

5.2 **Ordinal Variables**

   a) SAS/Stata Tasks.

   i)   Calculate the percentage distribution for *vigfreqwR*.

   ii) Calculate the quartiles for *vigfreqwR*.

   b) Write-Up Tasks.

   i)   What is the mode of *vigfreqwR*?

   ii) What is the median of *vigfreqwR*?

5.3 **Interval Variables**

   a) SAS/Stata Tasks.

   i)   Create a box plot and a histogram for *bmiR*, *age*, and *exfreqwR*.

   ii) Calculate the mean and standard deviation for *bmiR*, *age*, and *exfreqwR*.

      iii) Calculate the median for *bmiR*, *age*, and *exfreqwR*.

  b) Write-Up Tasks.

      i) Use the results to describe the distribution of *bmiR*, *age*, and *exfreqwR*. In your response, be sure to use all of the information (both figures as well as the mean and median) to discuss the shape of the distribution (e.g., whether each variable appears symmetric, skewed left, or skewed right).

5.4 Cross-Question Write-ups

  b) Write-Up Tasks

      i) Create a table similar to the tables shown in Literature Excerpt 5.1 and 5.2 based on the results you obtained in Question 5.1, 5.2, and 5.3. When creating the table, you can follow the conventions shown in either Literature Excerpt or use the style in your discipline. Either way, your goal will be that the table is "self-contained" (interpretable on its own).

      ii) Use the results in Question 5.1, 5.2, and 5.3 to write a few sentence description of the sample, focusing on the mode, median and/or mean values.

5.5 Weighted Values

  a) SAS/Stata Tasks.

      i) Calculate weighted proportions in each category for SEX, RACERPI2, and *vigfreqwR*.

      ii) Calculate the weighted mean and weighted standard deviation for *bmiR*, *age*, and *exfreqwR*.

  b) Write-Up Tasks.

      i) Create a new summary table and write a new description of the sample, based on the weighted values (similar to the table and description you wrote in Question 5.4).

      ii) Discuss how the unweighted and weighted results differ. Be sure to consider what you know about which groups were oversampled by the study as you discuss the differences.

COURSE EXERCISE

Use the techniques discussed in this chapter to examine and describe the variables in the dataset that you created in the course exercise to Chapter 4.

Begin by considering whether each of the variables you extracted for your analytic data set might fit the definition of each of the types of variables listed in Table 5.1. Consider

COURSE
EXERCISE
5

especially whether any variables might be considered of more than one type and how this may affect the interpretation of that variable.

Calculate graphs and measures of the center and spread of each variable. Be sure not to ask for analyses not appropriate to each variable's type(s). Discuss how each of the results informs you about each variable.

Create a table of descriptive statistics for your analytic data set, following the example tables shown in Literature Excerpts 5.1 and 5.2 or using the style in your discipline (either way, your goal will be that the table is "self-contained," meaning interpretable on its own). Write a one paragraph description of your sample based on this table.

If your data were collected with a complex survey design, calculate the weighted mean, weighted standard deviation, and weighted proportion for each variable in your data set. Create another table of these weighted descriptive statistics and revise your paragraph description of the sample to reflect the weighted values. Compare the unweighted and weighted results, and discuss the differences thinking about what you know of the study's sampling design (which subgroups were oversampled).

Chapter 6

SAMPLE, POPULATION AND SAMPLING DISTRIBUTIONS

CHAPTER 6: SAMPLE, POPULATION AND SAMPLING DISTRIBUTIONS

The concepts we discuss in this chapter provide an essential foundation that will carry through the rest of the book. We gather these concepts together in one chapter so that we can look at them in depth, and so that it will be easy for you to come back to them as needed, for review, as you read later chapters. In reviewing these basic concepts, we spend most of our time in this chapter considering the mean and standard deviation of a continuous variable. These basic concepts will extend to the other types of tests that we consider in later chapters. Before delving into these concepts, we begin by illustrating the two types of statistical inference that we will consider in this chapter and in future chapters.

6.1: STATISTICAL INFERENCE

In the social sciences, quantitative research generally examines the association between two or more variables, usually with some form of a regression model. Typically, a sample is used to draw inferences about a population using one of two approaches that we will examine in detail below: hypothesis tests and confidence intervals. You may have encountered these methods already and wondered about the meaning of the terms used when their results are reported and how the techniques are implemented. We offer two literature excerpts as examples, using them to illustrate the concepts we will cover in the remainder of the chapter.

6.1.1: Literature Excerpt 6.1

An article published by Jack Martin, Bernice Pescosolido, Sigrun Olafsdottir, and Jane McLeod in a 2007 issue of the *Journal of Health and Social Behavior* provides an example of hypothesis testing. The authors used the National Stigma Study-Children which was embedded within the 2002 General Social Survey to examine correlates of adults' preference for social distance from children with mental health problems (e.g., willingness to move next door to, to spend an evening with, to have their child share a classroom with, and to have their child make friends with a child in each of four vignettes designed to describe ADHD, depression, asthma, and "normal troubles").

Their main findings are shown in their Table 3 (see Literature Excerpt 6.1), which presents several regression models showing how a social distance preference is associated with several sets of variables. As you have likely seen in other social science publications, some of the numbers within the table are followed by one, two, or three asterisks, and a note at the bottom of the table reads: "*$p < .05$; **$p < .01$; ***$p < .001$ (one-tailed tests)." You may have wondered what exactly such results mean. We will study them in depth below. In short, these results follow a conventional approach for reporting hypothesis tests based on regression analyses. The asterisks summarize the results of the hypothesis test: Values with one or more asterisks provide support for the researchers' hypotheses; Values with no asterisks do not provide support for the

Literature Excerpt 6.1

Table 3. Unstandardized Estimates for the Regression (ordinary least squares) of Social Distance Preferences from Children with Mental Health Problems on Vignette Characteristics, Respondent Attributes, Causal Attributes, Problem Type, Perceived Dangerousness, and the Endorsement of Stigmatizing Beliefs, 2002 General Social Survey (N = 1,134)

	(1)	(2)	(3)	(4)	(5)	(6)	(7)
Vignette characteristics							
ADHD	.316***	.319***	.257***	.167***	.213***	.254***	.166**
Depression	.251***	.261***	.233***	.096	.089	.234***	.035
Asthma	-.197***	-.187***	.095	-.023	.094	.093	.011
14 years old	.076*	.078*	.073*	.084**	.073*	.071*	.080**
Female	-.065*	-.062*	-.034	-.030	-.014	-.032	-.012
Black	-.006	-.001	.034	.036	.034	.035	.037
Respondent attributes							
Age	—	.002	.002	.001	.002	.001	.001
Female	—	-.101**	-.081*	-.081**	-.081**	-.077*	-.078*
Black	—	.043	.030	.021	.043	.031	.040
Other race	—	.151*	.000	.057	.052	.078	.035
Family income	—	-.001	.001	.001	.001	.001	.001
Education	—	-.019**	-.006	-.007	-.005	-.006	-.005
South	—	.083*	.045	.051	.039	.044	.042
Size of place	—	.003	.001	.004	.004	.002	.005
Married	—	.070*	.045	.050	.061	.043	.057
Parent	—	.006	.018	.016	.016	.021	.016
Causal attribution							
Chemical imbalance	—	—	.039	.006	-.006	.041	-.009
Genetic or inherited problem	—	—	.017	-.004	.009	.020	-.001
Stressful circumstances	—	—	-.011	-.018	-.029	-.013	-.029
Way the individual was raised	—	—	.032	.037	.024	.031	.026

Table 3. Continued

	(1)	(2)	(3)	(4)	(5)	(6)	(7)
Lack of discipline in the home	—	—	.081***	.090***	.069**	.078***	.076**
Bad character	—	—	.105***	.112***	.099***	.105**	.106***
Violent TV or video games	—	—	.067**	.061**	.029	.064**	.030
Food or chemical allergies	—	—	-.086***	-.091***	-.076***	-.088***	-.083***
Problem type (label)							
Normal ups and downs	—	—	—	-.089***	—	—	-.069***
Mental illness	—	—	—	.078***	—	—	.016
Physical illness	—	—	—	.032	—	—	.018
Perceived dangerousness							
Violent toward self	—	—	—	—	.097***	—	.088**
Violent toward others	—	—	—	—	.134***	—	.112***
Stigma associated with mental health treatment							
Stigma scale	—	—	—	—	—	.047*	.038
Constant	1.694	1.823	1.037	1.276	.845	.923	1.00
R-squared	.104	.129	.215	.238	.259	.217	.268
F	21.68***	10.34***	12.66***	12.81***	14.88***	12.30***	13.43***

* $p<.05$; ** $p<.01$; *** $p<.001$ (one-tailed tests)

Source: Martin, Jack K., Bernice A. Pescosolido, Sigrun Olafsdottir, and Jane D. McLeod (2007). "The Construction of Fear: Americans' Preferences for Social Distance from Children and Adolescents with Mental Health Problems." *Journal of Health and Social Behavior*, 48: 50–67.

researchers' hypotheses. For example, the authors interpret the results in the first column of their table (Model 1) as follows (p. 59, rounding error in the original):

> In model 1, when compared to the reference category of a "normal troubles" child, behaviors associated with the diagnostic categories of ADHD and depression predict a significant desire to avoid social contact (b = .317 for ADHD, b = .253 for depression, $p < .001$). Americans also emerge as significantly less likely to desire social distance from the asthmatic child (b = −.196, $p < .001$). These results support the claim that behaviors associated with childhood mental disorders encourage a desire for social distance.

We will have much more to say about how these conclusions are drawn below and in future chapters (as well as how to understand the other words and numbers in the table) but for now, our goal is to have this type of result in mind as we discuss the basic concepts of hypothesis testing below (for example, the p in the authors' note is the p-value that we discuss below; the "one-tailed tests" they reference in their table note is one type of hypothesis tests that we will examine how to conduct below).

6.1.2: Literature Excerpt 6.2

A publication by Brennan Davis and Christopher Carpenter in the 2009 issue of the *American Journal of Public Health* provides an example of how to draw statistical inferences using confidence intervals. Although historically this approach has been less commonly used for reporting results in social science publications than hypothesis testing, it is increasingly being adopted. As we will begin to discuss below and will elaborate in future chapters, the confidence interval approach has several advantages. By providing a range of values for the association between two variables (the range being between the lower and upper values listed in the confidence interval) the confidence interval makes explicit the uncertainty in our inference from our single sample to the population. We will learn why this uncertainty exists in the Section 6.3, when we discuss the sampling distribution. We can also use the confidence interval bounds to make conclusions about the same hypotheses examined in the hypothesis testing approach (for the "two-tailed" type of hypotheses that we will define below, the hypothesis test and confidence interval approach will lead to exactly the same conclusions about the hypotheses); however, the confidence interval approach also allows us to see what conclusion would be made for many other hypothesis tests (not only the hypotheses laid out by the researchers who published the results). In this way, the confidence interval is more informative than a report of a single hypothesis test, because it emphasizes the range of conclusions that can be drawn from one set of results (for example, a researcher with a different perspective on the topic may be able to draw conclusions about her own hypotheses using such published confidence intervals, and thus help inform her future studies).

Taking a look at Literature Excerpt 6.2, we see that Davis and Carpenter report both hypothesis tests and confidence intervals in their Table 2. The table reports several regression

Literature Excerpt 6.2

Table 2. Association Between a School's Proximity to a Fast-Food Restaurant and Overweight, Obesity, and Body Mass Index (BMI) Among Its Students (N = 529367): California Healthy Kids Survey, 2002–2005

Indicator	Model 1: Overweight, AOR (95% CI)	Model 2: Obese, AOR (95% CI)	Model 3: BMI, b (95% CI)	Model 4: BMI, b (95% CI)	Model 5: BMI, b (95% CI)	Model 6: BMI, b (95% CI)
Fast-food restaurant within 0.5 miles of school (among the top LSR establishments)	1.06*** (1.02, 1.10)	1.07*** (1.02, 1.12)	0.10*** (0.03, 0.16)			
Other restaurant within 0.5 miles of school (not among the top LSR establishments)	1.04** (1.01, 1.08)	1.04* (1.0, 1.09)	0.08** (0.01, 0.14)			
Fast-food restaurant 0–0.25 miles from school				0.12*** (0.04, 0.20)		
Fast-food restaurant 0.25–0.5 miles from school				0.14*** (0.06, 0.23)		
Fast food restaurant 0.5–0.75 miles from school				0.06 (−0.04, 0.16)		

					Distance to nearest fast-food restaurant	
						-0.03*** (-0.05, -0.01)
No. of nearby fast-food restaurants						0.00 (0.00, 0.00)
R^2	0.05	0.06	0.10	0.10	0.10	0.10

Note:
CI = confidence interval; AOR = adjusted odds ratio; LSR = limited-service restaurants. We estimated logit models for overweight (model 1) and obese (model 2) youths, and for these models we present AORs. In model 1, obese youths were also considered to be overweight. We used ordinary least squares for the BMI outcome in models 3 through 6. CIs were adjusted for clustering at the school level. In addition to the variables shown, all models also included controls for the following student characteristics: a female indicator, grade indicators, age indicators, race/ethnicity indicators, and physical exercise indicators. All models also included indicator variables for school location type, including large urban, midsize urban, small urban, large suburban, midsize suburban, small suburban, town, and rural. A full set of parameter estimates is available from the author upon request.

*$P<.10$; **$P<.05$; ***$P<.01$.

Source: Davis, Brennan and Christopher Carpenter (2009). "Proximity of Fast-Food Restaurants to Schools and Adolescent Obesity." *American Journal of Public Health*, 99: 505–510.

models based on the California Healthy Kids Study of over half a million middle and high school students in the early 2000s. The researchers were interested in how the proximity of fast-food restaurants to schools associated with students' body mass index and their overweight and obese status. Hypothesis test results are shown by the asterisks following many of the values, and a note similar to the one we saw in Literature Excerpt 6.1 tells us that "* $P<.10$; ** $P<.05$; *** $P<.01$." The confidence intervals are in parentheses following the asterisks, and the column label says "95% CI" where CI stands for confidence interval (and we will learn below what 95% means). In interpreting their first set of results, the authors say (p. 506).

> Table 2 presents our main results, showing that youths who attended schools located near fast-food restaurants were heavier than were other students with similar observable characteristics who attended schools not located near fast-food restaurants. Models predicting youths' overweight (model 1) and obesity (model 2) show that a youth had 1.06 times the odds of being overweight (95% confidence interval [CI] = 1.02, 1.10) and 1.07 times the odds of being obese (95% CI = 1.02, 1.12) if the youth's school was near a fast-food establishment; both estimates were statistically significant."

The authors provide a conclusion about their own hypotheses based on these results (that proximity to fast-food restaurants is significantly associated with youths' overweight and obesity), but the confidence interval would allow us to consider other hypotheses (as we will learn to do below and in later chapters). The confidence interval further signals to us that the odds of overweight is not exactly 1.06 but may be anywhere from 1.02 to 1.10 and the odds of obesity is not exactly 1.07 but rather anywhere between 1.02 and 1.12 (odds is a term that is probably familiar to you from everyday conversation, but in Part 4 of the book we will consider in depth its meaning in regression models).

We now turn to unpacking the concepts that underlie these statistical inferences; as we do, keep these literature excerpts in mind to help you understand the relevance of the concepts for understanding the literature and for your own future research.

6.2: POPULATION AND SAMPLE DISTRIBUTIONS

Social scientists are usually interested in understanding society writ large, but testing our theories using information about every member of society is usually practically and economically infeasible. We instead rely on **samples** from **populations** to allow us to draw **inferences** about whether our theoretical expectations hold. Our samples are sometimes drawn from a population that approximates the larger society of interest to us (e.g., nationally representative samples of the U.S. population). Other times, the population from which we draw our sample is further restricted to reduce logistical and financial costs (e.g., a sample drawn to represent a particular state, city, school, or company). In each case, if we use a simple random sampling design (or a complex sampling design analyzed to appropriately account for its strata, clusters, and weights), we expect the distribution of a variable in the sample to mirror the distribution of the variable in the population.

Figures 6.1a and 6.1b show examples of two different hypothetical population distributions of continuous variables. We created these purposefully using statistical software so that the distribution on the top left, in Figure 6.1a, is symmetrical; and, the distribution on the top right, in Figure 6.1b, is skewed to the right. To make the examples more concrete, we imagine that the variable in the symmetric distribution is the number of words spoken by a population of 100,000 toddlers who live in a large city; and, that the variable in our skewed distribution is annual earnings in a population of 100,000 employees of a large corporation that has multiple locations across the country. We asked our statistical software to randomly draw 300 cases from each of these hypothetical population distributions, shown on the bottom left and bottom right (in Figure 6.1c and Figure 6.1d), to simulate what would happen if we actually drew samples from such a population. Notice that in both cases the **sample distribution** has a shape similar to its **population distribution** (symmetrical on the bottom left and skewed right on the bottom right).

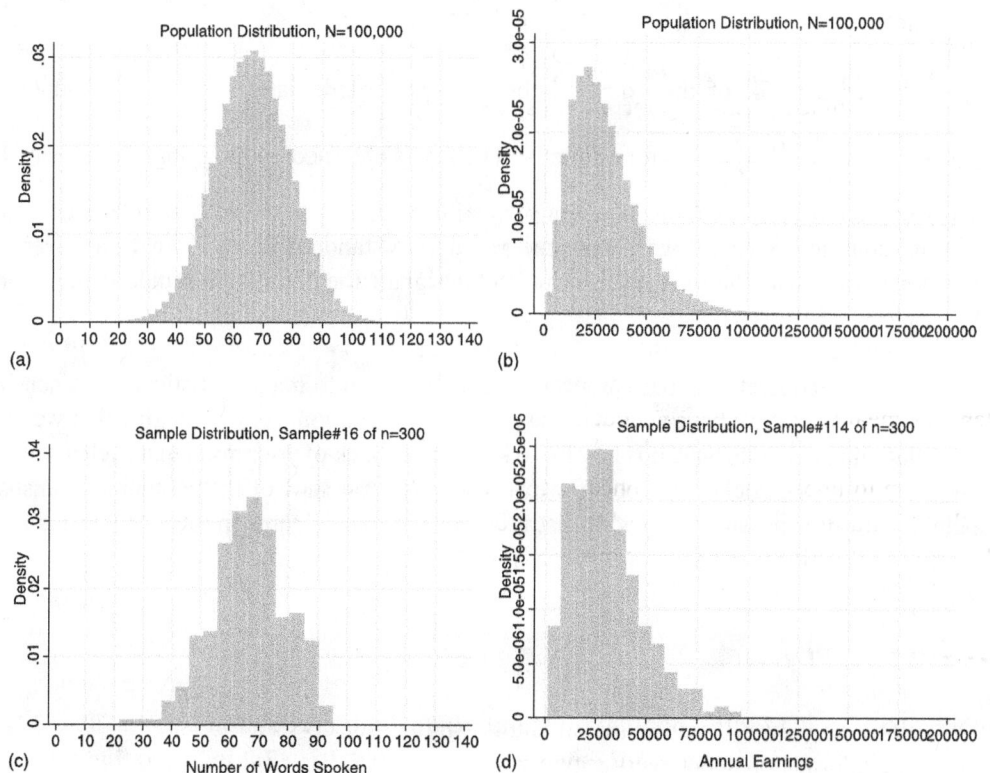

■ **Figure 6.1** Examples of Hypothetical Symmetric and Skewed Population and Sample Distributions

In fact, we can use the measures of central tendency and variation that we introduced in Chapter 5 to draw inferences about the central tendency and variation of the variable in the population. That is, rather than simply using these values to describe the characteristics of our sample, we can also use these values to tell us something about the characteristics of the population from which the sample was drawn. When we do so, we refer to the values based on the sample as **sample statistics**, which are calculated based on formulas called **estimators**, and we refer to the corresponding values in the population as **population parameters**. Sample statistics are quantities that can be calculated by sample data. Population parameters are unknown quantities (due to cost and feasibility constraints) that we estimate based on the sample data.

From this perspective, for example, we can think of the equation for the mean that we introduced in Chapter 5, $\overline{Y} = \frac{\sum_{i=1}^{n} Y_i}{n}$, as an estimator. The result obtained by plugging in values of Y and n from a particular sample is a sample estimate of the population parameter. It is common to use Greek symbols to denote population values. For example, the population mean is commonly denoted by a lowercase Greek m, μ, which is said "mu." A subscript Y can be used to designate the population mean of the variable Y. Thus, μ_Y represent the mean of Y in the population, a value that is unknown (due to cost and feasibility constraints) but which we estimate using the sample mean, $\overline{Y}$.

We can likewise think of the equation for the standard deviation that we introduced in Chapter 5, $s_Y = \sqrt{\frac{\Sigma(Y_i - \overline{Y})^2}{n-1}}$, as an estimator. The result obtained by plugging in values of $\overline{Y}$, Y and n from a particular sample is a sample estimate of the population standard deviation. Following common practice, we denote the population standard deviation with a lower case Greek s, σ, read "sigma". We use a subscript Y to designate the population standard deviation of the variable Y, σ_Y.

In order to make concrete the basic concepts we will rely on to make statistical inferences it is useful to imagine that we have access to the complete population. As we imagine that we know the population data in this way, it is helpful to keep in the back of your mind that such a situation would be rare in the social sciences (for example, as is the goal of the Decennial Census of Population; or, as is possible with administrative data for participants in social programs).

▪ Box 6.1

As noted in Chapter 5, the formula for the population standard deviation (Equation 6.3a in Table 6.1) differs from the formula for the sample standard deviation (Equation 6.3b in Table 6.1) in that we do not subtract one from the population size (the denominator is N not N-1). The subtraction of one from the denominator in the formula for the sample standard deviation reflected the fact that we had to estimate the sample mean in order to calculate the numerator of the sample standard deviation (i.e., to calculate the deviation of each observed value from the sample mean). For the population formula, however, we use the population mean, μ_Y, which is calculated based on population values. In other words, the formula for the population standard deviation is based just on known quantities (Y_i for every member of the population, N, and μ_Y) whereas the sample standard deviation is based on known and estimated quantities (Y_i and n are known but $\overline{Y}$ is estimated). We lose one **degree of freedom** when we use the estimate of $\overline{Y}$ when we calculate the sample standard deviation.

Imagine we did have information about every member of the population. How would we calculate the mean and standard deviation? The formula for the population mean is similar to the sample mean, but based on the total population size (N) rather than the sample size (n). That is, $\mu_Y = \dfrac{\sum_{i=1}^{N} Y_i}{N}$. As noted in Chapter 5, the formula for the standard deviation of Y in the population is also similar to the formula for the sample standard deviation of Y, and uses N rather than n: $\sigma_Y = \sqrt{\dfrac{\sum_{i=1}^{N}(Y_i - \mu_Y)^2}{N}}$. These formulas are summarized in the Table 6.1, where we show the standard deviation of Y itself as well as the square of the standard deviation (the variance of Y).

■ **Table 6.1: Formula for the Mean and Standard Deviation in the Population and Sample**

	Distribution Type			
	Population		Sample	
Mean	$\mu_Y = \dfrac{\sum_{i=1}^{N} Y_i}{N}$	(6.1a)	$\bar{Y} = \dfrac{\sum_{i=1}^{n} Y_i}{n}$	(6.1b)
Variance	$\sigma_Y^2 = \dfrac{\sum_{i=1}^{N}(Y_i - \mu_Y)^2}{N}$	(6.2a)	$s_Y^2 = \dfrac{\sum_{i=1}^{n}(Y_i - \bar{Y})^2}{n-1}$	(6.2b)
Standard Deviation	$\sigma_Y = \sqrt{\sigma_Y^2} = \sqrt{\dfrac{\sum_{i=1}^{N}(Y_i - \mu_Y)^2}{N}}$	(6.3a)	$s_Y = \sqrt{s_Y^2} = \sqrt{\dfrac{\sum_{i=1}^{n}(Y_i - \bar{Y})^2}{n-1}}$	(6.3b)

Source: This table is adapted from Wybraniec and Wilmoth (1999: 77).

We used these formulas to calculate the mean, variance and standard deviation for the hypothetical population and sample distributions shown in Figure 6.1.[1] The results are shown in Table 6.2.

As we would expect, the sample statistics are similar to but not identical to the population parameters. The sample distributions reflect their population distributions because we drew each sample randomly. The sample distributions differ somewhat from the population distributions because the sample contains just 300 of the total 100,000 population members. In our symmetric distribution, the population mean is 66.01 whereas the sample mean is 66.72. And, the population standard deviation is 12.97 whereas the sample standard deviation is 12.51. In our skewed distribution, the population mean is $29,978 whereas the sample mean is $30,430. And, the population standard deviation is $17,282 whereas the sample standard deviation is $17,580. If we drew a second sample of size 300 from each population, we would expect the new set of 300 population members we drew would differ, at least somewhat, from the original 300 members drawn into

■ **Box 6.2**

We emphasize that we were able to calculate the population values in Table 6.2 because we created these data sets. In practice, the population value is usually unknown because it is too expensive or otherwise impractical to obtain information about every member of the population.

■ **Table 6.2: Means and Standard Deviations for Hypothetical Populations and Samples shown in Figure 6.1**

	Distribution Type			
	Symmetric *Number of Words Spoken*		Skewed *Annual Earnings*	
	Population (N=100,000)	Sample (n=300)	Population (N=100,000)	Sample (n=300)
Mean	$\mu_Y = 66.01$	$\overline{Y} = 66.72$	$\mu_Y = 29{,}978$	$\overline{Y} = 30{,}430$
Variance	$\sigma_Y^2 = 168.34$	$s_Y^2 = 156.50$	$\sigma_Y^2 = 298{,}683{,}424$	$s_Y^2 = 309{,}056{,}400$
Standard Deviation	$\sigma_Y = 12.97$	$s_Y = 12.51$	$\sigma_Y = 17{,}282$	$s_Y = 17{,}580$

the first sample, and the calculation of the sample mean, standard deviation, and variance would be somewhat different. If we used a random process to draw the sample each time, the sample distributions should again reflect the respective population distribution. We will come back to these ideas below when we discuss the sampling distribution.

6.2.1: Theoretical Distributions

We created the symmetric and skewed population data shown in Figure 6.1 based on **theoretical distributions**. Statisticians have developed formulas for such theoretical distributions that allow them to calculate what proportion of values will fall above and below a particular value on a variable that follows a particular theoretical distribution. These theoretical distributions form the backbone of all of the methods of statistical inference that we will examine in future chapters of the book. In this section, we use one theoretical distribution—the normal distribution—to illustrate the value of using a theoretical distribution to tell us where a value falls within a distribution. (We will consider in Section 6.5 three other types of distributions that we will rely on for some statistics in future chapters.)

The Normal Distribution

We chose the normal distribution as an example of a theoretical distribution for two reasons. First, we use the normal distribution because some characteristics are normally distributed in the population (such as height and IQ). Second, many inferential methods rely on the normal distribution even when the population distribution is not normal, including several of the methods we will examine in later chapters. In this section, we show the benefit of using the normal distribution when the variable itself is normally distributed. In later sections, we will use similar techniques when our sample statistic (the sample mean) follows the normal distribution.

We asked our statistical software to create our hypothetical population data for the symmetric distribution (shown in Figure 6.1a) based on this normal distribution.[2] The normal distribution has a familiar **bell shaped curve**. Most of the cases in the hypothetical population shown in Figure 6.1a are found in the middle of the distribution. The curve falls off symmetrically from this center, such that the left and right sides of the curve are mirror images of each other. In contrast to a skewed distribution which has a long tail on one side (as in Figure 6.1b), in the normal distribution relatively few cases fall far in the left or right tail of the distribution (e.g., below 40 and above 95 in Figure 6.1a).

Although the normal distribution always follows this general bell shape, it can be shifted left or right depending on a variable's mean and stretched out or pushed in depending on a variable's standard deviation. We can draw many specific cases of the normal distribution that all follow this same shape, but each with a different center and spread. The top row of Figure 6.2 shows hypothetical examples of three variables drawn to follow a theoretical normal distribution but each with a different mean and standard deviation. On the left, in Figure 6.2a, is a set of hypothetical students' scores on a test of math achievement. In the middle, in Figure 6.2b, are diastolic blood pressure measures of a hypothetical sample of adults. On the right, in Figure 6.2c, are heights of a different hypothetical sample of adult women. Each of these distributions was created based on the theoretical normal distribution, but with a different mean and different standard deviation. Math achievement, on the left, was created to have the largest standard deviation (15.23) and thus looks most stretched out. Height, on the right, has the smallest standard deviation (1.67) and thus has the highest peak in the middle of the distribution. Diastolic blood pressure, in the middle, has a standard deviation between the other two examples (5), and is somewhat less stretched out than Figure 6.2a but somewhat more stretched out than Figure 6.2c. The center of each distribution also differs, with math achievement having the largest mean (98.34), diastolic blood pressure falling in the middle (82.6), and height having the smallest mean (63.8).

The Standard Normal Distribution

The standard normal distribution is another example of the normal distribution, but with mean of zero and standard deviation of one. As we will see below, we can convert any variable that follows another normal distribution (with a different mean and different standard deviation) to the standard normal distribution by subtracting that variable's mean from each of its values (known as **recentering**) and dividing the result by that variable's standard deviation (known as **rescaling**). We will see that one advantage of doing this is that we can more readily compare values from normally-distributed variables with different means and standard deviations after converting to the standard normal (by recentering and rescaling). Another advantage is that it is somewhat easier to determine what proportion of values will fall above and below a particular value on the variable if we use the standard normal. Rather than having to calculate this proportion for each unique mean and standard deviation, we can just do it once for the normal

Box 6.3

Notice that the curves in Figure 6.2 are drawn smoothly, rather than with a histogram as was done in Figure 6.1a. This smooth curve implies a theoretical distribution where every possible value for the continuous variable is represented rather than a population or sample distribution where only certain values of the continuous variable are represented. Furthermore, for the theoretical distributions in Figure 6.2, each value reflects the probabilities that result from the mathematical formula (Larsen and Marx 2006; Wackerly, Mendenhall, and Scheaffer 2008), whereas in Figure 6.1a we allow some variation from the theoretical ideal.

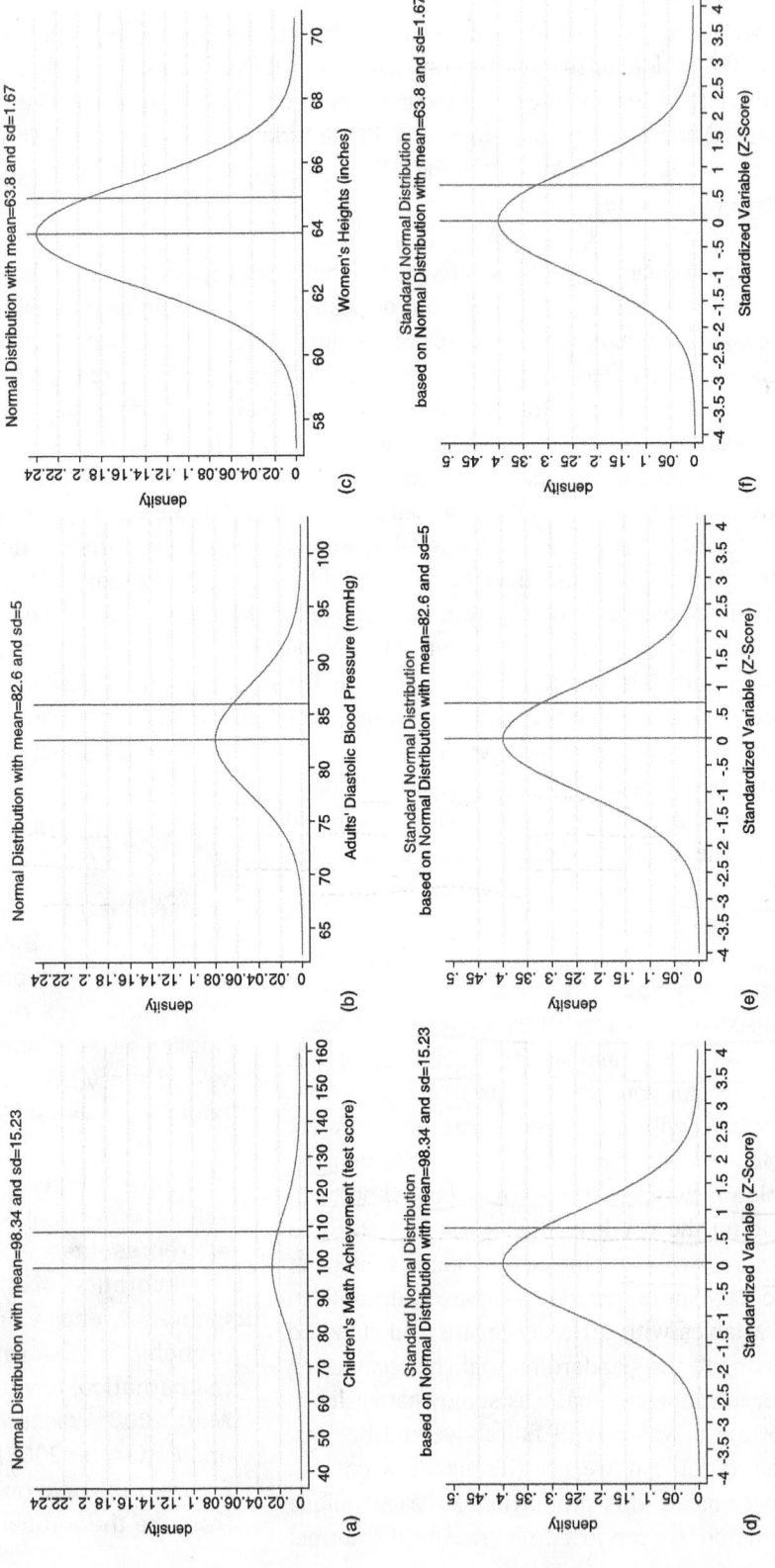

Figure 6.2 Three Hypothetical Examples of Normal Distributions in Their Raw Values and Standardized Values

Note. The graphs in Figure 6.2 were created with a modified version of the zdemo2 Stata command written by Philip B. Ender of the UCLA Academic Technology Services (UCLA Academic Technology Services n.d.).

distribution with mean of zero and standard deviation of one. Although today's computing power reduces the value of this advantage (since it is easy to ask the computer to calculate such proportions) we shall see that we can memorize the proportions associated with a few values in the standard normal distribution, and we will rely on these values regularly as we make statistical inferences.

Specifically, we calculate **standardized variables** to put variables that follow the normal distribution, but with different means and standard deviations, on common footing using the following formula:

$$Z = \frac{Y_i - \bar{Y}}{s_Y} \qquad (6.4)$$

where Z is the symbol typically used to denote a standard normal variable. Indeed, the resulting values are sometimes referred to as **Z-values** or **standard scores**. We used this formula to convert the variables in the three normal distributions in the top row of Figure 6.2, which each has its own mean and standard deviation, into standardized variables that now follow the **standard normal distribution** and have a mean of zero and a standard deviation of one (shown in the bottom row of Figure 6.2).

Note that the numerator in Equation 6.4 calculates how far above or below the mean each observed value on Y falls. The denominator of Equation 6.4 then puts this difference from the mean into standard deviation units, by dividing by the standard deviation. The resulting Z-values of the standard normal distribution have a mean of 0 and standard deviation of 1. This process allows us to use each variable's own mean as our reference point and each variable's own standard deviation as our yardstick in measuring distance, putting the different variables on equal footing.

Let's make this concrete, starting by calculating Z-values for the three middle values labeling the X axis in Figure 6.2c (*62, 64,* and *66*; see Table 6.3).

Thus, the height of *62* inches falls 1.08 inches below the average height of 63.8 (i.e., 62 − 63.8 = −1.8 in the numerator). This difference is 1.08 standard deviation units (i.e., $\frac{-1.8}{1.67} = -1.08$). Thus,

■ **Table 6.3: Examples of standard scores calculated based on Figure 6.2c**

Observed value of Y	Standardized value, Z, where $\bar{Y} = 63.8$ and $s_Y = 1.67$
62	$Z = \dfrac{Y_i - \bar{Y}}{s_Y} = \dfrac{Y_i - 63.8}{1.67} \quad = \dfrac{62 - 63.8}{1.67} = \dfrac{-1.8}{1.67} = -1.08$
64	$Z = \dfrac{Y_i - \bar{Y}}{s_Y} = \dfrac{Y_i - 63.8}{1.67} \quad = \dfrac{64 - 63.8}{1.67} = \dfrac{0.2}{1.67} = 0.12$
66	$Z = \dfrac{Y_i - \bar{Y}}{s_Y} = \dfrac{Y_i - 63.8}{1.67} \quad = \dfrac{66 - 63.8}{1.67} = \dfrac{2.2}{1.67} = 1.32$

we can say that the value of *62* falls 1.08 standard deviations below the mean. Likewise, the height of *64* falls 0.2 inches or 0.12 standard deviations above the mean. And, the height of *66* falls 2.2 inches or 1.32 standard deviations above the mean.

Let's now return to Figure 6.2 to demonstrate the usefulness of this standardization process for comparing variables with different means and standard deviations. The label on the X-axis of Figures 6.2a, 6.2b, and 6.2c give their units of measure. Math achievement is measured in test scores. Diastolic blood pressure is measured in mmHg. Height is measured in inches. As noted, in the bottom row of Figure 6.2 we show the distribution of the standardized version of each of the variables from the top row. Whereas the distributions in their actual units (test points, mmHg, and inches) look very different, their standardized distributions look very similar. This is because although the three variables' actual standard deviations are different, once we standardize each variable the standardized values all have a standard deviation of one. The two vertical lines in each graph are drawn at the mean and a value above the mean. Table 6.4 shows the actual and *Z*-value of each of the lines drawn to the right of the mean.

In their actual units, it is difficult to compare the three observed values. The value of 108.54 on test scores is larger than the 85.95 on blood pressure, which in turn is larger than the 64.92 in height. But, we know that one more point on a math achievement test may mean something very different from on more mmHg of blood pressure which in turn is quite different from one more inch of height.

The *Z*-values in Table 6.4 show us that, in fact, these values share something in common. Each of these values falls 0.67 standard deviations above its respective mean. This standardization process helps us compare "apples to apples" when variables have very different standard deviations. The *Z*-values tell us how far above or below the mean a value falls relative to its own standard deviation. In other words, for *Math Achievement* in the top row of Table 6.4, the shaded value of 10.20 is 0.67 of its standard deviation (15.23). For *Height* in the bottom row of Table 6.4, the shaded value of 1.12 is 0.67 of its standard deviation (1.67). That is, even though the deviations from the mean differ in absolute amounts (10.20 for *Math Achievement* and 1.12 for *Height*) they are both 0.67 relative to each variable's own standard deviation. So, the standardization process puts the variables on equal footing by using each variable's own mean

■ Table 6.4: Actual and *Z*-values shown with vertical lines to the right of the means in Figure 6.2

	Actual Value, Y	Standardized value, Z			
Math Achievement	108.54	$Z = \dfrac{Y_i - \bar{Y}}{s_Y} = \dfrac{Y_i - 98.34}{15.23}$	$= \dfrac{108.54 - 98.34}{15.23}$	$= \dfrac{10.20}{15.23}$	$= 0.67$
Blood Pressure	85.95	$Z = \dfrac{Y_i - \bar{Y}}{s_Y} = \dfrac{Y_i - 82.60}{5}$	$= \dfrac{85.95 - 82.60}{5}$	$= \dfrac{3.35}{5}$	$= 0.67$
Height	64.92	$Z = \dfrac{Y_i - \bar{Y}}{s_Y} = \dfrac{Y_i - 63.8}{1.67}$	$= \dfrac{64.92 - 63.8}{1.67}$	$= \dfrac{1.12}{1.67}$	$= 0.67$

as our reference point and each variable's own standard deviation as our yardstick in measuring distance. This is the first advantage of using the standard normal distribution.

As noted above, the second advantage of using the standard normal distribution is to make it easier to calculate the proportion of values that are more extreme than a particular value. We will see below that we will use these proportions regularly in statistical inference (for example to help us distinguish values that are typical from those that are quite unusual, under certain conditions). If we were to calculate the proportion of cases falling to the right of the values we examined in Table 6.4 (108.54 in Figure 6.2a; 85.95 in Figure 6.2b; 64.92 in Figure 6.2c), we would have to do so three separate times based on the normal distribution with each respective mean and standard deviation (98.34 and 15.23 in Figure 6.2a; 82.60 and 5 in Figure 6.2b; 63.8 and 1.67 in Figure 6.2c). But, once we convert the values to standard scores, and see that they are all values of 0.67 in the standard normal distribution, we can just calculate the proportion once (based on the standard normal distribution with mean of zero and standard deviation of one). In our case, it turns out that 25% of values fall above 0.67 in the standard normal distribution (we will see below how to ask SAS and Stata to make this calculation).

We also noted above that there are several common values that we will use repeatedly to interpret the standard normal distribution. These values reinforce what we already know about the bell-shaped curve of the normal distribution: That most of its values are fairly concentrated around the mean. We can now say more precisely that most values in the normal distribution fall within three standard deviations of the mean. About 68% of the values fall within one standard deviation of the mean; that is, between $\mu_Y - \sigma_Y$ and $\mu_Y + \sigma_Y$. About 95% of the values fall within two standard deviations of the mean; that is, between $\mu_Y - 2\sigma_Y$ and $\mu_Y + 2\sigma_Y$. And, nearly all (99.7%) of the values fall within three standard deviations of the mean; that is, between $\mu_Y - 3\sigma_Y$ and $\mu_Y + 3\sigma_Y$ (see Box 6.4). Whereas it is difficult for us to calculate in our head whether a specific value in a variable's natural units falls within these ranges, it is easy to tell if a Z-value is larger than the cutoffs of 1, 2, and 3 standard deviations. For example, it is not immediately clear how unusual a value of 151 on the math achievement test would be; but, we can quickly see that a Z-value of $Z = \dfrac{Y_i - \bar{Y}}{s_Y} = \dfrac{151 - 98.34}{15.23}$

= 3.46 falls more than than three deviations above the mean, suggesting that it is a relatively uncommon test score.

6.3: THE SAMPLING DISTRIBUTION

We have now examined two kinds of distributions—the population and sample distribution. We also considered how a theoretical distribution can help us determine what proportion of values is more extreme than a particular value in a sample or population distribution. There is another type of distribution in statistics—the **sampling distribution**—for which we will also use theoretical distributions to help us assign probabilities. However, sampling distributions are not distributions of values of variables. Instead, they are theoretical distributions of sample statistics. We will focus on the sampling distribution of one sample statistic—the mean—as an example in this chapter.

> ■ **Box 6.4**
>
> This is sometimes know as the **68–95–99.7 rule** or **empirical rule**. We will define the probability of falling within certain intervals of the mean based on the normal distribution more precisely below.

The sampling distribution is the distribution that we would construct if we sequentially drew many, many samples from the population, calculated a sample statistic for each of those samples, and plotted the sample statistics from all of the samples. In fact, the theoretical sampling distribution would include every possible sample from the population. This is a stretch in our thinking because the sampling distribution is something we would never actually construct in practice. Indeed, if we had the resources to draw numerous samples from the population, we would likely just survey every member of the population and obtain the population distribution directly. Even though we would never construct a real sampling distribution in practice, with today's computing power, we can ask the computer to mimic the process of constructing a sampling distribution. We will do so in this section (and you can do so in the chapter exercise) to help us make the sampling distribution more concrete.

If we never construct a sampling distribution in practice, you may wonder how and why it is so central to statistical inference? The utility of the sampling distribution is that statisticians are able to determine the theoretical distribution followed by the sampling distribution of particular estimators. For example, statisticians have shown that the sampling distribution for the mean $\bar{Y} = \frac{\sum_{i=1}^{n} Y_i}{n}$ follows a normal distribution. Once this theoretical distribution is known, statisticians can use the formulas for these distributions to attach values to the sample statistic we obtain from a single sample (and we can ask SAS and Stata to make these calculations for us).

Let's now look at how we can construct a hypothetical sampling distribution to help make it more concrete. We will extend the example population and sample distributions that we showed in Figure 6.1 in this way. Recall that the samples we showed in Figure 6.1c and Figure 6.1d were each drawn with $n = 300$ from our populations of $N = 100,000$ shown in Figure 6.1a and 6.1b. We created each hypothetical population using statistical software, and then asked the software to draw samples of size $n = 300$ from each hypothetical population. To create hypothetical *sampling distributions*, we repeated this process 500 times (so we had 500 samples, each drawn with size $n = 300$ from populations of size $N = 100,000$). In each sample, we also asked our statistical software to calculate the mean of the 300 sample members' values of Y. We did this for both the symmetric and skewed distributions shown in Figure 6.1a and 6.1b. To see the influence of different sample sizes on the sampling distribution, we repeated this process for samples of different sizes (in addition to $n = 300$, we used $n = 15$, $n = 30$, $n = 50$, $n = 100$, and $n = 1000$).

We graph the results in Figure 6.3 (for samples from the symmetric population distribution) and in Figure 6.4 (for samples from the skewed population distribution). Each of these figures represents a sampling distribution: The distribution of sample means calculated from many samples drawn randomly of the same size and from the same population.

Let's look closely at the sampling distribution of the samples of size 300. Table 6.5 shows the sample means for the first 10 and final 10 samples drawn from each type of population distribution. The relative frequency distribution for the sample means for all 500 samples drawn from each type of distribution are shown in Figure 6.3e (symmetric population distribution) and Figure 6.4e (skewed population distribution). Notice that the sample means in Table 6.5 range

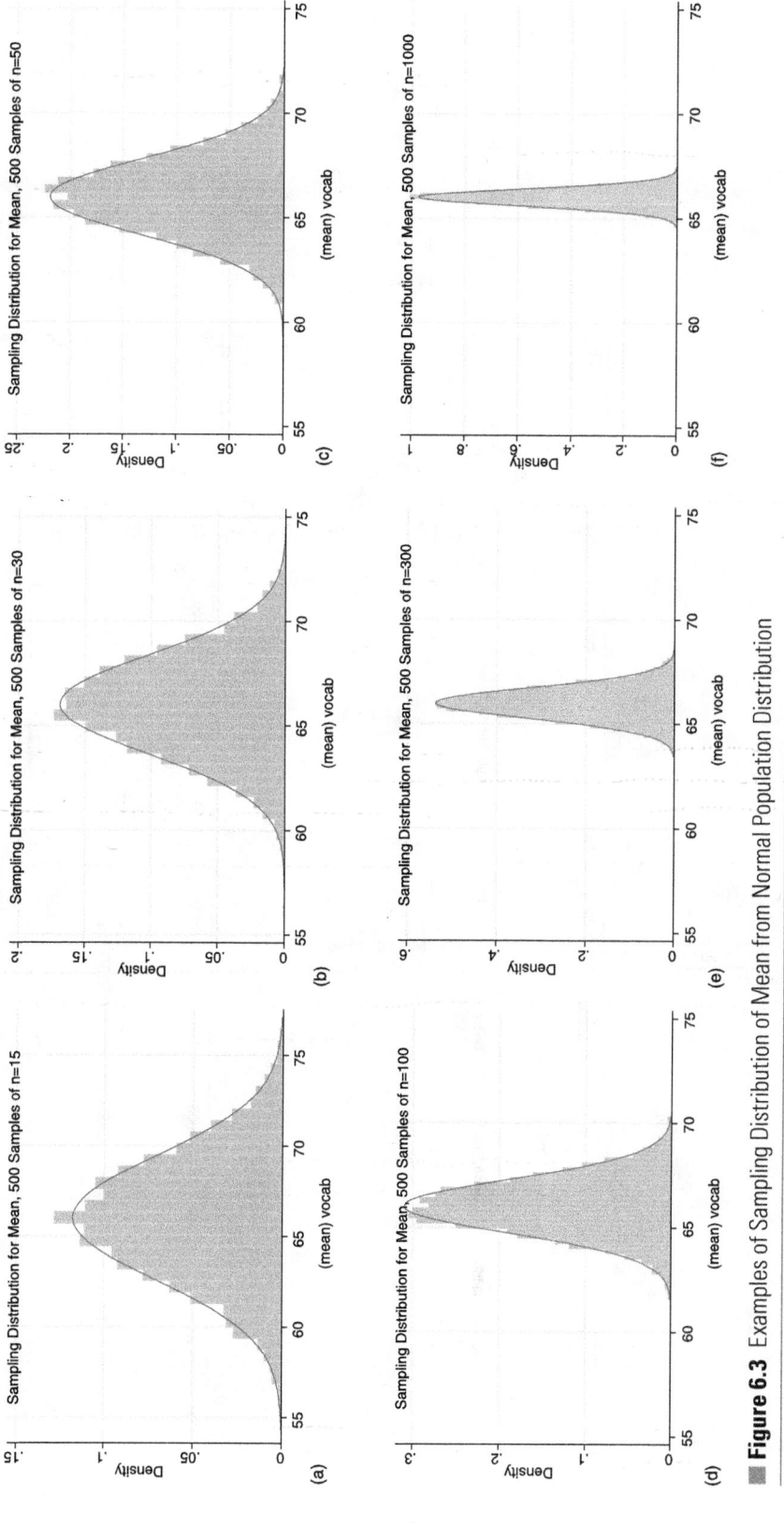

Figure 6.3 Examples of Sampling Distribution of Mean from Normal Population Distribution

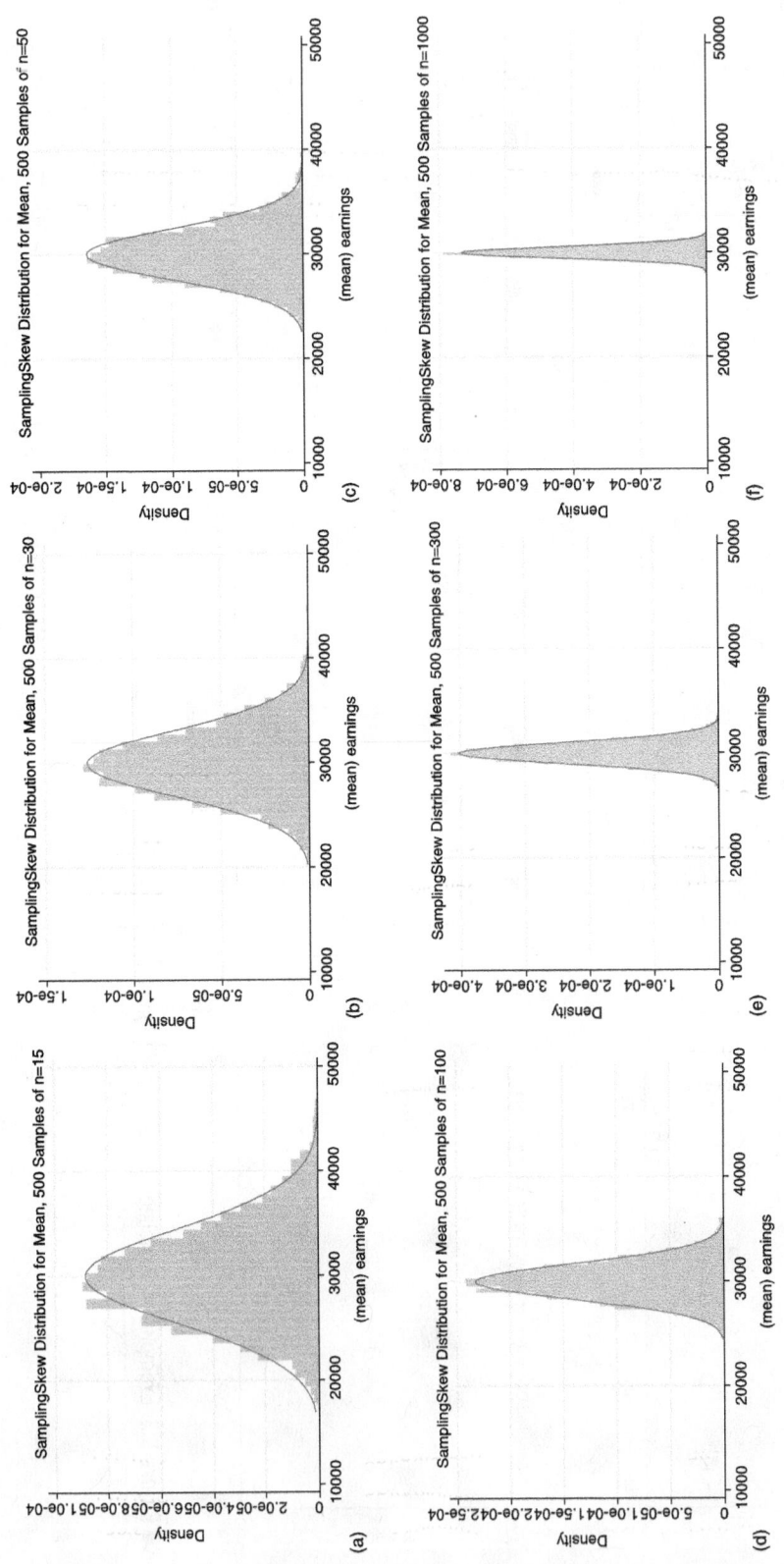

Figure 6.4 Examples of Sampling Distribution of Mean from Skewed Population Distribution

between about 65 and 67 for the symmetric distribution, hovering around the mean of 66.01 in the population (see again Table 6.2). Likewise, the relative frequency distribution shown in Figure 6.3e of the sample means from all 500 samples drawn from the symmetric distribution appear centered on 66. For the skewed population distribution, the sample means shown in Table 6.5 range between about $29,000 and $31,000 close to the mean of $29,978 in the population (see again Table 6.2). Likewise, the relative frequency distribution shown in Figure 6.4e of the sample means from all 500 samples drawn from the skewed distribution appear centered on about $30,000.

The graphs in Figure 6.3 and Figure 6.4 also show the relative frequency distributions for sets of 500 samples that we drew of different sizes ($n = 15$, $n = 30$, $n = 50$, $n = 100$, and $n = 1000$, in addition to $n = 300$) from the symmetric and skewed population distributions shown in Figure 6.1a and 6.1b. Notice that in both Figures 6.3 and 6.4, the distributions becomes more concentrated around the population mean as the size of the set of samples increases. In Figure 6.3a, when the samples were all drawn with $n = 15$, the relative frequency distribution is most spread out, with

▪ **Table 6.5: Sample means from first 10 and final 10 samples drawn from the population distributions shown in Figure 6.1a and Figure 6.1b**

Sample Means for Samples Drawn from:			
Symmetric Population Distribution (Figure 6.1a)		Skewed Population Distribution (Figure 6.1b)	
Sample#1	65.80	Sample#1	$30,159
Sample#2	65.57	Sample#2	$30,544
Sample#3	66.11	Sample#3	$29,310
Sample#4	65.88	Sample#4	$30,430
Sample#5	65.59	Sample#5	$30,511
Sample#6	66.72	Sample#6	$28,876
Sample#7	64.86	Sample#7	$31,210
Sample#8	67.00	Sample#8	$29,080
Sample#9	65.41	Sample#9	$30,665
Sample#10	66.36	Sample#10	$29,875
. . .		. . .	
Sample#491	67.03	Sample#491	$29,412
Sample#492	67.20	Sample#492	$30,688
Sample#493	65.36	Sample#493	$29,587
Sample#494	66.74	Sample#494	$30,082
Sample#495	65.54	Sample#495	$30,250
Sample#496	65.31	Sample#496	$30,544
Sample#497	66.70	Sample#497	$29,538
Sample#498	65.25	Sample#498	$29,277
Sample#499	65.60	Sample#499	$29,571
Sample#500	65.34	Sample#500	$30,931

the sample means appearing to range between about 55 and 75. In contrast, in Figure 6.3f, the sample means range just between about 65 and 67. We see something similar in Figure 6.4, where the sample means appear to range from nearly \$15,000 to \$45,000 in Figure 6.4a and between about \$28,000 and \$32,000 in Figure 6.4f.

How can we capture this difference in variation of the sample means in the sampling distributions for different sample sizes? Similar to using the standard deviation to capture the variation for a variable Y, we can use the standard deviation to capture the variation in a sampling distribution. When we do so we use a special name—the **standard error**—for the standard deviation. So, the standard error captures the amount of variation in sample statistics across samples drawn randomly of the same size from the same population. Normally, we would not be able to calculate the standard deviation of the sampling distribution directly (since we draw only one sample). However, when we know (or can assume) a theoretical distribution for our estimator, we can use formulas statisticians have derived to calculate the standard error.

For the sampling distribution for the estimator of the sample mean, statisticians have shown that $\bar{Y} = \frac{\sum_{i=1}^{n} Y_i}{n}$, is centered on the population mean, that is $\mu_{\bar{Y}} = \mu_Y$, and has a standard deviation (i.e., standard error) that is equal to the population standard deviation divided by the square root of the sample size, n, that is $\sigma_{\bar{Y}} = \frac{\sigma_Y}{\sqrt{n}}$. Table 6.6 shows the standard deviation of each of the sampling distributions shown in Figures 6.3 and 6.4 calculated using the population standard deviation from Table 6.2 and the size of each set of samples.

■ Table 6.6: Standard errors for sampling distributions shown in Figures 6.3 and 6.4

Samples of Size	Population Distribution with $\sigma_Y = 12.97$ (Figure 6.3)			Population Distribution with $\sigma_Y = 17{,}282$ (Figure 6.4)		
$n=15$	$\sigma_{\bar{Y}} = \frac{\sigma_Y}{\sqrt{n}} =$	$\sigma_{\bar{Y}} = \frac{12.97}{\sqrt{15}} =$	3.35	$\sigma_{\bar{Y}} = \frac{\sigma_Y}{\sqrt{n}} =$	$\sigma_{\bar{Y}} = \frac{17{,}282}{\sqrt{15}} =$	$4{,}462$
$n=30$	$\sigma_{\bar{Y}} = \frac{\sigma_Y}{\sqrt{n}} =$	$\sigma_{\bar{Y}} = \frac{12.97}{\sqrt{30}} =$	2.37	$\sigma_{\bar{Y}} = \frac{\sigma_Y}{\sqrt{n}} =$	$\sigma_{\bar{Y}} = \frac{17{,}282}{\sqrt{30}} =$	$3{,}155$
$n=50$	$\sigma_{\bar{Y}} = \frac{\sigma_Y}{\sqrt{n}} =$	$\sigma_{\bar{Y}} = \frac{12.97}{\sqrt{50}} =$	1.83	$\sigma_{\bar{Y}} = \frac{\sigma_Y}{\sqrt{n}} =$	$\sigma_{\bar{Y}} = \frac{17{,}282}{\sqrt{50}} =$	$2{,}444$
$n=100$	$\sigma_{\bar{Y}} = \frac{\sigma_Y}{\sqrt{n}} =$	$\sigma_{\bar{Y}} = \frac{12.97}{\sqrt{100}} =$	1.30	$\sigma_{\bar{Y}} = \frac{\sigma_Y}{\sqrt{n}} =$	$\sigma_{\bar{Y}} = \frac{17{,}282}{\sqrt{100}} =$	$1{,}728$
$n=300$	$\sigma_{\bar{Y}} = \frac{\sigma_Y}{\sqrt{n}} =$	$\sigma_{\bar{Y}} = \frac{12.97}{\sqrt{300}} =$	0.75	$\sigma_{\bar{Y}} = \frac{\sigma_Y}{\sqrt{n}} =$	$\sigma_{\bar{Y}} = \frac{17{,}282}{\sqrt{300}} =$	998
$n=1000$	$\sigma_{\bar{Y}} = \frac{\sigma_Y}{\sqrt{n}} =$	$\sigma_{\bar{Y}} = \frac{12.97}{\sqrt{1000}} =$	0.41	$\sigma_{\bar{Y}} = \frac{\sigma_Y}{\sqrt{n}} =$	$\sigma_{\bar{Y}} = \frac{17{,}282}{\sqrt{1000}} =$	547

Statisticians have also confirmed that, like our visual inspection of Figures 6.3 and 6.4 suggests, as sample size increases the sampling distribution of the sample mean follows a normal distribution. This is known as the **central limit theorem**. The rate at which the sampling distribution of the sample mean becomes normally distributed depends on the shape of the population distribution of Y. If Y itself is normally distributed, then the sample mean will follow a normal distribution, even in small samples. If Y is not normally distributed, then the sample mean will follow a normal distribution in larger samples. This convergence to the normal distribution will be faster to the extent that the population distribution is closer to a normal distribution. The graphs in Figures 6.3 and 6.4 overlay a smooth solid line showing a theoretical normal distribution on top of the relative frequency distributions of the sample means. These lines help us see that the sampling distribution for our symmetric (normally distributed) population variable is already quite normally distributed, even for a sample size of 15 (in Figure 6.3a). The sampling distributions from our skewed population distribution deviate somewhat from the normal distribution for the smallest sample size (in Figure 6.4a) but it looks similar to the normal distribution even for samples of size 50 and 100. Said another way, the sampling distributions in Figure 6.4 and Figure 6.3 look much more similar to each other than do the population distributions in Figure 6.1b versus Figure 6.1a and than do the sample distributions in Figure 6.1c and Figure 6.1d.

The central limit theorem tells us that—at least for large samples—the sampling distribution for the sample mean follows a normal distribution. The empirical rule tells us that nearly all of the observations from a normal distribution fall within three standard deviations of the mean. (About 68% within one standard deviation; about 95% within two standard deviations; and, nearly 100% within three standard deviations.) Putting these two concepts together, we expect that the sample statistics of the mean for nearly all of the samples we draw from a population will fall within three standard errors (i.e., $3 * \dfrac{\sigma_Y}{\sqrt{n}}$ using the formula from Table 6.6) of the mean of the sampling distribution.

Based on these same concepts, we further expect that when the sample size is large enough for the sampling distribution to follow a normal distribution, the values will follow the empirical distribution, with 68% of observations falling within one standard deviation of the mean, 95% within two standard deviations of the mean, and nearly all within three standard deviations of the mean. We can calculate these intervals, within one, two and three standard deviations of the mean using the population means from Table 6.2 (since we know the sampling distribution is centered on the population mean, see again Table 6.6). These values are shown in Table 6.7 for the symmetric distribution.

These intervals reinforce the observation that we made above that in Figure 6.3 and Figure 6.4 the sampling distribution became more concentrated on the mean as the sample size increased. For example, 95% of means calculated from samples of size $n = 1000$ are expected to fall between 65.19 and 66.83. In contrast, the interval is much wider when the sample size is $n = 15$. In the latter case, 95% of means calculated from samples of size $n = 15$ are expected to fall between 59.31 and 72.71.

Table 6.8 adds a third column to Table 6.1, summarizing the mean, variance, and standard deviation of the sampling distribution for the mean. We do so to reinforce the similarities and

■ **Table 6.7: Intervals based on the empirical rule for sampling distributions of sample shown in Figure 6.3 (Normal Population Distribution with $\mu_Y = 66.01$ and $\sigma_Y = 12.97$)**

68% of Observations

	$\mu_{\bar{Y}} - \sigma_{\bar{Y}}$	$\mu_{\bar{Y}} + \sigma_{\bar{Y}}$
$n=15$	$66.01 - 3.3488 = 62.66$	$66.01 + 3.3488 = 69.36$
$n=30$	$66.01 - 2.3680 = 63.64$	$66.01 + 2.3680 = 68.38$
$n=50$	$66.01 - 1.8342 = 64.18$	$66.01 + 1.8342 = 67.84$
$n=100$	$66.01 - 1.2970 = 64.71$	$66.01 + 1.2970 = 67.31$
$n=300$	$66.01 - 0.7488 = 65.26$	$66.01 + 0.7488 = 66.76$
$n=1000$	$66.01 - 0.4101 = 65.60$	$66.01 + 0.4101 = 66.42$

95% of Observations

	$\mu_{\bar{Y}} - 2\sigma_{\bar{Y}}$	$\mu_{\bar{Y}} + 2\sigma_{\bar{Y}}$
$n=15$	$66.01 - 2 * 3.3488 = 59.31$	$66.01 + 2 * 3.3488 = 72.71$
$n=30$	$66.01 - 2 * 2.3680 = 61.27$	$66.01 + 2 * 2.3680 = 70.75$
$n=50$	$66.01 - 2 * 1.8342 = 62.34$	$66.01 + 2 * 1.8342 = 69.68$
$n=100$	$66.01 - 2 * 1.2970 = 63.42$	$66.01 + 2 * 1.2970 = 68.60$
$n=300$	$66.01 - 2 * 0.7488 = 64.51$	$66.01 + 2 * 0.7488 = 67.51$
$n=1000$	$66.01 - 2 * 0.4101 = 65.19$	$66.01 + 2 * 0.4101 = 66.83$

99.7% of Observations

	$\mu_{\bar{Y}} - 3\sigma_{\bar{Y}}$	$\mu_{\bar{Y}} + 3\sigma_{\bar{Y}}$
$n=15$	$66.01 - 3 * 3.3488 = 55.96$	$66.01 + 3 * 3.3488 = 76.06$
$n=30$	$66.01 - 3 * 2.3680 = 58.91$	$66.01 + 3 * 2.3680 = 73.11$
$n=50$	$66.01 - 3 * 1.8342 = 60.51$	$66.01 + 3 * 1.8342 = 71.51$
$n=100$	$66.01 - 3 * 1.2970 = 62.12$	$66.01 + 3 * 1.2970 = 69.90$
$n=300$	$66.01 - 3 * 0.7488 = 63.76$	$66.01 + 3 * 0.7488 = 68.26$
$n=1000$	$66.01 - 3 * 0.4101 = 64.78$	$66.01 + 3 * 0.4101 = 67.24$

differences for the three kinds of distributions we have discussed in this chapter. The population distribution is a relative frequency distribution for Y that we could create if we could obtain information about all N members of the population. If we had this complete information, then we could calculate the population mean, variance and standard deviation using the formulas in Column 1 of Table 6.8. Due to monetary and logistical constraints, however, we typically draw a sample from the population. If we draw this sample randomly, we can use the relative frequency distribution of Y in the sample to approximate the relative frequency distribution of Y in the population. And, we can use the formulas for the sample mean, variance and standard deviation shown in Column 2 of Table 6.8 to estimate the population values. We know that these sample statistics will be similar to, but not exactly equal to, the population values, because they will depend on which members of the population are drawn into our particular sample. The sampling distribution is a relative frequency distribution of sample statistics which we could

■ **Table 6.8: Formula for the Mean and Standard Deviation in Population and Sample Distributions of Y and the Sampling Distribution for $\bar{Y}$**

	Distribution Type		
	Population	Sample	Sampling ($\bar{Y}$)	
Mean	$\mu_Y = \dfrac{\sum_{i=1}^{N} Y_i}{N}$	$\bar{Y} = \dfrac{\sum_{i=1}^{n} Y_i}{n}$	$\mu_{\bar{Y}} = \mu_Y$	(6.3a)
Variance	$\sigma_Y^2 = \dfrac{\sum_{i=1}^{N}(Y_i - \mu_Y)^2}{N}$	$s_Y^2 = \dfrac{\sum_{i=1}^{n}(Y_i - \bar{Y})^2}{n-1}$	$\sigma_{\bar{Y}}^2 = \dfrac{\sigma_Y^2}{n}$	(6.3b)
Standard Deviation	$\sigma_Y = \sqrt{\sigma_Y^2} = \sqrt{\dfrac{\sum_{i=1}^{N}(Y_i - \mu_Y)^2}{N}}$	$s_Y = \sqrt{s_Y^2} = \sqrt{\dfrac{\sum_{i=1}^{n}(Y_i - \bar{Y})^2}{n-1}}$	$\sigma_{\bar{Y}} = \sqrt{\sigma_{\bar{Y}}^2} = \sqrt{\dfrac{\sigma_Y^2}{n}} = \dfrac{\sigma_Y}{\sqrt{n}}$	(6.3c)

Source: This table is adapted from Wybraniec and Wilmoth (1999: 77).

construct if we drew many samples repeatedly from the population. This sampling distribution itself has a mean, variance, and standard deviation. The mean of the sampling distribution is equal to the population mean. And, the standard deviation of the sampling distribution, also known as the standard error, captures how much the sample statistics of the mean vary from sample to sample.

We will see in the next section the power of the two main points shown by these examples: (1) that the standard error decreases as the sample size increases and (2) that the sampling distribution of the mean becomes more normal as the sample size increases, even if the population distribution is not normal. Both of these help us make decisions about whether our theories are consistent with the data we observe empirically.

6.4: GENERAL CONCEPTS FOR STATISTICAL INFERENCE

We will use intervals like those that we calculated in Table 6.7 to make calculations for statistical inference. We relied on the population parameters (μ_Y and σ_Y) to construct the intervals in Table 6.7 even though these population parameters are rarely known. In this section, we will introduce the ideas of statistical inference by calculating intervals based on the sample estimate of the mean ($\bar{Y}$) rather than the population mean (μ_Y). For now, we will make the unlikely assumption that the standard deviation in the population (σ_Y) is known. In Section 6.5.1, we will show how to construct intervals based on the sample mean ($\bar{Y}$) and the sample standard deviation (s_Y). We will examine both of the approaches to statistical inference that we examined in Literature Excerpts 6.1 and 6.2: hypothesis tests and confidence intervals.

6.4.1: Hypothesis Testing

We follow several general steps when we conduct a hypothesis test, and we present the major concepts associated with each step in turn. These include:

(1) translate our substantive ideas, based on theory, concepts, or prior research, into statements called hypotheses;

(2) calculate a value called a test statistic which captures the location of our sample statistic in the sampling distribution;

(3) determine the probability that our calculated test statistic would occur given our hypotheses; and,

(4) relate this probability to a determined proportion of times that, by convention, we are resigned to making the wrong decision.

We introduce some terminology that goes along with the concepts associated with each of these steps.

Hypotheses

In inferential statistics our goal is to use sample statistics to draw inferences about the population. In the ideal situation, we use theory, concepts, and prior studies to develop expectations about the population before conducting our hypothesis test. We write these expectations as hypotheses. Usually, our hypotheses are about group differences (e.g., we might hypothesize that girls score better on tests of vocabulary than do boys) or associations between constructs (e.g., we might hypothesize that adults with more years of schooling earn more). We will examine such hypotheses beginning in Chapter 7. To introduce the basic ideas of hypothesis tests in this chapter, we consider hypotheses about a single mean. Doing so is somewhat artificial, because it is rare in the social sciences to make hypotheses about a single mean. But, this helps us lay out the basic ideas of hypothesis testing in a simple context. And, the ideas and formulas we introduce will carry over directly to tests we conduct in later chapters.

In general, in statistics, we state our hypotheses as expectations about the value of a population parameter. The most common **hypothesized value** for the population parameter is zero (we will see why this value is so common in future chapters). We always state two hypotheses. We use an **alternative hypothesis** to state our substantive ideas about what we expect based on theory, concepts, and prior studies. And, we use a **null hypothesis** to state the converse of what we expect (sometimes reflecting the status quo). We write these hypotheses in words and in symbols.

Table 6.9 provides an example of a null and alternative hypothesis about a population mean. The words in the bottom row state that we expect that the population mean differs from zero, based on theory, concepts or prior studies. This is our alternative hypothesis. The converse of this would be that the population mean is zero. This is our null hypothesis.

■ **Table 6.9: Examples of Two-Sided Hypotheses, with Hypothesized Value of Zero**

	Words	Symbols	
Null hypothesis:	The population mean is zero.	H_o:	$\mu_Y = 0$
Alternative hypothesis:	The population mean is not zero.	H_a:	$\mu_Y \neq 0$

■ **Box 6.5**

Some social scientists use the subscripts zero and one (H_0 and H_1) to designate the null and alternative hypotheses (rather than the letters o and a which we use). Some also refer to the alternative hypothesis as a **research hypothesis** to reinforce the fact that it is the hypothesis that we expect based on our theory, concepts and prior studies.

In symbols, we use H_o to designate the null hypothesis. And, we use H_a to designate the alternative hypothesis. We use our symbol for the population mean μ_Y to show that in our alternative hypothesis we expect that the population value differs from zero ($\mu_Y \neq 0$) and that in our null hypothesis we expect that the population value equals zero ($\mu_Y = 0$). Although we will often use a hypothesized value of zero throughout the book, to show a generic hypothesized value, potentially something other than zero, we will add a superscript asterisk to the population value, such as ($\mu_Y \neq \mu_Y^*$) and ($\mu_Y = \mu_Y^*$) where μ_Y^* designates any possible hypothesized value.

The hypotheses we just examined are referred to as **non-directional**, **two-sided**, or **two-tailed** hypotheses. These terms reflect the fact that we have not specified in our alternative hypothesis whether we expect that the population value is above or below the hypothesized value of zero. Rather, our alternative hypothesis simple states that the population mean is not equal to zero.

A **directional**, **one-sided**, or **one-tailed** hypothesis in contrast states that the population parameter either falls above or falls below the hypothesized value. Table 6.10 shows examples of such one-tailed hypotheses. In the first case (top two rows of Table 6.10), we write our alternative hypothesis as expecting that the population mean is greater than zero. Our null hypothesis is the converse (the population mean is less than or equal to zero). In the second case (bottom two rows of Table 6.10), we write our alternative hypothesis as expecting the population mean to be less than zero. Our null hypothesis is the converse (the population mean is greater than or equal to zero).

Below, we will use statistics to make a determination about whether we have enough evidence to **reject the null hypothesis** in favor of the alternative hypothesis. When we do not have enough evidence to reject the null hypothesis we say we **fail to reject the null hypothesis** rather than saying that we accept the null hypothesis (we will have more to say about this below).

■ **Table 6.10: Examples of One-Sided Hypotheses, with Hypothesized Value of Zero**

	Words	Symbols	
Null hypothesis:	The population mean is less than or equal to zero.	H_o:	$\mu_Y \leq 0$
Alternative hypothesis:	The population mean is greater than zero.	H_a:	$\mu_Y > 0$
Null hypothesis:	The population mean is equal to or greater than zero.	H_o:	$\mu_Y \geq 0$
Alternative hypothesis:	The population mean is less than zero.	H_a:	$\mu_Y < 0$

■ **Box 6.6**

You might be inclined to use the population mean of 66.01 from our hypothetical example as the hypothesized value. But, remember that we only know the population mean in this case because we designed a hypothetical population. In most cases, the population mean is unknown (indeed, that is generally the reason why we have drawn a sample and need to use it to estimate the population mean!).

■ **Table 6.11: Examples of Two-Sided Hypotheses, with Hypothesized Value of Fifty**

	Words	Symbols
Null hypothesis:	The mean number of words toddlers speak in the population is 50.	H_0: $\mu_Y = 50$
Alternative hypothesis:	The mean number of words toddlers speak in the population is not 50.	H_a: $\mu_Y \neq 50$

Let's consider an example based on our symmetric distribution from Figure 6.1a. Recall we imagined that the variable *Number of Words Spoken* measured the number of words that a population of toddlers (age two years old) speak. Consider that based on a large body of prior literature, we can determine that children typically speak about 50 words by this age. We could use this prior knowledge and set 50 as our hypothesized value. Suppose we also have reason to expect that our population of toddlers differs from this typical rate of language acquisition. If we had no additional information to specify a directional hypothesis, then we might lay out a non-directional (two-tailed) set of hypotheses (See Table 6.11).

If we had additional information about how the population from which our sample is drawn differs from the populations on which the prior literature is based, we might further specify a directional (one-tailed) hypothesis.

For example, perhaps our population comprises children whose parents have not completed a high school degree and we know from other studies that children receive less exposure to language when their parents have not finished high school. Then, we might state in our alternative hypothesis that the mean in our population is less than 50, as shown in Table 6.12.

■ **Table 6.12: First Example of One-Sided Hypothesis, with Hypothesized Value of Fifty**

	Words	Symbols
Null hypothesis:	The mean number of words spoken by toddlers in the population is 50 or more.	H_0: $\mu_Y \geq 50$
Alternative hypothesis:	The mean number of words spoken by toddlers in the population is less than 50.	H_a: $\mu_Y < 50$

Alternatively, perhaps our population comprises children across the country who attended a special enrichment program designed to enhance vocabulary. Then, we might hypothesize that the mean in our population is greater than 50, as shown in Table 6.13.

We will use the sample data shown in Figure 6.1c and Table 6.2 to evaluate these hypotheses below.

Locating our Sample Statistic in the Sampling Distribution

As mentioned above, we can use our sample statistic to evaluate our hypotheses. Our sample statistic is sometimes also referred to as a point estimate, because it is the single value that is our best guess of the value of the population parameter based on the information available in our sample from that population. In Table 6.2, our point estimate of the mean for the symmetric distribution is 66.72. This is our single best guess of the number of words spoken by toddlers in the population, based on our single sample. Of course, the estimate of 66.72 is bigger than our hypothesized value of 50. But, we know 66.72 is a sample statistic. The population mean is still unknown. In using the sample statistic to make an inference about the population mean we need to determine how unlikely a sample mean of 66.72 is if the population mean were really 50. We use statistics to quantify—and assign a probability value to—the chance that our sample statistic would be 66.72 if the population mean were 50.

The sampling distribution is fundamental to this process. To evaluate our hypotheses, we imagine constructing the sampling distribution under our null hypothesis (in our case, $\mu_Y = 50$ for the two-tailed hypothesis in Table 6.11), using the theoretical distribution that statisticians have determined our estimator follows (in our case, the normal distribution for the sample mean) and the value we calculated for the standard error (i.e., the standard deviation of the sampling distribution; in our case, $\sigma_{\bar{Y}}$, which we calculated to be 0.7488 for samples of $n = 300$ from our symmetric distribution in Table 6.6).

In Figure 6.5a, we show the theoretical normal distribution with a mean of 50 (our hypothesized value) and standard deviation of 0.7488 (the standard error). This is the sampling distribution under the null hypothesis. We include vertical bars that show the values that are two standard deviations above and below the hypothesized value of fifty (i.e., $50 - 2 * 0.7488 = 48.50$ and $50 + 2 * 0.7488 = 51.50$). Based on the empirical rule, if our null hypothesis that the population mean is 50 were true, then we would expect about 95% of sample statistics of the mean to fall between 48.50 and 51.50. A value smaller than 48.50 or larger than 51.50 would be

■ **Table 6.13: Second Example of One-Sided Hypothesis, with Hypothesized Value of Fifty**

	Words	Symbols	
Null hypothesis:	The mean number of words spoken by toddlers in the population is 50 or less.	H_o:	$\mu_Y \leq 50$
Alternative hypothesis:	The mean number of words spoken by toddlers in the population is greater than 50.	H_a:	$\mu_Y > 50$

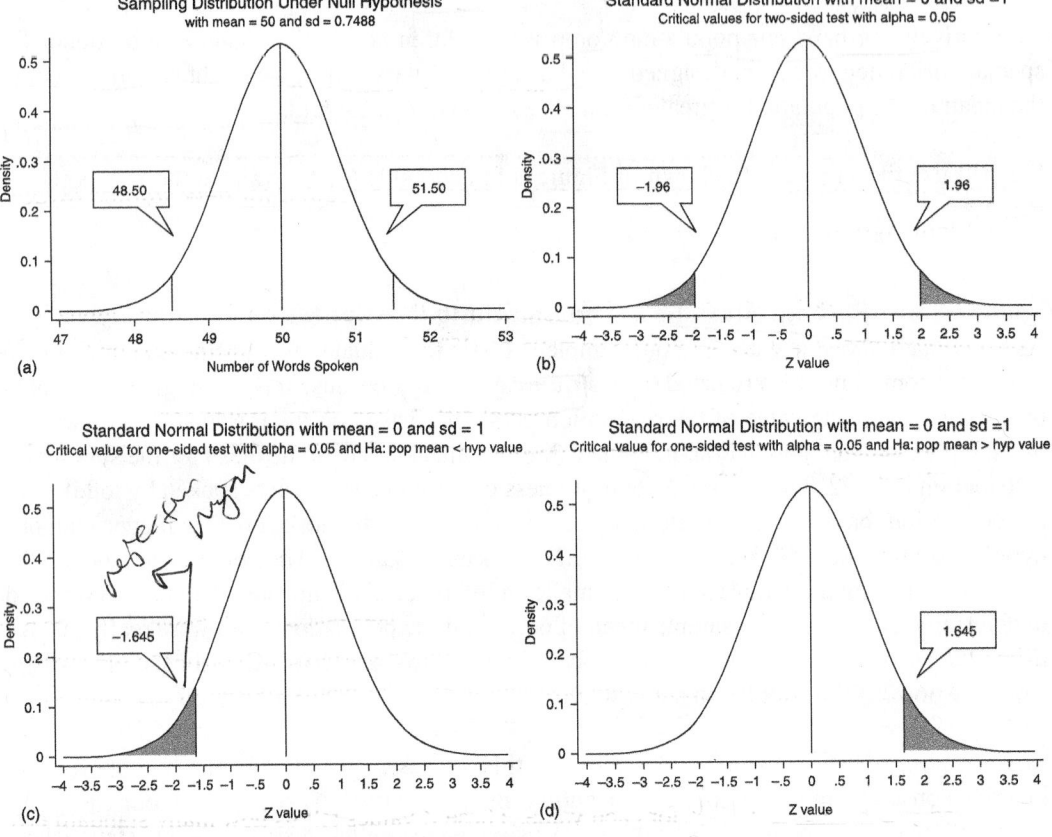

Figure 6.5 Examples of Critical Values and Alpha Levels

quite unusual if our null hypothesis were true. We know that 5% of the time, such values might be observed even if the population mean were in fact 50, but those would be rare cases (e.g., occurring in just 5 of 100 samples drawn). From Table 6.2, our point estimate of the population mean for the symmetric distribution is the sample mean, 66.72. This value falls outside the range of values that we would expect from 95% of sample statistics if our null hypothesis were true (i.e., 66.72 is greater than 51.50). Thus, our sample statistic (66.72) seems inconsistent with the null hypothesis that the mean number of words spoken by toddlers in the population from which our sample was drawn is 50.

This is the type of logic that we use when conducting a hypothesis test. We allow for some percentage of the time in which we would make an incorrect decision (i.e., 5% of the time in our case, where we could draw a sample with a mean estimate that is smaller than 48.50 or larger than 51.50 even if our null hypothesis were true). We refer to making this kind of incorrect decision as a **Type I error**. When we make a Type I error we "reject the null when the null is true." This phrase should make sense, given that we drew in Figure 6.5a a normal distribution *centered around our null hypothesis* and we know that 5% of the time we might draw samples that fall below 48.50 or above 51.50. Drawing one of these unusual samples would lead us to "reject the null" even though the null was true. We refer to the proportion of times we allow this

■ **Box 6.7**

The other type of error we might make, failing to reject the null hypothesis when it is in fact false, is referred to as a Type II error. Type II error is used less often in social science publications, although the related concept of power (rejecting the null hypothesis when it is in fact false) is used more often, especially to support proposals about the sample sizes needed for new studies (Kraemer and Thiemann 1987).

error to occur as the alpha level and denote it with the Greek symbol α (read "alpha"). By convention, alpha is usually set at 0.05 ($\alpha = .05$ or a 5% change of committing a Type I error).

When our sampling distribution follows the normal distribution, it is useful to convert our sample statistics to standardized values in order to conduct hypothesis tests. This conversion to standard scores makes it easier to see if our sample mean would be typical or unusual for our null hypothesis, given our sampling distribution. For example, we saw above that standardized values following a normal distribution should be bigger than two or less than negative two just 5% of the time.

In Figure 6.5b, we standardized the hypothetical sample means that we had shown in Figure 6.5a (the sampling distribution under the null hypothesis). In other words, we converted the values of 48.50 and 51.50 from their natural units (average number of words spoken in the sample) into Z-values based on the hypothesized value for the mean ($\mu_Y = 50$) and the standard error (the standard deviation of the sampling distribution, $\sigma_{\bar{Y}} = 0.7488$ for $n = 300$). That is, we calculate $Z = \dfrac{\bar{Y} - \mu_Y^*}{\sigma_{\bar{Y}}} = \dfrac{\bar{Y} - 50}{0.7488}$ for each value. These Z-values tell us how many standard error units a sample mean falls above or below the hypothesized value of the population mean. For example, a sample mean of 51.50 would fall $Z = \dfrac{51.50 - 50}{0.7488} = 2.00$ standard errors above the hypothesized value of the mean. Converting to standard scores makes it easier for us to quickly evaluate whether a sample mean is unusual or typical (given our hypothesized value and standard error and our knowledge that the sampling distribution for the sample mean follows a normal distribution).

Converting our sample statistics to standardized values also makes it easier to calculate precise probabilities, since we can use the standard normal distribution with mean zero and standard deviation of one (rather than the normal distribution with our specific hypothesized mean, in our case 50, and standard error, in our case 0.7488). In fact, we have been relying on the empirical rule to roughly define the interval in which we expect the middle 95% of the observations to fall. However, we can define this interval more precisely based on the theoretical normal distribution. We will similarly rely on other theoretical distributions to calculate probabilities in Section 6.5. In fact, the values which contain the middle 95% of the cases in the standard normal distribution are more precisely −1.96 and 1.96 (based on the theoretical normal distribution) rather than −2.00 and 2.00 (based on the empirical rule).[3] These values are shown with vertical lines in Figure 6.5b. The grey areas show the alpha level, with 2.5% of the observations falling below −1.96 and 2.5% of the observations falling above +1.96 standard errors from the mean.

We refer to values like −1.96 and 1.96 as **critical values.** These are the values above which the proportion of cases determined by our alpha level will fall. For the two-tailed hypothesis tests —like the example we just examined—there are two critical values because we divided our alpha level into the two tails (2.5% below 1.96 and 2.5% above 1.96).

There are always two critical values for two-tailed hypothesis tests. That is, under the two-tailed hypothesis test in Table 6.11, our alternative hypothesis simply stated that we expected the population mean to differ from 50. The population mean might either be smaller than 50 or the population mean might be larger than 50 in order to be consistent with our alternative hypothesis. Indeed, above we calculated the interval 48.50 and 51.50 that we expected to contain the middle 95% of sample statistics if our null hypothesis were true. Both values below 48.50 and values above 51.50 would be unusual if our null hypothesis that μ_Y = 50 were true.

For the one-tailed hypotheses shown in Tables 6.12 and 6.13, we place all of the alpha level in one tail and there is only one critical value. Specifically, for Table 6.12, the null hypothesis states that the mean is greater than or equal to 50 and the alternative hypothesis states that the mean is less than 50. So, sample statistics below the hypothesized value are consistent with the alternative hypothesis but sample statistics at or above the hypothesized value are not consistent with the alternative hypothesis. Likewise, in Table 6.13, the null hypothesis states that the mean is less than or equal to 50 and the alternative hypothesis states that the mean is greater than 50. So, in this case, sample statistics above the hypothesized value are consistent with the alternative hypothesis but sample statistics at or below the hypothesized value are not consistent with the alternative hypothesis.

If we use the formula $Z = \dfrac{\overline{Y} - \mu_Y^*}{\sigma_{\overline{Y}}}$ to calculate Z-values for all values in our sampling distribution then sample statistics that are smaller than the hypothesized value become negative and sample statistics that were larger than the hypothesized value become positive (compare Figure 6.5b and Figure 6.5a). This means that after we convert to standard scores, negative Z-values are consistent with the alternative hypothesis in Table 6.12 and positive Z-values are consistent with the alternative hypothesis in Table 6.13.

We place all of the alpha level in the tail consistent with the alternative hypothesis (the left tail for the alternative hypothesis in Table 6.12 since negative values are consistent with the alternative hypothesis; the right tail for the alternative hypothesis in Table 6.13 since positive values are consistent with our alternative hypothesis). Figures 6.5c and 6.5d show the result of doing so in the standard normal distribution with a conventional alpha level of 0.05. In Figure 6.5c, the critical value is −1.645. This is the value on the standard normal distribution below which 5% of the observations fall. The grey shaded area represents the full alpha of 0.05 (all 5% of the sample statistics that are unusual under the null hypothesis that $\mu_Y \geq 50$). In Figure 6.5d, the critical value is 1.645. This is the value on the standard normal distribution above which 5% of the observations fall. The grey shaded area represents the full alpha of 0.05 (all 5% of the sample statistics that are unusual under the null hypothesis that $\mu_Y \leq 50$).

3 Calculating Test Statistics and *p*-values

We just saw that we can place the alpha level in the tails of the sampling distribution under the null hypothesis in order to determine what values would be unusual if the null hypothesis were true. To make the comparison with our single sample point estimate easy, we convert the sample mean for our single sample to a Z-value and compare this calculated Z-value to the critical Z-value(s). This Z-value is known as our calculated **test statistic**. For tests based on the Z-distribution (and the *t*-distribution which we introduce in Section 6.5) the basic formula for a test statistic is:

$$test\ statistic = \frac{sample\ estimate - hypothesized\ population\ value}{standard\ error\ of\ the\ sample\ estimate}$$

In the case of testing a hypothesis about the population mean, it is:

$$Z = \frac{\bar{Y} - \mu_Y^*}{\dfrac{\sigma_Y}{\sqrt{n}}}$$

where μ_Y^* denotes our hypothesized value for the population mean (in our example 50).

To evaluate whether our sample statistic is unusual (given our sampling distribution under the null hypothesis) we use one of two approaches, both of which give equivalent results. One approach is to compare the calculated Z-value to the values above and below which we know 5% of the observations fall in the standard normal distribution (the critical values). If the **calculated value** that we obtain by plugging our sample values into the formula for the test statistic is more extreme than one of the critical values for a two-tailed alternative hypothesis (or the single critical value for a one-tailed alternative hypothesis), then we can reject the null hypothesis. Since in a two-tailed situation it is the magnitude (not the sign) of the calculated and critical values that matters, we sometimes write the decision rule for the two-tailed case as $|calculated\ Z| > |critical\ Z|$.

Alternatively, we can calculate the probability of observing a value more extreme than our calculated value, given our hypothesized value and standard error. This probability is known as the ***p*-value.** If the *p*-value is smaller than our alpha value then we can also conclude that our sample statistic would be unusual if the null were true and reject the null hypothesis. The *p*-value has the advantage of making clear how unusual our calculated Z-value would be if the null were true and allows us (or readers of our work) to see if we could reject the null hypothesis based on other alpha levels (although an alpha of 0.05 is most conventional, we might use a more stringent level such as .01 or a less stringent level such as .10 in some circumstances; we will discuss this issue further in Chapter 9).

We will have more to say about how to use SAS and Stata results to appropriately determine *p*-values for one-tailed tests in Chapter 8. For now, we focus on the *p*-value for a two-tailed hypothesis test. In this case, we calculate the *p*-value based on the probability of our calculated

■ Box 6.8

The two approaches of (1) comparing the calculated test statistic to the critical value and (2) comparing the p-value to the alpha value will give the same result. Relying on the p-value is common in the social sciences. In part, the p-value is useful because it is informative (e.g., if the p-value is 0.049 then our null hypothesis can be rejected if alpha is 0.05 but not if alpha is 0.01) and also because these values are provided in statistical output (whereas critical values usually are not). Indeed, many social science publications follow the convention of using asterisks to indicate p-value levels relative to common alpha values (e.g., * $p < .05$). In these cases, the more detailed information about the specific level of the p-value is not readily apparent to the reader.

For the standard normal distribution, however, it is easy to also compare our calculated value to the critical value(s) because the critical value(s) are always –1.96 and 1.96 for a two-tailed hypothesis test with alpha of 0.05 (and –1.645 for the one-tailed alternative hypothesis that the population value is less than the hypothesized value with alpha of 0.05; and 1.645 for the one-tailed alternative hypothesis that the population value is greater than the hypothesized value with alpha of 0.05). But, for the theoretical distributions we discuss in Section 6.5 this will generally not be the case (and thus p-values are easier to work with in those cases).

value falling in either tail of the distribution. That is, we sum the probability of observations being larger than our calculated value with a positive sign; and, the probability of values being smaller than our calculated value with a negative sign under the theoretical normal distribution.

If we consider the two-tailed hypothesis in Table 6.11, then our calculated Z-value would be:

$$Z = \frac{\bar{Y} - \mu_Y^*}{\frac{\sigma_Y}{\sqrt{n}}} = \frac{66.72 - 50}{0.7488} = 22.33$$

For our two-tailed test, since $|22.33| > |1.96|$, we can reject the null hypothesis that the mean number of words toddlers speak in the population is 50 and conclude that the mean number of words toddlers speak in the population is not equal to 50. In our example, our best single guess of the population value is our sample statistic of 66.72.

For the hypothesis tests that we consider in later chapters, SAS and Stata will automatically include the p-value associated with a test in the default output. But, we show in this chapter how we can ask SAS and Stata to show us the probability, using their calculations based on the theoretical standard normal distribution. The next to last row of Display A6 summarizes the syntax for a two-tailed hypothesis test. Notice that in both SAS and Stata the command includes 2* in the formula, which achieves the desired sum of the probability of values more extreme than our calculated value in both tails. Display B.6.1 shows our request to SAS and Stata to use this syntax to provide the p-value associated with our calculated Z-value of 22.33. This p-value is estimated to be 0.0000 in SAS and 0 in Stata (which does not mean the p-value is exactly zero, but quite small; so small that it is zero to four decimal places; an alternative way to write this that recognizes the p-value is not exactly zero would be <0.0001). As expected, this result is consistent with the result above based on the calculated and critical values. Because the *p*-value is smaller than the alpha value, we have evidence to reject the null hypothesis.

Normally, we would lay out only one alternative hypothesis—either the one in Table 6.11, the one in Table 6.12, or the one in Table 6.13. But, for instructional purposes, we can consider what our conclusion would be if we evaluated the one-tailed hypotheses based on our test statistic of 22.33. This calculated value is larger than the value of 1.645 which we saw above was the test statistic associated with the alternative hypothesis in Table 6.13. Thus, there would be evidence to reject the null hypothesis that the population mean is less than or equal to zero in favor of the alternative hypothesis that the population mean is greater than zero. In contrast, the calculated value of 22.33 is not more extreme than the critical value of −1.645 that we saw in Figure 6.5c was the test statistic associated with the alternative hypothesis in Table 6.12. Thus, there is not evidence to reject the null hypothesis that the population mean is greater than or equal to zero. These results should make intuitive sense: Our estimated sample mean is greater than 50, and we have evidence in favor of the one-tailed alternative hypothesis that the population mean is greater than 50 but we do not have evidence in favor of the one-tailed alternative hypothesis that the population mean is less than 50. This result reinforces the reason why a one-sided alternative should be based on prior theory, concepts or research rather than based on examining the estimates in the sample (i.e., don't set the alternative hypothesis based on the size or sign of the sample mean in your data).

We can also ask SAS and Stata to calculate *p*-values to evaluate these one-tailed hypotheses. In this case, we use the syntax in the top row of Display A6. We will have more to say about how to appropriately determine *p*-values for one-tailed tests based on the default SAS and Stata output in Chapter 8.

6.4.2: Confidence Intervals

Above we introduced the idea underlying a **confidence interval** when we calculated the interval that contained the middle 95% of observations in our sampling distribution. The general formula for the confidence interval is similar to the calculations we made above:

sample estimate $\pm Z_{\alpha/2} \times$ standard error of the sample estimate

where $Z_{\alpha/2}$ is the Z-value associated with a two-tailed alpha (divided into the two tails). For example, $Z_{\alpha/2} = 1.96$ for an alpha of .05.

In the case of hypothesis tests about the population mean, the confidence interval is:

$$\bar{Y} \pm Z_{\alpha/2} \times \sigma_{\bar{Y}}$$

We interpret the resulting values as: "We are 95% confident that the population mean falls between $\bar{Y} - Z_{\alpha/2} \times \sigma_{\bar{Y}}$ and $\bar{Y} + Z_{\alpha/2} \times \sigma_{\bar{Y}}$." This interpretation reflects the fact that the standard error $\sigma_{\bar{Y}}$ captures the variable in the sampling distribution and $\bar{Y}$ is our single best guess of the population mean which is the center of the sampling distribution. Thus, if we repeatedly drew random samples of the same size from the same population we would expect 95% of those samples' means to fall within the lower and upper bounds of the confidence interval.

The confidence interval approach has the advantage that it emphasizes the fact that our estimate of the mean is based on just a single sample. In other words, although the point estimate is our *best single* guess of the population mean, we should not conclude that the population mean is exactly the sample mean. The sample statistic would differ somewhat were we to draw a different sample. The confidence interval provides us with a *range* of values that represent our best *guesses* of the population value. Although many publications in the social sciences rely on the test statistic approach, the confidence interval approach is common in some subfields of the social sciences, as we will see in future chapters.

We can evaluate the hypotheses of a two-tailed hypothesis test with the confidence interval, and the results will be consistent with the test statistic approach for the same two-tailed hypothesis and same alpha level. In the confidence interval approach, if the hypothesized value, μ_Y^*, falls within the bounds of the confidence interval, then we fail to reject the null hypothesis. If the hypothesized value, μ_Y^*, falls outside the bounds of the confidence interval, then we reject the null hypothesis. This should make intuitive sense: If the hypothesized value falls within the range of our best guesses of the population value, then the hypothesized valued is a plausible value for the population mean. If the hypothesized value falls outside of the range of our best guesses of the population value, then the hypothesized valued is not a plausible value for the population mean.

In our example, for the two-tailed hypothesis test shown in Table 6.11 with an alpha of 0.05, we have:

$$\bar{Y} \pm Z_{\alpha/2} \times \sigma_{\bar{Y}} = 66.72 \pm 1.96 * 0.7488 = (66.72 - 1.47, 66.72 + 1.47) = (65.25, 68.19)$$

Thus, we are 95% confident that the mean number of words spoken by toddlers in the population falls between 65.25 and 68.19. Because our hypothesized value of 50 does not fall within this interval, we can reject the null hypothesis that the population mean is 50 in favor of the alternative hypothesis that the population mean differs from 50.

Note that if, instead of 50, we had set our hypothesized value to any value falling in the range of the confidence interval (such as 66, 67, or 68) then we would have failed to reject the null hypothesis. This reinforces why we say that we fail to reject the null hypothesis rather than accept the null hypothesis (i.e., if we accepted a single null hypothesis rather than failing to reject it, we would ignore the fact that other values can also not be rejected based on our sample data because their values also fall within the bounds of our confidence interval; in our example, 66, 67, and 68 are all larger than 65.25 but smaller than 68.19 thus we would fail to reject each of these as hypothesized values in a two-tailed null hypothesis).

6.5: OTHER COMMON THEORETICAL DISTRIBUTIONS

In this section, we briefly introduce three other theoretical distributions that are commonly used in the social sciences to conduct hypothesis tests and construct confidence intervals: the *t*-distribution, the *F*-distribution, and the chi-square distribution. We will draw on each of these distributions in Chapter 7 when we test hypotheses about associations between two variables, and we will draw on them again in Parts 3 and 4 of the book as we test hypotheses based on regression models (see Larsen and Marx 2006; Wackerly, Mendenhall, and Scheaffer 2008 for more details about these theoretical distributions).

6.5.1: The *t*-Distribution

The *t*-distribution is a bell-shaped distribution, very similar in shape to the standard normal distribution. The shape of the *t*-distribution, however, differs somewhat based on its degrees of freedom. As noted in Box 6.1, the degrees of freedom represent the cost to sample size of the number of parameters estimated by our model (in Box 6.1, we lost one degree of freedom when we used our estimate of the mean in the formula for the sample standard deviation). The degrees of freedom will be defined for each of the hypothesis tests that we consider in later chapters, and for a *t*-distribution will depend on the number of parameter estimates and the sample size. As the degrees of freedom become larger, the shape of the *t*-distribution converges to the shape of the *Z*-distribution. For smaller degrees of freedom, the *t*-distribution has "fatter tails" than the *Z*-distribution, meaning that it has more values that fall more than one, two and three standard deviations from the mean than does the standard normal distribution.

Examples with Various Degrees of Freedom

Figure 6.6 shows six examples of the *t*-distribution with 5, 10, 30, 60, 100, and 500 degrees of freedom. The *t*-distribution is drawn with the green curved line. For reference, the standard normal distribution is drawn with the black curved line. The vertical lines in each graph are drawn at the mean of the distribution, zero, as well as at the critical values on the *t*-distribution for a two-tailed hypothesis test with an alpha of .05. In other words, in each graph, 2.5% of the *t*-values fall below the leftmost vertical line and 2.5% of the *t*-values fall above the rightmost vertical line. These critical values are also listed below the horizontal axis.

Looking first at Figure 6.6a, we see what is meant by the "fatter tails" of the *t*-distribution with a relatively small (in this case 5) number of degrees of freedom. In the tails, the green line for the *t*-distribution is higher than the black line of the standard normal

■ **Box 6.9**

The graphs in Figures 6.6, 6.7, and 6.8 were created using the UCLA Stata Programs for Teaching written by the Statistical Consulting Group at UCLA's Academic Technology Services. The original programs are available at *http://www.ats.ucla.edu/stat/stata/ado/teach/*.

distribution, beginning around the value of −1.5 on the left and around the value of 1.5 on the right. As we saw above, in the standard normal distribution, the critical *Z*-values for a two-tailed test with alpha of .05 were −1.96 and 1.96. The critical values listed in Figure 6.6a for the *t*-distribution with 5 degrees of freedom are −2.57 and 2.57. Thus, a calculated *t*-value with 5 degrees of freedom would have to be larger to reject the null hypothesis than a calculated *Z*-value based on the standard normal distribution (greater in absolute value than 2.57 rather than 1.96).

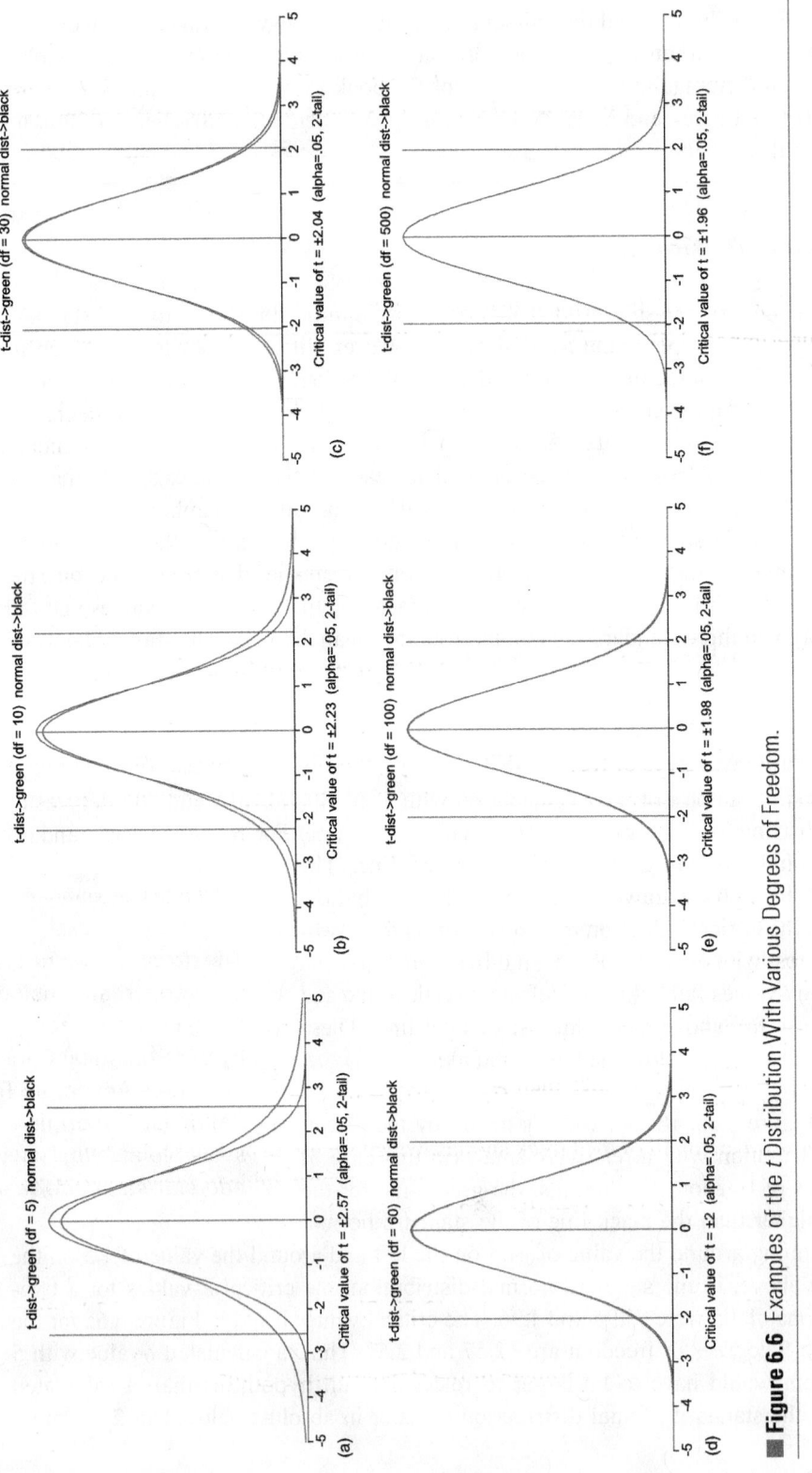

■ **Figure 6.6** Examples of the *t* Distribution With Various Degrees of Freedom.

t-dist->green (df = 5) normal dist->black

Critical value of t = ±2.57 (alpha=.05, 2-tail)

(a)

t-dist->green (df = 10) normal dist->black

Critical value of t = ±2.23 (alpha=.05, 2-tail)

(b)

t-dist->green (df = 30) normal dist->black

Critical value of t = ±2.04 (alpha=.05, 2-tail)

(c)

t-dist->green (df = 60) normal dist->black

Critical value of t = ±2 (alpha=.05, 2-tail)

(d)

t-dist->green (df = 100) normal dist->black

Critical value of t = ±1.98 (alpha=.05, 2-tail)

(e)

t-dist->green (df = 500) normal dist->black

Critical value of t = ±1.96 (alpha=.05, 2-tail)

(f)

Turning to Figure 6.6b, we see that the tails are still somewhat "fatter" for the t-distribution with 10 degrees of freedom, although less so than was the case with 5 degrees of freedom. With 10 degrees of freedom, the critical t-values for a two-tailed hypothesis test with an alpha of .05 are −2.23 and 2.23. Likewise, in Figure 6.6c with 30 degrees of freedom, the fatter tails of the t-distribution than the normal distribution are only slightly discernible in the graph, and the critical t-values are −2.04 and 2.04. For the larger degrees of freedom shown in the bottom row of Figure 6.6, the lines of the t and standard normal distribution are nearly identical. With 500 degrees of freedom, in Figure 6.6f, the critical value for the t-distribution is the same as the critical value of the standard normal distribution for a two-tailed test with an alpha of .05 (critical values of −1.96 and 1.96) and the black standard normal curve is superimposed on top of the green t-distribution curve such that the green curve is no longer visible.

Examples of Calculating *p*-values

As we just saw, there is not a single critical value for a two-tailed hypothesis test with an alpha of 0.05 across all t-distributions. Although the critical values converge to those of the standard normal distribution as the degrees of freedom get larger, they will differ for smaller degrees of freedom. As noted above, it is common to report p-values (as opposed to critical values) in publications. When SAS and Stata conduct a hypothesis test for us, they will list these p-values, specific to the degrees of freedom in our application. But, if we were to hand calculate a test statistic, we would need to determine the p-value ourselves. In the past, social scientists relied on tables which presented probabilities that statisticians had already calculated based on distributions with various degrees of freedom.[4] These days, it is also easy to ask SAS and Stata to calculate p-values for us. Display A.6 summarizes how to do so for the t-distribution, like we saw for the Z-distribution above.

As we noted above, we relied on the population standard deviation to calculate the standard error when we tested our null hypothesis that the number of words spoken in the population was 50 using the z-statistic. But, since the population standard deviation is rarely known, we need to estimate it using the sample information. When we substitute the sample standard deviation into the equation for the standard error, then we have an estimate the standard error.

That is, $\hat{\sigma}_{\bar{Y}} = \sqrt{\hat{\sigma}_{\bar{Y}}^2} = \sqrt{\dfrac{s_Y^2}{n}} = \dfrac{s_Y}{\sqrt{n}}$ rather than $\sigma_{\bar{Y}} = \sqrt{\sigma_{\bar{Y}}^2} = \sqrt{\dfrac{\sigma_Y^2}{n}} = \dfrac{\sigma_Y}{\sqrt{n}}$. Notice the hats (also

known as carets) now on top of all of the Greek sigmas, which we use to denote sample statistics rather than population values. We add this estimate to our summary table of means, variances and standard deviation in Table 6.14 as Equation 6.3d (next page).

In Table 6.2, we had shown that our sample based on size $n = 300$ drawn from the symmetric distribution had a standard deviation for Y of $s_Y = 12.51$. Plugging into Equation 6.3d gives

$\hat{\sigma}_{\bar{Y}} = \dfrac{s_Y}{\sqrt{n}} = \dfrac{12.51}{\sqrt{300}} = 0.7223$. This is an estimate of the standard error of the mean based on the

sample shown in Figure 6.1c. This estimate of the standard error is similar to, but slightly

■ Table 6.14: Formula for the Mean and Standard Deviation in Population and Sample Distributions of *Y* and the Sampling Distribution for Ȳ (*Adding the Estimated Standard Error*)

	Distribution Type		
	Population	Sample	Sampling (Ȳ)
Mean	$\mu_Y = \dfrac{\sum_{i=1}^{N} Y_i}{N}$	$\bar{Y} = \dfrac{\sum_{i=1}^{n} Y_i}{n}$	$\mu_{\bar{Y}} = \mu_Y$
Variance	$\sigma_Y^2 = \dfrac{\sum_{i=1}^{N}(Y_i - \mu_Y)^2}{N}$	$s_Y^2 = \dfrac{\sum_{i=1}^{n}(Y_i - \bar{Y})^2}{n-1}$	$\sigma_{\bar{Y}}^2 = \dfrac{\sigma_Y^2}{n}$ $\hat{\sigma}_{\bar{Y}}^2 = \dfrac{s_Y^2}{n}$
Standard Deviation	$\sigma_Y = \sqrt{\sigma_Y^2} = \sqrt{\dfrac{\sum_{i=1}^{N}(Y_i - \mu_Y)^2}{N}}$	$s_Y = \sqrt{s_Y^2} = \sqrt{\dfrac{\sum_{i=1}^{n}(Y_i - \bar{Y})^2}{n-1}}$	$\sigma_{\bar{Y}} = \sqrt{\sigma_{\bar{Y}}^2} = \sqrt{\dfrac{\sigma_Y^2}{n}} = \dfrac{\sigma_Y}{\sqrt{n}}$ $\hat{\sigma}_{\bar{Y}} = \sqrt{\hat{\sigma}_{\bar{Y}}^2} = \sqrt{\dfrac{s_Y^2}{n}} = \dfrac{s_Y}{\sqrt{n}}$ (6.3d)

Source: This table is adapted from Wybraniec and Wilmoth (1999: 77).

smaller than the true standard error of the sampling distribution which we calculated based on the population standard deviation, $\sigma_{\bar{Y}} = \dfrac{\sigma_Y}{\sqrt{n}} = \dfrac{12.97}{\sqrt{300}} = 0.7488.$.

We can also calculate a test statistic, similar to the z-statistic that we calculated above, but based on the estimate of the standard error. Specifically:

$$t = \frac{\bar{Y} - \mu_Y^*}{\hat{\sigma}_{\bar{Y}}} = \frac{\bar{Y} - \mu_Y^*}{\dfrac{s_Y}{\sqrt{n}}}$$

Where again μ_Y^* represents our hypothesized value of the population mean.

Based on Table 6.2, our sample mean $\bar{Y}$ is 66.72. Based on Table 6.11, our hypothesized value for the population mean μ_Y^* is 50. Plugging these values, along with the estimated standard error of 0.7223 into the formula for the test statistic gives:

$$t = \frac{\bar{Y} - \mu_Y^*}{\dfrac{s_Y}{\sqrt{n}}} = \frac{66.72 - 50}{\dfrac{12.51}{\sqrt{300}}} = \frac{66.72 - 50}{0.7223} = 23.15$$

This t statistic has $n-1$ degrees of freedom. One degree of freedom is lost due to our estimate of the standard deviation (i.e., $s_Y = \sqrt{\dfrac{\sum_{i=1}^{n}(Y_i - \bar{Y})^2}{n-1}}$). In our case, the degrees of freedom is $300 - 1 = 299$.

Display B.6.1 shows our request to SAS and Stata to calculate the probability of observing values more extreme than |23.15| in the standard normal distribution. The resulting two-tailed p-value is small, 0.0000 in SAS and 1.219e-68 in scientific notation in Stata. Thus, the p-value is less than an alpha of .05, and we can reject the null hypothesis that the number of words spoken by toddlers in the population is 50.

We can also calculate a confidence interval similar to the calculations we made above based on the t-distribution:

sample estimate $\pm t_{df,\alpha/2} \times$ estimated standard error of the sample estimate

where $t_{df,\alpha/2}$ is the t value associated with a two-tailed alpha (divided into the two tails) for a distribution with df degrees of freedom. When we are estimating the mean, we would have the equation $\bar{Y} \pm t_{df,\alpha/2} \times \hat{\sigma}_{\bar{Y}}$. For the example we just considered, we have $300-1=299$ degrees of freedom; thus, with a two-tailed alpha of .05 we have $t_{299,.05/2} = 1.9679$. Using our values of 66.72 for the sample mean and 12.51 for the sample standard deviation, we have:

$$\bar{Y} \pm t_{df,\alpha/2} \times \hat{\sigma}_{\bar{Y}} = 66.72 \pm 1.9679 \times \frac{12.51}{\sqrt{300}} = (65.30, 68.14)$$

We can use the confidence interval to draw conclusions about our hypotheses (e.g., since the confidence interval does not include our hypothesized value of 50, we can reject the null hypothesis that the population mean is 50). The confidence interval also allows us to make a statement about the expected range of values of the population parameter. This range is preferred over the point estimate because it does not imply that our sample statistic is exactly equal to the population parameter. In our example, we would say "We are 95% confident that the number of words spoken by toddlers in the population falls between 65.30 and 68.14."

6.5.2: The *F*-Distribution

Unlike the standard normal and *t*-distributions, the values in the *F*-distribution are non-negative and their shape is generally skewed to the right. Like the *t*-distribution, the shape of the *F*-distribution depends on its degrees of freedom; but, in the case of the *F*-distribution, there are two degrees of freedom, typically referred to as **numerator degrees of freedom** and **denominator degrees of freedom** (because, as we shall see in later chapters, test statistics that follow the *F*-distribution are ratios of two quantities—one in the numerator and one in the denominator—and each of these quantities has its own degrees of freedom). The shape of the *F*-distribution changes more substantially as the degrees of freedom change than was the case with the *t*-distribution. The *F*-distribution is highly skewed for small degrees of freedom, but becomes less skewed with larger degrees of freedom.

The *F* and *t*-distributions are related in a way that we will draw upon in later chapters. Specifically, when we conduct a hypothesis test that results in one numerator degree of freedom for the *F*-distribution there is an equivalent test of the same hypotheses based on the *t*-distribution. In these cases the *F*-value equals the square of the *t*-value for the equivalent hypothesis test.

Examples with Various Degrees of Freedom

Figure 6.7 illustrates six *F*-distributions with various numerator and denominator degrees of freedom that might be seen in social science applications. Examples with one numerator degrees of freedom, where $F = t^2$, are shown in Figures 6.7a and 6.7d. In these cases, the *F*-distribution is highly skewed. The distribution becomes somewhat less skewed for larger degrees of freedom. In our examples, the graph appears least skewed in Figure 6.7f.

Notice that the critical value for the examples of the *F*-distribution shown in Figure 6.7 vary depending on both the numerator and denominator degrees of freedom. In the two cases with one numerator degrees of freedom shown in Figures 6.7a and 6.7d, the critical *F*-values listed are the square of the critical *t*-values listed in Figure 6.6c and Figure 6.6e. We matched the *F*-distribution with the corresponding *t*-distribution whose degrees of freedom equals the denominator degrees of freedom of the *F*-distribution. That is, the *F*-distribution shown in Figure 6.7a (with 30 denominator degrees of freedom) corresponds to the *t*-distribution shown in Figure 6.6c (with 30 degrees of freedom); and, the square of the critical *t*-value (of 2.04 shown in Figure 6.6c), $F = t^2 = 2.04 * 2.04 = 4.16$, matches, within rounding error, the critical *F*-value (of 4.17 shown in Figure 6.7a). Likewise, the *F*-distribution shown in Figure 6.7d (with 100

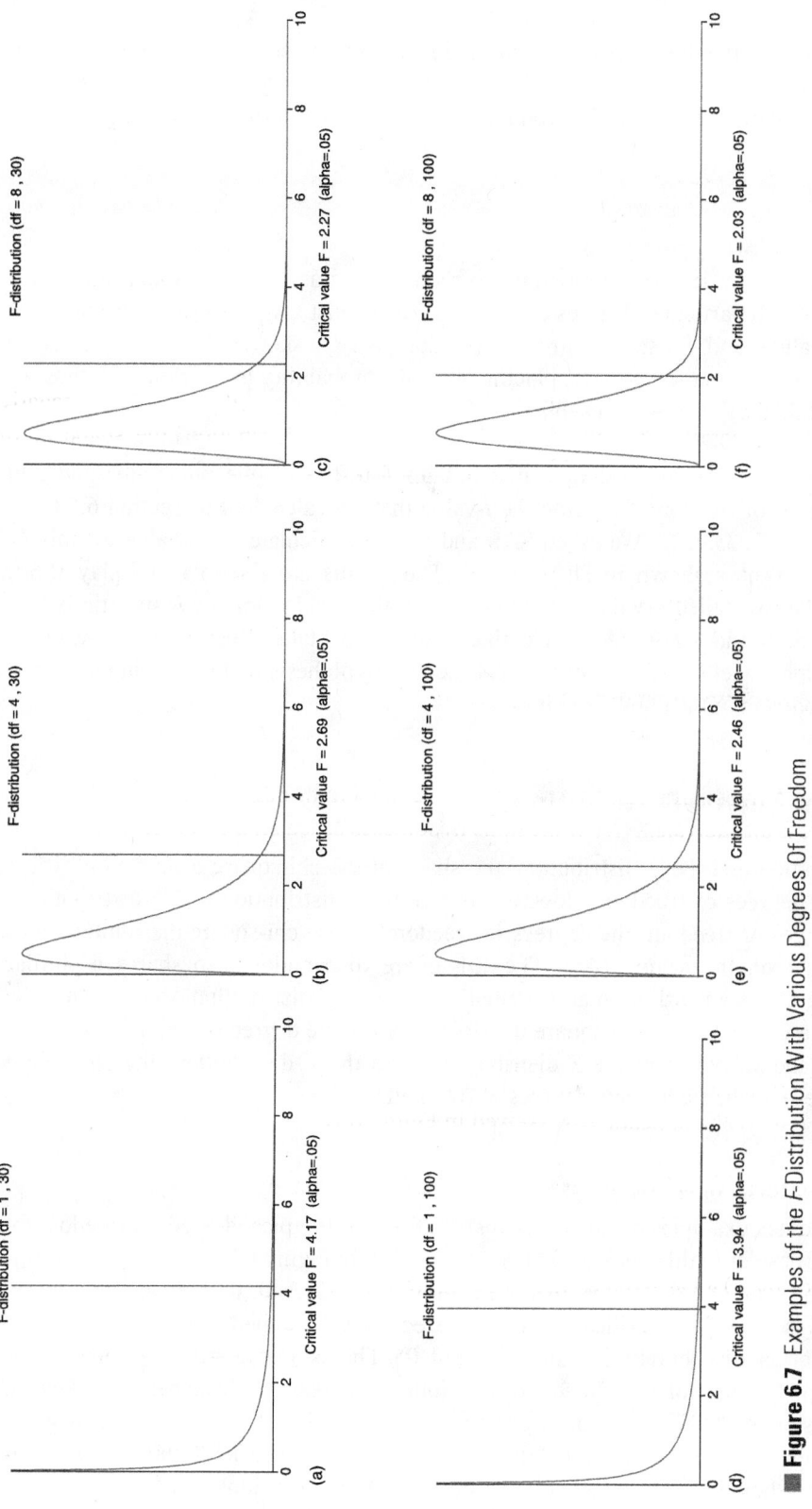

Figure 6.7 Examples of the *F*-Distribution With Various Degrees Of Freedom

denominator degrees of freedom) corresponds to the t-distribution shown in Figure 6.6e (with 100 degrees of freedom); and, the square of the critical t-value (of 1.98 in Figure 6.6e), $F = t^2 = 1.98 * 1.98 = 3.92$, again matches, within rounding error, the listed critical F-value (of 3.94 in Figure 6.7d).

Examples of Calculating p-values

As with the t-distribution, it is straightforward to request p-values from SAS and Stata for a calculated F-value with particular degrees of freedom. As we just saw, the F-distribution takes on only positive values; and, for small degrees of freedom, is right skewed. Most of the tests we will consider rely on a one-tailed p-value, placing all of the probability in the right tail, thus we focus on the one-tailed calculation in Display A.6.[5]

The t-test for our words spoken example matches an F-test with one numerator and 299 denominator degrees of freedom. Squaring the t-value that we calculated in Section 6.5.1, we have $F = t^2 = 23.15^2 = 535.9225$. We asked SAS and Stata to calculate the p-value for this F-statistic, using the syntax shown in Display A.6. The results are shown in Display B.6.1. Consistent with the two-tailed p-value for the t-statistic, the p-value for the F-statistic is tiny (again 0.0000 in SAS and 1.219e-68 in scientific notation in Stata). Because this p-value is smaller than an alpha level of .05, we could reject the null hypothesis that the mean number of words spoke by toddlers in the population is 50.

6.5.3: The Chi-Square Distribution

Like the t-distribution and the F-distribution, the shape of the chi-square distribution differs depending on its degrees of freedom. However, unlike the t-distribution and F-distribution's denominator degrees of freedom, the degrees of freedom for the chi-square distribution does not always depend on the sample size. The chi-square distribution also shares a similar relationship with the standard normal distribution as the F-distribution shares with the t-distribution. The values from a chi-square distribution with one degree of freedom are equal to the square of the values from the Z-distribution. Like the F-distribution, the chi-square distribution is skewed when it has few degrees of freedom.

Examples with Various Degrees of Freedom

Figure 6.8 provides six examples of chi-square distributions with typical degrees of freedom for the tests we will consider in this book (1, 2, 4, 9, 16, and 25). In Figure 6.8a, we see that the chi-square distribution with one degree of freedom is quite skewed. And, its critical value for an alpha level of .05 is equal to the critical Z-value squared for a two-tailed hypothesis test based on the standard normal distribution with alpha level of .05. That is, $\chi^2 = Z^2 = |1.96| * |1.96| = 3.84$. As the degrees of freedom of the chi-square distribution increase, it becomes less skewed. Indeed, the chi-square distribution converges to the normal distribution for large degrees of freedom (Larsen and Marx 2006; Wackerly, Mendenhall, and Scheaffer 2008); and, the chi-square distribution shown in Figure 6.8f, with 25 degrees of freedom, looks fairly symmetric.

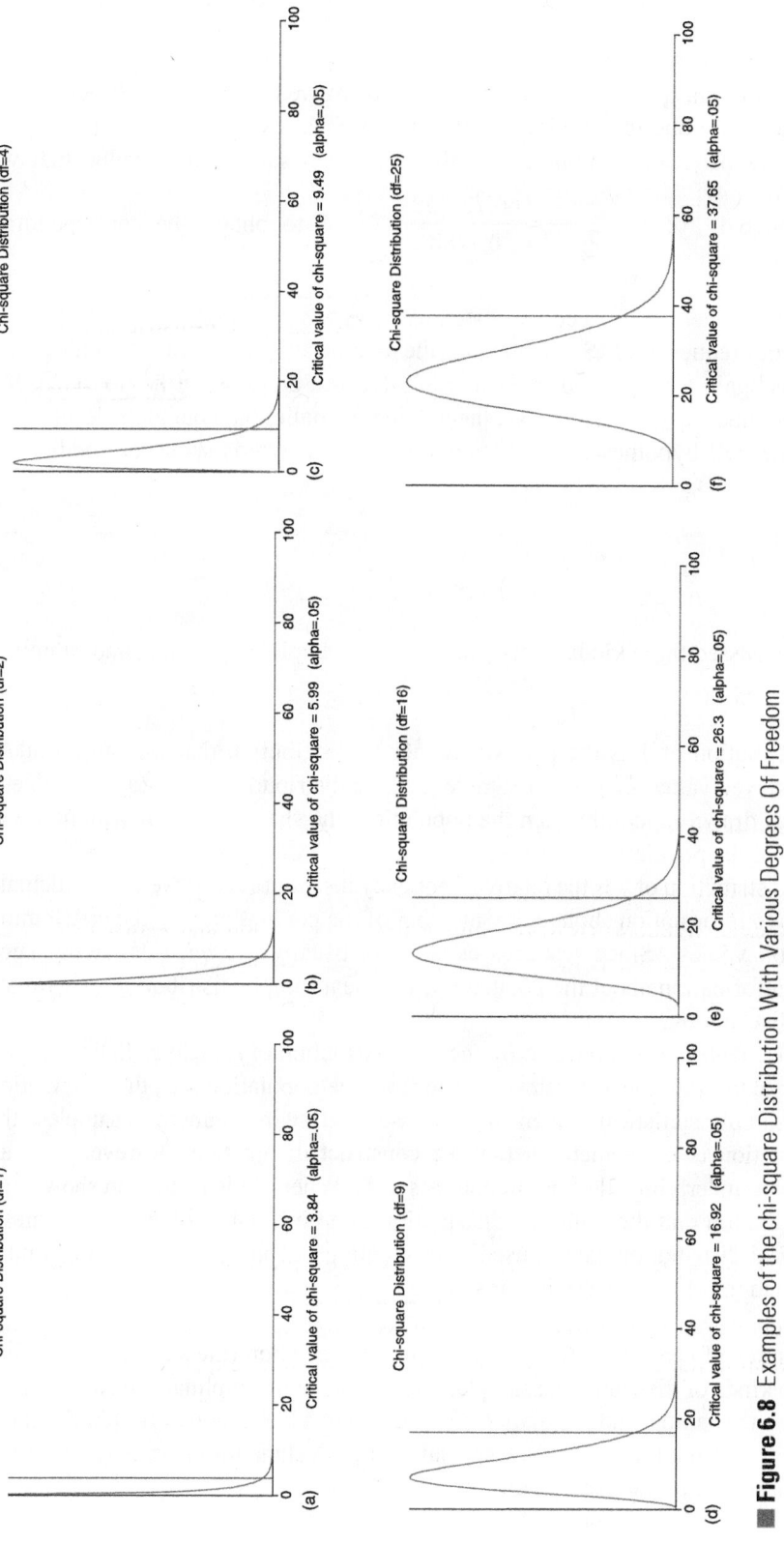

■ **Figure 6.8** Examples of the chi-square Distribution With Various Degrees Of Freedom

Examples of Calculating p-values

Similar to the F-distribution, the chi-square distribution is skewed right for small degrees of freedom and many tests are one-tailed, placing all of the probability in the right tail. Display A.6 shows how to calculate such one-tailed p-values. We can square the Z-value that we calculated in Section 6.4.1, $Z = \dfrac{\bar{Y} - \mu_Y^*}{\dfrac{\sigma_Y}{\sqrt{n}}} = \dfrac{66.72 - 50}{0.7488} = 22.33$, to obtain the corresponding

chi-square value with one degree of freedom. Specifically, $\chi^2 = Z^2 = 22.33 * 22.33 = 498.6289$. Display B.6.1 shows our request to SAS and Stata for the p-value associated with this chi-square value. The p-value is again tiny (0.0000 in SAS; 1.89e-110 in Stata's scientific notation). So, consistent with the Z-value we examined above, the p-value is smaller than our alpha level of .05 and we can reject the null hypothesis that the mean number of words spoke by toddlers in the population is 50.

SUMMARY 6

6.6: SUMMARY

In this chapter, we discussed three kinds of distributions: the sample, population, and sampling distributions.

■ The sample distribution of Y is the relative frequency distribution that we can calculate based on the observed values of Y in our sample (i.e., the distribution of the sample values). If the sample was drawn randomly from the population, the shape of this distribution will reflect the shape of the population distribution.

■ The population distribution of Y is the relative frequency distribution that we could calculate if we had access to information about every member of the population (i.e., the distribution of the population values). Since resource constraints usually prevent our having such comprehensive information about the population, we use a sample distribution to estimate the population distribution.

■ The sampling distribution is the relative frequency distribution of sample statistics that we would get were we to draw every possible sample from the population (i.e., the distribution of all possible sample statistics). Given the expense of drawing numerous samples, the sampling distribution is not something that we construct in practice. However, it is an essential construct underlying all of our hypothesis tests. When statisticians can show what theoretical distribution that the sampling distribution of an estimator follows, the formula for that theoretical distribution can be used to calculate probabilities of observing values more extreme than those we observe in our sample.

We can define measures of central tendency (the mean) and variation (the standard deviation) for each of the three kinds of distributions: sample, population, and sampling. We summarized these in Table 6.14 for the sample and population distribution of a continuous variable Y and the sample estimate of its population mean, $\bar{Y}$. A special term, the standard error, is used for the standard deviation of the sampling distribution.

If our Y variable follows the normal distribution, we know that 68% of the observations fall within one standard deviation of the mean, 95% within two standard deviations, and 99.7% within three standard deviations. Values that fall more than three standard deviations from the mean are unusual (even though we expect them 0.3% of the time). We can use standardized variables to help us identify such unusual values. The standard score is calculated by first finding the deviation from the mean of Y of each observed value of Y and then dividing by the standard deviation of Y; that is, $Z = \dfrac{Y_i - \bar{Y}}{s_Y}$.

The central limit theorem tells us that the sampling distribution for the sample mean follows a normal distribution. Thus, we can also rely on the above values to tell us whether a sample statistic falls far from a hypothesized value given the standard error of the sampling distribution. When we conduct hypothesis tests for the sample mean, our test statistic is a Z or t-statistic. In the rare case that we know the population standard deviation, we can calculate the standard error exactly and the test statistic follows the Z-distribution, $Z = \dfrac{\bar{Y} - \mu_Y^*}{\dfrac{\sigma_Y}{\sqrt{n}}}$. If we have to estimate the standard error using the sample standard deviation, then the test statistic follows the t-distribution, $t = \dfrac{\bar{Y} - \mu_Y^*}{\dfrac{s_Y}{\sqrt{n}}}$.

We also discussed the basic steps of a hypothesis test in this chapter, connecting them to the concepts of the sampling distribution, standard error, and standardized variable. In general, to conduct a hypothesis test we:

1. *List the null and alternative hypotheses about our expectation regarding the value of the population parameter being estimated (in our chapter examples, the hypothesized value of the population mean).* The alternative hypothesis is written based on our expectations drawn from theory, concepts, and prior studies. The null hypothesis is the converse of the alternative hypothesis.
2. *Calculate a test statistic.* For the test about the sample mean based on the Z-value and t-value that we considered in this chapter, this test statistic took on the common form of: (*sample statistic* minus *hypothesized value*) divided by the *standard error.*
3. *Determine the p-value* associated with the calculated test statistic given the test statistic's distribution (e.g., Z or t-distribution for the sample mean), being careful to consider both tails for a two-tailed test.
4. *Make a decision about the null hypothesis.* If the p-value is smaller than the alpha level then reject the null hypothesis. If the p-value is larger than the alpha level then fail to reject the null hypothesis.

Steps 3 and 4 could alternatively be conducted by calculating critical value(s), given the alpha level and the test statistic's theoretical distribution, and rejecting the null hypothesis if the calculated test statistic is more extreme than (one of) the critical value(s). For a two-tailed Z or t-test, the alpha level must be split into both tails to determine the critical values.

For a two-tailed test, Steps 2, 3, and 4 could also alternatively be completed by calculating a confidence interval (generally the point estimate plus and minus a multiple of the standard error). For the Z-distribution and alpha level of .05, the multiple is 1.96. If the confidence interval contains the hypothesized value, then we fail to reject the null hypothesis. If the confidence interval does not contain the hypothesized value, then we reject the null hypothesis. The confidence interval approach gives the same results as a two-tailed z-test or t-test, but has the advantage of making explicit that our point estimate would vary in different samples.

We focused on hypothesis tests of the sample mean based on the normal distribution in this chapter. However, we also introduced three other theoretical distributions (the t-distribution, F-distribution, and chi-square distribution) which we will rely on for statistical tests in future chapters.

KEY TERMS

Alpha level

Alternative hypothesis

Bell-shaped curve

Calculated value

Central limit theorem

Chi-square distribution

Confidence interval

Critical value

degrees of freedom

denominator degrees of freedom

Directional alternative hypothesis (also one-sided or one-tailed alternative hypothesis)

Empirical rule

Estimator

Hypothesized value

Inference

Non-directional alternative hypothesis (also two-sided or two-tailed alternative hypothesis)

Normal distribution

Null hypothesis

Numerator degrees of freedom

Outlier

p-value

Point estimate

Population

Population distribution

Population parameter

Sample

Sample distribution

Sampling distribution

Sample statistic

Standard error

Standard normal distribution

Standardized variable

t-distribution

Test statistic

Theoretical distribution

Type I error

Z-value (also standard score)

REVIEW QUESTIONS

6.1 Define the sample distribution, population distribution, and sampling distribution and discuss how they are related to one another.

6.2 What is a standardized value?

6.3 What is the empirical rule?

6.4 What is the central limit theorem?

6.5 What is a standard error? How is the standard error affected by sample size?

6.6 When are Z-values rather than t-values used to draw inferences about the sample mean?

6.7 What are null and alternative hypotheses?

6.8 Define the general concepts of alpha levels and critical values.

6.9 Define the general concepts of p-values and calculated values.

6.10 What is the general structure of the formulas for test statistics based on the Z and t-distributions?

6.11 What is a theoretical distribution?

6.12 Describe the basic shape of the normal distribution.

6.13 Describe the basic shape of the t-distribution and discuss how the t-distribution relates to the Z-distribution.

6.14 Describe the basic shape of the F-distribution and discuss how it relates to the t-distribution.

6.15 Describe the basic shape of the chi-square distribution and discuss how it relates to the Z-distribution.

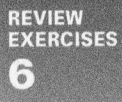

REVIEW EXERCISES

6.1 Imagine that you know that the standard deviation of math achievement tests in a population is 13.43.

a. What would be the standard error for the sampling distribution of the mean math achievement test score if the sample size were 50? 250? 700? 1500?

b. If the average math achievement test score in this population were 97.58, in what range would you expect 95% of sample means to fall, if they were calculated based on samples that were drawn randomly from this same population of size 50? 250? 700? 1500?

c. Given these expected ranges, for which of these sample sizes would you expect to draw a sample that would reject the null hypothesis that the population mean was 100?

6.2   Suppose that you measured the heights of a sample of 200 adults drawn randomly from all adult residents of a Southern city and found that the mean height was 71 inches with a standard deviation of 3.76.

   a. Where does a person with a height of 80 inches fall in this sample distribution, in standard deviation units?

   b. What is the standard score for a height of 62 inches based on this sample distribution?

   c. What is your single best guess of the population mean of adult residents of the city from which this sample was drawn?

   d. What is your estimate of the standard error of the sampling distribution of the mean for similarly-drawn samples of size 200 from this same population?

   e. In what range would you expect 95% of sample means to fall in this sampling distribution, based on the information in the single sample you drew?

   f. Based on the 95% confidence interval, can you reject the null hypothesis that the mean height in this Southern city is 67 inches (against the alternative hypothesis that the mean height in this Southern city is not equal to 67 inches).

   g. Calculate a test statistic to draw a conclusion about the null hypothesis that the mean height in this Southern city is 67 inches (against the alternative hypothesis that the mean height in this Southern city is not equal to 67 inches). Use the most appropriate of the following critical values to guide your decision:, $t_{19,.025} = 2.09$, $t_{199,.025} = 1.97$, $z_{.025} = 1.96$.

CHAPTER EXERCISE

In this chapter exercise, we will create figures and examine the means for the symmetric population distribution shown in Figure 6.1a and sample distributions similar to the sample distribution shown in Figure 6.1c.

To create the sample distribution, we will use Stata's sample command which allows us to draw a simple random sample from a population. If we use the, count option, we can specify the size of the sample we want to draw. For example, sample 100, count will draw a simple random sample of size n=100.

When we create these samples, it is also helpful to use the command set seed to determine the initial value that Stata will use when making the random draws. By setting the seed, we can ensure that our results will replicate if we run the program multiple times. The seed can be any positive integer. We often use set seed 123456789 because it is easy for us to remember across programs.

CHAPTER
EXERCISE

6

To begin, create the shell of a basic Stata .do file (refer to Display A.4.2—include the four commands that you always put at the start of a Stata program; be sure to open and close a log file; be sure to also save your .do file). Then add the syntax needed for the Stata tasks below.

6.1 Population, Sample and Sampling Distributions

a) Stata Tasks.

i) Reproduce the figures shown in Figure 6.1a and Figure 6.1b and the population mean and standard deviation from Table 6.2 using the following syntax:

```
use PopSym
histogram vocab, xlabel(0(10)140, grid)
graph export PopSym.wmf, replace
summarize vocab
drop _all
```

ii) Use syntax like the following to repeatedly draw *samples of size n=30, 100, and 1000* from the population, graph the variable *vocab* in the sample, and calculate the mean and standard deviation in the sample.

```
set seed 123456789
use PopSym
sample 30, count
histogram vocab, bin(15) xlabel (0(10)140, grid)
graph export SampleSym30_1.wmf, replace
summarize vocab
drop _all
```

You may want to pause after you draw your first sample of size 30 (i.e., after sample 30, count command) and browse the data to make concrete how you have drawn a sample from the original population.
Repeat the above syntax 10 times for each sample size (n=30, n=100 and n=1000).

iii) Calculate the *p*-value for the test statistic that you calculated in Write-up Task 6.1bvii, using the commands shown in Display A.6.

b) Write-Up Tasks.

i) By hand (or using a spreadsheet like Excel) calculate the average of the 10 means for each sample size that you drew (the average of the 10 means for samples of size n=30, the average of the 10 means for samples of size n=100, the average of the 10 means for samples of size n=100). Discuss how these averages compare to one another and to the population mean.

ii) Use Equation 6.3c and the population standard deviation found in 6.1ai to calculate the standard error for each size of sample (n=30, n=100, n=1000). Discuss the relative size of these standard errors across the three samples.

iii) Use the population mean and the standard error that you calculated in 6.1bii to calculate the bounds within which you would expect the middle 95% of the sampling distribution of the mean to fall for each size of sample (n=30, n=100, n=1000). Discuss how these bounds compare across the three sizes of samples (e.g., which size sample has the widest bounds). Discuss whether the actual values of sample means for the 10 samples that you drew actually fall within these bounds for each size of sample. If some of the sample means fall outside the bounds, discuss why you think this may be. Also discuss the relative size of the confidence intervals across the three samples.

iv) Suppose that you did not know the population standard deviation. How would the formula for the standard error differ from the formula that you used in 6.1bii? Use this formula to calculate the standard errors based on your 1st sample of each size (n=30, n=100, n=1000).

v) Suppose that you did not know the population mean. Use the standard errors that you calculated in 6.1biv along with the sample means from your 1st sample of each size (n=30, n=100, n=1000) to calculate 95% confidence intervals. Use the most appropriate of the following critical values: $t_{29,.05/2}$ = 2.045, $t_{99,.05/2}$ = 1.984, and $t_{999,.05/2}$ = 1.962.

vi) Suppose that you had made the following null and alternative hypotheses:

Words		Symbols
Null hypothesis:	The mean number of words toddlers speak in the population is 65.	H_o: $\mu_Y = 65$
Alternative hypothesis:	The mean number of words toddlers speak in the population is not 65.	H_a: $\mu_Y \neq 65$

What conclusion would you make about these hypotheses based on each set of results that you calculated in 6.1bv? Are the results across the three samples the same or different? Why do you think this may be?

vii) Show how to calculate the test statistic based on the first samples (the same samples you used in 6.1bv) for the hypotheses shown in 6.1bvi. *Calculate the p-values for these test statistics using the Stata commands shown in Display A.6.* What conclusion would you make based on these results (use alpha of .05)?

Chapter 7

BIVARIATE INFERENTIAL STATISTICS

CHAPTER 7: BIVARIATE INFERENTIAL STATISTICS

Statistical inference allows us to use a sample to inform us about a population. In the social science literature, statistical inference sometimes focuses on one variable at a time (typically examining whether the mean equals or differs from zero in the population). More often, however, statistical inference is made with bivariate and multivariate statistics. In this chapter, we will introduce statistical inference for bivariate associations between two variables. Bivariate analyses are often used in exploratory analyses as researchers prepare to conduct regression analyses. In publications, bivariate associations are generally reported early in the results section of an article, either to describe variables within two or more groups (e.g., to describe the analysis variables separately for men and women or among different racial-ethnic groups) or to report the **simple association** between two variables (with simple meaning that the association between the two variables is examined without considering any other variables). Within-group descriptions help us understand what characteristics are similar and what characteristics differ between the groups, often suggesting additional variables that should be taken into account in our **multivariate models** (where multivariate refers to two or more variables—often numerous variables—that are examined together, often with regression approaches, as we will examine in Part 3).

Not surprisingly, type of the two variables being examined affects the approach to statistical inference. We present commonly-used tests appropriate for one categorical and one continuous variable, two categorical variables, and two continuous variables. In the first case, for example, we might ask whether the means on a continuous variable (like income) are equal or different across groups of a categorical variable (like gender). In the second case, we might examine whether the frequency distributions for one categorical variable (like self-reported health) differ across groups of another categorical variable (like race-ethnicity). In the third case, we might examine the degree to which two continuous variables (for example years of education and earnings) are correlated (intuitively, the degree to which cases that fall above or below the mean on one variable fall in the same direction—above or below the mean—on the other variable). Before we turn to these three types of statistical inference, we will illustrate their use with four literature excerpts.

7.1: LITERATURE EXCERPTS

7.1.1: Literature Excerpt 7.1

Holly Furdyna, Belinda Tucker, and Angela James (2008) analyze telephone survey data from adults in over two-dozen U.S. cities to examine how the relative earnings of African American and white women to their spouses associates with their marital happiness. Given their focus on racial-ethnic differences, their Table 1 (shown in Literature Excerpt 7.1) shows means and proportions on their analysis variables not only for the full sample, but also separately for African American and white women. They present the statistics for continuous and categorical variables separately, with continuous variables in the top panel and categorical variables in the bottom panel of their table. Similar to what we saw in Chapter 5, they present the mean and standard deviation (as well as the range) for continuous variables and the percentage distribution for most categorical variables.[1] In addition, the last column of their table is labeled *Difference* at the top. The column is further labeled *t* in the top panel (for *t*-tests comparing means of continuous variables within two groups) and χ^2 in the bottom panel (for chi-square tests comparing the percentage distribution of one variable within two or more groups of another variable).

▦ Literature Excerpt 7.1

Table 1. Sample Characteristics for Key Variables

	Whole Sample (N = 431)			African American (n = 171)		White (n = 260)		Difference
	M	SD	Range	M	SD	M	SD	t
Respondent Characteristics								
Continuous variables								
Income ratio	0.84	1.08	.01–20	0.85	0.46	0.83	1.34	−0.24
Education	14.60	2.10	10–20	14.20	1.90	14.90	2.18	3.63***
Age	39.32	8.38	21–55	39.33	8.22	39.32	8.50	−0.01
Work-Family Gender Ideology[a]	7.57	1.41	3.67–10	7.44	1.58	7.66	1.27	1.60
Religiosity[b]	6.78	2.58	1–10	7.85	2.11	6.07	2.62	−7.45***
Importance of Marriage[c]	8.82	1.95	1–10	9.02	1.92	8.68	1.97	−1.77

	Whole Sample (N = 431) (%)	African American (n = 171) (%)	White (n = 260) (%)	Difference (χ^2)
Categorical variables				
High marital happiness[d]	55	44	62	13.00***
W/H income ratio levels[e]				
Level 1: Ratio < 1/2	28	20	32	
Level 2: 1/2 ≤ Ratio < 3/4	27	27	28	
Level 3: 3/4 ≤ Ratio < 1	18	19	17	
Level 4: Ratio ≥ 1	27	34	23	10.16*
Financial need[f]	37	43	24	4.60*
Educational difference[g] W > H	26	29	24	1.56
Parenthood[h]	80	91	73	19.23***
Median couple income[i]	66,190	62,500	70,000	

[a] Lower score indicates more traditional work-family gender ideology, higher score indicates more progressive/egalitarian.
[b] Higher score indicates stronger religiosity.
[c] Higher score indicates placing greater importance on marriage.
[d] 1 = reports "very happy" in marriage, 0 = does not report "very happy" in marriage.
[e] 1 = in focal income ratio level grouping, 0 = not in focal grouping.
[f] 1 = financial need, 0 = no financial need.
[g] 1 = more education than husband, 0 = same or less education than husband.
[h] 1 = one or more living children, 0 = no living children.
[i] Median couple income shown due to skewness of the income variable.
*p < .05.***p < .001.

Source: Furdyna, Holly E., Belinda Tucker, and Angela D. James. 2008. "Relative Spousal Earnings and Marital Happiness Among African American and White Women." *Journal of Marriage and Family*, 70: 332–344.

■ **Box 7.1**

Social scientists often use the phrase statistical significance as a shorthand summary of a hypothesis test. A test statistic is said to be statistically significant if its *p*-value is smaller than an alpha level. Similarly, values are often referred to as "significantly different" between two groups if a test statistic is statistically significant. In the quote from Literature Excerpt 7.1, for example, the authors say "Whites were significantly more likely than Blacks to report high marital happiness." As we move forward in the book, we will distinguish the concept of statistical significance (can we conclude that the two groups differ?) from substantive significance (how big is the difference between the two groups?).

We will discuss how to calculate the statistics and *p*-values (indicated by asterisks in the authors' table) in Sections 7.2 to 7.5 below. For now, we will consider how the authors use these results in the text to describe the main differences on their analytic variables by race-ethnicity. They begin with their outcome variable (marital happiness) and central predictor (relative earnings):

> African American and white participants differ on a number of key variables (see Table 1). Whites were significantly more likely than Blacks to report high marital happiness: 62% versus 44%, respectively ($\chi^2 = 13.00$, p < .001). Income ratio level distributions differed significantly by race ($\chi^2 = 10.16$, p < .05). African American wives were more likely than Whites to earn as much as or more than their husbands (Level 4: 34% vs. 23%) and Whites were more likely than African Americans to earn less than half of their husbands' earnings (Level 1: 32% vs. 20%). Notably, the women did not differ on the income ratio variable in continuous form (see Table 1, top) (p. 336).

Notice that the authors repeat in the text the specific levels of the within-group percentages to help the reader follow along from the table and to highlight the size of the differences. For example, the values allow us to see that the majority of white women report high marital happiness while the majority of African American women do not. And, the groups are reversed in which is most concentrated in the highest (African Americans) and lowest (whites) relative earnings' categories, with about one-third versus one-fifth of each group in these respective categories. They also demonstrate the utility of treating the income ratio (of wives to husbands earnings) categorically as well as continuously, as the percentage distribution across categories reveals differences between the two groups not evident in the within-group means of the continuous variable.

The authors go on to describe, in less detail, how the two groups differ on the additional variables used in their multivariate analyses.

> White wives earned more than African American wives and had significantly more education. African American women were more likely to have children and reported greater financial need and stronger religious beliefs. There were no racial differences in age, educational disparity, work-family gender ideology, or importance of marriage (p. 336).

These results suggest, for example, that the authors' multivariate models should account for the higher education levels and earnings of white than African American women, since these may affect their general mental health and relationships with their spouses (and thus their outcome of marital happiness) and might also help predict where their incomes' fall relative to their husbands (since women with more education and more earnings likely have more chances to earn more than their husbands than do those with less education and earnings). Number of children, financial need, and religious beliefs likewise also differ between the two groups, and would be important control variables to the extent that they also associate with both marital happiness and relative earnings. Interestingly other variables, including the educational difference between spouses, do not differ significantly between the two groups.

7.1.2: Literature Excerpt 7.2

A literature excerpt from Oldehinkel and colleagues (2008) also presents descriptive means and proportions within two groups, but these authors were interested in gender differences in youth developing depression following parental divorce. Their Table 1 (shown in Literature Excerpt 7.2) shows the within-gender means and standard deviations (for continuous variables) and percentages (for categorical variables) on the analytic variables gathered in their sample of Dutch youth. Similar to the authors in Literature Excerpt 7.1, these authors report either t-tests (for continuous variables) or chi-square tests (for categorical variables) which are denoted by the label χ^2/t at the top of their third column of numbers. The authors list p-values in the last column of numbers (labeled p). Only one p-value is smaller than the common alpha of .05; and, thus the authors conclude that only one difference is statistically significant between their gender groups: Girls report higher depression than do boys at their second time point (*YSR Depressive Problems T2*). The authors describe these results in the text as follows:

> None of the variables showed significant gender differences, except self-reported (YSR) depressive problems at T2, which were higher in girls (p. 288).

You may have noticed that Oldehinkel and colleagues' footnote to their Table 1 which reads "adjusted for unequal variances." We will discuss the meaning of this statement below.

7.1.3: Literature Excerpt 7.3

Literature Excerpt 7.3 provides an example of using a graph to show differences in the percentage distribution between two groups. As we have mentioned, such graphs can often help readers visualize the within-group patterns, since differences that are less salient in tables are often immediately apparent in graphs. Kan's (2007) Figure 1 (shown in Literature Excerpt 7.3) presents such a graph, depicting the percentage of men and women who occupy different categories of employment histories in their British sample. The graph makes clear that men in their sample are about twice as likely (or more) than women to fall in the first two categories (continuously full-time or mostly full-time employment) whereas women are about three times as likely (or more) to be in the final three categories (mostly part-time, mixed patterns, and

■ Literature Excerpt 7.2

Table 1.　Descriptive Statistics of the Variables Used in This Study, Separately for Girls and Boys

	Mean (SD) or %		Gender differences		
Variables	Girls	Boys	χ^2/t	df	p
Age at T1	10.58 (0.64)	10.61 (0.64)	−1.03	2147	.30
Age at T2	13.07 (0.62)	13.05 (0.59)	0.57	2014	.57
Parental depression (range 0–4)	0.73 (1.13)	0.70 (1.10)	0.61	2019	.54
Parental divorce	25.0%	23.2%	0.98	1	.32
Age at the time of the divorce	6.34 (3.80)	5.84 (3.64)	1.46	467	.14
YSR Depressive Problems T1	3.89 (3.18)	3.69 (3.23)	1.47	2108	.14
YSR Depressive Problems T2	4.16 (3.75)	2.87 (2.77)	8.73	1900[a]	<.001
CBCL Depressive Problems T1	2.36 (2.47)	2.54 (2.60)	−1.56	1987	.12
CBCL Depressive Problems T2	1.98 (2.50)	1.90 (2.47)	0.71	1816	.47

Note: YSR = Youth Self-Report, CBCL = Child Behavior Checklist.
[a] Adjusted for unequal variances.

Source: Oldehinkel, Albertine J., Johan Ormel, René Veenstra, Andres F. De Winter, and Frank C. Verhulst. 2008. "Parental Divorce and Offspring Depressive Symptoms: Dutch Developmental Trends During Adolescence." *Journal of Marriage and Family,* 70: 284–293.

■ Literature Excerpt 7.3

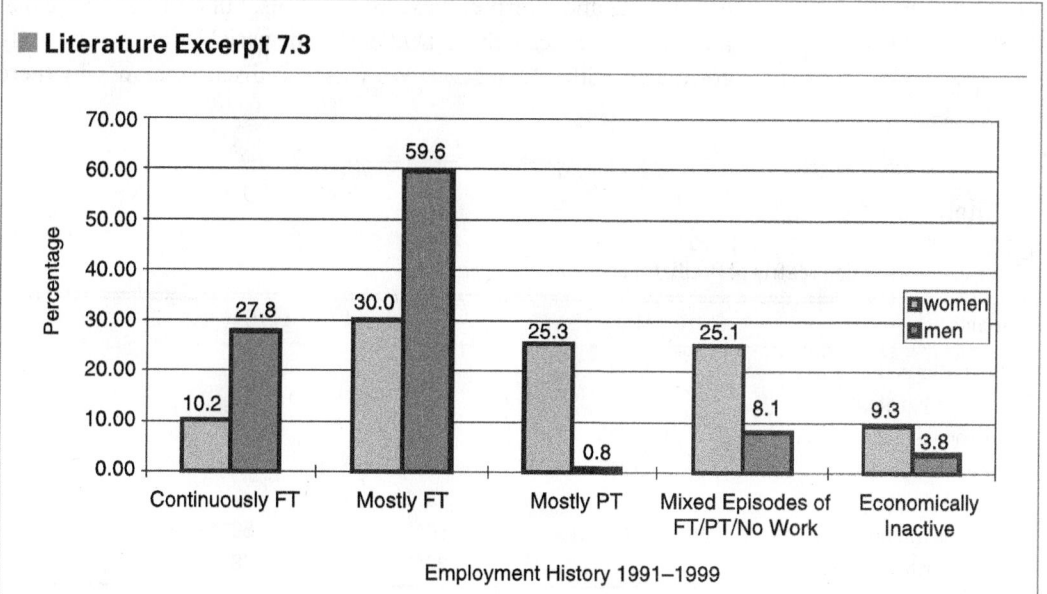

Figure 1: Employment History of Married/Cohabiting Men and Women, 1991–1999.

Source: Kan, Man Yee. 2007. "Work Orientation and Wives' Employment Careers: An Evaluation of Hakim's Preference Theory." *Work and Occupations,* 34: 430–462.

economically inactive). Although Kan does not report the test statistic which she may have used to test hypotheses, the descriptive pattern evident in the figure helps the reader visualize the substantively large ways in which the distribution of employment histories differs for men and women.

7.1.4: Literature Excerpt 7.4

Although sometimes social scientists will report the correlations among all of their analysis variables, such reports can become quite large for studies with many covariates and contemporary journal articles rarely publish them in their entirety. Some studies do more selectively report correlations. Literature Excerpt 7.4 provides an example of a correlation matrix[2] presented in a study by Deborah Capaldi, Mike Stoolmiller, Sara Clark, and Lee Owen (2002) of risks associated with contraction of a sexually-transmitted disease (STD) among boys from the Oregon Youth Study. The authors' Table 3 (shown in Literature Excerpt 7.4) provides a typical example of the format used for presenting such a correlation matrix. The authors' seven analytic variables are listed in the first column. In order to conserve space, the variables are designated by their corresponding number in the top row (the numbers can be linked to the variable names in the first column). Within the cells, the values of the correlations are listed. For example, the correlation between variable 1 (SES/income) and variable 2 (Parental monitoring) is .33. We will discuss below how to calculate and interpret these associations, but for now we see that the asterisks indicate that all but one of the variables are significantly correlated with one another. We will also discuss below why there

■ **Box 7.2**

We focus on the Pearson correlation in this chapter, since it is commonly used in most social science subfields. Other types of correlations are available, designed specifically for cases in which one or both of the variables are ordinal rather than interval (Chen and Popovich 2002).

■ **Literature Excerpt 7.4**

Table 3.   Correlation Matrix of Predictor and Outcome Variables

Variable	1	2	3	4	5	6	7
1. SES/income	—						
2. Parental monitoring	.33**	—					
3. Deviant-peer association	−.32**	−.61**	—				
4. Antisocial behavior	−.29**	−.55**	.86**	—			
5. Substance use	−.22**	−.48**	.69**	.72**	—		
6. Lifetime average sexual risk	−.17*	−.39**	.50**	.53**	.56**	—	
7. Contraction of an STD	−.05	−.22**	.22**	.22**	.28**	.22**	—

$*p < .05.$ $**p < .01.$

Source: Capaldi, Deborah M., Mike Stoolmiller, Sara Clark, and Lee D. Owen. 2002. "Heterosexual Risk Behaviors in At-Risk Young Men From Adolescence to Young Adulthood: Prevalence, Prediction and Association with STD Contraction." *Developmental Psychology*, 38: 394–406.

are dashes on the diagonal and no values shown in the top right of the table. Because the authors do not mention the type of correlation they calculate, we assume that they are the commonly reported Pearson correlations that we define below. As is typical in many social science subfields, they present these correlations for all of their study variables, even though some might not be considered continuous (e.g., *Contraction of an STD* is a dichotomous variable representing whether the youth had or had not contracted a sexually-transmitted disease).

7.2: ONE CATEGORICAL AND ONE INTERVAL VARIABLE

Literature Excerpts 7.1 and 7.2 both used a *t*-test to compare the means of a continuous variable between two groups. We will now examine the details of how to conduct this test. We also show how to use a confidence interval to provide a range of estimates of the difference in means between the two groups. We will also present the basic one-way analysis of variance *F*-test, which can be used to similarly test for mean differences when a categorical variable takes on more than two groups.

7.2.1: Two-sample *t*-test

We use the **two-sample *t*-test** as the first bivariate hypothesis test that we examine because it parallels the tests that we will conduct in regression analysis (in fact, we shall see in Chapter 10 that we can test the same hypothesis about the equivalence of the within-group means and obtain the same *t*-statistic from regression analysis as we do with a *t*-test presented in this section).

The *t*-test follows four basic steps common to many hypothesis tests, like those considered in Chapter 6:

1. Define the null and alternative hypotheses about the value that you expect for the parameter being estimated (in our case, the difference between the two groups' means).
2. Calculate a test statistic (often, as in our case, the point estimate of the parameter minus the hypothesized value, divided by the estimated standard error).
3. Determine the *p*-value associated with the calculated test statistic, given the test statistic's distribution (e.g., in our case, the *t*-distribution).
4. Reject the null hypothesis if the *p*-value is smaller than the pre-specified alpha level (usually 0.05).

> ■ **Box 7.3**
>
> As we saw in Chapter 6, the *Z*-distribution and *t*-distribution are commonly used distributions in statistics. And, in the remaining chapters of the book we will calculate *z*-statistics or *t*-statistics to evaluate additional hypotheses, beyond the hypothesis that the means in two groups are equivalent. However, the word *ttest* is commonly used in statistical packages for simple tests about the mean, as is evident in the name of the commands in SAS and Stata (see Display A.7.1).

Alternatively, at steps 3 and 4 you could calculate the critical value, given the test statistic's distribution and desired alpha level, and reject the null hypothesis if the calculated value is more extreme than the critical value. As noted in Chapter 6, these two approaches will provide equivalent results; but, p-values are easy to obtain with modern statistical software and more informative (making it easy for readers to evaluate whether the null hypothesis could be rejected at other alpha levels and giving an indication of how far the sample estimate falls from the hypothesized value).

In our case, we are evaluating the difference in means between two groups, and thus we can write our null hypothesis (H_o) and alternative hypothesis (H_a) as follows:

	Words	Symbols 1	Symbols 2
H_o	The mean of the continuous variable is the same in the two groups.	$\mu_1 = \mu_2$	$\mu_1 - \mu_2 = 0$
H_a	The mean of the continuous variable differs between the two groups.	$\mu_1 \neq \mu_2$	$\mu_1 - \mu_2 \neq 0$

where μ_1 represents the population mean on Y for the first group and μ_2 represents the population mean on Y for the second group. Notice that we express the null hypothesis from words to symbols in two ways. The first way matches more exactly how we say in words that the means are equal in the two groups, $\mu_1 = \mu_2$. The second way uses simple algebra (subtracting μ_2 from both sides) to re-write this expression to the equivalent form of $\mu_1 - \mu_2 = 0$. The alternative hypothesis is similarly depicted symbolically, but with the *not-equals* sign.

The advantage of the second way of depicting our null and alternative hypotheses with symbols is that the parameter being estimated reduces to a single quantity, the difference in the means ($\mu_1 - \mu_2$), and this quantity is what we estimate with our point estimate ($\bar{Y}_1 - \bar{Y}_2$) where $\bar{Y}_1$ represents the mean of our continuous variable in the first group ($\bar{Y}_1 = \dfrac{\sum_{i=1}^{n_1} Y_i}{n_1}$ with n_1 representing the number of sample members who are from the first group) and $\bar{Y}_2$ represents the mean of our continuous variable in the second group ($\bar{Y}_2 = \dfrac{\sum_{i=1}^{n_2} Y_i}{n_2}$ with n_2 representing the number of sample members who are from the second group).

The second way of depicting our null and alternative hypotheses also lists our hypothesized value of zero. We can use this point estimate and hypothesized value to begin to write our test statistic as follows (building on the general concept of the test statistic being the point estimate of the parameter minus the hypothesized value, divided by the estimated standard error):

$$test\ statistic = \frac{(\bar{Y}_1 - \bar{Y}_2) - 0}{\hat{\sigma}_{\bar{Y}_1 - \bar{Y}_2}} \tag{7.1}$$

To complete this formula, we need to determine how to estimate the standard error of the difference between the means, $\hat{\sigma}_{\bar{Y}1 - \bar{Y}2}$. We introduce two common ways to define this quantity. Both are available in SAS and Stata (in SAS they are both presented in the default output) and you may see both in the literature (as in Literature Excerpt 7.2). We will discuss below the relative merits of each approach.

Suppose first that we calculate our estimate of the variance of the sampling distribution introduced in Chapter 6 for each subgroup mean (the square root of which would be the standard errors of the subgroup means). That is:

	Group 1	Group 2
Variance of Subgroup Mean	$\hat{\sigma}^2_{\bar{Y}_1} = \dfrac{s^2_{Y1}}{n_1}$	$\hat{\sigma}^2_{\bar{Y}_2} = \dfrac{s^2_{Y2}}{n_2}$
Standard Deviation of Subgroup Mean	$\hat{\sigma}_{\bar{Y}_1} = \dfrac{s_{Y1}}{\sqrt{n_1}}$	$\hat{\sigma}_{\bar{Y}_2} = \dfrac{s_{Y2}}{\sqrt{n_2}}$
Standard Deviation of Y for Subgroup	$s_{Y1} = \sqrt{\dfrac{\sum_{i=1}^{n_1}(Y_i - \bar{Y}_1)^2}{n_1 - 1}}$	$s_{Y2} = \sqrt{\dfrac{\sum_{i=1}^{n_2}(Y_i - \bar{Y}_2)^2}{n_2 - 1}}$

One possible estimate of the variance of the difference in means would be the sum of the variance of the two subgroup means. The square root of this value would be the standard error of the difference in means:

$$\hat{\sigma}_{\bar{Y}_1 - \bar{Y}_2} = \sqrt{\frac{S^2_{Y1}}{n_1} + \frac{S^2_{Y2}}{n_2}} \qquad\qquad (7.2)$$

■ Box 7.4

This formula is based on the general formula for the variance of a linear combination of two variables (Wackerly, Mendenhall, and Scheaffer 2008):

Linear Combination: $aX1 + bX2$

Variance of Linear Combination: $a^2 Var(X1) + b^2 Var(X2) + 2ab Cov(X1, X2)$

In our case, the linear combination is $\bar{Y}_1 - \bar{Y}_2$. Thus, $a=1$ and $b=-1$ and the variance of our linear combination would be:

$$Var(\bar{Y}_1) + Var(\bar{Y}_2) - 2Cov(\bar{Y}_1, \bar{Y}_2)$$

If we assert that the two samples are independent (and thus $Cov(\bar{Y}_1, \bar{Y}_2)$ is zero), then the variance of the difference in means reduces to $Var(\bar{Y}_1) + Var(\bar{Y}_2)$.

■ Box 7.5

You may sometimes see references to a z-test to compare subgroup means. This Z-value relies on a similar estimate of the standard error of the difference between the means, but assumes that the population standard deviation of Y within each subgroup is known. That is, $\sigma_{\bar{y}_1 - \bar{y}_2} = \sqrt{\dfrac{\sigma^2_{Y1}}{n_1} + \dfrac{\sigma^2_{Y2}}{n_2}}$. Notice that the only difference between this equation and Equation 7.2 is that we have removed the hats from the variance symbols in the numerator (σ^2_{Y1} rather than s^2_{Y1}; σ^2_{Y2} rather than s^2_{Y2}) to denote that the variance is known rather than estimated.

We can substitute Equation 7.2 into the denominator of Equation 7.1 and then our test statistic is (Wackerly, Mendenhall, and Scheaffer 2008; see also SAS 2008b: 7409–7410; Stata 2009a: 2002):

$$t = \frac{(\bar{Y}_1 - \bar{Y}_2) - 0}{\sqrt{\dfrac{s_{Y1}^2}{n_1} + \dfrac{s_{Y2}^2}{n_2}}}$$

(7.3)

Although this formula for the t-statistic is simple and clearly draws on the formulas for the standard error of each mean, calculation of the degrees of freedom is complicated. Both SAS and Stata show the Satterthwaite degrees of freedom by default, which is calculated as follows (Wackerly, Mendenhall, and Scheaffer 2008; see also SAS 2008b: 7409–7410; StataCorp 2009a: 2002):

$$df = \frac{(\dfrac{s_{Y1}^2}{n_1} + \dfrac{s_{Y2}^2}{n_2})^2}{\dfrac{(\dfrac{s_{Y1}^2}{n_1})^2}{n_1 - 1} + \dfrac{(\dfrac{s_{Y2}^2}{n_2})^2}{n_2 - 1}}$$

(7.4)

Notice that this degrees of freedom can result in a non-integer value (with decimals).

An alternative estimate of the standard error of the difference in the means can be calculated if we assume that the standard deviations are the same in the two groups. If this assumption holds, then we can calculate a pooled standard deviation directly (Wackerly, Mendenhall, and Scheaffer 2008; see also SAS 2008b: 7409–7410; StataCorp 2009a: 2002):

$$\hat{\sigma}_{12} = \sqrt{\frac{(n_1 - 1)s_{Y1}^2 + (n_2 - 1)s_{Y2}^2}{n_1 + n_2 - 2}}$$

(7.5)

We can use this pooled standard deviation to calculate the following standard error of the difference in means, as an alternative to Equation 7.2:

$$\hat{\sigma}_{\bar{Y}_1 - \bar{Y}_2} = \sqrt{\frac{(n_1 - 1)s_{Y1}^2 + (n_2 - 1)s_{Y2}^2}{n_1 + n_2 - 2}} \sqrt{\frac{1}{n_1} + \frac{1}{n_2}}$$

(7.6)

Substituting Equation 7.6 into the denominator of Equation 7.1 we have the following alternative test statistic for the difference in subgroup means:

$$t = \frac{(\bar{Y}_1 - \bar{Y}_2) - 0}{\sqrt{\dfrac{(n_1 - 1)s_{Y1}^2 + (n_2 - 1)s_{Y2}^2}{n_1 + n_2 - 2}} \sqrt{\dfrac{1}{n_1} + \dfrac{1}{n_2}}}$$

(7.7)

This t-statistic has $n_1 + n_2 - 2$ degrees of freedom.

Which version of the *t*-test should you use? Some scholars prefer to first test the assumption that the variances (and equivalently standard deviations) are equal in the two groups. If they are, then they use Equation 7.7. If they are not, then they use Equation 7.3. The test of the equivalence of the variances relies on the fact that the ratio of the variance of *Y* in the two groups follows an *F*-distribution (Wackerly, Mendenhall, and Scheaffer 2008; see also StataCorp 2009a: 1692).

$$F = \frac{s_{Y1}^2}{s_{Y2}^2}$$

The null hypothesis is that the variances are equal in the two groups. The alternative hypothesis is that the variances differ between the two groups.

H_o The variances are equal in the two groups.
H_a The variances differ between the two groups.

The *p*-value of this calculated *F*-statistic and/or the critical *F*-value for an alpha of 0.05 can be examined in an *F* distribution with $n_1 - 1$ numerator and $n_2 - 1$ denominator degrees of freedom. The implementation of this test depends on which group is placed in the numerator. As we shall see below, SAS and Stata differ in this regard.

Some scholars do not like this approach, for example because the *F*-test is sensitive to whether the population distributions are truly normal; they recommend relying on the version of the two-sample *t*-test that assumed unequal variances (Moore 2010: 488–489). We present both since you will see both in publications and since some statistical packages provide both *t*-tests of equal means and the *F*-test of equal variances in the default output (such as SAS does). We will return to this topic of the assumption of equal variances in Part 3 as we study OLS regression and learn how to relax this assumption.

A Hypothetical Example

Table 7.1 shows a hypothetical example of the calculation of the two sample *t*-test, based on the two formulas shown above.

The example extends one from Chapter 6 of words spoken by toddlers to consider how the mean number of words spoken might differ for boys and girls. To illustrate the calculations, we imagine a sample with just 15 cases, six boys and nine girls. We show the calculations of the means and standard deviations within each gender, using a process similar to what we followed in Tables 5.1 and 5.2 of Chapter 5 to calculate the overall mean and standard deviation. We then plug the resulting values into the two formulas for the *t*-test and the *F*-test for equal variances.

The results show that the mean number of words spoken in the sample is 54.83 words for boys and 58.78 words for girls. Thus, the point estimate of the difference in means, $\bar{Y}_1 - \bar{Y}_2$, is –3.95. The variance for boys is somewhat larger than the variance for girls (46.17 versus 28.20), and the *F*-value of the ratio of the variances is $\frac{46.17}{28.20} = 1.6374$. Based on $6-1=5$ numerator and

■ **Table 7.1: Calculation of the two-sample _t_-test based on hypothetical data: Number of words spoken among two-year-old boys and girls**

	Boys				Girls		
	Words Spoken (Y_i)	Deviation from Mean $(Y_i - \bar{Y}_1)$	Deviation from Mean Squared $(Y_i - \bar{Y}_1)^2$		Words Spoken (Y_i)	Deviation from Mean $(Y_i - \bar{Y}_2)$	Deviation from Mean Squared $(Y_i - \bar{Y}_2)^2$
Case 1	44	−10.83	117.36	Case 3	52	−6.78	45.94
Case 2	51	−3.83	14.69	Case 4	53	−5.78	33.38
Case 5	53	−1.83	3.36	Case 6	55	−3.78	14.27
Case 9	59	4.17	17.36	Case 7	56	−2.78	7.72
Case 11	60	5.17	26.69	Case 8	59	0.22	0.05
Case 13	62	7.17	51.36	Case 10	60	1.22	1.49
				Case 12	62	3.22	10.38
				Case 14	64	5.22	27.27
				Case 15	68	9.22	85.05
Sum	329	0	230.83		529	0	225.56

Subgroup Means of Y

$$\bar{Y}_1 = \frac{\sum_{i=1}^{n_1} Y_i}{n_1} = \frac{329}{6} = 54.83 \qquad \bar{Y}_2 = \frac{\sum_{i=1}^{n_2} Y_i}{n_2} = \frac{529}{9} = 58.78$$

Subgroup Variances of Y

$$s_{Y1}^2 = \frac{\sum_{i=1}^{n_1}(Y_i - \bar{Y}_1)^2}{n_1 - 1} = \frac{230.83}{6-1} = 46.17 \qquad s_{Y2}^2 = \frac{\sum_{i=1}^{n_2}(Y_i - \bar{Y}_2)^2}{n_2 - 1} = \frac{225.56}{9-1} = 28.20$$

Assume Same Variance

$$t = \frac{(\bar{Y}_1 - \bar{Y}_2) - 0}{\sqrt{\frac{(n_1-1)s_{Y1}^2 + (n_2-1)s_{Y2}^2}{n_1 + n_2 - 2}}\sqrt{\frac{1}{n_1} + \frac{1}{n_2}}} = \frac{54.83 - 58.78}{\sqrt{\frac{(6-1)46.17 + (9-1)28.20}{6+9-2}}\sqrt{\frac{1}{6} + \frac{1}{9}}} = \frac{-3.95}{3.12} = -1.26$$

$$df = (n_1 + n_2 - 2) = (6 + 9 - 2) = 13$$

Allow Different Variances

$$t = \frac{(\bar{Y}_1 - \bar{Y}_2) - 0}{\sqrt{\frac{s_{Y1}^2}{n_1} + \frac{s_{Y2}^2}{n_2}}} = \frac{54.83 - 58.78}{\sqrt{\frac{46.17}{6} + \frac{28.20}{9}}} = \frac{-3.95}{3.29} - 1.20$$

$$df = \frac{(\frac{s_{Y1}^2}{n_1} + \frac{s_{Y2}^2}{n_2})^2}{\frac{(\frac{s_{Y1}^2}{n_1})^2}{n_1 - 1} + \frac{(\frac{s_{Y2}^2}{n_2})^2}{n_2 - 1}} = \frac{(\frac{46.17}{6} + \frac{28.20}{9})^2}{\frac{(\frac{46.17}{6})^2}{6-1} + \frac{(\frac{28.20}{9})^2}{9-1}} = 8.97$$

Test Equal Variances

$$F = \frac{s_{Y1}^2}{s_{Y2}^2} = \frac{46.17}{28.20} = 1.6374$$

$9-1=8$ denominator degrees of freedom, the associated p-value for this F-statistic is 0.51.[3] Thus, we fail to reject the null hypothesis that the variances are the same in the two groups.

The t-test assuming equal variances has a t-statistic of -1.26 with 13 degrees of freedom. The resulting p-values is 0.23, so we fail to reject the null hypothesis that the mean number of words spoken is the same for two-year-old boys and girls.[4]

The t-test allowing unequal variances gives a similar result. The t-statistic is -1.20 with 8.97 degrees of freedom (based on Satterthwaite's formula). The resulting p-value is 0.26, so we again fail to reject the null hypothesis that the mean is the same among two-year-old boys and girls.[5]

NSFH Example

We now turn to a real example, using the NSFH data. SAS and Stata both have `ttest` commands that allow us to request the two-sample t-test (see Display A.7.1). In its default output, SAS provides calculations based on both of the formulas, assuming equal and allowing unequal variances, as well as the F-test of the equality of variances.

Note however that SAS calculates $F = \dfrac{s_{Y1}^2}{s_{Y2}^2}$ by placing the larger of the two variances in the numerator. Thus, if Group 1 has the smaller variance, then the SAS F-statistic will be equal to the inverse of the Stata F-statistic ($F_{Stata} = \dfrac{1}{F_{SAS}}$ in this case, for example $2 = \dfrac{1}{0.5}$). The degrees of freedom are likewise reversed in this case, thus the numerator degrees of freedom in Stata become the denominator degrees of freedom in SAS, and vice versa.

In Stata, the t-test assuming equal variances is shown by default. The t-test allowing unequal variances can be requested with an option (`, unequal`) and a separate `sdtest` command tests the equality of the variances.

Display B.7.1 shows our use of these commands to test whether men and women in our NSFH distance example live a similar average distance from their mothers. In SAS, the command is `proc ttest; class M2DP01; var g1miles; run;` where the categorical variable for gender (*M2DP01*) is listed in the `class` statement and the continuous variable for distance (*g1miles*) is listed in the `var` statement. In Stata, we first request the default t-test assuming equal variances using `ttest g1miles, by(M2DP01)`. We next test for the equivalence of variances using `sdtest g1miles, by(M2DP01)`. Finally, we request the t-test allowing unequal variances with `ttest g1miles, by(M2DP01) unequal`.

■ Box 7.6

To simplify the examples in this chapter, we have further restricted the analytic sample for the NSFH distance example to cases in which the adult respondent has fewer than five brothers and fewer than five sisters. This is a simple way to address the fact that while most respondents have four or fewer siblings of each gender, a few reported nearly two dozen. We will consider other ways to deal with these skewed distributions in later chapters.

Men are listed first in the SAS and Stata output tables because they are coded with a lower value than women in the NSFH data set (with a *1* versus a *2*). The *t*-test will give the same results regardless of which group is listed first. The only difference will be on the sign of the difference and the sign of the *t*-value (i.e., $\bar{Y}_{woman} - \bar{Y}_{men} = 264.9 - 319.9 = -55$ with $t\frac{-55-0}{16.98} = -3.24$ when we assume equal variances).

Because of the volume of output shown, we circled the values of interest to us. Both SAS and Stata provide the point estimates of the subgroup means, and we see that men live an average distance of 320 miles from their mothers whereas women live an average of 265 miles from their mothers, a difference of about 55 miles. The *t*-value based on the assumption of equal variances is 3.24 with a *p*-value of 0.0012; and, the *t*-value based on allowing unequal variances is 3.17 with a *p*-value of 0.0015. Because both *p*-values are smaller than 0.05 we can reject the null hypothesis that the means are equal in favor of the alternative hypothesis that the means differ. That is, the difference between men and women in distance from mothers is significantly different from zero. The results of the *F*-test also show that we can reject the null hypothesis that the variances are equal (*F*-value of 1.25 with a *p*-value less than 0.0001). Thus, some would use this as evidence to report the *t*-test allowing unequal variances.

As noted, the SAS and Stata output contain some results that we will not consider in detail. The Stata output shows three *p*-values listed under three different alternative hypotheses. The alternative hypothesis in the middle is the one we are using (that the difference between the means is not equal to zero). The alternative hypothesis on the left indicates that the difference between the means is less than zero (Ha: diff < 0) and the alternative hypothesis on the right indicates that the difference between the means is greater than zero (Ha: diff > 0). As noted in Chapter 6, these two alternative hypotheses are called directional, one-sided, or one-tailed and we will discuss them in detail in Chapter 8.

We will also discuss in Chapter 8 the confidence intervals shown in the SAS and Stata output. Like the confidence intervals introduced in Chapter 7, these confidence intervals are formed by adding and subtracting a multiple of the estimated standard error from the point estimate.

In our NSFH example, for a 95% confidence interval of the difference in means with our large sample size, $t_{\alpha/2} = 1.96$ and we have the following when we assume equal variances:

$$54.9727 \pm 1.96 \times 16.9797 = (21.69, 88.25)$$

And the following when we allow for unequal variances:

$$54.9727 \pm 1.96 \times 17.3295 = (21.01, 88.94)$$

As was true in Chapter 7, the confidence interval approach leads to the same conclusion as a two-tailed hypothesis test of the same null hypothesis with the same alpha level. In our case, the hypothesized value of zero does not fall within the 95% confidence interval so we can reject the null hypothesis. The confidence interval approach again has the advantage of highlighting that the difference in means is estimated with error (since we have estimated the difference in the population using a single sample; other samples would give somewhat different results, and the expected variability across samples is captured in the standard error). In our case, we estimate that the difference in distance adult men and women live from their mother ranges anywhere between about 20 and 90 miles (rather than exactly 55 as based on the point estimate of the difference).

7.2.2: One-Way Analysis of Variance

When our categorical variable has more than two groups, we utilize **one-way analysis of variance** (also known as **ANOVA**) to test the null hypothesis that the mean is the same across subgroups versus the alternative that at least two groups' means differ.

To write the formula for this test, we will use the symbol, $\bar{Y}_g$, to refer to the **within-group** (i.e., **subgroup) mean**, where g indicates each group from $g=1$ to $g=G$ with G representing the total number of groups. We will now call $\bar{Y}$ the **overall mean** (sometimes referred to as **grand mean**). Recall that the numerator of our formula for the standard deviation (Equation 5.2) is: $\Sigma_{i=1}^{n}(Y_i-\bar{Y})^2$. Imagine now that instead of looking at how the individual values of Y deviate from the overall mean, we consider how the individual values of Y deviate from the mean within their subgroup (e.g., if we were considering incomes of non-Hispanic Blacks, non-Hispanic Whites, and Hispanics we would consider each person's income relative to the mean income in their racial-ethnic group). We can write this symbolically as: $\Sigma_{i=1}^{n}(Y_i-\bar{Y}_g)^2$. This is referred to as the sum of squared deviations "Within Groups" (or sometimes just the "Within Sum of Squares" or "Sum of Squares Within").

Let's return to the original term $\Sigma_{i=1}^{n}(Y_i-\bar{Y})^2$ from our equation for the standard deviation again. Now imagine that instead of looking at how the individual values of Y deviate from the overall mean, we consider how the subgroup means deviate from the overall mean (e.g., if we were considering incomes of non-Hispanic Blacks, non-Hispanic Whites, and Hispanics we would consider the mean income of each racial-ethnic group relative to the overall mean). We can write this symbolically as: $\Sigma_{i=1}^{n}(Y_g-\bar{Y})^2$ or equivalently $\Sigma_{g=1}^{G}n_g(Y_g-\bar{Y})^2$. This is referred to as the sum of squared deviations "Between Groups" (or sometimes just the "Between Sum of Squares" or "Sum of Squares Between").[6]

We can then write the F-value to test the null hypothesis that the means are equivalent across the two or more groups against the alternative that at least two group means differ as follows (Wackerly, Mendenhall, and Scheaffer 2008; see also StataCorp 2009a: 1287):

$$F = \cfrac{\left[\cfrac{\sum_{i=1}^{n}(\bar{Y}_g - \bar{Y})^2}{(G-1)}\right]}{\left[\cfrac{\sum_{i=1}^{n}(Y_i - \bar{Y}_g)^2}{n-G}\right]} = \cfrac{\left[\cfrac{\sum_{g=1}^{G}n_g(\bar{Y}_g - \bar{Y})^2}{(G-1)}\right]}{\left[\cfrac{\sum_{i=1}^{n}(Y_i - \bar{Y}_g)^2}{n-G}\right]} \qquad (7.8)$$

Where again G stands for the total number of groups. This F-statistic has G-1 numerator and n-G denominator degrees of freedom. Simply put, the F-statistic for a one-way ANOVA is just the ratio of the "between" sum of squares to the "within" sum of squares, each divided by their respective degrees of freedom.

Like Equation 7.7, the F-statistic shown in Equation 7.8 assumes the variances are equal in the two (or more) groups. In fact, when the F-statistic is calculated for a group with only two categories the t-test (assuming equal variances) and F-test will give equivalent results. In this case, $F = t^2$ and the p-values will be equivalent. We will show in Chapter 10 that one-way analysis of variance, like the t-test, can be conducted in a regression context. And, we will discuss in Chapter 14 how to relax the assumption that the variances are equal across groups.

A Hypothetical Example

It is straightforward to use the example shown in Table 7.1 to illustrate the calculation of the F-statistic based on Equation 7.8. Doing so also helps us reinforce the fact that one-way analysis of variance and the two-sample t-test (assuming equal variances) produce equivalent results when a grouping variable has only two categories.

We can fill in the values needed for Equation 7.8 based on the values we already calculated in Table 7.1. In our example, $n=15$ and $G=2$. We calculated the "within" sums of squares $\Sigma_{i=1}^{n}(Y_i-\bar{Y}_g)^2$ separately for the boys and girls already in Table 7.1, when we subtracted the group mean from each value and then squared the results before summing. We just need to add together our two sums to get the sum across all 15 cases: $\Sigma_{i=1}^{n}(Y_i-\bar{Y}_g)^2 = 230.83 + 225.56 = 456.39$. The "between sum of squares" is straightforward to calculate as well, especially using the version of the formula written $\Sigma_{g=1}^{G}n_g(\bar{Y}_g-\bar{Y})^2$. The overall mean can be calculated based on the sums we already used to calculate the within-group means (i.e., adding the two subgroup sums gives the total sum). That is, $\bar{Y} = \dfrac{\Sigma_{i=1}^{n}Y_i}{n} = \dfrac{329 + 529}{6 + 9} = 57.20$. Then, for the 6 boys, the squared deviation of their group mean (54.83) from the overall mean (57.2) is: $(\bar{Y}_g - \bar{Y})^2 = (54.83 - 57.20)^2 = (-2.37)^2$ $= 5.6169$. And, for the 9 girls, the the squared deviation of their group mean (58.78) from the overall mean (57.20) is: $(\bar{Y}_g - \bar{Y})^2 = (58.78 - 57.20)^2 = (1.58)^2 = 2.4964$. Since there are six boys and nine girls in the sample, $\Sigma_{i=1}^{n}(\bar{Y}_g-\bar{Y})^2 = \Sigma_{g=1}^{G}n_g(\bar{Y}_g-\bar{Y})^2 = 6 * 5.6169 + 9 * 2.4964 = 56.169$.

Plugging these results into Equation 7.8 we have:

$$F = \frac{\left[\dfrac{\sum_{i=1}^{n}(\bar{Y}_g - \bar{Y})^2}{(G-1)}\right]}{\left[\dfrac{\sum_{i=1}^{n}(Y_i - \bar{Y}_g)^2}{n-G}\right]} = \frac{\left[\dfrac{\sum_{g=1}^{G}n_g(\bar{Y}_g - \bar{Y})^2}{(G-1)}\right]}{\left[\dfrac{\sum_{i=1}^{n}(Y_i - \bar{Y}_g)^2}{n-G}\right]} = \frac{\dfrac{56.169}{(2-1)}}{\dfrac{456.39}{15-2}} = 1.60$$

This F-statistic follows the F-distribution with $2-1=1$ numerator and $15-2=13$ denominator degrees of freedom. The p-value associated with the calculated F-statistic of 1.60 is 0.23, thus we fail to reject the null hypothesis that the means differ in the two groups.[7]

As expected, these results match the results of our t-test above (within rounding error due to our hand calculations). Specifically, $t^2 = (1.26)^2 = 1.59$ and the p-value is 0.23 in both cases.

NSFH Examples

SAS and Stata both have commands that allow us to readily conduct one-way analysis of variance. In Stata, the command is simply `oneway` followed by the continuous variable and then the categorical variable. In SAS, the command is `proc ANOVA`, the categorical (classification) variable is indicated in a `class` statement, and the continuous variable is indicated in a `model` statement (see Display A.7.1).

Display B.7.2 and B.7.3 shows these commands implemented with our NSFH distance example, with *g1miles* as a continuous variable and gender (*M2DP01*; Display B.7.2) or number of sisters (*g2numsis*; Display B.7.3) as categorical variables. The results in Display B.7.2 further reinforce the fact that one-way analysis of variance and the two-sample t-test produce the same result for testing the null hypothesis that the means are equivalent in two groups. Display B.7.2 shows the results of requesting a one-way analysis of variance to examine whether the means of distance from the mother are the same or different for men and women, the same null and alternative hypothesis that we examined in Display B.7.1. As expected, the results are consistent. The t-statistic (assuming equal variances) in Display B.7.1 was 3.2376. This value squared equals the F-statistic shown in Display B.7.2 of 10.48 (i.e., $3.2376 * 3.2376 = 10.482054$). And, in both Display B.7.1 and B.7.2 the p-value is 0.0012.

Display B.7.3 shows that one-way analysis of variance can also be used to test hypotheses about whether means differs across the groups of a variable with more than two categories. In our case, we examine whether adults with different numbers of sisters varied in the distance they lived from their mother.[8] The results in Display B.7.3 provide an F-value of 2.57 with a p-value of 0.0363. Given the p-value is less than 0.05, we can reject the null hypothesis that the distance from the mother is the same for adults with different numbers of sisters.

In a paper, we would likely not only report this F-statistic, but also show the subgroup means (as was done in Literature Excerpts 7.1 and 7.2 for two groups; in our NSFH distance example, we would expand to five columns of subgroup means for the categories of zero to four sisters). SAS's `proc means` command and Stata's `summarize` command allow us to calculate such subgroup means. In SAS, we add a `class` statement to the `proc means` command that lists our categorical (classification) variable (in our case `class g2numsis;`). In Stata, we add the `bysort <categorical variable>:` option before our summarize command (in our case, `bysort g2numsis: summarize g1miles`). The results, also shown in Display B.7.3, reveal that the average distance from the mother varies from a low of 257 for adults with two sisters to a high of 332 for adults with three sisters, although there is no clear linear progression (from low to high or high to low distance as number of sisters increases). The ANOVA results tell us that the means differ among adults with different numbers of sisters but we cannot tell just from the ANOVA results which subgroup means, specifically, differ (e.g., does the mean of 257 for adults with two sisters differ significantly from them mean of 268 for adults with no sisters?). We will examine this association further in Part 3, where we show how to test the significance of differences in means between each pair of categories for such a multi-category variable and to test for the linearity of the associations.

7.3: TWO CATEGORICAL VARIABLES

When both variables are categorical, the t-test is not strictly appropriate (since we would need to calculate the mean of one of the categorical variables). Instead, social scientists commonly rely on the **Pearson Chi-Square** test to examine whether the distribution of one categorical variable varies depending on the levels of another categorical variable.

7.3.1: Cross-tabulation of Two Categorical Variables

We already used the cross-tabulation in Chapter 4 to help us verify that a created variable's values were distributed as expected in relation to an original variable's values. We will now use the cross-tabulation to examine more substantively interesting associations. Before we define the statistical test of association between two categorical variables, it is useful to first examine the cross-tabulation between the two variables in more detail and define some of its values.

The table below shows the cross-tabulation of two categorical variables. To make the concepts less abstract, we imagine that we have a sample of preschoolers of three different race-ethnicities (shown in the columns) who spend time in four different types of child care (shown in the rows). Rather than having just the single value n denoting the entire sample size, we now use subscripts on n to denote the number of cases that fall within each cell formed by the intersection of a row group and column type. The first value in the subscript is the row number; and, the second value in the subscript is the column number. For example, n_{11} denotes the number of cases that are from row 1 (center child care) and column 1 (Hispanic race-ethnicity). Similarly, n_{32} denotes the number of cases that use relative child care (row 3) and are of non-Hispanic Black race-ethnicity (column 2).

Hypothetical cross-tabulation of preschoolers' race-ethnicity and type of child care

| Type of Child Care | Race-Ethnicity | | | Row Total |
	Hispanic	Non-Hispanic Black	Non-Hispanic White	
Center	n_{11}	n_{12}	n_{13}	$n_{1.}$
Family Day Care	n_{21}	n_{22}	n_{23}	$n_{2.}$
Relative Care	n_{31}	n_{32}	n_{33}	$n_{3.}$
Nanny Care	n_{41}	n_{42}	n_{43}	$n_{4.}$
Column Total	$n_{.1}$	$n_{.2}$	$n_{.3}$	$n_{..}$

When a value is aggregated across all columns or across all rows we replace the column or row value in the subscript with a dot. Thus, $n_{.2}$ is the total number of cases of non-Hispanic Black race-ethnicity, aggregated across all types of child care. In our example, $n_{.2} = n_{12} + n_{22} + n_{32} + n_{42}$. Similarly, $n_{4.}$ represents the total number of cases who use nanny child care aggregated across all race-ethnicities. In our example, $n_{4.} = n_{41} + n_{42} + n_{43}$. The total sample size can be similarly represented with two dots $n_{..}$ (rather than just n) reflecting the fact that it is aggregated across both rows and columns (i.e., across all child care types and across all race-ethnicities).

When we first examined the percentage distribution in Chapter 5 for a single variable, the desired calculation was clear (the frequency in each of the variable's categories divided by the total sample size and multiplied by 100). But, when two variables are cross-tabulated, we can now calculate three types of percentages: **row percentages, column percentages** and/or **cell percentages**. We want to be careful that we know which are being presented by our statistical software (so we choose the desired values) and which makes sense to present in our manuscripts to reflect our research questions or hypotheses. In our example, the column percentages are the values commonly presented in tables such as those we examined in Literature Excerpts 7.1 and 7.2, since we are interested in how the distribution of several variables (shown in the rows) depends on the race-ethnicity (shown in the columns).

More specifically, the row percentage is the cell frequency divided by the row total and multiplied by 100. For example, in the first cell, the row percentage would be $\frac{n_{11}}{n_{1.}}*100$. Row percentages sum to 100 across the columns (e.g., in our case, $\frac{n_{11}}{n_{1.}}*100 + \frac{n_{12}}{n_{1.}}*100 + \frac{n_{13}}{n_{1.}}*100 = 100$). The column percentage is the cell frequency divided by the column total and multiplied by 100. For example, in the first cell, the column percentage would be $\frac{n_{11}}{n_{.1}}*100$. Column percentages sum to 100 down the rows (e.g., in our case, $\frac{n_{11}}{n_{.1}}*100 + \frac{n_{21}}{n_{.1}}*100 + \frac{n_{31}}{n_{.1}}*100 + \frac{n_{41}}{n_{.1}}*100 = 100$). The cell percentage is the cell frequency divided by the total sample size and multiplied by 100. For example, in the first cell, the cell percentage would be $\frac{n_{11}}{n_{..}}*100$. The cell percentages add to 100 across all cells.

The row and column totals are often referred to as the **marginal distributions**, whereas the distributions within columns or within rows are referred to as **conditional distributions** (conditional on a value of the other variable). In fact, if there are no missing cases on either variable, the marginal distributions will match the results we get from a one-way tabulation. The conditional distributions provide new information, and allow us to evaluate whether the percentage distribution of one variable differs depending on the level of another variable. If the differences are large enough, we can see them visually with the column and row percentages. We will show how to test the statistical significance of these differences more formally with the Pearson chi-square in the next section.

A Hypothetical Example

Table 7.2 provides a hypothetical example of the values of two categorical variables, the first with three groups and the second with two types.

▪ **Table 7.2   Values of Urbanicity and Gender in a Hypothetical Sample of 40 Cases**

Case	Urbanicity	Gender	Cell	Case	Urbanicity	Gender	Cell
1	Rural	Female	Rural-Female	21	Rural	Female	Rural-Female
2	Suburban	Female	Suburban-Female	22	Rural	Female	Rural-Female
3	Urban	Male	Urban-Male	23	Rural	Male	Rural-Male
4	Rural	Male	Rural-Male	24	Rural	Male	Rural-Male
5	Suburban	Male	Suburban-Male	25	Urban	Female	Urban-Female
6	Urban	Female	Urban-Female	26	Suburban	Male	Suburban-Male
7	Urban	Female	Urban-Female	27	Urban	Male	Urban-Male
8	Suburban	Female	Suburban-Female	28	Urban	Male	Urban-Male
9	Rural	Female	Rural-Female	29	Urban	Male	Urban-Male
10	Suburban	Female	Suburban-Female	30	Suburban	Female	Suburban-Female
11	Urban	Female	Urban-Female	31	Rural	Male	Rural-Male
12	Rural	Female	Rural-Female	32	Urban	Female	Urban-Female
13	Suburban	Male	Suburban-Male	33	Rural	Male	Rural-Male
14	Rural	Female	Rural-Female	34	Suburban	Male	Suburban-Male
15	Rural	Female	Rural-Female	35	Suburban	Female	Suburban-Female
16	Suburban	Female	Suburban-Female	36	Urban	Female	Urban-Female
17	Suburban	Male	Suburban-Male	37	Suburban	Male	Suburban-Male
18	Urban	Female	Urban-Female	38	Suburban	Female	Suburban-Female
19	Urban	Male	Urban-Male	39	Rural	Female	Rural-Female
20	Urban	Female	Urban-Female	40	Rural	Male	Rural-Male

We include in the table a column labeled cell in which we indicate the row-column combination for each case. This helps us tally up the number that fall in each cell, as shown in the next table.

	Gender	
Urbanicity	Male	Female
Urban	╫╫	╫╫ |||
Suburban	╫╫		╫╫ ||
Rural	╫╫		╫╫ |||

Note: ╫╫ represents a tally of five.

And, the table on the next page translates the tallies into numbers (i.e., the observed frequency in each cell).

■ Table 7.3: Observed cell frequencies

Urbanicity	Gender		Total
	Male	Female	
Urban	$n_{11} = 5$	$n_{12} = 8$	$n_{1.} = 13$
Suburban	$n_{21} = 6$	$n_{22} = 7$	$n_{2.} = 13$
Rural	$n_{31} = 6$	$n_{32} = 8$	$n_{3.} = 14$
Total	$n_{.1} = 17$	$n_{.2} = 23$	$n_{..} = 40$

Finally, the next table shows shows the row, column, and cell percentages (in that order) along with the frequency.

		Gender		
		Male	Female	Row Total
Urbanicity	Urban	5	8	13
		38.46	61.54	100.00
		29.41	34.78	32.50
		12.50	20.00	32.50
	Suburban	6	7	13
		46.15	53.85	100.00
		35.29	30.43	32.50
		15.00	17.50	32.50
	Rural	6	8	14
		42.86	57.14	100.00
		35.29	34.78	35.00
		15.00	20.00	35.00
	Column Total	17	23	40
		42.50	57.50	100.00
		100.00	100.00	100.00
		42.50	57.50	100.00

Focusing on the first cell, we can verify the calculations that we defined above. For example, in the first cell, the row percentage is $\frac{n_{11}}{n_{1.}} * 100 = \frac{5}{13} * 100 = 38.46$. We can also verify that $38.46 + 61.54 = 100$ as shown by the 100 listed for the second value in the top row of the final column. The column percentage in the first cell is $\frac{n_{11}}{n_{.1}} * 100 = \frac{5}{17} * 100 = 29.41$. We can verify that $29.41 + 35.29 + 35.29 = 100$ as shown by the 100 listed for the third value in the last row of the first column. Finally, the cell percentage in the first cell is $\frac{n_{11}}{n_{1..}} * 100 = \frac{5}{40} * 100 = 12.50$; and, the cell percentages sum to 100 across all cells, $12.50 + 20.00 + 15.00 + 17.50 + 15.00 + 20.00 = 100$.

Notice that the interpretation of each type of percentage is different, so again we want to be careful to pick the desired type for our application. The row percentage in the first cell is interpreted as: Among urban residents, about 38% are male. The column percentage in the first cell is interpreted as: Among men, about 29% live in urban areas. The cell percentage in the first cell is interpreted as: Among all cases, about 12.5% are men who live in urban areas.

Often, in a paper we would follow a process similar to that shown in the Literature Excerpts 7.1 and 7.2, using the categorical variable of substantive interest in our research questions as the column variable (gender in our current example; race-ethnicity in the Furdyna and colleagues paper; gender in the Oldehinkel and colleagues paper) and using each of our other variables as the row variable in successive two-way cross-tabulations, and showing column percentages.

NSFH Example

Display B.7.4 cross-tabulates the respondent's number of brothers and sisters in the NSFH distance example. We use the `proc freq` command and `tabulate` command that we introduced in Chapter 4 (see again Display A.4) but we now use options in Stata to request the row, column, and cell percentages (, `row column cell` ; see Display A.7.1).

A few preliminary comments are in order. First, recall again that we excluded cases with five or more brothers or five or more sisters from the cross-tabulation in this chapter to simplify the presentation (particularly important in this instance, since cross-tabulations with a dozen or more values on each variable become difficult to digest). Second, notice that both SAS and Stata put the values of the variable that we list first in the command into the rows (in our case *g2numbro*) and put the values of the variable that we list second in the command into the columns (in our case *g2numsis*). This is useful to remember because often tables in manuscripts are structured like Literature Excerpts 7.1 and 7.2 with the categorical variable of focus listed in the columns (so it should be the second variable in our SAS and Stata commands). If neither variable is of focus, then it is best to put the variable with fewer categories second in the command (because it is easier to read the SAS and Stata output with more rows and fewer columns than vice-versa). Third, notice that SAS and Stata both provide a key to help us interpret the percentages (circled in Display B.7.4). Importantly, the order differs between SAS and Stata (SAS puts the cell percentage second, below the frequency, whereas Stata lists it last).

We will begin by interpreting the values in the first cell. Here, the row percentage is 55.39. Thus, among adults who have no brothers, just over half have no sisters. Similarly, the column percentage is 53.69. Thus, among adults who have no sisters, about half have no brothers. The cell percentage is 19.61%. Thus, almost one-fifth of all adults have no brothers and no sisters. Taking a different example, we have circled the cell where the row of two brothers intersects with the column of four sisters. Here, we see that the row percentage is 5.67%. Thus, among adults who have two brothers, about 6% have four sisters. On the other hand, the column percentage is 24.44%. Thus, among adults who have four sisters, almost one-quarter have two brothers. Finally, the cell percentage is 1.12. Thus, just 1% of adults have two brothers and four sisters.

7.3.2: Pearson Chi-square Test

With the basic values defined above, it is straightforward to show how to test for statistically significant associations between the two variables using the Pearson chi-square (Agresti and Finlay 1999: 254; SAS 2008b: 1732–1733; StataCorp 2009a: 1894).

The null hypothesis for the Pearson chi-square test is that the two categorical variables are statistically independent of each other (we review this construct below). The alternative is that they are statistically associated with each other.

H_o The two variables are statistically independent.
H_a The two variables are statistically associated.

The test is constructed based on the difference between the observed number of cases in each cell and the number of cases we would expect to be in each cell if the two variables were indeed statistically independent of each other. To calculate the expected frequency in each cell, we start by defining the row and column frequencies more generally, with i indicating any of the I rows and j indicating any of the J columns. Then:

$$n_{i.} = \sum\nolimits_{j=1}^{J} n_{ij}$$

$$n_{.j} = \sum\nolimits_{i=1}^{I} n_{ij}$$

We then use these values to calculate the expected frequency in the cell:

$$f_e = \frac{n_{i.} * n_{.j}}{n_{..}}$$

This expected cell count is based on the basic probability theorem that the joint probability of two independent events is the product of their individual probabilities (Wackerly, Mendenhall, and Scheaffer 2008). Recall that this is often written with symbols as follows: $P(A \cap B) = P(A)P(B)$ if A and B are independent. If two events are not independent, then we write their joint probability as follows: $P(A \cap B) = P(A)P(B|A) = P(B)P(A|B)$. The vertical bar is read "given" thus we can read $P(B|A)$ as "the probability of B given A" and we can read $P(A|B)$ as "the probability of A given B". If two events are independent then the probability of one occurring does not differ depending on whether the other occurred. That is, if two events are independent then $P(B|A)$ is always the same, $P(B)$ and $P(A|B)$ is always the same, $P(A)$. If the two events are not independent, then the probability of one event depends on the other event (here $P(B|A)$ is not always the same and $P(A|B)$ is not always the same).

In our cross-tabulation, each cell can be thought of as an intersection of two events (in this case, one category of each variable). The individual probabilities, P(A) and P(B), are estimated with the marginal proportion of cases in each category: $\frac{n_{i.}}{n}$ and $\frac{n_{.j}}{n}$. We multiply these together to get the joint probability $\frac{n_{i.}}{n} * \frac{n_{.j}}{n} = \frac{n_{i.} * n_{.j}}{n * n}$ assuming independence. Because we are interested in the expected count for the chi-square, rather than the expected proportion, we multiply this value by n giving: $n * \dfrac{n_{i.} * n_{.j}}{n * n}$. One of the n's then cancels out of the numerator and denominator, and

we are left with: $\cancel{n} * \dfrac{n_{i.} * n_{.j}}{\cancel{n} * n} = \dfrac{n_{i.} * n_{.j}}{n}$.

Because of the way the expected frequencies are defined, the column and row percentage distributions based on the *expected* frequencies will be the same for the conditional distributions as in the marginal distribution. This reflects the definition of independence. If the probability of one variable—say number of sisters—does not depend on the level of another variable—say number of brothers—then the distribution of the percentage of sisters for people with no, one, two, three, or four brothers should be the same as the overall distribution of the percentage of sisters. In other words, the probability of having each number of sisters should not depend on the number of brothers, under independence. The same would be true for the conditional distribution of number of brothers within levels of number of sisters (these should be the same as the marginal distribution of number of brothers if the two variables are independent). In contrast, the conditional distributions based on the *observed* cell frequencies may differ from the marginal distributions, to the extent that the two variables are not actually independent. The Pearson chi-square tests whether the differences between the observed and expected frequencies are large enough to conclude that the two variables are not independent.

Specifically, the chi-square value is calculated for each case by subtracting this expected frequency (f_e) from the observed frequency (f_o), squaring the result, and dividing by the expected cell frequency. The resulting values are then summed across all cells (all rows and columns).

$$\chi^2 = \sum_{j=1}^{J} \sum_{i=1}^{I} \frac{(f_0 - f_e)^2}{f_e} \tag{7.9}$$

Examining the basic structure of this formula, we see that the chi-square value captures the degree to which the observed cell frequencies differ from the expected cell frequencies. If all observed cell frequencies match their expected cell frequencies then $(f_o - f_e)$ would be zero for each cell, their sum in the numerator would be zero, and thus the chi-squared value would be zero. But, to the extent that the observed cell frequencies differ from the expected cell frequencies the numerator will become larger. This will happen regardless of whether the observed value is smaller or larger than expected, since the difference is squared in the numerator.

The resulting χ^2 values from Equation 7.9 follow a chi-square distribution with $(r - 1) * (c - 1)$ degrees of freedom, where r is the number of rows and c is the number of columns, allowing for the calculation of a p-value (the probability of larger values than our calculated value).[9] If the p-value is less than 0.05 then we can reject the null hypothesis that the two variables are independent.

A Hypothetical Example

We return to the hypothetical example we used in Section 7.3.1 to demonstrate the calculation of row, column, and cell percentages to now test the independence of the two variables. Our hypothetical example is small, and it is worth noting that the chi-square test is not recommended when the expected count in one or more cells is small; usually a minimum expected cell count of five in every cell is recommended. We have designed the example to meet this minimum. And, we show in the NSFH example next how to ask SAS and Stata to show the expected cell counts so that you can verify that the criteria is met in an application as well.[10]

The following table shows how to first calculate the expected count in each cell, using the formula $f_e = \dfrac{n_{i.} * n_{.j}}{n_{..}}$. For example, in the first cell, the row count ($n_{i.}$) is 13, the column count ($n_{.j}$) is 17, and our total sample size (n) is 40; thus, $f_e = \dfrac{13*17}{40} = 5.525$.

■ **Table 7.4 Expected Cell Frequencies**

		Type		Observed Total
		One	Two	
Group	One	$\dfrac{13*17}{40} = 5.525$	$\dfrac{13*23}{40} = 7.745$	13
	Two	$\dfrac{13*17}{40} = 5.525$	$\dfrac{13*23}{40} = 7.475$	13
	Three	$\dfrac{14*17}{40} = 5.95$	$\dfrac{14*23}{40} = 8.05$	14
	Observed Total	17	23	40

We next calculate the cell values we will sum to calculate the chi-square ($\dfrac{(f_0 - f_e)^2}{f_e}$). In each cell, we subtract the expected cell frequency from Table 7.4 from the observed cell frequency in Table 7.3, square the result, and divide by the expected cell count.

		Type	
		One	Two
Group	One	$\dfrac{(5-5.525)^2}{5.525} = 0.0499$	$\dfrac{(8-7.475)^2}{7.475} = 0.0369$
	Two	$\dfrac{(6-5.525)^2}{5.525} = 0.0408$	$\dfrac{(7-7.475)^2}{7.475} = 0.0302$
	Three	$\dfrac{(6-5.95)^2}{5.95} = 0.0004$	$\dfrac{(8-8.05)^2}{8.05} = 0.0003$

Summing these values across the cells gives the Pearson chi-square value:

$\chi^2 = 0.0499 + 0.0408 + 0.0004 + 0.0369 + 0.0302 + 0.0003 = 0.1585.$

This value follows a chi-square distribution with $(r - 1) * (c - 1) = (3 - 1) * (2 - 1) = 2 * 1 = 2$ degrees of freedom. The p-value for a chi-square of 0.1585 with 2 degrees of freedom is 0.924.[11]

Because this *p*-value is larger than an alpha of .05, we fail to reject the null hypothesis that the two variables are independent.

NSFH Example

In SAS and Stata we again use the `proc freq` and `tabulate` commands to request the Pearson chi-square, now with the `chisq` and `chi2` options respectively (see Display A.7.1). We now use the `expected` option in each software package to show the expected cell count. And, we use the `nocol norow` and `nopercent` options in SAS to omit the row, column, and cell percentages, in order to reduce the volume of output and focus on the values essential to the calculation of the chi-square.

Display B.7.5 shows our use of these commands to request the chi-square statistic to test the null hypothesis that the number of brothers and number of sisters an adult has are independent. The Pearson chi-square is 628.3557 with 16 degrees of freedom since $(5 - 1) * (5 - 1) = 4 * 4 = 16$.[12] The *p*-value is listed as <0.0001. Because the *p*-value is less than an alpha of .05, we can reject the null hypothesis that the two variables are independent and conclude that they are associated.

Looking at the cross-tabulation in Display B.7.5 we can compare the observed to expected frequencies (and verify that no expected counts are below 5; in fact the smallest is 12.8 for the cell comprising four brothers and four sisters). It is not surprising that families which have more sons also have more daughters, and this association is reflected in the difference between the observed and expected counts. The observed counts are higher than the expected counts "on the diagonal" in the cells with the same number of brothers as sisters. For example, whereas if the variables were independent we would expect 762.4 cases in the cell with zero brothers and zero sisters, we instead see nearly 50% more than that amount of cases, at 1,156. In contrast, as we move farther from the diagonal, there are fewer cases observed than expected. For example, if the variables were independent, we would expect to see 425.2 cases with two brothers and no sisters. But, we observe just 297 cases in this cell.

7.4: TWO INTERVAL VARIABLES

As we discussed in reviewing the Literature Excerpts, it is uncommon to show an entire correlation matrix of all of the analytic variables used in a study in contemporary journal articles. But, correlations are often reported selectively in papers, either in smaller tables with some of the variables or in the text. The correlation coefficient is also important because we will draw on the correlation and its formula as we discuss how to interpret our regression results in future chapters.

7.4.1: Pearson Correlation

The **Pearson correlation** measures the degree of linear association between two interval variables. Although other types of correlations are available (see Chen and Popovich 2002), the Pearson correlation is so commonly used in the social sciences that, as we saw in Literature Excerpt 7.4, when correlations are reported without adjective, Pearson correlations are assumed. The Pearson correlation is useful for comparing the strength of association across sets of variables because its values are always bounded between -1 and 1. This allows social scientists to assess whether a correlation is larger than the typical size of associations in their subfield of work. As we discuss in Chapter 8, general benchmarks also exist for assessing the size of correlations as "big" or "small".

The Pearson correlation statistic is an estimate of a population correlation coefficient, which divides the covariation between two variables, say Y and X, by the standard deviation of each of those variables. The population correlation coefficient is commonly depicted with the Greek letter "rho" denoted ρ. In symbols it is written as follows:

$$\rho = \frac{cov(Y,X)}{\sigma_Y \sigma_X} \tag{7.10}$$

The sample estimate of the correlation coefficient is formed by substituting the sample estimate for the population covariance of Y and X and for the sample standard deviations of Y and X into Equation 7.10 (Wackerly, Mendenhall, and Scheaffer 2008; see also SAS 2010a: 19; StataCorp 2009a: 329):

$$r = \frac{\dfrac{\sum_{i=1}^{n}(Y_i - \bar{Y})(X_i - \bar{X})}{n-1}}{\sqrt{\dfrac{\sum_{i=1}^{n}(Y_i - \bar{Y})^2}{n-1}}\sqrt{\dfrac{\sum_{i=1}^{n}(X_i - \bar{X})^2}{n-1}}}$$

Because $\dfrac{1}{n-1}$ appears in the numerator and $\sqrt{\dfrac{1}{n-1}} * \sqrt{\dfrac{1}{n-1}}$ appears in the denominator, we can cancel out these terms, and the correlation formula reduces to:

$$r = \frac{\sum_{i=1}^{n}(Y_i - \bar{Y})(X_i - \bar{X})}{\sqrt{\sum_{i=1}^{n}(Y_i - \bar{Y})^2}\sqrt{\sum_{i=1}^{n}(X_i - \bar{X})^2}} \tag{7.11}$$

Examining this formula, we can see that the numerator should be larger to the extent that the two variables, Y and X, tend to fall on the same side of their respective means for each case. For example, if $Y_i - \bar{Y}$ and $X_i - \bar{X}$ are both large and positive for a case; or, if $Y_i - \bar{Y}$ and $X_i - \bar{X}$ are both large and negative for a case, then their product will be large and positive and will add a larger positive value to the sum in the numerator. On the other hand, if the deviations are of the same sign, but one is large and the other is small, then the contribution to the sum will be relatively small. As noted above, correlations can be negative in sign. This can occur if consistently across cases when one deviation (say $Y_i - \bar{Y}$) is positive then the other ($X_i - \bar{X}$) is negative. On the other hand, if large positive cross-products are balanced off by large negative cross-products, then the overall correlation will be small.

This sum of the cross-products of the deviations are divided by each variable's standard deviation, thus assuring that the correlation will fall between −1 and 1. As noted above, this facilitates comparison of correlations for a range of variables. Variables with larger standard deviations (like distance in miles or annual earnings in dollars) are put on common footing with variables with smaller standard deviations (like years of schooling or hourly wages). We will discuss this further in Chapter 8 when we consider rescaling and effect size.

It is essential to keep in mind that the Pearson correlation measures the degree of linear association between two variables. If two variables are associated with each other, but in a non-linear fashion, the Pearson correlation will understate (and may completely miss) their association. Figure 7.1 illustrates four patterns of association between two variables that we created to represent: (a) positive linear association, (b) negative linear association, (c) lack of association, and (d) non-linear association.

In Figure 7.1a the data points appear clustered around a positive sloping line. The lines show the means of Y and X, helping us to see that when X falls below the mean, Y also seems more likely to fall below its mean. And, when X falls above its mean, Y seems more likely to fall above its

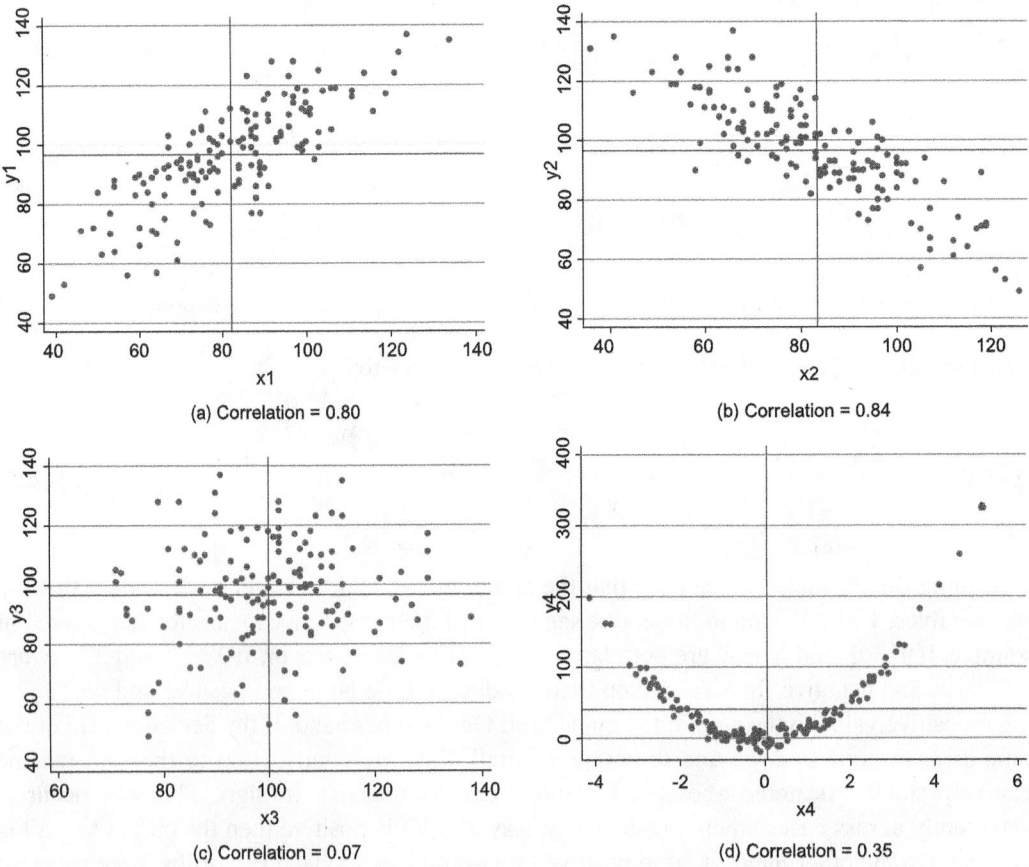

(a) Correlation = 0.80

(b) Correlation = 0.84

(c) Correlation = 0.07

(d) Correlation = 0.35

■ **Figure 7.1** Examples of Correlations for Different Patterns of Association mean. Consistent with this pattern, the correlation of these dots is large and positive, at 0.80. Figure 7.1b shows a similar pattern, but in a negative direction, with a correlation of −0.84. In contrast, Figure 7.1c looks like a scattered cloud of dots, with little association between Y and X. In this case, when X is below the mean Y appears equally likely to be above and below its mean. Consistent with this visual assessment, the correlation is small in Figure 7.1c (at 0.07). In Figure 7.1d, the dots seem tightly clustered around a U-shaped curve. The correlation is relatively modest (at 0.35), reflecting the fact that although Y and X are associated, the pattern is non-linear (when X falls slightly above its mean, Y does as well; but Y also consistently falls above its mean when X falls far below the mean). In Chapter 12 we will discuss how to use regression models to estimate non-linear associations such as those shown in Figure 7.1d.

Unlike what we will see for regression analyses, correlation does not treat one variable as the outcome and one variable as the predictor. Thus, it does not matter which variable we designate as Y and which variable we designate as X in Equation 7.11. If we reverse the designation, the result will be the same. That is:

$$r = \frac{\sum_{i=1}^{n}(Y_i - \bar{Y})(X_i - \bar{X})}{\sqrt{\sum_{i=1}^{n}(Y_i - \bar{Y})^2}\sqrt{\sum_{i=1}^{n}(X_i - \bar{X})^2}} = \frac{\sum_{i=1}^{n}(X_i - \bar{X})(Y_i - \bar{Y})}{\sqrt{\sum_{i=1}^{n}(X_i - \bar{X})^2}\sqrt{\sum_{i=1}^{n}(Y_i - \bar{Y})^2}}$$

This is why correlation matrices like the one shown in Literature Excerpt 7.4 show only one set of values, typically those below the diagonal. The values on the diagonal are omitted from such correlation matrices because the correlation of a variable with itself will always be one. That is, if we replace the X variable in Equation 7.11 with Y we have the following result:

$$r = \frac{\sum_{i=1}^{n}(Y_i - \bar{Y})(Y_i - \bar{Y})}{\sqrt{\sum_{i=1}^{n}(Y_i - \bar{Y})^2}\sqrt{\sum_{i=1}^{n}(Y_i - \bar{Y})^2}} = \frac{\sum_{i=1}^{n}(Y_i - \bar{Y})^2}{\sum_{i=1}^{n}(Y_i - \bar{Y})^2} = 1$$

Our null hypothesis typically is that two variables are uncorrelated in the population ($\rho = 0$) and the alternative that they are linearly related ($\rho \neq 0$). Since the alternative is nondirectional, the linear association can be either in a positive direction (if the correlation falls between 0 and 1) or a negative direction (if the correlation falls between 0 and −1).

| H_o | The two variables are uncorrelated. | $\rho = 0$ |
| H_a | The two variables are linearly related. | $\rho \neq 0$ |

These hypotheses can be evaluated with a test statistic that follows the t-distribution. Specifically, both SAS and Stata provide p-values based on the following formula (Wackerly, Mendenhall, and Scheaffer 2008; see also SAS 2010: 19; StataCorp 2009c:329):

$$t = \sqrt{n-2}\sqrt{\frac{r^2}{1-r^2}} \qquad (7.12)$$

with $n-2$ degrees of freedom.

Hypothetical Examples

Table 7.5 uses the Y variable that we examined in Table 7.1 – number of words spoken by 14 toddlers—and adds a second continuous X variable—vocabulary test scores of the mothers of those toddlers. We complete similar calculations for the mean and standard deviation of Y and X as we have used in previous examples. That is, we calculate the overall mean for each variable, each value's deviation from the mean, and these deviations squared. The sum of the deviations squared is used in the denominator of Equation 7.11. For the numerator of Equation 7.11, we also calculate the cross-product of the mean deviations of the two variables for each case, and sum

■ **Table 7.5: Calculation of the Pearson correlation coefficient: Hypothetical example of number of words spoken by fourteen toddlers and their mothers' vocabulary test scores**

	Toddlers' Number of Words Spoken			Mothers' Vocabulary Test Scores			
	Words Spoken (Y_i)	Deviation from Mean $(Y_i - \bar{Y})$	Deviation from Mean Squared $(Y_i - \bar{Y})^2$	Value (X_i)	Deviation from Mean $(X_i - \bar{X})$	Deviation from Mean Squared $(X_i - \bar{X})^2$	Cross-Product of Deviations from Mean $(Y_i - \bar{Y}) \times (X_i - \bar{X})$
Case 1	44	−13.20	174.24	100	−2.47	6.08	32.56
Case 2	51	−6.20	38.44	101	−1.47	2.15	9.09
Case 3	52	−5.20	27.04	84	−18.47	341.02	96.03
Case 4	53	−4.20	17.64	96	−6.47	41.82	27.16
Case 5	53	−4.20	17.64	101	−1.47	2.15	6.16
Case 6	55	−2.20	4.84	96	−6.47	41.82	14.23
Case 7	56	−1.20	1.44	86	−16.47	271.15	19.76
Case 8	59	1.80	3.24	95	−7.47	55.75	−13.44
Case 9	59	1.80	3.24	118	15.53	241.28	27.96
Case 10	60	2.80	7.84	96	−6.47	41.82	−18.11
Case 11	60	2.80	7.84	121	18.53	343.48	51.89
Case 12	62	4.80	23.04	103	0.53	0.28	2.56
Case 13	62	4.80	23.04	122	19.53	381.55	93.76
Case 14	64	6.80	46.24	107	4.53	20.55	30.83
Case 15	68	10.80	116.64	111	8.53	72.82	92.16
Sum	858	0	512.40	1537	0	1863.73	472.60

Mean

$$\bar{Y} = \frac{\sum_{i=1}^{n} Y_i}{n} = \frac{858}{15} = 57.20 \qquad \bar{X} = \frac{\sum_{i=1}^{n} X_i}{n} = \frac{1537}{15} = 102.47$$

Correlation

$$r = \frac{\sum_{i=1}^{n}(Y_i - \bar{Y})(X_i - \bar{X})}{\sqrt{\sum_{i=1}^{n}(Y_i - \bar{Y})^2}\sqrt{\sum_{i=1}^{n}(X_i - \bar{X})^2}} = \frac{472.60}{\sqrt{512.40} * \sqrt{1863.73}} = 0.4836$$

Test statistic

$$t = \sqrt{n-2}\sqrt{\frac{r^2}{1-r^2}} = \sqrt{15-2}\sqrt{\frac{0.4836^2}{1-0.4836^2}} = 1.99$$

these cross-products across all cases. Plugging these values into Equation 7.11 results in a correlation of 0.4836.

This correlation is fairly sizable, falling about mid-way between the range for positive correlations of 0 and 1. We can see why this is so by examining the deviations from the mean on both toddlers' number of words spoken and mothers' vocabulary test scores for each case in Table 7.5. To facilitate this, we sorted the values in the table in ascending order of the values of the number of words spoken by the children. The first 7 cases have words spoken that fall below the mean. The next 8 cases have words spoken that fall above the mean. Looking at the deviations of mothers' vocabulary scores from its mean, we see that in all 7 of the first 7 cases (Case 1 to Case 7) the value of mothers' vocabulary test scores also falls below its mean. And, in 6 of the 8 latter cases (from Case 8 to Case 15) the value of mothers' vocabulary test scores falls above its mean. Thus, in most cases, the cross-product for the numerator is positive (due to a positive deviation on toddlers' number of words spoken multiplied by a positive deviation on mothers' vocabulary test scores or a negative deviation on toddlers' number of words spoken multiplied by a negative deviation on mothers' vocabulary test scores). Still, the largest deviation from the mean of one variable is generally paired with a more modest deviation from the mean for the other variable (e.g., Case 1, 3, 7, 9, 11, and 13); thus, the positive correlation is of moderate value, falling about mid-way between 0 and 1.

Once the correlation is calculated, we use the sample size and correlation value to calculate the test statistic based on Equation 7.12. In our case, the t-value of 1.99 with $15 - 2 = 13$ degrees of freedom has a p-value of 0.068.[13] This p-value is just above the conventional cutoff of 0.05, so we cannot reject the null hypothesis that the variables are not linearly associated.[14]

NSFH Example

The `proc corr` command in SAS and the `pwcorr` command in Stata calculate the Pearson correlation (see Display A.7.1). In Display B.7.6, we asked SAS and Stata to calculate the correlation between the adult respondent's age (*g2age*) and his or her mother's age (*g1age*). Not surprisingly, these variables are highly correlated in our analytic sample, at 0.85. The associated p-value is less than 0.0001. Since the p-value is less than an alpha of 0.05, we can reject the null hypothesis that the correlation is zero in the population, and conclude that there is evidence of a linear association between mothers' ages and the ages of their adult children.

7.5: WEIGHTED STATISTICS

We discuss in this section ways to account for the sampling weights from a complex sampling design when calculating bivariate associations. We wait until later chapters to discuss strategies to more comprehensively account for strata and clusters when testing hypotheses about bivariate associations. We do so because neither SAS nor Stata has survey commands specifically designed to calculate Pearson correlations or to calculate two-sample t-tests or ANOVAs. In Parts 3 and 4 of the book, we will introduce the survey regression commands available in both SAS and Stata that comprehensively account for sampling weights, strata and clusters; as we shall see, many of the bivariate hypothesis tests that we examined in this chapter can also be conducted in a regression context. Knowing how to use the weight options, as we discuss in this section, will be useful in situations where you only need to adjust for weighting and when you collaborate with colleagues who use these options. However, it is important to keep in mind that hypothesis tests, even about bivariate associations, should be conducted with the survey commands that we cover in Parts 3 and 4 of the book if your sample also used clustering and/or stratification.

7.5.1: Weighted Subgroup Means and Standard Deviations

As we showed above, subgroup means can be calculated with the same formula as we used for the overall mean, but applied just to the cases in the subgroup. Likewise, weights are incorporated into the formula in the same fashion as we showed in Sections 5.6.1 and 5.6.3 of Chapter 5. Again, we assume relative weights (w_i^*, which have been normalized to sum to the observed sample size, for example by dividing each unadjusted weight by the average of the unadjusted weights).[15]

	Group 1	Group 2
Subgroup Weighted Mean	$weighted \ \bar{Y}_1 = \dfrac{\sum_{i=1}^{n_1} w_i^* \times Y_i}{n_1}$	$weighted \ \bar{Y}_2 = \dfrac{\sum_{i=1}^{n_2} w_i^* \times Y_i}{n_2}$
Subgroup Weighted Standard Deviation	$weighted \ s_{Y1}^2 = \sqrt{\dfrac{\sum_{i=1}^{n_1} w_i^* \times (Y_i - weighted \ \bar{Y}_1)^2}{n_1 - 1}}$	$weighted \ s_{Y2}^2 = \sqrt{\dfrac{\sum_{i=1}^{n_2} w_i^* \times (Y_i - weighted \ \bar{Y}_2)^2}{n_2 - 1}}$

■ Box 7.8

We emphasize again that these weight options adjust only for oversampling, and not for clustering or stratification. In fact, Stata distinguishes different types of weights and only allows for one type on the summarize command (referred to by Stata as analytic weights or `aweights`) to reinforce to users that this command does not adjust for the features of complex sampling designs (including sampling weights, which are referred to in Stata as probability weights or `pweights`; Sribney 2009).

SAS and Stata both provide options to incorporate weights in many of their commands, in addition to the survey commands that we introduced in Chapter 5. In each case, we add an option (a `weight` statement in SAS; the option [aw=<weight variable>] in Stata; see Display A.7.2) to the commands that we used for the unweighted subgroup means (`proc means` in SAS and `summarize` in Stata). As we did in Chapter 5, we add the option `vardef=weight` to `proc means` in SAS and we restrict the analyses to our distance subsample.

Display B.7.7. shows the results of our using these commands with the weight option when calculating the subgroup means of the distance from the mother (*g1miles*) within numbers of sisters (*g2numsis*). Compared to the unweighted means shown in Display B.7.3 we see that the weighted subgroup means are somewhat larger than the unweighted subgroup means. For example, adults with no sisters live an average of 288 miles from their mothers based on the weighted mean and an average of 268 miles from their mothers based on the unweighted mean; adults with four sisters live an average of 315 miles from their mothers based on the weighted mean and an average of 289 miles from their mothers based on the unweighted mean. The weighted standard deviations are also somewhat larger than the unweighted standard deviations (e.g., 616 versus 601 for cases with no sisters; 677 versus 658 for cases with four sisters).

As we discussed in Chapter 5, the relative size of the weighted and unweighted means will depend on whether cases with higher or lower values on the analytic variables (here *g1miles* and *g2numsis*) tend to have larger or smaller weights. In our situation, cases with lower values of *g1miles* tend to have smaller weights (e.g., the weights average 0.88 for adults who live within one hundred miles of their mothers) and cases with higher values of *g1miles* tend to have larger weights (e.g., the weights average 1.06 for adults who live one thousand miles or more from their mothers), consistent with our finding that the weighted means are larger than the unweighted means. The weights also are somewhat larger for cases with fewer sisters (averaging 0.95 for cases with no sisters and 0.84 for cases with four sisters).

7.5.2: Weighted Cross-tabulation

The formulas defined in Section 7.3.1 can be used to calculate the weighted observed frequency and weighted row, column, and cell percentages. However, now the calculation is based on the sum of the weights for the cases that fall in a cell rather than based on the actual tally of cases in a cell. For example, if 5 cases fell into the first cell, then the unweighted value of n_{11} would be 5. If these five cases had unadjusted weights of 0.50, 0.50, 1.00, 0.50, and 1.00 respectively, then the sum of their weights would be $0.50 + 0.50 + 1.00 + 0.50 + 1.00 = 3.50$. Thus, the weighted frequency in the cell would be 3.5.

In both SAS and Stata, we can again request weighted frequencies and percentages by adding options (the `weight` statement in SAS; [aw=<weight variable>] in Stata) to the commands we used for the unweighted cross-tabulation (`proc freq` in SAS and `tabulate` in Stata; see Display A.7.2). Display B.7.8 shows the results of our requesting the weighted cross-tabulation of number of brothers and number of sisters. In this case, comparing the weighted to the unweighted percentages (from Display B.7.4) shows that they are similar in many cases. For example, in the top cell (adults with no brothers and no sisters) the weighted frequency is 1156.019 versus the unweighted frequency of 1156. In this top cell, the cell percentage is 19.61, weighted and unweighted. The weighted row and column percentages are somewhat lower than the unweighted estimates (54.51 versus 55.39; 52.53 versus 53.69, respectively). In other applications, the weighted values might be higher than the unweighted values; the relative sizes of the weighted and unweighted statistics depend on the values of the weights for cases with different characteristics.

7.5.3: Weighted Correlation

Both SAS and Stata will calculate a weighted correlation, using the following formula with relative weights (Wackerly, Mendenhall, and Scheaffer 2008; see also SAS 2010a: 19; Stata 2009a: 329):

$$r = \frac{\sum_{i=1}^{n} w_i^* \times (Y_i - \bar{Y})(X_i - \bar{X})}{\sqrt{\sum_{i=1}^{n} w_i^* \times (Y_i - \bar{Y})^2} \sqrt{\sum_{i=1}^{n} w_i^* \times (X_i - \bar{X})^2}} \tag{7.13}$$

This formula is easily compared to Equation 7.10, revealing that the cross-product and squared deviations are multiplied by the sampling weight before they are summed. Thus, cases with larger weights (who were not oversampled) will contribute more to the sums than those with smaller weights (who were oversampled).

Weighted correlations are also easily requested in SAS and Stata with options on the correlation commands (`proc corr` in SAS and `pwcorr` in Stata). Again, SAS uses the `weight` statement; and, Stata uses the option [aw=<weight variable>] (see Display A.7.2). Display B.7.9 shows our addition of these options to the commands shown in Display B.7.6. The results reveal that the weighted correlation of mothers' ages with their adult children's ages is slightly larger than the unweighted correlation (0.87 versus 0.85). We will re-emphasize that, although the SAS and Stata output provide a p-value, it does not take into account clustering and stratification. In Part 3, we will introduce the survey regression commands that can be used to get the correct p-values if your data come from a complex design with stratification and clustering.

7.6: SUMMARY

In this chapter, we learned how to examine the bivariate association between two variables, including how to calculate means of a continuous variable and proportions of a categorical variable within subgroups of another categorical variable and how to calculate correlations between two continuous variables. We also learned how to test whether the pairs of variables were significantly associated with one another, including with the two-sample t-test for comparing the means of a continuous variable between two groups, the one-way analysis of variance (ANOVA) for comparing the means of a continuous variable across two or more groups, the Pearson chi-square test of independence for two categorical variables, and the Pearson correlation of linear association between two continuous variables. In addition, we showed how to calculate weighted subgroup means, weighted proportions in cross-tabulations, and weighted correlations. We emphasized that these weighted statistics only calculate the point estimates of these statistics, adjusting just for the oversampling of a complex sampling design but not for any stratification or clustering. In Part 3 of the book we will show how to adjust for these other aspects of the design, and relate those techniques back to this chapter in order to show how to conduct a two-sample t-test, a one-way ANOVA, and a Pearson chi-square test when your data were gathered based on a complex sampling design.

KEY TERMS

ANOVA

Cell percentage

Column percentage

Conditional distribution

Grand mean

Marginal distribution

Multivariate model

One-way analysis of variance

Overall mean

Pearson chi-square

Pearson correlation

Row percentage

Simple association

Statistical significance

Subgroup mean

Within-group mean

t-test

REVIEW QUESTIONS

7.1. How are bivariate statistics often used in social science publications?

7.2. What are the null and alternative hypotheses for the two-sample *t*-test discussed in this chapter?

7.3. What are the major differences between the two ways to calculate the test statistic for the two-sample *t*-test discussed in the chapter?

7.4. What are the null and alternative hypotheses for the one-way analysis of variance?

7.5. What are the null and alternative hypotheses for the Pearson chi-square test?

7.6. Describe how the observed frequencies are calculated and how they contribute to the size of the Pearson chi-square.

REVIEW
QUESTIONS
7

7.7. What are the null and alternative hypotheses for the Pearson correlation?

7.8. What are the minimum and maximum values of the Pearson correlation?

7.9. Describe what patterns of association might result in Pearson correlations close to −1, 0, and 1, and why the numerator in the formula for the Pearson correlation would lead to large or small values in each case.

7.10. Discuss how weights are incorporated into the calculation of subgroup means, cross-tabulations, and the Pearson correlation.

REVIEW EXERCISES 7

REVIEW EXERCISES

7.1. Imagine that you draw a random sample from a population of employees in a Western city. The 300 employees in the sample who have less than a high school degree average $16,500 in annual earnings with a standard deviation of $5,100. The 500 employees in the sample who have a high school degree or more earn an average of $24,750 per year, with a standard deviation of $4,000.

   a. First assume that the two groups have equal variances. Under this assumption, is there statistical evidence that the incomes of these two groups differ significantly from each other at an alpha of .05? In your response, be sure to explicitly state the null and alternative hypotheses. Use the most appropriate of the following critical values: $t_{798,.025} = 1.96$, $t_{299,.025} = 1.97$, $Z_{.025} = 1.96$

   b. Test the assumption that the two groups have equal variances (null) versus the possibility that the variances differ between the two groups (alternative). Use the most appropriate of the following critical values: $F_{299.499,.025} = 1.22$, $F_{499.299,0.25} = 1.23$.

   c. If you allow the two groups to have different variances, is there statistical evidence that the incomes of these two groups differ significantly from each other? Use the most appropriate of the following critical values: $t_{518,.025} = 1.96$, $t_{299,.025} = 1.97$, $Z_{.025} = 1.96$.

7.2. Consider the following observed cell frequencies from a cross-tabulation of family income status and type of child care used for preschoolers, based on a sample randomly drawn from parents in a mid-western state.

| | Type of Child Care | | |
	Relative or Nanny	Family Day Care	Center Care
Low-income	65	5	180
Middle-income	30	50	120
High-income	59	9	112

a. What are the observed frequencies in the marginal distributions of family income and type of care?
b. What is the expected frequency in each cell, assuming independence?
c. Are the expected frequencies large enough to justify calculation of the Pearson chi-square?
d. What is the Pearson chi-square value for testing the null hypothesis that the two variables are independent against the alternative that they are statistically associated?
e. What are the degrees of freedom for the Pearson chi-square?
f. Calculate and interpret the row percentage, column percentage and cell percentage for the cell containing high-income families who use center care.

7.3. Imagine that you collected the following information about the number of fast food meals eaten each month and body mass index in a sample of 14 students drawn randomly from a local college.

caseid	fastfood	bmi	caseid	fastfood	bmi
1	7	29	8	5	20
2	18	40	9	0	16
3	8	35	10	1	32
4	8	24	11	6	28
5	12	32	12	5	28
6	30	58	13	3	26
7	8	35	14	0	24

a. Calculate the mean monthly fast food consumption and mean body mass index in this sample.
b. For each variable, calculate the deviation between each of its observed values and its mean (28 deviations in all).
c. Based on the calculated deviations, do you expect to see a positive correlation, no correlation, or negative correlation between the two variables? Be sure to justify your response.
d. Calculate the Pearson correlation between the two variables.

7.4. Calculate the column and row percentages for the observed and expected cell counts shown in Display B.7.5. (You can verify your calculations of the column and row percentages for the observed counts based on Display B.7.4). Discuss how the conditional and marginal column and row percentages differ based on the observed cell counts and the expected cell counts.

CHAPTER EXERCISES

In these Chapter Exercises, you will write a SAS and a Stata batch program to calculate some bivariate inferential statistics ("SAS/Stata Tasks"). You will want to have Display A.7 handy as you write your batch programs. You will use the results to answer some questions related to the substance of what we learned in Chapter 7 ("Write-Up Tasks").

To begin, prepare the shell of a batch program, including the commands to save your output and helpful initial commands (e.g., In SAS, use the `libname` command to assign the SAS library where the formats can be found; In Stata, turn more off, drop any data in use, and close any open log; see Display A.4.2). Use the NHIS 2009 dataset that you created in Chapter 4. When you use/set the data, be sure to *exclude any cases with missing values on SEX, RACERPI2, exfreqwR, bmiR, or age.*

Use an alpha of .05 for all hypothesis tests. *Be sure to provide the steps that lead you to your write-up answers!*

7.1 One Categorical and One Interval Variable

a) SAS/Stata Tasks.

   i) Conduct two-sample *t*-tests for gender differences in the mean of the following three variables: (1) *age*, (2) *bmiR*, and (3) *exfreqwR* assuming equal variances.

   ii) Test whether there is statistical evidence that the variances are equal for males and females on these same three variables.

   iii) Conduct two-sample *t*-tests for gender differences in the mean of the following three variables: (1) *age*, (2) *bmiR*, and (3) *exfreqwR* assuming unequal variances.

b) Write-Up Tasks.

   i) Use the results for the *age* variable to make a conclusion about the following null and alternative hypotheses:

H_o	The mean age is the same for men and women.
H_a	The mean age differs between men and women

Base your conclusions on the results that assume equal variances. You can rely on the output for the *p*-value (circle and/or otherwise indicate where you found the *p*-value), but show how to calculate the *t*-statistic and degrees of freedom listed in the output. Treat men as Group 1 and women as Group 2.

ii) Use the results for the *age* variable to make a conclusion about the following null and alternative hypotheses:

H_o The variance of age is the same for men and women.
H_a The variance of age differs between men and women

You can rely on the output for the *p*-value (circle and/or otherwise indicate where you found the *p*-value), but show how to calculate the *F*-statistic and degrees of freedom listed in the output.

iii) List the *t*-statistic, degrees of freedom and *p*-value for the hypothesis you conducted in 7.1bi but now assuming unequal variances. Show how the *t*-statistic and degrees of freedom are calculated. How are the results similar to/different from what you found in 7.1bi?

7.2 Two Categorical Variables

a) SAS/Stata Tasks.

i) Crosstabulate *RACERPI2* and *SEX* and request row, column, and cell percentages.

ii) Crosstabulate *RACERPI2* and *SEX* and request the expected cell frequencies and the Pearson chi-square test.

b) Write-Up Tasks.

i) Interpret the row, column, and cell percentages in words for the cell that contains African American males.

ii) Show how to calculate the expected cell frequency in this same cell.

iii) What is the smallest expected cell frequency listed in the results? Is this an adequate minimum number for the Pearson chi-square test?

iv) Make a conclusion about whether race and gender are statistically independent (null) or statistically associated (alternative) based on the results.

7.3 Two Interval Variables

a) SAS/Stata Tasks.

i) Calculate the Pearson correlation between each pair of the following three variables: (1) *age*, (2) *bmiR*, and (3) *exfreqwR*.

b) Write-Up Tasks.

i) Based on the listed *p*-values, which of the pairs of variables are statistically uncorrelated (null) versus linearly related (alternative)?

7.4 Cross-Question Write-ups

b) Write-Up Tasks

    i) Create a table similar to the tables shown in Literature Excerpt 7.1 and 7.2 based on the results you obtained in Question 7.1 and 7.2. When creating the table, you can follow the conventions shown in either Literature Excerpt or use the style in your discipline. Either way, your goal will be that the table is "self-contained" (interpretable on its own).

    ii) Write a few sentence description of gender differences in the sample, referencing your table.

    iii) Create a table similar to the table shown in Literature Excerpt 7.3 based on the results you obtained in Question 7.3. When creating the table, you can follow the conventions shown in the Literature Excerpt or use the style in your discipline. Either way, your goal will be that the table is "self-contained" (interpretable on its own).

7.5 Weighted Statistics

a) SAS/Stata Tasks.

    i) Request weighted means for (1) *age*, (2) *bmiR*, and (3) *exfreqwR* within gender.

    ii) Request weighted proportions of race-ethnicity within gender.

b) Write-Up Tasks.

    i) Create a table as you did in Question 7.4, but include only the weighted means and weighted proportions (not significance tests).

    ii) Discuss how the weighted means and weighted proportions compare to the unweighted means and unweighted proportions.

Part 3

ORDINARY LEAST SQUARES REGRESSION

Chapter 8

BASIC CONCEPTS OF BIVARIATE REGRESSION

CHAPTER 8: BASIC CONCEPTS OF BIVARIATE REGRESSION

With basic concepts of descriptive and inferential statistics under our belt, we are now ready to tackle regression analysis. We will begin in this chapter with basic concepts of **bivariate regression** with one continuous dependent variable and one continuous independent variable.

Fundamentally, regression modeling involves the algebra and geometry of a function, starting with a straight line. Understanding this basic math aids interpretation of our results. Returning to this basic math will be quite helpful in understanding more complicated models as we move forward, and we will repeatedly revisit the strategies for interpretation that we introduce in this chapter.

Whereas a mathematical straight line function is deterministic, statistical models contain a systematic (straight line) and probabilistic component. Because of this, in regression, there are three basic parameters of the model: the intercept and slope of the straight line and the conditional variance of the distribution of values around that straight line. We will see that this is true in both the population and the sample.

■ **Box 8.1**

Some social scientists, especially in certain subfields, avoid using the term *effect* because it implies a causal relationship between the predictor and outcome. We will return to this issue in Chapter 13, but will at times use the term *effect*.

To test social science research questions, we need a reliable strategy for estimating the parameters of the model (the intercept, slope, and conditional variance). Ordinary least squares (OLS) is the most commonly used approach. We look in detail in this chapter at the least squares estimators and their standard errors and how to answer our research questions and evaluate our hypotheses using these estimates. We then discuss a number of strategies for evaluating the substantive size of statistically significant effects (see Box 8.1). In Part 4 of the book we will consider an alternative estimation strategy for the model parameters.

We will use two examples in this chapter, both taken from the NSFH. One uses the datafile we created in Chapter 4. We will learn the syntax to estimate a regression model in SAS and Stata based on *g1miles* and *g2earn* from that datafile. We will also use a second example taken from the NSFH, in which we examine how the hours of chores that employed women complete each week is predicted by their number of children and by their hours of paid work. The batch programs for creating this datafile from the NSFH and reproducing the in-text examples are provided on the textbook web site (*http://www.routledge.com/cw/gordon*). In this chapter, we use three versions of this "hours of chores" datafile:

(a) the *full sample* of 3,116 women who were currently employed;
(b) a *stylized sample* of 50 women that we created to illustrate the conditional regression equation;
(c) a *hypothetical* population and 5,000 *samples* drawn from the hypothetical population to illustrate the sampling distribution of the slope.

We will also use this hours of chores example in future chapters, when it illustrates a point better than our distance from the mother example.

8.1: ALGEBRAIC AND GEOMETRIC REPRESENTATIONS OF BIVARIATE REGRESSION

We start with basic concepts of a straight line, first in a graph and then in an equation, using geometry and algebra to reinforce the basic concepts. These basic mathematical concepts give us the building blocks we need in order to understand the regression model.

Regression models with a single predictor variable are typically referred to as **simple regression** or **bivariate regression** (bivariate because two variables are involved—the outcome variable, which we often call Y, and the predictor variable, which we often call X). At the heart of bivariate regression models is the geometry of a straight line. A straight line is defined by an **intercept**, which denotes the point at which the line intersects the Y axis, and a **slope**, which measures the amount that Y changes when X increases by 1. We can write this algebraically as $Y = \beta_0 + \beta_1 X$ and display this geometrically as shown in Figure 8.1.

The graph of the line makes clear that the slope, β_1, measures the amount of **linear association** between Y and X (see Box 8.2).

■ Box 8.2

For our regression models we follow the convention of using Greek letters to denote population parameters. We use subscripts to indicate associated predictor variables for the regression coefficients. In this chapter, we represent the intercept with the subscript zero and the single predictor with the subscript 1. In subsequent chapters, numbers 2 and above will designate additional predictor variables. Below, we will put "hats" on the Greek letters to denote sample estimates of these population parameters, such as $\hat{\beta}_0$. Keep in mind that other books and articles may use different notation (e.g., lowercase Roman letters, such as *a* and *b*, for the sample coefficients).

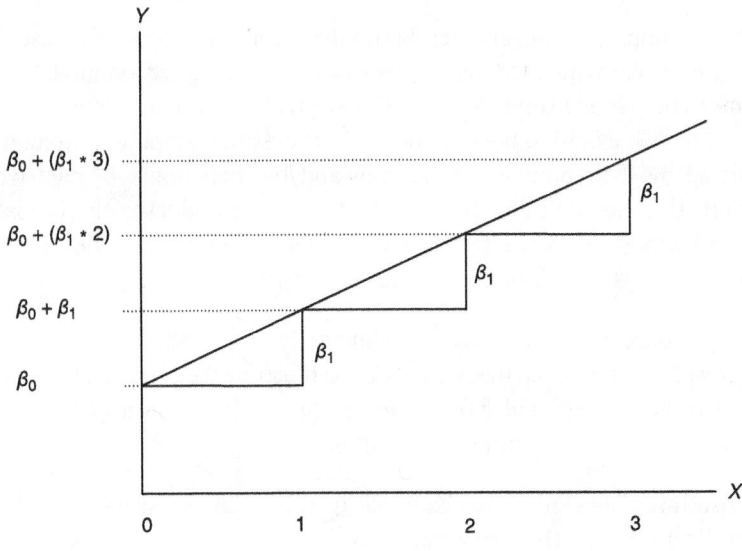

■ Figure 8.1

If $\beta_1 = 0$ then Y would not change when X increased. This result can be seen both algebraically and geometrically.

Geometrically, when $\beta_1 = 0$ our straight line plot becomes horizontal (see Fig. 8.2). Clearly, Y remains the same regardless of the values of X in this situation. In this "flat line" context, X and Y are unrelated.

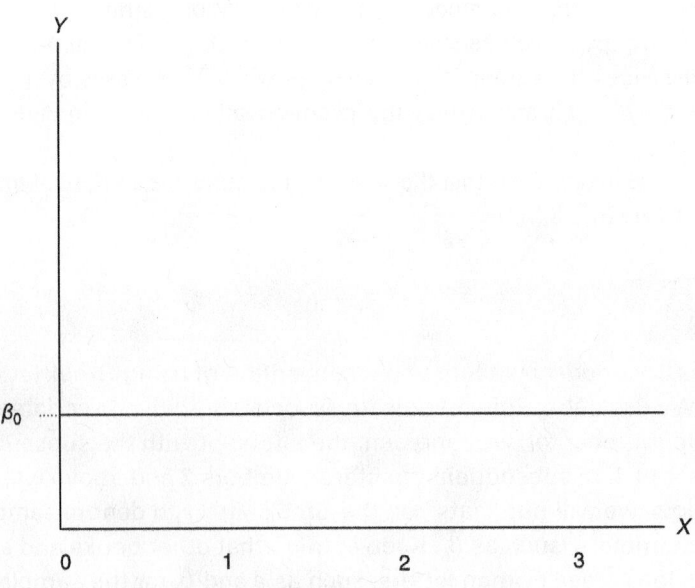

■ Figure 8.2

Algebraically, if $\beta_1 = 0$ then everything but the intercept "drops out" of the equation. That is, $Y = \beta_0 + \beta_1 X = \beta_0 + 0 * X = \beta_0$. No matter what the value of X, $Y = \beta_0$.

The regression equation defines the values along the line. We can substitute any X value into the equation to calculate its associated Y value. With any two pairs of X and Y values we can plot the straight line.

Suppose we have an equation with an intercept of 3 and a slope of 0.5. We would write this algebraically as $Y = 3 + 0.5X$. Substituting in the values 0, 1, 2, and 3 into the equation results in the following values of Y:

X	$Y = 3 + 0.5X$	Y
0	$Y = 3 + 0.5 * 0 = 3 + 0.0$	3.0
1	$Y = 3 + 0.5 * 1 = 3 + 0.5$	3.5
2	$Y = 3 + 0.5 * 2 = 3 + 1.0$	4.0
3	$Y = 3 + 0.5 * 3 = 3 + 1.5$	4.5

We can draw a simple graph of these values to show the line visually.

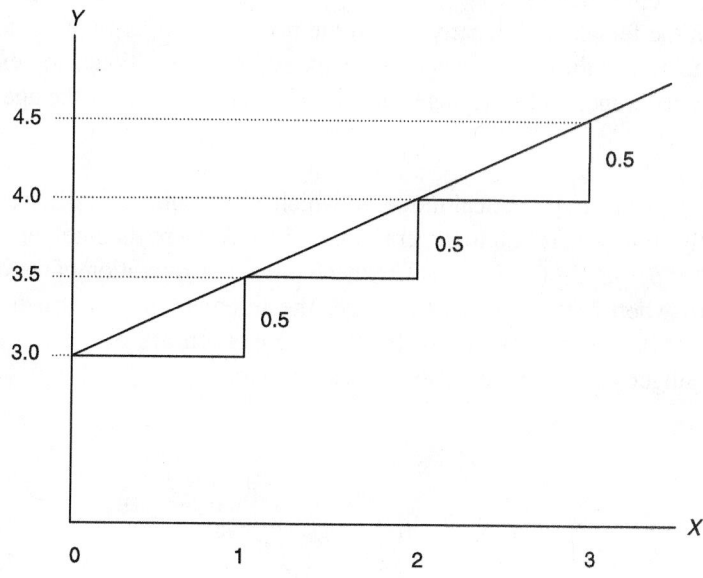

8.1.1: Interpretation of the Intercept

The interpretation of the intercept and slope are also made clear from the algebraic and geometric forms of the regression line.

In regression analysis, the focus is on the *Y intercept*, referred to simply as the *intercept* for short. The intercept provides the value of Y when $X = 0$. This interpretation always holds mathematically.

Although the intercept can always be calculated and interpreted in this way, and will always be shown in our SAS and Stata output, it may or may not make sense to interpret it substantively. In social science applications, the intercept is of little substantive interest when zero is not in the range of values for the X variable, either by definition or within the sample. For example:

Years of Education	With mandatory enrollment through middle or junior high school, the lower bound may be 6–9 years.
Legal Wages	With a minimum wage law, legal wages in many occupations cannot fall below a given level, such as $7.25 h.
SAT Scores	SAT scores are designed to range from 200 to 800.
Age in a Sample of Adults	Many surveys include age restrictions. Some include only adult respondents (e.g., sampling only persons over, say, 18 years of age). Others focus on older persons (e.g., sampling persons over, say, 65 years of age).

On the other hand, it is also helpful to keep in mind that zero need not be the minimum value for either Y or X. Although most introductions to the simple regression model use a graph like the one above in which only positive values of X and Y are depicted, the Xs and Ys can be less than zero. Consider, for example, a variable constructed to measure the difference in ages between two partners in a couple such as $age_{male} - age_{female}$. This difference will be positive when the male is older than the female and negative when the male is younger than the female. Perhaps we would want to relate these differences in ages across generations, for example with Y capturing the age difference in the younger generation and X capturing the age differences in the older generation.

The graph below depicts a hypothetical model in which the couples' age differentials would be reproduced exactly from generation to generation, i.e., $Y = X$. Here the intercept is zero and the slope is 1. Thus, $Y = \beta_0 + \beta_1 X = 0 + 1X = X$. The mechanical interpretation of the intercept in this case is "Y is zero when X is zero." In this case, the intercept would also have substantive meaning, telling us that when parents in the older generation are of the same age, then the partners in the younger generation are also of the same age.

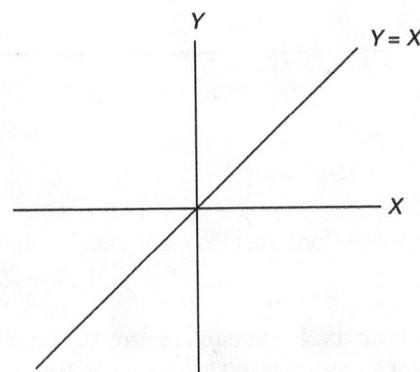

Other examples of variables including negative values might be measures of family income or business profits, in which debts and losses are allowed, or standardized values of a variable constructed using the formula we learned in Chapter 6:

$$Z = \frac{X_i - \bar{X}}{s_X}$$

(8.1)

Notice that Z takes on the value of zero when X is at its mean. We will see in Chapter 11 how subtracting the mean (or another value) from a predictor can be useful for interpretation.

8.1.2: Interpretation of the Slope

The slope measures how much the outcome variable, Y, changes for each one unit increase in X. We assume initially that the relationship between Y and X is a straight line. (We will allow for nonlinear relationships in Chapter 12.) *Because we are modeling a straight line, the amount of change on Y for a one unit increase in X does not depend on the starting value of X.* This is a simple but critical concept. We will come back to it several times later in the textbook so let's explore it in more detail in order to reinforce it.

We can see in Figure 8.1 that the change in Y when X goes from zero to 1 is equivalent to the change in Y when X goes from 1 to 2 which is equivalent to the change in Y when X goes from 2 to 3. We show this algebraically in the table below, explicitly writing the result of substituting each value of X into the equation. Then, the change in Y for a one-unit increase in X is the difference in the resulting value of Y for the current row and prior row:

	$Y = \beta_0 + \beta_1 X$		Change in Y when X increased by 1		
When $X = 0$	$Y = \beta_0 + \beta_1 * 0$	$= \beta_0$	—		
When $X = 1$	$Y = \beta_0 + \beta_1 * 1$	$= \beta_0 + \beta_1$	$(\beta_0 + \beta_1) - \beta_0$	$= \beta_0 - \beta_0 + \beta_1$	$= \beta_1$
When $X = 2$	$Y = \beta_0 + \beta_1 * 2$	$= \beta_0 + 2\beta_1$	$(\beta_0 + 2\beta_1) - (\beta_0 + \beta_1)$	$= (\beta_0 - \beta_0) + (2\beta_1 - \beta_1)$	$= \beta_1$
When $X = 3$	$Y = \beta_0 + \beta_1 * 3$	$= \beta_0 + 3\beta_1$	$(\beta_0 + 3\beta_1) - (\beta_0 + 2\beta_1)$	$= (\beta_0 - \beta_0) + (3\beta_1 - 2\beta_1)$	$= \beta_1$

Although the above result may seem obvious, we will use this technique of substituting different values of X and comparing the results as we work with more complicated models in future chapters. Thus, it is helpful to have this simpler case very clearly in mind.

This constant slope reflects the way in which we have written these models to be linear in X. When the model is linear, it allows for a very concise interpretation of the slope: "Y changes by β_1 units when X increases by 1." We will see in Chapter 12 and Part 4 that nonlinear models require lengthier explanations and interpretations.

In our linear model, what if we changed X by 2 units instead of 1 unit? How much would Y change then? We can use a similar table structure to work out this result. Now, we subtract from the result for Y in the current row the value of Y two rows prior (e.g., Y when $X = 2$ minus Y when $X = 0$, Y when $X = 3$ minus Y when $X = 1$).

	$Y = \beta_0 + \beta_1 X$	Change in Y when X increased by 2
When $X = 0$	$Y = \beta_0 + \beta_1 * 0 = \beta_0$	—
When $X = 1$	$Y = \beta_0 + \beta_1 * 1 = \beta_0 + \beta_1$	—
When $X = 2$	$Y = \beta_0 + \beta_1 * 2 = \beta_0 + 2\beta_1$	$(\beta_0 + 2\beta_1) - (\beta_0) \quad = (\beta_0 - \beta_0) + (2\beta_1) \quad = 2\beta_1$
When $X = 3$	$Y = \beta_0 + \beta_1 * 3 = \beta_0 + 3\beta_1$	$(\beta_0 + 3\beta_1) - (\beta_0 + \beta_1) \quad = (\beta_0 - \beta_0) + (3\beta_1 - \beta_1) \quad = 2\beta_1$

More generally, if we increase X by i units, then Y will change by $i\beta_1$ units. We will come back to this result near the end of the chapter.

8.2: THE POPULATION REGRESSION LINE

The algebraic and graphic straight lines we've been discussing so far are **deterministic**. Y is predicted exactly from the intercept and slope coefficients and the value of X. This model actually captures only one portion of the statistical regression model, what is often called the **systematic component**. The other portion of the statistical regression model is an error term. Adding this error term produces the statistical or **probabilistic** regression model:

$$Y_i = \beta_0 + \beta_1 X_i + \varepsilon_i \qquad (8.2)$$

where $\beta_0 + \beta_1 X_i$ is the systematic component and ε_i is the **nonsystematic** (also known as **random** or **stochastic**) **component**. This model is probabilistic rather than deterministic in that the exact value of Y that we observe depends not only on the fixed value calculated by plugging in the values of the intercept, slope, and X, but it also depends on the value of the error term. Later, we will make assumptions about the probability distribution of this error term. We refer to Equation 8.2 as the **population regression line**, assuming that we know or can calculate exactly the values of the intercept and slope (i.e., we know the values of Y and X for every member of the population). Later, we will learn how to estimate these parameters using a sample from the population. The sample regression model, like the population regression model, has both a systematic and stochastic component.

To help understand these systematic and random components of the regression model, we will examine them in a graph. The values predicted from the systematic portion of the equation are the points that plot the regression line. This portion of the population regression line is also known as the **expected value** of Y given X which is denoted as $E(Y|X_i)$. The expected value is essentially another name for the mean and as we shall see $E(Y|X_i)$ is the **conditional mean** of Y for a given level of X (see Box 8.3). It is calculated from the systematic portion of the regression line: $E(Y|X_i) = \beta_0 + \beta_1 X_i$. For example, $E(Y|X_i = 1) = \beta_0 + \beta_1 * 1 = \beta_0 + \beta_1$.

The expected value of Y calculated from the systematic portion of the regression model is the same for each member of the population with the same value of X. The error term allows population members with the same value of X to vary on Y. The error term represents the distribution of the observed Y around the conditional expected values at each level of X. It is important to note that this variation exists in the *population*. The population regression line is probabilistic. The error terms can be thought of as capturing many various forces that explain Y in addition to the predictor, X, that is in the regression equation. These might include variables

■ Box 8.3

The concept of "expected value" is intuitive. It is the value that we expect given the probability distribution of the variable. In calculating the expected value, we weight each possible value of the variable by the probability of observing that value. A value that is highly probable gets a higher weight (is more expected). A value that has a lower probability gets a lower weight (is less expected). This concept is easiest to illustrate with a discrete variable. Consider a hypothetical variable that can take on five values: zero with a probability 0.50, 1 with probability of 0.30, 2 with a probability of 0.10, 3 with a probability of .07, 4 with a probability of .03. Zero is most likely in this distribution, and so should be weighted highest in calculating the expected value. Four is least likely, and thus should receive the lowest weight. The expected value would be 0 * 0.50 + 1 * 0.30 + 2 * 0.10 + 3 * 0.07 + 4 * 0.03 = 0.83. The expected value is similarly calculated for continuous variables, but we integrate over the continuous values of the variable, each weighted by its probability, rather than summing.

that have not been considered by a particular theory, that are not available in the data, or that represent "pure" randomness in human behavior.

If these error terms were distributed approximately normally within each level of X, the model might look something like the graph shown below.

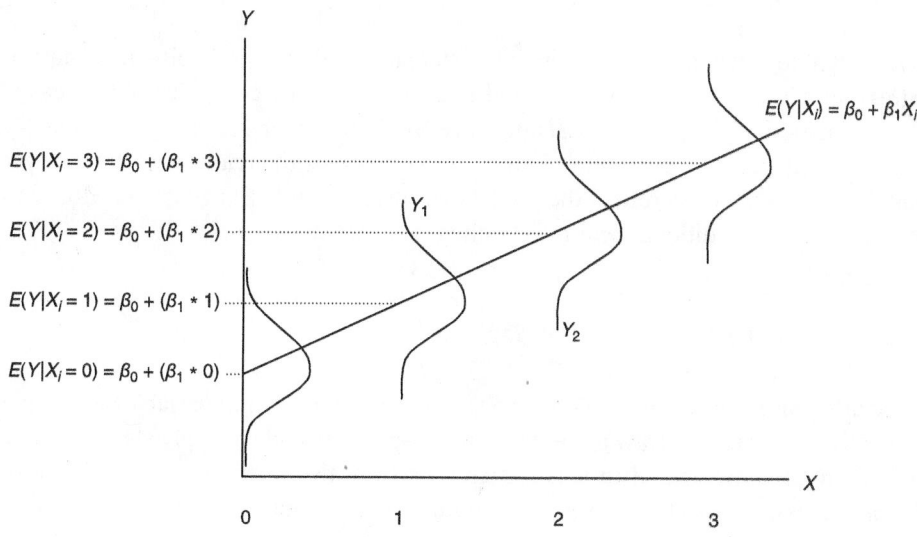

The figure depicts four **conditional distributions** of Y within four levels of X. Each conditional distribution is centered on a conditional mean which is determined by the systematic portion of the regression line. Each conditional distribution varies around that conditional mean, with the variability determined by the random portion of the regression line. For example, when $X = 0$, the distribution is centered around the conditional mean of $E(Y|X_i = 0) = \beta_0 + (\beta_1 * 0)$. And, when $X = 3$, the conditional distributed is centered around the conditional mean of $E(Y|X_i = 3) = \beta_0 + (\beta_1 * 3)$.

The line is drawn to represent a positive slope. Thus, the conditional means increase as X increases. The systematic portion of the regression model captures the fact that *on average* the values of Y move linearly upward with increasing X. However, the random component of the regression model allows for variability around these conditional averages. Because of the random component, it is not the case that *all* Ys at a higher level of X will have higher values than *all* Ys at a lower level of X. In fact, any two observed Ys, one at the higher level of X and one at the lower level of X, may reflect a reverse relationship from the conditional averages (i.e., higher Y at the smaller rather than the larger X value). The points Y_1 and Y_2 in the figure on page 247 depict this situation. Y_1 is in the upper tail of the conditional distribution at $X = 1$ and Y_2 is in the lower tail of the conditional distribution at $X = 2$. Thus, $Y_1 > Y_2$ even though $E(Y|X_i = 1) < E(Y|X_i = 2)$.

These conditional distributions of the Ys at various levels of X are fundamental to the standard regression model. The systematic and stochastic components of the regression model represent, respectively, the mean and variance of these conditional distributions; that is, the mean of each of these conditional distributions is $(Y|X_i) = \beta_0 + \beta_1 X_i$. The variance of each of these conditional distributions is the variance of ε_i which is typically denoted simply σ^2. We used this Greek symbol "sigma" for the variance with subscripts Y and X in Part 2 of the book. In the regression context, it is conventional to denote the **conditional variance** as σ^2 and to use explicit subscripts to denote other variances. For example, we will continue to denote the unconditional (or marginal) variance of Y as σ_Y^2.

It is important to keep in mind both the systematic and the probabilistic components of the regression model when we estimate and interpret the slope coefficients. It is easy to slip into deterministic language (e.g., "Earnings are \$10,000 higher for every additional year of schooling") when really we should use language that reminds the reader that the relationship is probabilistic, and our slopes reflect the conditional means (e.g., "Earnings are \$10,000 higher, on average, for every additional year of schooling").

8.3: THE SAMPLE REGRESSION LINE

In the social sciences, we can rarely observe the values of the desired variables for all members of a population. Instead, we draw a sample from a population and we apply statistics to describe a sample regression model and to make inferences from that sample regression model to the population regression model. In particular, the sample regression model is:

$$Y_i = \hat{\beta}_0 + \hat{\beta}_1 X_i + \hat{\varepsilon}_i \tag{8.3}$$

The ^ symbols or "hats" are used to distinguish the **population parameters** (e.g., β_1) from **sample estimates** (e.g., $\hat{\beta}_1$). The systematic or deterministic portion of this sample regression model is:

$$\hat{Y}_i = \hat{\beta}_0 + \hat{\beta}_1 X_i \tag{8.4}$$

The values $\hat{Y}_i$ are often referred to as the **fitted values, predicted values**, or **Y-hats**, and Equation 8.4 is called a **prediction equation**. We can substitute a value of X into this prediction equation, multiply by the estimated slope, and add the estimated intercept in order to obtain a predicted value for Y. The estimated error, $\hat{\varepsilon}_i$, is the difference between the observed sample value, Y_i, and the fitted value based on the sample regression, $\hat{Y}_i$, or $\hat{\varepsilon}_i = Y_i - \hat{Y}_i$. This can be seen by substituting Equation 8.4 into Equation 8.3 and rearranging the terms.[1] The variance of the errors—the conditional variance or $\hat{\sigma}^2$—is also estimated based on the sample. In Section 8.4, we will define the formula for calculating the estimate.

Figure 8.3 shows an example of the association between hours of chores and number of children, using the stylized sample of size n = 50 that we created based on the employed women in Wave 1 of the NSFH.[2] The example shows 10 observations within each level of number of children, illustrating the distribution of observed values around the conditional means. Two errors are shown, one above and one below the sample regression line (for case $i = 23$ and case $i = 36$ in the stylized sample). These two observed sample points also illustrate the fact that, although the average hours of chores is higher among households with more children, Case 23 with two children reported more chores than Case 36 with three children.

The reason why the observed value for Case 23 is higher than predicted and the observed value for Case 36 is lower than predicted may simply be pure random variation in human behavior. Or, there may be something that we could measure about each of these women that would help explain their deviations from the conditional means (for example, perhaps Case 36 works very long hours, and has less time left over to devote to chores than the average woman with three children; and perhaps Case 23 works only a few hours per week, and has more time left over to

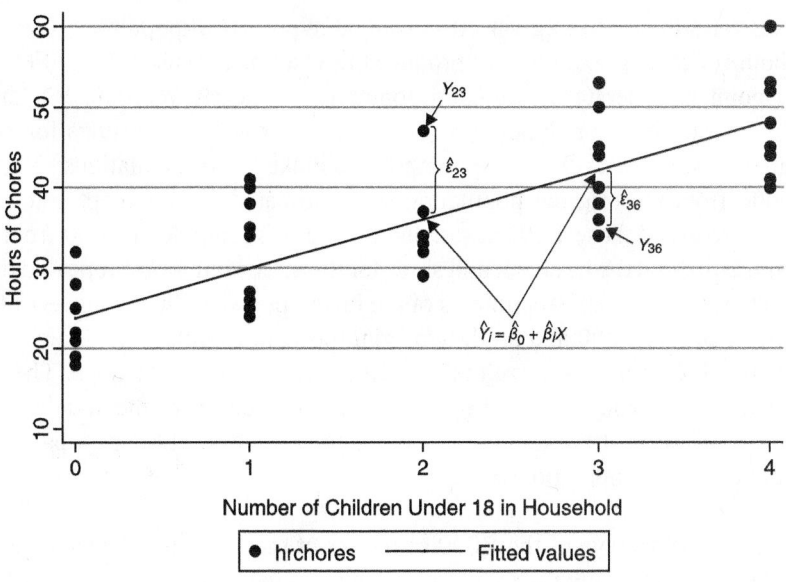

■ Figure 8.3

Source: Stylized sample from National Survey of Families and Households, Wave 1

devote to chores than the average woman with two children). In multiple regression, we can put additional predictors (such as hours of paid work) in the model that may explain some of this remaining conditional variation.

8.3.1: Sampling Distributions

Recall that an **estimator** is a formula that tells us how to calculate our best guess of the population parameter based on the information available in our sample from that population. The **estimate** is the value calculated from the formula for a particular sample.

Like all estimators, estimators for the population intercept, slope, and conditional standard deviation of a regression model have **sampling distributions**. This means that estimates of the population parameters of the regression line based on any sample that we draw randomly from the population ($\hat{\beta}_0 \hat{\beta}_1 \hat{\sigma}^2$) will differ to some degree from the actual population parameters ($\beta_0 \beta_1 \sigma^2$). Differences in estimates between repeated random samples, drawn in the same way from the same population, reflect sampling fluctuations (that is, most samples contain primarily the most typical values of the population, but some samples may happen to draw mostly unusual values of the population). Thus, as we saw in Part 2 an estimate of the sample mean based on the estimator $\dfrac{\sum_{i=1}^{n} Y_i}{n}$ will be close to but not exactly equal to the population mean. Similarly, the estimates of the intercept, slope, and conditional standard deviation will be close to but not necessarily exactly equal to the population parameters (with the expected closeness measured by the standard deviation of the sampling distribution for the estimator, the standard error, whose formula we will examine below).

Figure 8.4 illustrates this sampling variation using a hypothetical population created based on our NSFH "hours of chores" example. To produce this example, we used the NSFH observations as a starting point to generate a simulated population of nearly 700,000. We calculated the intercept and slope for this population. (We will discuss below the formulas for making these calculations; for now, we just rely on the computer to make these calculations.) We then drew a sample of 1,000 from the original population, and estimated the intercept and slope for this sample. We then returned those 1,000 cases, and drew a fresh sample of 1,000 from the original population, and estimated the intercept and slope for this new sample. We repeated this sampling 5,000 times. This produced 5,000 estimates of the intercept and 5,000 estimates of the slope, all based on samples of size 1,000 and all drawn from the same population. Figure 8.4 plots these 5,000 estimates to help us to visualize the sampling distribution of the slope. The mean of this sampling distribution should be close to the population value. And, the standard deviation of this sampling distribution (the standard error) estimates how close any particular sample estimate would be to this population value.

We also calculated the average of the 5,000 estimates of the slope and the average of the 5,000 estimates of the intercept to compare with the population value of the slope and intercept. And, we calculated the standard deviation of the 5,000 estimates of the slope and the standard deviation of the 5,000 estimates of the intercept to evaluate the standard error.

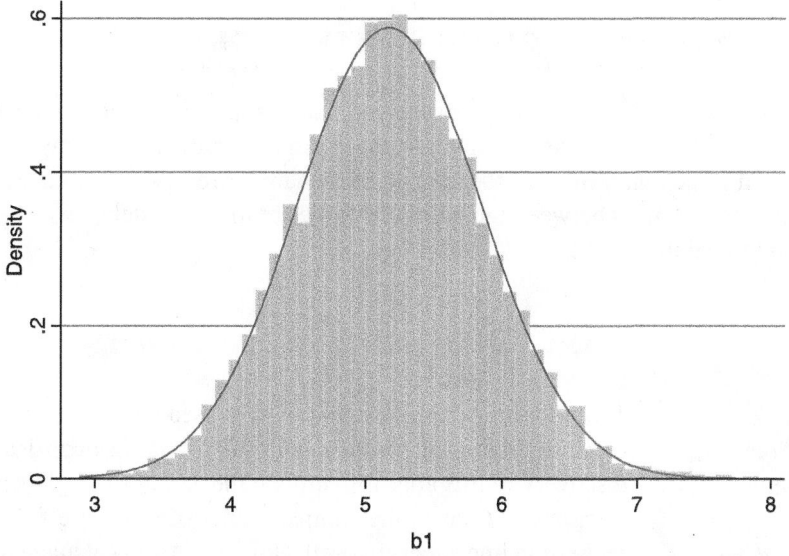

■ **Figure 8.4** Sampling distribution for slope with $n = 1,000$

	Population Value ($n = 699,765$)	Average of 5,000 Sample Estimates (each $n = 1,000$)	Standard Deviation of 5,000 Sample Estimates (each $n = 1,000$)
Intercept	27.96	27.95	0.8421
Slope	5.16	5.17	0.6777

The population value of the slope is 5.16. So, with each additional child in the household, the average hours of chores per week increases by about 5. The slope calculated in each sample of $n = 1,000$ is an estimate of this population slope. Figure 8.4 shows the sampling fluctuation in our estimate of the slope across the 5,000 random samples. This is a simulation of the sampling distribution of the estimator for the regression slope. Across our 5,000 samples, the slopes range from about 3 to 7.5 with a mean of 5.17, nearly exactly the population value of 5.16. The standard deviation of the sampling distribution of slopes is 0.68. We will discuss later assumptions about the distribution of the slope estimator, but for now we have superimposed a normal distribution line on the histogram. The sampling distribution of the slopes is quite close to this normal distribution. So, based on the empirical rule, about 95 percent of slopes should fall between $5.17 - 1.96 * 0.6777 = 3.84$ and $5.17 + 1.96 * 0.6777 = 6.50$, which appears to be the case in Figure 8.4.[3]

When we have only one sample, as we normally do, we cannot know if we have drawn a typical sample, whose estimate falls in the center close to the population parameter, or an unusual sample, whose estimate falls in the tails far from the population parameter. But, when the standard deviation of the sampling distribution is smaller (all else equal), then every sample's estimate will be close to the population parameter.

We will now turn to the formulas we used to estimate the slope and its standard error (i.e., the standard deviation of this sampling distribution) as well as the formulas for the intercept and conditional variance.

8.4 ORDINARY LEAST SQUARES ESTIMATORS

How do we calculate the value of the intercept and slope from a collection of data points? A standard approach is **OLS regression**. In OLS, the estimators provide the sample estimates of the intercept and slope that minimize the sum of the squared errors, $\hat{\varepsilon}_i$, which as we discussed above measure the distances between the observed values of the dependent variable, Y_i, and the estimated conditional means, $\hat{Y}_i$.

■ Box 8.4

Note that the intercept and slope for the stylized sample differ from those for the hypothetical population, shown on the previous page, because of the different ways each was created from the NSFH full sample of 3,116 employed women. The intercept and slope also differ in the full sample of 3,116 than in either the stylized sample or hypothetical population. (As we will see later, the intercept is 28.69 and the slope is 6.38 in the full sample of 3,116.)

8.4.1: The Least Squares Approach

Today, least squares is so commonly used that it is easy to lose sight of the incremental process and major breakthrough leading to the discovery of this approach around the end of the eighteenth century. Imagine looking at the sample points from Figure 8.3 without the regression line superimposed. How might you calculate the intercept and slope for a line that best summarizes the systematic linear trend that is clear from the data points?

The intercept and slope, calculated for the stylized sample in Figure 8.3, are 23.78 and 6.13, respectively (see Box 8.4). Figure 8.5 shows one guess we might draw by freehand, rounding the intercept and slope to 24 and 6, respectively. How might we choose between these two sets of values? Figure 8.5 indicates the same two observed values as we showed in Figure 8.3. The errors, representing the

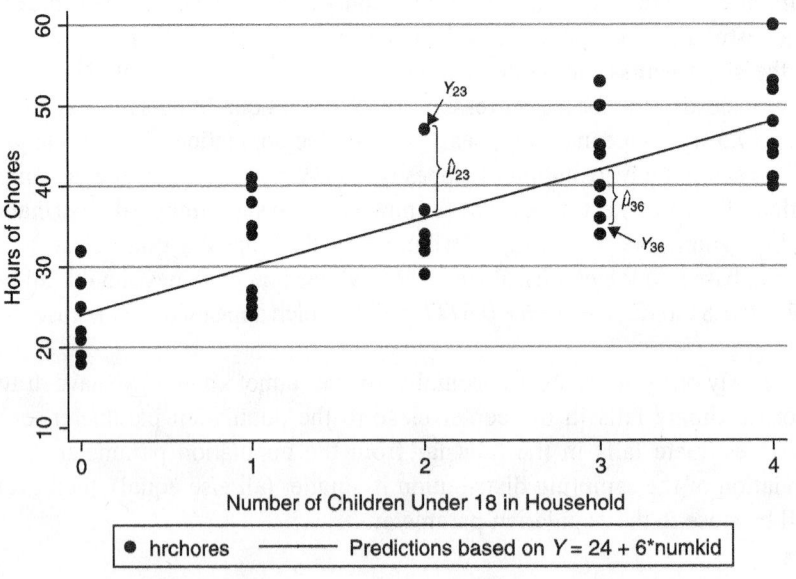

■ **Figure 8.5**

Source: Stylized sample from National Survey of Families and Households, Wave 1

difference between these observed values and the new fitted values, are now labeled $\hat{\mu}_{23}$ and $\hat{\mu}_{36}$. Perhaps we could use the errors to choose which line (the one in Figure 8.3 or in Figure 8.5) comes closest to the observed values? An intuitive choice might be to minimize the sum of these errors (which is smaller $\Sigma\hat{\varepsilon}_i$ or $\Sigma\hat{\mu}_i$?). Unfortunately, such a choice does not produce a unique solution.

During the eighteenth century, astronomers confronted a similar problem. In 1805, mathematician Adrien Marie Legendre published the method of least squares, which solved this problem. As quoted by noted statistician and historian Stephen Stigler (1986, 13), Legendre saw:

> an element of arbitrariness in any way of, as he put it, "distributing the errors among the equations," but that did not stop him from dramatically proposing a single best solution: "Of all the principles that can be proposed for this purpose, I think there is none more general, more exact, or easier to apply, than what which we have used in this work; it consists of making the sum of the squares of the errors a *minimum*. By this method, a kind of equilibrium is established among the errors which, since it prevents the extremes from dominating, is appropriate for revealing the state of the system which most nearly approaches the truth (Legendre 1805: 72–3).

The least squares approach has numerous advantages, including those mentioned in Legendre's quote as well as offering a single solution for the estimates of the intercept, slope, and conditional variance whose formulas can be derived in a straightforward manner by mathematicians.

We will not reproduce the derivations here. However, we will note conceptually that it starts with the formula for the squared errors:

$$\sum \hat{\varepsilon}_i^2 = \sum (Y_i - \hat{Y}_i)^2 = \sum (Y_i - (\hat{\beta}_0 + \hat{\beta}_1 X_i))^2$$

This formula has two unknown values, $\hat{\beta}_0$ and $\hat{\beta}_1$. Given our set of data, with observed values for X and Y, we would like to find the values of $\hat{\beta}_0$ and $\hat{\beta}_1$ that minimize these squared residuals. Using calculus, it is possible to differentiate these equations with respect to each unknown, set the result to zero, and solve for the unknown (for details, see Fox 2008; Kutner, Nachtsheim, and Neter 2004; Wooldridge 2009).

8.4.2: Point Estimators of the Intercept and Slope

Following are these closed form solutions for the intercept and slope in the bivariate regression model:

$$\hat{\beta}_1 = \frac{\sum (X_i - \bar{X})(Y_i - \bar{Y})}{\sum (X_i - \bar{X})^2} \tag{8.5}$$

$$\hat{\beta}_0 = \bar{Y} - \hat{\beta}_1 \bar{X} \tag{8.6}$$

Through the calculus derivation of the least squares estimators it can be shown that the estimated errors sum to zero. That is, $\Sigma\hat{\varepsilon}_i = \Sigma(Y_i - \hat{Y}_i) = 0$. Note that this applies to the errors, *not* the squared errors. The nonzero quantity of squared errors is what we minimize to estimate the intercept and slope. But, since the errors themselves sum to zero, across all sample points positive errors (above the regression line) balance out with negative errors (below the regression line).

It is also the case that if we substitute the sample mean of the predictor variable, $\bar{X}$, into the prediction equation, $\hat{Y}_i = \hat{\beta}_0 + \hat{\beta}_1 X$, the resulting $\hat{Y}_i$ will equal the sample mean of the outcome variable, $\bar{Y}$.[4] This is referred to as the sample regression line passing through the sample means.

8.4.3: Point Estimator of the Conditional Variance

The conditional variance is estimated based on the sample errors. For the bivariate regression model with one predictor the point estimator for the conditional variance is:

$$\hat{\sigma}^2 = \frac{\sum \hat{\varepsilon}_i^2}{n-2} = \frac{\sum (Y_i - \hat{Y}_i)^2}{n-2} = \frac{\sum (Y_i - (\hat{\beta}_0 + \hat{\beta}_1 X))^2}{n-2} \tag{8.7}$$

This value is also referred to as the **Mean Square Error** (MSE). Notice that the value in the numerator is the sum of the squared errors, which is what we minimize in least squares. This sum is divided by the sample size, less two, so the result is very nearly the simple average of the squared errors (hence the term Mean Square Error). The denominator is known as the **degrees of freedom**. The subtraction of 2 from the sample size accounts for the two estimates—the estimated intercept and the estimated slope—used in the calculation of $\hat{Y}_i$ for the numerator of Equation 8.7. As we discussed above, $\hat{\sigma}^2$ is an estimate of the conditional variance of the Ys at each level of X. The square root of this value is the estimate of the **conditional standard deviation**, commonly referred to as the **Root Mean Square Error** or **Root MSE**.

Recall that the error is the stochastic portion of the regression equation. Based on the other (systematic) portion of the sample regression equation, all observations at a given X level have the same fitted value estimated by:

$$\hat{Y}_i = \hat{\beta}_0 + \hat{\beta}_1 X_i$$

Thus, the conditional variation in Y is determined by the variation in the error term. Consequently, the Root MSE is an estimate of both the conditional standard deviation of the error term and the conditional standard deviation of the dependent variable.

If Y and X are strongly associated, then the standard deviation of the conditional distribution of the Ys given X will be considerably less than the standard deviation in the **unconditional distribution** of Y ($\hat{\sigma} < \hat{\sigma}_Y$). In other words, if there is a linear relationship between Y and X then, across observations, the observed values fall closer to the regression line than to the overall sample mean. The figure below depicts such conditional distributions. These distributions are centered on the estimated conditional means. And, their estimated conditional standard deviation is smaller than the unconditional standard deviation ($\hat{\sigma}_Y$) shown to the left.

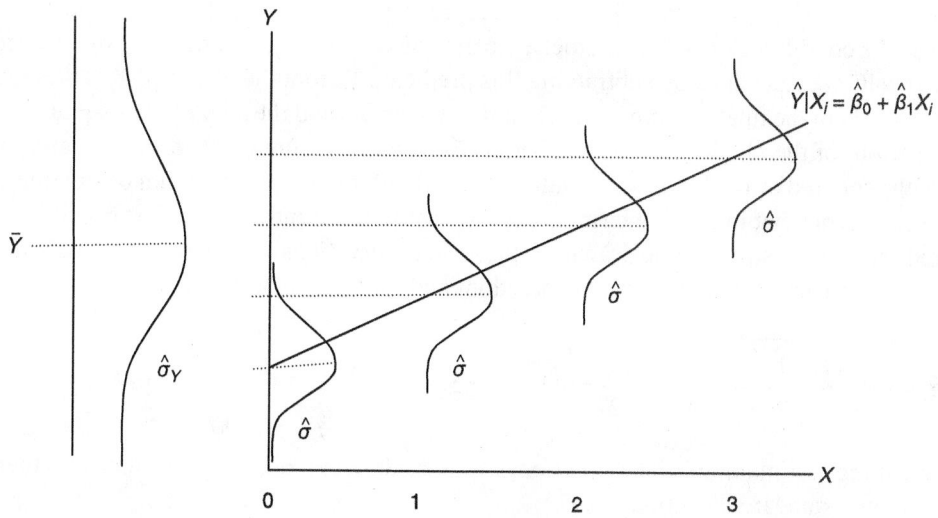

Below, we will ask SAS and Stata to calculate the conditional and unconditional standard deviations using our example of the distance the mother lives from her adult child. First, let's take a look at the results for our stylized example based on 50 cases created from the NSFH. Using the formula above, the prediction equation is estimated to be: $\hat{Y}_i = 23.78 + 6.13X$. We might also write this as $\widehat{hrchores}_i = 23.78 + 6.13 * numkid$ to make the variables in our example explicit. We can use what we learned above about the algebra and geometry of a straight line to say in words what these values represent. The intercept estimates that when a household contains no children, a woman will spend nearly 24 hours per week on chores, on average. With each additional child in the household, the woman spends about six additional hours per week on chores, on average.

Although we will rely on the computer to make these calculations throughout the textbook, it can be helpful to see an explicit set of calculations to help demystify the process. Appendix G provides a spreadsheet of these calculations for our stylized example. (The spreadsheet is available on the textbook web site *http://www.routledge.com/cw/gordon*) The first two columns contain the observed values of the Y and X variables, *hrchores* and *numkid*. The rows circled in green show the two observations highlighted in Figure 8.3. The third and fourth columns calculate the deviations of each of these observed values from their respective means (the means are shown at the bottom of columns 1 and 2). The fourth and fifth columns provide the product of these deviations, across Y and X and between X and itself. The sum of these products are shown below columns 5 and 6, and these are entered into the equations to make the calculations labeled *Slope* and *Intercept*.

$$\hat{\beta}_1 = \frac{\sum(X_i - \bar{X})(Y_i - \bar{Y})}{\sum(X_i - \bar{X})^2} = \frac{613}{100} = 6.13$$

$$\hat{\beta}_0 = \bar{Y} - \hat{\beta}_1\bar{X} = 36.04 - (6.13 * 2) = 23.78$$

The seventh column then uses the intercept and slope to predict the Ys based on the observed Xs (e.g., for case 23, the calculation is $23.78 + 6.13 * 2 = 36.04$; for case 36, the calculation is $23.78 + 6.13 * 3 = 42.17$). Notice that, as expected, within levels of number of children, the predicted value of Y is the same. These values represent the systematic portion of the regression line (i.e., the conditional mean). The stochastic portion of the model is estimated by the errors in the next column, calculated by subtracting this predicted $\hat{Y}_i$ from the observed Y_i. The square of these errors is in the final column, and the sum of the errors and the sum of their squares appear at the bottom of these columns. Notice that, as expected, the sum of the errors is zero, but the sum of the squared errors is a positive value. It is difficult to interpret this sum of squared errors in absolute terms, but in relative terms we know that it represents the smallest possible sum of squared errors for a straight line drawn for these 50 observations. The RMSE value divides this sum of squared errors by the degrees of freedom and then takes the square root.

$$\hat{\sigma} = \sqrt{\frac{\sum(Y_i - \hat{Y}_i)^2}{n-2}} = \sqrt{\frac{1614.2}{50-2}} = \sqrt{33.63} = 5.80$$

The resulting estimate of the conditional standard deviation, 5.80, is smaller than the unconditional standard deviation, 10.47.[5]

8.4.4 Standard Error of the Estimators of the Intercept and Slope

In social science applications, our ultimate goal is generally to answer our research questions or evaluate our hypotheses. We will see below that an essential ingredient for doing so is the standard error of our estimators, which allow us to calculate test statistics and confidence intervals. As discussed above, the standard error is the standard deviation of the sampling distribution for the estimator. A relatively large standard error means that in any given sample our estimate is more likely to fall further from the population value. A relatively small standard error means that in any given sample our estimate is more likely to fall closer to the population value.

Under least squares, the standard errors of the estimators of the intercept and slope are calculated with the following formulas (for details on the derivations, see Fox 2008; Kutner, Nachtsheim, and Neter 2004; Wooldridge 2009).

$$\sigma_{\hat{\beta}_1} = \frac{\sigma}{\sqrt{\Sigma(X_i - \bar{X})^2}} \tag{8.8}$$

$$\sigma_{\hat{\beta}_0} = \sigma\sqrt{\frac{\Sigma(X_i)^2}{n\Sigma(X_i - \bar{X})^2}}$$

Note that these formulas depend on the unknown conditional standard deviation, σ. By substituting the estimate of the conditional standard deviation, $\hat{\sigma} = \sqrt{\frac{\Sigma(Y_i - \hat{Y}_i)^2}{(n-2)}}$ we can estimate the standard errors for the intercept and slope.

$$\hat{\sigma}_{\hat{\beta}_1} = \frac{\hat{\sigma}}{\sqrt{\sum(X_i - \bar{X})^2}}$$

$$\hat{\sigma}_{\hat{\beta}_0} = \hat{\sigma}\sqrt{\frac{\sum(X_i)^2}{n\sum(X_i - \bar{X})^2}}$$

Our research questions typically involve hypothesis tests about the slope, so we are particularly concerned with how close our estimate of the slope is to the population value.

What does the formula for the standard error of the slope shown in Equation 8.8 tell us about the key components that affect its size?

■ The standard error of the slope is directly proportional to the conditional standard deviation. So, with all else held constant, *a larger conditional standard deviation would correspond to a larger standard error for the slope and thus less precision in our estimate of the slope.* In other words, to the extent that the observed Y_i do not cluster closely around the regression line, then our estimates of the slope will vary more from sample to sample.

■ The standard error of the slope is inversely proportional to the sum of the squared deviations of the X_i from their mean $\bar{X}$. Thus, all else equal, *greater variation in the observed values of the predictor variable will correspond to a smaller standard error for the estimates of the slope.* In other words, we can more precisely estimate the slope when we have good variability in the X values.

■ We can also see in the denominator of the equation for the standard error of the slope estimate that *as the sample size increases the standard error of the estimate of the slope decreases, all else equal.* This can be seen since each additional observation in the sample adds another squared difference between X_i and $\bar{X}$ to be summed in the denominator (i.e., the denominator contains the *variation* in the Xs not the *variance* of the Xs).

It is useful to keep these factors in mind as you plan a research project and interpret your results. You will be better able to estimate the association between your predictor of interest and the outcome if you have: (a) a larger sample size, (b) more variation on the predictor variable, and (c) a better fit around the regression line. The first two of these can be built into your study design. Using existing data sources is one way to obtain a larger sample size. Collaboration with peers and mentors or external funding may help you to increase the sample size if you collect your own data. Variation on the predictor variable can also be increased (or at least not unwittingly limited) through thoughtful study design. Using existing data sets may again be helpful. For example, national designs may provide the greatest variation on some variables, such as neighborhood income, which would be constrained in localized studies. Thinking carefully may also help you to avoid decisions that limit variation (e.g., design decisions such as drawing a sample from particular organizations or geographic areas, or restricting the age of sample members, may affect the variation of a predictor of interest). The closeness that the observed data fall to your regression line may seem harder to control, although reducing measurement error in your outcome variable and predictor, and relying on prior studies and solid theory to identify your predictors of interest, are good strategies.

8.4.5: The Standard OLS Assumptions

If our goal were description—finding the best fitting line for the sample data—then we could stop with the formulas for the **point estimates** of the slope and intercept. But, to draw inferences about the population parameters, as we typically want to do in the social sciences, we need some additional assumptions. We will examine these assumptions in greater detail in later chapters, especially Chapter 14. Here, we preview a few of them. If the OLS assumptions hold, it can be shown that the OLS estimators are unbiased and have the minimum standard error of all unbiased linear estimators (they are called the **Best Linear Unbiased Estimators, "BLUE"**).

■ **Box 8.5**

The idea of the OLS coefficient being best—having the smallest standard error—among all linear unbiased estimators is also referred to as it being **efficient**. When two estimation techniques both produce unbiased estimates, the technique that has the lower standard error is referred to as more efficient.

One important assumption of OLS is that we are modeling the conditional means of the outcome variable in relation to the predictor of interest (i.e., is the average value of Y larger [or smaller] within higher levels of X than within lower levels of X)? We allow for variation around these conditional means, so that any given individual at a particular level of X may have an observed value of Y that is higher or lower than the conditional mean. Still, it is important to be careful in discussing our findings to emphasize the distinction between prediction of averages and individual variation around those averages (i.e., the estimates should not be interpreted as though they reflect a deterministic relationship between X and Y).

The model is also assumed to be linear in the parameters, meaning that we do not raise our coefficients to a power or multiply coefficients together. We can model nonlinear associations between X and Y, however, and we will learn how to do so in Chapter 12. For example, we might expect a positive but diminishing association between children's reading achievement and family income: the difference in reading achievement for children from families with $10,000 and $20,000 of income may be larger than the difference in reading achievement for children from families with $110,000 and $120,000 in income. Or, we might expect that the association between age and verbal acuity is curvilinear, rising from childhood to middle adulthood, and then falling in older age. Incorrectly modeling such associations as though they are linear is not a problem inherent to regression analysis. Rather, it is the job of the researcher to conceptualize the relationship appropriately between the predictor and outcome, as linear or nonlinear (or check for nonlinear associations during model estimation) and to specify correctly the model to identify nonlinear relationships, if needed. We will learn how to do this in Chapter 12.

Our OLS model also assumes that the conditional variance is the same across levels of X. This has been implicit above, for example in the lack of a subscript on σ^2. Constant conditional variance is referred to as homoskedasticity. Nonconstant conditional variance is called heteroskedasticity and is often indicated by subscripting the conditional variance as σ_i^2. We will discuss how to identify and address heteroskedasticity in Chapter 14.

We will also deal with other assumptions of the model in later chapters. For example, when we add additional predictors to the model in multiple regression in Chapter 9 we assume that the predictors are not collinear (not perfectly correlated). We also assume that the error terms are not correlated across individuals, and in Chapter 18 touch on ways to address potential correlation and refer to additional advanced techniques for doing so (see Box 8.6). More broadly, we assume that we have correctly specified the model, including the issue of nonlinear relationships noted above, but also in other ways (such as including the correct set of variables in the model).

8.4.6: The Normality Assumption

We do not need to assume any particular form for the distribution of the outcome variable, and the residuals, in order for the OLS estimators to be BLUE. However, the normality assumption is commonly used to justify hypothesis testing. We will discuss problem of outliers and influential observations that often go along with non-normality in Chapter 14.

■ Box 8.6

For example, errors might not be independent if we include multiple members of the same family, multiple students from the same class, or multiple companies from the same city, rather than drawing samples of individuals, students, and companies completely randomly. As discussed in Chapter 2, clustering is sometimes used to reduce the costs of a study and we show one method for accounting for such clustering in Section 8.5. We briefly preview additional techniques for doing so in the roadmap in Chapter 18.

We are able to calculate confidence intervals and test hypotheses in the standard OLS regression model because we assume that the errors, ε_i, follow a normal distribution. The error term is the stochastic component in the regression equation. This means that assumptions about the distribution of the error term carry over into assumptions about the distribution of the outcome variable and assumptions about the distribution of the estimators of the intercept and the slope (because the Ys enter the formulas for the intercept and the slope, and the error is the stochastic portion of the Ys; the Xs are assumed given).

The normality assumption is sometimes summarized with notation such as the following:

$$\varepsilon_i \sim idN(0, \sigma^2)$$
$$Y_i|X \sim idN(\beta_0 + \beta_1 X_i, \sigma^2)$$

In words, this simply means that the errors are distributed ($\sim$) independently (id) and normally (N), with a mean of zero and variance of σ^2. We already noted above the assumptions of constant variance and independence. The zero mean of the errors means that positive errors balance out negative errors, so the systematic portion of the regression model accurately captures the conditional mean of Y. Because of this, and the fact that the errors comprise the stochastic portion of the regression model, the Ys are also distributed independently and normally with a variance of σ^2, but their mean is the conditional mean, $\beta_0 + \beta_1 X_i$, the systematic portion of the regression model.

The assumption of normal errors can be motivated by the conceptualization of the error term that we discussed earlier. Namely, if we think of the error term as capturing the sum of many excluded factors that impact Y, then the central limit theorem can provide a justification for the normality assumption.[6]

8.4.7: Hypothesis Testing about the Slope

Given our normality assumption, we can use standard techniques for hypothesis testing based on the normal distribution. We will describe these in detail below for the slope, but first let's review the general steps of hypothesis testing.

Review of Basic Concepts

As you know from Chapter 7, to conduct a hypothesis test, you follow four basic steps:

1. List the null and alternative hypotheses about the value that you expect for the parameter being estimated (in regression models, typically the slope).
2. Calculate a test statistic (typically, the point estimate of the parameter minus the hypothesized value, divided by the estimated standard error).
3. Determine the critical value given the test statistic's distribution (e.g., Z- or t-distribution) and a pre-specified alpha level (typically 0.05).
4. Reject the null hypothesis if the magnitude of the calculated test statistic is larger than the critical value.

Alternatively, at steps 3 and 4 you could calculate the p-value, given the test statistic's distribution, and reject the null hypothesis if the p-value is smaller than the alpha level.

Also recall that hypothesis tests can be one-sided or two-sided. In a **two-sided hypothesis test,** the null hypothesis states that the parameter equals a particular value (the **hypothesized value**) and the alternative hypothesis states that the parameter does not equal that value. In a **one-sided hypothesis test**, the null hypothesis states that the parameter is either "less than or equal to" or "greater than or equal to" a particular value (the hypothesized value) and the alternative hypothesis states that the parameter is "greater than" or "less than" a particular value. The hypothesized value is typically zero in regression. In the two-sided context this means that the alternative hypothesis typically states that the relationship is expected to not equal zero ($\neq 0$). In the one-sided context this means that the alternative hypotheses typically state that the relationship is expected to be positive (>0) or negative (<0).

Let's take a look at the standard normal distribution to reinforce these ideas. Figure 8.6 shows a hypothetical example of a two-sided hypothesis test based on the Z-distribution. Recall that with a two-sided test we split the alpha value between the two tails, as shown in the shaded areas in the figure. For the conventional $\alpha = 0.05$ the critical Z-value for a two-sided test is $|1.96|$. We show the negative value explicitly on the left in Figure 8.6. The probability to the left of that Z-value is 0.025. So, 2.5 percent of the Z-values are more negative than -1.96.

The Z-distribution is symmetric, and the shaded area on the right side of the figure similarly depicts the 2.5 percent of Z-values that are larger than 1.96.

In Figure 8.6, we also show a hypothetical calculated Z-value of -1.40. For a two-sided test, remember that the p-value is the proportion of Z-values that are more extreme than the absolute value of our Z-value. On the left, we show that 8 percent of Z-values are more negative than

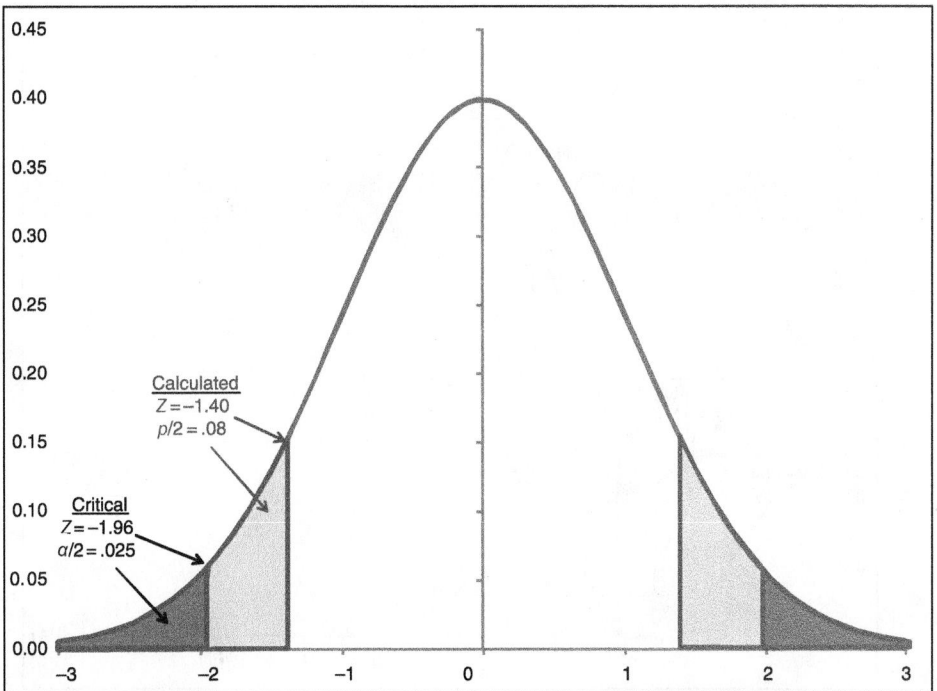

Figure 8.6

−1.40 (the sum of the light and dark gray areas on the left of the figure). The value 0.08 is half of the p-value. The other half is represented by the light and dark gray areas on the right side of the figure: an additional 8 percent of the Z-values are more positive than 1.40. So the p-value in our hypothetical example is 0.08 + 0.08 = 0.16.

To make a conclusion about our hypothesis test in this hypothetical case, we would either compare the calculated Z-value to the critical Z-value or compare the calculated p-value to the alpha level. Each comparison will lead us to the same conclusion:

1. The absolute value of the calculated Z-value |−1.40| is smaller than the absolute value of the critical Z-value |−1.96| thus we fail to reject.
2. The calculated p-value of 0.16 is larger than the alpha of 0.05 thus we fail to reject.

Figure 8.7 shows an example of a one-sided test. To illuminate the differences between the one-sided and two-sided cases, we assume that we have the same calculated Z-value of −1.40. In the one-sided case, we do not double the percentage of Z-values more extreme than our calculated Z-value. Rather, we concentrate on one tail. In our case, let's assume that our alternative hypothesis was that our point estimate would be negative. (We will have more to say about this below.) So, the p-value is the probability of being more negative than the calculated Z-value, which we saw above is 0.08. Notice that there is nothing shaded in the right tail of Figure 8.7. Thus, in this one-sided case, the p-value is 0.08.

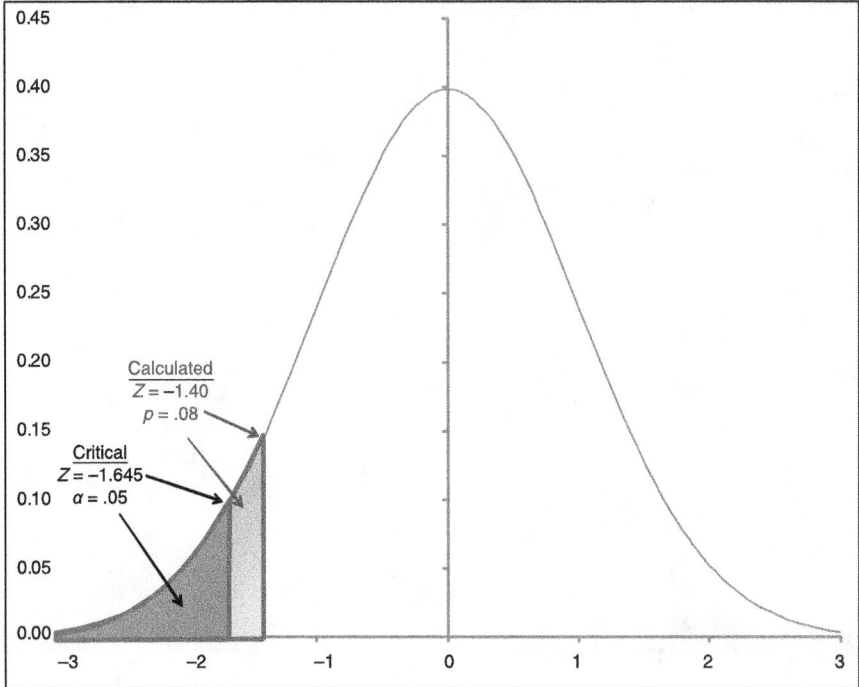

▪ Figure 8.7

In the one-sided case, we also do not split the alpha level between the two tails. We place it all in one tail. Again, in this case, since we assume that our alternative hypothesis was that our point estimate would be negative, we place the p-value in the left tail. The Z-value is now -1.645 because 5 percent of Z-values are more negative than -1.645.

In our hypothetical example, our conclusion about the test would be the same as in the two-sided case. We fail to reject the null hypothesis because $|-1.40| < |-1.645|$ and $0.08 > 0.05$. We will provide an example below of a case in which the one-sided and two-sided tests would lead to difference conclusions for the same point estimate.

Alternatively, we might calculate a **confidence interval** by adding and subtracting a multiple of the estimated standard error from the point estimate. As we saw in Chapter 7, the confidence interval approach leads to the same conclusion as a two-sided hypothesis test, with the same alpha level. In our case, we can test our null hypothesis by seeing whether the hypothesized value falls within these lower and upper bounds of the confidence interval. If the confidence interval contains the hypothesized value, then we fail to reject the null hypothesis. If we use $Z = 1.96$ for the multiplier of the estimated standard error, our decision will be the same as for the test statistic approach with a two-sided alternative and $\alpha = 0.05$. The resulting confidence interval is referred to as a 95 percent confidence interval, because it is based on the Z-value for an alpha of 5 percent. For a one-sided test, we must rely on the test statistic approach.

Generally, for the normal distribution, we could use the standard normal table to look up a critical Z-value for a given alpha level or to look up a p-value for a calculated Z-value. In regression analysis, we use the t-distribution instead of the Z-distribution, however, for tests about the slope and the intercept. Statistically, the t-distribution is needed because we used the estimated standard error of the slope given the conditional standard deviation was unknown. The degrees of freedom for the t-statistic is $n - 2$ in the bivariate regression case. However, as we saw in Chapter 6, the t becomes identical to the Z for large samples. Computer output will typically provide the exact t-values and associated p-values for the relevant degrees of freedom. If the sample is large (n greater than 60), we also know that t-values greater than about 2 will be significant at a two-sided 5 percent Type I error level, based on the empirical rule. This rough cutoff is useful when reviewing t-statistics that do not have p-values listed (e.g., in a book or journal article).

Confidence Interval Approach for the Slope

More precisely, the confidence interval for the slope can be constructed as $\hat{\beta}_1 \pm t_{\alpha/2} \, \hat{\sigma}_{\hat{\beta}_1}$ where $t_{\alpha/2}$ = 1.96 for $\alpha = 0.05$ and a large sample size.

As noted above, to test a null hypothesis about a population parameter against a two-sided alternative, we check whether the constructed confidence interval contains the hypothesized value of the population parameter. For the slope, we would proceed as follows.

$$H_0 : \beta_1 = \beta_1^*$$
$$H_a : \beta_1 \neq \beta_1^*$$

Decision rule:

> If β_1^* is contained within the bounds of the confidence interval, then do not reject the null hypothesis.
> If β_1^* is not contained within the bounds of the confidence interval, then reject the null hypothesis.

Recall that we do not accept the null hypothesis when we fail to reject. In either case of rejecting or failing to reject our null hypothesis, the range of slopes within the lower and upper bounds of the confidence interval provide our best estimates of the true population slope parameter.

This decision rule should make intuitive sense. If the hypothesized slope value is within the estimated range of values, then we cannot reject the hypothesis that the parameter takes on that null value. However, if the hypothesized slope value falls outside of the estimated range of values, then we can reject the null hypothesis that the parameter takes on the hypothesized value.

Test Statistic Approach for the Slope

For the test statistic approach, we define:

$$t = \frac{\hat{\beta}_1 - \beta_1^*}{\hat{\sigma}_{\hat{\beta}_1}}$$

where β_1^* is the hypothesized value of the slope under the null hypothesis (often zero) and $df = n - 2$ in bivariate regression.

Two-Sided Hypothesis Test

For a two-sided test, we then either contrast this t-statistic to the critical t-value for the given α and degrees of freedom (with α divided by two to include both tails) or we look up the p-value for our t-statistic and degrees of freedom (with the probability of the t-value being more extreme than our t-value being doubled to encompass both tails) and compare the calculated p-value to the selected α value. It is conventional to use $\alpha = 0.05$ and $t_{\alpha/2} = 1.96$ as the cutoffs.

As reviewed above, if the absolute value of the t-statistic is larger than the critical value (e.g., 1.96) or the p-value is less than the alpha value (e.g., .05) then we reject the null hypothesis; otherwise, we fail to reject the null hypothesis. In the latter case, we do not accept the null hypothesis. Under the test statistic approach, our best guess of the true population slope parameter is the point estimate $\hat{\beta}_1$.

As with the confidence interval, the decision rules for the hypothesis test should be intuitive. If our t-statistic is highly unusual (far in the tails of the sampling distribution constructed under the null hypothesis) then our findings are not consistent with the null hypothesis.

One-Sided Hypothesis Test

One-sided significance tests proceed similarly. Although we do not divide alpha into two tails.

Two-sided	One-sided (right tail)	One-sided (left tail)
$H_0: \beta_1 = \beta_1^*$ $H_a: \beta_1 \neq \beta_1^*$ Calculate p-value using the area to the right of the positive value of the calculated t-statistic and to the left of the negative value of the t-statistic.	$H_0: \beta_1 \leq \beta_1^*$ $H_a: \beta_1 > \beta_1^*$ Calculate p-value using the area to the right of the calculated t-statistic.	$H_0: \beta_1 \geq \beta_1^*$ $H_a: \beta_1 < \beta_1^*$ Calculate p-value using the area to the left of the calculated t-statistic.

When $\beta_1^* = 0$, then the one-sided "right tail" hypothesis corresponds to the situation where our theory suggests that our predictor and outcome variables are positively associated (i.e., $H_a: \beta_1 > 0$). Similarly, when $\beta_1^* = 0$, then the one-sided "left tail" hypothesis corresponds to the situation where our theory suggests that our predictor and outcome variable are negatively associated (i.e., $H_a: \beta_1 < 0$).

We will see below how to use SAS and Stata output to conduct a one-sided hypothesis test.

Zero as the Hypothesized Value

The typical hypothesis test in OLS regression is a two-sided test of the null hypothesis that $H_0: \beta_1 = 0$ versus the alternative that $H_a: \beta_1 \neq 0$.

The t-value and p-value provided in standard SAS and Stata output correspond to this test. This "straw man" test has a null hypothesis that Y is not linearly predicted by X and an alternative hypothesis that Y is linearly predicted by Y (either positively or negatively). Referring back to Figure 8.2, when the slope is zero, the relationship between X and Y is graphed as a horizontal line; in this situation, the conditional mean of Y is the same regardless of the level of X.

Sometimes enough prior research or theoretical clarity exists to specify in advance the expected direction of the relationship between the predictor and outcome. As noted above, if a positive association is expected, then the null hypothesis would be H_o: $\beta_1 \leq 0$ and the alternative hypothesis would be H_a: $\beta_1 > 0$. If a negative association is expected, then the null hypothesis would be H_o: $\beta_1 \geq 0$ and the alternative hypothesis would be H_a: $\beta_1 < 0$.

In these cases, if the estimated coefficient is consistent with the alternative hypothesis (the "correct sign"), we can calculate the one-sided p-value for a null hypothesized value of zero by dividing the p-value listed in SAS's output in half. A correct sign would be a positive estimate of the coefficient if our alternative hypothesis is H_a: $\beta_1 > 0$ and a negative estimate of the coefficient if our alternative hypothesis is H_a: $\beta_1 < 0$. If the estimated coefficient is not consistent with the alternative hypothesis ("wrong sign"), then we should subtract half of the listed p-value from one.

Example of Hypothesis Testing

Let's look at our NSFH distance example to put these approaches into practice. In Chapter 2, we initially stated our research questions in a nondirectional fashion: how does an adult's earnings relate to how near she lives to her mother? In this case, we would use a nondirectional or two-sided alternative.

H_o: Adults' earnings do not linearly predict the distance they live from their mothers.
H_a: Adults' earnings linearly predict the distance they live from their mothers.

In symbols, this is our standard hypothesis test, using the straw man hypothesized value of zero to represent no linear relationship:

H_o: $\beta_1 = 0$
H_a: $\beta_1 \neq 0$

SAS and Stata Syntax

We can ask SAS and Stata to estimate the slope and its standard error and to calculate the associated t-value and p-value using their basic regression commands.

	SAS	Stata
Basic Syntax	proc reg; model <depvar>=<indepvar>; run;	regress <depvar> <indepvar>

Notice the similar structure of the commands, mirroring our regression equation. The dependent variable is listed first (*depvar* on the left) followed by the independent variable (*indepvar* on the right). In SAS, the equals sign is included to separate the dependent from the independent variable, further mimicking how we write the equation. Both use a short word to reflect regression (reg or regress).[7] Following SAS convention, REG is a procedure (PROC). The command name should be paired with the word RUN; and, all variables must have been previously defined in a DATA step. SAS allows multiple model statements to be included in a single PROC REG, and we will use this approach in some cases. For example, we might type:

```
proc reg;
  model <depvar>=<indepvar1>;
  model <depvar>=<indepvar2>;
run;
```

Both SAS and Stata allow many more options, some of which we will learn later in this chapter and in future chapters (to access the documentation, type "REG procedure" in the SAS help index and type `help regress` in the Stata command window).

Prediction Equation

Display B.8.1 shows the commands for the regression of *g1miles* on *g2earn* and the resulting output. We show the full set of output, but we will focus for now on the elements circled in green. Each package shows the same calculated values, but in different positions. Near the top of both sets of output we see the sample size of 6,350. And, in the middle, the estimated Root MSE is 635.1 (rounded to the first decimal). Both then have tables which show the sample estimates of the intercept and slope (labeled `Coef.` in Stata and `Parameter Estimate` in SAS). Although SAS lists the intercept in the first row, and Stata in the last (labeled `_cons`), the estimated value is the same: 249.81 (rounded to two decimals).[8] The row for the slope is labeled with the predictor variable's name, *g2earn*. The estimate is 0.00113 (rounded to five decimals).[9]

Putting these estimates together we can write the prediction equation:

$$\hat{Y} = 249.81 + .00113 * X$$

or using the variable names

$$\overline{g1miles} = 249.81 + .00113 * g2earn$$

The slope is very small in size because one unit of change on the predictor—the adult child's earnings—represents a dollar change on annual earnings. As discussed above, we can multiply the coefficient estimate by a factor to convert to a more meaningful amount of change. For example, if we set $i = \$10,000$ as the amount of increase on X, then the amount of change on Y would be $0.0011333 * 10,000 = 11.333$. We can interpret this rescaled slope as: "The distance a mother lives from her adult child increases by over 11 miles, on average, with each additional \$10,000 the child earns." We will discuss below additional strategies for making substantively meaningful interpretations (but, as we will see, doing so will not affect our decision on the hypothesis test).

Two-Sided Hypothesis Test

Can we reject the null hypothesis that the slope is equal to zero? The SAS and Stata output list the estimated standard error to allow us to complete this test. Each also calculates a t-value and p-value based on the basic straw man hypothesis test (a null of no linear relationship against an alternative of some linear relationship, without specification of direction). In this case, $t = (\hat{\beta}_1 - 0)/\hat{\sigma}_{\hat{\beta}_1}$ $= (.0011333 - 0)/.00021852 = 5.19$ with $n - 2 = 6{,}350 - 2 = 6{,}348$ degrees of freedom.[10] The computer has done the work of looking up the p-value for this test statistic. Just based on the t-value, though, we should recognize that we can reject the null hypothesis. The t-distribution for our sample size of over 6,000 is very close to the normal and $t_{\alpha/2} = 1.96$ in this large sample. Our t-value of 5.19 is larger than this critical value. Likewise, the p-value is listed as less than .0001 in both sets of output. So, we can reject the null hypothesis. We do find evidence of a linear relationship between the respondent's earnings and the distance his or her mother lives away.

Notice that SAS labels the column containing the p-value "`Pr > |t|`" and Stata labels it "`P>|t|`." In both cases, placing the letter t within the two vertical lines represents the absolute value of t. This reminds us that SAS and Stata list the p-values for two-sided tests—the probability of a t-value larger than a t of the calculated magnitude with either positive or negative sign. In our case, it is the probability in a t-distribution with 6,348 degrees of freedom of a value larger than 5.19 or smaller than −5.19. This **two-sided p-value** is appropriate given the way we stated the alternative hypothesis above, without direction ($H_a: \beta_1 \neq 0$).

One-Sided Hypothesis Test

For our research question, it might have been possible to draw on conceptual ideas and prior empirical work to specify instead a directional alternative hypothesis. For example, children who earn more have more financial resources to allow a distant move and may be in higher status jobs where opportunities are available in distant locations.[11] Thus, we might have written the following research hypotheses:

H_0: Adults' earnings are unrelated to or negatively associated with the distance they live from their mothers.

H_a: Adults' earnings are positively associated with the distance they live from their mothers.

In symbols:

$H_0: \beta_1 \leq 0$
$H_a: \beta_1 > 0$

The alternative hypothesis denotes that positive estimates for the slope would be consistent with our expectations (a positive estimate would be of the "right sign"—greater than zero as in our alternative hypothesis). The null hypothesis indicates that an estimate of zero or an estimated negative value for the slope would not be consistent with our expectations (a negative estimate would be of the "wrong sign"—less than or equal to zero as in our null hypothesis).

Because SAS and Stata list two-sided *p*-values, we need to do some additional work to calculate a **one-sided *p*-value** and make a decision about such one-sided tests. This diagram illustrates the decision-making process for a one-sided test, based on statistical output.

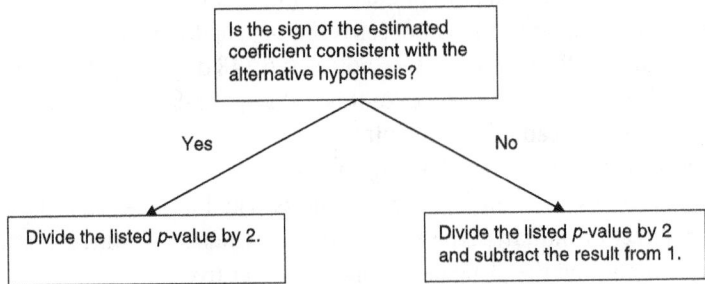

The resulting *p*-value is then compared to our alpha (typically 0.05) to make a decision about the one-sided null hypothesis. In our case, the sign is consistent with our alternative hypothesis (0.00113 is positive in sign), so we can divide the listed *p*-value in half. Doing so is unimportant in our example because the two-sided *p*-value is already quite small.

In cases of marginal significance, dividing the *p*-value in half can have greater importance. For example, if the listed two-sided *p*-value were 0.06, then it would not be significant at a conventional 5 percent alpha level. But, dividing it in half (to 0.03) would lead to rejection of the one-sided null hypothesis at a conventional 5 percent alpha level. Thus:

■ If you are able to state your hypothesis in a directional manner before examining the association in your data, then you should use a one-sided test.
■ If you are not able to state your hypothesis in a directional manner before examining the association in your data, you should use a two-sided test.

What if you specify a directional hypothesis a priori, and the estimated coefficient is the "wrong sign" (inconsistent with your alternative hypothesis) and shown to be statistically significant by SAS and Stata's two-sided test? In this case, if you use the decision rules above, you should convert this significant two-sided *p*-value to a nonsignificant one-sided *p*-value. For example, suppose we had an estimated coefficient that was negative in sign, our alternative hypothesis expected a positive sign, and the listed two-sided *p*-value was 0.04? Then, we should calculate the one-sided *p*-value to be $1 - (0.04/2) = 1 - 0.02 = 0.98$. This *p*-value indicates that we should fail to reject our original null hypothesis. In fact, the negative sign of the coefficient suggests that we were quite wrong in our alternative hypothesis, especially given its large magnitude relative to the estimated standard error (i.e., the fact that the estimate was in the wrong direction with a small two-sided *p*-value). This might be noted in discussing the findings, although it is not consistent with statistical methods to revise your original hypothesis to be consistent with the unexpected finding.

Confidence Interval Approach

Stata always includes a 95 percent confidence interval for the intercept and slope in its default output. We can ask SAS to report a confidence interval by adding the option /clb (Confidence Limits for the parameter estimates, sometimes also known as Betas). Display B.8.2 implements this option in SAS. The results from both packages are circled in green, and are the same within rounding. By hand, we can calculate them as follows:

$$\hat{\beta}_1 \pm t_{\alpha/2}\,\hat{\sigma}_{\hat{\beta}_1} = 0.0011333 \pm 1.96 * 0.00021852 = (0.000705, 0.001562)$$

Within rounding to four significant digits, our results match the packages.[12] Both packages and our hand calculations produce a lower bound of 0.000705 and an upper bound of 0.001562. As expected, this result does not contain the null value of zero and thus our decision is consistent with the two-sided hypothesis test (reject the null hypothesis). The results allow us to estimate that the coefficient falls between 0.000705 and 0.001562 with 95 percent confidence. Whether it actually contains the parameter in this sample is unknown, and the upper and lower limits of the confidence interval would differ from sample to sample.

8.4.8: Inference About the Intercept

Test statistics and confidence intervals for the intercept are constructed similarly.

As we saw at the beginning of this chapter, the intercept measures the point at which the regression line crosses the Y-axis (i.e., the conditional mean of Y when $X = 0$).

In our example, Display B.8.1 showed that the intercept is estimated to be 249.8116. Thus, adults with no earnings are estimated to live about 250 miles away from their mothers, on average.

As we discussed above, when $X = 0$ does not fall within the range of the X values, inference about the intercept will not be substantively meaningful. Similarly, the default hypothesis about the intercept included in computer printout tests $H_o: \beta_0 = 0$ against the alternative that $H_a: \beta_0 \neq 0$ may not be substantively meaningful in all applications (even though the SAS and Stata output will always conduct and present the results of this test in the default output). Even if $X = 0$ falls within the range of Xs, testing whether the conditional mean of Y when $X = 0$ is significantly above or below zero may not be substantively meaningful if zero is not a value in the range of Y (e.g., if the outcome was SAT scores). In other words, while testing whether the *slope* differs from zero is an important straw man test of X significantly linearly predicting Y, the substantive importance of testing whether the *intercept* equals zero will vary across applications.

For example, suppose we hypothesized that hours of paid work was negatively related to hours of chores. This raises two questions in relation to the interpretation of the intercept. First, is $X = 0$ a valid value? In our example, we can ask whether it makes sense to include those working no hours in the sample (i.e., can we think of a continuous progression from no work to increasing hours of work? Or, should we view the movement from nonemployment to employment as a distinct process from the hours worked once employed)? In the stylized example in Figure 8.8,

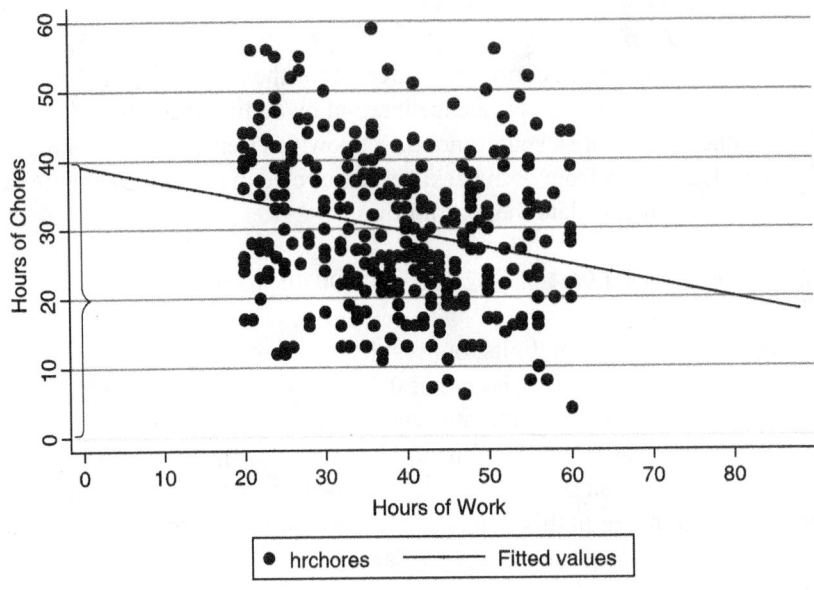

■ Figure 8.8

Source: Stylized sample from National Survey of Families and Households, Wave 1

we excluded women who worked fewer than 20 or more than 60 hours per week. Thus, $X = 0$ is not valid in this case (the sample points fall between 20 and 60 on the X axis). But, we allowed the sample line to extend to the point where the line would meet the Y axis, showing how a prediction could be made from the regression line when $X = 0$, even if no such values exist in the sample.

Second, even if zero is a valid value for the predictor, does it make sense to test whether the conditional mean is zero? Figure 8.9 illustrates the negative association between hours of work and hours of chores. Here, we included those who worked fewer than 20 hours per week (including the small number reporting zero hours in the survey week). Given our conceptualization of a negative association between hours of chores and hours of work, and our focus on women, does it make sense to test a null hypothesis of no hours spent on chores? The dashed line in Figure 8.9 shows a line with the sample slope as the estimated regression line, but shifted down so that it begins with an intercept of zero. The estimated negative slope would predict that women who worked more hours engaged in a negative level of chores, clearly not sensible. And, in fact, in the NSFH sample, only 1 percent of women report spending no hours per week on chores.

8.4.9: Substantive Interpretation

It is important to consider the substantive importance of the point estimates and confidence intervals for our coefficients, along with the results of our decisions about our null and alternative hypotheses.

Recall that when the sample size is larger, the standard error is smaller, and thus it is especially possible in larger samples to reject null hypotheses for substantively small associations. As a

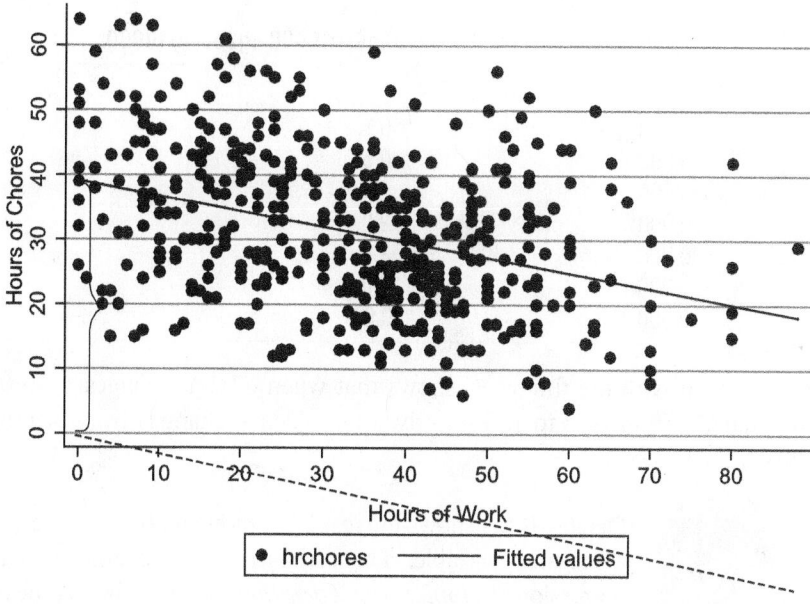

■ **Figure 8.9**

Source: Stylized sample from National Survey of Families and Households, Wave 1

consequence, it is important to ensure that findings that reject the null are substantively meaningful, especially when our sample sizes are large. In other words, for a substantively meaningful increase in X, is the estimated change in Y based on the point estimate or confidence interval of "real world" importance?

Reinterpreting for a Different Amount of Change

We discussed at the beginning of this chapter how to translate the slope into a more meaningful value if a one unit change in X is not substantively meaningful. We saw that the effect of X on Y for changes in X other than 1 can be easily calculated using the following rule: if we increase X by i units, then Y will change by $i\hat{\beta}_1$ units. In this case, we are reinterpreting the slope coefficient after estimating a regression model. When moving between different X and Y scalings, the significance of the effect of X on Y remains the same, but the ease with which the substantive relevance is seen may be clearer in some units of measurement than others.

Rescaling Before Estimation

We can also rescale X and/or Y before running the regression model to obtain the desired results directly from SAS and Stata. Although this does not affect our decisions about hypothesis tests, it can make the output easier to read. To rescale *g2earn* into units of $10,000 we could create a new variable that is equal to *g2earn10000* = *g2earn*/10000. An increase of 1 on this new variable represents a $10,000 change in earnings. The following table shows some example values to help make the correspondence between the values of the old and new variable concrete.

g2earn	g2earn10000=g2earn/10000
0	0.0
1,000	0.1
5,000	0.5
10,000	1.0
20,000	2.0
30,000	3.0
50,000	5.0
100,000	10.0

Comparing the fourth with the first rows shows that when *g2earn* changes from 0 to 10,000, *g2earn10000* changes from zero to 1. Similarly, when *g2earn* changes from 20,000 to 30,000 *g2earn10000* changes from 2 to 3.

■ **Box 8.7**

More explicitly, notice that if we multiply both the numerator and denominator by 10,000 in the original calculation of the *t*-value, the 10,000 cancels out:

$$t = \frac{\hat{\beta}_1 - 0}{\hat{\sigma}_{\hat{\beta}_1}} = \frac{.00113 * 10000 - 0}{.0002185 * 10000}$$

$$= \frac{.00113 * 10000}{.0002185 * 10000}$$

$$= \frac{.00113}{.0002185}.$$

If we had a nonzero hypothesized value, rather than zero, we would need to rescale it equivalently by 10,000, so the 10,000 would still cancel out of the numerator and denominator, even with a nonzero hypothesized value.

Display B.8.3 shows the results of re-estimating our models with such a rescaled variable. The estimated slope coefficient based on the regression of *g1miles* on *g2earn10000* reports directly the result 11.333 that we calculated above with our $i\hat{\beta}_1$ rule. Notice that in Display B.8.3, the estimated standard error is now also equivalent to the original estimate of the standard error multiplied by 10,000 (0.0002185 * 10,000 = 2.185). Because both the estimated coefficient and standard error are multiplied by the same factor, the *t*-value remains the same (5.19; see Box 8.7). Thus, our conclusion regarding our hypotheses remains unchanged by rescaling the coefficient estimate. Notice also that the intercept and its standard error remain the same as in our original model (compare Display B.8.3 to Display B.8.1). This result will hold in general. Unless a variable is involved in an interaction (as discussed in Chapter 11), rescaling one variable will affect only its own estimated coefficient and standard error, not the estimate of the intercept or estimates for other variables in the model.

In our case, the range of values on *g2earn* was quite large, making a one unit change very small relative to its overall variation, and thus the original coefficient estimate was tiny. It is also important to pay attention to cases in which a one unit change is very large relative to the variation on the predictor. For example, percentages are sometimes used to define contextual variables (e.g., percentage of neighbors who are the same race as the respondent, percentage of students receiving free lunch). If these variables are recorded as decimals, a one unit change will represent the maximal possible change on the variable and may exceed the actual observed range of the variable (i.e., zero to 1 represents 0 percent to 100 percent). In this case, estimates can look substantively larger than they actually are if they are not appropriately rescaled. For example, if we had a variable *psamerace* that captured the proportion of neighbors who are the same race as the respondent in decimals, we could create a new variable *psamerace10* = *psamerace* * 10 that would allow us to interpret the estimated coefficient as the average change in the outcome for a 10 percentage point increase on the predictor.

psamerace	psamerace10=psamerace*10
0.0	0
0.1	1
0.2	2
0.3	3
0.4	4
0.5	5
0.6	6
0.7	7
0.8	8
0.9	9
1.0	10

We can see that a change of zero to 1 on the new variable *psamerace10* represents a change from zero to 0.10 on the original variable *psamerace*.

The Algebra of Rescaling

There is another general way to figure out the rule that we deduced by examining the regression line in Section 8.1.2 (if we increase X by i units, then Y will change by $i\hat{\beta}_1$ units). If we define the following scale factors:

$$newY_i = rescaleY * Y_i$$
$$newX_i = rescaleX * X_i$$

The following relationships hold for the estimated slope coefficient and its standard error:

$$new\hat{\beta}_1 = \frac{rescaleY}{rescaleX} * \hat{\beta}_1$$

$$new\hat{\sigma}_{\hat{\beta}_1} = \frac{rescaleY}{rescaleX} * \hat{\sigma}_{\hat{\beta}_1}$$

The new X variable, *g2earn10000*, that we created above is created from the original X variable *g2earn* by multiplying by 1/10,000. That is, *g2earn10000* = 1/10,000 * *g2earn*. Thus, *rescaleX*=1/10,000. We did not rescale the Y value in this case, thus *rescaleY* = 1 (i.e., *newY*=1*Y*). Plugging into the formulas we get:

$$new\hat{\beta}_1 = \frac{1}{\frac{1}{10,000}} \hat{\beta}_1 = 10,000 * \hat{\beta}_1$$

$$new\hat{\sigma}_{\hat{\beta}_1} = \frac{1}{\frac{1}{10,000}} \hat{\sigma}_{\hat{\beta}_1} = 10,000 * \hat{\sigma}_{\hat{\beta}_1}$$

Thus, by multiplying the listed coefficient estimate and its standard error for *g2earn* by 10,000 we calculate the results that we would obtain if we ran the regression model using *g2earn10000*. Knowing this simple formula makes it easy to convert results so that they can be interpreted for different units of change, if other units are more substantively meaningful.

Standardized Slope Coefficient

The formula in Equation 8.5 is sometimes referred to as an **unstandardized regression coefficient**. A **completely standardized regression coefficient** would result if we rescaled both the X and the Y variables by dividing by their respective standard deviations (see Box 8.8). Such rescaled variables have standard deviation of 1. Variables whose values have been converted to Z- or standard normal-scores are examples of such rescaled variables and are sometimes referred to as standardized variables (see Equation 6.4). If we regressed the standardized Y value on the standardized X value, we call the resulting slope a standardized coefficient estimate. Such a standardized estimate of the slope may be especially useful for interpretation purposes if the original variables do not have substantively meaningful natural units (e.g., a sum of variables rated on scales such as 1 = *never*, 2 = *sometimes*, 3 = *often*, and 4 = *always*). In bivariate regression, the standardized slope is equivalent to the Pearson correlation. Recall that the *Pearson correlation* or r is a unitless measure of linear association between two variables, such as Y and X.

> **■ Box 8.8**
>
> Professional and journal style guides in the social sciences often use the Greek symbol β to designate a standardized coefficient. We have used the symbol β to indicate the unstandardized regression coefficient in the population. You should consult style guides, such as the American Sociological Association Style Guide (American Sociological Association 2007) and Publication Manual of the American Psychological Association (American Psychological Association 2009), and journal submission guidelines to choose the preferred conventions in your field or for a particular journal. We will provide some examples of these varying conventions in the literature excerpts in Chapters 9 and 10.

Based on our discussion above, it is straightforward to produce the formula that relates the standardized slope to the unstandardized slope. In this case, $newY_i = (1/s_y)Y_i$ and $newX_i = (1/s_x)X_i$.[13] Thus, $rescaleX = (1/s_x)$ and $rescaleY = 1/s_y$ and we can calculate the new slope as follows:

$$new\ \hat{\beta}_1 = \frac{rescaleY}{rescaleX} * \hat{\beta}_1 = \frac{\frac{1}{s_y}}{\frac{1}{s_x}}\hat{\beta}_1 = \frac{s_x}{s_y}\hat{\beta}_1$$

This new (rescaled) estimate of the slope is the estimate of the standardized slope coefficient.

Both SAS and Stata have commands to create standardized variables and calculate the estimates of the standardized regression coefficients. We will see how to request estimates of the standardized regression coefficients below.

We will first calculate them directly so we can see how to use the rescale formula. To obtain the standard deviations, we use Stata's command `summarize <varlist>` and the SAS statement `proc means; var <varlist>; run;` Display B.5.4 shows the results of running these commands for SAS and Stata to obtain the standard deviations of the variables *g1miles* and *g2earn*.

We can then plug these values into the formula to calculate by hand an estimate of the new slope (the standardized slope coefficient):

$$new\ \hat{\beta}_1 = \frac{s_x}{s_y}\hat{\beta}_1 = \frac{36475.81}{636.394} * .0011333 = .06496$$

Let's now replicate this process in SAS and Stata, by creating new rescaled variables that divide each variable by its respective standard deviation and estimate a regression model with the new standardized variables. Display B.8.5 shows our use of an expression with the division operator to create these new variables in SAS and Stata (see again Display A.4.1 and A.4.2) and our estimation of the regression model using these new variables. The estimate matches our hand calculation, within rounding error (0.06496 in SAS and 0.0649594 in Stata). Notice that the *t*-value is the same as before (5.19) as expected because the estimated standard error is rescaled by the same factor of s_x/s_y as the slope.

How do we interpret this new standardized estimate of the slope? Recall above that when we divided *g2earn* by 10,000 a one unit change on the new variable, *g2earn10000*, represented a $10,000 change on the original variable. Similarly, when we divide a predictor by its standard deviation, a one-unit change represents a one standard deviation change. For *g2earn*, the following table shows how values on *g2earnSD* relate to values on *g2earn* and *g2earn10000*.

g2earn	g2earn10000= g2earn/10000	g2earnSD= g2earn/36475.81
0	0.0	0.000
1,000	0.1	0.027
5,000	0.5	0.137
10,000	1.0	0.274
20,000	2.0	0.548
30,000	3.0	0.822
36,475.81	3.6	1.000
50,000	5.0	1.371
72,951.62	7.3	2.000
100,000	10.0	2.742
109,427.43	10.9	3.000
. . .	. . .	. . .

Thus, a change from 0 to 1 on *g2earnSD* corresponds to a change of one standard deviation (from zero to 36,475.81) on *g2earn*. And, a change from 1 to 2 on *g2earnSD* also corresponds to a change of one standard deviation (36,475.81 to 72,951.62) on *g2earn*.

Because we have also rescaled the outcome variable by dividing by its standard deviation, the slope estimate reflects by what fraction of a standard deviation the outcome variable will change when the predictor variable increases by one standard deviation. In our case, we might say "For each one standard deviation more that adults earn, they live about .065 of a standard deviation further away from their mothers on average."

Semistandardized Slope Coefficient

Sometimes, it is also useful to standardize only the outcome or only the predictor variable. This is done especially when one but not both of the variables is measured in units that have no intrinsic meaning (e.g., based on a rating scale or a sum of rating scale items). The results are referred to as semistandardized coefficient estimates (Stavig 1977).

We can use our formula to calculate the new coefficient estimate we would obtain if we only standardized the predictor or the outcome prior to re-estimating the regression. If we rescale X by dividing by its standard deviation but leave Y untouched, then we have $rescaleX=1/36475.81$ and $rescaleY=1$. Substituting into the equation $new\ \hat{\beta}_1 = (rescaleY/rescaleX)\hat{\beta}_1$ with our original slope of $\hat{\beta}_1 = .0011333$ gives us:

$$new\ \hat{\beta}_1 = \frac{1}{1/36475.81} * .0011333$$

$$= \frac{36,475.81}{1} * .0011333$$

$$= 41.34$$

This would be interpreted as "For each standard deviation more that adults earn they live about 41 miles further from their mothers, on average." If we rescale Y by dividing by its standard deviation but leave X untouched, then we have $rescaleY=1/636.394$ and $rescaleX = 1$. Substituting again, into the equation $new\ \hat{\beta}_1 = (rescaleY/rescaleX)\hat{\beta}_1$ gives us:

$$new\ \hat{\beta}_1 = \frac{(1/636.394)}{1} * .0011333$$

$$= \frac{1}{636.394} * .0011333$$

$$= 0.000001781$$

This number is tiny because it represents the amount of change on the outcome, in standard deviation units, for a one dollar increase in annual earnings. We might instead rescale earnings to $10,000 units while rescaling distance to standard deviation units. To do so, we use $rescaleY=1/636.394$ and $rescaleX=1/10,000$. Substituting again, into the equation $new\ \hat{\beta}_1 = (rescaleY/rescaleX)\hat{\beta}_1$ gives us:

$$new\ \hat{\beta}_1 = \frac{(1/636.394)}{(1/10,000)} * .0011333$$

$$= \frac{10,000}{636.394} * .0011333$$

$$= 0.01781$$

This would be interpreted as "For each $10,000 more that adults earn they live nearly 0.02 standard deviations further from their mothers, on average."

Although it is instructive to see how to hand-calculate the standardized variable and coefficient estimate, once you understand the process, you can use commands in SAS and Stata to obtain them directly. Stata has an option, `beta` which can be added to any regression command and SAS has the option `/stb` which can be added to any model statement. Stata's term "beta" reflects the fact that in some subfields it is conventional to use the greek symbol β or corresponding word *Beta* to denote the standardized slope. The SAS option can be remembered as shorthand for "standardized beta." Display B.8.6 shows these options implemented in SAS and Stata, and the results (0.06496 in SAS and 0.0649594 in Stata) match our earlier results (compare results of Display B.8.6 and Display B.8.5).

Finally, we use the command introduced in Chapter 7 to obtain the Pearson correlation in SAS and Stata and reinforce the fact that, in bivariate regression, the standardized coefficient estimate is equivalent to the Pearson correlation. The results, shown in Display B.8.7 again match the standardized estimates of the slope coefficient, within rounding (0.06496 in SAS and 0.0650 in Stata).

Reversing the Predictor and Outcome

As we interpret regression results, it is also important to keep in mind the asymmetric nature of the regression model. In regression modeling, we consider one variable to be the outcome variable and another variable (or set of variables in multiple regression) to be the predictor variable. The shorthand expression **"left-hand side"** and **"right-hand side"** of the equation reflects this asymmetry.

$$Y \;=\; \beta_0 + \beta_1 X + \varepsilon$$
Left-hand side   Right-hand side

The theoretical and conceptual undergirding of our model provide the basis for setting up, or specifying, this asymmetric relationship. It is these theories and conceptions that move us from a symmetric correlation relationship to an asymmetric regression model.

The asymmetric nature of regression, in contrast to the symmetric correlation coefficient, is evident if we reverse the predictor and outcome in our example (i.e., we regress *g2earn* on *g1miles*). The regression coefficient differs when we do so. It now reflects the amount of change in *g2earn* when *g1miles* increases by 1. Display B.8.8 shows the result of this regression. The coefficient estimate for *g1miles* can be interpreted as: "For each mile further the mother lives from her child, the child earns $3.72 more dollars per year, on average." Note that the *t*-value remains 5.19, so our conclusion based on our hypothesis test is the same. The coefficient estimate is quite different in Display B.8.8 than in Display B.8.1 (3.72324 versus 0.00113) because of the difference in standard deviations between the two variables (about 636 for miles and 36,476 for earnings). But, if we instead standardize both variables so that one unit of change represents one standard deviation for that variable, the coefficient is the same regardless of the order of the variables (and is equal to the Pearson correlation coefficient; see Display B.8.9 and compare slope to Display B.8.5). Likewise, if we reverse the order of the two variables in the variable lists asking SAS and Stata to calculate the correlation, the result is unchanged.[14]

These results bring out three major points:

1. We must always keep in mind the units of measurement of our variables when interpreting the substantive size of a coefficient estimate.
2. Which variable we choose to be the outcome will alter the size of the estimated slope coefficient (but not the statistical strength of the underlying relationship).
3. The basic OLS regression model cannot help us to decide which variable belongs on the left-hand versus the right-hand side.

As we move forward in Chapter 9, we will add more variables to the right-hand side, but keep the single outcome on the left. Our choices about which variable is the outcome and which are the predictors are up to us. Ideally, they are based on a specific theory or conceptual framework. But, ultimately, another researcher might reverse their order (and more sophisticated techniques exist to try to examine causal ordering; see roadmap in Chapter 18).

Effect Size

We saw different ways to rescale the slope estimates to aid interpretation, but we still did not answer the bottom line question of whether the association is big or small, substantively. For statistical significance, we have an exact critical value which is conventionally used to determine whether or not a t-statistic is statistically significant. What kinds of criterion can we use to determine if the size of the association is substantively meaningful? Although there is no hard-and-fast rule for doing so, the concept of **effect size** can be used to help us make such conclusions.

A quick scan of books and articles devoted to effect size will reveal numerous formulas which might appear unfamiliar on first blush, but actually are intimately related to the standardized and semistandardized slopes we have already discussed. In fact, effect size formulas are often grouped into those that capture linear relationships and those that capture group differences (Huberty 2002; McCartney and Rosenthal 2000). The Pearson correlation coefficient is the basic effect size measure in the linear relationship set. A measure conventionally referred to as Cohen's d is the basic effect size measure in the group difference set. It is defined as:

$$\frac{\bar{Y}_{Group_1} - \bar{Y}_{Group_2}}{s_Y} \tag{8.9}$$

Notice that this formula is nothing more than the difference in means on the outcome variable between two groups divided by the standard deviation of the outcome variable. We will use this formula directly in Chapter 10 when we introduce dummy variables to model predictor variables that indicate two or more groups. With continuous predictor variables, we can use this measure as an analogy for the semistandardized coefficient in which we keep the X variable in its natural units and standardize the Y variable. As we will emphasize below, it is important to think still about rescaling the X variable so that a one unit increase on the rescaled variable represents a meaningful amount of real world change when doing so.

Using effect sizes for interpretation has the same benefit as standardizing, discussed above. Effect sizes convert the size of the association into standard deviation units (see Box 8.9). Especially when the units of measure of the outcome do not have intrinsic meaning, this conversion can help you interpret the size of the effect. And, it can allow you more easily to compare associations across different variables that have different standard deviations. Whether to use the completely standardized or semistandardized measure will depend on your application. If your predictor variable does not have meaningful natural units, then the completely standardized measure may be preferred. If your predictor variable does have meaningful natural units, then the semistandardized measure may be helpful. We present an example of each below.

First, though, let's address the question of what size of an effect is meaningful. Recall that the Pearson correlation coefficient is bounded between zero and 1, in absolute value. Because the completely standardized coefficient in bivariate regression is equivalent to the Pearson correlation coefficient, it is also bounded between zero and 1, in absolute value. The semistandardized coefficient could be larger than 1 if a one-unit increase on the predictor variable is associated with more than a one standard deviation change on the outcome variable. But, the semistandardized effect is still interpreted as the fraction of a standard deviation that the outcome variable increases when the predictor variable increases by one (e.g., a semistandardized coefficient estimate of 1.5 would indicate that the outcome variable increases by one and a half standard deviations when the predictor variable increases by 1).

What is a large value for a completely standardized or semistandardized coefficient estimate? Guidelines developed by statistician Jacob Cohen (1969) are probably the most widely applied. Cohen recommended considering effect sizes of about 0.20 as small, 0.50 as medium, and 0.80 as large (Cohen 1992). This rule is widely used, particularly in some subfields, although some have argued that it is overused, especially given the limited empirical basis on which Cohen first developed the cutoffs (Huberty 2002; McCartney and Rosenthan 2000). Another alternative to using absolute cutoffs like Cohen's is to place effect sizes in the context of related literature on the outcome and predictor of interest or to compare the effect size for one predictor and outcome to effect sizes for other predictors. Researchers might also consider the real world costs and benefits of the predictor and outcome in interpreting the results. For example, McCartney and Rosenthal (2000) provide an example of a very small effect size that was interpreted as of practical importance because the outcome was mortality and the predictor was an inexpensive method for preventing heart attacks (daily aspirin use).

■ Box 8.9

In the multiple regression context which we will consider in the next chapter, effect size may also be calculated in other ways, including based on the value of R-squared. But, the analogy to Equation 8.9 is intuitive and as we show can be related to the semistandardized coefficient (and the dummy variable predictors we will discuss in Chapter 10). We encourage you to think carefully about how to characterize the size of effects in your particular applications, either in terms of the natural units of the variables, in comparison to real world benchmarks or in terms of the standard deviation of the variables.

How do our examples stack up using these guidelines? Above, we calculated the standardized coefficient estimate for our distance example to be 0.0649594. The semistandardized coefficient estimate was tiny for a $1 increase in annual earnings. It was larger, although still small, when we rescaled X so that a one-unit increase represented $10,000 in annual earnings (0.01781). Thus, in all of these cases (for a one standard deviation, a $1, and a $10,000 increase in annual earnings) the distance that the adult lives from his or her mother increases by less than one tenth of a standard deviation. All are small, based on Cohen's cutoffs. In Chapter 9 we will demonstrate how to place these effect sizes for earnings in the context of the size of effects of other predictor variables.

Both our predictor and our outcome in this distance example have meaningful natural units. Thus, we can also use real world benchmarks to evaluate the substantive importance of the estimated association. Recall that our unstandardized coefficient estimate was 11.33 when we rescaled earnings so that a one-unit increase reflected an increase of $10,000. Does a change of about 11 miles of distance for a $10,000 increase in annual earnings seem large? To answer this question, we might think about the practical consequence of 11 miles of distance for interactions between family members. Most of us would likely come to a similar conclusion based on these natural units of Y as we did with Cohen's cutoffs and the semistandardized slope: the association between earnings and distance, although statistically significant, seems substantively small (i.e., a change of 11 miles in average distance for a $10,000 increase in earnings is not large).

We can also convert the lower and upper bounds of our confidence intervals into standardized or semistandardized form to help us to assess the substantive size of an effect. The 95 percent confidence interval we calculated above was (0.000705, 0.001562). We can convert these bounds to units of $10,000 change in earnings by multiplying both numbers by 10,000. This results in a confidence interval of (7.05, 15.62). Thus, we might say that we have 95 percent confidence that the amount of increase in distance associated with a $10,000 increase in the adult's earnings falls between about 7 and 16 miles. We could also convert the bounds to semistandardized values by dividing by the standard deviation of distance (636.394). Since 7.05/636.394 = .011078 and 15.62/636.394 = .02454 we could say that we have 95 percent confidence that the amount of increase in distance associated with a $10,000 increase in the adult's earnings falls between about 0.01 and 0.03 of a standard deviation of distance. Completely standardizing the confidence interval bounds would involve multiplying the original values by the standard deviation of earnings and dividing by the standard deviation of distance. Since 0.000705*36475.81/636.394 = .0404 and 0.001562*36475.81/636.394 = .0895 we could say that we have 95 percent confidence that the amount of increase in distance associated with a standard deviation increase in the adult's earnings falls between about 0.04 and 0.09 of a standard deviation of distance. As with the point estimates, the confidence intervals suggest a small effect size.

The association we examined between number of children in the household and hours of chores, in contrast, seems larger in substantive size. Recall that in our stylized example of 50 cases above, we estimated that the women completed about six more hours of chores per week when one more child was in the household, on average. Across the seven days of the week this would represent nearly one more hour of chores per day. This seems a substantively larger amount of real world change than we saw in our distance example. For example, for women employed full-time, and allocating 8 hours to sleeping and 10 hours to work and commuting leaves six hours in a day; spending one more of those six remaining hours on chores seems a substantial change.

What about the effect size of the association between number of children and hours of chores? As noted above, the standard deviation of work hours is 10.47 in our stylized sample of 50. Thus, the semistandardized group difference between those having one fewer versus one more child is also sizable on Cohen's cutoffs. 6.13/10.47 = 0.58, somewhat larger than his criteria for a moderate association. The standard deviation of number of children is 1.43, thus the completely standardized coefficient estimate would be 6.13*1.43/10.47 = 0.84, a large effect by Cohen's cutoffs. Thus, in our stylized hours of chores example, we come to a similar conclusion based on examining the real world importance of the effect in its natural units and the relation to Cohen's cutoffs of the effect in its standardized units: the effect is moderate to large in size.[15]

8.5: COMPLEX SAMPLING DESIGNS

The techniques we presented in Section 7.5 accounted for sampling weights but not the clusters or strata that may also be present in a complex sampling design. We now present the survey regression commands available in Stata and SAS to adjust for these additional aspects of complex sampling designs. We begin by discussing why these adjustments are important and then show how to use the survey regression commands, relating back to the correlation coefficient introduced in Section 7.5. We will then revisit these survey regression commands in Chapter 10 (relating back to the *t*-tests and ANOVAs introduced in Chapter 7), in Chapter 14 (applying the commands to an OLS regression model with multiple predictors), and Chapter 17 (applying the commands to regression models for categorical outcomes with multiple predictors).

8.5.1: Addressing Complex Sampling Designs in Regression Models

We now have basic statistical concepts firmly in hand so that we can talk more specifically about how sampling weights, stratification, and clustering affect our analysis as well as the tradeoffs among different approaches meant to account for these aspects of complex sampling designs.

As we have discussed in this chapter, the regression coefficient and its standard error are central to regression analysis. Together, they allow us to determine whether we have enough evidence to reject our null hypothesis, usually based on whether the ratio of the coefficient to its standard error is larger than about two in absolute value. Thus, to ensure that this test gives us the most accurate answer, it is imperative that we correctly estimate the coefficient and standard error. On the one hand, if our analysis approach understates the standard error, then the denominator in this ratio will be "too small" and we may inaccurately reject our null hypothesis (i.e., commit a Type I error). On the other hand, if our analysis approach overstates the standard error, then the denominator in this ratio will be "too big" and we may inaccurately fail to reject our null hypothesis (i.e., commit a Type II error). The coefficient being overstated or understated would have similar consequences. We also saw in this chapter that the coefficient estimates the substantive size of the association between the predictor variable and the outcome. We would again like this coefficient to reflect the value in the population, and not be systematically larger or smaller than the true population parameter. Otherwise we would conclude that the population association is larger or smaller than its true value; this is the idea of bias introduced above.

Failing to take into account the oversampling, stratification, and clustering in a complex sampling design can lead to understating or overstating the coefficient and/or the standard error in the ways just described. The two major approaches to accounting for the complex sampling design are referred to as **design-based** and **model-based**. Design-based approaches modify the formulas for estimating the coefficient and standard error using the sampling weights and the indicators of strata and clusters. Model-based approaches rely on other strategies to account for design features, some of which we will learn in later chapters (such as adding additional predictor variables in the ways we will discuss in the next chapter, but using variables that define aspects of the survey design) and some of which we leave for your potential future study (such as the multilevel models which can help to account for the similarity of respondents drawn from the same cluster; we overview these models in Chapter 18 suggesting strategies for locating advanced courses and textbooks to learn about them). Although historically there was intense debate about which of these two approaches was best, increasingly statisticians and analysts are taking more of a middle ground, seeing benefits to each strategy (DuMouchel and Duncan 1983; Gelman 2007; Kailsbeek and Heiss 2000; Korn and Graubard 1991; Little 2004).

In fact, both the design-based and model-based approaches can produce unbiased estimates, although it is more difficult to be sure that the model-based approach has done so in practice (which is one reason why some have argued for the design-based approach). At the same time, the model-based approach is generally more efficient than the design-based approach (which is one reason why some have argued for the model-based approach). We consider the design-based approach for two main reasons: (1) the model-based approach requires advanced concepts, some of which we won't address until later chapters and some of which are part of the advanced topics we overview in Chapter 18; and (2) both Stata and SAS now have survey regression commands that allow us to readily implement the design-based approach (Baisden and Hu 2006; Kreuter and Valliant 2007). Chapter 18 provides resources for learning more about the model-based approach and the advanced techniques related to it.

Before turning to how we incorporate the features of the complex sampling design in SAS and Stata, let's consider again why we need to do so. For the simple regression model (with one predictor) that we introduced in this chapter, the consequences of oversampling are similar to those we discussed in Part 2. If the association of the outcome with the predictor differs between the groups that were oversampled and the groups not oversampled, then the estimate of the overall association between the outcome and predictor will be incorrect (biased) unless sampling weights are used.[16]

The consequences of clustering have to do with the OLS assumption (mentioned above) that the error terms not be correlated across individuals (see again Box 8.6). Typically, complex sampling designs in the social and health sciences use geographically-based clusters to reduce costs. To the extent that two people who live in the same cluster are more similar to each other than would be two randomly drawn people, who do not necessarily live near one another, then we violate one of our OLS assumptions. Usually, the consequence of violating this assumption is that our standard errors are smaller than they should be unless we use survey regression techniques (or other advanced techniques) to take into account the clustering. The extent to which clustering affects standard errors depends on the degree to which cluster members are similar to one another on the variables used in our analysis.[17]

Most discussions about the need to adjust for the features of a complex sampling design and strategies for doing so focus on the consequences of oversampling and clustering. However, to fully account for the complex sampling design, the strata also should be taken into account. Typically, adjusting for strata has the opposite effect as adjusting for clustering. Whereas adjusting for clustering usually increases standard errors, adjusting for strata usually decreases standard errors. Indeed, survey statisticians can use stratification when they design a study in order to improve the efficiency of estimates and thus we want to take advantage of these improved efficiencies in our analysis strategy.

8.5.2: SAS and Stata Commands for Survey Regression Analysis

We will return to the suite of SAS and Stata survey commands that we first introduced in Chapter 5, now using the regression commands in each of these suites. For Stata, we again use the `svyset` command to first tell Stata what variables contain the sampling weights and the indicators of clusters and strata. We then use the `svy` prefix before our `regress` command (StataCorp 2009b: 74–84). In SAS we use the `SURVEYREG` command (SAS Institute, 2008b: 6535–6611) with similar options as we used in Chapter 5 to designate the design features. Display A.8.2 summarizes these commands.

In Display B.8.10 we show these commands, replicating the model shown in Display B.8.3 but adjusting for the design features. Comparing the new results to the earlier display, we first can verify that the sample sizes match. The new results list the "domain" or "subpopulation" sample size as 6,350 which is the same sample size as shown in Display B.8.3. We can also verify that the weights sum to 6,350 (with rounding) which verifies that our adjustment creating relative weights achieved its goal. Focusing on the estimates of the coefficient and standard error, we see that both are biased upward when we fail to account for the features of the NSFH complex sampling design. The coefficient is 11.06 in Display B.8.10 versus 11.33 in Display B.8.3, indicating that our unweighted estimate slightly overstates the additional distance lived from the mother with each additional $10,000 in earnings. The standard error is also overstated when the design features are not adjusted (2.19 in Display B.8.3 versus 1.85 in Display B.8.10). Thus, the confidence interval is somewhat narrower in the new results (7.30 to 14.83) in contrast to the original results (7.04 to 15.62). The t-value is also somewhat larger in the new results (5.99 versus 5.19) reflecting the fact that the relative decrease in the standard error is larger than the relative decrease in the coefficient between the new and old results.

■ **Table 8.1:** Summary of coefficients and standard errors for regression of *g1miles* on *g2earn10000* with no, partial, and complete adjustment for the NSFH design features

Model adjusts for which design features?	$\hat{\beta}_1$	$\hat{\sigma}_{\hat{\beta}_1}$
None	11.33	2.19
Oversampling	11.06	3.61
Clustering	11.33	3.67
Stratification	11.33	3.15
All	11.06	1.85

Table 8.1 helps us further parse apart the consequences of adjusting for each aspect of the NSFH sampling design—the oversampling, clustering and stratification. We created this table by adjusting for each of these three design features on its own, and setting the results alongside the original results (from Display B.8.3 which adjusted for none of the three features) and the new results (from Display B.8.10 which adjusted for all three design features).

These results make clear that the changes to the coefficient estimate are due to applying the sampling weights to adjust for oversampling. In other words, the coefficient estimate is the same (11.33) when we adjust for no design features as when we adjust only for clustering or only for stratification. Likewise, the coefficient estimate is the same (11.06) when we adjust for only oversampling as when we adjust for all of the design features. These results reflect the fact that we discussed above that bias results when we do not adjust for any differential associations between the predictor and outcome in the groups that were and were not oversampled.

In contrast, the standard error is affected by each feature of the design, reflected in the different values of the standard error in each row of the table. The features of the design are interrelated (since the study's PSUs were drawn within strata and some aspects of oversampling occur within strata) and we see that whereas the standard errors when we adjust for just one design feature are each somewhat larger than the OLS standard errors (adjusting for no design features) the standard error is smallest when we adjust for all three design features.

8.5.3: Significance Tests for Correlations and Standardized Coefficients in Survey Regressions

The survey regression commands can be used to calculate *p*-values for the weighted correlations that we introduced in Section 7.5.3. However, SAS and Stata will not provide standardized coefficients directly when we use the survey regression commands. Thus, we can either use the weighted correlation syntax shown in Display A.7.2, standardize our outcome and/or predictor variables before estimating our regression model with the survey commands, or take the square-root of the *R*-squared values (which recall is the square of the correlation between the two variables from these bivariate regressions).

In Display B.8.11 we replicate the results from Display B.7.9, where we had calculated the weighted correlation between the adult respondents' ages and their mothers' ages. In Display

B.8.11 we re-estimate these weighted correlations by first standardizing each age variable before estimating the bivariate regression, using each variable's weighted mean and standard deviation. The results verify the weighted correlation of .867 that we had seen in Display B.7.9 and also provide a significance test for this correlation that is adjusted for the clustering and stratification of the NSFH sample design.

Display B.8.12 shows the survey regression results for the age variables in their natural units. In this case, the coefficients are unstandardized. But, the R-squared values match those from Display B.8.11. In all cases, the R-squared value is 0.7523 and if we take the square root of it, we get 0.867, the standardized coefficient (i.e., $\sqrt{0.7523} = 0.867$).

■ Box 8.10

Although in our large sample all of the p-values are quite small, rounding to values <.0001, you may notice that the t-values differ in Display B.8.11 when we regress *g1ageS* on *g2ageS* and when we regress *g2ageS* on *g1ageS*. Likewise, the F-values in Display B.8.11 and Display B.8.12 differ depending on which variable is the outcome and which is the predictor (although as expected, the t-value is the square root of the F-value within regressions). The fact that the t-value depends on which value is the outcome differs from what we saw for OLS regression, without adjustments for the complex sampling design. If you use this approach to calculate p-values for correlations, then the conservative approach is to report the larger of the two values (when they don't both round to zero as ours do here; Sribney 2005). If you are reporting standardized coefficients for regression results, you would report the p-value that results from the variable that you have defined as the outcome being on the "left hand side" of the equation.

8.6: SUMMARY

In this chapter, we introduced the basic concepts of regression in the bivariate context (with one outcome variable and one predictor variable). We presented the population regression line with algebra and graphs, emphasizing how each approach helps us to understand the interpretation of the intercept and slope. We also introduced the idea of conditional distributions, emphasizing that the population regression line has two components. The systematic component is the prediction equation determined by the intercept and slope and provides the mean of the conditional distributions. The random component is the error term and determines the variance of the conditional distributions. These error terms allow individual Ys within a given level of X to fall above or below the regression line (i.e., above or below the conditional means).

The sample regression line provides estimates of the conditional mean (the intercept and slope of the prediction equation) and conditional variance. Like all estimates of population parameters, these estimates have sampling distributions. In any one sample the estimate is unlikely to be exactly equal to the population parameter. The standard error is the standard deviation of the sampling distribution. The smaller the standard error, the closer a sample estimate is expected to fall to the population parameter. Because most of our research questions and hypothesis statements in the social sciences involve slopes, we looked in detail at the factors that affect the standard error of the estimator for the slope. These include the sample size, variation on the predictor variable, and strength of the relationship between the predictor and outcome.

We also considered how to evaluate our research questions (two-tailed tests) or hypothesis statements (one-tailed tests) using *t*-statistics and confidence intervals. For a two-tailed test, the confidence interval and *t*-statistic provide equivalent results. If the magnitude of the test statistic is larger than the critical value, then the confidence interval will not contain the hypothesized value. If the magnitude of the test statistic is smaller than the critical value, then the confidence interval will contain the hypothesized value. For a one-tailed test, we rely on the *t*-statistic, and reject the null hypothesis if the test statistic is more extreme than the critical value.

Regardless of our decision about rejecting or failing to reject the null hypothesis, the point estimate and confidence intervals provide our best guesses of the value of the population parameter. The confidence interval is superior to the point estimate in that it captures information about the uncertainty of our guess (the standard error of our estimate). For either point estimates or confidence intervals it is also important to consider the substantive size of the effect. We can rescale the predictor and/or outcome variables to aid in such interpretation. If the predictor and outcome variables have meaningful natural units, then we can rescale the predictor to an amount of change that has real world importance (e.g., $10,000 rather than $1 increase in annual earnings). Especially if the predictor and/or outcome variables do not have meaningful units, we can rescale based on their respective standard deviations. When we rescale both the predictor and outcome based on their standard deviations, we calculate a completely standardized coefficient estimate. When we rescale only one (the predictor or the outcome) we have a semistandardized coefficient estimate. The completely standardized and semistandardized coefficient estimates can be interpreted using the concept of effect size. They can be compared to cutoffs introduced by Jacob Cohen and, preferably, will also be considered in relation to other effect sizes in the literature and/or the effect sizes for other variables in a study.

KEY TERMS

Best Linear Unbiased Estimators (BLUE)

Bivariate Regression

Completely Standardized Regression Coefficient

Conditional Distribution
(also Conditional Mean, Conditional Standard Deviation, Conditional Variance)

Confidence Interval

Degrees Of Freedom

Deterministic

Effect Size

Estimate

Estimator

Expected Value

Fitted Value

Hypothesized Value

Intercept

Left-Hand Side/Right-Hand Side

Linear Association

Mean Square Error

Nonsystematic Component

One-Sided Hypothesis Test

One-Sided p-Value

Ordinary Least Squares (OLS) Regression

Point Estimate

Population Parameters

Population Regression Line

Predicted Values

Prediction Equation

Probabilistic

Random

Root Mean Square Error (or Root MSE)

Sample Estimates

Sampling Distributions

Semistandardized Regression Coefficient

Simple Regression

Slope

Stochastic

Systematic Component

Two-Sided Hypothesis Test

Two-Sided p-Value

Unconditional Distribution
(also Unconditional Mean, Unconditional Standard Deviation, Unconditional Variance)

Unstandardized Regression Coefficient

Y-Hat

REVIEW QUESTIONS

8.1 What does it mean, algebraically and geometrically, if the slope is equal to zero?

8.2 We can always mechanically interpret the intercept. What should we consider to determine if the intercept is substantively meaningful?

8.3 Write the general statement that we use to interpret the slope from a bivariate regression model (i.e., do so in the "general" case of Y as the outcome variable, X as the predictor variable and β_1 as the slope).

8.4 Write a general bivariate population regression equation and bivariate sample regression equation, including the error terms. Indicate which is the systematic and which the random component of each. Discuss what the systematic and random components represent in the conditional distributions associated with each regression equation.

8.5 Write the formulas for the point estimate of the slope, conditional variance, and standard error of the slope, in bivariate regression.

8.6 Will the conditional standard deviation be larger than, smaller than, or equal to, the standard deviation of the unconditional distribution of the outcome variable if the outcome and predictor variable are strongly associated? Why?

8.7 What are the three major factors that affect the size of the standard error of the slope in bivariate regression?

8.8 Write the formula for the test statistic of the slope in bivariate regression. What is the most common hypothesized value for the slope? Why? What are the null and alternative hypotheses about the slope tested in the default SAS and Stata output?

8.9 Write the formula for a 95 percent confidence interval about the slope. If you reject the null hypothesis in a two-sided hypothesis test, what do you expect to see in relation to the confidence interval?

8.10 What are the three ways discussed in the chapter to "change units" in order to interpret a slope in a more substantively meaningful way (e.g., in units of 10,000s of dollars rather than units of dollars, for example).

8.11 What are some strategies you can use to determine if a significant effect is substantively important (large or small)?

8.12 Define the standardized slope using the standard deviation of X, standard deviation of Y, and the unstandardized slope.

8.13 How do the standardized slope, unstandardized slope, and Pearson correlation change if we reverse which variable we use as the outcome and which variable we use as the predictor in bivariate regression?

REVIEW EXERCISES

REVIEW EXERCISES 8

8.1 Suppose that you estimate a bivariate regression of earnings on years of schooling and obtain the following estimates: $\hat{\beta}_0 = \$20,000$ and $\hat{\beta}_1 = \$5,000$.

    (a) Interpret the intercept.

    (b) Interpret the slope.

8.2 Suppose that you regress children's reading achievement scores on the number of books in the household and obtain the following estimates: $\hat{\beta}_0 = 70$ and $\hat{\beta}_1 = 0.60$.

    (a) Interpret the intercept.

    (b) Interpret the slope.

    (c) Reinterpret the slope for an increase of 10 books.

8.3 Show how to calculate the unstandardized regression coefficient based on the Pearson correlation coefficient, standard deviation of X, and standard deviation of Y.

8.4 Suppose you estimate an unstandardized slope coefficient of 0.5. If $\delta Y = 4$ and $\delta X = 2$, what is the completely standardized slope?

8.5 Suppose that $\hat{\beta}_1 = 0.035$ when we regress Y on X. Now, suppose we create a rescaled X variable, which is equal to the original X variable divided by 5. What would be the slope coefficient from the regression of Y on the new variable?

8.6 Write the formula for the standard error of the slope in bivariate regression and discuss what you might do as a researcher in planning a study in order to try to achieve a relatively small standard error.

8.7 What would happen to Equation 8.8 in the extreme case of no variation in the Xs? (That is, all X have the same value, and thus all X_i are equal to $\bar{X}$).

8.8 Does a positive slope coefficient from a simple regression model of Y on X mean that all observed Y values in the sample at $X = 11$ are larger than all observed Y values in the sample at $X = 10$, that the conditional mean predicted from the regression model at $X = 11$ is larger than the conditional mean predicted from the regression model at $X = 10$, or both? Why?

8.9 Consider a simple regression of Y on X based on a large sample size in which $\hat{\beta}_1 = 5$ and $\hat{\sigma}_{\hat{\beta}_1} = 2$.

    (a) Construct a 95 percent confidence interval for the slope.

    (b) Write a one-sentence interpretation of the confidence interval.

8.10 Suppose a colleague sends you a data set that contains two variables, a measure of mental health, and a measure of marital satisfaction. How would you determine which variable should be the dependent variable and which the independent variable?

8.11 Many social scientists would probably order the variables in our distance example as we have, predicting distance from the mother based on the adult's earnings. Can you think of some reasons for this order? Can you think of reasons for reversing the order (how might distance affect the adult's earnings)?

8.12 Consider a regression model with prediction equation $\hat{Y} = 2.32 + 4.59X$, and Root Mean Square = 2.32. Based on these results, what are the estimated mean and standard deviation for the conditional distribution of Y when $X = 0$ and when $X = 10$?

CHAPTER EXERCISE

In these Chapter Exercises, you will write a SAS and a Stata batch program to create a new variable, calculate some descriptive statistics, and estimate several bivariate regression models ("SAS/Stata Tasks"). You will want to have Displays A.4.1, A.4.2, and A.8 handy as you write your batch programs. You will use the results to answer some questions related to the substance of what we learned in Chapter 8 ("Write-Up Tasks").

To begin, prepare the shell of a batch program, including the commands to save your output and helpful initial commands (e.g., In SAS, use the `libname` command to assign the SAS library where the formats can be found; In Stata, turn *more* off and close open logs; see Display A.4.2). Use the NHIS 2009 dataset that you created in Chapter 4, but use an *if expression* to only keep cases that do not have missing values on the *age, exfreqwR and bmiR* variables (see Display A.4.1 and A.4.2).

8.1 Interpretation and Hypothesis Testing in Bivariate Regression

a) SAS/Stata Tasks.

  i) Regress *bmiR* on *age*.

  ii) In SAS, use the `/clb` option to request the 95% confidence intervals (recall that Stata calculates the confidence intervals by default).

b) Write-Up Tasks.

  i) Write the null and alternative hypotheses about the *slope* that are being tested by the *t*-value and *p*-value listed in the output. Why is this null hypothesis interesting? Write the steps for making a decision about these hypotheses (use alpha=.05). Interpret the point estimate of the slope.

  ii) Calculate by hand, and interpret, a 95% confidence interval for the slope. Note whether and how the confidence interval results relate to the *t*-test examined in Question 8.1bi.

  iii) Repeat the hypothesis test from Question 8.1bi, but use a one-sided alternative, based on the hypothesis that older adults have a higher body mass index. Be sure to write the null and alternative hypotheses and indicate the *t*-value and *p*-value for this test.

  iv) Write the null and alternative hypotheses about the intercept that are being tested by the *t*-value and *p*-value listed in the SAS and Stata output. You do not need to go through the steps of making a decision about this null hypothesis, but you should comment on whether this test is meaningful in this situation.

8.2 The Conditional Nature of Regression

a) SAS/Stata Tasks.

     i) Refer to the output from Question 8.1.

     ii) Calculate the unconditional standard deviation of *bmiR.*

  b) Write-Up Tasks.

     i) Write algebraically and present graphically the regression model estimated in Question 8.1. Calculate at least two predicted values for your graph (you can graph them roughly in freehand; the plot does not need to be exact).

     ii) What are the estimated mean and standard deviation for the conditional distribution of *bmiR* when *age* is 25? What about when *age* is 45? And when *age* is 65?

     iii) Compare the unconditional and conditional standard deviations of *bmiR* (Which is larger? What do their relative sizes suggest about the strength of the relationship between *bmiR* and *age*?).

8.3 Changing the Units of X

  a) SAS/Stata Tasks.

     i) Compute a new variable, *age10,* defined as age divided by 10. (*Remember: In SAS this new variable creation must happen in the DATA step!*).

     ii) Regress *bmiR* on this new variable.

  b) Write-Up Tasks.

     i) Based only on the output from Question 8.1, interpret the slope coefficient for a 10 year increase in age. Comment on the potential substantive meaning of this result. What other amounts of change might be substantively interesting?

     ii) Compare the slope from the regression of *bmiR* on the new variable (age divided by 10) to the slope you calculated in response to Question 8.3bi.

8.4 The Asymmetric Nature of Regression

  a) SAS/Stata Tasks.

     i) Correlate *bmiR* with *age.*

     ii) Regress *age* on *bmiR.*

     iii) Calculate the unconditional standard deviation of *age.*

  b) Write-Up Tasks.

     i) Show how to calculate the slope in the output from Question 8.1 and the slope in the output from this question (i.e., the new regression of *age* on *bmiR*) based on the Pearson correlation.

     ii) Briefly, discuss how you would decide which variable (*bmiR* or *age*) would be the dependent variable if you were writing a paper.

iii) Under what circumstances would the slope based on regressing *bmiR* on *age* equal the slope based on regressing *age* on *bmiR*?

8.5 Complex Sampling Designs

a) SAS/Stata Tasks.

i) Regress *bmiR* on *age* accounting for the complex sampling design features.

ii) Regress *age* on *bmiR* accounting for the complex sampling design features.

b) Write-Up Tasks.

i) Use the results from this question, and the earlier question, to: (a) calculate the weighted and unweighted correlation between age and body mass index and (b) test the null hypothesis that the two variables are uncorrelated. How do the weighted and unweighted results compare?

COURSE EXERCISE

COURSE EXERCISE 8

Using the data set you created in the course exercise to Chapter 4, regress one of your continuous outcomes on one of your continuous predictors. Before running the model, make your best guess of the expected direction of the association and justify your choice of outcome variable (can you think of a conceptual rational or an argument another scholar might make about reversing the order of the variables, so that a predictor becomes the outcome?).

Conduct a hypothesis test for the slope, using both a two-sided test for any linear relationship and a one-sided test using the direction you expect for the association as the alternative. Write a one-sentence interpretation of the slope estimate. If the outcome and predictor have natural units that are meaningful, consider rescaling them to other amounts of change (both by reinterpreting the original estimates and rescaling before a new estimation). Especially if the outcome and predictor do not have meaningful natural units, re-estimate the model after rescaling the outcome and predictor by their standard deviations. You should also use SAS and Stata's options to calculate the standardized slope. Based on the results, is the association substantively meaningful?

Comment on whether the intercept is meaningful in your case (e.g., is zero a valid value on your predictor variable, making the *Y*-intercept within range? Is zero a valid value on your outcome variable, making the null hypothesis relevant?). If the intercept is meaningful, write a one-sentence interpretation of it.

Calculate the unconditional standard deviation of your outcome variable and compare it to the estimate of the conditional standard deviation. What does this comparison suggest about how strongly the predictor and outcome variable are related?

Chapter 9

BASIC CONCEPTS OF MULTIPLE REGRESSION

CHAPTER 9: BASIC CONCEPTS OF MULTIPLE REGRESSION

Bivariate regression is often inadequate for social science theory given that we typically expect that more than one variable explains the outcome. For example, we wrote our research questions about distance to include not only the adult's earnings as a predictor of distance from the mother, but also the adult's age and number of brothers and sisters and the mother's age and years of schooling. We will add these additional variables, beyond earnings, to the model in this chapter (and in Chapter 10 we will add the adult's gender and race-ethnicity as predictors as well). In this chapter, we will focus on a basic understanding of how to interpret and test coefficients estimated from the model. In later chapters we will elaborate on this understanding, for example discussing in more detail how and why coefficient estimates change when other variables are added to the model.

9.1: ALGEBRAIC AND GEOMETRIC REPRESENTATIONS OF MULTIPLE REGRESSION

We will begin by examining a three-variable model, with one outcome variable and two predictors. Doing so allows us to understand the major concepts of multiple regression with simple algebra.

9.1.1: The Population Regression Model

The *population regression model* in multiple regression is a direct extension of the population regression model in simple regression:

$$Y_i = \beta_0 + \beta_1 X_{1i} + \beta_2 X_{2i} + \varepsilon_i$$

As in simple regression, this equation divides into a systematic and stochastic component; that is:

$$E(Y|X_{1i}, X_{2i}) = \beta_0 + \beta_1 X_{1i} + \beta_2 X_{2i}$$

is the systematic component—the conditional mean of Y for given levels of X_1 and X_2. The error ε_i is the random component and represents the distance that each case's outcome value, Y_i, falls from the conditional mean. Thus, the errors represent the additional variation in Y not explained by X_1 and X_2.

We can interpret the model parameters in a similar manner as we did in bivariate regression:

■ The intercept is the conditional mean of Y when both predictor variables equal zero. It is the point at which the regression function (now a plane) passes through the Y axis.
■ The slope of X_1 is the amount that the conditional mean of Y changes for a one-unit increase in X_1, controlling for X_2.
■ The slope of X_2 is the amount that the conditional mean of Y changes for a one-unit increase in X_2, controlling for X_1.

These interpretations can be made clear by manipulating the systematic portion of the regression function.

Intercept

Substituting $X_1 = 0$ and $X_2 = 0$ into the equation for the conditional mean leads to all the terms dropping out of the right-hand side of the equation except for the intercept.

$$E(Y|X_1 = 0, X_2 = 0) = \beta_0 + \beta_1 * 0 + \beta_2 * 0 = \beta_0$$

Slope

Let's consider first the slope of the X_1 variable. If we hold X_2 constant at a particular level, then that value is subsumed into the intercept and it is easy to see that the change in Y when we change X_1 by 1 is equal to β_1.

For example, let's hold X_2 constant at 3 and allow X_1 to vary between zero and 3. Following are the conditional means when these values are substituted into the systematic portion of the regression model.

Value of Xs are . . .		The conditional mean of Y equals . . .	
X_1	X_2		
0	3	$E(X_1 = 0, X_2 = 3) = \beta_0 + \beta_1 * 0 + \beta_2 * 3$	$= (\beta_0 + 3\beta_2)$
1	3	$E(X_1 = 1, X_2 = 3) = \beta_0 + \beta_1 * 1 + \beta_2 * 3$	$= (\beta_0 + 3\beta_2) + \beta_1$
2	3	$E(X_1 = 2, X_2 = 3) = \beta_0 + \beta_1 * 2 + \beta_2 * 3$	$= (\beta_0 + 3\beta_2) + 2\beta_1$
3	3	$E(X_1 = 3, X_2 = 3) = \beta_0 + \beta_1 * 3 + \beta_2 * 3$	$= (\beta_0 + 3\beta_2) + 3\beta_1$

Notice that because we hold X_2 constant at 3, each conditional mean contains the term $\beta_0 + 3\beta_2$. The value of X_1, which we vary, determines how much above or below $\beta_0 + 3\beta_2$ the conditional mean falls.

As we did for bivariate regression, we can also subtract conditional means in adjacent rows to see that when we increase X_1 by 1 the conditional mean changes by β_1, holding X_2 constant. This makes very concrete our standard one sentence interpretation of the slope in multiple regression.

Value of Xs are...		Difference in conditional mean between the current row and prior row is...		
X_1	X_2			
0	3			
1	3	$[(\beta_0 + 3\beta_2) + \beta_1] - [(\beta_0 + 3\beta_2)]$	$= \beta_0 + 3\beta_2 + \beta_1 - \beta_0 - 3\beta_2$	
			$\cancel{\beta_0} + \cancel{3\beta_2} + \beta_1 - \cancel{\beta_0} - \cancel{3\beta_2}$	$= \beta_1$
2	3	$[(\beta_0 + 3\beta_2) + 2\beta_1] - [(\beta_0 + 3\beta_2) + \beta_1]$	$= \beta_0 + 3\beta_2 + 2\beta_1 - \beta_0 - 3\beta_2 - \beta_1$	
			$\cancel{\beta_0} + \cancel{3\beta_2} + 2\beta_1 - \cancel{\beta_0} - \cancel{3\beta_2} - \beta_1$	$= 2\beta_1 - \beta_1 = \beta_1$
3	3	$[(\beta_0 + 3\beta_2) + 3\beta_1] - [(\beta_0 + 3\beta_2) + 2\beta_1]$	$= \beta_0 + 3\beta_2 + 3\beta_1 - \beta_0 - 3\beta_2 - 2\beta_1$	
			$\cancel{\beta_0} + \cancel{3\beta_2} + 3\beta1 - \cancel{\beta_0} - \cancel{3\beta_2} - 2\beta_1$	$= 3\beta_1 - 2\beta_1 = \beta_1$

We can also write what we will refer to as a **conditional regression equation**, in which we allow one of the variables to vary (by not holding it constant at a particular value) and fix the other variable at a particular value.

$$E(X_1, X_2 = 3) = \beta_0 + \beta_1 X_{1i} + \beta_2 * 3 = (\beta_0 + 3\beta_2) + \beta_1 X_{1i}$$

The result would be similar if we held X_2 constant at any other value. This would simply change the constant multiple of β_2 which we have subsumed into the intercept by holding X_2 constant. For example,

$$E(X_1, X_2 = 0) = \beta_0 + \beta_1 X_{1i} + \beta_2 * 0 \quad = \beta_0 + \beta_1 X_{1i}$$
$$E(X_1, X_2 = 6) = \beta_0 + \beta_1 X_{1i} + \beta_2 * 6 \quad = (\beta_0 + 6\beta_2) + \beta_1 X_{1i}$$

Our findings would be analogous if we held X_1 constant while allowing X_2 to vary (i.e., the value of β_1 would be subsumed in the intercept and Y would change by β_2 when X_2 increased by 1). For example:

$$E(X_1 = 0, X_2) = \beta_0 + \beta_1 * 0 + \beta_2 X_{2i} \quad = \beta_0 + \beta_2 X_{2i}$$
$$E(X_1 = 3, X_2) = \beta_0 + \beta_1 * 3 + \beta_2 X_{2i} \quad = (\beta_0 + 3\beta_1) + \beta_2 X_{2i}$$
$$E(X_1 = 6, X_2) = \beta_0 + \beta_1 * 6 + \beta_2 X_{2i} \quad = (\beta_0 + 6\beta_1) + \beta_2 X_{2i}$$

Generally, these conditional regression equations can be expressed as follows:

$$E(X_1, X_2 = m) = \beta_0 + \beta_1 X_{1i} + \beta_2 * m \quad = (\beta_0 + m\beta_2) + \beta_1 X_{1i}$$
$$E(X_1 = n, X_2) = \beta_0 + \beta_1 * n + \beta_2 X_{2i} \quad = (\beta_0 + n\beta_1) + \beta_2 X_{2i}$$

With three variables in the equation, we could still represent the relationships graphically using a plane that occupies three-dimensional space. But, with more than three predictor variables, this process of holding other variables constant while we allow one variable to vary will allow us to display our findings graphically. These conditional regression equations reduce the multiple regression plane to straight lines. Plotting them allows us to visualize the effect of one of the X variables while holding the other X variables constant, making clear the interpretation of each of the slope parameters. Such graphs often facilitate interpretation (especially when the association is nonlinear, as we will see in Chapter 12).

9.1.2: Example 9.1

Figure 9.1 presents to the following regression plane:

$$E(Y|X_{1i}, X_{2i}) = 10 + 2X_{1i} + 3X_{2i}$$

This equation shows that the plane has an intercept of 10, a slope of 2 for the first predictor variable, and a slope of 3 for the second predictor variable. Following our general discussion above, these parameters can be interpreted as follows:

▪ Intercept: the conditional mean of Y when both X_1 and X_2 are zero is 10.
▪ Slope of X_1: holding X_2 constant, Y increases by 2, on average, when X_1 increases by 1.
▪ Slope of X_2: holding X_1 constant, Y increases by 3, on average, when X_2 increases by 1.

These values are illustrated in Figure 9.1(a). In Figure 9.1(a), the top, left cell contains the value of 10 which is the value of Y when both predictors are zero. If we look across the rows, we see increments of 3 in Y corresponding to each increase of 1 in X_2. This is of course expected, given our interpretation of the slope for X_2 holding X_1 constant. Similarly, if we look down the columns, we see increments of 2 in Y corresponding to each increase of 1 in X_1. Again, this is expected given our interpretation of the slope for X_1 holding X_2 constant.

Conditional regression equations are illustrated in Figure 9.1(c) for the effect of X_2 when X_1 is held constant at zero, 3, and 6. The graph makes explicit that the rate of change of Y for a given change in X_2 is the same at all levels of X_1 (equal to β_2) but these parallel lines are shifted upward (downward) by the amount of β_1 for each unit of X_1. In Figure 9.1(c), since we hold X_1 constant at values that differ by three points each between adjacent lines (i.e., $X_1 = 0, 3, 6$), the distance between the lines is $\beta_1 * 3 = 2 * 3 = 6$.

Figure 9.1(d) is analogous, giving the effect of X_1 holding X_2 constant. The lines in Figure 9.1(d) are spaced farther apart than the lines in Figure 9.1(c) owing to the higher slope for X_2 than X_1. (The distance between lines is $\beta_2 * 3 = 3 * 3 = 9$ in Figure 9.1(d).) The difference in slopes for X_1 and X_2 is also clear from the steeper lines in Figure 9.1(c) than Figure 9.1(d).

Figure 9.1(b) provides a three-dimensional plot depicting how Y changes when we change both X_1 and X_2. For any $\{X_1, X_2\}$ point located at the base of the graph, the conditional mean of Y is

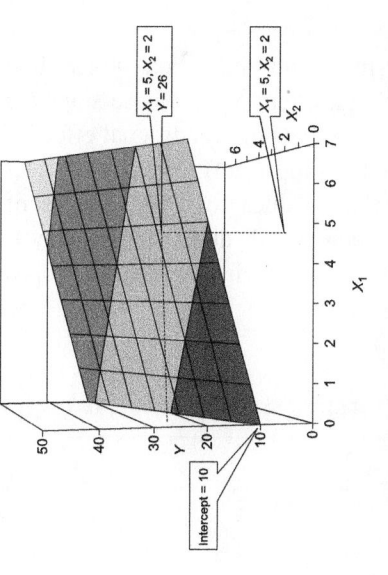

X_1	X_2							
	0	1	2	3	4	5	6	7
0	10	13	16	19	22	25	28	31
1	12	15	18	21	24	27	30	33
2	14	17	20	23	26	29	32	35
3	16	19	22	25	28	31	34	37
4	18	21	24	27	30	33	36	39
5	20	23	26	29	32	35	38	41
6	22	25	28	31	34	37	40	43
7	24	27	30	33	36	39	42	45

(a) Conditional Means of Y Given X_1 and X_2 $E(Y|X_1,X_2) = 10 + 2X_1 + 3X_2$

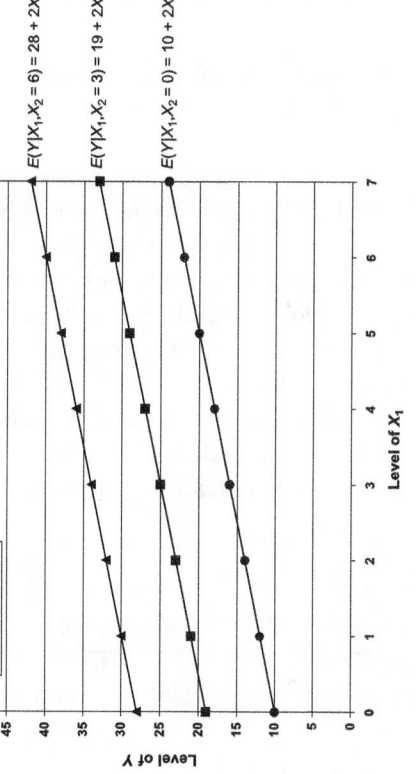

(b) Three-Dimensional Plot of Regression Plane for $E(Y|X_1,X_2) = 10 + 2X_1 + 3X_2$

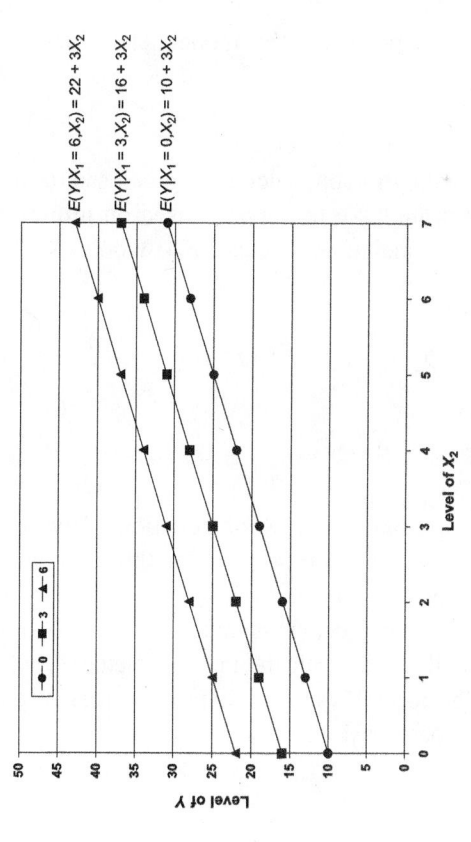

(c) Effect of X_2 holding X_1 Constant at 0, 3, and 6

(d) Effect of X_1 holding X_2 constant at 0, 3, and 6

■ **Figure 9.1** Illustration of Conditional Means and Conditional Regression Equations plotted in the response plane. This plot makes clear that the regression plane crosses the Y axis at the value of $Y = 10$. And, the figure shows the point {5,2} corresponding to a conditional mean of:

$$E(Y|X_1 = 5, X_2 = 2) = 10 + 2 * 5 + 3 * 2 = 26$$

The conditional regression equations we just examined make up this plane. Each line running from left to right in the plane represents the conditional effect of X_1, whose slope we know is 2. Each line running from front to back in the plane represents the conditional effect of X_2, whose slope we know is 3. At an angle (from bottom left to top right) we see the effect of simultaneously increasing X_1 and X_2. Looking back to the values in the diagonals of Figure 9.1(a) makes it clear that, as expected, Y changes by 5 when both X_1 and X_2 increase by 1. X_1 and X_2 are said to have *additive* effects on Y in this model (we add their two separate slopes when both change).

9.2: OLS ESTIMATION OF THE MULTIPLE REGRESSION MODEL

The sample **multiple regression model** with three variables is:

$$Y_i = \hat{\beta}_0 + \hat{\beta}_1 X_{1i} + \hat{\beta}_2 X_{2i} + \hat{\varepsilon}_i$$

The systematic portion of this model determines the fitted (predicted) values:

$$\hat{Y}_i = \hat{\beta}_0 + \hat{\beta}_1 X_{1i} + \hat{\beta}_2 X_{2i}$$

As in simple regression, calculus can be used to derive formulas for calculating the slopes and intercepts in multiple regression based on minimizing the sum of squared errors (Fox 2008; Kutner, Nachtsheim, and Neter 2004; Wooldridge 2009). In the model with two predictors we are now minimizing:

$$\sum \hat{\varepsilon}_i^2 = \sum (Y_i - \hat{Y})^2 = \sum (Y_i - (\hat{\beta}_0 + \hat{\beta}_1 X_{1i} + \hat{\beta}_2 X_{2i}))^2 \qquad (9.1)$$

9.2.1: Point Estimates and Standard Errors of the Intercept and Slope

Taking the partial derivative of Equation 9.1 with respect to each unknown parameter, setting each result to zero, and solving for the unknown allows statisticians to write formulas for the intercept and slope. Writing the formulas requires matrix algebra for models with several predictors, which is not essential for our purposes (for matrix presentations, see Fox 2008; Kutner, Nachtsheim, and Neter 2004; Wooldridge 2009). But, it is informative to write the formulas for the standard errors of the slopes in the model with two predictors, and relate these back to the formulas for the standard error of the slope that we examined in Equation 8.7.

$$\sigma_{\hat{\beta}_1} = \sqrt{\frac{\sigma^2}{\sum(X_{1i} - \overline{X}_1)^2(1 - r_{12}^2)}}$$

$$\sigma_{\hat{\beta}_2} = \sqrt{\frac{\sigma^2}{\sum(X_{2i} - \overline{X}_2)^2(1 - r_{12}^2)}}$$

(9.2)

As we did in bivariate regression, we estimate $\sigma_{\hat{\beta}_1}$ and $\sigma_{\hat{\beta}_2}$ by substituting $\hat{\sigma}^2$ for σ^2, since σ^2 is unknown. In general, in multiple regression:

$$\hat{\sigma}^2 = \frac{\sum \hat{\varepsilon}_i^2}{n - k} = \frac{\sum(Y_i - \hat{Y}_i)^2}{n - k}$$

and k = number of predictors in the model plus 1 for the intercept. In a model with two predictors, we have:

$$\hat{\sigma}^2 = \frac{\sum(Y_i - (\beta_0 + \hat{\beta}_1 X_{1i} + \hat{\beta}_2 X_{2i}))^2}{n - 3}$$

As in the bivariate case, σ^2 is assumed to be homoskedastic and measures the conditional variance of the errors (and thus the conditional variance of the Ys).

Comparing Equation 9.2 to Equation 8.7 shows that, as in bivariate regression, the standard error of the slope in multiple regression depends directly on the conditional standard deviation of the Ys and depends inversely on the variation of the predictor variable and the sample size.

The new term in the denominator $(1 - r_{12}^2)$ shows that, in multiple regression, the standard error of the slope for X_1 also depends on the Pearson correlation between X_1 and X_2. The larger the correlation between the two predictor variables, the larger the standard error. At one extreme, if the two predictor variables are uncorrelated ($r_{12} = 0$), then the new term in the denominator is $(1 - r_{12}^2) = 1 - 0 = 1$ and the formula reduces to the same equation as the bivariate case. At the other extreme, if the two predictor variables are perfectly correlated ($r_{12} = 1$), then the new term in the denominator becomes $(1 - r_{12}^2) = 1 - 1 = 0$. Dividing by zero is indeterminate (the standard error approaches infinity as the correlation approaches 1). We will examine the implications of such high correlation between predictors in Chapter 14, when we consider the topic of multicollinearity.

9.2.2: Interpreting and Rescaling the Variables

Our interpretation for each of the slope parameters in regression models with two predictor variables is the same as in the case of bivariate regression, except for the clause "holding the other variable(s) constant."

Additional results that we used to interpret the estimates in simple regression hold as well:

■ For linear models, the change in Y for a given increase in X does not depend on the starting value of X. (We will consider nonlinear models in Chapter 12.)
■ If we want to interpret a slope parameter for an increase of i units rather than an increase of 1 unit after estimation, then we multiply the relevant slope estimate by i.
■ We can also rescale a predictor variable prior to determining its slope so that we can read the new slope, based on the rescaled variable, directly from our output.
■ And, we can use the formulas discussed in Section 8.4.9, including the formulas for the standardized and semistandardized coefficient estimates.

9.2.3: Example 9.2

Display B.9.1 provides an example of a multiple regression in which we added the variable *g1yrschl* to the model predicting *g1miles* based on *g2earn*. We will consider additional values from the output later in the chapter, but for now focus on the parameter estimates and standard errors.

Statistical Significance of Point Estimates

First, let's consider the point estimates and hypothesis tests for each of the three rows in turn.

■ The intercept is estimated to be 78.35. This can be interpreted as follows: "Adults with no earnings whose mothers completed no schooling live nearly 80 miles away from their mothers, on average." Recall from Chapter 4 that some mothers do have no schooling and some adults have no earnings in the NSFH. As always, the default output includes a test of $\beta_0 = 0$ versus the alternative that $\beta_0 \neq 0$. We can mechanically reject this null hypothesis. The t-value of 2.25 exceeds 1.96 and the two-sided p-value of 0.025 is less than 0.05. But, recall that we have omitted adults who coreside with their mothers, therefore this null hypothesis is not strictly meaningful (although some adults report living as little as 1 mile from their mothers). Thus, in this case, the intercept is meaningful in terms of zero being a possible value for both predictors, but testing the null hypothesis that the intercept is zero is not meaningful, because zero is not a possible value for the outcome in our sample.
■ The point estimate for *g2earn* is 0.00102. The t-value of 4.39 has a two-sided p-value that is less than 0.0001. Because the t-value is larger than 1.96 and the p-value is smaller than 0.05, we can reject the null hypothesis of no linear relationship at a 5 percent alpha level. This estimate is slightly smaller than the value of 0.00113 seen in the bivariate regression in Chapter 8. In Chapter 13, we will have more to say about interpreting the change in a coefficient estimate when other variables are added to the model. The coefficient estimate can be interpreted as: "For each additional dollar earned annually, the adult lives 0.00102 miles farther away from his or her mother, on average, holding the mother's educational level constant."
■ The point estimate for *g1yrschl* is 15.92. The t-value of 5.36 has a two-sided p-value less than 0.0001. Because the t-value is larger than 1.96 and the p-value is smaller than 0.05, we can reject the null hypothesis of no linear relationship at a 5 percent alpha level. The

coefficient estimate can be interpreted as: "For each additional year of schooling the mother attained, she lives nearly 16 miles farther from her child, on average, controlling for the child's earnings."

If we had directional hypotheses, we would follow the same procedures as discussed in Section 8.4.7 to test them in multiple regression as in bivariate regression.

Substantive Size of Point Estimates

At first blush, the association between the mother's years of schooling and distance looks much larger than the association between the adult's earnings and distance. However, it is important to consider the variables' units of measurement to interpret the substantive size of these associations. As we discussed in Chapter 8, a dollar more in annual earnings is quite a small change. In multiple regression we can still translate the association into a more meaningful amount of change by multiplying the coefficient estimate by a factor i. Using a change in annual earnings of $i = \$10,000$, we calculate $i\beta = 10,000*0.00102 = 10.20$. Thus, the mother is expected to live about 10 miles farther away, on average, with each additional $\$10,000$ in the adult's earnings, controlling for the mother's years of schooling.

We can also rescale variables before estimating the regression model. Display B.9.2 shows the result of rescaling *g2earn* before running the regression, using the *g2earn10000* variable that we created in Chapter 8. Notice that rescaling earnings does not affect the intercept nor the coefficient estimate for years of schooling. Even though coefficient estimates can be reinterpreted for different units of change on the predictor after estimation (e.g., with the $i\beta$ formula), rescaling the variables to a meaningful amount of change will influence how "fast readers" (who sometimes turn straight to tables) interpret the findings. Quickly scanning the parameter estimates table in Display B.9.2 versus Display B.9.1, the rescaling makes the slope for the adult's earnings seem more on a par with the slope for the mother's schooling in Display B.9.2 than it did in Display B.9.1.

Although one year of schooling seems a more meaningful amount of change than $\$1$ of annual earnings, we also might want to rescale the mother's educational attainment to an amount of change that is a more natural benchmark for readers. For example, four years of schooling might be a relevant amount of "real world" change, representing the amount of time typically taken to complete high school or college.[1] We can multiply the coefficient estimate for *glyrschl* in Display B.9.1 by 4 to obtain $i\beta = 4*15.92 = 63.68$. We can also rescale the variable before estimation by creating a new variable *glyrschl4 = glyrschl/4*. The results, shown in Display B.9.3, match within rounding error our hand calculation. And, as expected, the intercept and the coefficient estimate for *glearn* match the values shown in Display B.9.1. We could interpret the rescaled slope for education as: "With each additional four years of schooling attained by the mother, she lives over 60 miles farther from her child, on average, controlling for the child's earnings."

Confidence Intervals

Confidence intervals for multiple regression, like bivariate regression, are shown in the default Stata output. In SAS, we can use the /clb option to obtain them, as we did in Chapter 8. The confidence intervals are calculated in the same way in multiple regression as in bivariate regression: we add and subtract 1.96 times the estimated standard error to the point estimate for a 95 percent confidence interval.

Looking for example at Display B.9.2, the following confidence intervals are displayed in the Stata output:

	$\hat{\beta} \pm t_{\alpha/2}\hat{\sigma}_{\hat{\beta}}$	Confidence Bounds
G2earn10000	10.22048 ± 1.96 * 2.329708	(5.65,14.79)
G1yrschl	15.92156 ± 1.96 * 2.970548	(10.10,21.75)
_cons	78.34818 ± 1.96 * 34.89219	(9.95,146.75)

For our two predictor variables, we could interpret these as "We are 95 percent confident that the coefficient for the adult respondent's earnings, in $10,000 units, falls between 5.65 and 14.79" and "We are 95 percent confident that the coefficient for the mother's years of schooling falls between 10.10 and 21.75." These confidence bounds are helpful because they make clear the level of uncertainty in our point estimate, stating our results as a range rather than a single value (e.g., "Each additional $10,000 in earnings is associated with the respondent living between 5 and 15 miles farther from the mother, holding mother's education constant" rather than "Each additional $10,000 in earnings is associated with the respondent living about 10 miles farther from the mother, holding mother's education constant.").

Standardized Coefficients

We can also calculate semistandardized or completely standardized coefficient estimates in multiple regression, using the same rescaling formula discussed in section 8.4.9 (i.e., completely standardized coefficient estimates are calculated by multiplying by the standard deviation of the predictor and dividing by the standard deviation of the outcome; semistandardized coefficient estimates are calculated by dividing by the standard deviation of the outcome).

The results for Display B.9.1 are as follows:[2]

	$\hat{\beta} * (s_X/s_Y)$	$\hat{\beta}/s_Y$
G2earn	0.001022 * (37492.04/645.0074) =0.059	0.001022/645.0074 =0.000
G1yrschl	15.92156 * (2.940383/645.0074) =0.073	15.92156/645.0074 =0.025

We can interpret these as we did in Chapter 8. For the completely standardized coefficient estimates, a one standard deviation increase in earnings is associated with the adult living 0.06 standard deviations farther from the mother, on average, holding mother's education constant. And, a one standard deviation increase in the mother's schooling is associated with a 0.07 standard deviation increase in the miles lived from the mother, on average, holding the adult's earnings constant. For the semistandardized coefficient estimates, a \$1 increase in earnings is associates with zero standard deviation change in distance lived from the mother, on average, holding the mother's education constant.[3] And, when the mother has one more year of schooling, the adult lives about 0.025 of a standard deviation further away, on average, holding earnings constant.

9.3: CONDUCTING MULTIPLE HYPOTHESIS TESTS

When we conduct more than one hypothesis test, we are increasingly vulnerable to making a Type I error—rejecting the null hypothesis when the null is true (Bland and Altman 1995; Shaffer 1995). This concern is especially important in the context of multiple regression, where we begin to consider how a number of different predictor variables are associated with the outcome variable and thus conduct multiple tests, for example testing whether the slopes for each of the predictors differs significantly from zero. For models with dozens of predictors, this amounts to dozens of individual tests. With today's computing power, it is easy to conduct many, many tests. In this section, we will provide an intuitive example of this issue and discuss one strategy for controlling the Type I error across such numerous individual hypothesis tests. In the following sections we will discuss alternative strategies for thinking about conducting multiple hypothesis tests and selecting from among alternative regression models.

The issue of controlling the Type I error when making multiple hypothesis tests should make sense intuitively. It is a natural extension of your understanding of how sampling error relates to the probability of rejecting the null when the null is true—a Type I error—in any individual test. We know that the level of alpha we use controls the Type I error rate. The p-value provides us with the probability that we would obtain a t-statistic more extreme than the one we obtained if the null were true, given the sampling distribution of our t-statistic. If we use an alpha level of .05, then we reject the null hypothesis if the p-value is less than .05, and say that we had a 5 percent chance of making a Type I error.

However, in multiple regression models, we begin to conduct tests for numerous slope coefficients. When we conduct many tests using the same sample, then it is likely that—by chance—across all the tests we will observe some of the extreme t-statistics that fall in the tails of the sampling distribution. Indeed, a few such extreme t-statistics are expected based on the standard deviation of the sampling distributions; the problem is that it may be tempting to interpret them as real rejections of the null hypothesis in applications (and with a single sample, we cannot distinguish Type I errors from valid rejections of the null hypothesis).

More concretely, imagine that we have a data set with five measured variables that we think associate with the outcome variable. Suppose that we conduct five individual hypotheses, all at the 0.05 alpha level. Across these multiple tests, the chance of making at least one Type I error is higher than 0.05. The exact probability of making at least one Type I error across the five tests depends on how the probabilities are related among tests. We can heuristically examine the probability of making at least one Type I error by assuming that the tests are independent (note that in the regression case this assumption won't hold but it makes it easy to understand the issue).

Recall from basic statistics that, if A and B are independent, then $P(A \cap B) = P(A)P(B)$. In words, the probability of both A and B happening is the probability of A times the probability of B, given that A and B are independent. Now, at alpha = .05, the probability that a test is correct with respect to Type I error (i.e., that when the null is true we fail to reject it) is $1-.05 = .95$. Under independence, we can multiply the individual probabilities for each test to get the probability that all tests are correct. This would be $0.95 * 0.95 * 0.95 * 0.95 * 0.95 = 0.95^5$ for five tests. Generally, it is 0.95^m where m is the number of tests. The probability of the complement of this outcome, that at least one of the tests has a Type I error, is $1-0.95^m$.

Number of Tests	Probability of at least one Type I error assuming independence of tests and alpha = .05 for each test
1	$1-0.95^1 = 0.05$
2	$1-0.95^2 = 0.10$
3	$1-0.95^3 = 0.14$
5	$1-0.95^5 = 0.23$
10	$1-0.95^{10} = 0.40$
30	$1-0.95^{30} = 0.79$
50	$1-0.95^{50} = 0.92$
100	$1-0.95^{100} = 0.99$

This makes clear that as the number of tests increases, the probability of making at least one Type I error can increase rapidly.

Bland and Altman (1995) provide a number of examples in which clinical trials were simulated by randomly assigning patient records into two groups that were not actually given different treatments, and seeing whether one group appeared to have superior outcomes in any hypothesis tests. Across numerous tests, some cases were identified in which the treatment group looked better than the control group on some outcomes (even though these groups in fact did not receive different treatments). For example, one case simulated a clinical trial for two alternative treatments of coronary artery disease. The patient records were randomly assigned to one of the two fictitious treatments. When patients were subdivided into those with more and less serious coronary artery disease, one of the treatment groups appeared superior, with longer survival times. As Bland and Altman note (1995, 310): "the finding would be easy to account for by saying that the superior 'treatment' had its greatest advantage for the most severely ill patients!" even though, in fact, the two groups had been randomly created and did not receive different treatments.

One way to account for this concern would be to adjust the alpha level of the test. If we decreased the alpha level for each individual test, we would make it harder to reject each individual null hypothesis, and reduce the chances of making at least one Type I error across the tests. For example, with $\alpha = 0.05$ for five independent tests $1-0.95^5 = 0.23$. But, with $\alpha = 0.01$ for five tests $1-0.99^5 = 0.05$. Such an adjustment was developed by Carlo Emilio Bonferroni (for more detailed discussion of this approach, and other adjustments, see Bland and Altman 1995;

Schochet 2008; Shaffer 1995). Under the **Bonferroni adjustment**, an overall Type I error probability is decided upon, say .05, and then this rate is divided by the number of tests to determine the alpha level for the individual tests. For example, for two tests at an overall alpha level of .05, we would use an alpha of .05/2 = .025 for each individual test. Bonferroni adjustments obviously become quite stringent in applications with many tests (e.g., .05/50 = .001).

Often, a Bonferroni-type adjustment is considered particularly important in cases in which the researcher is conducting **exploratory** rather than **confirmatory** research. In an exploratory study, the researcher may not have strong theoretical reasons to expect particular relationships between predictor variables and the outcome variable, but rather, may have collected data with numerous possible predictor variables and then looked to see which seem relevant empirically. When strong theoretical expectations are specified in advance, then the researcher can reduce the chances of overemphasizing results that are due to sampling error.

An interchange in the sociological literature provides an example of such a distinction (Schaefer 1982; House, LaRocco, and French 1982). In this interchange, the critiquer, Schaefer, raises the concern that the authors of the original paper, House, LaRocco, and French, conducted 225 separate analyses. With so many tests conducted, she raises the concern that surely the probability of a Type I error on at least one of the tests is nearly 100 percent. The authors responded by noting that when they went back and applied more stringent alpha levels using the Bonferroni adjustment, they still found a number of significant effects. And, most importantly, the pattern of these significant effects was consistent with their hypotheses. If the significant effects reflected pure sampling error, then they would be expected to occur as often for results that differed from their substantive expectations as for results consistent with their substantive expectations. And, they noted that their results replicated a prior study. If the results were due to sampling errors alone, it is unlikely that they would be seen across two different samples. This debate shows that a Bonferroni-type adjustment (or simply using a more conservative alpha level) may be helpful when conducting a very large number of hypothesis tests in a single study and that it is beneficial to ground hypotheses in prior research and theory whenever possible.

9.4 GENERAL LINEAR *F*-TEST

Multiple regression also introduces the possibility of making joint tests about more than one slope at the same time. For example, is at least one of the slopes in the model significant? Is at least one of the slopes in a subset of the predictors significant (for instance, at least one of the adult's characteristics and at least one of the mother's characteristics in our distance example)? Do two slope coefficients differ from one another? These tests are all subsumed under what is often called the **general linear *F*-test**.

The general linear *F*-test encompasses many situations in which joint hypotheses will be tested in multiple regression. Although conceptually this may seem similar to the Bonferroni-type adjustment, such approaches are distinct. Bonferroni-type adjustments deal with making a number of individual tests and controlling the Type I error across these tests. The general linear *F*-test considers hypotheses about more than one parameter simultaneously.

9.4.1: Basics of Decomposing the Sums of Squares

We already have considered in detail the sum of squared errors, $\Sigma(Y_i - \hat{Y}_i)^2$, which we minimize to obtain the ordinary least squares estimates. We will now abbreviate this quantity as SSE (for **Sum of Squared Errors**).[4] We also learned in Chapter 5 that the numerator in the calculation of the variance of a variable was the sum of the squared deviation of each observed value from the overall (unconditional) mean $\Sigma(Y_i - \bar{Y})^2$. We will call this quantity the **Total Sum of Squares**, or TSS. In this section, we will also examine how these two quantities are related, and define a third sum of squares, $\Sigma(\hat{Y}_i - \bar{Y})^2$ which is referred to as the **Model Sum of Squares**, or MSS.

These quantities are related to one another. $Y_i - \bar{Y} = (Y_i - \hat{Y}_i) + (\hat{Y}_i - \bar{Y})$ and TSS = SSE + MSS. Figure 9.2 shows these relationship visually.

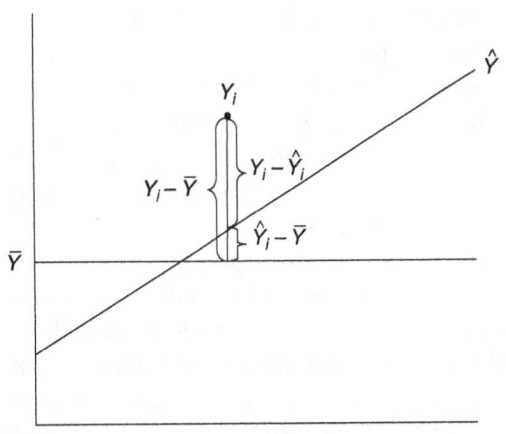

Total Sum of Squares (TSS) $\qquad \Sigma(Y_i - \bar{Y})^2$

Sum of Squares Errors (SSE) $\qquad \Sigma(Y_i - \hat{Y}_i)^2$

Model Sum of Squares (MSS) $\qquad \Sigma(\hat{Y}_i - \bar{Y})^2$

$$\text{TSS} = \text{SSE} + \text{MSS}$$

■ **Figure 9.2**

9.4.2: Overview of the General Linear *F*-test

Let's use our distance example to consider what it might mean to conduct multiple tests simultaneously. Consider the following set of models:

Model 1 $\quad \beta_0 + \varepsilon_i$

Model 2 $\quad \beta_0 + \beta_1 g2earn_i + \varepsilon_i$

Model 3 $\quad \beta_0 + \beta_1 g2earn_i + \beta_2 g1yrschl_i + \varepsilon_i$

Model 4 $\quad \beta_0 + \beta_1 g2earn_i \qquad\qquad\qquad + \beta_4 g2age_i + \beta_5 g2numbro_i + \beta_6 g2numsis_i + \varepsilon_i$

Model 5 $\quad \beta_0 + \beta_1 g2earn_i + \beta_2 g1yrschl_i + \beta_3 g1age_i + \beta_4 g2age_i + \beta_5 g2numbro_i + \beta_6 g2numsis_i + \varepsilon_i$

These models have the same outcome but differ in the set of predictor variables. We can use null hypotheses to produce one model from another, including complex hypotheses involving two or more slopes.

For example, comparing Model 3 with Model 2, we see that Model 3 contains two predictors, *g2earn* and *glyrschl* and Model 2 contains just one predictor, *g2earn*. If we placed a restriction on Model 3 based on a null hypothesis that $\beta_2 = 0$ then Model 2 would result. Comparing Model 3 to Model 1, we see that Model 1 has no predictors. So, we would need a joint null hypothesis that $\beta_1 = 0$ and $\beta_2 = 0$ in order to produce Model 1 from Model 3.

The process of placing the constraints on Model 3 to produce Model 2 and Model 1 are shown below.

Original Model 3	$glmiles_i = \beta_0 + \beta_1 g2earn_i + \beta_2 glyrschl_i + \varepsilon_i$
Place constraint $\beta_2 = 0$ on Model 3	$glmiles_i = \beta_0 + \beta_1 g2earn_i + 0 * glyrshl_i + \varepsilon_i$
	$\beta_0 + \beta_1 g2earn_i + \varepsilon_i$
Place constraints $\beta_1 = 0$ and $\beta_2 = 0$ on Model 3	$glmiles_i = \beta_0 + 0 * g2earn_i + 0 * glyrschl_i + \varepsilon_i$
	$\beta_0 + \varepsilon_i$

Notice that we explicitly substitute a zero for the coefficient listed in the constraint.

Model 1 is often referred to as the **intercept-only model**. Notice that it can be produced by any of the other models by constraining all of the slopes in each of the other models to zero. We will see below that the intercept-only model is used in a special case of the general linear *F*-test referred to as the **model** or **overall *F*-test**.

Whenever one model can be produced by placing constraints on the coefficients of another model, we refer to the models as **nested**. For example, we showed that Model 1 could be produced from Model 3 by constraining β_1 and β_2 to zero. And, Model 2 could be produced from Model 3 by constraining β_2 to zero. In this chapter, we will only consider constraints that a coefficient equals zero (in later chapters, we will consider other constraints, such as that two coefficients are equal). This means that, in this chapter, a nested model will contain a subset of the variables found in another model. As we just saw, Model 1 is nested in all of the other models. Model 2 is also nested in Models 3, 4, and 5. Model 3 and Model 4 are each nested in Model 5. But, Model 3 is not nested in Model 4. (Neither contains a subset of the variables in the other model. Model 3 contains one variable that is not in Model 4 and Model 4 contains three variables that are not in Model 3.)

In the terminology of the general linear *F*-test, the model with fewer variables is referred to as the **reduced (restricted** or **constrained) model** and the model with more variables is referred to as the **full (unrestricted** or **unconstrained) model**. For example, in comparing Model 3 to Model 2, Model 2 is the reduced model and Model 3 is the full model. Which is the reduced and which the full model is always relative to the particular test that you are conducting. For example, Model 3 could be a reduced model in comparison to Model 5 as a full model.

The general linear *F*-test involves four basic steps:

1. Fit the full model and obtain the error sum of squares SSE(*F*)
2. Fit the reduced model under the null hypothesis and obtain the error sum of squares SSE(*R*)
3. Calculate the *t*-statistic

$$F = \frac{\mathrm{SSE}(R) - \mathrm{SSE}(F)}{df_R - df_F} \div \frac{\mathrm{SSE}(F)}{df_F} \qquad (9.3)$$

Recall that for the F-distribution, there are two degrees of freedom, one associated with the numerator and one associated with the denominator. Here, the **numerator degrees of freedom** is $df_R - df_F$ and the **denominator degrees of freedom** is df_F. The degrees of freedom for the reduced and full models (df_R, df_F) are calculated as $n\text{-}k$ where k is the number of predictor variables in each model, plus one for the intercept.

4. Reject the null hypothesis if the F-value is greater than the critical F at the given alpha level and numerator and denominator degrees of freedom; otherwise do not reject.

As noted, the full (unrestricted) model and the reduced (restricted) model differ based on the constraints (restrictions) stated in the null hypothesis. The numerator degrees of freedom (differences in degrees of freedom between the restricted and unrestricted models) will always equal the number of restrictions in the null hypothesis. For example, if $H_o: \beta_1 = 0$ and $\beta_2 = 0$, then the numerator degrees of freedom would be two. And, for $H_o: \beta_1 = 0$ the numerator degrees of freedom would be one.

Notice that the latter null hypothesis $H_o: \beta_1 = 0$ is the same null hypothesis that we learned to test in Chapter 5 with the t-value. In fact, whenever there is just one restriction in the numerator, we will see that the calculated F-value equals the square of a t-value for the same null hypothesis (and the p-value for the calculated F-statistic will equal the two-sided p-value for the t-statistic). But, the F-test is more general than the t-test because we can also use it to test more complex hypotheses about multiple parameters at once (such as $H_o: \beta_1 = 0$ and $\beta_2 = 0$).

It is important to emphasize that nested models evaluated by a general linear F-test must have the same outcome and must be estimated on the same sample size. If some predictors are missing more cases than other predictors, we need to be sure to drop cases missing values on any predictors before estimating any model to assure that all models are estimated on the same sample size. We show how to do this in Example 9.6 below.

9.4.3: Model F-test

The *model* or *overall* F-test compares the estimated model to an intercept-only model, testing whether at least one of the slopes of the predictor variables in the full model is significant.[5] In this special case, we can rewrite the general linear F-test formula in terms of the total sum of squares and model sum of squares. We will consider the model F-test for the bivariate and multiple regression cases, because each provides some unique insights.

Bivariate Regression
We begin by examining the model F-test in bivariate regression.

General Results

The F-statistic for the model F-test in bivariate regression is identical to the square of the t-statistic for the slope coefficient. Both test whether the single slope coefficient is equal to zero. In the general linear F-test conceptualization, the null and alternative hypotheses result in the following full and reduced models for bivariate regression:

Reduced	$H_o: \beta_1 = 0$	$Y_i = \beta_0 + \varepsilon_i$
Full	$H_a: \beta_1 \neq 0$	$Y_i = \beta_0 + \beta_1 X_{1i} + \varepsilon_i$

As discussed above, we obtain the reduced model by placing the restrictions of the null hypothesis on the full model. In this case, we take the full model $Y_i = \beta_0 + \beta_1 X_{1i} + \varepsilon_i$ and constrain the slope coefficient to zero ($\beta_1 = 0$ in the null hypothesis). Thus, the reduced model is $Y_i = \beta_0 + 0 * X_{1i} + \varepsilon_i = \beta_0 + \varepsilon_i$.

As noted above, the reduced model is often referred to as an "intercept-only model." The null hypothesis reflects a horizontal line—the conditional means are all the same, regardless of the level of the predictor variable. Thus, in the intercept-only model, the predicted value for each case is the sample mean, $\bar{Y}$. Because of this, the SSE(R) is equal to the total sum of squares (TSS) for a model F-test when the reduced model is the intercept-only model.

Notationally, since $\hat{Y}_i = \bar{Y}$ in the reduced model, we can substitute $\bar{Y}$ for $\hat{Y}_i$ in the formula for SSE(R): $\Sigma(Y_i - \hat{Y}_i)^2 = \Sigma(Y_i - \bar{Y})^2$. The degrees of freedom for each model (full and reduced) is n-k where k represents the number of predictors, plus one for the intercept. Since the reduced model includes only the intercept, k is 1 and thus $df_R = n - 1$. Under the alternative hypothesis, the SSE(F) is equal to the sum of squared errors (SSE) for the model $Y_i = \beta_0 + \beta_1 X_{1i} + \varepsilon_i$. In this case, $k = 2$ for the calculation of degrees of freedom, since the model contains one predictor variable plus the intercept, so $df_F = n - 2$.

Plugging these results into the formula for the general linear F-test gives a special case of the general linear F-test for the overall (model) F-test. For the bivariate case:

$$F = \frac{SSE(R) - SSE(F)}{df_R - df_F} \div \frac{SSE(F)}{df_F} = \frac{TSS - SSE}{(n-1)-(n-2)} \div \frac{SSE}{n-2} = \frac{MSS}{1} \div \frac{SSE}{n-2} \quad (9.4)$$

We will see a similar overall F-test for multiple regression below, with the intercept-only model as the reduced model.

Note that the numerator degrees of freedom is one in this example.[6] Thus, the F-statistic is equal to the square of the t-statistic associated with the same null hypothesis (e.g., in this case, the square of the t-statistic for the single slope coefficient, β_1).

Example 9.3

We will first apply the general linear F-test to our hours of chores example in the full NSFH sample, and then below we will use it with the distance example. For hours of chores predicted by number of children, the full and reduced models would be:

Reduced	$H_o: \beta_1 = 0$	$hrchores_i = \beta_0 + \varepsilon_i$
Full	$H_a: \beta_1 \neq 0$	$hrchores_i = \beta_0 + \beta_1 numkid_{1i} + \varepsilon_i$

For instructional purposes, we will first use the general formula for the F-test, and explicitly estimate the reduced model and use Equation 9.3. Then, we will calculate the result with Equation 9.4. Let's start by estimating the full model, so we can see where to locate the total sum of squares (TSS), the SSE, and model sum of squares (MSS) in the ouput. Display B.9.4 shows the results. In Stata, the sums of squares are shown in the top left table. In SAS the sums of squares are in the table labeled "Analysis of Variance." The relevant column is labeled with the phrase "sums of squares" in SAS, and with the abbreviation SS in Stata. Both label the MSS row with the word Model. SAS uses Error and Stata uses Residual to label the row containing the SSE. And, Stata uses Total and SAS Corrected Total for the row containing TSS. With rounding, the values are MSS = 152,453, SSE = 2,206,415, and TSS = 2,358,868.

The intercept-only model can be run in SAS and Stata by omitting predictor variables from the regression command. In Stata `regress hrchores` and in SAS `proc reg; model hrchores=; run;`. The results are shown in Display B.9.5. Notice that, as expected, for this model the SSE equals the TSS, and as a result the MSS is zero.

The results from Display B.9.4 provide us with SSE(F) = 2,206,415 and $df_F = n - k = 3{,}116 - 2 = 3{,}114$. The results from Display B.9.5 provide us with SSE(R) = 2,358,868 and $df_R = 3{,}116 - 1 = 3{,}115$. Substituting into Equation 9.3 gives:

$$F = \frac{SSE(R) - SSE(F)}{df_R - df_F} \div \frac{SSE(F)}{df_F} = \frac{2{,}358{,}868 - 2{,}206{,}415}{(3{,}116 - 1) - (3{,}116 - 2)} \div \frac{2{,}206{,}415}{(3{,}116 - 2)} = 215.1629$$

with $(3{,}116 - 1) - (3{,}116 - 2) = 1$ numerator and $(3{,}116 - 2) = 3{,}114$ denominator degrees of freedom.

For this special case of the model or overall F-test, where the reduced model is an intercept-only model, we can also use Equation 9.4 to calculate the F-value directly from the TSS. This is convenient because we do not have to explicitly run the intercept-only model. All of the information we need is in sum of squares tables listed in Display B.9.4. Of course, this gives us the same result since TSS = SSE(R) for the intercept-only reduced model. Using just Display B.9.4 we can fill out Equation 9.4:

$$F = \frac{TSS - SSE}{(n-1) - (n-2)} \div \frac{SSE}{n-2} = \frac{2{,}358{,}868 - 2{,}206{,}415}{(3{,}116 - 1) - (3{,}116 - 2)} \div \frac{2{,}206{,}415}{(3{,}116 - 2)} = 215.1629$$

Because this overall or model F-test is commonly used, and can be calculated using the TSS for the reduced (intercept-only) model, it is always available in the SAS and Stata output. It appears in the right side of SAS's Analysis of Variance table, and is in the top right corner of the Stata output, just below the sample size (see black circles in Display B.9.4). SAS and Stata both show the associated p-value for this F-test, with one numerator and 3,114 denominator degrees of freedom (labeled `Prob > F` in Stata and `Pr > F` in SAS). In our case, the p-value is less than 0.0001, so we can reject the null hypothesis.

Recall that we mentioned that an F-test with one numerator degrees of freedom will be equivalent to a t-test for the same null hypothesis. In this case, our null is H_o: $\beta_1 = 0$, so the equivalent t-test should be the t-test for the *numkid* variable. We expected that the square of the t-value should equal the F-value. In this case, $t = 14.67$, so $t^2 = 14.67^2 = 14.67 * 14.67 = 215.21$. This matches the listed F-value, with rounding error.[7] Although the general linear F-test may seem redundant in this simple bivariate case (since we can use a t-statistic to test the same hypothesis), we will show many additional applications of it below and in subsequent chapters.

Multiple Regression

We now examine the model F-test for multiple regression.

General Results

The general linear F-test extends to the overall or model F-test for multiple regression in a straightforward fashion.

Reduced	H_o: $\beta_1 = \beta_2 = \ldots = \beta_p = 0$	$Y_i = \beta_0 + \varepsilon_i$
Full	H_a: at least one β_p $(p = 1, \ldots, p)$ is not equal to zero	$Y_i = \beta_0 + \beta_1 X_{1i} + \beta_2 X_{2i} + \ldots + \beta_p X_{pi} + \varepsilon_i$

Notice that the alternative is written as at least one of the slopes is not equal to zero. This is the complement to the null, which specifies that all of the slopes equal zero. If we reject the null, it could be that just one slope differs significantly from zero, that some differ from zero, or that all differ from zero. In multiple regression, if we reject the null hypothesis of the overall F-test, then we must inspect the individual t-tests for the individual slopes to see which differ significantly from zero.

In multiple regression, like bivariate regression, the reduced model of the model F-test is the intercept-only model. Thus, the formula for this application of the general linear F-test can be rewritten using the TSS.

$$F = \frac{\text{SSE}(R) - \text{SSE}(F)}{df_R - df_F} \div \frac{\text{SSE}(F)}{df_F} = \frac{\text{TSS} - \text{SSE}(X_1, \ldots, X_p)}{(n-1) - (n-k)} \div \frac{\text{SSE}(X_1, \ldots, X_p)}{n-k} \tag{9.5}$$

where p is the number of predictors and k is the number of predictors plus 1 (for the intercept). We use the notation $SSE(X_1, \ldots, p)$ for the full model because it can be helpful for clarity to list the variables in the model.

Example 9.4

Display B.9.6 shows the result of a multiple regression model predicting *hrchores* based on *numkid* and *hrwork*. The reduced model is the intercept-only model, shown in Display B.9.5, which is the same reduced model as we used above for the bivariate case. Substituting in the SSE(*R*) for this reduced model, or equivalently the TSS from Display B.9.6, results in the following *F*-value.

$$F = \frac{\text{TSS} - \text{SSE}(numkid, hrwork)}{(n-1)-(n-3)} \div \frac{\text{SSE}(numkid, hrwork)}{(n-3)}$$

$$= \frac{2{,}358{,}868 - 2{,}178{,}881}{(3{,}116-1)-(3{,}116-3)} \div \frac{2{,}178{,}881}{3{,}116-3} = 128.57506$$

where k = 3 because our full model has two predictors plus the intercept. The numerator degrees of freedom works out to 2.[8] The denominator degrees of freedom is $3{,}116 - 3 = 3{,}113$.

Notice that this overall *F*-test is again listed in SAS and Stata (circled in black in Display B.9.6). The *p*-value is listed as less than .0001, thus we can reject the null hypothesis that the slopes for *numkid* and *hrwork* are both zero and conclude that at least one differs from zero. Inspecting the *t*-values and two-sided *p*-values for these two variables in the SAS and Stata parameter estimates tables shows that we can reject the null hypothesis that the slope equals zero for each of them. In this case, because the numerator degrees of freedom of the *F*-test is larger than one, neither of these *t*-values squared equals the *F*-test.

9.4.4: Partial *F*-Test

We now examine how to use the general linear *F*-test to conduct a **partial *F*-test**.

General Results

The general linear *F*-test can also be used to test for the incremental or partial effect of a predictor variable, or set of predictor variables, given that one or more predictor variables are already included in the model. Logical sets of variables are common in applications, such as sets of variables measuring characteristics of the studied individual and his/her family, the sets of characteristics about each partner in a couple, or the set of characteristics about an individual's biological makeup, psychological makeup, and social network. In our distance example, we might consider the adult respondents' characteristics as one set of predictors and the mothers' characteristics as another set of predictors and specify the following reduced and full models:

Reduced	$H_o: \beta_3 = 0, \beta_4 = 0,$ $\beta_5 = 0, \beta_6 = 0$	$hrchores_i = \beta_0 + \beta_1 g1yrschl_i + \beta_2 g1age_i + \varepsilon_i$
Full	$H_a: \beta_3 \neq 0$ and/or $\beta_4 \neq 0$ and/or $\beta_5 \neq 0$ and/or $\beta_6 \neq 0$	$hrchores_i = \beta_0 + \beta_1 g1yrschl_i + \beta_2 g1age_i$ $+ \beta_3 g2earn_i + \beta_4 g2age_i$ $+ \beta_5 g2numbro_i + \beta_6 g2numsis_i + \varepsilon_i$

In these models, the full model includes characteristics of both the respondent and mother as predictors. The reduced model includes only the characteristics of the mother, testing the joint null hypothesis that the slopes for all of the respondents' characteristics equal zero against the alternative that the slope for at least one of the respondents' characteristics differs from zero.

Example 9.5

We will start with a simple example of the partial F-test using our hours of chores example. The reduced and full models might be:

Reduced $\quad H_0: \beta_2 = 0 \qquad hrchores_i = \beta_0 + \beta_1 numkid_i + \varepsilon_i$

Full $\qquad H_a: \beta_2 \neq 0 \qquad hrchores_i = \beta_0 + \beta_1 numkid_i + \beta_2 hrwork_i + \varepsilon_i$

We already have the SAS and Stata results for these reduced and full models, in Display B.9.4 and Display B.9.6, respectively. Display B.9.4 shows that for this reduced model, SSE(R) = 2,206,415. The reduced model contains one predictor in addition to the intercept, so $k = 2$ and $df_R = n - k = 3116 - 2 = 3114$. Display B.9.6 shows that for this full model, SSE(F) = 2,178,881. The full model contains two predictors in addition to the intercept, so $k = 3$ and $df_F = n - k = 3,116 - 3 = 3,113$. Substituting into the formula for the general linear F-test, and using the notation to indicate which variables are in the model as shown in Equation 9.5, provides:

$$F = \frac{SSE(R) - SSE(F)}{df_R - df_F} \div \frac{SSE(F)}{df_F} = \frac{SSE(X_1) - SSE(X_1, X_2)}{(n-2) - (n-3)} \div \frac{SSE(X_1, X_2)}{(n-3)}$$

$$F = \frac{SSE(numkid) - SSE(numkid, hrwork)}{(n-2) - (n-3)} \div \frac{SSE(numkid, hrwork)}{(n-3)}$$

$$= \frac{(2,206,415 - 2,178,881)}{(3,116-2) - 3,116-3)} \div \frac{2,178,881}{(3,116-3)} = 39.34$$

The numerator degrees of freedom is 1 and the denominator degrees of freedom is $3,116 - 3 = 3,113$.[9]

Given that the reduced model is not an intercept-only model, we should not expect the calculated F-value to match the F-values listed in the default output in Display B.9.4 or Display B.9.6 (circled in black). But, given that the numerator degrees of freedom is 1, the F-value should match the square of a t-value for the null hypothesis $H_o: \beta_2 = 0$. In our example, the second variable is *hrwork* and the null hypothesis $H_o: \beta_2 = 0$ is tested in the parameter estimates table of Display B.9.6. The square of the t-value listed for *hrwork* is $t^2 = -6.27^2 = 39.31$. This matches our F-value with rounding error. Because the p-value is so small in our case (<.0001) we cannot tell, but the p-value for the F-test is exactly the same as the two-sided p-value for *hrwork* in Display

B.9.6. Since this *p*-value is less than 0.05, we conclude we can reject the null hypothesis.

More on Decomposing the Model Sum of Squares

Before considering another application of the partial *F*-test, we will pause to visualize how the partial *F*-test is based on a decomposition of the sum of squares.

Figure 9.3 visualizes three models based on the *hrchores* outcome. In the middle is the model with two predictors, $X_1 = numkid$ and $X_2 = hrwork$. On the left is the model with just one predictor, $X_1 = numkid$. On the right is the model with just one predictor, $X_2 = hrwork$. We have already examined the sums of squares for two of these models in Display B.9.4 (predictor: *numkid*) and Display B.9.6 (predictors: *numkid* and *hrwork*). Display B.9.7 shows the results for a new regression with just *hrwork* as a predictor. Note that across all of these models, the outcome is *hrchores* and the sample size is 3,116, thus the results are appropriate for comparison with general linear *F*-tests.

At the bottom of Figure 9.3, below each of the model headings, the total sum of squares is listed. These values are taken from the last row of the sums of squares tables in the output of Display B.9.4, Display B.9.6, and Display B.9.7. In all cases, as expected, the TSS = 2,358,868. Because the total sum of squares captures variation around the unconditional mean, it is the same across all of the models (see Box 9.2).

At the top of Figure 9.3, under each model heading, is the MSS. These are taken from the top row of the sums of squares tables in the output.

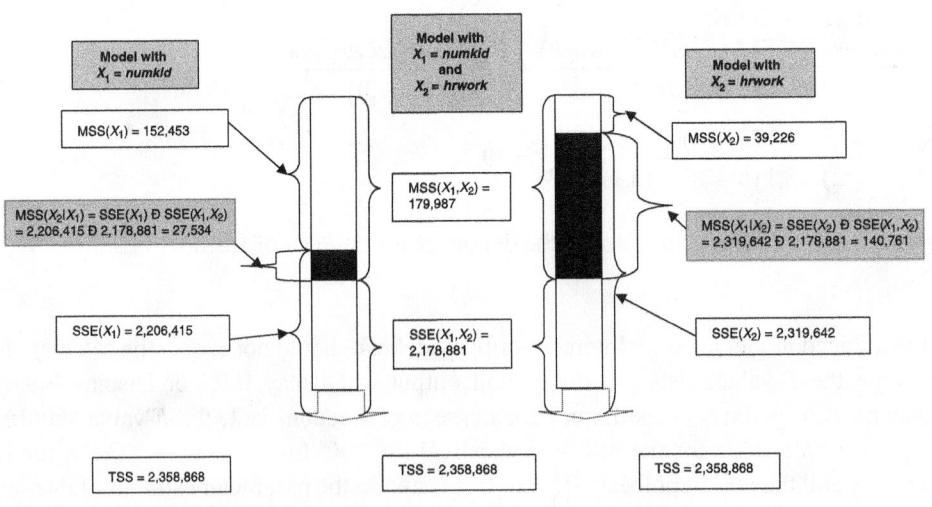

Figure 9.3 More on Decomposition of Sums of Squares

Note: The boxes are not drawn to scale

As noted above, we must be careful to be sure that the sample size remains the same across various models with different sets of predictors. Otherwise, the total sum of squares will change, because the unconditional mean will change at least slightly and we will have a different number of deviations from that mean to square and add to the sum. It is thus important to be careful to check that the sample size of your full and reduced models are the same whenever conducting general linear *F*-tests. As we remind you in the next example, this can easily be done with an *if* qualifier in SAS and Stata. Recall that SAS can also have several Model statements in a single PROC REG. Putting the Model statements together in the same PROC REG assures that the sample sizes will be the same, because SAS drops cases that are missing on any of the variables referred to in any models in the same PROC REG.

From Display B.9.4,

$$\text{MSS}(X_1) = \text{MSS}(numkid) = 152,453.$$

From Display B.9.6,

$$\text{MSS}(X_1, X_2) = \text{MSS}(numkid, hrwork) = 179,987.$$

From Display B.9.7,

$$\text{MSS}(X_2) = \text{MSS}(hrwork) = 39,226.$$

In the middle of Figure 9.3, under each model heading, is the SSE. These are taken from the middle row of the sums of squares tables in the output.

From Display B.9.4,

$$\text{SSE}(X_1) = \text{SSE}(numkid) = 2,206,415.$$

From Display B.9.6,

$$\text{SSE}(X_1, X_2) = \text{SSE}(numkid, hrwork) = 2,178,881.$$

From Display B.9.7,

$$\text{SSE}(X_2) = \text{SSE}(hrwork) = 2,319,642.$$

We can use algebra to relate these quantities to one another across models, drawing on the fact that TSS = SSE + MSS. One useful quantity is the additional sum of squares explained when we add one or more variables to a model. This quantity is sometimes referred to as the "extra sum of squares" (the extra amount explained by the model when the new variables are added). We denote this as $MSS(X_2|X_1)$ for a model in which X_1 was originally in the model and then we added X_2 (i.e., what amount of sum of squares is explained by X_2 given that X_1 is already in the model)? With variable names, in our example, we would write

$$MSS(X_2|X_1) = MSS(hrwork|numkid).$$

Because TSS = SSE + MSS, we can view this extra sums of squares equivalently as (a) the reduction in the sum of squares error, or (b) the increment to the model sum of squares, when we add the new variable or set of variables to the model. We will focus on the former, since this is the quantity that appears in the numerator of the general linear F-test: $SSE(R) - SSE(F)$. For $MSS(X_2|X_1)$, the reduced model contains only X_1 and the full model contains both X_1 and X_2, so

$$MSS(X_2|X_1) = SSE(X_1) - SSE(X_1, X_2).$$

With variable names,

$$MSS(hrwork|numkid) = SSE(numkid) - SSE(numkid, hrwork)$$

We can use Figure 9.3 to locate the relevant values for this formula. The reduced model is on the left, and the full model is the one in the middle. Substituting the SSE from the respective models into $MSS(hrwork|numkid) = SSE(numkid) - SSE(numkid, hrwork)$ results in 2,206,415 − 2,178,881 = 27,534. In Figure 9.3, this result is shown in the green box on the left. The solid rectangle visualizes how this value (27,534) captures the lower SSE in the full versus the reduced models (or equivalently the additional MSS in the full versus the reduced models). This is the amount of extra sums of squares explained by X_2 (hrwork) given X_1 (numkid) is already in the model.

Similarly, on the right, our reduced model contains just *hrwork* and we can also compare this model to the full model with both *numkid* and *hrwork*. Now, the extra sum of squares would be: $MSS(X_1|X_2) = SSE(X_2) - SSE(X_1, X_2)$. Written with the variable names, this would be

$$MSS(numkid|hrwork) = SSE(hrwork) - SSE(numkid, hrwork)$$
$$= 2,319,642 - 2,178,881 = 140,761.$$

In Figure 9.3, this result is shown in the green box on the right. The solid black rectangle on the right visualizes how this value (140,761) captures the lower SSE in the full versus reduced models (with just *hrwork*) or equivalently the additional MSS in the full versus the reduced models. This is the amount of extra sums of squares explained by X_1 (numkid) given X_2 (hrwork) is already in the model.

Comparing the values of the extra sums of squares, and the size of the black boxes, clearly X_1 (numkid) explains more additional variation in hrchores than does X_2 (hrwork).

Example 9.6

Let's now look at an example of the partial *F*-test with a larger set of predictors using our distance example. We will use as the reduced model the two-predictor model we estimated in Display B.9.1, which had *g2earn* and *g1yrschl* as predictors. We will add our other predictors to a full model (*g1age, g2age, g2numbro, g2numsis*).

Reduced $H_o: \beta_3 = 0, \beta_4 = 0,$ $hrchores_i = \beta_0 + \beta_1 g2earn_i + \beta_2 g1yrschl_i + \varepsilon_i$
                     $\beta_5 = 0, \beta_6 = 0$

Full $H_a: \beta_3 \neq 0$ $hrchores_i = \beta_0 + \beta_1 g2earn_i + \beta_2 g1yrschl_i$
           and/or $\beta_4 \neq 0,$ $\beta_3 g1age_i + \beta_4 g2age_i$
           and/or $\beta_5 \neq 0$ $\beta_5 g2numbro_i + \beta_6 g2numsis_i + \varepsilon_i$
           and/or $\beta_6 \neq 0$

Display B.9.8 shows the results of estimating the full model in SAS and Stata. Notice that we show explicitly how we used an *if* qualifier in SAS's DATA step and on Stata's use command to restrict the data set to cases not missing any values across the outcome and six predictor variables. We did this before running the restricted model in Display B.9.1 as well. Thus, both models are estimated on the same sample size of 5,475. Using the *if* qualifier in this case is important because there are cases that have missing values on one or more of the four new variables (*g1age, g2age, g2numbro, g2numsis*) but do not have missing values on the two original predictors (*g2earn, g1yrschl*). Thus, without this *if* qualifier, the reduced model shown in Display B.9.1 would have been estimated on a larger sample size and as a consequence its TSS would have differed from that of the full model shown in Display B.9.8.

We use the general linear *F*-test formula to conduct our hypothesis test. From the SAS output,[10] Display B.9.1 provides the SSE(*R*) = 2,255,081,902 and the degrees of freedom for the reduced model is $n - k = n - 3 = 5,475 - 3 = 5,472$ since *k* is 3 for the reduced model (two predictors plus the intercept). In Display B.9.8, the SSE(*F*) = 2,238,453,227 with degrees of freedom $n - k = n - 7 = 5,475 - 7 = 5,468$ since *k* is 7 for the full model (six predictors plus the intercept). Substituting into Equation 9.3 we get:

$$F = \frac{SSE(R) - SSE(F)}{df_R - df_F} \div \frac{SSE(F)}{df_F} = \frac{2,255,081,902 - 2,238,453,227}{(5,475-3)-(5,475-7)}$$

$$\div \frac{2,238,453,227}{(5,475-7)} = 10.15$$

The numerator degrees of freedom works out to 4.[11] As expected, this is the number of restrictions placed on the full model by the null hypothesis (the number of equals signs in the null hypothesis). The denominator degrees of freedom is $5,475 - 7 = 5,468$.

The reduced model in this example is not the intercept-only model, so the *F*-value we calculated does not match the *F*-value for the overall model *F*-test listed either in Display B.9.1 or Display B.9.8. The numerator degrees of freedom is also larger than 1, so the *F*-value does not match any *t*-value squared. We can use SAS and Stata's `test` commands to check our calculation and to obtain the p-value for the calculated F-value, with 4 numerator and 5,459 denominator degrees of freedom. The basic syntax is `test <varlist>` where in SAS the variables in the varlist are separated by commas. By default, when we include a variable in the variable list of the `test` command, SAS and Stata will include a constraint that its coefficient is zero in the null hypothesis.[12]

Display B.9.8 shows the commands and results of these tests. In both cases, the F-value matches our hand calculation of 10.15. Each lists four numerator and 5,468 denominator degrees of freedom for the test. And, both indicate that the associated p-value is less than .0001. Thus, at a 5 percent alpha level, we can reject the null hypothesis. We have evidence that at least one of the four new variables—*g1age, g2age, g2numbro, g2numsis*—has a coefficient that differs significantly from zero.

Examining the individual t-tests for these four variables in Display B.9.8 shows that we can reject the null hypothesis that the slope coefficient is zero for two variables, *g1age* and *g2numsis*. The null hypothesis for *g1age* could be written $H_o: \beta_3 = 0$ since it is the third variable in the model. The t-value for this variable is 3.17 with a two-sided p-value of 0.002. Since the t-value is larger than 1.96 and the p-value is smaller than 0.05, we can reject the null hypothesis at a 5 percent alpha level and conclude there is a linear relationship between *g1age* and *g1miles*. We could interpret this as: "When the mother is one year older, she lives over 4.5 miles farther from her child, on average, controlling for the adult's age, earnings, and number of brothers and sisters and for the mother's years of schooling."

The null hypothesis for *g2numsis* could be written $H_o: \beta_6 = 0$ since it is the sixth variable in the model. The t-value for this variable is 2.82 with a two-sided p-value of 0.005. Since the t-value is larger than 1.96 and the p-value is smaller than 0.05, we can reject the null hypothesis at a 5 percent alpha level and conclude there is a linear relationship between *g2numsis* and *g1miles*. We could interpret this as: "When adults have one more sister, they lives nearly 17 miles farther from their mothers, on average, controlling for their age, earnings, and number of brothers and for the mother's age and years of schooling."

As when we examined the associations of *g1miles* with *g2earn* and *g1yrschl* it is important to consider the substantive size of a one unit change in *g1age* and *g2numsis* when considering these statistically significant associations. At face value, the effect for *g2numsis* appears larger than the effect of *g1age* because its coefficient estimate is larger. But, we might prefer to rescale *g1age* since adding one more sister seems a greater substantive change than adding one year to the mother's age.

In fact, the standard deviation of *g1age* is 11.30 versus a standard deviation of 1.56 for number of sisters. Thus, a one unit change on *g2numsis* represents nearly two thirds of the variable's standard deviation. In contrast, a one-unit change on *g1age* represents less than a tenth of that variable's standard deviation. We could evaluate the effect of a standard deviation change on each variable by multiplying their respective coefficient estimates by their standard deviations using our formula $i\beta$. This results in 11.30 * 4.56 = 51.53 for *g1age* and 1.56 * 16.94 = 26.43 for *g2numsis*.

Thus, when we put the variables on a more even footing by standardizing, the association between the mother's age and distance is larger in magnitude than the association between the number of sisters and distance. Especially if we had a conceptual rationale for another unit of change, we might also rescale *glage* in its natural units and keep *glmiles* in its natural units (e.g., to report the coefficient estimate for a 10-year rather than one-year change on *glage* we could create a variable *glage10=glage/10* before estimating the regression or multiply the coefficient estimate from Display B.9.8 by 10, $10 * 4.56 = 45.6$).

9.4.5: Other Linear Constraints

In Chapters 10 and 11, we will consider the application of the general linear F-test to test other linear constraints, such as the equality of two coefficients and the sum of two coefficients.

9.5: *R*-SQUARED

We can also use the sums of squares to define **R-squared**, which is a commonly reported assessment of the goodness of fit of a regression model. For the ordinary least squares regression, there are various ways to write the R-squared formula (Long 1997, Chapter 4). We will use an equation that relates nicely to our discussion of the general linear F-test and decomposition of the sum of squares.

$$R^2 = \frac{\text{TSS} - \text{SSE}}{\text{TSS}} = 1 - \frac{\text{SSE}}{\text{TSS}}$$

Notice that the numerator of this R-squared formula is the numerator in the first term of the model F-test (Equation 9.4). Since $\text{TSS} = \text{MSS} + \text{SSE}$ we can also write the formula equivalently as:

$$R^2 = \frac{\text{MSS}}{\text{TSS}}$$

Rewritten this way it is clear that R-squared measures the proportion of the total variation in Y (around the unconditional mean) that is explained by the model (the variation around the conditional means). If there is a strong association between our predictor and outcome, then the variation around the conditional means should be considerably smaller than the variation around the unconditional means (see Section 8.4.3). We thus interpret R-squared as "The predictor variable(s) explain R-squared*100 percent of the total variation in the outcome variable." In the case of bivariate regression, R-squared is equal to the square of the Pearson correlation coefficient.[13]

9.5.1: Example 9.7

Let's first look at R-squared for our bivariate example predicting *glmiles* based on *g2earn*. In Display B.8.7 we saw that the correlation between these two variables was 0.0650. Thus, $r^2 = 0.0650^2 = .00423$. Looking back at Display B.8.1 we can read the MSS and TSS from the analysis of variance tables and calculated R-squared directly as:

$$R^2 = \frac{\text{MSS}}{\text{TSS}} = \frac{10,850,283}{2,571,327,990} = 0.00422$$

SAS and Stata also list the R-squared value in their default output (just to the right of the Root MSE in SAS and under the p-value for the model F-test in Stata). In Display B.8.1, both report an R-squared of 0.0042, again consistent with our hand calculations. We interpret the R^2 value as "The adult's earnings explain less than 1 percent (0.0042 * 100 = 0.42) of the variation in the distance his or her mother lives away."

Let's look as well at our stylized example of 50 cases, relating *hrchores* to *numkid* in Chapter 8 to see an example of a larger R-squared value. The Pearson correlation between these two variables in the stylized sample is 0.8364.[14] The square of this is $r^2 = 0.8364^2 = 0.8364 * 0.8364 = .6996$. This R^2 value would be interpreted as "The number of children in the household explains 70 percent of variation (0.6996 * 100 = 69.96) in the number of hours per week that employed women spend on chores." Consistent with our comparison of the size of the effects of *numkid* on *hrchores* and *g2earn* on *glmiles* in Chapter 8, comparing the R-squared values for these two models suggests that the association between number of children and hours of chores for employed women is much larger in our stylized example than the association between earnings and distance from mother for all adults.[15] (R-squared of .700 versus 0.004).

The ready interpretation of R-squared makes it widely used for assessing the fit of a regression model. However, R-squared is problematic in that it always increases if we add additional predictor variables to our model. Thus, if we chose models purely on the basis of R-squared, we would end up with more complicated models that have more predictor variables. In science, we usually prefer more parsimonious models (the model that explains the most variance with the fewest predictors). An **adjusted R-squared** is used to deal with this issue:

$$R_a^2 = 1 - \frac{\text{SSE} / (n - k)}{\text{TSS} / (n - 1)}$$

This formula recognizes that each variable added to the model reduces the degrees of freedom by 1 (i.e., moving from a model with two predictors to three predictors, k increases from 3 to 4). If a new variable added to a regression model does not help in explaining the variation in Y (i.e., if the increase in the MSS when the variable is added to the model is small), then it may not be sufficient to overcome the loss in a degree of freedom by adding the variable to the model.

9.5.2: Example 9.8

We can use the results from Display B.8.1 to also calculate the adjusted R-squared.

$$R_a^2 = 1 - \frac{2,560,477,708 / (6350 - 2)}{2,571,327,990 / (6350 - 1)} = .00406$$

This adjusted R-squared value is slightly smaller than the unadjusted R-squared value of 0.00422. The adjusted R-squared is listed in the SAS and Stata output of Display B.8.1, just below R-squared.

9.5.3: Example 9.9

Finally, we will look at an example of calculating R-squared for our multiple regression of *glmiles* on six predictors found in Display B.9.8. Here, R-squared is:

$$R^2 = 1 - \frac{\text{SSE}}{\text{TSS}} = 1 - \frac{2,238,453,227}{2,277,372,983} = .01709$$

and

$$R_a^2 = 1 - \frac{\text{SSE}/(n-k)}{\text{TSS}/(n-1)} = 1 - \frac{2,238,453,227/(5475-7)}{2,277,372,983/(5475-1)} = .01601$$

Again, the adjusted R-squared is moderately smaller than the unadjusted R-squared.

9.6: INFORMATION CRITERIA

Information criteria are increasingly used to select from alternative regression models, either in conjunction with the hypothesis testing approaches presented above or as part of an alternative approach, referred to as Bayesian (Weakliem 2004). Some scholars have critiqued the standard hypothesis testing approach, for example, because the choice of alpha level is arbitrary and because hypothesis tests are more likely to be rejected in larger sample sizes (thus leading to more complex models, with more predictors, especially in larger samples). Information criteria do not need an alpha level, are designed to penalize more complex models (with more predictors) over simpler models (with fewer predictors), and are less vulnerable to identifying more complex models in larger sample sizes.

Akaike's Information Criterion (AIC) and Bayesian Information Criterion (BIC) can be calculated in the ordinary least squares framework as follows (Fox 2008; Weakliem 2004):

$$\text{AIC} = n * \log\left(\frac{\text{SSE}}{n}\right) + 2k$$

$$\text{BIC} = n * \log\left(\frac{\text{SSE}}{n}\right) + k * log(n)$$

where n is the sample size and k is the number of predictors in the model plus one for the intercept (see Box 9.3).

For both AIC and BIC, models with smaller values are preferred. Guidelines for the strength of evidence favoring the model with the smaller value are also available based on the absolute difference in

> **■ Box 9.3**
>
> SAS and Stata both display the AIC and BIC based on a different formula, using what is called the log-likelihood. We will cover this concept in Chapter 15. In this chapter we present the formulas based on the SSE because they can be calculated based on the ordinary least squares regression results, although only one can be obtained with basic SAS and Stata commands (in SAS, by adding the option / `selection=cp aic` to the Model statement).

AICs or BICs between two models. Raftery (1995) recommended guidelines that refer to the strength of evidence in favor of the model with the smaller BIC. If the BIC difference is 0–2 then the evidence is weak, 2–6 is positive, 6–10 is strong, and greater than 10 is very strong evidence in favor of the model with the smaller BIC (Raftery 1995). Burnham and Anderson (2002, 70) recommend guidelines that refer to the strength of evidence for continuing to consider the model with the larger AIC. If the AIC difference is 0–2 then the evidence is "substantial," if it is 4–7 then the evidence is "considerably less," and if it is greater than 10 then it is "essentially none."

For the hours of chores examples, we can calculate the AIC and BIC based on the results in Displays B.9.4, B.9.5, B.9.6, and B.9.7.

Predictors	k	SSE	$AIC = n*\log\left(\dfrac{SSE}{n}\right) + 2k$	$BIC = n*\log\left(\dfrac{SSE}{n}\right) + k*\log(n)$
numkid	2	2,206,415	$= 3{,}116*\log\left(\dfrac{2{,}206{,}415}{3{,}116}\right) + 2*2$	$= 3{,}116*\log\left(\dfrac{2{,}206{,}415}{3{,}116}\right) + 2*\log(3116)$
			$= 20{,}452.981$	$= 20{,}465.07$
hrwork	2	2,319,642	$= 3{,}116*\log\left(\dfrac{2{,}319{,}642}{3{,}116}\right) + 2*2$	$= 3{,}116*\log\left(\dfrac{2{,}319{,}642}{3{,}116}\right) + 2*\log(3116)$
			$= 20{,}608.918$	$= 20{,}621.006$
numkid, hrwork	3	2,178,881	$= 3{,}116*\log\left(\dfrac{2{,}206{,}415}{3{,}116}\right) + 2*3$	$= 3{,}116*\log\left(\dfrac{2{,}178{,}881}{3{,}116}\right) + 3*\log(3116)$
			$= 20{,}415.852$	$= 20{,}433.985$

Based on these results, the preferred model is the multiple regression, with both number of children and hours of work as predictors. This model has the lowest values on both AIC and BIC. The absolute value of difference in BICs between this model and the next best fitting model (the bivariate model with only number of children as a predictor) is $|20{,}433.985 - 20{,}465.07| = 31.085$, providing very strong evidence that the multiple regression is preferred. The absolute value of difference in AICs between these same models is $|20{,}415.852 - 20{,}452.981| = 37.129$, providing no evidence in favor of the bivariate model with number of children as a predictor.

9.7: LITERATURE EXCERPT 9.1

We present a literature excerpt here that offers an example of how to present results from multiple regression in a manuscript. We will present several additional examples in Chapter 10, and future chapters. Across chapters, we draw our examples from a range of different fields and journals to help you get used to the somewhat different styles used by each discipline and journal. When you start to format your own results for a manuscript, be sure to check the style guide in your field (e.g., American Psychological Association 2009; American Sociological Association 2007) as well as the manuscript submission guidelines and recent articles in relevant journals.

The excerpt we examine in this chapter is taken from Dooley and Prause (2005) who studied how adverse changes in maternal employment during pregnancy (such as moving from adequate employment to unemployment, having a poverty-level wage, working part-time involuntarily, or being out of the labor force) were associated with child birth weight. Literature Excerpt 9.1 shows Table 3 from their paper, with the results of four regression models that they estimated to examine these associations. Because this is the first table of results we are looking at in detail since learning some of the substance of regression analysis, we will first make some general comments about the presentation of regression results in tables.

Indeed, tables provide a succinct summary of regression results. You will become skilled at how to "read" these tables as we move forward in the book. In fact, as you become more experienced with regression analyses, you will probably find that you increasingly turn to the tables in a journal article, rather than relying on the authors' text explanations of the findings.

Although specific content and symbols will vary from subfield to subfield, most tables follow a fairly similar structure. A title summarizes the contents of the table, usually including the name of the dependent variable and key independent variables for tables of regression results. In Dooley and Prause's table, these are "Birth Weight" and "Change in Employment Status." Dooley and Prause's title also tells us the sample size ($N = 1,165$) and reminds us that the outcome is measured in grams.

The notes at the bottom of the table provide us with key details. Most often, a note tells us which symbols are used to denote which levels of p-values. In Dooley and Prause's table, the first note tells us that a single asterisk is used to denote a p-value that is less than 0.05. And, a † symbol is used to denote a p-value that is less than 0.10. Sometimes authors will explicitly indicate whether p-values are one-sided or two-sided. When unstated, we must assume that the reported p-values are the default two-sided values. It is important to check for such table notes about which symbols are used for which significance levels, since the symbols used vary from author to author and journal to journal (as we will see in other literature excerpts).

Notes often also provide information about which values are included in the table. The second note to Dooley and Prause's table tells us that the numbers in parentheses in the table are t-ratios. We should expect to see that these t-ratios are larger than $|1.96|$ whenever we see an asterisk (because we know that t-ratios of 1.96 are associated with two-sided p-values less than 0.05 in large samples).

The first column of a table typically lists short names of the predictor variables. Then, the following columns provide coefficient estimates (and sometimes standard errors and/or t-values)

■ **Literature Excerpt 9.1**

Table 3. Association of Change in Employment Status and Birth Weight (in grams): Ordinary Least Squares Regression (N = 1,165)

Predictor Variable	Model 1 b	Model 1 Beta	Model 2 b	Model 2 Beta	Model 3 b	Model 3 Beta	Model 4 b	Model 4 Beta
Age (years)	−10.76 (−2.77)*	−.09	−12.07 (−3.11)*	−.10	−1.89 (−.57)	−.02	−2.37 (−.54)	−.02
Child sex (1 = male)	92.74 (3.04)*	.09	93.00 (3.06)*	.09	90.10 (3.53)*	.08	85.72 (3.44)*	.08
African American (1 = yes)	−158.59 (−3.76)*	−.11	−158.50 (−3.77)*	−.11	−141.23 (−4.00)*	−.10	−140.24 (−4.07)*	−.10
Weight prior to pregnancy (kg)	6.46 (5.07)*	.15	6.40 (5.05)*	.15	4.66 (4.37)*	.12	5.23 (4.99)*	.12
Alcohol use during pregnancy[a]								
Less than once/month	75.86 (1.88)†	.06	72.07 (1.79)†	.05	35.12 (1.04)	.03	43.92 (1.33)	.03
More than once/month	17.34 (.43)	.01	13.10 (.32)	.01	4.89 (.14)	.004	15.21 (.46)	.01
Smoking during pregnancy (1 = yes)	−205.57 (−5.32)*	−.16	−198.53 (−5.15)*	−.15	−199.08 (−6.16)*	−.15	−214.78 (−6.79)*	−.17
Change from adequate employment to[b]								
Unemployment	−185.32 (−2.40)*	−.07	−187.96 (−2.44)*	−.07	−137.72 (−2.13)*	−.05	−154.97 (−2.45)*	−.06
Poverty wage	−76.32 (−1.17)	−.03	−75.30 (−1.16)	−.03	−109.14 (−2.00)*	−.05	−91.73 (−1.72)†	−.04
Involuntary part-time	−418.05 (−2.53)*	−.07	−416.44 (−2.53)*	−.07	−184.24 (−1.33)	−.03	−193.36 (−1.43)	−.03
Out of the labor force	−46.95 (−1.08)	−.03	−52.43 (−1.21)	−.04	−85.20 (−2.34)*	−.06	−98.05 (−2.75)*	−.07
Trimester of first prenatal care visit[c]								
No prenatal care			−837.07 (−3.22)*	−.09	−333.69 (−1.52)	−.04	−386.33 (−1.80)†	−.04
Second or third visit			−50.92 (−1.10)	−.03	−29.65 (−.76)	−.02	−23.32 (−.61)	−.01
Missing			−227.32 (−1.94)*	−.06	−200.95 (−2.04)*	−.05	−178.93 (−1.86)†	−.04
Weeks of gestation					135.80 (22.01)*	.53	129.94 (21.38)*	.51
Weight gain during pregnancy (kg)							15.29 (7.48)*	.18
Constant	3,223.36		−3,273.53		−2,137.60		1,929.75	
F(df)	8.49 (11,1153)*		7.97 (14,1150)*		42.63 (15,1149)*		45.37 (16,1148)*	
Adjusted R^2	.066		.076		.349		.379	

† $p < .10$; * $p < .05$
Note: Numbers in parentheses are t-ratios.
[a] Relative to never used alcohol.
[b] Relative to remaining adequately employed.
[c] Relative to first prenatal care visit in the first trimester.

Source: Dooley, David and Joann Prause. 2005. "Birth Weight and Mothers' Adverse Employment Change." *Journal of Health and Social Behavior,* 46: 41–55.

for these predictor variables.[16] In Dooley and Prause's table, there are four additional columns of results for four models (we will have more to say about how to compare coefficient estimates across models in Chapter 13). The labels at the top of each column sometimes denote the meaning of the tabled values (sometimes supplemented in notes, as in Dooley and Prause's note about the *t*-ratio). In Dooley and Prause's table, the lower case *b* represents an unstandardized coefficient estimate and the word *Beta* represents a standardized coefficient estimate. Again, different professional styles and journals will have conventions for which symbols to use to represent which statistics. Tables also often present additional information from a multiple regression, such as the results of the overall *F*-test and *R*-squared. These results are provided in the final rows of Dooley and Prause's table.

Now that we understand the basic structure of the table, let's go back and look at a few specific results. First, we see that for Model 1, the overall *F*-test is significant (asterisk indicates a *p*-value less than 0.05). The numerator and denominator degrees of freedom are summarized in parentheses, as indicated in the row label F(df). For Model 1, there are 11 numerator and 1,153 denominator degrees of freedom. Counting the variables with coefficient estimates listed in Model 1, we see that there are 11 variables in the model (consistent with the 11 numerator degrees of freedom. In this model, $k = 11 + 1$, so the denominator degrees of freedom is $1,165-12 = 1,153$ (recall that the sample size of 1,165 is listed in the table title). We can surmise that this overall *F*-test has a null hypothesis that all 11 variables have coefficients equal to zero against an alternative hypothesis that at least one of the 11 variables has a coefficient that is different from zero. Because the calculated *F*-value is significant, we can reject the null hypothesis. We now want to examine the individual coefficient estimates to see which are significant.

We will focus for now on one of the significant predictor variables: weight prior to pregnancy (circled in green). The note next to the variable name reminds us that this variable is measured in kilograms (1 kg is about 2.2 lbs). The note in the title told us that the outcome variable is measured in grams. So, for every additional kilogram that the mother weighed prior to pregnancy, the newborn weighed about six and a half more grams, on average, controlling for the other variables in the model. Consistent with the asterisk indicating that the *p*-value is less than 0.05, the *t*-value in parentheses for this coefficient estimate is 5.07 (larger than 1.96).

Is this significant effect big or small? Given that the predictor and outcome have meaningful natural units, we can evaluate the size of the unstandardized coefficient estimate relative to real world benchmarks. In doing so, we may want to translate the coefficient estimate into a larger change in maternal prepregnancy weight. For example, multiplying the coefficient estimate by 10 reveals that an increase in maternal prepregnancy weight of 10 kilograms (or about 22 pounds) is associated with an increase in newborn birth weight of about 65 grams (which is one tenth of a pound). In the text, the authors note that babies are considered to be of low birth weight if they weigh less than 2,500 grams at birth, and the average birth weight in the sample is about 3,300 grams (pp. 144, 147). Thus, 65 grams represents less than 10 percent of the difference between being low birth weight and average weight in the sample.

328 ■ ■ ■   APPLIED STATISTICS FOR THE SOCIAL AND HEALTH SCIENCES

The authors also provide the completely standardized coefficient estimates in their table, which allow us to interpret the results from an effect size or unitless perspective. In this case, the standardized coefficient estimate is 0.15, small in general for an effect size. Relative to the other standardized coefficient estimates in the table it appears larger (although we will have more to say about how to interpret the other coefficient estimates in the next chapter, and the completely standardized coefficient is not appropriate for many of them). One good benchmark for comparison may be weeks of gestation, a strong correlate of birth weight. The completely standardized coefficient estimate for this variable is 0.53 in the first model where it is included (Model 3, see black circle). So, the effect size of maternal prepregnancy weight is nearly 30 percent of the effect size for weeks of gestation. Thus, in its natural units and by effect size benchmarks, the effect of maternal prepregnancy weight seems modest, although it seems somewhat larger relative to the effects of other variables.

SUMMARY
8

9.8: SUMMARY

In this chapter, we extended the concepts introduced in Chapter 8 for bivariate regression models to multiple regression models with two or more predictors. We discussed how tests of statistical significance and calculations of the substantive size of individual coefficients are quite similar to bivariate regression. We introduced the concept of conditional regression equations to aid in interpretation of multiple regression models. We also introduced several new ideas related to hypothesis testing, including being thoughtful about significance levels when conducting large numbers of individual hypothesis tests and using the general linear F-test to conduct hypotheses about several parameters simultaneously. We provided examples of how the general linear F-test is used to test whether there is evidence that any of the coefficients in the regression model differ from zero (overall F-test) and whether a subset of the coefficients in the regression model differ from zero (partial F-test). The general linear F-test can be used to compare nested models, in our case situations in which one model contains a subset of the variables in a larger model.

We ended by discussing measures that are often used to evaluate the performance of regression models: the R-squared and information criteria (AIC and BIC). R-squared summarizes the proportion of variation in the outcome variable explained by the set of variables in the model. Information criteria identify the regression model that best summarizes the data, allowing selection of the best model from many alternatives. Both R-squared and information criteria can be used to compare non-nested as well as nested models. The information criteria are also preferred by critics of classical hypothesis testing. Unlike classical hypothesis testing approaches, AIC and BIC do not rely on arbitrary significance levels (e.g., 5 percent Type I error rate in classical hypothesis testing). And, AIC and BIC are designed to identify simpler models (fewer variables in best fitting model) whereas classical hypothesis testing is more likely to identify more complex models (with more variables), especially when sample sizes are large.

KEY TERMS

Adjusted R-Squared

Akaike's Information Criterion (AIC)

Bayesian Information Criterion (BIC)

Bonferroni Adjustment

Conditional Regression Equation

Confirmatory

Denominator Degrees of Freedom

Exploratory

Full Model
(also Unrestricted Model, Unconstrained Model)

General Linear F-Test

Intercept-Only Model

Model F-Test
(also Overall F-Test)

Model Sum of Squares (MSS)

Multiple Regression Model

Nested

Numerator Degrees Of Freedom

Partial F-Test

R-Squared

Reduced Model
(also Restricted Model, Constrained Model

Sum of Squared Errors (SSE)

Total Sum of Squares (TSS)

REVIEW QUESTIONS

REVIEW
QUESTIONS
9

9.1. How do we interpret the intercept and the slope of each predictor variable in a multiple regression model with two predictors, X_1 and X_2, and the outcome of Y?

9.2. How does the formula for the standard error of the slope in multiple regression differ from the formula for the standard error of the slope in bivariate regression?

9.3. Write the four basic steps of the General Linear F-test.

9.4. Write the null hypothesis for the General Linear F-test that is found in standard SAS and Stata regression output. Write the alternative hypothesis and the full and reduced models associated with this test in the case of bivariate regression and multiple regression with two predictors (use Y as the outcome and X_1 and X_2 as the predictors). Be sure you can show how the reduced model is obtained by placing the constraints of the null hypothesis on the full model and that you are able to read the SSE's and df's from SAS and Stata output in order to conduct the F-test by hand.

9.5. What relationship do you expect to see between the numerator degrees of freedom in the General Linear F-test and the null hypothesis associated with that test? Under what circumstances do you expect the F-test to be equivalent to a t-test (and the t-value to equal the square root of the F-value)?

9.6. How do we interpret R-squared in the case of simple and multiple regression? How does R-squared relate to the Pearson correlation in simple regression?

REVIEW EXERCISES

REVIEW
EXERCISES
9

9.1. Verify the values in the conditional equations shown in Figure 9.1. What would be the expected change in Y if we simultaneously increased X_1 by 2 and X_2 by 3?

9.2. In Example 9.2, what would the estimates of the intercept and slope be if we used the two rescaled variables, *g2earn10000* and *g1yrschl4* as the predictors?

9.3. Consider the following regression models, predicting national female labor force participation rates based on the proportion of women with a secondary education, the ratio of children to women, and the percentage of the population that is female.

$femlfp = \beta_0$
$femlfp = \beta_0 + \beta_1 femeduc$
$femlfp = \beta_0 + \beta_1 femeduc + \beta_2 kidratio$
$femlfp = \beta_0 + \beta_3 pctfem$
$femlfp = \beta_0 + \beta_1 femeduc + \beta_2 kidratio + \beta_3 pctfem$

(a) Which models are nested?

(b) For each pair of nested models, write the null hypothesis that would need to be imposed on the full model in order to produce the reduced model.

9.4. Suppose that the unadjusted R-squared value from a regression of wages (WAGE) on years of work experience (EXPER) is 0.25.

(a) Interpret this R-squared value.

(b) What is the Pearson correlation (r) between WAGE and EXPER?

9.5. Suppose that you know that the Pearson correlation between two variables is 0.70. What percentage of variation do these two variables share?

9.6. If you have bivariate regression results in which the t-value for the slope is 4, what would be the overall (model) F-statistic for this simple regression model?

9.7. Refer to Literature Excerpt 9.1.

(a) Write the null and alternative hypotheses for the F-test presented in Model 1. Make a conclusion based on the presented results.

(b) Write the null and alternative hypotheses for the t-ratio for Age. Make a conclusion based on the presented results.

(c) Interpret the unstandardized coefficient estimate for Age in Model 1.

(d) Interpret the standardized coefficient estimate for Age in Model 1.

9.8. Suppose that you estimate a multiple regression model using the following variables:

DEPRESS	Depression scale (ranging from 0 to 105)
REDUC	Respondent's education level (ranging from 0 to 20)
REARNINC	Respondent's annual earned income (ranging from $1 to $800,000)
HRWORK	Respondent's hours spent at paid work/week (ranging from 1 to 95)
NUMKID	Number of persons <=18 in the household (ranging from 0 to 10)

And obtain the following results:

Source	SS	df	MS		
Model	33076.9637	4	8269.24092	Number of obs	= 5320
Residual	1515927.29	5315	285.216799	F(4, 5315)	= 28.99
				Prob > F	=0.0000
				R-squared	=0.0214
Total	1549004.25	5319	291.220954	Adj R-squared	= 0.0206
				Root MSE	= 16.888

depress	Coef.	Std. Err.	t	P>|t|	[95% Conf. Interval]
reduc	−.4999201	.0968659	−5.16	0.000	−.6898171 −.3100231
rearninc	−.0000506	8.40e−06	−6.03	0.000	−.0000671 −.0000342
hrwork	−.0078686	.0180722	−0.44	0.663	−.0432975 .0275603
numkid	.6742838	.1959539	3.44	0.001	.2901337 1.058434
_cons	23.72232	1.517835	15.63	0.000	20.74674 26.6979

(a)   Verify the value of R-squared and adjusted R-squared with a hand calculation.

(b)   Interpret the R-squared value.

(c)   Verify the calculation of the model F-value with a hand calculation. Be sure to write the null and alternative hypotheses and make a conclusion based on the displayed p-value.

(d)   Interpret the intercept. As you do so, comment on whether the intercept is meaningful for this regression model.

(e)   Interpret the point estimate for *reduc* using units of 4.

(f)   Verify the confidence interval bounds for *numkid* with a hand calculation and write a one-sentence interpretation of the interval.

(g)   Hand-calculate the AIC and BIC for this model.

(h)   Suppose you calculated a nested alternative model with nine predictors and obtained an SSE of 1,484,564.94. Would this model be preferred over the above model based on the AIC, BIC F-test and adjusted R-squared?

9.9. Imagine that you conducted an exploratory regression analysis with 10 predictor variables and you wanted to control the Bonferroni alpha level across the tests of the 10 slopes at 0.05. What would be the alpha level you should use for each individual slope t-test?

9.10. How are TSS = total sum of squares, MSS = model sum of squares, and SSE = sum of squared errors mathematically related?

CHAPTER EXERCISE

In this exercise, you will write a SAS and Stata batch program to estimate a multiple regression model, building on the batch program you wrote for Chapter 8.

Start with the batch program that you wrote for Chapter 8, using the NHIS 2009 data set with an *if expression* to only keep cases that do not have missing values on the *age*, *exfreqwR* and *bmiR* variables.

9.1   Interpretation and Hypothesis Testing in Multiple Regression

a)   SAS/Stata Tasks.

   i)   Regress *bmiR* on *age* and *exfreqwR*.

b)   Write-Up Tasks.

   i)   In one sentence, interpret the intercept from the output. Is the intercept meaningful for this model and data?

ii) In one sentence each, interpret the two slope estimates from the output

iii) Is each of the slope estimates statistically significantly different from zero? Is each of the slope estimates substantively large in size?

iv) Write the null and alternative hypotheses for the *F*-test listed in the SAS output. Based on the output, can we reject the null hypothesis (use alpha=.05)?

v) Interpret the *R*-squared value in one sentence.

vi) Compare the conditional standard deviation of *bmiR* in this multiple regression to the simple regression and the unconditional standard deviation of *bmiR* estimated in the chapter exercise for Chapter 8. What does the comparison suggest about the fit of the multiple regression? Is this consistent with the *R*-squared value?

COURSE EXERCISE

Re-estimate the model you developed in Chapter 8, adding one or more additional continuous predictors. Determine whether you can make directional hypotheses for any of these new predictors. Estimate the model and test your hypotheses about each slope, using two-sided or one-sided *p*-values as appropriate. In one sentence, interpret each point estimate. Request and hand calculate 95 percent confidence intervals, and interpret them, for each predictor.

Write a one-sentence interpretation of the intercept. With the new predictors added, is the intercept meaningful (i.e., is zero a valid value on all of the predictor variables?).

Write the null and alternative hypothesis for the model *F*-test listed in the output. Based on the output, is this test significant (use alpha = .05)? Hand-calculate this *F*-value.

Hand-calculate the *R*-squared value and verify your calculation using the output. Interpret the *R*-squared value in one sentence.

Determine a relevant reduced model to compare to your multiple regression model (the reduced model could be the bivariate model that you estimated in Chapter 8, or a model that includes a conceptually coherent subset of variables). Conduct the partial *F*-test for these full versus reduced models. Use the test command in SAS and Stata to confirm your hand calculation of the *F*-value and to obtain the *p*-value to make a decision based on the test. Be sure to explicitly write the null and alternative hypotheses, and the reduced and full models, for this test.

Hand-calculate AIC and BIC for the full and reduced models. Which model is preferred, based on the results?

Chapter 10

DUMMY VARIABLES

CHAPTER 10: USING DUMMY VARIABLES FOR NOMINAL AND ORDINAL PREDICTORS

Up until now, we have not examined the categorical predictors in our distance research questions, the respondent's gender and race-ethnicity. In this chapter, we will consider how to estimate and interpret models with such categorical predictors. We will begin by examining gender and race-ethnicity separately, and then estimate a full model with these categorical predictors and all of the continuous variables that we included in our final model in Chapter 9. Before detailing how to set up and interpret these models, however, we will take a look at a literature excerpt, to motivate the importance of models with categorical predictors, and how they relate to what we have learned already and what is still to come.

In a 1998 article in *Social Psychology Quarterly*, Jaya Sastry and Catherine Ross contemplate a possible western bias in prior studies of personal control and psychological well-being. Because Asian culture is more collectivist than western culture, they anticipate that Asians may report less personal control than non-Asians. Results of their analyses of a combination of US samples are reproduced in Literature Excerpt 10.1.

They interpret the results as follows:

> Asian Americans have significantly lower levels of personal control than do whites, the omitted group . . . Surprisingly, Asian ethnicity has a stronger relationship with the sense of control than does being black or being employed; these two variables have well-established relationships to perceived control (Sastry and Ross 1998: 108).

This excerpt illustrates the use of dummy variables to code categories of a predictor variable. Examining Sastry and Ross's table, a superscript *a* on the words *Asian* and *Black* denotes "Compared with white." Why do they interpret the results in this way? The table also shows that the unstandardized coefficient estimate (*b*) for Asian is −0.312 while the coefficient estimate for Black is −0.090. If both of these are compared with whites, as the footnote indicates, how can we tell if Asian Americans and Blacks differ from each other, on average, in personal control? In this chapter, we will answer these questions.

Note that Sastry and Ross's table includes a column labeled beta with the standardized coefficient estimates. They provide the standardized coefficient estimates for all variables. Some journals may encourage authors to do this. Or, authors may include them for all variables to be comprehensive, especially if it is easy to ask the software to calculate them. However, as we will make clear below, a one-unit change is always meaningful for dummy variables and completely standardized coefficient estimates do not make sense in this context. It is important, though, to evaluate the substantive size as well as the statistical significance of associations with dummy variables. We will illustrate how to do so below.

In general, we can use dummy variables in a regression model to test whether the mean of the outcome variable differs among categories of a predictor variable. Thus, we might examine research questions and hypotheses such as:

Table 2. Regression of Sense of Control on Ethnicity/Race, Socioeconomic Status, Household Status, and Sociodemographics: Domestic Survey

	b (S.E.)	Beta
Ethnicity/Race		
Asian[a]	−.312***	−.079
	(.044)	
Black[a]	−.090***	−.052
	(.020)	
Socioeconomic Status		
Household income[b]	.001***	.083
	(.000)	
Education	.049***	.251
	(.002)	
Employed	.068***	.065
	(.013)	
Household Status		
#of children	.001	.003
	(.006)	
Married	.039***	.038
	(.012)	
Sociodemographics		
Age	−.004***	−.141
	(.000)	
Female	−.014	−.013
	(.012)	
Intercept	.131	
R^2	.150	

Notes:
b = unstandardized coefficient; S.E. = standard error of b; beta = standardized coefficient
[a] Compared with white
[b] In thousands
+ $p < .10$, *$p < .05$, **$p < .01$, ***$p < .001$ (two-tailed test)

Source: Sastry, Jaya and Catherine E. Ross. 1998. "Asian Ethnicity and Sense of Personal Control." *Social Psychology Quarterly*, 61(2): 110.

"Do men and women differ in their average incomes?"

"Among persons of Hispanic origin living in the USA, do those from Puerto Rico, Mexico, and Cuba differ in their mean length of residence?"

"When teenage girls agree versus disagree with a statement that mothers should stay home to raise children do they ultimately attain fewer years of schooling in adulthood, on average?"

"Do for-profit hospitals provide lower average quality patient care than nonprofit hospitals?"

When our original variable has only two categories (such as gender), then there is only one difference between the two groups' means. When we have a variable with more than two categories, we are sometimes primarily interested in the contrast of one category with each of the other categories. For example, we might compare whites with each other racial-ethnic group. Other times, our hypotheses might be more detailed and include contrasts among other groups (e.g., hypotheses about how African Americans may differ from Hispanics and Asians). As we will see, contrasts with one group will be easily read from our regression model. If we are interested in additional contrasts among the other groups, we will discuss three approaches for making them:

(a) re-estimating the regression model with a slightly different set of variables;

(b) using a partial F-test (building on what we learned in Chapter 9);

(c) testing the significance of a linear combination of coefficient estimates (something we will learn to do in this chapter).

We will use one or more of these three approaches in the remaining chapters of the book as we interpret additional types of regression models. Although they produce the same results for a two-sided hypothesis test (thus in practice we will choose to use just one of them), looking at each in detail in this chapter offers insight into understanding dummy variable regression models. Knowing all three approaches also helps us to understand the various ways in which other researchers will present their results. And, understanding the three approaches in detail helps us to understand how to ask SAS and Stata to make the calculations for each approach.

In the remainder of this chapter, we first consider why we need a new strategy when one of the predictor variables is categorical. We will then look at the mechanics of defining dummy variables conceptually and in SAS and Stata. We will also look closely at regression equations with dummy variable predictors to help us to understand how to interpret their coefficients. We will start with a simple case with one dummy variable predictor. We will relate the results for this case to a *t*-test for the difference in means between two groups in order to solidify our understanding. We will next extend the model to cases in which we have: (a) multiple dummies representing one multicategory nominal or ordinal variable; and (b) multiple dummies representing two different nominal or ordinal variables. As we discuss the first case, we will examine in detail the three approaches to contrasting the means of all of the categories. As we discuss the second case, we will learn how to present the results in a table, including the sets of dummy variables as well as the continuous predictors we examined in Chapters 8 and 9. We end with an example from the literature to help us "put it all together."

10.1: WHY IS A DIFFERENT APPROACH NEEDED FOR NOMINAL AND ORDINAL PREDICTOR VARIABLES?

Thus far, we have been emphasizing our interpretation of the intercept and slope for models relating two interval-level variables to one another. But, when our predictor variable is nominal or ordinal, using a slope to relate this variable to the outcome is generally not appropriate.

As we discussed in Chapter 5, nominal variables, like a variable *race*, take on multiple categories, but the values lack both order and distance.

race:
1 = African American
2 = White
3 = Mexican American
4 = American Indian
5 = Other

The values could both be changed and reordered with no loss of information:

race2:
4 = American Indian
41 = Mexican American
59 = African American
124 = White
500 = Other

Clearly, it would not make sense to enter either the *race* or *race2* variable as a single predictor in a regression model.

Similarly, education is often captured with ordinal categories that indicate progression toward degree attainment:

hidegree:
1 = Less than high school
2 = High school degree
3 = Some college, no degree
4 = Associate's degree

5 = Bachelor's degree
6 = Some postgraduate study
7 = Graduate degree

These values represent order, but not necessarily distance. We may be able to equivalently use other values to preserve order but imply other distances, such as:

hidegree2:
 9 = Less than high school
12 = High school degree
13 = Some college, no degree
14 = Associate's degree
16 = Bachelor's degree
18 = Some postgraduate study
21 = Graduate degree

Although we will focus on nominal variables in this chapter, in Chapter 12 we will consider using dummy variables to test for nonlinear effects of such ordinal predictor variables, building on the techniques learned in this chapter.

10.2: HOW DO WE DEFINE DUMMY VARIABLES?

To deal with these issues, nominal and ordinal variables can be analyzed in regression models using sets of **dummy variables**. Each dummy variable indicates one of the levels of the original variable (hence, these are sometimes also called **indicator variables**). Commonly, dummy variables take on two values—0 and 1—where the 1 represents the category on the original variable that the dummy variable indicates and 0 represents all other categories. Other codings are possible, although the 0/1 coding is common in the social sciences and makes it easy to interpret the results, as we will see below (see Box 10.1).

▪ Box 10.1

One common alternative is effect coding. The effect variables are similar to dummies in that we create c-1 of them if a categorical variable has *c* categories and each effect variable is coded "1" to represent one of the original categories and "0" to represent all the other categories except the reference category. In the effect coding approach, the reference category is given the value "–1" on all of the effect variables. With this coding, the intercept represents the overall sample mean of the outcome (rather than the mean for the reference group). And, the coefficients of the effect variables capture the difference between the mean on the outcome for that category and the overall sample mean. In some models this coding can facilitate interpretation of the intercept, and effect coding is commonly used in Analysis of Variance models. But, dummy coding is more common for regression analysis in the social sciences. When correctly implemented, the two approaches provide equivalent results (the difference being in the interpretation).

Dummy variable is the most widely used term for this approach. But, some find it confusing or misleading. One of the definitions of "dummy" in Webster's Dictionary is "An imitation or copy of something, to be used as a substitute," and the term "dummy variable" likely reflects the fact that the variable takes the place of the original category. One of the earliest article-length treatments of dummy variables notes "The dummy variable is a simple and useful method for introducing into a regression analysis information contained in variables that are not conventionally measured on a numerical scale" (Suits 1957: 548). Unfortunately, the word "dummy" also has derogatory meanings which can make it difficult for students to get used to the term. As Suits (1957: 551) noted "One occasionally encounters suspicion of dummy variables and a feeling that somehow something not quite respectable is involved in their use . . . Perhaps part of the trouble lies in the use of the term 'dummy' variable." But, the term is conventional and any and all of the categories of the original variable can be defined with "dummies" (i.e., one category is not inferior to the others, in the derogatory sense of the term dummy).

As we will see in more detail below, we represent a single categorical variable with a *set* of dummy variables. These dummy variables should be thought of together as a set of variables that capture the multiple categories of the original variable. Removing one of the dummies or recoding one of the dummies affects the interpreting of the full set of dummies. For this reason, some scientists refer to them as **dummy** or **indicator terms** rather than as dummy or indicator variables.

The following table provides an example of five dummy variables used to indicate the categories of the *race* variable.

Original Variable	Set of Dummy Variables				
race	*aframer*	*white*	*mexamer*	*amind*	*other*
1 = African American	1	0	0	0	0
2 = White	0	1	0	0	0
3 = Mexican American	0	0	1	0	0
4 = American Indian	0	0	0	1	0
5 = Other	0	0	0	0	1

The table shows that a "1" on each dummy variable indicates one of the categories of the original variable. All other categories of the original variable have values of "0" on that dummy variable. For example, all cases coded "3" on *race* would be coded a "1" on the new variable named *mexamer*. And, all cases coded "1, 2, 4", and "5" on the original *race* variable would be coded "0" on the new variable named *mexamer*.

Because they are mutually exclusive (each represents one and only one of the original categories) and exhaustive (cover all of the original categories), any one of the new dummy variables is redundant with the remaining four dummy variables. For example, if we know that a case is coded a "0" on *white*, "0" on *mexamer*, "0" on *amind*, and "0" on *other*, then we can figure out that the case will be coded as "1" on *aframer*. Similarly, if we know that a case is coded a "0" on *white*, "1" on *mexamer*, "0" on *amind*, and "0" on *other*, then we can figure out that the case will be coded as "0" on *aframer*. Algebraically, any one of the dummy variables can be determined by the general equation:

$$X_1 = 1 - (X_2 + X_3 + X_4 + X_5)$$

where X_1 represents one of the variables and X_2 through X_5 represent the remaining four variables. In our example in this paragraph, *aframer* = 1 − (*white* + *mexamer* + *amind* + *other*) which works out to *aframer* = 1 − (0 + 0 + 0 + 0) = 1 − 0 = 1 in the first case and *aframer* = 1 − (0 + 1 + 0 + 0) = 1 − 1 = 0 in the second case described above.

As we will discuss further in Chapter 14, variables with this kind of redundancy cannot all be included together as predictors. Thus, we omit one of the dummy variables when we estimate a regression model. In general, to represent a variable with c categories requires c-1 dummy variables. In the *race* example, the original variable has c = 5 categories, thus we need *c − 1 = 5 − 1 = 4* dummy variables. The group whose dummy variable is excluded is often referred to as the **reference category**. Other frequently used terms, such as **omitted category** or **excluded category**, are also strictly correct, as we have left one of the dummies for one of the categories out of the model. However, these terms can be misleading in that they imply that this *omitted* or *excluded* category is not part of the analysis, when in fact it is central to our interpretation. Which one of the five dummies we omit is arbitrary. The decision on the reference category does not affect the results of the regression analysis, although as we will see below, the coefficient estimates for the four included dummies directly show us only four contrasts (between the mean of the category indicated and the mean of the reference category). For example, if *mexamer* were excluded, then the coefficient estimate for *white* would capture the difference in means between whites and Mexican Americans. But, as we will see below, the contrasts among all the categories can be easily recovered, regardless of which one dummy from the set is excluded from the model.

Although the decision about which category to make the reference category does not affect the overall results, it does affect the ease of interpretation of results. As just noted, the difference in outcome means between that reference group and each of the other categories can be directly read from the output and directly presented in tables, thus the contrasts with the reference category will be particularly salient in the default results (see Box 10.2). In addition, as we will see below, the standard errors will be larger for contrasts involving categories that contain few cases and unless the differences in means are relatively large in size, *t*-values will be small for these contrasts. When the reference category has small cell size, all of the individual *t*-tests listed in the default output may be insignificant, even though contrasts between some of the included categories with larger sample sizes may be significant. Again, because this default output will likely stand out to you and those who read your work, and may be what you highlight in tables, it is preferable to choose a category with a relatively larger sample size as a reference.

■ **Box 10.2**

Although one reference category must be selected to estimate the model, additional contrasts can be presented by using subscripts or superscripts (see Literature Excerpt 10.2 below for an example) or by including separate rows for each contrast.

In general, it is best to avoid seemingly easy choices, such as omitting the first or last category (and to be especially careful in cases when the software package will create dummy indicators and exclude one of them for you). A better decision is to use as a reference a category that is of particular substantive interest. Prior empirical evidence and conceptual models can often be used to roughly predict the ordering of means on the outcome for some or many of the categories. Thinking through such prior evidence and rationales can help you to choose to exclude the category whose mean on the outcome you anticipate will differ from the mean on the outcome of the greatest number of other categories or with the largest magnitude of differences (for some categories, you may not be able to make predictions based on prior evidence and theory; you can include the dummy for such categories and omit as a reference a category for which you can make predictions of significant contrasts). If two or more are candidates for exclusion, then you might choose the one with the larger sample size.

10.2.1: How Do We Construct Dummy Variables in SAS and Stata?

Dummy variables can be easily constructed in SAS and Stata. We will begin with a straightforward approach that uses the syntax we already know for generating variables. We will then use a more compact syntax explicitly designed for dummy variables and available in both SAS and Stata.[1]

In Display B.3.1 we saw that the race variable was called M484 in the raw data file, and that the values 97 and 99 indicated missing data (refusals and no answers, respectively). Display C.10 shows the BADGIR codebook results for M484 (and for M2DP01 the variable capturing the respondent's gender, which we will use below). The codebook tells us which values correspond to which categories. Display B.10.1 shows similar results for our analytic sample. Recall that we excluded from our analytic sample respondents who were born outside the USA and who reported that their mother lived outside the USA or lived with them. These exclusion criteria may selectively affect the races. In fact, comparing Display B.10.1 to Display C.10, we see that our analytic sample has a higher percentage of white than the total sample, and most subgroups (other than American Indians) are a smaller percentage in the analytic than the total sample. Some category sizes become quite small (fewer than 30 cases) in our analytic sample, thus making it difficult to estimate conditional means in these categories with precision. We might collapse together some categories on conceptual grounds (perhaps using the empirical techniques discussed below as support in initial models). For pedagogical reasons, we separate out one of the categories with a small sample (American Indian) and group together the remaining categories with 40 or fewer cases. This allows us to demonstrate the implications of small cell size for the standard error and the conceptual challenge of interpreting a heterogeneous *other* category.

Using the *If* Qualifier

One approach to creating the relevant dummy variables is to use the *if* qualifier. To do so, we need to have in mind the expressions that indicate either being in a category or not in a category. And, we want to pay careful attention to missing values. Table 10.1 shows how we would like each original category of the original M484 variable to be coded on the new set of dummy variables.

■ **Table 10.1: Example of Dummy Variable Coding**

Original Variable	New Dummy Variables				
M484	aframer	white	mexamer	amind	other
1 = African American	1	0	0	0	0
2 = White	0	1	0	0	0
3 = Mexican American	0	0	1	0	0
4 = Puerto Rican	0	0	0	0	1
5 = Cuban	0	0	0	0	1
6 = Other Hispanic	0	0	0	0	1
7 = American Indian	0	0	0	1	0
8 = Asian	0	0	0	0	1
9 = Other	0	0	0	0	1
97 = Refusal	.	.	.	.	.
99 = No Answer	.	.	.	.	.

For nominal variables such as race, we recommend choosing names for the dummy variables that reflect which original categories are coded a "1" on the new variable.

An alternative would be to use a name that contains the original variable name and category number (e.g., M484_1, M484_2, M484_3, M484_7, M484_45689). The latter can be useful in some cases (for example, in initial analyses of a variable with many categories, or ordinal variables where the numbers tie back to a meaningful rating scale). However, we find that using dummy variable names that reflect the category coded "1" usually make it easier to interpret output.

For the variable *aframer*, we can say, in words, that we would like to code the new variable a "1" if M484 is coded a "1". For all other values, except 97 and 99, we would like to code *aframer* a "0". We would like 97 and 99 to carry the value of '.' missing on *aframer*. One straightforward way to achieve this desired result in Stata is with the commands:

```
generate aframer=1 if M484==1
replace aframer=0 if M484~=1
replace aframer=. if M484>=97
```

In SAS, the comparable code would be:

```
if M484=1 then aframer=1;
if M484~=1 then aframer=0;
if M484>=97 then aframer=.;
```

We can verify that the results are what we desire by adding a table statement to the PROC FREQ command in SAS and by using the tabulate command in Stata to cross-tabulate the original variable with the new variable. Because the default results differ between the two packages, we add some options to obtain just what we need. Stata includes only the cell frequencies whereas SAS includes column, row, and overall percentages by default. Because for checking purposes we only need the cell frequencies, we can add an option in SAS to exclude the percentages. In SAS, we would type: `PROC FREQ; tables M484*aframer /NOCOL NOROW NOPERCENT; run;` We also add the option, `missing` in Stata, because by default Stata excludes cases missing on either variable from the cross-tabulation, and we want to be able to verify that the 97 and 99 values are coded '.' `missing` on the new dummy variable. Thus, in Stata we would type `tabulate M484 aframer, missing`. Display B.10.2 shows the results of creating and checking this variable.

The results show that, as desired, cases coded a "1" on the original variable are a "1" on the new *aframer* dummy. Cases that were a 99 on the original variable are missing on the new dummy (we can see this explicitly in Stata; in SAS, the bottom of the table notes that three cases are missing, and the 99s do not appear in the upper table). All other categories are coded a "0". We cannot overemphasize the importance of checking your code in this way. A little time spent verifying that the results are what you desire will pay off immensely in the long run, when you avoid having to redo work after fixing an early error (or worse yet, having to report that results presented or published were in error).

The dummy variables for *white*, *mexamer*, and *amind* can be constructed similarly, given that each indicates a single value on the original M484 variable. The *other* dummy requires a lengthier expression to indicate its multiple categories. In words, a "1" should be coded if M484 is between 4 and 6 or if M484 is an 8 or 9. A "0" should be coded if M484 is between 1 and 3 or is a 7. A '.' `missing` should be coded if M484 is a 97 or 99. The following translates these expressions from words into Stata code:

```
generate other=1 if (M484>=4 & M484<=6) | M484==8 | M484==9
replace other=0 if (M484>=1 & M484<=3) | M484==7
replace other=. if M484>=97
```

In SAS, the comparable code would be:

```
if (M484>=4 & M484<=6) | M484=8 | M484=9 then other=1;
if (M484>=1 & M484<=3) | M484=7 then other=0;
if M484>=97 then other=.;
```

Checking that your code achieves the correct results is particularly important with such lengthier expressions. We can again use a `PROC FREQ` in SAS and `tabulate` in Stata to do so. Display B.10.3 shows the results.

Using the True/False Evaluation

Both SAS and Stata also allow a simple syntax in which a new dummy variable is defined based on an expression that is either true or false. If the expression is true, then the new variable is coded a "1". If the expression is false, then the new variable is coded a "0". For example, for *aframer*, this expression would be stated in words as "Does M484 equal one?" For *other*, this expression would be stated in words as "Is M484 between 4 and 6 or an 8 or 9?". We can readily translate these statements into SAS or Stata syntax using the expressions we wrote above to code a "1" for each variable. In both SAS and Stata we write a statement with the new variable name on the left of the equals sign and the expression on the right. Missing data can be dealt with using an *if* qualifier.[2]

Dummy indicator for:	SAS	Stata
African American	`if M484<97 then aframer=(M484=1);`	`generate aframer=(M484==1) if M484<97`
White	`if M484<97 then white= (M484=2);`	`generate white= (M484==2) if M484<97`
Mexican American	`if M484<97 then mexamer=(M484=3);`	`generate mexamer=(M484==3) if M484<97`
American Indian	`if M484<97 then amind= (M484=7);`	`generate amind= (M484==7) if M484<97`
Other	`if M484<97 then other= ((M484>=4 & M484<=6)	M484=8	M484=9);`	`generate other= ((M484>=4 & M484<=6)///	M484==8	M484==9) if M484<97`

Let's take the dummy variable for *aframer* and see how it would be coded, based on the expression being true or false.

Original Variable M484	Is *if* qualifier true or false?	Is expression true or false? (Does M484 equal 1?)		New Dummy Variable *aframer*
	if M484<97	SAS M484=1	Stata M484==1	
1 = African American	True	True		1
2 = White	True	False		0
3 = Mexican American	True	False		0
4 = Puerto Rican	True	False		0
5 = Cuban	True	False		0
6 = Other Hispanic	True	False		0
7 = American Indian	True	False		0
8 = Asian	True	False		0
9 = Other	True	False		0
97 = Refusal	False	n/a		.
99 = No Answer	False	n/a		.

In the first row, when the original variable is coded "1", the expression "Is M484 less than 97" is true, so the expression "Does M484 equal 1?" is evaluated. Because the latter statement is also true, the new variable *aframer* is coded "1". In contrast, in the second row, when the original variable is coded "2", the first statement is again true but the second statement "Does *M484* equal 1" is false, thus the new variable *aframer* is coded "0". The new variable is similarly coded except in the last two rows. In these cases, the first statement "Is M484 less than 97" is false, thus the second statement is not evaluated and the new variable is coded a '.' `missing`.

When SAS or Stata executes the code, the value on the original variable for each case is examined in relation to the expressions. The following table provides an example of what the results might look like in the datafile for the original variable M484 and the new variable *aframer*:

id	M484	aframer	. . .
10101	4	0	. . .
10102	99	.	. . .
10103	2	0	. . .
20101	1	1	. . .
20102	1	1	. . .
30102	9	0	. . .
30103	3	0	. . .
. . .	. . .	. . .	. . .

10.3: INTERPRETING DUMMY VARIABLE REGRESSION MODELS

We will now manipulate the regression equations to help us to understand the general interpretation of dummy variable coefficients. We will also look at several examples to make this general discussion concrete. We will start with a simple case with one dummy variable predictor and then look at several extensions with multiple predictors. We will end with some conventional ways to present results for dummy variable predictors.

10.3.1: Single Dummy Variable Predictor

We will begin by manipulating the equation for a simple model with a single dummy variable predictor to help us to understand why we can interpret the coefficient of the dummy variable as the difference in means between the group coded "1" on the dummy variable and the reference group coded "0" on the dummy variable.

We will represent the dummy variable with the letter D to distinguish it from integer-level predictor variables which we have been denoting X in earlier chapters. Then, a model with a single dummy predictor can be represented as follows:

$$Y_i = \beta_0 + \beta_1 D_i + \varepsilon_i$$

Suppose that Y represents the variable *g1miles* from our prior examples (the distance in miles that an adult lives from his or her mother) and that D represents a dummy variable *female* which equals "1" to indicate women and "0" for men. It is conventional still to refer to β_0 as the intercept, but we will call β_1 the dummy variable coefficient (rather than the slope).

Recall that our original variable ($M2DP01$) has two levels (coded 1 = men and 2 = women). Thus, the number of categories, c, is two. We can create two dummy variables based on this original two-category variable: (a) dummy *male* which indicates the *M2DP01* category of 1 (men); and, (b) a dummy *female* which indicates the *M2DP01* category of 2 (women). Based on our rule, we need $c - 1 = 2 - 1 = 1$ of these dummy variables in the regression model. We'll start by including *female*, although we will see in Display B.10.4 below that the significance tests do not depend on which dummy variable we exclude (although interpretation of the default output does).

We can use our familiar process of writing expected values (conditional means) for particular levels of our predictor variable to understand how we interpret this model with the female dummy. Because we include just one dummy variable that takes on only two values in this simple model, there are only two possible expected values. When $D = 0$, then we have the expected value for men. When $D = 1$, then we have the expected value for women. Substituting in the values of D gives the following results:

$$E(Y|D_i = 0) = \beta_0 + \beta_1 \times 0 = \beta_0 \qquad \text{the average distance from the mother for men} \qquad (10.1)$$

$$E(Y|D_i = 1) = \beta_0 + \beta_1 \times 1 = \beta_0 + \beta_1 \qquad \text{the average distance from the mother for women} \qquad (10.2)$$

We can take the difference between these two results to help us to interpret the dummy variable coefficient β_1.[3]

In words: (the average distance from the mother for women) minus (the average distance from the mother for men)

In symbols: $(\beta_0 + \beta_1) - (\beta_0) = \beta_1$ $\qquad (10.3)$

So, how do we interpret β_0 and β_1 in this model with a single dummy variable predictor? As we just showed in Equation 10.1, the intercept (β_0) is the average distance from the mother for men. And, as we saw in Equation 10.3, the dummy variable coefficient (β_1) is the difference in average distance from the mother between women and men. As seen in Equation 10.2, in order to calculate the actual average for women, we need to add together the intercept (β_0) and the dummy variable coefficient (β_1).

Our typical null hypothesis about the slope in earlier chapters has been that it equals zero, which represented a horizontal line or no linear relationship between Y and X. How would we interpret the case in which the dummy variable coefficient, β_1, is zero? Looking back at Equation 10.2, if $\beta_1 = 0$, then the expected value for women would be $\beta_0 + \beta_1 = \beta_0 + 0 = \beta_0$. This is the same expected value as calculated for men in Equation 10.1. Thus, when the dummy variable coefficient is zero, the mean for women is the same as the mean for men. In general, our familiar process of calculating the t-statistic for the hypothesis that $\beta_1 = 0$ is still a meaningful hypothesis (although now it represents no difference in the mean on Y between the two groups, rather than no linear relationship between Y and X). We can use the same formulas we learned in Chapters 8 and 9 to calculate the coefficients, standard errors, and t-values for this test. The standard t-value (ratio of the coefficient to its standard error) and p-value that SAS and Stata will show will be a test of this null hypothesis that the dummy variable coefficient is zero (H_o: $\beta_1 = 0$; the means are the same in the two groups) against an alternative hypothesis that the dummy variable's coefficient is not zero (H_a: $\beta_1 \neq 0$; the means differ between the two groups). It is also possible to test directional hypotheses using the techniques discussed in Section 8.4.7.

In sum, in a simple model with a single dummy variable, we interpret the intercept as the average on the outcome for the reference category (in this case, men). And, we interpret the coefficient of the dummy variable as the difference in outcome means between the **included category** (in this case, women) and the reference category (in this case, men). If the dummy variable's coefficient is not significantly different from zero, then the outcome means for the two groups are statistically equivalent. If the dummy variable's coefficient is significant, then this means that we have statistical evidence that the included category (in this case, women) has a different average value on the outcome than does the reference category (in this case, men).

Let's now look at an example to make this concrete. Display B.10.4 contains the results of actually regressing *glmiles* on *female* in the NSFH data. We use the syntax explained above to create a dummy variable *female* based on evaluating the expression "Is *M2DP*01 equal to two?" (Recall that *M2DP*01 has no missing values; see again Display C.7). Notice that our command for the regression is the same as we have been using already for interval predictors, but we now use our dummy variable predictor (*female*).

The results give us the following estimated regression equation:

$$\hat{Y} = 323.76 - 59.39 \times female$$

Both the intercept and dummy coefficient differ significantly from zero. Their *t*-values (23.56 and −3.35) are both greater than our cutoff for a 5 percent two-sided test for our large sample (critical *t*-value of 1.96). And, both of the *p*-values are less than 0.05.

Using the general interpretation for the intercept and dummy coefficient that we just worked out, we would say:

On average, adult men live about 324 miles from their mothers.
Adult women live about 60 miles closer to their mothers than do men, on average.
Adult women, on average, live 323.76 − 59.39 = 264.37 miles from their mothers.

What happens if we switch the reference category from men to women? Display B.10.4 also contains the results of creating a new dummy variable called *male* and regressing *glmiles* on *male* in the NSFH data. Notice that our code is very similar to the code for the top model in Display B.10.4, although the expression used to define the dummy *male* now asks "Is M2DP01 equal to 1?" to indicate men, and the predictor variable in the regression command is *male* rather than *female*.

The results give us the following estimated regression equation:

$$\hat{Y} = 264.37 + 59.39 \times male$$

Several important points are made clear by comparing these results to those in the top panel of Display B.10.4:

- The dummy coefficient for *male* is identical in magnitude to the dummy coefficient for *female* but opposite in sign (59.39 and −59.39, respectively). Just as the mean for females is about 60 miles less than the mean for men, the mean for men is about 60 miles more than the mean for women.
- The intercept is now 264.37, which we had calculated based on the top panel of Display B.10.4 to be the average distance for women. So, as expected, with the dummy variable switched to *male*, the intercept is the average distance for women, who are now the reference category.
- The mean distance for men can be calculated as the intercept plus the dummy coefficient in the bottom panel of Display B.10.4. That is, 264.37 + 59.39 = 323.76. As expected, within rounding, this is the same mean distance for men as we read from the intercept in the top model of Display B.10.4, when men were the reference category.

Correspondence with a *t*-test for the Difference between Two Means

The simple regression model we just examined, with one dummy variable predictor, is directly analogous to the *t*-test for a difference in means between two groups that we learned in Chapter 7.[4] Let's conduct the same hypothesis test that we did in Display B.10.4 with a *t*-test to help relate our new concepts to these familiar concepts. We just saw that in the regression context, one way to write our null hypothesis was that the dummy variable coefficient (difference in means between the two groups) was zero. We can write our hypotheses for the *t*-test of the difference between two means equivalently as:

$$H_o: \mu_{male} - \mu_{female} = 0$$
$$H_a: \mu_{male} - \mu_{female} \neq 0$$

Display B.10.5 shows the results of conducting a *t*-test of these hypotheses with *M2DP*01 as our grouping variable. Recall that the *t*-test command calculates the mean on the interval-variable (here, *g1miles*) within each of the groups and the difference between these means. These match up to the values we saw in Display B.10.4. The mean for men (*M2DP*01 = 1, labeled MALE in Display B.10.5) is 323.76. The mean for women (*M2DP*01 = 2, labeled FEMALE in Display B.10.5) is 264.37.

The difference between the two means in Display B.10.5 is 59.39 and the *t*-value is 3.35. This is consistent with the results we saw in the dummy variable regression. The sign (positive) matches the bottom model in Display B.10.4 because the difference in means for the *t*-test is calculated by subtracting the higher-coded value (*M2DP*01 = 2, FEMALE) from the lower coded value (*M2DP*01 = 1, MALE).

If we can test the same hypothesis with the *t*-test for group means as with dummy-variable regression, why learn them both? As we have seen in earlier chapters, it is rare in the social sciences that we have data (such as experimental data) that make the two-group *t*-test (or simple dummy variable model) informative.[5] As we will see in the next series of sections, in the regression context we can extend the model by adding additional predictor variables to test more complex hypotheses and control for confounding variables. Social scientists often use *t*-tests for group means when initially describing data, but for testing central research hypotheses, they generally rely on the regression approach.

10.3.2: Nominal/Ordinal Variable with More than One Category

In this section, we will extend our concepts to models with multiple dummy variables representing an original categorical variable with more than two levels.

For example, a model that includes three dummy variables to represent four categories of a categorical variable can be written as follows:

$$Y_i = \beta_0 + \beta_1 D_{1i} + \beta_2 D_{2i} + \beta_3 D_{3i} + \varepsilon_i \tag{10.4}$$

Again, the outcome variable might be *g1miles* and the dummy variables might represent three of the race-ethnicity categories in the NSFH. For simplicity in this example, we will define the reference category as African Americans and exclude the relatively small number (100) of NSFH cases in our analytic sample who identified themselves as Puerto Rican, Cuban, other Hispanic, Asian, or Other. Thus, our example will take $D_1 = amind$, $D_2 = mexamer$, and $D_3 = white$. We already defined the relevant variables above, and reproduce the table below, shading the categories that we will drop from the data set before estimating the regression.

Original Variable	New Dummy Variables				
M484	aframer	white	mexamer	amind	other
1 = African American	1	0	0	0	0
2 = White	0	1	0	0	0
3 = Mexican American	0	0	1	0	0
4 = Puerto Rican	0	0	0	0	1
5 = Cuban	0	0	0	0	1
6 = Other Hispanic	0	0	0	0	1
7 = American Indian	0	0	0	1	0
8 = Asian	0	0	0	0	1
9 = Other	0	0	0	0	1
97 = Refusal	.	.	.	.	.
99 = No Answer	.	.	.	.	.

Notice that excluding these categories from the data set is different from excluding the *other* category to make it the reference category. When we drop cases coded 4 to 6, 8, 9, or missing, our data set will now be comprised of the subset of the cases who report being African American, white, Mexican American, or American Indian, and any three of the four dummies presented below can be used in a regression model.

Original Variable		New Dummy Variables		
M484	*aframer*	*white*	*mexamer*	*amind*
1 = African American	1	0	0	0
2 = White	0	1	0	0
3 = Mexican American	0	0	1	0
7 = American Indian	0	0	0	1

In Equation 10.4, the intercept represents the mean for the reference category (in our first example, African Americans). The dummy variable coefficients in Equation 10.4 assess the difference between the mean of this reference category and the mean of each of the categories indicated by the three included dummy variables. We can see this by writing the expected values.

$$
\begin{aligned}
E(Y|D_{1i} = 0, D_{2i} = 0, D_{3i} = 0) \\
= \beta_0 + \beta_1 \times 0 + \beta_2 \times 0 + \beta_3 \times 0 \\
= \beta_0
\end{aligned}
\qquad
\begin{aligned}
&\text{average distance} \\
&\text{from mother for} \\
&\text{African Americans}
\end{aligned}
\qquad (10.5)
$$

$$
\begin{aligned}
E(Y|D_{1i} = 1, D_{2i} = 0, D_{3i} = 0) \\
= \beta_0 + \beta_1 \times 1 + \beta_2 \times 0 + \beta_3 \times 0 \\
= \beta_0 + \beta_1
\end{aligned}
\qquad
\begin{aligned}
&\text{average distance from} \\
&\text{mother for American} \\
&\text{Indians}
\end{aligned}
\qquad (10.6)
$$

$$
\begin{aligned}
E(Y|D_{1i} = 0, D_{2i} = 1, D_{3i} = 0) \\
= \beta_0 + \beta_1 \times 0 + \beta_2 \times 1 + \beta_3 \times 0 \\
= \beta_0 + \beta_2
\end{aligned}
\qquad
\begin{aligned}
&\text{average distance from} \\
&\text{mother for} \\
&\text{Mexican Americans}
\end{aligned}
\qquad (10.7)
$$

$$
\begin{aligned}
E(Y|D_{1i} = 0, D_{2i} = 0, D_{3i} = 1) \\
= \beta_0 + \beta_1 \times 0 + \beta_2 \times 0 + \beta_3 \times 1 \\
= \beta_0 + \beta_3
\end{aligned}
\qquad
\begin{aligned}
&\text{average distance} \\
&\text{from mother} \\
&\text{for whites}
\end{aligned}
\qquad (10.8)
$$

Let's subtract the expected value for the reference category (African American) from the expected value for each of the included categories to see why this is the correct interpretation for the dummy variable coefficients, similarly to what we did above when we interpreted the single dummy for *female* in Equation 10.3.

Difference in expected value in words:	Difference in expected value in symbols:
American Indian minus African Americans	$(\beta_0 + \beta_1) - (\beta_0) = \beta_1$
Mexican Americans minus African Americans	$(\beta_0 + \beta_2) - (\beta_0) = \beta_2$
Whites minus African Americans	$(\beta_0 + \beta_3) - (\beta_0) = \beta_3$

These results make it explicit that each dummy variable coefficient captures how much higher or lower the outcome mean is for the included category than the outcome mean for the reference category.[6] A common mistake for students when interpreting models like this one is to interpret each of the dummies as the contrast of the group indicated by the dummy versus all other groups. The results above make clear that this interpretation is not correct. Rather, the comparison group is the reference category (in this case African Americans).[7]

Display B.10.6 shows the SAS and Stata code for creating these new dummy variables and the regression command which lists the names of the three dummy variables following the format that we used for equations with multiple predictors in Chapter 9. We list them in the order we associated them with our general dummies ($D_1 = amind$, $D_2 = mexamer$, and $D_3 = white$) so that it is easy to relate them to our general formulas.

Looking at the parameter estimates, we see that just one of the dummy variable coefficients is significantly different from zero (t-value greater than 1.96 and p-value less than 0.05): the coefficient for white, which is positive in sign. So, American Indians and Mexican American adults do not differ significantly from African American adults in the mean distance they live from their mothers. But, white adults live about 60 miles further away from their mothers than do African American adults, on average.

The actual predicted values are:

African Americans	240.97	
American Indians	$240.97 + 157.03 = 398.00$	(10.9)
Mexican Americans	$240.97 - 8.25 = 232.72$	(10.10)
Whites	$240.97 + 56.72 = 297.69$	

So, Mexican Americans live an average of 233 miles from their mothers. African Americans live just slightly further from their mothers, averaging 241 miles. Whites live further, nearly 300 miles on average from their mothers. The mean for American Indians is substantially larger than any other group, at nearly 400 miles.

But, American Indians have the smallest sample size and their estimate has the largest standard error (in Display B.10.6, $\hat{\sigma}_{\hat{\beta}1} = 129.49$ whereas $\hat{\sigma}_{\hat{\beta}2} = 54.48$ and $\hat{\sigma}_{\hat{\beta}3} = 24.77$). Thus, although the average distance they live from their mothers is estimated to be substantially larger than the three other groups, the estimate has considerable error. This reflects the different sample sizes among the groups. Recall that we excluded cases missing any variables (including the interval variables we will add to the model below), so the sample sizes are even smaller than what was seen in Display B.10.1. Among the 5,401 cases included in the regression model, there are just 25 American Indians as opposed to 166 Mexican Americans and 4,432 whites. The reference category, African American, has 778 cases. Seeing the implications of these sample sizes for the standard errors reinforces our comment above of not selecting a category with few cases as the reference category. And, it reinforces the general importance of selecting a data set or designing new data collection to contain sufficient sample sizes across the groups of interest (the NSFH data are not well suited to regression models that focus on American Indians).

Testing Differences in Means among the Included Groups

As mentioned above, we can recover the differences in means among all groups, based on the default output with any of the categories used as a reference. We do so by calculating the difference between the estimated coefficients for the two included dummy variables.

To start, we can use the predicted values (means within groups) that we figured out above (Equations 10.9 and 10.10) to calculate directly the difference in means between Mexican Americans and American Indians.

$$(\bar{X}_{mexamer} - \bar{X}_{aframer}) - (\bar{X}_{amind} - \bar{X}_{aframer})$$
$$(\bar{X}_{mexamer} - \bar{X}_{amind})$$
$$232.72 - 398.00$$
$$= -165.28 \tag{10.11}$$

This result (-165.28) should match the difference in coefficients between Mexican Americans and American Indians. Indeed, recall that our interpretations of the coefficient estimates mirror the difference in means written above. When African Americans are the reference category, the coefficient estimate for Mexican Americans ($\hat{\beta}_2$) reflects the difference in means between Mexican Americans and African Americans; and, the coefficient estimate for American Indians ($\hat{\beta}_1$) reflects the difference in means between American Indians and African Americans. Thus, we can calculate the difference in means between Mexican Americans and American Indians based on their respective coefficient estimates from the regression with African Americans as the reference category.

$$\hat{\beta}_2 - \hat{\beta}_1$$
$$(-8.25) - (157.03) = -165.28$$

This difference of -165.28 is larger than the difference between either group and African Americans. But, is this difference between the two included groups (Mexican Americans and American Indians) itself significantly different from zero? That is, does the average difference that Mexican Americans live from their mothers differ significantly from the average difference that American Indians live from their mothers?

In general, what if we also had hypothesized about the differences in means between the pairs of included groups as well as differences from the reference category mean? We might, for example, expect that white adults live further from their mothers than do American Indian and Mexican American adults, due to emphases on familial ties in American Indian and Mexican cultures.[8] We will now look at three strategies for testing for differences among the included groups (including whether the -165.28 calculated in Equation 10.11 is significant):

(a) re-estimating the regression model with a slightly different set of variables;
(b) using a partial F-test;
(c) testing the significance of a linear combination of coefficients.

We'll conclude by talking about the relative strengths and weaknesses of each approach.

Re-estimating the Model with a Different Reference Category

One way to test the differences in means among the included groups is to re-estimate the model with a different reference category, similar to the strategy we took above when we had a single dummy predictor. When we have more than one dummy predictor, this approach can become cumbersome because we may need to re-estimate the model multiple times, depending on the number of categories on our original variable. In this case, we have three included dummies, so there are three pairwise comparisons among them (American Indian versus Mexican American, American Indian versus white, and Mexican American versus white). We will capture two of these three contrasts the first time that we exclude a different dummy variable from the set. But, we'll need to re-estimate the model a third time to pick up the final contrast.

Importantly, as we will see, there is no need to re-estimate the model, since all of the information we need to contrast the included categories is available upon our first estimation (this is evident, for example, in the fact that the sum of squares and overall F-test will be the same across models which use different reference categories). But, it is pedagogically helpful for some students to see this concretely.

Display B.10.7 provides the results of re-estimating the regression model first with American Indians as the reference category, then with Mexican Americans as the reference category, and finally with whites as the reference category. Note that each time, we included three of the four dummy variables in this set. We must do so in order to get equivalent results as our initial model, from Display B.10.6.

First, notice that each regression model in Display B.10.7 repeats one of the coefficient estimates from Display B.10.6, but reversed in sign. This is because we are calculating the difference in means between the same pair of groups, but flipping the reference category.

For the contrast between American Indians and African Americans:

■ The coefficient estimate for *amind* was 157.03 in Display B.10.6 (with African Americans excluded). The coefficient estimate for *aframer* in the top model of Display B.10.7 (with American Indians excluded) is −157.03.

For the contrast between Mexican Americans and African Americans:

■ The coefficient estimate for *mexamer* was −8.25 in Display B.10.6 (with African Americans excluded). The coefficient estimate for *aframer* in the middle model of Display B.10.7 (with Mexican Americans excluded) is 8.25.

For the contrast between whites and African Americans:

■ The coefficient estimate for *white* was 56.72 in Display B.10.6 (with African Americans excluded). The coefficient estimate for *aframer* in the bottom model of Display B.10.7 (with whites excluded) is −56.72.

This is directly analogous to what we saw in the simple regression model for gender: when we switched the dummy variable that we excluded, the coefficient estimate was the same in magnitude, but opposite in sign. The same is true in these models with a set of dummies for a multicategory variable, but only one contrast remains the same when we switch the reference category. The other contrasts offer new comparisons among some of the originally included variables.

In the top model of Display B.10.7, because the group "American Indians" is now the reference category, we now have estimates of the difference in means between Mexican Americans and American Indians (−165.28) and between whites and American Indians (−100.31). Neither is significant under a two-sided test (both t-values less than 1.96 and p-values greater than 0.05). Notice that the former value of −165.28 is exactly the same amount as the difference in coefficient estimates we calculated in Equation 10.11. This re-emphasizes the fact that all of the information about the contrasts is captured in a single estimation of the model. What we could not read off of the original regression output in Display B.10.6, however, was whether this difference in average distance between Mexican Americans and American Indians was significant. Re-estimating the model with American Indians excluded in Display B.10.7 shows us that it is not (even though the difference is large in absolute terms, its standard error is also large, due to the small sample size of American Indians, making the t-value just −1.21).

The two values we just examined are also repeated in the middle and bottom models of Display B.10.7. The contrast of American Indians and Mexican Americans is found in the middle model, the same magnitude but reversed in sign from what we saw in the top model (the coefficient estimate for *amind* with Mexican Americans excluded is 165.28 in the middle model). Similarly, the contrast of whites and American Indians is found in the bottom model, the same magnitude but reverse sign from what we saw in the top model (the coefficient estimate for *amind* with whites excluded is 100.31 in the bottom model).

The middle and bottom panels also contain one new contrast that was not found in the top panel of Display B.10.7 nor in Display B.10.6. The difference between whites and Mexican Americans is just over 60 miles (64.97 in the middle model for *white* with Mexican Americans excluded; −64.97 in the bottom panel for *mexamer* with whites excluded). This difference is not significant for a two-sided test ($p = .197$).[9]

As noted, although this approach—re-estimating the regression model with a different excluded dummy variable—gives us all of the contrasts that we desire and is quite simple and concrete, it can become cumbersome. Depending on the number of dummy variables in the set, we must re-estimate the model several times and we obtain some redundant information in each re-estimation. We will now look at two different approaches, each of which can be implemented in SAS and Stata with commands that follow a single estimation of the model.

Using the Partial F-test

A second approach to testing hypotheses about differences between the included variables is with the partial F-test which we learned in Chapter 9. We can use the SAS and Stata test commands that we learned in that chapter, but first we will examine the logic of the partial F-test for our new application in this chapter and we will calculate one test "by hand" to make the logic concrete.

Recall that we used the partial F-test to compare a full and reduced model, where we wrote the reduced model by placing the restrictions of the null hypothesis on the full model. What are the restrictions when we are comparing the two included coefficients? Let's use the coefficients in Equation 10.4 to figure out what would need to be true for the means for American Indians and whites to differ. To do so, we will write the differences between the expected values for the included variables found in Equations 10.6 to 10.8 in words and with symbols:[10]

Difference in expected value in words	Difference in expected value in symbols	
American Indians minus Mexican Americans	$(\beta_0 + \beta_1) - (\beta_0 + \beta_2) = \beta_0 + \beta_1 - \beta_0 - \beta_2 = \beta_1 - \beta_2$	(10.12)
American Indian minus whites	$(\beta_0 + \beta_1) - (\beta_0 + \beta_3) = \beta_0 + \beta_1 - \beta_0 - \beta_3 = \beta_1 - \beta_3$	(10.13)
Mexican Americans minus whites	$(\beta_0 + \beta_2) - (\beta_0 + \beta_3) = \beta_0 + \beta_2 - \beta_0 - \beta_3 = \beta_2 - \beta_3$	(10.14)

Thus, for each pair of included groups, the difference in their means is captured by the difference between their respective dummy variables' coefficients. What if we wanted to test the null hypothesis that the difference in means between a pair of included groups is zero? For example, what if $H_o: \beta_1 = \beta_2$ (or equivalently $H_o: \beta_1 - \beta_2 = 0$)? Looking back at the expected values in Equations 10.6 and 10.7, we can see that if β_1 and β_2 are equivalent to one another, then the two groups' means must be the same, because we add that same value $\beta_1 = \beta_2$ to the intercept (β_0) to calculate each group's expected value. More concretely, suppose $\beta_0 = 30$ and $\beta_1 = \beta_2 = 10$. Then the expected value for American Indians would be: $\beta_0 + \beta_1 = 30 + 10 = 40$. And, the expected value for Mexican Americans would be: $\beta_0 + \beta_2 = 30 + 10 = 40$.

How do we use this null hypothesis ($H_o: \beta_1 = \beta_2$) to construct the partial F-test? Our full model is Equation 10.4. Our reduced model results from applying the restriction of the null hypothesis (that the coefficients for the first two dummy variables are equal) to this full model. If $\beta_1 = \beta_2$, then we can substitute a new symbol to represent this single coefficient in the model. Let's call it β_{12}.

$$Y_i = \beta_0 + \beta_{12}D_{1i} + \beta_{12}D_{2i} + \beta_3 D_{3i} + \varepsilon_i$$

We can now simplify this equation algebraically, because of the common term β_{12}:

$$Y_i = \beta_0 + \beta_{12}(D_{1i} + D_{2i}) + \beta_3 D_{3i} + \varepsilon_i$$

What does the new term $D_{1i} + D_{2i}$ imply? To make this clear, let's look back at the values of our dummy variables (reordered to match the order of the dummy variables in our regression model).

Original Variable	Dummy Indicator for:			
	American Indian	Mexican American	White	American Indian or Mexican American
M484	D_{1i}	D_{2i}	D_{3i}	$D_{1i} + D_{2i}$
7 = American Indian	1	0	0	1
3 = Mexican American	0	1	0	1
2 = White	0	0	1	0
1 = African American	0	0	0	0

So, we could think of $D_{1i} + D_{2i}$ as a new dummy indicator of being either American Indian or Mexican American. Suppose we explicitly defined a new variable $D_{12i} = D_{1i} + D_{2i}$, then we could estimate the following as our reduced model:

$$Y_i = \beta_0 + \beta_{12}D_{12i} + \beta_3 D_{3i} + \varepsilon_i$$

The sum of squared errors and degrees of freedom from this reduced model, along with the sum of squared errors and degrees of freedom from the full model (Equation 10.4), would be used to calculate a partial F-test of the null hypothesis that $H_o: \beta_1 - \beta_2 = 0$ (or equivalently $H_o: \beta_1 = \beta_2$) against the alternative that $H_a: \beta_1 - \beta_2 \neq 0$ (or equivalently $H_a: \beta_1 \neq \beta_2$).

Display B.10.8 shows the results of estimating the reduced model. The sums of squares error for the reduced model is 2,192,402,062 with degrees of freedom 5,398. The sum of squared errors for the full model is shown in Display B.10.6 as 2,191,808,493 with degrees of freedom 5,397. The difference in degrees of freedom between the two models is one, as expected (5,398 − 5,397 = 1) because there is one restriction in the null hypothesis (that the two coefficients are equivalent).

Substituting into our standard formula for the partial F-test provides the following result:

$$F = \frac{SSE(R) - SSE(F)}{df_R - df_F} \div \frac{SSE(F)}{df_F} = \frac{(2,192,402,062) - 2,191,808,493}{5,398 - 5,397}$$

$$\div \frac{2,191,808,493}{5,397} = 1.4616$$

Estimating the reduced model and calculating the F-value by hand like this is not time-saving, relative to our first approach (re-estimating the model with a different reference category). But, we can use the `test` command which we learned in Chapter 9, using the variable names to tell SAS and Stata what restriction to place on the full model (e.g., in the example we just calculated, where the null hypothesis is $H_o: \beta_1 = \beta_2$ we would write `test amind=mexamer`). Recall that SAS and Stata use the variable names on the test commands to refer to their associated coefficients, so `test amind=mexamer` is interpreted by SAS and Stata as "Test the null hypothesis that the coefficient for American Indians is equal to the coefficient for Mexican Americans." Because we ordered our predictor variables so that the first was American Indian and the second Mexican American, this null hypothesis can be written symbolically as $H_o: \beta_1 = \beta_2$.

Display B.10.9 shows the results of these test commands. The results confirm our calculation for the contrast of American Indians to Mexican Americans, providing a calculated F-value of 1.46. The p-value of 0.2267 is larger than 0.05. Thus, we fail to reject the null hypothesis that the means for American Indians and Mexican Americans are equivalent. The additional two tests also have p-values that are larger than 0.05, thus giving statistical evidence that the means do not differ significantly between American Indians and whites, $F(1,5397) = 0.62, p = 0.4326$, and between Mexican Americans and whites, $F(1,5397) = 1.66, p = 0.1972$.

Testing the Linear Combination of Coefficients

We will now consider a final approach for testing the difference in means among the included categories. To do so, we will introduce a new statistical concept: how to test the significance of a linear combination of coefficients. Generally, in our models, a **linear combination** will involve the addition of two coefficients or the subtraction of two coefficients.

We saw above that one way to write the null hypothesis when we tested the difference in means of our first two included variables was $H_o: \beta_1 - \beta_2 = 0$. This difference is a linear combination of coefficients. Statistical theory tells us how to calculate the standard error of a linear combination, and we can divide the difference in estimated coefficients by this standard error. The resulting value is a t-statistic, and thus we can use our standard procedures for calculating a p-value or comparing the calculated t-value to a critical t-value in order to make a conclusion about the null hypothesis.

The new statistical concept we need in order to implement this approach is the **variance–covariance matrix of the estimated regression coefficients**. We emphasized in Chapter 8 that the estimated regression coefficients have sampling distributions; that is, the estimate of the population parameter (the population regression coefficient) will differ somewhat when calculated on each successive sample that we might draw from the population. The variances of the regression coefficients capture that variation. We use the square root of these variances— the standard errors—whenever we calculate a t-statistic for an individual regression coefficient. As in a variance–covariance matrix for variables, the variances of the regression coefficients fall "on the diagonal" of the matrix. The parameter estimates also covary (in some applications, when the intercept is large, the slope is also large; in other applications, when the intercept is large, the slope is small; in yet other applications, the intercept and slope are hardly associated). The covariances—the values that fall "off the diagonal" of the matrix—capture this covariation among the coefficients. We use these covariances in the formula for the standard error of a linear combination of coefficients.

Display B.10.10 shows how to ask SAS and Stata for the variance–covariance matrix of the estimates. To see that a portion of this new variance–covariance matrix contains some familiar quantities, let's first compare the square root of the diagonal elements of this matrix with the standard errors in the model, which are displayed in Display B.10.6.

■ For *amind* the variance on the diagonal of the matrix (found by looking down the column labeled *amind* and across the row labeled *amind*) is 16,766.643. The square root of 16,766.643 is 129.49, which matches the standard error shown in Display B.10.6 for *amind*.

■ For *mexamer* the variance on the diagonal of the matrix is 2,968.4825. The square root of 2,968.4825 is 54.48, which matches the standard error shown in Display B.10.6 for *mexamer*.

■ For *white* the variance on the diagonal of the matrix is 613.63279. The square root of 613.63279 is 24.77, which matches the standard error shown in Display B.10.6 for *white*.

We also need the off-diagonal elements to calculate the standard error for the linear combination of coefficients. We find the covariance between the coefficients for *amind* and *mexamer* by reading down the column labeled *amind* and across the row labeled *mexamer*. This value is 522.0001. Notice that in our current model, all of these off-diagonal elements (covariances) are identical because we do not have any control variables in the model. In models with additional predictor variables (such as the model shown in Display B.10.12), the covariances would differ.

The formula for the **standard error of the difference** between two coefficients is (see Box 10.3):

$$\sqrt{\hat{\sigma}_{\hat{\beta}_1}^2 + \hat{\sigma}_{\hat{\beta}_2}^2 - 2\widehat{\text{cov}}_{\hat{\beta}_1 \hat{\beta}_2}}$$

where $\hat{\sigma}_{\hat{\beta}_1}^2$ is the estimated variance of the first estimated coefficient (in our case the variance of *amind* which we saw was 16,766.643), $\hat{\sigma}_{\hat{\beta}_2}^2$ is the estimated variance of the second estimated coefficient (in our case the variance of *mexamer* which we saw was 2,968.4825), and $\widehat{\text{cov}}_{\hat{\beta}_1 \hat{\beta}_2}$ is the estimated covariance between the first and second estimated coefficients (in our case the covariance of *amind* and *mexamer* which we saw was 522.0001). Thus, the standard error of the difference in this case is:

■ Box 10.3

This formula is based on the general formula for the variance of a linear combination of two variables:

Linear Combination: $aX_1 + bX_2$
Variance of Linear Combination: $a^2\text{Var}(X_1) + b^2\text{Var}(X_2) + 2ab\text{Cov}(X_1, X_2)$

Note that a and b can be 1 and they can be negative in sign. So, if we had $a = 1$ and $b = -1$, the resulting formula would be:

$\text{Var}(X_1) + \text{Var}(X_2) - 2\text{Cov}(X_1, X_2)$

which is a general version of the formula we used for the difference between two coefficients. Similarly, if $a = 1$ and $b = 1$ then the formula would be:

$\text{Var}(X_1) + \text{Var}(X_2) + 2\text{Cov}(X_1, X_2)$

which is a formula we can use if we need to test the sum of two coefficients (e.g., $\beta_1 + \beta_2$). For example, we could use this formula to calculate the standard error of the predicted value for women based on estimating Equation 10.2 (i.e., $\beta_0 + \beta_1$).

$$\sqrt{16,766.643 + 2,968.4825 - 2 \times 522.0001} = 136.71549$$

To calculate the *t*-value, we divide the difference in coefficient estimates by this standard error:

$$t = \frac{(\hat{\beta}_1 - \hat{\beta}_2) - 0}{\sqrt{\hat{\sigma}_{\hat{\beta}_1}^2 + \hat{\sigma}_{\hat{\beta}_2}^2 - 2 \times \widehat{cov}_{\hat{\beta}_1 \hat{\beta}_2}}} = \frac{[(157.0283) - (-8.254855)] - 0}{136.71549} = \frac{165.28315}{136.71549} = 1.208957$$

This *t*-value is smaller than the critical *t*-value of 1.96 for a 5 percent significance level in our large sample, thus we cannot reject our null hypothesis. Notice that the standard error and *t*-value match those seen in the middle panel of Display B.10.7 for the *amind* coefficient estimate (with Mexican American as the excluded category).

For testing linear combinations, Stata also offers a specific command called `lincom`. This command is useful because it calculates the difference in coefficient estimates, the standard error, the *t*-value, and the *p*-value, thus reducing the chances that we will make a calculation error and providing all of the details we would need for reporting results in a paper. Display B.10.11 shows the results of using the lincom command for all three contrasts among the included variables shown in Equations 10.12 to 10.14.

Again, these results match the corresponding contrasts found in Display B.10.7 when we re-estimated the model with a different reference category, emphasizing that all of the relevant contrasts can be tested after a single model estimation. This final linear combination approach is thus the preferred approach because it gives the complete information about all contrasts (coefficient estimates, standard errors, *t*-values, and *p*-values) available based on a single estimation of the model.

Summary of Approaches to Testing Contrasts Among Included Categories
We'll now take a closer look at the similarity in results across the three approaches, and then discuss their relative strengths. Let's start by summarizing the results for each approach, drawn from Display B.10.7, Display B.10.9, and Display B.10.11.

In words	In symbols	Approach 1: Re-estimating the Model (Display B.10.7)				Approach 2: Partial F test (Display B.10.9)		Approach 3: Linear Combination (Display B.10.11)			
		Diff	se	t-value	p-value	F-value	p-value	Diff	se	t-value	p-value
Mexican American minus American Indian	$\beta_2 - \beta_1$	−165.28	136.72	−1.21	0.23	1.46	0.23	−165.28	136.72	−1.21	0.23
White minus American Indian	$\beta_3 - \beta_1$	−100.31	127.81	−0.78	0.43	0.62	0.43	−100.31	127.81	−0.78	0.43
White minus Mexican American	$\beta_3 - \beta_2$	64.97	50.38	1.29	0.20	1.66	0.20	64.97	50.38	1.29	0.20

The table makes clear that the three approaches provide equivalent results, although the first and third approaches provide more information:

■ All approaches provide the same calculated test statistics. (Recall, for a test with one numerator degree of freedom, the square root of the F-value equals the t-value in magnitude. In the first row, $\sqrt{1.46} = 1.21$. In the second row, $\sqrt{0.62} = 0.79$. In the third row, $\sqrt{1.66} = 1.29$).
■ All approaches provide the same p-values for two-sided tests.
■ The first and third approaches also calculate the difference in coefficient estimates and the standard error of this difference.
■ The first and third approaches provide the direction of the difference and can be used to test directional hypotheses (one-sided tests) by adjusting the p-value based on whether its sign is consistent with the alternative hypothesis.

For most models, today's computing power is quick enough that re-estimating a model with a different reference category takes only a few minutes. But, for some data sets and for some of the more complicated types of model we will preview in Chapter 18, it can take days to re-estimate a model. In these situations, the second and third approaches are time-saving. The second and third approaches also provide compact code, which is helpful for organizing and proofing our batch programs. Each approach is also useful in the broader context of learning statistical methods for the social sciences. Approach 2 reinforces our understanding of the partial F-test. Approach 3 introduces the new concepts of the linear combination and variance–covariance matrix of the estimates which we will see again in future chapters and in reading the literature.

What approach should we use? If we only want to report the significance of contrasts among included variables, then the `test` command will give us the information and can be implemented in either SAS or Stata. If we want to report the exact difference between the included variables' coefficient estimates and the standard error of these differences, then Stata's `lincom` command is convenient. Alternatively, to obtain the difference in coefficient estimates and their standard errors, we can also re-estimate the model with a different reference category. This approach will not be time-consuming as long as our sample is not quite large and our model is fairly simple.

We will now end our discussion of dummy variable predictors with an example of including more than one multicategory predictor in the model and adding interval-level variables to the model with sets of dummy indicators. Because most of the interpretation follows what we have already discussed, we will focus on the presentation and interpretation of the results, using the `test` command to contrast the included categories.

10.3.3: More than One Nominal/Ordinal Predictor

Putting together our models from Section 10.3.1 and Section 10.3.2, we now estimate a model that predicts how far adults live from their mothers based both on their gender and their race-ethnicity.

$$Y_i = \beta_0 + \beta_1 D_{1i} + \beta_2 D_{2i} + \beta_3 D_{3i} + \beta_4 D_{4i} + \varepsilon_i \qquad (10.15)$$

To combine our two earlier models, we now represent *female* with D_4 and we maintain the use of D_1 for American Indians, D_2 for Mexican Americans, and D_3 for whites. As we will emphasize in the interpretation below, this model is additive. It assumes that the association between race and distance is the same for men and women. And, it assumes that the association between gender and distance is the same across races. We will discuss in Chapter 11 how to test and loosen this assumption.

Before we look at the results of estimating this model, let's look at the general expected values to help us understand the interpretations. We make these calculations by using the dummy variables to indicate each group, then adding together the effects that are relevant for each group.

	MEN	Average distance for:
1	$E(Y\|D_1 = 0, D_2 = 0, D_3 = 0, D_4 = 0) = \beta_0 + \beta_1 \times 0 + \beta_2 \times 0 + \beta_3 \times 0 + \beta_4 \times 0$ $= \beta_0$	African-American men
2	$E(Y\|D_1 = 1, D_2 = 0, D_3 = 0, D_4 = 0) = \beta_0 + \beta_1 \times 1 + \beta_2 \times 0 + \beta_3 \times 0 + \beta_4 \times 0$ $= \beta_0 + \beta_1$	American Indian men
3	$E(Y\|D_1 = 0, D_2 = 1, D_3 = 0, D_4 = 0) = \beta_0 + \beta_1 \times 0 + \beta_2 \times 1 + \beta_3 \times 0 + \beta_4 \times 0$ $= \beta_0 + \beta_2$	Mexican-American men
4	$E(Y\|D_1 = 0, D_2 = 0, D_3 = 1, D_4 = 0) = \beta_0 + \beta_1 \times 0 + \beta_2 \times 0 + \beta_3 \times 1 + \beta_4 \times 0$ $= \beta_0 + \beta_3$	White men
	WOMEN	
5	$E(Y\|D_1 = 0, D_2 = 0, D_3 = 0, D_4 = 1) = \beta_0 + \beta_1 \times 0 + \beta_2 \times 0 + \beta_3 \times 0 + \beta_4 \times 1$ $= \beta_0 + \beta_4$	African-American women
6	$E(Y\|D_1 = 1, D_2 = 0, D_3 = 0, D_4 = 1) = \beta_0 + \beta_1 \times 1 + \beta_2 \times 0 + \beta_3 \times 0 + \beta_4 \times 1$ $= \beta_0 + \beta_1 + \beta_4$	American Indian women
7	$E(Y\|D_1 = 0, D_2 = 1, D_3 = 0, D_4 = 1) = \beta_0 + \beta_1 \times 0 + \beta_2 \times 1 + \beta_3 \times 0 + \beta_4 \times 1$ $= \beta_0 + \beta_2 + \beta_4$	Mexican-American women
8	$E(Y\|D_1 = 0, D_2 = 0, D_3 = 1, D_4 = 1) = \beta_0 + \beta_1 \times 0 + \beta_2 \times 0 + \beta_3 \times 1 + \beta_4 \times 1$ $= \beta_0 + \beta_3 + \beta_4$	White women

In examining these expected values, we see that the interpretations are similar to our earlier examples with one categorical variable, although they now control for the other variable(s) in the model:

■ The intercept is the average on the outcome for the group coded zero on all of the included dummy variables, in this case African-American men (*amind* = 0, *mexamer* = 0, *white* = 0, *female* = 0). Equivalently, when all of the predictor variables are dummies, then, the intercept is the mean for the group that is indicated by the reference category of each of the original categorical variables (in the example, for race-ethnicity: African Americans; for gender: men).

▨ Looking within race-ethnicity and between genders, we see that the coefficient estimate for D_4 (which represents the *female* dummy variable) still captures the difference in means between women and men, but now holding constant race-ethnicity. So, holding race constant as African American, the difference between the expected value in row 5 (African-American women) and row 1 (African-American men) is β_4. The difference between the expected values in the remaining rows within race-ethnicity is similarly β_4 (row 6 minus row 2; row 7 minus row 3; row 8 minus row 4).

▨ Looking within gender and across race-ethnicity reveals that the coefficient estimates for each of the included dummy variables for race-ethnicity captures the difference between the indicated category and the excluded race-ethnicity (African Americans), but now controlling for gender. For example, the difference in expected values between row 6 (American Indian women) and row 5 (African-American women) is β_1; and, the difference in expected values between row 2 (American Indian men) and row 1 (African-American men) is β_1. So, controlling for gender, β_1 represents the average difference distance between American Indians and African Americans. Similarly, the difference between row 7 and row 5 and between row 3 and row 1 is β_2. And, the difference between row 8 and row 5 and between row 4 and row 1 is β_3.

▨ Finally, for contrasts among the included categories of race-ethnicity within gender, we would still test the equality of their coefficients (or equivalently that the difference between their coefficients is zero). For example, the difference in expected values between row 6 (American Indian women) and row 7 (Mexican-American women) is $\beta_1 - \beta_2$. Likewise, the difference between row 2 (American Indian men) and row 3 (Mexican-American men) is $\beta_1 - \beta_2$. Similarly, the difference between row 6 and row 8 and between row 2 and row 4 is $\beta_1 - \beta_3$. And, the difference between row 7 and row 8 and between row 3 and row 4 is $\beta_2 - \beta_3$.

10.3.4: Adding Interval Variables and Presenting the Results

We will now further extend the model by adding interval predictors, and interpret the results in a table and figure format similar to that we might use in a publication. The purpose of adding more variables to the model and putting these results in presentation format is to examine a more realistic model and practice presentation style, not to suggest the substantive relevance of these findings. In a publication, we would flesh out the conceptual rationale for our hypothesis tests, and add additional controls. We will look at a substantively interpretable example from the published literature in the final section of this chapter.

We can extend Equation 10.15 by adding the full list of interval variables we examined at the end of Chapter 9.

$$Y_i = \beta_0 + \beta_1 D_{1i} + \beta_2 D_{2i} + \beta_3 D_{3i} + \beta_4 D_{4i} + \beta_5 X_{5i} + \beta_6 X_{6i} + \beta_7 X_{7i} + \beta_8 X_{8i} + \beta_9 X_{9i} + \beta_{10} X_{10i} + \varepsilon_i$$

where $X_5 = g2earn$, $X_6 = g2age$, $X_7 = g2numbro$, $X_8 = g2numsis$, $X_9 = g1yrschl$, $X_{10} = g1age$.

This model is still additive, and the interpretation of the dummy variable coefficients remains as discussed above; however, we now will remind the reader in our interpretation that we have controlled for this fuller set of variables.

Display B.10.12 provides the results of estimating this equation in SAS and Stata. And, Table 10.2 shows how these results might be presented in a publication table.

Examining the results for our dummy variables, we see that, controlling for the respondent's race-ethnicity, earnings, age, number of bothers and number of sisters, and the mother's age and years of schooling, adult women live 34 miles closer to their mothers than do adult men, on average. Under a two-sided test, this effect is marginally significant, with a p-value less than 0.10.[11] Controlling for gender, the racial-ethnic groups do not differ significantly from one another in distance lived from the mother and other predictors.[12]

■ Table 10.2: Regression Model of Distance Adults Live from their Mothers (in miles)

	Coefficient (s.e.)
Respondent's Characteristics	
Race-ethnicity[a]	
American Indian	185.14
	(128.54)
Mexican American	61.85
	(55.32)
White	35.07
	(25.22)
Female	−33.79+
	(18.80)
Annual Earnings[b]	6.68*
	(2.51)
Age (years)	−0.04
	(1.65)
Number of Brothers	5.20
	(5.96)
Number of Sisters	18.56*
	(6.03)
Mother's Characteristics	
Years of Schooling	21.12*
	(3.28)
Age (years)	4.61*
	(1.44)
Intercept	−293.51
	(71.86)

Notes: Standard errors in parentheses. $n = 5,401$.
[a] Reference category is African American.
[b] In $10,000 increments, adjusted to 2007 dollars.
* $p < .05$. + $p < .10$ (two-sided tests).

Source: National Survey of Families and Households, Wave I.

Notice that the intercept in this model is −293.51, a value that is indicated to differ significantly from zero. This nonsensical negative value on distance reflects the mechanical interpretation of the intercept as the predicted value when all variables in the model equal zero. Although zero is a possible value on many variables, it is not possible in this sample of adults for *g2age* and *g1age*.[13] Thus, the estimated intercept is not interpretable and the hypothesis test that its value equals zero is not meaningful. It is useful to list the estimate in the table, however, so that more meaningful predictions can be made from the model, as we will illustrate below.

The table also shows that the significant associations seen in Chapter 9 for the respondent's earnings and number of sisters and mother's age and years of schooling remain significant once we also control for the respondent's race-ethnicity and gender.

We will use predictions from the model to illustrate the association of distance to one of these— mother's years of schooling—along with the differences of conditional means by gender. There are various strategies for making such predictions in multiple regression models with many predictors. We will discuss these various techniques in Chapter 12, as we use graphs more intensively to illustrate nonlinear effects. For now, we will use an approach in which we hold all variables constant at their sample means except one or two variables which we will vary systematically. For example, we could make predictors for men and women by substituting in values of 0 and 1 on the female variable and we could make predictions for different levels of the mother's years of schooling, for example, by substituting in values of 10 and 14 on *g1yrschl* and we could use the sample means for the remaining variables (obtained from the Stata summarize and SAS proc means commands introduced in Chapter 4).

For example, the full prediction equation is:

$$g1miles = -293.51 + 185.14 * amind + 61.85 * mexamer + 35.07 * white$$
$$-33.79 * female + 6.68 * g2earn10000 - 0.04 * g2age + 5.20 * g2numbro$$
$$+ 18.56 * g2numsis + 21.12 * g1yrschl + 4.61 * g1age$$

Substituting in the mean values for the interval variables other than *g1yrschl* (see Display B.10.13), and indicating the most common race-ethnicity in the data (white) results in:

$$g1miles = -293.51 + 185.14 * 0 + 61.85 * 0 + 35.07 * 1 - 33.79 * female$$
$$+ 6.68 * 3.075228 - 0.04 * 34.35271 + 5.20 * 1.432883 + 18.56 * 1.381781$$
$$+ 21.12 * g1yrschl + 4.61 * 60.13498$$

Now, all of the values are fixed, except for *female* and *g1yrschl*. We can work through the algebra to rewrite the equation as:

$$g1miles = 71.047519 - 33.79 * female + 21.12 * g1yrschl$$

Since *female* can only take on two values, we can further write this as two conditional regression equations:

female = 0 $glmiles = 71.047519 - 33.79 * 0 + 21.12 * glyrschl$
                                   $= 71.05 + 21.12 * glyrschl$

female = 1 $glmiles = 71.047519 - 33.79 * 1 + 21.12 * glyrschl$
                                   $= 37.26 + 21.12 * glyrschl$

These results are two regression lines, with the same slope (the coefficient estimate for *glyrschl*) but different intercepts. We need at least two points to plot each of these lines. One point is given by the intercept, but we will use two more typical values for the mother's years of schooling in the data set: 10 and 14.

female = 0		$glmiles = 71.05 + 21.12 * glyrschl$
	$glyrschl = 10$	$glmiles = 71.05 + 21.12 * 10 = 282.25$
	$glyrschl = 14$	$glmiles = 71.05 + 21.12 * 14 = 366.73$
female = 1		$glmiles = 37.26 + 21.12 * glyrschl$
	$glyrschl = 10$	$glmiles = 37.26 + 21.12 * 10 = 248.46$
	$glyrschl = 14$	$glmiles = 37.26 + 21.12 * 14 = 332.94$

We asked Stata to make additional predictions for us, for the levels of schooling from 8 to 16, and show the plot of the results in Figure 10.1.

This figure reinforces the fact that we are using an additive model. We have not allowed the effect of gender to differ by mother's years of schooling (nor allowed the effect of mother's years of schooling to differ by gender). The slope of each regression line is 21.12, the coefficient estimate

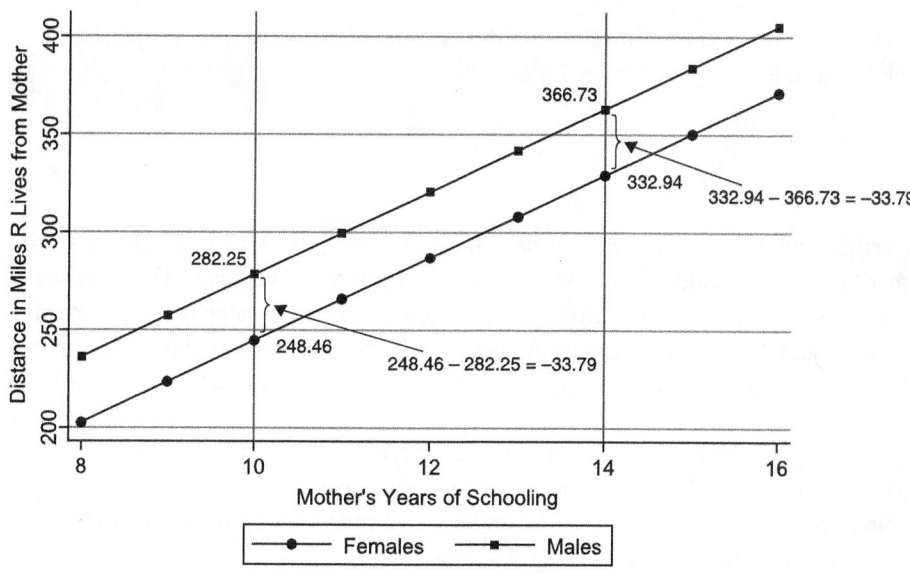

■ **Figure 10.1**

Source: National Survey of Families and Households, Wave 1

for *glyrschl*. And, the distance between the regression lines is −33.79, the coefficient estimate for *female*. We will examine how to allow for interactions in Chapter 11, and we will see that figures are often particularly useful in displaying results when interactions are significant.

We can use techniques similar to those used in Chapters 8 and 9 to evaluate the substantive magnitude of the marginally significant difference in average distances by gender. Because the predictor is a dummy indicator, a one-unit increase signifies a change from the category coded "0" to the category coded "1" (males to females using the *female* variable from the model in Display B.10.12). Rescaling the dummy variable for interpretation thus does not make sense (including dividing by the standard deviation to produce a completely standardized coefficient). But, it is possible to rescale the outcome variable for interpretation purposes. For example, we might divide the coefficient estimate of *female* by the standard deviation of *glmiles* to evaluate the effect size using a semistandardized coefficient estimate. This is directly analogous to Equation 8.9 where the numerator is the difference in group means on the outcome and the denominator is the outcome standard deviation.

Based on `Proc Means` in SAS and `summarize` in Stata we find that for the subsample of 5,401 in our current model, the standard deviation of *glmiles* was 637.5 (nearly the same as the value for the subsample used in Chapters 8 and 9). So, $\hat{\beta}_4/s_y = -33.79/637.5 = -0.053$. Thus, the difference in average miles from the mother by gender is small using Cohen's criteria. And, in the outcome's natural units, an average difference of about 33 miles for men versus women may seem substantively modest as well, at least for private transportation (although perhaps larger than the semistandardized result).

10.4: PUTTING IT ALL TOGETHER

We use two literature excerpts to reinforce the concepts learned in this chapter, and connect them back to those learned in Chapter 9.

10.4.1: Literature Excerpt 10.2

A 2005 article published in *Sociology of Education* by Kelly Raley, Michelle Frisco, and Elizabeth Wildsmith provides a nice example of testing substantively based hypotheses about a multicategory predictor variable, including the choice of reference category and presentation of tests among included variables. Examining their results helps us to verify our understanding of the interpretation of dummy variable models in a substantive context.

The authors used the NSFH to examine how children's living arrangements influence their educational outcomes. They took advantage of the rich information that parents reported about family transitions since the child's birth, gathered retrospectively in the NSFH, to classify children into five categories of *Family Experiences*:

■ those who were always living with two biological or adoptive parents (*two parent*);
■ those who were always living with one parent (*always single*);

■ those who at some point lived with a step-parent who was married to their biological parent (*married stepfamily*);

■ those who at some point lived with a cohabiting partner of their biological parent (*cohabiting stepfamily*);

■ those whose parents divorced but never repartnered or remarried (*divorced*).

As they point out, separating out cohabiting stepfamilies is important, given the rapid rise in this family form, but has been relatively neglected in the literature.

The authors anticipate that two mechanisms predict how family type, including cohabiting, will relate to educational success: family resources and family instability. Based on prior literature, they expect that children in cohabiting stepfamilies will have more resources (parental time and money) than children in single-parent families, but less than those in two-parent families. In contrast, they expect that children in cohabiting families will experience more family instability than single-parent and other families (more transitions, include dissolution of the partnership, and more conflict). If the latter mechanism (family instability) outweighs the former mechanism (family resources), then they expect that children in cohabiting families will have poorer educational outcomes than children in single-parent families.

Literature Excerpt 10.2 shows the results of the authors' OLS regression models using these prior family experiences to predict the mothers' reports of the child's current grades (*Grades*) and mothers' expectations for how much schooling the child would complete (*Mother's Educational Expectations*).

Before examining the results, we will first compare the basic layout and contents of this table to the example we examined in Literature Excerpt 9.1. Raley, Frisco, and Wildsmith use the notation B (rather than b) for unstandardized coefficient estimates, and do not present standardized coefficients. They also provide the level of the p-values (rather than using asterisks to designate significance), and do not provide the standard error or t-value.[14] The sample sizes are also listed for each model within the table (rather than in the title). The note mentions the analyses are weighted to address the data's complex sampling design in the way we discussed in Chapter 8. The contents of the table in Literature Excerpt 10.2 also shows the R-squared, but not the overall F-test.

For some details needed in substantive interpretation, we looked within the text of the article. There we saw that the child's *Grades* is reported by mothers on a 9-point scale, from 1 = mostly *F*s to 9 = mostly As. The variable averages between 7 and 7.3 across the five family experiences' categories. *Mother's Educational Expectations* for the child ranges from 1 to 7, with 1 indicating not finishing high school and 7 indicating completing a master's or doctorate degree. This variable has an average of 4 to 4.9 across the five family experiences' categories (pp. 149–50, 152).[15]

As just described, the authors have five categories of family experience. They explicitly defined these categories to be "mutually exhaustive and mutually exclusive" (p. 150). Thus, there are c = 5 categories on their original family experiences variable and they can include $c = 5 - 1 = 4$

▪ **Literature Excerpt 10.2**

Table 3.   OLS Estimates for a Model Predicting Parent's Educational Expectations and Grades at the First Interview

| | Mother's Educational Expectations | | | | Grades | | | |
| | Model 0 | | Model 1 | | Model 0 | | Model 1 | |
Variables	B	p-value	B	p-value	B	p-value	B	p-value
Family Experiences (two parent)								
Always single	−.85	.00	−.17	.53	−.55	.02	−.33	.19
Divorced	−.31	.07	.02	.90[a]	−.37	.02[b]	−.23	.13[a]
Married stepfamily	−.47	.02	−.32	.09	−.22	.21	−.24	.17[a]
Cohabiting stepfamily	−.64	<.01	−.40	.01	−.72	<.01	−.68	<.01
Race-Ethnicity (non-Hispanic white)								
Black			.37	.02			.29	.05
Hispanic			.31	.11			.39	.03
Other race			.34	.37			.68	.05
Female			.19	.05			.50	<.01
Grade level			−.01	.60			−.06	.01
Not in school			−1.77	<.01				
Mother's Education (less than high school)								
High school			.77	<.01			.33	.01
Some college			1.47	<.01			.62	<.01
College graduate			2.10	<.01			1.18	<.01
Missing			1.48	.02			.10	.86
Income (lowest quintile)								
20–39%			.27	.14			.17	.30
40–59%			.35	.07			.36	.05
60–79%			.66	<.01			.37	.04
80%+			1.18	<.01			.55	.00
Missing			.42	<.01			.03	.85
Unweighted Sample Size	1,161		1,161		1,100		1,100	
R^2		.02		.22		.03		.13

Note: Analyses are weighted.
[a] Significantly different from cohabiting stepfamilies, $p < .05$.
[b] Significantly different from cohabiting stepfamilies, $p < .10$.

Source: Raley, R. Kelly, Michelle L. Frisco, and Elizabeth Wildsmith. 2005. "Maternal Cohabitation and Educational Success." *Sociology of Education*, 78: 155.

dummy variables to indicate these categories. They tell us how they chose their reference category:

> Following common practice, we present models with two-parent families as the reference group. However, because our hypotheses are predictions about how children who experience

maternal cohabitation compare to others, we note when cohabiting stepfamilies are significantly different from the other groups (p. 153).

In their Table 3 (see again Literature Excerpt 10.2), the reference category is indicated by the word "*two parent*" next to *Family Experiences*. Looking at the other variables listed in their table, we can see that they similarly indicate the reference category for *Race-Ethnicity* (*non-Hispanic white*), *Mother's Education* (*less than high school*), and *Income* (*lowest quintile*). The indentation of their row headings helps us to distinguish the levels of these multicategory variables from other variables. They also include single dummy variables to indicate gender (*female*) and school enrollment status (*not in school*). As is often done in articles, they do not explicitly note the reference category for these single dummy variables, but by aligning them on the left, we can easily recognize that these represent original variables that have two categories.

Because the authors are particularly interested in contrasts with children living in cohabiting families, they use a superscript letter to indicate significant differences between the coefficients for cohabiting stepfamilies and the coefficients for the other included categories (*Always single, Divorced*, and *Married stepfamily*). As the notes to the authors' table describe, the superscript *a* indicates *p*-values less than .05 for these contrasts. The superscript *b* indicates *p*-values less than .10 for these contrasts.[16]

For each of their outcome variables, the authors present two models. Model 0 includes only the set of four *Family Experiences* dummies. Model 1 adds variables that they treat as controls (race-ethnicity, gender, grade level, school enrollment status, maternal education, and income). Because our interest in this chapter is in understanding the interpretation of the dummy variables, we will examine just one of the models (Model 1) in order to simplify the discussion. The estimates for the set of dummy coefficients are circled in green for these models in Literature Excerpt 10.2. We will discuss further in Chapter 13 how we could compare the results of the two models to see how the coefficient estimates for the dummy variables change when the control variables are added.

For *Mother's Educational Expectations* in Model 1, the *p*-values indicate that only one of the contrasts with the reference category (two-parent families) is significant: mothers who had cohabited with a partner expected their child to complete less education (.40 of a point less), on average, controlling for race-ethnicity, gender, grade level, school enrollment status, maternal education, and income. We conclude that this difference is significant because the *p*-value for this dummy variable (0.01) is less than an alpha of 0.05.

The superscript *a* for the *Divorced* variable indicates that mothers also reported lower educational expectations for children when they had cohabited with a partner than when they had divorced but not repartnered, on average with controls. The coefficient estimate for the contrast indicated by the superscript *a* is not explicitly shown in the table, but we can figure it out based on the values that are shown. The coefficient estimate for *Divorced* of 0.02 is the difference in means between the *Divorced* category and the reference category, *Two-Parent* families; that is, $\hat{Y}_{\text{Divorced}} - \hat{Y}_{\text{TwoParent}} = 0.02$. Similarly the *B* coefficient estimate for *Cohabiting Stepfamily* of -0.40 is the difference in means between the *Cohabiting Stepfamily* category and the reference category, *Two Parent* families; that is, $\hat{Y}_{\text{CohabitingStep}} - \hat{Y}_{\text{TwoParent}} = -0.40$. Thus, the difference between Cohabiting Stepfamilies and Divorced families is:

$$(\hat{Y}_{\text{CohabitingStep}} - \hat{Y}_{\text{TwoParent}}) - (\hat{Y}_{\text{Divorced}} - \hat{Y}_{\text{TwoParent}}) = -0.40 - (0.02) = -0.42$$

This difference between cohabiting and divorced families of -0.42 is slightly larger than the difference between cohabiting and two-parent families of -0.40.

Turning to the results for *Grades* in Model 1, we again see that only one of contrasts with the reference category (two-parent families) is significant: mothers reported lower grades for children when they had cohabited (the magnitude of the coefficient estimate is nearly 0.70 of a point on the scale). In addition, the superscript a's indicate that children in cohabiting families have significantly lower mother-reported grades than children in divorced families and married stepfamilies, on average with controls (differences of $[-0.68] - [-0.24] = -0.44$ and $[-0.68] - [-0.23] = -0.45$).

As the authors cover in detail in their discussion, there are many cautions to interpreting these results causally, even with their set of controls. Nonetheless, their results have important implications and appropriately using dummy variable models helped them to reveal these findings. Many studies have not separated cohabiting families from other families (sometimes because information was not collected to identify such families). The authors took advantage of the NSFH design (oversampling cohabiting families) in order to do so. The results indicate that this distinction is important, because children in cohabiting families often have lower education-related outcomes than children in other family types.[17] As the authors conclude: "Research that does not distinguish among different forms of unmarried-mother families is likely to assign the negative effects of cohabitation to experience in a single-parent family" (p. 158). The authors also conclude that the results "suggest that family instability has negative effects on educational outcomes over and above the negative effects that are due to the lower resources available to children in cohabiting stepfamilies" (p. 158), although they could not examine these mechanisms directly. (We will discuss how to do so in Chapter 13.) These results point to directions for future research (quantitative, qualitative, and mixed methods), including the importance of using designs that allow for separating out cohabiting families and for exploring the mechanisms through which children's educational outcomes may be limited by the composition of parents in their family.

10.4.2: Literature Excerpt 10.3

Our second literature excerpt, published in the journal *Public Health Reports*, provides an example of presenting confidence intervals for regression coefficients, a practice that is standard in public health but less common in social science journals. The authors, Leo Morales, Peter Guitierrez, and Jose Escarce were interested in extending the established finding that Hispanic children have higher blood lead levels than non-Hispanic children by exploring variation in blood lead levels among Hispanic children.

Literature Excerpt 10.3 shows Table 3 from the article which presents point estimates and confidence intervals from two multiple regression models predicting children's blood lead

▨ Literature Excerpt 10.3

Table 3. Continuous measure of lead among Mexican-American youth 1 to 17 years of age

| | \multicolumn{4}{c}{Blood lead levels µg/dl (β [95% CI])} |
	Model 1		Model 2	
Sex				
Male	0.63	[0.41, 0.85][a]	0.58	[0.37, 0.80][a]
Female		—		—
Age				
1 to 4	1.82	[1.43, 2.20][a]	1.76	[1.38, 2.13][a]
5 to 11	0.78	[0.53, 1.03][a]	0.81	[0.52, 1.09][a]
12 to 17		—		—
Generational status				
First	0.84	[0.30, 1.38][a]	0.66	[0.99, 1.22][b]
Second	0.08	[−0.31, 0.47]	0.00	[−0.42, 0.42]
Third or higher		—		—
Home language				
Spanish	0.79	[0.28, 1.30][a]	0.83	[0.28, 1.37][a]
Spanish and English	0.46	[−0.17, 1.10]	0.47	[−0.16, 1.09]
English		—		
Family income (poverty-income ratio)				
<50%	1.18	[0.60, 1.77][a]	1.19	[0.58, 1.81][a]
50% to 100%	0.96	[0.39, 1.52][a]	0.85	[0.29, 1.41][a]
100% to 200%	0.50	[0.13, 0.87][b]	0.34	[0.02, 0.67][b]
200% or more		—		—
Educational attainment of household head (years)				
6 or less	0.62	[0.14, 1.09][b]	0.57	[0.47, 1.10][b]
7 to 12	0.39	[0.04, 0.74][b]	0.28	[−0.10, 0.66]
13 or more		—		—
Age of housing				
Built before 1946			0.77	[0.17, 1.36][b]
Built 1946 to 1973			0.51	[0.08, 0.95][b]
Built 1974 or later				—
Drinking water				
Tap			0.48	[0.13, 0.82][a]
Well			0.50	[−0.69, 1.68]
Bottled				—

Note: Regressions also include indicators for region.
[a] $p < 0.01$
[b] $p < 0.05$
CI – confidence interval

Source: Morales, Leo S., Peter Guitierrez, and Jose J. Escarce. 2005. "Demographic and Socioeconomic Factors Associated with Blood Lead Levels among American Children and Adolescents in the United States." *Public Health Reports*, 120(4): 448–454.

levels. Let's first examine the similarities and differences between this table's layout and contents and those of Literature Excerpt 10.2 and Literature Excerpt 9.1. Most salient is that the authors present the point estimate and confidence interval, but not the standard error nor t-ratio, within the table. The notes tell us that all significance levels are indicated with superscript letters (a for $p < .01$ and b for $p < .05$). Scanning the results, we can see that the only cases which do not have a superscript letter are confidence intervals that include zero, as expected (i.e., second-generational status; Spanish and English home language; educational attainment of 7 to 12 in Model 2; and well drinking water).

All of the predictor variables are coded with dummy indicators of two or more categories. The authors explicitly list each reference category in the table. For example, the first variable is the child's sex. *Male* is the included category and *Female* the reference category. In Model 2, the point estimate tells us that males have average blood levels that are 0.58 µg/dl higher than females, controlling for the other variables in the model. The confidence interval tells us that males have blood levels that are between 0.37 and 0.80 µg/dL higher than females, controlling for the other variables in the model.

An example of a predictor variable with more than two categories is *Age of housing* which indicates structures *Built before 1946* and structures *Built 1946 to 1973* versus those *Built 1974 or later*, the reference category. The first point estimate tells us that children who live in homes built before 1946 have blood levels that are 0.77 µg/dl higher, on average, than children living in homes built after 1973, controlling for the other variables in the model. The first confidence interval tells us that children who live in homes built before 1946 have blood levels that are between 0.17 and 1.36 µg/dl higher than children living in homes built after 1973, controlling for the other variables in the model. The second point estimate tells us that children who live in homes built between 1946 and 1973 have blood levels that are 0.51 µg/dl higher, on average, than children living in homes built after 1973, controlling for the other variables in the model. The second confidence interval tells us that children who live in homes built between 1946 and 1973 have blood levels that are between 0.08 and 0.95 µg/dl higher than children living in homes built after 1973, controlling for the other variables in the model.

The results for the age of housing are estimated with less precision than the effect of gender, something made clear by the confidence intervals. Thus, although the point estimate for *Built before 1946* is larger than the point estimate for gender, the range of the confidence intervals is wider.

How large are these results, substantively? Looking to the Method section of the article tells us that blood levels are measured in micrograms per deciliter. Although the mean and standard deviation are not indicated, the authors report the range is 0.07 to 71.8 and that 10 was the CDC threshold for intervention at the time of publication (p. 449). Thus, the difference between boys and girls is about one twentieth of the intervention threshold.[18] The confidence interval bounds range about one third less than and larger than this point estimate. For age of housing, whereas the point estimates are close to (or slightly larger than) the point estimate for gender, they range from much smaller (as small as one one-hundredth of the CDC threshold) to much larger (over one tenth of the CDC threshold).[19]

10.5: COMPLEX SAMPLING DESIGNS

The survey regression commands introduced in Section 8.5 can be used with dummy variable predictors. We demonstrate their application in this section, which also allows us to show how these regression commands can be used to adjust for complex sampling designs when conducting the two-sample *t*-tests and analysis of variance tests that we introduced in Chapter 7.

10.5.1: Regression With a Single Dummy Predictor (Two-Sample *t*-test)

In Display B.10.14 we re-estimated the regression models shown in Display B.10.4 but now adjusted for the NSFH complex sampling design. As we showed in Display B.10.5, the OLS regression model with a single dummy predictor allows us to conduct the same test as a two-sample *t*-test assuming equal variances. Thus, the results in Display B.10.14 allow us to conduct this two-sample *t*-test with adjustments for the complex sampling design.

Comparing the new and original results, we see that the difference between men and women in terms of miles lived from their mothers was overstated before we adjusted for the complex sampling design. That is, whereas in Display B.10.4 we estimate the difference between men and women to be nearly 60 miles in Display B.10.14 it is just 44 miles. The standard error was also slightly overstated before adjusting for the complex sampling design (17.71 in the original results and 17.23 in the new results). Together, the new coefficient and standard error still allow us to reject the null hypothesis that the means for men and women are the same, although the *t*-value is smaller (−2.57 versus −3.35) and the *p*-value is larger (0.015 versus 0.001).

10.5.2: Regression With Multiple Dummy Predictors (Analysis of Variance)

We can also re-estimate the results from Display B.10.6 but adjusting for the NSFH complex sampling design features, to demonstrate the application of the survey regression commands with multiple dummy predictors and relate the results back to the test of analysis of variance introduced in Chapter 7. The results are shown in Display B.10.15. Recall that in this regression, African American adults are the reference group. Comparing the new and old results, we see that two contrasts are larger (American Indians versus African Americans and Mexican Americans versus African Americans) and one is smaller (whites versus African Americans) after we adjust for the complex survey design. All of the standard errors are larger in the new results, however, and in Display B.10.15 none of the significance tests are statistically significant (all of the *p*-values for the contrasts between the included groups and the reference category are larger than .05).

The results in Display B.10.15 also include an overall *F*-test which tests the same hypothesis as we introduced with analysis of variance in Chapter 7. The adjustment for complex sampling design is implemented somewhat differently in SAS and Stata, so the values are slightly different (1.66 in SAS and 1.56 in Stata). But, in both cases, the *p*-values associated with these *F*-statistics are larger than .05 (.18 and .22 respectively in SAS and Stata). Thus, we fail to reject the null hypothesis that the means are the same across all four racial-ethnic groups.

10.6: SUMMARY

Dummy variables allow us to use nominal and ordinal variables as predictors in regression models. Each dummy variable indicates one category of the original variable. If the original variable has c categories, then we can include $c - 1$ of these dummies in the regression model. The coefficient for each dummy variable captures the difference in means on the outcome variable between the indicated category and this reference category, adjusting for any other variables in the model.

When an original variable has more than two categories, we may be interested in testing hypotheses about the differences in means between pairs of the included categories. We can use one of three approaches to do so:

(a) re-estimating the regression model with a different reference category;
(b) using a partial F-test;
(c) testing the significance of a linear combination of coefficients.

These approaches provide equivalent results for two-sided hypothesis tests. Understanding each of them helps us to learn concepts and understand the literature, but we will use only one in practice. The second approach is easy to implement in SAS and Stata, although it does not calculate the difference in means between the included categories, nor the standard error of these differences. The first and third approaches calculate these values, in addition to the test statistics and p-values, and allow for directional (one-sided) tests. The first approach can be cumbersome, but is not unwieldy for small samples and relatively simple models. But, we recommend using the third approach (if you have access to Stata) because it produces the simplest and most complete results while reinforcing that all information is contained in a single estimation of the model.

KEY TERMS

Dummy Term (also Indicator Term)

Dummy Variable (also Indicator Variable)

Included Category

Linear Combination

Reference Category (also Omitted Category, Excluded Category)

Standard Error of the Difference

Variance–Covariance Matrix of the Estimated Regression Coefficients

REVIEW QUESTIONS

10.1. Conceptually, how do you define a set of dummy variables based on an original nominal or ordinal variable?

10.2. Why is one dummy variable excluded when you estimate a regression model? How do you choose this reference category?

10.3. In the case of an original variable with two categories and an original variable with three categories, how would the intercept and dummy variable coefficient(s) change if you changed the reference category?

10.4. What are the three approaches to testing the differences in means among the included groups?

10.5. Explain how the interpretation of the dummy coefficients relates to the difference between the predictions (the Y-hats) in a model that contains only dummy variables.

REVIEW EXERCISES

10.1. Suppose you estimated the following regression equation:

EARÑINGS = 32,000 – 12,000 * FEMALE

where EARNINGS is a respondent's annual earnings and FEMALE is a dummy variable coded 1 for women and 0 for men.

(a) How can you interpret the intercept and dummy coefficient from this model?

(b) What would the new prediction equation be if you regressed earnings on a new dummy variable, *MALE*, coded 1 for men and 0 for women?

10.2. Suppose you have sample data in which average household income was $50,000 per year for non-Hispanic white adults, $34,000 per year for non-Hispanic Black adults, and $40,000 for Hispanic adults. Write the prediction equations (including the intercept and slope) that you would see if you estimated separately each of the following regression models:

(a) Regress household income on two dummy variables indicating non-Hispanic white and non-Hispanic Black adults, with Hispanic adults as the reference category.

(b) Regress household income on two dummy variables indicating non-Hispanic white and Hispanic adults, with non-Hispanic Black adults as the reference category.

(c) Regress household income on two dummy variables indicating non-Hispanic Black and Hispanic adults, with non-Hispanic white adults as the reference category.

10.3. Suppose that you obtain a new software package and want to verify that you are correctly using its regression command. You know that in your data set the average number of days that low birthweight newborns stay in the hospital (NUMDAYS) is 15 for white babies and 30 for Latino babies. Write the prediction equations (including the intercept and slope) that you should obtain from the software package if you estimated separately each of the two following bivariate regression models:

(a) regress NUMDAYS on a dummy variable WHITE, coded "1" for white babies and "0" for Latino babies.

(b) regress NUMDAYS on a dummy variable LATINO, coded "1" for Latino babies and "0" for white babies.

10.4. Refer to Literature Excerpt 10.1. The authors present the items for the outcome variable, Sense of Control, in the Appendix (p. 117). Sense of Control is the average of eight items in which the respondent claims or denies control over good and bad outcomes. The average ranges from –2 to 2. The mean (standard deviation) of the outcome are 0.52 (0.51) for Asians and 0.68 (0.50) for non-Asians.

(a) Interpret the R-squared value.

(b) The article indicates that "marital status is coded (1) for respondents who are currently married or living together as married, and (0) for the divorced separated, widowed, or never married" (p. 107). Write the null and alternative hypotheses being tested for this Married variable.

(c) Interpret the unstandardized coefficient estimate for the Married variable.

(d) Calculate a semistandardized estimate for the Married variable, using the standard deviation of the outcome variable. (Because the authors only provided the standard deviation within the Asian and non-Asian subgroups, you can choose one of the group's standard deviations or calculate the semistandardized estimate once using each standard deviation.)

(e) Calculate and interpret a 95 percent confidence interval for the Married Variable using the unstandardized coefficients.

10.5. Refer to Model 2 of Literature Excerpt 10.3.

(a) Write the null and alternative hypotheses for each of the "Educational attainment of household head" dummy variables. Make a conclusion based on the presented results.

(b) Interpret the point estimates for each of the "Educational attainment of household head" dummy variables.

(c) Interpret the confidence intervals for each of the "Educational attainment of household head" dummy variables.

10.6. Below are SAS results from a hypothetical data set using the following variables:

WAGE	Outcome variable ranging from $2/hour to $15/hour
EDUC	Education level ranging from 8 to 13
UNION	Dummy variable (1 = in a union job; 0 = not in a union job)
JOBCLUB	Dummy variable (1 = got job from job club; 0 = didn't get job from job club)

Analysis of Variance					
Source	DF	Sum of Squares	Mean Square	F Value	Pr > F
Model	3	1881.98291	627.32764	145.71	<.0001
Error	996	4287.98767	4.30521		
Corrected Total	999	6169.97058			

Root MSE	2.07490	R-Square	0.3050	
Dependent Mean	8.20074	Adj R-Sq	0.3029	

Parameter Estimates					
Variable	DF	Parameter Estimate	Standard Error	t Value	Pr > |t|
Intercept	1	−0.97396	0.47246	−2.06	0.0395
educ	1	0.83490	0.04462	18.71	<.0001
jobclub	1	0.65761	0.15841	4.15	<.0001
union	1	1.19360	0.15553	7.67	<.0001

a) Write the prediction equation based on this model.

b) Interpret the point estimate for the *jobclub* variable.

c) Interpret the point estimate for the *union* variable.

d) Calculate and interpret the confidence interval for the *jobclub* variable.

e) Calculate and interpret the confidence interval for the *union* variable.

CHAPTER EXERCISE

In this exercise, you will write a SAS and a Stata batch program to estimate a multiple regression model, with dummy variables, building on the batch programs you wrote for Chapters 9 and 10.

CHAPTER
EXERCISE

10

Again, use the NHIS 1999 data set with an *if expression* to only keep cases that do not have missing values on the *age, exfreqwR,* and *bmiR* variables but now also exclude those missing on *SEX, HISPAN_I* and *RACERPI2* variables.

Note you will need to look back to your answers to the Chapter Exercise in Chapter 3 to identify the original missing variable codes for these variables, as well as the codes used to indicate each gender and race-ethnicity. Be careful to assure that cases with missing values on the original variables *SEX, HISPAN_I* and *RACERPI2* variables have been excluded and/or are '.' missing on your dummy variables. You can check this, and more generally check your dummy variables against the original variables, using the `tabulate` and `proc freq` commands.

Note: In all of the questions you can use *either* explicit coding of each level of the dummy variable using multiple lines of commands *or* the succinct dummy variable syntax.

In all cases, conduct two-sided hypothesis tests. Use a 5% alpha unless otherwise indicated.

10.1 Two-Category Original Variable

a) SAS/Stata Tasks:

   i) Create a dummy variable to indicate *women*. (Be careful to account for missing value codes).

   ii) Regress *bmiR* on this dummy variable (we will refer to this as *Regression #1* in the Write-Up Tasks).

   iii) Create another dummy variable to indicate *men*. (Be careful to account for missing value codes).

   iv) Regress *bmiR* on this dummy variable (we will refer to this as *Regression #2* in the Write-Up Tasks).

b) Write-Up Tasks.

   i) Interpret the point estimates of the intercept and slope in Regression #1.

   ii) Interpret the point estimates of the intercept and slope in Regression #2.

   iii) Discuss how Regression #1 and Regression #2 are related to each other (e.g., show how you could have figured out the intercept and slope for Regression #2 based only on Regression #1).

10.2 Multi-Category Original Variable

a) SAS/Stata Tasks.

   i) Create six dummy variables to indicate persons of: 1) Hispanic ancestry and any race, 2) non-Hispanic ancestry and white only race, 3) non-Hispanic ancestry and African American only race, 4) non-Hispanic ancestry and American Indian or Alaskan Native only race ("AIAN"), 5) non-Hispanic ancestry and Asian only race, and 6) non-Hispanic ancestry and multiple races. *(Be careful to account for missing value codes)*.

ii) Regress *bmiR* on *all six* dummy variables (we will refer to this as *Regression #3* in the Write-Up Tasks).

iii) Regress *bmiR* on *five of the six* dummy variables, using persons of *non-Hispanic white race-ethnicity* as the reference category (we will refer to this as *Regression #4*).

   (1) Use the test command to test whether there are *any differences* in the mean body mass index among the six race-ethnicity categories (we will refer to this as *Test #1* in the Write-Up Tasks).

   (2) Use the test command to test whether the mean body mass index differs between *each pair* of the five categories included in the regression model (ten tests all together; we will refer to this as *Test #2* in the Write-Up Tasks).

iv) Regress *bmiR* on *five of the six* dummy variables, using persons of *Hispanic race-ethnicity* as the reference category (we will refer to this as *Regression #5* in the Write-Up Tasks).

   (1) Use the Stata lincom command to test whether the means differ between *each pair* of the five categories included in the regression model (ten tests all together; we will refer to this as *Test #3* in the Write-Up Tasks).

b) Write-Up Tasks.

   i) Describe the results in Regression #3. Are they what you expected? How should you pick the reference category in a model with dummy variables?

   ii) Write the null and alternative hypotheses and a conclusion based on the results of the Test #1 command. Is this test shown in the output of any of the regressions (Regression #3, Regression #4, Regression #5)? If it is, why? If not, why not?

   iii) Interpret the point estimates of the intercept and dummy variable coefficients in the default output for Regression #4.

   iv) Interpret the point estimates of the intercept and dummy variable coefficients in the default output for Regression #5.

   v) Indicate which of the tests in Test #2 and Test #3 correspond to which of the tests in the default output of Regression #4 and Regression #5. Be sure to note whether any of the tests in Test #2 and Test #3 are not shown in either set of default output.

10.3 Complex Sampling Design

a) SAS/Stata Tasks.

   i) Regress *bmiR* on the *female* dummy variable, accounting for the NHIS complex sampling design (we will refer to this as *Regression #6* in the Write-Up Tasks).

   ii) Regress *bmiR* on *five of the six* dummy variables, using persons of *non-Hispanic white race-ethnicity* as the reference category, accounting for the NHIS complex sampling design (we will refer to this as *Regression #7*).

b) Write-Up Tasks.

   i) Compare the results of Regression #6 to Regression #1.

   ii) Compare the results of Regression #7 to Regression #4.

COURSE EXERCISE

Using the data set you created in the course exercise to Chapter 4, create a set of dummy variables to indicate one of your categorical predictor variables.

Choose one of the categories as a reference, and regress your continuous outcome variable on the remaining dummy variables. Use the `test` command in SAS and Stata and the `lincom` command in Stata to test the contrasts among the included categories. Before estimating the code, think about whether you could make directional hypotheses, in advance, about any of the pairwise contrasts (i.e., do you have enough theoretical basis or prior empirical evidence to expect that the mean for one group is larger than the mean for another group?). In cases where you can specify a directional hypothesis, use a one-sided hypothesis test.

Write the prediction equation and calculate the predicted value for each category on the original variable by substituting "0"s and "1"s for the dummy variables.

In one sentence, interpret the point estimates of the intercept and each dummy variable coefficient.

Calculate and interpret a 95 percent confidence interval for each dummy variable.

Chapter 11

INTERACTIONS

CHAPTER 11: INTERACTIONS

The models we have considered thus far have all involved additive relationships. The coefficient for one variable is the same, regardless of the level of another variable. In this chapter, we will discuss **interactions** between variables: situations in which the relationship between a predictor variable and the outcome variable differs depending on the level of another predictor variable.

We will begin by looking at interactions between dummy variables, an approach that might address questions such as "Is the gender gap in wages the same for African Americans and whites?" "Are the health benefits that distinguish married from single adults the same for women and men?" "Does the gap in educational attainment between teenage and adult mothers differ depending on their living arrangements (i.e., alone, extended family, married, cohabiting)?"

We will then consider interactions between a dummy variable and an interval variable, an approach that might address questions such as "Are the returns to education (the link between educational attainment and earnings) greater for whites than other race/ethnicity groups?" "Is the association between job satisfaction and complexity of job tasks stronger for people with a college degree than those with a high school degree?" "Is the link between the level of crime in a community and the level of social disorganization in a community weaker in suburban or rural areas than in urban areas?"

We will also present the **Chow Test** to measure the degree to which an entire regression model differs between two or more groups, extending these approaches to the multiple regression context. For example, if we build a model of educational attainment that includes parents' educational attainment, educational aspirations of peers in high school, and a youth's score on a standard achievement test in high school as predictors, are all of the coefficients in the model the same for boys and girls, or do some differ by gender?

We will end by considering interactions between two interval variables. This approach might be used for hypotheses such as "Job stress is associated with harsher parenting, but this association weakens with each additional increment of social support received from family and friends" or "Living in a community where adults have higher average educational attainment relates to the educational aspirations of youth, but more strongly when a higher proportion of neighborhood adults are the same race/ethnicity as the youth."

Interactions require more steps for interpretation than do additive models, and graphs are often useful in presenting the results succinctly. For each type of interaction, we will begin by using algebra to understand the interpretation of conditional regression equations. We separately examine three types of interaction (dummy by dummy variable, dummy by interval variable, and interval by interval variable) to facilitate understanding, although we will see that there are many similarities in specification and interpretation across these types. We will discuss how to estimate the models in SAS and Stata and how to graph the prediction equations and present the results using Excel.[1] We will use our hours of chores example, but we will include men as well as women in the sample so that we can consider gender differences in the overall number of hours spent on chores and in the effects of marital status, hours of paid work, and number of children.[2]

We will see that each type of interaction uses a product term between variables to capture the interaction, and that we can build on what we have learned about the general linear F-test and linear combinations to calculate conditional effects when interpreting the models. We introduce the concept of centering variables to aid in interpretation of models involving one or more interval predictors. We will also look at two literature excerpts to help us to understand why and how interactions are used in research, and how graphing the results can facilitate interpretation (see also Jaccard and Turrisi 2003 for a nice, detailed treatment of interactions in multiple regression).

11.1: LITERATURE EXCERPT 11.1

Peter Marsden, Arne Kalleberg, and Cynthia Cook published a study in the journal *Work and Occupations* in 1993 that examined gender differences in organizational commitment. The authors hypothesized not only that there might be an overall average difference in organizational commitment between men and women, captured by a dummy variable, but also why such differences might exist. They further speculated that the constructs that explain organizational commitment might differ for men and women. As they note:

> The final analyses that we report here examine the possibility that there may be gender differences in the processes leading to organizational commitment. If family roles compete more strongly with work roles among women than among men, for example, then we should expect some interactions of such variables with gender in their effects on commitment (p. 382).

They also expect gender differences in effects because prior research has found "the way in which age, autonomy, and occupational status are associated with job involvement differs between men and women" (p. 382).

The authors used the 1991 General Social Survey to examine their hypotheses. This nationally representative survey was an improvement over prior studies of gender differences in organizational commitment which focused on a single or small number of organizations, making it difficult to know the generalizability of the results. The outcome of organizational commitment was captured with six questions such as "I am willing to work harder than I have to in order to help this organization succeed" and "I find that my values and the organization's are similar" rated from 1 = *strongly disagree* to 4 = *strongly agree*. The sum of the organizational commitment items averaged 2.87 with a standard deviation of 0.54.

The authors measure 15 aspects of jobs and families that might predict organizational commitment, as well as two controls (race-ethnicity and education). They estimate regression models that allow them to examine how each of these 17 variables predicts organizational commitment for men and for women, and whether the effects of these 17 variables differ between men and women. Literature Excerpt 11.1 shows the results from their Table 5. They use a general linear *F*-test and find "at most, weak evidence of differences between men and women" across the 17 variables (The *F*-statistic reported in the table notes of 1.218 with 17 and 699 degrees of freedom and $p > 0.10$; see value circled in green in the Literature Excerpt).

Although most of the 17 variables have statistically equivalent effects for men and women, the authors use asterisks in the middle column of the table to indicate that the coefficient estimates for these three variables do differ significantly for men and women (see black circles in the Literature Excerpt). In each of these three cases, the predictor is associated with the outcome only for men and not for women (see green circles in Literature Excerpt).

■ For *Nonmerit reward criteria*, the association is significantly negative for men (−.135) but insignificant for women (−.010). Thus, if men perceive that nonmerit criteria (race, gender, and "favored relationship with the boss") are used in decisions about raises and promotions, then they report less organizational commitment (p. 385). Among women, perceptions of nonmerit criteria are not associated with organizational commitment.

■ For the dummy indicator of current marital status, men report higher organizational commitment when they are married (.145) but marital status is not associated with organizational commitment for women (−.011).

■ For school-age children, aged 12 or less, in the household, the association is marginally negative for men (−0.050) but not significant for women (0.027). Thus, men tend to report less organizational commitment when there are more children in the household, but number of children is not associated with organizational commitment for women.

We will learn below how the authors estimated this model, and how they are able to interpret the results as they do, as well as additional strategies for presenting results from models that include interactions.

■ **Literature Excerpt 11.1**

Table 5. Gender-Specific Regressions for Organizational Commitment (All Employed Respondents)

Explanatory Variables	Regression Coefficients		
	Women		Men
Work position			
Position in authority hierarchy	.015		.075**
Autonomy	.159**		.135**
Perceived quality workplace relations	.191**		.142**
Promotion procedures (dummy)	.072		.035
Nonmerit reward criteria	−.010	***	−.135**
Workplace size (log)	.002		−.012
Self-employed (dummy)	.314**		.273**
Career experiences			
Years with employer	.018		.012
Advances with this employer	.042		.053
Hours worked last week (or typical)	.001		.000
Compensation			
Annual earnings (log)	.023		−.040
Number of fringe benefits	.011		.026*
Family affiliations			
Currently married (dummy)	−.011	***	.145**
Number of persons aged 12 or less in household	.027	***	−.050†
Frequency of job-home conflict	−.056*		−.009
Sociodemographic controls			
White (dummy)	.044		−.120†
Years education	−.009		.004
Constant	1.450**		1.704**
R^2	.355		.385
N	369		366

Note: The gender-specific equations presented here are derived from an equation that includes interaction terms between gender and all other variables; R^2 for that equation is .364. F statistic for test of the hypothesis that there are no gender differences between equations is 1.218 on 17 and 699 degrees of freedom, p >.10.

† $p < .10$; * $p < .05$; ** $p < .01$; *** t statistic for gender difference in coefficients exceeds 2.0.

Source: Marsden, Peter V., Arne L. Kalleberg, and Cynthia R. Cook. 1993. "Gender Differences in Organizational Commitment: Influences of Work Positions and Family Roles." *Work and Occupations*, 20: 368–90.

11.2: INTERACTIONS BETWEEN TWO DUMMY VARIABLES

In Chapter 10, we considered additive models that included two sets of dummy variables constructed based on the levels of two different categorical variables. We will begin examining interactions by considering interactions between such dummy variables.

11.2.1: Review of Additive Model

We start with the additive model, so we can easily relate its results to the interaction model. We will predict hours spent on chores by indicators of being female and being married. We will begin with a simple conceptualization, and then further complicate it below. For gender, we might initially consider various social processes, including socialization practices, through which women learn how to accomplish housekeeping tasks and take responsibility for keeping an orderly home, resulting in adult women reporting spending more time each week on household chores than adult men. For marital status, we might initially expect that people who are married versus single reside in households with more need for chores (for example, the laundry to be done, amount of food to prepare, amount of shopping to be done, etc., all increase with one more person in the household).

We will specify this model as follows:

$$Y_i = \beta_0 + \beta_1 D_{1i} + \beta_2 D_{2i} + \varepsilon_i$$

where D_1 is a dummy variable *married* coded 1 = married and 0 = unmarried and D_2 is a dummy variable *female* coded 1 = female and 0 = male and Y_i is *hrchores*, the hours per week spent on chores. As we learned in Chapter 10, the intercept in this model provides the average number of hours per week spent on chores for men who do not have a spouse (the reference category on each dummy). The coefficient estimate for the first dummy indicates how many more or less hours married persons spend on chores, controlling for gender. And, the coefficient estimate for the second dummy indicates how many more or less hours women spend on chores, controlling for having a spouse.

Recall that in this additive model the difference in means between married and single persons is the same regardless of gender and the difference in means between men and women is the same regardless of marital status. In this simple model, with two dummy predictors of two separate variables, there are four possible expected values (conditional means) from the model, shown in Table 11.1.

■ **Table 11.1: Conditional Means with Two Dummy Variables (Additive Model)**

Unmarried Men	$E(Y \mid D_1 = 0, D_2 = 0)$	$= \beta_0 + \beta_1 * 0 + \beta_2 * 0$	$= \beta_0$
Married Men	$E(Y \mid D_1 = 1, D_2 = 0)$	$= \beta_0 + \beta_1 * 1 + \beta_2 * 0$	$= \beta_0 + \beta_1$
Unmarried Women	$E(Y \mid D_1 = 0, D_2 = 1)$	$= \beta_0 + \beta_1 * 0 + \beta_2 * 1$	$= \beta_0 + \beta_2$
Married Women	$E(Y \mid D_1 = 1, D_2 = 1)$	$= \beta_0 + \beta_1 * 1 + \beta_2 * 1$	$= \beta_0 + \beta_1 + \beta_2$

Thus, the effect of being married for men is β_1 (difference between row 2 and row 1). And, the effect of being married is also β_1 for women (difference between row 4 and row 3). If we compare row 3 to row 1 and row 4 to row 2, we similarly see that the effect of being female is the same among single persons as it is among married persons.

We can also see the constant effect of one variable within levels of the other variable by writing the conditional regression equations where we hold gender constant (at either 0 = *male* or 1 = *female*) and allow marital status to vary (between 0 = unmarried and 1 = married).

■ **Table 11.2: Conditional Regression Equation for Effect of Being Married Within Gender (Additive Model)**

Men	$E(Y|D_1, D_2 = 0)$	$= \beta_0 + \beta_1 * D_{1i} + \beta_2 * 0$	$= \beta_0 + \beta_1 D_{1i}$
Women	$E(Y|D_1, D_2 = 1)$	$= \beta_0 + \beta_1 * D_{1i} + \beta_2 * 1$	$= (\beta_0 + \beta_2) + \beta_1 D_{1i}$

These results show that the effect of being married (D_1) is the same for men and for women (β_1 in both cases). And, the interpretations of the conditional intercepts match the conditional means in Table 11.1. In each conditional regression equation, the intercept is the mean for people coded "0" on D_{1i}, that is unmarried people. So, the intercept for men in Table 11.2 matches the conditional mean in row 1 of Table 11.1 (unmarried men). And, the intercept for women in Table 11.2 matches the conditional mean in row 3 of Table 11.1 (unmarried women).

We can similarly write the conditional regression equations where we hold marital status constant (at 0 = unmarried or 1 = married) and allow gender to vary (between 0 = *male* and 1 = *female*).

■ **Table 11.3: Conditional Regression Equation for Effect of being Female within Marital Status (Additive Model)**

Unmarried	$E(Y|D_1 = 0, D_2)$	$= \beta_0 + \beta_1 * 0 + \beta_2 * D_{2i}$	$= \beta_0 + \beta_2 D_{2i}$
Married	$E(Y|D_1 = 1, D_2)$	$= \beta_0 + \beta_1 * 1 + \beta_2 * D_{2i}$	$= (\beta_0 + \beta_1) + \beta_2 D_{2i}$

These results show that the effect of being female (D_2) is the same for unmarried and married persons (β_2 in both cases). And, the interpretations of the conditional intercepts match the conditional means in Table 11.1. In Table 11.3, the intercept is the mean for people coded "0" on D_{2i}, that is, men. So, the intercept for unmarried persons in Table 11.3 matches the conditional mean in row 1 of Table 11.1 (unmarried men). And, the intercept for married persons in Table 11.3 matches the conditional mean in row 2 of Table 11.1 (married men).

11.2.2: Introduction of Interaction Model

Restricting the effect of each dummy to be the same within levels of the other variable is frequently inconsistent with theory and prior research. In our example, we might hypothesize that there is an interaction between marriage and gender in predicting hours spent on chores. As we noted above, a household with a married couple has greater chore demands (e.g., more laundry, cooking, etc.) than would a household comprised by either partner in that couple alone. But, there are also two people to accomplish those chores, and the total time spent on chores across the two people may be less than each would spend in their own households owing to shared tasks. For example, one larger meal can be cooked and shared for less than the time it takes to cook two separate meals. Various conceptual models and prior empirical studies suggest that women and men will not evenly divide such chores in the shared household. Rather, women will do more than men (West and Zimmerman 1987; Grossbard-Shechtman 1993). This suggests that married men should spend less time on chores than unmarried men, but married women should spend more time on chores than unmarried women. And, we should also see that the gender difference in time spent on chores is larger for married than unmarried persons.[3]

In regression models, we test for the presence of such interactions by introducing a **product term** into the regression model. This product term is a variable created by multiplying together the two predictor variables of interest. This product term is added to the regression model along with the two predictor variables of interest.

$$Y_i = \beta_0 + \beta_1 D_{1i} + \beta_2 D_{2i} + \beta_3 D_{1i} D_{2i} + \varepsilon_i$$

We can write the conditional means as we did before, by substituting in the four possible combinations of zeros and ones across the two separate dummy variables. We substitute in the appropriate value (0 or 1) within the product term as well as the individual variables.

Table 11.4: Conditional Means with Two Dummy Variables (Interaction Model)

Unmarried Men	$E(Y\|D_1=0, D_2=0)$	$= \beta_0 + \beta_1 * 0 + \beta_2 * 0 + \beta_3 * 0 * 0$	$= \beta_0$
Married Men	$E(Y\|D_1=1, D_2=0)$	$= \beta_0 + \beta_1 * 1 + \beta_2 * 0 + \beta_3 * 1 * 0$	$= \beta_0 + \beta_1$
Unmarried Women	$E(Y\|D_1=0, D_2=1)$	$= \beta_0 + \beta_1 * 0 + \beta_2 * 1 + \beta_3 * 0 * 1$	$= \beta_0 + \beta_2$
Married Women	$E(Y\|D_1=1, D_2=1)$	$= \beta_0 + \beta_1 * 1 + \beta_2 * 1 + \beta_3 * 1 * 1$	$= \beta_0 + \beta_1 + \beta_2 + \beta_3$

Comparing rows within this table makes clear that the effect of being married is no longer required to be the same for men and women and the effect of being female is no longer required to be the same for persons who are and are not married. For example, the difference in average hours of chores between married and unmarried men is β_1 but the difference in average hours of chores between married and unmarried women is $\beta_1 + \beta_3$. Similarly, the difference in average hours of chores between unmarried men and unmarried women is β_2 whereas the difference in average hours of chores between married men and married women is $\beta_2 + \beta_3$.

When we write these results in terms of conditional regression equations, we similarly see that now both the intercept and the effect of one dummy differs, depending on the level of the other dummy. First, holding gender constant at its two levels, and allowing marital status to vary results in the following two conditional regression equations. Notice that we again substitute the appropriate value into the product term for the variable that is held constant.

■ **Table 11.5: Conditional Regression Equation for Effect of being Married within Gender (Interaction Model)**

Men	$E(Y|D_1, D_2 = 0)$	$= \beta_0 + \beta_1 * D_{1i} + \beta_2 * 0 + \beta_3 * D_{1i} * 0$	$= \beta_0 + \beta_1 * D_{1i}$
Women	$E(Y|D_1, D_2 = 1)$	$= \beta_0 + \beta_1 * D_{1i} + \beta_2 * 1 + \beta_3 * D_{1i} * 1$	$= (\beta_0 + \beta_2) + (\beta_1 + \beta_3) * D_{1i}$

These equations let us directly calculate the result we saw, based on comparing the conditional means in Table 11.4. The effect of being married for men is β_1. The effect of being married for women is $\beta_1 + \beta_3$. The coefficient on the product term, β_3, captures the difference in the effect of being married between men and women. If $\beta_3 = 0$ then the effect of being married would be the same for men and women.

As in the additive model, the intercepts differ in the two conditional regression equations. In the first equation, β_0 is the average hours of chores for men who are coded a zero on D_1 (are unmarried). In the second equation, $\beta_0 + \beta_2$ is the average hours of chores for women who are coded "0" on D_1 (are unmarried). These match the predicted means we calculated above for rows 1 and 3 of Table 11.4.

We can similarly write the conditional regression equations where we hold marital status constant (at 0 = unmarried or 1 = married) and allow gender to vary (between 0 = *male* and 1 = *female*).

■ **Table 11.6: Conditional Regression Equation for Effect of being Female within Marital Status (Interaction Model)**

Unmarried	$E(Y|D_1 = 0, D_2)$	$= \beta_0 + \beta_1 * 0 + \beta_2 * D_{2i} + \beta_3 * 0 * D_{2i}$	$= \beta_0 + \beta_2 * D_{2i}$
Married	$E(Y|D_1 = 1, D_2)$	$= \beta_0 + \beta_1 * 1 + \beta_2 * D_{2i} + \beta_3 * 1 * D_{2i}$	$= (\beta_0 + \beta_1) + (\beta_2 + \beta_3) * D_{2i}$

These equations also directly calculate the results we saw above by comparing the predicted values from Table 11.4. The effect of being female for unmarried adults is β_2. The effect of being female for married adults is $\beta_2 + \beta_3$. The coefficient on the product term, β_3, captures the difference in the effect of being female between unmarried and married adults. If $\beta_3 = 0$, then the effect of being female would be the same for married and unmarried adults.

In terms of the intercept, in the first equation, β_0 is the average hours of chores for unmarried adults who are coded "0" on D_2 (are male). In the second equation, $\beta_0 + \beta_1$ is the average hours of chores for married adults who are coded "0" on D_2 (are male). These match the predicted means we calculated above for rows 1 and 2 of Table 11.4.

11.2.3: Creating the Product Term in SAS and Stata

We can easily create the product term needed to estimate these models in SAS and Stata using the general syntax for creating a new variable and the multiplication operator. We suggest choosing a name for the product term that signals the variables in the interaction. We recommend still restricting to 12 characters, to improve readability of output, and perhaps using symbols (like the underscore; in Stata, capitalization might also be used). It may be necessary to abbreviate the original variable names to restrict the name of the product term to 12 characters. For example, we could use the name *fem_marr* for the product term between *female* and *married*.

In SAS, we would create the variable with the command `fem_marr=female*married`; in Stata, we would similarly type `generate fem_marr=female*married` (see Box 11.1). The new variable will contain the result of multiplying the values of the two original variables together. Any variable coded '.' `missing` on either of the variables will be coded missing on the product term. For example, we might have in the data file:

MCASEID	female	married	fem_marr	...
54638	0	1	0	...
33865	0	1	0	...
76453	1	0	0	...
99857	0	.	.	...
26374	0	0	0	...
11948	1	1	1	...
95443	1	1	1	...
66730	1	0	0	...
22647	.	1	.	...
88740	0	0	0	...
.	.	.	.	.
.	.	.	.	.
.	.	.	.	.

11.2.4: Further Understanding the Product Term

It can be helpful for students to think of the product term between two dummy variables as an indicator for something unique about having a particular characteristic on both variables. We

---

▨ **Box 11.1**

Remember that in SAS the new variable creation must happen within the Data Step. All variables needed for any regression models estimated anywhere in the batch program, including product terms, must be created in the Data Step. In contrast, in Stata, the new variable creation can occur anywhere in the batch program, including just before the model using that variable. For example, product terms could be created in the line immediately preceding the interaction model. We usually put our variable creation in Stata together at the beginning of the batch program, because we find that it helps to organize our batch program for proofing.

allow the mean for people coded "1" on *both* dummies to differ from the mean for people coded "1" on only *one* of the dummies. We can see that by multiplying the two original dummies, the results are exactly equivalent to what we would have created if we had set out to make a dummy to indicate cases coded "1" on both dummies.

	Married?	Female?	Married* Female	Married and Female?
	D_1	D_2	$D_1{*}D_2$	D_3
Not Married/Male	0	0	0	0
Married/Male	1	0	0	0
Not Married/Female	0	1	0	0
Married/Female	1	1	1	1

Now, to calculate the mean we expect for people who are married and female, we cannot simply sum the basic effects of being married and being female captured by D_1 and D_2. Instead, we need to add in something unique about having both of the characteristics—being both married and being female. This uniqueness is captured by D_3.

The following table replicates the results we saw above, but now using the dummy indicator of being married and female. Although equivalent to what we have already seen, this table may be helpful to students who find it useful to think in terms of the indicator of something unique about people with both of the characteristics (here married and female) as they become familiar with the product term used in interactions.

Table 11.7: Conditional Means in Model with Indicator of being Married and Female

Unmarried Men	$E(Y\|D_1 = 0, D_2 = 0, D_3 = 0)$	$= \beta_0 + \beta_1 * 0 + \beta_2 * 0 + \beta_3 * 0$	$= \beta_0$
Married Men	$E(Y\|D_1 = 1, D_2 = 0, D_3 = 0)$	$= \beta_0 + \beta_1 * 1 + \beta_2 * 0 + \beta_3 * 0$	$= \beta_0 + \beta_1$
Unmarried Women	$E(Y\|D_1 = 0, D_2 = 1, D_3 = 0)$	$= \beta_0 + \beta_1 * 0 + \beta_2 * 1 + \beta_3 * 0$	$= \beta_0 + \beta_2$
Married Women	$E(Y\|D_1 = 1, D_2 = 1, D_3 = 1)$	$= \beta_0 + \beta_1 * 1 + \beta_2 * 1 + \beta_3 * 1$	$= \beta_0 + \beta_1 + \beta_2 + \beta_3$

This coding allows for something different about having both characteristics indicated by the two dummies for the original variable, as opposed to having just one of the characteristics.[4]

11.2.5: Example 11.1

Display B.11.1 shows the commands for creating the product term and estimating the interaction model in SAS and Stata. The estimated regression equation is:

$$\hat{Y}_i = 22.31 - 2.60D_{1i} + 10.20D_{2i} + 6.64D_{1i}D_{2i} \qquad (11.1)$$

Or, written with our variable names:

$$\widehat{hrchores}_i = 22.31 - 2.60married_i + 10.20female_i + 6.64fem\_marr_i$$

<table>
<tr><td>

■ Box 11.2

Our conceptual models might allow us to specify the direction of the interaction. For example, in our case, we hypothesized that the effect of being female on doing more chores should be accentuated among married persons. This implies that the product term should be positive. In our case, the product term is in fact positive, consistent with our hypothesis, so we could conduct a one-sided hypothesis test by dividing the p-value in half. If the sign on the product term was inconsistent with our hypothesis, then we would subtract half the p-value from one.

</td><td>

The default hypothesis test for *fem_marr* tests whether a significant interaction is present. As we discussed above, if the coefficient on the product term is zero ($\beta_3 = 0$), then the effect of each variable is the same within levels of the other variable. If the coefficient on the product term is not zero ($\beta_3 \neq 0$), then the effect of each variable differs within levels of the other variable (see Box 11.2). In our case, the *t*-value of 5.29 is greater than the critical *t* of 1.96 for our large sample, and the *p*-value is smaller than 0.05, so we can reject the null hypothesis.

Let's use the prediction equation (Equation 11.1) to calculated predicted values (Table 11.8) and the conditional regression equations, and then we will revisit the interpretation of the values in the prediction equation.

Table 11.8 shows that married men are estimated to spend the least amount of time on chores, on average, at about 20 hours per week. Unmarried men spend slightly more time on chores, at about 22 hours per week. Unmarried women spend nearly ten more hours per week on chores, at about 33 hours per week. And, married women spend the most time on chores, at over 36 hours per week.

</td></tr>
</table>

■ Table 11.8: Predicted Values (Y-hats) from Estimated Interaction Model with Two Dummy Variables

Unmarried Men	$(\hat{Y}|D_1 = 0, D_2 = 0)$	$= 22.31 - 2.60 * 0 + 10.20 * 0 + 6.64 * 0 * 0$	22.31
Married Men	$(\hat{Y}|D_1 = 1, D_2 = 0)$	$= 22.31 - 2.60 * 1 + 10.20 * 0 + 6.64 * 1 * 0$	19.71
Unmarried Women	$(\hat{Y}|D_1 = 0, D_2 = 1)$	$= 22.31 - 2.60 * 0 + 10.20 * 1 + 6.64 * 0 * 1$	32.51
Married Women	$(\hat{Y}|D_1 = 1, D_2 = 1)$	$= 22.31 - 2.60 * 1 + 10.20 * 1 + 6.64 * 1 * 1$	36.55

The conditional regression equations allow us to readily see the differences in effects within levels of the other variable, and will allow us to assess the significance of these **conditional effects**. We can again use the prediction equation, Equation 11.1, to hold one variable constant while allowing the other to vary.

Notice that we can read the coefficient estimates for one of the conditional regression equations—the equation for the category coded "0" on the other variable—directly from the SAS and Stata output. The other requires us to sum two coefficient estimates.

For the conditional equation that we can read directly off the output (men in Table 11.9; unmarried in Table 11.10), we can immediately see the results of the test of whether that

■ Table 11.9: Estimated Conditional Regression Equation for Effect of being Married, within Gender

Men $(\hat{Y}|D_1, D_2 = 0)$ $= 22.31 - 2.60 * D_{1i} + 10.20 * 0 + 6.64 * D_{1i} * 0$ $= 22.31 - 2.60D_{1i}$

Women $(\hat{Y}|D_1, D_2 = 1)$ $= 22.31 - 2.60 * D_{1i} + 10.20 * 1 + 6.64 * D_{1i} * 1$ $= (22.31 + 10.20) + (-2.60 + 6.64)D_{1i}$

$= 32.51 + 4.04D_{1i}$

■ Table 11.10: Estimated Conditional Regression Equation for Effect of being Female, within Marital Status

Unmarried $(\hat{Y}|D_1 = 0, D_2)$ $= 22.31 - 2.60 * 0 + 10.20 * D_{2i} + 6.64 * 0 * D_{2i}$ $= 22.31 + 10.20D_{2i}$

Married $(\hat{Y}|D_1 = 1, D_2)$ $= 22.31 - 2.60 * 1 + 10.20 * D_{2i} + 6.64 * 1 * D_{2i}$ $= (22.31 - 2.60) + (10.20 + 6.64) * D_{2i}$

$= 19.71 + 16.84D_{2i}$

conditional effect differs from zero. For men, the t-value for *married* (D_{1i}) from Display B.11.1 is -2.88, which is larger in magnitude than 1.96, and the associated p-value is smaller than 0.05. Thus, for men, we can reject the null hypothesis that the effect of being married is zero. Likewise, for the unmarried the t-value for *female* (D_{2i}) from Display B.11.1 is 11.15, which is larger than 1.96, and the associated p-value is smaller than 0.05. Thus, for unmarried persons, we can reject the null hypothesis that the effect of being female is zero.

Estimating the Conditional Regression Equation for Included Category

What about the conditional effect of being married for women? And, the conditional effect of being female for married persons? We can use the same three approaches we introduced in Chapter 10 to calculate the significance of these conditional effects:

(a) re-estimating the regression model using different reference categories;
(b) using a general linear F-test;
(c) testing the significance of a linear combination of coefficients.

Changing the Reference Category

If we re-estimate the model reversing the reference category for the conditioning variable, we will be able to read the other conditional equations from the default results (conditional regression equation for women in Table 11.9; conditional regression equation for married in Table 11.10). Display B.11.2 shows the results for doing this.

In the top panel, we created a new dummy indicator *male* and a new product term based on this variable called *male_marr*. When we use these new variables in the regression, substituting *male* for *female* and *male_marr* for *fem_marr*, we can read the conditional effect of being married for women directly from the output. The coefficient estimate for *married* is now 4.03, matching our hand calculation for the effect of being married among women in Table 11.9. The associated t-value of 4.63 is greater than 1.96 and the p-value is smaller than 0.05, indicating that the effect of being married is significantly different from zero for women, as it was for men. But, for women, the coefficient estimate is positive in sign, whereas for men it was negative in sign.

In the bottom panel of Display B.11.2, we create a new dummy indicator *unmarried* and a new product term based on this variable called *fem_unmarr*. When we use these new variables in the regression, substituting *unmarried* for *married* and *fem_unmarr* for *fem_marr*, we can read the conditional effect of being female for married persons directly from the output. The coefficient estimate for *female* is now 16.84, matching our hand calculation for the effect of being female among married adults in Table 11.10. The associated *t*-value of 19.58 is greater than 1.96 and the *p*-value is smaller than 0.05, indicating that the effect of being female is also significantly different from zero for married adults, as it was for unmarried adults. Both conditional effects of being female are positive in sign, but the **magnitude of the effect** is larger for married adults than unmarried adults.

General Linear *F*-test

We can also use a general linear *F*-test to test the conditional effects. Although the results will not provide us with the point estimate of the conditional effect, they will tell us whether our hand-calculated conditional effects are significantly different from zero. To request these tests in SAS and Stata, we mimic the way the conditional effects are written in Tables 11.5 and 11.6.

Conditional Effect of...	In symbols	In SAS and Stata
Married for Women (from Table 11.5)	$\beta_1 + \beta_3$	test married+fem_marr=0
Female for Married Persons (from Table 11.6)	$\beta_2 + \beta_3$	test female+fem_marr=0

The SAS and Stata commands will test the null hypothesis that the sum of the coefficients for the listed variables (*married* and *fem_marr* in the top row; *female* and *fem_marr* in the bottom row) equal zero, against the alternative that they are not equal to zero.

The results are shown in Display B.11.3. Notice that because these test the same conditional effects as shown in Display B.11.2, when we reverse the reference categories, the *F*-values should match the square of the respective *t*-value in Display B.11.2.

- For the conditional effect of being married for women, we had $t = 4.63$ in Display B.11.2 and we have $F = 21.44$ in Display B.11.3. As expected, $t^2 = 4.63 * 4.63 = 21.44$ which matches the *F*-value.
- For the conditional effect of being female for married adults, we had $t = 19.58$ in Display B.11.2 and we have $F = 383.30$ in Display B.11.3. As expected, $t^2 = 19.58 * 19.58 = 383.38$ which matches the *F*-value, within rounding error.
- The *p*-values for the *F*-tests in Display B.11.3 also match the respective two-sided *p*-values for the *t*-tests shown in Display B.11.2 (all $p < 0.0001$).

Linear Combination of Coefficients

We can also use the linear combination of coefficients approach that we learned in Chapter 10 to calculate the conditional effects. In this case, our linear combination involves the sum rather than the difference between two coefficients, and the formula for estimating the standard error of the sum of two coefficients is:

$$\sqrt{\hat{\sigma}^2_{\hat{\beta}_1} + \hat{\sigma}^2_{\hat{\beta}_2} + 2\widehat{cov}\,\hat{\beta}_1\hat{\beta}_2}$$

Notice that for the sum of two coefficients, we add rather than subtract twice the covariance between the coefficients in the formula (see Box 10.3 in Chapter 10 for additional details). We obtain the covariances using the /covb option in SAS and the estat vce option in Stata, as we did in Chapter 10. The results are shown in Display B.11.4.

For the hypothesis that H_0: $\beta_1 + \beta_3 = 0$ we calculate the relevant t-value using the following formula and results from Display B.11.4:

$$t = \frac{(\hat{\beta}_1 + \hat{\beta}_3) - 0}{\sqrt{\hat{\sigma}^2_{\hat{\beta}_1} + \hat{\sigma}^2_{\hat{\beta}_3} + 2\widehat{cov}_{\hat{\beta}_1\hat{\beta}_3}}} = \frac{(-2.60 + 6.64) - 0}{\sqrt{0.81770038 + 1.5770922 + (2*-0.81770038)}}$$

$$= \frac{4.03}{.8714309} = 4.62$$

Notice that the standard error in the denominator, and the final t-value, match the results shown in the top panel of Display B.11.2 where we reversed the dummy variable to estimate the conditional effect of being married for women directly.

Similarly, for the hypothesis that H_0: $\beta_2 + \beta_3 = 0$ we calculate the relevant t-value using the following formula and results from Display B.11.4:

$$t = \frac{(\hat{\beta}_2 + \hat{\beta}_3) - 0}{\sqrt{\hat{\sigma}^2_{\hat{\beta}_2} + \hat{\sigma}^2_{\hat{\beta}_3} + 2\widehat{cov}_{\hat{\beta}_2\hat{\beta}_3}}} = \frac{(10.20 + 6.64) - 0}{\sqrt{0.83731317 + 1.5770922 + (2*-0.83731317)}}$$

$$= \frac{16.84}{.86010408} = 19.58$$

Notice that the standard error in the denominator, and the final t-value, match the results shown in the bottom panel of Display B.11.2 where we reversed the dummy variable to estimate the conditional effect of being female for married persons directly.

In Stata, we can also use the lincom command to ask Stata to calculate the point estimate and standard error for a linear combination of coefficients for us. Display B.11.5 shows the results of doing so, which match our hand calculations above and the results in Display B.11.2. As we noted in Chapter 10, this approach is the preferable among the three, because it provides the fullest information (point estimate, standard error, t-value, and p-value) for the conditional effects after a single estimation, although the direct command is available only in Stata. In the remainder of the chapter, when we use the linear combination approach, we will use the Stata command.

11.2.6: Summary of Interpretation

In a model with an interaction between two dummy variables:

$$Y_i = \beta_0 + \beta_1 D_{1i} + \beta_2 D_{2i} + \beta_3 D_{1i} D_{2i} + \varepsilon_i$$

we interpret the results as follows.

- Intercept (β_0): average of the outcome variable for cases coded "0" on both dummies.
- Coefficient of First Dummy (β_1): conditional effect of first dummy when the second dummy is zero.
- Coefficient of Second Dummy (β_2): conditional effect of second dummy when the first dummy is zero.
- Coefficient of Product Term (β_3): difference in conditional effects (amount larger or smaller than the conditional effect of one dummy is for cases coded "1" versus "0" on the other dummy).

As we see below, if we add additional control variables to the model, then our interpretation of the coefficients for the dummy variables and product term remain the same, although we add the phrase "controlling for the other variables in the model." When other variables are in the model, the intercept may no longer be meaningful, if zero is not a valid value on some of those variables. We can also use the same three techniques presented above to test the conditional effect of the variable coded one on the other dummy, when controls are in the model.

11.2.7: Presenting Results and Interpreting their Substantive Size

We will end this section by showing how to calculate predicted values based on the coefficient estimates and graph the results. In Appendix H.11.1, we show how to use Excel to do this. Excel is simple to use, widely accessible, and can be used with coefficient estimates produced from any software package, including SAS and Stata (or coefficient estimates from a published article). We will use this technique in Chapter 12 as well, when we interpret nonlinear models estimated in OLS. SAS and Stata both also have dedicated commands for predicting values and graphing them such as the graph command we used in Part 2.

Figure 11.1 shows the chart which we created in Excel (again, see Appendix H.11.1 for the detailed steps for creating such a chart). The values calculated by Excel and plotted in the chart match those that we calculated "by hand" in Table 11.8. But, graphing the values can help the reader to visualize the interaction results. Figure 11.1 makes clear that the gender gap is wider for married than unmarried adults. Likewise, men do fewer chores when they are married than unmarried. Women do more chores when they are married than unmarried. The graph also helps us to visualize the substantive significance of the contrasts which we found were all statistically significant.[5] For example, among married adults, women spend an average of over 16 more hours on chores per week than do men. If this additional time on chores were equally distributed throughout the week, it would amount to more than two more hours spent on chores

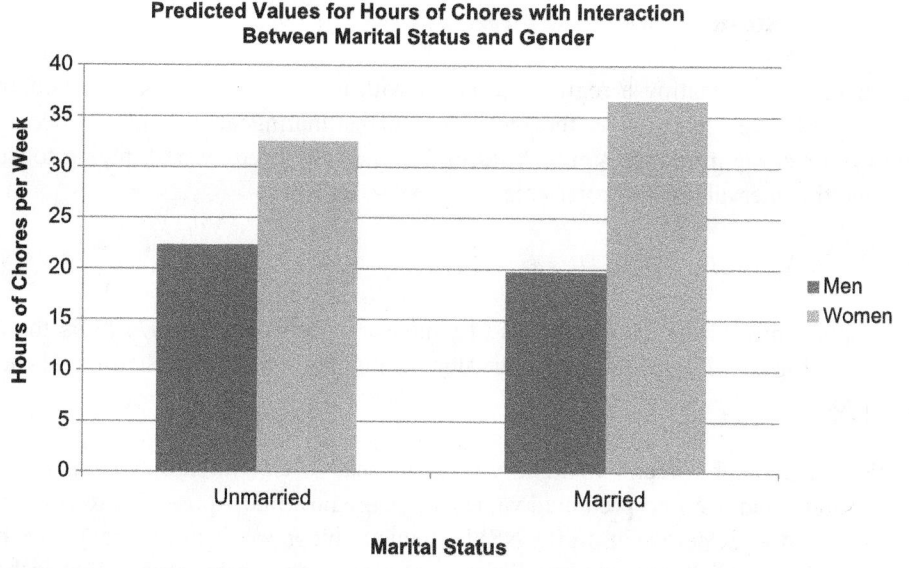

Predicted Values for Hours of Chores with Interaction Between Marital Status and Gender

■ **Figure 11.1** Example of Chart of Predicted Values, Created in Excel

per day for wives than husbands. This difference between wives and husbands is also over three quarters of the standard deviation of hours of chores (s_y = 25.16) in the sample of men and women combined. Thus, this effect size is between medium and large using Cohen's rules of thumb (16.84/25.16 = 0.67, between 0.50 and 0.80; see again Section 8.4.9).

11.3: INTERACTION BETWEEN A DUMMY AND AN INTERVAL VARIABLE

We will continue with our example of hours of chores per week as the outcome variable, but now we will focus on hours of paid work per week as a predictor and conceptualize ways in which we might think of gender moderating the relationship between hours of employment and hours of chores. One hypothesis might come from the "second shift" concept, expecting that women bear most of the burden of household chores, even if they are employed. We might hypothesize that, on average, men tend to spend a fairly limited and fixed amount of time on chores per week, and that they decide on this level of chores pretty independently from their hours of employment. Women, on the other hand, may take on as much of the burden of chores as they can, cutting back only when their paid work hours force them to do so. Under this hypothesis, the association between hours of employment and hours of chores should be negative for both genders, but stronger (have a steeper slope) for women than for men (see Box 11.3).

> ■ **Box 11.3**
>
> Note that the words *weaker* and *stronger* refer to the magnitude of the effect. In both cases the effect may be negative, but a weaker effect for women would mean that it was less negative for women than men and a stronger effect for women would mean that it was more negative for women than men.

11.3.1: Conditional Regression Equations

The mechanics of estimating a regression model with an interaction between a dummy and interval variable are the same as the mechanics of estimating an interaction between two dummy variables: we introduce a product term that is constructed by multiplying together the dummy and the interval predictor variable.

$$Y_i = \beta_0 + \beta_1 X_{1i} + \beta_2 D_{2i} + \beta_3 X_{1i} D_{2i} + \varepsilon_i \qquad (11.2)$$

where X_1 is an interval measure of hours of paid work per week, *hrwork*, D_2 is the dummy indicator of being *female*, and Y is our interval measure of hours spent on household chores per week, *hrchores*.

Unlike the interaction between two dummy variables that we examined in the previous section, where the model had just four predicted values, there are now many possible predictions across the hours of paid work per week. In the NSFH, the variable *hrwork* ranges from zero to 93 for men and from zero to 88 for women, the variable takes on nearly every value in between, although most values fall between 10 and 50 hours of work per week.[6]

Conditional Regression Equations for Interval Variable

We will begin by considering the conditional regression equations holding gender constant at its two levels and allowing *hrwork* to vary.

▨ **Table 11.11: Conditional Regression Equation for Hours of Paid Work within Gender (Interaction Model)**

Male	$E(Y \mid X_1, D_2 = 0)$	$= \beta_0 + \beta_1 * X_{1i} + \beta_2 * 0 + \beta_3 * X_{1i} * 0$	$= \beta_0 + \beta_1 * X_{1i}$
Female	$E(Y \mid X_1, D_2 = 1)$	$= \beta_0 + \beta_1 * X_{1i} + \beta_2 * 1 + \beta_3 * X_{1i} * 1$	$= (\beta_0 + \beta_2) + (\beta_1 + \beta_3) * X_{1i}$

This is very similar to what we saw above in Table 11.5 for the conditional effect of being married within gender. But now, with an interval predictor, β_3 captures any difference in the slope relating X (hours of paid work) to Y (hours of chores) for women versus men. And, β_2 captures any difference in the mean hours of chores where these lines cross the Y axis (when X_1 is zero).

It is also instructive to reinforce these interpretations by comparing the above result to the additive model that included a dummy variable and an interval variable. Recall from Chapter 10 that such a model results in two conditional regression equations that differed only in the intercept. In that case, the coefficient for the dummy variable measured the constant difference between the two parallel regression lines (see Section 10.3.4).

$$Y_i = \beta_0 + \beta_1 X_{1i} + \beta_2 D_{2i} + \varepsilon_i$$

■ **Table 11.12: Conditional Regression Equation for Hours of Paid Work within Gender (Additive Model)**

Male	$E(Y\|X_1, D_2 = 0)$	$= \beta_0 + \beta_1 * X_{1i} + \beta_2 * 0$	$= \beta_0 + \beta_1 * X_{1i}$
Female	$E(Y\|X_1, D_2 = 1)$	$= \beta_0 + \beta_1 * X_{1i} + \beta_2 * 1$	$= (\beta_0 + \beta_2) + \beta_1 * X_{1i}$

This model allows the intercepts to differ but constrains the association between X (hours of paid work) and Y (hours of chores) to be the same for men and women, resulting in parallel lines. Thus, adding the interaction term to this model allows us to examine not only whether being in one group versus the other (e.g., male versus female) shifts the regression line up or down but also whether the slope of the regression line is steeper or shallower for one group versus the other (e.g., males versus females).

If we also omitted the dummy variable for female, by restricting $\beta_2 = 0$, we would force men and women to have exactly the same regression line, $(Y\|X_1) = \beta_0 + \beta_1 X_{1i}$. It is helpful to keep this in mind because these are clearly nested models, and we will see below how we can use the general linear F-test to compare these models and statistically test whether allowing for different intercepts and different slopes improves the fit of the models.

Conditional Effects for Dummy Variable

As noted above, in the interaction model, if the lines are not parallel, then the difference between the groups captured by the dummy (in our case, men and women) is not constant. The difference will be larger at some levels of the interval variable than at other levels of the interval variable. The coefficient on the dummy variable captures the average difference between groups when the interval variable is zero (see again Table 11.11). Especially if zero is not a valid or meaningful value on the interval variable, we may want to examine the conditional effects of the dummy variable at other values of the interval variable.

■ **Table 11.13: Conditional Effect of Being Female within Hours of Paid Work Per Week**

Hours			
10	$E(Y\|X_1 = 10, D_2)$	$= \beta_0 + \beta_1 * 10 + \beta_2 * D_2 + \beta_3 * 10 * D_2$	$= (\beta_0 + 10\beta_1) + (\beta_2 + 10\beta_3)D_2$
20	$E(Y\|X_1 = 20, D_2)$	$= \beta_0 + \beta_1 * 20 + \beta_2 * D_2 + \beta_3 * 20 * D_2$	$= (\beta_0 + 20\beta_1) + (\beta_2 + 20\beta_3)D_2$
30	$E(Y\|X_1 = 30, D_2)$	$= \beta_0 + \beta_1 * 30 + \beta_2 * D_2 + \beta_3 * 30 * D_2$	$= (\beta_0 + 30\beta_1) + (\beta_2 + 30\beta_3)D_2$
40	$E(Y\|X_1 = 40, D_2)$	$= \beta_0 + \beta_1 * 40 + \beta_2 * D_2 + \beta_3 * 40 * D_2$	$= (\beta_0 + 40\beta_1) + (\beta_2 + 40\beta_3)D_2$
50	$E(Y\|X_1 = 50, D_2)$	$= \beta_0 + \beta_1 * 50 + \beta_2 * D_2 + \beta_3 * 50 * D_2$	$= (\beta_0 + 50\beta_1) + (\beta_2 + 50\beta_3)D_2$

So, in the first row, the effect of being female (D_2) is $\beta_2 + 10\beta_3$. This captures the difference in average hours of chores between women and men who are employed 10 hours per week.

Similarly, in the last row, the effect of being female (D_2) is $\beta_2 + 50\beta_3$. This captures the difference in average hours of chores between women and men who are employed for 50 hours per week.

11.3.2: Creating the Product Term in SAS and Stata

We can again create the product term easily in SAS and Stata using the general syntax for creating a new variable and the multiplication operator. Using a consistent convention for creating interactions within a project will help you to keep track of the interactions and read the output. The convention is up to you. We will again use the *fem_* at the beginning of the name of our product term, as we did for the interaction between gender and marital status. In SAS, we will create the variable with the command `fem_hrwork=female*hrwork;` In Stata, we will similarly type `generate fem_hrwork=female*hrwork`.

Similarly to the interaction between two dummy variables, the new variable will contain the result of multiplying the values of the two original variables together. Any variable coded '.' `missing` on either of the variables will be coded missing on the product term. For example, we might have in the data file:

MCASEID	female	hrwork	fem_hrwork	...
54638	0	25	0	...
33865	0	40	0	...
76453	1	0	0	...
99857	0	.	.	...
26374	0	0	0	...
11948	1	45	45	...
95443	1	30	30	...
66730	1	0	0	...
22647	.	50	.	...
88740	0	0	0	...
.	.	.	.	.
.	.	.	.	.
.	.	.	.	.

11.3.3: Calculating Conditional Regression Equations in SAS and Stata

In Section 11.2 we saw that the conditional effects for the category coded "0" on the dummy (e.g., men and unmarried adults in our example) could be read right off the regression output. And, there were three ways to obtain the significance of the other conditional effects:

(a) re-estimating the model with a different reference category;
(b) using the test commands to conduct general linear F-tests;
(c) calculating the standard error and t-value for a linear combination of coefficients.

We can use similar approaches for the conditional regression equations when we have an interaction between a dummy and interval variable. We will again present these approaches in some detail, to see the comparable results produced by these approaches in this new context.

In the remaining sections, we will use the third approach, with the Stata `lincom` command, because it succinctly gives us all the results we desire (point estimates, standard errors, *t*-values, *p*-values) after a single estimation.

Re-estimating the Regression Equation

For the conditional effect of the interval variable, we can re-estimate the model with the other category on the dummy variable as the reference. In our case, we could use the *male* dummy variable and a new product term `male_hrwork=male*hrwork`. This will allow us to read directly from the default output the conditional regression equation for women shown in Table 11.11.

For the conditional effects of being female within levels of hours of paid work, we can also re-estimate the model with a different level of hours of work indicated by the value of zero. In particular, we will *center* the conditioning variable so that zero represents the conditioning value.

Let's look at an explicit example to make this concrete. If we were interested in the condition of "Hours of Paid Work Per Week = 10," then we would center the hours of paid work variable by creating a new variable that subtracts the value of 10 from *hrwork* (i.e., `hrworkC10=hrwork–10`).

hrwork	hrworkC10 = hrwork – 10
0	–10
5	–5
10	0
15	5
20	10
25	15
30	20
35	25
40	30
45	35
50	40

Notice that a zero on the new variable, *hrworkC10*, represents a 10 on the original variable, *hrwork*. If we create a new product term with this centered variable and re-estimate the regression, then all the estimates will remain unchanged except the intercept and the coefficient estimate for the dummy variable in the interaction. The intercept will now be the average hours of chores for men who work 10 hours per week. And, the coefficient estimate for female will now represent the difference in average chores between women and men who work 10 hours per week.

To implement this approach, we need to follow three steps in SAS and Stata for each conditioning value:

1. Calculate the centered variable.
2. Create a product term using the new centered variable.
3. Estimate the regression model using the new centered variable and the new product term.

For example, for the level of 10 on hours of work, we would do the following.

	SAS	Stata
Variable Creation	```data interact; set "c:\hrchores\interact"; hrworkC10=hrwork–10; fem_hrwC10=female*hrworkC10; run;```	```generate hrworkC10=hrwork–10 generate fem_hrwC10=female*hrworkC10```
Regression Model	```proc reg; model hrchores=hrworkC10 female fem_hrwC10; run;```	```regress hrchores hrworkC10 /// female fem_hrwC10```

We purposefully showed the Data Step in SAS to emphasize that the new variable creation must happen within the Data Step (not interspersed with procedures, such as immediately before the relevant Proc Reg).

Using the Test Command

To use the **test** command to obtain the significance of the coefficients in the conditional regression equations, we mirror the ways in which we represented each coefficient in Tables 11.11 and 11.13 above.

For the effect of hours of work among women, the conditional effect shown in Table 11.11 was $\beta_1 + \beta_3$. The sum of the coefficient for the interval variable and the product term. The corresponding test command would be **test hrwork+fem_hrwork=0**. Based on this command, SAS and Stata would test the null hypothesis that the sum of the coefficients for these two variables was zero against the two-sided alternative that their sum differed from zero.

For the effect of being female within hours of paid work, we can use the following test statements, mirroring the conditional effects shown in Table 11.13.

Hours	Symbols	SAS/Stata Syntax
10	$\beta_2 + 10\beta_3$	test female+10*fem_hrwork=0
20	$\beta_2 + 20\beta_3$	test female+20*fem_hrwork=0
30	$\beta_2 + 30\beta_3$	test female+30*fem_hrwork=0
40	$\beta_2 + 40\beta_3$	test female+40*fem_hrwork=0
50	$\beta_2 + 50\beta_3$	test female+50*fem_hrwork=0

Note that the syntax for these test commands is exactly the same for SAS and Stata test. Each tests whether the sum of the coefficient for female and the indicated multiple of the coefficient for the product term equals zero against the alternative that the sum is not equal to zero.

Linear Combination of Coefficients

We can similarly mimic the conditional effects with the Stata lincom command. For the conditional effect of hours of work among women this would be lincom hrwork+fem_hrwork.

For the effect of being female within hours of paid work this would be:

Hours	Stata Syntax
10	lincom female+10*fem_hrwork
20	lincom female+20*fem_hrwork
30	lincom female+30*fem_hrwork
40	lincom female+40*fem_hrwork
50	lincom female+50*fem_hrwork

11.3.4: Example 11.2

We begin by estimating Equation 11.2 in SAS and Stata. Display B.11.6 shows the commands used to create the product term and estimate the regression, and the results. The estimated regression equation is:

$$\hat{Y}_i = 26.12 - 0.12X_{1i} + 16.99D_{2i} - 0.13X_{1i}D_{2i} \tag{11.3}$$

Or, written with our variable names:

$$\widehat{hrchores}_i = 26.12 - 0.12hrwork_i + 16.99female_i - 0.13fem\_hrwork_i$$

The default hypothesis test for **fem_hrwork** shown in SAS and Stata tests whether the interaction is significant. If we cannot reject the null hypothesis that the product term is zero ($H_o: \beta_3 = 0$), then the effect of each variable is statistically equivalent within levels of the other variable. If we can reject the null hypothesis that the product term is zero, then we have evidence that the effect of each variable differs within levels of the other variable ($H_a: \beta_3 \neq 0$). In our case, the t-value for *fem_hrwork* of -2.87 is greater in magnitude than the cutoff of 1.96 for our large sample, and the p-value is smaller than 0.05, so we can reject the null hypothesis.[7]

Conditional Regression Equations for Effect of Hours of Paid Work

We can use the prediction equation (Equation 11.3) to calculate predicted values and the conditional regression equations. Let's begin with the conditional regression equations for our interval variable, *hrwork*.

■ **Table 11.14: Estimated Conditional Regression Equation for Effect of Hours of Paid Work, Within Gender**

Men	$(\hat{Y}\|X_1, D_2 = 0)$	$= 26.12 - 0.12X_{1i} + 16.99 * 0 - 0.13 * X_{1i} * 0$	$= 26.12 - 0.12X_{1i}$
Women	$(\hat{Y}\|X_1, D_2 = 1)$	$= 26.12 - 0.12X_{1i} + 16.99 * 1 - 0.13 * X_{1i} * 1$	$= (26.12 + 16.99) - (0.12 + 0.13)X_{1i}$
			$= 43.11 - 0.25X_{1i}$

Notice that similar to the interaction of two dummy variables, we can read the coefficient estimates for one of the conditional regression equations—the equation for the category coded zero on the other variable, *men*—directly from the SAS and Stata output (see Box 11.4). The other (conditional regression equation for *women*) requires us to sum two coefficients to calculate the intercept and to sum two coefficients to calculate the slope.

■ **Box 11.4**

The conditional effect that we can read off the default output is sometimes referred to as the *main effect*. We find the term *conditional effect* preferable, however, because as we emphasize throughout the chapter, whenever an interaction is present, we must interpret the effect of one variable conditional on levels of the other variable in the interaction. Depending on the number of levels of the other variable, there may be numerous conditional effects.

For men, we can refer back to Display B.11.6 to see the results of the test of whether the conditional effect of hours of work differs from zero. The *t*-value for *hrwork* (X_{1i}) is −3.96, which is larger in absolute magnitude than 1.96, and the associated *p*-value is smaller than 0.05. Thus, for men, we can reject the null hypothesis that the effect of hours of work on hours of chores is zero.

For women, we hand-calculated the conditional effect in Table 11.14. To test whether this association between hours of work and hours of chores is significantly different from zero for women requires us to use one of the three strategies discussed above. Display B.11.7 presents the results of each of the three approaches, re-estimating the regression in the top panel, *F*-test in the middle panel, and linear combination in the bottom panel.

The first and third approaches provide the point estimate and standard errors, as well as the hypothesis test. The values are the same, with the estimate of the conditional effect of *hrwork* for women being estimated to be −0.25 in both cases. This matches, within rounding error, our hand calculation above.[8] As expected, the *F*-value in the second approach equals the square of the *t*-value from the first and third approaches ($t^2 = -8.18 * -8.18 = 66.91$), within rounding error. In all cases, the *p*-value is less than 0.05, indicating that we can reject the null hypothesis that the conditional effect of hours of work is zero among women.

Conditional Effects of Gender

We can similarly use Equation 11.3 to calculate the conditional effects of being female within hours of paid work.

The results show that the gender gap in hours of chores narrows as work hours increase. Among adults who work 10 hours per week, women spend nearly 16 more hours a week on chores than

■ Table 11.15: Estimated Effect of Being Female, Within Hours of Paid Work

Hours	Conditional Regression Equations		
10	$(\hat{Y}|X_1 = 10, D_2)$	$= 26.12 - 0.12 * 10 + 16.99 D_{2i} - 0.13 * 10 * D_{2i}$	$= (26.12 - 1.20) + (16.99 - 1.30) D_{2i}$ $= (24.92) + (15.69) D_{2i}$
20	$(\hat{Y}|X_1 = 20, D_2)$	$= 26.12 - 0.12 * 20 + 16.99 D_{2i} - 0.13 * 20 * D_{2i}$	$= (26.12 - 2.40) + (16.99 - 2.60) D_{2i}$ $= (23.72) + (14.39) D_{2i}$
30	$(\hat{Y}|X_1 = 30, D_2)$	$= 26.12 - 0.12 * 30 + 16.99 D_{2i} - 0.13 * 30 * D_{2i}$	$= (26.12 - 3.60) + (16.99 - 3.90) D_{2i}$ $= (22.52) + (13.09) D_{2i}$
40	$(\hat{Y}|X_1 = 40, D_2)$	$= 26.12 - 0.12 * 40 + 16.99 D_{2i} - 0.13 * 40 * D_{2i}$	$= (26.12 - 4.80) + (16.99 - 5.20) D_{2i}$ $= (21.32) + (11.79) D_{2i}$
50	$(\hat{Y}|X_1 = 50, D_2)$	$= 26.12 - 0.12 * 50 + 16.99 D_{2i} - 0.13 * 50 * D_{2i}$	$= (26.12 - 6.00) + (16.99 - 6.50) D_{2i}$ $= (20.12) + (10.49) D_{2i}$

do men. Among adults who work 50 hours per week, the gender difference is just over 10 hours per week.

Do these conditional gender gaps differ significantly from zero? We will use the three approaches outlined above to ask SAS and Stata to conduct hypothesis tests for the conditional effects of gender. The results are shown in Displays B.11.8 to B.11.10. Display B.11.8 shows the results of re-estimating the regression model after centering hours of work. Display B.11.9 shows the results of the **test** command. Display B.11.10 shows the results of the **lincom** command. The first and third approaches provide the point estimates of the effect of gender within each level of hours of paid work. The results match our hand calculations in Table 11.15 with rounding error.[9] The F-values from the second approach equal the square of the t-values from the first and third approaches.

Hours of paid work per week	F-value (Approach #2)	Square of t-value (Approach #1 and #3)
10	121.13	$t^2 = 11.01 * 11.01 = 121.22$
20	187.62	$t^2 = 13.70 * 13.70 = 187.69$
30	304.23	$t^2 = 17.44 * 17.44 = 304.15$
40	344.12	$t^2 = 18.55 * 18.55 = 344.10$
50	178.79	$t^2 = 13.37 * 13.37 = 178.76$

In all cases, the p-values are less than 0.05, so we can reject the null hypothesis that the gender difference is zero within each levels of hours of paid work.

11.3.5: Summary of Interpretation

In a model with an interaction between a dummy variable and an interval variable:

$$Y_i = \beta_0 + \beta_1 X_{1i} + \beta_2 D_{2i} + \beta_3 X_{1i} D_{2i} + \varepsilon_i$$

we interpret the results as follows.

- Intercept (β_0): average of the outcome variable for cases coded "0" on the dummy and zero on the interval variable. If zero is not a valid value on the interval variable, then the intercept is not meaningful.
- Coefficient of Interval Variable (β_1): conditional slope for interval variable for the category coded "0" on the dummy.
- Coefficient of Dummy Variable (β_2): conditional effect of dummy variable when the interval variable is zero. If zero is not a valid value on the interval variable, then this conditional effect is not meaningful.
- Coefficient of Product Term (β_3): difference in conditional effects for a one-unit change on the other variable (amount larger or smaller that the conditional slope is for cases coded "1" on the dummy; amount conditional effect of dummy changes as the interval variable increases by one).

As we see below, if we add additional control variables to the model, then our interpretation of these coefficient estimates remain the same, although we add the phrase "controlling for the other variables in the model." When other variables are in the model, the intercept may no longer be meaningful, if zero is not a valid value on some of those variables. We can use the same three techniques presented above to test the conditional effects, when controls are in the model.

11.3.6: Presenting Results and Interpreting their Substantive Size

We can use similar techniques as discussed in Appendix H.11.1 to present the results of an interaction between a dummy and interval variable in Excel. Figure 11.2 shows the results (see Appendix H.11.2 for details on creating this type of graph).

As with the interaction of two dummy variables, the graph helps us to visualize the conditional regression effects calculated above. The negative association between hours of paid work and hours of chores looks steeper for women than for men, as expected. Changing from 10 to 50 hours of paid work per week, women's weekly hours of chores decreases by 10 hours, whereas men's weekly hours of chores decrease by less than 5 hours. And, the gap between women and men narrows as hours of paid work increases, dropping from a gap of over 15 hours at 10 hours of weekly employment to a gap of about 10 hours at 50 hours of weekly employment.

These differences seem large in a real world sense. It is also straightforward to calculate their size relative to the standard deviation of hours of chores of 25.16. Appendix H.11.2 shows how we used Excel to calculate these differences in predicted values relative to the outcome standard

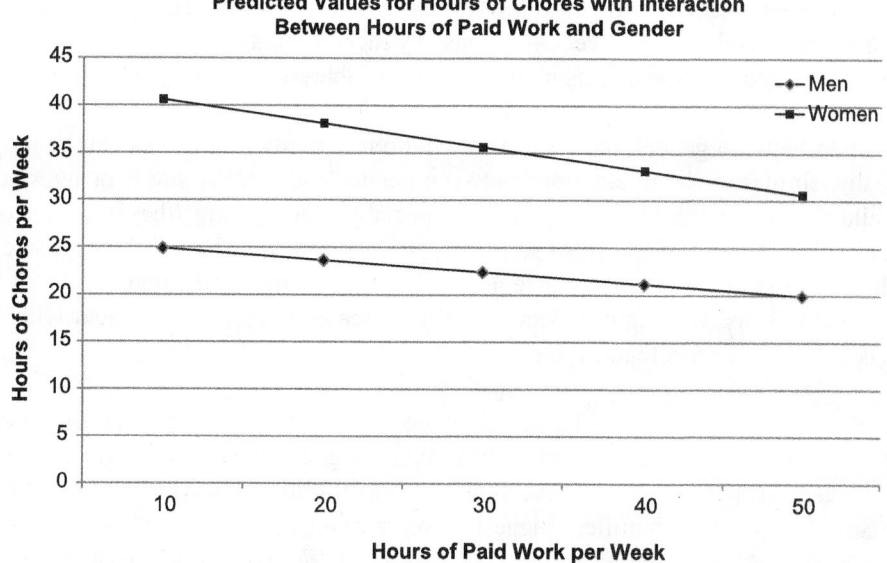

**Predicted Values for Hours of Chores with Interaction
Between Hours of Paid Work and Gender**

■ **Figure 11.2** Example of Line Graph of Dummy by Interval Interaction, Created in Excel

deviation, to create the semistandardized effects or approximate effect size. As shown in Display H.11.8, the gender gap drops from over 60 percent to just 40 percent of the standard deviation of hours of chores when we move from 10 to 50 hours of work per week. Using Cohen's rule of thumb, the approximate effect size drops from above to below the cutoff for medium size (see again Section 8.4.9). In terms of the conditional effects of hours of work, for a large increase in employment of 40 hours per week (from 10 to 50 hours), the effect size is under the medium cutoff, but twice as large for women (0.40) as for men (0.20).

In addition to using changes in hours of employment that have real world meaning in its natural units, we might also calculate fully standardized conditional effects for hours of paid work. The standard deviation of *hrwork* is 14.70.[10] We can calculate standardized conditional effects of hours of work for men and for women by multiplying the conditional effects by the ratio of the standard deviations of the predictor and outcome variables. The standardized effects are small for both genders. Among women, a one standard deviation increase in weekly hours of work is associated with a 0.15 standard deviation decrease in weekly hours of chores [$= (-0.12432 - 0.1256) * 14.70/25.16 = -0.15$]. Among men, a one standard deviation increase in weekly hours of work is associated with a 0.07 standard deviation decrease in weekly hours of chores ([$= (-0.12432) * 14.70/25.16 = -0.07$]; see also Display H.8.9 regarding calculating these standardized effects in Excel).

11.4: CHOW TEST

We can build on the concepts just introduced to examine whether a full multiple regression model differs between two groups. In our example, suppose that we theorized that hours spent on chores per week was determined jointly by the two variables considered above—marital status and hours of paid work per week—and also by race-ethnicity and the number of children in the household; and, that the effects of all of these variables differed by gender.[11]

An interaction between gender and number of children in predicting chores can be motivated conceptually, similar to the interactions between gender and marital status or hours of paid work. Children are a net addition to chores, especially when young (they require cooking, laundry, cleaning, driving to and from activities, etc., but can contribute little to these chores). We might anticipate that women complete more of the chores around the house associated with having children. Thus, we might expect that any increase in chores associated with having children is larger for women than for men.

▪ Box 11.5

For this example, we will exclude from the sample the relatively small number of families in the NSFH of other race-ethnicities. An alternative to excluding them from the sample would be to group them together in an *other* category, but it is difficult to develop hypotheses and interpret results for such a heterogeneous group. And, the example is simplified by using three homogeneous groups.

Similarly, we might look to literature on egalitarianism in African American families, suggesting less of a gender difference in chores within these families, and traditionalism in Mexican American families, suggesting more of a gender difference in chores within these families (see Box 11.5). We will use whites as the reference group since they are the largest category (with nearly three-quarters of the NSFH sample) and we expect them to differ from both African Americans and Mexican Americans, although in opposite ways. Because of these familial differences, we also expect greater differences by race-ethnicity in hours of chores among women than among men.

So, generally, we have a multiple regression model with five predictors.

$$Y_i = \beta_0 + \beta_1 D_{1i} + \beta_2 X_{1i} + \beta_3 X_{2i} + \beta_4 D_{3i} + \beta_5 D_{4i} + \varepsilon_i \tag{11.4}$$

where D_1 is a dummy indicator of marital status (*married*), X_1 is hours of paid work per week (*hrwork*), X_2 is number of children in the household (*numkid*), and D_3 and D_4 are a pair of dummy variables indicating African American (*aframer*) and Mexican American (*mexamer*) race-ethnicities, respectively, with whites being the reference category.

Not shown is D_2, the dummy indicator of gender (*female*). Because we expect all of the coefficients for all five predictors shown in Equation 11.4 to differ by gender, an intuitive approach to estimating the model would be to run the regression twice, once on the subsample of men and once on the subsample of women. This approach is the intuitive basis for what is referred to as a *Chow test* (Chow 1960; see Ghilagaber 2004 for a more recent treatment of the test and Giordano, Longmore, and Manning 2006; Jarrell and Stanley 2004; and Fairweather 2005 for recent applications). Alternatively, we could use our new understanding of product terms to specify a single model with the dummy for gender and interactions between gender and each of the five other predictors. Gujarati (1970a, 1970b) showed that this approach provides an equivalent F-test for any group differences in the full regression model as the Chow test. We will confirm this in our example below and see that these two approaches provide the same coefficient estimates although somewhat different standard errors. Both allow us to test whether any coefficients differ between the groups (in our case between men and women). But, the second approach also allows us to determine readily whether individual coefficients differ by gender.

11.4.1: Separate Regression Models Within Groups

We will write the separate regression equations for men and women using subscripts to differentiate the coefficients for men (M) and for women (W).

Men
$$Y_i = \beta_{M0} + \beta_{M1}D_{1i} + \beta_{M2}X_{1i} + \beta_{M3}X_{2i} + \beta_{M4}D_{3i} + \beta_{M5}D_{4i} + \varepsilon_i \quad (11.5)$$

Women
$$Y_i = \beta_{W0} + \beta_{W1}D_{1i} + \beta_{W2}X_{1i} + \beta_{W3}X_{2i} + \beta_{W4}D_{3i} + \beta_{W5}D_{4i} + \varepsilon_i \quad (11.6)$$

We will similarly use subscripts to designate the model run on the total sample (T) as:

Total Sample
$$Y_i = \beta_{T0} + \beta_{T1}D_{1i} + \beta_{T2}X_{1i} + \beta_{T3}X_{2i} + \beta_{T4}D_{3i} + \beta_{T5}D_{4i} + \varepsilon_i \quad (11.7)$$

We will estimate the gender-specific models in SAS or Stata by using a *by* option to estimate the regression model within the levels of gender (once for men and once for women). The data first need to be sorted by gender (so that cases coded "0" on the group variable are in the initial rows of the data file and cases coded "1" on the group variable are in the remaining rows of the data file). In SAS, the sorting takes place with the procedure `proc sort` and the `by` statement is used in both the `sort` and `reg` procedures. In Stata, the sorting can be combined with a `by` request using the `bysort` prefix preceding the `regress` command.

SAS

```
proc sort;
  by female;
run;

proc reg;
  model hrchores=married hrwork numkid aframer mexamer;
  by female;
run;
```

Stata

```
bysort female: regress hrchores married hrwork numkid aframer mexamer
```

11.4.2: The Fully Interacted Model and General Linear *F*-test

We can also write a single equation that captures Equations 11.5 and 11.6 (for men and women) using a straightforward extension of the concepts we have already considered for interactions.

This equation is called a **fully interacted model** and includes one product term between every variable in the model and the grouping variable (gender in our example).

Our hypothesis is that the entire model shown in Equation 11.4 is moderated by gender. This means that we have to allow all of the parameters in the model—the intercept, the coefficients for the three dummies and the slope coefficients for the two interval variables—to vary by gender. We can do so by adding a dummy variable indicating females to the model (to allow the intercept to vary by gender) and by adding five product terms, each created by multiplying the variable from the basic model by the female dummy (to allow the coefficients for the three dummies and the slopes for the two interval variables to vary by gender). In our example, we would have:

$$Y_i = \beta_0 + \beta_1 D_{1i} + \beta_2 X_{1i} + \beta_3 X_{2i} + \beta_4 D_{3i} + \beta_5 D_{4i}$$
$$+ \beta_6 D_{2i} + \beta_7 D_{2i} D_{1i} + \beta_8 D_{2i} X_{1i} + \beta_9 D_{2i} X_{2i} + \beta_{10} D_{2i} D_{3i} + \beta_{11} D_{2i} D_{4i} + \varepsilon_i \qquad (11.8)$$

Recall that D_2 is the dummy indicator for females.

Now, we can see that this specification produces the two desired conditional regression equations:

▨ **Table 11.16: Conditional Regression Equations within Gender**

Male	$E(Y \mid D_1, X_1, X_2, D_3, D_4, D_2 = 0)$	$= \beta_0 + \beta_1 D_{1i} + \beta_2 X_{1i} + \beta_3 X_{2i} + \beta_4 D_{3i} + \beta_5 D_{4i}$
		$+ \beta_6 * 0 + \beta_7 * 0 * D_{1i} + \beta_8 * 0 * X_{1i} + \beta_9 * 0 * X_{2i} + \beta_{10} * 0 * D_{3i} + \beta_{11} * 0 * D_{4i}$
		$= \beta_0 + \beta_1 D_{1i} + \beta_2 X_{1i} + \beta_3 X_{2i} + \beta_4 D_{3i} + \beta_5 D_{4i}$
Female	$E(Y \mid D_1, X_1, X_2, D_3, D_4, D_2 = 1)$	$= \beta_0 + \beta_1 D_{1i} + \beta_2 X_{1i} + \beta_3 X_{2i} + \beta_4 D_{3i} + \beta_5 D_{4i}$
		$+ \beta_6 * 1 + \beta_7 * 1 * D_{1i} + \beta_8 * 1 * X_{1i} + \beta_9 * 1 * X_{2i} + \beta_{10} * 1 * D_{3i} + \beta_{11} * 1 * D_{4i}$
		$= (\beta_0 + \beta_6) + (\beta_1 + \beta_7) D_{1i} + (\beta_2 + \beta_8) X_{1i} + (\beta_3 + \beta_9) X_{2i} + (\beta_4 + \beta_{10}) D_{3i} + (\beta_5 + \beta_{11}) D_{4i}$

The top row provides the conditional regression equation for men and the bottom row the conditional regression equation for women. Note that it is clear from this table that each of the product terms captures the difference between men and women on each of the model parameters: β_6 the difference in the intercept, β_7 the difference in the effect of being married (D_1), β_8 the difference in the effect of hours of paid work per week (X_1), β_9 the difference in the effect of number of children (X_2), β_{10} the difference in the effect of being African American versus white (D_3), and β_{11} the difference in the effect of being Mexican American versus white (D_4).

The conditional regression equations make clear that for the entire regression model to be the same for men and women, all of these coefficients, from β_6 through β_{11}, must equal zero. We can use the general linear F-test to test such a joint null hypothesis against the alternative that at least one of the coefficients, from β_6 through β_{11}, does not equal zero. If we reject the joint null hypothesis, then we can look at the individual coefficients for the *female* dummy and the product terms to see which individual coefficients differ significantly from zero.

Table 11.17 summarizes the null and alternative hypotheses and the full and restricted models of this general linear F-test.

■ Table 11.17: General linear F-test of gender differences based on fully interacted model

H_0	$\beta_6 = 0,\ \beta_7 = 0,\ \beta_8 = 0,\ \beta_9 = 0,\ \beta_{10} = 0,\ \beta_{11} = 0$
H_a	$\beta_6 \neq 0$ and/or $\beta_7 \neq 0$ and/or $\beta_8 \neq 0$ and/or $\beta_9 \neq 0$ and/or $\beta_{10} \neq 0$ and/or $\beta_{11} \neq 0$
	(that is, at least one of the coefficients from β_6 to β_{11} is not equal to zero)

Full
$$Y_i = \beta_0 + \beta_1 D_{1i} + \beta_2 X_{1i} + \beta_3 X_{2i} + \beta_4 D_{3i} + \beta_5 D_{4i}$$
$$+ \beta_6 D_{2i} + \beta_7 D_{2i} D_{1i} + \beta_8 D_{2i} X_{1i} + \beta_9 D_{2i} X_{2i} + \beta_{10} D_{2i} D_{3i} + \beta_{11} D_{2i} D_{4i} + \varepsilon_i$$

Reduced
$$Y_i = \beta_0 + \beta_1 D_{1i} + \beta_2 X_{1i} + \beta_3 X_{2i} + \beta_4 D_{3i} + \beta_5 D_{4i}$$
$$+ 0 * D_{2i} + 0 * D_{2i} D_{1i} + 0 * D_{2i} X_{1i} + 0 * D_{2i} X_{2i} + 0 * D_{2i} D_{3i} + 0 * D_{2i} D_{4i} + \varepsilon_i$$
$$= \beta_0 + \beta_1 D_{1i} + \beta_2 X_{1i} + \beta_3 X_{2i} + \beta_4 D_{3i} + \beta_5 D_{4i} + \varepsilon_i$$

The reduced model is the same as Equation 11.7. And, as we shall see, the full model (fully interacted model) has the same residual sums of squares as Equations 11.5 and 11.6 added together (see Box 11.6).

11.4.3: Example 11.3

Display B.11.11 shows the results of estimating the reduced model (Equation 11.7). Display B.11.12 shows the results of estimating Equations 11.5 and 11.6. Display B.11.13 shows the results of estimating the fully interacted model. Display B.11.13 also shows the results of asking

■ Box 11.6

It is worth examining how the conditional regression equation for men in Table 11.16 differs from the reduced model in Table 11.17, since in the abstract they look equivalent. First, one is based on constraining the values of a predictor (conditioning) and the other is based on constraining coefficients to zero (based on the null hypothesis). That is, in Table 11.16, we obtain the conditional regression equation for men by substituting in zeros for D_2 in the fully interacted model. In contrast, in Table 11.17, we obtain the reduced model by substituting in zeros for β_6 to β_{11} in the fully interacted model. Second, they are based on different subsamples. The full model in Table 11.17 is estimated using the total sample, with the dummy *female* and the product terms omitted. It assumes (based on the null hypothesis) that the coefficients do not differ by gender. Thus, if the null hypothesis is correct, the best estimates of the effects of our five predictors in Equation 11.4 are based on men and women combined. In contrast, the conditional regression equation for men in Table 11.16 based on the fully interacted model is equivalent to Equation 11.5, the model estimated just on the male subsample. It assumes (based on the alternative hypothesis) that the coefficients do differ by gender. Thus, if the alternative hypothesis is correct, the best estimates of our five predictors in Equation 11.4 are based on men and women separately.

SAS and Stata to calculate the general linear F-test shown in Table 11.17 which we will use to verify our hand calculations. Display B.11.14 uses Stata's `lincom` command to calculate the conditional effects for women, shown in Table 11.16.

We will begin by comparing the models, including verifying that the models run within gender are equivalent to the fully interacted model in terms of of the point estimates and residual sums of squares.

- The sum of the sample size of the regression model estimated on the male subsample and the sample size of the regression model estimated on the female subsample ($n_M + n_W = 2,849 + 2,971 = 5,820$ from Display B.11.12) is equal to the sample size of the total sample ($n_T = 5,820$ in Display B.11.11) and the fully interacted model (n = 5,820 in Display B.11.13). For Display B.11.12 versus Display B.11.11, this is expected, since the subsample models in Display B.11.12 simply selected two groups that comprise the full sample. For Display B.11.13 versus Display B.11.11, this verifies that the full and reduced models are estimated on the same sample, which as we emphasized in Chapter 9 is required for a general linear F-test.
- The sum of the residual sum of squares for the models run on the male and female subsamples ($SSE_M + SSE_W = 1,142,398.38 + 2,081,280.21 = 3,223,678.6$ in Display B.11.12) is also the same as the sums of squares error for the fully interacted model (SSE = 3,223,678.59 in Display B.11.13).
- And, the sum of the error degrees of freedom for the models run on the male and female subsamples (error df_M + error df_W = 2,843 + 2,965 = 5,808 in Display B.11.12) is the same as error degrees of freedom for the fully interacted model (error df = 5,808 in Display B.11.13).

Thus, both approaches (running models within gender or running a fully interacted model) give us equivalent inputs for the full model in the general linear F-test.

$$F = \frac{SSE(R) - SSE(F)}{df_R - df_F} \div \frac{SSE(F)}{df_F} = \frac{3,456,551.62 - 3,223,678.59}{5,814 - 5,808}$$
$$\div \frac{3,223,678.59}{5,808} = 69.93$$

This matches the result shown in Display B.11.13 for the F-test of the null hypothesis laid out in Table 11.17 (that the *female* dummy and the product terms all have coefficients equal to zero). The numerator degrees of freedom is $5,814 - 5,808 = 6$ which equals the number of constraints in the null hypothesis (six coefficients equal zero in the null hypothesis).

The test command in SAS and Stata provides the p-value for the F-test, which is less than 0.05. Thus, we reject the null hypothesis and conclude that at least one of the coefficients differs between men and women. An advantage of the fully interacted model over the models run within gender is that we can then look at the individual product terms and the *female* dummy to see which individual coefficients differ from zero.

The point estimates from the models run within gender match the point estimates for the fully interacted model (including the subsequent `lincom` commands for the conditional effects among women). The standard errors for the individual coefficients (and thus the t-values and p-values) differ somewhat. But, in our case, the conclusions for two-sided hypothesis tests are the same in both approaches (see Box 11.7).

■ **Table 11.18: Point Estimates and Significance Tests from Models Run within Gender and Fully Interacted Model**

	Within Gender		Fully Interacted Model		
	Men (Display B.11.12)	Women (Display B.11.12)	Men (Display B.11.13)	Difference (Display B.11.13)	Women (Display B.11.14)
married	−3.18*	1.30	−3.18*	4.48*	1.30
hrwork	−0.11*	−0.22*	−0.11*	−0.11*	−0.22*
numkid	1.45*	6.24*	1.45*	4.79*	6.24*
aframer	6.04*	4.06*	6.04*	−1.98	4.06*
mexamer	5.77*	14.26*	5.77*	8.49*	14.26*
intercept	25.18*	34.69*	25.18*	9.51*	34.69*

* $p < 0.05$ (two-tailed test).

11.4.4: Presenting Results

Appendix H.11.3 shows how to create a graph of the interaction between gender and hours of paid work, similar to the graph we showed in Figure 11.2, but using the fully interacted model. This illustrates how to make predictions with additional variables in the model, beyond those in the interaction.

Indeed, typically, in a manuscript, our hypotheses focus on a subset of the variables in a multiple regression model. Or, if we have numerous hypotheses, we focus on one at a time for interpretation. Graphs can be useful to aid in interpretation in these multiple regression contexts, similar to what we saw above in Section 11.2 and 11.3 with models that just included the two variables in the interaction. But, when we have additional variables in a multiple regression model, we are immediately confronted with the question: how should we deal with the other variables when we want to make predictions while varying just one or two variables? It makes

---

■ **Box 11.8**

We can think of this prediction as a thought experiment in which we examine the effects for the "average person" (with mean levels on all covariates). We systematically vary this average person's values on the predictors central to our research questions, to see what their outcome level would be if they had these characteristics. One disadvantage to this approach is that the mean may not be a meaningful value on some of the predictors. For dummy variables, the mean will be some value between zero and 1 whereas in reality each sample member takes on the exact values of zero or 1. Similarly, count variables can take on only integers, whereas the mean will be noninteger. One simple approach to deal with this might be to round such values to the closest meaningful value (see also Long 1997 and Long and Freese 2006 for other approaches).

---

sense to hold these variables constant, so that we can isolate the effect of changing the predictors we are focusing on interpreting (in our case, hours of work and gender). But, what values should we use? A number of alternative choices are available (Long 1997; Long and Freese 2006), but we will use one standard approach, in which we hold all other variables constant at their means (see Box 11.8).

Figure 11.3 shows the results of using this approach. Comparing the graphs in Figures 11.2 and 11.3 and the partially and fully standardized effects in Displays H.11.9 and H.11.11 with those in Figure 11.3 shows generally similar results, although the association between hours of work and hours of chores is a bit less steep in Figure 11.3 than Figure 11.2 (slope of −0.22 versus −0.25 for women).

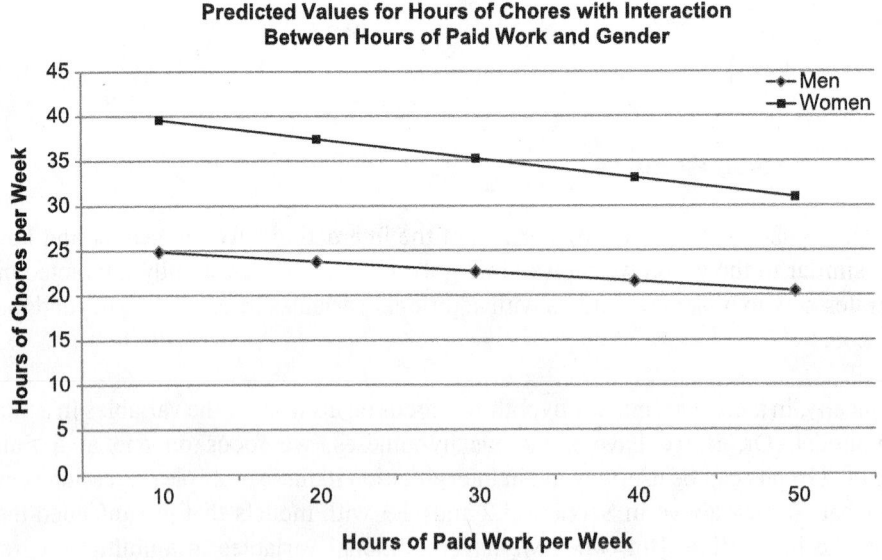

■ **Figure 11.3** Predicted Values from Fully Interacted Model

11.4.5: Summary of Interpretation

Following are general interpretations for a fully interacted model:

- Intercept (β_0): average of the outcome variable for cases coded "0" on all variables in the model. If zero is not a valid value on one or more predictors, then the intercept is not meaningful.
- Coefficient of individual variables: conditional effect of variable for the category coded "0" on the grouping variable.
- Coefficient of grouping variable: difference in intercept between category coded "1" and category coded "0" on the grouping variable. If zero is not a valid value on one or more predictors, then this coefficient is not meaningful.
- Coefficient of product terms: amount larger or smaller that the conditional effect for each variable is for cases coded "1" on the grouping variable.

We can use any of three techniques to test the conditional effects for the group coded "1" on the grouping variable (re-estimate the model with the other group as a reference on the grouping variable or use general linear F-tests or tests of linear combinations).

The standard calculation of the Chow test includes the dummy variable for the two groups in the null hypothesis. This captures whether the intercept differs between the groups. However, it will often make sense to exclude this dummy from the general linear F-test in the fully interacted model. As we have seen, if one or more of the product terms are significant, then the gender gap will vary within levels of the other variables. And, if zero is not a valid value on all predictors, then testing whether the Y intercept differs by gender is not meaningful.

It is also possible to specify a partially interacted model, rather than a fully interacted model, if we expect that some but not all effects will vary by the grouping variable. For example, we might expect some variables to have similar effects on hours of chores for men and women (such as the size of the house, which may affect the overall volume of chores).

And, a fully or partially interacted model can be set up for grouping variables with more than two groups. In this case, one group will be the reference and sets of product terms will be created using the dummy indicator of each of the remaining groups. These product terms, and the dummy indicators of each of the included groups, will be included in the full regression model (see Gujarati 1970b for an example).

11.4.6: Revisiting Literature Excerpt 11.1

Looking back at Literature Excerpt 11.1, we now understand how and why the authors estimated a fully interacted model to estimate the presented coefficient estimates that they describe in the note to their table (see sentence underlined in green). They indicate that an F-test for gender differences was insignificant (see sentence underlined in black). Because they report 17 numerator degrees of freedom for this test, and the gender-specific equations contain 17 predictors, it appears that they excluded the dummy variable for gender from this test. Excluding the gender dummy is consistent with their goal in this section of the paper to answer the question "Are correlates of commitment gender-specific?" (p. 382).

The fact that the authors do not use graphics to help to understand the interactions is consistent with the limited evidence of interactions by gender in terms of statistical and substantive significance.

As noted previously, just three of the 17 individual covariates had coefficient estimates that differed significantly by gender. We can use the reported descriptive statistics in the paper to fully standardize the two scale predictors and partially standardize the dummy predictor. Doing so shows that the significant differences are all small in size.

Predictor Variable	Unstandardized Interaction Coefficient	Standard Deviation of Predictor	Standardized Interaction Coefficient[a]
Nonmerit reward criteria	$-0.010 - (-0.135) = 0.125$	0.72	0.17
Currently married	$-0.011 - 0.145 = -0.156$	n/a	-0.29
Number of persons aged 12 or less in household	$0.027 - (-0.050) = 0.077$	0.91	0.13

Note: Standard deviation of outcome (organizational commitment) is 0.54 (p. 376). Standard deviation of predictor variables are taken from the paper's appendix.
[a] Completely standardized coefficient for 1st and 3rd predictor variables. Semistandardized coefficient for 2nd predictor variable (because it is a dummy variable).

And, as the authors note in the text, they had limited a priori hypotheses for how the 17 predictors might have different effects for men versus women. One interaction is consistent with prior research (association of marital status significant and positive for men and insignificant for women), but another is inconsistent with expectations (e.g., effect of number of children being significant and negative in sign for men and insignificant for women) and one has no "ready interpretation" (p. 383) from the authors (effect of nonmerit reward criteria significant and negative for men but insignificant for women).

11.5: INTERACTION BETWEEN TWO INTERVAL VARIABLES

Interactions between two interval variables often seem more complicated to interpret than interactions involving at least one dummy variable. But, as we will see, the concepts we've considered for interactions between two sets of dummy variables and between a dummy and interval variable extend directly to interactions between two interval variables.

11.5.1: Conditional Regression Equations

Setting up an interaction model for two interval variables proceeds similarly to interactions involving at least one dummy variable: we introduce a product term between the two interval variables into the model to test for an interaction.

We will continue with our example of hours of chores per week as the outcome, but now we will introduce an interaction between number of children and hours of paid work per week.

To begin, let's look at the additive version of the model:

$$Y_i = \beta_0 + \beta_1 X_{1i} + \beta_2 X_{2i} + \varepsilon_i$$

where X_1 measures hours of paid work per week (*hrwork*) and X_2 measures number of children in the household (*numkid*; see Box 11.9).

In this additive model, the association between hours of chores and hours of paid work does not depend on the number of children in the household. Likewise, the association between hours of chores and the number of children in the household does not depend on the hours of paid work. We can see this clearly by looking at the conditional regression equations (see Table 11.19).

■ **Box 11.9**

To simplify the presentation, we excluded families with more than four children from the sample throughout this chapter.

It is clear from these tables that the condition we place on one of the variables is absorbed in the intercept and the slope for the other variable is the same regardless of the condition. Thus, the conditional regression equations for an additive model with two interval variables produce many parallel lines. This result is similar to what we saw with an additive model with a dummy and interval variable in Section 10.3.4, but with only two parallel lines.

The interaction model introduces a product term between hours of paid work and number of children:

$$Y_i = \beta_0 + \beta_1 X_{1i} + \beta_2 X_{2i} + \beta_3 X_{1i} X_{2i} + \varepsilon_i \qquad (11.10)$$

■ **Table 11.19: Conditional Regression Equations (Additive Model)**

Effect of Hours of Paid Work Per Week (X_1), Conditional on Number of Children (X_2)

No Children	$E(Y\|X_1, X_2 = 0)$	$= \beta_0 + \beta_1 * X_{1i} + \beta_2 * 0$	$= \beta_0 + \beta_1 * X_{1i}$
One Child	$E(Y\|X_1, X_2 = 1)$	$= \beta_0 + \beta_1 * X_{1i} + \beta_2 * 1$	$= (\beta_0 + \beta_2) + \beta_1 * X_{1i}$
Two Children	$E(Y\|X_1, X_2 = 2)$	$= \beta_0 + \beta_1 * X_{1i} + \beta_2 * 2$	$= (\beta_0 + 2\beta_2) + \beta_1 * X_{1i}$
Three Children	$E(Y\|X_1, X_2 = 3)$	$= \beta_0 + \beta_1 * X_{1i} + \beta_2 * 3$	$= (\beta_0 + 3\beta_2) + \beta_1 * X_{1i}$
Four Children	$E(Y\|X_1, X_2 = 4)$	$= \beta_0 + \beta_1 * X_{1i} + \beta_2 * 4$	$= (\beta_0 + 4\beta_2) + \beta_1 * X_{1i}$

Effect of Number of Children (X_2), Conditional on Hours of Paid Work Per Week (X_1)

Hours paid work/week

10	$E(Y\|X_1 = 10, X_2)$	$= \beta_0 + \beta_1 * 10 + \beta_2 * X_{2i}$	$= (\beta_0 + 10\beta_1) + \beta_2 * X_{2i}$
20	$E(Y\|X_1 = 20, X_2)$	$= \beta_0 + \beta_1 * 20 + \beta_2 * X_{2i}$	$= (\beta_0 + 20\beta_1) + \beta_2 * X_{2i}$
30	$E(Y\|X_1 = 30, X_2)$	$= \beta_0 + \beta_1 * 30 + \beta_2 * X_{2i}$	$= (\beta_0 + 30\beta_1) + \beta_2 * X_{2i}$
40	$E(Y\|X_1 = 40, X_2)$	$= \beta_0 + \beta_1 * 40 + \beta_2 * X_{2i}$	$= (\beta_0 + 40\beta_1) + \beta_2 * X_{2i}$
50	$E(Y\|X_1 = 50, X_2)$	$= \beta_0 + \beta_1 * 50 + \beta_2 * X_{2i}$	$= (\beta_0 + 50\beta_1) + \beta_2 * X_{2i}$

Now it is clear from the conditional regression equations that if the interaction term is significant, then the effect of number of children depends on the hours of paid work per week and the effect of hours of paid work depends on the number of children (see Table 11.20).

■ **Table 11.20: Conditional Regression Equations (Interaction Model)**

Effect of Hours of Paid Work Per Week (X_1), Conditional on Number of Children (X_2)

No Children	$E(Y\|X_1, X_2 = 0)$	$= \beta_0 + \beta_1 * X_{1i} + \beta_2 * 0 + \beta_3 * X_{1i} * 0$	$= \beta_0 + \beta_1 * X_{1i}$
One Child	$E(Y\|X_1, X_2 = 1)$	$= \beta_0 + \beta_1 * X_{1i} + \beta_2 * 1 + \beta_3 * X_{1i} * 1$	$= (\beta_0 + \beta_2) + (\beta_1 + \beta_3) * X_{1i}$
Two Children	$E(Y\|X_1, X_2 = 2)$	$= \beta_0 + \beta_1 * X_{1i} + \beta_2 * 2 + \beta_3 * X_{1i} * 2$	$= (\beta_0 + 2\beta_2) + (\beta_1 + 2\beta_3) * X_{1i}$
Three Children	$E(Y\|X_1, X_2 = 3)$	$= \beta_0 + \beta_1 * X_{1i} + \beta_2 * 3 + \beta_3 * X_{1i} * 3$	$= (\beta_0 + 3\beta_2) + (\beta_1 + 3\beta_3) * X_{1i}$
Four Children	$E(Y\|X_1, X_2 = 4)$	$= \beta_0 + \beta_1 * X_{1i} + \beta_2 * 4 + \beta_3 * X_{1i} * 4$	$= (\beta_0 + 4\beta_2) + (\beta_1 + 4\beta_3) * X_{1i}$

Effect of Number of Children (X_2), Conditional on Hours of Paid Work Per Week (X_1)

Hours
paid work/week

10	$E(Y\|X_1 = 10, X_2)$	$= \beta_0 + \beta_1 * 10 + \beta_2 * X_{2i} + \beta_3 * 10 * X_{2i}$	$= (\beta_0 + 10\beta_1) + (\beta_2 + 10\beta_3) * X_{2i}$
20	$E(Y\|X_1 = 20, X_2)$	$= \beta_0 + \beta_1 * 20 + \beta_2 * X_{2i} + \beta_3 * 20 * X_{2i}$	$= (\beta_0 + 20\beta_1) + (\beta_2 + 20\beta_3) * X_{2i}$
30	$E(Y\|X_1 = 30, X_2)$	$= \beta_0 + \beta_1 * 30 + \beta_2 * X_{2i} + \beta_3 * 30 * X_{2i}$	$= (\beta_0 + 30\beta_1) + (\beta_2 + 30\beta_3) * X_{2i}$
40	$E(Y\|X_1 = 40, X_2)$	$= \beta_0 + \beta_1 * 40 + \beta_2 * X_{2i} + \beta_3 * 40 * X_{2i}$	$= (\beta_0 + 40\beta_1) + (\beta_2 + 40\beta_3) * X_{2i}$
50	$E(Y\|X_1 = 50, X_2)$	$= \beta_0 + \beta_1 * 50 + \beta_2 * X_{2i} + \beta_3 * 50 * X_{2i}$	$= (\beta_0 + 50\beta_1) + (\beta_2 + 50\beta_3) * X_{2i}$

Clearly, the slope of each variable can now differ, depending on the level of the other variable. In the top panel, each time we raise the number of children by one, we add β_3 to the effect of hours of paid work. Similarly, in the bottom panel, each time we raise the hours of paid work by 10, we add $10 * \beta_3$ to the effect of number of children.

11.5.2: Example 11.3

Display B.11.15 presents the estimates of Equation 11.10. Display B.11.16 presents the conditional effects of Table 11.20, calculated using the Stata `lincom` command.[12]

Based on Display B.11.15, we see that the interaction term is significantly different from zero. The t-value for *numk_hrw* is −6.63, greater in magnitude than 1.96, and the p-value is smaller than 0.05. Thus, the effect of each variable depends on the level of the other variable, meaning that the conditional regression equations are needed in order to interpret the results.

Display B.11.16 presents the conditional effects of hours of work, within number of children, on the left and the conditional effects of number of children, within hours of work, on the right. All of the conditional effects differ significantly from zero, with p-values less than 0.05. Thus, the association of one variable with the outcome is significant across levels of the other variable, but the steepness of the conditional slopes vary. For employment, we see that the effect of an additional hour of paid work ranges from −0.19 when no children are in the household to −0.70

when four children are in the household. For children, the effect of one more child ranges from 7.79 when the adult works 10 hours per week to 2.69 when the adult works 50 hours per week. We will examine the substantive magnitude of these associations further in the next section.

11.5.3: Presenting Results

Appendix H.11.4 shows how to adapt the steps for calculating predictions and graphing the results in Excel for this interaction between two interval variables.

Figure 11.4 shows how we used this approach to graph the effects of hours of work within levels of number of children. We graphed the conditional slopes for three rather than all five levels of number of children to make it easier for the eye to pick up the difference in steepness across the lines.

In Display H.11.12, we also calculated the partially (dividing by the standard deviation of *hrchores* of 25.16) and fully standardized (multiplying by the standard deviation of the predictor, *hrwork*, of 14.70 and dividing by the standard deviation of *hrchores* of 25.16) conditional effects. For hours of work, we show the unstandardized and partially standardized effects of a more substantively meaningful 10 hour rather than 1 hour change (columns I and J of Display H.11.12).

Most of the effects are fairly modest in size, although the effect of hours of work for adults with four children is approaching a medium size (−0.41). Ten more hours of paid work among these families is associated with an unstandardized 7 hour decrease in time spent on chores per week (about 1 hour less per day, if spread equally throughout the week).

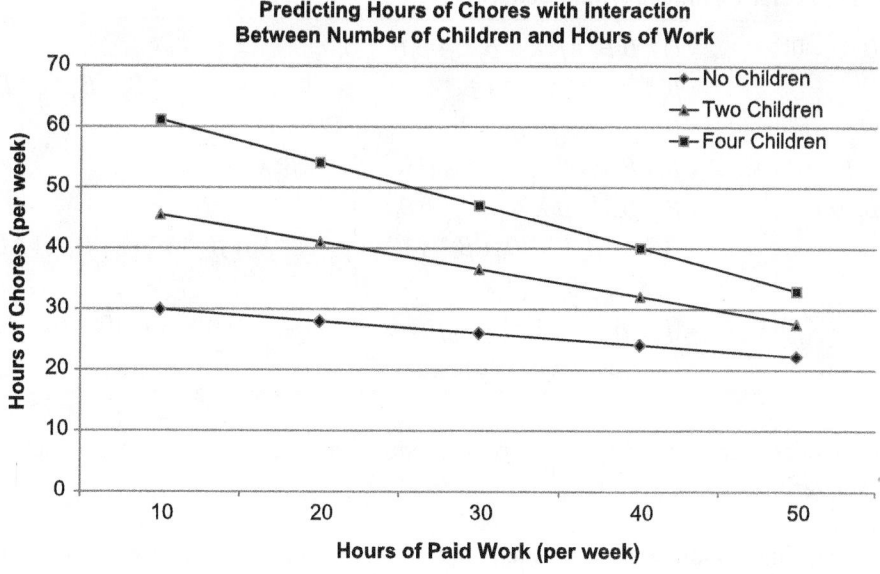

Figure 11.4 Presenting Interaction Between Two Interval Variables, Graph Created in Excel

11.5.4: Summary of Interpretation

Following are general interpretations for interactions between two interval variables:

- Intercept (β_0): average of the outcome variable for cases coded zero on both interval variables. If zero is not a valid value on at least one of the predictors, then the intercept is not meaningful.
- Coefficient of individual variables: conditional effect of one variable when the other variable is zero. These conditional effects are not meaningful if zero is not a valid value on the other variable.
- Coefficient of product terms: amount larger or smaller that the conditional effect is for one variable when the other variable in the interaction increase by one.

It is common to conduct interactions between interval variables one by one (as we will see in the next literature excerpt). We could also place the interval interaction between hours of paid work and number of children within our fully interacted model. This would lead to a three-way interaction. This three-way interaction makes conceptual sense in our example, since we might expect that the interaction between hours of work and number of children depends on gender.

$$
\begin{aligned}
Y_i = &\ \beta_0 + \beta_1 D_{1i} + \beta_2 X_{1i} + \beta_3 X_{2i} + \beta_4 D_{3i} + \beta_5 D_{4i} \\
&+ \beta_6 D_{2i} + \beta_7 D_{2i} D_{1i} + \beta_8 D_{2i} X_{1i} + \beta_9 D_{2i} X_{2i} \\
&+ \beta_{10} D_{2i} D_{3i} + \beta_{11} D_{2i} D_{4i} \\
&+ \beta_{12} X_{1i} X_{2i} + \beta_{13} D_{2i} X_{1i} X_{2i} + \varepsilon_i
\end{aligned}
\tag{11.9}
$$

The conditional regression equations based on this model are as follows.

■ Table 11.21: Conditional Regression Equations within Gender

Male $\quad E(Y\|D_1, X_1, X_2, D_3, D_4, D_2 = 0)$	$= \beta_0 + \beta_1 D_{1i} + \beta_2 X_{1i} + \beta_3 X_{2i} + \beta_4 D_{3i} + \beta_5 D_{4i}$
	$+ \beta_6 * 0 + \beta_7 * 0 * D_{1i} + \beta_8 * 0 * X_{1i} + \beta_9 * 0 * X_{2i} + \beta_{10} * 0 * D_{3i} + \beta_{11} * 0 * D_{4i}$
	$+ \beta_{12} X_{1i} X_{2i} + \beta_{13} * 0 * X_{1i} X_{2i}$
	$= \beta_0 + \beta_1 D_{1i} + \beta_2 X_{1i} + \beta_3 X_{2i} + \beta_4 D_{3i} + \beta_5 D_{4i} + \beta_{12} X_{1i} X_{2i}$
Female $\quad E(Y\|D_1, X_1, X_2, D_3, D_4, D_2 = 1)$	$= \beta_0 + \beta_1 D_{1i} + \beta_2 X_{1i} + \beta_3 X_{2i} + \beta_4 D_{3i} + \beta_5 D_{4i}$
	$+ \beta_6 * 1 + \beta_7 * 1 * D_{1i} + \beta_8 * 1 * X_{1i} + \beta_9 * 1 * X_{2i} + \beta_{10} * 1 * D_{3i} + \beta_{11} * 1 * D_{4i}$
	$+ \beta_{12} X_{1i} X_{2i} + \beta_{13} * 1 * X_{1i} X_{2i}$
	$= (\beta_0 + \beta_6) + (\beta_1 + \beta_7) D_{1i} + (\beta_2 + \beta_8) X_{1i} + (\beta_3 + \beta_9) X_{2i} + (\beta_4 + \beta_{10}) D_{3i} + (\beta_5 + \beta_{11}) D_{4i}$
	$+ (\beta_{12} + \beta_{13}) X_{1i} X_{2i}$

Now, each gender-specific conditional regression equation includes the interaction between the two interval variables.

The three-way interaction term is created in SAS and Stata using a three-variable product term (e.g., `fem_nk_hw=female*numkid*hrwork` in SAS; `generate fem_nk_hw=female*numkid*hrwork` in Stata).

If the coefficient on this three-way interaction term (β_{13}) is significantly different from zero, then the interaction between hours of paid work and number of children differs significantly between men and women. The conditional effect of this interaction can be read off the default output for men (β_{12}). For women, we could use Stata's lincom command to easily calculate ($\beta_{12} + \beta_{13}$) and its significance (or we could re-estimate the model with the *male* dummy and *male* product terms, or use the test command in SAS or Stata).

11.6: LITERATURE EXCERPT 11.2

We end with an example from the literature of an interaction between two interval variables.[13]

In 2007, Rory McVeigh and Julianna Sobolewski published a study in the *American Journal of Sociology* that aims to examine how socioeconomic characteristics relate to voting, especially how occupation and wealth relate to voting Democratic or Republican. As the authors state (p. 448):

> Social scientists have given substantial attention to relationships between voting and social class ... Most of this research assumes that, were it not for other factors, individuals possessing limited economic resources would naturally prefer candidates who promise to do more than their opponents to promote vertical redistribution of wealth. More prosperous voters, on the other hand, should prefer candidates who promote policies that will help them to preserve their accumulated wealth.

The authors add to this literature by considering not only income inequality within a single group (all Americans) but also between groups (between men and women and whites and nonwhites) and especially how these inequalities are linked to occupational segregation. In addition, whereas much of the literature has focused on individual voters, the authors look at local contexts (counties). They hypothesize that (p. 449):

> Republican candidates should receive the most electoral support in locations where large proportions of the community benefit from a conservative political agenda that preserve inequalities based on categorical distinctions. Support for Republican candidates should be especially strong in locations where there is a high degree of occupational segregation based on gender and racial categories, and where these categorical boundaries are most vulnerable to penetration.

The authors note in the article that "To facilitate interpretation of our interaction effects, we center all of our independent variables on their mean values" (p. 472). Thus, in the tables, the coefficient estimate of each variable involved in the interaction is its conditional effect when the other variable is at its mean (see Box 11.10). They also use graphs to help the reader to visualize significant interactions.

> ■ **Box 11.10**
>
> This can be a useful strategy for making the tables interpretable when zero is not a meaningful value on one or more of the variables in the interaction(s), although it is important to remember to adjust for this centering when calculating other conditional effects by hand or in SAS or Stata.

Although the authors test a number of interactions, we will focus on one presented in the first column of their Table 3 (see Literature Excerpt 11.2a). Notice that in this table, six models were run, each with one interaction between sex segregation and another variable. As we noted above, unless one of the variables in the interaction is a grouping variable, it is common to reduce complexity and facilitate interpretation by running separate models, each with a single interaction.

■ Literature Excerpt 11.2a

Table 3. Percentage Voting Republican in 2004 Presidential Election: Occupational Sex Segregation Interacting with Threats to Segregation, U.S. Counties

	Model 1	Model 2	Model 3	Model 4	Model 5	Model 6
Theoretical variables:						
Occupational sex segregation	13.927***	12.060***	13.104***	11.984***	10.862***	10.020***
	(2.742)	(2.729)	(2.793)	(2.737)	(2.746)	(2.769)
Occupational race segregation	.841	1.506	1.401	1.160	.846	1.327
	(.933)	(.956)	(.940)	(.950)	(.950)	(.949)
%women in labor force	−.001	−.007	.020	.014	.030	.008
	(.033)	(.034)	(.033)	(.033)	(.032)	(.033)
%nonwhite	−.119***	−.113***	−.116***	−.112***	−.118***	−.110***
	(.016)	(.016)	(.016)	(.016)	(.016)	(.016)
%nonwhite, squared	−.003***	−.003***	−.003***	−.003***	−.003***	−.003***
	(.0004)	(.0004)	(.0004)	(.0004)	(.0004)	(.0004)
%management	.241***	.256***	.291***	.256***	.225***	.198***
	(.049)	(.050)	(.049)	(.050)	(.048)	(.050)
%professional	.156**	.180***	.148**	.169**	.145**	.168**
	(.055)	(.055)	(.055)	(.056)	(.055)	(.055)
%construction and extraction	−.188***	−.177**	−.196***	−.206***	−.248***	−.194***
	(.058)	(.059)	(.058)	(.059)	(.061)	(.059)
%production workers	−.038	−.027	−.039	−.037	−.056	−.045
	(.032)	(.032)	(.031)	(.032)	(.031)	(.031)
%women with bachelor's degree	−.593***	−.561***	−.575***	−.609***	−.653***	−.603***
	(.041)	(.043)	(.041)	(.043)	(.041)	(.041)
%nonwhite with bachelor's degree	−.039**	−.034*	−.035*	−.036**	−.043**	−.039**
	(.014)	(.014)	(.014)	(.014)	(.014)	(.014)
Residential mobility	.160***	.157***	.156***	.161***	.166***	.162***
	(.027)	(.027)	(.027)	(.027)	(.027)	(.027)
Sex segregation × women labor force	.967***					
	(.249)					
Sex segregation × women with degree		.967***				
		(.224)				
Sex segregation × residential mobility			1.132***			
			(.194)			

Sex segregation × professional					.892**	
					(.339)	
Sex segregation × construction						.733
						(.456)
Sex segregation × production						−.853***
						(.211)
Control variables:						
Republican partisanship	3.844***	3.805***	3.844***	3.842***	3.885***	3.859***
	(.084)	(.084)	(.084)	(.085)	(.084)	(.085)
Unemployment, 2004	−.775***	−.779***	−.786***	−.812***	−.804***	−.800***
	(.097)	(.096)	(.099)	(.097)	(.097)	(.097)
Log of population density	−1.250***	−1.222***	−1.129***	−1.232***	−1.310***	−1.204***
	(.127)	(.129)	(.127)	(.128)	(.128)	(.130)
Median family income	.182***	.184***	.147***	.170***	.170***	.174***
	(.027)	(.028)	(.027)	(.027)	(.027)	(.027)
Income inequality	.016	.000	.017	.002	.014	.011
	(.049)	(.050)	(.050)	(.050)	(.050)	(.050)
%Evangelical	.068***	.067***	.064***	.066***	.065***	.065***
	(.009)	(.009)	(.009)	(.009)	(.009)	(.009)
%Catholic	−.049***	−.049***	−.049***	−.049***	−.049***	−.050***
	(.010)	(.009)	(.009)	(.009)	(.010)	(.010)
%married	.214***	.198***	.217***	.214***	.229***	.224***
	(.032)	(.032)	(.031)	(.032)	(.032)	(.032)
%part-time	.023	.029	.054	.043	.040	.032
	(.028)	(.028)	(.028)	(.028)	(.028)	(.028)
Median age	−.338***	−.326***	−.351***	−.317***	−.301***	−.303***
	(.044)	(.043)	(.044)	(.044)	(.043)	(.044)
Exposure CBSA sex segregation	11.075***	10.623***	10.396***	9.564***	8.626***	8.817***
	(2.515)	(2.488)	(2.457)	(2.474)	(2.484)	(2.541)
R^2	.868	.869	.870	.868	.868	.868

Note: Fixed effects estimates with controls for state-level effects (robust SE's in parentheses).
* $P < .05$.
** $P < .01$.
*** $P < .001$.

Source: McVeigh, Rory and Julianna M. Sobolewski. 2007. "Red Counties, Blue Counties, and Occupational Segregation by Sex and Race." *American Journal of Sociology*, 113: 446–506.

The interaction we focus on is circled in green in Literature Excerpt 11.2a. The conditional effects of the two variables in the interaction are circled in black. One is a measure of horizontal inequality (occupational sex segregation) which the authors measure by the *index of dissimilarity* in the county. The variable can range from zero to 1 and represents the "proportion of either men or women who would have to change occupations to produce a distribution where sex is completely uncorrelated with occupational categories" (p. 465). The other variable in the interaction is a variable that they view as a potential threat to occupational sex segregation: the percentage of the county's women who are in the labor force. The outcome is the percentage voting Republican among those who voted in the 2004 presidential election in the county.

The results reveal a positive and significant interaction (indicated by asterisks on 0.967). As noted, the authors centered the variables at their means before creating the product terms. So, when sex segregation is at its mean level, the percentage of women in the labor force is unrelated to voting Republican (−0.001). In contrast, the conditional effect of occupational sex segregation on voting when female labor force participation is at its mean level is significant (13.927 with asterisks). Scanning the table, this coefficient estimate appears quite large relative to the other values, but recall that occupational sex segregation ranges from zero to 1. Thus, this estimate indicates that when sex segregation changes from its minimum to maximum value in counties with average female labor force participation, the percentage voting Republican increases by 14 points, controlling for numerous other characteristics of the counties.

The authors' Figure 2, shown in Literature Excerpt 11.2b, presents conditional effects of occupational sex segregation within three levels of female labor for participation: 45 percent, 55 percent and 65 percent. Among counties with the greatest threat (65 percent women in the labor force) the figure

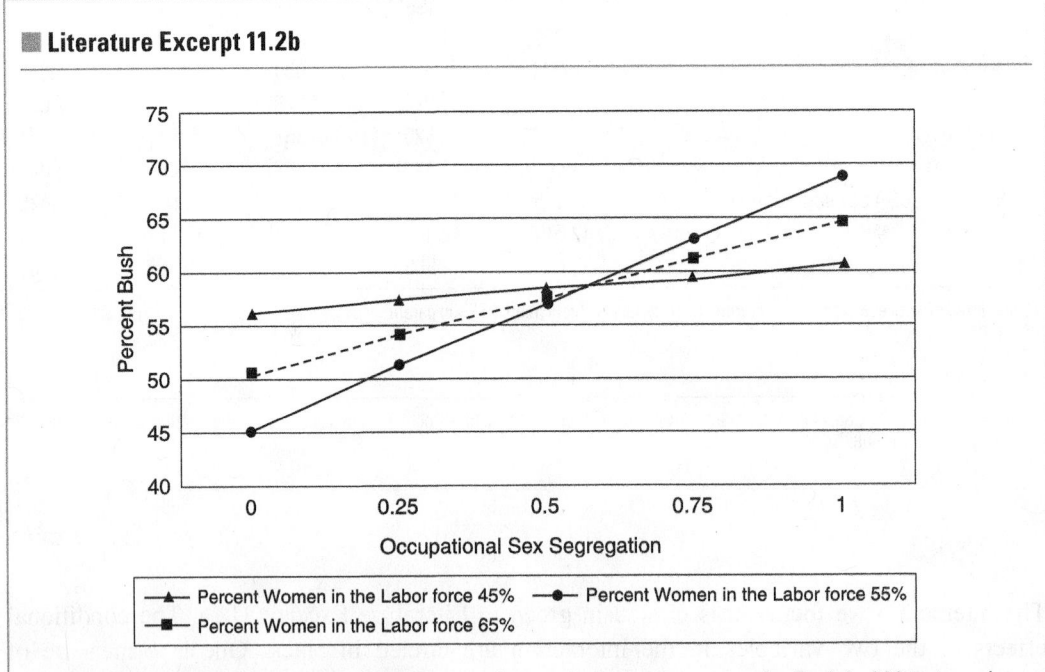

Literature Excerpt 11.2b

Figure 2 The effect of occupational sex segregation on the percentage vote for Bush in 2004 at varying levels of percentage women in the labor force

Source: McVeigh, Rory and Julianna M. Sobolewski. 2007. "Red Counties, Blue Counties, and Occupational Segregation by Sex and Race." *American Journal of Sociology,* 113: 446–506.

shows that moving from the minimal to the maximal level of sex segregation is associated with nearly a 25 point increase in the percentage of the counties' voters who voted Republican. In contrast, among counties with the lowest threat (45 percent women in the labor force) the increase in Republican voting associated with maximal change in sex segregation is less than 5 points.[14]

11.7: SUMMARY

In this chapter, we showed how to estimate and interpret interactions. Adding interactions to regression models allows us to test for moderation effects anticipated in our conceptual models. Estimating interactions is important to correctly specifying regression models. Depending on the form of the interaction, effects estimated on the full sample may understate, overstate, or fully mask the conditional effects within levels of the other variable.

Although we looked separately in the chapter at interactions between two dummy, a dummy and interval, and two interval variables, all follow a similar process of adding a product term to the regression model to capture the interaction. A significant coefficient estimate on the product term indicates statistical evidence for moderation. Calculating conditional effects (the association between one variable and the outcome within levels of the other variable) facilitates interpretation of the significant interaction. Three approaches can be used to test the significance of these conditional effects: (a) re-estimating the model after excluding a different reference category on a dummy variable or after recentering an interval variable, (b) using the general linear F-test, or (c) testing the linear combination of coefficients. Stata's `lincom` command provides an easy way to implement the third approach, and obtain all the information needed after a single estimation (the estimate, standard error, and significance of each conditional effect). We also used Excel to calculate predicted values and graph the conditional effects, and to calculate partially and fully standardized conditional effects. Such graphs and calculations are vital to the substantive interpretation of statistically significant effects. Finally, we showed how to estimate a fully interacted model and use the Chow test to examine whether an entire regression model differs within groups.

KEY TERMS

Chow Test

Conditional Effect(s)

Fully Interacted Model

Interaction(s)

Magnitude of (the) Effect (also weaker and stronger)

Product Term

SUMMARY 11

KEY TERMS 11

REVIEW QUESTIONS

11.1 For dummy*dummy interaction models:

(a) What is the difference between the conditional means and the conditional effects?

(b) How do you write each conditional effect based on the general regression equation and/or the prediction equation?

(c) How do you interpret each coefficient in the model (the values that you would see in the default SAS and Stata output), including the intercept?

(d) How would your results change if you used a different reference category on one or both dummy variables?

11.2 For dummy*interval interaction models:

(a) In a basic model, with one interval predictor (X), one dummy predictor (D), and the product term of the dummy times the interval predictor (D*X), how would you interpret the intercept and three variables' coefficients?

(b) How would you write the conditional regression equations for this model within the two levels of the dummy variable?

(c) How would you write the conditional regression equations for this model within levels of the interval predictor variable?

(d) What would be the null and alternative hypotheses, and the corresponding reduced and full models, for the Chow test based on this model?

(e) What would you expect the results to be if you reverse coded the dummy variable, omitting the category that had previously been coded "1", created a new interaction term based on this new reverse coded dummy, and re-estimated the model with the new dummy and new interaction term?

11.3 For interval*interval interaction models:

(a) How do you interpret the coefficients in a model with an interaction between two interval variables (the intercept, the coefficient for each of the predictor variables and the coefficient on the product term)?

(b) How would you write conditional regression equations (holding one variable constant at a particular value) based on the interval by interval interaction model?

REVIEW EXERCISES

11.1 Consider the research question: "Greater job stress is associated with harsher parenting, but this association weakens with each additional increment of social support received from family and friends." How would you set up a regression model to examine this research question?

11.2 Imagine that you hypothesize that the racial gap in earnings is smaller for women than for men (that is, the difference in average earnings between African Americans and whites is smaller for women than for men). You estimate the following prediction equation:

EARNINGS = 35,000 − 15,000 * FEMALE − 10,000 * AFRAMER + 10,000 * FEMALE * AFRAMER

in which FEMALE is coded "0" for men and "1" for women and AFRAMER is coded "0" for whites and "1" for African Americans.

(a) What are the estimates of the racial earnings gap for men and women based on this model (i.e., hint: write the conditional regression equations, holding gender constant at zero and one, and indicate the coefficient for AFRAMER in these equations).

(b) Calculate the four conditional means based on this prediction equation.

11.3 Suppose that you hypothesize that earnings is explained by a person's education level (EDUC, years of schooling) and experience (EXPER, years in the occupation) but that this regression model differs for men and women (FEMALE, 0 = men, 1 = women).

(a) Write the general equation for a fully interacted model that would test this hypothesis.

(b) Write the null and alternative hypotheses for the Chow test based on this fully interacted model.

(c) Write the reduced model that results from placing the constraints of the null hypothesis on the full model.

11.4 Refer to Model 2 in Literature Excerpt 11.2a. Note that the author's measure *% women with bachelor's degree* is: "a measure of the percentage of women ages 25 or older who have earned a bachelor's degree (including those who have also earned a graduate or professional degree" (p. 467).

(a) Interpret the coefficient estimate for *Occupational sex segregation* in Model 2.

(b) Interpret the coefficient estimate for *% women with bachelor's degree* in Model 2.

(c) Interpret the coefficient estimate for *Sex segregation × women with degree* in Model 2.

(d) Calculate the conditional effect of *Occupational sex segregation* when *% women with bachelor's degree* is 10 and 30 (recall that the variables in the interaction are centered; note that the mean of *% women with bachelor's degree* is 16.06).

11.5 Based on the two regression models shown below, do the following:

(a) Statistically compare Model 1 and Model 2 using the Chow test (use a cutoff of $F = 2.22$ for a significant test at alpha = 0.05). *Be sure to list the null and alternative hypotheses for the test.*

(b) Write the prediction equation based on Model 2. You may round all coefficients to two nonzero decimal places (e.g., round 0.00034561 to 0.00035).

(c) Based on the prediction equation that you wrote out in Question 11.5b, write the conditional regression equations for married and unmarried persons based on Model 2. You may round all coefficients to two nonzero decimal places (e.g., round 0.00034561 to 0.00035).

(d) Based on the results of Model 2, which coefficients in the conditional equations you wrote in Question 11.5c differ significantly for married versus unmarried persons? Justify your response by writing the relevant *t*-values and/or *p*-values (use a cutoff alpha of 0.05). Be sure to consider the intercept as well as the four predictor variables.

DEPRESS	Depression scale (ranging from 0 to 105)
REDUC	Respondent's education level (ranging from 0 to 20)
REARNINC	Respondent's annual earned income (ranging from $1 to $800,000)
HRWORK	Respondent's hours spent at paid work/week (ranging from 1 to 95)
NUMKID	Number of persons <=18 in the household (ranging from 0 to 10)
MARRY	Dummy indicator of respondent's marital status (1 = married, 0 = not married)
MRY_EDUC	Product of MARRY*REDUC
MRY_EARN	Product of MARRY*REARNINC
MRY_HRWK	Product of MARRY*HRWORK
MRY_NUMK	Product of MARRY*NUMKID

Model 1

```
. regress depress reduc rearninc hrwork numkid
```

Source	SS	df	MS		Number of obs	= 5320
					F(4, 5315)	= 28.99
Model	33076.9637	4	8269.24092		Prob > F	= 0.0000
Residual	1515927.29	5315	285.216799		R-squared	= 0.0214
					Adj R-squared	= 0.0206
Total	1549004.25	5319	291.220954		Root MSE	= 16.888

depress	Coef.	Std. Err.	t	P>|t|	[95% Conf.	Interval]
reduc	-.4999201	.0968659	-5.16	0.000	-.6898171	-.3100231
rearninc	-.0000506	8.40e-06	-6.03	0.000	-.0000671	-.0000342
hrwork	-.0078686	.0180722	-0.44	0.663	-.0432975	.0275603
numkid	.6742838	.1959539	3.44	0.001	.2901337	1.058434
_cons	23.72232	1.517835	15.63	0.000	20.74674	26.6979

Model 2

```
. regress depress reduc rearninc hrwork numkid marry mry_reduc mry_
earn mry_hrwk mry_numk
```

Source		SS	df	MS
Model		64439.3136	9	7159.92374
Residual		1484564.94	5310	279.579084
Total		1549004.25	5319	291.220954

```
Number of obs  = 5320
F(9, 5310)     = 25.61
Prob > F       = 0.0000
R-squared      = 0.0416
Adj R-squared  = 0.0400
Root MSE       = 16.721
```

depress		Coef.	Std. Err.	t	P>|t|	[95% Conf.	Interval]
reduc		−.2655434	.160663	−1.65	0.098	−.5805089	.0494222
rearninc		−.0000641	.0000134	−4.77	0.000	−.0000904	−.0000378
hrwork		−.012559	.0293056	−0.43	0.668	−.0700101	.0448921
numkid		1.862119	.3300898	5.64	0.000	1.215007	2.509231
marry		−.5102804	3.130079	−0.16	0.871	−6.64652	5.62596
mry_reduc		−.2853036	.2009015	−1.42	0.156	−.679153	.1085458
mry_earn		.0000308	.0000172	1.80	0.073	−2.83e−06	.0000644
mry_hrwk		.0043745	.0370308	0.12	0.906	−.0682211	.0769701
mry_numk		−1.46112	.4100886	−3.56	0.000	−2.265062	−.6571779
_cons		23.00074	2.479346	9.28	0.000	18.1402	27.86128

CHAPTER EXERCISE

CHAPTER
EXERCISE

11

In this exercise, you will write a SAS and a Stata batch program to estimate a multiple regression model, with interactions.

Again, use the NHIS 1999 data set with an *if expression* to only keep cases that do not have missing values on the *age, exfreqwR, bmiR, SEX, HISPAN_I* and *RACERPI2* variables.

In all cases, conduct two-sided hypothesis tests. Use a 5% alpha unless otherwise indicated.

11.1 Interaction Between Two Dummy Variables

a) SAS/Stata Tasks:

i) Create a dummy variable to indicate persons of Hispanic ancestry who are of any race-ethnicity.

ii) Create a dummy variable to indicate women.

iii) Create a product term interacting the dummy variables for *women* and for *Hispanic* persons.

iv) Calculate the mean of *bmiR* for each of the four sub-groups created by the two dummies (i.e., Hispanic/female, not Hispanic/female, Hispanic/male, not Hispanic/male). We will refer to these results as *Summarize #1* in the write-up.

 v) Regress *bmiR* on the two dummy variables (we will refer to this additive model as *Regression #1* in the Write-Up Tasks).

 vi) Regress *bmiR* on the two dummy variables and the product term (we will refer to this interaction model as *Regression #2* in the Write-Up Tasks).

  (1) Use the Stata lincom command to test the conditional effect of being *Hispanic* for women (we will refer to this lincom command as *Test #1* in the Write-Up Tasks).

  (2) Use the Stata lincom command to test the conditional effect of being *a woman* for Hispanic persons (we will refer to this lincom command as *Test #2* in the Write-Up Tasks).

b) Write-Up Tasks.

 i) Write the prediction equation for Regression #2. Calculate the four possible conditional means for Regression #2 by hand (Show your work!). Discuss how these means relate the results from Summarize #1.

 ii) Write the prediction equation for Regression #1. Calculate the four possible conditional means for Regression #1 by hand (Show your work!). Discuss how these means relate the results from Summarize #1.

 iii) Interpret the intercept, each dummy variable coefficient, and the product term in Regression #2. Which differ significantly from zero (annotate or list the relevant *t*- and *p*-values to identify how you are making your conclusions)?

 iv) Interpret the coefficients estimated in Test #1 and Test #2. Which differ significantly from zero (annotate or list the relevant *t*- and *p*-values to indicate how you are making your conclusions)?

 v) Show how to calculate the coefficients in Regression #2 and the coefficients estimated in Test #1 and Test #2 by hand using the results from Summarize #1.

11.2 Interaction Between a Dummy and Interval Variable

a) SAS/Stata Tasks.

 i) Create a product term interacting the dummy variable indicating *women* with the variable capturing *age*.

 ii) Regress *bmiR* on the *female* dummy, the *age* variable, and their interaction (we will refer to this interaction model as *Regression #3* in the Write-Up Tasks).

(1) Use the SAS and Stata `test` commands to conduct a Chow test that the intercept and slope for the association of *age* with *bmiR* differs for women and men (we will refer to this `test` command as *Test #3* in the Write-Up Tasks).

(2) Use the Stata `lincom` command to calculate the conditional slope of *age* for women (we will refer to this `lincom` command as *Test #4* in the Write-Up Tasks).

(3) Use the Stata `lincom` command to calculate the conditional effect of *being female* for persons age 30, age 40, and age 50 (we will refer to this `lincom` command as *Test #5* in the Write-Up Tasks).

iii) Regress *bmiR* on the *age* variable (we will refer to this as *Regression #4* in the Write-Up Tasks).

b) Write-Up Tasks.

i) Use Regression #3 and Regression #4 to calculate the *F*-value by hand for the Chow test that you asked SAS and Stata to conduct in Test #3. Verify that the value matches the value that you obtained from SAS and Stata. Write the null and alternative hypotheses for this test and make a conclusion using the SAS or Stata output (annotate or list the relevant *F* and *p*-values to indicate how you are making your conclusions).

ii) Calculate by hand the coefficient for the test that you asked Stata to conduct in Test #4.

iii) Calculate by hand the coefficients for the tests that you asked Stata to conduct in Test #5.

11.3 Interaction Between Two Interval Variables

a) SAS/Stata Tasks.

i) Create a product term interacting the *age* variable and the *exfreqwR* variable.

ii) Regress *bmiR* on the *age* variable, the *exfreqwR* variable, and their interaction (we will refer to this interaction model as *Regression #5* in the Write-Up Tasks).

(1) Use the Stata `lincom` command to calculate the conditional effects of *age* for people who exercise 0, 3, and 7 times per week (we will refer to this `lincom` command as *Test #6* in the Write-Up Tasks).

(2) Use the Stata `lincom` command to calculate the conditional effects of *exfreqwR* for people who are 30, 40 and 50 years old (we will refer to this `lincom` command as *Test #7* in the Write-Up Tasks).

b) Write-Up Tasks.

i) Based on the parameter estimates in Regression #5, is there evidence of an interaction between *age* and *exfreqwR* in predicting *bmiR*? Justify your response by stating the null and alternative hypotheses and the *t*-value and/or *p*-value.

ii) Calculate by hand the coefficients for the tests that you asked Stata to conduct in Test #6.

iii) Calculate by hand the coefficients for the tests that you asked Stata to conduct in Test #7.

COURSE EXERCISE

COURSE EXERCISE 11

Identify at least one interaction model that you might estimate, based on the data set that you created in the course exercise to Chapter 4. Ideally, think about conceptual reasons why you might expect interactions between some of the dummy and/or interval variables available in the data set. Alternatively, choose a few variables and explore whether interactions are identified empirically in the data set.

Create the product term between the two variables in your interaction. Estimate the interaction model, including both the variables and their interaction. Refer to the sections of the chapter summarizing how to interpret the coefficients based on each type of model, and write a one-sentence interpretation of each coefficient. Use the strategies outlined in the chapter to calculate and test the significance of conditional effects, depending on the types of variable in your model (dummy and/or interval). Follow the steps outlined in Appendices H.11.1 to H.11.4 to graph the results. Discuss whether the conditional effects that you graph are statistically significant and substantively meaningful.

Chapter 12

NONLINEAR RELATIONSHIPS

CHAPTER 12: NONLINEAR RELATIONSHIPS

To date, we have assumed that the association between an interval predictor variable and the outcome is linear. A one-unit increase in the predictor results in the same change in the outcome across all levels of the predictor. A nonlinear relationship, in contrast, allows the effect of the predictor to differ at different starting values. For example, the difference in school achievement may be greater between families with $11,000 and $10,000 annual incomes than families with $101,000 and $100,000 annual incomes. In this chapter we present techniques for modeling nonlinear relationships between the predictor and outcome within the context of OLS estimation and demonstrate how to use various nonlinear shapes to match our conceptual models. In Part 4 and Chapter 18, we will discuss additional strategies for modeling nonlinear relationships, outside of OLS.

12.1: NONLINEAR RELATIONSHIPS

12.1.1: Some Possible Shapes of Nonlinear Relationships

We will discuss three of the most common approaches to modeling nonlinear relationships within OLS in the social sciences (see Box 12.1):

(a) transforming X or Y using natural logs;[1]
(b) using a quadratic form of X;
(c) using dummy variables for X.

Figure 12.1 illustrates some possible nonlinear shapes associating X and Y. Notice that in the middle and bottom figures, the steepness of the slope varies, but it never changes sign, across the levels of X. In the middle two figures, the slope is always positive, and in the bottom two figures the slope is always negative. In contrast, in the top two figures, the slope reverses sign.

■ **Box 12.1**

We focus on these three because they are commonly used, but other transformations are possible. Some allow for an exploratory search for the best-fitting nonlinear curve associating a predictor with an outcome (e.g., developed by Box and Cox 1964 and Tukey 1977; see Fox 2008, for an introduction to transformations in general and their application in regression analysis). Other *spline* or *piecewise linear* models allow a linear relationship between the predictor and outcome that varies in steepness in different ranges of the predictor (Fox 2008; Gujarati 2003). These models can be quite useful in some contexts, but it is rare in the social sciences for theoretical models to suggest where the slopes would change, and the quadratic and logarithmic approaches are more commonly used.

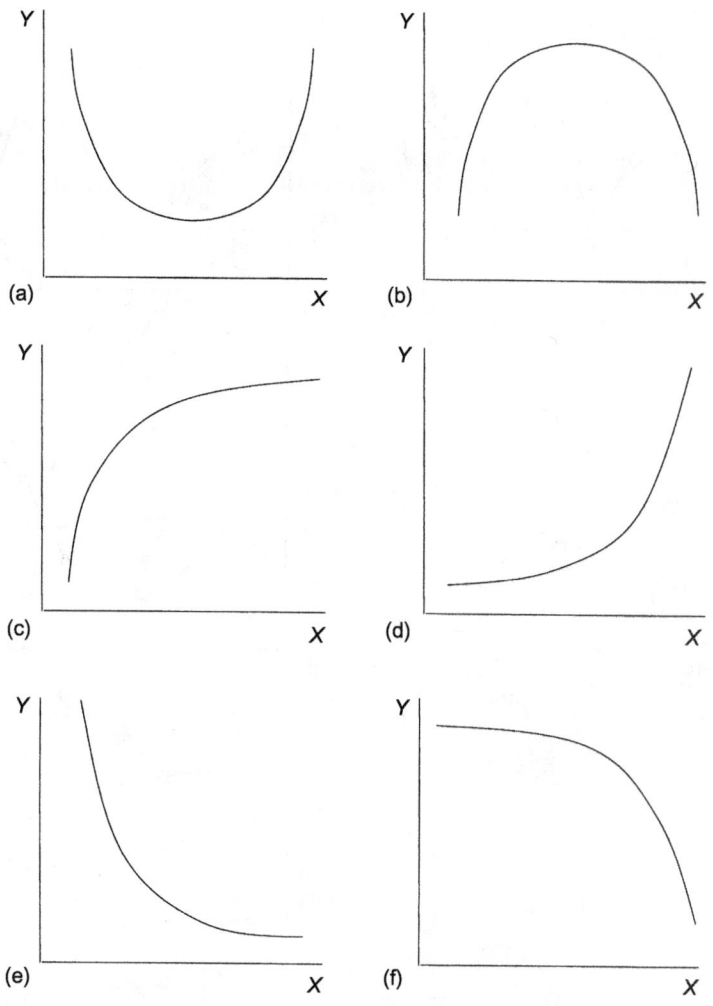

■ Figure 12.1 Some Possible Nonlinear Shapes Associating X with Y

In Figure 12.1(a), the slope starts out negative and then becomes positive. In Figure 12.1(b), the slope starts out positive and then becomes negative.

Figure 12.2 adds dashed lines drawn to just touch the curves at various points. These lines are referred to as **tangent lines**. They help us to visualize the slope at different levels of X. Starting in the bottom two figures, we see in Figure 12.2(e) that the slope begins steeply negative at lower values of X and then approaches zero at higher values of X. In contrast, in Figure 12.2(f), the slope begins near zero, and then becomes steeply negative. We refer to the association in Figure 12.2(e) as **decreasing at a decreasing rate** and the association in Figure 12.2(f) as **decreasing at an increasing rate**. In Figure 12.2(c), the slope begins steeply positive and then approaches zero. In Figure 12.2(d), the slope begins close to zero and then becomes steeply

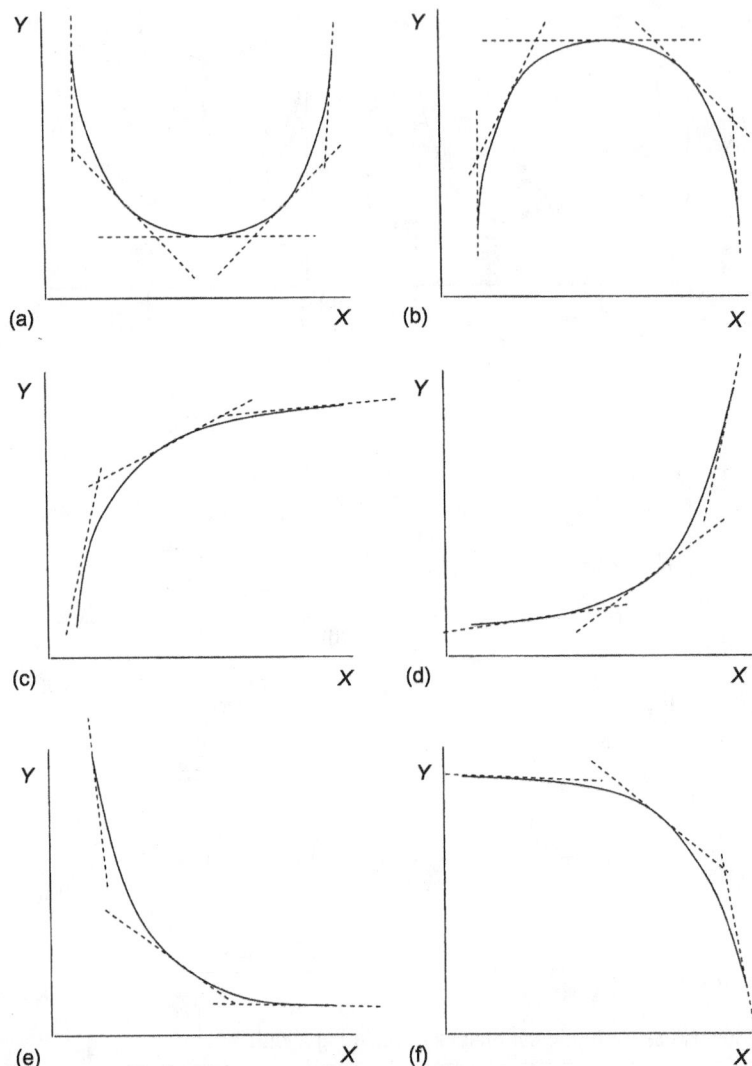

■ **Figure 12.2** Some Possible Nonlinear Shapes Associating *X* with *Y*. With Tangent Lines

positive. We refer to Figure 12.2(c) as **increasing at a decreasing rate** and Figure 12.2(d) as **increasing at an increasing rate**. The top two figures put together two of these types of association. In Figure 12.2(a), the association is decreasing at a decreasing rate at lower values of X and then increasing at an increasing rate at higher values of X. At some point in the middle, the slope becomes zero. In Figure 12.2(b), the association is increasing at a decreasing rate at lower values of X and decreasing at an increasing rate at higher values of X. At some point in the middle, the slope becomes zero.

We can imagine some substantive relationships that might produce shapes like those in Figure 12.2.

- In Figure 12.2(a), we might imagine associating financial or physical dependency as an outcome and age as a predictor. Children are quite dependent on adults for their physical needs, especially when very young. With the transition to adulthood, they become able to provide for their own needs. Then, with old age, they become increasingly dependent on others.
- In Figure 12.2(b), we could envision an association between income and age. Children have little personal income, especially during preschool and school age. As they move through adolescence and into adulthood, they begin to produce some earnings. At some point in middle age, their incomes peak and then begin to decline as they retire and enter old age.
- In Figure 12.2(c), we might think of predicting a positive developmental outcome (such as reading comprehension) based on family income. We might imagine that each increment to income associates more strongly with increased reading comprehension among lower than higher income families. At higher income levels, additional income may have very little association with reading comprehension.
- In Figure 12.2(e), we might similarly imagine associating a negative developmental outcome (such as problem behaviors) with family income. We might imagine that each increment to income associates more strongly with decreased problem behaviors among lower-income families. At higher-income levels, additional income may have very little association with behavior problems.
- In Figure 12.2(d), we can imagine associating earnings as the outcome with education as a predictor. We might expect that returns to education are larger at higher education levels (e.g., that the increment to earnings for adults with one additional year of graduate school is larger than the increment to earnings for adults with one additional year of high school).
- In Figure 12.2(f), we might imagine a negative association of health behavior, such as smoking or eating processed foods, with education, expecting that these behaviors might diminish more rapidly at higher than at lower levels of education.

Each of the graphs in Figure 12.2 shows a smooth relationship between X and Y. We might also have conceptual models that suggest nonlinear associations that are not smooth. For example, consider the example of returns to education that we posed for Figure 12.2(d). Rather than a smoothly increasing association between education and earnings, as shown in Figure 12.3(a), we might expect more of a stair-step type of association, as shown in Figure 12.3(b). Earnings may increase more with years of schooling associated with degree completion (e.g., from 11 to 12 and from 15 to 16) than those associated with one more year toward a degree (e.g., 10 to 11 and 14 to 15). Indeed, we might treat different categories of education as ordinal categories rather than interval numbers, like years of schooling.

12.1.2: Literature Excerpts

Four literature excerpts help to illuminate further how nonlinear associations might be used conceptually.[2]

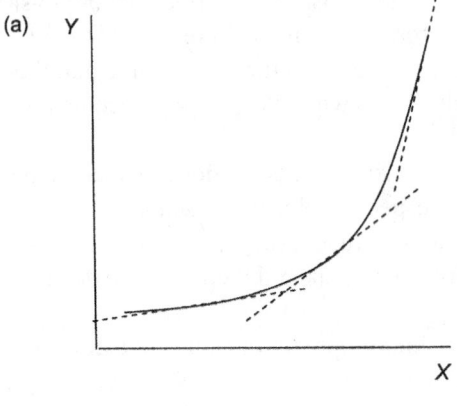

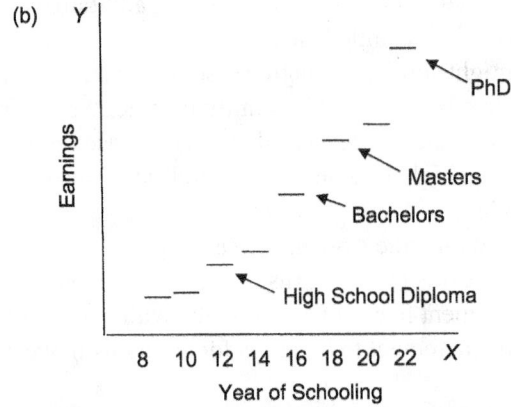

■ **Figure 12.3** Stair Step Nonlinear Relationship Between X and Y

Literature Excerpt 12.1: Age and Household Income

Andrea Willson (2003) examined the kind of age–income trajectory we conceptualized above, but focused particularly on women. She was interested in how women's income trajectories were influenced not only by their own employment but also by their marital status (which could give access to a husband's earnings and retirement benefits) and race. Her Figure 3, reproduced in Literature Excerpt 12.1, plots predicted values from a regression model that allows for a **curvilinear** association between age and household income. The plots show the predicted peak in income during middle age, with the association being especially curved for white married women who were always employed (top curve). In contrast, the association is slightly but less sharply curved for black women who were never married and not always employed (bottom curve). One of the conclusions from the figure is that income inequality is greatest in midlife and diminishes in older age (although as Willson points out, her outcome does not capture potential asset differentials in later life, which might reveal additional inequality in older age).

■ **Literature Excerpt 12.1**

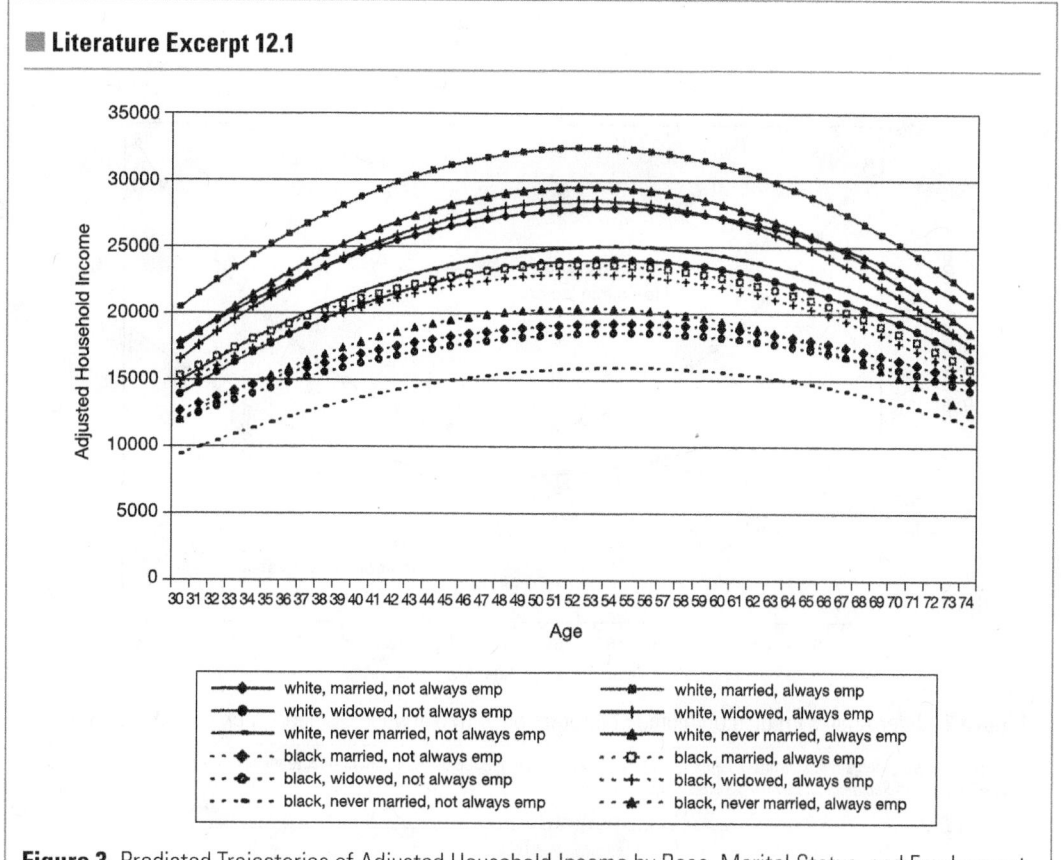

Figure 3 Predicted Trajectories of Adjusted Household Income by Race, Marital Status, and Employment Pattern

Source: Willson, Andrea E. 2003. "Race and Women's Income Trajectories: Employment, Marriage, and Income Security over the Life Course." *Social Problems*, 50: 87–110.

Literature Excerpt 12.2: Age and Social Contact

Cornwell, Laumann, and Schumm (2008) take up the often held notion that the elderly are socially isolated. As they note: "Contrary to the image of older adults as either helpless victims of modernization or authors of their own isolation, this line of research portrays older individuals as resilient to potentially isolating events like retirement and bereavement" (p. 186). Although they find that many associations with social connectedness are linear, they find that the association of age with the volume of contact with network members is curvilinear (see Literature Excerpt 12.2). They speculate about the reasons for the U-shaped pattern.

> Contact volume may decrease through the 50s and 60s because social roles begin to dissipate around this time. Contact volume is lowest for those in their late 60s and early 70s, but it may increase as respondents grow older and they adapt to the loss of social roles, friends, and family members (p. 193).

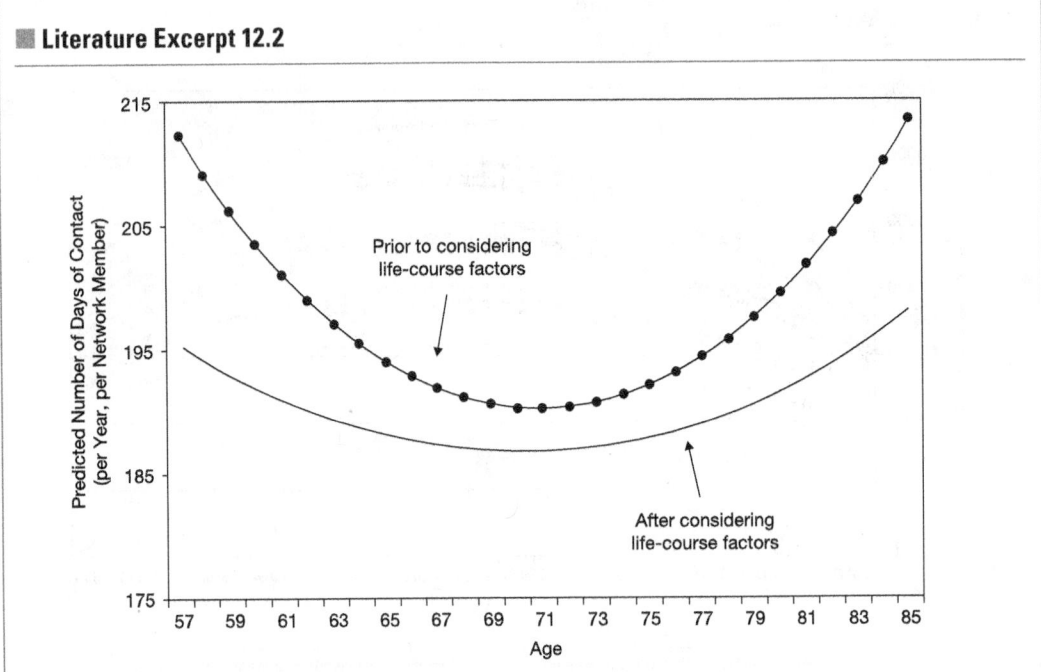

■ **Literature Excerpt 12.2**

Figure 2 Older Adult's Predicted Volume of Interaction with Network Members, per Year and by Age

Source: Cornwell, Benjamin, Edward O. Laumann, and L. Philip Schumm. 2008. "The Social Connectedness of Older Adults: A National Profile." *American Sociological Review*, 73: 185–203.

The authors note that their interpretation of this curvilinear association is speculative, since little prior conceptual and empirical work has anticipated or found such nonlinear relationships.

Literature Excerpt 12.3: Per Capita Income and Health

Pritchett and Summers (1996) consider the nonlinear way in which "wealthier is healthier" at the country level. Their Figure 1, reproduced in Literature Excerpt 12.3, shows that as per capita income increases, infant mortality declines and life expectancy increases, but these associations are particularly rapid at lower income levels. They interpret the association using techniques we will discuss below, noting that "The estimates imply that if income were 1 percent higher in the developing countries, as many as 33,000 infant and 53,000 child deaths would be averted annually" (p. 844).

Literature Excerpt 12.4: Number of Children and Women's Hourly Wage

Glauber (2007) examines the wage penalty associated with motherhood. She dummy-coded the number of children into five categories (grouping together women with four or more children), allowing for a relationship between children and hourly wage that could take any form, including

Literature Excerpt 12.3

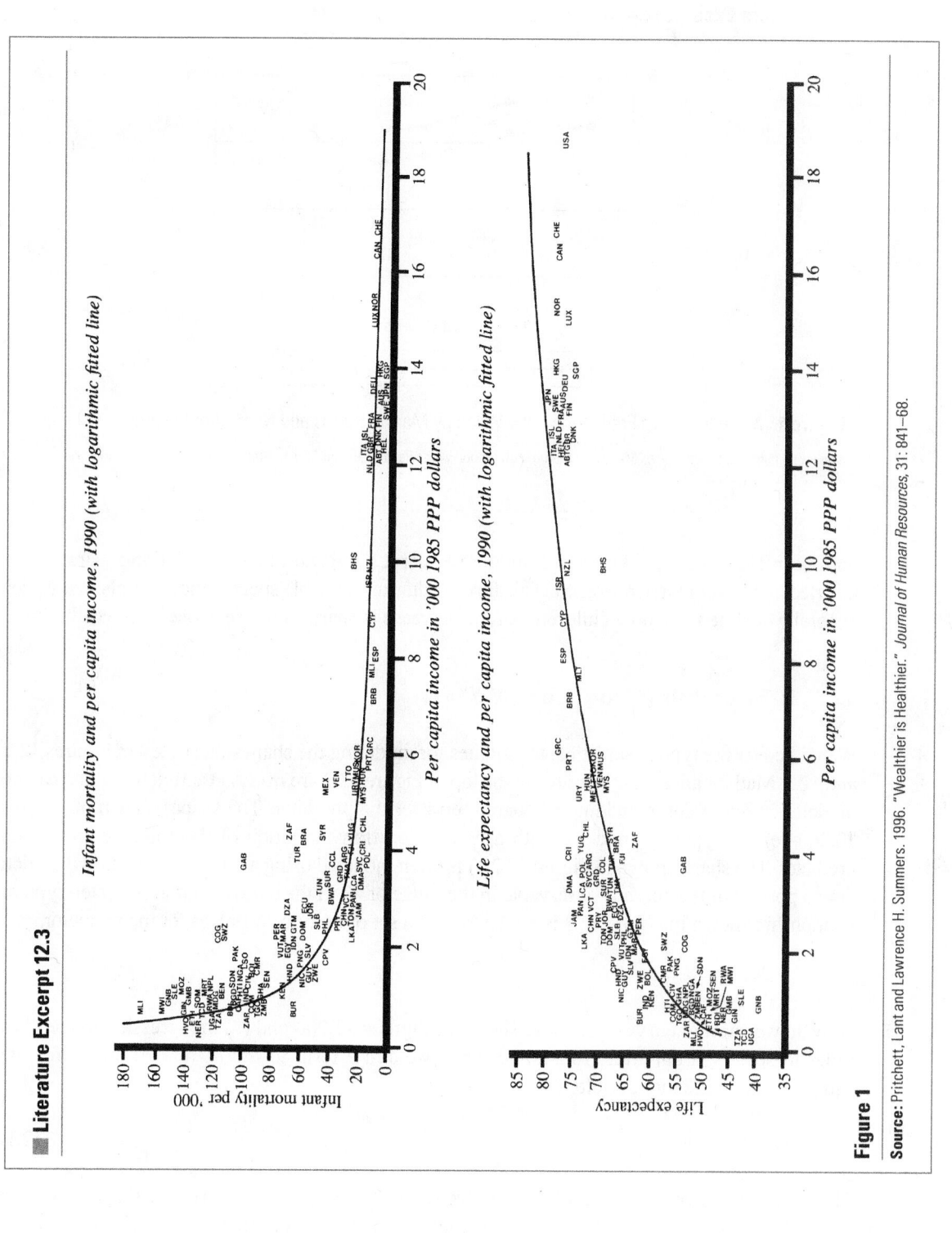

Figure 1

Source: Pritchett, Lant and Lawrence H. Summers. 1996. "Wealthier is Healthier." *Journal of Human Resources,* 31: 841–68.

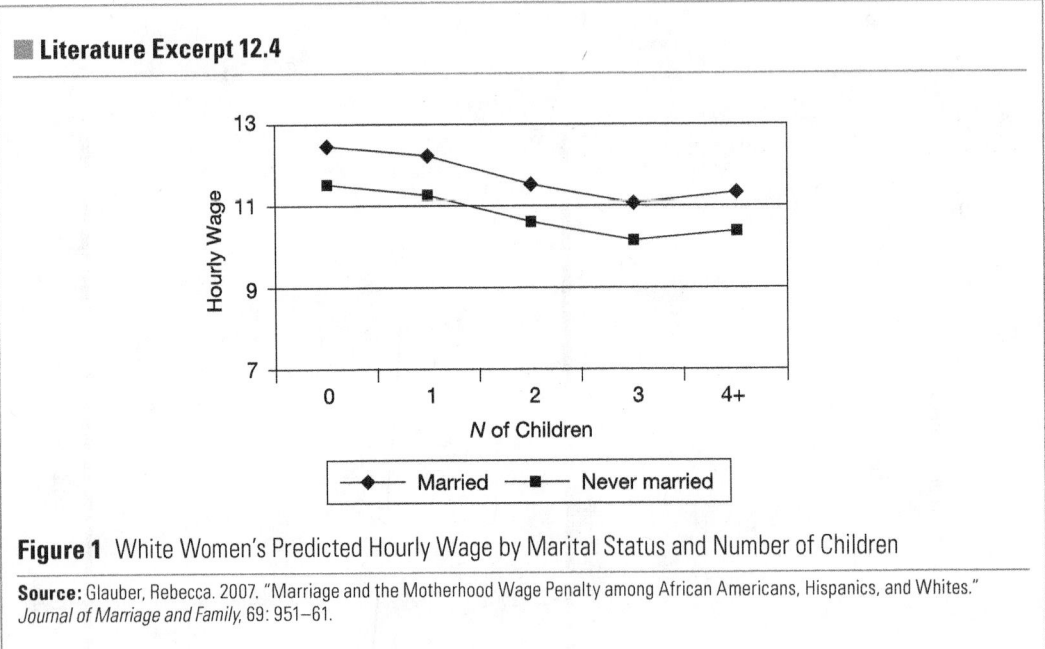

■ Literature Excerpt 12.4

Figure 1 White Women's Predicted Hourly Wage by Marital Status and Number of Children

Source: Glauber, Rebecca. 2007. "Marriage and the Motherhood Wage Penalty among African Americans, Hispanics, and Whites." *Journal of Marriage and Family*, 69: 951–61.

nonlinear. Her Figure 1, shown in Literature Excerpt 12.4, shows the association separately for married and never married women. This flexible dummy variable specification reveals that wages generally decline with more children, but the decrease is sharpest between one and two children.

12.1.3: Specifying Nonlinear Models

We will cover the typical statistical techniques for modeling the shapes illustrated in Figures 12.2 and 12.3. Mathematically, the figures in the top of Figure 12.2 are **quadratic** functions, and can be modeled in regression by adding a squared term for the predictor. The shapes shown in Figures 12.2(c)–(e) are typically modeled with a natural log transformation of the outcome and/or the predictor. The shape shown in Figure 12.2(f) is often modeled using a quadratic function in which only a portion of the curve is observable in the range of Xs in the data. And, the stair-step type of relationship shown in Figure 12.3 is modeled with a set of dummy variables for the predictor.

Quadratic Form

How do we capture curves like those shown in Figures 12.2(a) and (b) in regression models? In order to specify a quadratic functional form, we add a term to the regression model for the square of the predictor variable.

$$Y_i = \beta_0 + \beta_1 X_i + \beta_2 X_i^2 + \varepsilon_i \tag{12.1}$$

The U-shape shown in Figure 12.2(a) occurs when $\beta_2 > 0$ and the inverted U-shape shown in Figure 12.2(b) occurs when $\beta_2 < 0$. If $\beta_2 = 0$, then the model reduces to the linear functional form:

$$Y_i = \beta_0 + \beta_1 X_i + 0 * X_i^2 + \varepsilon_i$$
$$= \beta_0 + \beta_1 X_i + \varepsilon_i$$

This means that the linear model is nested within the quadratic model, and we can thus use a general linear F-test to test whether a quadratic form fits the data better than a linear form.

The value of X at which the slope becomes zero—the horizontal tangent lines in Figure 12.2—can be calculated using the formula $-\beta_1/2\beta_2$.[3] Calculating this point can be useful, to discern whether this point at which the slope changes direction is within the range of X values in the data set, or alternatively is to the left or to the right of the observed X values. Indeed, within applications, only a portion of the U or inverted-U may actually fit the data, such as in Figure 12.2(f).

As illustrated in Figure 12.2 and the examples, the slope is no longer constant in a regression model with a quadratic functional form. Thus, we can no longer make a general statement that a one-unit change in X is associated with a given expected change in Y. Indeed, clearly, it is possible for increases in X to be associated with decreases in Y over some range of the X values, to be associated with no change in Y at some point, and to be associated with increases in Y over another range of the X values. To illustrate these nonlinear relationships, it is often useful to calculate predicted values over the range of X in the sample and plot them, or to calculate predicted values at key values of X to display in a table or paper text. The slope at particular values of X can also be calculated using the equation $\beta_1 + 2\beta_2 X_i$.[4] Note that if $X_i = 0$, then this equation works to $\beta_1 + 2\beta_2 * 0 = \beta_1$. So, the coefficient for β_1 is the slope associating the predictor with the outcome when the predictor is zero. If zero is not a valid value on the predictor, then β_1 is not meaningful.

Logarithmic Transformation

The shapes in Figures 12.2(c)–(e) can be specified by taking the **natural log** of the outcome (12.2(c), 12.2(e)), predictor (12.2(d), 12.2(e)), or both (all three shapes).

With the **logarithmic transformations**, we model the linear association between the log of X and/or log of Y. We can then transform the coefficient estimates and predicted values back into the natural units of X and Y for interpretation, and reveal the nonlinear relationship between X and Y.

Models in which Y but not X is transformed are sometimes referred to as log-lin models (see Box 12.2). Similarly, models in which both Y and X are transformed are log-log models and models in which X but not Y is transformed are called lin-log models.

Percentage Change

To begin, let's firmly define four types of change: **absolute change, factor change, proportionate (or relative) change,** and **percentage change**. Factor change and percentage change are frequently used when interpreting models based on the

■ **Box 12.2**

This terminology for a model with a logged outcome in the regression context is especially common in economics, where such models are typical. In other fields, such as sociology, the term loglinear is often used for models of the cell frequencies in a contingency table.

logarithmic transformation in OLS. Recall that in the Literature Excerpt 12.3 we quoted the authors' interpretation of the effect, which referred to a 1 percent change rather than a one-unit change in the predictor. The following table provides general formulas and two examples for four types of change.

Type of Change	General Formula	Examples	
		$X_{new} = 102, X_{old} = 101$	$X_{new} = 2, X_{old} = 1$
Absolute	$X_{new} - X_{old}$	$102 - 101 = 1$	$2 - 1 = 1$
Factor	$\dfrac{X_{new}}{X_{old}}$	$\dfrac{102}{101} = 1.009901$	$\dfrac{2}{1} = 2$
Relative	$\dfrac{(X_{new} - X_{old})}{X_{old}}$	$\dfrac{(102-101)}{101} = 0.009901$	$\dfrac{(2-1)}{1} = 1$
Percentage	$\left[\dfrac{(X_{new} - X_{old})}{X_{old}}\right]*100$	$\left[\dfrac{(102-101)}{101}\right]*100 = 0.99\%$	$\left[\dfrac{(2-1)}{1}\right]*100 = 100\%$

Note that we wrote the table with Xs (change on predictor variables) but the results are the same for Ys (change on outcome variables).

The examples make clear that even when absolute change is the same for two different starting values (one unit of absolute change in our examples), factor, relative, and percentage change depend upon the starting value. In our example, an increase in 1 is a larger proportional change at smaller values of the variable (starting at 1) than at larger values of the variable (starting at 101).

Notice that relative and percentage change can be rewritten in terms of factor change.

Relative Change
$$\frac{(X_{new} - X_{old})}{X_{old}} = \frac{X_{new}}{X_{old}} - \frac{X_{old}}{X_{old}} = \frac{X_{new}}{X_{old}} - 1 = Factor\ Change - 1 \tag{12.2}$$

Percentage Change
$$\frac{X_{new} - X_{old}}{X_{old}}*100 = \left[\frac{X_{new}}{X_{old}} - \frac{X_{old}}{X_{old}}\right]*100 = \left[\frac{X_{new}}{X_{old}} - 1\right]*100 = (Factor\ Change - 1)*100 \tag{12.3}$$

Log-Lin Model
We write the log-lin regression model as follows:

$$\ln(Y_i) = \beta_0 + \beta_1 X_{1i} + \varepsilon_i \tag{12.4}$$

For interpretation, it is useful to exponentiate both sides of the equation resulting in:[5]

$$Y_i = \exp(\beta_0 + \beta_1 X_{1i} + \varepsilon_i) = e^{\beta_0 + \beta_1 X_{1i} + \varepsilon_i} \tag{12.5}$$

We write the prediction equation based on Equation 12.4 as $\widehat{\ln(Yi)} = \hat{\beta}_0 + \hat{\beta}_1 X_{1i}$. Thus, a prediction based on the estimated coefficients is in log Y units.

We need a few technical details to accurately transform these predictions back into the natural units of Y. It is intuitive to transform the predictions back to Y's natural units by taking the exponential of both sides of this prediction equation:

$$\hat{Y}_i = \exp(\hat{\beta}_0 + \hat{\beta}_1 X_{1i}) = e^{\beta_0 + \beta_1 X_{1i}} \tag{12.6}$$

But, if Y really follows a lognormal distribution, then it can be shown that the predicted values should in fact be adjusted for the estimate of the conditional variance (i.e., $\hat{\sigma}^2$ the mean square error; Greene 2008).

$$\hat{Y}_i = \exp(\hat{\sigma}^2/2)\exp(\hat{\beta}_0 + \hat{\beta}_1 X_{1i}) = e^{\hat{\sigma}^2/2} \, e^{\beta_0 + \beta_1 X_{1i}} \tag{12.7}$$

The larger the mean square error, the more this adjustment will affect the predictions.

Wooldridge (2009: 210–13) also recommends another adjustment which does not assume normality of the error terms:

$$\hat{Y}_i = \widehat{\exp(\varepsilon)}\exp(\hat{\beta}_0 + \hat{\beta}_1 X_{1i}) = \widehat{e^{(\varepsilon)}} e^{\beta_0 + \beta_1 X_{1i}} \tag{12.8}$$

where $\widehat{\exp(\varepsilon)}$ is estimated by calculating the residuals from Equation 12.4 and then exponentiating them and taking their average. This will produce a single value which is the estimate of $\widehat{\exp(\varepsilon)}$ that is used in adjusting the predictions for interpretation. We illustrate how to use this approach below.

Exact Interpretation of Coefficient

We can also examine change in predicted values as we did in earlier chapters to help us to interpret the coefficient estimates from the log-lin regression, although rather than considering the absolute change in the outcome, we will consider its factor changes (the ratio of predicted values rather than the difference in predicted values). The results are the same using either Equation 12.6, 12.7, or 12.8, so we will use the simpler 12.6. We substitute into the equation the generic notation for $X_1 = X$ and $X_1 = X + 1$ to denote a one-unit increase in X and rewrite the results using the laws of exponents.[6]

■ **Table 12.1: Expected Values at Two Levels of X**

$E(Y \mid X_1 = X + 1)$	$\exp(\beta_0 + \beta_1 (X + 1))$	$\exp(\beta_0 + \beta_1 X + \beta_1)$	$\exp(\beta_0)\exp(\beta_1 X)\exp(\beta_1)$
$E(Y \mid X_1 = X)$	$\exp(\beta_0 + \beta_1 X)$	$\exp(\beta_0 + \beta_1 X)$	$\exp(\beta_0)\exp(\beta_1 X)$

We can now calculate the factor change in the expected value: the ratio of the predicted value when X is incremented by 1 over the predicted value when X is at its original value.

$$\frac{E(Y|X_1 = X+1)}{E(Y|X_1 = X)} = \frac{\exp(\beta_0)\exp(\beta_1 X)\exp(\beta_1)}{\exp(\beta_0)\exp(\beta_1 X)} = \exp(\beta_1)$$

We can rewrite the final expression as follows:

$$E(Y|X_1 = X + 1) = \exp(\beta_1) * E(Y|X_1 = X)$$

This makes it clear that taking the exponential of the slope coefficients gives us the factor by which Y is expected to change, when X increases by 1. For example, if $\exp(\beta_1) = 1.25$, then we would say "Y is expected to be 1.25 times larger when X increases by 1." Thus, for the log-lin model, we can concisely interpret the nonlinear relationship between X and Y in terms of the factor change. It is sometimes convenient also to convert this factor change to relative or percentage change. Using Equations 12.2 and 12.3, relative change would be $\exp(\beta_1) - 1$ and percentage change would be $[\exp(\beta_1) - 1] * 100$. So, our factor change of 1.25 would be a relative change of 0.25 and a percentage change of 25 percent. We could say "Y is expected to be 25 percent larger when X increases by 1."

It is straightforward to show that the interpretation of the effect of a dummy variable is similar. For the model $\ln(Y_i) = \beta_0 + \beta_1 X_{1i} + \beta_2 D_{1i} + \varepsilon_i$, taking the exponential of β_2 gives the factor by which Y is expected to differ for cases indicated by $D_1 = 1$ versus cases indicated by $D_1 = 0$, holding X_1 constant. Subtracting 1 from this exponentiated value, and multiplying by 100, gives us the percentage by which cases indicated by $D_1 = 1$ differ on Y from cases coded $D_1 = 0$, holding X_1 constant.

In log-lin models, absolute change does not reduce to such a concise interpretation. For example based an Equation 12.6:

$$E(Y|X_1 = X + 1) - E(Y|X_1 = X) = [\exp(\beta_0)\exp(\beta_1 X)\exp(\beta_1)] - [\exp(\beta_0)\exp(\beta_1 X)]$$

To interpret the absolute change requires calculating predicted values for specific values of X and summarizing these various values in the text, a table, or a graph.

Approximate Interpretation of Coefficient

In publications, you may sometimes see authors interpret the coefficient estimate from a log-lin regression model as relative change, without exponentiating the value and subtracting one. This approximation holds when the coefficient estimate is small and the change in X is small. However, as is seen in the table below, clearly this approximation is adequate only for small coefficients and with today's computing power it is easy to make the exact calculations.

Value of Coefficient	Percentage Change Interpretation (%)	
β_1	Exact $[(\exp(\beta_1) - 1)]*100$	Approximate β_1*100
.05	5.13	5
.10	10.52	10
.25	29.40	25
.50	64.87	50
1.00	171.83	100

Log-Log and Lin-Log Models

In some models, we may also transform an interval *predictor* variable by taking its log.

lin-log $\quad Y_i = \beta_0 + \beta_1 \ln(X_{1i}) + \varepsilon_i$

log-log $\quad \ln(Y_i) = \beta_0 + \beta_1 \ln(X_{1i}) + \varepsilon_i$

One approach to interpretation for these models uses the same kind of approximation that we discussed for the log-lin model.

1. In log-log models, the coefficient for the logged predictor β_1 can be interpreted *approximately* as: a 1 percent increase in X is associated with a β_1 percent change in Y, all else constant.
2. In lin-log models, the coefficient for the logged predictor β_1 can be interpreted *approximately* as: a 1 percent increase in X is associated with a $\beta_1/100$ change in Y, all else constant.

The first interpretation above is used frequently in economics, and in subfields of other disciplines that intersect with economics. The effect of a 1 percent change in X on the percent change in Y captures elasticity, a central concept in economics. In addition, wages and incomes are typically positive values with a right skew and often become closer to the normal distribution with a log transformation. A recent paper published in the *American Journal of Sociology* provides an example. Sharkey (2008: 950–1) writes:

> Table 2 contains results from the basic model of intergenerational mobility, where the log of the average neighborhood income of parents predicts the log of average neighborhood income of children as adults. Under ordinary least squares (OLS), the intergenerational elasticity is .64 meaning a 1 percent change in the parent's neighborhood income is associated with a .64 percent change in the child's neighborhood income as an adult.

Alternatively, the results of log-log and lin-log models can be interpreted using predicted values. In log-log models, the values of X must be transformed into $ln(X)$ before making the predictions and the predicted values must be transformed back into the original units by taking the exponential of the predicted values (and adjusted, as shown in Equations 12.7 or 12.8). In lin-log models, the values of X must be transformed into $ln(X)$ before making the predictions, but the predicted values will be in the natural units of Y.

Dummy Variables

Dummy variables can be used to model an association between an interval or ordinal predictor and the outcome, allowing for a flexible relationship between the predictor and outcome. This approach is especially useful for ordinal variables, where there are a relatively small number of categories and substantial sample sizes in each category, such as the Literature Excerpt 12.4 which examined the number of children as a predictor. When categories are numerous and/or when substantive rationales apply, original categories can also be grouped to form larger categories. For example, in Literature Excerpt 12.4, mothers with four or more children were grouped together.

$$wage = \beta_0 + \beta_1 onekid + \beta_2 twokid + \beta_3 threekid + \beta_4 fourpkid + \varepsilon_i$$

Tests among the included categories can be conducted as discussed in Chapter 10 using a different reference category, test commands, or linear combinations (e.g., tests of $\beta_1 = \beta_2$ or equivalently $\beta_1 - \beta_2 = 0$).

When we use dummy variables to indicate the categories of ordinal or interval variables, we can also test the linearity of the relationship between the predictor and outcome (see Box 12.3). If the association is in fact linear, then the change in Y between adjacent categories of X should be equivalent across levels of X. For the model in Literature Excerpt 12.4 if the change is linear, we expect

$$(\beta_1) = (\beta_2 - \beta_1) = (\beta_3 - \beta_2) = (\beta_4 - \beta_3)$$

These constraints can be tested with a general linear F-test. (The last might be excluded in this example, since *fourpkid* groups together women with five and more children.)

12.1.4: Examples

We will now look at an example based on our NSFH distance outcome. We will illustrate the quadratic and logarithmic models by predicting distance based on the mother's years of schooling. We might expect that distance would associate with years of schooling with an "increasing at an increasing rate" shape. As noted previously, education may lead to greater distance. For example, education may associate with more job opportunities in distant areas and greater income for moves, especially at the highest education levels.[7] We will illustrate the dummy variable approach based on the adult's number of sisters. This variable is a count with a small number of values. Thus, its association with the outcome can be flexibly modeled with a small number of dummy variables. We might expect that an adult with more sisters can rely on these sisters to remain close to an aging parent, allowing the adult to live further away.[8] We will begin with a simple

■ Box 12.3

For interval variables, we might group several adjacent categories together to produce a large enough sample size for a dummy variable specification. For example, for age as a predictor, we might group age in 5- or 10-year intervals. Then, the dummies no longer capture a one-unit change on the predictor (rather, for example, a 5- or 10-unit change). But, using this approach can be helpful for visualizing the shape of the relationship between a predictor and outcome.

model where just the outcome and predictor of interest (mother's years of schooling; number of sisters) are in the model, but we will add the rest of the control variables from our data set when we discuss outliers and heteroskedasticity in Chapter 14.

Quadratic and Logarithmic Models

We can create the needed squared and logged variables using operators in SAS and Stata. The squared term can be calculated using the multiplication operator, which we used for interactions. But, now the variable is multiplied by itself. In both SAS and Stata the `log` command takes the natural log of the variable. When using the log transformation, it is important to remember that the log of a negative value and the log of zero are undefined. Because of these properties, logarithmic transformations are best applied to variables that naturally take on only positive values. For variables in which possible values also include zero, the transformation is sometimes taken after adding some constant, typically one (e.g., $\log X = \log(X + 1)$). This adjustment works well and conforms with the interpretations described above as long as there are not many zeros and the maximum value in the natural units is not small. Both *g1miles* and *g1yrschl* are non-negative; in our analytic data set *g1miles* does not contain zeros, but *g1yrschl* does contain zeros. So, our commands would be as follows.

	SAS	Stata
squared predictor	sqg1yrschl=g1yrschl*g1yrschl;	generate sqg1yrschl=g1yrschl*g1yrschl
logged predictor	logg1yrschl=log(g1yrschl+1);	generate logg1yrschl=log(g1yrschl+1)
logged outcome	logg1miles=log(g1miles);	generate logg1miles=log(g1miles)

Techniques for Choosing among Models

We estimate six models:

(a) a linear model, in which neither the outcome nor predictor are logged (which we'll refer to as lin-lin);
(b) a lin-log model;
(c) a quadratic model with a linear outcome (which we'll refer to as lin-sq);
(d) a log-lin model;
(e) a log-log model;
(f) a quadratic model with a logged outcome (which we'll refer to as log-sq).

We will estimate each model and then make predictions from the models to examine the shape of the estimated relationship.

Four of the models, the log-log, log-lin, lin-sq, or log-sq, might capture the expected "increasing at an increasing rate" association between the mother's years of schooling and distance. If each shows this association, which should we choose as the best? For nested models, we can use the general linear F-test to compare models. Only two sets of models are nested, however. The lin-sq model is nested within the lin-lin model and the log-sq model is nested within the log-lin model. In these cases, the t-test for the squared term conducts the general linear F-test of whether the quadratic form fits better than the linear form for the relationship.

As long as the two models have the same outcome variable, we can also compare the size of the adjusted R-squared values to compare them, even when not nested. We can also use AIC and BIC to compare non-nested models. In our case, we can use the adjusted R-squared to compare among each set of three models with the same outcome: the linear outcome (lin-lin, lin-log, lin-sq) and the log outcome (log-lin, log-log, log-sq).

It is not appropriate to compare the R^2 or adjusted R^2 values of models with different outcomes, including our non-logged versus logged outcomes. As a critique of early applications of models with logged outcomes emphasized:

> The authors make [the choice between the models with non-logged and logged outcomes] by comparing the R²s. But the R² yielded by estimation of [the logged model] is not the proportion of the variance of Y explained by the regression. It is rather the proportion of the variance of the logarithm of Y explained by the regression: logy, not Y, is the dependent variable. The two regression models are explaining different sources of variation, and the R²s are therefore in principle incomparable (Seidman 1976: 463).

It is possible to calculate a version of R^2 for the model with a logged outcome, by converting predictions based on the logged model back into their natural units and then regressing the outcome in its natural units on these predictions (for example, this is the approach suggested by Seidman 1976). The rescaling adjustments to the predicted values discussed above for log outcomes will not affect this R-squared value, so any of the predictions (Equations 12.6, 12.7, and 12.8) can be used to make the calculation.

Estimated Models

Display B.12.1 provides the SAS and Stata results for the three models with the nonlogged outcome. Display B.12.2 provides similar results for the three models with the logged outcome. Display B.12.3 shows how to calculate $\widehat{\exp(\varepsilon)}$ to adjust the predictions in logged units and to calculate the approximate R-squareds to compare the logged to the linear models. Finally, Display H.12.1 summarizes the results of the models in Excel, and calculates and graphs predicted values for specific levels of X.

More specifically, in Display B.12.1, we create the logged and squared terms for the predictor, and then regress *glmiles* on the three forms of the predictor: natural units (lin-lin), logged (lin-log), and quadratic (lin-sq). Because all of these models have the same outcome, we can compare the adjusted R-squared values. Although all of the values are quite small, the value for the quadratic model is largest (0.0082). In addition, we can test whether the quadratic model is preferred over the linear model using the significance of the squared variable, *sqg1yrschl*, in Display B.12.1.[9] It has a t-value of 3.55, which is larger than 1.96, giving us evidence that the model with the squared term explains more variation in distance than the linear model.

In Display B.12.2, we create the logged outcome, and regress it on the three forms of the predictor. The three models in this box have the same outcome, *logg1miles*, and thus may be compared on their adjusted *R*-squared values. Again, the adjusted *R*-squared values are all small in magnitude, but largest for the quadratic model (0.0223). In addition, the *t*-value for the squared term is significantly different from zero in the log-sq model (*t*-value of 3.98).

We can also compare the models with AIC and BIC, using the formulas from Chapter 9 (see next page). The results again indicate the quadratic models are preferred (have the smallest AIC and BIC).

So, the quadratic model is preferred for both the logged outcome and the outcome in its natural units. But, which of these two has the best fit? And, how different is the shape of these different models? In Display B.12.3 we show how to calculate the adjustment to the predicted values of the logged outcome and how to calculate its approximate *R*-squared value in the natural units of *Y*. We show the procedure for the *log-sq* model as an example. The process can be similarly implemented for the *log-lin* and *log-log* models.

There are several steps in Display B.12.3, including some new commands:

- Stata's `predict` command (alone and with the `, residuals` option) and SAS's `output` statement with the `predicted=` and `residual=` options. The predictions are calculated by SAS and Stata substituting into the prediction equation the value(s) of *X* for each case. For example, a case with *g1yrschl* = 12 and *sqg1yrschl* = 12 * 12 = 144 would have the following prediction based on the third model in Display B.12.2: log (*Y*) = 2.809548 − 0.0635735 * 12 + 0.0087078 * 144 = 3.3005892. Using these commands, rather than making hand calculations, is quite useful for large data sets and large models. In our data set, Stata and SAS calculate the predicted value for all 5,472 cases. SAS and Stata's commands work a bit differently.
  - In Display B.12.3, in Stata syntax, we type `predict logYhat` to ask Stata to calculate the predicted values and store them in the new variable that we call *logYhat*. We also type `predict logResid, residuals` to ask Stata to calculate the residuals and store them in the new variable that we call *logResid*. Stata adds the new variables to the existing data file, so it is easy to use them in further analyses.
  - In SAS, we need to save the predictions and residuals in a new data file. We can keep other variables we need in that data file as well (such as *g1miles* in our example) and then refer to that data file in future analyses. To do so, we type:

```
output out=predict(keep=g1miles logYhat logResid)
        predicted=logYhat residual=logResid;
```

  where `out=` tells SAS to create a new data file called *predict*, `keep=` tells SAS which variables to keep (in our example, *g1miles logYhat*, and *logResid*) `predicted=` asks SAS to calculate predicted values and store them in the new variable named *logYhat*, and `residual=` asks SAS to calculate residuals and store them in the new variable named *logResid*.

Model	k	SSE	$AIC = n*\log\left(\frac{SSE}{n}\right)+2k$	$BIC = n*\log\left(\frac{SSE}{n}\right)+k*\log(n)$
lin-lin	2	2,262,599,142	$=5472*\log\left(\frac{2{,}262{,}599{,}142}{5{,}472}\right)+2*2$ $=70{,}769.987$	$=5472*\log\left(\frac{2{,}262{,}599{,}142}{5{,}472}\right)+2*\log(5472)$ $=70{,}783.201$
lin-log	2	2,269,835,869	$=5472*\log\left(\frac{2{,}269{,}835{,}869}{5{,}472}\right)+2*2$ $=70{,}787.46$	$=5472*\log\left(\frac{2{,}269{,}835{,}869}{5{,}472}\right)+2*\log(5472)$ $=70{,}800.675$
lin-sq	3	2,257,385,363	$=5472*\log\left(\frac{2{,}257{,}385{,}363}{5{,}472}\right)+2*3$ $=70{,}759.363$	$=5472*\log\left(\frac{2{,}257{,}385{,}363}{5{,}472}\right)+3*\log(5472)$ $=70{,}779.185$
log-lin	2	31,239	$=5472*\log\left(\frac{31{,}239}{5{,}472}\right)+2*2$ $=9{,}536.3506$	$=5472*\log\left(\frac{31{,}239}{5{,}472}\right)+2*\log(5472)$ $=9{,}549.5654$
log-log	2	31,467	$=5472*\log\left(\frac{31{,}467}{5{,}472}\right)+2*2$ $=9{,}576.1433$	$=5472*\log\left(\frac{31{,}467}{5{,}472}\right)+2*\log(5472)$ $=9{,}589.3581$
log-sq	3	31,149	$=5472*\log\left(\frac{31{,}149}{5{,}472}\right)+2*3$ $=9{,}522.5629$	$=5472*\log\left(\frac{31{,}149}{5{,}472}\right)+3*\log(5472)$ $=9{,}542.3851$

- We then use the exponential function in SAS and Stata—exp—to convert the predicted values and residuals into their nonlogged natural units. We type `explogYhat=exp(logYhat);` and `explogResid=exp(logResid);` in SAS and `generate explogYhat=exp(logYhat)` and `generate explogResid=exp(logResid)` in Stata. Note that in SAS we must first set the new data set *predict*. We named the new destination data set, where we save the exponentiated values, *predict2*.
- To calculate the scaling value to adjust for the downward bias on the predictions we use the `proc means` command in SAS and the `summarize` command in Stata. The resulting coefficient estimate of 10.75774 is the value we will use momentarily to adjust our prediction equation for this *log-sq* model in Display H.12.1.
- The final regression model in Display B.12.3, which includes a constant term for the regression of *g1miles* on *explogYhat* provides the approximate R-squared value for the log-sq model in the natural units of Y: 0.0073.

Display H.12.1 uses Excel to summarize the results across the models, building on the techniques introduced in Appendix H.11. The R-squared values and coefficient estimates from each model are shown in cells A1 to G8. In cells A10 to G21, predictions are calculated for each model for values of *g1yrschl* ranging from 6 to 16.[10]

The prediction equation shown in the Excel formula bar shows the prediction for the values of *glyrschl*=12 which we hand-calculated in the first bullet above. But, in Excel, we take the exponential of this prediction and multiply by the scale factor from Display B.12.3 of 10.75774. We can confirm with a calculator that 10.75774 * exp(3.3005892) = 291.84 which is the result from the Excel formula.

We will walk through an example of each prediction equation in the text, to emphasize the importance of appropriately accounting for the transformations when making predictions. We must be sure to use the appropriate transformation on the right-hand side as well as the left-hand side of the equations. As we show below, it is easy to get the predictions right by thinking back to how each variable is created in SAS and Stata. We must also take care to make any adjustments to the prediction to translate back to its natural units. To get this right, it is helpful to write the outcome variable name, to emphasize if it is in its logged or natural units.[11]

Examples of prediction equations for g1yrschl = 12		$\widehat{\log g1 miles}$	$\widehat{g1 miles}$
Prediction Equation			
Lin-lin			
$\widehat{g1 miles} = 92.86 + 17.39 * g1yrschl$		–	301.54
$\widehat{g1 miles} = 92.86 + 17.39 * 12$			
Lin-log			
$\widehat{g1 miles} = 24.65 + 107.62 * \log g1yrschl$		–	300.69
$\widehat{g1 miles} = 24.65 + 107.62 * \log (g1yrschl + 1)$			
$\widehat{g1 miles} = 24.65 + 107.62 * \log (12 + 1)$			
Lin-sq			
$\widehat{g1 miles} = 293.78 - 25.70 * g1yrschl + 2.09 * sqg1yrschl$		–	286.34
$\widehat{g1 miles} = 293.78 - 25.70 * g1yrschl + 2.09 * g1yrschl * g1yrschl$			
$\widehat{g1 miles} = 293.78 - 25.70 * 12 + 2.09 * 12 * 12$			
Log-lin			
$\widehat{\log g1 miles} = 1.97 + 0.116 * g1yrschl$		3.36	10.8991*exp(3.36)
$\widehat{\log g1 miles} = 1.97 + 0.116 * 12$			313.78
Log-log			
$\widehat{\log g1 miles} = 1.28 + 0.814 * \log g1yrschl$			
$\widehat{\log g1 miles} = 1.28 + 0.814 * \log (g1yrschl + 1)$		3.37	11.102*exp(3.37)
$\widehat{\log g1 miles} = 1.28 + 0.814 * \log (12 + 1)$			322.83
Log-sq			
$\widehat{\log g1 miles} = 2.81 - 0.0636 * g1yrschl + 0.00871 * sqg1yrschl$			
$\widehat{\log g1 miles} = 2.81 - 0.0636 * g1yrschl + 0.00871 * g1yrschl * g1yrschl$		3.30	10.75774*exp(3.30)
$\widehat{\log g1 miles} = 2.81 - 0.0636 * 12 + 0.00871 * 12 * 12$			291.84

These results match the values in the row for *glyrschl* = 12 in Display H.12.1 (Row 17), within rounding error.

The predicted values for all levels of *glyrschl* are plotted in the six graphs in Display H.12.1. Three of the six plots look curvilinear to the eye: log-lin, lin-sq, and log-sq. These are three of the specifications that we anticipated might capture the expected "increasing at an increasing rate" relationship. These three models also show the largest adjusted R-squared values, although there is not a single best choice based on our model comparisons. Based on the within-outcome adjusted R-squares, and general linear F-test for the squared term, the *log-sq* model outperforms the *log-lin* model. But, the approximate R-squared in the natural Y units is slightly higher for the *log-lin* than for the *log-sq* model, and both are slightly lower than the value for the *lin-sq* model (0.0077 and 0.0075 in the fourth row in the Excel worksheet; 0.0082 in the third row of the Excel worksheet). Even so, we will see in Chapter 14 some other reasons to prefer logging the outcome.

Dummy Variable Flexible Forms

We now turn to our example of predicting distance based on number of sisters, using dummy variables to allow a flexible form of the relationship. The results are similar for the outcome in its natural units and log form and we will focus on the logged outcome.

Display B.12.4 shows the commands we used to create the seven dummy variables and the results of estimating the regression model using these dummies. We collapsed together adults with seven or more sisters, because fewer than 30 cases had each observed value above six, and use adults with no sisters as the reference category. We graph the predicted values based on this model in Display H.12.2. We use the technique shown in Display B.12.3 to calculate the scale factor for the exponentiated predicted values. The shape of the graph suggests that the flexible dummy specification is useful because the shape is not linear but is also not like any of the shapes shown in Figure 12.2. Distance is fairly constant, hovering around 300 miles, for adults with zero to three sisters, then it begins to fall for those with four to six sisters, and finally jumps to nearly 600 miles for those with seven or more sisters.

The figure suggests that we might further simplify the model by collapsing together some of the categories. We used the test command for each pair of included categories to see whether there was empirical support for such collapsing (e.g., `test g2numsis1=g2numsis2`; `test g2numsis1=g2numsis3`; `test g2numsis1=g2numsis4`, etc).

The following table summarizes the *p*-values for those tests.

	g2numsis0	g2numsis1	g2numsis2	g2numsis3	g2numsis4	g2numsis5	g2numsis6
g2numsis1	0.18						
g2numsis2	0.62	0.10					
g2numsis3	0.76	0.56	0.52				
g2numsis4	0.25	0.07	0.42	0.23			
g2numsis5	0.04	0.01	0.07	0.04	0.30		
g2numsis6	0.05	0.02	0.07	0.04	0.22	0.72	
g2numsis7p	0.03	0.07	0.02	0.05	0.01	0.00	0.00

The pattern of results suggests that adults with zero to three sisters could be grouped together. The means do not differ among the groups with zero to three sisters (solid green rule box), but each of these small sister sizes differs from those with five or six sisters (solid black box), at the alpha level of 0.07 or smaller. Likewise, adults with five and six sisters have statistically equivalent means (dashed black rule box). Those with seven or more sisters differ from all other groups (green dashed rule box), suggesting they should be a separate group. But, those with four sisters do not differ from any of groups, except those with seven or more sisters (unboxed values), making it unclear whether to group those with four sisters with the smaller or larger sister sizes. In cases like this, a judgment will have to be made, ideally with some conceptual rationale, and it is useful to examine how sensitive the results are to different choices about the four-sister category (e.g., grouping them with those with three or fewer sisters, grouping them with those with five or six sisters, leaving them as their own category). We will present the model which leaves adults with four sisters as their own category, which we found slightly better fitting and the most substantively revealing (in a paper, it might make sense to summarize in a footnote or paragraph the results of the alternative specifications).

The results of the collapsed model are presented in Display B.12.5 and the predicted values are calculated and plotted in Display H.12.3. In the collapsed model, like the original model, we still fail to reject the null hypothesis that those with four sisters differ from those with zero to three or those with five or six, and the predicted values shows that the group with four sisters live nearly 60 miles closer to their mothers than those with zero to three sisters and about 60 miles further from their mothers than those with five or six sisters, on average.

We can formally test that the model in Display B.12.5 is a better fit to the data than the model in Display B.12.4 using the general linear F-test. The null hypothesis is that $\beta_1 = \beta_2 = \beta_3 = 0$ (adults with zero to three sisters live the same average distance from their mothers) and $\beta_5 = \beta_6$ (adults with five or six sisters live the same average distance from their mothers). Imposing these constraints on the model in Display B.12.4 results in the model in Display B.12.5. We can use their respective sums of square errors and error degrees of freedom to calculate the F-value.

$$F = \frac{31,780.1391 - 31,761.1625}{5,468 - 5,464} \div \frac{31,761.1625}{5,464} = 0.816$$

This F-value, with 4 numerator and 5,464 denominator degrees of freedom, is not significant, with a p-value of 0.51 (see Box 12.4). This indicates that we cannot reject the null hypothesis that those with zero to three sisters live the same average distance from their mothers and that those with five or six sisters live the same average distance from their mothers. So, the model shown in Display B.12.5 is preferred over the model shown in Display B.12.4.

■ **Box 12.4**

As discussed in Chapter 6, the p-value can be requested from SAS and Stata (see again Display A.6 and Display B.6.1).

Overall, these results suggest that the linear effect of number of sisters that we reported previously (in Chapter 9) is not a good approximation of the actual relationship between number of sisters and distance from the mother. Adults who have three or fewer sisters live about the same average distance of nearly 300 miles from their mothers. Adults with four sisters live somewhat closer, at less than 240 miles. And, adults with five or six sisters live somewhat closer still, at about 170 miles. In contrast, those with seven or more sisters live substantially further away: close to 600 miles from their mothers on average. The vast majority of adults have zero to three sisters, and only 54 adults in the sample have seven or more sisters. It is possible that these very large families differ from other families in some way that explains this much greater distance. On the other hand, the graphs in Displays H.12.2 and H.12.3 should also give an analyst concerns about an influential observation (possibly a data error) that pulls the average distance upward among this small set of very large families. We will consider this possibility in Chapter 14.

12.2: SUMMARY

In this chapter, we showed how to specify several common forms of nonlinear relationships between an interval predictor and outcome variable using the quadratic function and logarithmic transformation. We discussed how these various forms might be expected by conceptual models and how to compare them empirically. We also learned how to calculate predictions to show the estimated forms of the relationships, and used Excel to facilitate these calculations and to graph the results. We also showed how to use dummy variables to estimate a flexible relationship between an ordinal or interval predictor and the outcome.

KEY TERMS

Absolute Change

Curvilinear

Decreasing at a Decreasing Rate

Decreasing at an Increasing Rate

Factor Change

Increasing at a Decreasing Rate

Increasing at an Increasing Rate

Logarithmic Transformation

Natural Log

Percentage Change

Proportionate (or Relative) Change

Quadratic

Tangent Lines

REVIEW QUESTIONS

12.1. How would you choose among three models that predicted an outcome variable with: (a) a linear predictor variable, (b) a logged predictor variable, and (c) a quadratic predictor variable?

12.2. How would you create a logged predictor variable when the predictor includes zero (but no negative values)?

    (a) How would you write the prediction equation when a linear outcome variable is regressed on this variable?

    (b) Suppose 5 was a valid value on the predictor. How would you make a prediction for this value of the predictor?

12.3. What are the approximate and exact interpretations of the coefficient estimate for a logged outcome variable when the predictor is in its natural units (log-lin model)?

12.4. What are the approximate interpretations for a model with a logged predictor when the outcome is also logged (log-log model) and when the outcome is not logged (lin-log model)?

12.5. How would you write a general prediction equation for a quadratic functional form?

    (a) Suppose 5 was a valid value on the predictor. How would you make a prediction for this value of the predictor?

    (b) What do the significance and sign of the coefficient estimate for the quadratic term tell us?

    (c) What are the formulas for calculating the slope at each level of X and for calculating the point at which the slope becomes zero?

12.6. How can you calculate the various types of change (absolute, factor, relative, and percentage) for two values?

REVIEW EXERCISES

12.1. Imagine that your collaborator regressed the log of respondents' earnings on their years of schooling, and obtained the following results:

LNÊARN = 5.31 + 0.22 * YRSCHL

(a) Help your collaborator interpret the coefficient for YRSCHL with a factor and percentage change approach (i.e., *calculate the factor and percentage change and interpret them in words*; use the *exact* not the approximate approaches).

12.2 Suppose that your collaborator regressed the log of income on a dummy indicator of being African American versus white and found that the coefficient for the African American dummy variable was –0.511.

(a) Help your collaborator interpret this coefficient with a factor and percentage change approach (i.e., *calculate the factor and percentage change and interpret them in words*; use the *exact* not the approximate approaches).

12.3 Consider the following regression equation:

EARÑINGS = 1,000 + 1,600 * AGE – 20 * SQAGE

where SQAGE is the square of AGE, AGE is measured in years, and EARNINGS is annual earnings.

(a) If you plotted predicted values from this prediction equation, would you expect to see a U- or inverted U-shape? Why?

(b) At what value of AGE does the slope switch directions?

(c) What are predicted earnings when AGE is 20, 40, and 60?

CHAPTER EXERCISE

In this exercise, you will write a SAS and a Stata batch program to estimate non-linear relationships.

Again, use the NHIS 1999 data set with an *if expression* to only keep cases that do not have missing values on the *age, exfreqwR, bmiR, SEX, HISPAN_I* and *RACERPI2* variables.

In all cases, conduct two-sided hypothesis tests. Use a 5% alpha unless otherwise indicated.

12.1 Non-linearity

a) SAS/Stata Tasks.

i) Summarize the *bmiR* and *age* variables to verify whether either variable has zero values.

ii) Create a logged version of each variable, adding one before logging if the original variable contains zeros.

iii) Create a quadratic term for the *age* variable.

iv) Regress the original non-logged *bmiR* variable on *age*, on the logged version of *age*, and both the linear and quadratic terms for *age*.

v) Regress the logged version of the *bmiR* variable on *age*, on the logged version of *age*, and both the linear and quadratic terms for *age*.

vi) Calculate the adjustment factor for making predictions for the log-log model.

vii) For the log-log model, calculate the R-squared values discussed in the chapter that approximate the R-squared value in Y units.

b) Write-Up Tasks.

i) Calculate AIC and BIC for each model.

ii) Based on the significance of individual coefficients, the AIC/BIC values, and the R-squared values for the models, which of the six models is preferred?

iii) Interpret the coefficient in the log-lin model using the approximate and exact approaches to interpretation.

iv) Interpret the coefficient in the log-log model using the approximate interpretation.

v) Using only the sign of the coefficient on the quadratic term, does the lin-sq model quadratic form have a U-shape or inverted U-shape? Calculate the value of age at which the slope becomes zero and calculate the slope of age for persons aged 30, 40 and 50.

vi) Based on the lin-log model, calculate the predicted body mass index for persons aged 30, 40 and 50.

COURSE EXERCISE

Identify at least one nonlinear relationship that you might estimate based on the data set that you created in the course exercise to Chapter 4. Ideally, think about conceptual reasons why you might expect a nonlinear relationship between one of the predictors

COURSE
EXERCISE

12

and outcomes. Alternatively, choose a predictor and explore whether a nonlinear relationship is identified empirically in the data set. Ideally, choose a continuous predictor to practice quadratic and logged models and choose a categorical predictor to practice examining stair-step-type models with dummy variables.

For your continuous predictor, estimate the six models discussed in the chapter (lin-lin, lin-log, lin-sq, log-lin, log-log, and log-sq models). Compare the performance of the models using individual t-tests (where appropriate), R-squared values, and AIC/BIC values. Plot predicted values from the preferred model, transforming the predictor and/or outcome as needed when making predictions.

For your categorical predictor, use dummy variables to flexibly estimate the relationships among the categories and outcome. Use tests among the dummy variables to potentially collapse groups. Calculate predicted values and graph the results.

Chapter 13

INDIRECT EFFECTS AND OMITTED VARIABLE BIAS

CHAPTER 13: INDIRECT EFFECTS AND OMITTED VARIABLE BIAS

Multiple regression is ideally suited to social science research because it allows researchers to adjust for confounding variables when experimental designs are not possible. But, such confounders are not always measured. When they are not, researchers can use their understanding of multiple regression to anticipate the direction of bias due to their omission. Multiple regression can also be used to determine whether the effect of a variable on the outcome operates through the mechanisms laid out in theories, by adding measures for those mechanisms to the model. But, care must be taken to interpret these mechanisms, because study designs often do not allow the direction of effects to be unambiguously determined.

13.1: LITERATURE EXCERPT 13.1

We begin with an excerpt from the literature that illustrates the use of multiple regression to adjust for confounders and to examine mediators. Stacey Brumbaugh and colleagues (2008) examined the predictors of attitudes toward gay marriage in three states that considered but ultimately rejected (Minnesota) or had recently passed (Arizona and Louisiana) changes to marriage laws. Called covenant marriage, these changes increase the bar for entering and exiting marriage, requiring counseling before marriage and extended waiting periods before fault-based divorce. The authors hypothesize that individuals are more likely to oppose gay marriage when they perceive a cultural weakening of heterosexual marriage as a threat. In their model, the people most threatened would be those who have a stake in marriage, such as married persons. They further expect and test for a mechanism for this effect: "Based on our threat model, we hypothesize that religious, political and social attitudes, especially attitudes regarding the deinstitutionalization of marriage and marriage promotion efforts, mediate the effects of marital, parenthood, and cohabitation histories on attitudes toward gay marriage" (p. 349). The authors also control for a number of sociodemographic and socioeconomic variables, which adjust for their potential effect on both the predictors of interest and the outcome. For example, they note that prior results associating race-ethnicity and attitudes about gay rights depend on whether and how researchers had adjusted for socioeconomic status.

Literature Excerpt 13.1 reproduces Table 3 from the paper. The organization of the results follows a standard strategy for presenting the effects of adding confounders and mediators. Model 1 begins with a set of sociodemographic controls (female, black, other race, and age) and dummy indicators for two of the three states included in the study. Model 2 adds controls for socioeconomic status (dummy indicators of education and employment and log family income). Model 3 adds dummy indicators of marital, cohabitation, and parenthood histories. Model 4 adds religious, political and social attitudes.

The table setup makes it easy to look across a row and see how a coefficient estimate changes when other variables enter the model. For example, we see that the coefficient estimate for the dummy indicator of female changes little across the models (being −0.42 in three of the models, and −0.44 in one model). In contrast, the coefficient estimate for black race-ethnicity (versus the white reference category) increases to 0.32 from 0.24 in Model 2 versus Model 1, remains at

■ Literature Excerpt 13.1

Table 3. Regression Models Predicting Attitudes Against Gay Marriage (N = 976)

Variable	Model 1 B	Model 1 pr^2	Model 2 B	Model 2 pr^2	Model 3 B	Model 3 pr^2	Model 4 B	Model 4 pr^2
Intercept	2.92***		1.73***		2.88***		−.02	
Sociodemographic controls								
Female	−.42***	(2.7%)	−.42***	(2.5%)	−.44***	(2.9%)	−.42***	(3.2%)
Black	.24*	(0.3%)	.32**	(0.6%)	.32**	(0.6%)	.22*	(0.4%)
Other race	−.18	(0.1%)	−.12	(0.0%)	−.07	(0.0%)	−.12	(0.0%)
Age	.02***	(5.6%)	.02***	(5.7%)	.01***	(0.8%)	.01**	(0.5%)
State context								
Arizona	−.06	(0.0%)	−.06	(0.0%)	−.04	(0.0%)	−.06	(0.0%)
Louisiana	.24**	(0.6%)	.23**	(0.5%)	.22**	(0.6%)	−.04	(0.0%)
Socioeconomic status								
High school			.52***	(1.1%)	.50***	(1.0%)	.44***	(1.0%)
Some college			.36**	(0.5%)	.36**	(0.5%)	.33**	(0.6%)
College			.33*	(0.4%)	.30*	(0.3%)	.21	(0.2%)
Postcollege			.07	(0.0%)	.11	(0.0%)	.17	(0.1%)
Employed full time			−.09	(0.1%)	−.05	(0.0%)	−.00	(0.0%)
Log family income			.08	(0.3%)	.02	(0.0%)	.00	(0.0%)
Income missing			−.32**	(0.5%)	−.21	(0.2%)	−.17	(0.2%)
Marital, cohabitation, and parenthood histories								
Divorced/separated					−.33***	(1.0%)	−.08	(0.0%)
Never married					−.36***	(0.7%)	−.15	(0.1%)
Child or children					.34***	(0.9%)	.24**	(0.6%)
Recently cohabited					−.52***	(3.4%)	−.20**	(0.6%)
Religious, political, and social attitudes								
Religiosity							.10*	(2.6%)
Political conservatism							.27***	(4.5%)
Attitudes toward divorce							.04***	(1.2%)
Perceived blameworthiness for family breakdown							.07***	(3.0%)
Attitudes toward covenant marriage							.02***	(0.7%)
F Statistic	15.80***		9.11***		11.05***		22.85***	
Nested *F*	N/A		3.18***		15.55***		52.81***	
R^2	.09		.11		.16		.35	
Adjusted R^2	.08		.10		.15		.3	

Note: In parentheses are the effect sizes, measured by squared partial correlation coefficients (pr^2), indicating the percentage of remaining variance explained.
* $p < .05$. ** $p < .01$.
*** $p < .001$, one-tailed tests.

Source: Brumbaugh, Stacey M., Laura A. Sanchez, Steven L. Nock and James D. Wright. 2008. "Attitudes Toward Gay Marriage in States Undergoing Marriage Law Transformation." *Journal of Marriage and Family,* 70: 345–59.

0.32 in Model 3, and then falls to 0.22 in Model 4. Turning to the coefficient estimates for the marital, cohabitational, and parenthood histories, these change considerably between Models 3 and 4. The coefficient estimates all fall in magnitude between Model 3 and Model 4, and become nonsignificant for the contrasts of *divorced/separated* and of *never married* with the reference category (*married or widowed*).

We will discuss below how to examine in more detail how and why a coefficient changes when another variable enters the model. In this literature excerpt, the pattern of coefficient estimates for black race-ethnicity is difficult to interpret because the difference between blacks and whites unexpectedly widens, rather than falls, with adjustments for socioeconomic status.[1] The pattern of marital, cohabitation, and parenthood histories is easier to interpret, and in line with the authors' expectations. Those with a higher stake in marriage, including those who are currently married, have not recently cohabited, and are not parents have more negative views toward gay marriage. These differences are reduced substantially when attitudes toward divorce and covenant marriage, the breakdown of the family, political conservatism, and religiosity are added to the model. This result can be interpreted as demonstrating that attitudes are a reason for the differences among those with different marital, parenthood, and cohabitation experiences, although as the authors note, the direction of association is difficult to determine with cross-sectional data. It is possible that attitudes predict family structure rather than family structure predicting attitudes. Justification for interpreting a variable as a confounder or mediator, and placing a variable as a predictor, mediator, or outcome, cannot be provided empirically by cross-sectional data. The researcher uses theory and prior empirical research to guide placement of variables in the model. More advanced techniques and longitudinal designs build on the basic concepts of OLS better to identify the ordering and causal nature of associations (see roadmap in Chapter 18).

13.2: DEFINING CONFOUNDERS, MEDIATORS, AND SUPRESSOR VARIABLES

Frequently, a coefficient estimate decreases in size when other variables are added to the model. Such a change is interpreted as reflecting spuriousness or mediation, depending on the conceptual model and study design. It is also possible for a coefficient estimate to increase when another variable is added to the model. Such change is typically interpreted as reflecting suppression.

13.2.1: Confounders

As we discussed in Chapter 8, regression models are asymmetrical. One variable is selected as the outcome and other variables are predictors of that outcome. This setup implies a causal association between the predictor and outcome. But, with observational data, it is difficult to justify a causal interpretation. We also saw in Chapter 8 that a bivariate regression coefficient is nothing more than a rescaled correlation coefficient. Simply selecting one variable as the outcome and the other as the predictor in a regression model does not elevate the association from correlational to directional.

Similarly, the well-known phrase *Correlation does not imply causation* holds for bivariate and multiple regression. If we use a dummy variable that indicates teenage motherhood to predict years of schooling in a bivariate regression with correlational data, and find a significant negative coefficient estimate, we cannot conclude that teenage parenthood causes adolescent girls to limit their schooling. Because we did not randomly assign young mothers to be teenage mothers or not, they may differ on many other characteristics that predict both their status as teenage mothers and the years of schooling they complete (such as growing up in a low-income neighborhood or a low-income family). If the association is really due to these other variables, then social programs and policies aimed at reducing teenage motherhood would not increase the years of schooling these girls complete. Rather, in this case, we would need to address the root cause—family and community background—to simultaneously reduce teenage motherhood and increase educational attainment.

Statistically, this situation is referred to as a **spurious relationship**. The other characteristics that predict both our predictor of interest and the outcome are referred to as **confounders** or **common causes** or **extraneous variables**. A spurious relationship exists when an apparent association between one variable and another is really due to a third variable. It is helpful to display this and other associations in this chapter visually.

Figures 13.1(a) and (b) help us visualize a spurious relationship using conventions we will follow throughout this chapter. The arrows point away from predictor variables toward outcomes. Throughout our examples, we will use the subscript 2 to denote our predictor of interest and the subscript 3 to depict the third variable, leaving the subscript 1 for our ultimate outcome of interest.

Figure 13.1(a) illustrates a directional relationship from X_2 (predictor) to Y (outcome). The lack of arrow between X_2 and Y in Figure 13.1(b) indicates that X_2 is no longer associated with Y once we account for X_3. Instead, the arrows from X_3 to X_2 and Y show that when X_3 changes, it produces change in both X_2 and Y. Ignoring X_3 makes it appear that X_2 leads to Y because both X_2 and Y covary with X_3; that is, X_2 and Y seem to "move together" because of their shared association with X_3.

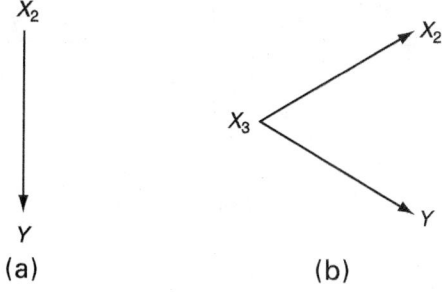

(a)   (b)

■ **Figure 13.1**

Table 13.1 provides a hypothetical example of what the regression results would look like in the case of a completely spurious association. In Model 1, *Years of Schooling* is predicted by *Age at First Birth* in a bivariate regression. The coefficient estimate is positive and significant. In Model 2, when we add a measure of *Parents' SES* to the model, the coefficient estimate for *Age at First Birth* falls to zero and is insignificant. Only *Parents' SES* significantly predicts *Years of Schooling* in Model 2.

■ **Table 13.1: Completely Spurious Association between Age at First Birth and Years of Schooling**

	Dependent Variable: Years of Schooling	
	Model 1	Model 2
Age at First Birth	0.16*	0.00
	(0.02)	(0.01)
Parents' SES	—	0.99*
		(0.01)
Intercept	7.64	10.48
	(0.31)	(0.10)

* $p < .05$—indicates excluded from model.

Source: Hypothetical data created for illustration purposes.

Although the word "spurious" is typically used to denote a situation in which a third variable completely explains away an association, as is illustrated in Table 13.1, it is also possible for an association to be reduced but not eliminated by adjusting for a confounder. In Table 13.2 we use hypothetical data to illustrate a partially spurious association between the predictor and outcome. In Model 2 of Table 13.2, when we control for *Parents' SES*, the coefficient estimate for *Age At First Birth* decreases but remains positive and significant. And, the association between *Parents' SES* and *Years of Schooling* is smaller in magnitude in Table 13.2 versus Table 13.1, reflecting the fact that in the second hypothetical example, we created the hypothetical data set to have a weaker association between *Parents' SES* and *Years of Schooling*.

■ **Table 13.2: Partially Spurious Association between Age at First Birth and Years of Schooling**

	Dependent Variable: Years of Schooling	
	Model 1	Model 2
Age at First Birth	0.16*	0.09*
	(0.02)	(0.01)
Parents' SES	—	0.59*
		(0.02)
Intercept	7.64	8.95
	(0.31)	(0.25)

* $p < .05$—indicates excluded from model.

Source: Hypothetical data created for illustration purposes.

13.2.2: Example 13.1

We will also use our NSFH hours of work variable to illustrate various types of association throughout the chapter. We will begin by estimating how men's ratings of their own health predict their hours of work, and examine to what extent the men's ages confound this association. We anticipate that older age predicts both poorer health and reduced work hours (or retirement). Hours of work and age are variables we considered in prior chapters. The health rating comes from a standard question, "Compared with other people your age, how would you describe your health?" which is rated on a scale from 1 = *very poor* to 5 = *excellent*.[2]

Display B.13.1 presents the results of estimating two models in SAS and Stata. The first model predicts hours of work in a bivariate regression based on the health rating. The second adds the respondent's age in a multiple regression model. For ease of comparison, and to demonstrate how we might table the results for a manuscript, we summarize the results below.

■ **Table 13.3: Predicting Hours of Work by Self-Reported Health in the NSFH, with and without Controls for Age**

	Dependent Variable: Hours of Work Per Week	
	Model 1	Model 2
Self-Reported Health	1.14*	1.02*
	(0.31)	(0.31)
Age (Years)	—	−0.10*
		(0.02)
Intercept	37.86	42.27
	(1.29)	(1.51)

* p < .05—indicates excluded from model.

Source: NSFH, Wave 1, Sample of Men, *n* = 3,742.

Model 1 shows that, before controlling for age, each additional point higher that the respondent rated his health is associated with over one additional hour of work per week. When age is controlled, the association drops by over 10 percent to one additional hour per week $[(1.02-1.14)/1.14 * 100 = -10.53]$. The results are consistent with our expectation that age is a confounder. We chose age because it is hard to argue that health influences age (except through altering the sample by attrition through death or very poor health).

13.2.3: Mediators

Mediation occurs when a third variable represents the mechanism through which an association between a predictor and outcome operates. The third variable is typically referred to as a **mediator**, an **intervening variable**, or a **proximal cause**.

Mediating relationships are often seen in elaborate conceptual models that do not simply suggest that two variables are related, but spell out how and why they are related. An empirical test that verifies not only the association between the two variables, but also the evidence for the intervening mechanisms, will provide more convincing support of the theory. Similarly, if two theories suggest two different mechanisms, we would ideally use an empirical model to test which explanatory framework is best reflected in the data.

$$X_2 \longrightarrow Y \qquad\qquad X_2 \longrightarrow X_3 \longrightarrow Y$$

(a)   (b)

▦ **Figure 13.2**

Going back to our example of teenage mothers, we can consider mechanisms that explain why those who share a household with their own parents complete more years of schooling. One reason might be because these young mothers receive help with childcare from their parents. Table 13.4 uses hypothetical data to show how such a mediating relationship might be revealed with regression analysis. In Model 1, *Coresidence with Parents* is positively and significantly associated with *Years of Schooling*. In Model 2, when we add *Hours of Parental Help with Child Care Per Week* to the model, the association with *Coresidence with Parents* falls to close to zero and is insignificant.

▦ **Table 13.4: Completely Mediating Association between Coresidence with Parents and Years of Schooling**

	Dependent Variable: Years of Schooling	
	Model 1	Model 2
Coresidence with Parents	1.32*	−0.03
	(0.08)	(0.08)
Hours of Parental Help with Child Care Per Week	—	0.20*
		(0.01)
Intercept	10.48*	7.96*
	(0.05)	(0.11)

* p < .05—indicates excluded from model.

Source: Hypothetical data created for illustration purposes.

Notice that the statistical pattern of results looks quite similar in Tables 13.1 and 13.4. A coefficient estimate for one variable that was significant in Model 1 becomes insignificant in Model 2. The statistical results do not tell us if the third variable is a confounder or a mediator. We determine its role in the model based on conceptual ideas about how the variable should operate and ideally based on careful measurement. For example, conceptually, we might consider the extent to which it is plausible for the parents' SES to be influenced by their daughter's teenage pregnancy (placing it in the middle intervening rather than prior confounding position). Methodologically, we might be careful to measure parents' SES when the daughter was born or in elementary school, so that it precedes the teenage pregnancy.

As with confounding, mediation may be partial rather than complete. We illustrate such partial mediation in Table 13.5.

In this case, the association between *Coresidence with Parents* and *Years of Schooling* drops substantially in size, but remains significant in Model 2. And, *Hours of Parental Help with Child Care Per Week* is less strongly associated with *Years of Schooling* than was the case in Table 13.4.

■ **Table 13.5: Partially Mediating Association between Coresidence with Parents and Years of Schooling**

| | Dependent Variable: Years of Schooling | |
	Model 1	Model 2
Coresidence with Parents	1.32*	0.53*
	(0.08)	(0.09)
Hours of Parental Help with Child Care Per Week	—	0.12*
		(0.01)
Intercept	10.48*	8.55
	(0.05)	(0.11)

* p < .05—indicates excluded from model.

Source: Hypothetical data created for illustration purposes.

13.2.4: A Note on Terminology: Mediation and Moderation

Students (and scholars) often confuse the terms mediation and **moderation**. The term moderation is another word used to describe the presence of an interaction. We say that X_3 moderates the relationship between X_2 and Y when an interaction exists. Moderation is depicted visually as follows:

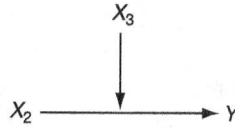

■ **Figure 13.3**

Examining common definitions of these words may help you to remember their meaning. One definition of moderate in Webster's dictionary is "to become less violent, severe, intense, or rigorous." One definition of mediate is "to effect (a result) or convey (a message, gift, etc.) by or as if by an intermediary." Baron and Kenny (1986) provide a clear and accessible clarification of the distinctions between these terms.

13.2.5: Calculating Direct and Indirect Effects

The geneticist Sewall Wright developed a method called **path analysis** that often goes hand in hand with diagrams like those shown above to depict the causal pathways among variables. As Wright (1921, 557) wrote in a seminal paper on the topic:

> The degree of correlation between two variables can be calculated by well-known methods, but when it is found it gives merely the resultant of all connecting paths of influence. The present paper is an attempt to present a method of measuring the direct influence along each separate path in such a system and thus of finding the degree to which variation of a given effect is determined by each particular cause.

Figure 13.4(a) below depicts the "resultant of all connecting paths of influence" and Figure 13.4(b) one of the "separate paths" that Wright's technique was designed to measure.

(a)   (b)

■ **Figure 13.4**

The association on the left is referred to as the **total effect** of X_2 on Y. The association in the top of Figure 13.4(b), depicted by the two arrows pointing from X_2 to X_3 and from X_3 to Y is referred to as the **indirect effect** of X_2 on Y through X_3. The bottom arrow in Figure 13.4(b), pointing from X_2 to Y, is referred to as the **direct effect** of X_2 on Y. The broader technique, referred to as path analysis, can incorporate much more complicated diagrams with multiple indirect pathways (e.g., indirect paths from X_2 to Y through X_4, X_5, X_6, etc.) and additional stages of connections (e.g., indirect paths from X_3 to Y; see Box 13.1).

Figures 13.4(a) and (b) depict several regression models. We will define each of these formally so we can see how to calculate the direct, indirect, and total effects. We are going to use a new notational convention to make this clear. We will use $\hat{\beta}$ to denote a coefficient estimate for a multiple regression and we will use b to denote a coefficient estimate from a bivariate regression.

We will use subscripts to indicate which variable is the outcome and predictor, referring to Y with the number 1, X_2 with the number 2, and X_3 with the number 3 and placing the outcome number first followed by the predictor in the subscript; for example, b_{12} would denote a bivariate regression with Y as the outcome and X_2 as the predictor.

We identify the regressions in Figures 13.4(a) and (b) using the arrows. Each arrow points from a predictor to an outcome. If an outcome has more than one arrow pointing to it, then the variables at the other end of the arrows are the predictors of a multiple regression. If an outcome has one arrow pointing to it, then the variable at the other end of that arrow is the single predictor in a bivariate regression. Notice that in Figure 13.4(b), X_3 is an outcome in one regression (an arrow points to it) and a predictor in another regression (an arrow points away from it).

■ **Box 13.1**

Many courses in path analysis and structural equation modeling are available, including through resources like summer courses at the University of Michigan (*http://www.icpsr.umich.edu/sumprog/*) and the University of Kansas (*http://www.quant.ku.edu/StatsCamps/overview.html*) and likely at your local university. Numerous texts on the topics are available as well (e.g., Bollen 1989; MacKinnon 2008; Iacobucci 2008).

■ **Table 13.6: Regression Models Used in Estimating Indirect and Direct Effects**

Figure 13.4(a)	$Y_i = b_1 + b_{12}X_{2i} + \hat{e}_{1i}$	(13.1)
Figure 13.4(b)	$Y_i = \hat{\beta}_1 + \hat{\beta}_{12}X_{2i} + \hat{\beta}_{13}X_{3i} + \hat{\varepsilon}_{1i}$	(13.2)
	$X_{3i} = b_3 + b_{32}X_{2i} + \hat{e}_{3i}$	(13.3)

We place these coefficients on the relevant paths below.

(a)   (b)

■ **Figure 13.5**

The indirect effect of X_2 on Y can be calculated by multiplying the coefficient estimates on the two paths associating X_2 to Y through X_3; that is, the indirect effect is $b_{32} * \hat{\beta}_{13}$. The direct effect of X_2 on Y is captured by the multiple regression coefficient estimate, $\hat{\beta}_{12}$. The total effect of X_2 on Y can be calculated as the sum of the direct and indirect effects, $\hat{\beta}_{12} + b_{32} * \hat{\beta}_{13}$. This result will be equal to the total effect as calculated by the bivariate regression coefficient estimate, b_{12}.

■ **Table 13.7: Calculating the Total, Direct, and Indirect Effects**

Total	$b_{12} = \hat{\beta}_{12} + b_{32} * \hat{\beta}_{13}$
Direct	$\hat{\beta}_{12}$
Indirect	$b_{32} * \hat{\beta}_{13}$

13.2.6: Example 13.2

We will again use our NSFH example of men's hours of work, but now we will look at health limitations as a mediator of the effect of self-reported health. The limitations measure is the sum of six dichotomous items about whether or not the respondent perceives that physical or mental conditions limit his or her ability to: care for personal needs, such as dressing, eating or going to the bathroom; move about inside the house; work for pay; do day-to-day household tasks; climb a flight of stairs; and walk six blocks. The mediation of some of the effect of overall health on work hours through health limitations can be shown in figures, as follows. (For now, we will leave respondent's age out of the model, but we will show the full model below.)

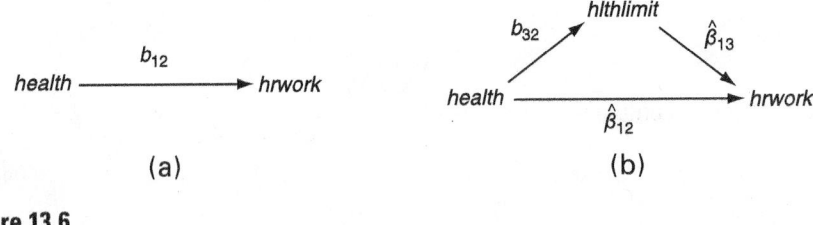

(a)   (b)

■ **Figure 13.6**

The results of using SAS and Stata to estimate the three regressions shown in the diagrams are presented in Display B.13.2. We summarize them below:

■ **Table 13.8: Regression Models Used in Estimating Indirect and Direct Effects of Men's Health on their Hours of Work, with Mediation through Health Limitations**

Figure 13.6(a)	$\widehat{hrwork}_i = 37.86 + 1.14 * health_i$
Figure 13.6(b)	$\widehat{hrwork}_i = 38.52 + 1.008 * health_i - 5.656 * hlthlimit_i$
	$\widehat{hlthlimit}_i = 0.12 - 0.0239 * health_i$

The values of the total, direct, and indirect effects can be calculated as follows:

■ **Table 13.9: Calculating the Total, Direct, and Indirect Effects of Men's Health on their Hours of Work, with Mediation through Health Limitations**

Total	$b_{12} = 1.14$
	$\hat{\beta}_{12} + b_{32} * \hat{\beta}_{13} = 1.008 + (-0.0239 * -5.656) = 1.14$
Direct	$\hat{\beta}_{12} = 1.008$
Indirect	$b_{32} * \hat{\beta}_{13} = -0.0239 * -5.656 = 0.135$

As expected, the sum of the direct and indirect effects equals the total effect.

13.2.7: Suppressor Variables

The example above is a case in which the indirect effect is of the same sign as the direct effect. As a consequence, the direct effect is smaller in magnitude than the total effect. It is also possible that the indirect effect may have the opposite sign as the direct effect. In these cases, the total effect may be close to zero, and adding the mediator variable to the model may reveal a significant association between the predictor of interest and the outcome. Mediators that have this type of effect are called **suppressor variables**.

■ **Literature Excerpt 13.2**

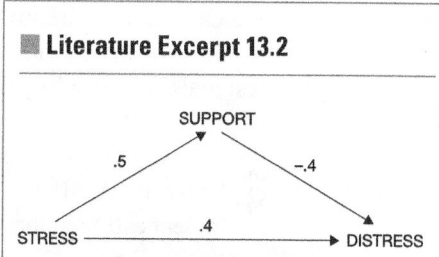

Figure 1B Additive Effect Buffering: The Resource as an Intervening, Suppressor Variable

Source: Wheaton, Blair. 1985. "Models for the Stress-Buffering Functions of Coping Resources." *Journal of Health and Social Behavior,* 26: 352–64.

Blair Wheaton (1985) provides an example of a suppressor variable in the field of medical sociology. Literature Excerpt 13.2 reproduces a figure that depicts a positive direct effect of stress on distress and a negative indirect effect of stress on distress through social support. As he notes:

> Probably the central analytical fact about this model is that the indirect effect through social support operates in a direction opposite to the overall causal effect of stress on distress (suggesting the term *suppressor variable* is appropriate) . . . The point here is that the total causal effect of stress on distress (.2) is less than its direct effect (.4). It is the total effect, not just the direct effect, that reflects the impact of stress. Thus, it is clear in this case that support acts to buffer this overall impact (p. 356, italics in the original).

The total effect of .2 is calculated based on the values on the arrows in Literature Excerpt 13.2, using the formulas we presented above (.4 + (5 * −.4) = .4 − .2 = .2).

Although researchers often think in terms of indirect effects that have the same sign as the direct effect, considering suppressor variables in our conceptual models and empirical work is important, especially because ignoring them can result in the overall association between a predictor of interest and outcome to be near zero (or of the "wrong sign").

13.2.8: A Note on the Meaning of Controlling

We can also use the regressions depicted above to help us to understand the meaning of controlling for other variables in multiple regression. In Equation 13.3, we regressed X_3 on X_2 as we calculated the indirect effect. The errors in this equation represent the variation in X_3 not explained by X_2. If we calculate these errors, and use them in a bivariate regression to predict Y, we will see that the resulting coefficient estimate equals $\hat{\beta}_{13}$ from Equation 13.2. Going through this process can make concrete the meaning of a multiple regression coefficient. When controlling for the other variable(s), we isolate the unique effect of one predictor on the outcome; that is, we answer the question: is the variation that the predictor does not share with other variables in the model related to the outcome?

We can use the `output` statement in SAS and the `predict` command in Stata to request the residuals from Equation 13.3 for our hours of work example. We then regress Y on these residuals. The results are in the top two rows of Display B.13.3.

We can similarly regress X_2 on X_3 and obtain the errors, which represent the variation in X_2 not explained by X_3. If we regress Y on these residuals, we will obtain the multiple regression coefficient estimate for X_2 from Equation 13.2. These results are shown in the bottom two rows of Display B.13.3.

Comparing the results in Display B.13.3 with those in the multiple regression shown in the middle panel of Display B.13.2 confirms that our residual regressions reproduce the multiple regression coefficients.

- ▦ In Display B.13.2, the coefficient for *Health* in the multiple regression (middle panel) is 1.008126. In Display B.13.3, the top panel shows the commands for creating the residuals from a regression of *Health* on *HlthLimit*. These residuals reflect the variation in *Health* not explained by *HlthLimit*. The results of the regression of *hrwork* on these residuals is shown in the top panel of Display B.13.3. The coefficient, 1.008126, matches the coefficient estimate for *Health* from the multiple regression in Display B.13.2.
- ▦ In Display B.13.2, the coefficient for *HlthLimit* in the multiple regression (middle panel) is −5.655881. In Display B.13.3, the bottom panel shows the commands for creating the residuals from a regression of *HlthLimit* on *Health*. These residuals reflect the variation in *HlthLimit* not explained by *Health*. The results of the regression of *hrwork* on these residuals is shown in the bottom panel of Display B.13.3. The coefficient, −5.655881, matches the coefficient estimate for *HlthLimit* from the multiple regression in Display B.13.2.

13.3: OMITTED VARIABLE BIAS

What if we believe part of the effect of health on hours of work operates through health limitations, but we do not have a measure of health limitations? How might we think through the potential effect of omitting the health limitations measure from our model? Or, what if we think that a portion of the association between health and hours of work is really due to age as a common cause, but we did not collect the study participants' ages? How might we think through the potential effect of omitting age from our model? **Omitted variable bias** is defined exactly the same as the indirect effect ($b_{32} * \hat{\beta}_{13}$), although because we typically do not have a measure of the omitted variable, we consider just the signs of the arrows on the direct and indirect pathways to anticipate the consequences of lacking this measure.

Table 13.10 can be used to assess the direction of the bias based on thinking through the signs on the pathways. The columns indicate the anticipated sign on the association between the included and excluded predictor variables. The rows indicate the anticipated sign of the association between the excluded predictor variable and the outcome. The product of the column and row signs are shown in the cells.

■ **Table 13.10: Expected Direction of Omitted Variable Bias**

		Direction of Association Between the *Included* and *Excluded Predictor* Variables	
		Positive (+)	Negative (–)
Direction of Association Between *Excluded Predictor* Variable and *Outcome* Variable	Positive (+)	+ + = positive	+ – = negative
	Negative (–)	– + = negative	– – = positive

So, if the sign of the association between the excluded variable is in the same direction with both the included predictor and outcome, then the omitted variable bias will be positive. If the sign of the association between the excluded variable and the included predictor and outcome are in different directions, then the omitted variable bias will be negative.

We can combine the expected direction of the omitted variable bias with the expected direction of the direct effect of the included variable to produce an assessment of whether we will likely understate or overstate the direct effect of the included variable due to omitted variable bias.

Typical indirect effects, like our example of health limitations mediating the association of health with hours of work, fall on the diagonal of Table 13.11. Omitting the indirect effect overstates the direct effect of the predictor of interest. This is sometimes referred to as biasing the effect away from zero. Suppression effects fall off the diagonal. The direct effect and indirect effect have opposite signs, and so omitting the suppressor variable leads to an understatement of the direct effect of the predictor of interest. This is sometimes referred to as bias toward zero. In cases in which the indirect effect of a suppressor variable is larger than the direct effect, the sign on the coefficient estimate for the predictor of interest will be in the wrong direction, relative to its expected direct effect.

These tables can be helpful if a reviewer of your research raises a question about a variable that you left out of the model or if you realize too late that you should have measured an important concept. If the variable is conceptualized as having an indirect effect of the same sign as the

■ Table 13.11: Expected Misstatement of the Magnitude of the Direct Effect of Included Variable

		Direction of Omitted Variable Bias	
		Positive	Negative (–)
Direction of *Direct Effect* of Included Variable	Positive	*positive + positive* overstate (bias away from zero)	*positive + negative* understate (bias toward zero) or incorrect direction (wrong sign)
	Negative	*negative + positive* understate (bias toward zero) or incorrect direction (wrong sign)	*negative + negative* overstate (bias away from zero)

direct effect, then omitting it overstates the direct effect of your predictor of interest. But, if the variable is conceptualized as having an indirect effect of opposite sign as the direct effect, then omitting it understates the direct effect of your predictor of interest.

Notice that the tables above can be used to think about the direction of omitted variable bias for confounders as well as mediators. For example, if a confounding excluded variable is expected to be associated in the same direction with the predictor of interest and the outcome, then the omitted variable bias will be positive. If the estimated effect of the predictor of interest with the outcome is also positive, then the omitted variable may be biasing the estimated effect upward.

13.4: SUMMARY

In this chapter, we examined how adding variables to a multiple regression model affects the coefficients and their standard errors. Multiple regression allows us to estimate the pathways that our theoretical frameworks suggest link variables and to adjust for confounders in our observational data. In many cases, adding a variable will lead to the coefficient estimate for our predictor of interest to decrease in magnitude, either because of adding a common cause it shares with the outcome (spuriousness) or because of adding an intervening variable that links it to the outcome (mediation). In some cases, adding a variable will lead the coefficient estimate of interest to increase in magnitude (suppression). It is useful to think carefully about potential suppressors, since omitting them can lead to an underestimation of the direct effect of our predictor of interest. Distinguishing between confounders and mediators cannot be determined by the empirical methods we study in this book. Conceptual rationales and measurement decisions determine their placement in the model (e.g., assuring that confounders precede and mediators follow predictors of interest logically and operationally). In cross-sectional data, the direction of arrows will often be debatable.

KEY TERMS

Confounder (also Common Cause, Extraneous Variable)

Direct Effect

Indirect Effect

Mediation

Mediator (also Proximal Cause, Intervening Variable)

Moderation

Omitted Variable Bias

Path Analysis

Spurious Relationship

Suppressor Variables

Total Effect

REVIEW QUESTIONS

13.1   How can you calculate the direct and indirect effects in a path diagram in which the effect of X_2 on Y is partially mediated by X_3?

13.2   How can you calculate the total effect based on the direct and indirect effects?

13.3   How can you draw examples of path diagrams in which omitted variable bias overstates the direct effect of X_2 on Y away from zero in a *positive* direction, in which omitted variable bias overstates the direct effect of X_2 on Y away from zero in a *negative* direction, and in which omitted variable bias understates the direct effect of X_2 on Y (toward zero)?

REVIEW EXERCISES

13.1.   Refer to Brumbaugh and colleagues Table 3 presented in Literature Excerpt 13.1. Compare the coefficients for the *Female* and *Age* variables in Model 2 versus Model 3 (when marital, cohabitation, and parenthood histories are added to the model). Discuss whether you would interpret the changes in coefficients for these two variables as *mediation, suppression*, and/or *confounding*. What else might you need to know in order to make a determination?

13.2. Refer to Dooley and Prause's Table 3 presented in Literature Excerpt 9.1.

    (a) Compare the coefficients for *Age* in Model 2 and Model 3. What do the results suggest is the possible direction of correlations among *Age, Weeks of Gestation*, and *Birth Weight*?

    (b) Compare the coefficients for *Weight prior to pregnancy* in Model 3 and Model 4. What do the results suggest is the possible direction of correlations among *Weight prior to pregnancy, Weight gain during pregnancy*, and *Birth Weight*?

13.3. Suppose that a researcher anticipates that the association between stress and distress may be suppressed because persons who are exposed to stressors may elicit social support from their social networks and social support reduces distress.

    (a) *Calculate the indirect effect* of stress on distress through social support using the results found in the table below.

    (b) *Comment* on whether the researcher's expectation about the suppressor effect is confirmed.

    (c) As you answer the question, be sure to *fill out the diagram*, by writing variable names in the boxes and coefficients in the circles.

Predictor Variable	Outcome Variable		
	Social Support	Distress	Distress
Stress	0.52*	1.80*	0.61*
	(0.03)	(0.01)	(0.08)
Social Support	—	-2.29*	—
		(0.01)	
Intercept	-26.08	-79.76	-19.98
	(3.40)	(0.49)	(7.81)

* $p<.05$

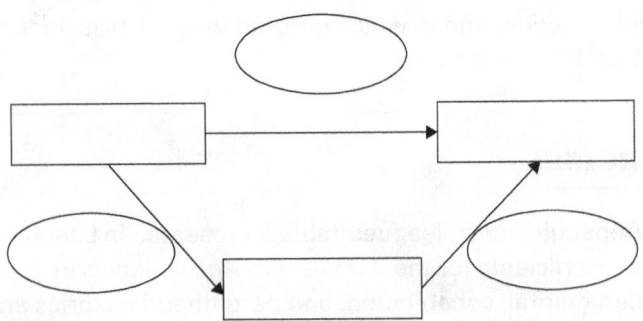

13.4. Consider the three regression model results presented below.

(a) Calculate the missing coefficient for the bivariate regression of SATMATH on FEMALE (cell labeled **A** below) based on the other coefficients listed in the table.

(b) As you answer the question, be sure to fill out the diagram by writing variable names in the boxes and coefficients in the circles.

Predictor Variable	Outcome Variable		
	SATMATH	SATMATH	NUMMATH
FEMALE	**A**	−98.16	−2.51
NUMMATH	—	28.83	—
Intercept	473.51	358.30	4.00

* $p<.05$

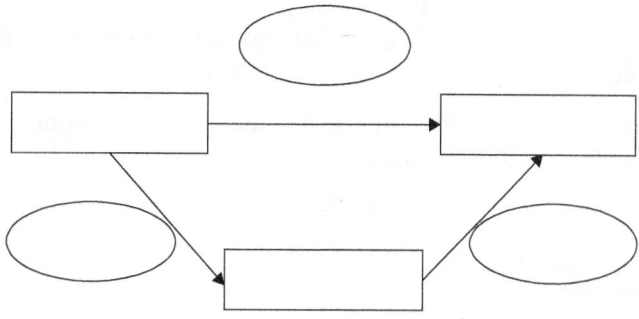

CHAPTER EXERCISE

In this exercise, you will write a SAS and a Stata batch program to estimate a mediated relationship.

We will again use the NHIS 1999 data set but in this question we will focus on the questions about days of work missed and the twelve questions about functional limitation in addition to body mass index. Thus, when you use the data include an *if expression* to only keep cases that do not have missing values on *bmiR, WKDAYR,* and the twelve variables that begin with *FL* (refer back to your notes from the chapter exercise in Chapter 3; For this chapter exercise, we will treat values at or above 4 on the twelve functional limitations variables as missing).

In all cases, conduct two-sided hypothesis tests. Use a 5% alpha unless otherwise indicated.

13.1 Total, Direct and Indirect Effects

a) SAS/Stata Tasks.

   i) After using the data with non-missing values, verify that *WKDAYR* and the twelve functional limitations variables have only valid values (0 to 366 for *WKDAYR* and 0 "not at all difficult to 3 "very difficult" for the twelve functional limitations variables).

   ii) Create a new variable, *FLsum*, that is the sum of the twelve functional limitations variables.

   iii) Regress *WKDAYR* on *bmiR* (We will refer to this as *Regression #1*).

   iv) Regress *WKDAYR* on *bmiR* and *FLsum* (We will refer to this as *Regression #2*).

   v) Regress *FLsum* on *bmiR* (We will refer to this as *Regression #3*).

b) Write-Up Tasks.

   i) Use Regression 2 and Regression 3 to calculate the total, direct, and indirect effects.

   ii) Comment on how the total effect calculated in Question 13.1.bi relates to the coefficient in Regression 1.

COURSE EXERCISE

COURSE EXERCISE 13

Identify at least one confounding and at least one mediating relationship that you might estimate based on the data set that you created in the course exercise to Chapter 4. Ideally, think about conceptual reasons why you might expect that one variable confounds or mediates the effect of another variable.

For the meditational relationship, estimate the regression models needed to calculate the total, direct, and indirect effects. Calculate each of these effects based on the results.

For the confounding relationship, show how the coefficient estimate for your predictor of interest changes when you add the confounding variable to the regression model. What is the direction of bias when this variable is omitted from the regression model? How is it related to the outcome and predictor of interest?

Using the commands shown in Display B.13.3, show how you can reproduce the multiple regression coefficients by regressing the outcome on the residuals.

OUTLIERS, HETEROSKEDASTICITY, AND MULTICOLLINEARITY

CHAPTER 14: OUTLIERS, HETEROSKEDASTICITY, AND MULTICOLLINEARITY

In this chapter we discuss several violations of model assumptions in OLS, and strategies for identifying and dealing with them. In particular, we consider how extreme data points can influence point estimates and how heteroskedasticity and multicollinearity can influence standard errors. Extreme data points can arise for various reasons, one of which is mis-specification of the form of the relationship between the predictor and outcome (e.g., as linear rather than nonlinear). Heteroskedasticity means that the assumption of constant conditional variance is violated. Multicollinearity is an extreme case of expected correlations among predictors. Indeed, some correlation among predictors is needed in order to benefit from multiple regression's ability to reduce bias: adding variables to a multiple regression model will not change the coefficient estimate of our predictor of interest unless the new variables are correlated at least to some degree with our predictor. At the same time, correlation among the predictors increases the standard errors of the coefficients. Very high correlation among predictor variables, or multicollinearity, will make our coefficient estimates quite imprecise.

14.1: OUTLIERS AND INFLUENTIAL OBSERVATIONS

A historical perspective by one of the developers of a widely used diagnostic for influential observations provides a nice introduction to this section:

> My own ideas on diagnostics grew out of theoretical work on robust estimation and applied work on econometric models. One model we were working on just did not agree with economic theory. After looking at residuals and some plots without noting anything, I questioned the economic theory. The economists said our estimated model could not be right, so I checked all of the data again. One observation had been entered incorrectly several iterations back and it seemed to me that I should have had a better clue to that problem long before I questioned the economic theory. Leaving each observation out one-at-a-time was easy to talk about and after a few weeks of programming easy to do in practice (Welsch 1986: 404).

This quote highlights the intimate relationship between diagnosing influential observations and model testing, as well as how influential observations might arise (data entry error) and can be diagnosed (examining how excluding a single case affects the estimates).

14.1.1: Definition of Outliers and Influential Observations

An **outlier** is a value that falls far from the rest of the values on a variable. In a regression context, we typically are especially interested in outliers on the outcome variable. In some cases, outliers may go hand in hand with the outcome variable not being normally distributed. For instance, in our distance example, we know that the outcome variable of miles from the mother is highly skewed, with many zero values but some adults living thousands of miles from the mother. In a univariate context where the variable is expected to be normally distributed, outliers are often identified as values falling more than two standard deviations above or below the mean. Although we expect about 5 percent of observations to fall in this range by chance, a larger number of outliers or very extreme outliers may suggest non-normality or errors in the data.

An **influential observation** is an observation whose inclusion in or exclusion from the data file greatly changes the results of the regression analysis. These observations can be extreme because they fall relatively far from the mean across the predictor variables and because they fall relatively far from the conditional regression line (regression surface in multiple regression). It is extremely important to watch for such influential observations to avoid reporting results that depend on a single or small number of observations.

As illustrated in Literature Excerpt 14.1 an observation may be an outlier and not influential or influential but not an outlier. In Figure 1a, point A' is an outlier on Y but not influential. Point is A'' influential but not an outlier on Y. In Figure 1b, point A' is both an outlier and influential. Figures 1c and 1d further visualize how the slope of the regression line might change when a single point is included or excluded. In Figure 1c, when point A is excluded, the estimate of the slope is zero, but when A is included, the slope is positive (the regression line is pulled upward by the influential observation). In Figure 1d, when point A is excluded, the estimate of the slope is positive, but when A is included, the slope is zero (the regression line is pulled downward by the influential observation).

14.1.2: Possible Reasons for Outliers and Influential Observations

One reason for outliers and influential observations is data errors. Thus, it is always important to check for data entry and data management errors. We have emphasized in earlier chapters the importance of verifying that the distribution of values match codebooks in existing data, that missing data values are appropriately recoded, and that the distribution of values on created variables conform with desired results. Skipping these steps at the data management stage can lead to identification of outliers at the analysis stage (or if overlooked at the analysis stage, potentially reporting erroneous results). If you are using existing data, it is also helpful to stay

■ **Literature Excerpt 14.1**

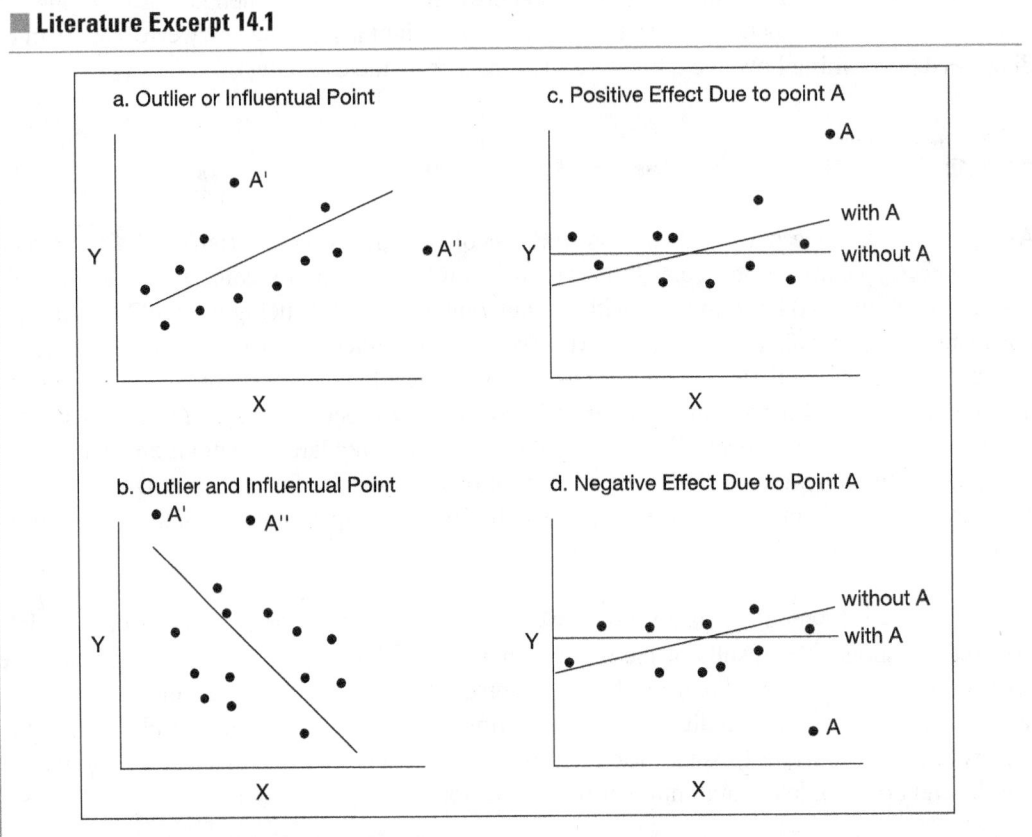

Figure 1 Examples of Outliers and Influential Points

Source: Chatterjee, Sangit and Mustafa Yilmaz. (1992). "A Review of Regression Diagnostics for Behavioral Research." *Applied Psychological Measurement,* 16: 209–27.

in contact with the study staff, where possible (for example, signing up to listservs where data corrections and new data releases are announced). When you collect your own data, it is important to first carefully collect data (to reduce reporting errors from respondents), then to carefully enter the data (to reduce keystroke errors), and finally to examine the distribution of variables (to identify extreme values that should be verified against the raw data).

Another reason for outliers and influential observations is that the model is not specified correctly. When the relationship between a predictor and outcome is curvilinear, but a linear relationship between the predictor and outcome is estimated, diagnostics on the linear model may identify apparent influential observations that are no longer influential once a nonlinear model is estimated. The extreme cases may also conform to a different model than the other cases (perhaps suggesting an interaction or other subgroup analysis is needed).

The Lyons (2007) article that we examined in Chapter 1 provides an example. The table reproduced in Literature Excerpt 1.1b had columns labeled *Excluding Outliers.* In the text,

Lyons notes that three influential observations were identified using some of the techniques we describe in the next section. These were three communities that had "unusually high levels of antiwhite hate crime given their affluence and racial (white) homogeneity" and were all located on Chicago's southwest side (p. 844). When these cases were omitted from the analysis, the expected association was revealed (antiwhite hate crime was higher in poorer areas with high residential mobility). As Lyon's notes "thorough explanation for these different patterns in the southwest warrants qualitative exploration beyond the scope of the present study" (p. 844) but he speculates about the potential reasons for these three cases conforming to a different model in the discussion. He notes that all three communities are areas with high antiblack hate crime that is explained well by his defended communities model. He speculates that the high antiwhite crime could be retaliatory for current antiblack crime, or due to historical racial tensions in these areas. He also speculates that whites may be more ready to define and report acts as racially motivated in these areas (p. 849).

Another alternative to excluding outlying cases or conducting subgroup analyses would be to transform the outcome, as we did using the log transformation in Chapter 12. In fact, two of our Literature Excerpts examining nonlinear relationships in Chapter 12 used a log transformation of the outcome (Glauber 2007; Pritchett and Summers 1996; Willson 2003 used another—square root—transformation because she found the log transformation too severe).

Yet another alternative to deal with outliers would be to move to a model that makes different assumptions about the distribution of the outcome; that is, values that seem unusual in a normal distribution may not be unusual for other distributions. In Chapter 18, we will provide a roadmap to models designed for count outcomes which often have long right tails. In fact, our fourth Literature Excerpt in Chapter 12, Cornwell, Laumann, and Schumm 2008, used one of these models (Poisson regression) for their count outcome.

14.1.3: Identifying Outliers and Influential Observations

Many diagnostic measures have been developed with cutoff values to use as a general guide in identifying influential observations (see Chatterjee and Hadi 1986; Fox 1991; Belsey, Kuh, and Welsch 1980). We will cover five that are used frequently in the literature: (a) hat values, (b) studentized residuals, (c) Cook's distance, (d) DFFITS, and (e) DFBETAs.

The first two diagnostic measures do not measure influence, per se, but the potential for influence based on an outlying value on the outcome (studentized residuals) or the predictors (hat values). The latter three measure the change in the predicted values or coefficient estimates when a case is excluded from versus included in the estimation sample.

Each of these diagnostics is calculated for every case in the data set. Suggested cutoffs are available to identify extreme values for each diagnostic, although it is generally recommended that these be used along with graphs to identify extreme values in the context of a given data set (Chatterjee and Hadi 1986; Welsch 1986). We will illustrate how to use such cutoffs and graphs below.

The first diagnostic considers how unusual each observation is on the predictor variables and the second considers how far each observation falls from the fitted regression line (surface).

■ **Hat values** (h_i) measure the distance of the X-values for the ith case from the means of the X-values for all n cases. Hat values fall between zero and 1, and a larger hat value indicates that the case falls far from the center (means) of the predictors in multidimensional space. The hat value is sometimes called a measure of **leverage** because observations that are distant from the center of the X variables have the potential to greatly alter the coefficient estimates from the model. For moderate to large sample sizes, $2(k-1)/n$ or $3(k-1)/n$ has been suggested as a cutoff for identifying high leverage (where k is the number of predictors plus one for the intercept, and thus the cutoff is two or three times the number of predictors divided by the sample size; Chatterjee and Hadi 1986; Hoaglin and Kempthorne 1986).

■ **Studentized residuals** are the estimated errors we are familiar with ($\hat{e}_i = Y_i - \hat{Y}_i$) scaled by the root mean square error and hat value.

$$t_i^* = \frac{Y_i - \hat{Y}_i}{\hat{\sigma}_i \sqrt{1 - h_i}}$$

In the formula, $\hat{\sigma}_i$ is the mean square error for the regression model when the ith residual is excluded from the estimation sample and h_i is the hat value. The studentized residuals follow a t-distribution with n-k degrees of freedom (where k is the number of predictors in the model plus one for the intercept). Values larger than 2 or 3 in absolute value are generally taken to be extreme, since about 95 percent of observations should fall within the range of -2 and 2.

■ **Standardized residuals** may be calculated similarly.

$$t_i = \frac{Y_i - \hat{Y}_i}{\hat{\sigma} \sqrt{1 - h_i}}$$

Here, $\hat{\sigma}$ is the usual root mean square error for the regression model when all cases are included in the estimation sample.

Three other measures directly assess influence: how results from the regression differ when the observation is included or omitted.

■ **Cook's distance** combines the standardized residuals and hat values in a single calculation:

$$D_i = \frac{t_i^2}{k-1} * \frac{h_i}{(1 - h_i)}$$

Because t_i is squared in the numerator, Cook's distance is always positive in value. A cutoff of $4/n$ has been suggested to flag potentially influential observations.

■ **DFFITS** is similar to Cook's distance, but calculated based on the studentized residual:

$$DFFIT_i = t_i^* \sqrt{h_i/(1-h_i)}$$

Cook's distance and DFFITS can identify different values as influential, because the DFFITS measures the influence on both the coefficients and conditional variance (because t_i^* uses $\hat{\sigma}_i$), while Cook's distance captures only the influence on the coefficients (because t_i uses $\hat{\sigma}$).

The word DFFIT comes from "difference in fit," and can be remembered as an abbreviation of this phrase.[1]

For large data sets, the cutoff for high DFFITS is that the absolute value of the DFFITS is greater than $2\sqrt{(k-1)/n}$ where k is equal to the number of parameters in the model plus 1 for the intercept. For smaller data sets, a cutoff of 1 or 2 has also been suggested (Chatterjee and Hadi 1986).[2]

■ **DFBETAS** provide a standardized measure of the difference between a parameter estimate when all n cases are used to estimate the regression ($\hat{\beta}_k$) and when the ith case is omitted from the sample prior to running the regression ($\hat{\beta}_{ki}$).

$$DFBETA_i = \frac{(\hat{\beta}_k - \hat{\beta}_{ki})}{\hat{\sigma}_{\hat{\beta}_k}}$$

Thus, DFBETA can be remembered as "difference in beta." A separate DFBETA is calculated for each predictor variable included in the model. For large data sets, when the absolute value of DFBETA is larger than $2\sqrt{n}$ there may be high influence (Chatterjee and Hadi 1986).

Table 14.1 summarizes the diagnostic measures and their cutoffs.

■ **Table 14.1: Summary of Diagnostic Measures of Outlying and Influential Observations**

Name	Definition	Cutoff Values	
Hat value	Measures how far observations fall from center of the predictor variables. Also known as leverage.	$2(k-1)/n$	$3(k-1)/n$
Studentized or standardized residuals	Scaled residuals from regression model. (Scaling factor differs slightly between two versions)	2	3
Cook's distance	Combined measure based on standardized residuals and hat values.	$4/n$	
DFFITS	Capture changes in the "fit" of the regression, both the coefficients and conditional variance, when a case is excluded from the sample.	1 or 2	$2\sqrt{(k-1)/n}$
DFBETAS (one for each predictor in model)	Capture how each coefficient changes when a case is excluded from the sample.	$2/\sqrt{n}$	

Note: k is the number of predictors plus one for the intercept. n is the sample size. Most measures can be negative or positive in sign, so take the absolute value (use abs () function in SAS and Stata) before evaluating their magnitude relative to the cutoffs.

14.1.4: Strategies for Addressing Outliers and Influential Observations

As noted above, a common approach to dealing with non-normality of the outcome variable within the context of OLS is to take the log of the outcome variable. Obviously, this approach won't work in all cases (e.g., variables with numerous zeros or negative values, or dichotomous outcomes). But in some cases it does a good job of normalizing the outcome variable and reducing outliers.

Another common approach to dealing with influential cases in OLS is to see how these cases differ from other cases and to refine the model accordingly. When the influential cases are few in number, not an obvious data entry error, or have no apparent substantive meaning, it is possible simply to examine how sensitive the findings are to the inclusion or exclusion of the outlying observations. In the case of the Lyons (2007) Literature Excerpt mentioned above, the three outlying cases hung together in a substantive way, but were too few in number to be separately analyzed, so they were excluded from the presented results but mentioned in the results and discussion sections.

14.1.5: Example 14.1

We will use our distance example to illustrate the process of identifying and addressing outliers in practice. As we noted above, although cutoffs exist for considering diagnostic values extreme, there is no hard-and-fast procedure for identifying and addressing outliers. There are many decision points where different researchers might make somewhat different choices. We try to convey this fluid process in our example. It is typically useful to use graphs of the variables and multiple diagnostic values to try to get a full picture of potential outliers and their actual influence. In practice, we are typically concerned with being sure that our results are not sensitive to the inclusion or exclusion of one or more influential observations (including those that are data entry errors) and that we have not mis-stated an association when it applies differently to some subset of the data. We may need to take several different approaches to looking for and addressing outliers before we are confident that these problems are not present. We would typically present the final result that we conclude best represents the data, but summarize in a footnote, paragraph, or appendix, what we did to come to this conclusion. In examining outliers (and heteroskedasticity in the next section) we will estimate a multiple regression similar to the one we estimated in Table 10.2, but allowing for the nonlinear associations of *g1yrschl* and *g2numsis* with *g1miles*, and including the *other* racial-ethnic group.

Graphing the Variables

Graphing the variables in the data set, especially the outcome and central predictors, is an important general first step in any project. Graphs can also be specifically useful in identifying outliers. Univariate plots can be examined for extreme values that fall far from the remainder of the distribution. Histograms and box plots, and stem-and-leaf plots for small data sets, are useful for this purpose. Scatterplots can be used to plot the outcome against the predictor to see if some values fall far from the major cloud of data, suggesting potential influence.

Univariate Plots

As introduced in Chapter 5, the `proc univariate` command in SAS provides a number of useful plots (including a histogram or stem-and-leaf plot and a box plot). We use the following command to request plots of the outcome (in natural units and logged form) and two central predictors (mother's schooling and number of sisters).

```
proc univariate plots;
  var g1miles logg1miles g1yrschl g2numsis;
run;
```

In Stata we use the `stem` command for stem-and-leaf plots, the `histogram` command for histograms, and the `graph` command for box plots. We find box plots particularly helpful for examining potential outliers, although you should experiment with which graph works best for you.[3]

Stem-and-Leaf	Histogram	Box Plot
stem g1miles	histogram g1miles	graph box g1miles
stem logg1miles	histogram logg1miles	graph box logg1miles
stem g1yrschl	histogram g1yrschl	graph box g1yrschl
stem g2numsis	histogram g2numsis	graph box g2numsis

Recall that in a box plot, the top of the box is the 75th percentile and the bottom of the box is the 25th percentile. The horizontal line through the middle of the box is the median. Dots represent outliers, which are defined in the box plot as values more than 1.5 times the interquartile range above or below the box (recall the interquartile range is the difference between the value at the 75th and the 25th percentiles). Whiskers extend from the box to the largest and smallest values that are not outliers.

Figure 14.1 provides a box plot of a standard normal variable for reference. Notice that some outliers are present, even for a normal variable (because we expect 5 percent of the values to fall

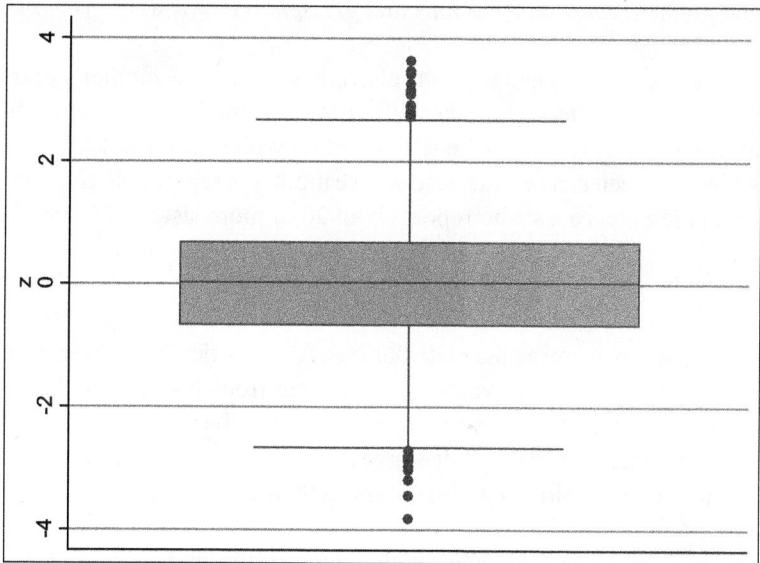

■ **Figure 14.1** Box Plot for a Standard Normal Variable

beyond about two standard deviations above and below the mean). In Figure 14.1, a few values are nearly four standard deviations above and below the mean.

Figure 14.2 presents the box plots of our four variables, using the Stata results. The boxes for *logg1miles* (Figure 14.2(b)) and *g1yrschl* (Figure 14.2(c)) look the most symmetric, and *logg1miles* has no outliers. *g1yrschl* has some outliers, especially the small values between zero and five years of schooling. In contrast *g1miles* and *g2numsis* both are skewed upward (skewed right) with some outliers falling far from the rest of the data (see Figures 14.2(a) and (d)). The top values on *g1miles* is one respondent who reports living 9,000 miles from his mother. The next closest value is 6,000 miles. On *g2numsis*, one respondent reports 20 and one respondent reports 22 sisters. The next closest value is 11. These results reinforce the benefit of the log transformation of the outcome for better approximating a normal distribution of the outcome in our case (compare Figures 14.2(a) and (b)) and suggest the potential for outliers and influential observations in the models that we estimated in earlier chapters with the nonlogged outcome and *g1yrschl* and *g2numsis* as continuous predictors.

Scatterplots

In SAS we can use the `proc gplot` statement to create scatterplots. For example, to graph *g1miles* on the *Y* axis and *g1yrschl* on the *X* axis, we would type:

```
proc gplot;
  plot g1miles*g1yrschl;
run;
```

In Stata, we can create scatterplots using `graph twoway scatterplot` followed by the name of our outcome and a predictor variable. For example, `graph twoway scatterplot g1miles g1yrschl` would graph *g1miles* on the *Y* axis and *g1yrschl* on the *X* axis.[4]

We plotted the nonlogged and logged versions of *g1miles* against the mother's years of schooling and the adult's number of sisters, and show the results from Stata in Figure 14.3. The plots with *g1miles* in its natural units are on the left and those with *g1miles* in logged form are on the right. As shown by the green arrows, the case whose mother is reported to live 9,000 miles away (Figures 14.3(a) and (c)) and cases who report about 20 or more sisters (Figures 14.3(c) and (d)) stand out.

Diagnostic Values

Graphs can also be used to examine the distribution of diagnostic values. Regardless of whether values fall above or below cutoffs, values that fall far from the rest of the data are worth examining. Sets of cases that fall above the cutoff can also be examined to see whether they share a common characteristic that might suggest how a model could be modified to reduce their influence and/or how sensitive the results are to their exclusion.

In SAS, we can request all of the diagnostics with options on the model statement (`/r influence`). By default, the table of values is simply listed in the ouput. But, we can use an `ods` statement to

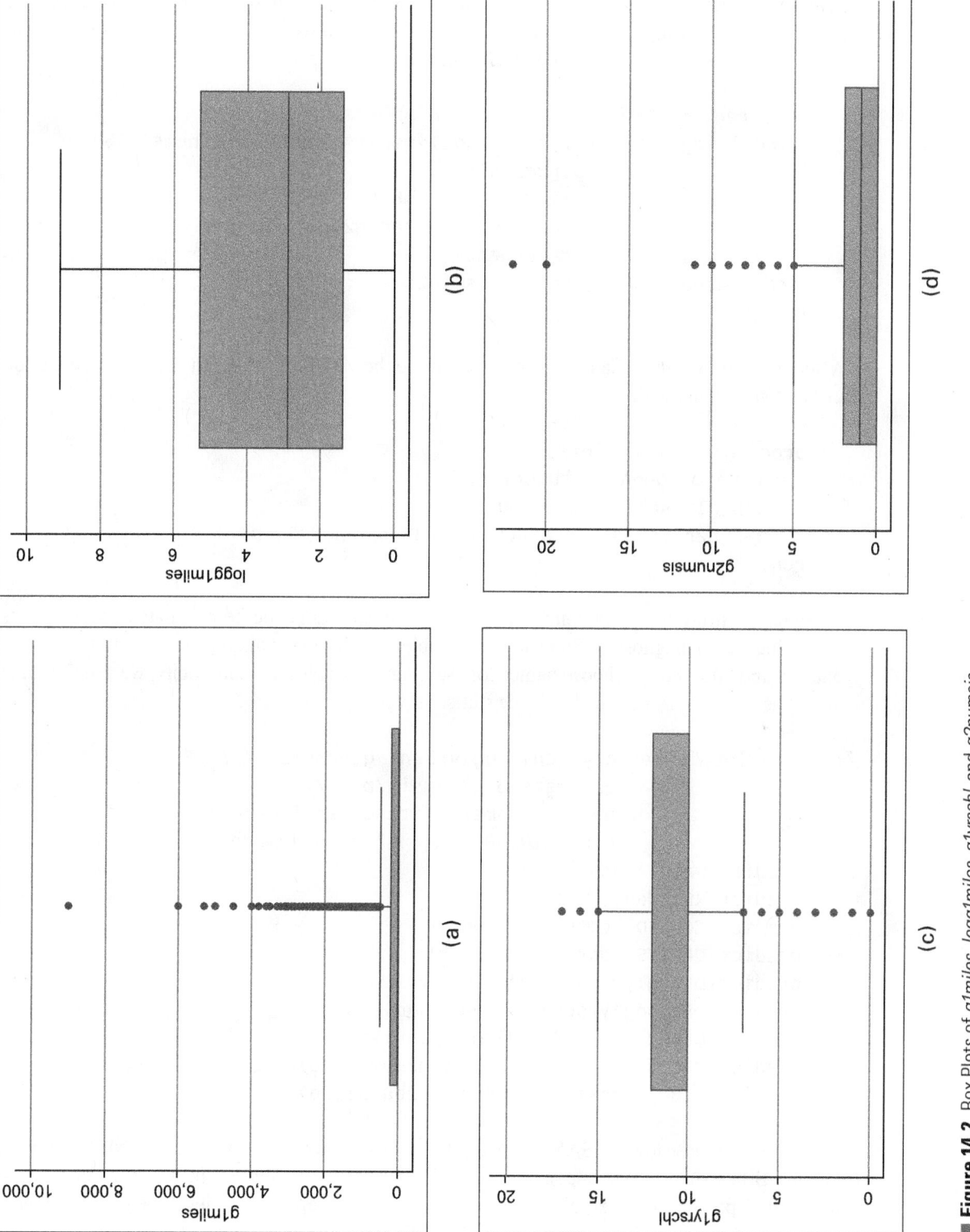

Figure 14.2 Box Plots of *g1miles, logg1miles, g1yrschl,* and *g2numsis*

save the diagnostics in a data file to examine.[5] SAS names these statistics by default, with names that map clearly onto the names we used above, and we will use these names in Stata as well (e.g., the *DFBETAS* are named *DFB_* followed by the variable name).

```
proc reg;
  model logg1miles=g1yrschl sqg1yrschl g2numsis4 g2numsis56
                   g2numsis7p
                   amind mexamer white other female
                   g2earn10000 g1age g2age g2numbro
                   /r influence;
  ods output outputstatistics=influence;
run;
```

After creating the output data file, we can examine the values of the diagnostics using the proc univariate command.

```
proc univariate plots;
  var HatDiagonal RStudent CooksD DFFITS
    DFB_g1yrschl DFB_sqg1yrschl
    DFB_g2numsis4 DFB_g2numsis56 DFB_g2numsis7p;
run;
```

In Stata, we use the predict command to request each diagnostic be calculated, with options indicating which diagnostics. Stata adds a variable containing the diagnostic value to the current data set and allows us to choose names for these new variables. For simplicity, we use the same names as SAS chooses for its influence statistics.

```
regress logg1miles g1yrschl sqg1yrschl g2numsis4 ///
                   g2numsis56 g2numsis7p ///
                   amind mexamer white other female ///
                   g2earn10000 g1age g2age g2numbro
  predict HatDiagonal, hat
  predict RStudent, rstudent
  predict CooksD, cooksd
  predict DFFITS, dfits
  predict DFB_g1yrschl, dfbeta(g1yrschl)
  predict DFB_sqg1yrschl, dfbeta(sqg1yrschl)
  predict DFB_g2numsis4, dfbeta(g2numsis4)
  predict DFB_g2numsis56, dfbeta(g2numsis56)
  predict DFB_g2numsis7p, dfbeta(g2numsis7p)
```

We can use expressions in SAS and Stata to identify whether the values exceed the cutoffs. Display B.14.1 shows these calculations and summarizes the results. For most of the diagnostics, less than 5 percent of cases fall above the cutoff. The exceptions are leverage (*HatDiagonal*) with about 6 percent of cases above 3 and DFFITS with just over 5 percent above the cutoff.

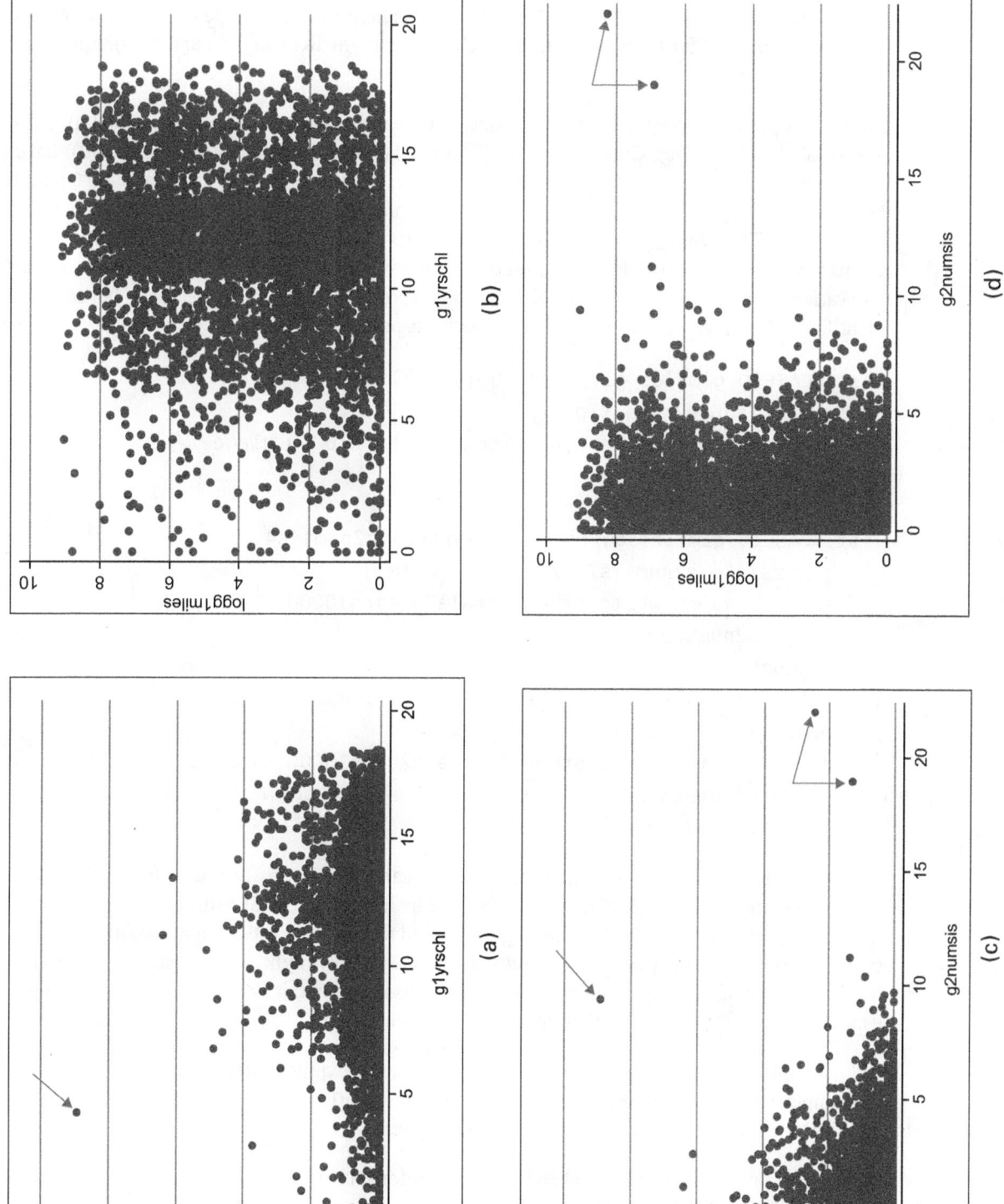

■ **Figure 14.3** Scatterplots of *g1miles* and *logg1miles* with *g1yrschl* and *g2numsis*

Because these cutoffs are only rough guides, it is also helpful to graph the diagnostic values to see whether any fall far from the rest. We use proc univariate in SAS and the graph box command in Stata to create box plots of the results.

Figure 14.4 presents box plots for the six diagnostic values. The hat value (Figure 14.4(a), with *Y* axis labeled *Leverage*), Cook's distance (Figure 14.4(c)), and DFFITS (Figure 14.4(d)) have values that clearly fall from the rest of the distribution (above about 0.10, above about 0.04, and below about −0.40, respectively). We use the list command to examine the cases that fall beyond these values. The syntax is list <variable list> if <expression> in Stata and proc print; var <variable list>; where <expression>; run; in SAS. We listed each of the variables in the regression model using an expression to identify the cases beyond the identified extreme value. For example, in Stata we typed:

```
list MCASEID g1miles g1yrschl sqg1yrschl g2numsis4 ///
    g2numsis56 g2numsis7p ///
    amind mexamer white other female g2earn10000 g1age ///
    g2age g2numbro ///
    if HatDiagonal>0.10
list MCASEID g1miles g1yrschl sqg1yrschl g2numsis4 ///
    g2numsis56 g2numsis7p ///
    amind mexamer white other female g2earn10000 g1age ///
    g2age g2numbro ///
    if CooksD>0.04
list MCASEID g1miles g1yrschl sqg1yrschl g2numsis4 ///
    g2numsis56 g2numsis7p ///
    amind mexamer white other female g2earn10000 g1age ///
    g2age g2numbro ///
    if DFFITS<-0.40
```

The results (not shown in a box) reveal that the same two cases are identified as extreme across these measures. Both of these cases have earnings of nearly $1 million/year. A box plot (not shown) revealed that earnings are highly skewed to the right. Although we are not focusing on earnings in this chapter, these results suggest that we might want to log or otherwise transform earnings to reduce outliers (and, as discussed above, it is common to log earnings, especially in substantive fields that intersect with economics).

In addition to examining cases whose diagnostic values are quite extreme relative to the rest of the sample, we also examined cases that fell above the cutoff on any of the diagnostics, creating a variable *anyhi*. For example, in Stata we would type:[6]

```
generate anyhi=HatDiagonal3Hi==1 |RStudentHi==1| ///
    CooksDHi==1|DFFITSHi==1| ///
    DFB_g1yrschlHi==1 |DFB_sqg1yrschlHi==1| ///
    DFB_g2numsis4Hi==1|DFB_g2numsis56Hi==1| ///
    DFB_g2numsis7pHi==1
```

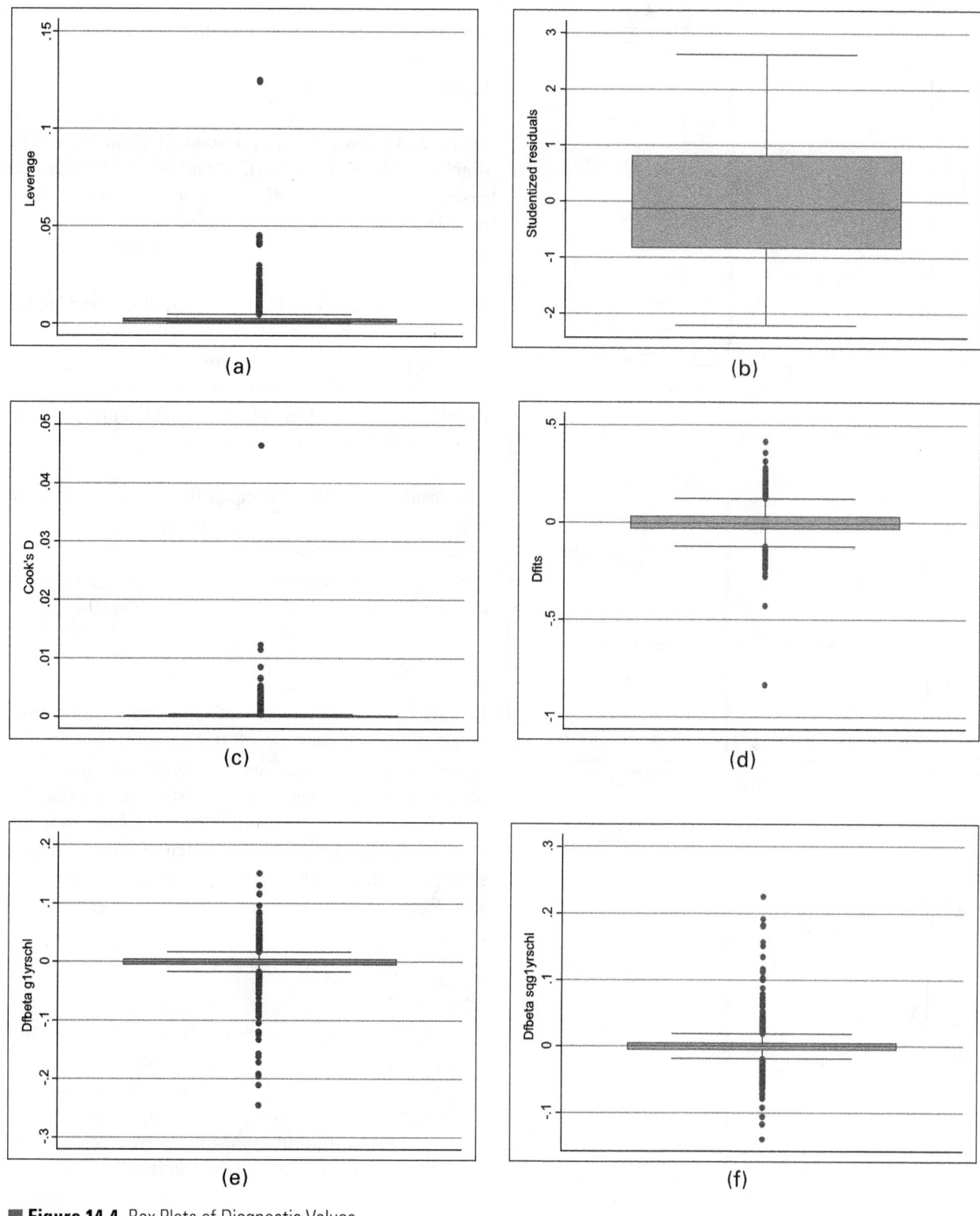

Figure 14.4 Box Plots of Diagnostic Values

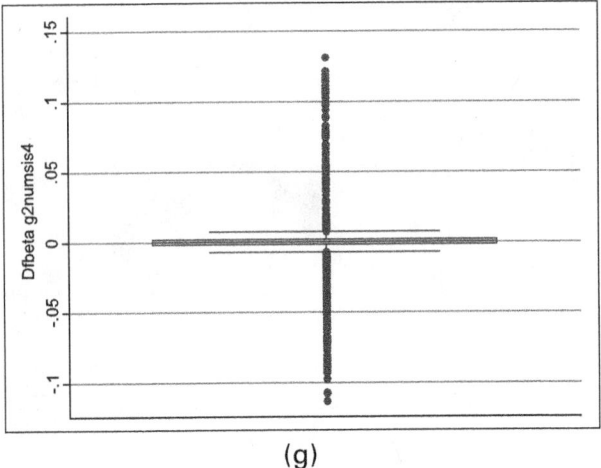

(g)

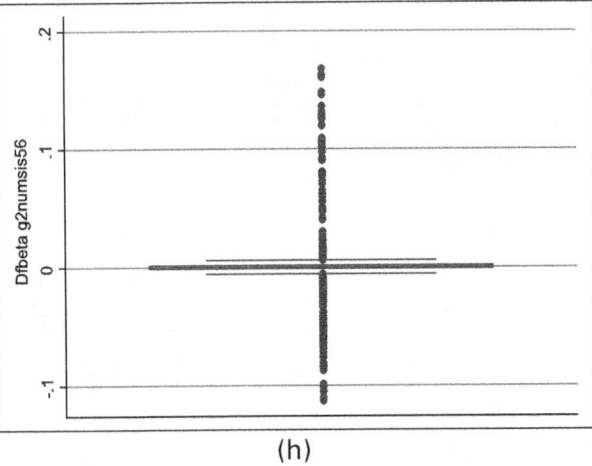

(h)

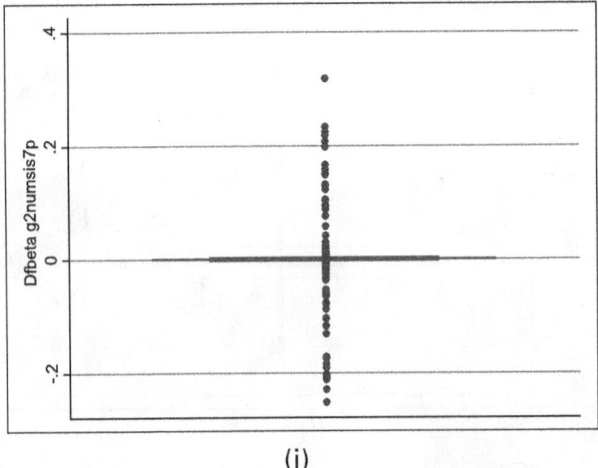

(i)

■ **Figure 14.4** Box Plots of Diagnostic Values—Cont'd

We created box plots separately for cases coded "0" and "1" on this *anyhi* dummy variable. The results are in Figure 14.5. In each panel, the graph on the left is a box plot for the cases coded "0" on *anyhi* and the graph on the right is a box plot for cases coded "1" on *anyhi*. The graphs on the right show that outlying and influential cases tend to have high values on *g1miles* (Figure 14.5(a)), both low and high values on *g1yrschl* (Figure 14.5(b)), and high values on *g2numsis* (Figure 14.5(c)).

We also summarized all of the predictor variables for the subset of the sample identified as an outlier or influential observation on any diagnostic measure versus those not so identified (see Box 14.1). The results are listed in Display B.11.2, and summarized in Table 14.2 below.

The results show that the cases that are extreme on at least one diagnostic on average have mothers with fewer years of schooling (9.89 versus 11.65), more sisters (across dummies *g2numsis4*, *g2numsis56*, and *g2numsis7p*, $0.24 + 0.21 + 0.07 = 0.52$ versus $0.01 + 0.01 + 0.00 = 0.02$), and are more likely to be nonwhite (1-*white* is $1-0.51 = 0.49$ versus $1-0.86 = 0.14$).

In fact, all of the cases of American Indian and other ethnicities and all of the cases with seven or more sisters are identified as outliers or influential observations by at least one diagnostic measure (i.e., the mean is 0.00 for the subgroup *anyhi* = 0 for the variables *g2numsis7p*, *amind*, and *other*). Each of these groups is small, containing about 70 or less cases in the entire data set. When we examined the individual diagnostics for

■ **Box 14.1**

In SAS, the diagnostics must be merged into the original data file to make these calculations, as shown at the top of Display B.14.2. Typically, when merging two files, you will use the by option and merge on an identifier (e.g., by MCASEID). Because we know that both data files are sorted in the same order in this case, we do not need a by variable on the merge.

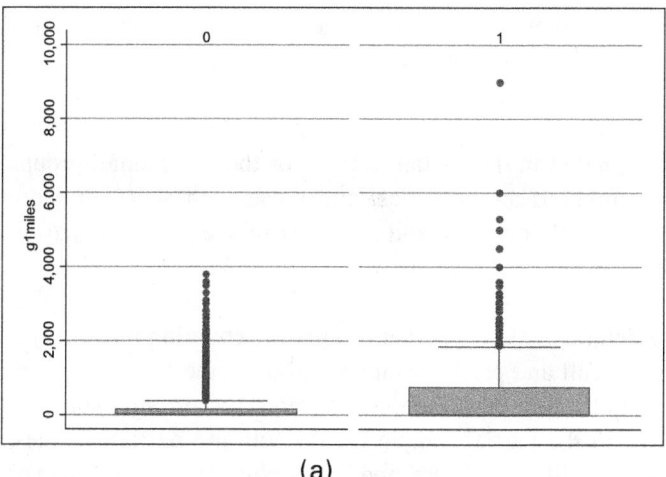

(a)

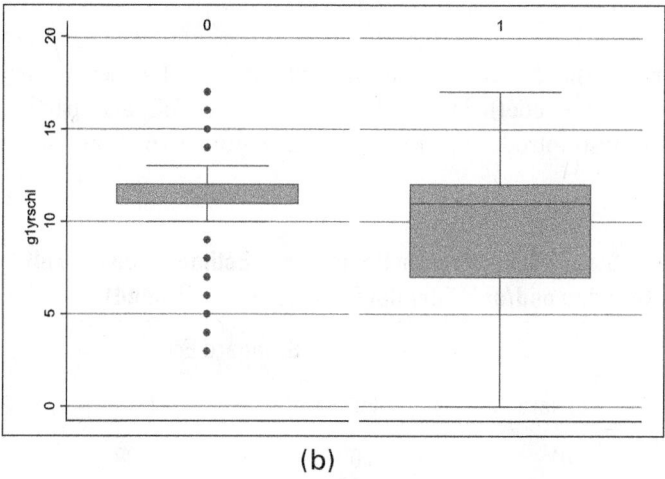

(b)

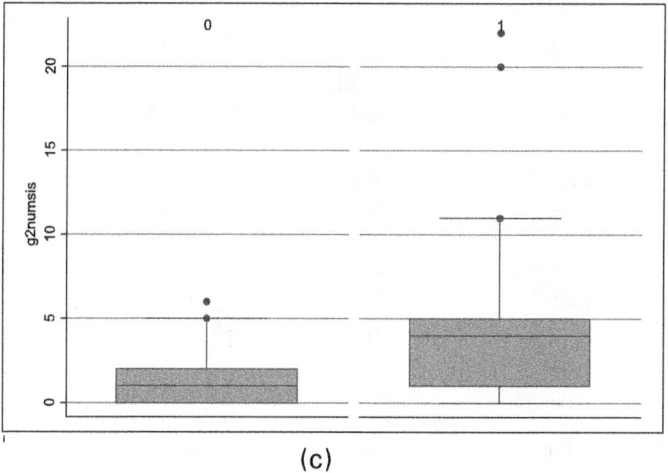

(c)

■ **Figure 14.5** Box Pots of *g1miles*, *g1yrschl*, and *g2numsis* for Cases that Do and Do Not Fall above the Cutoff on any Diagnostics

■ **Table 14.2: Means for Predictor Variables Among Cases Without and With any Extreme Values Across Diagnostics**

	anyhi = 0	anyhi = 1
	(n = 4,694)	(n = 778)
g1yrschl	11.65	9.89
sqg1yrschl	141.97	118.37
g2numsis4	0.01	0.24
g2numsis56	0.01	0.21
g2numsis7p	0.00	0.07
amind	0.00	0.03
mexamer	0.01	0.15
white	0.86	0.51
other	0.00	0.09
female	0.60	0.63
g2earn10000	3.04	3.24
g1age	59.94	60.95
g2age	34.26	34.47
g2numbro	1.30	2.21

these cases (not shown), we saw that all have hat values that fall above the cutoff, reflecting their rareness in the data set. In addition, the DFBETA for *g2numsis7p* is above the cutoff for nearly every case with seven or more sisters, indicating that the coefficient estimate is highly sensitive to which of this small set of cases are in the sample. As we discuss below, one decision we might make in the face of these results would be to say that the NSFH data are not well suited for examining American Indian and the heterogeneous other race-ethnicities and families with numerous siblings, and to exclude these subgroups from analyses.

Before discussing decision-making in more detail, we examine an additional concrete way to examine the sensitivity of the results to a set of outlying and influential observations: re-estimating the regression model after excluding the cases that we have identified as having outliers and/or influential observations across the diagnostics.[7] Display B.14.3 shows the original multiple regression model estimated on the full sample. Display B.11.4 shows the multiple regression estimated on the partial sample, with outliers and influential observations excluded (*anyhi* = 0). We summarize the results below, in Table 14.3, for the full and partial samples (*anyhi* = 0).

Notice that the coefficients are not estimated in the partial sample for the three small groups mentioned above (American Indians, other race-ethnicities, and those with seven or more sisters) because all of the cases are coded a "1" on *anyhi* and thus are excluded from the partial sample (the notation "—" in the table indicates that they are excluded).

The coefficient estimates for the predictors of focus (mother's years of schooling and number of sisters) are fairly similar between the full and partial samples, although the standard errors are larger, especially for the dummy indicators of numbers of sisters. These rising standard errors reflect the smaller sample sizes in the partial sample (in the full and partial samples, respectively, there are 245 versus 62 cases with four sisters; and 200 versus 40 cases with five or six sisters).

We can also get a concrete picture of the effect of outlying and influential observations by plotting predicted values based on the coefficients estimated for the full and partial samples, using procedures similar to those introduced in Chapter 12. Figure 14.6 shows such graphs.[8]

■ **Table 14.3: Coefficient Estimates and Standard Errors from Regressions Estimated on the Full Sample and the Partial Sample (With Outlying and/or Influential Observations Excluded)**

	Coefficient		Standard Error	
	Full	Partial	Full	Partial
g1yrschl	−0.05	−0.01	0.05	0.08
sqg1yrschl	0.008**	0.008*	0.00	0.00
g2numsis4	−0.03	−0.07	0.16	0.29
g2numsis56	−0.28	−0.33	0.18	0.36
g2numsis7p	0.99**	—	0.33	—
amind	1.15*	—	0.48	—
mexamer	−0.15	−0.46	0.21	0.34
white	0.41**	0.59**	0.09	0.10
other	0.97**	—	0.29	—
female	−0.07	0.02	0.07	0.07
g2earn10000	0.04**	0.07**	0.01	0.01
g1age	0.01+	0.01*	0.01	0.01
g2age	0.01*	0.02*	0.01	0.01
g2numbro	0.04+	0.06*	0.02	0.02
_cons	1.12	0.08	0.37	0.54

Sample size is 5,472 for full sample and 4,694 for partial sample, with cases above cutoffs for outliers or influential observations excluded.
— Excluded.
** $p < 0.01$, * $p < 0.05$, + $p < 0.10$, two-sided p-values.

The results are strikingly similar in the full and partial samples, even with the much reduced sample sizes, although obviously the cases with seven or more siblings are not in the partial data file. This gives us confidence in the general form of the association for these two predictors of focus. We would need to make a choice for a manuscript about which results to present. We could present the full sample results, and note that the result for seven or more sisters is quite sensitive to which cases are included. Or, we might decide to exclude cases with seven or more sisters, perhaps noting that a design that specifically oversampled adults from very large families would be needed, to better estimate distance for that group. A similar decision might be made to exclude adults of American Indian and other race-ethnicities, given that their relatively small representation in the sample makes it difficult to obtain accurate estimates for these groups.

14.2: HETEROSKEDASTICITY

As discussed in Chapter 8, the OLS model assumes that the variance of the errors are homoskedastic—constant across levels of X. If the error variances are in fact different at different levels of X, then they are referred to as **heteroskedastic**.

The OLS estimators are not biased under heteroskedasticity (i.e., the expected value of the estimate $\hat{\beta}_1$ equals the population parameter β_1). However, the OLS estimates are no longer the *best* (lowest variance) estimators. Rather, it is possible to use another estimator that is also unbiased but will have a lower variance than the OLS estimator. Depending on the form of heteroskedasticity, it is possible that the standard errors of some predictors are underestimated and that the standard errors for some predictor variables are overestimated in OLS (Hayes and Cai 2007).

14.2.1: Possible Reasons for Heteroskedasticity

If the reason for heteroskedasticity can be identified, then it is possible to correct for the nonconstant variance through various modeling techniques. For example, a common culprit in aggregate data is that the variances may depend on the size of the group (e.g., state, city, employer, school) on which calculations of means and proportions are made. The variance will be smaller for the groups with the largest size. Figure 14.7 provides an example of heteroskedasticity in state-level data in which violent crime rates were regressed on the percentage of the state's families with below-poverty incomes. The plot of the errors against the population size looks like a reverse fan, with the widest spread at the smallest population sizes. Another typical example is consumer expenditure data: if we regress expenditures on income, we often see increasing conditional variance with increasing income, explained by the larger discretionary income among persons with higher incomes (Downs and Rocke 1979).

Until the 1980s, nonconstant variance was commonly dealt with using strategies to test for heteroskedasticity, identify the source of the differences in conditional variances, and adjust for them. For example, a technique called *weighted least squares* allows researchers to weight each case in the calculation of the sum of squared residuals depending on the source of

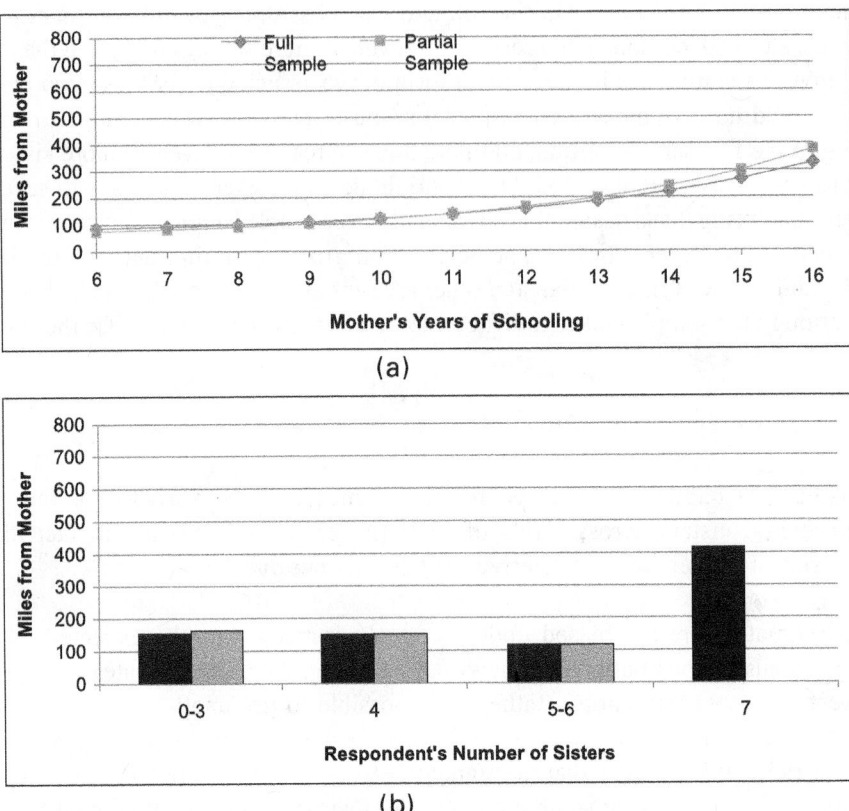

(a)

(b)

■ **Figure 14.6** Graph of Predicted Values from Multiple Regression in Full Sample and Partial Sample (with Outliers and Influential Observations Excluded)

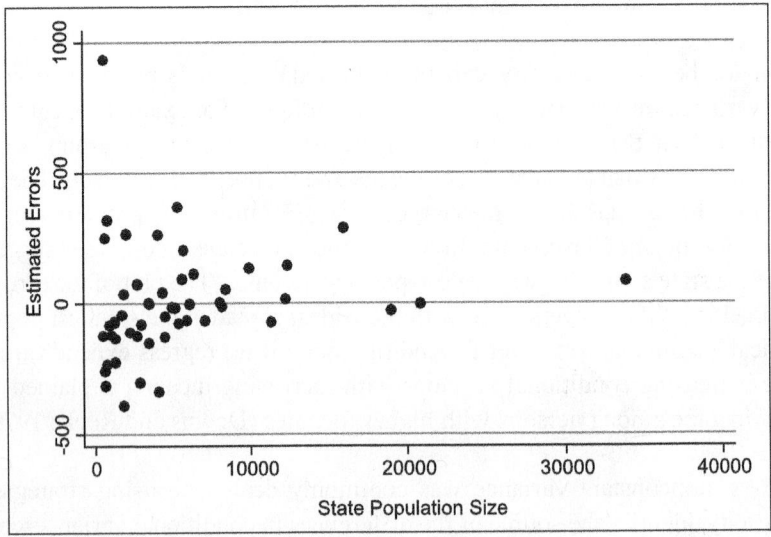

■ **Figure 14.7** Heteroskedastic Errors from Regression of State Violent Crime Rate on Percentage of Families in Poverty in 2000

heteroskedasticity. In aggregate data, like our state-level example, cases with larger sample size would receive a lower weight. The problem with this approach is that at times there is not an obvious culprit producing nonconstant variance, and even when one culprit is identified, it is unknown whether all sources of heteroskedasticity have been addressed when an adjustment for one source of heteroskedasticity is made (Hayes and Cai 2007). Transformations of Y, such as the log transformation, may also reduce heteroskedasticity; however, again, such a transformation may not correct for all sources of heteroskedasticity.

14.2.2: Heteroskedasticity-Consistent Standard Errors

Today, general adjustments for heteroskedasticity of unknown form are possible and can be calculated in most statistical packages, including SAS and Stata. These **heteroskedasticity-consistent standard errors** are also sometimes referred to as **robust standard errors, heteroskedasticity robust standard errors, White standard errors,** or **Huber-White standard errors.** With recent developments, they are increasingly referred to with the letter HC followed by a number (e.g., HC0). These values are easier to calculate and broader in scope than earlier approaches to correcting for heteroskedasticity. As Hayes and Cai (2007, 711) put it:

> The appeal of this method lies in the fact that, unlike such methods as [Weighted Least Squares], it requires neither knowledge about nor a model of the functional form of the heteroskedasticity. It does not require the use of an arbitrary transformation of Y, and no intensive computer simulation is necessary.

In fact, all of the values needed to calculate the heteroskedasticity-consistent standard errors are available in a standard estimation of OLS.

In the bivariate context, we can write HC0 by substituting the value σ_i^2 for σ^2 in the formula for the standard error of the regression slope (Equation 5.8). We convert to a variance by squaring the result and multiplying the top and bottom by $\Sigma(X_i - \bar{X})^2$.

$$\sigma_{\hat{\beta}_i}^2 = \frac{\sum (X_i - \bar{X})^2 \sigma_i^2}{\left[\sum (X_i - \bar{X})^2\right]^2}$$

Under homoskedasticity, because $\sigma_i^2 = \sigma^2$ this formula reduces to the usual formula for the estimated variance of the OLS coefficient:

$$\sigma_{\hat{\beta}_i}^2 = \frac{\sum (X_i - \bar{X})^2 \sigma_i^2}{\left[\sum (X_i - \bar{X})^2\right]^2} = \frac{\sigma^2 \sum (X_i - \bar{X})^2}{\left[\sum (X_i - \bar{X})^2\right]^2} = \frac{\sigma^2}{\sum (X_i - \bar{X})^2}$$

The heteroskedasticity-consistent variances can be estimated by using the estimated errors for each observation based on the sample regression equation (i.e., the $\hat{\varepsilon}_i^2$):

$$\text{HC0} = \frac{\sum (X_i - \bar{X})^2 \hat{\varepsilon}_i^2}{\left[\sum (X_i - \bar{X})^2 \right]^2}$$

The square root of this number is the heteroskedasticity-consistent standard error.

Recently, researchers increasingly use a slightly different calculation that adjusts for the hat values:

$$\text{HC3} = \frac{\sum (X_i - \bar{X})^2 * (\hat{\varepsilon}_i^2 / (1 - h_i)^2)}{\left[\sum (X_i - \bar{X})^2 \right]^2}$$

Additional variants HC1, HC2, and HC4 are available, although recent simulations by Long and Ervin (2000) found HC3 to have superior performance. Importantly, their simulations showed that HC3 performed well in small as well as large samples and that HC3 was not inferior to the OLS standard errors when the homoskedasticity assumption held. Based on their results, the authors recommend that researchers routinely report HC3 standard errors, rather than the traditional OLS standard errors.

T-values for coefficients can be calculated in the usual fashion based on this heteroskedasticity-consistent standard error:

$$t = \frac{\hat{\beta}_1 - \beta_1^*}{\sqrt{\text{HC3}}}$$

where $\hat{\beta}_1$ is the standard OLS parameter estimate and β_1^* is the hypothesized value, typically zero for our "straw man" hypothesis.

The formula for the heteroskedasticity-consistent standard error can be extended to multiple regression in a straightforward fashion and the procedure for calculating t-values is the same, although matrix algebra is required to write the formula (see Hayes and Cai 2007 and Long and Ervin 2000 for the matrix formulas).

14.2.3: Calculating Heteroskedasticity-Consistent Standard Errors in SAS and Stata

SAS 9.2 and Stata 11 calculate the various heteroskedasticity-consistent standard errors. For earlier releases of SAS, Hayes and Cai (2007) wrote macros to calculate the various heteroskedasticity-consistent standard errors and to use them to calculate t-values and p-values in SAS. The web site for downloading the macros is provided in Appendix I (and via a link on the textbook web site *http://www.routledge.com/cw/gordon*).

Example 14.2
Display B.14.5 presents the HC3 standard errors for the full sample multiple regression presented in Display B.14.3. We summarize the resulting coefficient estimates and standard errors from these two models (Display B.14.3 and Display B.14.5) in Table 14.4.

■ **Table 14.4: OLS and Heteroskedasticity-Consistent Standard Errors**

| | Coefficient | | Standard Error | | |
	OLS	HC3	OLS	HC3	Difference
g1yrschl	−0.05	−0.05	0.05	0.05	0.00
sqg1yrschl	0.008**	0.008**	0.00	0.00	0.00
g2numsis4	−0.03	−0.03	0.16	0.16	0.00
g2numsis56	−0.28	−0.28	0.18	0.18	0.00
g2numsis7p	0.99**	0.99**	0.33	0.37	0.04
amind	1.15*	1.15**	0.48	0.40	−0.08
mexamer	−0.15	−0.15	0.21	0.20	−0.01
white	0.41**	0.41**	0.09	0.09	0.00
other	0.97**	0.97**	0.29	0.32	0.03
female	−0.07	−0.07	0.07	0.07	0.00
g2earn10000	0.04**	0.04**	0.01	0.01	0.00
g1age	0.01+	0.01+	0.01	0.01	0.00
g2age	0.01*	0.01*	0.01	0.01	0.00
g2numbro	0.04+	0.04*	0.02	0.02	0.00
_cons	1.12	1.12	0.37	0.38	0.01

Sample size is 5,472.

OLS = Model with standard calculation of standard errors. HC3 = Model with heteroskedasticity-consistent standard errors using the HC_3 formula.

** $p < 0.01$, * $p < 0.05$, + $p < 0.10$, two-sided p-values.

As expected, the coefficient estimates are the same in both models, but the summarized p-values sometimes differ because the standard errors differ. The coefficient for *amind* is now significant at $p < 0.01$ rather than $p < 0.05$. The coefficient for *g2numbro* is now significant at $p < 0.05$ rather approaching significance at $p < 0.10$. The standard errors change the most for variables that contain the smallest groups in the data set, although in some cases the standard errors for these variables are larger (other race-ethnicities and adults with seven or more sisters) and in some cases smaller (American Indian race-ethnicities) under the HC3 calculation.

14.3: MULTICOLLINEARITY

We end this chapter by considering multicollinearity. We have seen that the multiple regression model allows us to obtain estimates of the direct effect of a predictor variable on the outcome, parsing out the portion due to confounders and the flows through indirect pathways. It is also the case that when the predictor variables are themselves correlated, it can be difficult to separate out their unique effects on the outcome variable, depending on the degree of the correlation. At the extreme, if two predictor variables are perfectly correlated, then they are indistinguishable and we cannot disentangle their separate influences on the outcome variable. The situation of high correlation among predictor variables is referred to as **multicollinearity**.

14.3.1: Diagnosing Multicollinearity

Several approaches can be taken to diagnose multicollinearity. We will discuss three of them: (a) Variance Inflation Factors, (b) significant model F but no significant individual coefficients, and (c) rising standard errors in models with controls.

Variance Inflation Factors

We have already seen the formula which is used to define the **Variance Inflation Factor** (VIF). Recall that in a model with two predictors X_2 and X_3 the standard error and variance of the coefficients are:[9]

$$\text{Standard Error } \hat{\sigma}_{\hat{\beta}_{12}} = \sqrt{\frac{\hat{\sigma}^2}{\sum (X_{2i} - \bar{X}_2)^2 (1 - r_{23}^2)}} \qquad \hat{\sigma}_{\hat{\beta}_{13}} = \sqrt{\frac{\hat{\sigma}^2}{\sum (X_{3i} - \bar{X}_3)^2 (1 - r_{23}^2)}}$$

$$\text{Variance } \hat{\sigma}_{\hat{\beta}_{12}}^2 = \frac{\hat{\sigma}^2}{\sum (X_{2i} - \bar{X}_2)^2 (1 - r_{23}^2)} \qquad \hat{\sigma}_{\hat{\beta}_{13}}^2 = \frac{\hat{\sigma}^2}{\sum (X_{3i} - \bar{X}_3)^2 (1 - r_{23}^2)}$$

The VIF is defined as the right-hand term in the denominator:

$$\text{VIF} = \frac{1}{(1 - r_{23}^2)}$$

Substituting the VIF into the formula for the variance of the coefficient estimates makes the name clear, as the VIF is the factor by which the variance increases due to the correlation between the predictors.

$$\hat{\sigma}_{\hat{\beta}_{12}}^2 = \frac{\hat{\sigma}^2}{\sum (X_{2i} - \bar{X}_2)^2} * \text{VIF} \qquad \hat{\sigma}_{\hat{\beta}_{13}}^2 = \frac{\hat{\sigma}^2}{\sum (X_{3i} - \bar{X}_3)^2} * \text{VIF}$$

Thus, when the two predictor variables are uncorrelated and VIF = 1, the VIF has no impact on the estimated variance of the coefficient. However, as the correlation between the two predictor variables increases, the VIF will get larger, and, all else equal, the estimated variance of the coefficient will increase as well.

Substituting the extreme values of the correlation into the VIF formula can also be instructive.

When the two predictor variables are uncorrelated, then $r_{23}^2 = 0$ and thus:

$$\text{VIF} = \frac{1}{(1 - 0)} = \frac{1}{1} = 1$$

When the two predictor variables are perfectly correlated, then $r_{23}^2 = 1$ and thus:

$$\text{VIF} = \frac{1}{(1 - 1)} = \frac{1}{0} = \infty$$

OUTLIERS, HETEROSKEDASTICITY, AND MULTICOLLINEARITY ■ ■ ■ 505

So, increasing correlation between the predictor variables will make the estimated variance of the coefficients, and thus their standard errors, larger. As a consequence, t-values will be smaller, and it will be harder to reject the null hypothesis that the coefficient is zero. As the correlation approaches the extreme of 1, the standard errors will "blow up," approaching infinity. In SAS and Stata, if two variables are perfectly correlated, the software will drop one variable from the model and report this problem in the results.

The formula for the VIF can be generalized to multiple regression models with more than two predictor variables:

$$\text{VIF} = \frac{1}{(1 - R_j^2)}$$

where R_j^2 is the R-squared value from a regression of one of the predictor variables, call it X_j, on the remaining predictor variables. Note that when there are more than two predictor variables, the VIF is different for each predictor variable in the model.

Since we commonly report standard errors of coefficients, rather than variances of coefficients, it is often useful to take the square root of the VIF for interpretation. A VIF of 4 would be interpreted as follows: the estimated variance of the coefficient for this predictor variable is four times larger, and the standard error for the coefficient for this predictor variable is $\sqrt{4} = 2$ times larger, due to the variation that this predictor variable shares with the other predictor variables in the model, all else equal.

A cutoff value of 4 or 10 is sometimes given for regarding a VIF as high. But, it is important to evaluate the consequences of the VIF in the context of the other elements of the standard error, which may offset it (such as sample size; O'Brien 2007). We discuss below various remedies for multicollinearity.

Significant Model F but No Significant Individual Coefficients

A telltale sign of high multicollinearity is having a significant model F-value but no significant t-values for individual coefficients in the model. Think about what this means: jointly, the coefficients in the model are significant (the rejection of the null for the model F tells us that at least one of the individual coefficients differs significantly from zero). But, no individual coefficient is significant. These contradictory findings are indicative of the fact that the predictors are so highly correlated in the model that it is impossible to isolate their individual impact on the outcome. However, the variance that they share is also shared by the outcome variable (together, they reduce the SSE). In fact, in this kind of situation, if we include only one of the collinear variables in the model, then that variable will be revealed as significant (and similarly for all of the collinear variables).

Rising Standard Errors in Models with Controls

Another sign of multicollinearity relates to the VIF, but is diagnosed without actually calculating the VIFs: seeing the standard errors become substantially larger in models with additional controls. Watching for this sign of multicollinearity can be useful when examining published results that report standard errors.

Example 14.3

We will first use a hypothetical example to demonstrate the three signs of multicollinearity. In this model, a teenage mother's years of schooling is predicted by her report during middle school of how far she thought she would go in school (*higrade7*) and how important school was to her (*impschl7*).

For instructional purposes, we will show how to calculate the VIFs by hand after regressing one predictor on the other predictor. And, we will also ask SAS and Stata to calculate the VIFs (with the `/vif` option in SAS and the `estat vif` command in Stata). Display B.14.6 shows the results.

First, notice that in the multiple regression predicting years of school (*yrschl*) based on *higrade7* and *impschl7* that the overall model F is significant ($F(2,997) = 9.66, p < 0.05$). But, neither variable has a large t-value (t-value of −1.10 for *higrade7*; t-value of 1.51 for *impschl7*). The VIFs are quite large at 105.89. (The VIF is shown in the last column of the `Parameter Estimates` table in SAS and in a new output table in Stata.) And, the regression of *higrade7* on *impschl7* in the bottom panel of the table shows that the R-squared is quite high, at 0.9906, reflecting the fact that we defined the variables to share nearly all of their variance. Plugging into the VIF formula gives:

$$VIF = \frac{1}{(1 - 0.9906)} = 106.38$$

Within rounding error, this result is equivalent to the value calculated by SAS and Stata.[10]

Display B.14.7 shows the regression of *yrschl* on *higrade7* and *impschl7* in bivariate regressions, revealing that each is significantly positively associated with the outcome when considered on its own. We put the values side by side in a table below to see the change in the coefficient estimates and standard errors between the bivariate and multiple regression.

▪ **Table 14.5: Predicting Years of Schooling in Bivariate and Multiple Regression Models**

	Dependent Variable: Years of Schooling		
Expected Highest Grade (7th Grade Report)	0.18* (0.043)	—	−0.48 (0.44)
Importance of School (7th Grade Report)	—	1.80* (0.42)	6.56 (4.35)
Intercept	8.24 (0.65)	8.17 (0.64)	8.25 (0.65)

* $p < .05$—indicates excluded from model.

Source: Hypothetical data created for illustration purposes.

Notice that the standard errors are about 10 times larger in the multiple than the bivariate regression, in line with $\sqrt{VIF} = \sqrt{105.89} = 10.29$, so, even without seeing the VIFs or the overall F-test, we can identify a problem with multicollinearity in this table simply by noticing the very large increase in the standard errors between the bivariate and multiple regressions. By examining the standard errors in publications, you can watch for such problems (and this is one reason why it is so useful to report the standard errors in tables). Also, notice that the coefficient estimates have changed markedly between the bivariate and multiple regressions. The sign of the coefficient estimate for expected highest grade has even changed sign. This reflects the very imprecise estimate of the coefficient estimates in the multiple regression with such a high level of multicollinearity.

Example 14.4

We will also use our multiple regression results from the NSFH hours of work example, with health, health limitations, and age as predictors, to demonstrate the three signs of multicollinearity. The results of estimating the full regression model and requesting VIFs in SAS and Stata are in Display B.14.8. We summarize them below, alongside the results from Displays B.13.1 and B.13.2 from Chapter 13.

■ **Table 14.6: Predicting Mens' Hours of Work in the NSFH**

	Dependent Variable: Hours of Work Per Week			
	Model 1 (Display B.13.1)	Model 2 (Display B.13.1)	Model 3 (Display B.13.2)	Model 4 (Display B.14.8)
Self-Reported Health	1.144* (0.31)	1.017* (0.31)	1.008* (0.31)	0.896* (0.31)
Age (Years)	—	-0.105* (0.02)	—	-0.103* (0.02)
Health Limitations	—	—	-5.656* (2.45)	-5.125* (2.44)
Intercept	37.86 (1.29)	42.27 (1.51)	38.52 (1.32)	42.80 (1.53)

* p<.05—indicates excluded from model.

Source: NSFH, Wave 1, Sample of Men, $n = 3{,}742$.

Notice that the standard errors for our predictors change very little across the models. This is consistent with the fact that the VIFs are all quite low (ranging from 1.01 to 1.04 for the three predictors; see again Display B.14.8).

Notice also that in this case the VIFs differ across the variables, since there are more than two predictors in the model. In Display B.14.9, we show one of the regressions of a predictor (*g2age*) on the other two predictors (*Health* and *HlthLimit*) that is needed to calculate the VIF for *g2age* ($VIF = 1/(1-0.0073) = 1.01$).

14.3.2: Remedies for Multicollinearity

If multicollinearity appears to be a problem with your data, what can you do? A high VIF in and of itself may not require action, especially if you have a large sample size and substantial variation on the relevant predictor; that is, as we discussed in Chapters 8 and 9, the correlation among the predictors is only one of several components that contribute to the variance of a coefficient in a multiple regression. If we increase sample size, increase variation in X, or reduce conditional variance, then the estimated variance of the coefficient will decrease (all else constant). Thus, with a large sample size, ample variation in the predictors, and small conditional variance, it may be possible still to see significant t-ratios even with relatively high correlation among the predictors. It is important to consider these offsetting components when evaluating multicollinearity and choosing possible remedies for it. Still, if you see a significant overall model F-value with no significant t-values, or see that standard errors increase dramatically between the bivariate and multiple regression models, then you may need to take steps to address it. As you think about potential multicollinearity in your model, we recommend that you consider two key questions:

1. Are the predictor variables indicators of the same or different constructs?
2. How strongly are the predictor variables correlated in the real world as opposed to your sample (and why)?

Same Construct/Strongly Correlated

The two predictors we looked at that had a severe multicollinearity problem in our hypothetical example—expected highest grade and importance of school—are an example of this kind of situation.

If the variables are really multiple indicators of the same construct, then you will likely want to combine the multiple indicators into a single measure. Sometimes researchers do this in an ad hoc fashion simply by picking the indicators that seem to measure the same thing and summing these variables. A better approach is to use confirmatory factor analysis or item response theory to verify that the variables measure the same thing and to produce the summary measure (Andrich 1988; Harrington 2008; Long 1983; Ostini and Nering 2006).[11]

Another common ad hoc approach to this problem is to use a single indicator at a time in the model. This has the benefit of allowing the researcher to see if the pattern of results is replicated across the multiple indicators of the same construct. However, the disadvantage is that to the extent that the variables really do indicate a single construct, then each individual indicator of the construct will have greater measurement error than would a combined measure developed through one of the approaches just discussed.

Different Constructs/Strongly Correlated

If the predictors are strongly correlated but conceptually do not seem to indicate the same construct, then combining them into a single summary measure does not make sense. Similarly, if they measure distinct constructs, then including a single indicator at a time into the model will lead to omitted variable bias.

Often, high correlations among measures of different constructs arise because the two predictors go together so strongly in the population that, even though it is theoretically interesting to think of the two independently, it is hard in reality to think of varying one of the predictors independently of the other. In other words, ask yourself: in the population, is it possible to hold one of the predictors constant while varying the other predictor (or, will one predictor almost always change when you vary the other)? An example of this situation is a father's and mother's education. In the USA, spouses and partners tend to have similar educational attainment. However, we might develop a conceptual framework regarding why the mother's versus father's educational attainment might have different associations with an outcome (like child development).

So, what can you do in this situation? If an experimental study can be constructed, then the researcher can manipulate the levels of the key predictor variables so that they are uncorrelated in the sample. Of course, this may not be possible in many social science studies (e.g., we cannot ethically or practically take men and women of different educational levels and then partner them together). If an experimental study is not feasible, then a very large sample and substantial variation on each predictor (e.g., mother's and father's education) may be required to overcome the variance inflation created by the strong correlation between predictor variables.

Different Constructs/Not Strongly Correlated

If the two variables measure distinct constructs and you don't think they are strongly correlated in the population, then consider whether your sampling strategy creates more correlation between the two variables than exists in the population. Sometimes a sample has been drawn for only a subgroup of the population and the correlation among key variables is higher in that subgroup than in the full population. For example, in a study that uses family income and neighborhood income as predictors of children's vocabulary scores, if the samples are drawn from economically homogeneous areas, then there will be higher correlation between the two measures of income than would be the case in a nationally representative sample. If a study aimed to separate the effects of each type of income, then a nationally representative data source might be needed.

Same Construct/Not Strongly Correlated

If you think that the two variables indicate the same thing, then they should be correlated in the population. If you later realize that they would not be correlated in the population, then you would need to revisit your conceptual framework to consider whether they do indeed measure the same thing.

14.4: COMPLEX SAMPLING DESIGNS

We now illustrate the use of the survey regression commands to adjust for the NSFH complex sampling design using the regression model with numerous predictors from Display B.14.3. Display B.14.10 shows the new results, which we also summarize in Table 14.7 alongside the original results.

▨ **Table 14.7: Coefficient Estimates and Standard Errors from Regressions Estimated with and without Adjustments for the Complex Sampling Design**

	Coefficient		Standard Error	
	Adjusted for Complex Sampling Design?		Adjusted for Complex Sampling Design?	
	No	Yes	No	Yes
g1yrschl	−0.047	−0.058	0.049	0.051
sqg1yrschl	0.008 **	0.009 **	0.002	0.002
g2numsis4	−0.027	−0.142	0.157	0.169
g2numsis56	−0.279	−0.389 *	0.177	0.144
g2numsis7p	0.985 **	1.029 **	0.328	0.331
amind	1.145 *	1.171 **	0.480	0.367
mexamer	−0.146	−0.155	0.210	0.184
white	0.411 **	0.420 **	0.094	0.103
other	0.969 **	1.255 **	0.294	0.268
female	−0.072	−0.029	0.070	0.062
g2earn10000	0.037 **	0.038 **	0.009	0.007
g1age	0.010	0.009	0.005	0.005
g2age	0.014 *	0.011	0.006	0.006
g2numbro	0.042	0.063 **	0.022	0.021

Notes. Sample size is 5,472.

** $p < 0.01$, * $p < 0.05$, two-sided p-values.

The results show that, in our case, adjustment for the complex sampling design generally leads to coefficients that are somewhat larger in magnitude, with the exception of the coefficients for *female, g1age*, and *g2age*. Among the standard errors, seven are smaller in size, four are larger in size, and three round to the same value when the complex sampling design is accounted for. Together, the changes in coefficients and standard errors lead to three changes in our conclusions about whether coefficients differ significantly from zero: two coefficients which were not statistically significant now are (the dummy for five or six sisters and the coefficient for number of brothers) and one coefficient which was statistically significant now is not (the coefficient for the adult respondent's age).

Which results should we present in a paper? Because the NSFH was gathered with a complex sampling design it is preferable to show the results that adjust for the design features. These results account for the oversampling of certain subgroups, thus producing coefficients that better reflect the true values in the population. And, the standard errors adjust for the fact that adults who live in the sample's primary sampling units may be more similar to each other (which would mean the unadjusted standard errors are too small) at the same time that adults within the study's strata may also share similarities (which would mean the unadjusted standard errors are too large).

As our example illustrates, the adjustments for the complex sampling design will not uniformly lead to larger or smaller coefficients and standard errors, nor will these adjustments always produce hypothesis tests that are more or less statistically significant. In other words, adjusting for the complex sampling design will not always favor, or work against, our finding evidence for our hypotheses. The adjustments will, however, lead to more accurate point estimates, conclusions about our hypotheses, and confidence interval estimates.

14.5: SUMMARY

SUMMARY
14

In this chapter, we discussed some common problems that can arise in estimating regression models (outliers and influential observations, heteroskedasticity, and multicollinearity). You should regularly check for these issues throughout a project and correct them where needed. A mis-specified model can go hand in hand with these problems; thus you must often go back and forth between specifying alternative conceptual models and checking for violations of model assumptions. For example, cases may be influential (greatly affect the regression estimates) when the form of the relationship is mis-specified as linear rather than nonlinear. Outlying cases may also influence the estimated form of the relationship.

We discussed using diagnostic measures to identify outlying and influential cases, and various strategies for dealing with them. We also presented contemporary formulas for estimating standard errors to adjust for heteroskedasticity, even when the form of such nonconstant variance is unknown. These heteroskedasticity-consistent standard errors can be easily estimated in SAS and Stata. We also introduced three strategies for identifying multicollinearity and suggested ways to think carefully about whether predictors indicate the same or distinct constructs and how they are correlated in the population (as opposed to your sample) when making decisions about how to address multicollinearity. Careful study planning can allow you to increase the components of the standard error that offset multicollinearity (e.g., larger sample size, more variation on X, lower conditional standard deviation).

KEY TERMS

KEY TERMS
14

Cook's distance

DFBETA

DFFITS

Hat value (also Leverage)

Heteroskedasticity

Heteroskedasticity-Consistent Standard Errors (also Robust Standard Errors, Heteroskedasticity Robust Standard Errors, White Standard Errors, Huber–White Standard Errors)

Influential Observation

Multicollinearity

Outlier

Studentized Residual (also Standardized Residual)

Variance Inflation Factor

REVIEW QUESTIONS

REVIEW QUESTIONS 14

14.1. What is the difference between an outlier and an influential observation? How might you proceed if you identified some outliers and influential observations in your dataset?

14.2. What is the major difference in the formulas for heteroskedasticity-consistent standard errors and OLS standard errors? What are the differences in the assumptions for these standard errors?

14.3. What are three telltale signs of multicollinearity?

14.4. What is the formula for calculating the VIF and how does it relate to the formula for the standard error of the slope in multiple regression? In a regression model with two predictors, how does the VIF change as the correlation between the two predictors becomes smaller (approaches and then equals zero) and becomes larger (approaches and then equals one)?

REVIEW EXERCISES

REVIEW EXERCISES 14

14.1. What other components of the standard error of the slope could compensate for a high VIF? In your response, be sure to *write the general formula* for the standard error of the slope in *multiple regression* and to be specific *about how each component* in this formula affects the standard error of the slope.

14.2. Write the *general equation* for the VIF.

(a) *Interpret the VIF* for the NUMKID variable in the results shown below.

(b) *Why* is the VIF for MARRY *identical* to the VIF for NUMKID in this model?

Analysis of Variance					
Source	DF	Sum of Squares	Mean Square	F Value	Pr > F
Model	2	167.26747	83.63373	0.46	0.6325
Error	7639	1394622	182.56604		
Corrected Total	7641	1394789			

Root MSE	13.51170	R-Square	0.0001
Dependent Mean	40.80764	Adj R-Sq	−0.0001
Coeff Var	33.11071		

Parameter Estimates						
Variable	DF	Parameter Estimate	Standard Error	t-Value	Pr > |t|	Variance Inflation
Intercept	1	40.83340	0.25175	162.20	<.0001	0
marry	1	0.17007	0.31834	0.53	0.5932	1.04711
NUMKID	1	−0.11647	0.13094	−0.89	0.3738	1.04711

CHAPTER EXERCISE

In this exercise, you will write a SAS and a Stata batch program to examine outliers, heteroskedasticity, and multicollinearity.

Use the NHIS 1999 data set with an *if expression* to only keep cases that do not have missing values on the *age, exfreqwR, bmiR, SEX, HISPAN_I* and *RACERPI2* variables.

Include the syntax that you wrote in Chapter 10 to create the dummy indicator of females and the six dummy variables to indicate persons of: 1) Hispanic ancestry and any race, 2) non-Hispanic ancestry and white only race, 3) non-Hispanic ancestry and African American only race, 4) non-Hispanic ancestry and American Indian or Alaskan Native only race ("AIAN"), 5) non-Hispanic ancestry and Asian only race, and 6) non-Hispanic ancestry and multiple races.

In all cases, conduct two-sided hypothesis tests. Use a 5% alpha unless otherwise indicated.

14.1 Outliers and Influential Observations

    a) SAS/Stata Tasks.

        i) Regress *bmiR* on *age*.

CHAPTER
EXERCISE
14

ii) Calculate the hat values, studentized residuals, Cook's Distance, DFFITS and DFBETAs. (Note you will have only one DFBETA because there is only one predictor in the model.)

iii) Create dummy variables to indicate which cases have extreme values on each of the five diagnostic measures (use the cutoffs shown in Display A.14).

iv) Create a dummy variable to indicate cases that are coded one on at least one of the five dummy variables you just created. Re-estimate the regression model for the subgroup with no values above the cutoffs on the five diagnostics and for the subgroup with at least one value above the cutoffs of the five diagnostics.

v) Summarize the *bmiR* and *age* variables for the subgroup with no values above the cutoffs on the five diagnostics and for the subgroup with at least one value above the cutoffs of the five diagnostics.

b) Write-Up Tasks.

i) Describe the difference in the coefficient estimates in the regression results for the subgroups with and without outliers/influential observations. What do the results from the summarize command suggest about which cases have extreme values? How might you present and interpret these findings in a paper?

14.2 Heteroskedasticity-Consistent Standard Errors

a) SAS/Stata Tasks.

i) Estimate a multiple regression model with *bmiR* as the outcome and with the following predictor variables: *age, exfreqwR*, the dummy indicator of women, and five of the dummy indicators of race-ethnicity (use persons of Hispanic race-ethnicity as the reference category).

ii) Re-estimate this multiple regression model and request HC3 heteroskedasticity-consistent standard errors.

b) Write-Up Tasks.

i) Discuss how the coefficient, standard error, and *t*-test for the results differ between the models estimated in Question 14.2.ai and Question 14.2.aii.

14.3 Multicollinearity

a) SAS/Stata Tasks.

i) Calculate the Pearson correlation between *bmiR* and *age*.

ii) Regress *age* on the following predictor variables: *exfreqwR*, the dummy indicator of women, and five of the dummy indicators of race-ethnicity (exclude persons of Hispanic ethnicity).

    iii) Re-estimate the regression models from Question 14.4.ai and from Question 14.2.ai and ask SAS and Stata to calculate the variance inflation factors.

  b) Write-Up Tasks.

    i) Show how to calculate the variance inflation factors based on the Pearson correlation and the regression of *age* on the other predictors.

14.4 Complex Sampling Designs

  a) SAS/Stata Tasks.

    i) Re-estimate the multiple regression from 14.2ai but accounting for the complex sampling design.

  b) Write-Up Tasks.

    i) Compare the weighted and unweighted results of the multiple regression model.

COURSE EXERCISE

COURSE
EXERCISE
14

Choose one of the multiple regression models that you estimated in earlier chapters, including at least one continuous predictor variable.

Use diagnostic measures to identify potentially outlying or influential observations. Examine the cases with high values, and make a decision about how to proceed based on the results (e.g., do any with extreme values appear to be data entry errors? Do the results suggest that you should be running subgroup analyses? Do the results suggest that you should exclude a subset of cases from your models?).

Re-estimate your model with heteroskedasticity-consistent standard errors. How different are the results from those with the OLS standard errors assuming homoskedasticity?

Calculate the VIF for each of your predictor variables. Estimate bivariate regressions of your outcome on each of your predictors, and compare the standard errors to those in the multiple regression model (i.e., how much do the standard errors increase in the multiple regression versus the bivariate regressions?). Conduct the model F-test. If it is significant, is at least one of the individual t-tests significant? If any of these procedures indicate problematically high levels of multicollinearity in your model, think about which strategy for addressing multicollinearity best fits your situation. If you were to collect new data to examine your research questions, what would be important for avoiding problems with multicollinearity in your particular situation?

Part 4

THE GENERALIZED LINEAR MODEL

Chapter 15

INTRODUCTION TO THE GENERALIZED LINEAR MODEL WITH A CONTINUOUS OUTCOME

CHAPTER 15: INTRODUCTION TO THE GENERALIZED LINEAR MODEL WITH A CONTINUOUS OUTCOME

The OLS regression model that we studied in Part 3 is powerful and widely used. However, many social science applications use outcome variables that are not continuous and do not follow the conditional normal distribution assumed for hypothesis testing in OLS models. These include dichotomous outcomes such as demographic characteristics (marital status, poverty status), participation in social programs (receipt of cash assistance, coverage by public health insurance), and health status (overweight status, contraction of a sexually transmitted disease). And, they include nominal outcomes such as choice of type of school (public school, private parochial, and private nonsectarian), type of child care arrangements (none, relative, friend, center) or labor force status (not employed and not looking for work, not employed and looking for work, employed). They also include multi-category ordinal outcomes, that we have seen are sometimes treated as continuous, such as highest educational degree (less than high school degree, high school degree, bachelor's degree, master's degree, PhD degree) and responses to a likert scale (e.g., ratings from *1=strongly disagree, 2=agree, 3=neutral, 4=agree,* to *5=strongly agree*).

We introduce the generalized linear model in this chapter as a framework to extend what we have learned about the standard linear regression model with a continuous outcome to models for other kinds of outcome variables. We will consider dichotomous, ordinal and nominal outcomes in Chapters 16 and 17. In Chapter 18, we provide a roadmap of additional models that allow for other types of outcomes (including count variables that are often right-skewed). We use the generalized linear model framework because it helps us understand that the various models are not as unrelated as they might seem at first glance. The basic concepts of the generalized linear model approach also provide insight into how and why we use alternative approaches for non-continuous outcomes. And, it is helpful to have grounding in these concepts, since you may see them when reading the literature or in future courses.

The basic elements of the generalized linear model are familiar to us already: All generalized linear models consist of a systematic and random component, similar to the systematic and random components of the OLS regression model that we already considered in depth in Part 3. But, generalized linear models have three new features:

(1) We will rely on **maximum likelihood estimation** rather than ordinary least squares estimation.
(2) We will introduce a new **link function** concept which will provide us with flexibility for specifying nonlinear models.
(3) We may use a different distributional assumption than normality for the random component.

These new features of the generalized linear model allow us to define a broad array of models appropriate for many different kinds of outcome variables, including but also extending beyond continuous outcomes.

In the remainder of this chapter, we will discuss these three new aspects of the models and illustrate them with a linear regression model, showing that we can obtain basic estimates identical to those we saw in OLS regression using the generalized approach. We begin by introducing the main concepts of maximum likelihood estimation and showing a detailed example based on the normal distribution. As we do so, we introduce new techniques for testing hypotheses for models estimated using maximum likelihood. We then show how to estimate a generalized linear model in SAS and Stata, discussing the new concept of a "link" from the systematic part of the regression model to the mean of our outcome variable. We begin in the next section with a literature excerpt which demonstrates the utility of the generalized linear model in the social sciences.

15.1: LITERATURE EXCERPT 15.1

In the November 2005 issue of the *Journal of Marriage and Family*, Zheng Wu wrote about the use of generalized linear models in family studies. The entire article is an accessible introduction to the approach (a nice complementary reading to this chapter). Within it, Wu provides an example of an analysis based on the generalized linear model, in which he draws on data from the Canadian General Social Survey to analyze adults' reports of their number of close friends. This outcome is highly skewed, with a range of 0 to 96 although 85% of respondents report 10 or fewer friends. Wu shows estimates based on the generalized linear model that mirror the OLS approach (treating his outcome as conditionally normally distributed) as well as estimates that allow for alternative distributions appropriate for a count-type outcome like Wu's that is right-skewed (these alternative distributions are called the Poisson and Negative Binomial; although we won't cover these distributions in detail in this book, Chapter 18 provides a general overview of the models based on them and references that detail them).

We reproduce Wu's Table 4 in Literature Excerpt 15.1. The left column of numbers provides results for the linear model that mirror an OLS regression analysis. The middle and right columns present results that instead assume the errors follow a Poisson or Negative Binomial distribution.

■ Literature Excerpt 15.1

Table 4. Regression Coefficients From Linear, Poisson, and Negative Binomial Models of Close Friends, the 1990 General Social Survey, Statistics Canada

Independent Variable	Linear	Poisson	Negative Binomial
Marital status			
Separated/divorced	−3.065 (1.611)	−0.377 (0.041)	−0.383 (0.138)
Widowed	−1.449 (1.200)	−0.174 (0.030)	−0.205 (0.103)
Never married	−1.055 (1.665)	−0.135 (0.039)	−0.139 (0.138)
Married/cohabiting[a]			
Female (*yes* = 1)	−4.728 (0.777)	−0.513 (0.018)	−0.501 (0.062)
Age	−0.042 (0.069)	−0.005 (0.002)	−0.005 (0.006)
Children	−0.155 (0.142)	−0.018 (0.003)	−0.008 (0.011)
Siblings	0.089 (0.113)	0.010 (0.003)	0.010 (0.009)
Living alone (*yes* = 1)	1.074 (1.141)	0.133 (0.029)	0.151 (0.100)
Income	−0.285 (0.131)	−0.032 (0.003)	−0.027 (0.010)
Education	0.097 (0.139)	0.011 (0.003)	0.018 (0.011)
Health	0.927 (0.404)	0.104 (0.010)	0.106 (0.033)
Church attendance	0.372 (0.206)	0.042 (0.005)	0.042 (0.017)
Intercept	12.258 (5.282)	2.548 (0.124)	2.389 (0.425)

Note: Standard errors are in parentheses.
[a] Reference category.

Source: Wu, Zheng. 2005. "Generalized Linear Models in Family Studies" *Journal of Marriage and Family,* 67: 1029–1047.

The "Linear" coefficients can be interpreted in the same way as we learned in Part 3. For example, the coefficient of −4.728 for the *Female* variable indicates that adult women report over four fewer close friends than do adult men, on average and controlling for the other variables in Wu's model. We will see below that the coefficients estimated with maximum likelihood follow a z-distribution and that we can calculate a z-statistic using the same basic formula that we learned in Chapter 7 ($z = \dfrac{point\, estimate - hypothesized\, value}{standard\ error\ of\ the\ estimate}$). With the standard error of 0.777 shown in parentheses for *Female* we can determine that the point estimate of −4.728 differs significantly from zero. That is, $z = \dfrac{-4.728 - 0}{0.777} = -6.08$ is more negative than the critical value that we know is −1.96 for a z-value with two-sided alpha of 0.05. Age is also negatively associated with number of close friends (each additional year of age is associated with .04 fewer friends) although this association is not statistically significant ($z = \dfrac{-0.042 - 0}{0.069} = -.61$ which is not more negative than the −1.96 critical value for a z-value with two-sided alpha of 0.05).

In the article, Wu uses some of the additional techniques for hypothesis testing and fit assessment that we discuss below (and in Chapter 16) to determine that the Negative Binomial model is more appropriate for these data than the linear model. Importantly, in some cases, the Negative Binomial model leads to different conclusions about statistical significance than does the linear model. For example, whereas *Church attendance* is statistically significant in the Negative Binomial model $(z = \dfrac{0.042 - 0}{0.017} = 2.47$ which is larger than the critical value of 1.96) it is not statistically significant in the linear model $(z = \dfrac{0.372 - 0}{0.206} = 1.81$ which is smaller than the critical value of 1.96). However, like the models we discuss in Chapters 16 and 17, the coefficients from the Negative Binomial (and Poisson) models cannot be interpreted directly in the units of the outcome (although the exponential of the coefficients can, similar to what we saw in Chapter 12; see Long 1997 for details). In other words, it is not correct to say that adults who fall one point higher on the measure of church attendance average 0.042 more friends based on the Negative Binomial model. However, we can say that adults who fall one point higher on the measure of church attendance average $e^{0.042} = 1.04$ times more friends based on the Negative Binomial model. We will see in Chapters 16 and 17 how to transform such coefficients so that they are interpretable (at least for the set of models we consider in those chapters).

15.2: MAXIMUM LIKELIHOOD ESTIMATION

We begin by introducing the basic concepts and procedures involved in **maximum likelihood estimation**, the technique we will use to estimate various types of generalized linear models (see Eliason 1993 and Fox 2010 for accessible but more detailed introductions to maximum likelihood techniques).[1]

In Part 3, we relied on ordinary least squares to estimate the parameters of the regression model. The best estimates were produced when we minimized the squared errors between the observed Ys and their conditional means (based on the estimated regression line). An alternative approach that produces equivalent results asks the question: What value of the intercept and slope are most likely to have produced the data we have in hand (given an assumption about the theoretical distribution that produced the data)? This alternative approach is called maximum likelihood estimation. It is the workhorse of many advanced statistical techniques, so it is worth understanding in some detail how it does what it does.

15.2.1: Calculating the Density of Values of Y Given the Population Parameters

In this section, we will first illustrate the concepts of maximum likelihood estimation with the unconditional sample mean, assuming a normal distribution (see Fox 2008, Appendix D for an excellent discussion of the concepts of maximum likelihood that is more advanced than the presentation in this text, but still quite accessible). We will ask the question: What value of the mean of Y—μ_Y—is most likely to have produced the data we have in hand (given we have observed the specific values of Y—Y_i—in our data). We will start by assuming that the variable Y has normally distributed errors. (For now, we will set aside the fact that we have already learned that $\bar{Y} = \dfrac{\sum_{i=1}^{n} Y_i}{n}$ is a good estimator for μ_Y. We will come back to this formula below). We will then consider a simple regression model with one continuous predictor, again assuming the errors are distributed normally. Here we will ask the question: What value of the conditional mean of Y—$E(Y|X)$—is most likely to have produced the data we have in hand (each pair of Y_i and X_i for each case) and an assumption that the errors are normally distributed (conditional on X).

To start, we will refresh and expand upon our discussion of theoretical distributions in Chapter 6. We will begin by examining these distributions in the way that they are commonly used in probability theory. That is, we assume we know the parameters of the distribution (like the mean and standard deviation for a normal distribution) and we calculate the probability of observing particular values based on this distribution (i.e., some specific value of Y). We then examine how we typically use these distributions in statistics. That is, we assume we know the data (e.g., the values of Y in our sample) and we want to use the theoretical distribution to calculate the likelihood that the parameters (like the mean and standard deviation in the normal distribution) take on some value in the population.

Recall that in Figure 6.2 we showed a number of bell-shaped curves that followed the normal distribution with different means and standard deviations. These came from the family of normal distributions, which all follow this same general shape (but with different means and standard deviations). The **density function** is the mathematical equation which we used to plot these normal distributions (see Box 15.1). A density function tells us the chances of observing a particular value on a variable.

■ Box 15.1

The density function is related to but not exactly the same as a probability function (Wackerly, Mendenhall, and Scheaffer 2008). For a discrete variable, we can calculate the probability of each of its possible values exactly, based on its theoretical probability function (e.g., the binomial distribution which we consider in Chapter 16 is an example of a discrete probability function). For a continuous variable, the probability is not defined for each specific value of the variable. Rather, we define probabilities for continuous variables as the area under the density function. Thus, we think of the probability of a value falling between two values. The total area under the density function is one (mathematically, we say that the density function integrates to one). Equation 15.1 provides an example of the density function for the normal distribution. We are already familiar with concepts of probability for the normal distribution. We represent alpha values and p-values by shading the area under the curve of the normal distribution to the left or right of some value (e.g., see again Figure 6.5). We also already understand that this total area under the curve is one; for example, we know that the normal distribution is symmetric, with fifty percent of observations expected to fall on each side of the mean; and, we know that if we have the probability to the left a particular value we can subtract that value from one to get the probability to the right of that value).

The density function for the normal distribution looks complicated at first glance, but when we break apart its pieces, it is straightforward to use the formula to calculate values with a calculator or spreadsheet. The general density function for the normal distribution is:

$$f\left(Y\middle|\mu_Y,\sigma_Y\right)=\frac{1}{\sigma_Y\sqrt{2\pi}}\exp\left(\frac{-\left(Y_i-\mu_Y\right)^2}{2\sigma_Y^2}\right)$$

(15.1)

where $\pi\approx 3.1416$ and $\dfrac{1}{\sqrt{2\pi}}\approx 0.3989$.[2]

The left hand side of Equation 15.1—$f(Y|\mu_Y, \sigma_Y)$—can be read as follows: What is the density (f) of a possible value (Y) given ("|", the vertical bar) a particular value of the unconditional mean (μ_Y) and a particular value of the unconditional standard deviation (σ_Y)?

The right hand side of Equation 15.1—

$$\frac{1}{\sigma_Y\sqrt{2\pi}}\exp\left(\frac{-\left(Y_i-\mu_Y\right)^2}{2\sigma_Y^2}\right)$$

—contains the two population parameters, μ_Y and σ_Y, as well as the value of Y, Y_i, and a number of constants (including π) as well as mathematical operators that we know how to use (like the square root, square, division, and exponential).

Once we choose a value for the mean and standard deviation (which is indicated in the left side of Equation 15.1; as we noted above the symbols $|\mu_Y, \sigma_Y$ means "given a particular value of the unconditional mean and unconditional standard deviation") then everything in the equation becomes constant, except for the difference between a possible value of Y and the mean in the numerator. For example, suppose we set the mean to be 35 and the standard deviation to be 10. Then we would have the following specific density function:

$$f\left(Y\middle|\mu_Y=35,\sigma_Y=10\right)=\frac{1}{10*\sqrt{2\pi}}\exp\left(\frac{-\left(Y_i-35\right)^2}{2*10^2}\right)=.0399*\exp\left(\frac{-\left(Y_i-35\right)^2}{200}\right)$$

Now, we can plug in various values of Y into this specific equation to calculate their densities in a normal distribution with a mean of 35 and a standard deviation of 10. For example, the density for a value of 15 from a normal distribution with a mean of 35 and a standard deviation of 10 is:

$$f\left(Y=15\middle|\mu_Y=35,\sigma_Y=10\right)=.0399*\exp\left(\frac{-\left(15-35\right)^2}{200}\right)=.0399*\exp\left(\frac{-400}{200}\right)=.00540$$

Based on what we know about the normal distribution, we expect the density to be highest at the mean and to then drop to smaller values as we move one, two, and three standard deviations from the mean.[3] Table 15.1 (next page) shows the value of the density for select values of Y between 5 and 65 when we set the mean to 35 and the standard deviation to 10. The density is largest at the

■ **Table 15.1: Values of the density for a normal distribution with mean of 35 and standard deviation of 10**

Value of Y	Density		
5	$=.0399*\exp\left(\dfrac{-(5-35)^2}{200}\right)$	$=.0399*\exp\left(\dfrac{-900}{200}\right)$	$=.00044$
15	$=.0399*\exp\left(\dfrac{-(15-35)^2}{200}\right)$	$=.0399*\exp\left(\dfrac{-400}{200}\right)$	$=.00540$
25	$=.0399*\exp\left(\dfrac{-(25-35)^2}{200}\right)$	$=.0399*\exp\left(\dfrac{-100}{200}\right)$	$=.02420$
35	$=.0399*\exp\left(\dfrac{-(35-35)^2}{200}\right)$	$=.0399*\exp\left(\dfrac{0}{200}\right)$	$=.03990$
45	$=.0399*\exp\left(\dfrac{-(45-35)^2}{200}\right)$	$=.0399*\exp\left(\dfrac{-100}{200}\right)$	$=.02420$
55	$=.0399*\exp\left(\dfrac{-(55-35)^2}{200}\right)$	$=.0399*\exp\left(\dfrac{-400}{200}\right)$	$=.00540$
65	$=.0399*\exp\left(\dfrac{-(65-35)^2}{200}\right)$	$=.0399*\exp\left(\dfrac{-900}{200}\right)$	$=.00044$

mean value of 35, and decreases modestly by one standard deviation from the mean (at the values of $\mu_Y - \sigma_Y = 35 - 10 = 25$ and $\mu_Y + \sigma_Y = 35 + 10 = 45$) and then decreases sharply by two and three standard deviations of the mean (at the values of $\mu_Y - 2\sigma_Y = 35 - 20 = 15$ and $\mu_Y + 2\sigma_Y = 35 + 20 = 55$ and the values of $\mu_Y - 3\sigma_Y = 35 - 30 = 5$ and $\mu_Y + 3\sigma_Y = 35 + 30 = 65$).

Figure 15.1 plots density values not only for the seven values shown in Table 15.1 but for the full range of values from 0 to 70. We placed vertical lines in Figure 15.1 at the mean value of 35 as well as one and two standard deviations above and below the mean (at 15, 25, 45, and 55). The density clearly peaks at the mean and falls off in the expected bell shaped pattern from the mean.

15.2.2: Calculating the Density with Population Parameters Given a Sample of Ys

As we noted above in the likelihood approach to statistics we use the formula for the density in an alternative way from the approach we just followed. Rather than taking the mean and

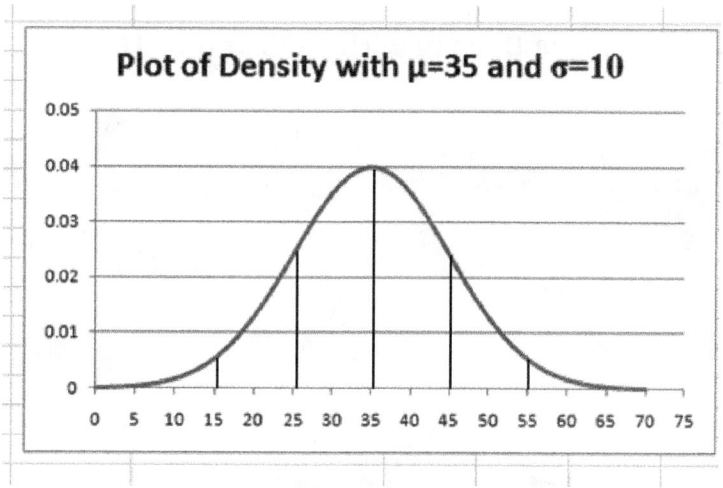

Figure 15.1 The Normal Density with $\mu_Y = 35$ and $\sigma_Y = 10$

standard deviation as known and calculating the densities for varying values of Y —$f(Y|\mu_Y, \sigma_Y)$—we take each Y as known and calculate its density for various possible values of the mean and standard deviation—$f(\mu_Y, \sigma_Y|Y)$.[4] Notice how we have shifted the mean and standard deviation to the left and Y to the right of the conditioning symbol—the vertical line. So now we are calculating the likelihood of a specific mean and standard deviation given the data. Doing so allows us to figure out what values of the parameters are most likely to have generated a particular observation (Y) or an entire sample of observations (Ys).

Calculating the Density for a Single Observation

To begin to understand this process, Figure 15.2 shows three density functions based on the normal distribution with three different means. All three figures use a standard deviation of 10. But, the top figure uses a mean of 25, the middle figure a mean of 35, and the bottom figure a mean of 45. The vertical line in each graph shows the density for the observed value of $Y = 35$ given the standard deviation of 10 and each of the three possible values of the mean. If each of the distributions represented three different populations, all with standard deviations of 10 but with these three different means, then the chances of drawing a value of $Y = 35$ from the population is clearly greatest for the middle population (where the vertical line is tallest), and smaller for the top and bottom populations (where the vertical lines are shorter). In other words, more members of the middle population have a value of 35, so our chances of drawing that value in a random sample are higher than in the top or bottom population where fewer members have a value of 35.

Box 15.2

To simplify the examples, we hold the standard deviation constant at one value and then vary possible values for the mean. In practice, it is possible to find the maximum across all possible combinations of the mean and standard deviation (i.e., allowing both the mean and standard deviation to vary). We will illustrate maximizing over two values when we demonstrate the maximization process for regression in Section 15.2.4.

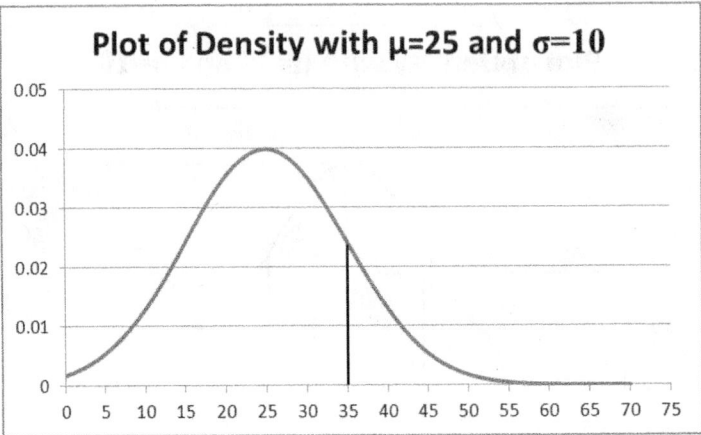

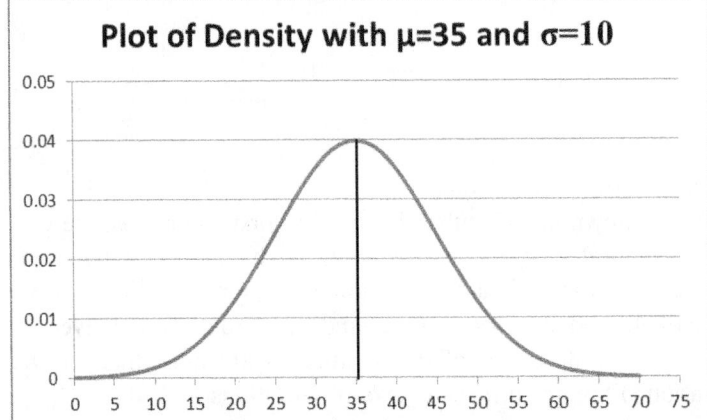

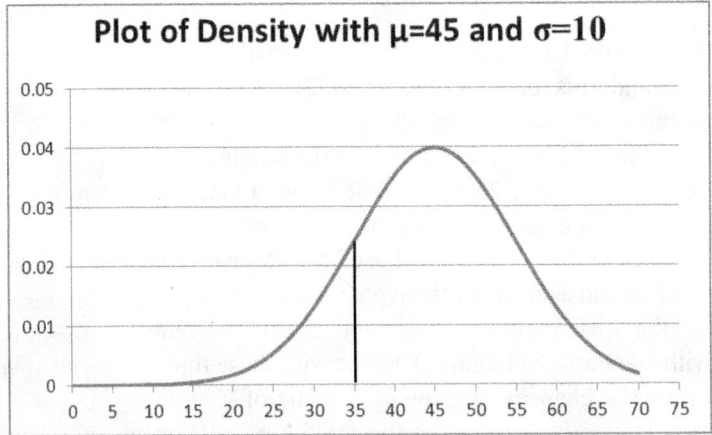

■ Figure 15.2 Illustration of Density for $Y=35$ from Normal Distributions With Means of 25, 35, and 45, and Standard Deviations of 10

Calculating the Likelihood for an Entire Set of Observations

We can extend this idea to an entire sample rather than just a single observation. In this case, we can use the density function to figure out what value of the mean (μ_Y) is most likely to have generated that entire sample of observations (assuming the errors follow a normal distribution). To do so, we calculate the density for each sample point. Then, if we assume the observations are independent, we can multiply them together to determine their joint density, which is the likelihood. We do this across different possible values for the parameters (like the possible values of 25, 35, and 45 shown for the means in Figure 15.2). We then see which values of the parameters resulted in the largest accumulated value across all observations (the densities for all observations multiplied together).

For example, suppose we have a small data set which contains the following values: {33,34,34,35,35,35,36,36,37}. We can use the maximum likelihood approach to ask the question: If we assume these observations were drawn from a population in which the errors follow a normal distribution with standard deviation of 10, what value of the mean is most likely?

Table 15.2 (next page) shows the densities for these observations. Each individual density is calculated based on the formula in the right hand side of Equation 15.1. For example, for the first observation, $Y=33$, in the top left cell we have:

$$f\left(\mu_Y = 25 \middle| Y = 33, \sigma_Y = 10\right) = \frac{1}{10 * \sqrt{2\pi}} \exp\left(\frac{-\left(Y_i - 25\right)^2}{2 * 10^2}\right) = 0.399 * \exp\left(\frac{-\left(33 - 25\right)^2}{200}\right) = .02897$$

And in the top middle cell we have:

$$f\left(\mu_Y = 35 \middle| Y = 33, \sigma_Y = 10\right) = \frac{1}{10 * \sqrt{2\pi}} \exp\left(\frac{-\left(Y_i - 35\right)^2}{2 * 10^2}\right) = 0.399 * \exp\left(\frac{-\left(33 - 35\right)^2}{200}\right) = .03910$$

And in the top right cell we have:

$$f\left(\mu_Y = 45 \middle| Y = 33, \sigma_Y = 10\right) = \frac{1}{10 * \sqrt{2\pi}} \exp\left(\frac{-\left(Y_i - 45\right)^2}{2 * 10^2}\right) = 0.399 * \exp\left(\frac{-\left(33 - 45\right)^2}{200}\right) = .01942$$

■ Box 15.3

The likelihood function tells us the chances we would observe the data we have in hand across all possible values of the parameter. This function is at a maximum for the value of the parameter that is most likely to have generated our sample data. The likelihood function is not the same as a probability function. Although likelihood values fall between zero and one, they do not sum to one across all possible values of the parameter (where the sum would be an integral if the function is continuous).

▦ **Table 15.2: Likelihood For a Set of Sample Observations Based on Normal Distributions with Means of 25, 35, and 45 and Standard Deviations of 10**

Y	$f(\mu_Y = 25 \mid Y, \sigma_Y = 10)$	$f(\mu_Y = 35 \mid Y, \sigma_Y = 10)$	$f(\mu_Y = 45 \mid Y, \sigma_Y = 10)$
33	0.028969155	0.039104269	0.019418605
34	0.026608525	0.039695255	0.021785218
34	0.026608525	0.039695255	0.021785218
35	0.024197072	0.039894228	0.024197072
35	0.024197072	0.039894228	0.024197072
35	0.024197072	0.039894228	0.024197072
36	0.021785218	0.039695255	0.026608525
36	0.021785218	0.039695255	0.026608525
37	0.019418605	0.039104269	0.028969155
Likelihood	2.67798×10^{-15}	2.41064×10^{-13}	2.67798×10^{-15}
Log-Likelihood	−33.5537126	−29.0537126	−33.5537126

The next to last row of Table 15.2, labeled **Likelihood** shows the product of the densities within each column. For example,

$Likelihood(\mu_Y = 25 \mid Y, \sigma_Y = 10) =$
0.028969155 ∗ 0.026608525 ∗ 0.026608525 ∗
0.024197072 ∗ 0.024197072 ∗ 0.024197072 ∗
0.021785218 ∗ 0.021785218 ∗ 0.019418605
$= 2.67798 \times 10^{-15}$

This calculation tells us how likely it would be to jointly observe all of the observations in our data file if the mean were 25 and the standard deviation were 10. Not surprisingly, given that we are multiplying together small values, the likelihood is quite small. In fact, all of the likelihoods in Table 15.2 are shown in scientific notation, with the number of decimal places shown by the notation $\times 10^{-15}$ and $\times 10^{-13}$. Thus, 2.67798×10^{-15} represents 0.00000000000000267798.

Because the likelihood for the mean of 35 has fewer decimal places ($\times 10^{-13}$) than the likelihoods when the mean is 25 or 45 (which have $\times 10^{-15}$), the likelihood when $\mu_Y = 35$ is the largest of the three. We can rewrite these values explicitly with the decimals to make this concrete:

$Likelihood(\mu_Y = 25 \mid Y, \sigma_Y = 10) =$	2.67798×10^{-15}	=0.00000000000000267798
$Likelihood(\mu_Y = 35 \mid Y, \sigma_Y = 10) =$	2.41064×10^{-13}	=0.000000000000241064
$Likelihood(\mu_Y = 45 \mid Y, \sigma_Y = 10) =$	2.67798×10^{-15}	=0.00000000000000267798

Again, among these three possible values for the mean, 35 is most likely because it has the largest likelihood. But, largest is relative. All of the likelihoods are small absolutely.

The last row of Table 15.2 is labeled **Log-Likelihood** and shows the log of the likelihoods in the row above. For example, $\ln(2.67798 \times 10^{-15}) = -33.5537126$. These log-likelihoods are easier to read than the likelihoods because they do not use scientific notation. Mathematically, it is also often easier to work with the log-likelihood than the likelihood, because we can then move from products to summations.[5] And, one of the tests for joint hypotheses we will examine below is easily calculated from the log-likelihoods. As a result, the log-likelihoods, rather than likelihoods, are usually reported in publications. The value of the parameter that maximizes the function is the same, regardless of whether we work with the likelihood or log-likelihood function. For log-likelihoods, we are looking for the largest negative value. Indeed, because likelihoods take on values between 0 and 1, their log (the log-likelihoods) will be zero or negative. Thus, although all of the log-likelihoods are again relatively small (negative) we are looking for the one that is relatively largest (least negative). In our case, consistent with the likelihoods, the log-likelihood is largest (least negative) for a mean of 35.

Log-Likelihood$(\mu_Y = 25 | Y, \sigma_Y = 10) =$	$\ln(2.67798 \times 10^{-15})$	$= -33.5537126$
Log-Likelihood$(\mu_Y = 35 | Y, \sigma_Y = 10) =$	$\ln(2.41064 \times 10^{-13})$	$= -29.0537126$
Log-Likelihood$(\mu_Y = 45 | Y, \sigma_Y = 10) =$	$\ln(2.67798 \times 10^{-15})$	$= -33.5537126$

The Likelihood Function

If we were to calculate the likelihoods across all possible values of the parameter(s) given a single set of data and assumed theoretical distribution we would have a **likelihood function**. The top panel of Figure 15.3 shows the likelihood function for our small data set, across all possible values of the mean (we limit the values to between 0 and 70 for display purposes; the likelihood could be calculated for any value from negative infinity to positive infinity, but in our case by 0 and 70 the likelihood has already approached zero). The bottom panel of Figure 15.3 shows the log-likelihood function. Notice that both functions peak at the mean value of 35. We will return to these figures in the next section as we discuss how statistical packages like SAS and Stata calculate estimates based on the maximum likelihood approach.

15.2.3: Iterative Searches and Closed Form Solutions

The process we went through in Section 15.2.2 is one approach sometimes used to find maximum likelihood estimates. This process is referred to as an **iterative search**. Typically, we let the computer do the work for us, mirroring the process we followed with our hand calculations. Computer programmers write programs that select a starting point (**start value**) on a likelihood function where the likelihood (and log-likelihood) is first calculated. The programmer includes a rule for moving a particular distance in a particular direction away from the starting point and calculating the likelihood (and log-likelihood) at this new location. Movement based on the rule is continued until it is determined that a maximum has been reached (called **convergence**). The green arrows in Figure 15.3 show a possible starting point and direction for a move. The

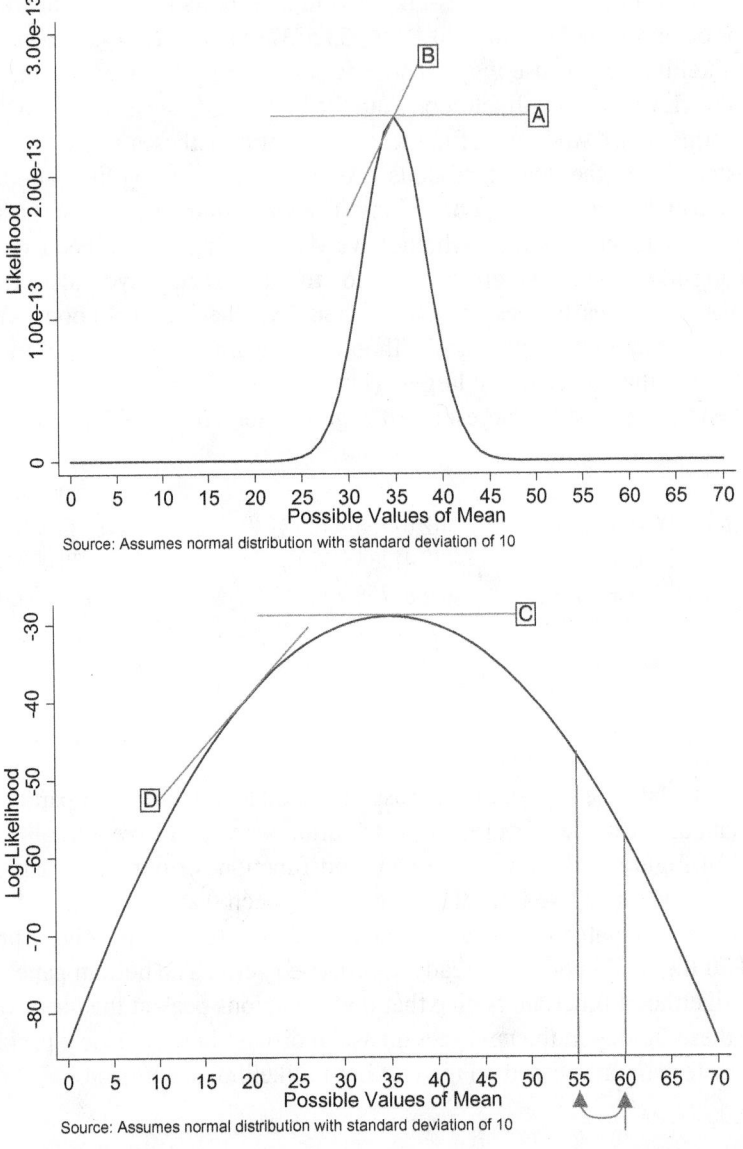

■ **Figure 15.3** Likelihood and Log-Likelihood Functions for Observations{33, 34, 34, 35, 35, 35, 36, 36, 37}

vertical green lines shows the height of the log-likelihood at the starting point and the new point. Many different rules exist for determining start values, what direction and how far to move, and how to determine that a maximum is reached. The models we will use in Chapters 16 and 17 have well-established algorithms that computer programmers use to tell the computer how to make these calculations. Unless your sample size is quite small or there is little variation on some of your predictor or outcome variables, you should get quick convergence from SAS and Stata for these models.[6]

In Chapter 5 we learned to calculate the unconditional sample mean using the formula $\bar{Y} = \dfrac{\sum_{i=1}^{n} Y_i}{n}$. For our small data set we could calculate:

$$\bar{Y} = \frac{\sum_{i=1}^{n} Y_i}{n} = \frac{33 + 34 + 34 + 35 + 35 + 35 + 36 + 36 + 37}{9} = 35$$

In fact, this formula for the sample mean is also the maximum likelihood estimator of the population mean. That is, this formula will always find the value of the mean for which the likelihood (and log-likelihood) are highest, given the sample data and the assumption that the errors follow a normal distribution in the population.

Statisticians derive this formula using calculus. Although we will not show the full derivation, the intuition is useful. Looking back at Figure 15.3, notice that we include horizontal lines labeled A and C at the peak of each curve. These peaks are easy for us to see visually. It turns out there is also a straightforward way to figure them out using mathematics.

The lines A and C in Figure 15.3 are tangent lines; they just touch each curve at their maxima. The lines labeled B and D in Figure 15.3 are also tangent lines, just touching the curve at points lower than the maxima. Note that lines A and C are flat whereas lines B and D slope upward. If we drew tangents at other points along the curve, they would also slope upward (like B and D) or downward. In fact, the maximum occurs at the point where the slope of the tangent line to the curve is zero (i.e., where the tangent is a flat line). For some likelihood functions, mathematicians can determine the value of the maximum point by taking the derivative of the log-likelihood function, setting it equal to zero, and solving for the desired parameter. Taking the derivative of the likelihood function based on the normal distribution, setting it equal to zero, and solving for the mean results in the formula $\dfrac{\sum_{i=1}^{n} Y_i}{n}$. When it is possible to write an equation to calculate the maximum likelihood estimate in this way, it is called a **closed-form solution**. As we will see in Chapters 16 and 17, for many generalized linear models it is not possible to calculate a closed-form solution. In these cases, we rely on the computer to conduct an iterative search.

15.2.4: Estimating a Linear Regression Model Using Maximum Likelihood

The density function that we use to calculate likelihoods for regression is similar to the density used for the unconditional mean that we wrote above, although in regression we now have a conditional mean (rather than an unconditional mean) of Y and a conditional standard deviation (rather than an unconditional standard deviation) of Y. We can denote these values as we did in Chapter 8 for a simple regression model (with one predictor). The conditional mean is the systematic portion of the regression model, $\beta_0 + \beta_1 X$. And, the conditional standard deviation is σ. Replacing μ_Y with $\beta_0 + \beta_1 X$ and replacing σ_Y with σ in Equation 15.1

results in the following density function for simple (bivariate) regression based on the normal distribution:

$$f\left(\beta_0,\beta_1 \middle| Y, X, \sigma\right) = \frac{1}{\sigma\sqrt{2\pi}} \exp\left(\frac{-\left(Y_i - \left(\beta_0 + \beta_1 X\right)\right)^2}{2\sigma^2}\right) \tag{15.2}$$

This density is written as we will use it in the likelihood function, with the two regression coefficients unknown (on the left side of the vertical bar) and with the observed Xs and Ys in the data known (on the right side of the vertical bar). To simplify our example below, we also assume the conditional standard deviation is known. That is, we read $f(\beta_0, \beta_1 | Y, X, \sigma)$ as the density for particular values of the intercept and slope given our data (Y and X variables) and an assumed conditional standard deviation. To calculate the likelihood, we then multiply the individual densities together across all observations calculated for a specific value of the intercept and slope and the assumed value of the standard deviation. In practice, the maximum likelihood estimate of σ is also identified through this process.

We will use the data shown in Table 15.3 as an example. We created this data file to follow a regression line with an intercept of 24 and a slope of 6, and a conditional standard deviation of 1.1812, with errors that follow the normal distribution (conditional on X).

▦ **Table 15.3: Hypothetical Dataset for Simple Linear Regression Designed to have an Intercept of 24, a Slope of 6, and a Conditional Standard Deviation of 1.1812**

Values of X	Values of Y								
0	22	23	23	24	24	24	25	25	26
1	28	29	29	30	30	30	31	31	32
2	34	35	35	36	36	36	37	37	38
3	40	41	41	42	42	42	43	43	44
4	46	47	47	48	48	48	49	49	50

Because of this, we know that we should choose 24 as the most likely value of the intercept and 6 as the most likely value of the slope in our hand calculations. But what if we did not know these were the values that generated the data, and we only had the values of X and Y? We can make these hand calculations to choose the most likely parameters by choosing a value for the intercept and slope, plugging those values into Equation 15.2, and then repeatedly plugging in each pair of values of X and Y. Once we have the densities for each observation, we then multiply them together to calculate the likelihood (and log the likelihood to calculate the log-likelihood).

For example, if we initially choose a value of 18 for the intercept and a value of 6 for the slope, we obtain the following result for the first cell value in Table 15.3 where $X = 0$ and $Y = 22$:

$$f\left(\beta_0 = 18, \beta_1 = 6 \middle| Y = 22, X = 0, \sigma = 1.1812\right) = \frac{1}{1.1812\sqrt{2\pi}} \exp\left(\frac{-\left(22 - \left(18 + 6*0\right)\right)^2}{2*1.1812^2}\right) = .05793916$$

Alternatively, if we choose an intercept of 24 and a slope of 6 (and assumed a conditional standard deviation of 1.1812), then the calculation for the first cell value $X = 0$ and $Y = 22$ is:

$$f\left(\beta_0 = 24, \beta_1 = 6 \middle| Y = 22, X = 0, \sigma = 1.1812\right) = \frac{1}{1.1812\sqrt{2\pi}} \exp\left(\frac{-\left(22 - \left(24 + 6*0\right)\right)^2}{2*1.1812^2}\right) = .07365511$$

We would make similar calculations for each of the 45 observations and then multiply the 45 values together to calculate the likelihood. We would repeat this process for each set of values of the intercept and slope.

Figure 15.4 shows the results of following this process repeatedly for many different possible values of the intercept and slope. To show the results with two dimensions, in Figure 15.4a we show calculations in which we always used an intercept of 24 but varied the value of the slope; and, in Figure 15.4b we show calculations in which we always used a slope of 6 but varied the value of the intercept. As expected, each log-likelihood function peaks at the correct value of the parameter that we know generated the data. That is, Figure 15.4a peaks at a slope of 6. And, Figure 15.4b peaks at an intercept of 24.

Figure 15.5 graphs the log-likelihood function in three-dimensions, showing how the value of the log-likelihood changes as we vary both the intercept and slope. Again, as expected, the function peaks at the point where the slope is 6 and the intercept is 24. When either the slope of the intercept (or both) are set at different values, the log-likelihood is lower.

This process is an example of an iterative search for the maximum likelihood estimates of the intercept and slope in bivariate regression assuming the errors follow a normal distribution (conditional on X). In this case, as with the unconditional sample mean, statisticians are able to calculate closed-form solutions for the formulas for the intercept and slope. Similar to what we saw in Section 15.2.3, the maximal value on the likelihood function occurs where a tangent line drawn to the likelihood function has a slope of zero. Mathematically, it is possible to take the derivative of the likelihood function based on the density shown in Equation 15.2, set it equal to zero, and solve for the intercept and slope. As with the unconditional mean, the maximum likelihood formulas for the intercept and slope that we use to calculate the conditional mean match the OLS formulas (i.e., they are $\hat{\beta}_1 = \dfrac{\Sigma\left(X_i - \bar{X}\right)\left(Y_i - \bar{Y}\right)}{\Sigma\left(X_i - \bar{X}\right)^2}$ and $\hat{\beta}_0 = \bar{Y} - \hat{\beta}_1\bar{X}$).

a. Log-Likelihood at Varying Values of Slope, with Intercept at $\beta_0 = 24$

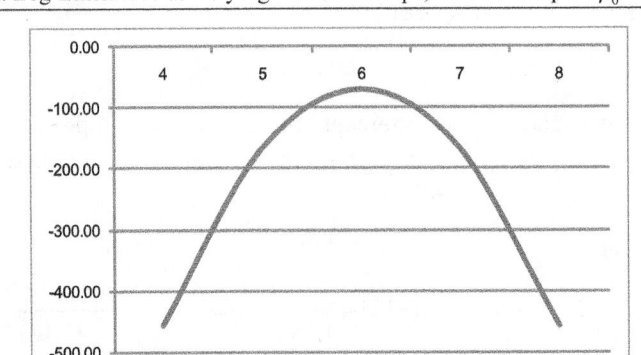

b. Log-Likelihood at Varying Values of Intercept, with Slope at $\beta_1 = 6$

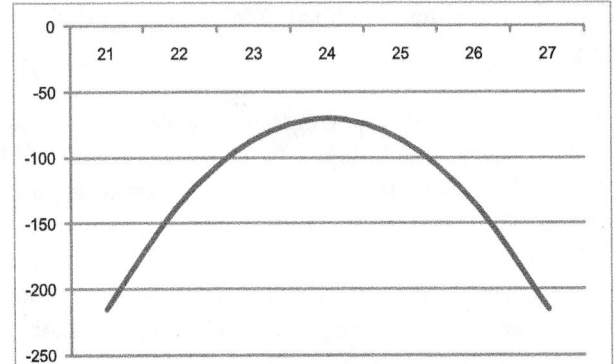

■ **Figure 15.4** Log-Likelihoods for Possible Values of the Slope and Intercept, with Conditional Standard Deviation of 1.1812

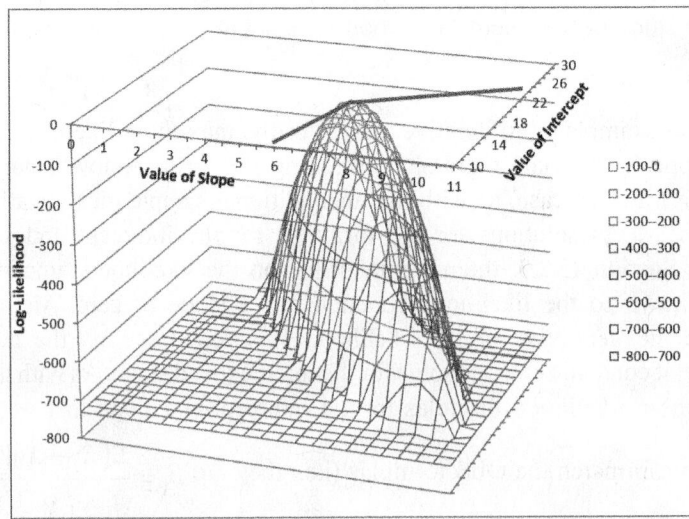

■ **Figure 15.5** Illustration of Log-Likelihood Function Varying Both Intercept and Slope

15.3: HYPOTHESIS TESTING WITH MAXIMUM LIKELIHOOD ESTIMATION

Hypothesis testing with maximum likelihood estimation proceeds similarly to what we have already learned for ordinary least squares estimation. As we have already mentioned above, however, we rely on the z-statistic rather than the t-statistic for tests of individual coefficients; and, we will similarly rely on the χ^2 rather than F-statistic for testing hypotheses about multiple parameters simultaneously. As we will see below, there are two types of χ^2 tests that are commonly used to examine hypotheses based on maximum likelihood techniques: the Wald χ^2 and the Likelihood-Ratio χ^2. The Wald χ^2 is also sometimes reported for tests of individual coefficients (rather than the z-statistic).

15.3.1: Testing a Hypothesis about a Single Parameter

The z-test

Statistical theory shows that maximum likelihood estimators are distributed "asymptotically normally," meaning that when the sample size is large, the sampling distribution for the estimator follows the normal distribution.[7] This property allows us to use a familiar technique for assessing the significance of an individual parameter:

$$z = \frac{\hat{\beta}_1 - \beta_1^*}{\hat{\sigma}_{\hat{\beta}_1}}$$

As in OLS regression, social science applications usually test the null hypothesis of $H_o: \beta_1^* = 0$ against the alternative that $H_a: \beta_1^* \neq 0$ because this tests whether there is any linear association between the predictor and the outcome. To test this hypothesis based on our maximum likelihood estimates we can either: 1) calculate a p-value associated with our calculated z-value which we will then compare to the alpha level (usually alpha of 0.05) or 2) relate the calculated z-value to a critical z-value to make a decision about the hypothesis (e.g., calculated z-values greater than 1.96 or less than −1.96 will be significant at the 5% two-tailed level).

> **■ Box 15.4**
>
> In maximum-likelihood estimation the variances of the slopes are estimated using the second derivative of the likelihood function. The square roots of these variances are the standard errors.

It is also straightforward to calculate confidence intervals using the estimated coefficients and standard errors. Similar to OLS regression, the confidence interval will be calculated as $\hat{\beta}_1 + z * \hat{\sigma}_{\hat{\beta}_1}$ where we use a z-value rather than a t-value since the maximum likelihood estimators are normally distributed (asymptotically). For a two-sided alternative and alpha of .05 we would use $\hat{\beta}_1 \pm 1.96 * \hat{\sigma}_{\hat{\beta}_1}$. As we discussed for OLS regression, the confidence interval is superior to a hypothesis test because it gives a plausible range of values for the parameter (rather than a single point estimate) while still allowing us to test the null hypothesis that the parameter is zero (if zero is contained within the confidence interval, then we fail to reject the null hypothesis; if zero is not contained within the confidence interval, then we reject the null hypothesis).

The Wald χ^2 test

As we noted above, for models estimated with maximum likelihood, tests for single parameters are sometimes conducted with the Wald chi-square rather than the z-test. We will see below that the tests lead to identical conclusions. Which statistic is reported is based on conventions in disciplines and subfields, researchers training and familiarity with the statistics (and sometimes default settings in computer software).

As we saw in Chapter 6, the z-test and chi-square for a single hypothesis with one degree of freedom are related by $z^2 = \chi^2$. Similar to what we saw for the t-test and F-test under the OLS regression model, this is true for the Wald χ^2 and the z-test presented above for the null hypothesis of $H_o: \beta_1^* = 0$ against the alternative hypothesis that $H_a: \beta_1^* \neq 0$. Namely:

$$z^2 = Wald\,\chi^2 = \frac{\left(\hat{\beta}_1 - \beta_1^*\right)^2}{\hat{\sigma}^2_{\hat{\beta}_1}}$$

The p-value will be the same for the z-test and the *Wald* χ^2 test of the same null and alternative hypotheses, thus they will lead to identical conclusions about the hypotheses. We will see below that SAS and Stata differ in which statistic they report in their default output for tests of individual coefficients (Stata provides z-values and SAS provides *Wald* χ^2 values). But, we can easily translate between the two either by taking the square or the square root.

Which should you report? This decision varies by conventions in your discipline or subfield. By reading the journals in your area, and talking to colleagues and mentors, you can determine which statistic authors typically report when they use maximum likelihood estimation.

15.3.2: Testing Joint Hypotheses

As was the case in the OLS regression model, we are often interested in testing joint hypotheses about multiple parameters simultaneously when we estimate models based on maximum likelihood. For example, like the model F-test in OLS regression, we may want to test the joint null hypothesis that the coefficients for all of the predictor variables in the model are zero. Or, like the Chow test in OLS regression, we may want to test the significance of the coefficients for a dummy grouping variable and the set of interactions with that dummy grouping variable.

In models estimated with maximum likelihood, there are several statistics that can be used to test these kinds of joint hypotheses. We will focus on two tests commonly used in the social sciences: an extension of the Wald chi-square that we just considered and the likelihood ratio test. Like the general linear F-test that we covered for OLS regression, the Wald chi-square and likelihood ratio test are quite useful because they can be applied to any nested models (see Long 1997 for an excellent extended discussion of these and additional tests).

The Likelihood Ratio Test

For joint hypotheses, students often find the likelihood ratio test simpler to comprehend than the *Wald* χ^2 so we will present the techniques and intuition for the likelihood ratio test first.

Mechanics of the Likelihood Ratio Test

The procedure for conducting the likelihood ratio test is very similar to the procedure we followed when conducting a general linear *F*-test. We estimate the model once without the constraint(s) of the null hypothesis (full model) and once with the constraint(s) of the null hypothesis (reduced model). For example, in a simple model with one predictor and the hypothesis $H_o\!:\!\beta_1^* = 0$ versus $H_a\!:\!\beta_1^* \neq 0$ we would estimate the model once with the predictor, X, included and once with the predictor, X, excluded (the latter model is the intercept-only model that we considered in Chapter 9). To similarly conduct a test like the OLS model *F*-test in multiple regression, we could estimate a full model with our complete set of predictor variables and a reduced model with only an intercept.

We draw on the log-likelihoods calculated for each of these estimated models to construct the Likelihood Ratio χ^2. We will refer to the log-likelihood value from the full model as $lnL(M_{full})$. We will refer to the log-likelihood value for the reduced model as $lnL(M_{reduced})$. Then, the Likelihood Ratio χ^2 is twice the difference in the log-likelihoods between the full and reduced models.

$$LR\chi^2 = 2[lnL(M_{full}) - lnL(M_{reduced})] = 2lnL(M_{full}) - 2lnL(M_{reduced})$$

The $LR\chi^2$ follows the chi-square distribution with degrees of freedom equal to the number of constraints in the null hypothesis (i.e., the degrees of freedom will be the number of predictor variables in the full model for a test that mirrors the model *F*-test). $LR\chi^2$ will never be negative since the likelihood for the reduced model cannot be larger than the likelihood for the full model.[8] Thus, the values calculated by the formula are consistent with the values of a chi-square distribution, which are always positive.

Intuition of the Likelihood Ratio Test

Examining the intuition behind the $LR\chi^2$ test can help us understand the meaning of the test and reinforce the idea of the likelihood function. Specifically, since the full and reduced models are nested, differing only by the constraints, they are on the same likelihood function. In other words, think of the iterative process we followed above to calculated likelihoods and log-likelihoods. Imagine that we calculated the log-likelihood once by plugging in the values listed in the null hypothesis (e.g., using a value of zero for the coefficient(s) of our predictor variable(s)). Then, imagine we calculated the log-likelihood again by plugging in the values listed in the alternative hypothesis (i.e., using the maximum likelihood estimates for the coefficient(s) of our predictor variable(s)).

If the constraints of the null hypothesis (in this text, generally that the coefficients for all predictor variables are zero) are consistent with our data, then the likelihood should not be much smaller for the reduced model than for the full model. On the other hand, if the constraints are not consistent with the data, then the likelihood should be much smaller for the reduced model than for the full model.

The Wald Chi-Square Test

The Wald chi-square test that we used above to test a single hypothesis can be extended to test multiple constraints simultaneously. This *Wald* χ^2 is based on a concept similar to our familiar *z*-tests and *t*-tests: If the constraint(s) are not valid, then the estimated coefficient(s) should differ from the constrained value(s) more than would be explained by sampling variability alone, with sampling variability captured by the standard error of the slope.

Figure 15.6 shows some different possible shapes of likelihood functions. The line in green is quite flat while the line in grey is very peaked, and the line in black is somewhere in between. When the log-likelihood function is flat (like the green line), then it is hard to find the maximum—a tangent line drawn to the likelihood function would be nearly horizontal for many possible values of the slope that are close to the maximum. In contrast, when the log-likelihood is quite curved near the peak (like the grey line), then it is easy to distinguish log-likelihoods below the maximum from the maximum.

The rate of change in the slope captures the degree of flatness or peakedness in the function. If the log-likelihood function is quite peaked then its slope is changing rapidly. If the log-likelihood function is more flat, then its slope is changing slowly. Statisticians calculate this rate of change based on the second derivative of the likelihood function. These values determine the variance (and standard error) of the estimates. The variance is found in the denominator of the *Wald* χ^2 statistic (its square root, the standard error, is found in the denominator of the *z*-statistic).

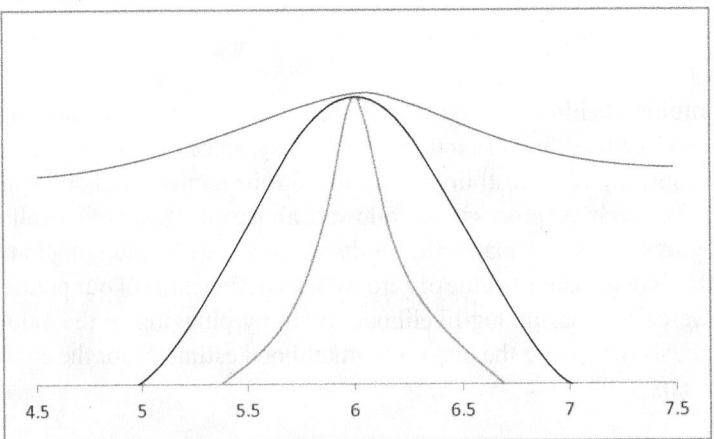

▦ **Figure 15.6** Illustration of Likelihood Functions with Different Shapes

$$Wald\,\chi^2 = \frac{\left(\hat{\beta}_1 - \beta_1^*\right)^2}{\hat{\sigma}_{\hat{\beta}_1}^2}$$

Thus, the square of the distance between the maximum likelihood estimate of the slope and the hypothesized value of the slope is weighted by the inverse of the variance of the estimate. The denominator will be large—and thus result in smaller chi-square values—if the likelihood function is flat (and thus it is hard to find a maximum). The denominator will be small—and thus result in larger chi-square values—if the likelihood function is peaked (and thus it is easy to find a maximum).

The *Wald* χ^2 formula that we just examined applies to tests of a single parameter. The formula for the *Wald* χ^2 for joint hypotheses about multiple constraints is more complicated and involves matrix notation. Although we will not consider its formula here, it is based on the same concept as discussed above of weighting the distance between each of the coefficients and their constrained values by the variances of the coefficients.

Choosing between the Wald χ^2 and Likelihood Ratio χ^2

The Wald chi-square and likelihood ratio tests are "asymptotically equivalent" (i.e., in large samples, they converge toward the same result). In the past, the choice between them was typically based on ease of computation (although this is less of a concern with modern statistical packages) as well as common practice in a field. Again, you can look to journals, colleagues, and mentors in your field to figure out what values are commonly reported.

■ **Box 15.5**

The **deviance** is another statistic that is often included in default statistical output based on maximum likelihood estimation and sometimes reported in publications. The deviance is calculated as $-2lnL(M_{full})$. When Nelder and Wedderburn (1972) introduced the generalized linear model, they discussed two extreme models—a "minimal" and "complete model"—that might be useful comparisons for an estimated model. The minimal model is the intercept-only model (which we often use as a reduced model when calculating the Likelihood Ratio χ^2 or *Wald* χ^2). The complete model is a model that fits the data perfectly because it fits one parameter for each case (i.e., the predicted values of Y equals the observed value of Y for every case). The deviance statistic compares the estimated model with the complete model.

15.4: THE GENERALIZED LINEAR MODEL

Now that we have introduced the technique that we will use to estimate generalized linear models—maximum likelihood estimation—we will return to the basic concepts of the generalized linear model, especially the link function. And, we will demonstrate how to estimate the generalized linear model for a linear regression model, matching the OLS results we saw in Part 3.

Nelder and Wedderburn (1972) introduced the term *generalized linear model* and a monograph by McCullagh and Nelder (1983) and GLIM computer software (Nelder 1975) centralized and popularized the approach.[9] As Nelder and Wedderburn (1972: 382) noted about the potential usefulness of this model in the classroom:

> [Generalized linear models] give a consistent way of linking together the systematic elements in a model with the random elements. Too often the student meets complex systematic linear models only in connection with normal errors, and if [s]he encounters probit analysis this may seem to have little to do with the linear regression theory [s]he has learnt. By isolating the systematic linear component the student can be introduced to . . . [continuous and categorical] independent variates, and transformations, quite independently of the added complications of errors and associated probability distributions.

Literature Excerpt 15.2 shows a variety of links and distributions as laid out by Nelder (1975) in the early 1970s. We will consider in this chapter the linear model, which falls in the top left cell of the table based on the Identity link and the Normal distribution. We will consider in Chapter 16 the logit and probit models with are based on the Logit and Probit links and the Binomial distribution. In Chapter 17, we will consider extensions of these models using a Multinomial distribution and more general logit link. Other models are mentioned in Chapter 18's roadmap, such as the Poisson model based on the Log link and Poisson distribution.

15.4.1: The Systematic Portion of the Model

Nelder and Wedderburn (1972) used the term "linear" to refer to the systematic portion of the regression model. For example, the systematic portion of any model with one continuous and one dummy variable predictor might be written:

$$\eta = \beta_0 + \beta_1 X_1 + \beta_2 D_1 \tag{15.3}$$

The use of the Greek η—pronounced "eta"—on the left hand side—rather than $E(Y)$ which we used in Part 3—is purposeful.[10]

The systematic portion of the model linearly predicts a value that is linked to the conditional mean of our outcome variable through a function (called the **link function**; Nelder and Wedderburn 1972, p. 372). This link is needed because our outcome variables are often constrained in the values they can take on (e.g., only certain categories, like a dichotomous, ordinal, or nominal variable, or only positive values, like a count variable). The predictions from Equation 15.3 are not constrained. So, if we used $\beta_0 + \beta_1 X_1 + \beta_2 D_1$ to directly predict a constrained outcome then we would likely calculate some values that fall outside the

▪ **Literature Excerpt 15.2**

Link		Distribution			
		Normal	Poisson	Binomial	Gamma
Identity	$\eta = \mu$	(i) (ii)		╳	(vi)
Log	$\eta = \log \mu$		(iii)	╳	
Inverse	$\eta = 1/\mu$			╳	
Square root	$\eta = \sqrt{\mu}$			╳	
Logit	$\eta = \log \dfrac{p}{1-p}$	╳	╳	(iv)	╳
Probit	$\eta = \varPhi(p)$	╳	╳	(v)	╳
Complementary log log	$\eta = \log(-\log(1-p))$	╳	╳		╳

(i) Linear regression with quantitative independent variates and Normal errors assumed.
(ii) Constant-fitting to multiway tables of quantitative variates with Normal errors assumed.
(iii) Log-linear models applied to contingency tables of counts.
(iv) Constant-fitting on a logit scale to multiway tables of proportions.
(v) Probit analysis of dose-response curves and surfaces.
(vi) The estimation of variance components from independent mean squares.

Source: Nelder, J.A. (1975). Announcement by the Working Party on Statistical Computing: GLIM (Generalized Linear Interactive Modeling Program). *Applied Statistics,* 24(2): 259–261. *Note:* The original was changed by replacing Y with η to be consistent with the notation used in the textbook.

possible values of the outcome variable. Letting η take on any value and then transforming the η values to the values needed for our outcome variable (with the link function) deals with this issue.

For example, if Y can take on only positive values (like our *glmiles* variable in our NSFH distance example) then we could use a log link—$\eta = \ln(E(Y))$. As we did in Chapter 12, we can use the exponential function to equivalently write such an equation as $\exp(\eta) = E(Y)$. Thus, we can take the exponential of the values produced by the systematic portion of the regression model ($\beta_0 + \beta_1 X_1 + \beta_2 D_1$ in Equation 15.3) to transform back to the natural units of Y. Because the exponential of a negative value is a positive value (between 0 and 1) this link assures that the transformed values will be positive, as desired.

A strength of the generalized linear model is that it allows us to continue to separate out model into two major components—a systematic and a random portion. We can also continue to use what we have already learned about the right hand side of the equation in OLS regression across models appropriate for different kinds of outcome variables. For example,

1. We can define dummy predictor variables and interpret them relative to a reference category.
2. We can define interactions between dummy and/or interval predictor variables.
3. We can define quadratic terms and logs of predictor variables.
4. We can interpret coefficients in multiple regression models as the effect for a predictor variable controlling for other variables in the model.

But, as we will discuss further below, and especially in Chapters 16 and 17, the difference from OLS is that unless we use the identity link, extra steps are needed to interpret the findings in meaningful ways. This is because the changes represented by the coefficients in the systematic portion of the model and the predictions from the systematic portion of the model are in terms of η rather than Y. We will learn how to use commands in SAS, Stata, and Excel to reduce the work involved in making such interpretations.

15.4.2: The Random Component of the Model

The random component of the generalized linear model describes the distribution of our outcome variable. Numerous distributions are allowed, many of which are appropriate for various outcomes that we cannot assume follow a normal distribution, conditional on the predictors (see again Literature Excerpt 15.2). For example, as we will consider in detail in Chapter 16, a binomial distribution results from a series of Bernoulli trials in which a variable takes on one of two values, and thus is appropriate for a dichotomous outcome. The multinomial distribution is similarly appropriate for multi-category outcomes. And, a logistic distribution can be used to model the random component for an ordinal outcome.

Every distribution has a central tendency. For the normal distribution, we have already considered estimating the central tendency, including the unconditional mean, $E(Y) = \mu_Y$, based

on $\bar{Y} = \dfrac{\sum_{i=1}^{n} Y_i}{n}$ (Chapter 5) and the conditional mean, $E(Y|X) = \beta_0 + \beta_1 X$ based on

$\hat{\beta}_1 = \dfrac{\Sigma(X_i - \bar{X})(Y_i - \bar{Y})}{\Sigma(X_i - \bar{X})^2}$ and $\hat{\beta}_0 = \bar{Y} - \hat{\beta}_1 \bar{X}$ (Chapter 8).

In the generalized linear model, the central tendency of a theoretical distribution (referred to as θ) is linked to the prediction from the systematic portion of the model (η from Equation 15.3) through a function (referred to as the link, for example the log). We can use the inverse of this function (like the exponential) to transform predictions based on the systematic portion of the model (which can take on any value) to the conditional mean of the outcome variable in its natural units (which can take on only certain values).

The link function in the standard linear regression model is quite simple. This is because if our outcome is truly distributed normally (conditional on the predictors), then it can take on any value in its natural units. Thus, we can use what is called an **identity link** for a linear regression model. The identity link sets the conditional mean of Y directly equal to the prediction from the systematic portion of the model. That is $\eta = E(Y)$. Substituting into Equation 15.3 we have:

$$E(Y) = \eta = \beta_0 + \beta_1 X_1 + \beta_2 D_1$$

As in ordinary least squares regression, we can assume a normal distribution for the random component of this linear regression model (conditional on the Xs).

15.4.3: Estimating the Generalized Linear Model in SAS and Stata

SAS and Stata both have dedicated commands for estimating the generalized linear model. We use options to specify the desired distribution and link. In Stata, the basic syntax is

```
glm <depvar> <indepvar>, family(<distribution>) link(<link>)
```

Stata uses the word "family" for the option to specify the distribution, since each theoretical distribution is really a whole family of distributions each with its own parameters (for example, as discussed in Chapter 6, the theoretical normal distribution comprises a family of distributions each with its own mean and standard deviation).

In SAS, the command is

```
proc genmod;
  model <depvar>=<indepvar> / dist=<distribution> link=<link>;
run;
```

For a basic linear regression model with a continuous outcome, we can use the word *normal* for the distribution and the word *identity* for the link in both Stata and SAS. In Chapters 16 and 17 we will learn the words to use to request additional distributions and links. Both packages use maximum likelihood estimation as the default technique for calculating parameter estimates.

Basic Model Estimates

Display B.15.1 shows the results of our re-estimating the first bivariate regression model we examined in Chapter 8, a regression of *g1miles* on *g2earn*, using the generalized linear model with an identity link, normal distribution, and maximum likelihood estimation. Comparing the coefficients with those in Chapter 8 (Display B.8.1) confirms that they match (within rounding) the results we saw under OLS estimation. Both OLS and the comparable generalized linear model estimate the intercept to be 249.8116 and the slope to be 0.0011. The output in Display B.15.1 circled in green confirms that the estimates used a normal (also referred to as Gaussian) distribution with an identity link and maximum likelihood estimation. The log-likelihood, circled in black, is reported to be −49990.7771. As expected, this value is negative, but because SAS and Stata used maximum likelihood estimation, we know that this is the least negative log-likelihood among all possible values for the intercept and slope.[11]

Testing Hypotheses for Individual Coefficients

In Display B.15.1, the p-values for the *g2earn* variable and the intercept in both Stata and in SAS are the smallest values each statistical packages shows (0.000 in Stata and <.0001 in SAS). Because they are so small, we cannot verify in this output that they are in fact identical. But, we can verify that the square of the z-values equal the *Wald* χ^2 values. For the slope, the square of the z-value from Stata, $(5.19)^2 = 26.9361$, matches within rounding the SAS chi-square value of 26.91. For the intercept, we also see that the square of the z-value from Stata, $(24.31)^2 = 590.9761$, matches within rounding the SAS chi-square value of 590.94.

Because the p-value of $< .0001$ for *g2earn* is less than an alpha of .05, we reject the null hypothesis that $\beta_1^* = 0$ in favor of the alternative $\beta_1^* \neq 0$. Thus, earnings is a statistically significant predictor of distance. Hypothesis testing and assessment of the substantive size of associations proceed as we are familiar from OLS.[12] Because we estimated a linear regression model with an identity link, the coefficient of 0.0011 can be interpreted as follows: "For each additional dollar of annual earnings, adult respondents live 0.0011 miles farther from their mothers, on average." Given a change of one dollar in annual earnings is quite small substantively, we might instead interpret this for, say, a $10,000 change in annual earnings. To do so after estimation, we can use the rule introduced in Chapter 8 that "if we increase X by i units, then Y is expected to change by $i\hat{\beta}_1$ units." In our case, for each additional $10,000 adult respondents' earn, we expect that they will live about $10000 * 0.0011 = 11$ miles farther from their mothers, on average. This rescaled value allows us to determine that although the association between earnings and distance is statistically significant, it is substantively small (an 11 mile difference for a $10,000 change in annual earnings).

Testing Joint Hypotheses

We will use the full sample hours of chores example from Chapter 9 to demonstrate use of the *Wald* χ^2 and *LR* χ^2 to test joint hypotheses. Display B.15.2 contains the results of the reduced model, an intercept-only model for hours of chores. Display B.15.3 contains the results of the full model, the regression of hours of chores on number of children and hours of work. The constraints from the null hypothesis are $H_o: \beta_1 = 0, \beta_2 = 0$. The alternative is $H_a: \beta_1 \neq 0$ and/or $\beta_2 \neq 0$.

In Stata, we can use the `test` command that we learned in Chapter 9 following a `glm` estimation, although Stata reports a *Wald* χ^2 rather than an *F*-value after a model that was estimated by maximum likelihood. The likelihood ratio test can be conducted using Stata's `lrtest` command. To use `lrtest` we need to store the estimates from our full and reduced regression models with the `estimates store <name>` command. We can choose any names to store the estimates; For simplicity, we use the name `reduced` for our reduced model and the name `full` for our full model. Then, the `lrtest` command references these stored results (`lrtest full reduced`).

To request these tests in SAS, we add a `contrast` statement after the model statement for the *full* model. The syntax differs from what we learned in Chapter 6 for the SAS `test` command: To test that a parameter has a coefficient equal to zero, we list the variable name followed by the value one. Multiple constraints are separated by commas. By default, the $LR\ \chi^2$ is calculated. We can request the *Wald* χ^2 by adding the option /`wald` to the `contrast` statement. And, we can use a label for the test to distinguish the two statistics. For example, `contrast "intercept only – wald" numkid 1, hrwork 1 /wald`; would calculate the Wald chi-square statistics to test that the coefficients for *numkid* and *hrwork* both equal zero in the multiple regression model.

First, note that, as expected, the coefficient estimates match those that we saw in Chapter 9 when we estimated the model using OLS (Display B.6.5 and Display B.9.6). Next, let's calculate the Likelihood Ratio chi-square statistic by hand to verify one of the new results. The log-likelihood for the full model in Display B.15.3 is −14626.3383. The log-likelihood for the reduced model is in Display B.15.2, −14749.9974. As expected the log-likelihood is larger (less negative) for the full than the reduced model, but is the difference statistically significant? The Likelihood Ratio chi-square answers this question for us. Twice the difference in the log-likelihoods is:

$$LR\chi^2 = 2 * ((-14626.3383) - (-14749.9974)) = 247.3182$$

This matches the results in the SAS and Stata output (circled in green in Display B.15.3), and the output shows us that the *p*-value is less than 0.0001. Since this *p*-value is smaller than an alpha of 0.05, we can reject the null hypothesis ($H_o : \beta_1 = 0,\ \beta_2 = 0$) and conclude that at least one of the two slopes differs significantly from zero. In fact, the individual *z* and *Wald* χ^2 tests have *p*-values that are quite small for both *numkid* and for *hrwork*.

The results of the *Wald* χ^2 test of the joint null hypothesis that both slopes are zero are circled in black in Display B.15.3. Recall that the $LR\chi^2$ and *Wald* χ^2 are asymptotically equivalent, meaning that they approach the same value as the sample size becomes infinitely large. Consistently, the *Wald* χ^2 = 257.40 in our sample of size 3,116 is in "the same ballpark" as the Likelihood Ratio chi-square of 419. The *p*-value for the *Wald* χ^2 test is small (<.0001) as was the case for the $LR\chi^2$, again indicating that we can reject the null hypothesis that both slope coefficients are zero in favor of the alternative hypothesis that at least one slope is not equal to zero.

15.5: SUMMARY

This chapter introduced the generalized linear model using linear regression with a continuous outcome. The generalized linear model unifies approaches for various types of outcomes in a single framework, including not only such continuous variables but also dichotomous, ordinal, nominal and other kinds of outcomes. Like OLS, the generalized linear model has random and systematic components, but distributions other than normal can be used for the random component and links can be used to transform the unbounded predictions from the systematic portion of the model to bounded values on the actual outcomes (such as two values for a dichotomy or positive integers for a count variable). The generalized linear model is estimated with maximum likelihood rather than ordinary least squares. Sometimes maximum likelihood estimation requires a search for the estimate (iterative search); other times a closed form solution exists. For the generalized linear model with a normal distribution and identity link examined in this chapter a closed form solution exists, and the formulas for the regression coefficients match the OLS formulas. In Chapters 16 and 17 the models will be estimated by SAS and Stata using an iterative search. We also introduced in this chapter several statistics for testing hypotheses in the generalized linear model, including the z-test, the *Wald* χ^2 and the Likelihood Ratio χ^2.

KEY TERMS

Asymptotic

Closed-Form Solution

Convergence

Density Function

Deviance

Iterative Search

Likelihood

Likelihood Function

Link Function

Log-Likelihood

Maximum Likelihood Estimation

Start Value

REVIEW QUESTIONS

15.1   What is a density function?

15.2   What is a likelihood and a log-likelihood?

15.3   What is a likelihood function?

15.4 What is the basic objective of maximum likelihood estimation?

15.5 What is the difference between an iterative search and a closed form solution?

15.6 What are the similarities and differences between the Likelihood Ratio χ^2 and the *Wald* χ^2?

15.7 When and how are the *z*-statistic and *Wald* χ^2 statistic related to each other?

15.8 What are the three main ways in which the generalized linear model differs from OLS regression?

15.9 What are some techniques we learned for OLS regression that can also be used in the generalized linear model?

15.10 What is a link function?

15.11 What distributional assumption and link are used to obtain coefficient estimates identical to OLS regression using the generalized linear model approach?

REVIEW EXERCISES

REVIEW EXERCISES 15

These exercises are meant to help you see inside the black box of how the computer calculates densities and likelihoods. You may take the most away from these exercises if you write the general formula and then show how to substitute in and make "hand" (calculator) calculations for several values. Then, additional calculations can be made by programming the formula into Excel (or another software package). Setting up the spreadsheet formulas and referencing various values to make the calculations often helps demystify to you how statistical software is making similar calculations.

15.1 Calculate by hand the density for the values 60, 80, 100, 120 and 140 from a normal distribution with mean of 100 and standard deviation of 15.

15.2 Imagine that you have a small data set with the values {3,4,4,5,5,5,6,6,7}. Assume that you know that the standard deviation is 1. Which of the following values of the mean is most likely to have generated the data: 3, 5, or 7? Justify your response based on the values of the likelihood and the log-likelihood.

15.3 Suppose you have a hypothetical data set like the following:

Values of X	Values of Y					
10	122	123	124	124	125	126
11	128	129	130	130	131	132
12	134	135	136	136	137	138

Which of the following values of the intercept and slope were most likely to have generated these data, assuming a standard deviation of 1.3693: (a) intercept=64, slope=6, (b) intercept=63, slope=6, or (c) intercept=64, slope=5?

CHAPTER EXERCISE

CHAPTER EXERCISE 15

In this exercise, you will write a SAS and a Stata batch program to estimate a generalized linear model.

Start with the NHIS 2009 data set that was created in Chapter 4 with an *if expression* to only keep cases that *do not have missing values on the age, exfreqwR and bmiR variables.*

15.1 The Generalized Linear Model with a Continuous Outcome

a) SAS/Stata Tasks.

   i) Use the SAS genmod and Stata glm commands to estimate a generalized linear model that regresses *bmiR* on *age* assuming an identity link and normally distributed errors. Call this Regression #1.

   ii) Use the SAS genmod and Stata glm command to estimate an "intercept only" generalized linear model with *bmiR* as the outcome, assuming an identity link and normally distributed errors. Call this Regression #2.

   iii) Use the SAS genmod and Stata glm command to estimate a generalized linear model that regresses *bmiR* on *age* and *exfreqwR* assuming an identity link and normally distributed errors. Call this Regression #3.

   iv) Compare Regression #3 to Regression #2 using the Wald chi-square test and the likelihood ratio test.

b) Write-Up Tasks.

   i) Compare the coefficient estimates in Regression #1 to the results you obtained in the chapter exercise to Chapter 8. What do you see?

   ii) Compare the coefficient estimates in Regression #3 to the results you obtained in the chapter exercise to Chapter 9. What do you see?

   iii) Show how to calculate by hand the z-test and the Wald chi-square test for the hypothesis that $\beta_1 = 0$ in Regression #1.

iv) Show how to calculate by hand the likelihood ratio test comparing Regression #3 to Regression #2.

v) Based on the SAS and Stata results can you reject the null hypothesis comparing Regression #3 to Regression #2 using the Wald chi-square test? What about based on the likelihood ratio test? Be sure to write the null and alternative hypotheses and justify your conclusions.

COURSE EXERCISE

Replicate the models that you estimated in the course exercises for Chapter 8 and Chapter 9 using a generalized linear model with an identity link and assuming normally distributed errors. Compare the coefficient estimates in the OLS models and generalized linear models. Use the Wald chi-square and the likelihood ratio test to compare the estimated models to an intercept only model.

COURSE
EXERCISE
15

Chapter 16

DICHOTOMOUS OUTCOMES

CHAPTER 16: DICHOTOMOUS OUTCOMES

Dichotomous outcome variables are common in the social sciences. The generalized linear model is ideal for such situations. Researchers can choose a distribution (the binomial) and a link (logit or probit) appropriate for a two-category outcome variable. The techniques presented in Chapter 15 can be used for hypothesis testing; and, in this chapter, we present additional techniques for assessing model fit using R-squared values and information criteria. We also introduce strategies for creating and graphing predictions and for transforming the coefficients for interpretation. These are important because the coefficients based on the logit and probit links cannot be directly interpreted in meaningful ways and because the logit and probit links allow the association between the predictor and outcome to be non-linear. We begin by examining a literature example to demonstrate the usefulness of these models and follow by discussing how the OLS model can be used, but is limited, with a dichotomous outcome.

▨ **Box 16.1**

Indeed, in a full-text search of JSTOR citations in the areas of education, health sciences, psychology and sociology from 2000 to 2005 we found that whereas over 10,000 citations included the word "regression" almost half as many—nearly 5,000—included the phrase "logit" or "logistic regression" (although just under 3,000 articles explicitly referenced "OLS" or "ordinary least squares" or "linear regression" some authors may use the word "regression" without modifier to refer to OLS). The predominance of the use of logit over probit models for dichotomous outcomes was evident in that nine times as many articles referenced the word logit or the phrase "logistic regression" than the word probit; that is, just over 500 articles included the word "probit."

16.1: LITERATURE EXCERPT 16.1

In a 2007 issue of *Social Forces*, Brian Goesling analyzed the association between educational attainment and self-reported health using the National Health Interview Surveys (NHIS). Because of his interest in changes over time, he drew on NHIS surveys conducted annually between 1982 and 2004. Health was assessed in each survey with a standard question in which respondents reported whether their health was fair, poor, good, very good, or excellent. Goesling presents results in which he dichotomized this variable to indicate fair or poor (= 1) versus good, very good or excellent (= 0) health. Education was assessed by respondents reports of their highest level of formal schooling. Goesling recoded this variable into college graduate (16 or more years; the reference group), high school graduate (12 to 15 years), and less than a high school degree (less than 12 years). Survey year was coded with integers ranging from 0 (which represented the year 1982) to 22 (which represented the year 2004). Respondent age was coded into three groups: 30–49, 50–69, and 70 or older. In some models, Goesling also adjusted for gender, race-ethnicity, marital status, and region of the country.

Goesling reports two sets of results that illustrate the main models we consider in this chapter. One set is based on the logistic regression model which is the generalized linear model assuming a binomial distribution and a logit link. The other set is based on a linear probability model, which we also consider below and is an OLS regression model with a dichotomous outcome. Goesling's analyses demonstrate how we can use techniques which we learned in Part 3, such as interactions, with generalized linear models. Specifically, he includes in his models an interaction between survey year and the dummy indicators of less than high school degree and high school graduate (with college graduate as the reference). Because survey year was coded with a zero for 1982, when these interactions are in the model, the coefficients for the education dummy variables estimate the level of health disparities between those with less versus more education in 1982. The interactions capture how these disparities widened or narrowed over time (through 2004). The survey year variable itself captures how self-reported health changed over time (from 1982 to 2004) for the reference education group (college graduates).

We show Goesling's Table 2 in Literature Excerpt 16.1a. The "unadjusted" results are without controls. The "adjusted" results control for gender, race-ethnicity, marital status, and region of

■ **Literature Excerpt 16.1a**

Table 2. Logistic Regression Results

Age Group	Independent Variable	Unadjusted		Adjusted	
		B	SE	b	SE
70+	Education: < 12	.870***	(.042)	.824***	(.043)
	Education: 12–15	.237***	(.044)	.286***	(.044)
	Year	−.020***	(.003)	−.023***	(.003)
	Year × < 12	.018***	(.003)	.016***	(.003)
	Year × 12–15	.014***	(.003)	.012***	(.003)
50–69	Education: < 12	1.837***	(.032)	1.709***	(.032)
	Education: 12–15	.722***	(.032)	.725***	(.032)
	Year	−.017***	(.002)	−.018***	(.002)
	Year × < 12	.013***	(.002)	.010***	(.003)
	Year × 12–15	.013***	(.002)	.011***	(.002)
30–49	Education: < 12	2.402***	(.036)	2.224***	(.037)
	Education: 12–15	1.055***	(.035)	1.022***	(.036)
	Year	.015***	(.003)	.008**	(.003)
	Year × < 12	−.019***	(.003)	−.015***	(.003)
	Year × 12–15	.001	(.003)	−.001	(.003)

Notes: Numbers in parentheses are robust standard errors. Models were estimated separately by age group. See text for details.
*$p < .05$ **$p < .01$ ***$p < .001$ (two-tailed tests)

Source: Goesling, B. 2007. "The Rising Significance of Education for Health?" *Social Forces*, 85: 1621–1644.

the country. We can interpret the statistical significance and direction of associations based on the results in this table. But, because the model uses the logit link, we cannot immediately assess the substantive significance of the results. (We shall see in a moment how Goesling uses one of the techniques we will learn below to assess the size of significant associations.) All but one of the coefficients in Goesling's Table 2 is statistically significant. For the older age groups, the directions of associations are the same. The coefficients for the dummy variables *Education: < 12* and *Education: 12–15* are both positive, indicating that in 1982 (the survey year coded zero) less educated respondents were more likely to report fair or poor health (coded one on the outcome) versus good, very good, or excellent (coded zero on the outcome) than were respondents who had at least a college degree. The interaction terms are both positive for these older age groups, indicating that the gap between the less and more educated respondents widened over time. The year variable itself is negative indicating that the reference education group (college graduates) was less likely to report poor health at the later than earlier survey years.

For the younger age group (aged 30–49), the dummy variables *Education: < 12* and *Education: 12–15* are again both positive, indicating that in this age group the health disparity by education was also evident in 1982. But, one interaction is not significantly different from zero (*Year x 12–15*) and the other is negative in sign (*Year x < 12*) indicating that the health disparity either stayed

■ **Literature Excerpt 16.1b**

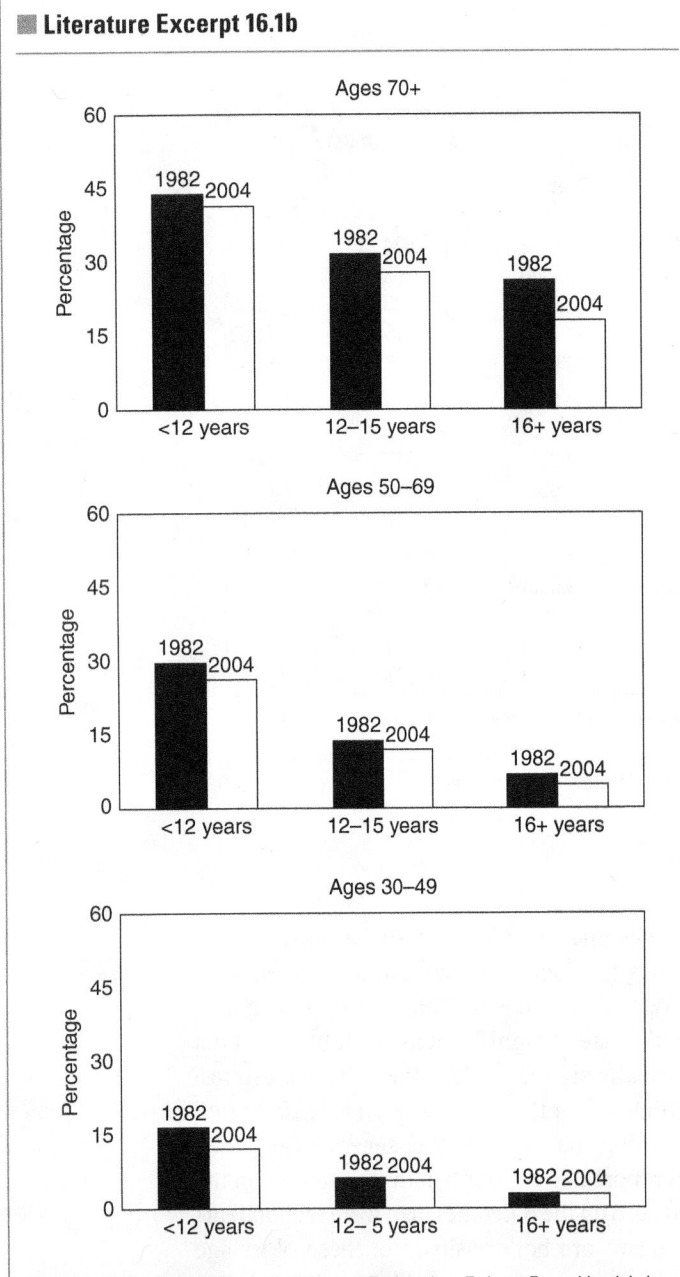

Figure 1 Predicted Probabilities of Reporting Fair or Poor Health by Education Level, Age Group and Survey Year

Source: Goesling, B. 2007. "The Rising Significance of Education for Health?" *Social Forces*, 85: 1621–1644.

the same or narrowed over time for this younger age group. And, for the younger age group, the coefficient for the *Year* variable is positive indicating that the reference education group (college graduates) was more likely to report fair or poor health at later than earlier survey years.

Although these different patterns are intriguing, it is hard to fully interpret them without knowing their magnitude. How big were the health disparities in the early 1980s? How much have they widened or narrowed over time? Goesling's Figure 1 (shown in Literature Excerpt 16.1b) uses the technique of calculating and plotting "predicted probabilities" which we will show how to do below. This is similar to our use of predicted values in Part 3, but now the values represent the probability of being coded one on the outcome that the model predicts for someone with various characteristics on the predictor variables (in this example, the predicted probability is more specifically the predicted probability of reporting fair or poor health). As we have seen in earlier chapters, such predictions can be made for any combination of values of the predictors, although researchers usually select representative values that best demonstrate the main findings. Goesling shows predictions within each of his three education levels and each of his three age groups for the first (1982) and last (2004) survey years.

The graphs verify that health disparities by education are evident in each age group and time period (i.e., the pairs of bars on the left, for respondents with less than a high school degree, are higher than the pairs of bars in the middle, for respondents with a high school degree, which are higher still than the pairs of bars on the right, for respondents with a college degree or more). The bars also show that health tended to improve over time (within each pair of bars, the lighter bar is lower than the darker bar). For the oldest age group (top graph in Literature Excerpt 16.1b), the difference by survey year is clearly largest for the most educated, consistent with the widening health disparities by education in this age group. In contrast, in the youngest age group (bottom graph in Literature Excerpt 16.1b) the difference by survey year is clearly largest for the least educated, consistent with the narrowing health disparities by education in this age group.

The predicted probabilities also allow us to assess the absolute and relative magnitude of these differences. Not surprisingly, the oldest age group is more likely to report fair or poor health than the youngest age group (the predicted percentages—the predicted probabilities multiplied by 100—are about 15% or more in the oldest group and about 15% or less in the youngest group). The absolute magnitude of the disparities is larger in the oldest group (among those 70 and older, about 40% of the least educated report fair or poor health in 2004 in contrast to about 20% of the most educated in this same year, a different of 20 percentage points). But, because the level of fair or poor health is so low for the most educated thirty and forty year-olds, the relative disparity is sizable in this age group (among thirty and forty year-olds, over 15% of the least educated report fair or poor health in 1982 in contrast to less than 5% of the most educated; although a difference of just 10 percentage points, it is relatively larger than we saw for the oldest: 15/5 = 3 versus 40/20 = 2).

In Literature Excerpt 16.1c we show Goesling's Table 3 which reports the linear probability models, which are OLS regression results with the dummy outcome variable. For these models, Goesling recoded the outcome so that 100 (rather than one) represents fair or poor health while zero still represents good, very good, or excellent health, so that the coefficients in Table 3 are in percentage point (rather than probability) units.

Goesling interprets the results for the linear regression model as largely similar to those of OLS regression (which we will see below can sometimes be the case). Specifically, the sign and significance of the results in Goesling's Table 3 are the same as the results in his Table 2 for the

---

■ **Box 16.2**

When we have a dichotomous variable as an outcome, it is useful to have language to distinguish absolute change in the level of the probability from the percentage change in the outcome. The conventional approach is to use the phrase percentage points to refer to the absolute change in the level of the probability. An example illustrates how we can use this "percentage points" phrase and the confusion that results when we are not careful with our language. For example, suppose that in a given industry the predicted probability of being unemployed is 0.02 for managers and 0.08 for clerical workers. An imprecise way to report this finding would be to say that "Our model predicts that the probability of being unemployed is 6% higher for clerical workers than managers" because the language "6%" implies percentage change (and in our case percentage change is actually $\frac{(0.08 - 0.02)}{0.02} * 100 = 300\%$). A more precise way to report the absolute change would be to say that "Our model predicts that unemployment is 6 percentage points higher for clerical workers than for managers."

■ **Literature Excerpt 16.1c**

Table 3. Linear Probability Models

Age Group	Independent Variable	Unadjusted		Adjusted	
		B	SE	b	SE
70+	Education: < 12	18.011***	(.713)	16.809***	(.710)
	Education: 12–15	4.328***	(.718)	5.259***	(.715)
	Year	–.320***	(.052)	–.366***	(.051)
	Year × < 12	.268***	(.053)	.229***	(.053)
	Year × 12–15	.192***	(.052)	.163**	(.051)
50–69	Education: < 12	29.161***	(.354)	26.649***	(.354)
	Education: 12–15	7.897***	(.277)	7.786***	(.278)
	Year	–.120***	(.022)	–.140***	(.021)
	Year × < 12	.045	(.029)	–.015	(.029)
	Year × 12–15	.073***	(.020)	.029	(.020)
30–49	Education: < 12	19.663***	(.274)	18.035***	(.271)
	Education: 12–15	4.438***	(.120)	4.108***	(.120)
	Year	.076***	(.010)	.023*	(.010)
	Year × < 12	–.214***	(.022)	–.175***	(.022)
	Year × 12–15	.037***	(.010)	.022*	(.010)

Notes: Numbers in parentheses are robust standard errors. Models were estimated separately by age group. See text for details.
*p < .05 **p < .01 ***p < .001 (two-tailed tests)

Source: Goesling, B. 2007. "The Rising Significance of Education for Health?" *Social Forces*, 85: 1621–1644.

oldest age group, although there are a couple of differences for the younger age groups. For the middle age group, the interactions between the education dummies and year variable are no longer significant. And, for the youngest age group, the interaction between the dummy for high school graduate and survey year (*Year x 12–15*) is now significantly positive.

Although Goesling does not plot the predicted values based on his Table 3, we can more easily interpret the substantive size of the significant linear probability model coefficients because they are already in probability units. For example, for the youngest age group, the coefficient for *Education: < 12* of 18.035 indicates that among thirty and forty year olds 18 percentage points more reported fair or poor health in 1982 if they did not have a high school degree than if they had a college degree. This difference had narrowed by –.175*22 = –3.85 percentage points by 2004.

16.2: LINEAR PROBABILITY MODEL

We will now consider in detail the **linear probability model** used by Goesling. This model was especially common before statistical packages made it easy to estimate models designed for dichotomous outcomes because it simply estimates a standard OLS regression model with a dichotomous outcome. This model is referred to as the linear probability model because we interpret the effect of the predictor variables on the probability of the outcome category coded one versus the outcome category coded zero. For ease of discussion, and following convention, we will refer to this as the probability of a **success**. The category coded zero on the outcome is referred to as a **failure**. Even though these terms are evaluative, the category coded one on the outcome (the "success") need not be desirable (it could be high school dropout, unemployment, or even death).

If an outcome variable in OLS regression is a dichotomous dummy variable, then the unconditional mean of this variable is simply the proportion coded a one on the outcome. This proportion is an estimate of the probability of begin coded a one on the outcome in the population, often written as $\hat{\pi}$.

$$\hat{\pi} = \widehat{\Pr}(Y = 1) = \frac{\sum_{i=1}^{n} Y_i}{n}$$

Since the Ys are coded one if the outcome is a success and zero if the outcome is a failure, the sum of the Ys—$\sum_{i=1}^{n} Y_i$—is simply the number of successes in the sample. Dividing by the sample size—n—we have the proportion of successes in the sample.

Similarly, the conditional means based on an OLS regression analysis represent the proportion coded one on the outcome within levels of the predictor variable. We can thus write our standard model as:

$$\hat{Y}|X, D = \hat{\pi}|X, D = \widehat{\Pr}(Y = 1|X, D) = \hat{\beta}_0 + \hat{\beta}_1 X + \hat{\beta}_2 D$$

In this model, $\hat{\beta}_1$ measures the change in the predicted probability of being in the category coded one on the outcome for a one unit increase in X, holding D constant. And, $\hat{\beta}_2$ measures the amount by which the predicted probability of being in the category coded one on the outcome differs for cases coded one on D versus those cases coded zero on D, holding X constant.

16.2.1: NSFH Distance Example

We will use our NSFH distance example for illustrations in this chapter and Chapter 17. Recall that the NSFH miles outcome variable is quite skewed: The mean miles respondents live from the mother is substantially larger than the median (291 versus 18 respectively) due to the skewed distribution. Although it is possible that the conditional distributions are less skewed than the unconditional distribution, this suggests to us that modeling it based on the conditional means and assuming a normal distribution for hypothesis testing, as we did in Part 3, may not be ideal.

In this chapter and the next chapter we examine alternative ways we might code this miles variable. Social scientists sometimes estimate a similar series of models for conceptual reasons in real applications. For example, as we have noted previously, for a measure of education the number of years of schooling completed has different meaning than the highest degree attained. Likewise, clinical researchers often focus on dichotomous measures of mental health diagnosis whereas medical sociologists often prefer continuous symptom sums. Specifying the outcome variable in different ways also allows us to see if our results are sensitive to any particular specification (examining such alternative specifications is referred to as conducting **sensitivity analyses**).

One way to categorize a continuous outcome variable is to define cutoffs based on the empirical distribution (e.g., based on percentiles, such as dividing the distribution into four groups based on the quartiles). This has the advantage of dividing the variable into similarly-sized groups, but the disadvantage is that the cutoffs may not have substantive meaning. An alternative is to define cutoffs using substantive criteria. For example, in Literature Excerpt 16.1, Goesling used cutoffs of 12 and 16 on his years of schooling variable to categorize respondents into three groups: those who likely had less than a high school degree, a high school degree, and a college degree or more. In our distance example, we might use various substantively meaningful distances, such as an approximate walking distance (e.g., one mile or so), short driving distance (e.g., 15 miles), longer driving distance (e.g., 45 miles), half-day drive (e.g., 200 miles), or full-day drive (e.g., 500 miles). For now, we will use a dichotomy of whether the mother lives within 45 miles of the respondent (coded zero) versus more than 45 miles from the respondent (coded one). A substantial number of respondents (over 3000, over 60% of the analytic sample) live within 45 miles of their mothers. We will explore some of the other alternative cutoffs in Chapter 17 when we look at multi-category outcomes.

Display B.16.1 shows the syntax that we used to create this variable (using the compact dummy variable syntax we learned in Chapter 10) and the results of regressing this new variable on respondent's earnings (as rescaled to $10,000 units in earlier chapters) using OLS estimation. All of the values in the results can be interpreted in the way we learned in Part 3. Thus, the t-value of 6.63 (greater than a critical t of 1.96 for a large sample size and 5% two-sided alpha) and p-value of <.0001 (less than an alpha of 0.05) tell us that earnings are significantly associated with the probability of living more than 45 miles from the mother. The coefficient of 0.0116 tells us that an increase of $10,000 in respondents' annual earnings is associated with an over one point (0.0116*100 = 1.16) increase in the percentage living more than 45 miles from the mother, on average.

16.2.2: Advantages of the Linear Probability Model

The linear probability model has an advantage over the logit and probit models that we will examine below in that it is easy to interpret. As we just saw, the coefficients can be directly interpreted in terms of the predicted probability of being coded one on the outcome. For example, in a recent paper examining the use of health services as an outcome, Decker (2005: p. 956) noted that she used the linear probability model for this reason: "Logit models produce results very similar to those presented here using a linear specification. The linear model is used only to ease presentation." In contrast, we will need to translate the coefficients and predictions from the logit and probit models in order to interpret them in terms of predicted probabilities. When researchers focus only on the significance and sign of coefficients, and do not take the time to translate the logit and probit coefficients into predicted probabilities, they ignore the substantive significance of their models (or lack thereof). The linear probability model makes it less likely researchers will stop before such substantive interpretation (and makes it easy for readers to understand the substantive size of effects based only on the presented coefficients).

16.2.3: Problems with the Linear Probability Model

On the other hand, there are numerous problems with using OLS regression estimates with a dichotomous outcome. The linear probability model violates two of the assumptions of the standard linear regression model (homoskedasticity of the error term; normality of the error term, for hypothesis testing), and it also can produce predicted probabilities that are below zero or above one and may not fit with hypotheses about nonlinear relationships (as discussed below).

Nonsensical Predictions

Probabilities should fall between zero and one. But, one of the often cited problems with the linear probability model is the fact that the model may predict probabilities outside of this range. For example, in the model we just looked at based on the NSFH data, two cases with very high annual earnings of nearly $1 million have predicted probabilities above one (i.e., there is a more than 100% predicted probability that these very high earners live more than 45 miles from their mothers). Specifically, if we write the prediction equation from Display B.16.1 as $\widehat{g1milesD45} = 0.3539566 + 0.0116146 * g2earn10000$ and substitute in the value of 100 for $g2earn10000$ to represent a person earning $1 million per year (since $g2earn10000$ is recalled to $10000 units) then we have $\widehat{g1milesD45} = 0.3539566 + 0.0116146 * 100 = 1.52$.

Although the very restricted pair of values for the dichotomous outcome variable makes these nonsensical predictions particularly striking, a similar problem can occur with interval level outcome variables in OLS whose valid values do not cover the entire range of numbers from negative to positive infinity (e.g., predicting out-of-range years of schooling when the values should only range from 9 to 20). Typically, out of range predictions occur only for a small set of observations with unusual values relative to the other observations in the sample. But, they are troubling to researchers.

Non-normality

Clearly, the dichotomous outcome variable is not normally distributed. This is obviously true for the unconditional distribution since the dichotomous outcome has only two values rather than a normally-distributed range of values. It is also true for the conditional distribution of Y given the Xs and the conditional errors. That is, within any X value, there are only two possible errors, because there are only two observed Y values, 0 and 1, and (as we saw in Chapter 8) the predicted Y value is the same within observations with the same X value.

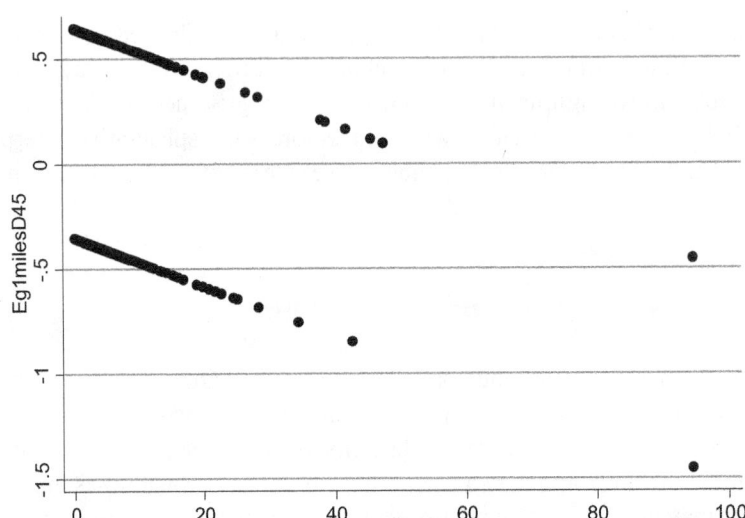

▦ **Figure 16.1** Plot of Errors for NSFH Distance Example Based on Linear Probability Model

For example, using the prediction equation based on the regression model shown in Display B.16.1 ($\widehat{g1milesD45}$ = 0.3539566 + 0.0116146 ∗ *g2earn10000*) we can predict the probability that an adult who earns \$100,000 per year lives more than 45 miles from the mother. Since we represent \$100,000 with *g2earn10000* = 10 we have $\widehat{g1milesD45}$ = 0.3539566 + 0.0116146 ∗ 10 = .4701026. But, the observed values for *g1milesD45* are only two values, zero or one. Thus, there are only two errors for persons who earn \$100,000 per year. If *g1milesD45* is observed to be zero, then the error is: 0 − .4701026 = −.4701026. If *g1milesD45* is observed to be one, then the error is: 1 − .4701026 = .5298974. Figure 16.1 shows a plot of such errors against *g2earn10000* showing these two values of the error within each level of earnings. In contrast, with a continuous outcome variable as in the standard linear regression model, we expect to have a range of values for the outcome within each level of the predictor (see again Section 8.4).

Heteroskedasticity

Mathematically, the variance of a binary variable depends on the probability of success in the population. That is, if the probability of a success is π then it can be shown that the variance is $\pi(1 - \pi)$. Because of this, in linear probability models the conditional variance of the outcome depends on the level of the predictors.

For example, as we just saw, the prediction equation for Display B.16.1 is $\widehat{g1milesD45}$ = 0.3539566 + 0.0116146 ∗ *g2earn10000*. We calculated above that the predicted probability of living more than 45 miles from the mothers was 0.4701026 for a respondent who earned \$100,000 per year. The estimated variance associated with this conditional probability would be $\hat{\pi}(1 - \hat{\pi})$ = 0.4701026 ∗ (1 − 0.4701026) = .24910615. For a respondent who earns \$10,000 per year (*g2earn10000* = 1), the predicted probability would be $\widehat{g1milesD45}$ = 0.3539566 + 0.0116146 ∗ 1 = .3655712. The estimated variance associated with this conditional probability would be $\hat{\pi}(1 - \hat{\pi})$ = 0.3655712 ∗ (1 − 0.3655712)

= .2319289. Because the conditional variance depends in this way on the level of the X values it is always heteroskedastic in a linear probability model.

Functional Form

When we discussed modeling nonlinearities within the context of standard linear regression models, we considered logging the outcome and predictor variables, which could allow us to model diminishing effects. We conceptually motivated this concept by imagining that we were predicting child outcomes based on the log of family income, noting that another $1000 added relatively more to family income for lower income families than higher income families and thus we might expect the association with child outcomes to be larger when we increased incomes for lower income than higher income families. Because of the floor at zero and ceiling at one for probabilities, similar hypotheses about nonlinear relationships are often applicable when the outcome is dichotomous. For example, we might hypothesize that each additional year of schooling has a larger impact on the propensity to work for those with high school and some college levels of education than those with college and post-graduate levels of education and than those with junior high or lower levels of education.

In sum, there are four major problems with the linear probability model. It violates the OLS assumption of heteroskedasticity and the assumption of conditional normality used for hypothesis testing in OLS. And, the linear probability model can produce out of range predictions and forces the association between the outcome and predictor to be linear (even though we may expect the association to be nonlinear for conceptual reasons and because the possible values for the probability of success on a dichotomous outcome are bounded by zero and one). Because alternative approaches that do not suffer from these problems can now be readily applied with modern statistical packages, researchers today do not generally rely on the linear probability model. In some subfields, however, the linear probability model is still used (especially if, as in the quote above, the researcher has estimated a logit or probit model to confirm similar results and reports the linear probability model results for ease of interpretation).

16.3: GENERALIZED LINEAR MODEL

The generalized linear model allows us to move away from the conditional normality assumption that is used for hypothesis testing in the standard linear regression model and to specify a functional form that is appropriate for predicting probabilities and a link that assures that predictions fall between 0 and 1.

With a dichotomous outcome variable, it is common to assume the **Bernoulli distribution** (and related **binomial distribution**) in the generalized linear model. The Bernoulli distribution models the success or failure for each case in the data. In the generalized linear model, the probability of a success is made an appropriate function of the explanatory variables, as we shall see below.

The link function in the generalized linear model allows us to address the problems with functional form and nonsensical predictions evident in the linear probability model. As we saw in Chapter 15, in the systematic portion of the generalized linear model, values can range from negative infinity to positive infinity. But, the values of the probability, π, can only range from 0 to 1. Using the identity link could thus result in nonsensical predictions, as we saw with the linear probability model. However, we can define a function of π which ranges from negative infinity to positive infinity, and use that as the link rather than the identity link. For dichotomous outcomes, we use either the logit or probit link to achieve this goal.

16.3.1: Logit Link

The logit link is popular because its core is the **odds** which is commonly used in day-to-day situations. The results of a logit model can be easily translated to odds for a familiar interpretation. Specifically, the **logit link** is:

$$\eta = \text{logit}(\pi) = \ln\left(\frac{\pi}{1-\pi}\right)$$

(16.1)

We refer to the resulting values $\ln\left(\frac{\pi}{1-\pi}\right)$ as logits or **log odds**.

Let's break down this function of the probability to see why this is a sensible link function. The ratio within parentheses, $\frac{\pi}{1-\pi}$, is the odds. As noted, odds are likely familiar to you from their use in various day-to-day contexts. As is evident from the formula, they are defined as the ratio of the probability of a success, π, to the probability of its complement, a failure, $1 - \pi$. In general usage, odds are not divided out but stated in ratio form (e.g., the odds of winning are 2-to-1). Table 16.1 (next page) provides examples

Moving from the first to last column of Table 16.1 accomplishes our goal of taking a variable that is constrained to just the values of zero and one to a variable that can take on any value from negative infinity to positive infinity. The first two columns show the probability of a success and the probability of a failure, including values in increments of .10 from zero to one. In the next two columns, we see that by writing the odds, we move from the probability values that range from zero to one to odds divided out which range from zero to positive infinity. Then, by taking the log of the odds, the odds between 0 and 1 become negative values. Thus, the full range of log odds is negative infinity to positive infinity, values that we can map directly to the systematic portion of the regression model.

Several features of the log odds are important. First, note the symmetry around the probability value of 0.5. For example, the log odds for a probability of success of 0.2 is the same magnitude as the log odds for the probability of success of 0.8, but reversed in sign (-1.3863 and 1.3863). And, the values which have reversed signs in log odds are reversed ratios for the odds (e.g., $\frac{1}{4}$ vs

■ **Table 16.1: Examples of Probabilities, Odds, and Log Odds**

Probability of

Success Pr(Y=1)	Failure Pr(Y=0)	Odds (Common Usage)	Odds (Divided Out)	Log Odds
0	1	$\frac{0}{1}$	0	negative infinity
.1	.9	$\frac{.1}{.9} = \frac{1}{9}$	.1111	−2.1972
.2	.8	$\frac{.2}{.8} = \frac{1}{4}$	.2500	−1.3863
.3	.7	$\frac{.3}{.7} = \frac{3}{7}$	.4286	−0.8473
.4	.6	$\frac{.4}{.6} = \frac{2}{3}$	.6667	−0.4055
.5	.5	$\frac{.5}{.5} = \frac{1}{1}$	1.0000	0
.6	.4	$\frac{.6}{.4} = \frac{3}{2}$	1.5000	0.4055
.7	.3	$\frac{.7}{.3} = \frac{7}{3}$	2.3333	0.8473
.8	.2	$\frac{.8}{.2} = \frac{4}{1}$	4.0000	1.3863
.9	.1	$\frac{.9}{.1} = \frac{9}{1}$	9.0000	2.1972
1	0	$\frac{1}{0}$	infinity	infinity

$\frac{4}{1}$ in the odds; −1.3863 vs 1.3863 in log odds). Finally, notice that the odds are equal to one when the log odds are zero and the probability of success is 0.50.

Figure 16.2 graphs values from Table 16.1, but also includes all the other possible values between zero and one. Specifically, Figure 16.2a and Figure 16.2b simply plot the probability π against itself and against the odds. Then, Figure 16.2c plots the probability against the log odds.

Note the S-shape of this logit curve in Figure 16.2c. The shape is fairly linear between probability of about 0.20 and 0.80. It is most curved at the extreme probability (0 to 0.2 and 0.8 to 1). As a result, if the actual predicted probabilities in your data set all fall within the more linear region (between about 0.20 and 0.80) then interpretation of the coefficients from a logit model will be simpler (because the association is fairly linear) than if the probabilities fall in the non-linear region (less than 0.20 or above 0.80).[1]

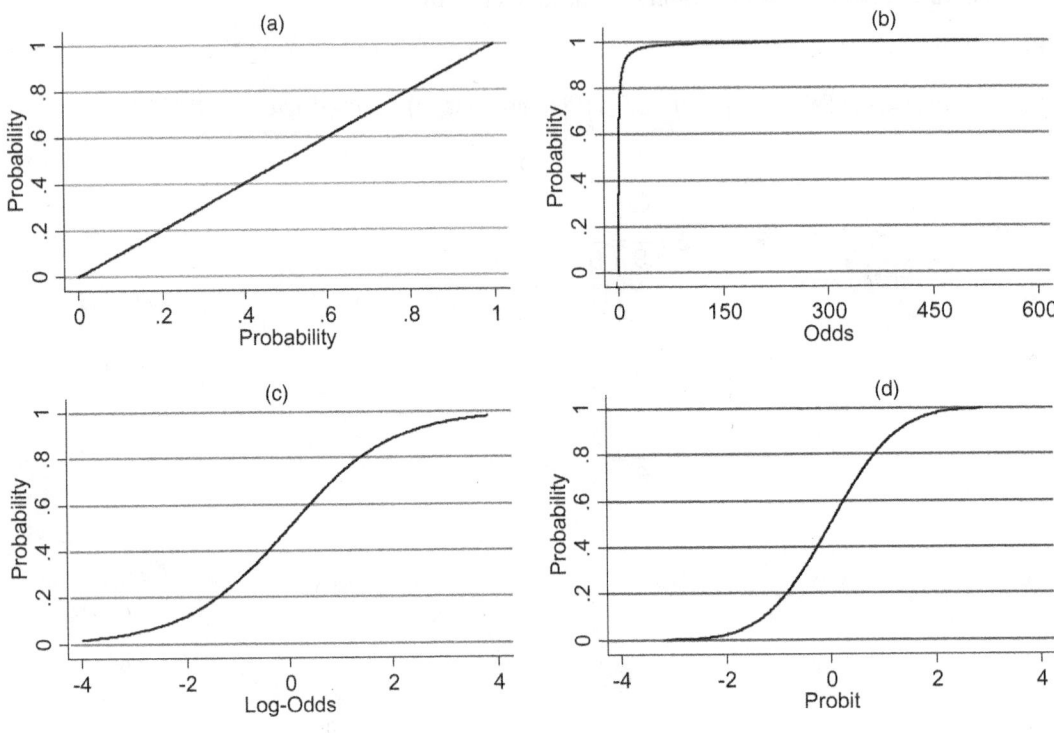

■ **Figure 16.2** Figure of Logit and Probit Transformations

Source: Based on 1000 uniformly distributed values ranging from 0 to 1.

16.3.2: Probit Link

The probit model is derived like the logit model, except that we use a different link:

$$\eta = \text{probit}(\pi) = \Phi^{-1}(\pi) \tag{16.2}$$

where Φ^{-1} is the inverse of the cumulative normal distribution function. The formula Φ^{-1} translates the probability into a Z-value. We refer to the values $\Phi^{-1}(\pi)$ as probits or Z-scores. The probit is cumulative in that it sums the probability of all values up to and including the current value of Z. The process is an inverse in the sense that we do the opposite of what we do when we take a Z-value and look up a p-value. That is, we take a probability and looking up an associated Z-value.[2]

Table 16.2 shows some examples of Z-values associated with various probabilities.

The logit link that we discussed above is actually also the inverse of a cumulative distribution function (the cumulative logistic, hence sometimes logit models are referred to as **logistic regression**). A plot of the probit transformation has a similar S shape as we just saw for the logit (see Figure 16.2d). Like the logit function, the probit function is also symmetric. In fact,

■ **Table 16.2:** *Z*-values associated with probabilities

π	*Z*-value
0	negative infinity
.1	−1.28
.2	−0.84
.3	−0.52
.4	−0.25
.5	0.00
.6	0.25
.7	0.52
.8	0.84
.9	1.28
1	positive infinity

the logit and probit distributions are quite similar around probability values of 0.5, with the greatest differences occurring in the tails (compare Figure 16.2c and Figure 16.2d). Because of this similarity between the two distributions, estimated models based on the logit and probit link will be very similar unless the Y variable is quite "unbalanced" (mainly zeros or mainly ones in the data).

16.3.3: The Binomial Distribution

The formula for the **binomial distribution** is straightforward, and helps reinforce the concepts of maximum likelihood, so we will examine it in detail here. The binomial distribution defines the probability for the *number* of successes in a sample, where a success is defined by the researcher (again, it need not be a positive event; it could be the number of persons who are unemployed, the number of persons with heart disease, or the number of high school dropouts).

The variable in the binomial distribution—the number of successes—is the sum of the outcome of a series of **Bernoulli trials**. A Bernoulli trial is simply each observation of either a success or failure. The name "trial" brings to mind a distinct process (e.g., tossing of a coin). However, in most social science applications, the trial is simply the observation for each person in the sample of their success/failure status however it is defined in the particular study (i.e., unemployed/employed, has heart disease/does not have heart disease, high school dropout/not a high school dropout, etc).

There are two keys to the binomial distribution based on the sum of the outcomes of such Bernoulli trials:

■ **Box 16.3**

Because of assumptions statisticians make for each model, the logit estimates are typically about 1.6 to 1.8 times the probit estimates for the same data and predictor variables. These assumptions have no practical consequence. If we were to change the assumptions, the size of the coefficients would change. However, because the standard errors change by the same factor as the coefficients, the significance of the coefficients would remain the same. The probabilities that we predict from the model also remain the same. But, it is important to remember that we cannot use the relative size of coefficients in the logit and probit models as evidence that one model is better than the other. In the standard specification in SAS and Stata, it will almost always be the case that the logit coefficients are larger than the probit coefficients.

◼ The trials (observations) must be independent. This criterion is usually met in statistical samples through random sampling.

◼ The trials (observations) must follow the same probability of a success (π). That is, each time we make an observation, we should have the same probability of seeing a success. For a fair coin, if we define a success as observing a heads, then the probability of success at each trial would be 0.5. In a social science example, the probability of observing an unemployed person might be, say, 0.04.[3]

As we saw in Chapter 15 for the normal distribution, probability theory takes the parameter (here π) as known and uses the theoretical distribution (here the binomial distribution) to figure out the probability of an observed value (here the number of successes). In statistics, we ask what value of the parameter (π) most likely produced that data that we have in hand, assuming the number of success in our application follows a binomial distribution. We will consider an example of each approach here.

A Simple Example of the Binomial Distribution

Let's consider a simple example with unemployment status as the outcome in a sample of three people where we assume the unconditional probability of unemployment in the population from which they were drawn is .04. The binomial distribution calculates the probability for each possible value of the number of these three people to have a success (in our case to be "unemployed"). That is, it asks the question: What would be the probability of observing that:

◼ none of the three people is unemployed
◼ one of the three people is unemployed
◼ two of the three people are unemployed
◼ all three of the three people are unemployed

where a success is defined as unemployment and π, the probability of a success, is 0.04?

To figure out the probability of the four outcomes (number of people with a success) we need to calculate the joint probability of the three individual results that define each number of successes (e.g., a value of one means one person is unemployed and two people are employed). From probability theory, we know that if events are independent, then we can multiply their individual probabilities to determine their joint probability. We also know from statistical theory that the probability of the complement of an event (a failure; in our case, being employed) is one minus the probability of that event. In our case, the probability of a failure (being employed) is $1 - 0.04 = 0.96$. This is all we need to know in order to figure out the probabilities of the first and last outcomes:

◼ none of the three people are unemployed: $0.96 * 0.96 * 0.96 = 0.884736$.
◼ all three of the three people are unemployed: $0.04 * 0.04 * 0.04 = 0.000064$.

For the second and third outcomes, there are several different ways we would observe each number of successes (one or two people unemployed). Probability theory tells us that we can calculate the overall probability by summing these distinct results.

■ **Table 16.3**

Ways We Can Observe One Person Unemployed

Person 1	Person 2	Person 3	Probability
unemployed	employed	employed	0.04*0.96*0.96 = 0.036864
employed	unemployed	employed	0.96*0.04*0.96 = 0.036864
employed	employed	unemployed	0.96*0.96*0.04 = 0.036864

Probability of Observing One Person Unemployed	0.036864+0.036864+0.036864 = 3*0.036864 = 0.110592

Ways We Can Observe Two People Unemployed

Person 1	Person 2	Person 3	Probability
unemployed	unemployed	employed	0.04*0.04*0.96 = 0.001536
employed	unemployed	unemployed	0.96*0.04*0.04 = 0.001536
unemployed	employed	unemployed	0.04*0.96*0.04 = 0.001536

Probability of Observing Two People Unemployed	0.001536+0.001536+0.001536 = 3*0.001536 = 0.004608

We have now determined the probability of all of the possible number of successes in our small sample of three people:

- none of the three people is unemployed $\qquad$ 0.884736
- one of the three people is unemployed $\qquad$ 0.110592
- two of the three people are unemployed $\qquad$ 0.004608
- all three of the three people are unemployed $\quad$ 0.000064

As expected, given that we've exhaustively considered all of the possible outcomes (number of successes), these four probabilities sum to one (0.884736 + 0.110592 + 0.004608 + 0.000064 = 1).

General Formula for the Binomial Distribution

We can now move from this specific example to readily understand the formula for the density function of the binomial distribution:

$$f\left(s|\pi,N\right) = \Pr\left(s|\pi,N\right) = \frac{N!}{s!\left(N-s\right)!}\pi^s\left(1-\pi\right)^{N-s} \qquad (16.3)$$

where N is the sample size and s is the number of successes in a particular outcome.

Let's examine each component of this equation to fully understand the formula and relate it back to our concrete example. We will begin with the rightmost section:

$$\pi^s(1-\pi)^{N-s}$$

This just tells us to multiply together the probability of a success (π) the number of times that there are successes in this outcome (s times). And, it tells us to multiply together the probability of the complement of the success ($1-\pi$) the number of times that there are not successes in this outcome ($N{-}s$ times). What is this for our four outcomes?

■ **Table 16.4**

Outcome (number of successes)	s	N	π	$\pi^s(1 - \pi)^{N-s}$		
none of the people is unemployed	0	3	.04	$0.04^0(1 - 0.04)^{3-0}$	$= .96^3$	$= .88473$
one of the people is unemployed	1	3	.04	$0.04^1(1 - 0.04)^{3-1}$	$= .04 * .96^2$	$= .03686$
two of the people are unemployed	2	3	.04	$0.04^2(1 - 0.04)^{3-2}$	$= .04^2 * .96^1$	$= .00153$
all three of the people are unemployed	3	3	.04	$0.04^3(1 - 0.04)^{3-3}$	$= .04^3$	$= .00006$

Notice that these values match exactly the probabilities we calculated for the 1st and 4th outcomes. For the 2nd and 3rd outcomes, they match the three individual probabilities that we had to sum to get the outcome probability in Table 16.3. We have to return to the 1st element in the binomial distribution formula to match the sums for the 2nd and 3rd outcome.

Specifically, the first element in the binomial distribution formula is:

$$\frac{N!}{s!(N-s)!}$$

This may be familiar to you as a combinatorics formula. The symbol ! (read factorial) may also be familiar to you from basic math; it tells us to multiply together the value times each value smaller than itself, down to one (i.e., $N! = N * (N - 1) * (N - 2) * (N - 3) \ldots * 3 * 2 * 1$ and by definition $0! = 1$). The result tells us how many combinations of size s we can form from N distinct objects. For example, with $s = 2$ and $N = 4$ the formula would tell us how many pairs we could form from 4 distinct objects.[4] That is, $\frac{4!}{2!(4-2)!} = \frac{4!}{2!2!} = \frac{4*3*2*1}{2*1*2*1} = 6.$

Getting back to our unemployment example, we can now calculate the first portion of the formula and see that the full formula produces exactly the final results that we calculated above for each outcome (number of successes):

Outcome (number of successes)	s	N	$\frac{N!}{s!(N-s)!}$	
none of the three people is unemployed	0	3	$\frac{3!}{0!(3-0)!} =$	$\frac{3*2*1}{1*3*2*1} = 1$
one of the three people is unemployed	1	3	$\frac{3!}{1!(3-1)!} =$	$\frac{3*2*1}{1*2*1} = 3$
two of the three people are unemployed	2	3	$\frac{3!}{2!(3-2)!} =$	$\frac{3*2*1}{2*1*1} = 3$
all three of the three people are unemployed	3	3	$\frac{3!}{3!(3-3)!} =$	$\frac{3*2*1}{3*2*1*1} = 1$

So, the first part of the binomial formula calculates the number of ways we can obtain the outcome. In our example, there was one way to obtain for the 1st and 4th outcomes (s = 0 and s = 3) and three ways to obtain for the 2nd and 3rd outcomes (s = 1 and s = 2).

Putting together the two pieces of the binomial formula, then:

Outcome (number of successes)	$\dfrac{N!}{s!(N-s)!}\pi^s(1-\pi)^{N-s}$
none of the three people is unemployed	1*.884736 = .884736
one of the three people is unemployed	3*.036864 = .110592
two of the three people are unemployed	3*.001536 = .004608
all three of the three people are unemployed	1*.000064 = .000064

Maximum Likelihood Estimation with the Binomial Distribution

We just used the binomial distribution to calculate the probability of observing a certain number of successes within a population given that we know the probability of a success in the population. In our example the probability of unemployment in the population was taken to be 0.04.

In statistics, however, we have the reverse problem: We have collected some data and know the number of successes in that particular sample. We want to estimate the probability of success in the population that was most likely to have generated this number of successes in the sample. The probability of success is the population parameter we seek to estimate in this case. We can use maximum likelihood estimation based on the binomial formula to select the value for the parameter that makes the data we observe in our sample most likely.

Similar to what we saw for the normal distribution, the unknown is now the population parameter. Rewriting what's on the left hand side of the equals sign so that s and N are known, but π is unknown, we obtain the likelihood function:

$$L\left(\pi|s,N\right) = \frac{N!}{s!\left(N-s\right)!} = \pi^s\left(1-\pi\right)^{N-s} \qquad (16.4)$$

Note that the equation on the right is exactly the same as what saw in Equation 16.3, but the left portion differs, now reading that we are defining the likelihood for the parameter (probability, π) given the data (the sample size, N, and number of successes, s). In other words, we will plug into the formula the number of successes (s) and the sample size (N) of the data that we have in hand, and calculate likelihoods by varying the value of the parameter (π). The value of the parameter (π) that has the largest likelihood is most likely to have generated the data.

Hypothetical Example of Calculating the Likelihood

Let's look at an example and follow an iterative process (calculate several of the likelihoods directly) to understand what they represent. Suppose we have a sample of N = 10 of which s = 6 people are unemployed. We want to know: What value of the parameter is most likely to have generated the data? In our case, what is the most likely probability of being unemployed in the population from which this sample was drawn? Let's take several possible values for π and calculate the likelihood based on the likelihood function we just defined. Notice that because

s and N are both known, the first portion of the equation $\left(\dfrac{N!}{s!(N-s)!}\right)$ reduces to a single number (210 in this case) across all calculations.

Possible Value of π	s	N	Likelihood: $L(\pi\|s=6, N=10) = \dfrac{10!}{6!(10-6)!}\,\pi^6(1-\pi)^{10-6} = 210\,\pi^6(1-\pi)^4$		
0	6	10	$L(\pi=0\|s=6, N=10)$	$= 210 * 0^6(1-0)^4$	$= .000000$
.1	6	10	$L(\pi=.1\|s=6, N=10)$	$= 210 * .1^6(1-.1)^4$	$= .000138$
.2	6	10	$L(\pi=.2\|s=6, N=10)$	$= 210 * .2^6(1-.2)^4$	$= .005505$
.3	6	10	$L(\pi=.3\|s=6, N=10)$	$= 210 * .3^6(1-.3)^4$	$= .036757$
.4	6	10	$L(\pi=.4\|s=6, N=10)$	$= 210 * .4^6(1-.4)^4$	$= .111477$
.5	6	10	$L(\pi=.5\|s=6, N=10)$	$= 210 * .5^6(1-.5)^4$	$= .205078$
.6	6	10	$L(\pi=.6\|s=6, N=10)$	$= 210 * .6^6(1-.6)^4$	$= .250823$
.7	6	10	$L(\pi=.7\|s=6, N=10)$	$= 210 * .7^6(1-.7)^4$	$= .200121$
.8	6	10	$L(\pi=.8\|s=6, N=10)$	$= 210 * .8^6(1-.8)^4$	$= .088080$
.9	6	10	$L(\pi=.9\|s=6, N=10)$	$= 210 * .9^6(1-.9)^4$	$= .011160$
1	6	10	$L(\pi=1\|s=6, N=10)$	$= 210 * 1^6(1-1)^4$	$= .000000$

Based on these calculations, it appears the likelihood is highest when $\pi = 0.60$. The value of the likelihood at that point is .2508. Figure 16.3 shows a graph of these values (with additional calculations between these 11 points) confirming the peak at $\pi = 0.60$ and reinforcing that the likelihood is a function. The likelihood function calculates how likely it is that each possible value of the parameter generated the data in our sample. As with the normal distribution, the slope of the function is zero at the maximum (see the green horizontal tangent line in Figure 16.3). Statisticians can take the derivative of the likelihood function, set it equal to zero, and solve for the unknown value π. In the case of the unconditional probability of success, the result is a closed-form solution, our typical definition of the sample proportion:

$$\hat{\pi} = \frac{s}{N}$$

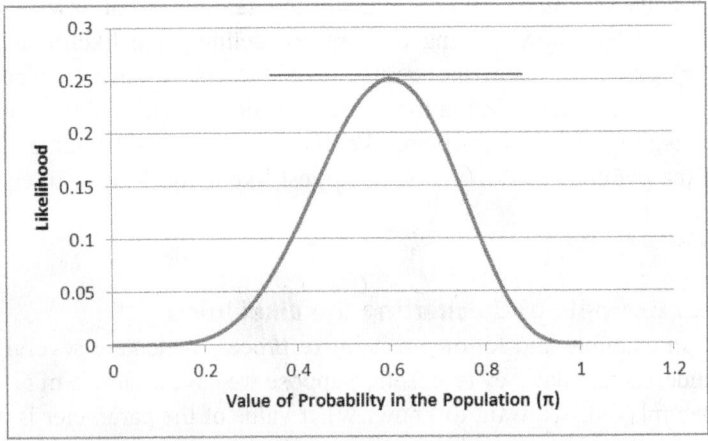

■ **Figure 16.3** Likelihood Function for Values of π When $N = 10$ and $s = 6$

In our case, $\hat{\pi} = \dfrac{s}{N} = \dfrac{6}{10} = 0.60$. In this case, we could have used this formula to calculate the estimated probability, rather than using an iterative search. However, for the conditional probabilities modeled by the logit and probit regression models there is no closed form solution. Thus, SAS and Stata will follow an iterative search for the coefficient estimates that allow us to predict the conditional probabilities.

16.3.4: NSFH Distance Example

The logit and probit models can be estimated in SAS and Stata using the commands for the generalized linear model that we introduced in Chapter 15, but specifying a binomial distribution and logit or probit link. Because logit and probit models are so popular, SAS and Stata also have dedicated commands for them. These commands are optimized for these models and provide some results unique to them, as we will discuss below. For now, though, we will use the generalized linear model commands, to show how these models parallel the estimation of the standard regression model in the generalized linear model framework that we showed in Chapter 15.

Display B.16.2 and Display B.16.3 show the syntax and results for the basic generalized linear model (`proc genmod` in SAS and `glm` in Stata). Notice that in both SAS and Stata we use the word `binomial` to indicate the binomial distribution and the word `logit` or `probit` to request the appropriate link.

Notice that notes in the output (circled in green) verify that the packages used maximum likelihood estimation with a binomial distribution (referred to as `Bernoulli` in Stata) and `logit` (Display B.16.2) or `probit` (Display B.16.3) link. The log likelihoods are similar for the two models (−3635.35 for the logit and −3636.69 for the probit). Both sets of results indicate that the null hypothesis that the coefficient for *g2earn10000* is zero can be rejected at alpha 0.05 (with *Z*-values in Stata larger than 1.96, comparable *Wald* χ^2 values in SAS larger than 1.96*1.96=3.84, and *p*-values smaller than 0.05).

As expected, the coefficient for the logit model is larger than the coefficient for the probit model. The ratio of the two is $\dfrac{0.0554104}{0.0308123} = 1.80$, which is within the expected range of 1.6 to 1.8 (see again Box 16.3). We will have more to say below about how to interpret these coefficients.

16.4: GOODNESS OF FIT

A challenge in maximum likelihood is that there is no single measure, like *R*-squared or adjusted *R*-squared in OLS, which is a standard for assessing goodness of fit. In terms of quantifying model fit, we will discuss several different measures sometimes used, to give you a sense of the variation you may encounter when reading the literature and your options when you are writing a paper. We recommend that you examine the literature in your subfield or a journal to which you are submitting a paper to see if one measure is preferred in your field over others.

16.4.1: Pseudo *R*-squared Measures

Why are there so many pseudo *R*-squared measures for maximum likelihood models? There are several ways that the *R*-squared in OLS can be calculated, for example based on the sums of squares or based on the *F*-value. Although these various approaches to calculating *R*-squared in OLS produce identical results, in maximum likelihood the measures that have been derived from these various approaches produce different results. We focus on three common pseudo *R*-squared values here (see Long 1997 and Long and Freese 2005 for discussion of additional *R*-squared values, not covered here). Like *R*-squared in OLS, each has a regular and "adjusted" version.

A "Count" *R*-squared Measure Based on the Accuracy of Model Predictions

The first *R*-squared value we will consider is analogous to the conceptualization of the *R*-squared in OLS as the proportional reduction in errors in predicting the Ys (Agresti & Finlay 2009). The formula we considered in Chapter 9 reflected this conceptualization, examining the error in prediction unexplained by our model (the difference between the observed Ys and predicted Ys based on our model) relative to the amount of error remaining if we predicted every Y using the overall sample mean (the difference between the observed Ys and the unconditional sample mean).

The count *R*-squared is similarly based on the accuracy of model predictions. In a model with a dichotomous outcome, how many observations are correctly predicted to be zeros? How many observations are correctly predicted to be ones? To calculate this *R*-squared value, we need the predicted probabilities from the model and some cutoff for determining when a predicted probability indicates a zero and when a predicted probability indicates a one.

Predicted Probabilities

Because the logit and probit models do not use an identity link, we must transform the value predicted linearly by the systematic portion of our model in order to calculate the probability that is nonlinearly predicted by the model.

More specifically, let's set our logit link from Equation 16.1 above equal to the systematic portion of the regression model.

$$\ln\left(\frac{\hat{\pi}}{1-\hat{\pi}}\right) = \hat{\eta} = \hat{\beta}_0 + \hat{\beta}_1 X \tag{16.5}$$

These values are **predicted logits**.

And similarly our probit model is based on Equation 16.2:

$$\Phi^{-1}(\hat{\pi}) = \hat{\eta} = \hat{\beta}_0 + \hat{\beta}_1 X \tag{16.6}$$

These values are **predicted probits**.

In both cases, the systematic portion of our regression model linearly predicts the logit or probit of the probability of a success on the outcome, but nonlinearly predicts the probability itself. Thus, we must transform the linear prediction from the model—the predicted logits or predicted probits—in order to determine the predicted probability.

For the logit model, we can solve for the probability. To make it easier to follow the calculations, let's substitute $\widehat{logit}$ for $\hat{\beta}_0 + \hat{\beta}_1 X$ in Equation 16.5 and then solve for $\hat{\pi}$ in order to see how we can convert the predicted logits into predicted probabilities.

$$\ln\left(\frac{\hat{\pi}}{1-\hat{\pi}}\right) = \widehat{logit} \tag{16.7}$$

$$\frac{\hat{\pi}}{1-\hat{\pi}} = \exp(\widehat{logit})$$

$$\hat{\pi} = (1-\hat{\pi})\exp(\widehat{logit})$$

$$\hat{\pi} = \exp(\widehat{logit}) - \hat{\pi}\exp(\widehat{logit})$$

$$\hat{\pi} + \hat{\pi}\exp(\widehat{logit}) = \exp(\widehat{logit})$$

$$\hat{\pi}(1 + \exp(\widehat{logit})) = \exp(\widehat{logit})$$

$$\hat{\pi} = \frac{\exp\left(\widehat{logit}\right)}{1+\exp\left(\widehat{logit}\right)} \tag{16.8}$$

Substituting back $\hat{\beta}_0 + \hat{\beta}_1 X$ for $\widehat{logit}$ we have the following formula:

$$\hat{\pi} = \frac{\exp\left(\hat{\beta}_0 + \hat{\beta}_1 X\right)}{1+\exp\left(\hat{\beta}_0 + \hat{\beta}_1 X\right)}$$

So, we can convert the predicted logit (the prediction from the systematic portion of our regression model) back into a probability by taking its exponential and dividing by one plus its exponential. If we have a more complicated model, with additional predictor variables, then we simply have a longer equation for the predicted logit (e.g., $\widehat{logit} = \hat{\beta}_0 + \hat{\beta}_1 X_1 + \hat{\beta}_2 X_2 + \hat{\beta}_3 D_1 + \hat{\beta}_4 D_2 + \hat{\beta}_5 D_3$).

Understanding this set of results helps to solidify our understanding of the logit model. The systematic portion of our model predicts linearly the logit, or log odds. We can transform the predicted log odds back into a probability by taking the exponential of the predicted log odds and dividing by one plus the exponential of the predicted log odds. The difference between the first and last formulas in this derivation (Equation 16.7 and Equation 16.8) can sometimes be confusing, especially since one involves subtraction and the other addition in the denominator. It is helpful to solidly understand that each version of the formula serves a different purpose: Equation 16.7 calculates a logit from a probability (with the desired result of translating the values of the probability, π, that are constrained between zero and one to values of the logit, that can fall anywhere between negative infinity to positive infinity, as shown in Table 16.1). Equation 16.8 calculates a probability from a logit (with the desired result of translating the values of the logit that are predicted from our model, and can fall anywhere between negative infinity to positive infinity, into predicted probabilities, π, that are constrained between zero and one, as desired).

For the probit model, we directly reference the cumulative distribution function.[5] This time, let's substitute $\widehat{probit}$ for $\hat{\beta}_0 + \hat{\beta}_1 X$ in Equation 16.6 so we can solve for $\hat{\pi}$ to see how we can convert the predicted probits into predicted probabilities.

$$\Phi^{-1}(\hat{\pi}) = \widehat{probit}$$

$$\hat{\pi} = \Phi(\widehat{probit})$$

Substituting back $\hat{\beta}_0 + \hat{\beta}_1 X$ for $\widehat{probit}$ gives

$$\hat{\pi} = \Phi(\hat{\beta}_0 + \hat{\beta}_1 X)$$

Thus, we simply reverse the process we followed when we converted probabilities to probits (Z-values). Now, we look for the probability associated with a given value of Z.[6]

Cutoff for Determining Accuracy of Prediction

The predicted probabilities from our model ($\hat{\pi}$) can range anywhere between zero and one. In contrast, the observed values for our outcome take on only two values, zero and one. That is, our model predicts the conditional probability of success (e.g., unemployment) for observations that have a certain set of values on the predictor variables. Our data gives the actual status on the outcome (e.g., unemployed or employed) for each observation. To assess the accuracy of our model, we must have some rule for determining which predicted probabilities should be treated as a match with zero and which should be treated as a match with one. A common rule takes 0.5 as a cutoff. If the predicted probability from our model for a particular observation is less than 0.5, we call it a predicted failure ($\hat{Y}_i = 0$). If the predicted probability from our model for a particular observation is greater than or equal to 0.5, we call it a predicted success ($\hat{Y}_i = 1$). Once we have converted the predicted probabilities to zeros and ones, we can construct a **classification table** to see how well our model predicts our observed failures (0s) and successes (1s).

	Classification Table Observed Outcome		
Predicted Outcome	Success $Y=1$	Failure $Y=0$	Row Total
Success ($\hat{Y}_i = 1$)	n_{11}	n_{10}	$n_{1.}$
Failure ($\hat{Y}_i = 0$)	n_{01}	n_{00}	$n_{0.}$
Column Total	$n_{.1}$	$n_{.0}$	n

This table displays the number of successes (ones) correctly predicted, n_{11}, and the number of failures (zeros) correctly predicted n_{00}. It also displays the number of cases that our model incorrectly predicted to be successes (ones), n_{10}, and the number of cases our model incorrectly predicted to be failures (zeros), n_{01}.

The Count Pseudo R-squared

A simple pseudo R-squared can be easily calculated from this classification table:

$$Count\,R^2 = \frac{n_{11} + n_{00}}{n}$$

This formula simply gives us the percentage of observations in the sample that are correctly predicted by the model.

Let's look at a simple example based on predicting the dichotomized miles variable from our NSFH distance example based on the respondent's earnings (we will show how to obtain these values below).

■ **Table 16.5**

	Classification Table Observed Outcome		
Predicted Outcome	Success Y=1	Failure Y=0	Row Total
Success ($\hat{Y}_i = 1$)	60	42	102
Failure ($\hat{Y}_i = 0$)	2072	3298	5370
Column Total	2132	3340	5472

The table shows that very few cases are predicted to be ones based on the model. Plugging these numbers into the formula for count R-squared gives the following result.

$$Count\,R^2 = \frac{n_{11} + n_{00}}{n} = \frac{60 + 3298}{5472} = 0.6137$$

So, overall, 61% of cases are correctly predicted, but most of the correct classifications are observed no's (failures).

An Adjusted Count Pseudo R-squared

Although simple and appealing, the count pseudo R-squared is problematic because it ignores the fact that, without turning to our estimated model, we may be able to correctly guess many of the observed values. In fact, without estimating our model, we could look at the marginal distribution of our outcome variable, and predict that everyone has the value that is observed most often in our sample. We cannot do worse than 50% correct with this simple guess.

For example, in the classification table that we just examined, there are more observed zeros than ones, (3340 zeros and 2132 ones). If we guessed that all of the observations are a zero, then we would be correct 61% of the time (3340/5472).

Thus, the following adjustment to the count pseudo R-squared is often used:

$$Adjusted\, Count\, R^2 = \frac{\left(n_{11}+n_{00}\right)-\max\left(n_{.0},n_{.1}\right)}{n-\max\left(n_{.0},n_{.1}\right)}$$

Where $\max(n_{.0}, n_{.1})$ is the maximum (observed) column marginal (the larger of the number of 1s or the number of 0s observed). *Adjusted Count R^2* is often interpreted as the percentage by which the model reduces errors in predictions over our simple guess.

In our example, this adjustment substantially reduces the pseudo R-squared value:

$$Adjusted\, Count\, R^2 = \frac{\left(60+3298\right)-3340}{5472-3340} = 0.0084$$

Percentage Reduction of Likelihood

Now we will present two other R-squared values that mirror two additional ways that we calculate R-squared in OLS regression. The calculation of the OLS R-squared that we focused on in Chapter 8 follows the percentage of variation explained approach:

$$R^2 = \frac{TSS-SSE}{TSS} = 1 - \frac{SSE}{TSS}$$

A common maximum likelihood measure of fit that is analogous to this explained variation approach substitutes log likelihoods in the places of the sums of squares. Specifically, we substitute the log likelihood for the intercept-only model which we considered in Chapter 15 in the denominator. And, we substitute the log likelihood for the model of interest, with an intercept and one or more predictors, in the numerator. We refer to this as McFadden's pseudo R-squared and it is calculated as:

$$McFadden's\, pseudo\, R^2 = 1 - \frac{lnL\left(M_{full}\right)}{lnL\left(M_{intercept\,only}\right)}$$

where M_{full} is the estimated model and $M_{intercept\,only}$ is an intercept-only model. This pseudo R-square is the value reported by default for Stata's dedicated logit and probit commands.

Like R-squared in OLS, McFadden's pseudo R^2 increases as we add predictor variables to the model. Thus, analogous to the adjusted R-squared in OLS, an adjustment has been proposed that restricts *McFadden's pseudo R²* to increase only if the log likelihood increases by more than 1 for each parameter added to the model:

$$McFadden's\ pseudo\ Adj\ R^2 = 1 - \frac{lnL(M_{full}) - (k-1)}{lnL(M_{intercept\ only})}$$

where k is the number of predictors in the model plus 1 for the intercept.

We can use the *R*-squared measures to evaluate the relative size of the log likelihoods across various models. Larger log-likelihoods for an estimated model, and thus larger pseudo *R*-squared values, are preferred. A value of zero on the unadjusted McFadden's pseudo *R*-squared occurs for the intercept-only model (or when all of the coefficients for the predictor variables are estimated to equal zero). In typical applications, McFadden's pseudo *R*-squared would not reach the maximum value of one (only a "fully saturated" model with one parameter per observation would do so).

A Transformation of the Likelihood Ratio

The final pseudo *R*-squared value that we will consider is analogous to a formula for calculating *R*-squared in OLS regression based on the model *F*-statistics. In maximum likelihood, we calculate this pseudo *R*-squared value based on the likelihood ratio test statistic that we defined in Chapter 15:

$$LR\chi^2 = 2[lnL(M_{full}) - lnL(M_{reduced})] = 2lnL(M_{full}) - 2lnL(M_{reduced})$$

where M_{full} and $M_{reduced}$ are full and reduced models, with the reduced model written based on placing the constraints of a null hypothesis on the full model. If we take M_{full} to be the estimated model and $M_{reduced}$ to be an intercept-only model, then another *R*-squared measure can be written based on the $LR\chi^2$. That is:

$$LR\chi^2 = 2[lnL(M_{full}) - lnL(M_{intercept\ only})] = 2lnL(M_{full}) - 2lnL(M_{intercept\ only})$$

and then:

$$Maximum\ Likelihood\ R^2 = R^2_{ML} = 1 - \exp\left[\frac{-LR\chi^2}{n}\right]$$

We include the notation R^2_{ML} so we can easily reference this version of the *R*-squared below.

The minimum of *Maximum Likelihood R²* is zero, since it approaches zero when all of the predictor variables in the estimated model have estimated coefficients of zero and thus $L(M_{full}) = L(M_{reduced})$. But, the maximum possible value of *Maximum Likelihood R²* is not one, but rather is:

$$1 - \exp\left[\frac{2 * lnL(M_{intercept\,only})}{n}\right]$$

An adjusted measure which can reach one is:[7]

$$Cragg \;\&\; Uhler's\; R^2 = \frac{1 - \exp\left[\dfrac{-LR\chi^2}{n}\right]}{1 - \exp\left[\dfrac{2 * lnL(M_{intercept\,only})}{n}\right]}$$

Summary

Numerous pseudo R-squared values have been proposed for maximum likelihood, analogous to the various formulas that can be used to calculate R-squared in OLS. Unfortunately, in maximum likelihood these different formulas lead to different results. And, in most cases, there is no simple interpretation of the pseudo R-squared values. In the three cases we considered here, each pseudo R-squared has an unadjusted and adjusted version, although the adjustments serve different purposes, and whereas two adjustments will reduce the value of R-squared (adjusting for a simple guess, adjusting for the number of parameters in the model) one will increase its value (adjusting the value so that it can reach one). In all cases, the pseudo R-squared values are bounded between zero and one, and higher scores are preferred. They are most useful for evaluating between models, than as an absolute assessment of fit. In other words, between two nested models that are estimated on the same sample with the same outcome, the model with the higher R-squared value would be preferred.

16.4.2: Information Measures

The information criteria that we presented for OLS regression in Chapter 9 are also available for maximum likelihood estimation, but based on different formulas. Recall that some researchers prefer these information measures to R-squared and pseudo R-squared measures because they reflect an alternative approach to model selection which puts the two models being compared on more equal footing (Burnham and Anderson 2002; Fox 2008). It is also the case that unlike R-squared, the basic information criteria—not just an adjusted version—account for the number of predictors in the model, thus advantaging more parsimonious models. Information criteria also have the advantage that we may use them to compare non-nested models. Recall that information measures are calculated such that *smaller (or more negative) values are preferred.*

Bayesian Information Criterion (BIC)

We will introduce three formula for calculating a Bayesian Information Criterion (the BIC is also sometimes called the Schwarz criterion after Gideon Schwarz who was one of the early developers of this approach, based on a statistical approach known as Bayesian theory; Schwarz 1978). We provide all three criteria in order to help us understand the values we may see across different publications and that we will see in our SAS and Stata output. Although each of these formula give a different value when calculated for a given model, they all lead to the same difference when we use them to compare two models. It is this difference that we will focus on, using the guidelines introduced in Section 9.6 to evaluate the degree of evidence in favor of the model with the smaller BIC value.

Specifically, the three BIC formulas are:

$$-2lnL(M_{full}) + k * \ln(n) \tag{16.9}$$

$$-2lnL(M_{full}) - (n - k) * \ln(n) \tag{16.10}$$

$$-LR\chi^2(M_{full}) + (k - 1) * \ln(n) \tag{16.11}$$

where k is the number of predictor variables in the model plus 1 and n is the sample size.

Although these formulas are distinct, it is clear that they are all based on the same elements. The first two formula have the same first term ($-2lnL(M_{full})$) and the third formula begins with a term that we know depends on this value $-LR\chi^2(M_{full})$. All of the equations end with the same term $\ln(n)$ and this final term is multiplied by a value that depends on k. It is straightforward to show that if we compare the same two models based on each of the three formulas that the resulting difference in BICs between the two models will be the same (you can try this in Review Exercise 16.1). In the case of comparing the estimated model to an intercept-only model, the result will be $-LR\chi^2(M_{full}) + \ln(n)$ in all cases.

Thus, regardless of which of the three formulas we use, we will reach the same conclusion based on the decision rules that we introduced in Section 9.6. Recall that the rules were recommended by Raftery (1995) and that they allow us to evaluate the evidence *in favor of the model with the smaller BIC value*. If the difference in BIC values is between 0 and 2, then the evidence in favor of the model with the smaller BIC value is "weak." If the difference is 2 to 6, then the evidence is "positive." If the difference is 6 to 10, then the evidence is "strong." If the difference is above 10, then the evidence is "very strong" (in favor of the model with the smaller BIC value).

Akaike Information Criterion (AIC)
We will show two formulas for calculating the Akaike Information Criterion (this information criterion is named after its developer Hirotugu Akaike; Akaike 1974) because we may come across results based on each of these in publications, and we will see them in the statistical output we examine below.

Specifically, the two AIC formula are:

$$-2lnL(M_{full}) + 2k \tag{16.12}$$

$$\frac{-2lnL(M_{full}) + 2k}{n} \tag{16.13}$$

Where again M_{full} is the estimated model and k is the number of predictor variables in the model plus 1 for the intercept.[8]

Differences between the AIC values based on the first formula (Equation 16.12) can be evaluated based on the criteria that we introduced in Section 9.6. Results based on the second formula can easily be converted to the first by multiplying by the sample size. Recall that the rules were recommended by Burnham and Anderson (2002) and that they allow us to evaluate the evidence *in favor of continuing to consider the model with the larger AIC value*. If the difference in AIC values is between 0 and 2, then the evidence in "substantial." If the difference is 4 to 7, then the evidence is "considerably less." If the difference is greater than 10, then the evidence is "essentially none" (for continuing to consider the model with the larger AIC value).

Although the criteria for BIC and for AIC differ in their orientation and cut-points (and the criteria for AIC have gaps—e.g., what should we conclude if the difference is 3?), notice that they both indicate that a difference in the information criteria of 10 or more is the most convincing evidence. Although their orientation is different, they also actually point to the same conclusion in this situation of a difference that is larger than 10, since one tells us that we should prefer the model with the smaller information criteria in these cases and the other tells us that we should stop considering the model with the larger information criteria in these cases.

16.4.3: Obtaining Fit Statistics from SAS and Stata

AIC and BIC values were displayed in SAS and Stata's output for the `genmod` and `glm` commands (see again Display B.16.2 and Display B.16.3). Although we could rely on these results, for the remainder of the chapter, we will turn to SAS and Stata commands that are dedicated to estimating the generalized linear models with the binomial distribution and logit and probit links respectively.[9] Although the `genmod` and `glm` commands help us see how to implement the generalized linear model framework, the dedicated commands are optimized for these distributions and links, and will provide some results specific to these models.

In particular, we will focus on the `proc logistic` command in SAS and the `logit` and `probit` commands in Stata. These commands will calculate several of the fit statistics discussed above. In Stata, we can also use a set of commands written by sociologists J. Scott Long and Jeremy Freese to calculate additional fit statistics (Long and Freese 2005 discuss these commands in detail). The `spost` commands are not included in the official release of Stata, but they can be easily loaded by typing `net search spost` in the Stata command line. Display B.16.4 shows the end of the results we see when we type `net search spost`. Clicking on the circled result will install the programs needed to run the commands.[10]

The syntax of the `logit` and `probit` commands parallels the syntax for Stata's other regression command. As in the `regress` syntax, after the command we list the dependent variable followed by a list of independent variables, all separated by spaces. Among the Stata `spost` commands is a command called `fitstat` which will calculate numerous *R*-squared values and information criteria for us. We type it following a regression command and it will calculate the values based on that regression.

SAS has a dedicated `proc logistic` command that estimates a logit model by default. When the outcome is a dummy variable coded 0 and 1, the word `descending` is needed immediately after `proc logistic` to ensure that the cases coded a one on the outcome are treated as "successes." The model statement for `proc logistic` parallels the syntax for `proc reg` (see Display A.16). An option `/link=probit` may be placed at the end of the model statement, following the list of predictors, to request a probit model. The option `/rsquare` requests R-squared values. We also use the `/clparm=wald` option so that SAS displays confidence intervals for the coefficients (Confidence intervals for the coefficients are displayed by Stata in the default output).

Display B.16.5 illustrates the use of these commands in SAS and Stata to estimate a logit model regressing the dummy indicator of whether the NSFH respondent lives more than 45 miles of the mother based on the respondent's annual earnings (rescaled in $10,000 units).

First, notice that the results match those seen in Display B.16.2 including the coefficients, standard errors, Z-values and p-values, and the log-likelihood (SAS presents -2 `Log L` in the `proc logistic` output, but we can calculated the log-likelihood as $\frac{7270.699}{-2} = -3635.35$ for the estimated model, with `Intercept` and `Covariates`). Next, notice that the logit commands include a likelihood-ratio chi-squared test. In Stata, it is in a similar position as the overall F-test in the standard regress output. This value, labeled `LR chi2(1)` compares the estimated model to an intercept-only model. The value matches the value in the `fitstat` output that is labeled `LR(1)`. In SAS the likelihood-ratio chi-squared test is found in the table labeled `Testing Global Null Hypothesis: BETA=0`).

The Stata `fitstat` output shows each of the AIC and BIC values that we defined in the last rows of the `fitstat` output. They are calculated as follows:

BIC Values

Equation 16.9	$-2lnL(M_{full}) + k * \ln(n)$	$= -2 * -3635.35 + 2 * \ln(5472)$	$= 7287.91$
Equation 16.10	$-2lnL(M_{full}) - (n-k) * \ln(n)$	$= -2 * -3635.35 - (5472-2) * \ln(5472)$	$= -39811.78$
Equation 16.11	$-LR\chi2(M_{full}) + (k-1) * \ln(n)$	$= -1 * 46.2154 + (2-1) * \ln(5472)$	$= -37.61$

AIC Values

Equation 16.12	$-2lnL(M_{full}) + 2k$	$= -2 * -3635.35 + 2 * 2$	$= 7274.7$
Equation 16.13	$\dfrac{-2lnL(M_{full}) + 2k}{n}$	$= \dfrac{-2 * -3635.35 + 2 * 2}{5472}$	$= 1.33$

These values are all found in the Stata `fitstat` output. The value labeled `AIC` in `fitstat` is 1.329 (Equation 16.13) and the values labeled `AIC*n` and `AIC used by Stata` are 7274.699 (Equation 16.12). The value labeled `BIC` in the Stata `fitstat` output is −39,811.776 (Equation 16.10), the value labeled `BIC'` in the Stata `fitstat` output is −37.608 (Equation 16.11), and the value labeled

BIC used by Stata in the Stata fitstat output is 7287.914 (Equation 16.9). SAS shows one AIC value (7274.699, which matches Equation 16.12) and one BIC value (7287.914, which matches Equation 16.9; this value is labeled SC for Schwarz Criterion). The other information criteria can be hand-calculated based on the SAS output.[11]

Stata and SAS also provide one or more of the R-squared values that we introduced above. In place of the R-squared value that would normally be in the standard Stata regress output we see a value labeled pseudo R2 which is based on the McFadden's pseudo R-squared formula (see also the value labeled McFadden's R2 in the fitstat output). The adjusted McFadden's pseudo R-squared is to the right of McFadden's pseudo R-squared in the fitstat output. SAS provides the maximum likelihood R-squared, both the unadjusted (labeled R-Square) and adjusted (labeled Max-rescaled R-square) versions. These are labeled ML (Cox-Snell) R2 in the fitstat output, and Cragg and Uhler's R-squared is found next to it.

These values can be hand calculated as follows, showing how the McFadden's R-squared values can be determined based on the SAS output:[12]

R-squared values

McFadden's pseudo R^2

$$1 - \frac{lnL(M_{full})}{lnL(M_{intercept\,only})} \quad = \quad 1 - \frac{-3635.35}{-3658.457} \quad = .0063$$

McFadden's pseudo Adj R^2

$$1 - \frac{lnL(M_{full}) - (k-1)}{lnL(M_{intercept\,only})} \quad = \quad 1 - \frac{-3635.35 - (2-1)}{-3658.457} \quad = .0060$$

Maximum Likelihood R^2

$$1 - \exp\left[\frac{-LR\chi^2}{n}\right] \quad = \quad 1 - \exp\left[\frac{-1 * 46.2154}{5472}\right] \quad = .0084$$

Cragg & Uhler's R^2

$$\frac{1 - \exp\left[\frac{-LR\chi^2}{n}\right]}{1 - \exp\left[\frac{2 * lnL(M_{intercept\,only})}{n}\right]} \quad = \quad \frac{1 - \exp\left[\frac{-1 * 46.2154}{5472}\right]}{1 - \exp\left[\frac{2 * -3658.457}{5472}\right]} \quad = .0114$$

Stata's fitstat output also lists the Count R-squared (labeled *Count R2* in the fitstat output) and the Adjusted Count R-squared (to the right of Count R-squared in the output). Display B.16.6 shows results of Stata's post-estimation estat class command which also calculates the Count R-squared and shows the classification table on which it is based. In SAS, we can request similar results using the option / ctable pprob=0.50.[13] The values in the classification table match those shown in Table 16.5. We designed our layout in Table 16.5 to mirror the Stata layout, so the correspondence is easy to see. In SAS, the correctly predicted values are grouped together under the label Correct and those incorrectly predicted are grouped together under the label Incorrect; and, the label Event represents the successes and the label Non-Event represents the failures. Both SAS and Stata show the Count R-squared of 61.4 (labeled

`Percentages/Correct` in SAS and `Correctly Classified` in Stata), matching what we calculated above.

For our example, all of the measures of fit seem fairly low, with the exception of the unadjusted Count *R*-squared. However, the pseudo *R*-squared values and information criteria are most useful in assessing fit relative to another model. Display B.16.7 shows the results of estimating a model with more than one predictor, using the same set of predictors as we used in Chapter 14 (Table 14.3). We asked SAS and Stata to include the measures of information criteria and *R*-squared that we examined above. The `fitstat` command makes it easy to compare the fit statistics for this full model to the reduced bivariate model with only *g2earn10000* as a predictor in Display B.16.5. To make this comparison we modified the `fitstat` command in Display B.16.5 to read `fitstat, saving(biv)`. This stores the results in Stata's memory (the name in parentheses can be up to five letters; we used *biv* to stand for bivariate). Then, we type `fitstat, using(biv)` after the regression with numerous predictors. Notice that the `fitstat` results are now in a single column for each model in Display B.16.7. The "Current logit" is the regression with numerous predictors. The "Saved logit" is the bivariate regression. And the difference compares the two.[14]

The results consistently show that the regression model with numerous predictors fits better than the bivariate regression model. The *R*-squared values are all larger and the information measures are all smaller for the "Current logit" than the "Saved logit." The `fitstat` output provides a summary statement based on the cutoffs we presented in Section 9.6, saying that the difference in BICs of 78.150 provides very strong support for the current model (with numerous predictors). Still, the absolute fit of the model with more predictors seems minimal. The *R*-squared values (other than the unadjusted Count *R*-squared) are all still quite small in absolute terms.

16.4.4: Outliers and Influential Observations

The concepts of outliers and influential observations that we discussed for the standard linear regression model have been extended to the logit and probit models. We will discuss two of these (see Hosmer, Taber, and Lemeshow 1991 and Long and Freese 2005 for accessible discussion of these diagnostics and Pregibon 1981 and Lemeshow and Hosmer 1982 for detailed treatments).

The Pearson residual, like the residual we considered in OLS regression, is based on the difference between the observed and predicted value for each observation, although in the logit and probit models the observed values will be only 0 and 1 and the predicted probabilities will range between 0 and 1. This difference is divided by the standard deviation of the predicted probability to produce the Pearson residual.

$$r_i = \frac{Y_i - \hat{\pi}_i}{\sqrt{\hat{\pi}_i \left(1 - \hat{\pi}_i\right)}}$$

A standardized Pearson residual adjusts for a measure of leverage similar to the hat-value introduced in Chapter 14.

$$rstd_i = \frac{Y_i - \hat{\pi}_i}{\sqrt{\hat{\pi}_i \left(1 - \hat{\pi}_i\right)\left(1 - h_i\right)}}$$

where h_i is the distance of the Xs from their means weighted by the variance, $\hat{\pi}_i(1 - \hat{\pi}_i)$.

A measure similar to Cook's distance in OLS which assesses how much of an influence an observation has on the fitted values is referred to as C.

$$C = \frac{r_i^2 h_i}{\left(1 - h_i\right)^2}$$

Standard cutoff values are not available for these values, so we need to rely on examining the distribution to look for extreme values as we did in Chapter 14.

As with OLS, if you have collected your own data, you should look at these extreme cases and see if they may be data entry errors (even if you haven't collected your own data, you may want to verify that the values for these extreme cases are in the possible range given in the data documentation). If you haven't collected your own data, or you check the observations and they are not data entry errors, then you can conduct a sensitivity analysis, and re-estimate your model after excluding the extreme observations and/or consider how the extreme cases differ from other cases similar to the strategy we followed in Chapter 14. Examining the parameter estimates in the model estimated on the full data and the model estimated on the partial sample, excluding the extreme observations, can indicate the degree to which your substantive conclusions change when the influential observations are omitted. And, considering how the extreme cases differ from others may lead to new conceptual insights.

16.4.5: Locating Outliers and Influential Observations in SAS and Stata

The output statement in SAS and the predict command in Stata calculate the Pearson residual (Stata also calculates the standardized Pearson residuals) and C as well as other diagnostic measures, similar to the commands we used in Chapter 14.[15] In Stata, the syntax is predict <new variable name>, residuals and predict <new variable name>, rstandard and predict <new variable name>, dbeta respectively. The separate predict commands follow a regress command. In SAS the syntax is output out=<data set name> reschi=<new variable name> c=<new variable name>; The new variables are included along with the original variables in the new dataset that we called *influence*. In SAS, the output statement directly follows a model statement within a proc reg.

Figure 16.4 shows box plots of the standardized Pearson residuals and C values. The results are similar to those we saw in Chapter 14. Both the Pearson residuals and the C values point to the

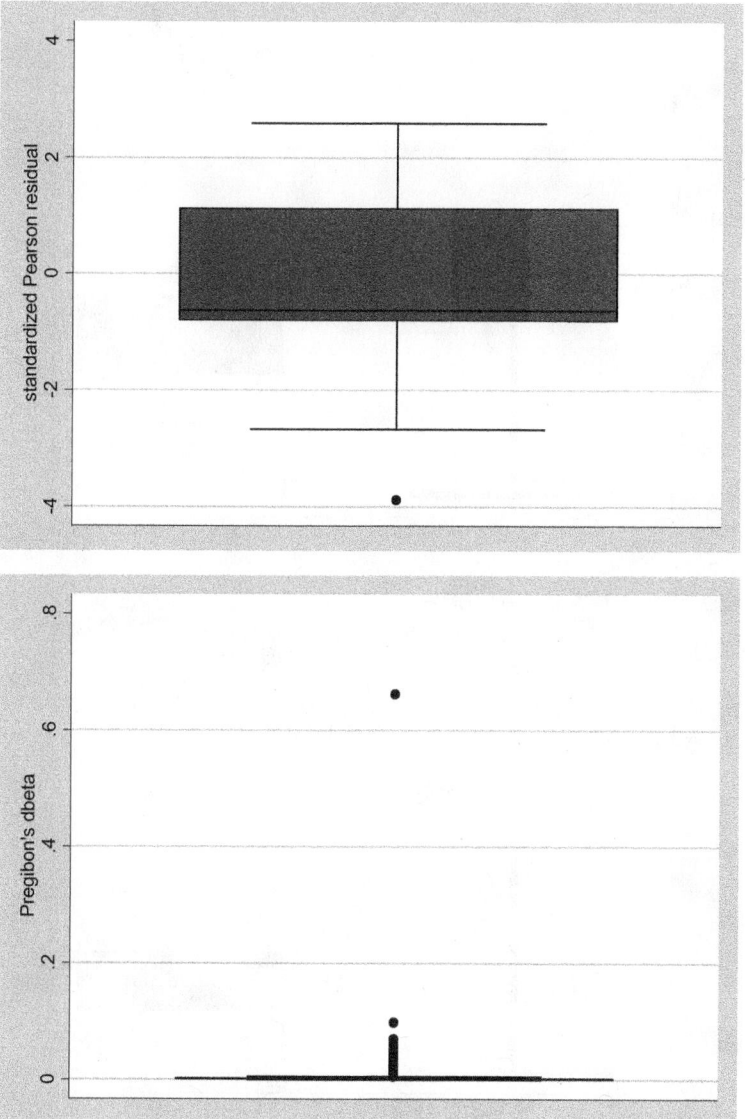

■ **Figure 16.4** Outliers and Influential Observations: Box Plots of Pearson Residuals and C values

same extreme value, less than -3 on the Pearson residuals and greater than 0.60 on C. This case has a large value of nearly \$1 million on annual earnings. The distribution of the Pearson residual is otherwise symmetric, and all of the remaining values are below three in absolute value. In contrast, the distribution of C shows a long tail. When we examined the means of the values in this tail, adults who reported being American Indian and having seven or more sisters appeared to be over-represented. Figure 16.5 shows a box plot of the C values by these dummy variables confirming that many of the cases in the tail fall into these two categories. As discussed in Chapter 14, in a real application, you might decide to exclude the American Indian

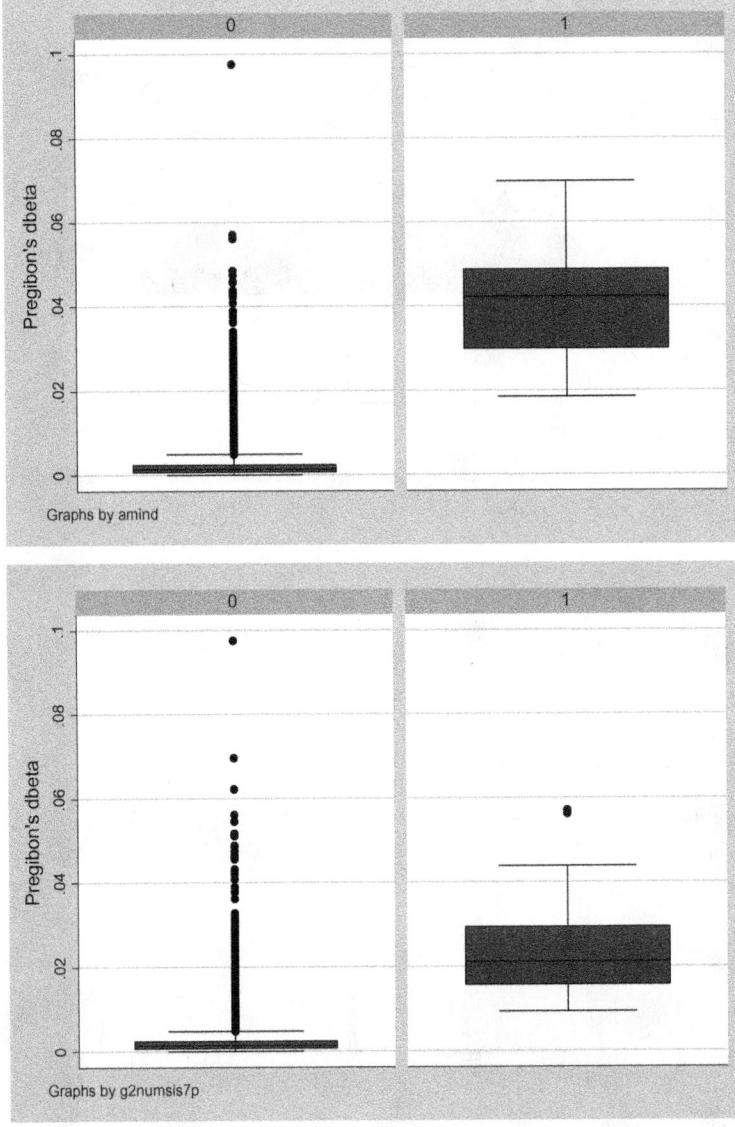

◼ **Figure 16.5** Influential Observations, by Status as American Indian and Having a Large Number of Sisters

adults and those with seven or more sisters, or offer a caveat about the small numbers in these categories.

16.5: INTERPRETATION

Once the model is established, through assessments of fit and potential influential values, the substantive magnitude of significant associations can be evaluated through interpretation of coefficients and predicted probabilities. Unlike OLS estimates, the logit and probit coefficients must always be transformed before they can be interpreted substantively, since they reflect changes in logits or probits rather than in probability units.

We cover two strategies for interpretation. One is calculating and tabulating or graphing predicted probabilities. The other is taking the difference between predicted probabilities when a predictor is at some level and then increased by some amount. These two approaches are clearly interrelated. One helps us visualize the association. The other quantifies the amount of change (in the case of continuous variables, the slope) underlying that visual depiction. As we saw with non-linear associations in OLS (Chapter 12), when we are in the non-linear region of the S curve of the logit and probit function (see again Figure 16.2), the amount of change will depend on the starting value of X. If we carefully examine the association, this non-linearity should be evident both visually and in different amounts of change when we use various starting values for our predictor of interest and/or when we hold the other predictor variables constant at different values.

We also introduce below a broader set of options for making predictions than the approaches we used in earlier chapters since different approaches are used in different subfields and provide somewhat different results. We refer to these as "predict then average," "average then predict," and "predict ideal types" (Long 1997: 69).[16] We discuss their relative strengths and limitations below.

We also discuss below an approach for interpreting the coefficients from the logit model that parallels the factor and percentage change interpretation of the log-linear model. We then introduce the use of discrete change and marginal effects for interpretation and see that, unlike relationships in OLS regression, the two approaches give us different results for non-linear regions of the slope. Your task in any application will be to choose from among these various interpretive approaches to present in a paper a concise yet complete way to get across the main findings for each predictor of interest.

16.5.1: Predicted Probabilities

As we saw in Literature Excerpt 16.1, predicted probabilities are often used in the interpretation of models with dichotomous outcomes. Reporting these predicted probabilities in figures, tables or the text solidifies for the reader the magnitude, or substantive significance, of any statistically significant effects. Knowing the range of predicted probabilities can also tell us whether a particular result falls on a region of the probability curve where the effect is largely linear (simplifying interpretation) or if the result falls on a region of the probability curve where the effect is largely nonlinear (complicating interpretation).

As we saw above, the basic process of calculating predicted probabilities is an extension of the process we followed to calculate predicted values in OLS regression, with the additional step of translating the predicted logit or probit into a predicted probability. The challenge for the researcher is choosing interesting probabilities to predict.

Predicted Probabilities for Every Case

Predicted probabilities can be calculated for every case in the datafile by substituting into the prediction equation their observed values on each predictor and then translating the result into a probability. Doing this by hand is time-consuming and error prone but Stata and SAS will do this for us.

Locating Linear Regions

One way to use these predicted probabilities is to calculate the range of predicted probabilities across all observations. As we saw above, when the range of predicted probabilities is between about .2 and .8 then the association will be fairly linear. If all predicted probabilities in your dataset fall within a linear region, then summarizing the result will be simplified.

"Predict then Average"

The predicted probabilities can also be used to help interpret the substantive significance of the result by averaging predictions within levels of predictor variables. In regression models with many predictors, cases with the same value on one predictor will have different-values on other predictors which will lead them to have somewhat different predicted probabilities. We can average these predicted values and compare them to the average of the predicted values for all cases with another value on that predictor.

If the predictor variable of interest, or a small number of related variables of interest, are dichotomous or take on only a few values, then a chart or table may be used to show the average predictions within levels of the predictor variables. In some cases, these predictions might also be reported in the text of a paper.

For continuous predictors graphs often best show the association. However, because the average of the predicted probabilities will be unreliable if only one or a few observations take on a specific level of a continuous predictor variable (e.g., few cases will have exactly, say, $11,051 annual earnings) we often group levels of the predictor (e.g., ages are often grouped by 5s or 10s). In our example below, we group respondents' earnings mostly into intervals of $10,000 increments.

Modified "Predict then Average"

Researchers can also allow all sample members to retain their original values on all variables other than the one of interest and then successively vary the value of the variable of interest, taking the resulting mean of the predicted probabilities. This approach represents a thought experiment: What if I gave everyone in the sample some level of the predictor, say 12 years of schooling. What would their predicted earnings be, given their other observed characteristics? And, what if I gave everyone in the sample a different level of the predictor, say 16 years of schooling? Then what would their predicted earnings be, given their other observed characteristics? This approach can be especially useful if few observed variables take on any given value of the predictor variable (such as in the case of a continuous variable like income).

It also adjusts the predictions for the fact that those with varying levels on the predictor of interest differ on other variables.

SAS and Stata Syntax

Similar to our request for diagnostics above, we can use the `score` statement in SAS and the `predict` command in Stata to request predicted values for all cases. In Stata the syntax is `predict <new variable name>, p`.[17] In SAS, the syntax is `score out=<data set name>` In Stata, the predicted probabilities are added to the data set already in memory. In SAS, a copy of the data including a new variable that contains the predicted probabilities (named *p_1* by default) is written to a new data set. Once we have these predictions, we can examine the minimum and maximum values to see if some of them fall in the non-linear regions of the S-shaped logit curve and we can average their values within levels of some of our predictors.

In our example, we will focus on the association between the adult respondent's earnings and distance and, for interpretation, limit our attention to cases that have annual earnings between none and $80,000.[18] Thus, we first summarize the predicted values for all cases and then for cases that fall within this earnings range. Display B.16.8 shows the results. In both cases, the min and max values on the predicted probabilities fall below .20 and the overall predicted probabilities also contain cases above .80. This suggests that the association between earnings and distance covers some of the non-linear region of the S-shaped curve.

Because annual earnings is a continuous value and takes on over 500 different-values in the data set, we collapsed income categories before averaging. We include 0 as its own value (it contains nearly 1000 cases) and then used $10,000 intervals up to $80,000. We use the mid-points (e.g., $5,000, $15,000, . . ., $75,000) to label these intervals. Similar to what we did in Chapter 14, we then used the `bysort` command in Stata and the `by` statement within `proc means` following a `proc sort` in SAS to summarize the predicted probabilities within these categories. The results are shown in Display B.16.9. We can also use a graph to help us see the pattern of results. Display H.16.1 uses Excel to do this. We use a bar rather than a line chart since the earnings categories represent intervals of $10,000. The results suggest that the predicted probability rises most consistently and steadily in the range between about $15,000 and $55,000; it appears fairly flat between zero and $25,000 and between $55,000 and $65,000.

Display B.16.10 shows how to implement the modified predict then average approach in SAS and Stata. To conserve space, we show three example predictions (for earnings of $0, $5000, and $15,000). In Stata, we use the `margins` command with the option , `at()` to request predicted probabilities at each desired level of earnings.[19] Within the `at()` option, we tell Stata what value we would like it to use for *g2earn10000* when making predictions.[20] When we do so, it is important to enter the variables recognizing any transformation or rescaling. In this case, because we use *g2earn10000* rather than *g2earn* in the model we use then values of 0.5 and 1.5 rather than 5000 or 15000 in the `at()` option. We made the remaining predictions with similar code.

In SAS, we can again use the score command, like we did in Display B.16.8, but because we want to assign each person the same value of *g2earn10000* to score, we create several copies of the data set. This is manageable because we use a single filename (rather than full path) for these new data sets (so they are saved only temporarily, and don't take up hard drive space permanently) and SAS allows multiple score commands within a single proc logistic command. Once we have the new data sets with the predicted probabilities, we can use proc means to calculate the average value.

The results are shown in Display B.16.10. Stata shows the predicted probability under the column labeled "Margin." In SAS, the same value is shown in the "Mean" column of the proc means output. The results show us that the predicted probability of living more than 45 miles from the mother would be .367 if all adults in the sample had no earnings, .371 if all adults had $5000 in earnings, and .378 if all adults had $15000 in earnings.

Display H.16.2 graphs these values (as well as the values we predicted at additional levels of earnings) in Excel. The graph still shows a positive trend, but it is attenuated in the modified "predict then average" versus the "predict then average" approach. Not surprisingly, this suggests that adults with different levels of earnings differ on the other predictors (mothers' years of schooling and age, adult's age, gender, race-ethnicity, and number of brothers and sisters). When we use the "predict then average" approach the means partially reflect the differences in these other covariates. When we use the modified "predict then average" approach, the covariates are kept the same for each level of earnings, because we repeatedly make predictions for each sample case as if they had each level of earnings.

"Average then Predict"

Like the modified "predict then average" approach, the "average then predict" approach has the advantage of using the same levels on the other predictors as we vary the level of the predictor of interest. But, an objection to this approach is that the means may not represent real values on the predictors (e.g., the mean of a dichotomous variable indicating cohabitation might be .15, whereas all observed values of that variable are either zero or one; or, the median of completed years of schooling might be 12.23 whereas someone in the data can only have integer values, like 12 or 13). To deal with this problem, researchers can round averages to the nearest meaningful value (e.g., round .15 to zero; round 12.32 to 12) or look at the percentage distribution to determine the modal or median value. However, even with rounding, this "average then predict" approach has the disadvantage that the set of sample means, modes, or medians across all the variables may not represent a real combination of X values in the sample or population. This is in contrast to modified "predict then average" approach in which the predictions are based on each observed case's actual values across the predictors.

Display B.16.11 and Display B.16.12 shows how to use Stata's margins command and SAS's score command to request these predictions. In Stata, we use three options for the margins command in these displays. The option noatlegend suppresses the command from listing the values of the predictors. We use this option for predictions after the first because the brief output is easier to read, after we verify the means once in the first set of output. The at() option allows us to hold one or more variables constant at specific values. If multiple variables are held constant at specific values, they are separated by spaces. We use (mean) _all in Display B.16.11 to ask margins to hold all variables except those specified in the at() option at their means. In Display B.16.12, we round the predictor variables to their nearest actual value and specify all of those values explicitly.

It is again important to enter the variables recognizing any transformation or rescaling. For example, we use values like 1.5 and 2.5 rather than 15000 or 25000 for *g2earn10000*. And, in Display B.16.12 we choose to hold *glyrschl* constant at 11 and then calculate 11 * 11 = 121 for the value of *sqglyrschl*. In addition, only one of the set of mutually-exclusive dummies representing the multi-category race-ethnicity variable is held constant at one in Display B.16.12 (*white*). The remaining dummies are held constant at zero.

> **■ Box 16.4**
>
> If we wanted to hold race-ethnicity constant at the reference category, African American, then we would indicate zeros for all of the included categories (amind=0 mexamer=0 white=0 other=0).

In SAS, in Display B.16.11 we use an output statement on the proc means command to ask SAS to create a new data file that contains the means for each of our predictor variables.[21] We then create versions of this new data file in which we assign earnings to each desired value and ask SAS to score each of these new data files. Finally, we use proc means to show the predicted probability created by the score command.[22] In Display B.16.12 we follow a similar process, but we reassign the values of all of the predictors to rounded values in a data step and then use this new data file as input for the score command.

The results in Display B.16.11 show that someone who had the average characteristics of the sample across all the controls would have a predicted probability of living more than 45 miles from the mother of .362 if that person also had no earnings and .366 if that person had $5000 in earnings. The results in Display B.16.12 provide similar results, although we rounded the values to integers so that they reflected possible values on the controls.[23] These results show that someone who had these "rounded average" characteristics of the sample across all the controls would have a predicted probability of living more than 45 miles from the mother of .346 if that person also had no earnings and .350 if that person had $5000 in earnings.

Display H.16.3 and Display H.16.4 table and graph the predicted probabilities. Because the values of the other predictors are very similar in the two approaches, it is not surprising that the predictions and graphs in these two boxes are quite similar. Like Display H.16.2, these graphs show a modest positive trend of increasing average probabilities of living more than 45 miles from the mother as the respondents' earnings increase.

"Predict Ideal Types"

Another common approach to prediction uses "ideal types." When such types fit well with your particular research question, they can make the findings more concrete to the reader. And, ideal types address the common complaint mentioned above with the "average then predict" approach that no sample cases may actually have the average value on all predictors. In fact, in our data file no case has the set of rounded average values of the predictor variables listed in Display B.16.12. In contrast, we can choose ideal types to present real cases.

We illustrate the "ideal type" approach by using SAS and Stata to predict two extreme cases: one that has a set of characteristics that nearly all associate with living far from the mother and the other that has a set of characteristics that nearly all associate with living close to the mother. We identified a set of possible values and then modified them a bit so that we identified configurations that were actually observed by at least one case in the data file. Display B.16.13 shows the results. Given that we chose two cases that reflect the extremes in the data, it is not surprising that the difference in predicted probabilities is much larger than what we saw when we only allowed earnings to vary and held the other variables constant. In particular, the predicted probability of living more than 45 miles from the mother is .18 for an African American female who is 20 years old, earns $5000 per year, has one brother and fewer than four sisters, and whose mother is 40 years old and has 9 years of schooling. In contrast, the predicted probability of living more than 45 miles from the mother is .67 for a white male who is 50 years old, earns $55000 per year, has two brothers and fewer than four sisters, and whose mother is 80 years old and has 16 years of schooling.

16.5.2: Logit Model: Factor Change Interpretation

For the logit—but not the probit—model we can also use a factor change interpretation based on the odds. This is one reason why the logit model is more attractive than the probit model to some researchers. Like our interpretation approach for the log-linear model, this interpretation for the logit model is based on the exponential of the coefficients.

Recall that, for the logit model, we can interpret the coefficients as having linear effects on the log odds. However, few of us find the log odds a meaningful value. If we take the exponential of the coefficients, we can interpret the factor effect on the odds, which is more meaningful (although still not as concrete in meaning as predicted probabilities).

$$\ln\left(\frac{\hat{\pi}}{1-\hat{\pi}}\right) = \hat{\beta}_0 + \hat{\beta}_1 X$$

$$\frac{\hat{\pi}}{1-\hat{\pi}} = \exp(\hat{\beta}_0 + \hat{\beta}_1 X)$$

The value on the left hand side is the predicted odds. It is calculated by exponentiating the predicted log odds, as shown in the right hand side of the equation.

Let's substitute $\widehat{odds}$ for $\frac{\hat{\pi}}{1-\hat{\pi}}$ and examine the ratio of the expected values when X is at its initial value and when X is incremented by 1, similar to what we did when we interpreted the log-linear model in Chapter 12.

$$\frac{\left(\widehat{odds}\middle| X+1\right)}{\left(\widehat{odds}\middle| X\right)} = \frac{\exp\left(\hat{\beta}_0 + \hat{\beta}_1\left(X+1\right)\right)}{\exp\left(\hat{\beta}_0 + \hat{\beta}_1 X\right)}$$

$$= \frac{\exp\left(\hat{\beta}_0 + \hat{\beta}_1 X + \hat{\beta}_1\right)}{\exp\left(\hat{\beta}_0 + \hat{\beta}_1 X\right)}$$

$$= \frac{\exp\left(\hat{\beta}_0\right) * \exp\left(\hat{\beta}_1 X\right) * \exp\left(\hat{\beta}_1\right)}{\exp\left(\hat{\beta}_0\right) * \exp\left(\hat{\beta}_1 X\right)}$$

$$= \exp\left(\hat{\beta}_1\right)$$

This exponential of the coefficient is often called an **odds ratio** because the left hand side of this equation is the ratio of two odds.

We can rewrite the final result to show this clearly:

$$\frac{\left(\widehat{odds}\middle| X+1\right)}{\left(\widehat{odds}\middle| X\right)} = \exp\left(\hat{\beta}_1\right)$$

Now, if we multiply both sides by $(\widehat{odds}|X)$ we have:

$$(\widehat{odds}|X+1) = (\widehat{odds}|X) * \exp(\hat{\beta}_1)$$

And thus it is easy to see why we can interpret $\exp(\hat{\beta}_1)$ as follows:

"For a one unit increase in X, the odds are expected to change by a factor of $\exp(\hat{\beta}_1)$ holding all other variables constant."

The strength of this approach is that we can interpret this constant factor change, regardless of the level of the predictor of interest and regardless of the specific level at which we have held constant the other predictor variable(s). That is, we have a one sentence interpretation, similar to linear associations in OLS regression. But, it is essential to remember that this constant factor change in the odds does *not* correspond to a constant factor change (or constant absolute change) in the probabilities. It is often useful to use the factor odds interpretation in conjunction with predicted probabilities so that the substantive meaning of the associations in terms of probabilities can be assessed along with their constant factor change in the odds.

Because we are now interpreting with factor change in the odds, rather than absolute change in the log odds, it is helpful to keep several points in mind. First, the sign of coefficients and the magnitude of odds ratios have a simple relationship:

1. If the coefficient is negative, then the odds ratio will be between 0 and 1.
2. If the coefficient is positive, then the odds ratio will be greater than 1.
3. If the coefficient is zero, then the odds ratio will be 1.

These results reflect the factor change interpretation of the odds ratios. If we multiply the original odds by a factor that falls above zero but below one, then the new odds will be smaller than the original odds. If we multiply the original odds by a factor that is larger than one, then the new odds will be larger than the original odds. If we multiply the original odds by a factor of one, then the new odds will be equal to the original odds. Thus, our "straw man" of no association—a coefficient of zero—corresponds to an odds ratio of 1.

Second, inverses must be taken to compare the magnitude of positive and negative associations. For example, we are used to recognizing that two coefficients of the same magnitude but opposite sign represents the same level of association but in opposite directions. For example, if we had a coefficient for a dummy variable that was 1.099; then, if we reverse coded that dummy variable, we would expect a coefficient of -1.099. When we exponentiate these two coefficients to interpret them in terms of odds ratios, we have a factor change in the odds of $\exp(1.099) = 3.00$ in the first case and have a factor change in the odds of $\exp(-1.099) = 0.33$ in the second case. These factor changes are inverses of one another: That is a factor odds effect of $\frac{1}{3} = 0.33$ is equivalent in magnitude to a factor odds effect of $\frac{3}{1} = 3$.

Third, similar to what we did with the log-linear model, we can also interpret the effect in terms of percentage change rather than factor change using the following formula:

$$(\exp(\hat{\beta}_1) - 1) * 100$$

This can be interpreted as:

"For a one unit increase in X, the odds are expected to change by $(\exp(\hat{\beta}_1) - 1) * 100$ percent, holding all other variables constant."

Confidence intervals for the odds ratios can also be calculated by exponentiating the bounds of the confidence intervals for the coefficient. We can interpret these intervals as:

"We are 95% confident that the odds change by between $\exp(\hat{\beta}_1 - 1.96 * \hat{\sigma}_{\hat{\beta}_1})$ and $\exp(\hat{\beta}_1 + 1.96 * \hat{\sigma}_{\hat{\beta}_1})$ when X increase by one, on average, holding all other variables constant."

Display B.16.14 contains the results of asking Stata to present the odds ratios using the , or option. SAS presents odds ratios in the default output for proc logistic, which are also shown in the display.[24] For *g2earn10000* the odds ratio is 1.032392. This can be interpreted as: "For a $10,000 increase in the respondent's annual earnings, the odds of living more than 45 miles from the mother are expected to increase by a factor of 1.03, holding constant the respondent's gender, race-ethnicity, age, and number of brothers and sisters and the mother's age and years of schooling." The percentage change is calculated as (1.032392-1)*100 = 3.2392. This can be interpreted as "For a $10,000 increase in the respondent's annual earnings, the odds of living more than 45 miles from the mother are expected to increase by 3%, holding constant the respondent's gender, race-ethnicity, age, and number of brothers and sisters and the mother's age and years of schooling."

Display B.16.14 also shows confidence intervals for the odds ratios. For example, for earnings we would say: "We are 95% confident that the odds of living more than 45 miles from the mother change by between 1.01 and 1.05 times when annual earnings increase by $10,000, holding all other variables constant."

16.5.3: Change In Probability For Given Change In X

The actual predicted probabilities we calculated above are useful for visualizing the substantive importance of a result. But, without additional manipulation, they don't give us the usual slope interpretation: How much does the probability change for a given change in X? We will consider two approaches to calculating these slopes for the probability curve: marginal effects and discrete change.

Marginal Effect

The marginal effect measures the "instantaneous" slope of the function relating the predictor and outcome variables, holding all other variables constant.[25] For linear relationships in our standard linear regression model, this marginal effect is simply the coefficient of the predictor variable, thereby giving us the simple interpretation that "holding all other variables constant, a one unit increase in X is associated with a β change in Y, on average." However, as we know, nonlinear relationships do not have this simple interpretation. When the curve is non-linear, the slope depends on the starting value of X. This is particularly true for logit and probit models when the probabilities are below 0.20 or greater than 0.80 (see again Figure 16.2).

Calculating the Marginal Effect

In fact, the marginal effect for models with a dichotomous outcome depends on the level of all the predictor variables and their coefficients:

$$\text{Marginal Effect} = f(\eta)\beta_k$$

Where $f(\eta)$ is the probability density function evaluated at the predicted η given a particular set of predictor variables and β_k is the coefficient for one of our k predictor variables. Note that we only need to calculate $f(\eta)$ once and then we can multiply the result times each of the coefficients.

To define specific marginal effects for the probit and logit models, we can substitute in the appropriate probability density functions.

For the probit model:

$$\text{Marginal Effect} = \phi(\eta)\beta_k$$

where ϕ is the probability density function of the standard normal.

For the logit model:

$$\text{Marginal Effect} = \frac{\exp(\eta)}{\left[1+\exp(\eta)\right]^2}\beta_k$$

There are three important points to keep in mind about the marginal effect:

■ The marginal effect on the probability will always have the same *sign* as the coefficient. Thus, the sign of the coefficient can always be interpreted in the default output.

■ The *magnitude* of the effect on the probability cannot be determined from the size of the coefficient in the default output. Instead, it depends on where we evaluate the marginal effect since its value is also determined by the coefficients and levels of other predictor variables in the model through $f(\eta)$.

■ The most common way for marginal effects on probabilities to be reported is to hold the other variables constant at their means, i.e., presenting *marginal effects at the mean*.

For the logit model we have been using as an example, let's calculate the marginal effects at the mean. We prefer having our statistical package do this for us, since it can carry out the values to more digits and avoid computational errors, but working out the computation at least once solidifies our understanding of the calculations underlying the values in our statistical output. This process is simpler than it may seem at first glance, because the value $f(\eta)$ is the same for all coefficients. In our logit example, we have the following results.[26]

The first column of Table 16.6 contains the coefficients from the logit model with numerous predictors shown in Display B.16.7. The second column contains the means of the predictor variables obtained from Stata's `summarize` command (We use a value of one for the intercept). The third column shows the product of each predictor variable's coefficient with its mean. The value of η is the sum of these products. Since this is a logit model, the value of $f(\eta) = \frac{\exp(\eta)}{\left[1+\exp(\eta)\right]^2}$. That is,

$f(\eta) = \frac{\exp(-0.468)}{\left[1+\exp(-0.468)\right]^2} = 0.237$. The fourth column multiplies each predictor variable's

coefficient by $f(\eta)$. For example, for *g2earn10000* we multiply $0.032 * 0.237 = .007584$ to obtain the marginal effect at the mean for the annual earnings variable, rescaled in $10,000 units.

Limitations of the Marginal Effect

Literally, this calculation of the marginal effects gives us the expected change in the probability for an infinitesimally small change in the predictor variable of interest. For continuous variables, a one unit change may be a small enough amount o change to make this calculation appropriate.

■ **Table 16.6: Examples of Calculating Marginal Effects**

	Coefficient	Mean of Predictor Variable	Coefficient* Mean of Predictor Variable	Marginal Effect at Mean f(η)β_k
Intercept	−2.326	1.000	−2.326	−0.5507
g1yrschl	−0.061	11.401	−0.699	−0.0145
sqg1yrschl	0.008	138.617	1.046	0.0018
g2numsis4	0.060	0.045	0.003	0.0142
g2numsis56	−0.246	0.037	−0.009	−0.0582
g2numsis7p	0.607	0.010	0.006	0.1438
amind	0.824	0.005	0.004	0.1952
mexamer	−0.233	0.030	−0.007	−0.0551
white	0.374	0.810	0.303	0.0885
other	0.669	0.013	0.009	0.1583
female	−0.022	0.603	−0.013	−0.0053
g2earn10000	0.032	3.071	0.098	0.0075
g1age	0.013	60.088	0.809	0.0032
g2age	0.008	34.294	0.262	0.0018
g2numbro	0.033	1.433	0.048	0.0079
			$\eta=$ −0.468	
			f(η)= 0.237	

For example, we might interpret the marginal effect at the mean for earnings as: "At the average levels of all other predictor variables, a $10,000 increase in annual earnings is associated with nearly a one percentage point (0.0075*100 = 0.75) increase in the chance of living more than 45 miles from the mother." For a continuous variable like earnings, when the effect on the probability is nearly linear, this marginal effect calculated at the mean gives a good approximation of the more general effect of the predictor variable. However, when the effect is in a very nonlinear region, the marginal effect at the mean will not give a good summary.

In addition, the marginal effect is not strictly interpretable for dummy variables, whose values can only change from 0 to 1 (i.e., the concept of infinitesimal change is not appropriate). In our example, the values of the marginal effect for the dummy indicators of number of sisters, race-ethnicities, and gender are not strictly meaningful. It is important to keep this in mind, since statistical output will often calculate the marginal effect for all predictor variables, regardless of whether the concept of an infinitesimally small change is appropriate and regardless of whether this small change occurs in a linear or non-linear region of the probability curve.

Discrete Change in the Probability

The **discrete change** is an alternative approach for interpreting dummy variables and for interpreting continuous variables in nonlinear regions of the probability curve (see Long 1997 and Long and Freese 2005). This approach is closely related to the predicted probabilities we already calculated to visualize the effects: The discrete change considers the change in the probability when we allow a variable of interest to take on two different values and we hold all other variables constant.

The marginal effect and discrete change will not be equivalent if the probability curve is in a nonlinear region. When the probability curve is in a nonlinear region, the discrete change will depend on the values we choose for the control variable(s), the starting value we choose for the variable of interest, and how much we allow the variable of interest to change. Thus, unlike the standard linear regression model, marginal effects and discrete change will not always give the same interpretation for logit and for probit models.

What Values Should We Use to Hold Constant the Other Variable(s)?

Similar to the choices we discussed above for predicted probabilities, there is no single answer to the question "What values should we use to hold constant the other variable(s)?" We can "predict then average" or "average then predict" or use "ideal types." If we "average then predict" we can use sample means of variables or we can use the rounded means or modal value or median value. We must also make choices about what value to start at and how much to change on our predictor of interest.

What Values Should We Use for the Variable of Interest?

For *dummy variables* we will always calculate the discrete change starting at 0 and ending at 1.

For continuous variables some common options are (see Long 1997):

■ **Centered Discrete Change.** Center the change at the mean of the variable, and use the mean less ½ as the starting point and the mean plus ½ as the ending point.
■ **Standard Deviation Change.** Center the change at the mean of the variable, and use the mean less half the standard deviation as the starting point and the mean plus half the standard deviation as the ending point.
■ **Maximal Change.** Start at the minimum value and end at the maximum value of the variable.

Other starting and ending points can be selected if they are meaningful for your substantive application (e.g., in our example, for annual earnings, we might use the values of $5000 to $75000 in $10,000 increments, as we predicted above).

For our example, we can easily calculate discrete change based on the predicted probabilities that we already calculated. For instance, using the "rounded average then predict" results gives the following discrete changes when we subtract the value of the predicted probability at the original level of the predictor from the value of the predicted probability at the new level of the predictor.

Respondent's Earnings	Predicted Probability	Discrete Change
0	0.3464	—
5000	0.3500	0.0036
15000	0.3573	0.0073
25000	0.3647	0.0074
35000	0.3721	0.0074
45000	0.3796	0.0075
55000	0.3871	0.0075
65000	0.3947	0.0076
75000	0.4023	0.0076

For example, the difference in predicted probabilities between the first two rows is 0.3500 − 0.3464 = 0.0036. And, the difference in predicted probabilities between the second two rows is 0.3573 − 0.3500 = 0.0073.

Notice that almost all of these discrete changes are between 0.0073 and 0.0076 which is nearly identical to the marginal effect we calculated above of 0.0075. The consistency in discrete change and marginal effect for earnings in our case is consistent with the graphs in Appendix H.16 which show that over much of the range of earnings the associations is approximately linear. (The first change from 0 to $5000 of 0.0036 is about half that of the other changes of $10,000 units because a change from 0 to $5000 is only an increase of $5000).

It is also helpful to relate these predicted probabilities back to odds ratios to see that the factor change in the odds can remain the same even as the absolute change in the predicted probabilities differs. To show this, we need to remind ourselves that the predicted probabilities reflect the predicted probability of success. Thus, one minus the predicted probability is the predicted probability of failure. And, the ratio of these two predictions is the odds. The table below shows the predicted probabilities we examined above but also calculates the predicted probability of failure, predicted odds, and predicted odds ratios based on them.[27]

Respondent's Earnings	Predicted Probability of Success	Predicted Probability of Failure	Predicted Odds	Predicted Odds Ratio (Odds at New Earnings/Odds at Original Earnings Level
0	0.3464	0.6536	0.5300	
5000	0.3500	0.6500	0.5385	—
15000	0.3573	0.6427	0.5560	1.0324
25000	0.3647	0.6353	0.5740	1.0324
35000	0.3721	0.6279	0.5926	1.0324
45000	0.3796	0.6204	0.6118	1.0324
55000	0.3871	0.6129	0.6316	1.0324
65000	0.3947	0.6053	0.6520	1.0324
75000	0.4023	0.5977	0.6732	1.0324

Note: Predicted odds ratios only shown for changes of earnings in $10,000 increments.

Note that the predicted odds ratio is constant even though we saw above that the discrete change varies.

The spost commands written by Long and Freese (2005) includes a command called prchange which calculates numerous types of change for us, including the marginal effects and the discrete changes defined above.[28] Display B.16.15 provides the results based on issuing this command after our logit model. The , fromto option after prchange shows the predicted probabilities as well as the change. The marginal effects are in the last column. Notice that the marginal effects match, within rounding error, our calculations above.

As noted above, marginal effects are not appropriate for dummy variables. Instead, for the dummy variables in our model, the probabilities and changes in the 1st to 3rd columns and the 4th to 6th columns of the top row of Display B.16.15 provide the desired results (changing from the minimum to maximum value, or equivalently from 0 to 1). For example, we bolded the row for the dummy indicator of *female*. For females the discrete change when we move from zero to one (the 6th column in the top row of Display B.16.15 labeled 0->1) is −0.0053, indicating that females are just over half a percentage point less likely to live more than 45 miles from the mother than are males based on our model, holding the other variables constant at their means.

For continuous variables, we could use the marginal effect. But, the prchange output also gives us additional choices that may be useful in our application. We bolded the row of output for earnings, *g2earn10000*. For earnings, the column labeled min->max provides a value of 0.5583 for the discrete change, indicating if we move from the smallest to largest values of earnings in our sample ($0 to about $950,000) while holding the other variables constant at their means then the predicted percentage of adults living more than 45 from their mothers increased by 56 points. The column labeled 0->1 represents an increase of $10,000 on the rescaled *g2earn10000*, thus its value of 0.0074 is very similar to the discrete changes we calculated for particular values of earnings above. The centered discrete change (in the column labeled −+1/2) is also close to this value (0.0075) since it too represents an increase of one unit, but starting 0.5 units below the mean and ending 0.5 units above the mean (for earnings, the mean is 3.070573 thus this discrete change is calculated starting at $3.070573 - 0.5 = 2.570573$ and ending at $3.070573 + 0.5 = 3.570573$). The centered standard deviation change labeled −+sd/2 begins at the mean less half a standard deviation and ends at the mean plus half a standard deviation (for earnings, the mean is 3.070573 and the standard deviation is 3.749562 thus this discrete change is calculated starting at $3.070573 - (0.5 * 3.749562) = 1.195792$ and ending at $3.070573 + (0.5 * 3.749562) = 4.945354$). This discrete change is 0.0283, indicating that for a one standard deviation increase in earnings the percentage of adults living more than 45 miles from their mothers is nearly 3 percentage points higher, holding the other variables constant at their means.

16.6: SUMMARY

In this chapter, we used the generalized linear model to specify models appropriate for outcomes that take on only two values. These models use a binomial distribution for the random component and either a logit or probit link to associate the systematic component to the probability. The logit and probit models will generally give similar results, although the logit model is more popular in the social and health sciences because the exponentials of its coefficients can be interpreted as odds ratios. Both of these models are preferred to the OLS model for dichotomous outcome variables because the assumptions of OLS are violated for binary outcomes (e.g., the conditional errors are not normally distributed and do not have constant variance) and because of likely out of range predictions and because we may conceptually expect non-linear associations between predictors and probabilities. Logit and probit models overcome these problems, but they require some additional work for interpretation. The linear probability model which applies OLS to a dichotomous outcome is simpler to interpret, although it violates two of the OLS assumptions. We covered three approaches for calculating predicted probabilities (predict then average, average then predict, and predict ideal type). And, we discussed the use of marginal effects and discrete change for re-interpreting coefficients in terms of changes in probabilities. Numerous measures have been suggested for assessing model fit for models with dichotomous outcomes. We covered several pseudo R-squared measures as well as two information criteria (AIC and BIC) and measures to locate outliers (standardized Pearson residuals) and influential observations (C).

KEY TERMS

Adjusted Count R-squared

Average Then Predict

Bernoulli Trial

Binomial Distribution

Classification Table

Count R-Squared

Cragg & Uhler's R-squared

Discrete Change

Failure

Linear Probability Model

Log Odds

Logit Link

Logistic Regression

Marginal Effect

Maximum Likelihood R-squared

Mcfadden's Adjusted Pseudo R-squared

Mcfadden's Pseudo R-squared

Odds

Odds Ratio

Pearson Residual

Predict Ideal Types

Predict Then Average

Predicted Logit

Predicted Probit

Probit Link

Sensitivity Analysis

Success

REVIEW QUESTIONS

16.1   What is a linear probability model? What are its advantages and disadvantages?

16.2   What is the formula for the logit link? How do we refer to its values?

16.3   What is the formula for the probit link? How do we refer to its values?

16.4   How do the logit and probit link achieve our goal of converting values that can only fall between 0 and 1 to values that range from negative infinity to positive infinity?

16.5   Write the formula for the binomial distribution and discuss what each major piece of the formula accomplishes.

16.6   Write the formula for converting predicted logits into predicted probabilities.

16.7   Write the formula for converting predicted probits into predicted probabilities.

16.8 Why are there so many different *R*-squared values for maximum likelihood estimation?

16.9 Discuss the advantages and disadvantages of the three main strategies for predicting values discussed in the chapter (predict then average, average then predict, and ideal types).

16.10 Discuss how values of odds ratios relate to values of coefficients, focusing on coefficient values that are negative, zero, and positive.

16.11 When will the marginal effect be similar in value to the discrete change?

16.12 For what types of variables are marginal effects appropriate?

REVIEW EXERCISES

16.1. Show algebraically that the difference in BICs would work out to the same value for all three formulas shown in the chapter (Equation 16.9, Equation 16.10, and Equation 16.11) in the simplest case when you compare a full model with one predictor to a reduced intercept-only model.

16.2. Calculate the odds and the log-odds for the following probabilities: 0.20, 0.50, and 0.80. Comment on how the results relate to the theoretical minimum and maximum of probabilities, odds, and log-odds.

16.3. Suppose that you interview 15 10th grade boys and that 5 of these boys report to you that they belong to a gang. Which of the following probabilities of an adolescent boy being in a gang do these results suggest is more likely in the population from which this sample was drawn: .33 or .50? Calculate the likelihoods for these two values using the likelihood function based on the binomial distribution in justifying your response.

16.4. Suppose that you estimated a regression model using ordinary least squares with a dummy indicator of adults' marital status as the outcome (0=not married, 1=married) and a continuous measure of years of schooling (range: 9 to 22) as the predictor. Suppose that you obtained the following statistically significant coefficient estimates for the prediction equation: $\hat{\beta}_0 = -0.10$ for the intercept and $\hat{\beta}_1 = 0.04$ for the slope. Respond to the following:

(a) Interpret the slope coefficient.

(b) Write the prediction equation.

(c) Calculate and interpret the predicted values when education is the following values: 9, 12, 16, and 22.

(d) Write the general name for using ordinary least squares with a dichotomous outcome, like this; and, in four brief sentences, comment on the major problems with this model, including any violations of the assumptions for least squares.

16.5. Consider that a colleague of yours has estimated a logit model predicting whether couples' divorce (dummy coded 0=stay married, 1=divorce) and obtains for the predictor variable POVERTY (dummy coded 0=family income above poverty line and 1=family income below poverty line) a coefficient of 0.693, a standard error of 0.295, a Z-value of 2.35 with a p-value of 0.019. The intercept in the equation is 0.05. Respond to the following:

(a) Does your colleague have evidence that the chances of a couple divorcing differs significantly for poor and non-poor families? Use an alpha of .05 in making your conclusion and justify your response based on both the Z-value and the p-value.

(b) Interpret the estimated coefficient for POVERTY with a factor change approach. Be sure to show how to calculate the factor change in your response.

(c) If your colleague re-estimated the model using probit, rather than logit, should she expect the coefficient for POVERTY to be larger or smaller (justify your response)?

(d) Write the prediction equation based on her results.

(e) What is the predicted probability of divorce for poor and non-poor families? Be sure to show all of your work.

CHAPTER EXERCISE

In this exercise, you will write a SAS and a Stata batch program to estimate a logit model.

Start with the NHIS 2009 dataset that was created in Chapter 4 with an *if expression* to only keep cases that *do not have missing values on the age, exfreqwR, SEX, and bmiR variables*.

16.1 Evaluating the Fit of a Logit Model

a) SAS/Stata Tasks.

i) Create a dummy variable to indicate females (as you did in Chapter 7).

ii) Create a dummy variable to indicate whether the respondent is *overweight* (coded *1* if *bmiR* is at or above 25 and 0 if *bmiR* is below 25).

iii) Use proc logistic in SAS and logit in Stata to regress the *overweight* dummy on the *female* dummy. Call this Regression #1.

iv) Use the `rsquare` option in SAS. Use the `fitstat` command in Stata after Regression #1 and save the results with the name *reg1*.

v) Use `proc logistic` in SAS and `logit` in Stata to regress the *overweight* dummy on the *female* dummy as well as *age* and *exfreqwR*. Call this Regression #2.

vi) Use the `rsquare` option in SAS. Use the `fitstat` command after Regression #2 and ask fitstat to compare the new results to the results saved in *reg1*.

vii) Use the `/ctable` option in SAS and the `estat class` command in Stata to request the classification table after Regression #2.

b) Write-Up Tasks.

i) Calculate by hand and interpret the Count *and* Adjusted Count *R*-squared values for Regression #2 based on the provided table of observed and predicted outcomes.

ii) For Regression #2, briefly summarize the pseudo *R*-squared values listed by the `fitstat` command (you need only discuss the pseudo *R*-squared values that are covered in the chapter).

iii) Indicate whether Regression #1 or Regression #2 is preferred based on the BICs. Be sure to comment on the relative size of each of the two BICs and their difference. (You do not need to calculate the BICs; you may read them off the fitstat output).

16.2 Interpreting the Coefficients of a Logit Model

a) SAS/Stata Tasks.

i) Ask Stata to show the odds ratios for Regression #2. (The odds ratios are already in the SAS default output).

ii) Based on Regression #2, use the `prchange, fromto` command to calculate discrete and marginal change in Stata for each variable, holding the other variables constant at their means.

iii) Ask SAS and Stata to calculate the unconditional means for the varables *age*, *exfreqwR,* and *female*.

b) Write-Up Tasks.

i) Use the factor change in odds approach to interpret the effects of each of the three predictor variables in the logit model. Calculate the odds ratios by hand (write the formula out and calculate them with your calculator rather relying on SAS and Stata) and interpret each result.

ii) Based on the predicted probabilities shown in the prchange output, show how to calculate and interpret in words the discrete change between men and women in Regression #2, while holding age and frequency of exercise constant at their overall sample means. Interpret the result.

iii) Show how to calculate by hand the marginal effect at the mean (using the mean values of each of the predictors) for the *age* variable in Regression #2.

iv) Can this marginal effect for age be interpreted in a meaningful way? If yes, interpret it. If no, state why not.

v) Can the marginal effect for the dummy variable indicating females that is shown in the prchange output be interpreted in a meaningful way? If yes, interpret it. If no, state why not.

COURSE EXERCISE

If you included dichotomous outcome variables in your data set, use one or more of them as an outcome in logit and probit models. Otherwise, if you can dichotomize one of the continuous outcome variables that you used in earlier chapters in a conceptually meaningful way, then do so, and compare the results of the dichotomized outcome to your earlier results. In either case, estimate several models that you can compare with the R-squared and information criteria discussed in the chapter. Interpret the coefficients in your models using odds ratios (for logit models) as well as predicted probabilities, discrete change, and marginal change.

Chapter 17

MULTI-CATEGORY OUTCOMES

CHAPTER 17: MULTI-CATEGORY OUTCOMES

In this chapter, we discuss how to extend the logit model that we introduced for dichotomous outcomes in Chapter 16 (what we will now refer to as a **binary logit model**) to outcomes with more than two categories. When the outcome is nominal, we have the multinomial logit model.

■ Box 17.1

There are probit versions of models for nominal and ordinal outcomes (multinomial probit and ordered probit; see Long 1997; Wooldridge 2002), however the logit models are more commonly used than the probit models in the social and health sciences. For example, our search of articles published between 2000 and 2005 in JSTOR's education, health sciences, psychology and sociology collections revealed 112 models that contained the phrase "ordered logit" or "ordered logistic" versus 104 that contained the phrase "ordered probit" and fully 309 contained the phrase "multinomial logit" or "multinomial logistic" versus just 14 that contained the phrase "multinomial probit."

■ Box 17.2

Our goal in this book has been to provide an accessible introduction to these models that meets the needs of the heterogenous group of graduate students found in many departments' statistics sequences (ranging from students who see themselves as unlikely to use quantitative methods in their own work and feeling high levels of math anxiety to those who are eager to learn everything they can about quantitative methods and are quite comfortable with math). Thus, we have intentionally limited the "bells and whistles" about each technique and the statistical packages that implement them. We encourage you to look to the references we provide throughout the book to learn these "bells and whistles" if you go on to use the techniques as you do your own work. They should be less overwhelming to learn once you have the foundation of understanding offered in this book. You should also now have the basic tools needed to extend your understanding of regression to additional models, including those we review in Chapter 18. Again, we offer numerous citations and suggested strategies for learning these techniques.

When the outcome is ordinal, we have the ordered logit model. With these models along with those we examined in earlier chapters, you will have the basic skills needed to use and understand regression analyses of a wide range of outcomes, including continuous (with OLS), dichotomous (with logit or probit), nominal (with multinomial logit) and ordinal (with ordered logit).

17.1: MULTINOMIAL LOGIT

The multinomial logit model is a direct extension of the logit model for dichotomous outcomes that we examined in Chapter 16. With two outcome categories, we had just one pair to compare. But, with a nominal outcome variable that has more than two categories, we can imagine comparing every pair of categories (ideally with theoretical expectations about what predicts a sample member occupying one category versus another).

For example, if the outcome were type of non-parental child care classified as: (1) relatives, (2) family day care providers, and (3) child care centers, then we can imagine conceptualizing how parents might choose between each pair (relatives versus family day care, relatives versus centers and family day care versus centers). On the one hand, since care by relatives and family day care providers tend to take place in homes whereas center care takes place in stand-alone facilities, we can imagine that parents who prefer home-like settings may be more likely to use relatives and family day care providers than centers. On the other hand, because centers often offer the most opportunities for children to socialize with others, and family day care providers usually offer somewhat more such opportunities than relatives, parents who prefer such socialization opportunities may be most likely to choose centers and least likely to choose relatives, with family day care providers falling in between. Likewise, because cost tends to be highest for centers followed by family day care providers followed by relatives, families with the lowest incomes may be most like to use relatives and least likely to use centers. We will now turn to a literature excerpt which provides another example of a multinomial logit model, as well as illustrating its empirical results and interpretation.

17.1.1: Literature Excerpt

Rukmalie Jayakody and Ariel Kalil (2002) used the multinomial logit model to study *social fathers*, men who act like a father to a child even though they are not the child's biological father. They used information from nearly 800 African American preschoolers (ages 3 to 6 years old) whose mothers participated in a welfare-to-work program in Georgia in the early 1990s.

Because they anticipated differences between social fathers who had a romantic relationship with the child's mother and those who did not, they examined three categories of their outcome variable: (1) children who had no social father (2) children who had a social father who was the mother's romantic partner, and (3) children who had a social father who was a male relative (typically a grandfather or uncle). For example, the authors anticipated that male relatives would differ from romantic partners because of their longer relationship history with the child and because they would be less likely to be seen as a source of competition for the mother's attention.

To answer their research questions regarding what characteristics predicted a child having no social father, a romantic partner social father, or a male relative social father, Jayakody and Kalil estimated a multinomial logit model. As is the case with a logit model for a dichotomous outcome, predicted probabilities facilitate interpretation of the substantive importance of associations that are statistically significant. Thus, the authors presented not only coefficients from the model (their Table 2 shown in Literature Excerpt 17.1a) but also predicted probabilities in either a table (their Table 3 shown in Literature Excerpt 17.1b) or a figure (their Figure 1 shown in Literature Excerpt 17.1c).

Because the outcome variable had three categories, there are three possible pairwise contrasts among the outcome categories: (1) romantic partner social father versus no social father (2) male relative social father versus no social father, and (3) romantic partner social father versus male relative social father. The authors used characteristics of the child, the mother, and the child's biological father to predict which of these outcome categories each child in the study occupied. As we will discuss below, it is common to choose a reference outcome category in multinomial logit models (similar to the reference category for a set of dummy predictor variables).[1] Jayakody and Kalil used the category of "no social father" as their reference outcome category. As a result, the coefficients in their Table 2 (Literature Excerpt 17.1a) can be interpreted

Literature Excerpt 17.1a

Table 2. Multinomial Logit Results: Correlates of Having a Social Father

	Romantic Partner Social Father		Male Relative Social Father	
	b	SE	b	SE
Constant	−1.02	.432	−.608	.479
Characteristics of the mother				
Never married (divorced or separated = 0)	.150	.219	−.09	.243
High school graduate (no = 0)	−.097	.195	.315	.232
Number of children	−.151	.120	−.287*	.136
Number of moves	.314**	.119	−.163	.141
Excellent or very good health (no = 0)	.132	.085	.060	.098
Had some earnings (no = 0)	−.112	.229	.037	.253
CES-D scale	.004	.009	−.004	.254
Characteristics of the child				
Girl (boy = 0)	−.311	.183	−.199	.209
Age 3 (4–6 = 0)	−.612*	.270	.032	.271
Biological father characteristics				
Lives in same state (no = 0)	−.146	.220	−.485*	.242
Has other child(ren) (no = 0)	.898***	.190	.767***	.216
Gives money (no = 0)	.662**	.246	.382	.294
Absent father involvement	−.495***	.137	−.274	.160

Note: Not having a social father is the comparison group. SE = standard error; CES-D = Center for Epidemiological Studies-Depression.
*p < .05. **p < .01. ***p < .001.

Source: Jayakody, Rukmalie and Ariel Kalil. 2002. "Social Fathering in Low-Income, African American Families with Preschool Children." *Journal of Marriage and Family*, 64: 504–516.

■ Literature Excerpt 17.1b

Table 3. Predicted Probabilities for Multinomial Logit

	Does Not Have a Social Father	Romantic Partner Social Father	Male Relative Social Father
Number of children			
One	0.47	0.32	0.21
Two	0.52	0.30	0.17
Three or more	0.57	0.29	0.14
Number of residential moves			
None	0.50	0.26	0.24
One	0.47	0.34	0.19
Two or more	0.43	0.42	0.15
Age of child			
3	0.55	0.22	0.24
4–6	0.46	0.34	0.20
Biological father characteristics			
Lives in other state	0.43	0.31	0.26
Lives in same state	0.49	0.32	0.19
No other children	0.57	0.25	0.17
Has other child(ren)	0.36	0.40	0.24
Does not give money	0.50	0.30	0.20
Gives money	0.37	0.42	0.21

Source: Jayakody, Rukmalie and Ariel Kalil. 2002. "Social Fathering in Low-Income, African American Families with Preschool Children." *Journal of Marriage and Family,* 64: 504–516.

■ Literature Excerpt 17.1c

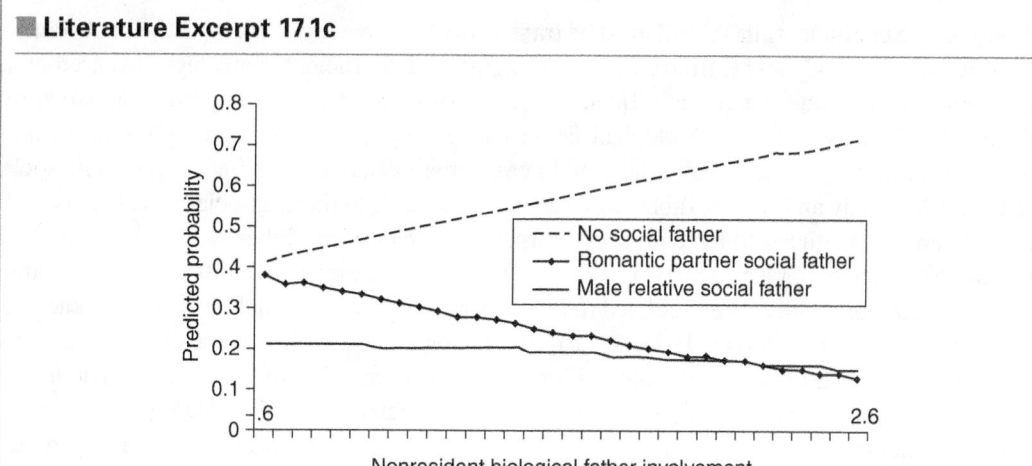

Figure 1 Predicted Probabilities of Having a Social Father by Nonresident Biological Father Involvement

Source: Jayakody, Rukmalie and Ariel Kalil. 2002. "Social Fathering in Low-Income, African American Families with Preschool Children." *Journal of Marriage and Family,* 64: 504–516.

similarly to the logit coefficients that we examined for a dichotomous outcome in Chapter 16, except that we now have two outcome categories shown in the table ("romantic partner social father" and "male relative social father" as labels to the table columns, each analogous to the "success" category in Chapter 16) and one reference outcome category ("no social father" analogous to the "failure" category in Chapter 16, as indicated in the table note which says "Not having a social father is the comparison group").

We can interpret the sign and significance of the coefficients in their Table 2 like we did the coefficients for a dichotomous logit model in Chapter 16. Specifically, based on the asterisks in the first column of numbers of their Table 2 we see that five variables significantly predict whether a child has a social father who is the mother's romantic partner versus no social father. The positive coefficients indicate that children are more likely to have a social father who is romantically involved with the mother than no social father when the mother has moved more often and when the biological father has other children and gives the study child money. The negative coefficients indicate that children are less likely to have a social father who is the mother's romantic partner versus no social father when they are younger (age 3 versus ages 4 to 6) and when the biological father is more involved in their lives.

We can similarly see in the third column of numbers of Jayakody and Kalil's Table 2 that three variables significantly predict whether a child has a social father who is a male relative versus no social father. The positive coefficient with asterisks indicates that (like having a social father who is the mother's romantic partner) children are more likely to have a social father who is a male relative than no social father when their biological father has other children. The negative coefficients with asterisks indicate that children are less likely to have a social father who is a male relative than no social father when their mother has more children and when their biological father lives in the same state.

As noted, the coefficients in Table 2 must be transformed before we can evaluate their substantive significance. Jayakody and Kalil transform the significant coefficients for categorical predictors into predicted probabilities in their Table 3 (Literature Excerpt 17.1b).[2] For example, we know from Table 2 that whether the biological father had other children significantly predicted both having a romantic partner social father and having a male relative social father versus no social father. In Jayakody and Kalil's Table 3, we see the magnitude of these associations. That is, 57% of children are predicted to have no social father if the biological father has no other children versus 36% if the biological father has other children, a difference of over 20 percentage points. Likewise, 25% of children are predicted to have a romantic partner social father if the biological father has no other children versus 40% if the biological father has other children, again a difference of over 20 percentage points. Finally, the difference in predicted percentage is also positive, but smaller—just 7 points—for having a social father who is a male relative based on whether or not the biological father has other children. Specifically, 17% of children are predicted to have a male relative social father if the biological father has no other children versus 24% if the biological father has other children.

The variable *Absent father involvement* was also significant in Table 2 (see again Literature Excerpt 17.1a). Because involvement is a continuous variable (On page 508 of the text, the authors tell us that it is a standardized scale ranging from −0.6 to 2.6 comprising items such as whether the biological father bought things for and spent time with the child), the authors plotted predicted probabilities at various levels of this covariate in their Figure 3 (Literature Excerpt 17.1c). Looking back at their Table 2, recall that this covariate significantly predicted whether children had a romantic partner social father versus no social father but did not significantly predict whether children had a male relative social father versus no social father. Consistent with this result, in the author's Figure 3 (see again Literature Excerpt 17.1c), there is little association between the nonresident biological father's involvement and the predicted probability of occupying the outcome category of "male relative social father" (the solid line in Figure 3). That is, about 20% of children are predicted to have a social father who is a male relative, regardless of the level of involvement of their biological fathers. In contrast, having no social father is positively related to the biological father's involvement (dashed line in the authors' Figure 3) and having a romantic partner social father is negatively related to the biological father's involvement (solid line with diamonds in the authors' Figure 3). More specifically, when the biological father is relatively uninvolved, about 40% of children are predicted to have no social father and to have a social father who is the mother's romantic partner. In contrast, when the biological father is highly involved, less than 20% of children are predicted to have a social father who is a romantic partner whereas about 70% of children are predicted to have no social father.

17.1.2: Mathematical Formulas

We now turn to the details of estimating and interpreting multinomial logit models such as the one just considered in Literature Excerpt 17.1. We will see that it is straightforward to extend the binomial distribution, logit link, and predicted probabilities from the binomial to the multinomial case.

Multinomial Distribution

Although we will not work through a detailed example as we did in Chapter 16, it is useful to recognize that we can write the probability density function for a multinomial distribution that is very similar to the probability density function for the binomial distribution which we considered in Section 16.3.3. The probability density function for the multinomial distribution is defined as follows (Fox 2008; Hoffmann 2004; Larsen and Marx 2006):

$$f\left(n_1, \ldots, n_c \mid \pi_1 \ldots, \pi_c, N\right) = \frac{N!}{n_1! n_2! \ldots n_c!} \pi_1^{n_1} \pi_2^{n_2} \ldots \pi_c^{n_c} \tag{17.1}$$

where $c = 1$ to C, C is the total number of categories, N is the total sample size, n_c is the sample size in category c, and $\sum_{c=1}^{C} n_c = N$.

Equation 17.1 reduces to the probability density function for the binomial distribution that we showed in Equation 16.3 when $C = 2$. That is, we can rewrite the left side of Equation 17.1 as follows for two categories.

$$= \frac{N!}{n_1! n_2!} \pi_1^{n_1} \pi_2^{n_2}$$

Since we define the dichotomous outcome so that each case must fall in one and only one of the two categories (the categories are mutually exclusive and exhaustive), we know that $n_2 = N - n_1$ and $\pi_2 = 1 - \pi_1$. Substituting these values we have:

$$= \frac{N!}{n_1!(N - n_1)!} \pi_1^{n_1} (1 - \pi_1)^{N - n_1}$$

If we further redefine $n_1 = s$ and $\pi_1 = \pi$ then we have:

$$= \frac{N!}{s!(N - s)!} \pi^s (1 - \pi)^{N - s}$$

This multinomial distribution can be used for the random component of a generalized linear model with a multi-category outcome, similar to our use of the binomial distribution for the random component of a generalized linear model with a dichotomous outcome (Fox 2008; Hoffman 2004).

Multinomial Logit Link

We can also extend the logit link to allow for multiple categories.

Recall that in Equation 16.1 we defined the logit link for the dichotomous outcome as follows:

$$\eta = \text{logit}(\pi) = \ln\left(\frac{\pi}{1 - \pi}\right)$$

With only two outcome categories, our discussion was simplified by defining one of the two categories as a success and the other as a failure. Since every case fell into one and only one of these two categories, a failure was the complement of a success and the probability of a failure was one minus the probability of a success.

When we have a nominal outcome with multiple categories, it is still the case that the probabilities must sum to one across all categories, because we define the variable such that every case falls into one and only one of the categories (the categories are still mutually exclusive and exhaustive). But, now we have more than two probabilities, and none are by definition the complement of another.

In the multi-category case, we will use c to index the categories and use C to denote the total number of categories. And, we will place a subscript on each probability to denote to which category it corresponds (e.g., π_1 is the probability of falling into the first category, π_2 is the probability of falling into the second category, and π_c is the probability of falling into the cth category). We can write mathematically the fact that the probabilities must sum to one across all categories as follows: $\sum_{c=1}^{C} \pi_c = 1$.

If we extend the concept of the odds to be the ratio of the probability of any one category to another, then we can imagine writing the log of the odds (logit) for each pair of categories.[3] Consider our example above of families that use one of three types of child care: (1) relative care, (2) family day care, or (3) center care. Then, we could write three different logits to compare each of the three pairs of categories:

Relative care   Vs.   Center care $= \ln\left(\dfrac{\pi_1}{\pi_3}\right)$

Family day care   Vs.   Center care $= \ln\left(\dfrac{\pi_2}{\pi_3}\right)$

Relative care   Vs.   Family day care $= \ln\left(\dfrac{\pi_1}{\pi_2}\right)$

Recall that in Table 16.1 we saw that the log-odds were the same magnitude but opposite in sign for complementary probabilities. For example, the log odds for a probability of success of 0.2 was the same magnitude as the log odds for the probability of success of 0.8, but reversed in sign (-1.3863 and 1.3863). In fact, since we know the probability of a failure is the complement of the probability of the success, we can write the following equation for the dichotomous (or binary logit) case:

$$= \ln\left(\frac{\pi}{1-\pi}\right) + \ln\left(\frac{1-\pi}{\pi}\right) = 0$$

Or, equivalently:

$$\ln\left(\frac{\pi}{1-\pi}\right) = -\ln\left(\frac{1-\pi}{\pi}\right)$$

This equation makes clear to us that if we reverse coded the *outcome* and re-estimated the model, while keeping all the predictor variables the same, we would expect to see coefficients of the same magnitude but opposite in sign.

When our outcome takes on more than two categories, a similar relationship holds (Long 1997).[4,5] That is,

$$\ln\left(\frac{\pi_1}{\pi_3}\right) - \ln\left(\frac{\pi_2}{\pi_3}\right) - \ln\left(\frac{\pi_1}{\pi_2}\right) = 0$$

Or, equivalently:

$$\ln\left(\frac{\pi_1}{\pi_3}\right) - \ln\left(\frac{\pi_2}{\pi_3}\right) = \ln\left(\frac{\pi_1}{\pi_2}\right) \tag{17.2}$$

Because of this relationship, one set of log odds is redundant. In other words, once we know two of the three log odds we can figure out the third. Similar redundancies hold for models with more than three categories.

As a consequence of this redundancy we use one category as a **reference outcome category** when we estimate the multinomial logit model, similar to our using one category as a reference when we create a set of dummy predictor variables.[6] Similar to the terminology we used for dummy predictor variables, we will refer to the outcome categories that we see listed in our output as the **included outcome categories**. Included outcome categories are the outcome categories that will be listed in our SAS and Stata ouput, analogous to our use of the term "included categories" for the dummy variable categories that are shown in our SAS and Stata output.

As with choosing a reference category for a set of dummy variables, which category we use as the outcome reference category is arbitrary in the sense that our choice will not affect the overall fit of the model nor the probabilities predicted from the model. And, similar to what we learned for dummy predictor variables, we can recover contrasts between the included outcome categories from a single estimation of the model. At the same time, because the contrasts with the reference outcome category are what we will see in the default output (and may be the results we want to focus on in our tables) it is useful to choose a reference category with a relatively large subsample size and with conceptual interest in comparison to most of the other categories. We will discuss below how to recover additional contrasts among the included outcome categories; and, in Section 17.3 below we will illustrate some strategies for presenting the results.

We can now show the link for the generalized linear model. Specifically, we equate the log odds for each included outcome category relative to the reference outcome category to the systematic portion of the regression model. For our example above, with the third category as the reference outcome category, we would have:

> ### Box 17.3
>
> The *Spost* commands written for Stata by Long and Freese (2006) include a number of commands that facilitate interpretation of multinomial logit models. In addition to the strategies we discuss below, the `listcoef` command will provide the contrasts between included outcome categories and `mlogplot` will plot odds ratios and discrete change coefficients.

Relative care	Vs.	Center care	$\ln\left(\dfrac{\pi_1}{\pi_3}\right) = \beta_{0,1v3} + \beta_{1,1v3}X$	(17.3)
Family day care	Vs.	Center care	$\ln\left(\dfrac{\pi_2}{\pi_3}\right) = \beta_{0,2v3} + \beta_{1,2v3}X$	(17.4)

Notice that we have added values to the subscripts of the coefficients in the systematic portion of these regression models to indicate the included and reference category. We put these values after the coefficient number, which still is zero for the intercept and ranges from one to k for the k predictor variables. For example, $\beta_{0,1v3}$ is the intercept for the contrast of Category 1 (Relative

Care) to Category 3 (Center Care). And, $\beta_{1,2v3}$ is the coefficient for the predictor variable (X) for the contrast of Category 2 (Family Day Care) to Category 3 (Center Care).

As was the case in the logit model, these coefficients predict the log-odds, and thus they are unlikely to help us evaluate the substantive magnitude of the association (since most of us are unfamiliar with the meaning of various magnitudes of log-odds). That is, $\beta_{1,2v3}$ captures the amount by which the log-odds of being in Category 2 versus Category 3 are expected to change as X increases by one unit. We will see below how to interpret the results in more substantively meaningful ways, using odds ratios and predicted probabilities.

In the default output, only the coefficients for the contrasts of each included outcome category with the reference outcome category are provided. We may also be interested in other contrasts between the included outcome categories. Using Equation 17.2 we can derive the contrasts between the included outcome categories. That is, we already saw that:

$$\ln\left(\frac{\pi_1}{\pi_3}\right) - \ln\left(\frac{\pi_2}{\pi_3}\right) = \ln\left(\frac{\pi_1}{\pi_2}\right)$$

We can substitute into this equation the systematic portions of the regression models shown in Equations 17.3 and 17.4 to show that:

$$\left(\beta_{0,1v3} + \beta_{1,1v3}X\right) - \left(\beta_{0,2v3} + \beta_{1,2v3}X\right) = \ln\left(\frac{\pi_1}{\pi_2}\right)$$

Multiplying the negative term through and then collecting the intercepts and slopes together, we have:

$$\beta_{0,1v3} + \beta_{1,1v3}X - \beta_{0,2v3} + \beta_{1,2v3}X = \ln\left(\frac{\pi_1}{\pi_2}\right)$$

$$\left(\beta_{0,1v3} - \beta_{0,2v3}\right) + \left(\beta_{1,1v3}X - \beta_{1,2v3}X\right) = \ln\left(\frac{\pi_1}{\pi_2}\right) \tag{17.5}$$

$$\left(\beta_{0,1v3} - \beta_{0,2v3}\right) + \left(\beta_{1,1v3} - \beta_{1,2v3}\right)X = \ln\left(\frac{\pi_1}{\pi_2}\right)$$

Thus, for the contrast of Category 1 to Category 2, the intercept is the difference between the intercepts for the contrasts of Category 1 to Category 3 and Category 2 to Category 3. Likewise, for the contrast of Category 1 to Category 2, the slope is the difference between the slopes for the contrasts of Category 1 to Category 3 and Category 2 to Category 3.

As we will see below, we can obtain the coefficients for these contrasts in three ways that are parallel to the three strategies that we used to obtain contrasts between included dummy predicted variables. That is, we can be obtain the contrasts by: (1) re-running the model with a different reference outcome category, (2) using the `test` command (in SAS and Stata), or (3) using the `lincom` command (in Stata).[7]

It is also straightforward to extend the logic we used in Chapter 16 to see that the exponential of the coefficients from a multinomial logit model are odds ratios. Consider Equation 17.3 for example where we had: $\ln\left(\dfrac{\pi_1}{\pi_3}\right) = \beta_{0,1v3} + \beta_{1,1v3}X$. If we take the exponential of both sides of this equation

we have: $\dfrac{\pi_1}{\pi_3} = \exp\left(\beta_{0,1v3} + \beta_{1,1v3}X\right)$. The ratio on the left is the odds of occupying Category 1 versus Category 3. If we increment the predictor X by one we can write a similar equation:

$\dfrac{\pi_1}{\pi_3}\bigg|(X+1) = \exp(\beta_{0,1v3} + \beta_{1,1v3}(X+1))$. Now, as we did in Chapter 16, we can write the ratio

of the odds when X is incremented by one to the odds when X is at its original value and simplify.

$$\frac{\left(\dfrac{\pi_1}{\pi_3}\bigg|X+1\right)}{\left(\dfrac{\pi_1}{\pi_3}\bigg|X\right)} = \frac{\exp(\beta_{0,1v3} + \beta_{1,1v3}(X+1))}{\exp(\beta_{0,1v3} + \beta_{1,1v3}X)}$$

$$= \frac{\exp(\beta_{0,1v3} + \beta_{1,1v3}X + \beta_{1,1v3})}{\exp(\beta_{0,1v3} + \beta_{1,1v3}X)}$$

$$= \frac{\exp(\beta_{0,1v3}) * \exp(\beta_{1,1v3}X) * \exp(\beta_{1,1v3})}{\exp(\beta_{0,1v3}) * \exp(\beta_{1,1v3}X)}$$

$$= \exp(\beta_{1,1v3})$$

As we saw in Chapter 16, the exponential of the coefficient can be referred to as an odds ratio because the left hand side of this equation is the ratio of two odds.

Similar to what we did in Chapter 16, we can again rewrite the final result:

$$\frac{\left(\dfrac{\pi_1}{\pi_3}\bigg|X+1\right)}{\left(\dfrac{\pi_1}{\pi_3}\bigg|X\right)} = \exp(\beta_{1,1v3})$$

as follows:

$$\left(\frac{\pi_1}{\pi_3}\bigg|X+1\right) = \left(\frac{\pi_1}{\pi_3}\bigg|X\right) * \exp(\beta_{1,1v3})$$

And thus it is easy to see why we can interpret $\exp(\beta_{1,1v3})$ as follows:

> "For a one unit increase in X, the odds of occupying Category 1 versus Category 3 are expected to change by a factor of $\exp(\beta_{1,1v3})$, holding any other variables in the model constant."

We can similarly interpret the coefficients for other contrasts. For example, $\exp(\beta_{1,2v3})$ would be interpreted as follows:

> "For a one unit increase in X, the odds of occupying Category 2 versus Category 3 are expected to change by a factor of $\exp(\beta_{1,2v3})$, holding any other variables in the model constant."

As was true for the binary logit model, the advantage of the factor change interpretation in the multinomial logit context is that the factor change does not depend on the starting value of X. This is why we have a simple single sentence interpretation for factor change. As we will see in the next section, the change in probabilities will depend on the starting value of X, especially when the predicted probabilities fall in the more non-linear regions (e.g., below 0.20 or above 0.80 on the cumulative logistic S curve).

Confidence intervals for the odds ratios can also be calculated by exponentiating the bounds of the confidence intervals for the coefficient. We can interpret these intervals as:

> "We are 95% confident that the odds of occupying Category 1 versus Category 3 change by between $\exp(\hat{\beta}_{1,1v3} - 1.96 * \hat{\sigma}_{\hat{\beta}_{1,1v3}})$ and $\exp(\hat{\beta}_{1,1v3} + 1.96 * \hat{\sigma}_{\hat{\beta}_{1,1v3}})$ when X increases by one, holding all other variables constant."

And

> "We are 95% confident that the odds of occupying Category 2 versus Category 3 change by between $\exp(\hat{\beta}_{1,2v3} - 1.96 * \hat{\sigma}_{\hat{\beta}_{1,2v3}})$ and $\exp(\hat{\beta}_{1,2v3} + 1.96 * \hat{\sigma}_{\hat{\beta}_{1,2v3}})$ when X increases by one, holding all other variables constant."

Predicted Probabilities

Recall that in the binary logit model we could predict the probabilities based on the following equation:

$$\hat{\pi} = \frac{\exp(\hat{\beta}_0 + \hat{\beta}_1 X)}{1 + \exp(\hat{\beta}_0 + \hat{\beta}_1 X)} \tag{17.6}$$

A similar equation can be used to predict probabilities based on the multinomial logit model. If the last category, C, is taken as the reference outcome category, then we can write the equation for predicting the probability of any category (c) from a multinomial logit as follows:

$$\hat{\pi}_c = \frac{\exp(\hat{\beta}_{0,cvC} + \hat{\beta}_{1,cvC}X)}{1 + \sum_{c=1}^{C-1} \exp(\hat{\beta}_{0,cvC} + \hat{\beta}_{1,cvC}X)} \tag{17.7}$$

Notice that Equation 17.7 differs from Equation 17.6 in three principal ways. First, the predicted probability has a subscript, c, indicating one of the outcome variable's C categories. Second, the coefficients have a subscript, cvC, indicating the contrast of one of the outcomes to the final category as reference. Third, the second term in the denominator is now a sum across all but one of the categories (from $c=1$ to $C-1$).

Equation 17.7 assumes that the coefficients for the reference outcome category are set to zero (that is why the first term in the denominator is a one). We could use other constraints, but the choice will not affect the probabilities predicted by the model and zero for the reference outcome category's coefficients is commonly used (Long 1997: 153). With this assumption, the predicted probability for the reference outcome category becomes:

$$\hat{\pi}_{c=C} = \frac{\exp(0 + 0 * X)}{1 + \sum_{c=1}^{C-1} \exp(\hat{\beta}_{0,cvC} + \hat{\beta}_{1,cvC}X)} = \frac{1}{1 + \sum_{c=1}^{C-1} \exp(\hat{\beta}_{0,cvC} + \hat{\beta}_{1,cvC}X)}$$

since $\exp(0) = 1$.

Although we have written the formulas in this section with the final category omitted, which category we choose to be this reference is arbitrary (indeed, given the outcome is nominal, which category is the "last" category is arbitrary). The predicted probabilities will not depend on which category is used as the reference outcome category (and as noted above, we can retrieve the coefficients for contrasts among the included outcome categories from a single estimation).

17.1.3: Strengths and Limitations

The multinomial logit model is well suited for nominal data. However, the number of possible pairwise comparisons increases quickly as the number of outcome categories increases. For three categories, there are three pairwise comparisons (i.e., Category 1 vs. Category 2; Category 1 vs. Category 3; and, Category 2 vs. Category 3). For four categories, there are six pairwise comparisons (i.e., Category 1 vs. Category 2; Category 1 vs. Category 3; Category 1 vs. Category 4; Category 2 vs. Category 3; Category 2 vs. Category 4; and Category 3 vs. Category 4). For five, there are 10. For six, there are 15. And so on.[8] It can become challenging to comprehend and present the results with so many categories.[9]

Ultimately, the number of categories also complicates conceptualization, as we ideally will have a basis for expecting contrasts between pairs of categories based on theory or prior research. For example, in our child care example, we could further subdivide the outcome categories, for example subdividing centers into those located in schools, those located in churches, those run as non-profit organizations, and those run as private enterprises. We could likewise separate relative caregivers into different types of relatives (e.g., partners versus grandparents versus aunts/uncles, etc). However, we would ideally have a conceptual rationale for doing so. For instance, if we were examining parental choices, we might expect highly religious parents to choose church-based centers. Or, we might expect parents who emphasize the importance of early childhood experiences in getting children ready for school to choose school-based settings. Or, we might expect couples who emphasize exclusive parental care of children to choose partners over other relatives as caregivers. However, if our conceptual model emphasized differences between parents who prefer home-based to other care settings and parents who prefer relatives to non-relatives, then our original three categories suffice.

There are statistical tests that you can use to help justify combining categories. For example, if no predictor variables significantly affect the odds of being in one category versus another, then those two categories might be combined (Caudill 2000; Long 1997: 162–163). The *Wald* χ^2 and *LR* χ^2 tests introduced in Chapter 16 can be used to test these hypotheses, as we demonstrate below. However, as we saw in Chapter 12 for dummy predictor variables, it is possible to obtain empirical results from such tests that do not point in a clear direction (for example, we might find empirical evidence that Category 1 and Category 2 can be combined, but also that only Category 1 and Category 3 could be combined but not Category 2 and Category 3). When we rely on such empirical justification for collapsing categories, we are also vulnerable to combining categories based on sample evidence when sample sizes are small (even if the categories are conceptually quite distinct) or not combining categories based on sample evidence when sample sizes are large (even if the categories are conceptually quite similar and substantive predictions for both categories based on the model are quite similar). Thus, in advance of estimating models (and in advance of selecting secondary data or collecting primary data) we encourage you to work at thinking through the conceptual rationale for defining your outcomes as you do (have you covered all of the relevant choices for your application) and for selecting your predictors (how and why do you expect each predictor to relate to contrasts between each pair of outcomes).

The multinomial logit model makes an assumption known as the **independence of irrelevant alternatives** (sometimes referred to as the **IIA assumption**). Hausman and McFadden (1984: 1221) define the assumption as follows: "the ratio of the probabilities of choosing any two alternatives is independent of the attributes or the availability of a third alternative." They use a generalized specification test developed by Hausman to test this assumption. The test is implemented by first estimating the full model with all outcome categories, then re-estimating the model with one of the outcome categories excluded, and finally comparing the results with a chi-square statistic. This statistic can sometimes be negative, a result that sometimes is taken as evidence that the assumption holds (Hausman and McFadden 1984; Long and Freese 2005; Wills 1987).

Although this test is still used in applications, Cheng and Long (2007) concluded that the Hausman test (and other common tests of the IIA assumption) is "unsatisfactory for applied work" (598). They recommend defining outcome categories conceptually so that they meet the IIA assumption as stated by McFadden (1974): "cases where the outcome categories 'can plausibly be assumed to be distinct and weighed independently in the eyes of each decision maker.' " (Cheng and Long 2007: 598). Again, this suggests the importance of using theory (and prior research) to guide the definition of the outcome categories (although some may disagree about what are "plausibly" distinct and independent outcomes).

17.1.4: NSFH Example

We will continue with the NSFH distance example that we used in Chapter 16, with distance from the mother as the outcome, the adult respondent's earnings as our key predictor, and other controls in the model. To estimate a multinomial logit model we collapse the *g1miles* outcome variable into three categories that might be conceptually interesting in an application, distinguishing those who live *within an hour or so drive* (1 to 45 miles), *within about a day's drive* (46 to 500 miles) and *farther than a day's drive* (greater than 500 miles) from the mother.

This three category outcome variable can be created using the general SAS and Stata commands for variable creation (and of course, in SAS, the new variable must be created within the data step).

SAS	Stata
| ```
if g1miles>0 & g1miles<=45 then g1milesN=23;
if g1miles>45 & g1miles<=500 then g1milesN=273;
if g1miles>500 & g1miles<=9000 then g1milesN=1500;
``` | ```
generate g1milesN=23 if g1miles>0 & g1miles<=45
replace g1milesN=273 if g1miles>45 & g1miles <=500
replace g1milesN=1500 if g1miles>500 & g1miles<=9000
``` |

These categories each have sizable sub-samples. Over 3,000 of the adults in the NSFH live within 45 minutes of their mothers, over 1,000 live between 46 and 500 miles of their mother, and nearly 900 live between 501 and 9000 miles of their mothers.

■ Box 17.4

We use the approximate midpoint of the lower two categories as the values of our categories: "23" as the midpoint of 0 to 45 and "273" as the midpoint of 46 to 500. For the highest category, we used the approximate average for cases who live more than 500 miles from their mothers, which is "1500" miles. We use these values, rather than 1, 2, and 3, to reinforce the fact that the values themselves are arbitrary. We simply need three separate values to represent the three separate categories. We have not covered in this book the commands to label the values with words to represent the meaning of the category (e.g., "within 45 miles"), although doing so would also facilitate interpretation of the output (see Acock 2008; Delwiche and Slaughter 2003).

Estimation in SAS and Stata

Stata's dedicated command to estimate a multinomial logit model is called `mlogit`. Its syntax is similar to Stata's other regression commands, although multinomial logit has an additional option called `baseout` which lets us specify which outcome category should be used as the reference. Displays B.17.1 and B.17.2 show the results of this command for two different choices of the reference outcome category. In Display B.17.1, we used the smallest outcome category ("23" representing the adults who live 0 to 45 miles from their mother). In Display B.17.2 we used the largest outcome category ("1500" representing the adults who live 501 to 9000 miles from their mother).

Notice that Stata indicates which category is the base outcome and then lists a separate set of results for each included outcome category. That is, the coefficients for each predictor variable and the intercept are first listed for one included outcome category and then listed for the second included outcome category. Specifically, in the Stata output of Display B.17.1, the category "23" is indicated as the base outcome and coefficients for the contrasts between each included outcome category ("273" and "1500") and that reference outcome category are shown. Likewise, in the Stata output of Display B.17.2, the category "1500" is indicated as the base outcome and coefficients for the contrasts between each included outcome category ("23" and "273") and that reference outcome category are shown.

Displays B.17.1 and B.17.2 also show how to estimate the multinomial logit model in SAS. We use the `proc logistic` command that we used in Chapter 16 for a binary logit model, but add the option `/link=glogit` on the model statement and the option `ref="<value>"` to indicate the reference category (`<value>` is one of the outcome categories, such as `ref="23"` in Display B.17.1 and `ref="1500"` in Display B.17.2). Notice that SAS lists the results differently than Stata. Whereas Stata grouped the intercept and coefficients together for each included outcome category, SAS lists the coefficients for the two included outcome categories together for each predictor variable. But, the coefficients match when we line them up.

Specifically, SAS lists the predictor variables in the first column and the included outcome categories in the second column (alternating between "1500" and "273" in Display B.17.1 and alternating between "273" and "23" in Display B.17.2). Looking at the two coefficients for *g2earn10000* in the SAS output of Display B.17.1, we see that each matches a coefficient in the Stata output of Display B.171. In SAS, the coefficient for *g2earn10000* next to the included outcome category of "1500" is 0.0272; this corresponds to the coefficient for *g2earn10000* in Stata in Display B.17.1 is found in the "1500" section, which has a value of 0.0272359. Similarly, in SAS in Display B.17.1, the coefficient for *g2earn10000* next to the included outcome category of "273" is 0.0351; This corresponds to the coefficient for *g2earn10000* in Stata's "273" section, which is 0.0351328.

Across Displays B.17.1 and B.17.2, we obtain the coefficients for all three contrasts among the three outcome categories. One set of contrasts is included in both sets of output and one set of contrasts is unique to each set of output. That is, the coefficients for the contrasts between the categories "23" and "1500" are shown in both sets of output: "1500" versus the base of "23" in Display B.17.1 and "23" versus the base of "1500" in Display B.17.2. The coefficients in these results are the same magnitude but reversed in sign. For example, the coefficient for *g2earn10000* in the "1500" section (Stata) or row (SAS) is 0.0272 of Display B.17.1 (with rounding); and, it is −0.0272 in the "23" section (Stata) or row (SAS) of Display B.17.2 (with rounding). In Display B.17.1, we also obtain the coefficients for the contrast between the outcome categories of "273" and "23." And, in Display B.17.2, we also obtain the contrasts between the outcome categories of "273" and "1500."

As noted above, there are several ways in which we can obtain contrasts between included categories that are not shown in default output. That is, in addition to re-estimating the model with a different reference outcome category (as we illustrated in Displays B.17.1 and B.17.2) we could have just estimated one of the two models (either the one shown in Display B.17.1 or Display B.17.2) and then (1) hand-calculated the other contrasts and obtained their significance with SAS or Stata's `test` command or (2) used Stata's `lincom` command to calculate the contrast and its significance. In the case of the multinomial logit model, it may be simpler to re-estimate the model with a different reference category, especially when a model has numerous predictors, rather than to write the `test` or `lincom` commands for each of the contrasts that must be conducted.[10] But, it is instructive to make these calculations at least once, to solidify our understanding of the relationship among the coefficients for each pair of contrasts and our recognition that which outcome category we use as a reference is arbitrary.

As an illustration, we calculated by hand the coefficient for the *g2earn10000* variable for the contrast between the included outcome categories shown in Display B.17.1. We then asked SAS and Stata to test the significance of this contrast with the `test` command (which calculates a *Wald* χ^2 value and associated *p*-value following a multinomial logit model) and we asked Stata to show the coefficient, its standard error, and its *Z*-value and *p*-value with the `lincom` command. Because the test we are conducting has one degree of freedom (reflecting the one equals sign in the null hypothesis), the *Wald* χ^2 should equal the square of the *Z*-value and the *p*-values should be the same (as we discussed in Chapter 15).

Table 17.1 (next page) shows the hand calculation and the syntax and results. Notice that because we have a separate coefficient for each included category for each predictor, we need to reference both the outcome category and the predictor in these commands. In Stata, we put the value that represents the outcome category in square brackets in front of the variable name (e.g., `[273] g2earn10000` for the coefficient of the earnings variable for category "273"; `[1500] g2earn10000` for the coefficient of the earnings variable for category "1500"). In SAS, we list the value that represents the outcome category at the end of the variable name, following the underscore (e.g., `g2earn10000_273` for the coefficient of the earnings variable for category "273"; `g2earn10000_1500` for the coefficient of the earnings variable for category "1500").

As shown in Equation 17.5, subtracting the coefficients for *g2earn10000* that are listed for the two included outcome categories in Display B.17.1 provides the coefficient for the contrast between the two included outcome categories. Note that we put the coefficient from the "1500" section on the right in the subtraction so that it will be the new reference outcome category.[11] Thus, the result matches the coefficient for *g2earn10000* for the "273" included outcome category of Display B.17.2 (0.00790).

■ Table 17.1: Coefficient for *g2earn10000* for the Contrast between Included Outcome Categories Shown in Display B.17.1

Hypotheses
$H_o: (\beta_{g2earn10000,273\,v23} - \beta_{g2earn10000,1500\,v23}) = 0$
$H_a: (\beta_{g2earn10000,273\,v23} - \beta_{g2earn10000,1500\,v23}) \neq 0$

Hand Calculation

$0.0351 - 0.0272 = .0079$

Stata Calculations

test **command**	Syntax	`test [273]g2earn10000=[1500]g2earn10000`

	Results	`(1)  [273]g2earn10000 - [1500]g2earn10000 = 0`
		`        chi2( 1) =    0.57`
		`     Prob > chi2 =    0.4518`

lincom **command**	Syntax	`lincom [273]g2earn10000 - [1500]g2earn10000`
	Results	`(1)  [273]g2earn10000 - [1500]g2earn10000 = 0`

```
g1milesN |  Coef.        Std. Err.   z          P>|z|
-------- +-------------------------------------------
(1)      |  .0078969     .0104959    0.75       0.452
```

SAS Calculations

test **command**	Syntax	`test g2earn10000_273=g2earn10000_1500;`
	Results	

Linear Hypotheses Testing Results			
Label	Wald Chi-Square	DF	Pr > ChiSq
Test 1	0.5661	1	0.4518

The test of our null hypothesis can be evaluated with SAS and Stata's `test` command output. These results both give a *Wald χ^2* value that rounds to 0.57 (0.5661 in SAS) with the same *p*-value (of 0.4518). Thus, we fail to reject the null hypothesis and conclude that the coefficients for *g2earn10000* for the two included outcome categories in Display B.17.1 do not differ significantly from each other. This means that, the chance of being in outcome category "273" versus "1500" does not depend on earnings, controlling for the other variables in the model. This is what we see explicitly in Display B.17.2 where we can read the coefficient of *g2earn10000* for the contrast of the included category "273" versus the reference category of "1500" directly off the output. Consistent with the `test` command results, the *p*-value for *g2earn10000* in the "273" section (Stata) or row (SAS) is 0.4518 (0.452 with rounding in Stata).

Especially if we needed to calculate many contrasts between included outcome categories, doing so by hand is time-consuming and error ridden (not only because we may make a mistake in reading the coefficients from the output or in plugging the values into our calculator but also because of rounding error due to our use of the rounded values shown in the SAS and Stata output). Stata's `lincom` command (shown in Table 17.1) avoids these problems, because it will calculate all the information we need for each contrast, including the value of the coefficient as well as its standard error (0.0104959), the Z-value ($(0.0078969 - 0)/0.0104959 = .7523795$), and p-value (0.452). These results match the results shown for *g2earn10000* in the "273" outcome category section of the Stata output of Display B.17.2, emphasizing that the results for all contrasts among outcome categories can be obtained from a single estimation. Note also that we can confirm that the chi-squared statistic shown from the `test` command and the Z-statistic shown from the `lincom` command are testing the same hypothesis by showing that the chi-square is equal to the Z-value squared ($.7523795 * .7523795 = 0.566$) and the p-values are the same (0.452 with rounding).

We could repeat the `lincom` command for every predictor variable and the intercept in order to obtain the complete set of results for the contrast of "273" with "1500" based just on the single estimation shown Display B.17.1. However, with modern computing speed, in most cases it will be simpler to repeat the `mlogit` command with a different base outcome, as we do in Display B.17.2.

Interpretation

As noted above, additional work is needed to move our interpretation of the results beyond the sign and significance of the coefficients. We begin in this section by considering the independence of irrelevant alternatives (IIA) assumption and by testing whether there is statistical evidence to collapse any of the outcome categories, although as noted above, there is debate about whether and how to use these tests and we recommend using them in conjunction with a conceptual rationale for whether the outcome categories fully encompass the set of relevant and distinct choices for your application. We then provide examples of requesting these tests from SAS and Stata and interpreting using odds ratios, predicted probabilities, and discrete change.

■ Box 17.5

Although calculating the odds ratios, predicted probabilities, and discrete change for numerous outcomes and predictors is possible with the commands we present in this chapter, interpretation is complicated in the multinomial logit context by the sheer volume of results. If you use the multinomial logit model in applications, especially with many outcome categories and numerous predictor variables, you may want to build on what you learn in this chapter by consulting sources such as Fox and Andersen (2006), Liao (1994), Long (1997), and Long and Freese (2006).

Hausman Test

In Stata, Long and Freese's `mlogtest` command with the `hausman` option will test the IIA assumption after a multinomial logit model has been conducted. As of this writing, SAS's `proc logistic` command did not have a test for the IIA assumption.[12]

Display B.17.3 shows how to use the Stata command to request the test after we specify a multinomial logit model; we repeated this test three times, with each of the three outcome

---

■ Box 17.6

The IIA assumption can be tested with a macro written for another SAS procedure, proc mdc, where "mdc" stands for multinomial discrete test and allows for a number of additional models for multi-category outcomes to be tested. The Hausman test is implemented as a macro rather than as a built-in SAS command. Given recent concerns about the Hausman test (see again Cheng and Long 2007), given that implementing the test in SAS requires introducing a new command and complex macro that will typically require some reformatting of your data, we do not include it in the book. A SAS program called "ExampleIIA.sas" is available on the course web site that illustrates how to use the command and macro with the NSFH distance example.

---

categories as the reference. For each model, two chi-square values are listed, one for each of the included outcome categories. Because each outcome category is included in two of the three multinomial logits, each outcome category is listed twice. As noted in the Stata output, the null hypothesis is that the odds for the listed included outcome category versus the reference outcome category are independent of the other categories. For example, there is evidence that the IIA assumption holds for the category "23." The Chi-square value of 0.958 has a *p*-value of 1.00, so we fail to reject the null hypothesis.

The other two outcome categories have negative chi-square values (−9.994 for outcome category "273" and −8.502 for outcome category "1500"). As noted above, this is not an uncommon result. Although it is sometimes taken as evidence that the IIA assumption is not violated, Cheng and Long (2007) argue that, generally, the Hausman test (and other IIA tests) is not useful in part due to the fact that such negative results can occur in applied contexts.

Without guidance from empirical results, we must evaluate the IIA assumption conceptually, and argue that the categories are "distinct" and can be "weighed independently" by decision-makers. In our case, we would need to argue that adults are able to make choices between living within an hour or so drive (1 to 45 miles) versus a day's drive (46 to 500 miles) from the mother independently from their decision to live farther than a day's drive (greater than 500 miles). Of course such an argument is hard to definitively make based just on conceptual grounds. We will return in the final "Putting it All Together" section of this chapter to a summary of results across our NSFH distance example from various model specifications, which will help us put this assumption in context.

Combining Categories

The Long and Freese mlogtest command can also be used to test whether there is empirical evidence for combining outcome categories. The *Wald* χ^2 version of the test is requested with the combine option. The $LR\chi^2$ test is requested with the lrcomb option. In SAS, we can request the *Wald* χ^2 version of the test using the SAS test command.

Display B.17.4 shows our use of these commands in our NSFH distance example. As noted in the Stata output, the null hypothesis is that there is evidence that the two outcomes can be combined because all of the coefficients associated with the contrast between the particular pair of outcome categories is zero. In SAS, our code shows explicitly that we are conducting a joint test of the difference between the coefficients for each pair of outcome categories. In the first SAS test command shown in Display B.17.4, we explicitly list the difference between coefficients for the two included categories (e.g., g1yrschl_23-g1yrschl_273, sqg1yrschl_23-sqg1yrschl_273 and so on for each predictor variable). In the second and third SAS test commands in Display B.17.4, we subtract zero from the coefficient of each included category since these coefficients are already relative to the reference outcome category (e.g., g1yrschl_23-0, sqg1yrschl_23-0 and so on for each predictor variable in the second test command; g1yrschl_273-0, sqg1yrschl_273-0 and so on for each predictor variable in the third test command). Because there is one difference for each of our 14 predictor variables, the degrees of freedom for the test should be 14, which is what we see in the output.

The output also shows us that the null hypothesis that these differences in coefficients for all predictor variables are zero can be rejected for all pairs of outcomes based on both the *Wald* χ^2 and the $LR\chi^2$. The largest *p*-value lists is 0.010 (with rounding) and thus all values are less than an alpha of .05. For example, in both SAS and Stata, for the contrast of category "23" with category "273" the *Wald* χ^2 is 131.046 with 14 degrees of freedom. Because the *p*-value of 0.000 is less than an alpha of 0.05 we reject the null hypothesis that the categories can be combined. Similarly, the $LR\chi^2$ in Stata for this same contrast is 140.233 with 14 degrees of freedom and a *p*-value of 0.000.

These results provide empirical evidence for retaining all three outcome categories in our analyses. As noted above, we also encourage you to think conceptually about the categories. In our case, we might argue that it is plausible that the correlates of a decision to move "far" away (farther than a day's drive from the mother) versus stay "close" (within an hour's drive of the mother) might differ from correlates of a decision to move "mid-way" (more than an hour but within a day's drive of the mother) versus staying "close" (within an hour's drive of the mother).

Odds Ratios

We can add the option rrr following our list of independent variables in Stata to request odds ratios.[13] If we want to see both the coefficients and the odds ratios, we can ask Stata to present the results of the most recently estimated model with odds ratios by repeating the mlogit command with the rrr option but no variables listed (i.e., mlogit, rrr). This syntax and the results are shown in Display B.17.5 and Display B.17.6. In SAS, the odds ratios are included in the default output.

We will use the coefficients for the *g2earn10000* variable to verify the calculation of these odds ratios and to illustrate their interpretation. For example, the odds ratio for the included outcome category in the "273" section (Stata) or row (SAS) in Display B.17.5 was calculated by taking the exponential of the corresponding coefficient in Display B.17.1. That is exp(.0351) = 1.036 which matches the value shown in Display B.17.5, within rounding. We can interpret this odds ratio as: "For a $10,000 increase in annual earnings, the odds of the adult living within a day's drive ("273") versus within an hour's drive ("23") of the mother are expected to change by a factor of 1.04 holding constant the mother's schooling and age and the respondent's race-ethnicity, gender, age, and number of brothers and sisters." Likewise, we can verify the calculation of the odds ratio of 0.973 for the included outcome category in the "23" section (Stata) or row (SAS) of Display B.17.6 is exp(−.0272) = .973. We interpret this result as follows: "For a $10,000 increase in annual earnings, the odds of the adult living more than a day's drive ("1500") versus living within an hour's drive ("23") of the mother are expected to change by a factor of 0.97, holding constant the mother's schooling and age and the respondent's race-ethnicity, gender, age, and number of brothers and sisters." We can also find the odds ratio for the contrast between category "273" and "1500" in Display B.17.6. Looking back to Display B.17.2 the coefficient for *g2earn10000* was 0.0079 and exp(0.0079) = 1.0079 matches the results shown in the "273" section (Stata) or row (SAS) of Display B.17.6, within rounding. We interpret this result as follows: "For a $10,000 increase in annual earnings, the odds of the adult living within a day's drive ("273") versus living more than a day's drive ("1500") of the mother are expected to change by a factor of 1.008, holding constant the mother's schooling and age and the respondent's race-ethnicity, gender, age, and number of brothers and sisters."

We can also use the confidence intervals shown in Displays B.17.5 and B.17.6 to interpret the results with confidence intervals rather than as point estimates. For example, the confidence interval bounds in Display B.17.5 for the *g2earn10000* variable in the "273" section (Stata) or row (SAS) are 1.015 and 1.057. Thus, we can say: "We are 95% confident that the odds of the adult living within a day's drive ("273") versus within an hour's drive ("23") change by between 1.015 and 1.057 when annual earnings increases by $10,000, holding constant the mother's schooling and age and the respondent's race-ethnicity, gender, age, and number of brothers and sisters."

Predicted Probabilities

Stata's `margins` command and SAS's `score` command can be implemented to calculate predicted probabilities for the multinomial logit model similar to the approach we took in Chapter 16. In Stata, we can also use the `prchange` command that we introduced in Chapter 16.[14] Of course, now for any set of values we choose for the predictors we can calculate three different predicted probabilities: one the predicted probability of occupying the first category ("23"), another the predicted probability of occupying the second category ("273"), and the third the predicted probability of occupying the third category ("1500"). In Stata's margins command, we can request each outcome category with the option `predict(outcome(<value>))` where we substitute the appropriate category value for `<value>`. In SAS, the `score` command will calculate a predicted probability for every outcome category, using the value that represents the category in the default variable name (e.g., *p_23* represents category "23," *p_273* represents category "273," and *p_1500* represents category "1500").

Display B.17.7 shows our request for predicted probabilities of occupying each category when *g2earn10000* is zero with the rest of the predictors held at their mean values, rounded to integers so that they represent possible values on each variable (this is the "rounded average then predict" approach introduced in Chapter 16; The other approaches discussed in Chapter 16, including "predict then average" and "ideal types" could also be used).[15] As in Chapter 16, for Stata, we show the full results for the first prediction and the brief results with `noatlegend` for the second and third predictions. In both SAS and Stata, in the first page of Display B.17.7, we see that the predicted probability of occupying category "23" (that is living within within an hour's drive of the mother) is .6534 for a 34-year-old white female who has no earnings, less than four sisters, one brother, and has a mother who is 60 years old and has 11 years of schooling (see covariate levels in the at option). A similar adult has a predicted probability of .2218 of living within a day's drive of the mother (category "273"). And, a similar adult has a predicted probability of .1248 of living more than a day's drive of the mother. Note that these three predicted probabilities sum to one, as expected (.6534 + .2218 + .1248 = 1). The second and third pages of Display B.17.7 show similar results but based on earnings of $5,000 and $15,000.

As we discussed in Chapter 16, it is often helpful to present the predicted probabilities in a table or graph for easier interpretation. Display H.17.1 uses Excel to do so, for the three sets of values calculated in Display B.17.7 and Display B.17.8 as well as additional levels of earnings through $75,000. In Display H.17.1, the line plotting the predicted probability of living between 46 and 500 miles of the mother (farther than an hour but within a day's drive) is shown with triangle markers. The line for the predicted probability of living between 501 and 9000 miles of the mother (farther than a day's drive) is drawn with diamonds. And, the line for the predicted probabilities of living within 45 miles (less than an hour's drive) is drawn with squares.

The results show that adults are most likely to live within an hour of the mother (line with square markers in Display H.17.1; at least 60% are predicted to live 0 to 45 miles from the mother). Around one-quarter live farther than an hour but within a day's drive (triangle markers in Display H.17.1; 22 to 26 percent live between 46 and 500 miles away from the mother). And, just over 10% live farther than a day's drive (12 to 14 percent live between 501 and 9000 miles away).

Discrete Change

The differences in predicted probabilities shown in Display H.17.1 are measures of discrete change. For example, if we use the term "typical" to represent an adult with the rounded mean values used in our predictions, then we could say that the difference in predicted probabilities between those who live within an hour (top line with square markers) versus those who live farther but still within a day's drive (middle line with triangle markers) is about ten percentage points smaller among typical adults with earnings of $75,000 per year versus those with no earnings (0.59660 − 0.26356 = .33304 as opposed to 0.65336 − 0.22178 = .43159). The difference in the two lower lines in Display H.17.1 widens, although more modestly. The difference is about 12 percentage points for adults who earn $75,000 per year (0.26356 − 0.1398333 = .1237267) versus about 10 percentage points for adults who earn $0 per year (0.22178 − 0.1248455 = .0969345).

We also asked Excel to calculate the discrete changes for each $10,000 increment in annual earnings listed in Display H.17.1. The lines in the graph in Display H.17.1 look quite linear, consistent with the similar amounts of discrete change in predicted probabilities for a $10,000 increment in earnings for the typical adult, regardless of starting income level. Consistent with the slight widening of the distance between the two bottom lines in the graph in Display H.17.1, and the fact that the line with triangles looks somewhat steeper than the line with diamonds, the discrete change for each $10,000 increment in earnings for the typical adult is larger for living more than an hour but within a day's drive (triangles) versus more than a day's drive (diamonds;

nearly 0.006 versus 0.002). The sign of the discrete change for the top line (squares) is negative, consistent with its downward slope, and the magnitude of the discrete change for the top line is even greater than the bottom two lines (nearly -0.008), reflecting its somewhat greater steepness.

The Spost `prchange` command will also calculate discrete change for us. Display B.17.8 shows the results. We bolded the results for the *g2earn10000* variable. We also bolded the mean (3.07057) and standard deviation (3.74956) of earnings shown in the output. The results show that as earnings increases from about $12,000 ((3.07057 $-$ 0.5 * 3.74956) = 1.19579) to about $50,000 ((3.07057 + 0.5 * 3.74956) = 4.94535) an adult with average characteristics is predicted to be three percentage points (.60220402 $-$ .63054317 = $-$.02833915) less likely to live within an hour of the mother. Likewise, for this same change, the average adult would be expected to be two percentage points more likely to live within a day's drive of the mother and about one percentage point more likely to live more than a day's drive from the mother.

Overall, the substantive size of the significant association between earnings and distance from the mother still seems modest in the multinomial logit context as was true for the linear and binary logit models which we considered earlier. We now turn to the ordered logit model, which provides us with the final model we will consider in detail in this text and the final approach we will take to modeling our NSFH distance example.

17.2: ORDERED LOGIT

A multinomial logit model could be used with an ordinal outcome variable. However, as we noted above, the multinomial logit model can become unwieldy as the number of outcome categories increases. And, if the covariates have a similar effect for each set of adjacent pairwise contrasts, then we can more efficiently estimate a model with a single coefficient for each covariate. This model is the ordered logit model.

17.2.1: Literature Excerpt

Shannon Davis and Lisa Pearce use the national Children of the NLSY79 data set to examine how adolescents' egalitarian work-gender attitudes predict their expectations for how much schooling they will complete. Because educational expectations were measured with three ordered categories in their data set: (1) expect to attend only high school, (2) expect to attend college, and (3) expect to attend graduate or professional school, the authors used an ordered logit model to examine their hypotheses. A central hypothesis in their study is that adolescents with more egalitarian work-gender attitudes will expect to complete more schooling, and that this association will be stronger for girls than for boys.

The authors present odds ratios based on their ordered logit model in their Table 2 (see Literature Excerpt 17.2a). Similar to the binary and multinomial logit models, the odds ratio in the ordered logit model is calculated as the exponential of the estimated coefficient from the systematic portion of the model. Although we will have more to say below about how to precisely interpret these odds ratios, for now we can use our familiar interpretation of the direction of association. That is, an odds ratio greater than 1 represents a positive association and an odds ratio less than 1 represents a negative association. The three variables relevant to the authors' central hypotheses are in the first three rows of their Table 2 (*Work-family gender ideology, Male*, and *Work-Family Gender Ideology X Male*). Note that their measure of *work-family gender ideology* is coded so that higher score reflect more egalitarian attitudes. To test their hypothesis of moderation, Model 3 in the final column of the table adds the interaction between work-family gender ideology and gender. The results show that there is an interaction between work-family gender ideology and gender, as expected (asterisks on odds ratio of 0.56). And, the direction of this association is consistent with the authors' expectations. Since the dummy for gender is coded so that males are indicated with a *1* and females are indicated with a *0*, we see that *Work-family gender ideology* is significantly positively associated with educational expectations for girls (asterisks on the odds ratio of 2.74), and that this association is weaker for adolescent boys (since the interaction *Work-family gender ideology X Male* of 0.56 is less than 1).

To help us better interpret the substantive meaning of this interaction, the authors' Figure 2 (Literature Excerpt 17.2b) plots the predicted probabilities based on the adolescents' gender and their work-family gender ideology scores. The authors used an "ideal type" approach to the predictions, and the table notes indicate what values they chose to hold constant the covariates.

▪ Literature Excerpt 17.2a

Table 2.   Ordered Logistic Regression of Educational Expectations ($N = 1,419$)

	Model 1	Model 2	Model 3
Work-family gender ideology	—	2.08***	2.74***
		(0.15)	(0.20)
Male	0.87	1.07	6.20*
	(0.11)	(0.12)	(0.86)
Work-Family Gender Ideology X Male	—	—	0.56*
			(0.28)
Race/ethnicity[a]			
Black	0.86	0.84	0.84
	(0.12)	(0.12)	(0.13)
Other race/ethnicity	0.68*	0.68*	0.67*
	(0.16)	(0.16)	(0.16)
Mother's education[b]			
Less than high school	0.70*	0.74	0.73
	(0.17)	(0.17)	(0.17)
Some college	1.74***	1.70***	1.69***
	(0.14)	(0.14)	(0.14)
Father's education[b]			
Less than high school	0.80	0.79	0.79
	(0.17)	(0.17)	(0.17)
Some college	1.17	1.21	1.23
	(0.16)	(0.16)	(0.16)

Missing	0.89	0.87	0.88
	(0.14)	(0.14)	(0.14)
Family income (logged)	1.00	1.00	1.00
	(0.01)	(0.01)	(0.01)
Family structure[c]			
Two-parent stepfamily	0.92	0.86	0.87
	(0.16)	(0.17)	(0.17)
Mother only	0.74*	0.70*	0.71*
	(0.14)	(0.14)	(0.14)
Other family type	0.71	0.68	0.69
	(0.21)	(0.21)	(0.21)
Mother currently employed	1.12	1.04	1.03
	(0.14)	(0.14)	(0.14)
Mother's expectations	1.39***	1.37***	1.37***
	(0.06)	(0.06)	(0.06)
GPA	1.22***	1.22***	1.22***
	(0.03)	(0.03)	(0.03)
GPA missing	0.82	0.86	0.85
	(0.13)	(0.13)	(0.13)
Self-esteem	2.19***	1.82***	1.82***
	(0.14)	(0.15)	(0.15)
Religious affiliation[d]			
Mainline Protestant	1.51*	1.44	1.43
	(0.20)	(0.20)	(0.20)
Other Protestant	0.89	0.90	0.89
	(0.20)	(0.20)	(0.20)
Catholic	1.06	1.01	1.02
	(0.15)	(0.15)	(0.16)
Other religion	1.22	1.19	1.23
	(0.20)	(0.21)	(0.21)
No religion	0.78	0.78	0.79
	(0.18)	(0.18)	(0.18)
Religious service attendance	1.07*	1.07*	1.07*
	(0.03)	(0.03)	(0.03)
Constant (expect to attend college)	4.42	6.04	6.90
Constant (expect to attend graduate / professional school)	7.09	8.75	9.63
Pseudo-R^2	.1317	.1409	.1424

Note: Values are odds ratios (standard errors). Standard errors are robust estimates clustered by family.
[a]Reference category is White.
[b]Reference category is high school graduate.
[c]Reference category is two biological parent household.
[d]Reference category is conservative Protestant.
*$p < .05$; **$p < .01$; ***$p < .001$ (two-tailed test).

Source: Davis, Shannon N. and Lisa D. Pearce. 2007. "Adolescents' Work-family Gender Ideologies and Educational Expectations." *Sociological Perspectives,* 50: 249–271.

■ **Literature Excerpt 17.2b**

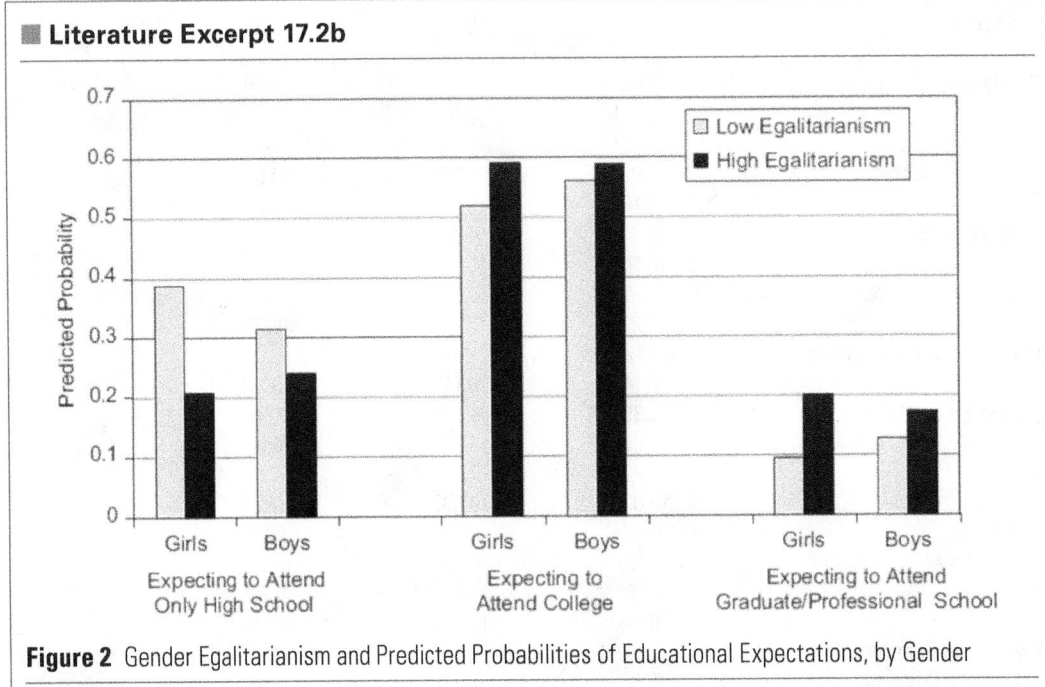

Figure 2 Gender Egalitarianism and Predicted Probabilities of Educational Expectations, by Gender

Note: Predicted probabilities calculated from ordinal logistic regression coefficients for respondents who are White, conservative, Protestant children of employed mothers living with both biological parents, who both have a high school education, where family income, mother's expectations, GPA, self-esteem, and church attendance are at their sample means.

Source: Davis, Shannon N. and Lisa D. Pearce. 2007. "Adolescents' Work-family Gender Ideologies and Educational Expectations." *Sociological Perspectives*, 50: 249–271.

For purposes of the predictions shown in Figure 2, the authors defined "Low Egalitarianism" as one standard deviation below the mean (3.04 − 0.43 = 2.61) and they defined "High Egalitarianism" as one standard deviation above the mean (3.04 + 0.43 = 3.47; Davis and Pearce, 2007: 257, 261).

In their Figure 2, the authors show the predicted probabilities of the lowest outcome category on the left (*Expecting to Attend Only High School*), of the middle outcome category in the middle (*Expecting to Attend College*), and the highest outcome category on the right (*Expecting to Attend Graduate/Professional School*). The lighter bars show the predicted probabilities for adolescents with low egalitarianism; the darker bars show the predicted probabilities for adolescents with high egalitarianism. In each set of four bars, we see that the difference in predicted probabilities by level of egalitarianism goes in the same direction for girls and boys, but the difference is larger for girls.

That is, for the predicted probabilities of "Expecting to Attend Only High School," we see that the model predicts that nearly four-in-ten girls who report low egalitarianism (and the other characteristics shown in the Figure note) expect to attend only high school in contrast to about two-in-ten girls who report high egalitarianism. Among boys, the model predicts that just over three-in-ten who report low egalitarianism expect to attend only high school in contrast to well over two-in-ten who report high egalitarianism. Thus, the difference by level of egalitarianism is larger for girls (a discrete change of nearly 20 percentage points for girls versus less than 10 percentage points for boys). Focusing within levels of egalitarianism, we likewise see that the gender difference reverses between the low and high egalitarianism categories. Looking again in the section of the chart reporting predicted probabilities of "Expecting to Attend Only High School," we see that among adolescents with low egalitarian attitudes (grey bars), girls are more likely than boys to expect to attend only high school; but, among adolescents with high egalitarian attitudes (black bars), girls are less likely than boys to expect to attend only high school.

Similar larger differences by egalitarianism for girls and reversal of gender differences within egalitarianism are evident for the other two outcome categories. For example, for the predicted probabilities of "Expecting to Attend Graduate/Professional School," nearly one-in-ten girls who report low egalitarianism (and the other characteristics shown in the Figure note) expect to attend graduate or professional school in contrast to about two-in-ten girls who report high egalitarianism. Among boys, about 15% of those who report low egalitarianism expect to attend graduate or professional school in contrast to about 18% who report high egalitarianism. Thus, the difference by level of egalitarianism is larger for girls (a discrete change of nearly 10 percentage points for girls versus about 5 percentage points for boys). And, looking again in the section of the chart reporting the predicted probabilities of "Expecting to Attend Graduate/Professional School," the gender difference reverses in the categories of low and high egalitarianism: Among adolescents with low egalitarian attitudes (grey bars), girls are less likely than boys to expect to attend graduate or professional school; but, among adolescents with high egalitarian attitudes (black bars), girls are more likely than boys to expect to attend graduate/professional school.

17.2.2: Mathematical Formulas

Like the multinomial logit model, the ordered logit is a natural extension of the binary logit model. But, in the case of the ordered logit model, just one coefficient is estimated for each predictor variable. The multiple, ordered levels of the outcome variable are incorporated into the model using separate intercepts, as we will see below.

> ■ **Box 17.7**
>
> Other models can be used to model ordinal outcomes (Agresti 2010; Long 1997). In this larger context, the model we discuss in this chapter is also referred to as a proportional odds model.

Specifically, the ordered logit model relies on **cumulative logits**. Like the logits we have already considered, the cumulative logits take the log of a ratio of two probabilities. However, rather than considering the probability of falling in a single category, the cumulative logits consider the probability of falling in any of the categories below and including a particular category relative to the probability of falling above that category. For example, if we had six categories, $c = 1$ to 6, we could define six cumulative logits:

	Cumulative Logit	
Category	Words	Notation
1	Log of the ratio of the probability of falling at or below category 1 to the probability of falling above category 1.	$\ln\left(\dfrac{\pi_{c\leq 1}}{\pi_{c>1}}\right)$
2	Log of the ratio of the probability of falling at or below category 2 to the probability of falling above category 2.	$\ln\left(\dfrac{\pi_{c\leq 2}}{\pi_{c>2}}\right)$
3	Log of the ratio of the probability of falling at or below category 3 to the probability of falling above category 3.	$\ln\left(\dfrac{\pi_{c\leq 3}}{\pi_{c>3}}\right)$
4	Log of the ratio of the probability of falling at or below category 4 to the probability of falling above category 4.	$\ln\left(\dfrac{\pi_{c\leq 4}}{\pi_{c>4}}\right)$
5	Log of the ratio of the probability of falling at or below category 5 to the probability of falling above category 5.	$\ln\left(\dfrac{\pi_{c\leq 5}}{\pi_{c>5}}\right)$
6	Log of the ratio of the probability of falling at or below category 6 to the probability of falling above category 6.	$\ln\left(\dfrac{\pi_{c\leq 6}}{\pi_{c>6}}\right)$

These cumulative logits are then set equal to the systematic portion of the regression model, with separate intercepts used to allow the cumulative logit to differ for each category.

■ **Table 17.2: Equating the Cumulative Logit to the Systematic Portion of the Regression Model**

Category	Cumulative Logit		Systematic Portion of Model
1	$\ln\left(\dfrac{\pi_{c\leq 1}}{\pi_{c>1}}\right)$	=	$\beta_{0,1} + \beta_1 X$
2	$\ln\left(\dfrac{\pi_{c\leq 2}}{\pi_{c>2}}\right)$	=	$\beta_{0,2} + \beta_1 X$
3	$\ln\left(\dfrac{\pi_{c\leq 3}}{\pi_{c>3}}\right)$	=	$\beta_{0,3} + \beta_1 X$
4	$\ln\left(\dfrac{\pi_{c\leq 4}}{\pi_{c>4}}\right)$	=	$\beta_{0,4} + \beta_1 X$
5	$\ln\left(\dfrac{\pi_{c\leq 5}}{\pi_{c>5}}\right)$	=	$\beta_{0,5} + \beta_1 X$
6	$\ln\left(\dfrac{\pi_{c\leq 6}}{\pi_{c>6}}\right)$	=	$\beta_{0,6} + \beta_1 X$

Notice that unlike the multinomial logit model, there is only one subscript on the coefficient for our predictor variable X. This reflects the fact that in the ordered logit model we do not allow the effect of covariates to differ across outcome categories. However, there are two subscripts on the intercept. Each category, c, has its own intercept, $\beta_{0,c}$, which allows for the multiple outcome categories. If we represent the value of c more generally with c_i then we can write

$$\ln\left(\frac{\pi_{c \le c_i}}{\pi_{c > c_i}}\right) = \beta_{0,c_i} + \beta_1 X \tag{17.8}$$

As with the binary and multinomial logit models, we can interpret the exponential of the coefficients estimated from our model with a factor change approach. Specifically, if we take the exponential of both sides of Equation 17.8 we have:

$$\left(\frac{\hat{\pi}_{c \ge c_i}}{\hat{\pi}_{c < c_i}}\right) = \exp(\hat{\beta}_{0,c_i} + \hat{\beta}_1 X)$$

If we write a similar equation after incrementing X by one, we have

$$\frac{\hat{\pi}_{c \ge c_i}}{\hat{\pi}_{c < c_i}} \mid X + 1 = \exp(\hat{\beta}_{0,c_i} + \hat{\beta}_1(X+1))$$

The ratio of these two predicted cumulative odds is:

$$\frac{\dfrac{\hat{\pi}_{c \ge c_i}}{\hat{\pi}_{c < c_i}} \mid X + 1}{\dfrac{\hat{\pi}_{c \ge c_i}}{\hat{\pi}_{c < c_i}} \mid X} = \frac{\exp(\hat{\beta}_{0,c_i} + \hat{\beta}_1(X+1))}{\exp(\hat{\beta}_{0,c_i} + \hat{\beta}_1 X)}$$

$$= \frac{\exp(\hat{\beta}_{0,c_i} + \hat{\beta}_1 X + \hat{\beta}_1)}{\exp(\hat{\beta}_{0,c_i} + \hat{\beta}_1 X)}$$

$$= \frac{\exp(\hat{\beta}_{0,c_i}) * \exp(\hat{\beta}_1 X) * \exp(\hat{\beta}_1)}{\exp(\hat{\beta}_{0,c_i}) * \exp(\hat{\beta}_1 X)} \tag{17.9}$$

$$= \exp(\hat{\beta}_1)$$

The strength of this interpretation approach, as in the case of binary and multinomial logit models, is that (unlike change in probabilities) factor change does not depend on the starting point on X. If there are other variables in our model, the factor change also does not depend on exactly what value we hold all other variables constant at (as long as they are held constant at some level as we vary X). Because of this, we can write a single sentence interpretation of factor change.

In practice, the model is often estimated with the reverse orientation, so that the probability of being at or above the highest category is in the numerator. When the model is oriented in this way, a positive coefficient will indicate that the chances of being in the higher categories on the outcome relative to the lower categories on the outcome increases as the predictor increases. The default Stata output is shown in this way and when we use the `descending` option in SAS `proc logistic`, as we did in Chapter 16, then the SAS output will also be oriented in this way.

Specifically, we can interpret $\exp(\hat{\beta}_1)$ as follows:

"For a one unit increase in X, the odds of the outcome falling in category $c > c_i$ versus the category $c \leq c_i$ are expected to change by a factor of $\exp(\beta_1)$, holding any other variables in the model constant."

This can also be said more succinctly as follows:

"For a one unit increase in X, the odds of the outcome falling in the higher versus the lower categories of the outcome are expected to change by a factor of $\exp(\beta_1)$, holding any other variables in the model constant."

Confidence intervals for the odds ratios can also be calculated by exponentiating the bounds of the confidence intervals for the coefficient. We can interpret these intervals as:

"We are 95% confident that the odds of occupying higher versus lower categories on the outcome change by between $\exp(\hat{\beta}_1 - 1.96 * \hat{\sigma}_{\hat{\beta}_1})$ and $\exp(\hat{\beta}_1 + 1.96 * \hat{\sigma}_{\hat{\beta}_1})$ when X increases by one, on average, holding all other variables constant."

Notice that this factor change interpretation is the same regardless of the category, because the category-specific intercepts cancel out in Equation 17.9. Thus, regardless of whether we substitute in $\hat{\beta}_{0,1}$ or $\hat{\beta}_{0,2}$ or $\hat{\beta}_{0,3}$ or $\hat{\beta}_{0,4}$ or $\hat{\beta}_{0,5}$ or $\hat{\beta}_{0,6}$ for $\hat{\beta}_{0,c_i}$ in Equation 17.9 the formula will reduce to the same factor change interpretation. In other words, the effect of the covariate on the odds is the same across all categories. This is known as the **proportional odds assumption** and we will have more to say about its strengths and limitations below.

The final formula we will consider is the formula for calculating predicted probabilities based on the ordered logit model. As was the case for binary and multinomial logit models, the amount that the probability changes with an increase in X may depend on the starting value of X (especially in non-linear regions of the logit S curve). So, it is important to examine several sets of specific predicted probabilities (at different starting levels of X and for different levels of the other variables in the model) when interpreting the model. The formulas used in calculating predicted probabilities are similar to the formulas used for binary and multinomial logit models. But, there are three new elements, which we will elaborate on below:

(1) We need to understand how to use the cumulative probabilities (i.e., the probability of being at or below a category of interest) to calculate the probability of falling in each category.

(2) We need to understand how to interpret the values we see in the output, since we generally will not see intercepts directly in the output, but rather cutpoints separating intercepts.
(3) We need to understand how the model deals with the cumulative probabilities for the lowest and highest categories (since the probability of being below the lowest category is zero and the probability of being above the highest category is zero).

To start, since we will predict cumulative probabilities for the model, we need to keep in mind that it is easy to figure out the probability of falling in any single category based on subtracting cumulative logits. For example, $\pi_{c=4} = \pi_{c\leq4} - \pi_{c\leq3}$. And, since our categories are mutually exclusive and exhaustive, and $\sum_{c=1}^{C}\pi_c = 1$, it must be that once we have figured out all but one of the cumulative probabilities for an ordinal variable, we can deduce the remaining probabilities. In our case, $\sum_{c=1}^{6}\pi_c = (\pi_{c\leq1}) + (\pi_{c\leq2} - \pi_{c\leq1}) + (\pi_{c\leq3} - \pi_{c\leq2}) + (\pi_{c\leq4} - \pi_{c\leq3}) + (\pi_{c\leq5} - \pi c_{\leq4}) + (\pi_{c\leq6} - \pi_{c\leq5}) = 1$

This suggests that there will be a redundancy in the equations laid out in Table 17.2. In order to estimate the model, we need to deal with this redundancy (we had to deal with a similar redundancy when we chose one outcome category as reference for the multinomial logit). SAS and Stata estimate what are referred to as **cutpoints** or **thresholds** which separate the various intercepts. They estimate *C-1* of these cutpoints for an outcome variable with *C* outcome categories. Although the choice of how to estimate the intercepts and/or cutpoints does not affect the model as a whole (e.g., the coefficients for the predictor variables; the predicted probabilities from the model), different approaches will lead to different values shown in the output for the cutpoints (or intercepts; Fox 2008; Long 1997).[16] We present here the approach used by Stata. The approach used by SAS is very similar, although the cutpoints will be opposite in sign of those reported by Stata.

Specifically, Stata estimates *c-1* cutpoints that separate the categories (StataCorp 2009c). The probability of falling in a category is defined relative to these cutpoints. The probability of falling in the middle categories is defined in relation to two of these cutpoints. Because, as we noted above, the probability of falling below the lowest category and the probability of falling above the highest category are both zero, the probabilities for these categories are defined only in relation to one cutpoint. The probability of falling in the first category is defined in relation to only the first estimated cutpoint. The probability of falling in the last category is defined in relation to only the last estimated cutpoint.

More explicitly, Stata writes the predicted probabilities for the middle categories as follows.

$$\hat{\pi}_{c=c_i} = \frac{1}{1+\exp(-\hat{k}_{c_i} + \hat{\beta}_1 X)} - \frac{1}{1+\exp(-\hat{k}_{c_i-1} + \hat{\beta}_1 X)}$$

where $\hat{k}$ represents the estimated cutpoints. As noted, for an outcome with *C* categories there are *C-1* estimated cutpoints. The cutpoint below the lowest estimated cutpoint (needed on the right hand side of the equation for Category 1) is taken to be negative infinitiy. The cutpoint above the largest estimated cutpoint (needed on the left hand side of the equation for Category C) is taken to be positive infinity.

Table 17.3 (below) translates this general equation to our specific case of a possible outcome variable with six categories. In the table, the value on the right for Category 1 is zero because the cutpoint below the lowest estimated cutpoint is defined as negative infinity. Because the cutpoint is multiplied by negative one in the formula, this translates to the exponential of positive infinity in the denominator ($\dfrac{1}{1+\exp(-1*-\infty+\hat{\beta}_1 X)}$). Since the exponential of positive infinity is positive infinity, we have one divided by positive infinity, or zero.

■ Table 17.3: Predicted Probabilities Based on Stata's Estimation

Category			Equation
1	$\hat{\pi}_{c=1}$	=	$\dfrac{1}{1+\exp(-\hat{k}_1+\hat{\beta}_1 X)} - 0$
2	$\hat{\pi}_{c=2}$	=	$\dfrac{1}{1+\exp(-\hat{k}_2+\hat{\beta}_1 X)} - \dfrac{1}{1+\exp(-\hat{k}_1+\hat{\beta}_1 X)}$
3	$\hat{\pi}_{c=3}$	=	$\dfrac{1}{1+\exp(-\hat{k}_3+\hat{\beta}_1 X)} - \dfrac{1}{1+\exp(-\hat{k}_2+\hat{\beta}_1 X)}$
4	$\hat{\pi}_{c=4}$	=	$\dfrac{1}{1+\exp(-\hat{k}_4+\hat{\beta}_1 X)} - \dfrac{1}{1+\exp(-\hat{k}_3+\hat{\beta}_1 X)}$
5	$\hat{\pi}_{c=5}$	=	$\dfrac{1}{1+\exp(-\hat{k}_5+\hat{\beta}_1 X)} - \dfrac{1}{1+\exp(-\hat{k}_4+\hat{\beta}_1 X)}$
6	$\hat{\pi}_{c=6}$	=	$1 - \dfrac{1}{1+\exp(-\hat{k}_5+\hat{\beta}_1 X)}$

The value on the left for Category 6 is one because the cutpoint above the highest estimated cutpoint is defined as positive infinity. Again, because the cutpoint is multiplied by negative one in the formula, this translates to the exponential of negative infinity in the denominator ($\dfrac{1}{1+\exp(-1*\infty+\hat{\beta}_1 X)}$). Since the exponential of negative infinity is zero, we have $\dfrac{1}{1+0}=1$.

Predicted probabilities can be hand calculated from the SAS output using formulas like those shown in Table 17.3, except that the values of the cutpoints are not multiplied by −1 in the denominator. For example, in the first and second rows of Table 17.3 we would replace $\dfrac{1}{1+\exp(-\hat{k}_1+\hat{\beta}_1 X)}$) with $\dfrac{1}{1+\exp(\hat{k}_1^*+\hat{\beta}_1 X)}$ where $\hat{k}_1^*$ is the SAS estimate of the cutpoint (SAS Institute 2008b: 3324).

17.2.3: Strengths and Limitations

As noted above, the ordered logit model makes a proportional odds assumption. It assumes that the factor change in the odds when a predictor variable changes is the same regardless of outcome category. The advantage of this assumption is that it simplifies interpretation. However, this assumption may be problematic if we expect that, for example, a covariate may have a stronger effect on the odds of moving between certain categories of an outcome versus others. For example, if an outcome were a likert-type measure capturing whether parents *strongly disagree, disagree, agree*, or *strongly agree* with corporal punishment, we might expect that the association being parental education and whether the parent *disagrees* versus *agrees* would differ from whether the parent *agrees* versus *strongly agrees*. We might hypothesize that education mostly has an effect of leading parents to be more likely to disagree and less likely to agree with this statement; however, we might hypothesize that education will have little effect on the strength of disagreement or agreement (i.e., less effect on whether the parent *strongly disagrees* versus *disagrees* and less effect on whether the parent *strongly agrees* versus *agrees* and more of an effect on whether the parent *disagrees* versus *agrees*). If the proportional odds assumption seems conceptually inappropriate for an application, one alternative is to estimate a multinomial logit model (since as we saw above it allows covariate effects to differ across categories). Other advanced models also relax this assumption (for example see Agresti 2010; Long 1997; Peterson and Harrell 1990; Williams 2006; and Wooldridge 2002).

Various tests of the proportional odds assumption are available (see Long 1997). We present below the Brant test which is included in the Long and Freese suite of *SPost* commands and a score test which is included in the default SAS output. The brant test is described in detail by Long (1997, 143–145). The test produces *Wald* χ^2 values for each covariate as well as an overall model *Wald* χ^2. These are based on the difference between the coefficients obtained by the ordered logit model and coefficients obtained by estimating a series of binary logit models that mimic the ordered logit. Each binary logit defines an outcome variable that is coded one for cases with a value on the outcome above category c and coded zero for cases with a value on the outcome at or below category c. This binary logit is repeated C-1 times. Then the results are combined to construct the *Wald* χ^2 values. The null hypothesis for each *Wald* χ^2 is that the coefficients do not differ. Thus, a significant overall *Wald* χ^2 test indicates that the proportional odds assumption is rejected for the model as a whole. The individual covariate *Wald* χ^2 values provide information about which specific predictor variables violate the assumption. A disadvantage of this test, as we will see in our example below, is that there may be insufficient cases in some categories to support the binary logit models.

17.2.4: NSFH Example

For the ordered logit model, we further subdivided the NSFH *glmiles* outcome variable into six categories.[17] We divided respondents who lived within about an hour's drive of the mother into three groups: (1) those who lived within one mile of the mother, (2) those who lived between 2 and 15 miles of the mother, and (3) those who lived between 16 and 45 miles of the mother. We also subdivided those who lived within a day's drive into: (4) those who lived about a half day's drive (46 to 200 miles) and (5) those who lived more than a half day's drive (201 to 500 miles). In addition, we retained the farthest category of: (6) living more than a day's drive from the mother (between 501 and 9000 miles). These six categories would lead to 15 pairwise contrasts in total for a multinomial logit model, an often unwieldy number of contrasts to digest and interpret.[18] Thus, if the proportional odds assumption holds, the complexity of the model is greatly reduced by using the ordered logit rather than the multinomial logit model.

We can again use standard SAS and Stata syntax to create this new six-category variable (and, as usual, the new variable must be created within the data step in SAS).

SAS	Stata
`if g1miles>0 & g1miles<=1 then g1mileso=1;`	`generate g1mileso=1 if g1miles>0 & g1miles<=1`
`if g1miles>1 & g1miles<=15 then g1mileso=8;`	`replace g1mileso=8 if g1miles>1 & g1miles<=15`
`if g1miles>15 & g1miles<=45 then g1mileso=30;`	`replace g1mileso=30 if g1miles>15 & g1miles<=45`
`if g1miles>45 & g1miles<=200 then g1mileso=123;`	`replace g1mileso=123 if g1miles>45 & g1miles<=200`
`if g1miles>200 & g1miles<=500 then g1mileso=350;`	`replace g1mileso=350 if g1miles>200 & g1miles<=500`
`if g1miles>500 & g1miles<=9000 then g1mileso=1500;`	`replace g1mileso=1500 if g1miles>500 & g1miles<=9000`

These categories each have sizable sub-samples in our NSFH data set. All of the categories have at least 450 cases, with the largest number of respondents (nearly 2,000) living between 2 and 15 miles of their mothers.

Estimation in SAS and Stata

The ordered logit model can be implemented in both SAS and Stata. In SAS, we use the same `proc logistic` command with the `descending` option as we used for binomial and multinomial logit. With more than two outcome categories, the ordered logit model is fit by default (so we omit the `/glogit` option used for multinomial logit). Stata has a dedicated command for ordered logit called `ologit`. The results of estimating the ordered logit model with these commands are shown in Display B.17.9. Note that SAS defines the cutpoints as the negative of their definition in Stata. But, the SAS and Stata estimates of the cutpoints and coefficients match to three decimal places.

Interpretation

We will now consider how to interpret these results. We begin with a test of the proportional odds assumption. We then calculate odds ratios, predicted probabilities, and discrete change.

■ **Box 17.8**

You can also use the commands introduced in Chapter 16 to request *R*-squared values and information criteria and to examine outliers and influential observations.

Testing the Proportional Odds Assumption

One approach to testing the proportional odds assumption is the `brant` command included among the *SPost* commands written by Long and Freese (2005). As noted above, this command can fail when some of the underlying binary logit models cannot be estimated (usually due to small sample size). When this happens, the command returns the message "*not all independent variables can be retained in all binary logits; brant test cannot be computed.*" This occurred in our case. We were able to obtain the test results when we excluded the variables that created the problem (*g2numsis7p* and *amind*; recall from Chapter 14 that very few cases are coded a one on these two covariates, which can sometimes produce estimation problems in binary logit models).

The results (shown in Display B.17.10) indicate that the overall test is significant (*Wald* χ^2=87.23 with *p*-value=0.000 and thus less than an alpha of 0.05) as are the individual tests for three variables (*white* with *Wald* χ^2=20.22 and *p*-value=0.000; *g2earn10000* with *Wald* χ^2=11.24 and *p*-value=0.024; and *g1age* with *Wald* χ^2=12.90 and *p*-value=0.012).

SAS includes a test of the proportional odds assumption in its default output. The result also shows that the assumption is rejected (with a chi-square of 92.6263 and a *p*-value of .0015).

This suggests that the ordered logit model (at least with the outcome category groupings we used here) is not ideal for these data. We examine this six category outcome with the multinomial logit model in the next "Putting it All Together" section. For now, we will continue with interpretation of the estimated model, to illustrate each aspect of interpretation introduced above.

Odds Ratios

As noted above, we can interpret the exponential of the coefficient from an ordered logit model with a factor change approach. We can request the odds ratios in Stata by adding the `or` option after our independent variables list or with the command `ologit, or` after estimating an ordered logit model. SAS includes the odds ratios in its default output. Display B.17.11 shows the results. For *g2earn10000* the result of taking the exponential of its coefficient from Display B.17.9 is exp(0.0246575) = 1.024964. This matches exactly the value shown in Display B.17.11 of 1.024964. We interpret this result as: "For a $10,000 increase in respondents' annual earnings, the odds of occupying the higher versus lower categories of distance from the mother are expected to change by a factor of 1.025, holding constant the mother's schooling and age and the respondent's race-ethnicity, gender, age, and number of brothers and sisters."[19]

Both SAS and Stata also show confidence intervals for the odds ratios in Display B.17.11. We can interpret these as: "For a $10,000 increase in respondents' annual earnings, we are 95% confident that the odds of occupying the higher versus lower categories of distance from the mother change by a factor of between 1.01 and 1.04, holding constant the mother's schooling and age and the respondent's race-ethnicity, gender, age, and number of brothers and sisters."

Predicted Probabilities

We can use the Stata `margins` command and SAS `score` command to predict probabilities for ordered logit, similar to what we did in Display B.17.7 for the multinomial logit model. Specifically in Stata, we again use the option `predict(outcome(<value>))` where `<value>` is the number for the outcome category that we want to predict. We specify the levels of the covariates using the `at` option. We must repeat this command for each outcome category; to conserve space we suppress the covariate values after the first command using the `noatlegend` option. In SAS, the predicted probabilities are automatically named as *p_<value>* with the value that refers to our outcome categories (in our case, there are six variables generated, *p_1, p_8, p_30, p_123, p_350,* and *p_1500*).

We show the results in Display B.17.12 for requesting predicted probabilities for the same values we used in multinomial logit for the "rounded" version of the "average then predict" approach (a 34-year-old white female who has no earnings, less than four sisters, one brother, and has a mother who is 60 years old and has 11 years of schooling) for each of our six categories. With six outcome categories, a table is useful to summarize the results, even for just one set of covariates. Table 17.4 does so. The results show that the modal predicted probability of living more than a mile but less than 15 miles from the mother, which is occupied by a predicted 38% of 34-year-old white females who have no earnings, less than four sisters, one brother, and who have a mother who is 60 years old and has 11 years of schooling. Adults are fairly evenly spread across the remaining categories, with predicted probabilities of between 12 and 15% in each category, except for the category of about a day's drive (201 to 500 miles) which just 7% of adults with these characteristics are predicted to occupy.

■ **Table 17.4: Predicted Probabilities for a 34-year-old White Female Who has No Earnings, Less Than Four Sisters, One Brother, and Has a Mother Who is 60 Years Old and has 11 Years of Schooling**

Category Value	Approximate Category Meaning	Predicted Probability
1	Within one mile of the mother	.147
8	Up to a half hour (2 to 15 miles)	.384
30	Up to an hour (16 and 45 miles)	.119
123	Up to half day's drive (46 to 200 miles)	.143
350	About a day's drive (201 to 500 miles)	.074
1500	More than a day's drive (501 and 9000 miles)	.133

In Display H.17.2 we show the predicted probabilities for other levels of earnings and graph these results in Excel. Because of the number of lines needed to illustrate six categories, we use two graphs, one of which shows the categories that have declining predicted probabilities as earnings increases and the other of which shows the categories that have increasing predicted probabilities as earnings increases. The results show that by separating the smallest category that we had originally examined (within 45 miles) in two we see that the predicted probabilities are declining with increasing earnings only in the two smallest categories (within one mile and two to fifteen miles).

Discrete Change

In terms of discrete change, we see in Display H.17.2 that for both of the smallest categories ("within one mile" and "two to fifteen miles"), the predicted probabilities change by about two percentage points as annual earnings increase from none to \$75,000 (0.12504 − 0.146713 = −.022 and 0.3593 − 0.38382 = −0.025). In contrast, the predicted probabilities change little for the category of 16 to 45 miles (0.12225 − 0.11922 = 0.003), increase by about one percentage point for the categories of 46 to 200 and 201 to 500 miles (0.15406 − 0.14293 = 0.011 and 0.0835216 − 0.0742982 = 0.009), and increase by over two percentage points for the category 501 to 9000 miles (0.15583 − 0.13302 = 0.023).[20]

In addition to the discrete changes just examined when annual earnings changes from none to \$75,000, Display H.17.2 also presents the discrete changes for each \$10,000 increase in annual earnings. As for the multinomial logit model, these values reinforce the quite linear associations between earnings and the probabilities seen in the graphs in Display H.17.2 and also reinforce the similarity in changes between the first and second and the fourth and fifth categories. That is, the discrete change for a \$10,000 increase in earnings is about −0.003 for the first and second categories; and, it is just over 0.001 for the fourth and fifth categories.

In Stata, we can also use the `prchange` command to request discrete change (and the underlying predicted probabilities that are used to calculate the discrete change with the `fromto` option). The bolded results show, for example, that as earnings increases from about \$12,000 to about \$50,000 an adult with average characteristics is predicted to be about one percentage point (.1235231 − .13388607 = −.01036297) less likely to live within one mile of the mother.

17.3: PUTTING IT ALL TOGETHER

To help integrate what we have learned, we will now look across the various types of regression models that we have estimated throughout the book with our NSFH distance from the mother example. We first present the coefficient estimates and significance tests from across models in a single table, so that we can look for consistency in the pattern of significance across models. For the earnings predictor variable, we then present predicted values from the models in graphs, so that we can look for consistency in the shape and substantive size of associations between predictors and outcomes across models. We additionally use these graphs to discuss the importance of considering the inherently non-linear patterns of association in the logit-based models as we interpret our results. In this section, we also revisit the assumptions of the multinomial and ordered logit models, adding to what we considered in earlier sections by reporting tests for both the three-category and six-category versions of the variables for both types of models. Finally, we consider how we might choose which set of results to present in a paper (reminding ourselves that we chose a small set of straightforward predictors from just one wave of the NSFH for this example and thus we would expand the set of variables before submitting this work for publication in substantive scholarly outlets).

17.3.1: Pattern of Significance

Table 17.5 presents the coefficients from six different regression models. We use the miles from the mother outcome variable in its natural units as well as the dichotomous, the three-category and the six-category versions of the variable (using both multinomial logit and ordered logit). For the multinomial logit models, to simplify the presentation we only show contrasts between each of the higher categories and the smallest category.[21] We number each column to make it easier to refer to specific results.

The set of predictors that we present is similar to the full model that we have considered throughout the book, although we collapsed together two sets of categories with small sample sizes. Specifically, we grouped American Indians with the "Other" race-ethnicity category; and, we omit the coefficients for the "Other" variable from Table 17.5 since it is difficult to interpret results for this heterogeneous group of "Other" race-ethnicities.[22] We also grouped adults with seven or more sisters together with those who have five or six sisters, creating a category of adults with five or more sisters.

In order to make it easier to discern similarities in the pattern of significance across models, we bolded coefficients with p-values less than .05 in Table 17.5. This bolding makes it easy to see that the most consistent result, in terms of statistical significance, is for annual earnings. In all models, adults who earn more live farther from their mothers, on average, controlling for their race-ethnicity, gender, age, and number of brothers and sisters as well as for their mothers' ages and years of schooling. Of course, we cannot readily discern the size of these associations from the logit coefficients. We will examine substantive size for the earnings variable below.

The next most consistent results, in terms of statistical significance, are for the contrast of whites to the reference race-ethnicity, African Americans, and the square term on mothers' years of schooling. For both of these predictors, eight of the eleven coefficients are statistically significant. For race-ethnicity, we see that in most cases, our results indicate that whites are predicted to live farther from their mothers than are African Americans, controlling for their gender, annual earnings, age, and number of brothers and sisters as well as for their mothers' ages and years of schooling. The exceptions are for the OLS model (Column 1) and two contrasts of the six-category multinomial logit model (Column 5: the contrasts of those who live 2–15 miles and those who live within 1 mile of their mothers; Column 8: the contrast of those who live 201–500 miles with those who live within 1 mile of their mothers). For mothers' years of schooling, in most cases there is a significant squared term, with the exception being three contrasts in the six-category multinomial logit model (between those who live 2–15 miles, 16–45 miles, 46–200 miles, and the reference of 1 mile from the mother, shown in Columns 5, 6, and 7).

Finally, both the respondents' ages and the mothers' ages have statistically significant coefficients in a few models. Adjusting for the other variables in the model, adults with older mothers live

Table 17.5: Regression Models of Distance Adults Live From their Mothers

	OLS	Binary Logit	Multinomial Logit (Ref: <=45 Miles)		Multinomial Logit (Ref: 1 Mile)					Ordered Logit	Ordered Logit
	Miles	>45 Miles	46–500 Miles	>500 Miles	2–15 Miles	16–45 Miles	46–200 Miles	201–500 Miles	>500 Miles	3-category	6-category
	(1)	(2)	(3)	(4)	(5)	(6)	(7)	(8)	(9)	(10)	(11)
Respondent's											
Race-ethnicity[a]											
Mexican American	37.26	−0.24	−0.27	−0.18	−0.14	0.14	−0.11	−0.62	−0.23	−0.24	−0.15
	(57.01)	(0.21)	(0.27)	(0.30)	(0.23)	(0.32)	(0.36)	(0.45)	(0.34)	(0.21)	(0.16)
White	31.32	**0.37***	**0.47***	**0.24***	0.13	**0.47***	**0.84***	0.32	**0.39***	**0.32***	**0.33***
	(25.58)	**(0.09)**	**(0.11)**	**(0.12)**	(0.12)	**(0.16)**	**(0.16)**	(0.17)	**(0.15)**	**(0.09)**	**(0.07)**
Female	−29.56	−0.02	0.06	−0.14	0.03	−0.04	0.06	0.10	−0.13	−0.07	−0.06
	(18.89)	(0.06)	(0.07)	(0.08)	(0.10)	(0.12)	(0.11)	(0.13)	(0.11)	(0.06)	(0.05)
Annual Earnings[b]	**6.71***	**0.03***	**0.03***	**0.03***	**0.06***	**0.05***	**0.08***	**0.09***	**0.07***	**0.02***	**0.02***
	(2.53)	**(0.01)**	**(0.01)**	**(0.01)**	**(0.02)**	**(0.02)**	**(0.02)**	**(0.02)**	**(0.02)**	**(0.01)**	**(0.01)**
Age (years)	0.38	0.01	0.01	0.01	0.00	**0.03***	0.01	0.02	0.02	0.01	**0.01***
	(1.66)	(0.01)	(0.01)	(0.01)	(0.01)	**(0.01)**	(0.01)	(0.01)	(0.01)	(0.01)	**(0.005)**
Number of Brothers	9.30	0.03	0.03	0.05	−0.02	0.02	0.01	0.04	0.04	0.04	0.03
	(5.83)	(0.02)	(0.02)	(0.03)	(0.03)	(0.04)	(0.03)	(0.04)	(0.03)	(0.02)	(0.02)
Number of Sisters[c]											
Four sisters	−16.98	0.06	0.11	−0.02	−0.12	−0.06	0.22	−0.39	−0.10	0.02	−0.01
	(42.46)	(0.14)	(0.16)	(0.20)	(0.20)	(0.26)	(0.23)	(0.32)	(0.25)	(0.14)	(0.12)
Five or more sisters	44.28	−0.06	−0.31	0.23	−0.01	−0.35	−0.51	−0.19	0.17	0.01	−0.07
	(43.26)	(0.15)	(0.19)	(0.18)	(0.19)	(0.28)	(0.28)	(0.30)	(0.23)	(0.14)	(0.13)
Mother's											
Years of Schooling	−11.19	−0.06	−0.07	−0.06	0.03	0.04	−0.03	−0.09	−0.04	−0.05	−0.03
	(13.21)	(0.04)	(0.05)	(0.06)	(0.06)	(0.08)	(0.08)	(0.09)	(0.08)	(0.04)	(0.04)
Years of Schooling Squared	**1.55***	**0.01***	**0.01***	**0.01***	0.00	0.002	0.01	**0.01***	**0.01***	**0.01***	**0.01***
	(0.61)	**(0.002)**	**(0.002)**	**(0.003)**	(0.003)	(0.004)	(0.004)	**(0.004)**	**(0.004)**	**(0.002)**	**(0.002)**
Age (years)	**3.99***	**0.01***	0.01	**0.02***	−0.01	**−0.02***	0.01	−0.004	0.01	0.01	0.01
	(1.46)	**(0.005)**	(0.01)	**(0.01)**	(0.01)	**(0.01)**	(0.01)	(0.01)	(0.01)	(0.01)	(0.004)

Notes: Standard errors in parentheses. N = 5,472.
[a] Reference category is African American. "Other" category is included in the models but not presented. [b] In $10,000 increments, adjusted to 2007 dollars.
[c] Reference category is three or fewer sisters.
* $p < .05$ (two-sided tests). Cells with $p < .05$ also bolded.

Source: National Survey of Families and Households, Wave I.

farther away based on the OLS and logit models (Columns 1 and 2) and based on one multinomial logit contrast (In Column 4, adults with older mothers are more likely to live ">500 miles" than "<=45 miles" away). For the remaining significant coefficient, however, adults with older mothers are less likely to occupy a farther than a closer category (In Column 6, adults with older mothers are less likely to live "16–45 Miles" than "1 Mile" away), with the other variables in the model held constant. In terms of the adult respondent's own age, two contrasts indicate that older respondents are more likely to live farther from their mothers, adjusting for the other variables in the model. Specifically, in the six-category multinomial logit model, older adults are more likely to live "16–45 Miles" versus "1 Mile" from their mother (Column 6); and, in the six-category ordered logit model, older adults are more likely to occupy father than closer categories of distance from their mother (Column 11).[23]

17.3.2: Multinomial Logit and Ordered Logit Assumptions

Before examining graphs illustrating the shape and the substantive size for the earnings variable, we pause to re-examine the assumptions of the multinomial logit and ordered logit models. As noted earlier in the chapter, one option to address the violation of the proportional odds assumption would be to instead use the multinomial logit model (another option would be to move to other models that are appropriate for ordinal outcomes but do not assume proportional odds, as we discuss in Chapter 18). It is also possible that the proportional odds assumption would not be violated for the three-category versus six-category version of the outcome.

In Table 17.6, we show the tests of the independence of irrelevant alternatives assumption for the multinomial logit models. And, in Table 17.7 we show the Brant test of the proportional odds

▦ **Table 17.6: Tests of the Assumption of Independence of Irrelevant Alternatives in the Multinomial Logit Models**

	Chi-square Value	Degrees of Freedom	p-value
Three-category Outcome			
<=45 Miles	0.22	12	1.00
46–500 Miles	4.21	13	.989
>500 Miles	0.67	12	1.00
Six-category Outcome			
1 Mile	1.99	48	1.00
2–15 Miles	−3.52	48	n/a
16–45 Miles	1.07	48	1.00
46–200 Miles	−6.03	48	n/a
201–500 Miles	−6.96	48	n/a
>500 Miles	−4.78	48	n/a

Notes: Results based on *Spost* commands written by Long and Freese (2006). n/a indicates that the p-value cannot be calculated when the Chi-square value is negative. The negative Chi-square values indicate that the test assumptions are not met for these outcomes.

▪ Table 17.7: Tests of the Proportional Odds Assumption of the Ordered Logit Models

	Chi-square Value	Degrees of Freedom	p-value
Three-category Outcome			
Overall	**26.61**	**12**	**.01**
Individual Predictors			
Respondent's			
Race-ethnicity[a]			
Mexican American	0.15	1	.70
White	**6.85**	**1**	**.01**
Female	**4.60**	**1**	**.03**
Annual Earnings[b]	**4.45**	**1**	**.04**
Age (years)	0.03	1	.85
Number of Brothers	0.04	1	.83
Number of Sisters[c]			
Four sisters	0.43	1	.51
Five or more sisters	**6.31**	**1**	**.01**
Mother's			
Years of Schooling	0.53	1	.47
Years of Schooling Squared	0.36	1	.55
Age (years)	0.03	1	.86
Six-category Outcome			
Overall	**95.28**	**48**	**.00**
Individual Predictors			
Respondent's			
Race-ethnicity[a]			
Mexican American	2.66	4	.62
White	**20.48**	**4**	**.00**
Female	5.10	4	.28
Annual Earnings[b]	**11.27**	**4**	**.02**
Age (years)	6.50	4	.17
Number of Brothers	1.73	4	.79
Number of Sisters[c]			
Four sisters	4.53	4	.34
Five or more sisters	**9.74**	**4**	**.05**
Mother's			
Years of Schooling	1.68	4	.79
Years of Schooling Squared	1.73	4	.79
Age (years)	**12.69**	**4**	**.01**

Notes: Results based on Brant test (Long 1997; Long and Freese 2006). Lines with p-values <.05 are bolded.
[a] Reference category is African American. "Other" category is included in the models but not presented. [b] In $10,000 increments, adjusted to 2007 dollars. [c] Reference category is three or fewer sisters.

assumption for the ordered logit models. Turning first to the multinomial logit results, we see that the *p*-values are all large for the three-category outcome in Table 17.6, indicating that the independence of irrelevant alternatives assumption is not violated. Recall that in Display B.17.3 some of the Chi-square values for the three-category outcome were negative. The models underlying the results in Table 17.6 differ from those for Display B.17.3 only in our collapsing the smallest race-ethnicity and number of sisters' categories as noted above; thus, this collapsing has the added benefit of resulting in all positive chi-square values in the top panel of Table 17.6. However, we do still see four negative Chi-square values for the six-category outcome. As discussed above, Cheng and Long (2007) conclude that the Hausman test should not be used in applied work; thus, if we wanted to present this model, we would argue on conceptual grounds that the six distance categories are distinct options that adults could be weighed independently from one another.

In Table 17.7 we see that the proportional odds assumption is still violated for the three-category outcome as was the case for the six-category outcome. The overall test is significant for both versions of the outcome. And, the tests are significant for four individual predictors (for the three-category outcome: white, female, earnings, and five or more sisters; for the six-category outcome: white, earnings, five or more sisters, and mothers' ages).

We will keep these results in mind as we summarize the findings below.

17.3.3: The Shape and Size of Significant Associations for Annual Earnings Across Models

In this section, we graph predicted values to illustrate the shape and size of significant associations for annual earnings. In an application, we would follow a similar process for the other predictor variables. We use two of the strategies for predictions introduced in Chapter 16: "average then predict" and "predict ideal types." For ideal types, we use similar extremes as we introduced in Chapter 16, one ideal type has characteristics that our model identifies as predicting living *close* to the mother (an African American female who is 20 years old, has one brother and fewer than four sisters, and whose mother is 40 years old and has 9 years of schooling) and the other ideal type has characteristics that our model identifies as predicting living *far* from the mother (a white male who is 50 years old, has two brothers and fewer than four sisters, and whose mother is 80 years old and has 16 years of schooling).

We present plots of predicted values in Figures 17.1 to 17.4 and we present specific predicted values and discrete change in Table 17.8. For the OLS models, predicted values are the predicted means of distance in miles from the mother. For the binary logit models, the predicted values are predicted probabilities of living more than 45 miles from the mother. For the multinomial logit and ordered logit models, the predicted values are predicted probabilities of occupying each of the three or six categories of the outcome.

We will begin by examining the figures, but will refer to Table 17.8 as we discuss some of the results. We'll first overview the contents of the four figures, and then look at them in detail.

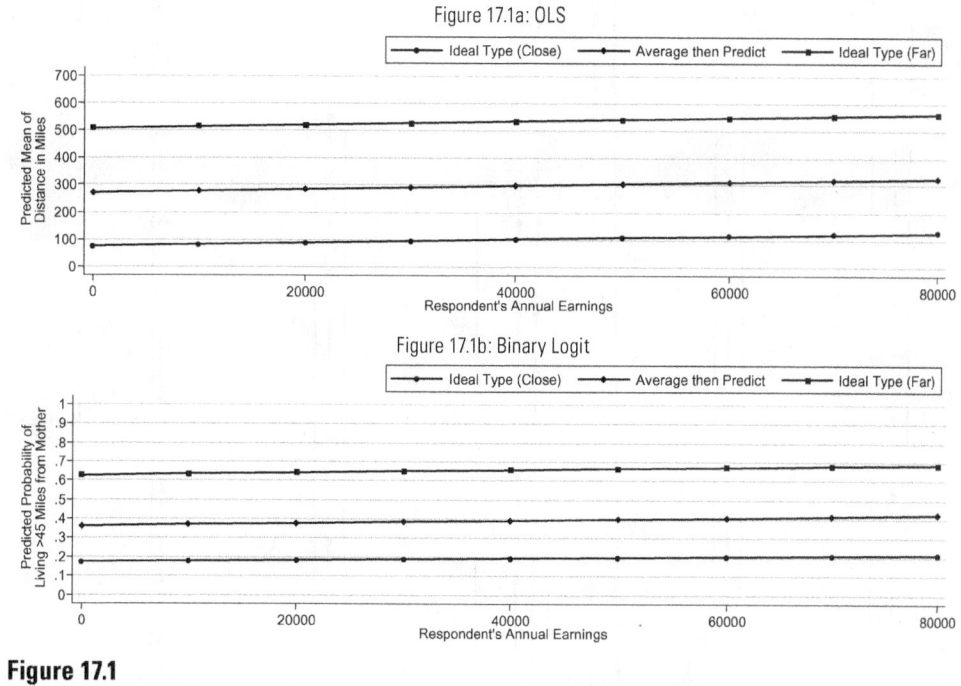

Figure 17.1

Figure 17.1 provides plots of the predicted means and predicted probabilities of success from the OLS and binary logit models. In these and the remaining figures, we use a circle marker on the line for the "close" ideal type, a diamond marker for the "average" person, and a square marker for the "far" ideal type. Figure 17.2 provides the predicted probabilities of each of the three categories of the three-category outcome, showing plots from the multinomial logit model on the left and from the ordered logit model on the right. Because there are now three lines for each of our three sets of predictions, we show results in the top row for the "close" ideal type, in the middle row for the "average" person, and in the bottom row for the "far" ideal type; and we distinguish the three categories using a short-dashed line (Category 1, <–45 Miles), solid line (Category 2: 46–500 Miles), and long-dashed line (Category 3: > 500 Miles). Figures 17.3 and 17.4 present the results for the six-category outcome. They are set up similarly to Figure 17.2, although in order to make the graphs easier to read, we present the first two of the six categories in Figure 17.3 and the last four of the six categories in Figure 17.4.

Continuous and Dichotomous Outcomes

Turning first to the OLS results in Figure 17.1a, we draw out two main points. First, each of three lines looks linear to our eyes. Second, the lines look parallel to our eyes, with the line for the "far" ideal type (with square markers) always highest, the line for the "average" person (with diamond markers) always in the middle and the line for the "close" ideal type (with circle

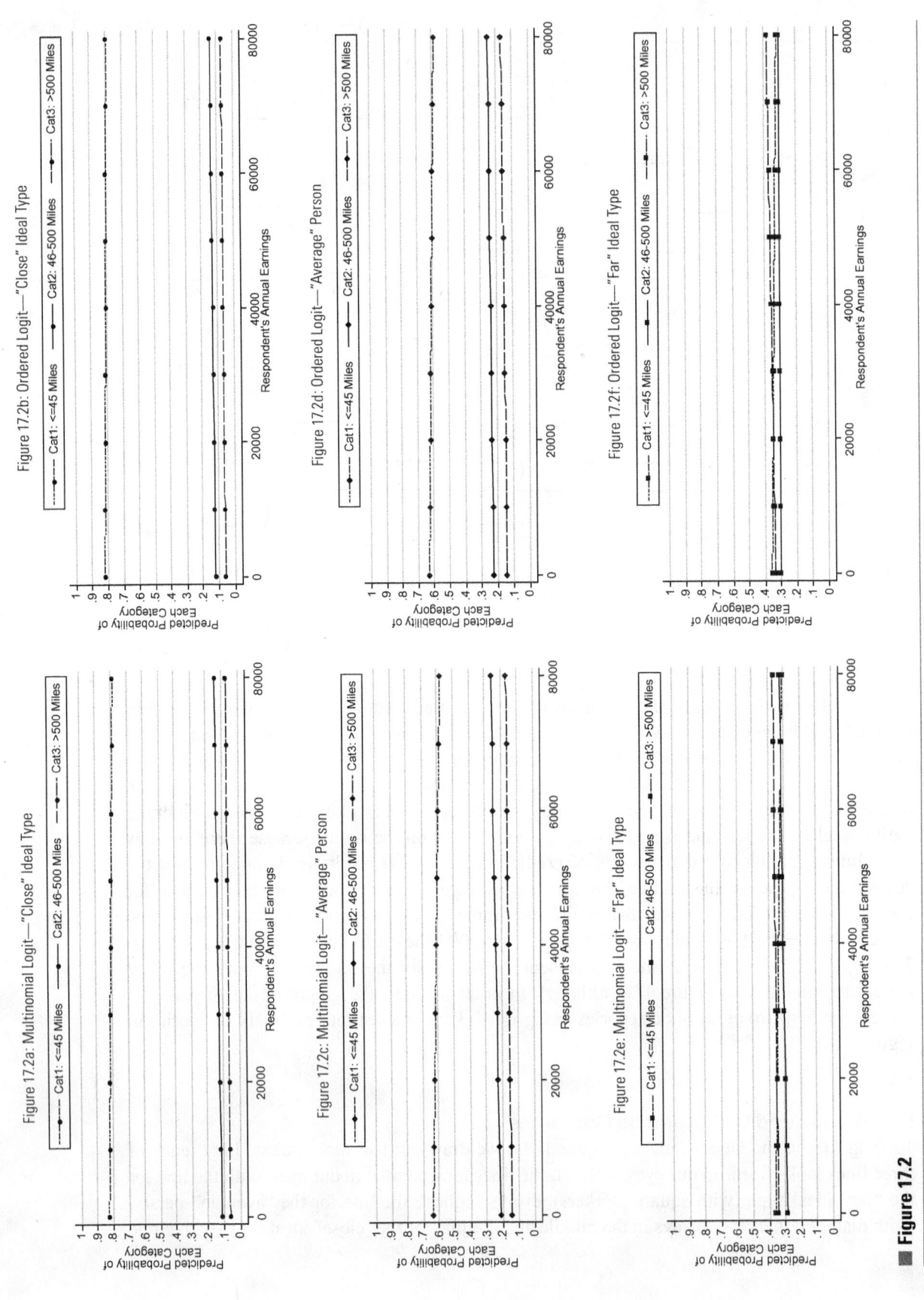

Figure 17.2

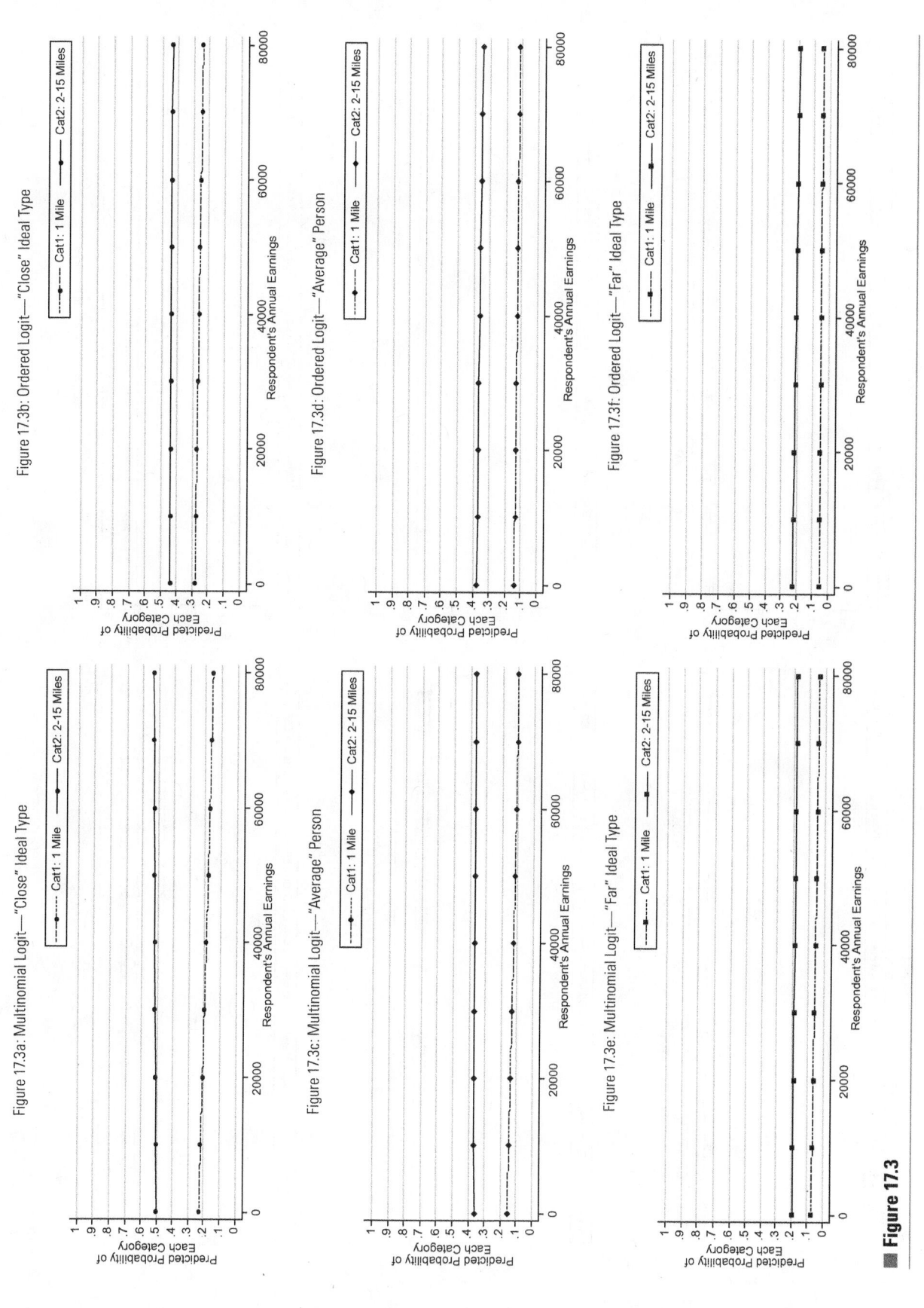

Figure 17.3b: Ordered Logit—"Close" Ideal Type

Figure 17.3d: Ordered Logit—"Average" Person

Figure 17.3f: Ordered Logit—"Far" Ideal Type

Figure 17.3a: Multinomial Logit—"Close" Ideal Type

Figure 17.3c: Multinomial Logit—"Average" Person

Figure 17.3e: Multinomial Logit—"Far" Ideal Type

Figure 17.3

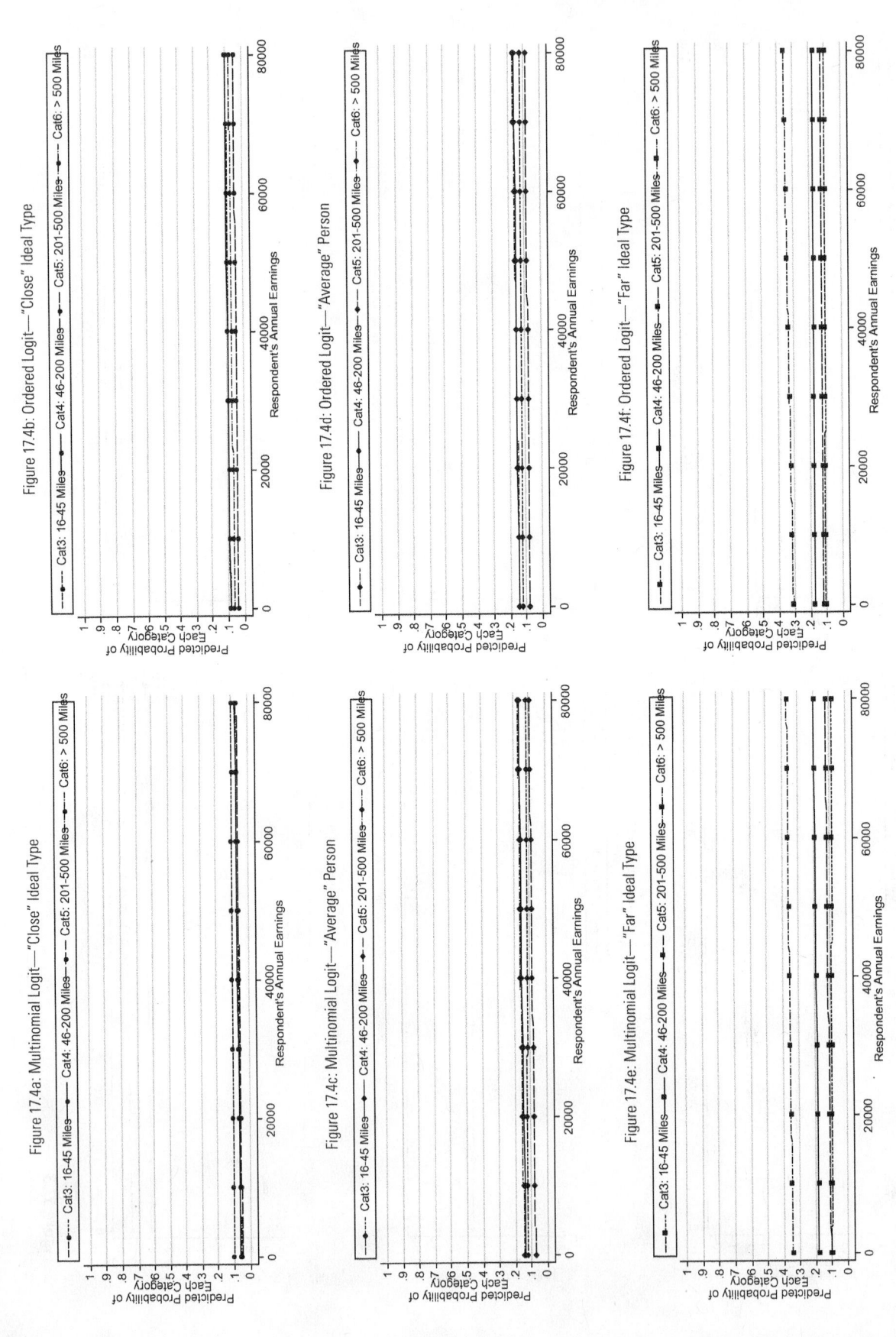

Figure 17.4b: Ordered Logit—"Close" Ideal Type

Figure 17.4d: Ordered Logit: "Average" Person

Figure 17.4f: Ordered Logit—"Far" Ideal Type

Figure 17.4a: Multinomial Logit—"Close" Ideal Type

Figure 17.4c: Multinomial Logit—"Average" Person

Figure 17.4e: Multinomial Logit—"Far" Ideal Type

Figure 17.4

■ Table 17.8: Predicted Values and Discrete Change when Annual Earnings is $20,000 and $30,000 and Other Variables are at One of Three Levels

	Level of Other Variables: Close[a]			Level of Other Variables: Average			Level of Other Variables: Far[b]		
	Level of Earnings		Discrete Change[c]	Level of Earnings		Discrete Change[c]	Level of Earnings		Discrete Change[c]
	$20,000	$30,000		$20,000	$30,000		$20,000	$30,000	
OLS (Miles)	87.46	94.17	6.71	283.97	290.68	6.71	522.29	528.99	6.71
Binary Logit (> 45 Miles)	.183	.187	.00477	.377	.385	.00747	.643	.650	.00724
Multinomial Logit (three-category)									
<=45 Miles	.817	.812	-.00487	.624	.617	-.00748	.350	.343	-.00695
46–500 Miles	.120	.124	.00353	.225	.230	.00519	.298	.303	.00446
>500 Miles	.062	.064	.00133	.151	.153	.00230	.352	.354	.00250
Ordered Logit (three-category)									
<=45 Miles	.814	.811	-.00340	.621	.615	-.00527	.348	.343	-.00505
46–500 Miles	.125	.127	.00211	.231	.234	.00244	.305	.305	-.0000229
>500 Miles	.061	.062	.00129	.148	.151	.00284	.347	.352	.00508
Multinomial Logit (six-category)									
1 Mile	.209	.199	-.00982	.139	.131	-.00750	.0650	.0609	-.00408
2–15 Miles	.509	.513	.00455	.364	.365	.000519	.191	.189	-.00148
16–45 Miles	.102	.102	-.000260	.121	.120	-.00121	.0966	.0947	-.00184
46–200 Miles	.0647	.0666	.00190	.144	.147	.00312	.186	.188	.00228
201–500 Miles	.0543	.0564	.00209	.0800	.082	.00246	.111	.113	.00237
> 500 Miles	.0620	.0635	.00154	.152	.155	.00261	.351	.354	.00275
Ordered Logit (six-category)									
1 Mile	.270	.266	-.00480	.132	.129	-.00278	.0526	.0514	-.00121
2–15 Miles	.438	.438	-.000279	.367	.364	-.00334	.214	.211	-.00356
16–45 Miles	.0910	.0921	.00113	.121	.122	.000338	.107	.106	-.000951
46–200 Miles	.0920	.0935	.00156	.151	.152	.00143	.178	.177	-.000348
201–500 Miles	.0418	.0427	.000852	.0805	.0818	.00123	.125	.126	.000686
> 500 Miles	.0667	.0683	.00154	.149	.152	.00312	.323	.328	.00538

Notes: [a] African American female who is 20 years old, has one brother and fewer than four sisters, and whose mother is 40 years old and has 9 years of schooling. [b] White male who is 50 years old, has two brothers and fewer than four sisters, and whose mother is 80 years old and has 16 years of schooling. [c] Discrete change is calculated based on predicted values carried to more digits than shown in the table.

markers) always lowest. These results are as we expect for OLS. Since we have not used any of the techniques to allow a non-linear relationship that were introduced in Chapter 12, we expect to see a linear association between earnings and average distance from the mother. And, since we have not used the techniques introduced in Chapter 11 to allow any interactions with other variables, the distance separating the three lines is always the same, reflecting the shift upward or downward of the intercept depending on at what level we choose to hold constant the other variables.

As expected, Table 17.8 shows the same result for the OLS results (top row). There are three examples of discrete change for a $10,000 increase in earnings in the OLS model.[24] We illustrate the results with predicted means for earnings at $20,000 and $30,000 for each of our three levels of the other variables ("close" ideal type, "average" person, and "far" ideal type). As we saw in Figure 17.1, the predicted means for distance are lower for the "close" ideal type, in the middle for the "average" person, and highest for the "far" ideal type. But, in each case, the discrete change when earnings increase from $20,000 to $30,000 is 6.71. For OLS, if we took the predicted mean from any other point on any of the three lines in Figure 17.1 and compared it with the predicted mean at a level of earnings $10,000 lower, then the difference would be 6.71 miles. As discussed in earlier chapters, most people would likely agree that this is a small effect, based on their general daily experiences. It is also small in statistical effect size terms (just one one-hundredth of the standard deviation of earnings which is 645).

The graph in Figure 17.1b shows the results from our binary logit model, plotting the predicted probabilities of adults living more than 45 miles from their mothers. To our eyes, these lines also look fairly linear and parallel, similar to Figure 17.1a. But, if we turn to Table 17.8 we can see that the amount of discrete change in the predicted probabilities actually depends on the level at which we hold the other variables in the model. In the second row of Table 17.8, with the binary logit results, we see that the discrete changes are similar in size for the "average" person (.00747) and "far" ideal type (.00724) but smaller for the "close" ideal type (.00477). Likewise, discrete change would differ if we used the same level for other predictors but started at a different level of earnings. For example, the discrete change in predicted probabilities for a person with the "close" ideal type characteristics but $70,000 versus $60,000 in annual earnings is .00516 which is larger than the discrete change seen for this same "close" ideal type in the logit model in Table 17.8 (.00477).

Three-Category Outcome

We now turn to Figure 17.2 which shows the results for our three-category outcome variable. The first point we will take away from this figure is that, to our eyes, the results are quite similar for the multinomial logit model (on the left) and the ordered logit model (on the right). Indeed, the graphs look more different across the rows, from the top to the middle to the bottom of each column. These differences across rows reflect the results of holding the other variables constant at different levels ("close" ideal type in the top row, "average" person in the middle row, and "far" ideal type in the bottom row). To see why, let's focus on the short-dashed line which shows the predicted probabilities for the first category, living within 45 miles of the mother. As expected, people with the "close" ideal type characteristics are most likely to fall in this category: The predicted probabilities for the short-dashed line in the top graphs hover around .80. In the middle graphs, the predicted probabilities of living within 45 miles of the mother for the "average" person hover around .60. And, in the bottom graphs, this short-dashed line is at about one-third.

Table 17.8 provides some specific predicted probabilities to make these results even more concrete. The third row of numbers in the table give the predicted probabilities for occupying the "<=45 Miles" category from the multinomial logit model. Translating to percentages by multiplying by 100, we can say that among people with the "close" ideal type characteristics who earn $20,000 per year, 81.7% are predicted to live within 45 miles of their mothers. For a person with average characteristics who earns $20,000, 62.4% are predicted to live this distance from their mothers. Among people with "far" characteristics who earn $20,000 per year, 35% are predicted to live within 45 miles of their mothers. These line up with the levels of about .80, .60, and .33 seen in Figure 17.2 for the dashed lines across the three types.

Before leaving Table 17.8, we can also see in that same 3rd row of numbers that the discrete change differs depending on which of the three types we examine. For the "close" ideal type, as earnings increase from $20,000 to $30,000 the predicted probability of living within 45 miles of the mother decreases by .00487. For the "average" person and the "far" ideal type, the discrete change in predicted probability of living within 45 miles of the mother as income increases from $20,000 to $30,000 is larger (−.00748 and −.00695, respectively).

Staying with Table 17.8, we also see more precisely how similar the results are for the ordered logit and multinomial logit models. Comparing the three rows of predictions for the three-category multinomial logit model to the three rows of predicted probabilities for the three-category ordered logit model, we see that the values are generally the same to two decimals.

■ **Box 17.9**

The non-linearity inherent in the logit model also means that we have to think carefully about the results of non-significant interactions. That is, even though we may fail to reject the null hypothesis that the coefficient of an interaction term differs from zero in a logit model, the size of the difference in predicted probabilities between two groups will depend on the level of all other variables in the model (including the variables in the interaction). Testing interactions in logit models is further complicated by the heteroskedasticity inherent in these models. Allison (1999) first raised this concern about comparing groups in logit (and probit) models and introduced a strategy to address this issue when testing interactions in these models. Long (2009) provides a different strategy to address this issue, and one which we find is quite useful even beyond testing for interactions. Specifically, Long (2009) suggests using the standard errors of predicted probabilities to test for differences between groups at different levels of the other variables. These standard errors are available in the Stata margins command that we used in Chapters 16 and 17 and Long (2009) provides additional Stata commands that make it easier to test the differences between predicted probabilities and to plot the different predicted probabilities with confidence intervals for two groups within levels of another variable.

These results suggest that at least for the predictions we examine on this three-category outcome, the results are not sensitive to the violation of the proportional odds assumption in the ordered logit model (see again Table 17.6).

Turning back to Figure 17.2, we emphasize again how important it is to carefully choose the levels of covariates when presenting results. In our case, the three sets of results we examine all show the decline in predicted probabilities of living within 45 miles of the mother as earnings increase, and the increases in predicted probabilities of both living "46–500 Miles" and ">500 Miles" from the mother as earnings increase. However, because the percentage who occupy each category is close to one-third in the "far" category, the lines are much more compressed in the graphs in the bottom row of Figure 17.2, and the order of the categories changes across levels of earnings (In Figures 17.2e and 17.2f, at the lowest level of earnings, adults are most likely to live within 45 miles of their mothers; but, at the highest level of earnings adults are most likely to live more than 500 miles from the mother).

Stepping back, most would probably also still agree that the substantive size of the associations is fairly small, across all of the graphs in Figure 17.2. For example, between the extremes of earnings (zero and $80,000) the changes in the predicted probabilities are never more than 5 points.

Six-Category Outcome

We now turn our attention to the final two figures, which show the results for the six-category version of the outcome. The main conclusions from the binary logit and three-category outcome are still evident in these Figures. That is, although the lines look fairly linear to our eye, the discrete changes shown in Table 17.8 make clear that the amount of change depends on the levels we hold constant the other variables (and, discrete change will also depend on what level we choose to start at for earnings). For example, in Table 17.8 the discrete change when earnings increase from $20,000 to $30,000 in the 9th row (for "1 Mile" from the mother) is −.00982 for the "close" ideal type versus −.00750 for the "average" person and −.00408 for the "far" ideal type. In addition, the graphs in Figures 17.3 and 17.4 look more similar between columns within rows (comparing the multinomial logit and ordered logit results for the same level of the predictors) than across rows within columns (comparing the results for the same model when we use different levels for the predictors). However, in Table 17.8, we see more differences in specific predicted probabilities between the multinomial and ordered logit models for the six-category outcome than we saw in the three-category outcome. For example, the predicted probability of living "1 Mile" from the mother is .209 for the "close" ideal type at the $20,000 earnings level in the multinomial logit model but .270 for the same levels of the predictors in the ordered logit model.

For the six-category version of the outcome, the lines are especially compressed for the four farthest categories for the "close" ideal type (shown in the top row of Figure 17.4). Less than 10 percent of adults with the "close" characteristics are predicted to occupy each of these categories, leading to considerable overlap in the lines.[25] Still, the overall association is small.

The largest discrete change associated with going from no earnings to $80,000 in earnings again never appears to be more than 5 points.

Stepping Back

If we were presenting these findings in a paper, we would repeat a similar process of examining predicted probabilities and discrete change for other predictor variables. But, taking just these results for the earnings variable all together, we would focus on the results for the multinomial logit model with the three-category outcome for presentation. Conceptually, we defined these three categories to represent a distance of about an hour's drive (<=45 miles), more than an hour but within a day's drive (46–500 miles), and more than a day's drive (> 500 miles). We expect these categories reflect the kinds of tradeoffs in practical access to their mother that adults may evaluate as they consider where to live. Although as we noted above, Cheng and Long (2007) discourage use of the empirical test for the independence of irrelevant alternatives, we are in the ideal situation with the three-category outcome in that the empirical results are consistent with this conceptual rationale (as we do not reject the independence of irrelevant alternatives assumption for any categories of this version of the outcome in Table 17.6). In a figure, we would lean toward presenting the results from Figure 17.2c, for the "average person," since the lines were not compressed. We would likely also present examples of predicted probabilities and discrete change for the two extreme ideal types, similar to those shown in Table 17.8 but for the larger change (from $0 to $80,000) to emphasize the relatively small substantive size of the associations, even for the largest change on earnings for both of the two extreme "ideal types."

17.3.4: Summary

In this section, we illustrated how to summarize the results from various models in order to choose which to present in a paper; and, we emphasized some of the key differences in interpretation between the OLS and logit models. We will again note that our NSFH distance example is simplified, and were we aiming to publish about the question of explaining how far adults live from their mothers we would consider additional covariates and take advantage of the multiple waves of the NSFH (see again Section 2.3). However, even in simplified form, this section illustrates the types of decisions you would need to make as you grapple with how to present your findings in a paper.

Before ending this section, we will also reinforce again that we have limited the book to a few of the most commonly used models for categorical outcomes, although many more models exist. These include models that relax the assumptions of the multinomial and ordered logit models and that are appropriate for additional types of outcomes (e.g., models for counts of the number of times an event occurs, which are often highly skewed). We also discuss in Chapter 18 strategies you can use to learn these models, including through advanced coursework. We encourage you to build on the basic concepts introduced in this book to learn these advanced models, especially those that are implemented frequently in your subfield (so that you can understand the articles that you read and apply the models in your own work).

17.4: COMPLEX SAMPLING DESIGNS

We end this chapter by demonstrating how to estimate logit models adjusting for complex sampling design features. The general syntax, shown in Display A.17.2, is very similar to the syntax for accounting for complex sampling design features in the standard linear regression model, which we showed in Display A.8.2. The syntax also parallels the syntax for estimating logit models in SAS and Stata. Specifically, in SAS, the command is now `proc surveylogistic` (rather than `logistic`) for all three types of models (binary logit, multinomial logit, ordered logit) and we use the option `/link=glogit` to obtain the multinomial logit results. We use the same commands as we have in other SAS models to specify the complex sampling design features. In Stata, the command names are the same for the three types of models (`logit`, `mlogit`, and `ologit`), but we now precede them with the `svy` command. And, before estimating any survey model, we `svyset` the data to specify the complex sampling design features.

To demonstrate these commands, we re-estimated three of the models shown in Table 17.5: (1) the binary logit (2) the three-category multinomial logit, and (3) the three-category ordered logit. The results are shown in Displays B.17.14, B.17.15, and B.17.16. Comparing the results for our earnings predictor, we see that in all cases earnings is significantly associated with distance, as was true in Table 17.5. In most cases, the coefficients and standard errors round to the same value (within two decimals), although the coefficients in the binary logit and one multinomial logit contrast now round to 0.04 rather than 0.03.

Even though this set of results is similar with and without adjustments, we prefer the results that account for the complex sampling design, since they adjust for the oversampling, clustering and stratification built into the NSFH design. We can use many of the commands that we introduced in Part 4 to interpret the results of logit models following these survey logit commands, including `prchange, margins`, and `predict` in Stata (although not all commands have been extended to work with complex survey data).

17.5: SUMMARY

SUMMARY 17

This chapter introduced regression models for multi-category outcomes, including the multinomial logit model for nominal outcomes and the ordered logit model for ordinal outcomes. We showed how each model uses a link similar to the logit model introduced in Chapter 16 for dichotomous outcomes. For the multinomial logit model, the link is the log of the ratio of the probabilities of occupying any two of the categories (e.g., $\ln\left(\frac{\pi_1}{\pi_3}\right), \ln\left(\frac{\pi_2}{\pi_3}\right)$, and $\ln\left(\frac{\pi_1}{\pi_2}\right)$). For the ordered logit model, the link is the log of the ratio of the cumulative probability to its complement (e.g., $\ln\left(\frac{\pi_{c\le1}}{\pi_{c>1}}\right), \ln\left(\frac{\pi_{c\le2}}{\pi_{c>2}}\right)$, and $\ln\left(\frac{\pi_{c\le3}}{\pi_{c>3}}\right)$). The exponential of coefficients from multinomial and ordered logit models can be interpreted as factor change in the odds, similar to binary logit. And, we use similar formulas as we did for the binary logit model to calculate predicted probabilities for the multi-category models.

The multinomial logit and ordered logit models both have strengths and limitations. The ordered logit model is a simple extension of the binary logit model. However, it constrains the effect of covariates on the odds to be constant across outcome categories, known as the proportional odds assumption. The multinomial logit is more flexible in that it estimates a coefficient for each covariate for each pair of outcome categories. However, as the number of categories increase, the number of coefficients estimated by the multinomial logit model increases greatly and can become unwieldy to digest and interpret. Collapsing categories based on theory and prior research, or based on chi-square tests of the data in an application, can be used to simplify the multinomial logit model. The multinomial logit model also assumes that no two categories are so similar that they do not represent distinct categories that can be weighed independently by decision makers. Although tests of this assumption are available, they may not be useful in applied contexts; again, a strong conceptual rationale for the model is recommended.

KEY TERMS

Binary Logit

Cumulative Logit

Cumulative Probability

Independence of Irrelevant Alternatives Assumptions (also IIA Assumption)

Multinomial Distribution

Multinomial Logit

Ordered Logit

Proportional Odds Assumption

Reference Outcome Category

Threshold (also Cutpoint)

REVIEW QUESTIONS

17.1 Write the link for the multinomial logit and the ordered logit models and discuss how they relate to the link for the binary logit model.

17.2 Write the formulas for predicting probabilities for the multinomial logit and ordered logit models and discuss how they relate to the formula for predicting probabilities based on the binary logit model.

17.3 Show why a factor change interpretation can be used in the multinomial logit and ordered logit models.

17.4 Discuss some strengths and limitations of the multinomial and ordered logit models.

17.5 Discuss how you would evaluate whether the assumptions of the multinomial and ordered logit models are met.

REVIEW EXERCISES

17.1. Suppose that you estimate a multinomial logit model predicting one of three types of child care used by families (center, family day care, or relative care) based on the mother's years of schooling, using relative care as the reference outcome category. Imagine that the coefficient for mother's years of schooling is 0.69 for the outcome category of centers and 0.41 for the outcome category of family day care.

(a) Calculate the coefficients that you would obtain if you instead used centers as the reference outcome category.

(b) Re-express all four coefficients (the original two coefficients and the two coefficients you calculated in (a) as odds ratios.

17.2. Suppose that you estimated a multinomial logit model with a categorical variable indicating mothers' employment status as the outcome (1=not employed, 2=employed part-time, 3=employed full-time) and father's annual earnings as the predictor (rescaled to $10,000 units, Range: 1 to 20). Suppose that you obtained the following statistically significant coefficient estimates for the prediction equations, with mother not employed as the reference outcome category: $\hat{\beta}_{0,2v1} =$ 1.10 for the intercept and $\hat{\beta}_{1,2v1} = -0.10$ for the slope of father's earnings with part-time employment as the outcome; and, $\hat{\beta}_{0,3v1} = 1.19$ for the intercept and $\hat{\beta}_{1,3v1} = -0.11$ for the slope of father's earnings with full-time employment as the outcome. Respond to the following:

(a) Calculate the predicted probability for being in each outcome category for mothers whose husbands earn $30,000 per year.

(b) Calculate the predicted probability for being in each outcome category for mothers whose husbands earn $40,000 per year.

(c) Calculate and interpret the discrete change in the predicted probability of each outcome that is associated with a $10,000 increase in earnings, starting at $30,000.

CHAPTER EXERCISE

CHAPTER
EXERCISE
17

In this exercise, you will write a SAS and a Stata batch program to estimate a multinomial logit model and an ordered logit model. You will also use the survey commands to estimate logit models.

Start with the NHIS 2009 dataset that was created in Chapter 4 with an *if expression* to only keep cases that *do not have missing values on the age, exfreqwR, SEX, and bmiR variables*.

17.1 Multinomial Logit Model

a) SAS/Stata Tasks.

i) Create a dummy variable to indicate *females* (as you did in Chapter 16).

ii) Create a categorical variable named *bmiC* with the following categories: (1) body mass index below 18.5 (underweight), (2) body mass index at or above 18.5 and less than 25 (healthy weight), (3) body mass index at or above 25 and less than 30 (overweight), and (4) body mass index at or above 30 (obese).

iii) Use proc logistic with the /link=glogit option in SAS and mlogit in Stata to regress *bmiC* on the *female* dummy and the *age* and *exfreqwR* variables. Re-estimate the model two times, once with the 3rd outcome category and once with the 4th outcome category as the reference.

iv) In Stata, use the mlogtest, hausman command after both of the multinomial logit models to test the irrelevance of independent alternatives assumption.

v) In Stata, re-display the results for the model with the fourth category (obese) as the baseline, but show odds ratios with the rrr option. (Odds ratios are already in the default SAS output).

vi) In Stata, use the prchange, fromto command to request predicted probabilities, discrete change, and marginal effects.

b) Write-Up Tasks.

i) What do you conclude about the independence of irrelevant alternatives assumption, based on the output from the mlogtest, hausman command?

    ii) Use the factor change in odds approach to interpret the effects of being female in the model with the fourth category (obese) as the reference. Calculate the odds ratios by hand (write the formula out and calculate the odds ratios with your calculator rather than relying on SAS and Stata) and interpret each result.

    iii) Based on the predicted probabilities shown in the prchange output, show how to calculate and interpret in words the discrete change between men and women for each outcome category, while holding age and frequency of exercise constant at their overall sample means. Interpret the results.

17.2 Ordered Logit Model

a) SAS/Stata Tasks.

    i) Use proc logistic in SAS and ologit in Stata to regress *bmiC* on the the *female* dummy and the *age* and *exfreqwR* variables.

    ii) In Stata, use the brant command to test proportional odds assumption. (The test of proportional odds is already in the default SAS output).

    iii) In Stata, re-display the results showing odds ratios with the or option. (Odds ratios are already in the default SAS output).

    iv) In Stata, use the prchange, fromto command to request predicted probabilities, discrete change, and marginal effects.

b) Write-Up Tasks.

    i) What do you conclude about the proportional odds assumption, based on the output from SAS and Stata?

    ii) Use the factor change in odds approach to interpret the effect of being female. Calculate the odds ratios by hand (write the formula out and calculate the odds ratios with your calculator rather than relying on SAS and Stata) and interpret the result.

    iii) Based on the predicted probabilities shown in the prchange output, show how to calculate and interpret in words the discrete change between men and women, while holding age and frequency of exercise constant at their overall sample means. Interpret the results.

17.3 Complex Sampling Designs

a) SAS/Stata Tasks.

    i) Use the survey commands in SAS and Stata to re-estimate the logit model that you estimated in Question 16.1

    ii) Use the survey commands in SAS and Stata to re-estimate the multinomial logit that you estimated in Question 17.1, with the fourth category (obese) as the baseline.

iii) Use the survey commands in SAS and Stata to re-estimate the ordered logit that you estimated in Question 17.2.

b) Write-Up Tasks.

   i) Create a table summarizing the results from the survey commands and the original results, similar to Table 17.5.

   ii) Discuss how the results from the survey commands compare to the original results.

COURSE EXERCISE

If you included nominal and/or ordinal outcome variables in your data set, use one or more of them as an outcome in multinomial logit and ordered logit models. Otherwise, if you can categorize one of the continuous outcome variables that you used in earlier chapters in a conceptually meaningful way, then do so, and compare the results of the categorized outcome to your earlier results. In the multinomial and ordered logit models, test the assumption of the model (independence of irrelevant alternatives for multinomial logit; proportional odds for ordered logit), interpret the results using odds ratios, and interpret the results using predicted probabilities and discrete change.

Part 5

WRAPPING UP

Chapter 18

ROADMAP TO ADVANCED TOPICS

CHAPTER 18: ROADMAP TO ADVANCED TOPICS

In this final chapter, we will revisit the literature excerpts from Chapter 1 to help "put together" what we have learned about regression analysis. And, we will provide a roadmap to additional statistical topics that you may need or encounter as you read the literature and conduct your own projects as well as providing you with strategies for learning about these topics.

18.1: REVISITING LITERATURE EXCERPTS FROM CHAPTER 1

To help us link back to where we started, and put together what we have learned, we will begin by revisiting the four literature excerpts that we presented in Chapter 1. With more understanding under your belt now, you can interpret the findings we examined in Chapter 1 in some greater detail, and also better distinguish basic regression concepts that you now understand from advanced topics that you may want to study.

18.1.1: Revisiting Literature Excerpt 1.3

We will take the excerpts from Chapter 1 in reverse order, and begin with Literature Excerpt 1.3. Recall that this excerpt was publishing by Christine Li-Grining and examined correlates of preschoolers' "effortful control." Looking back at her Table 3, several features should be more familiar and interpretable now than they were when we first looked at this table in Chapter 1.

For example, in her column labels, she indicated that she listed the R-squared value, B (unstandardized coefficient), SE B, and β (standardized coefficient), all of which we now know how to interpret. She also reports a ΔR^2 value, which is the change in R-squared and a complementary approach to capturing the additional variation explained by a subset of variables to the partial F-test that we covered in Chapter 6 (in fact, she reports the partial F-test for the set of five *Risk factors and child-mother interaction* in the text, which are $F(5,423) = 3.76$, $p < .01$ for *Delayed gratification* and $F(5,421) = 6.21$, $p < .001$ for *Executive control*, p. 215).[1]

Let's go ahead and interpret a few of her results in more detail.

- We know that the R-squared values are the percentage of variation in the outcome explained by the set of *Child characteristics*. So, child age, gender, race, and negative emotionality explain 19 percent of the variation in *Delayed gratification* and 42 percent of the variation in *Executive control*.
- Comparing the row of coefficient estimates (Bs) to the row of standard errors (SE Bs) we can see that the coefficient estimates with asterisks are all at least twice their standard errors, and those without asterisks are all less than twice their standard errors, as expected.
- Standardized coefficients are provided that help us to interpret the substantive size of significant effects, but for dummy variables, partially standardized coefficients would be more appropriate, something we know now how to calculate. For example, partially standardizing the significant gender coefficient (circled in green in Literature Excerpt 1.3)

would involve dividing by the standard deviation of the outcome, which is reported to be 0.72 (p. 213). The result is $-0.27/0.72 = -0.38$.[2] Thus, boys score over one quarter point lower than girls on delayed gratification, a difference of nearly four tenths of a standard deviation. This is a small to moderate effect, relative to Cohen's cutoffs, but seems more substantial relative to other predictors. For example, the difference between boys and girls is about three quarters the size of the standardized change associated with one more year of age ($0.35/0.72 = 0.49$).

18.1.2: Revisiting Literature Excerpt 1.2

Our second literature excerpt from Chapter 1 was by Stephen Vaisey, who examined how a sense of collective belonging developed within communes during the 1970s. Looking back at his Table 2 (Literature Excerpt 1.2b) we see that he presented unstandardized coefficients (b), standardized coefficients (β) and t-values (t) as well as R-squared and adjusted R-squared values.

Based on the R-squared values, we see that the set of variables in the model explain a substantial amount of the variation in the outcome—over three quarters. Three of the variables have coefficients that differ significantly from zero: authority, investment, and strength of moral order, with t-values larger than 2.00.[3] As we noted in Chapter 1, one of these significant variables has a sign which is the reverse of its simple correlation with the outcome (authority; see again Literature Excerpt 1.2a). We now know that it would be helpful if Vaisey had provided the coefficient estimates and standard errors from a bivariate regression, and the standard errors from the multiple regression, to help us to learn more about this sign reversal for authority. Indeed, an Appendix Table A2 in Vaisey's article suggests that multicollinearity may be a concern, with several correlations between predictor variables being 0.70 or larger. The variable authority is itself correlated above 0.70 with four other variables: *Spatiotemporal*, *Investment*, *Moral order*, and *Previous group*.

18.1.3: Revisiting Literature Excerpt 1.4

The fourth literature excerpt from Chapter 1 was by Baker and colleagues (2010) who examined barriers to child immunization perceived by Hmong parents.

Looking back at their Table 2 (in Literature Excerpt 1.4) we now understand that the significant associations were identified because the listed p-values were less than an alpha of .05. By providing the actual p-values, rather than using asterisks to denote significance levels, the authors allow us to determine what the conclusions would be based on more or less stringent alpha levels (for example if we wanted to make the Bonferroni adjustment in Chapter 9 using the number of t-tests shown in their Table 2–30—then we would use an alpha of $\frac{.05}{30} = .0017$ and find, for example, that the p-value in the top row and final column of .015 is no longer significant with this Bonferroni adjustment).

We also now understand that both unstandardized (b) and standardized (B) associations are shown, with the standardized coefficients being useful in interpreting the substantive size of associations for continuous predictors. We also now know how to use the descriptive information presented elsewhere in the paper to help us interpret the size of associations in additional ways, although doing so may lead us to desire additional information not presented by the authors (e.g., the standard deviations of the three subscales of barriers to immunization). And, we understand how to interpret the unstandardized coefficients for *Language* and *Type of Nonemergency Health Care* relative to their reference categories (e.g., parents who speak *Hmong or mostly Hmong* score 7.40 points higher on the barriers to Access subscale than do *English and mostly English*, on average, holding constant income, education, age of arrival in the U.S., years in the U.S., and type of nonemergency health care).

We also now know, for example, that the R^2 values in the table notes provide the percentage of the variation in each subscale explained by the set of predictor variables and the F-tests tell us that at least one of the predictors has a coefficient that differs significantly from zero in each of the three regression models.

The authors conduct some additional analyses in the paper—including structural equation modeling—which we did not cover in the book; but, as we will point out in the next "Roadmap" section, builds on what we have learned.

18.1.4: Revisiting Literature Excerpt 1.1

We will end with the Lyons article, which was the first excerpt that we considered in Chapter 1. We will not reinterpret his results in detail, because he in fact uses one of the advanced topics that we include in our roadmap next (negative binomial regression, appropriate for count outcomes like his number of hate crimes). But, we will use his results as a bridge to that roadmap, and to help us to see how much of the basic concepts of regression analysis that we learned in this book are transferable knowledge that you can build upon in learning such advanced techniques.

Indeed, even though he is using a different type of regression, much of what we see in his tables is consistent with what we learned. He presents a series of models in his Table 6 (Literature Excerpt 1.1a) and Table 8 (Literature Excerpt 1.1b) which allow us to see how the coefficient estimates and standard errors change as different variables are included in the model. He introduces several interactions which are product terms between two predictor variables, and he uses predicted values to interpret the significant interaction (his Table 7, in Literature Excerpt 1.1a).

In general, much of what you have learned translates to advanced topics in regression analysis. You have the foundation on which to build, depending on which advanced topics are particularly relevant in your field and for your research interests.

18.2: A ROADMAP TO STATISTICAL METHODS

In this section, we provide a roadmap to many commonly used techniques that complement or extend beyond the foundation we have provided. We have tried to cover many common techniques, although we have left some out to keep the roadmap manageable (e.g., we do not cover the *fuzzy set analysis* technique used by Vaisey in Literature Excerpt 1.2, or important topics related to regression modeling such as *multiple imputation, social network analysis*, and *meta-analysis*). In an attempt to make the roadmap useful but not overwhelming, we have focused on the comparative strengths of each technique. Table 18.1 summarizes the situations in

■ Table 18.1: Some Key Situations that Lend Themselves to Different Models

Continuous Dependent Variable

Ordinary Least Squares (OLS)	Continuous Outcome

Categorical Dependent Variable

Logit/Probit	Dichotomous outcome
Ordered Logit/Probit	Ordinal outcome
Multinomial Logit	Nominal outcome, person characteristics as predictors
Conditional Logit	Nominal outcome, outcome category characteristics as predictors
Poisson Regression	Count outcome (e.g., number of hospital visits, number of symptoms, number of arrests); conditional variance constrained
Negative Binomial Regression	Count outcome (e.g., number of hospital visits, number of symptoms, number of arrests); conditional variance allows for "overdispersion" and "underdispersion"
Log-Linear Models	Finding a simple structure to explain the pattern of counts in a cross-classification table

Limited Dependent Variable

Censored Regression	All persons have X values; Y values missing for some persons
Truncated Regression	X and Y not observed for some persons
Sample Selection	Like censored and truncated problems, although the selection (why some persons have missing data) is modeled
Event History Analysis	Time until an event; duration or survival analysis

Systems of Equations

Structural Equation Modeling	Writing a theoretical model as a path of direct and indirect effects (mediation) and estimating multiple equations simultaneously, allowing for correlated errors
Multilevel Models	Nested structure (children clustered within classes clustered within schools; time points clustered within persons)

Measurement Theory

Factor Analysis and Item Response Theory	Identifying the dimensions (concepts) measured by items
Latent Class Analysis	Identifying groups (classes) indicated by items

Additional Topics

Sampling Theory	Samples other than simple random sample (weights to adjust for oversampling; adjustments for clustered samples)
First Difference and Fixed Effects Models	Using longitudinal data (or other clustered data) to adjust for stable characteristics of persons (or other units)
Propensity Score Models	Approach to adjusting for bias in nonexperimental studies in which a comparison group is constructed to best "match" the treatment group or the chances of being in the treatment group are controlled

which each is often used. We hope that this will help you to identify which techniques might be useful in your field or your work. We suggest strategies to locate courses and resources for learning more about any that you identify as relevant to you (indeed, entire courses are often devoted to each topic we consider in the roadmap!).

18.2.1: Categorical Outcomes

As we saw in Chapter 14, a number of problems can arise when a non-normal outcome variable produces outlying and influential cases in OLS regression. In Part 4 we introduced models that are specifically designed for dichotomous, ordinal, and nominal outcomes. As we noted, numerous additional models exist for categorical outcomes, some of which loosen assumptions of the models we considered (Agresti 2010; Long 1997; Maddala 1983; Peterson and Harrell 1990; Williams 2006; Wooldridge 2002).

Before previewing these models, it is helpful to remind ourselves that whether a variable is nominal or ordinal or interval is not always clear cut, conceptually or in common practice. Often, the same variable can be (or is) treated in different ways. For example, we can think of (and measure) years of education as an interval variable, where one more always measures one more year spent in school. Or, we could think of (and measure) educational attainment as an ordinal variable, perhaps collapsing data into highest degree attained (e.g., junior high, high school, two-year college, four-year college, masters/JD, PhD/MD). If a researcher had focused on a sample that only covered a limited range of the educational distribution (e.g., say welfare recipients who primarily had a high school diploma or not) or had particular theoretical interest in a single contrast, education might be further collapsed to a dichotomous variable.

Dichotomous Outcomes

We already considered the **logit** and **probit** models for dichotomous outcomes. They assume that the outcome takes on two values, produced by a binomial distribution. They can be interpreted in terms of the probability of the category coded one on the outcome (e.g., how are earnings associated with the probability of being married?), although some extra effort are involved in translating to probability units for interpretation (see Long 1997 and Long and Freese 2006). The logit model can also be interpreted in terms of odds (e.g., how are earnings related to the odds of being married relative to not being married?), and such interpretations are common in some subfields (including health).

Ordinal Outcomes

The **ordered logit** and **ordered probit** models are appropriate for outcome variables that have a natural order, but in which the distance between adjacent categories is unknown.

The standard linear regression model is appropriate for such outcome variables only if the true distances between outcome categories are about equal. If they are not, then results from the standard linear regression model applied to such outcome variables can be misleading (even though Likert scales are sometimes analyzed with OLS, like the *Health* outcome that we analyzed in Chapters 13 and 14). We considered the ordered logit model in Chapter 17. The ordered probit model can be similarly derived as a natural extension of probit models.

Nominal Categories

There are also additional models for outcomes that do not have a natural order beyond the **multinomial logit** model that we considered in Chapter 17, such as the **conditional logit** models. The difference between these two models is that the multinomial logit uses characteristics of the individual to predict the probability of being in the outcome categories while the conditional logit uses characteristics of the outcome to predict the probability of being in the outcome category. For example, consider the study of an unmarried young adult's residential choice (e.g., living with their parents, living alone, or living with room-mates). With a multinomial logit, we might predict their choice based on their own characteristics, such as their gender and their school/work status. With a conditional logit, we might predict their choice based on characteristics of their options, such as the financial cost to them of living in each setting and their anticipated freedom to "do what they want" in each setting. The multinomial logit is more common in the social sciences than the conditional logit, although the conditional logit model fits with a number of interesting theoretical questions (but data are often less available on characteristics associated with the outcome categories). It is also possible to combine the models, if characteristics of both the individuals making choices and the alternatives are available (Agresti 2002).

18.2.2: Censored and Truncated Samples

There are also models for "limited dependent variables" which are continuous for much of their range, but censored or truncated in some way (see Long 1997 and Long and Freese 2006). These models fall into two major categories:

1. Censored dependent variables: all study participants have observations for all the predictor variables. But, for some participants, the value of the outcome variable is unknown. Often these unknown outcome variables are missing if the true value of the outcome falls below some censoring value, hence the term censored dependent variable. For example, wages might not be observed for persons earning below the minimum wage. Often, the outcome variable is assumed to be some value (e.g., zero on the censoring value) for the censored participants.
2. Truncated dependent variables: participants are excluded from the sample (have neither predictor nor outcome) based on their true value on the outcome.

These problems are similar to the problem of **sample selection** in which peoples' chances of participating in the study are related to their value on the outcome variable.

If we estimate a standard linear regression model on the available data, then our parameter estimates will be biased.

There are three major approaches to these models:

1. The **tobit** model adjusts for censoring using the probability of a person being censored. Censoring can happen "from above," "from below," or both.
2. The **truncated regression model** adjusts the expected value from the regression model for the fact that we observe only a portion of the distribution.
3. **Sample selection models** not only adjust for the censoring or truncation, but also model the mechanism of selection. The most well known of these approaches is **Heckman's selection model** (Heckman 1979; see also Stolzenberg and Relles 1997, and Bushway, Johnson, and Slocum 2007). In short, a probit model is estimated in which the probability of being in the sample is modeled. Then a transformation of the predicted value from this probit is included in the regression of the outcome of interest on the predictor variables in the truncated sample. Below we preview the way in which researchers increasingly use propensity scores to adjust for measured differences between groups (Mueser, Troske, and Gorislavsky 2007).

18.2.3: Count Outcomes

Models for count outcomes share something in common with the models we have already considered—like the models for ordinal and nominal outcomes, they attempt to recognize more appropriately the measurement form of the outcome variable. Like the censored and truncated regression models, extensions of models for count outcomes adjust for an overabundance of zero counts in the data or for the failure to observe persons with zero counts.

The major models are: (a) the **Poisson** regression model (b) the **Negative Binomial** regression model (c) the zero modified count model, and (d) the truncated count model. Poisson and negative binomial regression models have become especially common in social science when researchers analyze count outcomes.

Each of these adjusts for some cautions of the others: the Negative Binomial adjusts for a restriction that the conditional variance must equal the conditional mean in the Poisson regression model (allowing for something referred to as underdispersion and overdispersion; see again Literature Excerpt 1.1). The zero modified and truncated count models adjust for censoring and truncation, respectively.

18.2.4: Log-Linear Models

We have already considered a basic concept of log-linear models: We logged the outcome variable to allow for a nonlinear relationship with the predictor variables. Log-linear models also rely on the log transformation but use the Poisson rather than normal distribution and move away from the dependent and independent variable structures. Instead, the objective is to analyze the counts in the cells of a cross-classification table (e.g., a cross-tabulation of race against education) to determine if a simple underlying structure can explain the pattern of counts (Agresti 2007).

18.2.5: Structural Equation Models

Structural equation models allow several regression models, with different outcomes, to be estimated simultaneously (Bollen 1989). This can allow us to capture better a complete theoretical model building on the basic concepts of path analysis that we learned in Chapter 10 (e.g., pathways of direct and indirect effects). Through this simultaneous estimation, we can also allow for errors across equations to be correlated. Structural equation modeling is sometimes associated with the computer package LISREL (Scientific Software International 2009), although many other packages for estimating SEM models are available (e.g., AMOS, EQS, MPlus).

18.2.6: Multilevel Models

In recent years, multilevel models, sometimes referred to as hierarchical linear models (HLMs), have become increasingly popular in the social sciences (Bickel 2007; Rabe-Hesketh and Skrondal 2005; Raudenbush and Bryk 2002). These models allow the appropriate analysis of data which has a natural nested structure, for example students clustered within classrooms clustered within schools or times of measurement clustered within persons. These models are important because they can adjust for the lack of independence within the clusters (i.e., OLS standard errors would typically be too small if the clustering were ignored). They also allow theoretically interesting cross-level effects to be estimated.

18.2.7: First Difference and Fixed Effects Models

We can also capitalize on clustered data, including longitudinal data with individuals clustered over time, to adjust for unmeasured characteristics of the units of study that might otherwise bias our results. One way to do this is with first difference or fixed effects models (Allison 2005; Wooldridge 2009). The intuition is that by taking a difference in measures for the same individual, we adjust for any pre-existing (time-constant) characteristics of the individual that affect their measure at both time points, and see if what remains can be explained by the predictor variable(s) of interest.

18.2.8: Propensity Score Models

Propensity score analysis is increasingly used for non-experimental evaluations and social science research (Imbens and Wooldridge 2009; Williamson, Morley, Lucas, and Carpenter 2011). Several general approaches are common, including propensity score matching and propensity score weighting. Propensity score matching mimics the experimental context by constructing a comparison group from those who were not treated. Without random assignment, some of those who were not treated may differ from those who were treated in important ways that affect their outcomes. The matching approach identifies the non-treated persons who are most similar to each treated person. Although popularized for evaluations, this approach can also be used in social science contexts in which we compare two groups (e.g., married to unmarried persons; gang members to non-gang members; high school graduates to high school dropouts) and are concerned about selective differences between the two groups that may affect their outcomes. Contemporary matching approaches predict treatment status and then use the predicted probability of treatment to make the match. Propensity score weighting approaches similarly predict treatment status, but then adjust for the probability of treatment in a regression context. Like OLS regression, propensity score approaches only adjust for measured confounds. However, propensity score approaches can perform better than OLS, especially when the predictor variables have complex non-linear and interactive associations with the outcomes (Black and Smith 2002; Sanders Smith, and Zhang 2007).

18.2.9: Survey Methods/Complex Data Analysis

As we have emphasized throughout the book, if your data were gathered with a complex sampling design, you should account for the design features in your analyses.

Most frequently, people do not have a uniform chance of being part of the sample, but instead some are oversampled (e.g., the NSFH that we have analyzed in this book oversampled persons from certain racial/ethnic backgrounds and with certain kinds of household composition). This beneficially increases sample size for these subgroups, but simple descriptive statistics will not reflect the population unless this oversampling is accounted. As we have seen, sampling weights are often created to produce statistics that are representative of the original targeted population. Typically, these weights are the inverse of the probability of selection.

In addition, samples are often clustered, typically in multiple sample stages. As we have discussed most typically, clustering occurs to save costs—most national samples first choose "primary sampling units" and then select smaller sampling units within these, and finally select households and/or individuals. For example, they might first sample cities and then census tracts within cities and then households. This lowers the costs of the survey by focusing the survey teams' efforts on smaller geographic areas. It also avoids the problem of not having a listing of all persons in the USA to sample from (e.g., once a census tract is chosen, the survey team goes out to "enumerate" (list) every living space in that census tract).

After completing the book, you should now better understand why regression models estimated on complex samples should account for the fact that persons who live in a cluster are often more alike than persons randomly sampled from the population. This nonindependence of errors violates an OLS assumption. Typically, standard errors will be underestimated if this non-independence is not addressed.

We also saw in Part 1 of the book that complex sampling designs often organize people into subpopulations, called strata, such as those defined by regions of the U.S., urbanicity of the area, or racial-ethnic composition. PSUs and people can be drawn separately within strata, for example to assure adequate representation from each subpopulation. Typically, stratification reduces standard errors, and standard errors will be overestimated if strata are not taken into account.

We noted in Chapter 8 that two broad approaches exist for addressing complex sampling designs: a design-based and a model-based approach. We have demonstrated the design-based approach in the book. The model-based approach builds on the multiple regression techniques we have learned by adding predictor variables that designate design features (e.g., oversampled groups) and uses the multilevel modeling techniques we discussed above to adjust for clustering. A challenge to implementing the model-based approach is that the design features must be correctly specified (including any non-linear associations with the outcome and interactions with other predictor variables). It is also possible to extend the heteroskedasticity-consistent robust standard errors that we discussed in Chapter 14 can be used to adjust standard errors for clustered samples (Wooldridge 2009).

18.2.10: Event History Analysis

Event history analysis (sometimes also called survival analysis or duration analysis) is appropriate when the outcome variable is the time until an event occurs (Blossfeld and Rohwer 2002; Yamaguchi 1991). For example: What predicts the length of time until a dating couple becomes engaged? What predicts the length of time until a company dissolves? What predicts the length of time until a person dies? These approaches are more appropriate than OLS for such questions because, for example, they adjust for the fact that some of the people who have not had the event at the time of the last interview may still have the event in the future.

18.2.11: Measurement Theory/Psychometrics

Errors in the measurement of variables can distort or cloud relationships. Ideally, we should be able to distinguish poor measurement of our key concepts from lack of relationships among the true concepts. Psychometric models allow us to devise better measures. As discussed in Chapter 14, commonly used techniques are exploratory and confirmatory factor analyses and item response theory models (Andrich 1988; Harrington 2008; Long 1983; Ostini and Nering 2006).

Factor analysis uses correlations among variables to identify whether particular sets of variables tap underlying dimensions. Confirmatory differs from exploratory factor analysis in that you would explicitly lay out in advance which variables map onto which dimensions. As an example, social support is often divided into affective (expressing caring, "being there," spending time together) and instrumental (loaning money, watching one another's children, providing a job tip) dimensions. Item response theory models also identify whether items capture particular dimensions, but are not focused on correlations. For example, the Rasch measurement model differs from the factor analysis approach in that it analyzes the joint order of persons and items assuming that items "lower" on the dimension are answered positively by more persons than items "higher" on the dimension. For example, we might hypothesize that "providing a job tip" would be "lower" on the dimension of instrumental social support (observed more often) than "loaning money." Applying Rasch analyses and confirmatory factor models can greatly improve measures of key constructs, allowing models to test better for theoretical relationships.

Latent class analysis also uses observed variables to specify latent constructs, but in this case the latent constructs are categorical. Typically, the observed variables are categorical as well and the latent classes offer a way to reduce down to a few key response patterns the numerous cells formed by cross-classifying several multi-category variables (Collins and Lanza 2010). Cluster analysis is a similar approach, although latent class analysis has been shown to outperform it and latent class analysis has been incorporated within multi-equation regression modeling contexts (Magidson and Vermunt 2002; Muthén and Muthén 2007).

18.3: A ROADMAP TO LOCATING COURSES AND RESOURCES

As noted above, we have painted broad brush strokes in this roadmap, and to actually understand and apply the techniques would require substantial additional reading and training. Here we offer some suggestions for locating courses and resources for doing so. We have also only "dipped our toe" into the capabilities of the SAS and Stata software, and provided a smattering of references to other advanced software. Thus, we also provide some suggestions about courses and resources for learning about these powerful statistical packages below.

18.3.1: Statistics

We have provided references to books and journal articles throughout the book that offer a starting point for reading about advanced topics. Most likely, though, you will want to take a course or otherwise interact with instructors and peers as you learn an advanced topic. One way to do so is to take courses at your own university or other universities in your area. In checking for courses, it is often helpful to look at course offerings in departments outside of your discipline (including the statistics department), since much of statistics training crosses disciplinary boundaries and the limited number of faculties in any one department generally cannot cover all advanced topics (although, if available, taking a course in or close to your discipline can help you to understand how to apply it to research questions in your field). You will likely want to check for courses in fields such as human development, education, public health, social work, and public policy (if available in your geographic area) as well as departments such as sociology, psychology, economics, and political science.

Short courses are also offered by organizations and individuals that allow you to immerse yourself in a topic, typically over a day or two or a week or two. For example, ICPSR has long offered summer programs in quantitative methods, ranging from basic introductory statistics to a number of the advanced topics in our roadmap (ICPSR 2009). The University of Kansas's Quantitative Psychology program offers regular five-day summer programs on a range of advanced topics (University of Kansas 2009). Some individual faculties regularly offer short courses as well. For example, University of Pennsylvania sociology professor Paul Allison offers regular courses at locations across the country on longitudinal data analysis, event history analysis, categorical data analysis, and missing data analysis through his *Statistical Horizons* company (Allison 2009). Other resources may be found online (for example professor Alan Reifman at Texas Tech University often posts an annual compilation of summer statistics programs at *reifmanintrostats.blogspot.com*

18.3.2: Statistical Software

There are also numerous resources for learning statistical software, locally and nationally. You may want to start by checking with your local computing department (or those at other universities in your area) to see whether they offer basic courses in statistical programming. Most statistical software companies also offer their own training resources. For example, Stata offers NetCourses, which are taught over the Internet on a variety of topics, as well as onsite training and affiliated short courses (StataCorp 2009c). SAS offers live web-based courses, e-learning, onsite training, and other training opportunities (SAS 2009). Specialized software companies also offer training (e.g., see again Scientific Software International 2009). Numerous excellent online resources and user communities also exist (one excellent example is the UCLA Statistical Computing Group, 2009 which offers detailed publicly accessible resources specific to SAS, Stata, and SPSS). Various listservs and online forums are also available.

18.4: SUMMARY

SUMMARY
18

In this chapter, we revisited the literature excerpts from Chapter 1 to reinforce what we have learned (and have yet to learn) about regression models. We provided a roadmap of advanced topics that relate to or build upon the foundation of regression techniques taught in this book. And, we offered suggestions about where and how to get additional training in statistics and statistical computing. We hope that these offer you a range of resources to turn to as you begin to apply statistical analyses and regression modeling in your own research!

KEY TERMS

KEY TERMS
18

Conditional Logit

Heckman's Selection Model

Latent Class Analysis

Negative Binomial

Ordered Probit

Poisson

Propensity Score Models

Sample Selection

SUMMARY OF SAS AND STATA COMMANDS

The following displays summarize SAS and Stata commands used in the book.

The displays are organized by chapter, with each chapter's display summarizing the commands introduced in that chapter.

The displays are numbered with this appendix letter (A) followed by the chapter number and, where needed, a number representing the order where the commands were discussed in the chapter. For example Display A.4.1 summarizes the first set of SAS and Stata commands introduced in Chapter 4.

■ Display A.3 Basic File Types in SAS and Stata

Type	Format	Content	Usual Extension	
			SAS	Stata
data	plain text	**The information you want to analyze (but not yet in a format SAS or Stata can analyze)** ■ must be "read" by SAS or Stata before it can be used in analyses ■ organized in rows of observations and columns of variables ■ can be viewed by any text editor (e.g., Notepad, Textpad) or word processing software (e.g., WordPerfect, MS Word)	.dat .raw .txt	.dat .raw .txt
	SAS/Stata format	**The information you want to analyze (saved in a format SAS or Stata can analyze)** ■ can be viewed in SAS's spreadsheet utility called the "Table Editor" or Stata's spreadsheet called the "Data Browser" ■ cannot be viewed or used by other software (unless converted)	.sas7bdat	.dta
batch program	plain text	**The analyses you want SAS or Stata to conduct** ■ written in SAS or Stata syntax using SAS or Stata commands ■ can be written using any text editor (SAS and Stata also have built in editors) ■ can also be written or viewed using a word processor but do not save these files in the word processor's format or they will not be readable by SAS or Stata (they must "plain" or "ascii" text) files ■ be sure to **save** your batch programs frequently as you write them!	.sas	.do
results	plain text rich text	**The results of the analyses SAS or Stata has conducted for you** ■ can be viewed in the SAS output window or Stata results window ■ SAS has a separate "Log" window which reviews submitted statements, lists any messages and errors that occurred while SAS tried to run those statements, and summarizes how long it took to run the statements; this window is generally of temporary interest as you "debug" (look for errors in) a batch program ■ SAS' results (output window) can be saved in rich text format using the "ods" command (more on this in Chapter 4) so that the results can be viewed and edited in any word processor ■ Stata combines the review of commands, error messages, and processing speed with the results in a single results window. Stata's results can be saved in a Stata-specific .smcl format, although we will use the plain text (with the .log extension) since they are easy to read in any software	.log .rtf	.log .smcl

■ **Display A.4.1. Common Operators in SAS and Stata**

	Meaning	SAS Letters	SAS Symbols	Stata Symbols
Comparison Operators				
	Equal to	EQ	=	=
	Not equal to	NE	~=	~=
				!=
	Greater than	GT	>	>
	Greater than or equal to	GE	>=	>=
	Less than	LT	<	<
	Less than or equal to	LE	<=	<=
Logical Operators				
	And	AND	&	&
	Or	OR	|	|
	Not	NOT	~	~
				!
Arithmetic Operators				
	Multiplication	n/a	*	*
	Division	n/a	/	/
	Addition	n/a	+	+
	Subtraction	n/a	−	−

Notes:
- The & symbol (read ampersand) is typically found above the number 7 on the keyboard.
- On many keyboards, the | symbol (read vertical bar or pipe) is found on the key above the enter key (above the backward slash \). On the keyboard, it usually appears as two separate small lines, one above each other, although it appears as one solid vertical line on the screen.
- The ~ symbol (read tilde) is usually found on the top left of the keyboard.
- SAS can use either the letters or symbols. The letters may be easier to interpret at first, although using the symbol is more parallel to Stata.
- There are some additional symbols allowed in each language (see the respective help pages for each package). For simplicity, we include only one in most cases.
- To avoid unexpected results, put "or" expressions in parentheses and precede each variable name with an operator. For example, if (var1=6 | var1=7) not "if var1=6 | 7".

Display A.4.2 Summary of SAS and Stata Commands for Reading and Saving Data and for Creating and Checking Variables

	SAS	Stata
Locate formats	`libname library "<path>";`	n/a

Save results	`ods rtf body=<"path and filename.rtf">;`
	 `. . .`
	 `ods rtf close;`
		`log using <filename>, replace text`
		 `. . .`
		 `log close`

Read and save data	`data <path and data filename>;`
	 `set <path and data filename>`
	 `(keep= <variable list>);`
	 `if <expression>;`
	 `run;`
		`use <variable list> using <data filename> ///`
		 `if <expression>`
		 `. . . .`
		 `save <data filename>, replace`

Check raw data against codebook	`proc freq; tables <variable list>; run;`	`codebook <variable list>, tabulate (400)`
Cross-tab created and original variables	`proc freq; tables <var1>*<var2> /missing; run;`	`tabulate <var1> <var2>, missing`

Create and modify variables	`if <expression> then <variable name> =`
	 `expression;`
		`generate <variable name> = <expression> ///`
		 `if <expression>`
		 `replace <variable name> = <expression> if <expression>`

Add comments	`/* comment */`
	 `* comment ;`
		`/* comment */`
		 `* comment`
		 `// comment`

Notes	* You supply words in angle brackets <>
	 * Highlighted text is optional.
	
	 * In SAS, variable creation and modification must occur within the DATA Step (between the word DATA and Run).
	 * SAS statements must end with a semi-colon.
	 * SAS is not case sensitive. You can type statements, data filenames, and variable names in lowercase and/or uppercase.
		* Stata commands do not need a semi-colon at the end, but if you want to space a command over multiple lines you can use continuation comments (///) at the end of each continuing line (see examples above in "Read and Save Data" and "Create and Modify Variables" and in Display B.4.7).
		 * Stata is case sensitive. Commands must be typed in all lowercase. Variable names must be typed with lowercase and/or capitals to match how you named them or how they were named in the raw data.
		 * Add the following to the start of your batch program to facilitate debugging:
		
		 `version 11`
		 `set more off`
		 `capture drop _all`
		 `capture log close`
		
		 * Version 11 could be further specified with decimals (e.g., Version 11.1) to more precisely account for updates between major releases.

Display A.4.3 Summary of SAS and Stata Commands for Reading *ascii* Data and for Merging Data.

	SAS	Stata
Read ASCII data	data <path and data filename>; infile<path and data filename> lrecl = <number>; input <list of variables and their locations>; run;	infix <list of variables and their locations> using <data filename> ... save <data filename>, replace
Merge data	data <path and data filename>; merge <path and data filename> (keep= <variable list>) <path and data filename> (keep= <variable list>); by <merge variable name>; run;	use <variable list> using <data filename> merge 1:1 <merge variable name> using <filename> save <data filename>, replace
Notes	* You supply words in angle brackets <> * Highlighted text is optional.	

APPENDIX A

■ Display A.5.1. Summary of SAS and Stata Commands Introduced in Chapter Five (Basic Descriptive Statistics)

	SAS	Stata
Frequency and percentage distribution	proc freq; tables <variable list>; run;	tabl <variable list>
Percentiles	proc means p1 p5 p10 p25 p50 p75 p90 p95 p99; var <variable list>; run;	centile <var1>, centile(<desired percentile>)
Median	proc means p50; var <variable list>; run;	centile <var1>, centile(50)
Mean and standard deviation	proc means mean std min max; var <variable list>; run;	summarize <variable list>
Box plot	proc sgplot; vbox <var1>; run;	graph box <var1> graph export <filename>.wmf, replace
Box plot (without SAS Graph)	proc univariate plots; var <variable list>; run;	n/a
Histogram	proc sgplot; histogram <var1>; run;	histogram <var1>; graph export <filename>.wmf, replace
Histogram (without SAS Graph)	proc univariate plots; var <variable list>; run;	n/a

Note. Shaded text is optional. Text in angular brackets is user-supplied

Display A.5.2. Summary of SAS and Stata Commands Introduced in Chapter Five (Basic Descriptive Statistics) that Account for Complex Sample Designs

	SAS	Stata
Store the complex design features for future svy commands	n/a	svyset <psu variable> [pw=<weight variable>], /// strata(<stratum variable>) /// singleunit (certainty)
Weighted proportion	proc surveymeans mean rate=<data set name>; class <variable list>; var <variable list>; domain <subgroup variable>; cluster <psu variable>; strata <stratum variable>; weight <weight variable>; run;	svy, subpop(<subgroup variable>): tabulate <var1>
Weighted mean	proc surveymeans mean rate=<data set name>; var <variable list>; domain <subgroup variable>; cluster <psu variable>; strata <stratum variable>; weight <weight variable>; run;	svy, subpop(<subgroup variable>): mean <var1>
Weighted standard deviation	proc means mean std vardef=weight; var <variable list>; where <subgroup variable>=1; weight <weight variable>; run;	svy, subpop(<subgroup variable>): mean <var1> /// if <subgroup variable>==1 estat sd
Comments	The *psu variable* designates the primary sampling units. The *weight variable* contains the sampling weights. The *stratum variable* designates the strata. The options "singleunit(certainty)" in Stata and "rate=<data set name>" in SAS account for certainty PSUs. The *subgroup variable* takes on the value 0 for cases not to be included in the analysis and takes on the value 1 for cases to be included in the analysis (StataCorp 2009a: 53). In SAS additional levels of the domain can be specified, and in Stata some svy commands allow the use of the ", over" option for additional levels. In Stata, weighted proportions and weighted means should be requested for one variable at a time. otherwise, the "tabulate" command will produce cross-tabulations. And, the "mean" command will drop cases missing on any of the variables in a variable list. In SAS, one or more variables can be listed in a single variable list. Stata's "estat sd" command must follow a request for a weighted mean.	

Note. Shaded text is optional. Text in angular brackets is user-supplied.

▪ Display A.6 Summary of SAS and Stata Commands Introduced in Chapter Six (Sample, Population, and Sampling Distributions)

	SAS	Stata
Obtain probability of a value more extreme than calculated test statistic (one tail)		
Z distribution	pz=(1-probnorm(abs(<z value>))); put "p-value for z:" pz 5.4;	di (1-normal(abs(<z value>)))
t distribution	pt=(1-probt(abs(<t value>),<df>)); put "p-value for t:" pt 5.4;	di ttail(<df>,abs(<t value>))
F distribution	pf=(1-probf(<F value>,<df1>,<df2>)); put "p-value for f:" pf 5.4;	di Ftail(<df1>,<df2>,<F value>)
χ^2 distribution	pc=(1-probchi(<chi-sq value>,<df>)); put "p-value for Chi-square:" pc 5.4;	di chi2tail(<df>,<chi-sq value>)
Obtain probability of a value more extreme than calculated test statistic (both tails)		
Z distribution	pz=2*(1-probnorm(abs(<z value>))); put "p-value for z:" pz 5.4;	di 2*(1-normal(abs(<z value>)))
t distribution	pt=2*(1-probt(abs(<t value>),<df>)); put "p-value for t:" pt 5.4	di 2*(ttail(<df>,abs(<t value>)))

Notes: In SAS, the desired commands should be placed between the following syntax:

```
data _null_; file print; <commands>; run;
```

For example:

```
data _null_;
    file print;
    pf=(1-probf(1.60,1,13));
    put "p-value for f:" pf 5.4;
run;
```

■ **Display A.71. Summary of SAS and Stata Commands Introduced in Chapter Seven (Basic Inferential Statistics)**

	SAS	Stata

Two-sample t-test, assuming equal variances	`proc ttest;`
	`  class <twocatvar>;`
	`  var <var1>;`
	`run;`
		`ttest <var1>, by(<twocatvar>)`

Two-sample test for equal variances		`sdtest <var1>, by(<twocatvar>)`
Two-sample t-test, allowing unequal variances		`ttest <var1>, by(<twocatvar>) unequal`

Request sub-group means	`proc means;`
	`  var <var1>;`
	`  class <cat1>;`
	`run;`
		`bysort <cat1>: summarize <var1>`

One-way analysis of variance	`proc anova;`
	`  class <cat1>;`
	`  model <var1>=<cat1>;`
	`run;`
		`oneway <var1> <cat1>`

Request row, column and cell percentages	`proc freq;`
	`  tables <rowcat>*<colcat>;`
	`run;`
		`tabulate <rowcat> <colcat>, row column cell`

Pearson product moment chi-square	`proc freq;`
	`  tables <rowcat>*<colcat>`
	`  / chisq expected norow nocol nopercent;`
	`run;`
		`tabulate <rowcat> <colcat>, chi2 expected`

Pearson correlation, with p-values	`proc corr;`
	`  var <var1> <var2>;`
	`run;`
		`pwcorr <var1> <var2>, obs sig`

Notes:	*var1* and *var2* stand for continuous variables. *twocatvar* stands for a two-category variable. *rowcat*, *colcat*, and *cat1* stand for categorical variables with two or more categories; *rowcat* stands for row category and *colcat* stands for column category in a cross-tabulation. (in both SAS and Stata cross-tabulation results present better if the variable with the larger number of categories is listed first)	

Shaded text is optional. Text in angular brackets is user-supplied

Note. Shaded text is optional. Text in angular brackets is user-supplied

■ Display A.7.2. Summary of SAS and Stata Commands Introduced in Chapter Seven (Basic Inferential Statistics) that Account for Complex Sample Designs

	SAS	Stata

Weighted sub-group means and standard deviations	proc means mean std vardef=weight;
	  var <var1>;
	    class <cat1>;
	    weight <weight variable>;
	    where <subgroup variable>==1;
	
	run;
		bysort <cat1>: summarize <var1> [aw=<weight variable>] ///
		  if <subgroup variable>==1

Weighted cross-tabulation	proc freq;
	  tables <rowcat>*<colcat>;
	  weight <weight variable>;
	  where <subgroup variable>==1;
	run;
		tabulate <rowcat> <colcat> [aw=<weight variable>], row column cell ///
		  if <subgroup variable>==1

Weighted correlation	proc corr ;
	  var <var1> <var2>;
	  weight <weight variable>;
	  where <subgroup variable>==1;
	run;
		pwcorr <var1> <var2> [aw=<weight variable>] ///
		  if <subgroup variable>==1, obs sig

Comments	The subgroup variable indicates the analytic sample. The weight variable contains the sampling weights. var1 and var2 stand for continuous variables. rowcat, colcat, and cat1 stand for categorical variables with two or more categories; rowcat stands for row category and colcat stands for column category in a cross-tabulation. (in both SAS and Stata cross-tabulation results present better if the variable with the larger number of categories is listed first)	

■ **Display A.8 Summary of SAS and Stata Commands Introduced in Chapter Eight (Basic Concepts of Bivariate Regression)**

	SAS	Stata

Calculate sample means and standard deviations	`proc means;`
	`  var <variable list>;`
	`run;`
		`summarize <variable list>`

Calculate Pearson correlation coefficients	`proc corr;`
	`  var <variable list>;`
	`run;`
		`correlate <variable list>`

Estimate one bivariate regression model	`proc reg;`
	`  model <depvar>=<indepvar>;`
	`run;`
		`regress <depvar> <indepvar>`

Estimate two bivariate regression models	`proce reg;`
	`  model <depvar>=<indepvar1>;`
	`  model <depvar>=<indepvar2>;`
	`run;`
		`regress <depvar> <indepvar1>`
		`regress <depvar> <indepvar2>`

Request 95% confidence interval	`proc reg;`
	`  model <depvar>=<indepvar> / clb;`
	`run;`
		`* in default output *`

Request standardized coefficients	`proc reg;`
	`  model <depvar>=<indepvar> / stb;`
	`run;`
		`regress <depvar> <indepvar>, beta`

■ **Display A.9 Summary of SAS and Stata Commands Introduced in Chapter Nine (Basic Concepts of Multiple Regression)**

	SAS	Stata

Estimate one multiple regression model	`proc reg;`
	`  model <depvar>=<variable list>;`
	`run;`
		`regress <depvar> <variable list>`

Estimate "intercept-only" model	`proc reg;`
	`  model hrchores=;`
	`run;`
		`regress hrchores`

Conduct general linear F test	`test <variable list>;`
	
	`** in SAS, the variables in the`
	`variable list for the test command`
	`are separated by commas.`
	`** conducts test based on most`
	`recently estimated regression`
	`model.`
		`test <variable list>`
		
		`** in Stata, the variables in the`
		`variable list are not separated by`
		`commas.`
		`** conducts test based on most`
		`recently estimated regression`
		`model.`

APPENDIX A

■ Display A.10. Summary of SAS and Stata Commands Introduced in Chapter Ten (Dummy Variables)

	SAS	Stata

Succinct syntax to create dummy variable	`if <expression> then`
	`<varname> = <true/false expression>;`
	
	The true/false expression should evaluate to "true" for the cases that should be coded a '1' on the new dummy variable and should evaluate to "false" for the cases that should be coded a '0' on the new dummy variable. The shaded "if" qualifier can be used to be sure that cases with missing value codes are coded '.' missing on the new variable.
		`generate <varname> = <true/false expression> if <expression>`

Request variance-covariance matrix of coefficients	`proc reg;`
	`  model <depvar> = <variable list> /covb;`
	`run;`
		`regress <depvar> <variable list>`
		`  estat vce`

Calculate linear combination of coefficients	N/A	`regress <depvar> <variable list>` `  lincom <indepvar1> - <indepvar2>`

■ **Display A.11. Summary of SAS and Stata Commands Introduced in Chapter Eleven (Interactions)**

	SAS	Stata
Create a product term to test for an interaction	`<interact> = <var1>*<var2>;`	`generate <interact> = <var1>*<var2>`
Test conditional effect of one variable within levels of the other variable		

Re-estimating	`<var2c> = <var2> - <level2>;`
	`<interactc> = <var1>*<var2c>;`
	`proc reg;`
	`model <depvar> = <var1> var2c interactc>;`
	`run;`
		`generate <var2c> = <var2> - <level2>`
		`generate <interactc> = <var1>*<var2c>`
		`regress <depvar> <var1> var2c interactc>`

test command	`test <var1> + <level2>*<interact> = 0;`	`test <var1> + <level2>*<interact> = 0`
lincom command	n/a	`lincom <var1> + <level2>*<interact>`

Conduct Chow test	`proc reg;`
	`model <depvar> = <variable list> <groupvar>`
	`<interaction list>;`
	`test <group var> <interaction list>;`
	`run;`
		`regress <depvar> <variable list> ///`
		`<groupvar> <interaction list>`
		`test <group var> <interaction list>`

Notes:

All variable creation in SAS must happen in the data step.
var1   = name of one variable in the interaction
var2   = name of the other variable in the interaction
level2   = level of other variable for calculating conditional effect of one variable (e.g., to calculate the conditional effect of hours of work for families with two children, level2=2)
groupvar   = a variable defining two subgroups for a fully interacted model
variable list = list of variables (other than groupvar) in a fully interacted model
interaction list = list of product terms created by multiplying together each variable with the groupvar

Display A.12. Summary of SAS and Stata Commands Introduced in Chapter Twelve (Nonlinear Relationships)

	SAS	Stata
Create squared predictor	`<sqvar1> = <var1> * <var1>;`	`generate <sqvar1> = <var1> * <var1>`
Create logged predictor or outcome	`<logvar1> = log(var1);`	`generate <logvar1> = log(var1)`

Estimate quadratic model	`proc reg;`
	`  model <depvar> = <var1> <sqvar1>;`
	`run;`
		`regress <depvar> <var1> <sqvar1>`

Estimate log-log model	`proc reg;`
	`  model <logdepvar> = <logindepvar>;`
	`run;`
		`regress <logdepvar> <logindepvar>`

Estimate log-lin model	`proc reg;`
	`  model <logdepvar> = <indepvar>;`
	`run;`
		`regress <logdepvar> <indepvar>`

Calculate adjustment for predictions and R-squared in natural units	`/* obtain predicted value, in log units */`
	`proc reg;`
	`  model <logdepvar> = <indepvar>;`
	`  output out=predict (keep=<depvar> logYhat logResid)`
	`    predicted=logYhat residual=logResid;`
	`run;`
	
	`/* Transform predicted values back to natural units */`
	`data predict2;`
	`  set predict;`
	`  explogyhat=exp(logYhat);`
	`  explogResid=exp(logResid);`
	`run;`
	
	`/* Coefficient from the following regression is adjustment`
	`factor for predicted values */`
	`proc means data=predict2;`
	`  var explogResid;`
	`run;`
	
	`/* R-squared from the following regression is R-squared`
	`in natural units of Y */`
	`proc reg data=predict2;`
	`  model <devpar>=explogYhat;`
	`run;`
		`/* obtain predicted values, in log units */`
		`regress <logdepvar> <indepvar>`
		`predict logYhat`
		`predict logResid, residuals`
		
		`/* Transform predicted values back to natural units */`
		`generate explogyhat=exp(logYhat)`
		`generate explogResid=exp(logResid)`
		
		`/* Coefficient from the following regression is`
		`adjustment factor for predicted values */`
		`summarize explogResid // adjustment`
		
		`/* R-squared from the following regression is`
		`R-squared in natural units of Y */`
		`regress <depvar> explogYhat // R-squared`

Note:

The log of zero or negative values is undefined. A positive value may be added to the variable prior to transformation to deal with such values (if these values are not numerous and the maximum value on the variable is not small). Care must be taken to add this value back following transformation of predicted values into their natural units.

■ Display A.13. Summary of SAS and Stata Commands Introduced in Chapter Thirteen (Indirect Effects and Omitted Variable Bias)

	SAS	Stata
Estimating total effect	```proc reg; model <depvar> = <indepvar>; run;```	`regress <depvar> <indepvar>`
Estimating direct effect	```proc reg; model <depvar> = <indepvar> <medvar>; run;```	`regress <depvar> <indepvar> <medvar>`
Estimating extra regression for calculating indirect effect	```proc reg; model <medvar> = <indepvar>; run;```	`regress <medvar> <indepvar>`
Notes: indepvar = predictor of interest medvar = mediating variable		

■ **Display A.14. Summary of SAS and Stata Commands Introduced in Chapter Fourteen (Outliers, Heteroskedasticity, and Multicollinearity)**

	SAS	Stata
Outlying and Influential Observations		
| Graph individual variables | ```
proc univariate plots;
  var <variable list>;
run;
``` | ```
stem <variable name>
histogram <variable name>
graph box <variable name>
``` |
| Create scatterplots | ```
proc gplot;
  plot <var1>*<var2>;
run;
``` | ```
graph twoway scatterplot <var1> <var2>
``` |
| Calculate diagnostic measures | ```
proc reg;
  model <depvar> = <variable list> /r influence;
  ods output outputstatistics=<influence>;
run;
``` | ```
regress <depvar> <variable list>
predict HatDiagonal, hat
predict RStudent, rstudent
predict CooksD, cooksd
predict DFFITS, dffts
predict DFB_<indepvar1>, dfbeta(<indepvar1>)
predict DFB_<indepvar2>, dfbeta(<indepvar2>)
predict DFB_<indepvar3>, dfbeta(<indepvar3>)
``` |
| | Notes: In Stata, to calculate DFBETAS, the code "predict DFB_<indepvar1>, dfbeta (<indepvar1>)" should be repeated for each variable in the variable list. | |
| Compare diagnostic measures to cutoffs | ```
data <influence2>;
  set <influence>;
  HatDiagonal3Hi  =HatDiagonal        >3*(k-1)/n;
  RStudentHi      =abs(RStudent)      >2;
  CooksDHi        =CooksD             >4/n;
  DFFITSHi        =abs(DFFITS)        >2*sqrt((k-1)/n);
  DFB_indepvar1Hi =abs(DFB_indepvar1) >2/sqrt(n);
  DFB_indepvar2Hi =abs(DFB_indepvar2) >2/sqrt(n);
  DFB_indepvar3Hi =abs(DFB_indepvar3) >2/sqrt(n);
run;
``` | ```
generate HatDiagonal3Hi  =HatDiagonal        >3*(k-1)/n
generate RStudentHi      =abs(RStudent)      >2
generate CooksDHi        =CooksD             >4/n
generate DFFITSHi        =abs(DFFITS)        >2*sqrt((k-1)/n)
generate DFB_indepvar1Hi =abs(DFB_indepvar1) >2/sqrt(n)
generate DFB_indepvar2Hi =abs(DFB_indepvar2) >2/sqrt(n)
generate DFB_indepvar3Hi =abs(DFB_indepvar3) >2/sqrt(n)
``` |
| | Notes: In the formula for the cutoffs, substitute the number of predictors in your model plus one for the intercept for k and substitute the sample size on which your regression is estimated for n. Repeat the command for DFB variables for each independent variable in your model. | |

(Continued)

■ Display A.14. Summary of SAS and Stata Commands Introduced in Chapter Fourteen (Outliers, Heteroskedasticity, and Multicollinearity) (continued)

	SAS	Stata
Outlying and Influential Observations (continued)		
Identify cases with any extreme values	`anyhi = HatDiagonal3Hi=1	RStudentHi=1` `	CooksDHi=1	DFFITSHi=1` `	DFB_indepvar1Hi=1	DFB_indepvar2Hi=1` `	DFB_indepvar3Hi=1;`	`generate anyhi = HatDiagonal3Hi==1	RStudentHi==1 ///` `	CooksDHi==1	DFFITSHi==1 ///` `	DFB_indepvar1Hi==1	DFB_indepvar2Hi==1 ///` `	DFB_indepvar3Hi==1`

Summarize and regress cases with and without extreme values	`data <influence3>;`
	`  merge <original file name> <influence2>;`
	`run;`
	`proc sort data=<influence3>; by <anyhi>; run;`
	`proc means data=<influence3>;`
	`  var <variable list>;`
	`  by <anyhi>;`
	`run;`
	`proc reg data=<influence3>;`
	`  model <depvar> = <variable list>;`
	`  by <anyhi>;`
	`run;`
		`bysort <anyhi>: summarize <variable list>`
		`bysort <anyhi>: regress <depvar> <variable list>`

List cases	`proc print;`
	`  var <variable list>;`
	`  where <expression>;`
	`run;`
		`list <variable list> if <expression>`

Heteroskedasticity		

Calculate heteroskedasticity-consistent standard errors	`%include "c:\nsfh_distance\sas\hcreg.sas";`
	`%HCREG (data = <filename>, dv = <depvar>, iv =`
	`<variable list>);`
		`regress <depvar> <variable list>, vce(hc3)`

Multicollinearity		

Calculate variance inflation factors	`proc reg;`
	`  model <depvar> = <variable list> /vif;`
	`run;`
		`regress <depvar> <variable list>`
		`estat vif`

■ Display A.15 Summary of SAS and Stata Commands Introduced in Chapter Fifteen (Introduction to the Generalized Linear Model with a Continuous Outcome)

	SAS	Stata

Estimate a generalized linear model	proc genmod ;
	  Model <depvar>=<variable list>
	      / dist=<distribution> link=<link>;
	run;
		glm <depvar> <variable list>, ///
		    family(<distribution>) link(<link>)

Estimate a linear regression model (mirroring OLS)	proc genmod ;
	  Model <depvar>=<variable list>
	      / dist=normal link=identity;
	run;
		glm <depvar> <variable list>, ///
		    family(normal) link(identity)

Request a Wald χ^2 test	proc genmod;
	  Model <depvar>=<variable list>
	      / dist=<distribution> link=<link>;
	  contrast "wald" <var1> 1, <var2> 1, . . . <vark> 1 /
	  wald;
	run;
		test <variable list>

Request a Likelihood Ratio χ^2 test	proc genmod;
	  Model <depvar>=<variable list>
	      / dist=<distribution> link=<link>;
	  contrast "LR" <var1> 1, <var2> 1, . . . <vark> 1;
	run;
		<estimate reduced model>
		estimates store reduced
		
		<estimate full model>
		estimates store full
		
		lrtest full reduced

Display A.16 Summary of SAS and Stata Commands Introduced in Chapter Sixteen (Dichotomous Outcomes)

	SAS	Stata
Basic Model Estimation		

Estimate a logit model—generalized linear model syntax	`proc genmod descending;`
	`  Model <depvar>=<indep variable list>`
	`  / dist=binomial link=logit;`
	`run;`
		`glm <depvar> <indep variable list>, ///`
		`  family(binomial) link(logit)`

Estimate a logit model—dedicated syntax	`proc logistic descending;`
	`  Model <depvar>=<indep variable list>;`
	`run;`
		`logit <depvar> <indep variable list>`

Request odds ratios	*odds ratios already in default output*	`logit <depvar> <indep variable list>`, *or*

Request confidence intervals	`proc logistic descending;`
	`  Model <depvar>=<indep variable list>`
	`  / clparm=wald;`
	`run;`
		confidence intervals already in default output

Estimate a probit model—generalized linear model syntax	`proc genmod descending;`
	`  Model <depvar>=<indep variable list>`
	`  / dist=binomial link=probit;`
	`run;`
		`glm <depvar> <indep variable list>, ///`
		`  family(binomial) link(probit)`

Estimate a probit model—dedicated syntax	`proc logistic descending;`
	`  Model <depvar>=<indep variable list>`
	`  / link=probit;`
	`run;`
		`probit <depvar> <indep variable list>`

Request confidence intervals	`proc logistic descending;`
	`  Model <depvar>=<indep variable list>`
	`  / link=probit clparm=wald;`
	`run;`
		confidence intervals already in default output

Predicted Probabilities		

Range of Predicted Probabilities	`proc logistic descending data= <dataname>;`
	`  Model <depvar>=<indep variable list>;`
	`  Score out=<predall>;`
	`run;`
	`proc means data=<predall>; var p_1; run;`
		`logit <depvar> <indep variable list>`
		`predict <Pdepvar>, p`
		`summarize <Pdepvar>`

"Predict then Average"	`proc sort data=<predall>;`
	`  by <group var>;`
	`run;`
	`proc means data=<predall>;`
	`  var p_1;`
	`  by <group var>;`
	`run;`
		`bysort <group var>: summarize <Pdepvar>`

(continued)

APPENDIX A

Display A.16 Summary of SAS and Stata Commands Introduced in Chapter Sixteen (Dichotomous Outcomes) (continued)

	SAS	Stata
| Modified "Predict then Average" | ```
data <predm0>;
  set <dataname>;
  <var1>=<value>;
run;

proc logistic descending data=<dataname>;
  Model <depvar>=<indep variable list>;
  Score data=<predm0> out=<predm0s>;
run;
proc means data=<predm0s>; var p_1; run;
``` | `margins, at( <var1>=<value> )` |
| "Average then Predict" | ```
proc means data=<dataname>;
  var <indep variable list>;
  output out=<predmean> mean=;
run;

data <preda0>;
  set <predmean>;
  <var1>=<value>;
run;

proc logistic descending data=<dataname>;
  Model <depvar>=<indep variable list>;
  Score data=<preda0> out=<preda0s>;
run;

proc means data=<preda0s>; var p_1; run;
``` | `margins, at( (mean) _all <var1>=<value> )` |
| "Average then Predict" with Rounded Values or "Ideal Types" | ```
data <predideal1>;
  set <predmean>;
  <var1>=<value>;
  <var2>=<value>;
  <vark>=<value>;
run;

proc logistic descending data=<predideal1>;
  Model <depvar>=<indep variable list>;
  Score data=<predideal1> out=<predideal1s>;
  proc means data=<predideal1s>; var p_1; run;
``` | `margins, at( <var1>=<value> <var2>=<value> <vark>=<value> )` |

(continued)
```

■ **Display A.16 Summary of SAS and Stata Commands Introduced in Chapter Sixteen (Dichotomous Outcomes) (continued)**

	SAS	Stata
Identify Outliers and Influential Observations		
Request Diagnostics for Outliers and Influential Observations	output out=<data set name> reschi=<new variable name> c=<new variable name>;	predict <new variable name>, residuals predict <new variable name>, rstandard predict <new variable name>, dbeta
R-squared, Information Criteria, Marginal Effects and Discrete Change		

Request Classification Table	proc logistic descending;
	  Model <depvar>=<indep variable list>
	  / ctable pprob=0.50;
	run;
		estat class

Request R-squared Values and Information Criteria	proc logistic descending;
	  Model <depvar>=<indep variable list>
	  / rsquare;
	run;
	
	information criteria already in default output
		fitstat, saving(<name>)
		fitstat, using(<name>)

Request Discrete Change and Marginal Effect	*see footnote in chapter about proc qlim*	prchange, fromto
Notes:	Each of the commands for predicted probabilities, identifying outliers and influential observations, R-squared, information criteria, marginal effects and discrete change must follow an estimated regression model. They make calculations based on the most recently estimated model. The "fitstat" and "prchange" commands are not part of the general release of Stata. Type "net search spost" in the Stata command window to install them (and other spost commands written by Scott Long and Jeremy Freese). In Stata, use "noatlegend" with the margins command for brief output. In SAS, we explicitly use the "data=<dataname>" option to specify data set names in proc logistic when we request predicted probabilities. This is because we are creating new data sets either with the "score" or "output" commands or with an additional "data" step. By default SAS uses the most recently created data set for a "proc," unless we explicitly provide a datset name with the "data=<dataname>" option. This <dataname> will be your analytic data file that contains the dependent variable and independent variables on which you want to estimate a regression model. We use the prefix "pred" for the data sets we create as input and outputs from the "score" command and as output on the "output" command on additional data steps, although you can choose whatever names you like for these data sets. If you specify just a filename, without a path, then these data sets will only be created temporarily (which is usually desirable for predicted probabilities; in our examples in Appendix B, we create numerous temporary data files and summarize their results within the program, so that we do not need to save them permanently). In SAS, also note that "p_1" is the default name for the predicted probability of a success used by the "score" command.

Note. Shaded text is optional. Text in angular brackets is user-supplied.

■ Display A.17.1 Summary of SAS and Stata Commands Introduced in Chapter Seventeen (Multi-Category Outcomes)

	SAS	Stata
Basic Model Estimation		
Estimate a multinomial logit model	```proc logistic descending ref="<value>";
Model <depvar>=<variable list>
/link=glogit;
run;```	`mlogit <depvar> <variable list>, baseout(<value>)`
Estimate an ordered logit model	```proc logistic descending;
Model <depvar>=<variable list>;
run;```	`ologit <depvar> <variable list>`
Interpretation		
Odds ratios	*odds ratios already in default output*	mlogit, rrr ologit, or
Tests for contrasts of individual variables between pairs of included outcome categories in multinomial logit	```proc logistic descending ref="<value3>";
Model <depvar>=<variable list>
/link=glogit;
<Label1>: test <var1>_<value1>-<var1>_<value2>
;```	```mlogit <depvar> <variable list>, baseout(<value>)
test [<value1>]<var1> = [value2]<var1>
lincom [<value1>]<var1> - [value2]<var1>```
Chi-square tests for combining categories in multinomial logit	```proc logistic descending ref="<value3>";
Model <depvar>=<variable list>
/link=glogit;
<Label1>: test   <var1>_<value1>-<var1>_<value2>
<var2>_<value1>-<var2>_<value2>
<vark>_<value1>-<vark>_<value2>
;
<Label2>: test   <var1>_<value1>-0
<var2>_<value1>-0
<vark>_<value1>-0
;
<Label3>: test   <var1>_<value2>-0
<var2>_<value2>-0
<vark>_<value2>-0
;
run;```	mlogtest, combine mlogtest, lrcomb

(continued)

Display A.17.1 Summary of SAS and Stata Commands Introduced in Chapter Seventeen (Multi-Category Outcomes) (continued)

	SAS	Stata
Hausman test of IIA for multinomial logit	n/a	mlogtest, hausman
Test of proportional odds for ordered logit	*proportional odds test already in default output*	brant, detail

Predicted probabilities	proc means data=<dataname>;
	  var <indep variable list>;
	  output out=<predmean> mean=;
	run;
	
	data <preda0>;
	  set <predmean>;
	  <var1>=<value>;
	run;
	
	proc logistic descending data=<dataname>;
	  Model <depvar>=<indep variable list>;
	  Score data=<preda0> out=<preda0s>;
	run;
	
	proc means data=<preda0s>; var p_1; run;
		margins, predict(outcome(<value>)) ///
		  at(<var1>=<value> <var2>=<value> <vark>=<value>)

Discrete change Marginal effect	n/a	prchange, fromto

(continued)

■ Display A.17.1 Summary of SAS and Stata Commands Introduced in Chapter Seventeen (Multi-Category Outcomes) (continued)

	SAS	Stata
Notes:	Each of the commands for interpretation must follow an estimated regression model. These commands make calculations based on the most recently estimated model. "mlogtest" and "brant" are not part of the general release of Stata. Type "net search spost" in the Stata command window to install them (and other spost commands written by Scott Long and Jeremy Freese). Use "noatlegend" with the margins command for brief output. In SAS, we explicitly use the "data=<dataname>" option to specify data set names in proc logistic when we request predicted probabilities. This is because we are creating new data sets either with the "score" or "output" commands or with an additional "data" step. By default SAS uses the most recently created data set for a "proc," unless we explicitly provide a datset name with the "data=<dataname>" option. This <dataname> will be your analytic data file that contains the dependent variable and independent variables on which you want to estimate a regression model. We use the prefix "pred" for the data sets we create as input and outputs from the "score" command and as output on the "output" command on additional data steps, although you can choose whatever names you like for these data sets. If you specify just a filename, without a path, then these data sets will only be created temporarily (which is usually desirable for predicted probabilities; in our examples in Appendix B, we create numerous temporary data files and summarize their results within the program, so that we do not need to save them permanently). In SAS, also note that "p_<value>" is the default name for each predicted probability used by the "score" command where <value> is the valued assigned to each outcome category. In SAS, in the test command for multinomial logit, we refer to the coefficients for various included outcome categories with an underscore followed by their value. For example, <var1>_<value1> could be "age_1" to represent the coefficient of a variable age in the equation for the first included category. Note that the values are the values actually assigned to your categories (e.g., if the included categories were labeled 100 and 200, then the references to an age variable would be "age_100" and "age_200").	

Note. Shaded text is optional. Text in angular brackets is user-supplied.

APPENDIX A

■ **Display A.17.2. Summary of SAS and Stata Commands Introduced in Chapter Seventeen (Multi-Category Outcomes) that Account for Complex Sample Designs**

	SAS	Stata
Store the complex design features	n/a	svyset <psu variable> [pw=<weight variable>] /// , strata (<stratum variable>) /// singleunit (certainty)

Survey Binary Logit	proc surveylogistic rate=<data set name>;
	  model <depvar>(descending)=<indepvarlist>;
	    domain <subgroup variable>;
	    cluster <psu variable>;
	    strata <stratum variable>;
	    weight <weight variable>;
	run;
		svy, subpop(<subgroup variable>): logit <depvar> <indepvarlist>

Survey Multinomial Logit	proc surveylogistic rate=<data set name>;
	  model <depvar>(descending)=<indepvarlist>
	    / link=glogit;
	    domain <subgroup variable>;
	    cluster <psu variable>;
	    strata <stratum variable>;
	    weight <weight variable>;
	run;
		svy, subpop (<subgroup variable>): mlogit <depvar> <indepvarlist> ///
		, baseout(23)

Survey Ordered Logit	proc surveylogistic rate=<data set name>;
	  model <depvar>(descending)=<indepvarlist>;
	    domain <subgroup variable>;
	    cluster <psu variable>;
	    strata <stratum variable>;
	    weight <weight variable>;
	run;
		svy, subpop (<subgroup variable>): ologit <depvar> <indepvarlist>

Comments	The *weight variable* contains the sampling weights.	

Note. Shaded text is optional. Text in angular brackets is user-supplied.

EXAMPLES OF DATA CODING, AND OF THE SAS AND STATA INTERFACE, COMMANDS, AND RESULTS, BASED ON THE NATIONAL SURVEY OF FAMILIES AND HOUSEHOLDS

The following are summaries of data coding for the National Survey of Families and Households and of the SAS and Stata interface, commands, and results from the examples used throughout the text (using both the distance and hours of chores examples drawn from the NSFH).

The programs and results are also available on the course web site.

Each display is numbered with this appendix letter (B), the chapter number and a number to signify the order in which the display is referenced in the chapter. For example B.5.3 would be the third display referenced in Chapter 5.

Display B.3.1 Summary of Variables in Analytic Data File for NSFH Distance Example

	Created Variable Name	Original Variable Name	Description	Missing Data Codes	Notes
Main Interview * Household Composition					
	—	MCASEID	Case Number	n/a	—
	g2age	M2BP01	Age Of Respondent	97,98	Years
	—	M2DP01	Sex Of Respondent	n/a	—
Main Interview * Social Background					
	—	M484	Which Group Describes R (Race)	97,99	—
	—	M497A	Country/State Live When Born	995,997 998,999	1–51, 990=U.S. 996=always lived here
	g1yrschl	M502	Highest Grade School Mother Completed	98,99	25=GED
Self-Administered Primary Respondent * Attitudes					
	—	E1301	Mother Living Or Deceased	7,8,9	1=still living
	g1age	E1302	Age of R's Mother	96,97 98,99	Years
	g1miles	E1305	How Far Away R Mother Lives	9996,9997 9998,9999	Miles 9994=Foreign Country 9995=Mother Live w/R
	g2numbro	E1332A	Number Living Brothers R Has	97,98,99	96=Inapplicable (zero)
	g2numsis	E1332B	Number Living Sisters R Has	97,98,99	96=Inapplicable (zero)
Weights and Constructed Variables					
	g2earn	IREARN	R Total Earnings	9999997 9999998 9999999	1986 dollars
	—	WEIGHT	Individual Case Weight	n/a	—
From Sudaan.doc					
	—	Stratum	Indicator of Stratum	n/a	—
	—	PSU	Indicator of Primary Sampling Unit	n/a	—

■ Display B.4.1 Locating Data, Programs and Results in Stata

(a) Writing a program in Stata's Do-File Editor

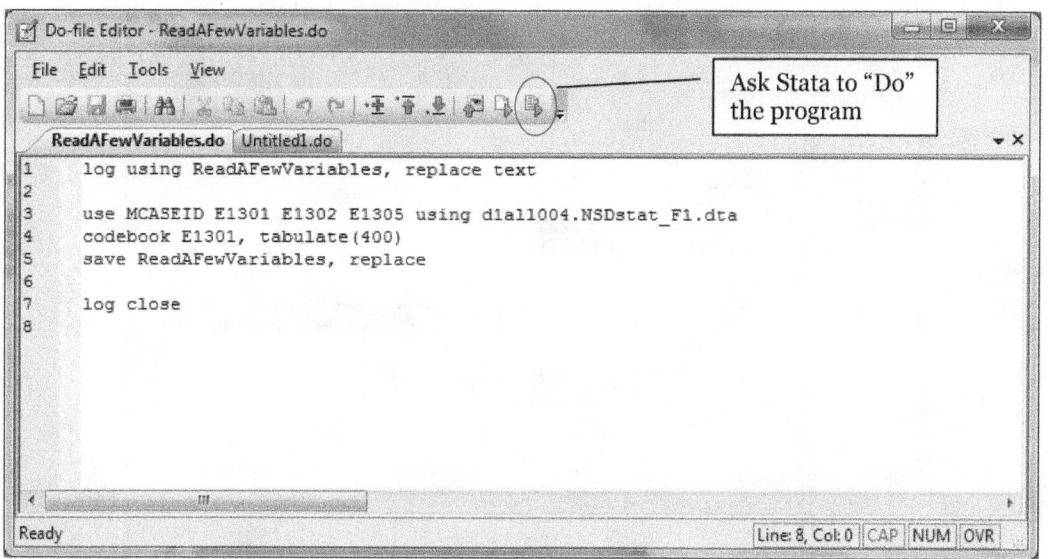

(b) Running programs and viewing results in Stata

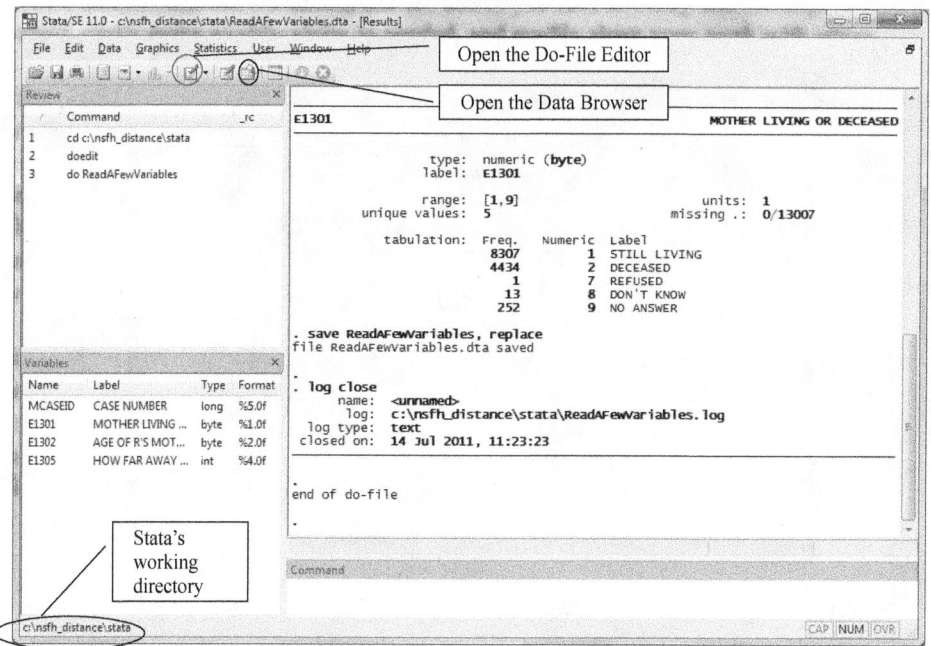

■ Display B.4.2 Locating Data, Programs, and Results Files in SAS

(a) Writing a program in SAS's enhanced editor and viewing messages

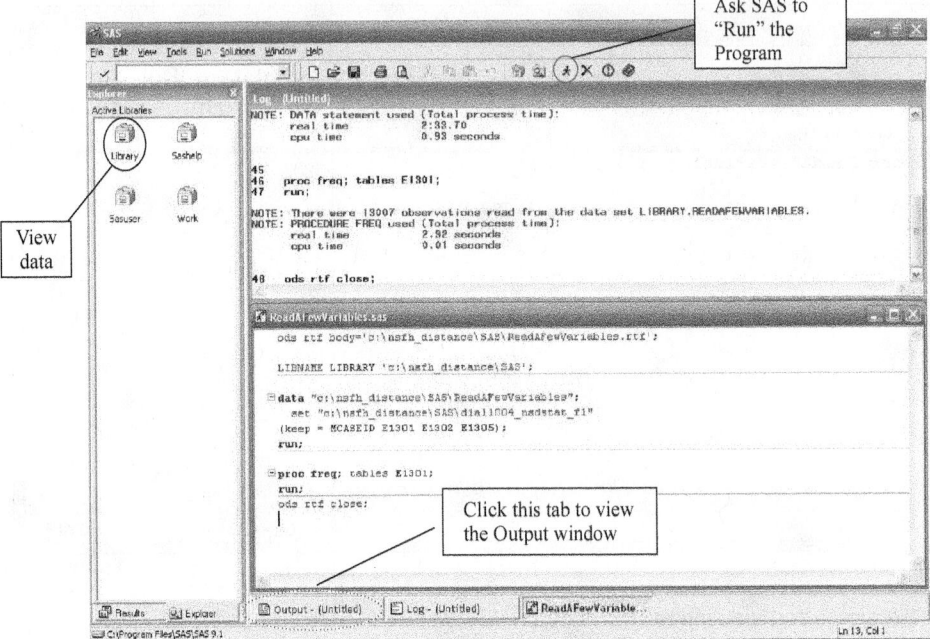

(b) Viewing data in SAS

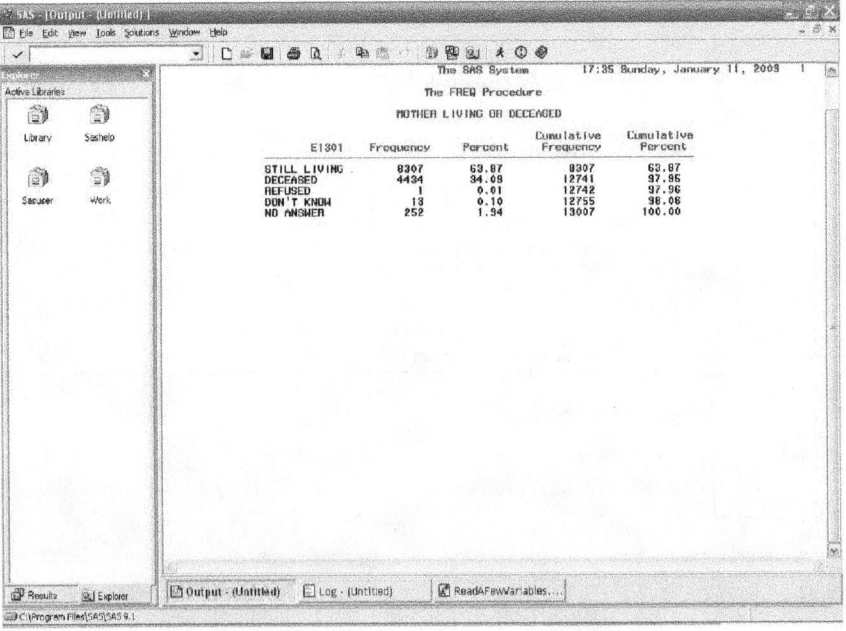

■ **Display B.4.3 Viewing Data in SAS and Stata**

(a) Viewing data in Stata

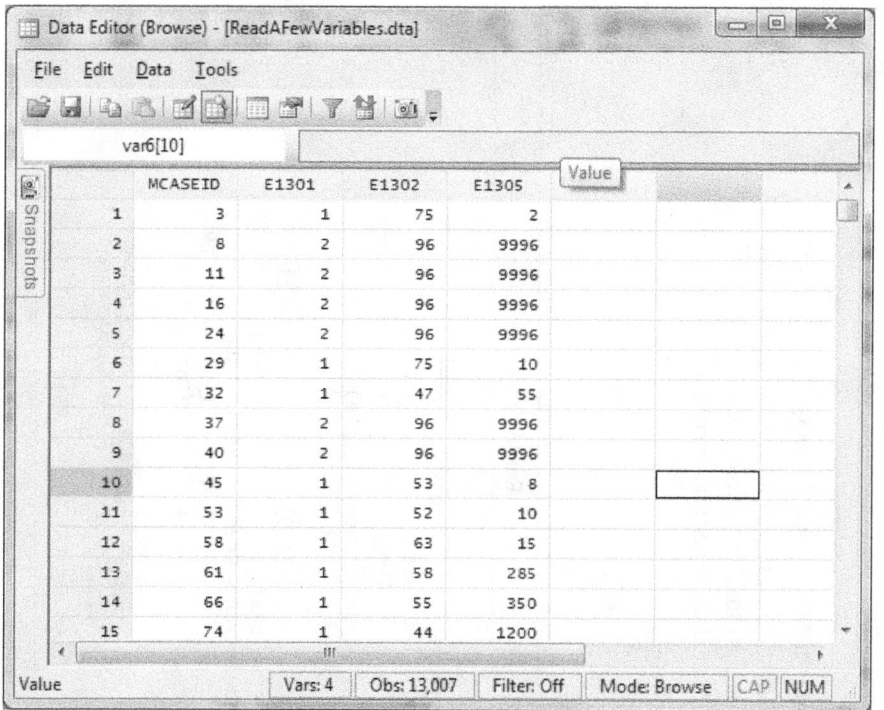

(b) Viewing data in SAS

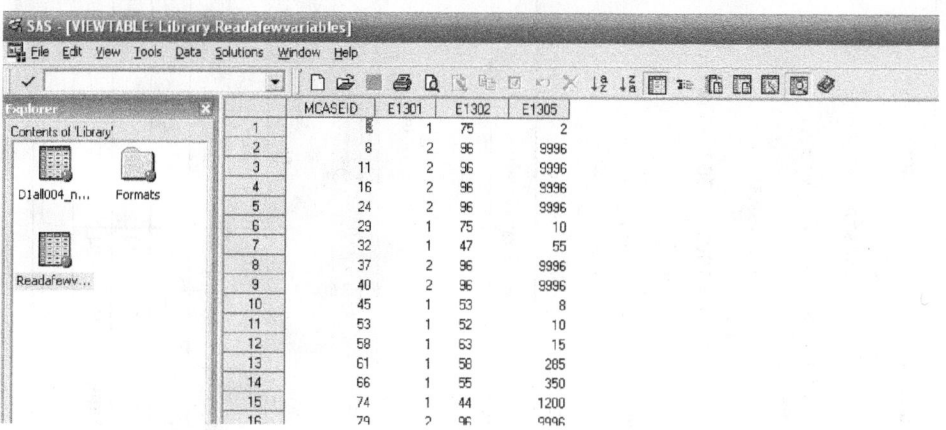

Display B.4.4 Program to Read A Few Variables from the NSFH Wave 1 Data File

	SAS	Stata
	ReadAFewVariables.sas	ReadAFewVariables.do

Program File	<pre>ods rtf body="c:\nsfh_distance\SAS\
	ReadAFewVariables.rtf";
	LIBNAME LIBRARY "c:\nsfh_distance\SAS";
	
	data "c:\nsfh_distance\SAS\
	  ReadAFewVariables";
	  set "c:\nsfh_distance\SAS\
	  d1a11004_nsdstat_f1"
	  (keep = MCASEID E1301 E1302 E1305);
	run;
	
	proc freq; tables E1301;
	run;
	ods rtf close;</pre>
		<pre>log using ReadAFewVariables, replace text
		use MCASEID E1301 E1302 E1305 using d1a11004.NSDstat_F1.dta
		codebook E1301, tabulate(400)
		save ReadAFewVariables, replace
		log close</pre>

	ReadAFewVariables.rtf	ReadAFewVariables.log
Results File	MOTHER LIVING OR DECEASED 	E1301	Frequency	Percent	Cumulative Frequency	Cumulative Percent
---	---	---	---	---
STILL LIVING	8307	63.87	8307	63.87
DECEASED	4434	34.09	12741	97.95
REFUSED	1	0.01	12742	97.96
DON'T KNOW	13	0.10	12755	98.06

NO ANSWER	252	1.94	13007	100.00		<pre>---
						E1301 MOTHER LIVING OR DECEASED
						--- 	
						
						          type: numeric (byte)
						         label: E1301
						
						         range: [1,9] units: 1
						unique values: 5 missing .: 0/13007
						    tabulation: Freq. Numeric Label
						                 8307 1 STILL LIVING
						                 4434 2 DECEASED
						                    1 7 REFUSED
						                   13 8 DON'T KNOW
						                  252 9 NO ANSWER</pre>

■ Display B.4.5 Example of Checking New Variable Creation in Stata

```
log using CheckingCreatedVariables, replace text
use MCASEID IREARN M502 using d1all004.NSDstat_F1.dta
generate g1yrschl=M502 if M502<98
replace g1yrschl=12 if M502==25

tabulate g1yrschl M502, missing
generate g2earn=IREARN*207.342/109.6 if IREARN<9999997
save CheckingCreatedVariables, replace
log close
```

	M502 (HIGHEST GRADE SCHOOL MOTHER COMPLETED)											
g1yrschl	0	1	2	3	4	15	16	17	25	98	99	Total
0	290	0	0	0	0	. . .	0	0	0	0	0	0	290
1	0	27	0	0	0	. . .	0	0	0	0	0	0	27
2	0	0	63	0	0	. . .	0	0	0	0	0	0	63
3	0	0	0	189	0	. . .	0	0	0	0	0	0	189
4	0	0	0	0	190	. . .	0	0	0	0	0	0	190
5	0	0	0	0	0	. . .	0	0	0	0	0	0	187
6	0	0	0	0	0	. . .	0	0	0	0	0	0	482
7	0	0	0	0	0	. . .	0	0	0	0	0	0	258
8	0	0	0	0	0	. . .	0	0	0	0	0	0	1,494
9	0	0	0	0	0	. . .	0	0	0	0	0	0	359
10	0	0	0	0	0	. . .	0	0	0	0	0	0	648
11	0	0	0	0	0	. . .	0	0	0	0	0	0	522
12	0	0	0	0	0	. . .	0	0	0	(4)	0	0	4,128
13	0	0	0	0	0	. . .	0	0	0	0	0	0	259
14	0	0	0	0	0	. . .	0	0	0	0	0	0	613
15	0	0	0	0	0	. . .	134	0	0	0	0	0	134
16	0	0	0	0	0	. . .	0	688	0	0	0	0	688
17	0	0	0	0	0	. . .	0	0	282	0	0	0	282
.	0	0	0	0	0	. . .	0	0	0	0	(2,155 | 39)	2,194
Total	290	27	63	189	190	. . .	134	688	282	4	2,155	39	13,007

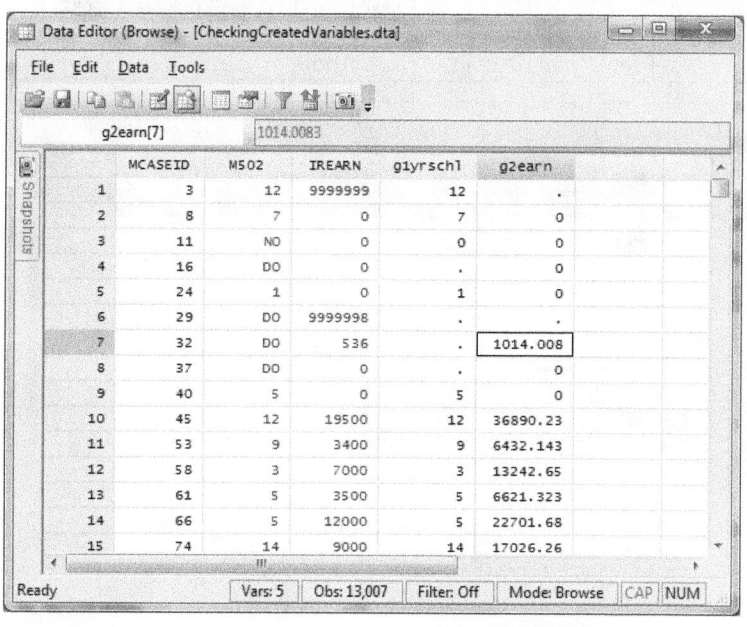

■ Display B.4.6 Example of Checking New Variable Creation in SAS

```
ods rtf body="c:\nsfh_distance\SAS\CheckingCreatedVariables.rtf";

LIBNAME LIBRARY "c:\nsfh_distance\SAS";

data "c:\nsfh_distance\SAS\CheckingCreatedVariables";
  set "c:\nsfh_distance\SAS\d1all004_nsdstat_f1"
(keep = MCASEID IREARN M502);

if M502<98 then g1yrschl=M502;
if M502=25 then g1yrschl=12;

if IREARN<9999997 then g2earn=IREARN*207.342/109.6;

run;

proc freq; tables g1yrschl*M502 /missing;
run;
ods rtf close;
```

Frequency	M502 (HIGHEST GRADE SCHOOL MOTHER COMPLETED)												
	0	1	2	3	4	...	15	16	17	25	98	99	Total
.	0	0	0	0	0	...	0	0	0	0	2155	39	2194
0	290	0	0	0	0	...	0	0	0	0	0	0	290
1	0	27	0	0	0	...	0	0	0	0	0	0	27
2	0	0	63	0	0	...	0	0	0	0	0	0	63
3	0	0	0	189	0	...	0	0	0	0	0	0	189
4	0	0	0	0	190	...	0	0	0	0	0	0	190
5	0	0	0	0	0	...	0	0	0	0	0	0	187
6	0	0	0	0	0	...	0	0	0	0	0	0	482
7	0	0	0	0	0	...	0	0	0	0	0	0	258
8	0	0	0	0	0	...	0	0	0	0	0	0	1494
9	0	0	0	0	0	...	0	0	0	0	0	0	359
10	0	0	0	0	0	...	0	0	0	0	0	0	648
11	0	0	0	0	0	...	0	0	0	0	0	0	522
12	0	0	0	0	0	...	0	0	0	4	0	0	4128
13	0	0	0	0	0	...	0	0	0	0	0	0	259
14	0	0	0	0	0	...	0	0	0	0	0	0	613
15	0	0	0	0	0	...	134	0	0	0	0	0	134
16	0	0	0	0	0	...	0	688	0	0	0	0	688
17	0	0	0	0	0	...	0	0	282	0	0	0	282
Total	290	27	63	189	190	...	134	688	282	4	2155	39	13007

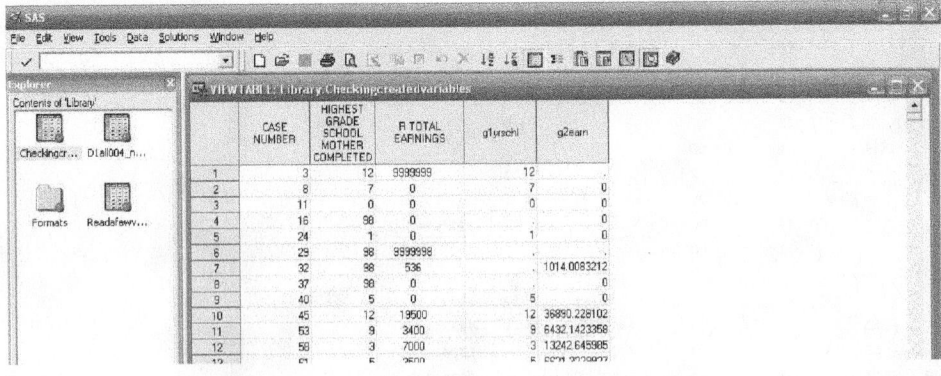

Display B.4.7 Program to Create Full Analytic Data File

	SAS	Stata
Commands	(see code below)	(see code below)

SAS

```
ods rtf body="c:\nsfh_distance\SAS\CreateData.rtf";

LIBNAME LIBRARY "c:\nsfh_distance\SAS";

data "c:\nsfh_distance\SAS\CreateData";
set "c:\nsfh_distance\SAS\d1al1004_nsdstat_f1"
    (keep = MCASEID M2BP01 M2DP01 M484 M497A M502
    E1301 E1302 E1305 E1332A E1332B IREARN);

if    E1301=1 &
      (M497A<=51 | M497A=990 | M497A=996) &
      E1305~=9994 & E1305~=9995;

if M2BP01<97        then g2age=M2BP01;

if M502<98          then g1yrsch1=M502;
if M502=25          then g1yrsch1=12;

if E1302<96         then g1age=E1302;

if E1305<9996       then g1miles=E1305;

if E1332A<97        then g2numbro=E1332A;
if E1332A=96        then g2numbro=0;

if E1332B<97        then g2numsis=E1332B;
if E1332B=96        then g2numsis=0;
/* Adjust earnings from 1986 to 2007 dollars with the
CPI ftp://ftp.bls.gov/pub/special.requests/cpi/
cpiai.txt */
if IREARN<9999997 then g2earn=IREARN*207.342/109.6;

run;

proc freq;
run;

ods rtf close;
```

Stata

```
version 11
capture drop _all
capture log close
set more off

log using CreateData, replace text

use MCASEID M2BP01 M2DP01 M484 M497A M502      ///
    E1301 E1302 E1305 E1332A E1332B IREARN      ///
    using d1al1004.NSDstat_F1.dta               ///
    if E1301==1 &                               ///
    (M497A<=51 | M497A==990 | M497A==996) &      ///
    E1305~=9994 & E1305~=9995

generate g2age=M2BP01      if M2BP01<97

generate g1yrsch1=M502     if M502<98
replace g1yrsch1=12        if M502==25

generate g1age=E1302       if E1302<96

generate g1miles=E1305     if E1305<9996

generate g2numbro=E1332A   if E1332A<97
replace g2numbro=0         if E1332A==96

generate g2numsis=E1332B   if E1332B<97
replace g2numsis=0         if E1332B==96

/* Adjust earnings from 1986 to 2007 dollars with the
CPI ftp://ftp.bls.gov/pub/special.requests/
cpi/cpiai.txt*/
generate g2earn=IREARN*207.342/109.6 ///
    if IREARN<9999997

codebook, tabulate(600)

save CreateData, replace

log close
```

■ Display B.4.8 Program to Create Full Analytic Data File with Complex Survey Design Features

	SAS	Stata
| Commands | ```
ods rtf body='c:\nsfh_distance\SAS\CreateDataSvy.rtf';

LIBNAME LIBRARY 'c:\nsfh_distance\SAS';

data "c:\nsfh_distance\SAS\CreateDataSvy";
  merge  "c:\nsfh_distance\SAS\d1a11004_nsdstat_f1"
         (keep = MCASEID M2BP01 M2DP01 M484 M497A M502
         E1301 E1302 E1305 E1332A E1332B IREARN WEIGHT)
         "c:\nsfh_distance\SAS\sudaan";
  by MCASEID;

DistanceSample=0;
if  E1301=1 &
    (M497A=51 | M497A=990 | M497A=996) &
    E1305~=9994 & E1305~=9995
    then DistanceSample=1;

adjweight=WEIGHT/10000;
StratumC=Stratum;
if Stratum>=100 then StratumC=999;

if M2BP01<97        then g2age=M2BP01;

if M502<98          then g1yrsch1=M502;
if M502=25          then g1yrsch1=12;

if E1302<96         then g1age=E1302;

if E1305<9996       then g1miles=E1305;

if E1332A<97        then g2numbro=E1332A;
if E1332A=96        then g2numbro=0;

if E1332B<97        then g2numsis=E1332B;
if E1332B=96        then g2numsis=0;

/* Adjust earnings from 1986 to 2007 dollars with the CPI
ftp://ftp.bls.gov/pub/special.requests/cpi/cpiai.txt */

if IREARN<9999997 then g2earn=IREARN*207.342/109.6;

run;

proc freq;
run;

ods rtf close;
run;
``` | ```
version 11
capture drop _all
capture log close
set more off

log using CreateDataSvy, replace text

use MCASEID M2BP01 M2DP01 M484 M497A M502    ///
    E1301 E1302 E1305 E1332A E1332B IREARN WEIGHT  ///
    using d1a11004.NSDstat_F1.dta

merge 1:1 MCASEID using sudaan

generate DistanceSample=0
replace  DistanceSample=1                     ///
    if E1301==1 &                             ///
    (M497A==51 | M497A==990 | M497A==996) &   ///
    E1305~=9994 & E1305~=9995

generate adjweight=WEIGHT/10000

generate g2age=M2BP01        if M2BP01<97

generate g1yrsch1=M502       if M502<98
replace  g1yrsch1=12         if M502==25

generate g1age=E1302         if E1302<96

generate g1miles=E1305       if E1305<9996

generate g2numbro=E1332A     if E1332A<97
replace  g2numbro=0          if E1332A==96

generate g2numsis=E1332B     if E1332B<97
replace  g2numsis=0          if E1332B==96

// Adjust earnings from 1986 to 2007 dollars with the CPI
// ftp://ftp.bls.gov/pub/special.requests/cpi/cpiai.txt

generate g2earn=IREARN*207.342/109.6 if IREARN<9999997

codebook, tabulate(600)

save CreateDataSvy, replace

log close
``` |

■ Display B.4.9 Program to Read the *ascii* Data File (*sudaan .dat*)

	SAS	Stata
| | ```
ods rtf body='c:\nsfh_distance\SAS\sudaan.rtf';

data 'c:\nsfh_distance\SAS\sudaan';
infile 'c:\nsfh_distance\sas\sudaan.dat' lrecl = 13;
input MCASEID 1-5 Stratum 6-8 PSU 9-11 NewLA 12-13;
run;
``` | ```
version 11
set more off
capture drop _all
capture log close

log using sudaan, replace text

infix MCASEID 1-5 Stratum 6-8 PSU 9-11 NewLA 12-13 ///
      using sudaan.dat
``` |
| Commands | ```
proc freq;
    tables Stratum PSU NewLA;
run;

ods rtf close;
``` | ```
codebook Stratum, tabulate(400)
codebook PSU, tabulate(400)
codebook NewLA, tabulate(400)

save sudaan, replace

log close
``` |

Display B.4.10 Program to Create SAS "Rate" Data File for Certainty PSUs

	SAS	Stata
| Commands | ```
proc sort data="c:\nsfh_distance\SAS\CreateDataSvy";
  by stratumC;
run;

data "c:\nsfh_distance\SAS\rate";
  set "c:\nsfh_distance\SAS\CreateDataSvy";
  keep stratumC _rate_;
  by stratumC;
  if first.stratumC;
  if stratumC<100 then _rate_=0;
    else _rate_=1;
run;
``` | n/a |
```

Display B.4.11 Example of Errors in SAS and Stata Editor Windows

(a) Example errors is SAS enhanced editor

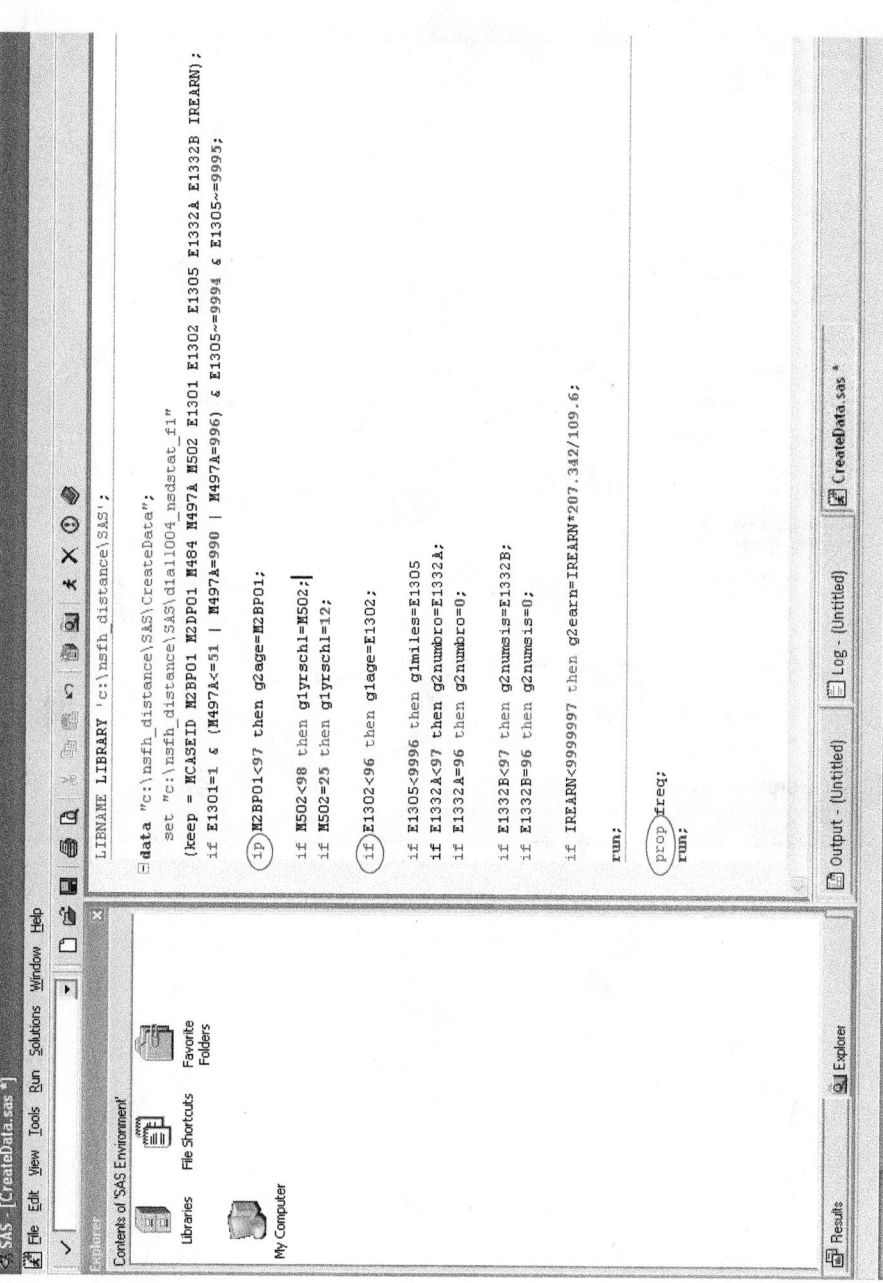

```
LIBNAME LIBRARY 'c:\nsfh distance\SAS';

data "c:\nsfh distance\SAS\CreateData";
    set "c:\nsfh distance\SAS\dia11004_nsdstat_f1"
    (keep = MCASEID M2BP01 M2DP01 M484 M497A M502 E1301 E1302 E1305 E1332A E1332B IREARN);
    if E1301=1 & (M497A<=51 | M497A=990 | M497A=996) & E1305~=9994 & E1305~=9995;

    iP M2BP01<97 then g2age=M2BP01;

    if M502<98 then g1yrschl=M502;
    if M502=25 then g1yrschl=12;

    if E1302<96 then g1age=E1302;

    if E1305<9996 then g1miles=E1305
    if E1332A<97 then g2numbro=E1332A;
    if E1332A=96 then g2numbro=0;

    if E1332B<97 then g2numsis=E1332B;
    if E1332B=96 then g2numsis=0;

    if IREARN<9999997 then g2earn=IREARN*207.342/109.6;

run;

prop freq;
run;
```

Explorer

Contents of 'SAS Environment'

Libraries   File Shortcuts

My Computer

Favorite Folders

Results   Explorer

Output - (Untitled)   Log - (Untitled)   CreateData.sas *

(b) Example errors in Stata Do-file Editor

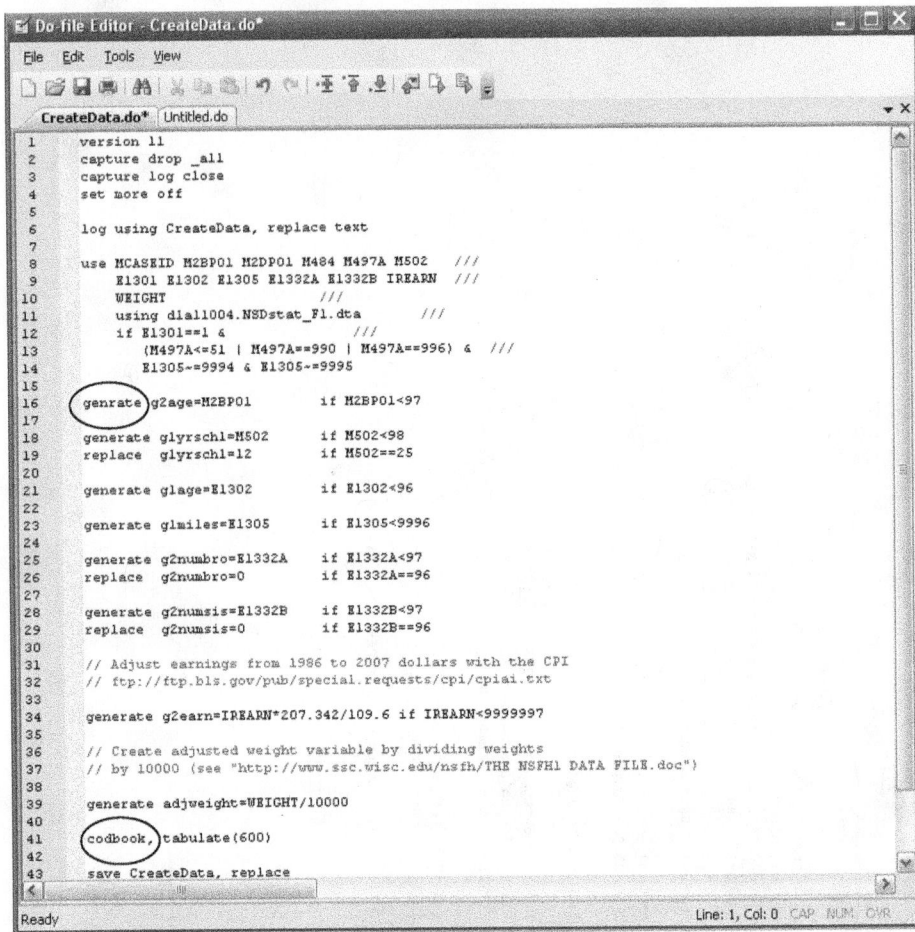

■ **Display B.4.12 Example of Errors in SAS Log Window**

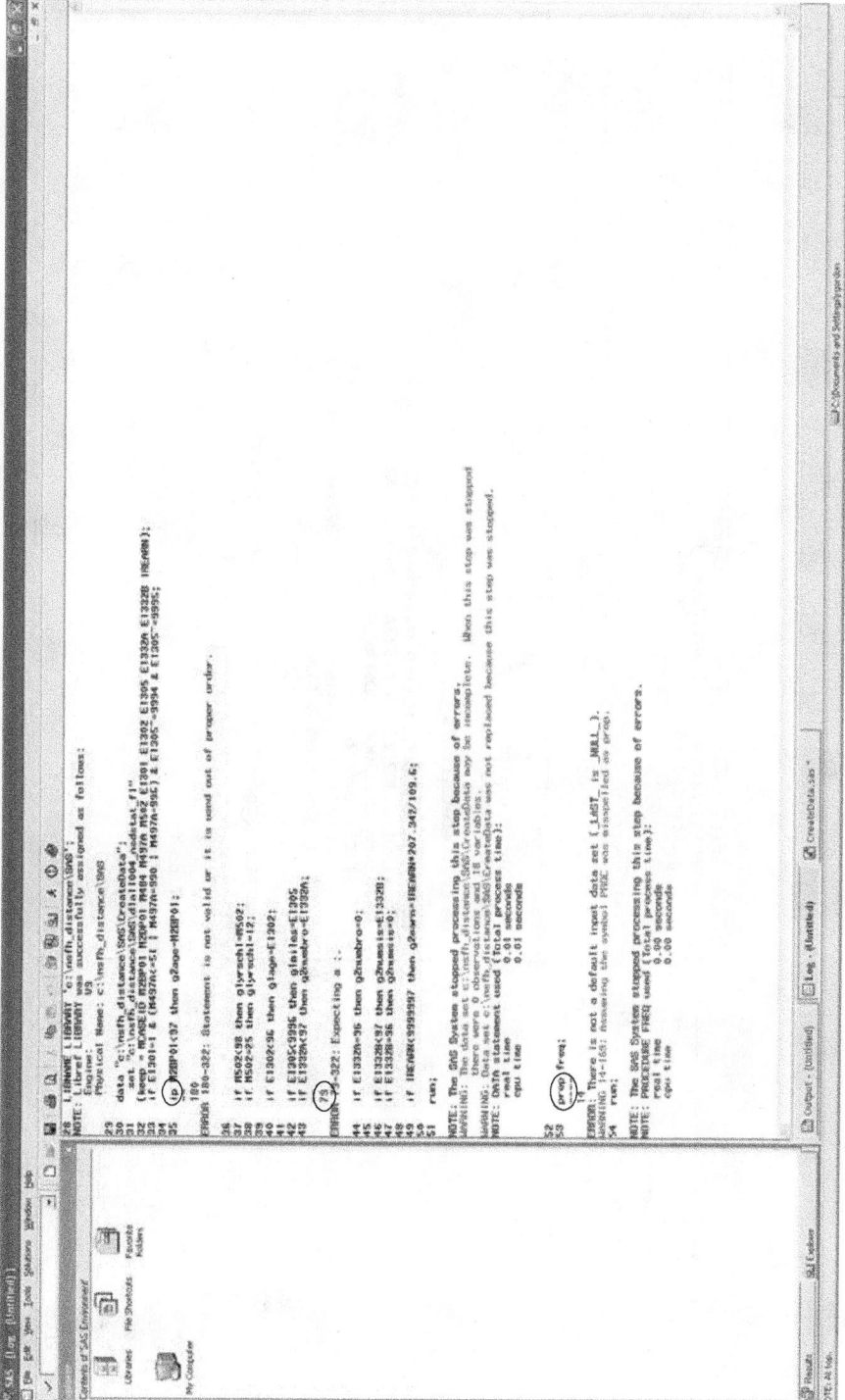

■ **Display B.4.13 Example of Error Message in Stata**

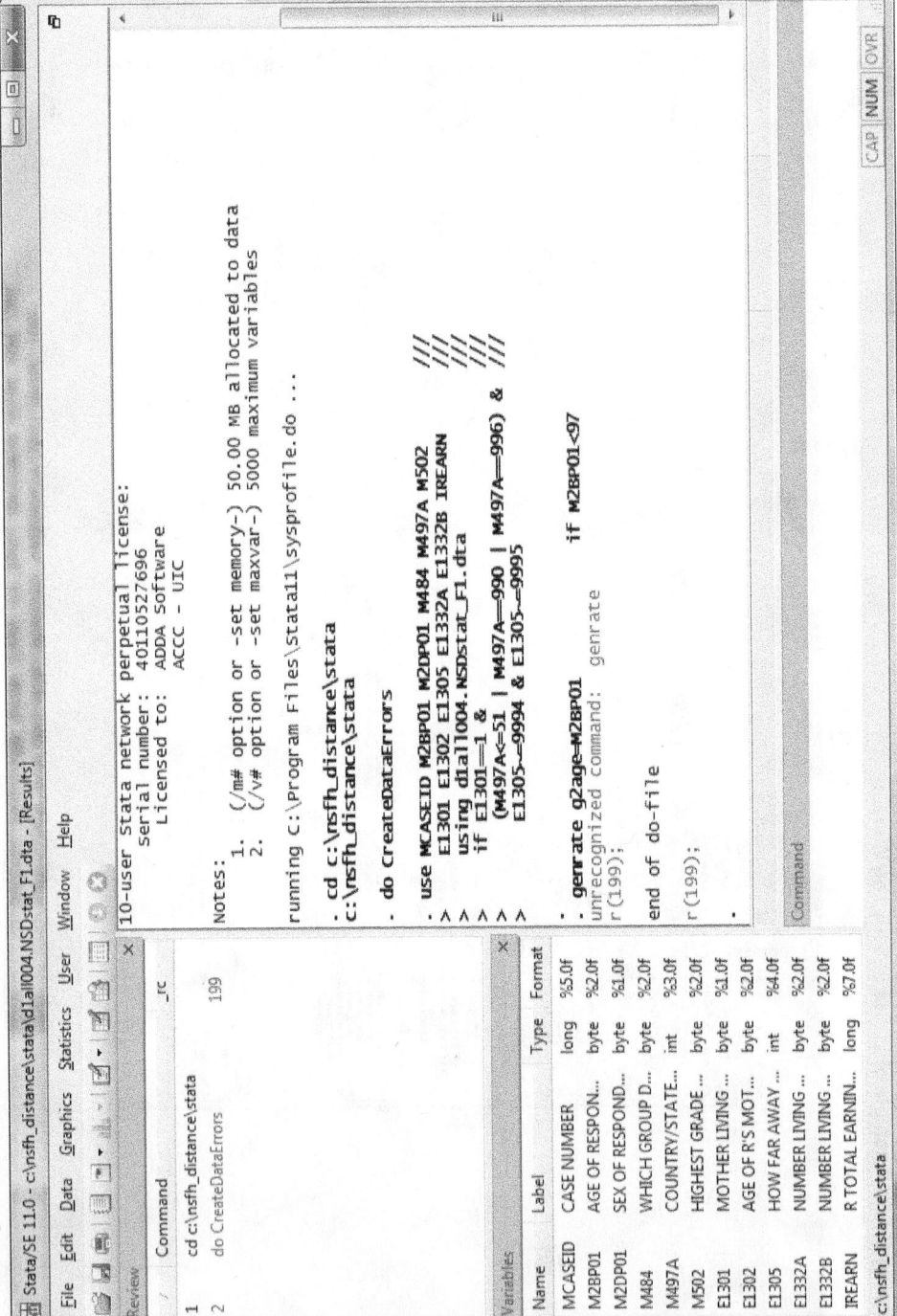

Display B.5.1. Frequency Distribution of Gender (*M2DP01*) and of Race-Ethnicity (*M484*) from the NSFH Distance Dataset

	SAS	Stata
Commands	```proc freq; tables M2DP01 M484; run;```	```tabl M2DP01 M484```

Results

SAS

SEX OF RESPONDENT

M2DP01	Frequency	Percent	Cumulative Frequency	Cumulative Percent
MALE	2785	40.36	2785	40.36
FEMALE	4116	59.64	6901	100.00

WHICH GROUP DESCRIBES R (RACE)

M484	Frequency	Percent	Cumulative Frequency	Cumulative Percent
BLACK	1165	16.88	1165	16.88
WHITE/NOT HISPANIC	5384	78.02	6549	94.90
MEX/CHICANO/ MEX.AM	218	3.16	6767	98.06
PUERTO RICAN	40	0.58	6807	98.64
CUBAN	5	0.07	6812	98.71
OTHER HISPANIC	34	0.49	6846	99.20
AMERICAN INDIAN	31	0.45	6877	99.65
ASIAN	20	0.29	6897	99.94
OTHER	1	0.01	6898	99.96
NO ANSWER	3	0.04	6901	100.00

Stata

```
-> tabulation of M2DP01
```

SEX OF RESPONDENT	Freq.	Percent	Cum.
MALE	2,785	40.36	40.36
FEMALE	4,116	59.64	100.00
Total	6,901	100.00	

```
-> tabulation of M484
```

WHICH GROUP DESCRIBES R (RACE)	Freq.	Percent	Cum.
BLACK	1,165	16.88	16.88
WHITE/NOT HISPANIC	5,384	78.02	94.90
MEX/CHICANO/MEX.AM	218	3.16	98.06
PUERTO RICAN	40	0.58	98.64
CUBAN	5	0.07	98.71
OTHER HISPANIC	34	0.49	99.20
AMERICAN INDIAN	31	0.45	99.65
ASIAN	20	0.29	99.94
OTHER	1	0.01	99.96
NO ANSWER	3	0.04	100.00
Total	6,901	100.00	

APPENDIX B

■ Display B.5.2. Frequency Distribution of Mother's Years of School (*g1yrschl*) from the NSFH Distance Dataset

SAS

Commands:

```
proc freq;
 tables g1yrschl;
run;
```

Results:

g1yrschl	Frequency	Percent	Cumulative Frequency	Cumulative Percent
0	44	0.70	44	0.70
1	3	0.05	47	0.75
2	17	0.27	64	1.02
3	53	0.84	117	1.86
4	53	0.84	170	2.70
5	58	0.92	228	3.62
6	178	2.83	406	6.44
7	119	1.89	525	8.33
8	632	10.03	1157	18.37
9	216	3.43	1373	21.79
10	402	6.38	1775	28.17
11	366	5.81	2141	33.98
12	2796	44.38	4937	78.37
13	177	2.81	5114	81.17
14	437	6.94	5551	88.11
15	94	1.49	5645	89.60
16	461	7.32	6106	96.92
17	194	3.08	6300	100.00

Stata

Commands:

```
tab1 g1yrschl
```

Results:

g1yrschl	Freq.	Percent	Cum.
0	44	0.70	0.70
1	3	0.05	0.75
2	17	0.27	1.02
3	53	0.84	1.86
4	53	0.84	2.70
5	58	0.92	3.62
6	178	2.83	6.44
7	119	1.89	8.33
8	632	10.03	18.37
9	216	3.43	21.79
10	402	6.38	28.17
11	366	5.81	33.98
12	2,796	44.38	78.37
13	177	2.81	81.17
14	437	6.94	88.11
15	94	1.49	89.60
16	461	7.32	96.92
17	194	3.08	100.00
Total	6,300	100.00	

Display B.5.3. Quartiles of Mother's Years of Schooling (*g1yrschl*) from the NSFH Distance Dataset

	SAS	Stata
Commands	```proc means p25 p50 p75; var g1yrschl; run;```	```centile g1yrschl, centile(25 50 75)```
| Results | **Analysis Variable : g1yrschl**<br><br>Lower Quartile: 10.0000000<br>Median: 12.0000000<br>Upper Quartile: 12.0000000 | ```
                                                   -- Binom. Interp.--
Variable    Obs    Percentile    Centile    [95% Conf. Interval]
g1yrschl    6300       25          10          10          10
                       50          12          12          12
                       75          12          12          12
``` |

APPENDIX B
```

Display B.5.4. Frequency Distribution of Number of Brothers (g2numbro) and Number of Sisters (g2numsis) from the NSFH Distance Dataset

SAS

Commands

```
proc freq;
tables g2numbro g2numsis;
run;
```

Results

g2numbro	Frequency	Percent	Cumulative Frequency	Cumulative Percent
0	2117	32.08	2117	32.08
1	1918	29.07	4035	61.15
2	1251	18.96	5286	80.10
3	640	9.70	5926	89.80
4	323	4.89	6249	94.70
5	166	2.52	6415	97.21
6	92	1.39	6507	98.61
7	48	0.73	6555	99.33
8	30	0.45	6585	99.79
9	8	0.12	6593	99.91
10	3	0.05	6596	99.95
11	1	0.02	6597	99.97
12	1	0.02	6598	99.98
19	1	0.02	6599	100.00

g2numsis	Frequency	Percent	Cumulative Frequency	Cumulative Percent
0	2185	33.24	2185	33.24
1	1909	29.04	4094	62.28
2	1201	18.27	5295	80.54
3	618	9.40	5913	89.95
4	317	4.82	6230	94.77
5	171	2.60	6401	97.37
6	98	1.49	6499	98.86
7	42	0.64	6541	99.50
8	16	0.24	6557	99.74
9	11	0.17	6568	99.91
10	3	0.05	6571	99.95
11	1	0.02	6572	99.97
20	1	0.02	6573	99.98
22	1	0.02	6574	100.00

Stata

Commands

```
tab1 g2numbro g2numsis
```

Results

```
-> tabulation of g2numbro
```

g2numbro	Freq.	Percent	Cum.
0	2,117	32.08	32.08
1	1,918	29.07	61.15
2	1,251	18.96	80.10
3	640	9.70	89.80
4	323	4.89	94.70
5	166	2.52	97.21
6	92	1.39	98.61
7	48	0.73	99.33
8	30	0.45	99.79
9	8	0.12	99.91
10	3	0.05	99.95
11	1	0.02	99.97
12	1	0.02	99.98
19	1	0.02	100.00
Total	6,599	100.00	

```
-> tabulation of g2numsis
```

g2numsis	Freq.	Percent	Cum.
0	2,185	33.24	33.24
1	1,909	29.04	62.28
2	1,201	18.27	80.54
3	618	9.40	89.95
4	317	4.82	94.77
5	171	2.60	97.37
6	98	1.49	98.86
7	42	0.64	99.50
8	16	0.24	99.74
9	11	0.17	99.91
10	3	0.05	99.95
11	1	0.02	99.97
20	1	0.02	99.98
22	1	0.02	100.00
Total	6,574	100.00	

Display B.5.5. Box Plot of Mother's Age (*g1age*) from the NSFH Distance Dataset

	SAS	Stata
| Commands | ```
proc sgplot;
    vbox g1age;
run;
``` | ```
graph box g1age
graph export box_g1age.emf, replace
``` |
| Results | | |

■ **Display B.5.6. Histogram of Mother's Age (*g1age*) from the NSFH Distance Dataset**

	SAS	Stata

Commands	`proc sgplot;`
	`    histogram g1age;`
	`run;`
		`histogram g1age`
		`graph export hist_g1age.emf, replace`

Results	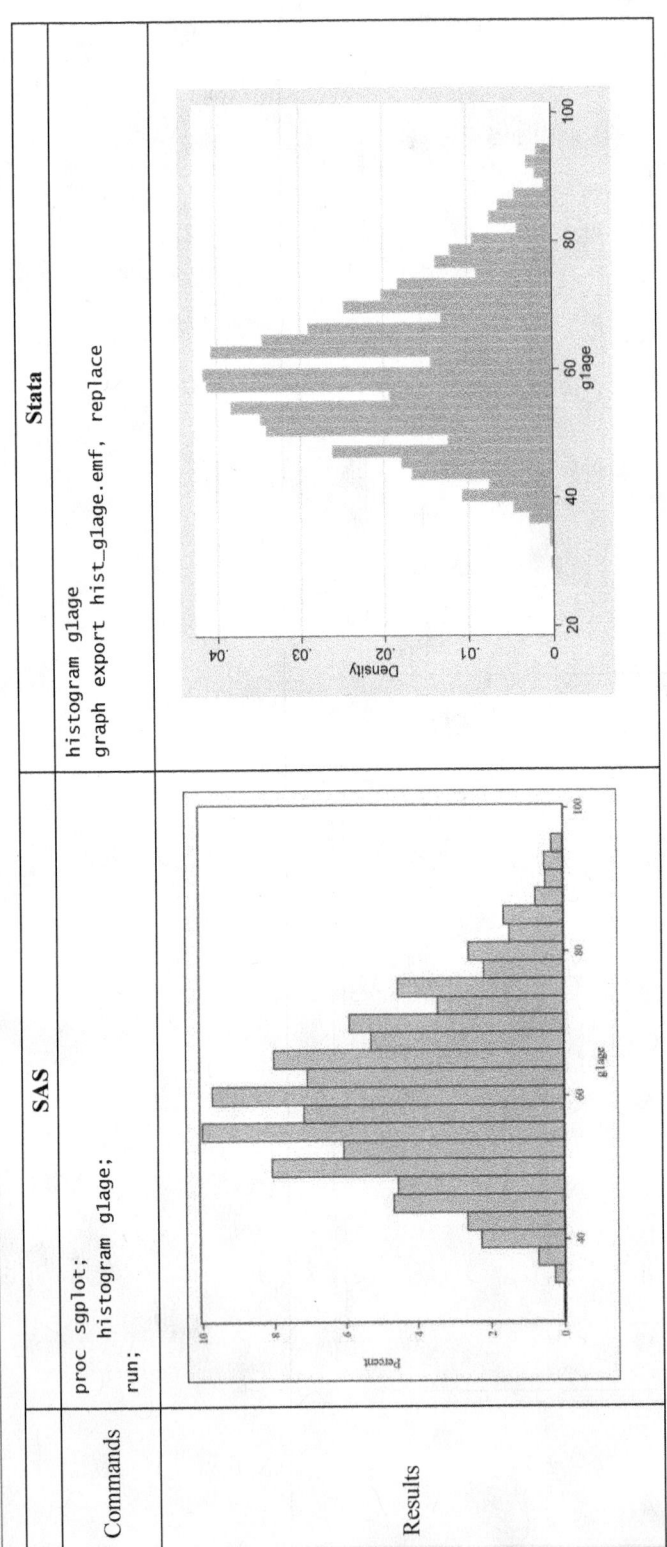	

■ Display B.5.7. Adjusted Histogram of Mother's Age (*g1age*) from the NSFH Distance Dataset

	SAS	Stata
Commands	n/a	`histogram g1age, width(5)` `graph export hist5_g1age.emf, replace`
Results	n/a	

Display B.5.8. Mean and Standard Deviation of Mother's Age (*g1age*) from the NSFH Distance Dataset

	SAS	Stata

Commands	`proc means;`
	`    var g1age;`
	`run;`
		`summarize g1age`

Results		

SAS

Variable	N	Mean	Std Dev	Minimum	Maximum
g1age	6801	60.5200706	11.5783997	29.0000000	95.0000000

Stata

Variable	Obs	Mean	Std. Dev.	Min	Max
g1age	6801	60.52007	11.5784	29	95

■ **Display B.5.9.** **Box Plots of Respondent's Age (*g2age*), Mother's Distance Away (*g1miles*), and Respondent's Earnings (*g2earn*) from the NSFH Distance Dataset**

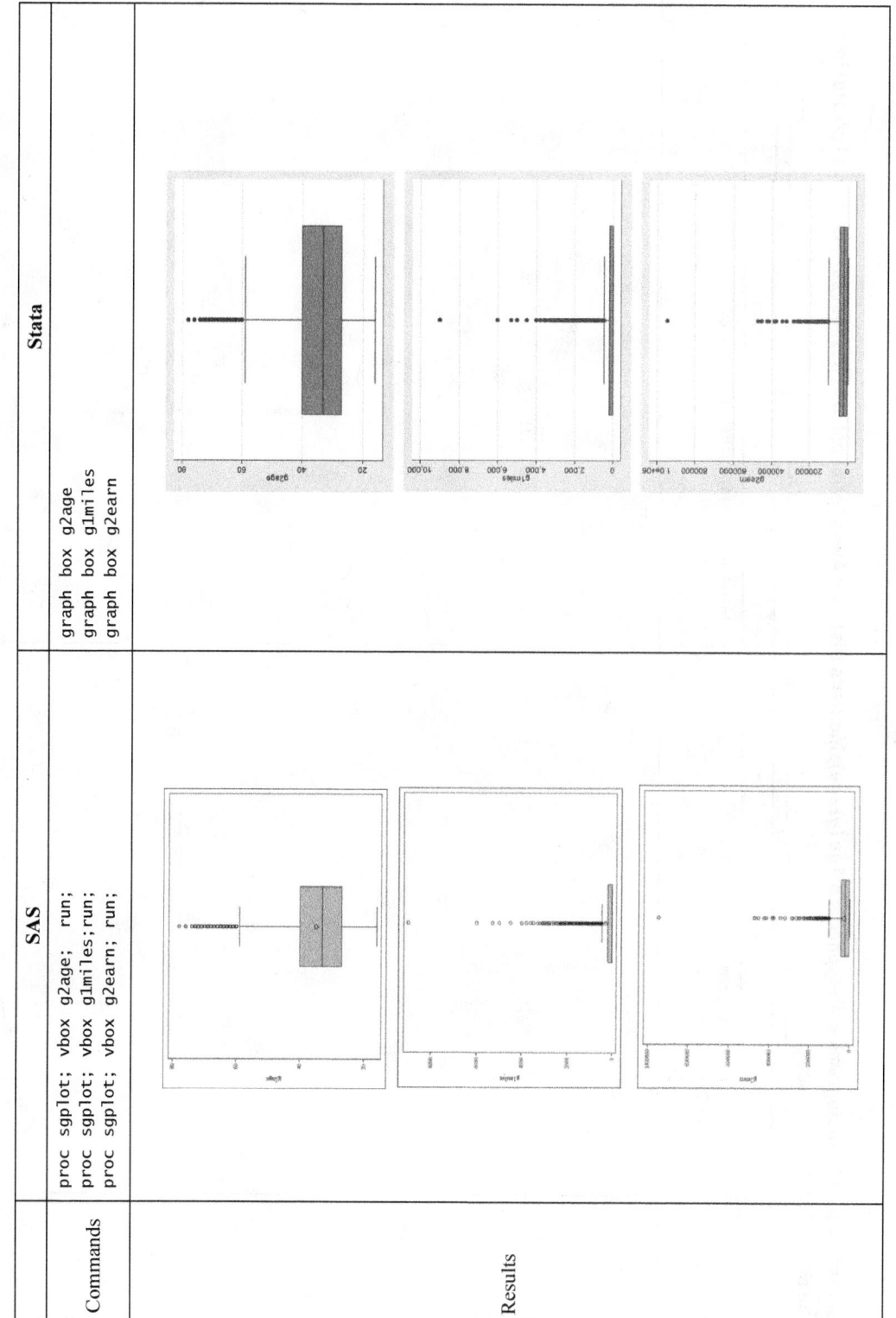

Commands	SAS	Stata
| | ```
proc sgplot; vbox g2age;  run;
proc sgplot; vbox g1miles;run;
proc sgplot; vbox g2earn; run;
``` | ```
graph box g2age
graph box g1miles
graph box g2earn
``` |
| Results | | |

APPENDIX B

■ **Display B.5.10. Histograms of Respondent's Age (*g2age*), Mother's Distance Away (*g1miles*), and Respondent's Earnings (*g2earn*) from the NSFH Distance Dataset**

	SAS	Stata

Commands	`proc sgplot; histogram g2age; run;`
	`proc sgplot; histogram g1miles; run;`
	`proc sgplot; histogram g2earn; run;`
		`histogram g2age, width(5)`
		`histogram g1miles`
		`histogram g2earn`

Results		

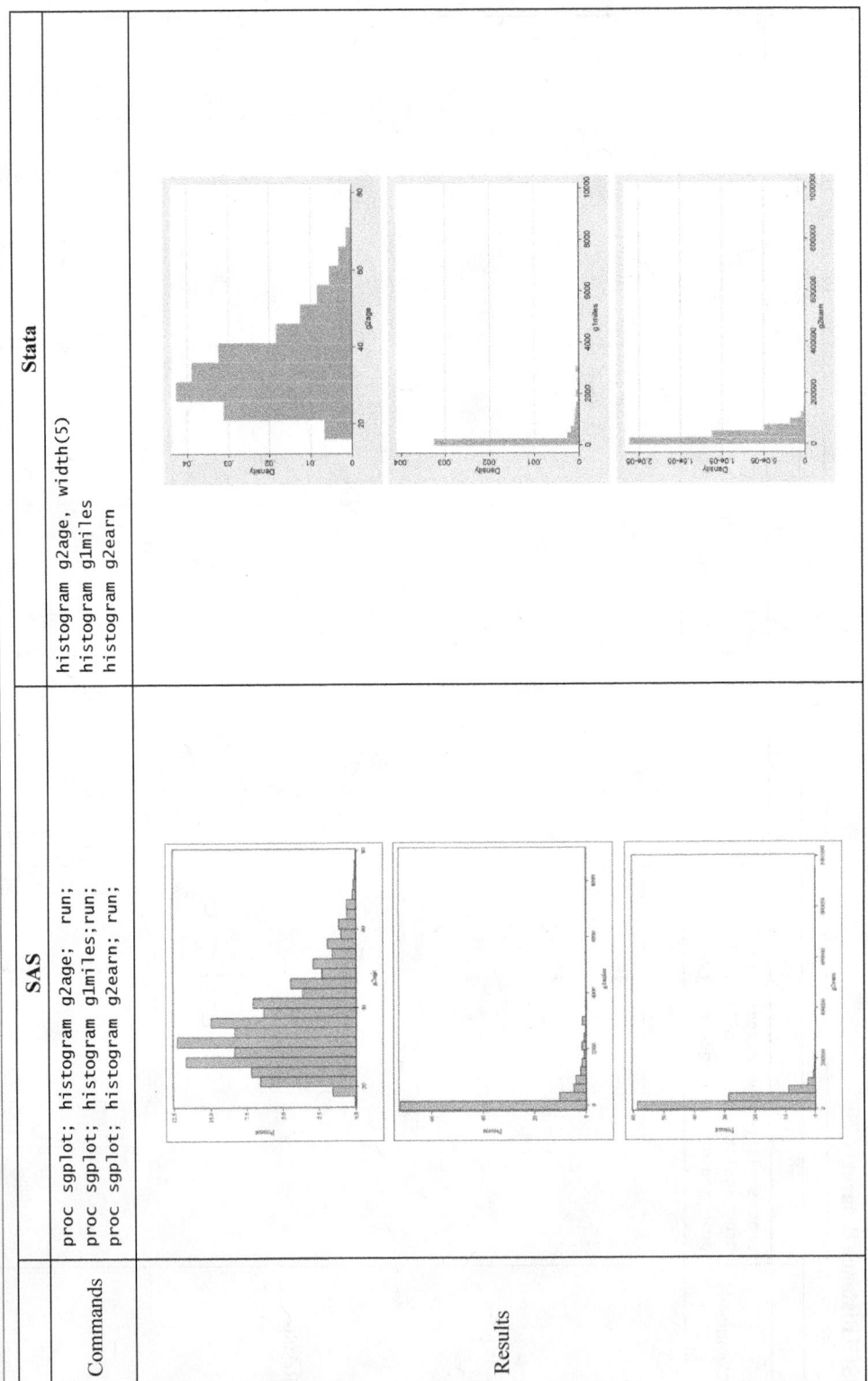

■ Display B.5.11. Means, Medians and Standard Deviations of Mother's Age (*g1age*), Respondent's Age (*g2age*), Mother's Distance Away (*g1miles*), and Respondent's Earnings (*g2earn*) from the NSFH Distance Dataset

	SAS	Stata
Commands	proc means n mean std min max p50; var g1age g2age g1miles g2earn; run;	summarize g1age g2age g1miles g2earn centile g1age g2age g1miles g2earn, centile(50)

SAS Results

Variable	N	Mean	Std Dev	Minimum	Maximum	50th Pctl
g1age	6801	60.5200706	11.5783997	29.0000000	95.0000000	60.0000000
g2age	6900	34.8368116	10.4165612	16.0000000	78.0000000	33.0000000
g1miles	6809	279.9706271	631.3679937	1.0000000	9000.00	15.0000000
g2earn	6433	29614.27	36351.57	0	945903.28	22701.68

Stata Results

```
. summarize g1age g2age g1miles g2earn

    Variable |     Obs        Mean    Std. Dev.     Min        Max
-------------+--------------------------------------------------------
       g1age |    6801    60.52007     11.5784       29         95
       g2age |    6900    34.83681    10.41656       16         78
     g1miles |    6809    279.9706     631.368        1       9000
      g2earn |    6433    29614.27    36351.57        0   945903.3

                                                  -- Binom. Interp. --
    Variable |     Obs  Percentile    Centile    [95% Conf. Interval]
-------------+--------------------------------------------------------
       g1age |    6801          50         60       59         60
       g2age |    6900          50         50       33         33
     g1miles |    6809          50         15       15         20
      g2earn |    6433          50   22701.68  22701.68   24593.49
```

■ **Display B.5.12. Weighted Means of Mother's Age (*g1age*), Respondent's Age (*g2age*), Mother's Distance Away (*g1miles*), and Respondent's Earnings (*g2earn*) from the NSFH Distance Dataset**

Commands

SAS

```
proc surveymeans mean
rate="c:\nsfh_distance\SAS\rate";
   var g1age g2age g1miles g2earn;
   domain DistanceSample;
   cluster PSU;
   strata StratumC;
   weight adjweight;
run;
```

Stata

```
svyset PSU [pw=adjweight], strata(Stratum) singleunit(certainty)
svy, subpop(DistanceSample): mean g1age
svy, subpop(DistanceSample): mean g2age
svy, subpop(DistanceSample): mean g1miles
svy, subpop(DistanceSample): mean g2earn
```

Results

SAS

DistanceSample	Variable	Mean	Std Error of Mean
1	g1age	61.874922	0.181003
	g2age	36.038573	0.164641
	g1miles	311.319126	17.665606
	g2earn	32332	480.001946

Stata

	Mean	Linearized Std. Err.	[95% Conf. Interval]	
g1age	61.87492	.1810034	61.50623	62.24361

	Mean	Linearized Std. Err.	[95% Conf. Interval]	
g2age	36.03857	.1646408	35.70321	36.37394

	Mean	Linearized Std. Err.	[95% Conf. Interval]	
g1miles	311.3191	17.66561	275.3355	347.3028

	Mean	Linearized Std. Err.	[95% Conf. Interval]	
g2earn	32331.74	480.0019	31354.01	33309.47

■ **Display B.5.13. Weighted Proportions of Gender (*M2DP01*) and of Race-Ethnicity (*M484*) from the NSFH Distance Dataset**

	SAS	Stata

Commands	`proc surveymeans mean`
	`rate="c:\nsfh_distance\SAS\rate";`
	`    class M2DP01 M484;`
	`    var M2DP01 M484;`
	`    domain DistanceSample;`
	`    cluster PSU;`
	`    strata StratumC;`
	`    weight adjweight;`
	`run;`
		`svyset PSU [pw=adjweight], strata(Stratum) singleunit(certainty)`
		
		`svy, subpop(DistanceSample): tabulate M2DP01`
		`svy, subpop(DistanceSample): tabulate M484`

Results

SAS:

Distance Sample	Variable	Level	Mean	Std Error of Mean
1	M2DP01	MALE	0.465314	0.006558
		FEMALE	0.534686	0.006558
	M484	BLACK	0.101066	0.004803
		WHITE/NOT HISPANIC	0.854470	0.007832
		MEX/CHICANO/MEX.AM	0.024783	0.007247
		PUERTO RICAN	0.004512	0.000408
		CUBAN	0.000885	0.000107
		OTHER HISPANIC	0.006490	0.001126
		AMERICAN INDIAN	0.004212	0.000730
		ASIAN	0.003045	0.000711
		OTHER	0.000274	0.000273
		REFUSED	.	
		NO ANSWER	0.000263	0.000113

Stata:

```
Number of strata    =    68    Number of obs      =     13007
Number of PSUs      =   100    Population size    = 13008.156
                               Subpop. no. of obs =      6901
                               Subpop. size       = 6275.6037
                               Design df          =        32

M2DP01 | proportions
-------+------------
  MALE |      .4653
FEMALE |      .5347
-------+------------
 Total |          1
-------+------------

Number of strata    =    68    Number of obs      =     13007
Number of PSUs      =   100    Population size    = 13008.156
                               Subpop. no. of obs =      6901
                               Subpop. size       = 6275.6037
                               Design df          =        32

    M484 | proportions
---------+------------
   BLACK |      .1011
WHITE/NO |      .8545
MEX/CHIC |      .0248
PUERTO R |      .0045
   CUBAN |    8.9e-04
OTHER HI |      .0065
AMERICAN |      .0042
   ASIAN |       .003
   OTHER |    2.7e-04
 REFUSED |          0
NO ANSWE |    2.6e-04
---------+------------
   Total |          1
---------+------------
```

▪ Display B.5.14. Weighted Standard Deviations of Mother's Age (*g1age*), Respondent's Age (*g2age*), Mother's Distance Away (*g1miles*), and Respondent's Earnings (*g2earn*) from the NSFH Distance Dataset

	SAS	Stata

Commands	```
	proc means mean std vardef=weight;
	     var g1age g2age g1miles g2earn;
	     where DistanceSample=1;
	     weight adjweight;
	run;
	``
		``
		svyset PSU [pw=adjweight], strata(Stratum) singleunit(certainty)
		svy, subpop(DistanceSample): mean g1age if DistanceSample==1
		estat sd
		svy, subpop(DistanceSample): mean g2age if DistanceSample==1
		estat sd
		svy, subpop(DistanceSample): mean g1miles if DistanceSample==1
		estat sd
		svy, subpop(DistanceSample): mean g2earn if DistanceSample==1
		estat sd
		``

Results	Variable, Mean, Std Dev: g1age 61.8749222 12.1367617 g2age 36.0385729 11.1215791 g1miles 311.3191261 660.6151614 g2earn 32331.74 39497.57	Mean / Std. Dev. g1age | 61.87492 12.13765 g2age | 36.03857 11.12239 g1miles | 311.3191 660.6637 g2earn | 32331.74 39500.64

■ Display B.6.1. Requesting p-values from SAS and Stata

	SAS	Stata
| Commands | ```
data _null_;
    file print;

    pz=2*(1-probnorm(abs(22.33)));
        put "p-value for z:" pz 5.4;

    pz=(1-probnorm(abs(22.33)));
        put "p-value for z:" pz 5.4;

    pt=2*(1-probt(abs(23.15),299));
        put "p-value for t:" pt 5.4;

    pf=(1-probf(535.9225,1,299));
        put "p-value for f:" pf 5.4;

    pc=(1-probchi(498.6289,1));
        put "p-value for chi-square:" pc 5.4;

run;
``` | ```
di  2*(1-normal(abs(22.33)))

di  (1-normal(abs(22.33)))

di  2*(ttail(299,abs(23.15)))

di  Ftail(1,299,535.9225)

di  chi2tail(1,498.6289)
``` |
| Results | ```
p-value for z: .0000
p-value for z: .0000
p-value for t: .0000
p-value for f: .0000
p-value for chi-square: .0000
``` | ```
di  2*(1-normal(abs(22.33)))
.
di  (1-normal(abs(22.33)))
0
di  2*(ttail(299,abs(23.15)))
.
1.219e-68
di  Ftail(1,299,535.9225)
1.219e-68
di  chi2tail(1,498.6289)
1.89e-110
``` |

■ **Display B.7.1. Two-sample t-test of Miles from Mother (*g1miles*) by Respondent's Gender (*M2DP01*) from the NSFH Distance Dataset (Subsample with Fewer than Five Brothers and Fewer than Five Sisters)**

	SAS	Stata

Commands	```proc ttest;
	    class M2DP01;
	    var g1miles;
	run;```
		``ttest g1miles, by(M2DP01)
		ttest g1miles, by(M2DP01) unequal
		sdtest g1miles, by(M2DP01)```

Results

SAS

M2DP01	N	Mean	Std Dev	Std Err	Minimum	Maximum
MALE	2381	319.9	678.7	13.9092	1.0000	6000.0
FEMALE	3446	264.9	606.8	10.3366	1.0000	6000.0
Diff (1-2)		54.9727	637.2	16.9797		

M2DP01	Method	Mean	95% CL Mean		Std Dev	95% CL Std Dev	
MALE		319.9	292.6	347.2	678.7	660.0	698.6
FEMALE		264.9	244.7	285.2	606.8	592.8	621.5
Diff (1-2)	Pooled	54.9727	21.6863	88.2592	637.2	625.8	648.9
Diff (1-2)	Satterthwaite	54.9727	20.9988	88.9466			

Method	Variances	DF	t Value	Pr > |t|
Pooled	Equal	5825	3.24	0.0012
Satterthwaite	Unequal	4736.6	3.17	0.0015

Stata

Two-sample t test with equal variances

Group	Obs	Mean	Std. Err.	Std. Dev.	[95% Conf.	Interval]
MALE	2381	319.9005	13.90921	678.7069	292.625	347.1759
FEMALE	3446	264.9277	10.3366	606.7859	244.6613	285.1942
combined	5827	287.3904	8.353617	637.6716	271.0142	303.7666
diff		54.97272	16.97966		21.68627	88.25917

diff = mean(MALE) - mean(FEMALE)   t = 3.2376
Ho: diff = 0   degrees of freedom = 5825

Ha: diff < 0   Ha: diff != 0   Ha: diff > 0
Pr(T < t) = 0.9994   Pr(|T| > |t|) = 0.0012   Pr(T > t) = 0.0006

Two-sample t test with unequal variances

Group	Obs	Mean	Std. Err.	Std. Dev.	[95% Conf.	Interval]
MALE	2381	319.9005	13.90921	678.7069	292.625	347.1759
FEMALE	3446	264.9277	10.3366	606.7859	244.6613	285.1942
combined	5827	287.3904	8.353617	637.6716	271.0142	303.7666
diff		54.97272	17.3295		20.99884	88.9466

diff = mean(MALE) - mean(FEMALE)   t = 3.1722
Ho: diff = 0   Satterthwaite's degrees of freedom = 4736.64

Ha: diff < 0   Ha: diff != 0   Ha: diff > 0
Pr(T < t) = 0.9992   Pr(|T| > |t|) = 0.0015   Pr(T > t) = 0.0008

(continued)

■ Display B.7.1. Two-sample t-test of Miles from Mother (*g1miles*) by Respondent's Gender (*M2DP01*) from the NSFH Distance Dataset (Subsample with Fewer than Five Brothers and Fewer than Five Sisters)(continued)

	SAS	Stata
| Results | **Equality of Variances** | ```
Variance ratio test

    Group |     Obs      Mean    Std. Err.   Std. Dev.   [95% Conf.  Interval]
----------+---------------------------------------------------------------------
     MALE |    2381   319.9005   13.90921    678.7069     292.625    347.1759
   FEMALE |    3446   264.9277   10.3366     606.7859     244.6613   285.1942
----------+---------------------------------------------------------------------
 combined |    5827   287.3904    8.353617   637.6716     271.0142   303.7666
---------------------------------------------------------------------------------
    ratio = sd(MALE) / sd(FEMALE)                                f = 1.2511
Ho: ratio = 1                               degrees of freedom = 2380, 3445

  Ha: ratio < 1              Ha: ratio != 1             Ha: ratio > 1
Pr(F < f) = 1.0000      2*Pr(F > f) = 0.0000        Pr(F > f) = 0.0000
``` |

SAS — Equality of Variances

Method	Num DF	Den DF	F Value	Pr > F
Folded F	2380	3445	1.25	<.0001
```

■ **Display B.7.2. Analysis of Variance of Miles from Mother (*g1miles*) by Respondent's Gender (*M2DP01*) from the NSFH Distance Dataset (Subsample with Fewer than Five Brothers and Fewer than Five Sisters)**

	SAS	Stata

Commands	`proc anova;`
	`  class M2DP01;`
	`    model g1miles=M2DP01;`
	`run;`
		`oneway g1miles M2DP01`

Results	(see table below)	(see table below)

SAS

Source	DF	Sum of Squares	Mean Square	F Value	Pr > F
Model	1	4255240	4255240	10.48	0.0012
Error	5825	2364742190	405964		
Corrected Total	5826	2368997431			

Stata

Analysis of Variance

Source	SS	df	MS	F	Prob > F
Between groups	4255240.37	1	4255240.37	10.48	0.0012
Within groups	2.3647e+09	5825	405964.325		
Total	2.3690e+09	5826	406625.031		

■ Display B.7.3. Analysis of Variance and Subgroup Means of Miles from Mother (*g1miles*) by Number of Sisters (*g2numsis*) from the NSFH Distance Dataset (Subsample with Fewer than Five Brothers and Fewer than Five Sisters)

SAS

ANOVA Commands

```
proc anova;
    class g2numsis;
    model g1miles=g2numsis;
run;
```

ANOVA Results

Source	DF	Sum of Squares	Mean Square	F Value	Pr > F
Model	4	4168297	1042074	2.57	0.0363
Error	5822	2364829134	406188		
Corrected Total	5826	2368997431			

Commands

```
proc means;
    var g1miles;
    class g2numsis;
run;
```

Results

Analysis Variable : g1miles

g2numsis	N Obs	N	Mean	Std Dev	Minimum	Maximum
0	2153	2128	268.3735902	601.3912721	1.0000000	5300.00
1	1817	1797	314.9003895	664.3439733	1.0000000	6000.00
2	1110	1102	257.3793103	603.5002560	1.0000000	6000.00
3	544	536	331.5559701	733.6270772	1.0000000	4000.00
4	270	264	289.0265152	658.2163443	1.0000000	3200.00

Stata

ANOVA Commands

```
oneway g1miles g2numsis
```

ANOVA Results

Analysis of variance

Source	SS	df	MS	F	Prob > F
Between groups	4168297.04	4	1042074.26	2.57	0.0363
Within groups	2.3648e+09	5822	406188.446		
Total	2.3690e+09	5826	406625.031		

Commands

```
bysort g2numsis: summarize g1miles
```

Results

```
-> g2numsis = 0
```

Variable	Obs	Mean	Std. Dev.	Min	Max
g1miles	2128	268.3736	601.3913	1	5300

```
-> g2numsis = 1
```

Variable	Obs	Mean	Std. Dev.	Min	Max
g1miles	1797	314.9004	664.344	1	6000

```
-> g2numsis = 2
```

Variable	Obs	Mean	Std. Dev.	Min	Max
g1miles	1102	257.3793	603.5003	1	6000

```
-> g2numsis = 3
```

Variable	Obs	Mean	Std. Dev.	Min	Max
g1miles	536	331.556	733.6271	1	4000

```
-> g2numsis = 4
```

Variable	Obs	Mean	Std. Dev.	Min	Max
g1miles	264	289.0265	658.2163	1	3200

Display B.7.4. Cross-Tabulation of Number of Brothers (*g2numbro*) and Number of Sisters (*g2numsis*) with Row, Column, and Cell Percentages from the NSFH Distance Dataset (Subsample with Fewer than Five Brothers and Fewer than Five Sisters)

SAS

Commands

```
proc freq;
  tables  g2numbro*g2numsis;
run;
```

Results

Table of g2numbro by g2numsis

Key: Frequency / Percent / Row Pct / Col Pct

g2numbro	g2numsis 0	1	2	3	4	Total
0	1156	492	271	135	33	2087
	19.61	8.35	4.60	2.29	0.56	35.41
	55.39	23.57	12.99	6.47	1.58	
	53.69	27.08	24.41	24.82	12.22	
1	522	662	377	152	88	1801
	8.86	11.23	6.40	2.58	1.49	30.56
	28.98	36.76	20.93	8.44	4.89	
	24.25	36.43	33.96	27.94	32.59	
2	297	405	277	119	66	1164
	5.04	6.87	4.70	2.02	1.12	19.75
	25.52	34.79	23.80	10.22	5.67	
	13.79	22.29	24.95	21.88	24.44	
3	138	176	116	86	47	563
	2.34	2.99	1.97	1.46	0.80	9.55
	24.51	31.26	20.60	15.28	8.35	
	6.41	9.69	10.45	15.81	17.41	
4	40	82	69	52	36	279
	0.68	1.39	1.17	0.88	0.61	4.73
	14.34	29.39	24.73	18.64	12.90	
	1.86	4.51	6.22	9.56	13.33	
Total	2153	1817	1110	544	270	5894
	36.53	30.83	18.83	9.23	4.58	100.00

Stata

Commands

```
tabulate g2numbro g2numsis, row column cell
```

Results

Key: frequency / row percentage / column percentage / cell percentage

g2numbro	g2numsis 0	1	2	3	4	Total
0	1,156	492	271	135	33	2,087
	55.39	23.57	12.99	6.47	1.58	100.00
	53.69	27.08	24.41	24.82	12.22	35.41
	19.61	8.35	4.60	2.29	0.56	35.41
1	522	662	377	152	88	1,801
	28.98	36.76	20.93	8.44	4.89	100.00
	24.25	36.43	33.96	27.94	32.59	30.56
	8.86	11.23	6.40	2.58	1.49	30.56
2	297	405	277	119	66	1,164
	25.52	34.79	23.80	10.22	5.67	100.00
	13.79	22.29	24.95	21.88	24.44	19.75
	5.04	6.87	4.70	2.02	1.12	19.75
3	138	176	116	86	47	563
	24.51	31.26	20.60	15.28	8.35	100.00
	6.41	9.69	10.45	15.81	17.41	9.55
	2.34	2.99	1.97	1.46	0.80	9.55
4	40	82	69	52	36	279
	14.34	29.39	24.73	18.64	12.90	100.00
	1.86	4.51	6.22	9.56	13.33	4.73
	0.68	1.39	1.17	0.88	0.61	4.73
Total	2,153	1,817	1,110	544	270	5,894
	36.53	30.83	18.83	9.23	4.58	100.00
	100.00	100.00	100.00	100.00	100.00	100.00
	36.53	30.83	18.83	9.23	4.58	100.00

■ **Display B.7.5. Pearson Chi-Square for Cross-Tabulation of Number of Brothers (*g2numbro*) and Number of Sisters (*g2numsis*) from the NSFH Distance Dataset (Subsample with Fewer than Five Brothers and Fewer than Five Sisters)**

SAS

Commands

```
proc freq;
    tables g2numbro*g2numsis
    / chisq expected norow nocol nopercent;
run;
```

Results

Table of g2numbro by g2numsis

g2numbro Frequency expected	g2numsis 0	1	2	3	4	Total
0	1156 762.35	492 643.38	271 393.04	135 192.62	33 95.604	2087
1	522 657.88	662 555.21	377 339.18	152 166.23	88 82.503	1801
2	297 425.19	405 358.84	277 219.21	119 107.43	66 53.322	1164
3	138 205.66	176 173.56	116 106.03	86 51.963	47 25.791	563
4	40 101.91	82 86.01	69 52.543	52 25.751	36 12.781	279
Total	2153	1817	1110	544	270	5894

Statistic	DF	Value	Prob
Chi-Square	16	628.3557	<.0001
Likelihood Ratio Chi-Square	16	614.4236	<.0001
Mantel-Haenszel Chi-Square	1	422.8753	<.0001
Phi Coefficient		0.3265	
Contingency Coefficient		0.3104	
Cramer's V		0.1633	

Stata

Commands

```
tabulate g2numbro g2numsis, chi2 expected
```

Results

```
+-------------------+
| key               |
|-------------------|
| frequency         |
| expected frequency|
+-------------------+
```

g2numbro	g2numsis 0	1	2	3	4	Total
0	1,156 762.4	492 643.4	271 393.0	135 192.6	33 95.6	2,087 2,087.0
1	522 657.9	662 555.2	377 339.2	152 166.2	88 82.5	1,801 1,801.0
2	297 425.2	405 358.8	277 219.2	119 107.4	66 53.3	1,164 1,164.0
3	138 205.7	176 173.6	116 106.0	86 52.0	47 25.8	563 563.0
4	40 101.9	82 86.0	69 52.5	52 25.8	36 12.8	279 279.0
Total	2,153 2,153.0	1,817 1,817.0	1,110 1,110.0	544 544.0	270 270.0	5,894 5,894.0

Pearson chi2(16) = 628.3557   Pr = 0.000

Display B.7.6. Pearson Correlation of Mother's Age (*g1age*) and Respondent's Age (*g2age*) from the NSFH Distance Dataset (Subsample with Fewer than Five Brothers and Fewer than Five Sisters)

	SAS	Stata
| Commands | ```
proc corr;
    var g1age g2age;
run;
``` | ```
pwcorr g1age g2age, obs sig
``` |
| Results | **Pearson Correlation Coefficients**<br>Prob > \|r\| under H0: Rho=0<br>Number of Observations<br><br>　　　　　　g1age　　　g2age<br>g1age　1.00000　0.85101<br>　　　　　　　　　　　<.0001<br>　　　　5827　　　5826<br><br>g2age　0.85101　1.00000<br>　　　　<.0001<br>　　　　5826　　　5893 | ```
          |    g1age    g2age
----------+-----------------
    g1age |   1.0000
          |
          |     5827
          |
    g2age |   0.8510   1.0000
          |   0.0000
          |     5826     5893
``` |
```

Display B.7.7. Weighted subgroup Means of Miles from Mother (*g1miles*) by Number of Sisters (*g2numsis*) from the NSFH Distance Dataset (Subsample with Fewer than Five Brothers and Fewer than Five Sisters)

	SAS	Stata

Commands	`proc means mean std vardef=weight;`
	`    var g1miles;`
	`    class g2numsis;`
	`    weight adjweight1;`
	`    where DistanceSample=1;`
	`run;`
		`bysort g2numsis: summarize g1miles [aw=adjweight1] if DistanceSample==1`

SAS Results

Analysis Variable : g1miles

g2numsis	N Obs	Mean	Std Dev
0	2128	288.3867183	615.9734653
1	1797	355.5414668	703.3372021
2	1102	286.9257597	617.1027949
3	536	416.6741133	844.1912605
4	264	314.6269926	676.848626

Stata Results

```
-> g2numsis = 0

    Variable |     Obs       Weight        Mean    Std. Dev.   Min      Max
    ---------+----------------------------------------------------------------
     g1miles |    2128   2127.99995    288.3867    615.9735     1     5300

-> g2numsis = 1

    Variable |     Obs       Weight        Mean    Std. Dev.   Min      Max
    ---------+----------------------------------------------------------------
     g1miles |    1797   1796.99993    355.5415    703.3372     1     6000

-> g2numsis = 2

    Variable |     Obs       Weight        Mean    Std. Dev.   Min      Max
    ---------+----------------------------------------------------------------
     g1miles |    1102   1101.99994    286.9258    617.1028     1     6000

-> g2numsis = 3

    Variable |     Obs       Weight        Mean    Std. Dev.   Min      Max
    ---------+----------------------------------------------------------------
     g1miles |     536   535.999969    416.6741    844.1913     1     4000

-> g2numsis = 4

    Variable |     Obs       Weight        Mean    Std. Dev.   Min      Max
    ---------+----------------------------------------------------------------
     g1miles |     264   263.999992     314.627    676.8485     1     3200
```

▪ **Display B.7.8. Weighted Cross-tabulation of Number of Brothers (*g2numbro*) and Number of Sisters (*g2numsis*) from the NSFH Distance Dataset (Subsample with Fewer than Five Brothers and Fewer than Five Sisters)**

SAS

Commands

```
proc freq;
  tables g2numbro*g2numsis;
  weight adjweight2;
  where DistanceSample=1;
run;
```

Results

Table of g2numbro by g2numsis

g2numbro		g2numsis					Total
Frequency / Percent / Row Pct / Col Pct		0	1	2	3	4	
0		1156.02 / 19.61 / 54.51 / 52.53	504.617 / 8.56 / 23.79 / 27.23	296.256 / 5.03 / 13.97 / 26.80	133.077 / 2.26 / 6.27 / 27.14	30.8013 / 0.52 / 1.45 / 12.59	2120.77 / 35.98
1		550.377 / 9.34 / 30.01 / 25.01	696.966 / 11.83 / 38.00 / 37.61	374.029 / 6.35 / 20.40 / 33.83	131.337 / 2.23 / 7.16 / 26.78	81.2027 / 1.38 / 4.43 / 33.20	1833.91 / 31.11
2		324.341 / 5.50 / 27.81 / 14.74	414.948 / 7.04 / 35.58 / 22.39	259.925 / 4.41 / 22.29 / 23.51	105.532 / 1.79 / 9.05 / 21.52	61.4719 / 1.04 / 5.27 / 25.14	1166.22 / 19.79
3		128.551 / 2.18 / 25.12 / 5.84	154.302 / 2.62 / 30.16 / 8.33	113.028 / 1.92 / 22.09 / 10.22	77.9185 / 1.32 / 15.23 / 15.89	37.8604 / 0.64 / 7.40 / 15.48	511.66 / 8.68
4		41.24 / 0.70 / 15.77 / 1.87	82.1042 / 1.39 / 31.40 / 4.43	62.3399 / 1.06 / 23.84 / 5.64	42.5298 / 0.72 / 16.27 / 8.67	33.228 / 0.56 / 12.71 / 13.59	261.442 / 4.44
Total		2200.53 / 37.34	1852.94 / 31.44	1105.58 / 18.76	490.393 / 8.32	244.564 / 4.15	5894 / 100.00

Stata

Commands

```
tabulate g2numbro g2numsis [aw=adjweight2] if DistanceSample==1 ///
, row column cell
```

Results

```
+-----------------------+
| Key                   |
|-----------------------|
|       frequency       |
|    row percentage     |
|   column percentage   |
|    cell percentage    |
+-----------------------+
```

			g2numsis			
g2numbro	0	1	2	3	4	Total
0	1,156.019 / 54.51 / 52.53 / 19.61	504.61717 / 23.79 / 27.23 / 8.56	296.2558 / 13.97 / 26.80 / 5.03	133.07663 / 6.27 / 27.14 / 2.26	30.801329 / 1.45 / 12.59 / 0.52	2,120.77 / 100.00 / 35.98 / 35.98
1	550.37656 / 30.01 / 25.01 / 9.34	696.96585 / 38.00 / 37.61 / 11.83	374.02944 / 20.40 / 33.83 / 6.35	131.33651 / 7.16 / 26.78 / 2.23	81.202698 / 4.43 / 33.20 / 1.38	1,833.911 / 100.00 / 31.11 / 31.11
2	324.34125 / 27.81 / 14.74 / 5.50	414.94767 / 35.58 / 22.39 / 7.04	259.92469 / 22.29 / 23.51 / 4.41	105.53202 / 9.05 / 21.52 / 1.79	61.471858 / 5.27 / 25.14 / 1.04	1,166.2175 / 100.00 / 19.79 / 19.79
3	128.55064 / 25.12 / 5.84 / 2.18	154.30211 / 30.16 / 8.33 / 2.62	113.02804 / 22.09 / 10.22 / 1.92	77.9184984 / 15.23 / 15.89 / 1.32	37.860369 / 7.40 / 15.48 / 0.64	511.65966 / 100.00 / 8.68 / 8.68
4	41.239992 / 15.77 / 1.87 / 0.70	82.104241 / 31.40 / 4.43 / 1.39	62.339862 / 23.84 / 5.64 / 1.06	42.529827 / 16.27 / 8.67 / 0.72	33.2280195 / 12.71 / 13.59 / 0.56	261.44194 / 100.00 / 4.44 / 4.44
Total	2,200.527 / 37.34 / 100.00 / 37.34	1,852.937 / 31.44 / 100.00 / 31.44	1,105.578 / 18.76 / 100.00 / 18.76	490.3935 / 8.32 / 100.00 / 8.32	244.56427 / 4.15 / 100.00 / 4.15	5,894 / 100.00 / 100.00 / 100.00

■ **Display B.7.9. Weighted Correlation of Mother's Age (*g1age*) and Respondent's Age (*g2age*) from the NSFH Distance Dataset (Subsample with Fewer than Five Brothers and Fewer than Five Sisters)**

	SAS	Stata
| Commands | ```
proc corr ;
    var g1age g2age;
    weight adjweight3;
    where DistanceSample=1;
run;
``` | ```
pwcorr g1age g2age [aw=adjweight3] if DistanceSample==1, obs sig
``` |
| Results | Pearson Correlation Coefficients, N = 5826<br>Prob > \|r\| under H0: Rho=0<br><br>| | g1age | g2age |<br>\|---\|---\|---\|<br>| g1age | 1.00000 | 0.86736<br><.0001 |<br>| g2age | 0.86736<br><.0001 | 1.00000 | | ```
         |    g1age    g2age
---------+----------------
   g1age |  1.0000
         |    5826
         |
   g2age |  0.8674   1.0000
         |  0.0000
         |    5826     5826
``` |
```

■ **Display B.8.1 Regression of Distance from Mother on Respondent's Earnings**

	SAS	Stata
| Commands | ```
proc reg;
  Model g1miles=g2earn;
run;
``` | ```
regress g1miles g2earn
``` |

SAS Results

Number of Observations Read	6350
Number of Observations Used	6350

Analysis of Variance

Source	DF	Sum of Squares	Mean Square	F Value	Pr > F
Model	1	10850283	10850283	26.90	<.0001
Error	6348	2560477708	403352		
Corrected Total	6349	2571327990			

Root MSE	635.09989	R-Square	0.0042
Dependent Mean	283.47102	Adj R-Sq	0.0041
Coeff Var	224.04403		

Parameter Estimates

Variable	DF	Parameter Estimate	Standard Error	t Value	Pr > |t|
Intercept	1	249.81157	10.27798	24.31	<.0001
g2earn	1	0.00113	0.00021852	5.19	<.0001

Stata Results

```
      Source |       SS       df       MS              Number of obs =    6350
-------------+------------------------------           F(  1,  6348) =   26.90
       Model |  10850282.2     1  10850282.2           Prob > F      =   0.0000
    Residual | 2.5605e+09  6348  403351.876           R-squared     =   0.0042
-------------+------------------------------           Adj R-squared =   0.0041
       Total | 2.5713e+09  6349  404997.321           Root MSE      =   635.1
```

```
------------------------------------------------------------------------------
     g1miles |      Coef.   Std. Err.      t    P>|t|     [95% Conf. Interval]
-------------+----------------------------------------------------------------
      g2earn |   .0011333   .0002185     5.19   0.000     .000705    .0015617
       _cons |   249.8116   10.27798    24.31   0.000    229.6632   269.9599
------------------------------------------------------------------------------
```

■ Display B.8.2 Regression of Distance from Mother on Respondent's Earnings: Confidence Interval

	SAS	Stata

Commands	`proc reg;`
	`  model g1miles=g2earn /clb;`
	`run;`
		`regress g1miles g2earn`

SAS Results

Number of Observations Read	6350
Number of Observations Used	6350

Analysis of Variance

Source	DF	Sum of Squares	Mean Square	F Value	Pr > F
Model	1	10850283	10850283	26.90	<.0001
Error	6348	2560477708	403352		
Corrected Total	6349	2571327990			

Root MSE	635.09989	R-Square	0.0042
Dependent Mean	283.47102	Adj R-Sq	0.0041
Coeff Var	224.04403		

Parameter Estimates

Variable	DF	Parameter Estimate	Standard Error	t Value	Pr > |t|	95% Confidence Limits	
Intercep	1	249.81157	10.27798	24.31	<.0001	229.66325	269.95989
g2earn	1	0.00113	0.00021852	5.19	<.0001	0.00070498	0.00156

Stata Results

```
      Source |       SS       df       MS              Number of obs =    6350
-------------+------------------------------           F(  1,  6348) =   26.90
       Model |  10850282.2      1  10850282.2           Prob > F      =  0.0000
    Residual |  2.5605e+09   6348  403351.876           R-squared     =  0.0042
-------------+------------------------------           Adj R-squared =  0.0041
       Total |  2.5713e+09   6349  404997.321           Root MSE      =  635.1

-------------+----------------------------------------------------------------
     g1miles |      Coef.   Std. Err.      t    P>|t|     [95% Conf. Interval]
-------------+----------------------------------------------------------------
      g2earn |   .0011333   .0002185     5.19   0.000     .000705    .0015617
       _cons |   249.8116   10.27798    24.31   0.000    229.6632   269.9599
```

◼ Display B.8.3 Regression of Distance from Mother on Respondent's Earnings: Rescaled Earnings to $10,000 Units

	SAS	Stata

Commands	`LIBNAME LIBRARY 'c:/nsfh_distance/SAS';`
	`data Rescale10000;`
	`    set "c:/nsfh_distance/SAS/`
	`    CreateData";`
	`    if g1miles~=.& g2earn~=.;`
	`    g2earn10000=g2earn/10000;`
	`run;`
	`proc reg;`
	`    Model g1miles=g2earn10000;`
	`run;`
		`use CreateData if g1miles~=. & g2earn~=.`
		`generate g2earn10000=g2earn/10000`
		`regress g1miles g2earn10000`

Results:

SAS

Number of Observations Read	6350
Number of Observations Used	6350

Analysis of Variance

Source	DF	Sum of Squares	Mean Square	F Value	Pr > F
Model	1	10850283	10850283	26.90	<.0001
Error	6348	2560477708	403352		
Corrected Total	6349	2571327990			

Root MSE	635.09989	R-Square	0.0042
Dependent Mean	283.47102	Adj R-Sq	0.0041
Coeff Var	224.04403		

Parameter Estimates

Variable	DF	Parameter Estimate	Standard Error	t Value	Pr > |t|
Intercept	1	249.81157	10.27798	24.31	<.0001
g2earn10000	1	11.33347	2.18517	5.19	<.0001

Stata

```
      Source |       SS       df       MS              Number of obs =    6350
-------------+------------------------------           F(  1,  6348) =   26.90
       Model |  10850282.2     1  10850282.2           Prob > F      =  0.0000
    Residual |  2.5605e+09  6348   403351.876           R-squared     =  0.0042
-------------+------------------------------           Adj R-squared =  0.0041
       Total |  2.5713e+09  6349   404997.321           Root MSE      =   635.1

------------------------------------------------------------------------------
     g1miles |      Coef.   Std. Err.      t    P>|t|     [95% Conf. Interval]
-------------+----------------------------------------------------------------
 g2earn10000 |   11.33347    2.185166     5.19   0.000     7.049807    15.61713
       _cons |   249.8116    10.27798    24.31   0.000     229.6632    269.9599
------------------------------------------------------------------------------
```

■ Display B.8.4 Standard Deviations of Distance from Mother and Respondent's Earnings

	SAS	Stata
Commands	proc means; var g1miles g2earn; run;	summarize g1miles g2earn
Results		

SAS Results:

Variable	N	Mean	Std Dev	Minimum	Maximum
g1miles	6350	283.4710236	636.3939981	1.0000000	9000.00
g2earn	6350	29699.16	36475.81	0	94590328

Stata Results:

Variable	Obs	Mean	Std. Dev.	Min	Max
g1miles	6350	283.471	636.394	1	9000
g2earn	6350	29699.16	36475.81	0	945903.3

■ Display B.8.5 Regression of Distance from Mother on Respondent's Earnings: Standardized Coefficient using Rescaled Variables

Commands

SAS

```
LIBNAME LIBRARY 'c:\nsfh_distance\SAS';

data RescaleSD;
  set "c:\nsfh_distance\SAS\CreateData";
  if g1miles~=. & g2earn~=.;
  g1milesSD=g1miles/636.394;
  g2earnSD=g2earn/36475.81;
run;

proc reg;
  Model g1milesSD=g2earnSD;
run;
```

Stata

```
use CreateData   if g1miles~=. & g2earn~=.

generate g1milesSD=g1miles/636.394
generate g2earnSD=g2earn/36475.81
regress g1milesSD g2earnSD
```

Results

SAS

Number of Observations Read	6350
Number of Observations Used	6350

Analysis of Variance

Source	DF	Sum of Squares	Mean Square	F Value	Pr > F
Model	1	26.79100	26.79100	26.90	<.0001
Error	6348	6322.20896	0.99594		
Corrected Total	6349	6348.99996			

Root MSE	0.99797	R-Square	0.0042
Dependent Mean	0.44543	Adj R-Sq	0.0041
Coeff Var	224.04403		

Parameter Estimates

Variable	DF	Parameter Estimate	Standard Error	t Value	Pr > |t|
Intercept	1	0.39254	0.01615	24.31	<.0001
g2earnSD	1	0.06496	0.01252	5.19	<.0001

Stata

Source	SS	df	MS		
Model	26.7909973	1	26.7909973	Number of obs =	6350
Residual	6322.20892	6348	.995937133	F(1, 6348) =	26.90
				Prob > F =	0.0000
Total	6348.99992	6349	.999999987	R-squared =	0.0042
				Adj R-squared =	0.0041
				Root MSE =	.99797

g1milesSD	Coef.	Std. Err.	t	P>|t|	[95% Conf. Interval]
g2earnSD	.0649594	.0125246	5.19	0.000	.040407 .0895118
_cons	.3925423	.0161503	24.31	0.000	.3608822 .4242024

Display B.8.6 Regression of Distance from Mother on Respondent's Earnings: Standardized Coefficients Calculated by SAS and Stata

	SAS	Stata
Commands	```proc reg;`` `  Model g1miles=g2earn /stb;`` `run;```	```regress g1miles g2earn, beta```

SAS

Commands

```
proc reg;
  Model g1miles=g2earn /stb;
run;
```

Results

Number of Observations Read	6350
Number of Observations Used	6350

Analysis of Variance

Source	DF	Sum of Squares	Mean Square	F Value	Pr > F
Model	1	10850283	10850283	26.90	<.0001
Error	6348	2560477708	403352		
Corrected Total	6349	2571327990			

Root MSE	635.09989	R-Square	0.0042
Dependent Mean	283.47102	Adj R-Sq	0.0041
Coeff Var	224.04403		

Parameter Estimates

Variable	DF	Parameter Estimate	Standard Error	t Value	Pr > |t|	Standardized Estimate
Intercept	1	249.81157	10.27798	24.31	<.0001	0
g2earn	1	0.00113	0.00021852	5.19	<.0001	0.06496

Stata

Commands

```
regress g1miles g2earn, beta
```

Results

Source	SS	df	MS
Model	10850282.2	1	10850282.2
Residual	2.5605e+09	6348	403351.876
Total	2.5713e+09	6349	404997.321

```
Number of obs =   6350
F(  1,  6348) =  26.90
Prob > F      = 0.0000
R-squared     = 0.0042
Adj R-squared = 0.0041
Root MSE      = 635.1
```

g1miles	Coef.	Std. Err.	t	P>|t|	Beta
g2earn	.0011333	.0002185	5.19	0.000	.0649594
_cons	249.8116	10.27798	24.31	0.000	

Display B.8.7 Correlation of Distance from Mother and Respondent's Earnings

	SAS	Stata
| Commands | ```
proc corr;
   var g1miles g2earn;
run;
``` | ```
correlate g1miles g2earn
``` |
| Results | Pearson Correlation Coefficients, N = 6350<br>Prob > \|r\| under H0: Rho=0<br><br>| | g1miles | g2earn |<br>|---|---|---|<br>| g1miles | 1.00000 | 0.06496<br><0001 |<br>| g2earn | 0.06496<br><0001 | 1.00000 | | ```
             | g1miles   g2earn
-------------+-----------------
     g1miles | 1.0000
      g2earn | 0.0650    1.0000
``` |
```

Display B.8.8 Regression of Respondent's Earnings on Distance from Mother

	SAS	Stata

Commands	`proc reg;`
	`  Model g2earn=g1miles;`
	`  run;`
		`regress g2earn g1miles`

Results

SAS

Number of Observations Read	6350
Number of Observations Used	6350

Analysis of Variance

Source	DF	Sum of Squares	Mean Square	F Value	Pr > F
Model	1	3564500542	3564500542	26.90	<.0001
Error	6348	8.411601E12	1325078994		
Corrected Total	6349	8.447246E12			

Root MSE	36402	R-Square	0.0042
Dependent Mean	29699	Adj R-Sq	0.0041
Coeff Var	122.56789		

Parameter Estimates

Variable	DF	Parameter Estimate	Standard Error	t Value	Pr > |t|
Intercept	1	28644	500.08351	57.28	<.0001
g1miles	1	3.72324	0.71786	5.19	<.0001

Stata

Source	SS	df	MS
Model	3.5645e+10	1	3.5645e+10
Residual	8.4116e+12	6348	1.3251e+09
Total	8.4472e+12	6349	1.3305e+09

Number of obs = 6350
F(1, 6348) = 26.90
Prob > F = 0.0000
R-squared = 0.0042
Adj R-squared = 0.0041
Root MSE = 36402

g2earn	Coef.	Std. Err.	t	P>|t|	[95% Conf. Interval]	
g1miles	3.723237	.717864	5.19	0.000	2.315981	5.130492
_cons	28643.73	500.0835	57.28	0.000	27663.4	29624.06

■ Display B.8.9 Regression of Rescaled Earnings on Rescaled Miles

	SAS	Stata
Commands	```proc reg;` `Model g2earnSD=g1milesSD;` `run;```	```regress g2earnSD g1milesSD```

Results

SAS

Number of Observations Read	6350
Number of Observations Used	6350

Analysis of Variance

Source	DF	Sum of Squares	Mean Square	F Value	Pr > F
Model	1	26.79100	26.79100	26.90	<.0001
Error	6348	6322.20826	0.99594		
Corrected Total	6349	6348.99926			

Root MSE	0.99797	R-Square	0.0042
Dependent Mean	0.81422	Adj R-Sq	0.0041
Coeff Var	122.56789		

Parameter Estimates

Variable	DF	Parameter Estimate	Standard Error	t Value	Pr > |t|
Intercept	1	0.78528	0.01371	57.28	<.0001
g1milesSD	1	0.06496	0.01252	5.19	<.0001

Stata

Source	SS	df	MS
Model	26.7909952	1	26.7909952
Residual	6322.20842	6348	.995937055
Total	6348.99942	6349	.999999909

```
Number of obs =   6350
F( 1, 6348)   =  26.90
Prob > F      = 0.0000
R-squared     = 0.0042
Adj R-squared = 0.0041
Root MSE      = .99797
```

g2earnSD	Coef.	Std. Err.	t	P>|t|	[95% Conf. Interval]	
g1milesSD	.0649594	.0125246	5.19	0.000	.040407	.0895118
_cons	.7852802	.01371	57.28	0.000	.7584039	.8121564

Display B.8.10. Regression of Distance from Mother on Respondent's Earnings (Rescaled to $10,000 units) with Adjustments for the NSFH Complex Sampling Design

	SAS	Stata
| Commands | ```
proc surveyreg rate="c:\nsfh_distance\SAS\rate";
    model g1miles=g2earn10000 /clparm;
    domain DistanceSample;
    cluster PSU;
    strata StratumC;
    weight adjweight;
run;
``` | ```
svyset PSU [pw=adjweight], strata(Stratum) singleunit(certainty)
svy, subpop(DistanceSample): regress g1miles g2earn10000
``` |

SAS Results:

Domain Summary

Number of Observations in Domain	6350
Sum of Weights in Domain	6350.0

Estimated Regression Coefficients

Parameter	Estimate	Standard Error	t Value	Pr > |t|	95% Confidence Interval	
Intercept	278.334841	20.6769313	13.46	<.0001	237.063513	319.606168
g2earn10000	11.060531	1.8474969	5.99	<.0001	7.372911	14.748150

Stata Results:

```
Survey: Linear regression

Number of strata  =  68        Subpop. no. of obs  =      6350
Number of PSUs    = 100        Subpop. size        = 6349.9997

                          Linearized
   g1miles |    Coef.    Std. Err.     t    P>|t|   [95% Conf. Interval]
-----------+----------------------------------------------------------
g2earn10000| 11.06053   1.847375    5.99   0.000    7.297551   14.82351
     _cons | 278.3348   20.67557   13.46   0.000    236.2201   320.4496

Note: strata with single sampling unit treated as certainty units.
```

B52 ■ ■ ■ APPLIED STATISTICS FOR THE SOCIAL AND HEALTH SCIENCES

APPENDIX B

Display B.8.11. Significance Test for Weighted Correlation of Mother's Age (g1age) and Respondent's Age (g2age) from the NSFH Distance Dataset (Subsample with Fewer than Five Brothers and Fewer than Five Sisters).

Commands

SAS

```
g1ageS=(g1age-61.64621)/12.59308;
g2ageS=(g2age-35.89338)/11.46265;

proc surveyreg rate="c:\nsfh_distance\SAS\rate";
  model g1ageS=g2ageS /clparm;
  domain DistanceSample;
  cluster PSU;
  strata StratumC;
  weight adjweight3;
run;
proc surveyreg rate="c:\nsfh_distance\SAS\rate";
  model g2ageS=g1ageS /clparm;
  domain DistanceSample;
  cluster PSU;
  strata StratumC;
  weight adjweight3;
run;
```

Stata

```
svyset PSU [pw=adjweight], strata(Stratum) singleunit(certainty)

gen g1ageS=(g1age-61.64621)/12.59308
gen g2ageS=(g2age-35.89338)/11.46265

svy, subpop(DistanceSample): regress g1ageS g2ageS
svy, subpop(DistanceSample): regress g2ageS g1ageS
```

Results

SAS

Estimated Regression Coefficients

Parameter	Estimate	Standard Error	t Value	Pr > |t|
Intercept	0.00000032	0.00802714	0.00	1.0000
g2ageS	0.86735960	0.00600689	144.39	<.0001

Estimated Regression Coefficients

Parameter	Estimate	Standard Error	t Value	Pr > |t|
Intercept	-0.0000003	0.00826553	-0.00	1.0000
g1ageS	0.8673593	0.00788569	109.99	<.0001

Stata

g1ageS	Coef.	Linearized Std. Err.	t	P>|t|
g2ageS	.8673596	.0060065	144.40	0.000
_cons	3.18e-07	.0080266	0.00	1.000

g2ageS	Coef.	Linearized Std. Err.	t	P>|t|
g1ageS	.8673593	.0078852	110.00	0.000
_cons	-2.59e-07	.008265	-0.00	1.000

Display B.8.12. Significance Test for Weighted Correlation of Mother's Age (g1age) and Respondent's Age (g2age) from the NSFH Distance Dataset (Subsample with Fewer than Five Brothers and Fewer than Five Sisters).

Commands

SAS

```
proc surveyreg rate="c:\nsfh_distance\SAS\rate";
    model g1age=g2age /clparm;
    domain DistanceSample;
    cluster PSU;
    strata stratumC;
    weight adjweight3;
run;
proc surveyreg rate="c:\nsfh_distance\SAS\rate";
    model g2age=g1age /clparm;
    domain DistanceSample;
    cluster PSU;
    strata stratumC;
    weight adjweight3;
run;
```

Stata

```
svyset PSU [pw=adjweight], strata(Stratum) singleunit(certainty)

svy, subpop(DistanceSample): regress g1age g2age
svy, subpop(DistanceSample): regress g2age g1age
```

```
Number of strata    =     68    Number of obs       =      13007
Number of PSUs      =    100    Population size     =  14060.419
                               Subpop. no. of obs  =       5826
                               Subpop. size        =  5826.0002
                               Design df           =         32
                               F(  1,     32)      =   20852.23
                               Prob > F            =     0.0000
                               R-squared           =     0.7523
```

g1age	Coef.	Linearized Std. Err.	t	P>|t|
g2age	.9528973	.0065989	144.40	0.000
_cons	27.44351	.2506471	109.49	0.000

Survey: Linear regression

```
Number of strata    =     68    Number of obs       =      13007
Number of PSUs      =    100    Population size     =  14060.419
                               Subpop. no. of obs  =       5826
                               Subpop. size        =  5826.0002
                               Design df           =         32
                               F(  1,     32)      =   12099.62
                               Prob > F            =     0.0000
                               R-squared           =     0.7523
```

g2age	Coef.	Linearized Std. Err.	t	P>|t|
g1age	.7895	.0071774	110.00	0.000
_cons	-12.77631	.4213395	-30.32	0.000

Results

SAS

Fit Statistics

R-square	0.7523

Tests of Model Effects

Effect	Num DF	F Value	Pr > F
Model	1	20849.7	<.0001

Estimated Regression Coefficients

Parameter	Estimate	Standard Error	t Value	Pr > |t|
Intercept	27.4435074	0.25066242	109.48	<.0001
g2age	0.9528973	0.00659928	144.39	<.0001

Fit Statistics

R-square	0.7523

Tests of Model Effects

Effect	Num DF	F Value	Pr > F
Model	1	12098.1	<.0001

Estimated Regression Coefficients

Parameter	Estimate	Standard Error	t Value	Pr > |t|
Intercept	-12.776305	0.42136530	-30.32	<.0001
g1age	0.789500	0.00717783	109.99	<.0001

■ Display B.9.1 Regression of Distance from Mother on Respondent's Earnings and Mother's Years of Schooling

	SAS	Stata

Commands	`proc reg;`
	`  Model g1miles=g2earn g1yrschl;`
	`run;`
		`regress g1miles g2earn g1yrschl`

SAS Results

Number of Observations Read	5475
Number of Observations Used	5475

Analysis of Variance

Source	DF	Sum of Squares	Mean Square	F Value	Pr > F
Model	2	22291081	11145541	27.04	<.0001
Error	5472	2255081902	412113		
Corrected Total	5474	2277372983			

Root MSE	641.96022	R-Square	0.0098
Dependent Mean	291.22721	Adj R-Sq	0.0094
Coeff Var	220.43277		

Parameter Estimates

Variable	DF	Parameter Estimate	Standard Error	t Value	Pr > |t|
Intercept	1	78.34818	34.89219	2.25	0.0248
g2earn	1	0.00102	0.00023297	4.39	<.0001
g1yrschl	1	15.92156	2.97055	5.36	<.0001

Stata Results

Source	SS	df	MS		Number of obs = 5475
Model	22291080.9	2	11145540.4		F(2, 5472) = 27.04
Residual	2.2551e+09	5472	412112.921		Prob > F = 0.0000
					R-squared = 0.0098
Total	2.2774e+09	5474	416034.524		Adj R-squared = 0.0094
					Root MSE = 641.96

g1miles	Coef.	Std. Err.	t	P>|t|	[95% Conf. Interval]
g2earn	.00102	.000233	4.39	0.000	.0005653 .0014788
g1yrschl	15.92156	2.970548	5.36	0.000	10.09811 21.74502
_cons	78.34818	34.89219	2.25	0.025	9.945613 146.7507

Display B.9.2 Regression of Distance from Mother on Respondent's Earnings and Mother's Years of Schooling: Earnings Rescaled to $10,000 Units

	SAS	Stata

Commands	proc reg;
	  Model g1miles=g2earn10000 g1yrschl;
	  run;
		regress g1miles g2earn10000 g1yrschl

SAS Results

Number of Observations Read	5475
Number of Observations Used	5475

Analysis of Variance

Source	DF	Sum of Squares	Mean Square	F Value	Pr > F
Model	2	22291081	11145541	27.04	<.0001
Error	5472	2255081902	412113		
Corrected Total	5474	2277372983			

Root MSE	641.96022	R-Square	0.0098
Dependent Mean	291.22721	Adj R-Sq	0.0094
Coeff Var	220.43277		

Parameter Estimates

Variable	DF	Parameter Estimate	Standard Error	t Value	Pr > |t|
Intercept	1	78.34818	34.89219	2.25	0.0248
g2earn10000	1	10.22048	2.32971	4.39	<.0001
g1yrschl	1	15.92156	2.97055	5.36	<.0001

Stata Results

Source	SS	df	MS		
Model	22291080.9	2	11145540.5		
Residual	2.2551e+09	5472	412112.921		
Total	2.2774e+09	5474	416034.524		

Number of obs = 5475
F(2, 5472) = 27.04
Prob > F = 0.0000
R-squared = 0.0098
Adj R-squared = 0.0094
Root MSE = 641.96

g1miles	Coef.	Std. Err.	t	P>|t|	[95% Conf. Interval]
g2earn10000	10.22048	2.329708	4.39	0.000	5.653329 14.78763
g1yrschl	15.92156	2.970548	5.36	0.000	10.09811 21.74502
_cons	78.34818	34.89219	2.25	0.025	9.945613 146.7507

Display B.9.3 Regression of Distance from Mother on Respondent's Earnings and Mother's Years of Schooling: Schooling Rescaled to 4-Year Units

Commands

SAS

```
g1yrsch14=g1yrsch1/4;
. . .
proc reg;
  Model g1miles=g2earn g1yrsch14;
run;
```

Stata

```
generate g1yrsch14=g1yrsch1/4
regress g1miles g2earn g1yrsch14
```

Results

Stata

Source	SS	df	MS		
Model	22291080.9	2	11145540.4		
Residual	2.2551e+09	5472	412112.921		
Total	2.2774e+09	5474	416034.524		

Number of obs = 5475
F(2, 5472) = 27.04
Prob > F = 0.0000
R-squared = 0.0098
Adj R-squared = 0.0094
Root MSE = 641.96

g1miles	Coef.	Std. Err.	t	P>|t|	[95% Conf. Interval]
g2earn	.001022	.000233	4.39	0.000	.0005653 .0014788
g1yrsch14	63.68624	11.88219	5.36	0.000	40.39242 86.98006
_cons	78.34818	34.89219	2.25	0.025	9.945613 146.7507

SAS

Number of Observations Read	5475
Number of Observations Used	5475

Analysis of Variance

Source	DF	Sum of Squares	Mean Square	F Value	Pr > F
Model	2	22291081	11145541	27.04	<.0001
Error	5472	2255081902	412113		
Corrected Total	5474	2277372983			

Root MSE	641.96022	R-Square	0.0098
Dependent Mean	291.27721	Adj R-Sq	0.0094
Coeff Var	220.43277		

Parameter Estimates

Variable	DF	Parameter Estimate	Standard Error	t Value	Pr > |t|
Intercept	1	78.34818	34.89219	2.25	0.0248
g2earn	1	0.00102	0.00023297	4.39	<.0001
g1yrsch14	1	63.68624	11.88219	5.36	<.0001

Notes

The variable creation in SAS must take place in the DATA step.

Display B.9.4 Regression of Hours of Chores on Number of Children (Full NSFH Sample of 3,116 Employed Women)

	SAS	Stata
| Commands | ```
proc reg;
  Model hrchores=numkid;
run;
``` | `regress hrchores numkid` |

SAS Results

Number of Observations Read	3116
Number of Observations Used	3116

Analysis of Variance

Source	DF	Sum of Squares	Mean Square	F Value	Pr > F
Model	1	152453	152453	215.16	<.0001
Error	3114	2206415	708.54674		
Corrected Total	3115	2358868			

Root MSE	26.61854	R-Square	0.0646
Dependent Mean	34.45250	Adj R-Sq	0.0643
Coeff Var	77.26156		

Parameter Estimates

Variable	DF	Parameter Estimate	Standard Error	t Value	Pr > |t|
Intercept	1	28.69373	0.61767	46.45	<.0001
numkid	1	6.38361	0.43519	14.67	<.0001

Stata Results

Source	SS	df	MS		
Model	152453.437	1	152453.437		
Residual	2206414.53	3114	708.546735		
Total	2358867.97	3115	757.260986		

Number of obs = 3116
F(1, 3114) = 215.16
Prob > F = 0.0000
R-squared = 0.0646
Adj R-squared = 0.0643
Root MSE = 26.619

hrchores	Coef.	Std. Err.	t	P>|t|	[95% Conf. Interval]
numkid	6.383609	.435193	14.67	0.000	5.530315 7.236903
_cons	28.69373	.6176739	46.45	0.000	27.48264 29.90482
```

■ Display B.9.5 Intercept-only Model for Hours of Chores (Full NSFH Sample of 3,116 Employed Women)

	SAS	Stata

Commands	`proc reg;`
	`  model hrchores=;`
	`run;`
		`regress hrchores`

Results

SAS:

Number of Observations Read	3116
Number of Observations Used	3116

Analysis of Variance

Source	DF	Sum of Squares	Mean Square	F Value	Pr > F
Model	0	0	.	.	.
Error	3115	2358868	757.26099		
Corrected Total	3115	2358868			

Root MSE	27.51838	R-Square	0.0000
Dependent Mean	34.45250	Adj R-Sq	0.0000
Coeff Var	79.87337		

Parameter Estimates

Variable	DF	Parameter Estimate	Standard Error	t Value	Pr > |t|
Intercept	1	34.45250	0.49297	69.89	<.0001

Stata:

Source	SS	df	MS	
Model	0	0	.	Number of obs = 3116
Residual	2358867.97	3115	757.260986	F(0, 3115) = 0.00
				Prob > F = .
Total	2358867.97	3115	757.260986	R-squared = 0.0000
				Adj R-squared = 0.0000
				Root MSE = 27.518

hrchores	Coef.	Std. Err.	t	P>|t|	[95% Conf. Interval]
_cons	34.4525	.4929741	69.89	0.000	33.48592 35.41909

Display B.9.6 Regression of Hours of Chores on Number of Children and Hours of Paid Work (Full NSFH Sample of 3,116 Employed Women)

	SAS	Stata

Commands	`proc reg;`
	`Model hrchores=numkid hrwork;`
	`run;`
		`regress hrchores numkid hrwork`

Results

SAS

Number of Observations Read	3116
Number of Observations Used	3116

Analysis of Variance

Source	DF	Sum of Squares	Mean Square	F Value	Pr > F
Model	2	179987	89993	128.58	<.0001
Error	3113	2178881	699.92965		
Corrected Total	3115	2358868			

Root MSE	26.45618	R-Square	0.0763
Dependent Mean	34.45250	Adj R-Sq	0.0757
Coeff Var	76.79031		

Parameter Estimates

Variable	DF	Parameter Estimate	Standard Error	t Value	Pr > |t|
Intercept	1	36.24366	1.35126	26.82	<.0001
numkid	1	6.15556	0.43406	14.18	<.0001
hrwork	1	−0.21040	0.03355	−6.27	<.00011

Stata

Source	SS	df	MS		
Model	179986.973	2	89993.4863	Number of obs = 3116
Residual	2178881	3113	699.929649	F(2, 3113) = 128.58
				Prob > F = 0.0000
Total	2358867.97	3115	757.260986	R-squared = 0.0763
				Adj R-squared = 0.0757
				Root MSE = 26.456

hrchores	Coef.	Std. Err.	t	P>|t|	[95% Conf. Interval]
numkid	6.155562	.4340641	14.18	0.000	5.304481	7.006642
hrwork	-.2104033	.0335466	-6.27	0.000	-.276179	-.1446275
_cons	36.24366	1.351263	26.82	0.000	33.5942	38.89311

APPENDIX B

Display B.9.7 Regression of Hours of Chores on Hours of Paid Work (Full NSFH Sample of 3,116 Employed Women)

	SAS	Stata

Commands	`proc reg;`
	`  model hrchores=hrwork;`
	`run;`
		`regress hrchores hrwork`

SAS Results

Number of Observations Read	3116
Number of Observations Used	3116

Analysis of Variance

Source	DF	Sum of Squares	Mean Square	F Value	Pr > F
Model	1	39226	39226	52.66	<.0001
Error	3114	2319642	744.90747		
Corrected Total	3115	2358868			

Root MSE	27.29299	R-Square	0.0166
Dependent Mean	34.45250	Adj R-Sq	0.0163
Coeff Var	79.21919		

Parameter Estimates

Variable	DF	Parameter Estimate	Standard Error	t Value	Pr > |t|
Intercept	1	43.18768	1.29926	33.24	<.0001
hrwork	1	-0.25025	0.03449	-7.26	<.0001

Stata Results

Source	SS	df	MS
Model	39226.104	1	39226.104
Residual	2319641.87	3114	744.907472
Total	2358867.97	3115	757.260986

Number of obs = 3116
F(1, 3114) = 52.66
Prob > F = 0.0000
R-squared = 0.0166
Adj R-squared = 0.0163
Root MSE = 27.293

hrchores	Coef.	Std. Err.	t	P>|t|	[95% Conf. Interval]	
hrwork	-.2502534	.0344861	-7.26	0.000	-.3178712	-.1826357
_cons	43.18768	1.299256	33.24	0.000	40.6402	45.73517

APPENDIX B

■ **Display B.9.8 Regression of Distance from Mother on Respondent's Earnings, Mother's Years of Schooling, Respondent and Mother's Age, and Respondent's Number of Brothers and Sisters**

Commands

SAS

```
LIBNAME LIBRARY 'c:\sfh_distance\SAS';
data CreateData;
    set "c:\nsfh_distance\SAS\createData";
    if g1miles~=. & g2earn~=. & g1yrschl~=.
    & g1age~=. & g2age~=. & g2numbro~=. &
    g2numsis~=.;
run;
proc reg;
    Model g1miles=g2earn g1yrschl g1age g2age
          g2numbro g2numsis;
    test g1age g2age, g2numbro, g2numsis;
run;
```

Stata

```
use CreateData if g1miles~=. & g2earn~=.     ///
                & g1yrschl~=. & g1age~=.     ///
                & g2age~=. & g2numbro~=. & g2numsis~=.
regress g1miles g2earn g1yrschl g1age g2age  ///
        g2numbro g2numsis
test g1age g2age g2numbro g2numsis
```

Results

SAS

Number of Observations Used: 5475

Analysis of Variance

Source	DF	Sum of Squares	Mean Square	F Value	Pr > F
Model	6	38919757	6486626	15.85	<.0001
Error	5468	2238453227	409373		
Corrected Total	5474	2277372983			

Root MSE	639.82287	R-Square	0.0171
Dependent Mean	291.22721	Adj R-Sq	0.0160
Coeff Var	219.69886		

Parameter Estimates

Variable	DF	Parameter Estimate	Standard Error	t Value	Pr > |t|
Intercept	1	-275.28450	67.89939	-4.05	<.0001
g2earn	1	0.00082868	0.00023716	3.49	0.0005
g1yrschl	1	21.20263	3.13213	6.77	<.0001
g1age	1	4.55911	1.44023	3.17	0.0016
g2age	1	-0.13125	1.65018	-0.08	0.9366
g2numbro	1	4.48160	5.96686	0.75	0.4526
g2numsis	1	16.94382	6.00851	2.82	0.0048

Test 1 Results for Dependent Variable g1miles

Source	DF	Mean Square	F Value	Pr > F
Numerator	4	4157169	10.15	<.0001
Denominator	5468	409373		

Stata

```
      Source |       SS       df       MS              Number of obs =    5475
-------------+------------------------------           F(  6,  5468) =   15.85
       Model | 38919756.6      6  6486626.11           Prob > F      =  0.0000
    Residual | 2.2385e+09   5468  409373.304           R-squared     =  0.0171
-------------+------------------------------           Adj R-squared =  0.0160
       Total | 2.2774e+09   5474  416034.524           Root MSE      =  639.82

     g1miles |     Coef.   Std. Err.      t    P>|t|    [95% Conf. Interval]
-------------+----------------------------------------------------------------
      g2earn |   .0008287   .0002372     3.49  0.000    .0003638    .0012936
    g1yrschl |   21.20263   3.132135     6.77  0.000    15.0624     27.34286
       g1age |   4.559107   1.440233     3.17  0.002    1.735677    7.382537
       g2age |   -.131249   1.650181    -0.08  0.937   -3.366261    3.103763
    g2numbro |   4.481604   5.96686      0.75  0.453   -7.215816    16.17902
    g2numsis |   16.94382   6.008505     2.82  0.005    5.164763    28.72289
       _cons |  -275.2845   67.89939    -4.05  0.000   -408.3943   -142.1747

. test g1age g2age g2num

 (1)  g1age = 0
 (2)  g2age = 0
 (3)  g2numbro = 0
 (4)  g2numsis = 0

       F(  4,  5468) =   10.15
            Prob > F =    0.0000
```

■ Display B.10.1 Codebook for M484 in Analytic Data File

	SAS	Stata
Commands	`proc freq; run;`	codebook

Results

SAS

WHICH GROUP DESCRIBES R (RACE)

M484	Frequency	Percent	Cumulative Frequency	Cumulative Percent
BLACK	1165	16.88	1165	16.88
WHITE/NOT HISPANIC	5384	78.02	6549	94.90
MEX/CHICANO/MEX.AM	218	3.16	6767	98.06
PUERTO RICAN	40	0.58	6807	98.64
CUBAN	5	0.07	6812	98.71
OTHER HISPANIC	34	0.49	6846	99.20
AMERICAN INDIAN	31	0.45	6877	99.65
ASIAN	20	0.29	6897	99.94
OTHER	1	0.01	6898	99.96
NO ANSWER	3	0.04	6901	100.00

Stata

```
M484                       WHICH GROUP DESCRIBES R (RACE)

                type:  numeric (byte)
               label:  M484

               range:  [1,99]                     units:  1
       unique values:  10               missing .:  0/6901

         tabulation:   Freq.   Numeric   Label
                        1165      1      BLACK
                        5384      2      WHITE/NOT
                                         HISPANIC
                         218      3      MEX/CHICANO/MEX.AM
                          40      4      PUERTO RICAN
                           5      5      CUBAN
                          34      6      OTHER HISPANIC
                          31      7      AMERICAN INDIAN
                          20      8      ASIAN
                           1      9      OTHER
                           3     99      NO ANSWER
```

Display B.10.2 Creating and Checking *aframer* Dummy Variable

SAS

Commands

```
LIBNAME LIBRARY "c:\nsfh_distance\SAS";

data CheckAfrAmer;

set "c:\nsfh_distance\SAS\CreateData";

if M484=1 then aframer=1;
if M484~=1 then aframer=0;
if M484>=97 then aframer=.;

run;

proc freq;
tables M484*aframer /NOCOL NOROW
NOPERCENT;
run;
```

Results

Table of M484 by aframer

M484(WHICH GROUP DESCRIBES R (RACE))	aframer		
Frequency	0	1	Total
BLACK	0	1165	1165
WHITE/NOT HISPANIC	5384	0	5384
MEX/CHICANO/MEX.AM	218	0	218
PUERTO RICAN	40	0	40
CUBAN	5	0	5
OTHER HISPANIC	34	0	34
AMERICAN INDIAN	31	0	31
ASIAN	20	0	20
OTHER	1	0	1
NO ANSWER	0	0	0
Total	5733	1165	6898

Frequency Missing = 3

Stata

Commands

```
use CreateData

generate aframer=1 if M484==1
replace aframer=0 if M484~=1
replace aframer=. if M484>=97
tabulate M484 aframer, missing
```

Results

WHICH GROUP DESCRIBES R (RACE)	aframer			Total
	0	1	.	
BLACK	0	1,165	0	1,165
WHITE/NOT HISPANIC	5,384	0	0	5,384
MEX/CHICANO/MEX.AM	218	0	0	218
PUERTO RICAN	40	0	0	40
CUBAN	5	0	0	5
OTHER HISPANIC	34	0	0	34
AMERICAN INDIAN	31	0	0	31
ASIAN	20	0	0	20
OTHER	1	0	0	1
NO ANSWER	0	0	3	3
Total	5,733	1,165	3	6,901

Display B.10.3 Creating and Checking *other* Dummy Variable

Commands

SAS

```
LIBNAME LIBRARY "c:\nsfh_distance\SAS";

data CheckOther;
    set "c:\nsfh_distance\SAS\CreateData";

if (M484>=4 & M484<=6) | M484=8 | M484=9
    then other=1;
if (M484>=1 & M484<=3) | M484=7 then
    other=0;
if M484>=97 then other=.;

run;

proc freq;
    tables M484*other /NOCOL NOROW
        NOPERCENT;
run;
```

Stata

```
use CreateData

generate other=1 if (M484>=4 & M484<=6) ///
    | M484==8 | M484==9
replace other=0 if (M484>=1 & M484<=3) | M484==7
replace other=. if M484>=97

tabulate M484 other, missing
```

Results

SAS

Table of M484 by other

M484(WHICH GROUP DESCRIBES R (RACE)) Frequency	other 0	1	Total
BLACK	1165	0	1165
WHITE/NOT HISPANIC	5384	0	5384
MEX/CHICANO/MEX.AM	218	0	218
PUERTO RICAN	0	40	40
CUBAN	0	5	5
OTHER HISPANIC	0	34	34
AMERICAN INDIAN	31	0	31
ASIAN	0	20	20
OTHER	0	1	1
NO ANSWER	0	0	0
Total	6798	100	6898

Frequency Missing = 3

Stata

WHICH GROUP DESCRIBES R (RACE)	other 0	1	.	Total
BLACK	1,165	0	0	1,165
WHITE/NOT HISPANIC	5,384	0	0	5,384
MEX/CHICANO/MEX.AM	218	0	0	218
PUERTO RICAN	0	40	0	40
CUBAN	0	5	0	5
OTHER HISPANIC	0	34	0	34
AMERICAN INDIAN	31	0	0	31
ASIAN	0	20	0	20
OTHER	0	1	0	1
NO ANSWER	0	0	3	3
Total	6,798	100	3	6,901

■ Display B.10.4 Regression of *g1miles* on Gender Dummies in the NSFH

Regression of *g1miles* on *female* in the NSFH.

	SAS	Stata
Variable Creation	`female=(M2DP01==2);`	`generate female=(M2DP01==2)`

Regression Model	`proc reg;`
	`   model g1miles=female;`
	`run;`
		`regress g1miles female`

Select Results — SAS

Parameter Estimates

Variable	DF	Parameter Estimate	Standard Error	t Value	Pr > |t|
Intercept	1	323.75559	13.74255	23.56	<.0001
female	1	-59.38793	17.70771	-3.35	0.0008

Select Results — Stata

g1miles	Coef.	Std. Err.	t	P>|t|
female	-59.38793	17.70771	-3.35	0.001
_cons	323.7556	13.74255	23.56	0.000

Regression of *g1miles* on *female* in the NSFH.

	SAS	Stata
Variable Creation	`male=(M2DP01==1);`	`generate male=(M2DP01==1)`

Regression Model	`proc reg;`
	`   model g1miles=male;`
	`run;`
		`regress g1miles male`

Select Results — SAS

Parameter Estimates

Variable	DF	Parameter Estimate	Standard Error	t Value	Pr > |t|
Intercept	1	264.36766	11.16715	23.67	<.0001
male	1	59.38793	17.70771	3.35	0.0008

Select Results — Stata

g1miles	Coef.	Std. Err.	t	P>|t|
male	59.38793	11.16715	3.35	0.001
_cons	264.3677	17.70771	23.67	0.000

Comments: *Don't forget: In SAS, variable creation must occur in the data step!*

Display B.10.5 t-test of *g1miles* by *M2DP01* in the NSFH

	SAS	Stata
t-test	```proc ttest; class M2DP01; var g1miles; run;```	```ttest g1miles, by(M2DP01)```

SAS — Select Results

Statistics

Variable	M2DP01	N	Lower CL Mean	Mean	Upper CL Mean	Std Err
g1miles	MALE	2148	294.35	323.76	353.16	14.996
g1miles	FEMALE	3253	243.9	264.37	284.84	10.44
g1miles	Diff (1–2)		24.674	59.388	94.102	17.708

T-Tests

Variable	Method	Variances	DF	t Value	Pr > |t|
g1miles	Pooled	Equal	5399	3.35	0.0008
g1miles	Satterthwaite	Unequal	4097	3.25	0.0012

Stata — Select Results

Two-sample t-test with equal variances

Group	Obs	Mean	Std. Err.	[95% Conf. Interval]	
MALE	2148	323.7556	14.99641	294.3466	353.1646
FEMALE	3253	264.3677	10.44012	243.8978	284.8375
combined	5401	287.9865	8.674792	270.9804	304.9926
diff		59.38793	17.70771	24.67367	94.10218

diff = mean(MALE) − mean(FEMALE)   t = 3.3538
Ho: diff = 0   degrees of freedom = 5399

Ha: diff < 0   Ha: diff != 0   Ha: diff > 0
Pr(T < t) = 0.9996   Pr(|T| > |t|) = 0.0008   Pr(T > t) = 0.0004

Display B.10.6 Regression of *g1miles* on *amind*, *mexamer*, and *white* in the NSFH

	SAS	Stata
Variable Creation	`LIBNAME LIBRARY 'c:\nsfh_distance\SAS';` `data CreateData;` `  set "c:\nsfh_distance\SAS\CreateData";` `  if g1miles~=. & g2earn~=. & g1yrsch1~=.` `    & g1age~=. & g2age~=. & g2numbro~=. &` `    g2numsis~=.` ` & ((M484>=1 & M484<=3)	M484==7);`  ` if M484<97 then aframer=(M484=1);` ` if M484<97 then white= (M484=2);` ` if M484<97 then mexamer= (M484=3);` ` if M484<97 then amind= (M484=7);`  `run;`	`use CreateData if g1miles~=. & g2earn~=. & g1yrsch1~=.   //` `  & g1age~=. & g2age~=. & g2numbro~=. //` ` & g2numsis~=. & ((M484>=1 & M484<=3)	M484==7)`  `generate aframer= (M484==1) if M484<97` `generate white= (M484==2) if M484<97` `generate mexamer= (M484==3) if M484<97` `generate amind= (M484==7) if M484<97`

Regression Model	`proc reg;`
	`  model g1miles=amind mexamer white;`
	`run;`
		`regress g1miles amind mexamer white`

Stata Select Results

Source	SS	df	MS
Model	2946571.39	3	982190.464
Residual	2.1918e+09	5397	406116.082
Total	2.1948e+09	5400	406436.123

```
Number of obs =    5401
F( 3,  5397) =    2.42
Prob > F     =  0.0643
R-squared    =  0.0013
Adj R-squared = 0.0008
Root MSE     =  637.27
```

g1miles	Coef.	Std. Err.	t	P>|t|	[95% Conf. Interval]	
amind	157.0283	129.4861	1.21	0.225	-96.81669	410.8732
mexamer	-8.254855	54.48378	-0.15	0.880	-115.0651	98.55535
white	56.71736	24.77161	2.29	0.022	8.154998	105.2797
_cons	240.9717	22.84732	10.55	0.000	196.1818	285.7617

SAS Select Results

Number of Observations Read	5401
Number of Observations Used	5401

Analysis of Variance

Source	DF	Sum of Squares	Mean Square	F Value	Pr > F
Model	3	2946571	982190	2.42	0.0643
Error	5397	2191808493	406116		
Corrected Total	5400	2194755064			

Root MSE	637.27238	R-Square	0.0013
Dependent Mean	287.98648	Adj R-Sq	0.0008
Coeff Var	221.28552		

Parameter Estimates

Variable	DF	Parameter Estimate	Standard Error	t Value	Pr > |t|
Intercept	1	240.97172	22.84732	10.55	<.0001
amind	1	157.02828	129.48607	1.21	0.2253
mexamer	1	-8.25485	54.48378	-0.15	0.8796
white	1	56.71736	24.77161	2.29	0.0221

■ Display B.10.7 Regression of *g1miles* on Race-Ethnicity Dummies in the NSFH, with Different Reference Categories

American Indian is Reference Category

	SAS	Stata
Commands	model g1miles=aframer mexamer white;	regress g1miles aframer mexamer white

SAS — Select Results — Parameter Estimates

Variable	DF	Parameter Estimate	Standard Error	t Value	Pr > |t|
Intercept	1	398.00000	127.45448	3.12	0.0018
aframer	1	-157.02828	129.48607	-1.21	0.2253
mexamer	1	-165.28313	136.71549	-1.21	0.2267
white	1	-100.31092	127.81344	-0.78	0.4326

Stata — Select Results

g1miles	Coef.	Std. Err.	t	P>|t|
aframer	-157.0283	129.4861	-1.21	0.225
mexamer	-165.2831	136.7155	-1.21	0.227
white	-100.3109	127.8134	-0.78	0.433
_cons	398	127.4545	3.12	0.002

Mexican American is Reference Category

	SAS	Stata
Commands	model g1miles=amind aframer white;	regress g1miles amind aframer white

SAS — Select Results — Parameter Estimates

Variable	DF	Parameter Estimate	Standard Error	t Value	Pr > |t|
Intercept	1	232.71687	49.46193	4.70	<.0001
amind	1	165.28313	136.71549	1.21	0.2267
aframer	1	8.25485	54.48378	0.15	0.8796
white	1	64.97221	50.37971	1.29	0.1972

Stata — Select Results

g1miles	Coef.	Std. Err.	t	P>|t|
amind	165.2831	136.7155	1.21	0.227
aframer	8.254855	54.48378	0.15	0.880
white	64.97221	50.37971	1.29	0.197
_cons	232.7169	49.46193	4.70	0.000

White is Reference Category

	SAS	Stata
Commands	model g1miles=amind mexamer aframer;	regress g1miles amind mexamer aframer

SAS — Select Results — Parameter Estimates

Variable	DF	Parameter Estimate	Standard Error	t Value	Pr > |t|
Intercept	1	297.68908	9.57250	31.10	<.0001
amind	1	100.31092	127.81344	0.78	0.4326
mexamer	1	-64.97221	50.37971	-1.29	0.1972
aframer	1	-56.71736	24.77161	-2.29	0.0221

Stata — Select Results

g1miles	Coef.	Std. Err.	t	P>|t|
amind	100.3109	127.8134	0.78	0.433
mexamer	-64.97221	50.37971	-1.29	0.197
aframer	-56.71736	24.77161	-2.29	0.022
_cons	297.6891	9.572497	31.10	0.000

Display B.10.8 Regression of *g1miles* on *amindmex* and *white* in the NSFH

	SAS	Stata
Variable Creation	`if M484<97 then amindmex= (M484=7 | M484=3);`	`generate amindmex= (M484==7 | M484==3) if M484<97`

Regression Model	`proc reg;`
	`  model g1miles=amindmex white;`
	`run;`
		`regress g1miles amindmex white`

Select Results

SAS

Number of Observations Read	5401
Number of Observations Used	5401

Analysis of Variance

Source	DF	Sum of Squares	Mean Square	F Value	Pr > F
Model	2	2353002	1176501	2.90	0.0553
Error	5398	2192402062	406151		
Corrected Total	5400	2194755064			

Root MSE	637.29962	R-Square	0.0011
Dependent Mean	287.98648	Adj R-Sq	0.0007
Coeff Var	221.29498		

Parameter Estimates

Variable	DF	Parameter Estimate	Standard Error	t Value	Pr > |t|
Intercept	1	240.97172	22.84830	10.55	<.0001
amindmex	1	13.37906	51.46347	0.26	0.7949
white	1	56.71736	24.77267	2.29	0.0221

Stata

Source	SS	df	MS		
Model	2353001.59	2	1176500.79	Number of obs =	5401
				F(2, 5398) =	2.90
				Prob > F =	0.0553
Residual	2.1924e+09	5398	406150.808	R-squared =	0.0011
				Adj R-squared =	0.0007
Total	2.1948e+09	5400	406436.123	Root MSE =	637.3

g1miles	Coef.	Std. Err.	t	P>|t|	[95% Conf. Interval]	
amindmex	13.37906	51.46347	0.26	0.795	-87.51011	114.2682
white	56.71736	24.77267	2.29	0.022	8.152923	105.2818
_cons	240.9717	22.8483	10.55	0.000	196.1798	285.7636

Display B.10.9 Using the Test Command to Test the Difference in Means among the Included Categories

	SAS	Stata

Regression Model and Test Commands	```proc reg;```
	 ```model g1miles=amind mexamer white;```
	 ```test amind=mexamer;```
	 ```test amind=white;```
	 ```test mexamer=white;```
	 ```run;```
		```regress g1miles amind mexamer white```
		 ```test amind=mexamer```
		 ```test amind=white```
		 ```test mexamer=white```

Select Results

SAS:

Test 1 Results for Dependent Variable g1miles

Source	DF	Mean Square	F Value	Pr > F
Numerator	1	593570	1.46	0.2267
Denominator	5397	406116		

Test 2 Results for Dependent Variable g1miles

Source	DF	Mean Square	F Value	Pr > F
Numerator	1	250146	0.62	0.4326
Denominator	5397	406116		

Test 3 Results for Dependent Variable g1miles

Source	DF	Mean Square	F Value	Pr > F
Numerator	1	675452	1.66	0.1972
Denominator	5397	406116		

Stata:

```
. test amind=mexamer

 (1)  amind - mexamer = 0

       F(  1,  5397) =    1.46
            Prob > F =    0.2267

. test amind=white

 (1)  amind - white = 0

       F(  1,  5397) =    0.62
            Prob > F =    0.4326

. test mexamer=white

 (1)  mexamer - white = 0

       F(  1,  5397) =    1.66
            Prob > F =    0.1972
```

■ Display B.10.10 The Variance–Covariance Matrix of the Estimated Regression Coefficients

	SAS	Stata

New Commands	`proc reg;`
	`    model g1miles=amind mexamer white /covb;`
	`run;`
		`regress g1miles amind mexamer white`
		`estat vce`

Select Results	**Covariance of Estimates**
	
	| Variable
		Intercept	amind	mexamer	white |
					|---|---|---|---|---|
					| Intercept | 522.00010494 | -522.0001049 | -522.0001049 | -522.0001049 |
					| amind | -522.0001049 | 16766.643371 | 522.00010494 | 522.00010494 |
					| mexamer | -522.0001049 | 522.00010494 | 2968.4825245 | 522.00010494 |
					| white | -522.0001049 | 522.00010494 | 522.00010494 | 613.63279484 |
						Covariance matrix of coefficients of regress model
						
						``
						        e(V)
							amind mexamer white _cons
							-------------+--
							       amind
								16766.643
								     mexamer
									522.0001 2968.4825
									       white
										522.0001 522.0001 613.63279
										       _cons
											-522.0001 -522.0001 -522.0001 522.0001
											``

Comments	In SAS, we request the variance–covariance matrix of the estimated regression coefficients with an **option** following the model statement. The option is **covb** which can be remembered as a shorthand for "**cov**ariance" of the "**b**etas." As with all options, the word **covb** needs to be separated with a **forward slash "/"** from the last predictor variable listed in the model statement.	In Stata, we request the variance–covariance matrix of the estimated regression coefficients with a **command** following the regression command. The command is **estat** (a general command for "postestimation statistics"). The subcommand **vce** asks Stata to list the variance covariance estimates.

■ Display B.10.11 The Stata *lincom* Command

	Stata
| New Commands | ```
regress glmiles amind mexamer white
   lincom mexamer-amind
   lincom white-amind
   lincom white-mexamer
``` |
| Select Results | ```
. lincom mexamer-amind

(1)  - amind + mexamer = 0

  glmiles |     Coef.   Std. Err.      t    P>|t|    [95% Conf. Interval]
----------+----------------------------------------------------------------
      (1) |  -165.2831   136.7155   -1.21   0.227    -433.3007   102.7344

. lincom white-amind

(1)  - amind + white = 0

  glmiles |     Coef.   Std. Err.      t    P>|t|    [95% Conf. Interval]
----------+----------------------------------------------------------------
      (1) |  -100.3109   127.8134   -0.78   0.433    -350.8769   150.255

. lincom white-mexamer

(1)  - mexamer + white = 0

  glmiles |     Coef.   Std. Err.      t    P>|t|    [95% Conf. Interval]
----------+----------------------------------------------------------------
      (1) |   64.97221    50.37971   1.29   0.197     -33.79235  163.7368
``` |
| Comments | In Stata, we use the **lincom** command to calculate and test the significance of linear combinations of coefficients. As with the **test** command, we use the variable name to indicate to Stata which coefficient is of interest. We will generally use simple linear combinations that take the sum or difference of two coefficients, although more complicated linear combinations are possible (see **help lincom** in Stata). |

■ Display B.10.12 Regression of *g1miles* on *amind*, *mexamer*, *white*, and *female* in the NSFH

	SAS	Stata

Regression Model and Test Commands	`proc reg;`
	`  model g1miles=amind mexamer white female`
	`    g2earn g2age g2numbro g2numsis`
	`    g1yrschl g1age;`
	
	`  test amind=mexamer;`
	`  test amind=white;`
	`  test mexamer=white;`
	`run;`
		`regress g1miles amind mexamer white female ///`
		`    g2earn g2age g2numbro g2numsis ///`
		`    g1yrschl g1age`
		
		`test amind=mexamer`
		`test amind=white`
		`test mexamer=white`

SAS — Parameter Estimates

Variable	DF	Parameter Estimate	Standard Error	t Value	Pr > |t|
Intercept	1	-293.50824	71.86251	-4.08	<.0001
amind	1	185.14082	128.53760	1.44	0.1498
mexamer	1	61.84987	55.31577	1.12	0.2636
white	1	35.06974	25.22134	1.39	0.1644
female	1	-33.79229	18.79857	-1.80	0.0723
g2earn	1	0.00066760	0.00025048	2.67	0.0077
g2age	1	-0.03834	1.65004	-0.02	0.9815
g2numbro	1	5.20427	5.96187	0.87	0.3827
g2numsis	1	18.56337	6.03220	3.08	0.0021
g1yrschl	1	21.11644	3.27596	6.45	<.0001
g1age	1	4.60571	1.44147	3.20	0.0014

Test 1 Results for Dependent Variable g1miles

Source	DF	Mean Square	F Value	Pr > F
Numerator	1	326914	0.82	0.3657
Denominator	5390	399494		

Test 2 Results for Dependent Variable g1miles

Source	DF	Mean Square	F Value	Pr > F
Numerator	1	558148	1.40	0.2373
Denominator	5390	399494		

Test 3 Results for Dependent Variable g1miles

Source	DF	Mean Square	F Value	Pr > F
Numerator	1	104437	0.26	0.6092
Denominator	5390	399494		

Stata

Source	SS	df	MS		
Model	41483650.7	10	4148365.07	Number of obs = 5401
Residual	2.1533e+09	5390	399493.769	F(10, 5390) = 10.38
				Prob > F = 0.0000
Total	2.1948e+09	5400	406436.123	R-squared = 0.0189
				Adj R-squared = 0.0171
				Root MSE = 632.06

g1miles	Coef.	Std. Err.	t	P>|t|	[95% Conf. Interval]
amind	185.1408	128.5376	1.44	0.150	-66.84484	437.1265
mexamer	61.84987	55.31577	1.12	0.264	-46.59139	170.2911
white	35.06974	25.22134	1.39	0.164	-14.37427	84.51376
female	-33.7923	18.79857	-1.80	0.072	-70.64509	3.060504
g2earn	.0006676	.0002505	2.67	0.008	.0001766	.0011586
g2age	-.038338	1.650044	-0.02	0.981	-3.273091	3.196415
g2numbro	5.204269	5.961866	0.87	0.383	-6.483399	16.89194
g2numsis	18.56337	6.032196	3.08	0.002	6.737823	30.38891
g1yrschl	21.11644	3.275965	6.45	0.000	14.69423	27.53866
g1age	4.605706	1.441466	3.20	0.001	1.77985	7.431563
_cons	-293.5082	71.86251	-4.08	0.000	-434.3878	-152.6287

```
(1) amind - mexamer = 0
    F( 1, 5390) =    0.82
      Prob > F =  0.3657
(1) amind - white = 0
    F( 1, 5390) =    1.40
      Prob > F =  0.2373
(1) mexamer - white = 0
    F( 1, 5390) =    0.26
      Prob > F =  0.6092
```

Select Results

◼ Display B.10.13 Means for Interval Predictors

	SAS	Stata

Commands	`proc means;`
	`  var g2earn g2age g2numbro g2numsis`
	`      g1yrschl g1age;`
	`run;`
		`summarize g2earn g2age g2numbro g2numsis //`
		`          g1yrschl g1age`

Select Results

SAS:

Variable	N	Mean	Std Dev	Minimum	Maximum
g2earn	5401	30752.28	37626.16	0	945903.28
g2age	5401	34.3527125	10.0265673	16.0000000	76.0000000
g2numbro	5401	1.4328828	1.5660708	0	19.0000000
g2numsis	5401	1.3817812	1.5511505	0	22.0000000
g1yrschl	5401	11.4141826	2.9210752	0	17.0000000
g1age	5401	60.1349750	11.3189828	29.0000000	95.0000000

Stata:

variable	Obs	Mean	Std. Dev.	Min	Max
g2earn	5401	30752.28	37626.16	0	945903.3
g2age	5401	34.35271	10.02657	16	76
g2numbro	5401	1.432883	1.566071	0	19
g2numsis	5401	1.381781	1.551151	0	22
g1yrschl	5401	11.41418	2.921075	0	17
g1age	5401	60.13498	11.31898	29	95

■ Display B.10.14. Regression of *g1miles* on Gender Dummies in the NSFH, Accounting for the NSFH Complex Sampling Design

	SAS	Stata

Regression of *g1miles* on *female* in the NSFH, accounting for the NSFH complex sampling design

Commands (SAS):
```
proc surveyreg rate="c:\nsfh_distance\SAS\rate";
    model g1miles=female /clparm;
    domain DistanceSample;
    cluster PSU;
    strata StratumC;
    weight adjweight;
run;
```

Commands (Stata):
```
svyset PSU [pw=adjweight], strata(Stratum) singleunit(certainty)
svy, subpop(DistanceSample): regress g1miles female
```

Results (SAS): Estimated Regression Coefficients

Parameter	Estimate	Standard Error	t Value	Pr > |t|
Intercept	344.482293	19.8145489	17.39	<.0001
female	-44.215601	17.2314359	-2.57	0.0125

Results (Stata):

g1miles	Coef.	Linearized Std. Err.	t	P>|t|
female	-44.2156	17.23038	-2.57	0.015
_cons	344.4823	19.81334	17.39	0.000

Regression of *g1miles* on *male* in the NSFH, accounting for the NSFH complex sampling design

Commands (SAS):
```
proc surveyreg rate="c:\nsfh_distance\SAS\rate";
    model g1miles=male /clparm;
    domain DistanceSample;
    cluster PSU;
    strata StratumC;
    weight adjweight;
run;
```

Commands (Stata):
```
svyset PSU [pw=adjweight], strata(Stratum) singleunit(certainty)
svy, subpop(DistanceSample): regress g1miles male
```

Results (SAS): Estimated Regression Coefficients

Parameter	Estimate	Standard Error	t Value	Pr > |t|
Intercept	300.266692	20.3365517	14.76	<.0001
male	44.215601	17.2314359	2.57	0.0125

Results (Stata):

g1miles	Coef.	Linearized Std. Err.	t	P>|t|
male	44.2156	17.23038	2.57	0.015
_cons	300.2667	20.33531	14.77	0.000

■ Display B.10.15. Regression of *g1miles* on *amind, mexamer,* and *white* in the NSFH, Accounting for the NSFH Complex Sampling Design

	SAS	Stata

Commands	`proc surveyreg rate="c:\nsfh_distance\SAS\rate";`
	`    model g1miles=amind mexamer white  /clparm;`
	`    domain DistanceSample;`
	`    cluster PSU;`
	`    strata stratumC;`
	`    weight adjweight;`
	`run;`
		`svyset PSU [pw=adjweight], strata(Stratum) singleunit(certainty)`
		`svy, subpop(DistanceSample): regress g1miles amind mexamer white`

Results

SAS

Tests of Model Effects

Effect	Num DF	F Value	Pr > F
Model	3	1.66	0.1837
Intercept	1	101.96	<.0001
amind	1	0.72	0.4002
mexamer	1	0.06	0.8080
white	1	2.63	0.1094

Estimated Regression Coefficients

Parameter	Estimate	Standard Error	t Value	Pr > |t|	95% Confidence Interval	
Intercept	270.343053	26.773084	10.10	<.0001	216.90375	323.782352
amind	181.786745	214.711687	0.85	0.4002	-246.77958	610.353065
mexamer	22.056496	90.416388	0.24	0.8080	-158.41537	202.528361
white	54.926914	33.852861	1.62	0.1094	-12.64368	122.497508

Stata

Survey: Linear regression

```
Number of strata   =      68      Number of obs      =      13007
Number of PSUs     =     100      Population size    =  14256.883
                                  Subpop. no. of obs =       5401
                                  Subpop. size       =  5401.0002
                                  Design df          =         32
                                  F(   3,     30)    =       1.56
                                  Prob > F           =     0.2201
                                  R-squared          =     0.0007
```

g1miles	Coef.	Linearized Std. Err.	t	P>|t|	[95% Conf. Interval]	
amind	181.7867	214.6724	0.85	0.403	-255.4866	619.0601
mexamer	22.05649	90.39983	0.24	0.809	-162.0819	206.1949
white	54.92691	33.84666	1.62	0.114	-14.01648	123.8703
_cons	270.3431	26.76818	10.10	0.000	215.8181	324.8681

Note: strata with single sampling unit treated as certainty units.

Display B.11.1 Regression of *hrchores* on *married, female,* and *fem_marr* in the NSFH

	SAS	Stata
Variable Creation	`fem_marr=female*married;`	`generate fem_marr=female*married`

Regression Model	`proc reg;`
	`  model hrchores=married female fem_marr;`
	`run;`
		`regress hrchores married female fem_marr`

SAS — Select Results

Number of Observations Read	6054
Number of Observations Used	6054

Analysis of Variance

Source	DF	Sum of Squares	Mean Square	F Value	Pr > F
Model	3	297807	99269	169.97	<.0001
Error	6050	3533423	584.03690		
Corrected Total	6053	3831230			

Root MSE	24.16686	R-Square	0.0777
Dependent Mean	27.72382	Adj R-Sq	0.0773
Coeff Var	87.17001		

Parameter Estimates

Variable	DF	Parameter Estimate	Standard Error	t Value	Pr > |t|
Intercept	1	22.31421	0.69677	32.03	<.0001
married	1	-2.60489	0.90427	-2.88	0.0040
female	1	10.19964	0.91505	11.15	<.0001
fem_marr	1	6.63953	1.25582	5.29	<.0001

Stata — Select Results

Source	SS	df	MS		
Model	297806.971	3	99268.9903	Number of obs =	6054
Residual	3533423.25	6050	584.036902	F(3, 6050) =	169.97
				Prob > F =	0.0000
				R-squared =	0.0777
Total	3831230.23	6053	632.947336	Adj R-squared =	0.0773
				Root MSE =	24.167

hrchores	Coef.	Std. Err.	t	P>|t|	[95% Conf. Interval]
married	-2.604886	.9042679	-2.88	0.004	-4.377573 -.8321986
female	10.19964	.9150482	11.15	0.000	8.405821 11.99346
fem_marr	6.63953	1.255823	5.29	0.000	4.177669 9.101391
_cons	22.31421	.6967666	32.03	0.000	20.9483 23.68013

Display B.11.2 Regression of *hrchores* on *married, female,* and *fem_marr* in the NSFH: Reversing Reference Category on Conditioning Variable

	SAS	Stata
	Conditional Effect of Being Married for Women	
Variable	`if female~=. then male=female=0;` `male_marr=male*married;`	`generate male=female==0 if female~=.` `generate male_marr=male*married`
Regression	`proc reg;` `  model hrchores=married male male_marr; run;`	`regress hrchores married male male_marr`

Select Results

SAS:

Parameter Estimates

Variable	DF	Parameter Estimate	Standard Error	t Value	Pr > |t|
Intercept	1	32.51386	0.59315	54.82	<.0001
married	1	4.03464	0.87143	4.63	<.0001
male	1	−10.19964	0.91505	−11.15	<.0001
male_marr	1	−6.63953	1.25582	−5.29	<.0001

Stata:

Source	SS	df	MS		
Model	297806.971	3	399268.9903		
Residual	3553423.25	6050	584.036902		
Total	3831230.23	6053	632.947336		

Number of obs = 6054
$F_{(3, 6050)}$ = 169.97
Prob > F = 0.0000
R-squared = 0.0777
Adj R-squared = 0.0773
Root MSE = 24.167

hrchores	Coef.	Std. Err.	t	P>|t|	[95% Conf. Interval]
married	4.034644	.8714309	4.63	0.000	2.326329 5.742959
male	−10.19964	.9150482	−11.15	0.000	−11.99346 −8.405821
male_marr	−6.63953	1.255823	−5.29	0.000	−9.101391 −4.177669
_cons	32.51386	.5931521	54.82	0.000	31.35107 33.67664

(continued)

■ Display B.11.2 Regression of *hrchores* on *married*, *female*, and *fem_marr* in the NSFH: Reversing Reference Category on Conditioning Variable (Continued)

	SAS	Stata
	Conditional Effect of Being Female for Married Adults	
Variable	`if married~=. then unmarried=married=0;` `fem_unmarr=female*unmarried;`	`generate unmarried=married=0 if married~=.` `generate fem_unmarr=female*unmarried`

Regression	`proc reg;`
	`  model hrchores=unmarried female fem_unmarr;`
	`run;`
		`regress hrchores unmarried female fem_unmarr`

SAS — Select Results

Parameter Estimates

Variable	DF	Parameter Estimate	Standard Error	t Value	Pr > |t|
Intercept	1	19.70933	0.57638	34.19	<.0001
unmarried	1	2.60489	0.90427	2.88	0.0040
female	1	16.83917	0.86010	19.58	<.0001
fem_unmarr	1	-6.63953	1.25582	-5.29	<.0001

Stata — Select Results

Source	SS	df	MS		
Model	297806.971	3	99268.9903	Number of obs = 6054	F(3, 6050) = 169.97
Residual	3533423.25	6050	584.036902	Prob > F = 0.0000	R-squared = 0.0777
				Adj R-squared = 0.0773	
Total	3831230.23	6053	632.947336	Root MSE = 24.167	

hrchores	Coef.	Std. Err.	t	P>|t|	[95% Conf. Interval]
unmarried	2.604886	.9042679	2.88	0.004	.8321986 4.377573
female	16.83917	.8601041	19.58	0.000	15.15306 18.52528
fem_unmarr	-6.63953	1.255823	-5.29	0.000	-9.101391 -4.177669
_cons	19.70933	.5763824	34.19	0.000	18.57941 20.83924

■ Display B.11.3 Regression of *hrchores* on *married, female*, and *fem_marr* in the NSFH: General Linear F-test

	SAS	Stata
| Regression Model | ```
proc reg;
    model hrchores=married female fem_marr;
    test married+fem_marr=0;
    test female+fem_marr=0;
run;
``` | ```
regress hrchores married female fem_marr
test married+fem_marr=0
test female+fem_marr=0
``` |

SAS

Parameter Estimates

Variable	DF	Parameter Estimate	Standard Error	t Value	Pr > |t|
Intercept	1	22.31421	0.69677	32.03	<.0001
married	1	−2.60489	0.90427	−2.88	0.0040
female	1	10.19964	0.91505	11.15	<.0001
fem_marr	1	6.63953	1.25582	5.29	<.0001

Test 1 Results for Dependent Variable hrchores

Source	DF	Mean Square	F Value	Pr > F
Numerator	1	12519	21.44	<.0001
Denominator	6050	584.03690		

Test 2 Results for Dependent Variable hrchores

Source	DF	Mean Square	F Value	Pr > F
Numerator	1	223862	383.30	<.0001
Denominator	6050	584.03690		

Stata

```
      Source |       SS       df       MS              Number of obs =    6054
-------------+------------------------------           F( 3,  6050) =  169.97
       Model |  297806.971      3  99268.9903           Prob > F      =  0.0000
    Residual |  3553423.25   6050  584.036902           R-squared     =  0.0777
-------------+------------------------------           Adj R-squared =  0.0773
       Total |  3831230.23   6053  632.947336           Root MSE      =  24.167

    hrchores |      Coef.   Std. Err.      t    P>|t|     [95% Conf. Interval]
-------------+----------------------------------------------------------------
     married | -2.604886   .9042679    -2.88   0.004    -4.377573   -.8321986
      female |  10.19964   .9150482    11.15   0.000     8.405821    11.99346
    fem_marr |   6.63953   1.255823     5.29   0.000     4.177669    9.101391
       _cons |  22.31421   .6967666    32.03   0.000     20.9483     23.68013

 (1) married + fem_marr = 0
       F(1,  6050) =   21.44
            Prob > F =    0.0000

 (1) female + fem_marr = 0
       F(1,  6050) =  383.30
            Prob > F =    0.0000
```

Select Results

APPENDIX B

■ Display B.11.4 Regression of *hrchores* on *married*, *female*, and *fem_marr* in the NSFH: Linear Combination of Coefficients

	SAS	Stata

Regression Model	`proc reg;`
	`  model hrchores=married female fem_marr / covb;`
	`run;`
		`regress hrchores married female fem_marr`
		`estat vce`

Select Results

SAS

Number of Observations Read	6054
Number of Observations Used	6054

Analysis of Variance

Source	DF	Sum of Squares	Mean Square	F Value	Pr > F
Model	3	297807	99269	169.97	<.0001
Error	6050	3533423	584.03690		
Corrected Total	6053	3831230			

Root MSE	24.16086	R-Square	0.0777
Dependent Mean	27.72382	Adj R-Sq	0.0773
Coeff Var	87.17001		

Parameter Estimates

Variable	DF	Parameter Estimate	Standard Error	t Value	Pr > |t|
Intercept	1	22.31421	0.69677	32.03	<.0001
married	1	-2.60489	0.90427	-2.88	0.0040
female	1	10.19964	0.91505	11.15	<.0001
fem_marr	1	6.63953	1.25582	5.29	<.0001

Covariance of Estimates

Variable	Intercept	married	female	fem_marr
Intercept	0.485483709	-0.485483709	-0.485483709	0.485483709
married	-0.485483709	0.817700376	0.485483709	-0.817700376
female	-0.485483709	0.485483087	0.837313167	-0.837313167
fem_marr	0.485483087	-0.817700376	-0.837313167	1.570922228

Stata

```
  Source |       SS         df        MS            Number of obs =    6054
---------+-------------------------------          F( 3,  6050)  =  169.97
   Model | 297806.971        3   99268.9903        Prob > F      =  0.0000
Residual | 353423.25      6050   584.036902        R-squared     =  0.0777
---------+-------------------------------          Adj R-squared =  0.0773
   Total | 3831230.23     6053   632.947336        Root MSE      =  24.167

hrchores |  Coef.     Std. Err.      T     P>|t|    [95% Conf. Interval]
---------+----------------------------------------------------------------
 married | -2.604886   .9042679    -2.88   0.004   -4.377573   -.8321986
  female | 10.19964    .9150482    11.15   0.000    8.405821    11.99346
fem_marr |  6.63953    1.255823     5.29   0.000    4.177669    9.101391
   _cons | 22.31421    .6967666    32.03   0.000   20.9483     23.68013

    estat vce

Covariance matrix of coefficients of regress model

   e(V) |   married     female     fem_marr     _cons
---------+--------------------------------------------------
 married | .81770038
  female | .48548371   .83731317
fem_marr | -.81770038  -.83731317  1.5770922
   _cons | -.48548371  -.48548371   .48548371   .48548371
```

■ Display B.11.5 Regression of *hrchores* on *married*, *female*, and *fem_marr* in the NSFH: Stata *lincom* Command

	SAS	Stata
Regression Model	n/a	regress hrchores married female fem_marr lincom married+fem_marr lincom female+fem_marr Source | SS df MS Number of obs = 6054 F(3, 6050) = 169.97 Model | 297806.971 3 99268.9903 Prob > F = 0.0000 Residual | 3553423.25 6050 584.036902 R-squared = 0.0777 Adj R-squared = 0.0773 Total | 3831230.23 6053 632.947336 Root MSE = 24.167 hrchores | Coef. Std. Err. T P>|t| [95% Conf. Interval] married | -2.604886 .9042679 -2.88 0.004 -4.377573 -.8321986 female | 10.19964 .9150482 11.15 0.000 8.405821 11.99346 fem_marr | 6.63953 1.255823 5.29 0.000 4.177669 9.101391 _cons | 22.31421 .6967666 32.03 0.000 20.9483 23.68013 (1) married + fem_marr = 0 hrchores | Coef. Std. Err. T P>|t| [95% Conf. Interval] (1) | 4.034644 .8714309 4.63 0.000 2.326329 5.742959 lincom female+fem_marr (1) female + fem_marr = 0 hrchores | Coef. Std. Err. T P>|t| [95% Conf. Interval] (1) | 16.83917 .8601041 19.58 0.000 15.15306 18.52528
Select Results	n/a	

■ Display B.11.6 Regression of *hrchores* on *hrwork, female* and *fem_hrwork* in the NSFH

	SAS	Stata
Variable Creation	`fem_hrwork=female*hrwork;`	`generate fem_hrwork= female*hrwork`

Regression Model	`proc reg;`
	`  model hrchores=hrwork female fem_hrwork;`
	`run;`
		`regress hrchores hrwork female fem_hrwork`

Select Results

SAS:

Number of Observations Read	6054
Number of Observations Used	6054

Analysis of Variance

Source	DF	Sum of Squares	Mean Square	F Value	Pr > F
Model	3	328274	109425	188.99	<.0001
Error	6050	3502956	579.00099		
Corrected Total	6053	3831230			

Root MSE	24.06244	R-Square	0.0857
Dependent Mean	27.72382	Adj R-Sq	0.0852
Coeff Var	86.79338		

Parameter Estimates

Variable	DF	Parameter Estimate	Standard Error	t Value	Pr > |t|
Intercept	1	26.12448	1.42428	18.34	<.0001
hrwork	1	-0.12432	0.03142	-3.96	<.0001
female	1	16.99004	1.83148	9.28	<.0001
fem_hrwork	1	-0.12560	0.04382	-2.87	0.0042

Stata:

```
      Source |       SS       df       MS              Number of obs =    6054
-------------+------------------------------           F(  3,  6050) =  188.99
       Model |  328274.257     3  109424.752           Prob > F      =  0.0000
    Residual |  3502955.97  6050  579.000987           R-squared     =  0.0857
-------------+------------------------------           Adj R-squared =  0.0852
       Total |  3831230.23  6053  632.947336           Root MSE      =  24.062

    hrchores |      Coef.   Std. Err.      t    P>|t|     [95% Conf. Interval]
-------------+----------------------------------------------------------------
      hrwork |  -.1243169   .0314199    -3.96   0.000    -.1859111   -.0627226
      female |   16.99004   1.831485     9.28   0.000     13.39968     20.5804
  fem_hrwork |  -.1256042   .0438182    -2.87   0.004    -.2115036   -.0397048
       _cons |   26.12448   1.424276    18.34   0.000     23.33239    28.91657
```

■ Display B.11.7 Regression of *hrchores* on *hrwork*, *female* and *fem_hrwork* in the NSFH: Conditional Regression Equations for Effect of Hours of Paid Work among Women

SAS	Stata
Approach #1: Re-estimating Regression	

`male_hrwork=male*hrwork;`
 `...`
 `proc reg;`
 `model hrchores=hrwork male male_hrwork;`
 `run;`
	`generate male_hrwork=male*hrwork`
	 `regress hrchores hrwork male male_hrwork`

SAS — Parameter Estimates

Variable	DF	Parameter Estimate	Standard Error	t Value	Pr > |t|
Intercept	1	43.11452	1.15142	37.44	<.0001
hrwork	1	−0.24992	0.03054	−8.18	<.0001
male	1	−16.99004	1.83148	−9.28	<.0001
male_hrwork	1	0.12560	0.04382	2.87	0.0042

Stata

```
   hrchores |     Coef.  Std. Err.      t    P>|t|   [95% Conf. Interval]
------------+----------------------------------------------------------
     hrwork | -.2499211  .0305422   -8.18  0.000   -.3097947   -.1900475
       male | -16.99004  1.831485   -9.28  0.000   -20.5804    -13.39968
male_hrwork |  .1256042  .0438182    2.87  0.004    .0397048     .2115036
      _cons |  43.11452  1.151423   37.44  0.000    40.85732    45.37172
```

SAS	Stata
Approach #2: F-Test	

`proc reg;`
 `model hrchores=hrwork female fem_hrwork;`
 `test hrwork+fem_hrwork=0;`
 `run;`
	`regress hrchores hrwork female fem_hrwork`
	 `test hrwork+fem_hrwork=0`

SAS — Test 1 Results for Dependent Variable hrchores

Source	DF	Mean Square	F Value	Pr > F
Numerator	1	38769	66.96	<.0001
Denominator	6050	579.00099		

Stata

```
(1)  hrwork + fem_hrwork = 0

     F(1, 6050) =   66.96
          Prob > F =  0.0000
```

SAS	Stata
Approach #3: Linear Combination	
n/a (or use /covb and hand calculate)	`regress hrchores hrwork female fem_hrwork` `lincom hrwork+fem_hrwork`

SAS — n/a

Stata

```
   hrchores |     Coef.  Std. Err.      t    P>|t|   [95% Conf. Interval]
------------+----------------------------------------------------------
        (1) | -.2499211  .0305422   -8.18  0.000   -.3097947   -.1900475
```

■ **Display B.11.8. Regression of *hrchores* on *hrwork*, *female* and *fem_hrwork* in the NSFH: Conditional Effect of Gender within Hours of Paid Work (Approach #1: Re-Estimation).**

	SAS	Stata
Variable Creation and Regression Model	(see code and output below)	(see code and output below)

SAS

```
hrworkC10=hrwork-10;
hrworkC20=hrwork-20;
hrworkC30=hrwork-30;
hrworkC40=hrwork-40;
hrworkC50=hrwork-50;

fem_hrwC10=female*hrworkC10;
fem_hrwC20=female*hrworkC20;
fem_hrwC30=female*hrworkC30;
fem_hrwC40=female*hrworkC40;
fem_hrwC50=female*hrworkC50;
...

proc reg;
  model hrchores=hrworkC10 female fem_hrwC10;
  model hrchores=hrworkC20 female fem_hrwC20;
  model hrchores=hrworkC30 female fem_hrwC30;
  model hrchores=hrworkC40 female fem_hrwC40;
  model hrchores=hrworkC50 female fem_hrwC50;
run;
```

Parameter Estimates

Variable	DF	Parameter Estimate	Standard Error	t Value	Pr > |t|
Intercept	1	24.88131	1.12982	22.02	<.0001
hrworkC10	1	-0.12432	0.03142	-3.96	<.0001
female	1	15.73400	1.42960	11.01	<.0001
fem_hrwC10	1	-0.12560	0.04382	-2.87	0.0042

Parameter Estimates

Variable	DF	Parameter Estimate	Standard Error	t Value>	Pr > |t|
Intercept	1	23.63814	0.84964	27.82	<.0001
hrworkC20	1	-0.12432	0.03142	-3.96	<.0001
female	1	14.47796	1.05697	13.70	<.0001
fem_hrwC20	1	-0.12560	0.04382	-2.87	0.0042

Stata

```
generate hrworkC10=hrwork-10
generate hrworkC20=hrwork-20
generate hrworkC30=hrwork-30
generate hrworkC40=hrwork-40
generate hrworkC50=hrwork-50

generate fem_hrwC10=female*hrworkC10
generate fem_hrwC20=female*hrworkC20
generate fem_hrwC30=female*hrworkC30
generate fem_hrwC40=female*hrworkC40
generate fem_hrwC50=female*hrworkC50

regress hrchores hrworkC10 female fem_hrwC10
regress hrchores hrworkC20 female fem_hrwC20
regress hrchores hrworkC30 female fem_hrwC30
regress hrchores hrworkC40 female fem_hrwC40
regress hrchores hrworkC50 female fem_hrwC50
```

```
  hrchores |    Coef.   Std. Err.     t    P>|t|    [95% Conf. Interval]
 hrworkC10 | -.1243169  .0314199   -3.96  0.000   -.1859111   -.0627226
    female |   15.734   1.429602   11.01  0.000    12.93147    18.53653
fem_hrwC10 | -.1256042  .0438182   -2.87  0.004   -.2115036   -.0397048
     _cons |  24.88131  1.129823   22.02  0.000    22.66646    27.09617
```

```
  hrchores |    Coef.   Std. Err.     t    P>|t|    [95% Conf. Interval]
 hrworkC20 | -.1243169  .0314199   -3.96  0.000   -.1859111   -.0627226
    female |  14.47796  1.056974   13.70  0.000    12.40591     16.55
fem_hrwC20 | -.1256042  .0438182   -2.87  0.004   -.2115036   -.0397048
     _cons |  23.63814  .8496356   27.82  0.000    21.97256    25.30373
```

APPENDIX B

■ Display B.11.8. Regression of *hrchores* on *hrwork*, *female* and *fem_hrwork* in the NSFH: Conditional Effect of Gender within Hours of Paid Work (Approach #1: Re-Estimation). (Continued)

```
    hrchores |      Coef.   Std. Err.      t    P>|t|     [95% Conf. Interval]
-------------+----------------------------------------------------------------
   hrworkC30 | -.1243169   .0314199    -3.96   0.000    -.1859111   -.0627226
      female |  13.22192   .7580464    17.44   0.000     11.73588    14.70796
  fem_hrwC30 | -.1256042   .0438182    -2.87   0.004    -.2115036   -.0397048
       _cons |  22.39498   .6039071    37.08   0.000     21.2111     23.57885
```

```
    hrchores |      Coef.   Std. Err.      t    P>|t|     [95% Conf. Interval]
-------------+----------------------------------------------------------------
   hrworkC40 | -.1243169   .0314199    -3.96   0.000    -.1859111   -.0627226
      female |  11.96587   .6450443    18.55   0.000     10.70136    13.23039
  fem_hrwC40 | -.1256042   .0438182    -2.87   0.004    -.2115036   -.0397048
       _cons |  21.15181   .4527355    46.72   0.000     20.26428    22.03933
```

```
    hrchores |      Coef.   Std. Err.      t    P>|t|     [95% Conf. Interval]
-------------+----------------------------------------------------------------
   hrworkC50 | -.1243169   .0314199    -3.96   0.000    -.1859111   -.0627226
      female |  10.70983   .8009605    13.37   0.000     9.139664    12.28
  fem_hrwC50 | -.1256042   .0438182    -2.87   0.004    -.2115036   -.0397048
       _cons |  19.90864   .4926231    40.41   0.000     18.94292    20.87435
```

Select Results

Variable	DF	Parameter Estimate	Standard Error	t Value	Pr > |t|
		Parameter Estimates			
Intercept	1	22.39498	0.60391	37.08	<.0001
hrworkC30	1	-0.12432	0.03142	-3.96	<.0001
female	1	13.22192	0.75805	17.44	<.0001
fem_hrwC30	1	-0.12560	0.04382	-2.87	0.0042

Variable	DF	Parameter Estimate	Standard Error	t Value	Pr > |t|
		Parameter Estimates			
Intercept	1	21.15181	0.45274	46.72	<.0001
hrworkC40	1	-0.12432	0.03142	-3.96	<.0001
female	1	11.96587	0.64504	18.55	<.0001
fem_hrwC40	1	-0.12560	0.04382	-2.87	0.0042

Variable	DF	Parameter Estimate	Standard Error	t Value	Pr > |t|
		Parameter Estimates			
Intercept	1	19.90864	0.49262	40.41	<.0001
hrworkC50	1	-0.12432	0.03142	-3.96	<.0001
female	1	10.70983	0.80096	13.37	<.0001
fem_hrwC50	1	-0.12560	0.04382	-2.87	0.0042

Display B.11.9. Regression of *hrchores* on *hrwork*, *female* and *fem_hrwork* in the NSFH: Conditional Effect of Gender within Hours of Paid Work (Approach #2: F-test)

Regression Model

SAS

```
proc reg;
    model hrchores=hrwork female fem_hrwork;
    test female+10*fem_hrwork=0;
    test female+20*fem_hrwork=0;
    test female+30*fem_hrwork=0;
    test female+40*fem_hrwork=0;
    test female+50*fem_hrwork=0;
run;
```

Stata

```
regress hrchores hrwork female fem_hrwork
    test female+10*fem_hrwork=0
    test female+20*fem_hrwork=0
    test female+30*fem_hrwork=0
    test female+40*fem_hrwork=0
    test female+50*fem_hrwork=0
```

Select Results

SAS

Test 1 Results for Dependent Variable hrchores

Source	DF	Mean Square	F Value	Pr > F
Numerator	1	70134	121.13	<.0001
Denominator	6050	579.00099		

Test 2 Results for Dependent Variable hrchores

Source	DF	Mean Square	F Value	Pr > F
Numerator	1	108634	187.62	<.0001
Denominator	6050	579.00099		

Test 3 Results for Dependent Variable hrchores

Source	DF	Mean Square	F Value	Pr > F
Numerator	1	176148	304.23	<.0001
Denominator	6050	579.00099		

Test 4 Results for Dependent Variable hrchores

Source	DF	Mean Square	F Value	Pr > F
Numerator	1	199246	344.12	<.0001
Denominator	6050	579.00099		

Test 5 Results for Dependent Variable hrchores

Source	DF	Mean Square	F Value	Pr > F
Numerator	1	103520	178.79	<.0001
Denominator	6050	579.00099		

Stata

```
(1)  female + 10 fem_hrwork = 0
        F( 1, 6050) =  121.13
            Prob > F =  0.0000

(1)  female + 20 fem_hrwork = 0
        F( 1, 6050) =  187.62
            Prob > F =  0.0000

(1)  female + 30 fem_hrwork = 0
        F( 1, 6050) =  304.23
            Prob > F =  0.0000

(1)  female + 40 fem_hrwork = 0
        F( 1, 6050) =  344.12
            Prob > F =  0.0000

(1)  female + 50 fem_hrwork = 0
        F( 1, 6050) =  178.79
            Prob > F =  0.0000
```

■ Display B.11.10 Regression of *hrchores* on *hrwork*, *female* and *fem_hrwork* in the NSFH: Conditional Effect of Gender within Hours of Paid Work (Approach #3: Linear Combinations)

	SAS	Stata
Regression Model	n/a	regress hrchores hrwork female fem_hrwork lincom female+10*fem_hrwork lincom female+20*fem_hrwork lincom female+30*fem_hrwork lincom female+40*fem_hrwork lincom female+50*fem_hrwork
Select Results	n/a	(1) female + 10 fem_hrwork = 0 hrchores | Coef. Std. Err. T P>|t| [95% Conf. Interval] (1) | 15.734 1.429602 11.01 0.000 12.93147 18.53653 (1) female + 20 fem_hrwork = 0 hrchores | Coef. Std. Err. T P>|t| [95% Conf. Interval] (1) | 14.47796 1.056974 13.70 0.000 12.40591 16.55 (1) female + 30 fem_hrwork = 0 hrchores | Coef. Std. Err. T P>|t| [95% Conf. Interval] (1) | 13.22192 .7580464 17.44 0.000 11.73588 14.70796 (1) female + 40 fem_hrwork = 0 hrchores | Coef. Std. Err. T P> t [95% Conf. Interval] (1) | 11.96587 .6450443 18.55 0.000 10.70136 13.23039 (1) female + 50 fem_hrwork = 0 hrchores | Coef. Std. Err. T P>|t| [95% Conf. Interval] (1) | 10.70983 .8009605 13.37 0.000 9.139664 12.28

■ Display B.11.11 Regression of *hrchores* on *married*, *hrwork*, *numkid*, *aframer*, and *mexamer* in the NSFH: Total Sample

	SAS	Stata

Regression Model	`proc reg;`
	`model hrchores=married hrwork numkid`
	`aframer mexamer;`
	`run;`
		`regress hrchores married hrwork numkid aframer mexamer`

Stata — Select Results

	Number of obs = 5820
	F(5, 5814) = 95.30
	Prob > F = 0.0000
	R-squared = 0.0757
	Adj R-squared = 0.0750
	Root MSE = 24.383

Source	SS	df	MS
Model	283291.065	5	56658.2129
Residual	3456551.62	5814	594.522122
Total	3739842.68	5819	642.695082

hrchores	Coef.	Std. Err.	t	P>|t|	[95% Conf. Interval]
married	-3.068214	.6809263	-4.51	0.000	-4.403083 -1.733345
hrwork	-.2943945	.0216851	-13.58	0.000	-.3369054 -.2518836
numkid	4.364196	.322211	13.54	0.000	3.732542 4.995849
aframer	5.221268	.8679679	6.02	0.000	3.519727 6.922808
mexamer	8.918807	1.647446	5.41	0.000	5.689201 12.14841
_cons	36.06816	.9996316	36.08	0.000	34.10851 38.02781

SAS — Select Results

Number of Observations Read	5820
Number of Observations Used	5820

Analysis of Variance

Source	DF	Sum of Squares	Mean Square	F Value	Pr > F
Model	5	283291	56658	95.30	<.0001
Error	5814	3456552	594.52212		
Corrected Total	5819	3739843			

Root MSE	24.38282	R-Square	0.0757
Dependent Mean	27.79553	Adj R-Sq	0.0750
Coeff Var	87.72210		

Parameter Estimates

Variable	DF	Parameter Estimate	Standard Error	t Value	Pr > |t|
Intercept	1	36.06816	0.99963	36.08	<.0001
married	1	-3.06821	0.68093	-4.51	<.0001
hrwork	1	-0.29439	0.02169	-13.58	<.0001
numkid	1	4.36420	0.32221	13.54	<.0001
aframer	1	5.22127	0.86797	6.02	<.0001
mexamer	1	8.91881	1.64745	5.41	<.0001

APPENDIX B

■ Display B.11.12 Regression of *hrchores* on *married, hrwork, numkid, aframer,* and *mexamer:* Separately for Males and Females

	SAS	Stata
| Regression Model | ```
proc sort; by female; run;
proc reg;
   model hrchores=married hrwork numkid
                  aframer mexamer;
   by female;
run;
``` | bysort female: regress hrchores married hrwork /// numkid aframer mexamer |

Males

Stata output:

```
      Source |       SS       df       MS              Number of obs =    2849
-------------+------------------------------           F( 5,  2843) =   17.75
       Model |  35661.778      5  7132.3556            Prob > F      =  0.0000
    Residual | 1142398.38   2843 401.828484            R-squared     =  0.0303
-------------+------------------------------           Adj R-squared =  0.0286
       Total | 1178060.16   2848 413.644718            Root MSE      = 20.046

    hrchores |      Coef.   Std. Err.      t    P>|t|     [95% Conf. Interval]
-------------+----------------------------------------------------------------
     married | -3.184859   .8664546     -3.68   0.000    -4.883803  -1.485916
      hrwork |  -.109475   .0269866     -4.06   0.000    -.1623902  -.0565598
      numkid |  1.445786   .4002116      3.61   0.000     .6610514   2.23052
     aframer |  6.041829   1.084095      5.57   0.000     3.916138   8.16752
     mexamer |  5.768344   1.849813      3.12   0.002     2.141233   9.395456
       _cons |  25.18235   1.303018     19.33   0.000     22.62739   27.73731
```

SAS Parameter Estimates (Males):

Variable	DF	Parameter Estimate	Standard Error	t Value	Pr > |t|
Intercept	1	25.18235	1.30302	19.33	<.0001
married	1	-3.18486	0.86645	-3.68	0.0002
hrwork	1	-0.10947	0.02699	-4.06	<.0001
numkid	1	1.44579	0.40021	3.61	0.0003
aframer	1	6.04183	1.08409	5.57	<.0001
mexamer	1	5.76834	1.84981	3.12	0.0018

Females

Stata output:

```
      Source |       SS       df       MS              Number of obs =    2971
-------------+------------------------------           F( 5,  2965) =   59.11
       Model |  207458.514     5  41491.7028           Prob > F      =  0.0000
    Residual | 2081280.21  2965 701.949481            R-squared     =  0.0906
-------------+------------------------------           Adj R-squared =  0.0891
       Total | 2288738.73  2970  770.6191             Root MSE      = 26.494

    hrchores |      Coef.   Std. Err.      t    P>|t|     [95% Conf. Interval]
-------------+----------------------------------------------------------------
     married |  1.297806   1.010148      1.28   0.199    -.6828562   3.278467
      hrwork | -.2151042   .0344651     -6.24   0.000    -.2826822  -.1475262
      numkid |  6.240049   .4831701     12.91   0.000     5.292666   7.187432
     aframer |  4.063293   1.256962      3.23   0.001     1.598687   6.527899
     mexamer |  14.26334   2.638858      5.41   0.000     9.089161   19.43752
       _cons |  34.69164   1.506367     23.03   0.000     31.738     37.64527
```

SAS Parameter Estimates (Females):

Variable	DF	Parameter Estimate	Standard Error	t Value	Pr > |t|
Intercept	1	34.69164	1.50637	23.03	<.0001
married	1	1.29781	1.01015	1.28	0.1990
hrwork	1	-0.21510	0.03447	-6.24	<.0001
numkid	1	6.24005	0.48317	12.91	<.0001
aframer	1	4.06329	1.25696	3.23	0.0012
mexamer	1	14.26334	2.63886	5.41	<.0001
```

Display B.11.13 Regression of *hrchores* on *married, hrwork, numkid, aframer,* and *mexamer* in the NSFH: Fully Interacted Model

SAS

Regression

```
proc reg;
model hrchores=married hrwork numkid
aframer mexamer female
fem_marr fem_hrwork
fem_numkid fem_aframer
fem_mexamer;

test female,fem_marr,fem_hrwork,fem_numkid,
fem_aframer,fem_mexamer;
run;
```

Select Results

Parameter Estimates

Variable	DF	Parameter Estimate	Standard Error	t Value	Pr > |t|
Intercept	1	25.18235	1.53141	16.44	<.0001
married	1	-3.18486	1.01833	-3.13	0.0018
hrwork	1	-0.10947	0.03172	-3.45	0.0006
numkid	1	1.44579	0.47036	3.07	0.0021
aframer	1	6.04183	1.27412	4.74	<.0001
mexamer	1	5.76834	2.17405	2.65	0.0080
female	1	9.50929	2.03457	4.67	<.0001
fem_marr	1	4.48267	1.35788	3.30	0.0010
fem_hrwork	1	-0.10563	0.04410	-2.39	0.0167
fem_numkid	1	4.79426	0.63705	7.53	<.0001
fem_aframer	1	-1.97854	1.69489	-1.17	0.2431
fem_mexamer	1	8.49500	3.19986	2.66	0.0079

Test 1 Results for Dependent Variable hrchores

Source	DF	Mean Square	F Value	Pr > F
Numerator	6	38812	69.93	<.0001
Denominator	5808	555.04108		

Stata

Regression

```
regress hrchores married hrwork numkid aframer mexamer ///
        female fem_marr fem_hrwork fem_numkid ///
        fem_aframer fem_mexamer

test female fem_marr fem_hrwork fem_numkid
     fem_aframer fem_mexamer
```

Select Results

```
                                      Number of obs =    5820
                                      F( 11,  5808) =   84.54
                                      Prob > F      =  0.0000
                                      R-squared     =  0.1380
                                      Adj R-squared =  0.1364
                                      Root MSE      =  23.559

     Source |     SS        df        MS
------------+---------------------------------
      Model | 516164.093    11    46924.0084
   Residual | 3223678.59  5808    555.04108
------------+---------------------------------
      Total | 3739842.68  5819    642.695082

   hrchores |    Coef.    Std. Err.     t    P>|t|   [95% Conf. Interval]
------------+------------------------------------------------------------
    married | -3.184859   1.018329   -3.13   0.002   -5.18163   -1.188556
     hrwork |  -.109475   .0317168   -3.45   0.001  -.1716517   -.0472982
     numkid |  1.445786   .4703616    3.07   0.002   .5237018    2.36787
    aframer |  6.041829   1.274117    4.74   0.000   3.544085    8.539573
    mexamer |  5.768344   2.174053    2.65   0.008   1.506391    10.0303
     female |  9.509286   2.034569    4.67   0.000   5.520772    13.4978
   fem_marr |  4.482665   1.357879    3.30   0.001   1.820716    7.144615
 fem_hrwork | -.1056292   .0441044   -2.39   0.017  -.1920904   -.0191681
 fem_numkid |  4.794263   .6370517    7.53   0.000   3.545404    6.043122
fem_aframer | -1.978536   1.694894   -1.17   0.243  -5.301159    1.344087
fem_mexamer |  8.494996   3.198859    2.66   0.008   2.224041    14.76595
      _cons |  25.18235   1.531414   16.44   0.000   22.18021    28.18449
```

```
.test female fem_marr fem_hrwork fem_numkid fem_aframer fem_mexamer
(1)  female = 0
(2)  fem_marr = 0
(3)  fem_hrwork = 0
(4)  fem_numkid = 0
(5)  fem_aframer = 0
(6)  fem_mexamer = 0
       F(6,  5808) =  69.93
            Prob > F =   0.0000
```

APPENDIX B

■ Display B.11.14 Regression of *hrchores* on *married, hrwork, numkid, aframer,* and *mexamer* in the NSFH: Conditional Regression for Women from Fully Interacted Model

	Stata

Regression Model	`regress hrchores married hrwork numkid aframer mexamer ///`
	`        female fem_marr fem_hrwork fem_numkid fem_aframer fem_mexamer`
	
	`lincom married+fem_marr`
	`lincom hrwork+fem_hrwork`
	`lincom numkid+fem_numkid`
	`lincom aframer+fem_aframer`
	`lincom mexamer+fem_mexamer`
	`lincom _cons+female`

Select Results	`( 1)  married + fem_marr = 0` ` hrchores	Coef. Std. Err. t P>|t| [95% Conf. Interval]` ` (1) |1.297806 .8982444 1.44 0.149 -.4630881 3.058699`  `(1) hrwork + fem_hrwork = 0`  ` hrchores	Coef. Std. Err. t P>|t| [95% Conf. Interval]` ` (1) |-.2151042 .0306471 -7.02 0.000 -.2751839 -.1550244`  `(1) numkid + fem_numkid = 0`  ` hrchores	Coef. Std. Err. t P>|t| [95% Conf. Interval]` ` (1) |6.240049 .4296449 14.52 0.000 5.397785 7.082313`  `(1) aframer + fem_aframer = 0`  ` hrchores	Coef. Std. Err. t P>|t| [95% Conf. Interval]` ` (1) |4.063293 1.117717 3.64 0.000 1.872152 6.254434`  `(1) mexamer + fem_mexamer = 0`  ` hrchores	Coef. Std. Err. t P>|t| [95% Conf. Interval]` ` (1) |14.26334 2.346528 6.08 0.000 9.663272 18.86341`  `(1) female + _cons = 0`  ` hrchores	Coef. Std. Err. t P>|t| [95% Conf. Interval]` ` (1) |34.69164 1.339493 25.90 0.000 32.06573 37.31754`

■ **Display B.11.15 Regression of *hrchores* on *hrwork* and *numkid* in the NSFH: Interaction Model**

	SAS	Stata
Variable Creation	`numk_hrw=numkid*hrwork;`	`generate numk_hrw=numkid*hrwork`

Regression Model	`proc reg;`
	`  model hrchores=hrwork numkid numk_hrw;`
	`run;`
		`regress hrchores hrwork numkid numk_hrw`

SAS Select Results

Number of Observations Read	6054
Number of Observations Used	6054

Analysis of Variance

Source	DF	Sum of Squares	Mean Square	F Value	Pr > F
Model	3	258894	86298	146.15	<.0001
Error	6050	3572336	590.46874		
Corrected Total	6053	3831230			

Root MSE	24.29956	R-Square	0.0676
Dependent Mean	27.72382	Adj R-Sq	0.0671
Coeff Var	87.64868		

Parameter Estimates

Variable	DF	Parameter Estimate	Standard Error	t Value	Pr > |t|
Intercept	1	31.89119	1.11564	28.59	<.0001
hrwork	1	-0.19367	0.02678	-7.23	<.0001
numkid	1	9.06985	0.80394	11.28	<.0001
numk_hrw	1	-0.12751	0.01924	-6.63	<.0001

Stata Select Results

```
      Source |       SS       df       MS              Number of obs =    6054
-------------+------------------------------           F(  3,  6050) =  146.15
       Model |  258894.349     3  86298.1165           Prob > F      =  0.0000
    Residual | 3572335.88  6050  590.46874             R-squared     =  0.0676
-------------+------------------------------           Adj R-squared =  0.0671
       Total | 3831230.23  6053  632.947336            Root MSE      =    24.3

    hrchores |      Coef.   Std. Err.      t    P>|t|     [95% Conf. Interval]
-------------+----------------------------------------------------------------
      hrwork |  -.193674    .026785    -7.23   0.000    -.2461821   -.1411658
      numkid |  9.069852    .8039375   11.28   0.000     7.493849    10.64586
    numk_hrw |  -.127512    .0192373   -6.63   0.000    -.165224    -.0897999
       _cons |  31.89119    1.115636   28.59   0.000     29.70415    34.07824
```

■ **Display B.11.16 Regression of *hrchores* on *hrwork* and *numkid* in the NSFH: Conditional Effects**

Regression Model	Conditional Effects of Hours of Work	Conditional Effects of Number of Children
	lincom hrwork+numk_hrw*0 lincom hrwork+numk_hrw*1 lincom hrwork+numk_hrw*2 lincom hrwork+numk_hrw*3 lincom hrwork+numk_hrw*4	lincom numkid+numk_hrw*10 lincom numkid+numk_hrw*20 lincom numkid+numk_hrw*30 lincom numkid+numk_hrw*40 lincom numkid+numk_hrw*50

Select Results

Conditional Effects of Hours of Work

```
(1) hrwork = 0

 hrchores |    Coef.  Std. Err.      t    P>|t|  [95% Conf. Interval]
      (1) | -.193674   .026785   -7.23   0.000   -.2461821  -.1411658

(1) hrwork + numk_hrw = 0

 hrchores |    Coef.  Std. Err.      t    P>|t|  [95% Conf. Interval]
      (1) | -.321186    .02145  -14.97   0.000   -.3632355   -.2791364

(1) hrwork + 2 numk_hrw = 0

 hrchores |    Coef.  Std. Err.      t    P>|t|  [95% Conf. Interval]
      (1) | -.4486979  .030707  -14.61   0.000   -.5088945   -.3885014

(1) hrwork + 3 numk_hrw = 0

 hrchores |    Coef.  Std. Err.      t    P>|t|  [95% Conf. Interval]
      (1) | -.5762099  .0465391 -12.38   0.000   -.6674431   -.4849768

(1) hrwork + 4 numk_hrw = 0

 hrchores |    Coef.  Std. Err.      t    P>|t|  [95% Conf. Interval]
      (1) | -.7037219  .062573  -10.95   0.000   -.8296891   -.5777547
```

Conditional Effects of Number of Children

```
(1) numkid + 10 numk_hrw = 0

 hrchores |    Coef.  Std. Err.      t    P>|t|  [95% Conf. Interval]
      (1) | 7.794732   .6292909  12.39   0.000   6.561098    9.028367

(1) numkid + 20 numk_hrw = 0

 hrchores |    Coef.  Std. Err.      t    P>|t|  [95% Conf. Interval]
      (1) | 6.519613   .4687363  13.91   0.000   5.600723    7.438503

(1) numkid + 30 numk_hrw = 0

 hrchores |    Coef.  Std. Err.      t    P>|t|  [95% Conf. Interval]
      (1) | 5.244493   .3426887  15.30   0.000   4.572701    5.916285

(1) numkid + 40 numk_hrw = 0

 hrchores |    Coef.  Std. Err.      t    P>|t|  [95% Conf. Interval]
      (1) | 3.969373   .2986177  13.29   0.000   3.383976    4.55477

(1) numkid + 50 numk_hrw = 0

 hrchores |    Coef.  Std. Err.      t    P>|t|  [95% Conf. Interval]
      (1) | 2.694253   .3673208   7.33   0.000   1.974174    3.414333
```

■ Display B.12.1 Models Relating Distance to Mother's Years of Schooling: Outcome in Natural Units

	SAS	Stata
Variable Creation	`loglyrsch1=log(glyrsch1+1);` `sqglyrsch1=glyrsch1*glyrsch1;`	`generate logglyrsch1=log(glyrsch1+1)` `generate sqglyrsch1=glyrsch1*glyrsch1`

Regression Model	`proc reg;`
	  `model glmiles=glyrsch1;`
	  `model glmiles=logglyrsch1;`
	  `model glmiles=glyrsch1 sqglyrsch1;`
	`run;`
		`regress glmiles glyrsch1`
		`regress glmiles logglyrsch1`
		`regress glmiles glyrsch1 sqglyrsch1`

Stata Select Results:

```
      Source |       SS         df       MS              Number of obs =    5472
-------------+------------------------------             F( 1,  5470) =    34.59
       Model |  14307139.9       1   14307139.9          Prob > F      =   0.0000
    Residual |  2.2626e+09     5470   413637.869         R-squared     =   0.0063
-------------+------------------------------             Adj R-squared =   0.0061
       Total |  2.2769e+09     5471   416177.35          Root MSE      =   643.15

------------------------------------------------------------------------------
     glmiles |      Coef.   Std. Err.      t    P>|t|     [95% Conf. Interval]
-------------+----------------------------------------------------------------
    glyrsch1 |    17.3926    2.95732     5.88   0.000     11.59508    23.19013
       _cons |   92.86328   34.81817     2.67   0.008     24.60582    161.1207
------------------------------------------------------------------------------
```

SAS Select Results:

Analysis of Variance

Source	DF	Sum of Squares	Mean Square	F Value	Pr > F
Model	1	14307140	14307140	34.59	<.0001
Error	5470	2262599142	413638		
Corrected Total	5471	2276906282			

Parameter Estimates

Variable	DF	Parameter Estimate	Standard Error	t Value	Pr > |t|
Intercept	1	92.86328	34.81817	2.67	0.0077
glyrsch1	1	17.39260	2.95732	5.88	<.0001

(continued)

Display B.12.1 Models Relating Distance to Mother's Years of Schooling: Outcome in Natural Units (Continued)

Select Results (continued)

Source	SS	df	MS		
Model	7070413.39	1	7070413.39	Number of obs =	5472
Residual	2.2698e+09	5470	414960.854	F(1, 5470) =	17.04
				Prob > F =	0.0000
				R-squared =	0.0031
				Adj R-squared =	0.0029
Total	2.2769e+09	5471	416177.35	Root MSE =	644.17

g1miles	Coef.	Std. Err.	t	P>|t|	[95% Conf. Interval]
logg1yrschl	107.6181	26.07152	4.13	0.000	56.50752 158.7286
_cons	24.65057	65.1465	0.38	0.705	-103.0625 152.3636

Source	SS	df	MS		
Model	19520918.9	2	9760459.43	Number of obs =	5472
Residual	2.2574e+09	5469	412760.169	F(2, 5469) =	23.65
				Prob > F =	0.0000
				R-squared =	0.0086
				Adj R-squared =	0.0082
Total	2.2769e+09	5471	416177.35	Root MSE =	642.46

g1miles	Coef.	Std. Err.	t	P>|t|	[95% Conf. Interval]
g1yrschl	-25.69624	12.47849	-2.06	0.040	-50.15905 -1.233428
sqg1yrschl	2.094442	.589306	3.55	0.000	.9391676 3.249716
_cons	293.7769	66.37331	4.43	0.000	163.6588 423.895

Analysis of Variance

Source	DF	Sum of Squares	Mean Square	F Value	Pr > F
Model	1	7070413	7070413	17.04	<.0001
Error	5470	2269835869	414961		
Corrected Total	5471	2276906282			

Parameter Estimates

Variable	DF	Parameter Estimate	Standard Error	t Value	Pr > |t|
Intercept	1	24.65058	65.14650	0.38	0.7052
logg1yrschl	1	107.61806	26.07152	4.13	<.0001

Analysis of Variance

Source	DF	Sum of Squares	Mean Square	F Value	Pr > F
Model	2	19520919	9760459	23.65	<.0001
Error	5469	2257385363	412760		
Corrected Total	5471	2276906282			

Parameter Estimates

Variable	DF	Parameter Estimate	Standard Error	t Value	Pr > |t|
Intercept	1	293.77688	66.37331	4.43	<.0001
g1yrschl	1	-25.69624	12.47849	-2.06	0.0395
sqg1yrschl	1	2.09444	0.58931	3.55	0.0004

Display B.12.2 Models Relating Distance to Mother's Years of Schooling: Logged Outcome

SAS

Variable Creation

```
logg1miles=log(g1miles);
```

Regression Model

```
proc reg;
  model logg1miles=g1yrschl;
  model logg1miles=logg1yrschl;
  model logg1miles=g1yrschl sqg1yrschl;
run;
```

Select Results

Model 1 — Analysis of Variance

Source	DF	Sum of Squares	Mean Square	F Value	Pr > F
Model	1	631.71941	631.71941	110.61	<.0001
Error	5470	31239	5.71104		
Corrected Total	5471	31871			

Parameter Estimates

Variable	DF	Parameter Estimate	Standard Error	t Value	Pr > |t|
Intercept	1	1.97424	0.12938	15.26	<.0001
g1yrschl	1	0.11557	0.01099	10.52	<.0001

Model 2 — Analysis of Variance

Source	DF	Sum of Squares	Mean Square	F Value	Pr > F
Model	1	404.56553	404.56553	70.33	<.0001
Error	5470	31467	5.75257		
Corrected Total	5471	31871			

Parameter Estimates

Variable	DF	Parameter Estimate	Standard Error	t Value	Pr > |t|
Intercept	1	1.27593	0.24256	5.26	<.0001
logg1yrschl	1	0.81406	0.09707	8.39	<.0001

Model 3 — Analysis of Variance

Source	DF	Sum of Squares	Mean Square	F Value	Pr > F
Model	2	721.84162	360.92081	63.37	<.0001
Error	5469	31149	5.69561		
Corrected Total	5471	31871			

Parameter Estimates

Variable	DF	Parameter Estimate	Standard Error	t Value	Pr > |t|
Intercept	1	2.80955	0.24656	11.40	<.0001
g1yrschl	1	-0.06357	0.04635	-1.37	0.1703
sqg1yrschl	1	0.00871	0.00219	3.98	<.0001

Stata

Variable Creation

```
generate logg1miles=log(g1miles)
```

Regression Model

```
regress logg1miles g1yrschl
regress logg1miles logg1yrschl
regress logg1miles g1yrschl sqg1yrschl
```

Select Results

Model 1

```
   Source |       SS       df       MS              Number of obs =    5472
----------+------------------------------          F( 1,  5470) =  110.61
    Model | 631.719424      1  631.719424          Prob > F      =  0.0000
 Residual | 31239.4079   5470  5.71104349          R-squared     =  0.0198
----------+------------------------------          Adj R-squared =  0.0196
    Total | 31871.1273   5471  5.82546652          Root MSE      =  2.3898

logg1miles |   Coef.    Std. Err.     t    P>|t|    [95% Conf. Interval]
-----------+----------------------------------------------------------
  g1yrschl | .1155714   .0109887   10.52  0.000    .0940292    .1371136
     _cons | 1.974236   .1293759   15.26  0.000   1.720608    2.227864
```

Model 2

```
   Source |       SS       df       MS              Number of obs =    5472
----------+------------------------------          F( 1,  5470) =   70.33
    Model | 404.565542      1  404.565542          Prob > F      =  0.0000
 Residual | 31466.5618   5470  5.75257071          R-squared     =  0.0127
----------+------------------------------          Adj R-squared =  0.0125
    Total | 31871.1273   5471  5.82546652          Root MSE      =  2.3985

logg1miles |   Coef.    Std. Err.     t    P>|t|    [95% Conf. Interval]
------------+----------------------------------------------------------
logg1yrschl | .8140615   .0970719    8.39  0.000    .6237619    1.004361
      _cons | 1.275927   .2425596    5.26  0.000    .8004137    1.75144
```

Model 3

```
   Source |       SS       df       MS              Number of obs =    5472
----------+------------------------------          F( 2,  5469) =   63.37
    Model | 721.841633      2  360.920816          Prob > F      =  0.0000
 Residual | 31149.2857   5469  5.69560901          R-squared     =  0.0226
----------+------------------------------          Adj R-squared =  0.0223
    Total | 31871.1273   5471  5.82546652          Root MSE      =  2.3865

logg1miles |    Coef.    Std. Err.     t    P>|t|    [95% Conf. Interval]
------------+----------------------------------------------------------
  g1yrschl  | -.0635735   .0463536   -1.37  0.170   -.154445    .027298
 sqg1yrschl |  .0087078   .0021891    3.98  0.000    .0044163    .0129993
      _cons |  2.809548   .2465555   11.40  0.000   2.326202    3.292895
```

■ Display B.12.3 Calculating $\widehat{\exp(\varepsilon)}$ and Approximate R-squareds: Example for *log-sq* model

SAS

Calculate Predictions

```
proc reg;
    model logg1miles=g1yrschl sqg1yrschl;
    output out=predict(keep=g1miles logYhat
    logResid)predicted=logYhat residual=logResid;
run;

data predict2;
    set predict;
    explogYhat=exp(logYhat);
    explogResid=exp(logResid);
run;
```

Calculate $\overline{\exp(\varepsilon)}$

```
proc means data=predict2;
    var explogResid;
run;
```

Mean Results

Analysis Variable: explogResid				
N	Mean	Std Dev	Minimum	Maximum
5472	10.7577435	26.1452245	0.0143307	606.5467606

Estimate R-squared

```
proc reg data=predict2;
    model g1miles=explogYhat;
run;
```

Regression Results

Root MSE	642.76634	R Square	0.0075
Dependent Mean	291.14912	Adj R-Sq	0.0073
Coeff Var	220.76877		

Parameter Estimates					
Variable	DF	Parameter Estimate	Standard Error	t Value	Pr > |t|
Intercept	1	160.35487	22.17333	7.23	<.0001
explogYhat	1	4.52556	0.70585	6.41	<.0001

Stata

Calculate Predictions

```
regress logg1miles g1yrschl sqg1yrschl
predict logYhat
predict logResid, residuals
generate explogYhat=exp(logYhat)
generate explogResid=exp(logResid)
```

Calculate $\overline{\exp(\varepsilon)}$

```
summarize explogResid
```

Mean Results

```
Variable |   Obs      Mean    Std. Dev.    Min       Max
---------+--------------------------------------------------
explogResid| 5472    10.75774  26.14523   .0143307  606.5466
```

Estimate R-squared

```
regress g1miles explogYhat
```

Regression Results

```
   Source |      SS       df       MS              Number of obs =    5472
----------+------------------------------          F( 1,  5470) =   41.11
    Model | 16983584.2      1  16983584.2          Prob > F      =  0.0000
 Residual | 2.2599e+9    5470  413148.574          R-squared     =  0.0075
----------+------------------------------          Adj R-squared =  0.0073
    Total | 2.2769e+09   5471  416177.35           Root MSE      =  642.77

  g1miles |    Coef.   Std. Err.     t    P>|t|   [95% Conf. Interval]
----------+----------------------------------------------------------
explogYhat| 4.52556   .7058474    6.41   0.000    3.141819    5.909302
    _cons | 160.3549  22.17332    7.23   0.000    116.8864    203.8234
```

Display B.12.4 Using a Dummy Variable Specification for Number of Sisters

	SAS	Stata

Create Variables	`g2numsis1=g2numsis=1;`
	`g2numsis2=g2numsis=2;`
	`g2numsis3=g2numsis=3;`
	`g2numsis4=g2numsis=4;`
	`g2numsis5=g2numsis=5;`
	`g2numsis6=g2numsis=6;`
	`g2numsis7p=g2numsis>=7;`
		`generate g2numsis1=g2numsis==1`
		`generate g2numsis2=g2numsis==2`
		`generate g2numsis3=g2numsis==3`
		`generate g2numsis4=g2numsis==4`
		`generate g2numsis5=g2numsis==5`
		`generate g2numsis6=g2numsis==6`
		`generate g2numsis7p=g2numsis>=7`

Estimate Regression	`proc reg data=nonlinear;`
	`  model logg1miles=g2numsis1 g2numsis2`
	`    g2numsis3 g2numsis4 g2numsis5 g2numsis6`
	`    g2numsis7p;`
	`run;`
		`regress logg1miles g2numsis1 g2numsis2 g2numsis3 ///`
		`   g2numsis4 g2numsis5 g2numsis6 g2numsis7p`

Regression Results

SAS

Number of Observations Read	5472
Number of Observations Used	5472

Analysis of Variance

Source	DF	Sum of Squares	Mean Square	F Value	Pr > F
Model	7	109.96480	15.70926	2.70	0.0085
Error	5464	31761	5.81280		
Corrected Total	5471	31871			

Root MSE	2.41098	R-Square	0.0035
Dependent Mean	3.29182	Adj R-Sq	0.0022
Coeff Var	73.24148		

Parameter Estimates

Variable	DF	Parameter Estimate	Standard Error	t Value	Pr > |t|
Intercept	1	3.28466	0.05584	58.82	<.0001
g2numsis1	1	0.10992	0.08191	1.34	0.1797
g2numsis2	1	-0.04876	0.09454	-0.52	0.6060
g2numsis3	1	0.03772	0.12230	0.31	0.7578
g2numsis4	1	-0.18858	0.16384	-1.15	0.2498
g2numsis5	1	-0.45919	0.21950	-2.09	0.0365
g2numsis6	1	-0.58571	0.29153	-2.01	0.0446
g2numsis7p	1	0.71156	0.33281	2.14	0.0326

Stata

Source	SS	df	MS	
Model	109.964799	7	15.709257	Number of obs = 5472
Residual	31761.1625	5464	5.8128043	F(7, 5464) = 2.70
				Prob > F = 0.0085
Total	31871.1273	5471	5.82546652	R-squared = 0.0035
				Adj R-squared = 0.0022
				Root MSE = 2.411

logg1miles	Coef.	Std. Err.	t	P>|t|	[95% Conf. Interval]
g2numsis1	.109918	.0819074	1.34	0.180	-.0506532 .2704891
g2numsis2	-.0487583	.0945361	-0.52	0.606	-.2340868 .1365702
g2numsis3	.0377221	.1222995	0.31	0.758	-.2020336 .2774778
g2numsis4	-.188578	.163842	-1.15	0.250	-.5097735 .1326175
g2numsis5	-.4591877	.2194971	-2.09	0.036	-.8894893 -.028886
g2numsis6	-.5857075	.2915286	-2.01	0.045	-1.15722 -.0141953
g2numsis7p	.7115629	.328107	2.14	0.033	.0591213 1.364004
_cons	3.284659	.0558431	58.82	0.000	3.175184 3.394134

Display B.12.5 Using a Dummy Variable Specification for Number of Sisters, Collapsed Model

	SAS	Stata
Create Variables	`g2numsis56 =g2numsis=5	g2numsis=6;`	`gen g2numsis56=g2numsis==5	g2numsis==6`

Estimate Regression	`proc reg data=nonlinear;`
	`model logg1miles=g2numsis4 g2numsis56`
	`   g2numsis7p;`
	`run;`
	
	`test g2numsis4=g2numsis56;`
	`test g2numsis4=g2numsis7p;`
	`test g2numsis56=g2numsis7p;`
	`run;`
		`regress logg1miles g2numsis4 g2numsis56 g2numsis7p`
		`test g2numsis4=g2numsis56`
		`test g2numsis4=g2numsis7p`
		`test g2numsis56=g2numsis7p`

SAS Regression Results:

Parameter Estimates

Variable	DF	Parameter Estimate	Standard Error	t Value	Pr>|t|
Intercept	1	3.31437	0.03419	96.95	<.0001
g2numsis4	1	-0.21829	0.15777	-1.38	0.1665
g2numsis56	1	-0.53382	0.17386	-3.07	0.0021
g2numsis7p	1	0.68185	0.32985	2.07	0.0388

Test 1 Results for Dependent Variable logg1miles

Source	DF	Mean Square	F Value	Pr > F
Numerator	1	10.96229	1.89	0.1697
Denominator	5468	5.81202		

Test 2 Results for Dependent Variable logg1miles

Source	DF	Mean Square	F Value	Pr > F
Numerator	1	35.85169	6.17	0.0130
Denominator	5468	5.81202		

Test 3 Results for Dependent Variable logg1miles

Source	DF	Mean Square	F Value	Pr > F
Numerator	1	162.83736	10.81	0.0010
Denominator	5468	5.81202		

Stata Regression Results:

```
      Source |       SS       df       MS              Number of obs =    5472
-------------+------------------------------           F(  3,  5468) =    5.22
       Model | 90.9882392      3   30.3294131          Prob > F      =  0.0013
    Residual | 31780.1391   5468   5.81202251          R-squared     =  0.0029
-------------+------------------------------           Adj R-squared =  0.0023
       Total | 31871.1273   5471   5.82546652          Root MSE      =  2.4108

  logg1miles |      Coef.   Std. Err.      t    P>|t|     [95% Conf. Interval]
-------------+----------------------------------------------------------------
   g2numsis4 |  -.2182923   .1577696    -1.38   0.167    -.5275836    .0909989
  g2numsis56 |  -.5338165   .1738644    -3.07   0.002    -.8746599   -.1929731
  g2numsis7p |   .6818486   .3298466     2.07   0.039     .0352181    1.328479
       _cons |   3.314373   .0341865    96.95   0.000     3.247354    3.381392

. test g2numsis4=g2numsis56

 (1)  g2numsis4 - g2numsis56 = 0

       F(  1,  5468) =    1.89
            Prob > F =    0.1697

. test g2numsis4=g2numsis7p

 (1)  g2numsis4 - g2numsis7p = 0

       F(  1,  5468) =    6.17
            Prob > F =    0.0130

. test g2numsis56=g2numsis7p

 (1)  g2numsis56 - g2numsis7p = 0

       F(  1,  5468) =   10.81
            Prob > F =    0.0010
```

Display B.13.1 Regression of Mens' Hours of Work on their Self-Reported Health, with and without Controls for Age

	SAS	Stata

Commands	`proc reg;`
	`  model hrwork=Health;`
	`  model hrwork=Health g2age;`
	`run;`
		`regress hrwork Health`
		`regress hrwork Health g2age`

Results (Model 1)

SAS — Parameter Estimates

Variable	DF	Parameter Estimate	Standard Error	t Value	Pr > |t|
Intercept	1	37.86048	1.28924	29.37	<.0001
Health	1	1.14351	0.30536	3.74	0.0002

Stata

```
Source |       SS       df       MS              Number of obs =    3742
-------+------------------------------           F( 1, 3740)   =   14.02
 Model | 2833.01506      1  2833.01506           Prob > F      =  0.0002
Residual|755569.781   3740 202.024006            R-squared     =  0.0037
-------+------------------------------           Adj R-squared =  0.0035
 Total |758402.796   3741 202.727291             Root MSE      =   14.214

 hrwork |    Coef.   Std. Err.     t    P>|t|    [95% Conf. Interval]
--------+------------------------------------------------------------
 Health | 1.143507   .3053625    3.74  0.000    .548133    1.7422
  _cons | 37.86048   1.289238   29.37  0.000    35.3328   40.38816
```

Results (Model 2)

SAS — Parameter Estimates

Variable	DF	Parameter Estimate	Standard Error	t Value	Pr > |t|
Intercept	1	42.26619	1.51318	27.93	<.0001
Health	1	1.01681	0.30504	3.33	0.0009
g2age	1	-0.10497	0.01907	-5.50	<.0001

Stata

```
Source |       SS       df       MS              Number of obs =    3742
-------+------------------------------           F( 2, 3739)   =   22.22
 Model | 8907.66109      2  4453.83055           Prob > F      =  0.0000
Residual|749495.135   3739 200.453366            R-squared     =  0.0117
-------+------------------------------           Adj R-squared =  0.0112
 Total |758402.796   3741 202.727291             Root MSE      =   14.158

 hrwork |    Coef.   Std. Err.     t    P>|t|    [95% Conf. Interval]
--------+------------------------------------------------------------
 Health | 1.016814   .3050426    3.33  0.001    .418475    1.61488
  g2age | -.104973   .0190688   -5.50  0.000   -.1423593  -.0675867
  _cons | 42.26619   1.513182   27.93  0.000    39.29944   45.23293
```

■ Display B.13.2 Regression Models Used in Estimating Indirect and Direct Effects of Men's Health on their Hours of Work, with Mediation through Health Limitations

Commands

SAS

```
proc reg;
    model hrwork=Health;
    model hrwork=Health HlthLimit;
    model HlthLimit=Health;
run;
```

Stata

```
regress hrwork Health
regress hrwork Health HlthLimit
regress HlthLimit Health
```

Results — Model 1

SAS

Parameter Estimates

Variable	DF	Parameter Estimate	Standard Error	t Value	Pr > |t|
Intercept	1	37.86048	1.28924	29.37	<0001
Health	1	1.14351	0.30536	3.74	0.0002

Stata

Source	SS	df	MS
Model	2833.01506	1	2833.01506
Residual	755569.781	3740	202.024006
Total	758402.796	3741	202.727291

Number of obs = 3742
F(1, 3740) = 14.02
Prob > F = 0.0002
R-squared = 0.0037
Adj R-squared = 0.0035
Root MSE = 14.214

hrwork	Coef.	Std. Err.	t	P>|t|	[95% Conf. Interval]
Health	1.143507	.3053625	3.74	0.000	.548133 1.7422
_cons	37.86048	1.289238	29.37	0.000	35.3328 40.38816

Results — Model 2

SAS

Parameter Estimates

Variable	DF	Parameter Estimate	Standard Error	t Value	Pr > |t|
Intercept	1	38.52018	1.31985	29.19	<0001
Health	1	1.00813	0.31078	3.24	0.0012
HlthLimit	1	-5.65588	2.45198	-2.31	0.0211

Stata

Source	SS	df	MS
Model	3906.67985	2	1953.33993
Residual	754496.117	3739	201.790884
Total	758402.796	3741	202.727291

Number of obs = 3742
F(2, 3739) = 9.68
Prob > F = 0.0001
R-squared = 0.0052
Adj R-squared = 0.0046
Root MSE = 14.205

hrwork	Coef.	Std. Err.	t	P>|t|	[95% Conf. Interval]
Health	1.008126	.3107785	3.24	0.001	.3988139 1.617438
HlthLimit	-5.655881	.451979	-2.31	0.021	-10.46323 -.848535
_cons	38.52018	1.319854	29.19	0.000	35.93248 41.10789

Results — Model 3

SAS

Parameter Estimates

Variable	DF	Parameter Estimate	Standard Error	t Value	Pr > |t|
Intercept	1	0.11664	0.00859	13.57	<0001
Health	1	-0.02394	0.00204	-11.76	<0001

Stata

Source	SS	df	MS
Model	1.24132056	1	1.24132056
Residual	33.5635748	3740	.008974218
Total	34.8048953	3741	.009303634

Number of obs = 3742
F(1, 3740) = 138.32
Prob > F = 0.0000
R-squared = 0.0357
Adj R-squared = 0.0354
Root MSE = .09473

HlthLimit	Coef.	Std. Err.	t	P>|t|	[95% Conf. Interval]
Health	-.0239363	.0020352	-11.76	0.000	-.0279265 -.019946
_cons	.1166407	.0085927	13.57	0.000	.0997938 .1334875

Display B.13.3 Understanding Controlling for with Regression on Residuals for X_3

	SAS	Stata
| Commands | ```
proc reg data=HoursOfChoresMediate;
  model Health=HlthLimit;
  output out=prede2i (keep=hrwork e2i)
    r=e2i;
run;

proc reg data=prede2i;
  model hrwork=e2i;
run;
``` | ```
regress Health HlthLimit
predict e2i, residuals
regress hrwork e2i
``` |

Stata Results (first):

```
      Source |       SS       df       MS              Number of obs =    3742
                                                        F( 1,  3740)  =   10.50
       Model |  2123.38643      1   2123.38643          Prob > F      =  0.0012
    Residual |   756279.41   3740  202.213746           R-squared     =  0.0028
                                                         Adj R-squared =  0.0025
       Total |  758402.796   3741  202.727291           Root MSE      =   14.22

      hrwork |      Coef.   Std. Err.      t    P>|t|     [95% Conf. Interval]
         e2i |   1.008126    .311104     3.24   0.001     .3981759   1.618076
       _cons |    42.6093   .2324628   183.30   0.000     42.15353   43.06507
```

SAS Results (first):

		Parameter Estimates			
Variable	DF	Parameter Estimate	Standard Error	t Value	Pr>|t|
Intercept	1	42.60930	0.23246	183.30	<.0001
e2i	1	1.00813	0.31110	3.24	0.0012

	SAS	Stata
| Commands | ```
proc reg;
  model HlthLimit=Health;
  output out=prede3i (keep=hrwork e3i)
    r=e3i;
run;

proc reg data=prede3i;
  model hrwork=e3i;
run;
``` | ```
regress HlthLimit Health
predict e3i, residuals
regress hrwork e3i
``` |

Stata Results (second):

```
      Source |       SS       df       MS              Number of obs =    3742
                                                        F( 1,  3740)  =    5.30
       Model |  1073.66477      1   1073.66477          Prob > F      =  0.0214
    Residual |  757329.132   3740   202.49442           R-squared     =  0.0014
                                                         Adj R-squared =  0.0011
       Total |  758402.796   3741  202.727291           Root MSE      =   14.23

      hrwork |      Coef.   Std. Err.      t    P>|t|     [95% Conf. Interval]
         e3i |  -5.655881   2.456249    -2.30   0.021     -10.4716  -.8401623
       _cons |    42.6093   .2326241   183.17   0.000     42.15322   43.06538
```

SAS Results (second):

		Parameter Estimates			
Variable	DF	Parameter Estimate	Standard Error	t Value	Pr>|t|
Intercept	1	42.60930	0.23262	183.17	<.0001
e3i	1	-5.65588	2.45625	-2.30	0.0214

APPENDIX B

APPENDIX B

Display B.14.1 Calculating Diagnostic Values

SAS

Request Diagnostics

```
proc reg data=miles;
model logg1miles=g1yrschl sqg1yrschl g2numsis4
      g2numsis56 g2numsis7p amind
      mexamer white other female
      g2earn10000 g1age g2age g2numbro
      /r infiuence;
ods output outputstatistics=infiuence;
run;
```

Use Cutoffs to Identify High Values

```
data influence2;
set influence;
HatDiagonal3Hi =HatDiagonal>3*14/5472;
RStudentHi=     abs(RStudent)>2;
CooksDHi=       CooksD>4/5472;
DFFITSHi= abs(DFFITS)>2*sqrt(14/5472);
DFB_g1yrschlHi = abs(DFB_g1yrschl)>2/sqrt(5472);
DFB_sqg1yrschlHi= abs(DFB_sqg1yrschl)>2/sqrt(5472);
DFB_g2numsis4Hi= abs(DFB_g2numsis4)>2/sqrt(5472);
DFB_g2numsis56Hi= abs(DFB_g2numsis56)>2/sqrt(5472);
DFB_g2numsis7pHi= abs(DFB_g2numsis7p)>2/sqrt(5472);
run;
```

Sum High Values

```
proc means data=influence2;
var HatDiagonal3Hi RStudentHi CooksDHi
    DFFITSHi DFB_g1yrschlHi DFB_sqg1yrschlHi
    DFB_g2numsis4Hi DFB_g2numsis56Hi
    DFB_g2numsis7pHi;
run;
```

Variable	N	Mean	Std Dev	Minimum	Maximum
HatDiagonal3Hi	5472	0.0575658	0.2329418	0	1.0000000
RStudentHi	5472	0.0135234	0.1155117	0	1.0000000
CooksDHi	5472	0.0467836	0.2111944	0	1.0000000
DFFITSHi	5472	0.0506213	0.192433	0	1.0000000
DFB_g1yrschlHi	5472	0.0383772	0.1921227	0	1.0000000
DFB_sqg1yrschlHi	5472	0.0498904	0.2177383	0	1.0000000
DFB_g2numsis4Hi	5472	0.0314327	0.1745001	0	1.0000000
DFB_g2numsis56Hi	5472	0.0279605	0.1648748	0	1.0000000
DFB_g2numsis7pHi	5472	0.0098684	0.0988576	0	1.0000000

Stata

Request Diagnostics

```
regress logg1miles g1yrschl sqg1yrschl g2numsis4
        g2numsis56 g2numsis7p amind
        mexamer white other female
        g2earn10000 g1age g2age
        g2numbro

predict HatDiagonal, hat
predict RStudent, rstudent
predict CooksD, cooksd
predict DFFITS, dfits
predict DFB_g1yrschl, dfbeta(g1yrschl)
predict DFB_sqg1yrschl, dfbeta(sqg1yrschl)
predict DFB_g2numsis4, dfbeta(g2numsis4)
predict DFB_g2numsis56, dfbeta(g2numsis56)
predict DFB_g2numsis7p, dfbeta(g2numsis7p)
```

Use Cutoffs to Identify High Values

```
generate HatDiagonal3Hi    =HatDiagonal>3*14/5472
generate RStudentHi        =abs(RStudent)>2
generate CooksDHi          =CooksD>4/5472
generate DFFITSHi          =abs(DFFITS)>2*sqrt(14/5472)
generate DFB_g1yrschlHi    =abs(DFB_g1yrschl)>2/sqrt(5472)
generate DFB_sqg1yrschlHi  =abs(DFB_sqg1yrschl)>2/sqrt(5472)
generate DFB_g2numsis4Hi   =abs(DFB_g2numsis4)>2/sqrt(5472)
generate DFB_g2numsis56Hi  =abs(DFB_g2numsis56)>2/sqrt(5472)
generate DFB_g2numsis7pHi  =abs(DFB_g2numsis7p)>2/sqrt(5472)
```

Sum High Values

```
summarize HatDiagonal3Hi RStudentHi CooksDHi DFFITSHi
          DFB_g1yrschlHi DFB_sqg1yrschlHi DFB_g2numsis4Hi
          DFB_g2numsis56Hi DFB_g2numsis7pHi
```

Variable	Obs	Mean	Std. Dev.	Min	Max
HatDiagona~i	5472	.0575658	.2329418	0	1
RStudentHi	5472	.0135234	.1155117	0	1
CooksDHi	5472	.0467836	.2111944	0	1
DFFITSHi	5472	.0506213	.219243	0	1
DFB_g1yrsc~i	5472	.0383772	.1921227	0	1
DFB_sqg1yr~i	5472	.0498904	.2177383	0	1
DFB_g2nu~4Hi	5472	.0314327	.1745001	0	1
DFB_g2nu~6Hi	5472	.0279605	.1648748	0	1
DFB_g2nu~pHi	5472	.0098684	.0988576	0	1

■ Display B.14.2 Summary Statistics by *anyhi*

SAS

Commands

```
data influence3;
  merge miles influence2;
run;
proc sort data=influence3; by anyhi; run;
proc means data=influence3;
  var g1yrschl sqg1yrschl g2numsis4 g2numsis56
      g2numsis7p amind mexamer white other
      female g2earn10000 g1age g2age g2numbro;
  by anyhi;
run;
```

Results

anyhi=0

Variable	N	Mean	Std Dev	Minimum	Maximum
g1yrschl	4694	11.6516830	2.4922425	3.0000000	17.0000000
sqg1yrschl	4694	141.9716660	56.9249794	9.0000000	289.0000000
g2numsis4	4694	0.0132084	0.1141782	0	1.0000000
g2numsis56	4694	0.0085215	0.0919277	0	1.0000000
g2numsis7p	4694	0	0	0	0
amind	4694	0	0	0	0
mexamer	4694	0.0102258	0.1006152	0	1.0000000
white	4694	0.8596080	0.3474303	0	1.0000000
other	4694	0	0	0	0
female	4694	0.5988496	0.4901836	0	1.0000000
g2earn10000	4694	3.0421728	2.9186966	0	25.1610274
g1age	4694	59.9443971	11.1694472	29.0000000	95.0000000
g2age	4694	34.2645931	9.9245113	16.0000000	76.0000000
g2numbro	4694	1.3046442	1.3951270	0	9.0000000

anyhi=1

Variable	N	Mean	Std Dev	Minimum	Maximum
g1yrschl	778	9.8856041	4.5470257	0	17.0000000
sqg1yrschl	778	118.3740360	85.1018177	0	289.0000000
g2numsis4	778	0.2352185	0.4244082	0	1.0000000
g2numsis56	778	0.2056555	0.4044398	0	1.0000000
g2numsis7p	778	0.0694087	0.2543114	0	1.0000000
amind	778	0.0321337	0.1764685	0	1.0000000
mexamer	778	0.1516710	0.3589324	0	1.0000000
white	778	0.5102828	0.5002158	0	1.0000000
other	778	0.0912596	0.2881632	0	1.0000000
female	778	0.6272494	0.4838476	0	1.0000000
g2earn10000	778	3.2419257	6.8925063	0	94.5903285
g1age	778	60.9511568	12.0444342	30.0000000	95.0000000
g2age	778	34.4704370	10.5143048	17.0000000	73.0000000
g2numbro	778	2.2095116	2.1941919	0	19.0000000

Stata

Commands

```
bysort anyhi: summarize g1yrschl sqg1yrschl
                        g2numsis4 g2numsis56
                        g2numsis7p amind
                        mexamer white other
                        female g2earn10000 g1age
                        g2age g2numbro
```

Results

-> anyhi = 0

Variable	Obs	Mean	Std. Dev.	Min	Max
g1yrschl	4694	11.65168	2.492242	3	17
sqg1yrschl	4694	141.9717	56.92498	9	289
g2numsis4	4694	.0132084	.1141782	0	1
g2numsis56	4694	.0085215	.0919277	0	1
g2numsis7p	4694	0	0	0	0
amind	4694	0	0	0	0
mexamer	4694	.0102258	.1006152	0	1
white	4694	.859608	.3474303	0	1
other	4694	0	0	0	0
female	4694	.5988496	.4901836	0	1
g2earn10000	4694	3.042173	2.918697	0	25.16103
g1age	4694	59.9444	11.16945	29	95
g2age	4694	34.26459	9.924511	16	76
g2numbro	4694	1.304644	1.395127	0	9

-> anyhi = 1

Variable	Obs	Mean	Std. Dev.	Min	Max
g1yrschl	778	9.885604	4.547026	0	17
sqg1yrschl	778	118.374	85.10182	0	289
g2numsis4	778	.2352185	.4244082	0	1
g2numsis56	778	.2056555	.4044398	0	1
g2numsis7p	778	.0694087	.2543114	0	1
amind	778	.0321337	.1764685	0	1
mexamer	778	.151671	.3589324	0	1
white	778	.5102828	.5002158	0	1
other	778	.0912596	.2881632	0	1
female	778	.6272494	.4838476	0	1
g2earn10000	778	3.241926	6.892506	0	94.59033
g1age	778	60.95116	12.04443	30	95
g2age	778	34.47044	10.5143	17	73
g2numbro	778	2.209512	2.194192	0	19

Display B.14.3 Multiple Regression on Full Sample

Commands

SAS

```
proc reg data=miles;
  model logg1miles=g1yrschl sqg1yrschl
    g2numsis4 g2numsis56
    g2numsis7p amind
    mexamer white other
    female g2earn10000
    g1age g2age g2numbro;
run;
```

Stata

```
regress logg1miles g1yrschl sqg1yrschl g2numsis4
    g2numsis56 g2numsis7p
    amind mexamer white other
    female g2earn10000
    g1age g2age g2numbro
```

Results

SAS

Parameter Estimates

Variable	DF	Parameter Estimate	Standard Error	t Value	Pr > |t|
Intercept	1	1.11740	0.36508	3.06	0.0022
g1yrschl	1	-0.04726	0.04877	-0.97	0.3326
sqg1yrschl	1	0.00822	0.00225	3.66	0.0003
g2numsis4	1	-0.02737	0.15664	-0.17	0.8613
g2numsis56	1	-0.27900	0.17650	-1.58	0.1140
g2numsis7p	1	0.98506	0.32826	3.00	0.0027
amind	1	1.14527	0.47983	2.39	0.0170
mexamer	1	-0.14627	0.21035	-0.70	0.4868
white	1	0.41083	0.09437	4.35	<.0001
other	1	0.96906	0.29356	3.30	0.0010
female	1	-0.07250	0.06968	-1.04	0.2982
g2earn10000	1	0.03740	0.00932	4.01	<.0001
g1age	1	0.01005	0.00539	1.87	0.0621
g2age	1	0.01442	0.00612	2.35	0.0186
g2numbro	1	0.04218	0.02152	1.96	0.0500

Stata

Source	SS	df	MS
Model	1530.79748	14	109.342677
Residual	30340.3298	5457	5.55989185
Total	31871.1273	5471	5.82546652

Number of obs = 5472
$F(14, 5457)$ = 19.67
Prob > F = 0.0000
R-squared = 0.0480
Adj R-squared = 0.0456
Root MSE = 2.3579

logg1miles	Coef.	Std. Err.	t	P>|t|	[95% Conf. Interval]	
g1yrschl	-.0472574	.048767	-0.97	0.333	-.1428602	.0483454
sqg1yrschl	.0082153	.0022461	3.66	0.000	.003812	.0126187
g2numsis4	-.0273686	.156636	-0.17	0.861	-.334377	.2797005
g2numsis56	-.279005	.1765034	-1.58	0.114	-.625022	.0670121
g2numsis7p	.985055	.3282596	3.00	0.003	.3415353	1.628575
amind	1.145266	.47983	2.39	0.017	.2046076	2.085924
mexamer	-.1462737	.2103489	-0.70	0.487	-.5586414	.266094
white	.4108335	.0943698	4.35	0.000	.225831	.5958359
other	.9690582	.293564	3.30	0.001	.3935557	1.54561
female	-.0724955	.0696832	-1.04	0.298	-.2091024	.0641113
g2earn10000	.0374032	.0093177	4.01	0.000	.0191369	.0556696
g1age	.0100507	.0053863	1.87	0.062	-.0005086	.0206099
g2age	.0144181	.0061237	2.35	0.019	.0024131	.026423
g2numbro	.0421847	.0215228	1.96	0.050	-8.53e-06	.0843779
_cons	1.117402	.365079	3.06	0.002	.4017015	1.833102

Display B.14.4 Multiple Regression on Partial Sample (with Outliers and Influential Observations Excluded)

Commands	
``` proc reg data=infiuence3; model logg1miles=g1yrschl sqg1yrschl g2numsis4 g2numsis56 mexamer white female g2earn10000 g1age g2age g2numbro; by anyhi; run; ```	``` bysort anyhi: regress logg1miles g1yrschl sqg1yrschl /// g2numsis4 g2numsis56 /// mexamer white female g2earn10000 /// g1age g2age g2numbro ```

Results

anyhi=0

Parameter Estimates

Variable	DF	Parameter Estimate	Standard Error	t Value	Pr > |t|
Intercept	1	0.08020	0.53581	0.15	0.8810
g1yrschl	1	-0.01033	0.08020	-0.13	0.8975
sqg1yrschl	1	0.00783	0.00348	2.25	0.0245
g2numsis4	1	-0.07464	0.28542	-0.26	0.7937
g2numsis56	1	-0.32919	0.35814	-0.92	0.3580
mexamer	1	-0.46111	0.33773	-1.37	0.1722
white	1	0.59151	0.09860	6.00	<.0001
female	1	0.02331	0.07320	0.32	0.7502
g2earn10000	1	0.07116	0.01265	5.63	<.0001
g1age	1	0.01328	0.00572	2.32	0.0202
g2age	1	0.01640	0.00644	2.55	0.0110
g2numbro	1	0.05895	0.02381	2.48	0.0133

-> anyhi = 0

Source	SS	df	MS		
Model	1807.83975	11	164.349068		
Residual	23144.4657	4682	4.94328615		
Total	24952.3055	4693	5.31691999		

Number of obs = 4694
F(11, 4682) = 33.25
Prob > F = 0.0000
R-squared = 0.0725
Adj R-squared = 0.0703
Root MSE = 2.2234

logg1miles	Coef.	Std. Err.	t	P>|t|	[95% Conf.	Interval]
g1yrschl	-.0103337	.080199	-0.13	0.897	-.1675614	.1468941
sqg1yrschl	.0078314	.0034796	2.25	0.024	.0010096	.0146531
g2numsis4	-.0746374	.2854243	-0.26	0.794	-.6342034	.4849286
g2numsis56	-.3291949	.3581387	-0.92	0.358	-1.031315	.3729254
mexamer	-.461109	.3377253	-1.37	0.172	-1.12321	.2009917
white	.5915109	.0985972	6.00	0.000	.398214	.7848078
female	.0233067	.0731999	0.32	0.750	-.1201995	.166813
g2earn10000	.0711568	.012648	5.63	0.000	.0463607	.0959528
g1age	.0132813	.0057172	2.32	0.020	.0020728	.0244897
g2age	.0164005	.0064434	2.55	0.011	.0037683	.0290326
g2numbro	.0589484	.0238129	2.48	0.013	.012264	.1056328
_cons	.0802039	.5358109	0.15	0.881	-.9702378	1.130646

■ Display B.14.5 Multiple Regression for Full Sample with Heteroskedasticity-Consistent Standard Errors (HC3)

Commands

SAS

```
proc reg;
  model logg1miles=g1yrschl sqg1yrschl g2numsis4
    g2numsis56 g2numsis7p amind mexamer white other
    female g2earn10000 g1age g2age g2numbro
    /hcc hccmethod=3;
run;
```

Stata

```
regress logg1miles g1yrschl sqg1yrschl g2numsis4
  g2numsis56 g2numsis7p amind mexamer white other
  female g2earn10000 g1age g2age g2numbro
  , vce(hc3)
```

Select Results

SAS

Parameter Estimates

Variable	DF	Parameter Estimates	Standard Error	t value	Pr > |t|	Heteroscedasticity Consistent Standard Error	Heteroscedasticity Consistent t value	Heteroscedasticity Consistent Pr > |t|
Intercept	1	1.11740	0.36508	3.06	0.0022	0.38286	2.92	0.0035
g1yrschl	1	−0.04726	0.04877	−0.97	0.3326	0.05220	−0.91	0.3653
sqg1yrschl	1	0.00822	0.00225	3.66	0.0003	0.00239	3.44	0.0006
g2numsis4	1	−0.02737	0.15664	−0.17	0.8613	0.15556	−0.18	0.8604
g2numsis56	1	−0.27900	0.17650	−1.58	0.1140	0.18432	−1.51	0.1302
g2numsis7p	1	0.98506	0.32826	3.00	0.0027	0.36850	2.67	0.0075
amind	1	1.14527	0.47983	2.39	0.0170	0.40449	2.83	0.0047
mexamer	1	−0.14627	0.21035	−0.70	0.4868	0.20479	−0.71	0.4751
white	1	0.41083	0.09437	4.35	<.0001	0.09484	4.33	<.0001
other	1	0.96906	0.29356	3.30	0.0010	0.32057	3.02	0.0025
female	1	−0.07250	0.06968	−1.04	0.2982	0.07214	−1.00	0.3150
g2earn10000	1	0.03740	0.00932	4.01	<.0001	0.01183	3.16	0.0016
g1age	1	0.01005	0.00539	1.87	0.0621	0.00537	1.87	0.0612
g2age	1	0.01442	0.00612	2.35	0.0186	0.00607	2.38	0.0176
g2numbro	1	0.04218	0.02152	1.96	0.0500	0.02134	1.98	0.0481

HCC Approximation Method: HC3

Stata

Linear regression

```
                                    Number of obs =   5472
                                    F( 14, 5457) =    19.55
                                    Prob > F      =   0.0000
                                    R-squared     =   0.0480
                                    Root MSE      =   2.3579
```

		Robust HC3				
logg1miles	Coef.	Std. Err.	t	P>|t|	[95% Conf.	Interval]
g1yrschl	−.0472574	.052199	−0.91	0.365	−.1495883	.0550735
sqg1yrschl	.0082153	.0023876	3.44	0.001	.0035348	.0128959
g2numsis4	−.0273686	.155564	−0.18	0.860	−.332336	.2775989
g2numsis56	−.279005	.1843165	−1.51	0.130	−.6403388	.0823289
g2numsis7p	.985055	.3685039	2.67	0.008	.2626404	1.70747
amind	1.145266	.4044861	2.83	0.005	.3523117	1.93822
mexamer	−.1462737	.2047908	−0.71	0.475	−.5477454	.2551979
white	.4108335	.0948416	4.33	0.000	.2249061	.5967608
other	.9690582	.3205739	3.02	0.003	.3406054	1.597511
female	−.0724955	.0721381	−1.00	0.315	−.213915	.0689239
g2earn10000	.0374032	.0118305	3.16	0.002	.0142108	.0605957
g1age	.0100507	.0053679	1.87	0.061	−.0004725	.0205738
g2age	.0144181	.0060699	2.38	0.018	.0025186	.0263175
g2numbro	.0421847	.021343	1.98	0.048	.0003438	.0840256
_cons	1.117402	.382864	2.92	0.004	.3668358	1.867968

Display B.14.6 Calculation of Variance Inflation Factors in *Hypothetical Data Set*

SAS

Commands

```
proc reg; model yrsch1=higrade7 impsch17 /vif;
run;
proc reg; model higrade7=impsch17; run;
```

Results

Analysis of Variance

Variable	DF	Sum of Squares	Mean Square	F Value	Pr > F
Model	2	34.68852	17.34276	9.66	<.0001
Error	997	1790.51348	1.79590		
Corrected Total	999	1825.19900			

Parameter Estimates

Variable	DF	Parameter Estimate	Standard Error	t Value	Pr > |t|	Variance Inflation
Intercept	1	8.25317	0.64637	12.77	<.0001	0
higrade7	1	-0.48197	0.43731	-1.10	0.2707	105.88741
impsch17	1	6.56431	4.34626	1.51	0.1313	105.88741

Results

Root MSE	0.09700	R-Square	0.9906
Dependent Mean	15.17502	Adj R-Sq	0.9905
Coeff Var	0.63922		

Parameter Estimates

Variable	DF	Parameter Estimate	Standard Error	t Value	Pr > |t|
Intercept	1	0.16405	0.04650	3.53	0.0004
impsch17	1	9.89148	0.03057	323.54	<.0001

Stata

Commands

```
regress yrsch1 higrade7 impsch17
estat vif
regress higrade7 impsch17
```

Results

```
      Source |       SS       df       MS              Number of obs =    1000
-------------+------------------------------           F( 2,   997) =    9.66
       Model |  34.6855227     2  17.3427614           Prob > F      =  0.0001
    Residual |  1790.51348   997  1.79590118           R-squared     =  0.0190
-------------+------------------------------           Adj R-squared =  0.0170
       Total |  1825.199     999  1.82702603           Root MSE      =  1.3401

      yrsch1 |      Coef.   Std. Err.      t    P>|t|     [95% Conf. Interval]
-------------+----------------------------------------------------------------
    higrade7 |  -.4819722   .4373145    -1.10   0.271    -1.340135    .3761902
    impsch17 |   6.564307   4.346258     1.51   0.131    -1.964557    15.09317
       _cons |   8.253167   .6463679    12.77   0.000     6.984769    9.521565

    Variable |       VIF       1/VIF
-------------+----------------------
    higrade7 |    105.89    0.009444
    impsch17 |    105.89    0.009444
-------------+----------------------
    Mean VIF |    105.89

      Source |       SS       df       MS              Number of obs =    1000
-------------+------------------------------           F( 1,   998) =
       Model |  984.958958     1  984.958958           Prob > F      =  0.0000
    Residual |  9.39063078   999  .00940945            R-squared     =  0.9906
-------------+------------------------------           Adj R-squared =  0.9905
       Total |  994.3495589   999  .995344934          Root MSE      =  .097

    higrade7 |      Coef.   Std. Err.      t    P>|t|     [95% Conf. Interval]
-------------+----------------------------------------------------------------
    impsch17 |   9.891479   .0305727   323.54   0.000     9.831484    9.951473
       _cons |   .164046    .0464975     3.53   0.000     .0728021    .25529
```

■ Display B.14.7 Bivariate Regression of Years of Schooling and Educational Expectations in *Hypothetical Data Set*

	SAS	Stata
Commands	`proc reg; model yrsch1=higrade7; run;` `proc reg; model yrsch1=impsch17; run;`	`regress yrsch1 higrade7` `regress yrsch1 impsch17`

Results

Stata (first model)

Source	SS	df	MS		
Model	30.5888705	1	30.5888705	Number of obs =	1000
Residual	1794.61013	998	1.79820654	F(1, 998) =	17.01
				Prob > F =	0.0000
				R-squared =	0.0168
Total	1825.199	999	1.82702603	Adj R-squared =	0.0158
				Root MSE =	1.341

yrsch1	Coef.	Std. Err.	t	P>|t|	[95% Conf. Interval]
higrade7	.175393	.0425256	4.12	0.000	.0919432 .2588428
_cons	8.239408	.6467184	12.74	0.000	6.970324 9.508492

Stata (second model)

Source	SS	df	MS		
Model	32.5041055	1	32.5041055	Number of obs =	1000
Residual	1792.69489	998	1.79628747	F(1, 998) =	18.10
				Prob > F =	0.0000
				R-squared =	0.0178
Total	1825.199	999	1.82702603	Adj R-squared =	0.0168
				Root MSE =	1.3403

yrsch1	Coef.	Std. Err.	t	P>|t|	[95% Conf. Interval]
impsch17	1.796889	.4224157	4.25	0.000	.9679642 2.625814
_cons	8.174101	.6424435	12.72	0.000	6.913406 9.43796

SAS (first model) — Parameter Estimates

Variable	DF	Parameter Estimate	Standard Error	t Value	Pr > |t|
Intercept	1	8.23941	0.64672	12.74	<.0001
higrade7	1	0.17539	0.04253	4.12	<.0001

SAS (second model) — Parameter Estimates

Variable	DF	Parameter Estimate	Standard Error	t Value	Pr > |t|
Intercept	1	8.17410	0.64244	12.72	<.0001
impsch17	1	1.79689	0.42242	4.25	<.0001

■ Display B.14.8 Variance Inflation Factors in NSFH Example

	SAS	Stata

Commands	```proc reg;```
	``` model hrwork=Health HlthLimit g2age /vif;```
	```run;```
		```regress hrwork Health HlthLimit g2age```
		```estat vif```

Results — SAS:

Parameter Estimates

Variable	DF	Parameter Estimate	Standard Error	t Value	Pr > |t|	Variance Inflation
Intercept	1	42.79665	1.53352	27.91	<.0001	0
Health	1	0.89608	0.31030	2.89	0.0039	1.04161
HlthLimit	1	-5.12471	2.44470	-2.10	0.0361	1.03865
g2age	1	-0.10337	0.01908	-5.42	<.0001	1.00734

Results — Stata:

```
      Source |       SS       df       MS              Number of obs =    3742
-------------+------------------------------           F(  3,  3738) =   16.29
       Model |  9787.71371     3  3262.57124           Prob > F      =  0.0000
    Residual |  748615.083  3738  200.271558           R-squared     =  0.0129
-------------+------------------------------           Adj R-squared =  0.0121
       Total |  758402.796  3741  202.727291           Root MSE      =  14.152

      hrwork |      Coef.   Std. Err.      t    P>|t|     [95% Conf. Interval]
-------------+----------------------------------------------------------------
      Health |   .8960821    .310296     2.89   0.004     .2877161    1.504448
   HlthLimit |  -5.124713   2.444696    -2.10   0.036    -9.917782   -.3316449
       g2age |  -.1033697   .0190755    -5.42   0.000    -.1407692   -.0659703
       _cons |   42.79665   1.533518    27.91   0.000     39.79003    45.80326

    estat vif

    Variable |      VIF       1/VIF
-------------+----------------------
      Health |      1.04    0.960053
   HlthLimit |      1.04    0.962785
       g2age |      1.01    0.992709
-------------+----------------------
    Mean VIF |      1.03
```

■ Display B.14.9 Results for Handcalculating Variance Inflation Factor for *g1age* in NSFH Example

	SAS	Stata

Commands	`proc reg;`
	`   model g2age=Health HlthLimit;`
	`run;`
		`regress g2age Health HlthLimit`

Stata Results

```
      Source |       SS          df       MS
-------------+---------------------------------
       Model | 4042.11187         2  2021.05593
    Residual | 550385.217      3739  147.201181
-------------+---------------------------------
       Total | 554427.329      3741  148.202975
```

```
Number of obs =    3742
F( 2, 3739)   =   13.73
Prob > F      =  0.0000
R-squared     =  0.0073
Adj R-squared =  0.0068
Root MSE      =  12.133
```

```
       g2age |    Coef.   Std. Err.      t    P>|t|   [95% Conf. Interval]
-------------+-------------------------------------------------------------------
      Health | -1.083913   .2654336   -4.08   0.000   -1.604322   -.5635043
   HlthLimit |  5.138519   2.094216    2.45   0.014    1.032602    9.244437
       _cons |  41.37054   1.127277   36.70   0.000    39.16041    43.58068
```

SAS Results

Root MSE	12.13265	R-Square	0.0073
Dependent Mean	36.95778	Adj R-Sq	0.0068
Coeff Var	32.82841		

Parameter Estimates

Variable	DF	Parameter Estimate	Standard Error	t Value	Pr > |t|
Intercept	1	41.37054	1.12728	36.70	<.0001
Health	1	-1.08391	0.26543	-4.08	<.0001
HlthLimit	1	5.13852	2.09422	2.45	0.0142

■ Display B.14.10. Multiple Regression on Full Sample, Accounting for the NSFH Complex Sampling Design

Commands

SAS

```
proc surveyreg rate="c:\nsfh_distance\SAS\rate";
    model logg1miles=g1yrschl sqg1yrschl g2numsis4
        g2numsis56 g2numsis7p amind mexamer white other
        female g2earn10000 g1age g2age g2numbro /clparm;
    domain DistanceSample;
    cluster PSU;
    strata StratumC;
    weight adjweight;
run;
```

Stata

```
svyset PSU [pw=adjweight], strata(Stratum) singleunit(certainty)

svy, subpop(DistanceSample): regress logg1miles
    g1yrschl sqg1yrschl g2numsis4 g2numsis56 g2numsis7p
    amind mexamer white other female g2earn10000
    g1age g2age g2numbro                          ///
                                                  ///
                                                  ///
```

Results

SAS

Estimated Regression Coefficients

Parameter	Estimate	Standard Error	t Value	Pr > |t|	95% Confidence Interval	
Intercept	1.3894284	0.36733285	3.78	0.0003	0.6562290	2.1226279
g1yrschl	-0.0586634	0.05136935	-1.14	0.2575	-0.1611971	0.0438702
sqg1yrschl	0.0090359	0.00216198	4.18	<.0001	0.0047205	0.0133512
g2numsis4	-0.1416901	0.16939711	-0.84	0.4059	-0.4798082	0.1964279
g2numsis56	-0.3891089	0.14424630	-2.70	0.0088	-0.6770257	-0.1011921
g2numsis7p	1.0285889	0.33156372	3.10	0.0028	0.3667850	1.6903929
amind	1.1714041	0.36710755	3.19	0.0022	0.4386544	1.9041539
mexamer	-0.1554789	0.18428438	-0.84	0.4018	-0.5233120	0.2123543
white	0.4198251	0.10311698	4.07	0.0001	0.2140027	0.6256475
other	1.2553111	0.26869038	4.67	<.0001	0.7190029	1.7916194
female	-0.0287472	0.06199953	-0.46	0.6444	-0.1524988	0.0950044
g2earn10000	0.0378061	0.00750545	5.04	<.0001	0.0228251	0.0527870
g1age	0.0086816	0.00516125	1.68	0.0972	-0.0016203	0.0189635
g2age	0.0114808	0.00613401	1.87	0.0656	-0.0007627	0.0237244
g2numbro	0.0626572	0.02085984	3.00	0.0037	0.0210208	0.1042937

Stata

Survey: Linear regression

Number of strata	=	68
Number of PSUs	=	100

Number of obs	=	13007
Population size	=	14247.64
Subpop. no. of obs	=	5472
Subpop. size	=	5472
Design df	=	32
F(14, 19)	=	41.50
Prob > F	=	0.0000
R-squared	=	0.0467

logg1miles	Coef.	Linearized Std. Err.	t	P>|t|	[95% Conf. Interval]	
g1yrschl	-.0586634	.0513146	-1.14	0.261	-.1631879	.0458611
sqg1yrschl	.0090359	.0021597	4.18	0.000	.0046367	.013435
g2numsis4	-.1416901	.1692167	-0.84	0.409	-.4863733	.202993
g2numsis56	-.3891089	.1440927	-2.70	0.011	-.6826161	-.0956017
g2numsis7p	1.028589	.3312106	3.11	0.004	.3539351	1.703243
amind	1.171404	.3667166	3.19	0.003	.424427	1.918381
mexamer	-.1554789	.1840881	-0.84	0.405	-.5304541	.2194964
white	.4198251	.1030072	4.08	0.000	.2100064	.6296438
other	1.255311	.2684042	4.68	0.000	.7085896	1.802033
female	-.0287472	.0619335	-0.46	0.646	-.1549016	.0974072
g2earn10000	.0378061	.0074975	5.04	0.000	.0225343	.0530779
g1age	.0086816	.0051558	1.68	0.102	-.0018203	.0191835
g2age	.0114808	.0061275	1.87	0.070	-.0010004	.0239621
g2numbro	.0626572	.0208376	3.01	0.005	.0202124	.1051021
_cons	1.389428	.3669416	3.79	0.001	.6419928	2.136864

Note: strata with single sampling unit treated as certainty units.

Display B.15.1 Regression of Distance from Mother On Respondent's Earnings using the Generalized Linear Model with Identity Link and Normal Distribution

	SAS	Stata
| Syntax | ```
proc genmod ;
  Model g1miles=g2earn / dist=normal link=identity;
run;
``` | ```
glm g1miles g2earn, family(normal) link(identity)
``` |

Stata output:

```
Iteration 0:     log likelihood = -49990.777

Generalized linear models                No. of obs      =      6350
Optimization     : ML                    Residual df     =      6348
                                         Scale parameter = 403351.9
Deviance        =  2560477708            (1/df) Deviance = 403351.9
Pearson         =  2560477708            (1/df) Pearson  = 403351.9

Variance function: V(u) = 1                          [Gaussian]
Link function    : g(u) = u                          [Identity]

                                         AIC             = 15.74576
Log likelihood   = -49990.77714          BIC             = 2.56e+09

                            OIM
g1miles |      Coef.   Std. Err.      z    P>|z|   [95% Conf. Interval]
g2earn  |   .0011333   .0002185     5.19   0.000   .0007051    .0015616
_cons   |   249.8116  10.27798     24.31   0.000   229.6671    269.956
```

SAS output:

Model Information

Data Set	WORK.GSSCH15
Distribution	Normal
Link Function	Identity
Dependent Variable	g1miles

Number of Observations Read	6350
Number of Observations Used	6350

Criteria For Assessing Goodness Of Fit

Criterion	DF	Value	Value/DF
Deviance	6348	2560477707.6	403351.8758
Scaled Deviance	6348	6350.0000	1.0003
Pearson Chi-Square	6348	2560477707.6	403351.8758
Scaled Pearson X2	6348	6350.0000	1.0003
Log Likelihood		-49990.7771	
Full Log Likelihood		-49990.7771	
AIC (smaller is better)		99987.5543	
AICC (smaller is better)		99987.5581	
BIC (smaller is better)		100007.8229	

Algorithm converged.

Analysis Of Maximum Likelihood Parameter Estimates

Parameter	DF	Estimate	Standard Error	Wald 95% Confidence Limits		Wald Chi-Square	Pr > ChiSq
Intercept	1	249.8116	10.2764	229.6703	269.9529	590.94	<.0001
g2earn	1	0.0011	0.0002	0.0007	0.0016	26.91	<.0001
Scale	1	634.9999	5.6347	624.0515	646.1403		

Note: The scale parameter was estimated by maximum likelihood.

Display B.15.2 Regression of Hours of Chores, Intercept Only Model, using the Generalized Linear Model with Identity Link and Normal Distribution

	SAS	Stata

Commands	`proc genmod;`
	`  model hrchores= / dist=normal link=identity;`
	`run;`
		`glm hrchores, family(normal) link(identity)`
		`estimates store reduced`

Stata — Results

```
Iteration 0:   log likelihood = -14749.997

Generalized linear models              No. of obs      =      3116
Optimization     : ML                  Residual df     =      3115
                                       Scale parameter =   757.261
Deviance         =   2358867.97        (1/df) Deviance =   757.261
Pearson          =   2358867.97        (1/df) Pearson  =   757.261

Variance function: V(u) = 1            [Gaussian]
Link function    : g(u) = u            [Identity]

                                       AIC             =  9.467906
Log likelihood   =   -14749.99739      BIC             =   2333810

             |              OIM
    hrchores |     Coef.   Std. Err.      z    P>|z|   [95% Conf. Interval]
-------------+----------------------------------------------------------------
       _cons |   34.4525   .4929741   69.89   0.000   33.48629   35.41871
```

SAS — Results

Model Information

Data Set	WORK.GSSCH15
Distribution	Normal
Link Function	Identity
Dependent Variable	hrchores

Number of Observations Read	3116
Number of Observations Used	3116

Criteria For Assessing Goodness Of Fit

Criterion	DF	Value	Value/DF
Deviance	3115	2358867.9705	757.2610
Scaled Deviance	3115	3116.0000	1.0003
Pearson Chi-Square	3115	2358867.9705	757.2610
Scaled Pearson X2	3115	3116.0000	1.0003
Log Likelihood		-14749.9974	
Full Log Likelihood		-14749.9974	
AIC (smaller is better)		29503.9948	
AICC (smaller is better)		29503.9986	
BIC (smaller is better)		29516.0834	

Algorithm converged.

Analysis Of Maximum Likelihood Parameter Estimates

Parameter	DF	Estimate	Standard Error	Wald 95% Confidence Limits		Wald Chi-Square	Pr > ChiSq
Intercept	1	34.4525	0.4929	33.4864	35.4186	4885.77	<.0001
Scale	1	27.5140	0.3485	26.8393	28.2056		

Notes: The scale parameter was estimated by maximum likelihood.

APPENDIX B

■ Display B.15.3 Regression of Hours of Chores on Number of Children and Hours of Work, using the Generalized Linear Model with Identity Link and Normal Distribution

SAS

Syntax

```
proc genmod;
  model hrchores=numkid hrwork / dist=normal link=identity;
  contrast "intercept only - LR" numkid 1, hrwork 1;
  contrast "intercept only - wald" numkid 1, hrwork 1 /wald;
run;
```

Results

Model Information

Data Set	WORK.GSSCH15
Distribution	Normal
Link Function	Identity
Dependent Variable	hrchores

Number of Observations Read	3116
Number of Observations Used	3116

Criteria For Assessing Goodness Of Fit

Criterion	DF	Value	Value/DF
Deviance	3113	2178880.9978	699.9296
Scaled Deviance	3113	3116.0000	1.0010
Pearson Chi-Square	3113	2178880.9978	699.9296
Scaled Pearson X2	3113	3116.0000	1.0010
Log Likelihood		-14626.3383	
Full Log Likelihood		-14626.3383	
AIC (smaller is better)		29260.6766	
AICC (smaller is better)		29260.6895	
BIC (smaller is better)		29284.8539	

Algorithm converged.

Analysis Of Maximum Likelihood Parameter Estimates

Parameter	DF	Estimate	Standard Error	Wald 95% Confidence Limits		Wald Chi-Square	Pr > ChiSq
Intercept	1	36.2437	1.3506	33.5965	38.8908	720.12	<.0001
Scale	1	6.1556	0.4339	5.3052	7.0059	201.30	<.0001
hrwork	1	-0.2104	0.0335	-0.2761	-0.1447	39.38	<.0001
Scale	1	26.4434	0.3350	25.7950	27.1082		

Note: The scale parameter was estimated by maximum likelihood.

Contrast Results

Contrast	DF	Chi-Square	Pr > ChiSq	Type
intercept only - LR	2	247.32	<.0001	LR
intercept only - Wald	2	257.40	<.0001	Wald

Stata

Syntax

```
glm hrchores numkid hrwork, family(normal) link(identity)
estimates store full

lrtest full reduced
test numkid hrwork
```

Results

```
Iteration 0:    log likelihood = -14626.338
```

Generalized linear models	No. of obs	=	3116
Optimization : ML	Residual df	=	3113
	scale parameter	=	699.9296
Deviance = 2178880.998	(1/df) Deviance	=	699.9296
Pearson = 2178880.998	(1/df) Pearson	=	699.9296

```
Variance function:  V(u) = 1              [Gaussian]
Link function    :  g(u) = u              [Identity]
```

		AIC	=	9.389819
Log likelihood = -14626.33832		BIC	=	2153839

hrchores	Coef.	OIM Std. Err.	z	P>|z|	[95% Conf. Interval]
numkid	6.155562	.4340641	14.18	0.000	5.304811 7.006312
hrwork	-.210403 3	.0335466	-6.27	0.000	-.2761534 -.1446531
_cons	36.24366	1.351263	26.82	0.000	33.59523 38.89208

```
.  estimates store full

.  lrtest full reduced

Likelihood-ratio test                        LR chi2(2)    =     247.32
(Assumption: reduced nested in full)         Prob > chi2   =     0.0000

.  test numkid hrwork

( 1)  [hrchores]numkid = 0
( 2)  [hrchores]hrwork = 0

           chi2( 2) =     257.15
         Prob > chi2 =    0.0000
```

Note Some SAS output omitted to conserve space.

■ Display B.16.1 Linear probability model for *g1miles* dichotomized at 45

	SAS	Stata

Syntax	`if g2miles ne . then g1milesD45=g1miles>45;`
	
	`proc reg;`
	`  model g1milesD45=g2earn10000;`
	`run;`
		`generate g1milesD45=g1miles>45 if g1miles~=.`
		
		`regress g1milesD45 g2earn10000`

SAS Results

Number of Observations Read	5472
Number of Observations Used	5472

Analysis of Variance

Source	DF	Sum of Squares	Mean Square	F Value	Pr > F
Model	1	10.37606	10.37606	43.97	<.0001
Error	5470	1290.95434	0.23601		
Corrected Total	5471	1301.33041			

Root MSE	0.48580	R-Square	0.0080
Dependent Mean	0.38962	Adj R-Sq	0.0078
Coeff Var	124.68685		

Parameter Estimates

Variable	DF	Parameter Estimate	Standard Error	t Value	Pr > |t|
Intercept	1	0.35396	0.00849	41.70	<.0001
g2earn10000	1	0.01161	0.00175	6.63	<.0001

Stata Results

```
      Source |       SS       df       MS              Number of obs =    5472
-------------+------------------------------           F(  1,  5470) =   43.97
       Model |  10.3760647     1  10.3760647           Prob > F      =  0.0000
    Residual | 1290.95434  5470  .23600279             R-squared     =  0.0080
-------------+------------------------------           Adj R-squared =  0.0078
       Total | 1301.33041  5471  .237859698            Root MSE      =  .4858

  g1milesD45 |     Coef.   Std. Err.      t    P>|t|    [95% Conf. Interval]
-------------+----------------------------------------------------------------
 g2earn10000 |   .0116146   .0017517     6.63   0.000    .0081806    .0150485
       _cons |   .3539566   .0084888    41.70   0.000    .3373152    .3705979
```

Comment: Reminder: The new variable creation in SAS must occur in the data step.

APPENDIX B

Display B.16.2 Logit model for *g1miles* dichotomized at 45 using the generalized linear model commands

Syntax

SAS

```
proc genmod descending;
  Model g1milesD45=g2earn10000
    / dist=binomial link=logit;
run;
```

Stata

```
glm g1milesD45 g2earn10000, family(binomial) link(logit)
```

Results

SAS

Model Information

Data Set	WORK.GSSCH16
Distribution	Binomial
Link Function	Logit
Dependent Variable	g1milesD45

Number of Observations Read	5472
Number of Observations Used	5472
Number of Events	2132
Number of Trials	5472

Response Profile

Ordered Value	g1milesD45	Total Frequency
1	1	2132
2	0	3340

PROC GENMOD is modeling the probability that g1milesD45="1".

Criteria For Assessing Goodness Of Fit

Criterion	DF	Value	Value/DF
Log Likelihood		-3635.3497	
Full Log Likelihood		-3635.3497	
AIC (smaller is better)		7274.6995	
AICC (smaller is better)		7274.7017	
BIC (smaller is better)		7287.9143	

Algorithm converged.

Analysis Of Maximum Likelihood Parameter Estimates

Parameter	DF	Estimate	Standard Error	Wald 95% Confidence Limits		Wald Chi-Square	Pr> ChiSq
Intercept	1	-0.6201	0.0387	-0.6959	-0.5444	257.21	<.0001
g2earn10000	1	0.0554	0.0087	0.0384	0.0725	40.60	<.0001
Scale	0	1.0000	0.0000	1.0000	1.0000		

Stata

```
Iteration 0:   log likelihood = -3640.1916
Iteration 1:   log likelihood = -3635.3504
Iteration 2:   log likelihood = -3635.3497
Iteration 3:   log likelihood = -3635.3497

Generalized linear models                No. of obs      =     5472
Optimization     : ML                    Residual df     =     5470
                                         Scale parameter =        1
Deviance         =  7270.699488          (1/df) Deviance = 1.329196
Pearson          =  5563.211013          (1/df) Pearson  = 1.01704

Variance function: V(u)  = u*(1-u)                        [Bernoulli]
Link function:     g(u)  = ln(u/(1-u))                    [Logit]

                                         AIC             = 1.329441
Log likelihood   = -3635.349744          BIC             = -39811.78
```

g1milesD45	Coef.	OIM Std. Err.	z	P>|z|	[95% Conf. Interval]	
g2earn10000	.0554104	.0086962	6.37	0.000	.0383661	.0724547
_cons	-.6201414	.0386675	-16.04	0.000	-.6959283	-.5443544

Notes

The scale parameter was held fixed.

■ Display B.16.3 Probit model for *g1miles* dichotomized at 45 using the generalized linear model commands

SAS

Syntax

```
proc genmod descending;
    Model g1milesD45=g2earn10000
/ dist=binomial link=probit;
run;
```

Results

Model Information

Data Set	WORK.GSSCH16
Distribution	Binomial
Link Function	Probit
Dependent Variable	g1milesD45

Number of Observations Read	5472
Number of Observations Used	5472
Number of Events	2132
Number of Trials	5472

Response Profile

Ordered Value	g1milesD45	Total Frequency
1	1	2132
2	0	3340

PROC GENMOD is modeling the probability that g1milesD45='1'.

Criteria For Assessing Goodness of Fit

Criterion	DF	Value	Value/DF
Log Likelihood		-3636.6852	
Full Log Likelihood		-3636.6852	
AIC (smaller is better)		7277.3704	
AICC (smaller is better)		7277.3726	
BIC (smaller is better)		7290.5852	

Algorithm converged.

Analysis Of Maximum Likelihood Parameter Estimates

Parameter	DF	Estimate	Standard Error	Wald 95% Confidence Limits		Wald Chi-Square	Pr > ChiSq
Intercept	1	-0.3759	0.0227	-0.4204	-0.3314	274.51	<.0001
g2earn10000	1	0.0308	0.0048	0.0215	0.0402	41.79	<.0001
Scale	0	1.0000	0.0000	1.0000	1.0000		

Notes

Stata

Syntax

```
glm g1milesD45 g2earn10000, family(binomial) link(probit)
```

Results

```
Iteration 0:   log likelihood = -3639.7532
Iteration 1:   log likelihood = -3636.6853
Iteration 2:   log likelihood = -3636.6852

Generalized linear models          No. of obs      =        5472
Optimization     : ML              Residual df     =        5470
                                   Scale parameter =           1
Deviance         =  7273.370417    (1/df) Deviance = 1.329684
Pearson          =  5633.82711     (1/df) Pearson  = 1.02995

Variance function : V(u) = u*(1-u)                 [Bernoulli]
Link function     : g(u) = invnorm(u)              [Probit]

                                   AIC             =   1.329929
Log likelihood   = -3636.685209    BIC             =   -39809.1
```

	Coef.	OIM Std. Err.	z	P>|z|	[95% Conf. Interval]
g1milesD45					
g2earn10000	.0308123	.0047666	6.46	0.000	.02147 .0401546
_cons	-.3759041	.0226882	-16.57	0.000	-.420372 -.3314361

Notes

The scale parameter was held fixed.

▪ Display B.16.4 Installing the S-Post .ado files

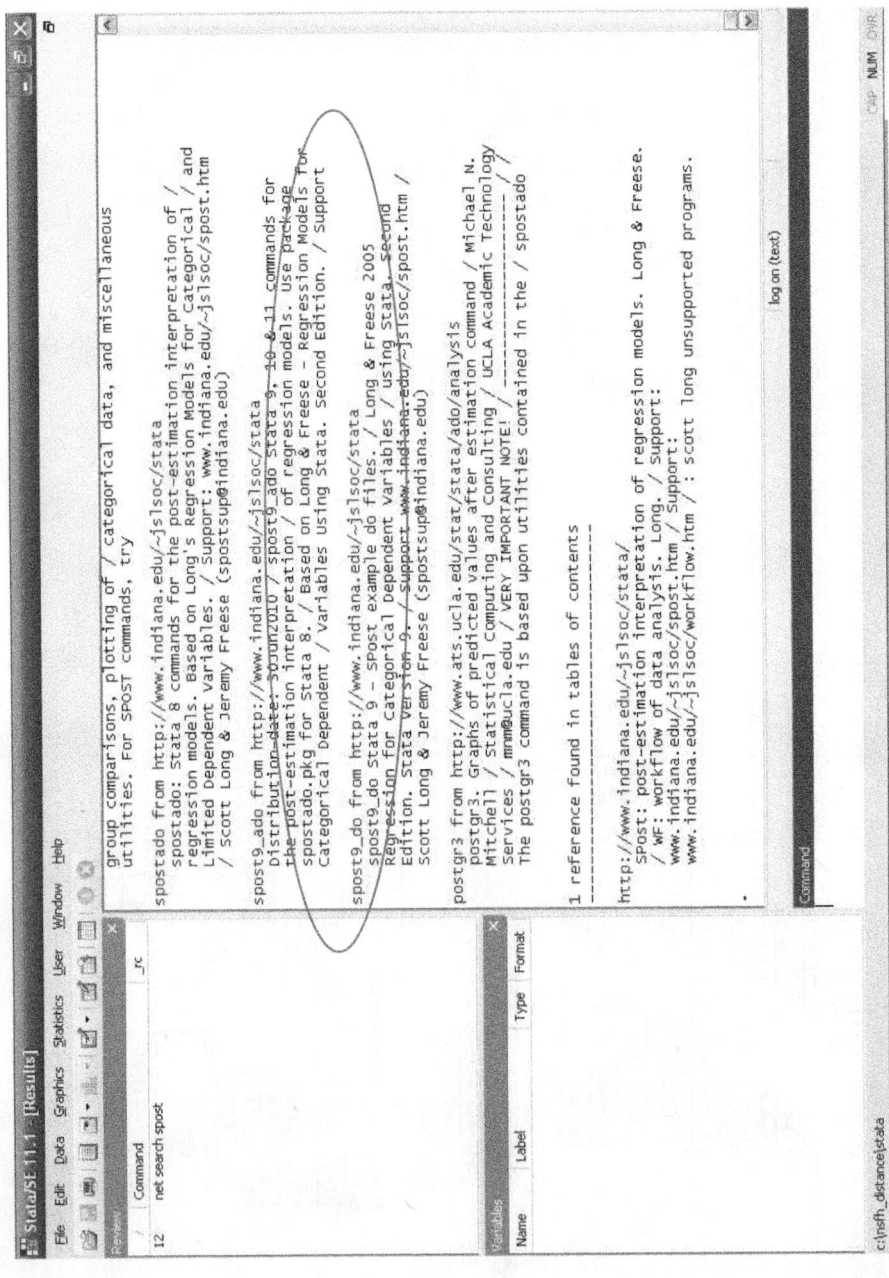

■ Display B.16.5 Logit model for *g1miles* dichotomized at 45 using SAS's *proc logistic* command and Stata's *logit* command

	SAS – proc logistic	Stata – logit
Syntax	``` proc logistic descending; Model g1milesD45=g2earn10000 / rsquare clparm=wald; run; ```	``` logit g1milesD45 g2earn10000 fitstat ```

Stata – logit (Results)

```
Iteration 0:   log likelihood = -3658.4575
Iteration 1:   log likelihood = -3635.6393
Iteration 2:   log likelihood = -3635.3498
Iteration 3:   log likelihood = -3635.3497

Logistic regression                        Number of obs  =     5472
                                           LR chi2(1)     =    46.22
                                           Prob > chi2    =   0.0000
Log likelihood = -3635.3497                Pseudo R2      =   0.0063
```

g1milesD45	Coef.	Std. Err.	z	P>|z|	[95% Conf. Interval]
g2earn10000	.0554104	.0086962	6.37	0.000	.0383661 .0724547
_cons	-.6201414	.0386675	-16.04	0.000	-.6959283 -.5443544

```
.  fitstat

  Measures of Fit for logit of g1milesD45

Log-Lik Intercept Only:    -3658.457   Log-Lik Full Model:    -3635.350
D(5470):                    7270.699   LR(1):                    46.215
                                       Prob > LR:                 0.000
McFadden's R2:                 0.006   McFadden's Adj R2:         0.006
ML (Cox-Snell) R2:             0.008   Cragg-Uhler(Nagelkerke) R2:0.011
McKelvey & Zavoina's R2:       0.013   Efron's R2:                0.009
Variance of y*:                3.333   Variance of error:         3.290
Count R2:                      0.614   Adj Count R2:              0.008
AIC:                           1.329   AIC*n:                  7274.699
BIC:                      -39811.776   BIC':                    -37.608
BIC used by Stata:          7287.914   AIC used by Stata:      7274.699
```

SAS – proc logistic (Results)

Response Profile

Ordered Value	g1milesD45	Total Frequency
1	1	2132
2	0	3340

Probability modeled is g1milesD45=1.

Testing Global Null Hypothesis: BETA=0

Test	Chi-Square	DF	Pr > ChiSq
Likelihood Ratio	46.2154	1	<.0001
Score	43.6306	1	<.0001
Wald	40.5995	1	<.0001

Model Fit Statistics

Criterion	Intercept Only	Intercept and Covariates
AIC	7318.915	7274.699
SC	7325.522	7287.914
-2 Log L	7316.915	7270.699

R-Square	0.0084	Max-rescaled R-Square	0.0114

Analysis of Maximum Likelihood Estimates

Parameter	DF	Estimate	Standard Error	Wald Chi-Square	Pr > ChiSq
Intercept	1	-0.6201	0.0387	257.2105	<.0001
g2earn10000	1	0.0554	0.00870	40.5995	<.0001

Wald Confidence Interval for Parameters

Parameter	Estimate	95% Confidence Limits	
Intercept	-0.6201	-0.6959	-0.5444
g2earn10000	0.0554	0.0384	0.0725

Display B.16.6 Classification Tables

	SAS – proc logistic	Stata - logit

Syntax	`proc logistic descending data= GSsch16;`
	`   Model g1milesD45=g2earn10000`
	`        / ctable pprob=0.50;`
	`run;`
		`logit g1milesD45 g2earn10000`
		`estat class`

Results — SAS:

Classification Table

| Prob Level | Correct | | Incorrect | | Percentages | | | | |
	Event	Non-Event	Event	Non-Event	Correct	Sensi-tivity	Speci-ficity	False POS	False NEG
0.500	60	3298	42	2072	61.4	2.8	98.7	41.2	38.6

Results — Stata:

Logistic model for g1milesD45

Classified	True D	~D	Total
+	60	42	102
-	2072	3298	5370
Total	2132	3340	5472

Classified + if predicted Pr(D) >= .5
True D defined as g1milesD45 != 0

Sensitivity	Pr(+| D)	2.81%
Specificity	Pr(-|~D)	98.74%
Positive predictive value	Pr(D| +)	58.82%
Negative predictive value	Pr(~D| -)	61.42%
False + rate for true ~D	Pr(+|~D)	1.26%
False - rate for true D	Pr(-| D)	97.19%
False + rate for classified +	Pr(~D| +)	41.18%
False - rate for classified -	Pr(D| -)	38.58%
Correctly classified		61.37%

Display B.16.7 Logit Model with Multiple Predictors, Showing Fit Statistics

Syntax

SAS

```
proc logistic descending data= GSsch16;
Model g1milesD45=g1yrschl sqg1yrschl g2numsis4
g2numsis56 g2earn10000 g1age g2age g2numbro
female mexamer white other
/ rsquare ctable pprob=0.50 clparm=wald;
run;
```

Stata

```
logit g1milesD45 g1yrschl sqg1yrschl g2numsis4 g2numsis56 g2numsis7p ///
      amind mexamer white other female g2earn10000 g1age g2age g2numbro
fitstat, using(biv)
```

Results

SAS

Analysis of Maximum Likelihood Estimates

Parameter	DF	Estimate	Standard Error	Wald Chi-Square	Pr > ChiSq
Intercept	1	-2.3255	0.3372	47.5620	<.0001
g1yrschl	1	-0.0614	0.0450	1.8591	0.1727
sqg1yrschl	1	0.00755	0.00205	13.6111	0.0002
g2numsis4	1	0.0600	0.1407	0.1818	0.6698
g2numsis56	1	-0.2458	0.1660	2.1926	0.1387
g2numsis7p	1	0.6072	0.2850	4.5403	0.0331
amind	1	0.8243	0.4146	3.9519	0.0468
mexamer	1	-0.2326	0.2134	1.1886	0.2756
white	1	0.3737	0.0874	18.2872	<.0001
other	1	0.6687	0.2576	6.7351	0.0095
female	1	-0.0222	0.0625	0.1261	0.7225
g2earn10000	1	0.0319	0.00930	11.7370	0.0006
g1age	1	0.0135	0.00481	7.8345	0.0051
g2age	1	0.00764	0.00543	1.9753	0.1599
g2numbro	1	0.0333	0.0193	2.9876	0.0839

Wald Confidence Interval for Parameters

Parameter	Estimate	95% Confidence Limits	
Intercept	-2.3255	-2.9864	-1.6646
g1yrschl	-0.0614	-0.1495	0.0268
sqg1yrschl	0.00755	0.00354	0.0116
g2numsis4	0.0600	-0.2157	0.3357
g2numsis56	-0.2458	-0.5711	0.0795
g2numsis7p	0.6072	0.0487	1.1657
amind	0.8243	0.0116	1.6369
mexamer	-0.2326	-0.6508	0.1856
white	0.3737	0.2024	0.5449
other	0.6687	0.1637	1.1736
female	-0.0222	-0.1447	0.1003
g2earn10000	0.0319	0.0136	0.0501
g1age	0.0135	0.00404	0.0229
g2age	0.00764	-0.00301	0.0183
g2numbro	0.0333	-0.00446	0.0711

Stata

```
Iteration 0:   log likelihood = -3658.4575
Iteration 1:   log likelihood = -3540.9234
Iteration 2:   log likelihood = -3540.3269
Iteration 3:   log likelihood = -3540.3265

Logistic regression

                            Number of obs  =     5472
                            LR chi2(14)    =   236.26
                            Prob > chi2    =   0.0000
                            Pseudo R2      =   0.0323

Log likelihood = -3540.3265
```

g1milesD45	Coef.	Std. Err.	z	P>|z|	[95% Conf.	Interval]
g1yrschl	-.0613528	.0449975	-1.36	0.173	-.1495463	.0268407
sqg1yrschl	.0075459	.0020453	3.69	0.000	.0035371	.0115547
g2numsis4	.0599758	.1406575	0.43	0.670	-.2157078	.3356593
g2numsis56	-.2457783	.1659821	-1.48	0.139	-.5710973	.0795406
g2numsis7p	.6071793	.2849525	2.13	0.033	.048826	1.165676
amind	.8242522	.4146279	1.99	0.047	.0115965	1.636908
mexamer	-.2326321	.2133756	-1.09	0.276	-.6508406	.1855764
white	.3736567	.0873773	4.28	0.000	.204003	.5449131
other	.6686562	.25765	2.60	0.009	.1636714	1.173641
female	-.022198	.062512	-0.36	0.723	-.1447192	.1003232
g2earn10000	.0318782	.009305	3.43	0.001	.0136408	.0501157
g1age	.0134683	.0048118	2.80	0.005	.0040374	.0228992
g2age	.0076362	.0054333	1.41	0.160	-.0030129	.0182853
g2numbro	.033314	.0192737	1.73	0.084	-.0044618	.0710898
_cons	-2.325522	.3372021	-6.90	0.000	-2.986426	-1.664618

(continued)

Display B.16.7 Logit Model with Multiple Predictors, Showing Fit Statistics (continued)

Results

Model Fit Statistics

Criterion	Intercept Only	Intercept and Covariates
AIC	7318.915	7110.653
SC	7325.522	7209.764
-2 Log L	7316.915	7080.653

Testing Global Null Hypothesis: BETA=0

Test	Chi-Square	DF	Pr > ChiSq
Likelihood Ratio	236.2619	14	<.0001
Score	231.4046	14	<.0001
Wald	218.8010	14	<.0001

Classification Table

Prob Level	Correct Event	Correct Non-Event	Incorrect Event	Incorrect Non-Event	Correct	Sensitivity	Specificity	False POS	False NEG
0.500	414	3021	319	1718	62.8	19.4	90.4	43.5	36.3

Stata

```
. fitstat, using(biv)

Measures of Fit for logit of g1milesD45
```

	Current logit	Saved logit	Difference
Model:			
N:	5472	5472	0
Log-Lik Intercept Only	-3658.457	-3658.457	0.000
Log-Lik Full Model	-3540.327	-3635.350	95.023
D	7080.653(5457)	7270.699(5470)	
LR	236.262(14)	46.215(1)	190.046(13)
Prob > LR	0.000	0.000	0.000
McFadden's R2	0.032	0.006	0.026
McFadden's Adj R2	0.028	0.006	0.022
ML (Cox-Snell) R2	0.042	0.008	0.034
Cragg-Uhler(Nagelkerke) R2	0.057	0.011	0.046
McKelvey & Zavoina's R2	0.056	0.013	0.043
Efron's R2	0.043	0.009	0.033
Variance of y*	3.486	3.333	0.153
Variance of error	3.290	3.290	0.000
Count R2	0.632	0.614	0.018
Adj Count R2	0.054	0.008	0.046
AIC	1.299	1.329	-0.030
AIC*n	7110.653	7274.699	-164.046
BIC	-39889.926	-39811.776	-78.150
BIC'	-115.758	-37.608	-78.150
BIC used by Stata	7209.764	7287.914	-78.150
AIC used by Stata	7110.653	7274.699	-164.046

```
Difference of 78.150 in BIC' provides very strong support for current
model.

Note: p-value for difference in LR is only valid if models are nested.
```

Display B.16.8 Range of Predicted Probabilities

	SAS	Stata
| Syntax | ```
proc logistic descending data= GSsch16;
Model g1milesD45=g1yrschl sag1yrschl g2numsis4
g2numsis56 g2numsis6 amind mexamer white other
female g2earn10000 g1age g2age g2numbro;
Score out=predall;
run;

proc means data=predall;
var p_1;
run;
proc means data=predall;
var p_1;
where g2earn10000>=0 & g2earn10000<=8;
run;
``` | ```
logit g1milesD45 g1yrschl sag1yrschl g2numsis4 g2numsis56  g2numsis7p //
       amind mexamer white other female g2earn10000 g1age g2age g2numbro;
predict Prg1milesD45, p
summarize Prg1milesD45
summarize Prg1milesD45 if g2earn10000>=0 & g2earn10000<=8
``` |
| Results | Analysis Variable : P_1 Predicted Probability: g1milesD45=1<br><br>| N | Mean | Std Dev | Minimum | Maximum |<br>| 5472 | 0.3896199 | 0.1005114 | 0.1250362 | 0.9438272 |<br><br>Analysis Variable : P_1 Predicted Probability: g1milesD45=1<br><br>| N | Mean | Std Dev | Minimum | Maximum |<br>| 5182 | 0.3824857 | 0.0953900 | 0.1250362 | 0.7278326 | | ```
. summarize Prg1milesD45

    Variable |    Obs       Mean     Std. Dev.      Min        Max
-------------+-------------------------------------------------------
Prg1milesD45 |   5472    .3896199     .1005115   .1250354   .9438273

. summarize Prg1milesD45 if g2earn10000>=0 & g2earn10000<=8

    Variable |    Obs       Mean     Std. Dev.      Min        Max
-------------+-------------------------------------------------------
Prg1milesD45 |   5182    .3824856     .0953901   .1250354   .7278327
``` |
```

APPENDIX B

Display B.16.9 "Predict then Average"

	SAS	Stata
Syntax	(see below)	(see below)
Results	(see below)	(see below)

Syntax

SAS

```
if g2earn10000=0       then g2earnC=0;
if g2earn10000>0 & g2earn10000<=1 then g2earnC=0.5;
if g2earn10000>1 & g2earn10000<=2 then g2earnC=1.5;
if g2earn10000>2 & g2earn10000<=3 then g2earnC=2.5;
if g2earn10000>3 & g2earn10000<=4 then g2earnC=3.5;
if g2earn10000>4 & g2earn10000<=5 then g2earnC=4.5;
if g2earn10000>5 & g2earn10000<=6 then g2earnC=5.5;
if g2earn10000>6 & g2earn10000<=7 then g2earnC=6.5;
if g2earn10000>7 & g2earn10000<=8 then g2earnC=7.5;

...

proc sort data=predall; by g2earnC; run;
proc means data=predall; var p_1; by g2earnC; run;
```

Stata

```
generate g2earnC=0       if g2earn10000==0
replace  g2earnC=0.5     if g2earn10000>0 & g2earn10000<=1
replace  g2earnC=1.5     if g2earn10000>1 & g2earn10000<=2
replace  g2earnC=2.5     if g2earn10000>2 & g2earn10000<=3
replace  g2earnC=3.5     if g2earn10000>3 & g2earn10000<=4
replace  g2earnC=4.5     if g2earn10000>4 & g2earn10000<=5
replace  g2earnC=5.5     if g2earn10000>5 & g2earn10000<=6
replace  g2earnC=6.5     if g2earn10000>6 & g2earn10000<=7
replace  g2earnC=7.5     if g2earn10000>7 & g2earn10000<=8

bysort g2earnC: summarize Prg1milesD45
```

Results

SAS

g2earnC=0

Analysis Variable : P_1 Predicted Probability: g1milesD45=1

N	Mean	Std Dev	Minimum	Maximum
975	0.3542034	0.0949629	0.1250362	0.6770448

g2earnC=0.5

Analysis Variable : P_1 Predicted Probability: g1milesD45=1

N	Mean	Std Dev	Minimum	Maximum
746	0.3595864	0.0926140	0.1288832	0.6620050

g2earnC=1.5

Analysis Variable : P_1 Predicted Probability: g1milesD45=1

N	Mean	Std Dev	Minimum	Maximum
665	0.3541377	0.0859214	0.1295528	0.6370764

g2earnC=2.5

Analysis Variable : P_1 Predicted Probability: g1milesD45=1

N	Mean	Std Dev	Minimum	Maximum
738	0.3669034	0.0863034	0.1301163	0.6397704

Stata

-> g2earnC = 0

Variable	Obs	Mean	Std. Dev.	Min	Max
Prg1milesD45	975	.3542033	.094963	.1250354	.6770448

-> g2earnC = .5

Variable	Obs	Mean	Std. Dev.	Min	Max
Prg1milesD45	746	.3595863	.0926141	.1288824	.6620049

-> g2earnC = 1.5

Variable	Obs	Mean	Std. Dev.	Min	Max
Prg1milesD45	665	.3541376	.0859215	.1295519	.6370764

-> g2earnC = 2.5

Variable	Obs	Mean	Std. Dev.	Min	Max
Prg1milesD45	738	.3669033	.0863035	.1301154	.6397704

(continued)

Display B.16.9 "Predict then Average" (continued)

Results

SAS

g2earnC=3.5

Analysis Variable : P_1 Predicted Probability: g1milesD45=1

N	Mean	Std Dev	Minimum	Maximum
743	0.3955669	0.0884911	0.1787687	0.7278326

g2earnC=4.5

Analysis Variable : P_1 Predicted Probability: g1milesD45=1

N	Mean	Std Dev	Minimum	Maximum
507	0.4189633	0.0899319	0.1790564	0.6970432

g2earnC=5.5

Analysis Variable : P_1 Predicted Probability: g1milesD45=1

N	Mean	Std Dev	Minimum	Maximum
370	0.4314980	0.0881802	0.1703144	0.6654266

g2earnC=6.5

Analysis Variable : P_1 Predicted Probability: g1milesD45=1

N	Mean	Std Dev	Minimum	Maximum
285	0.4356745	0.0824921	0.1952481	0.6581025

g2earnC=7.5

Analysis Variable : P_1 Predicted Probability: g1milesD45=1

N	Mean	Std Dev	Minimum	Maximum
153	0.4707365	0.0924980	0.1956282	0.6995254

Stata

```
-> g2earnC = 3.5

    Variable |     Obs        Mean    Std. Dev.        Min         Max
Prg1milesD45 |     743    .3955669    .0884911    .1787677    .7278327

-> g2earnC = 4.5

    Variable |     Obs        Mean    Std. Dev.        Min         Max
Prg1milesD45 |     507    .4189633     .089932    .1790553    .6970432

-> g2earnC = 5.5

    Variable |     Obs        Mean    Std. Dev.        Min         Max
Prg1milesD45 |     370     .431498    .0881803    .1703133    .6654267

-> g2earnC = 6.5

    Variable |     Obs        Mean    Std. Dev.        Min         Max
Prg1milesD45 |     285    .4356745     .082922     .195247    .6581025

-> g2earnC = 7.5

    Variable |     Obs        Mean    Std. Dev.        Min         Max
Prg1milesD45 |     153    .4707365    .0924981    .1956271    .6995254
```

Display B.16.10 Modified "Predict then Average"

	SAS	Stata
Syntax	(see code below)	(see code below)
Results	(see tables below)	(see output below)

SAS — Syntax

```
data predm0; set GSsch16; g2earn10000=0;run;
data predm_5; set GSsch16; g2earn10000=0.5; run;
data predm1_5; set GSsch16; g2earn10000=1.5;run;

proc logistic descending data= GSsch16;
Model g1milesD45=g1yrsch1 sqg1yrsch1 g2numsis4
  g2numsis56 g2numsis7p amind mexamer white other
  female g2earn10000 g1age g2age g2numbro;
  Score data=predm0 out=predm0s;
  Score data=predm_5 out=predm_5s;
  Score data=predm1_5 out=predm1_5s;
run;

proc means data=predm0s; var p_1; run;
proc means data=predm_5s; var p_1; run;
proc means data=predm1_5s; var p_1; run;
```

SAS — Results

Analysis Variable : P_1 Predicted Probability: g1milesD45=1

N	Mean	Std Dev	Minimum	Maximum
5472	0.3669834	0.0906493	0.1214969	0.7020352

Analysis Variable : P_1 Predicted Probability: g1milesD45=1

N	Mean	Std Dev	Minimum	Maximum
5472	0.3705622	0.0909794	0.1232084	0.7053586

Analysis Variable : P_1 Predicted Probability: g1milesD45=1

N	Mean	Std Dev	Minimum	Maximum
5472	0.3777611	0.0916151	0.1266938	0.7119401

Stata — Syntax

```
margins,  at(g2earn10000=0)
margins,  at(g2earn10000=0.5)
margins,  at(g2earn10000=1.5)
```

Stata — Results

```
Predictive margins                         Number of obs    =    5472
Model VCE  : OIM

Expression  : Pr(g1milesD45), predict()
at          : g2earn10000       =        0

             |           Delta-method
             |    Margin  Std. Err.      z    P>|z|   [95% Conf. Interval]
       _cons |  .3669833   .009093   40.36  0.000    .3491613   .3848053
```

```
Predictive margins                         Number of obs    =    5472
Model VCE  : OIM

Expression  : Pr(g1milesD45), predict()
at          : g2earn10000       =       .5

             |           Delta-method
             |    Margin  Std. Err.      z    P>|z|   [95% Conf. Interval]
       _cons |  .3705622  .0084087   44.07  0.000    .3540814   .3870429
```

```
Predictive margins                         Number of obs    =    5472
Model VCE  : OIM

Expression  : Pr(g1milesD45), predict()
at          : g2earn10000       =      1.5

             |           Delta-method
             |    Margin  Std. Err.      z    P>|z|   [95% Conf. Interval]
       _cons |  .3777611  .0072705   51.96  0.000    .3635111    .392011
```

Display B.16.11 "Average then Predict"

	SAS	Stata

Syntax	`proc means data=GSSch16;`
	`  var g1yrschl sqg1yrschl g2numsis4`
	`  g2numsis56 g2numsis7p amind mexamer white other`
	`  female g2earn10000 g1age g2age g2numbro;`
	`  output out=predmean mean=;`
	`run;`
	
	`data preda0;set predmean;g2earn10000=0;run;`
	`data preda_5;set predmean; g2earn10000=0.5;run;`
	
	`proc logistic descending data=GSSch16;`
	`  Model g1milesD45= g1yrschl sqg1yrschl g2numsis4`
	`  g2numsis56 g2numsis7p amind mexamer white other`
	`  female g2earn10000 g1age g2age g2numbro;`
	`  Score data=preda0 out=preda0s;`
	`  Score data=preda_5 out=preda_5s;`
	`run;`
	
	`proc means data=preda0s; var p_1; run;`
	`proc means data=preda_5s; var p_1; run;`
		`margins, at((mean) _all g2earn10000=0)`
		`margins, at((mean) _all g2earn10000=0.5)  noatlegend`

Stata Results

```
Adjusted predictions                           Number of obs  =  5472
Model VCE    : OIM

Expression   : Pr(g1milesD45), predict()
at           : g1yrschl      =  11.40058  (mean)
               sqg1yrschl    =  138.6166  (mean)
               g2numsis4     =  .0447734  (mean)
               g2numsis56    =  .0365497  (mean)
               g2numsis7p    =  .0098684  (mean)
               amind         =  .0045687  (mean)
               mexamer       =  .0303363  (mean)
               white         =  .8099415  (mean)
               other         =  .0129751  (mean)
               female        =  .6028874  (mean)
               g2earn10000   =         0
               g1age         =  60.08754  (mean)
               g2age         =  34.29386  (mean)
               g2numbro      =  1.433297  (mean)
```

	Margin	Delta-method Std. Err.	z	P>|z|	[95% Conf. Interval]
_cons	.3622172	.0092928	38.98	0.000	.3440036 .3804307

```
Adjusted predictions                           Number of obs  =  5472
Model VCE    : OIM

Expression   : Pr(g1milesD45), predict()
```

	Margin	Delta-method Std. Err.	z	P>|z|	[95% Conf. Interval]
_cons	.3659074	.0086043	42.53	0.000	.3490433 .3827714

SAS Results

Analysis Variable : P_1 Predicted Probability: g1milesD45=1

N	Mean	Std Dev	Minimum	Maximum
1	0.3622172	.	0.3622172	0.3622172

Analysis Variable : P_1 Predicted Probability: g1milesD45=1

N	Mean	Std Dev	Minimum	Maximum
1	0.3659074	.	0.3659074	0.3659074

Display B.16.12 "Average then Predict" with Rounded Values

Syntax

SAS

```
data predround;
  set predmean;
  g1yrsch1=11;    sqg1yrsch1=121;    g2numsis4=0;
  g2numsis56=0;   g2numsis7p=0;      amind=0;
  mexamer=0;      white=1;           other=0;
  female=1;       g2earn10000=3;     g1age=60;
  g2age=34;       g2numbro=1;
run;

data predr0;  set predround;  g2earn10000=0;run;
data predr_5; set predround;  g2earn10000=0.5;run;

proc logistic descending data=GSSch16;
Model g1milesD45= g1yrsch1 sqg1yrsch1 g2numsis4
  g2numsis56 g2numsis7p amind mexamer white other
  female g2earn10000 g1age g2age g2numbro;
Score data=predr0 out=predr0s;
Score data=predr_5 out=predr_5s;

proc means data=predr0s; var p_1; run;
proc means data=predr_5s; var p_1; run;
```

Stata

```
margins, at(g2earn10000=0      g1yrsch1=11 sqg1yrsch1=121
  g2numsis4=0 g2numsis56=0 g2numsis7p=0
  amind=0 mexamer=0 white=1 other=0 female=1
  g1age=60 g2age=34 g2numbro=1)
margins, at(g2earn10000=0.5 g1yrsch1=11 sqg1yrsch1=121
  g2numsis4=0 g2numsis56=0 g2numsis7p=0
  amind=0 mexamer=0 white=1 other=0 female=1
  g1age=60 g2age=34 g2numbro=1) noatlegend
```

Results

Stata

```
Adjusted predictions                    Number of obs  =   5472
Model VCE  : OIM

Expression :  Pr(g1milesD45), predict()
at         :  g1yrsch1        =      11
              sqg1yrsch1      =     121
              g2numsis4       =       0
              g2numsis56      =       0
              g2numsis7p      =       0
              amind           =       0
              mexamer         =       0
              white           =       1
              other           =       0
              female          =       1
              g2earn10000     =       0
              g1age           =      60
              g2age           =      34
              g2numbro        =       1
```

	Margin	Delta-method Std. Err.	z	P>|z|	[95% Conf. Interval]	
_cons	.3464128	.0109397	31.67	0.000	.3249713	.3678542

```
Adjusted predictions                    Number of obs  =   5472
Model VCE  : OIM
Expression :  Pr(g1milesD45), predict()
```

	Margin	Delta-method Std. Err.	z	P>|z|	[95% Conf. Interval]	
_cons	.3500304	.0106083	33.00	0.000	.3292385	.3708222

SAS

Analysis Variable : P_1 Predicted Probability: g1milesD45=1

N	Mean	Std Dev	Minimum	Maximum
1	0.3464128	.	0.3464128	0.3464128

Analysis Variable : P_1 Predicted Probability: g1milesD45=1

N	Mean	Std Dev	Minimum	Maximum
1	0.3500304	.	0.3500304	0.3500304

Display B.16.13 "Ideal Types"

	SAS	Stata

Syntax	`data predideal1; set predmean;`
	`g1yrsch1=9;  sqg1yrsch1=81;  g2numsis4=0;`
	`g2numsis56=0;  g2numsis7p=0;  amind=0;`
	`mexamer=0;  white=0;  other=0;`
	`female=1;  g2earn10000=0.5;  g1age=40;`
	`g2age=20;  g2numbro=1;`
	`run;`
	
	`data predideal2; set predmean;`
	`g1yrsch1=16;  sqg1yrsch1=256;  g2numsis4=0;`
	`g2numsis56=0;  g2numsis7p=0;  amind=0;`
	`mexamer=0;  white=1;  other=0;`
	`female=0;  g2earn10000=5.5;  g1age=80;`
	`g2age=50;  g2numbro=2;`
	`run;`
	
	`proc logistic descending data=GSSch16;`
	`Model g1milesD45= g1yrsch1 sqg1yrsch1 g2numsis4`
	`  g2numsis56 g2numsis7p amind mexamer white other`
	`  female g2earn10000 g1age g2age g2numbro;`
	`Score data=predideal1 out=predideal1s;`
	`Score data=predideal2 out=predideal2s;`
	`run;`
	
	`proc means data=predideal1s; var p_1; run;`
	`proc means data=predideal2s; var p_1; run;`
		`margins, at(g2earn10000=0.5 g1yrsch1=9  sqg1yrsch1=81`
		`  g2numsis4=0 g2numsis56=0 g2numsis7p=0`
		`  amind=0 mexamer=0 white=0 other=0 female=1`
		`  g1age=40 g2age=20 g2numbro=1)`
		
		`margins, at(g2earn10000=5.5 g1yrsch1=16 sqg1yrsch1=256`
		`  g2numsis4=0 g2numsis56=0 g2numsis7p=0`
		`  amind=0 mexamer=0 white=1 other=0 female=0`
		`  g1age=80 g2age=50 g2numbro=2)`

Results	Analysis Variable : P_1 Predicted Probability: g1milesD45=1
	
	| N
		Mean	Std Dev	Minimum	Maximum |
					|---|---|---|---|---|
					| 1 | 0.1753802 | . | 0.1753802 | 0.1753802 |
						`Adjusted predictions                    Number of obs   =     5472`
						`Model VCE  : OIM`
						
						`Expression  :  Pr(g1milesD45), predict()`
						`at          :  g1yrsch1        =        9`
						`               sqg1yrsch1      =       81`
						`               g2numsis4       =        0`
						`               g2numsis56      =        0`
						`               g2numsis7p      =        0`
						`               amind           =        0`
						`               mexamer         =        0`
						`               white           =        0`
						`               other           =        0`
						`               female          =        1`
						`               g2earn10000     =       .5`
						`               g1age           =       40`
						`               g2age           =       20`
						`               g2numbro        =        1`
						
						`              Delta-method`
						`       Margin   Std. Err.      z    P>|z|   [95% Conf. Interval]`
						`_cons  .1753802  .0151588    11.57   0.000   .1456694   .2050909`

(continued)

Display B.16.13 "Ideal Types" (continued)

	SAS	Stata

Stata

```
Adjusted predictions                         Number of obs   =    5472
Model VCE : OIM

Expression : Pr(g1milesD45), predict()
at         : g1yrschl           =       16
             sqg1yrschl         =      256
             g2numsis4          =        0
             g2numsis56         =        0
             g2numsis7p         =        0
             amind              =        0
             mexamer            =        0
             white              =        1
             other              =        0
             female             =        0
             g2earn10000        =      5.5
             g1age              =       80
             g2age              =       50
             g2numbro           =        2
```

	Margin	Delta-method Std. Err.	z	P>|z|	[95% Conf. Interval]
_cons	.6680717	.0215665	30.98	0.000	.6258022 .7103412

SAS

Results

Analysis Variable : P_1 Predicted Probability: g1milesD45=1

N	Mean	Std Dev	Minimum	Maximum
1	0.6680716	.	0.6680716	0.6680716

▪ Display B.16.14 Odds Ratio Interpretation of Logit Model

	SAS	Stata

Syntax	`proc logistic descending;`
	`  Model g1milesD45=g1yrschl sqg1yrschl`
	`g2numsis4 g2numsis56 g2numsis7p`
	`amind mexamer white other female`
	`g2earn10000 g1age g2age g2numbro;`
	`run;`
		`logit g1milesD45 g1yrschl sqg1yrschl g2numsis4 g2numsis56 g2numsis7p //`
		`amind mexamer white other female g2earn10000 g1age g2age g2numbro, or`

SAS — Results

Odds Ratio Estimates

Effect	Point Estimate	95% Wald Confidence Limits	
g1yrschl	0.940	0.861	1.027
sqg1yrschl	1.008	1.004	1.012
g2numsis4	1.062	0.806	1.399
g2numsis56	0.782	0.565	1.083
g2numsis7p	1.835	1.050	3.208
amind	2.280	1.012	5.139
mexamer	0.792	0.522	1.204
white	1.453	1.224	1.724
other	1.952	1.178	3.234
female	0.978	0.865	1.106
g2earn10000	1.032	1.014	1.051
g1age	1.014	1.004	1.023
g2age	1.008	0.997	1.018
g2numbro	1.034	0.996	1.074

Stata — Results

```
Iteration 0:   log likelihood = -3658.4575
Iteration 1:   log likelihood = -3540.9234
Iteration 2:   log likelihood = -3540.3269
Iteration 3:   log likelihood = -3540.3265

Logistic regression                        Number of obs  =      5472
                                            LR chi2(14)    =    236.26
                                            Prob > chi2    =    0.0000
Log likelihood = -3540.3265                 Pseudo R2      =    0.0323
```

g1milesD45	Odds Ratio	Std. Err.	z	P>|z|	[95% Conf. Interval]	
g1yrschl	.9404914	.0423198	-1.36	0.173	.8610986	1.027204
sqg1yrschl	1.007574	.0020608	3.69	0.000	1.003543	1.011622
g2numsis4	1.061811	.1493516	0.43	0.670	.8059708	1.398862
g2numsis56	.7820956	.1298139	-1.48	0.139	.5649052	1.08279
g2numsis7p	1.835247	.5229583	2.13	0.033	1.049887	3.208091
amind	2.280175	.9454241	1.99	0.047	1.011664	5.139254
mexamer	.79245	.1690884	-1.09	0.276	.5216071	1.203912
white	1.453038	.1269626	4.28	0.000	1.224338	1.724458
other	1.951613	.5028331	2.60	0.009	1.177827	3.233745
female	.9780466	.0611396	-0.36	0.723	.8652652	1.105528
g2earn10000	1.032392	.0096064	3.43	0.001	1.013734	1.051393
g1age	1.013559	.004877	2.80	0.005	1.004046	1.023163
g2age	1.007665	.005475	1.41	0.160	.9969917	1.018454
g2numbro	1.033875	.0199266	1.73	0.084	.9955482	1.073678

Display B.16.15 Discrete Change and Marginal Effects with Long and Freese's (2005) prchange command

Stata

Syntax

```
logit g1mi1esD45 g1yrsch1 sqg1yrsch1 g2numsis4 g2numsis56 g2numsis7p ///
amind mexamer white other female g2earn10000 g1age g2age g2numbro
prchange, fromto
```

Results

	from: x=min	to: x=max	dif: min->max	from: x=0	to: x=1	dif: 0->1
g1yrsch1	0.5576	0.3076	-0.2500	0.5576	0.5425	-0.0152
sqg1yrsch1	0.1804	0.6608	0.4804	0.1804	0.1815	0.0011
g2numsis4	0.3845	0.3988	0.0143	0.3845	0.3988	0.0143
g2numsis56	0.3873	0.3308	-0.0565	0.3873	0.3308	-0.0565
g2numsis7p	0.3837	0.5333	0.1496	0.3837	0.5333	0.1496
amind	0.3842	0.5873	0.2030	0.3842	0.5873	0.2030
mexamer	0.3868	0.3333	-0.0535	0.3868	0.3333	-0.0535
white	0.3164	0.4021	0.0857	0.3164	0.4021	0.0857
other	0.3831	0.5479	0.1648	0.3831	0.5479	0.1648
female	**0.3883**	**0.3830**	**-0.0053**	**0.3883**	**0.3830**	**-0.0053**
g2earn10000	**0.3622**	**0.9205**	**0.5583**	**0.3622**	**0.3696**	**0.0074**
g1age	0.2918	0.5006	0.2088	0.2180	0.2203	0.0023
g2age	0.3526	0.4627	0.1101	0.3253	0.3269	0.0017
g2numbro	0.3739	0.5293	0.1554	0.3739	0.3817	0.0078

	from: x-1/2	to: x+1/2	dif: -+1/2	from: x-1/2sd	to: x+1/2sd	dif: -+sd/2	MargEfct
g1yrsch1	0.3924	0.3779	-0.0145	0.4067	0.3640	-0.0427	-0.0145
sqg1yrsch1	0.3842	0.3860	0.0018	0.3312	0.4420	0.1108	0.0018
g2numsis4	0.3780	0.3922	0.0142	0.3837	0.3866	0.0029	0.0142
g2numsis56	0.4146	0.3565	-0.0581	0.3906	0.3797	-0.0109	-0.0582
g2numsis7p	0.3162	0.4590	0.1429	0.3780	0.3923	0.0142	0.1438
amind	0.2932	0.4861	0.1929	0.3786	0.3917	0.0132	0.1952
mexamer	0.4130	0.3580	-0.0550	0.3899	0.3804	-0.0094	-0.0551
white	0.3419	0.4302	0.0883	0.3679	0.4026	0.0347	0.0885
other	0.3096	0.4667	0.1571	0.3762	0.3941	0.0179	0.1583
female	**0.3878**	**0.3825**	**-0.0053**	**0.3864**	**0.3838**	**-0.0026**	**-0.0053**
g2earn10000	**0.3814**	**0.3889**	**0.0075**	**0.3711**	**0.3994**	**0.0283**	**0.0075**
g1age	0.3835	0.3867	0.0032	0.3673	0.4033	0.0360	0.0032
g2age	0.3842	0.3860	0.0018	0.3761	0.3942	0.0181	0.0018
g2numbro	0.3812	0.3891	0.0079	0.3790	0.3913	0.0124	0.0079

Display B.17.1 Multinomial Logit Model, with First Category as Reference

Syntax

```
proc logistic descending ref="23";
    model g1milesN=g1yrschl sqg1yrschl
g2numsis4 g2numsis56 g2numsis7p
amind mexamer white other female
g2earn10000 g1age g2age g2numbro
/ link=glogit;
run;
```

```
mlogit g1milesN g1yrschl sqg1yrschl g2numsis4 g2numsis56 ///
    g2numsis7p amind mexamer white other female ///
    g2earn10000 g1age g2age g2numbro, baseout(23)
```

Results

Analysis of Maximum Likelihood Estimates

Parameter	g1milesN	DF	Estimate	Standard Error	Wald Chi-Square	Pr > ChiSq
Intercept	1500	1	-3.6883	0.4744	60.4385	<.0001
Intercept	273	1	-2.5661	0.4003	41.0897	<.0001
g1yrschl	1500	1	-0.0483	0.0627	0.5954	0.4403
g1yrschl	273	1	-0.0664	0.0535	1.5408	0.2145
sqg1yrschl	1500	1	0.00846	0.00278	9.2969	0.0023
sqg1yrschl	273	1	0.00673	0.00243	7.6903	0.0056
g2numsis4	1500	1	-0.0180	0.1996	0.0081	0.9283
g2numsis4	273	1	0.1094	0.1636	0.4467	0.5039
g2numsis56	1500	1	-0.0249	0.2159	0.0133	0.9081
g2numsis56	273	1	-0.4280	0.2145	3.9802	0.0460
g2numsis7p	1500	1	1.0388	0.3318	9.8019	0.0017
g2numsis7p	273	1	0.1714	0.3789	0.2046	0.6510
amind	1500	1	0.5462	0.5901	0.8567	0.3547
amind	273	1	0.9955	0.4641	4.6012	0.0319
mexamer	1500	1	-0.1677	0.2985	0.3158	0.5742
mexamer	273	1	-0.2720	0.2689	1.0232	0.3118
white	1500	1	0.2373	0.1192	3.9616	0.0466
white	273	1	0.4717	0.1078	19.1635	<.0001
other	1500	1	0.6998	0.3359	4.3391	0.0372
other	273	1	0.6482	0.3099	4.3759	0.0365
female	1500	1	-0.1431	0.0839	2.9080	0.0881
female	273	1	0.0608	0.0737	0.6803	0.4095
g2earn10000	1500	1	0.0272	0.0113	5.8581	0.0155
g2earn10000	273	1	0.0351	0.0102	11.8278	0.0006
g1age	1500	1	0.0174	0.00657	7.0251	0.0080
g1age	273	1	0.0109	0.00570	3.6751	0.0552
g2age	1500	1	0.0105	0.00736	2.0497	0.1522
g2age	273	1	0.00555	0.00644	0.7407	0.3894
g2numbro	1500	1	0.0444	0.0259	2.9381	0.0865
g2numbro	273	1	0.0250	0.0231	1.1763	0.2781

Multinomial logistic regression

Number of obs = 5472
LR chi2(28) = 265.94
Prob > chi2 = 0.0000
Pseudo R2 = 0.0261

Log likelihood = -4966.6604

g1milesN	Coef.	Std. Err.	z	P>|z|
273				
g1yrschl	-.0663818	.0534776	-1.24	0.214
sqg1yrschl	.0067297	.0024267	2.77	0.006
g2numsis4	.1093711	.1636456	0.67	0.504
g2numsis56	-.4279864	.2145211	-2.00	0.046
g2numsis7p	.1713995	.3789291	0.45	0.651
amind	.9955118	.4640967	2.15	0.032
mexamer	-.2720187	.2689009	-1.01	0.312
white	.471429	.1077626	4.38	0.000
other	.6482224	.3098773	2.09	0.036
female	.0607938	.073708	0.82	0.409
g2earn10000	.0351328	.0102155	3.44	0.001
g1age	.010923	.0056978	1.92	0.055
g2age	.0055462	.0064443	0.86	0.389
g2numbro	.0250212	.0230698	1.08	0.278
_cons	-2.566056	.4003131	-6.41	0.000
1500				
g1yrschl	-.0483417	.0626532	-0.77	0.440
sqg1yrschl	.0084633	.0027757	3.05	0.002
g2numsis4	-.0179532	.1996462	-0.09	0.928
g2numsis56	-.0249064	.2158764	-0.12	0.908
g2numsis7p	1.038751	.3317895	3.13	0.002
amind	.5461822	.5900912	0.93	0.355
mexamer	-.1677198	.2984516	-0.56	0.574
white	.2373228	.1192355	1.99	0.047
other	.6997673	.3359352	2.08	0.037
female	-.1430825	.0839055	-1.71	0.088
g2earn10000	.0272359	.0112529	2.42	0.016
g1age	.0174026	.0065658	2.65	0.008
g2age	.0105328	.007357	1.43	0.152
g2numbro	.044438	.0259249	1.71	0.087
_cons	-3.688322	.744266	-7.77	0.000

(g1milesN==23 is the base outcome)

Display B.17.2 Multinomial Logit Model in Stata, with Last Category as Reference

Syntax

```
proc logistic descending ref="1500";
model g1milesN=g1yrschl sqg1yrschl
g2numsis4 g2numsis56 g2numsis7p
amind mexamer white other female
g2earn10000 g1age g2age g2numbro
/ link=glogit;
run;
```

```
mlogit g1milesN g1yrschl sqg1yrschl g2numsis4 g2numsis56 ///
g2numsis7p amind mexamer white other female ///
g2earn10000 g1age g2age g2numbro, baseout(1500)
```

Results

Multinomial logistic regression

Number of obs = 5472
LR chi2(28) = 265.94
Prob > chi2 = 0.0000
Pseudo R2 = 0.0261

Log likelihood = -4966.6604

g1milesN	Coef.	Std. Err.	z	P>|z|
23				
g1yrschl	.0483417	.0626534	0.77	0.440
sqg1yrschl	-.0084643	.0027757	-3.05	0.002
g2numsis4	.0179532	.1996463	0.09	0.928
g2numsis56	.0249064	.2158764	0.12	0.908
g2numsis7p	-1.038751	.3317906	-3.13	0.002
amind	-.5461822	.5900913	-0.93	0.355
mexamer	.1677198	.2984526	0.56	0.574
white	-.2373228	.1192356	-1.99	0.047
other	-.6997673	.3359354	-2.08	0.037
female	.1430825	.0839055	1.71	0.088
g2earn10000	-.0272359	.0112529	-2.42	0.016
g1age	-.0174026	.0065658	-2.65	0.008
g2age	-.0105328	.007357	-1.43	0.152
g2numbro	-.044438	.0259249	-1.71	0.087
_cons	3.688322	.474428	7.77	0.000
273				
g1yrschl	-.0180401	.0723182	-0.25	0.803
sqg1yrschl	-.0017336	.0031735	-0.55	0.585
g2numsis4	.1273243	.2253572	0.56	0.572
g2numsis56	-.40308	.2731752	-1.48	0.140
g2numsis7p	-.8673519	.4161338	-2.08	0.037
amind	.4493296	.6290316	0.71	0.475
mexamer	-.1042989	.3720554	-0.28	0.779
white	.23442	.1439932	1.63	0.104
other	-.0515449	.3873511	-0.13	0.894
female	.2038763	.0948765	2.15	0.032
g2earn10000	.0078969	.0104959	0.75	0.452
g1age	-.0064796	.0075167	-0.86	0.389
g2age	-.0049866	.0084224	-0.59	0.554
g2numbro	-.0194169	.0299496	-0.65	0.517
_cons	1.122265	.5485284	2.05	0.041

(g1milesN==1500 is the base outcome)

Analysis of Maximum Likelihood Estimates

Parameter	g1milesN	DF	Estimate	Standard Error	Wald Chi-Square	Pr > ChiSq
Intercept	273	1	1.1222	0.5485	4.1858	0.0408
Intercept	23	1	3.6883	0.4744	60.4385	<.0001
g1yrschl	273	1	-0.0180	0.0723	0.0622	0.8030
g1yrschl	23	1	0.0483	0.0627	0.5954	0.4403
sqg1yrschl	273	1	-0.00173	0.00317	0.2985	0.5848
sqg1yrschl	23	1	-0.00846	0.00278	9.2969	0.0023
g2numsis4	273	1	0.1273	0.2254	0.3192	0.5721
g2numsis4	23	1	0.0180	0.1996	0.0081	0.9283
g2numsis56	273	1	-0.4031	0.2732	2.1772	0.1401
g2numsis56	23	1	0.0249	0.2159	0.0133	0.9081
g2numsis7p	273	1	-0.8674	0.4161	4.3445	0.0371
g2numsis7p	23	1	-1.0388	0.3318	9.8019	0.0017
amind	273	1	0.4493	0.6290	0.5103	0.4750
amind	23	1	-0.5462	0.5901	0.8567	0.3547
mexamer	273	1	-0.1043	0.3721	0.0786	0.7792
mexamer	23	1	0.1677	0.2985	0.3158	0.5742
white	273	1	0.2344	0.1440	2.6504	0.1035
white	23	1	-0.2373	0.1192	3.9616	0.0466
other	273	1	-0.0515	0.3874	0.0177	0.8941
other	23	1	-0.6998	0.3359	4.3391	0.0372
female	273	1	0.2039	0.0949	4.6176	0.0316
female	23	1	0.1431	0.0839	2.9080	0.0881
g2earn10000	273	1	0.00790	0.0105	0.5661	0.4518
g2earn10000	23	1	-0.0272	0.0113	5.8581	0.0155
g1age	273	1	-0.00648	0.00752	0.7431	0.3887
g1age	23	1	-0.0174	0.00657	7.0251	0.0080
g2age	273	1	-0.00499	0.00842	0.3505	0.5538
g2age	23	1	-0.0105	0.00736	2.0497	0.1522
g2numbro	273	1	-0.0194	0.0299	0.4203	0.5168
g2numbro	23	1	-0.0444	0.0259	2.9381	0.0865

Display B.17.3 Results of Hausman Test of Independent of Irrelevant Alternatives (IIA) Assumption in Stata

| Syntax | ```
mlogit g1milesN g1yrschl sqg1yrschl g2numsis4 g2numsis56 g2numsis7p amind mexamer white other female ///
       g2earn10000 g1age g2age g2numbro, baseout(23)
       mlogtest, hausman
mlogit g1milesN g1yrschl sqg1yrschl g2numsis4 g2numsis56 g2numsis7p amind mexamer white other female ///
       g2earn10000 g1age g2age g2numbro, baseout(273)
       mlogtest, hausman
mlogit g1milesN g1yrschl sqg1yrschl g2numsis4 g2numsis56 g2numsis7p amind mexamer white other female ///
       g2earn10000 g1age g2age g2numbro, baseout(1500)
       mlogtest, hausman
``` |
| Results | ```
Reference Outcome Category: 23

**** Hausman tests of IIA assumption (N=5472)

Ho: Odds(Outcome-J vs Outcome-K) are independent of other alternatives.

Omitted |    chi2     df    P>chi2   evidence
--------+---------------------------------------
    273 |  -9.994    14      ---       ---
   1500 |  -8.502    14      ---       ---

Note: If chi2<0, the estimated model does not
meet asymptotic assumptions of the test.

Reference Outcome Category: 273

**** Hausman tests of IIA assumption (N=5472)

Ho: Odds(Outcome-J vs Outcome-K) are independent of other alternatives.

Omitted |    chi2     df    P>chi2   evidence
--------+---------------------------------------
     23 |   0.958    14    1.000    for Ho
   1500 |  -8.502    14      ---       ---

Note: If chi2<0, the estimated model does not
meet asymptotic assumptions of the test.

Reference Outcome Category: 1500

**** Hausman tests of IIA assumption (N=5472)

Ho: Odds(Outcome-J vs Outcome-K) are independent of other alternatives.

Omitted |    chi2     df    P>chi2   evidence
--------+---------------------------------------
     23 |   0.958    14    1.000    for Ho
    273 |  -9.994    14      ---       ---

Note: If chi2<0, the estimated model does not
meet asymptotic assumptions of the test.
``` |

Display B.17.4 Tests for Combining Categories

```
mlogit g1milesN g1yrschl sqg1yrschl g2numsis4 g2numsis56 ///
       g2numsis7p amind mexamer white other female ///
       g2earn10000 g1age g2age g2numbro, baseout(1500)
mlogtest, combine
mlogtest, lrcomb
```

Syntax

```
proc logistic descending ref="1500";
   model g1milesN=g1yrschl sqg1yrschl g2numsis4 g2numsis56
   g2numsis7p amind mexamer white other female
   g2earn10000 g1age g2age g2numbro
   / link=glogit;

Combine_23_273: test
g1yrschl_23-g1yrschl_273,          white_23-white_273,
sqg1yrschl_23-sqg1yrschl_273,      other_23-other_273,
g2numsis4_23-g2numsis4_273,        female_23-female_273,
g2numsis56_23-g2numsis56_273,      g2earn10000_23-g2earn10000_273,
g2numsis7p_23-g2numsis7p_273,      g1age_23-g1age_273,
amind_23-amind_273,                g2age_23-g2age_273,
mexamer_23-mexamer_273,            g2numbro_23-g2numbro_273
;

Combine_23_1500: test
g1yrschl_23-0,         white_23-0,
sqg1yrschl_23-0,       other_23-0,
g2numsis4_23-0,        female_23-0,
g2numsis56_23-0,       g2earn10000_23-0,
g2numsis7p_23-0,       g1age_23-0,
amind_23-0,            g2age_23-0,
mexamer_23-0,          g2numbro_23-0
;

Combine_273_1500: test
g1yrschl_273-0,        white_273-0,
sqg1yrschl_273-0,      other_273-0,
g2numsis4_273-0,       female_273-0,
g2numsis56_273-0,      g2earn10000_273-0,
g2numsis7p_273-0,      g1age_273-0,
amind_273-0,           g2age_273-0,
mexamer_273-0,         g2numbro_273-0
;
run;
```

Results

Linear Hypotheses Testing Results			
Label	Wald Chi-Square	DF	Pr > ChiSq
Combine_23_273	131.0453	14	<.0001
Combine_23_1500	176.2455	14	<.0001
Combine_273_1500	29.2689	14	0.0096

```
**** Wald tests for combining alternatives (N=5472)
Ho: All coefficients except intercepts associated with a given
pair
of alternatives are 0 (i.e., alternatives can be combined).
Alternatives tested          chi2      df    P>chi2
-
    23-    273             131.046     14    0.000
    23-   1500             176.246     14    0.000
   273-   1500              29.269     14    0.010
-

**** LR tests for combining alternatives (N=5472)
Ho: All coefficients except intercepts associated with a given
pair of alternatives are 0 (i.e., alternatives can be collapsed).
Alternatives tested          chi2      df    P>chi2
-
    23-    273             140.233     14    0.000
    23-   1500             181.450     14    0.000
   273-   1500              29.679     14    0.008
-
```

Display B.17.5 Multinomial Logit Model in Stata, Odds Ratios Reported with First Category as Reference

Syntax								

```
mlogit g1milesN g1yrschl sqg1yrschl g2numsis4 g2numsis56 //
       g2numsis7p amind mexamer white other female ///
       g2earn10000 g1age g2age g2numbro, baseout(23) rrr
```

Multinomial logistic regression

Number of obs	=	5472
LR chi2(28)	=	265.94
Prob > chi2	=	0.0000
Pseudo R2	=	0.0261

Log likelihood = -4966.6604

g1milesN	RRR	Std. Err.	z	P>|z|	[95% Conf. Interval]	
273						
g1yrschl	.9357735	.0500429	-1.24	0.214	.8426564	1.039181
sqg1yrschl	1.006752	.0024431	2.77	0.006	1.001975	1.011552
g2numsis4	1.115576	.1825592	0.67	0.504	.8094758	1.537428
g2numsis56	.6518203	.1398292	-2.00	0.046	.4280822	.992954
g2numsis7p	1.186965	.4497755	0.45	0.651	.5647976	2.494496
amind	2.706109	1.255896	2.15	0.032	1.089696	6.720245
mexamer	.76184	.2048594	-1.01	0.312	.4497539	1.290484
white	1.602785	.1727202	4.38	0.000	1.29762	1.979716
other	1.912139	.5925284	2.09	0.036	1.041721	3.509841
female	1.06268	.078328	0.82	0.409	.9197336	1.227843
g2earn10000	1.035757	.0105808	3.44	0.001	1.015225	1.056704
g1age	1.010983	.0057604	1.92	0.055	.9997556	1.022336
g2age	1.005562	.0064802	0.86	0.389	.9929406	1.018343
g2numbro	1.025337	.0236543	1.08	0.278	.9800077	1.072763
1500						
g1yrschl	.9528081	.0596965	-0.77	0.440	.8427038	1.077298
sqg1yrschl	1.008499	.0027993	3.05	0.002	1.003028	1.014001
g2numsis4	.982207	.1960939	-0.09	0.928	.6641464	1.452587
g2numsis56	.9754012	.2105661	-0.12	0.908	.6388943	1.489147
g2numsis7p	2.825687	.9375332	3.13	0.002	1.474702	5.414318
amind	1.726648	1.01888	0.93	0.355	.543147	5.488964
mexamer	.8455907	.2523679	-0.56	0.574	.4711051	1.517758
white	1.26785	.1511728	1.99	0.047	1.003632	1.601627
other	2.013284	.676333	2.08	0.037	1.042213	3.889141
female	.8666826	.0727194	-1.71	0.088	.7352577	1.021599
g2earn10000	1.02761	.0115636	2.42	0.016	1.005194	1.050526
g1age	1.017555	.0066811	2.65	0.008	1.004544	1.030734
g2age	1.010588	.0074349	1.43	0.152	.9961209	1.025266
g2numbro	1.04544	.0271029	1.71	0.087	.9936465	1.099934

(g1milesN=23 is the base outcome)

Results			

Odds ratios shown in default output (see Display B.17.1 for syntax)

Effect	g1milesN	Odds Ratio Estimates Point Estimate	95% Wald Confidence Limits	
g1yrschl	1500	0.953	0.843	1.077
g1yrschl	273	0.936	0.843	1.039
sqg1yrschl	1500	1.008	1.003	1.014
sqg1yrschl	273	1.007	1.002	1.012
g2numsis4	1500	0.982	0.664	1.453
g2numsis4	273	1.116	0.809	1.537
g2numsis56	1500	0.975	0.639	1.489
g2numsis56	273	0.652	0.428	0.993
g2numsis7p	1500	2.826	1.475	5.414
g2numsis7p	273	1.187	0.565	2.494
amind	1500	1.727	0.543	5.489
amind	273	2.706	1.090	6.720
mexamer	1500	0.846	0.471	1.518
mexamer	273	0.762	0.450	1.291
white	1500	1.268	1.004	1.602
white	273	1.603	1.298	1.980
other	1500	2.013	1.042	3.889
other	273	1.912	1.042	3.510
female	1500	0.867	0.735	1.022
female	273	1.063	0.920	1.228
g2earn10000	1500	1.028	1.005	1.051
g2earn10000	273	1.036	1.015	1.057
g1age	1500	1.018	1.005	1.031
g1age	273	1.011	1.000	1.022
g2age	1500	1.011	0.996	1.025
g2age	273	1.006	0.993	1.018
g2numbro	1500	1.045	0.994	1.100
g2numbro	273	1.025	0.980	1.073

Display B.17.6 Multinomial Logit Model in Stata, Odds Ratios Reported with Last Category as Reference

Syntax

```
mlogit g1milesN g1yrschl sqg1yrschl g2numsis4 g2numsis56 ///
        g2numsis7p amind mexamer white other female ///
        g2earn10000 g1age g2age g2numbro, baseout(1500) rrr
```

```
Multinomial logistic regression                Number of obs   =    5472
                                                LR chi2(28)     =  265.94
                                                Prob > chi2     =  0.0000
Log likelihood = -4966.6604                     Pseudo R2       =  0.0261
```

g1milesN	RRR	Std. Err.	z	P>|z|	[95% Conf. Interval]	
23						
g1yrschl	1.049529	.0657566	0.77	0.440	.9282476	1.186657
sqg1yrschl	.915724	.0027524	-3.05	0.002	.9861926	.9969816
g2numsis4	1.018115	.203263	0.09	0.928	.6884268	1.505692
g2numsis56	1.025219	.2213207	0.12	0.908	.6715253	1.565204
g2numsis7p	.3538963	.1174194	-3.13	0.002	.1846951	.6781045
amind	.5791567	.3417554	-0.93	0.355	.1821837	1.841123
mexamer	1.182605	.3529516	-0.56	0.574	.6588651	2.122673
white	.7887366	.0940455	-1.99	0.047	.6243649	.9963812
other	.4967009	.1668594	-2.08	0.037	.2571261	.959497
female	1.153825	.0968122	1.71	0.088	.9788575	1.360067
g2earn10000	.9731317	.0109505	-2.42	0.016	.951904	.9948327
g1age	.9827479	.0064526	-2.65	0.008	.9701822	.9954764
g2age	.9895225	.0072799	-1.43	0.152	.9753564	1.003894
g2numbro	.9565349	.0247981	-1.71	0.087	.9091457	1.006394
273						
g1yrschl	.9821217	.0710253	-0.25	0.803	.8523303	1.131677
sqg1yrschl	.9982679	.003168	-0.55	0.585	.9920779	1.004496
g2numsis4	1.135785	.2559574	0.56	0.572	.7302505	1.766529
g2numsis56	.6682586	.1825517	-1.48	0.140	.3912167	1.141489
g2numsis7p	.4200624	.1748022	-2.08	0.037	.1858233	.9495713
amind	1.567261	.9858568	0.71	0.475	.4567817	5.377421
mexamer	.900956	.3352056	-0.28	0.779	.4345196	1.86809
white	1.264175	.1820327	1.63	0.104	.953323	1.676388
other	.949761	.367891	-0.13	0.894	.445294	2.029216
female	1.226146	.1163325	2.15	0.032	1.018083	1.476731
g2earn10000	1.007928	.0105791	0.75	0.452	.9874053	1.028878
g1age	.9935413	.0074681	-0.86	0.389	.9790114	1.008287
g2age	.9950258	.0083805	-0.59	0.554	.9787352	1.011588
g2numbro	.9807704	.0293736	-0.65	0.517	.9248563	1.040065

(g1milesN=1500 is the base outcome)

Results

Odds ratios shown in default output (see Display B.17.2 for syntax)

Odds Ratio Estimates

Effect	g1milesN	Point Estimate	95% Wald Confidence Limits	
g1yrschl	273	0.982	0.852	1.132
g1yrschl	23	1.050	0.928	1.187
sqg1yrschl	273	0.998	0.992	1.004
sqg1yrschl	23	0.992	0.986	0.997
g2numsis4	273	1.136	0.730	1.767
g2numsis4	23	1.018	0.688	1.506
g2numsis56	273	0.668	0.391	1.141
g2numsis56	23	1.025	0.672	1.565
g2numsis7p	273	0.420	0.186	0.950
g2numsis7p	23	0.354	0.185	0.678
amind	273	1.567	0.457	5.377
amind	23	0.579	0.182	1.841
mexamer	273	0.901	0.435	1.868
mexamer	23	1.183	0.659	2.123
white	273	1.264	0.953	1.676
white	23	0.789	0.624	0.996
other	273	0.950	0.445	2.029
other	23	0.497	0.257	0.959
female	273	1.226	1.018	1.477
female	23	1.154	0.979	1.360
g2earn10000	273	1.008	0.987	1.029
g2earn10000	23	0.973	0.952	0.995
g1age	273	0.994	0.979	1.008
g1age	23	0.983	0.970	0.995
g2age	273	0.995	0.979	1.012
g2age	23	0.990	0.975	1.004
g2numbro	273	0.981	0.925	1.040
g2numbro	23	0.957	0.909	1.006

■ Display B.17.7 Predicted Probabilities from Multinomial Logit Model

Syntax

```
data predm10;
set predround;
g2earn10000=0;
run;
proc logistic descending data=GSSch17;
Model g1milesN=g1yrsch1 sqg1yrsch1 g2numsis4
g2numsis56 g2numsis7p amind
mexamer white other female
g2earn10000 g1age g2age g2numbro
/link=glogit;
Score data=predm10 out=predm10s;

proc means data=predm10s;
var p_23 p_273 p_1500;
run;
```

Variable	N	Mean	Std Dev	Minimum	Maximum
P_23	1	0.6533727	.	0.6533727	0.6533727
P_273	1	0.2217818	.	0.2217818	0.2217818
P_1500	1	0.1248455	.	0.1248455	0.1248455

```
margins, predict(outcome(23))  at(g2earn10000=0 g1yrsch1=11 sqg1yrsch1=121    ///
g2numsis4=0 g2numsis56=0 g2numsis7p=0                                           ///
amind=0 mexamer=0 white=1 other=0 female=1                                     ///
g1age=60 g2age=34 g2numbro=1)
margins, predict(outcome(273)) noatlegend at(g2earn10000=0 g1yrsch1=11         ///
sqg1yrsch1=121 g2numsis4=0 g2numsis56=0                                        ///
g2numsis7p=0 amind=0 mexamer=0 white=1 other=0                                 ///
female=1 g1age=60 g2age=34 g2numbro=1)
margins, predict(outcome(1500)) noatlegend at(g2earn10000=0 g1yrsch1=11        ///
sqg1yrsch1=121 g2numsis4=0 g2numsis56=0                                        ///
g2numsis7p=0 amind=0 mexamer=0 white=1 other=0                                 ///
female=1 g1age=60 g2age=34 g2numbro=1)
```

Results

```
Expression  : Pr(g1milesN==23), predict(outcome(23))
at          : g1yrsch1        =     11
              sqg1yrsch1      =    121
              g2numsis4       =      0
              g2numsis56      =      0
              g2numsis7p      =      0
              amind           =      0
              mexamer         =      0
              white           =      1
              other           =      0
              female          =      1
              g2earn10000     =      0
              g1age           =     60
              g2age           =     34
              g2numbro        =      1
```

	Margin	Delta-method Std. Err.	z	P>|z|	[95% Conf. Interval]
_cons	.6533726	.0109556	59.64	0.000	.6319001 .6748452

	Margin	Delta-method Std. Err.	z	P>|z|	[95% Conf. Interval]
_cons	.2217818	.0093495	23.72	0.000	.2034572 .2401064

	Margin	Delta-method Std. Err.	z	P>|z|	[95% Conf. Interval]
_cons	.1248455	.00708	17.63	0.000	.110969 .1387221

(continued)

Display B.17.7 Predicted Values from Multinomial Logit Model (continued)

Syntax

```
margins, predict(outcome(23)) noatlegend at(g2earn10000=0.5 g1yrschl=11  ///
        sqg1yrschl=121 g2numsis4=0 g2numsis56=0                          ///
        g2numsis7p=0 amind=0 mexamer=0 white=1 other=0                   ///
        female=1 g1age=60 g2age=34 g2numbro=1)                           ///
margins, predict(outcome(273)) noatlegend at(g2earn10000=0.5 g1yrschl=11 ///
        sqg1yrschl=121 g2numsis4=0 g2numsis56=0                          ///
        g2numsis7p=0 amind=0 mexamer=0 white=1 other=0                   ///
        female=1 g1age=60 g2age=34 g2numbro=1)                           ///
margins, predict(outcome(1500)) noatlegend at(g2earn10000=0.5 g1yrschl=11 ///
        sqg1yrschl=121 g2numsis4=0 g2numsis56=0                          ///
        g2numsis7p=0 amind=0 mexamer=0 white=1 other=0                   ///
        female=1 g1age=60 g2age=34 g2numbro=1)                           ///


data predm10_5;
set predround;
   g2earn10000=0.5;
run;

proc logistic descending data=GSSch17;
   Model g1milesN=g1yrschl sqg1yrschl g2numsis4
   g2numsis56 g2numsis7p amind
   mexamer white other female
   g2earn10000 g1age g2age g2numbro
   /link=glogit;
   Score data=predm10_5 out=predm1_5s;
run;

proc means data=predm1_5s;
var p_23 p_273 p_1500;
run;
```

Results

		Delta-method			[95% Conf. Interval]	
	Margin	Std. Err.	z	P>|z|		
_cons	.6497069	.0106236	61.16	0.000	.6288851	.6705288

		Delta-method			[95% Conf. Interval]	
	Margin	Std. Err.	z	P>|z|		
_cons	.2244458	.0091578	24.51	0.000	.2064967	.2423948

		Delta-method			[95% Conf. Interval]	
	Margin	Std. Err.	z	P>|z|		
_cons	.1258473	.0069632	18.07	0.000	.1121996	.139495

Variable	N	Mean	Std Dev	Minimum	Maximum
P_23	1	0.6497070	.	0.6497070	0.6497070
P_273	1	0.2244458	.	0.2244458	0.2244458
P_1500	1	0.1258472	.	0.1258472	0.1258472

(continued)

■ Display B.17.7 Predicted Values from Multinomial Logit Model (continued)

Syntax

```
data predml1_5;
set predround;
g2earn10000=1.5;
run;

proc logistic descending data=GSsch17;
Model glmilesn=glyrsch1 sqglyrsch1 g2numsis4
g2numsis56 g2numsis7p amind
mexamer white other female
g2earn10000 glage g2age g2numbro
/link=glogit;
Score data=predml1_5 out=predml1_5s;
run;

proc means data=predml1_5s;
var p_23 p_273 p_1500;
run;
```

```
margins, predict(outcome(23)) noatlegend at(g2earn10000=1.5 glyrsch1=11      ///
         sqglyrsch1=121 g2numsis4=0 g2numsis56=0                             ///
         g2numsis7p=0 amind=0 mexamer=0 white=1 other=0                      ///
         female=1 glage=60 g2age=34 g2numbro=1)
margins, predict(outcome(273)) noatlegend at(g2earn10000=1.5 glyrsch1=11     ///
         sqglyrsch1=121 g2numsis4=0 g2numsis56=0                             ///
         g2numsis7p=0 amind=0 mexamer=0 white=1 other=0                      ///
         female=1 glage=60 g2age=34 g2numbro=1)
margins, predict(outcome(1500)) noatlegend at(g2earn10000=1.5 glyrsch1=11    ///
         sqglyrsch1=121 g2numsis4=0 g2numsis56=0                             ///
         g2numsis7p=0 amind=0 mexamer=0 white=1 other=0                      ///
         female=1 glage=60 g2age=34 g2numbro=1)
```

Results

Variable	N	Mean	Std Dev	Minimum	Maximum
P_23	1	0.6423201	.	0.6423201	0.6423201
P_273	1	0.2298283	.	0.2298283	0.2298283
P_1500	1	0.1278516	.	0.1278516	0.1278516

```
             |            Delta-method
             |   Margin   Std. Err.      z    P>|z|    [95% Conf. Interval]
       ------+----------------------------------------------------------------
       _cons |  .6423201   .0102414    62.72  0.000     .6222473    .662393
```

```
             |            Delta-method
             |   Margin   Std. Err.      z    P>|z|    [95% Conf. Interval]
       ------+----------------------------------------------------------------
       _cons |  .2298283    .00897     25.62  0.000     .2122473    .2474092
```

```
             |            Delta-method
             |   Margin   Std. Err.      z    P>|z|    [95% Conf. Interval]
       ------+----------------------------------------------------------------
       _cons |  .1278516   .0068527    18.66  0.000     .1144206    .1412826
```

APPENDIX **B**

■ Display B.17.8 Discrete Change and Marginal Effects from Stata's *prchange* command following *mlogit*

Syntax

```
mlogit g1milesN g1lyrschl sqg1lyrschl g2numsis4 g2numsis56 g2numsis7p //
   amind mexamer white other female g2earn10000 g1age g2age g2numbro, baseout(1500)
prchange, fromto
```

Results

```
mlogit: Changes in Probabilities for g1milesN
```

g2earn10000

	Avg|Chg|	23	273	1500
from:x=min	0	.63939476	.2142857	.14631952
to:x=max	0	.07513892	.6987727	.2260738
dif:min->max	.3761056	-.56425584	.48450157	.07975428
from:x-1/2	0	.62025106	.22751674	.15223219
to:x+1/2	0	.6126914	.23277994	.15452869
dif:-+1/2	.00503979	-.0075966	-.00526319	.00229651
from:x-1/2sd	0	**.63054317**	**.2038613**	**.14907071**
to:x+1/2sd	0	**.60220402**	**.24011749**	**.15767848**
dif:-+sd/2	.0188276	**-.02833915**	**.01973136**	**.00860777**
MargEfct	.00503989	-.00755984	.00526327	.00229657

```
...
```

	23	273	1500
Pr(y|x)	.61647868	.23014042	.15338089

	g1lyrschl	sqg1lyrschl	g2numsis4	g2numsis56	g2numsis7p
x=	11.4006	138.617	.044773	.03655	.009868
sd_x=	2.94021	62.2587	.206825	.187671	.098858

	amind	mexamer	white	other	female
x=	.004569	.030336	.809942	.012975	.602887
sd_x=	.067444	.171527	.39383	.113177	.489344

	g2earn10000	g1age	g2age	g2numbro
x=	3.07057	60.0875	34.2939	1.4333
sd_x=	3.74956	11.3023	10.0098	1.56628

Results for other predictor variables omitted.

Display B.17.9 Ordered Logit Model in SAS and Stata

Syntax

SAS

```
proc logistic descending;
model g1mileso=g1yrschl sqg1yrschl
g2numsis4 g2numsis56 g2numsis7p
amind mexamer whiteother female
g2earn10000 g1age g2age g2numbro;
run;
```

Stata

```
ologit g1mileso g1yrschl sqg1yrschl g2numsis4 g2numsis56 g2numsis7p ///
amind mexamer white other female g2earn10000 g1age g2age g2numbro
```

Results

SAS

Analysis of Maximum Likelihood Estimates

Parameter		DF	Estimate	Standard Error	Wald Chi-Square	Pr > ChiSq
Intercept	1500	1	-3.4149	0.2826	146.0231	<.0001
Intercept	350	1	-2.8816	0.2816	104.6969	<.0001
Intercept	123	1	-2.1583	0.2806	59.1736	<.0001
Intercept	30	1	-1.6627	0.2800	35.2640	<.0001
Intercept	8	1	0.2202	0.2793	0.6215	0.4305
g1yrschl		1	-0.0241	0.0373	0.4175	0.5182
sqg1yrschl		1	0.00583	0.00171	11.5987	0.0007
g2numsis4		1	-0.00931	0.1192	0.0061	0.9378
g2numsis56		1	-0.2579	0.1353	3.6352	0.0566
g2numsis7p		1	0.6982	0.2479	7.9335	0.0049
amind		1	0.7456	0.3622	4.2379	0.0395
mexamer		1	-0.1413	0.1622	0.7588	0.3837
white		1	0.3301	0.0722	20.9016	<.0001
other		1	0.6991	0.2223	9.8945	0.0017
female		1	-0.0622	0.0531	1.3728	0.2413
g2earn10000		1	0.0247	0.00735	11.2604	0.0008
g1age		1	0.00660	0.00409	2.5984	0.1070
g2age		1	0.0120	0.00465	6.6089	0.0101
g2numbro		1	0.0290	0.0164	3.1503	0.0759

Stata

Ordered logistic regression

```
Number of obs   =     5472
LR chi2(14)     =   271.70
Prob > chi2     =   0.0000
Log likelihood = -9005.8197          Pseudo R2       =   0.0149
```

g1mileso	Coef.	Std. Err.	z	P>|z|	[95% Conf.	Interval]
g1yrschl	-.024021	.0383954	-0.63	0.532	-.0992745	.0512325
sqg1yrschl	.0058305	.0017546	3.32	0.001	.0023916	.0092694
g2numsis4	-.0093334	.1187023	-0.08	0.937	-.2419856	.2233188
g2numsis56	-.2580936	.1380119	-1.87	0.061	-.5285919	.0124046
g2numsis7p	.6981641	.2617234	2.67	0.008	.1851957	1.211133
amind	.7451709	.3410499	2.18	0.029	.0767254	1.413617
mexamer	-.141281	.1631091	-0.87	0.386	-.4609689	.1784069
white	.3301434	.0730166	4.52	0.000	.1870335	.4732532
other	.6992725	.223854	3.12	0.002	.2605266	1.138018
female	-.0621412	.0531161	-1.17	0.242	-.1662468	.0419644
g2earn10000	.0246575	.0074019	3.33	0.001	.0101501	.0391649
g1age	.0066016	.0040881	1.61	0.106	-.0014109	.0146141
g2age	.0119556	.0046421	2.58	0.010	.0028573	.0210539
g2numbro	.0290346	.0163694	1.77	0.076	-.0030488	.061118
/cut1	-.2197333	.2851794			-.7786746	.339208
/cut2	1.663156	.2857951			1.103008	2.223305
/cut3	2.15882	.2864267			1.597434	2.720206
/cut4	2.882052	.2874971			2.318568	3.445537
/cut5	3.415402	.2884828			2.849987	3.980818

■ Display B.17.10 Test of Proportional Odds Assumption for the Ordered Logit Model

Syntax

```
ologit g1mileso g1yrschl sqg1yrschl g2numsis4 g2numsis56 ///
       mexamer white other female g2earn10000 ///
       g1age g2age g2numbro
brant, detail
```

included in default SAS proc logistic output

Results

. brant, detail

Estimated coefficients from j-1 binary regressions

	y>1	y>8	y>30	y>123	y>350
g1yrschl	-.0122838	-.04687558	-.06761943	-.06366301	-.03076105
sqg1yrschl	.0051241	.00653249	.00777103	.00762252	.00639044
g2numsis4	-.08069809	.04169888	.04066566	-.20568928	-.08466266
g2numsis56	-.23728317	-.39603445	-.27682716	-.07193915	.02019594
mexamer	-.17299911	-.08332967	-.2664076	-.33509681	-.15673692
white	.28622109	.39412227	.3360407	.07001459	.09414982
other	.72968437	.73260846	.63354283	.4924946	.50916217
female	.00252315	-.03896935	-.02328522	-.08524584	-.1738782
g2earn10000	.06378774	.02534065	.03108362	.02009589	.00985586
g1age	-.00395698	.00481548	.01366315	.01049165	.01498304
g2age	.00971551	.015492	.00742929	.01103589	.00831514
g2numbro	.00905388	.04138834	.03833616	.04824819	.04820967
_cons	.81795076	-1.5923928	-2.2494581	-2.6439634	-3.5100086

Brant Test of Parallel Regression Assumption

variable	chi2	p>chi2	df
All	87.23	0.000	48
g1yrschl	1.61	0.807	4
sqg1yrschl	1.69	0.792	4
g2numsis4	4.63	0.328	4
g2numsis56	6.24	0.182	4
mexamer	2.83	0.586	4
white	20.22	0.000	4
other	0.93	0.921	4
female	5.02	0.285	4
g2earn10000	11.24	0.024	4
g1age	12.90	0.012	4
g2age	6.67	0.154	4
g2numbro	2.23	0.693	4

A significant test statistic provides evidence that the parallel regression assumption has been violated.

Score Test for the Proportional Odds Assumption		
Chi-Square	DF	Pr > ChiSq
92.6263	56	0.0015

Display B.17.11 Ordered Logit Model in Stata, with Odds Ratios Reported

	Syntax
Syntax	included in default SAS proc logistic output	ologit, or

Results

Stata output:

Ordered logistic regression

```
Number of obs   =     5472
LR chi2(14)     =   271.70
Prob > chi2     =   0.0000
Pseudo R2       =   0.0149
```

Log likelihood = -9005.8197

g1mileso	Odds Ratio	Std. Err.	z	P>|z|	[95% Conf. Interval]	
g1yrschl	.976652	.0374841	-0.63	0.532	.9054941	1.052568
sqg1yrschl	1.005848	.0017648	3.32	0.001	1.002394	1.009313
g2numsis4	.99071	.1175995	-0.08	0.937	.7850675	1.250219
g2numsis56	.7725229	.1066173	-1.87	0.061	.5894343	1.012482
g2numsis7p	2.010059	.5260795	2.67	0.008	1.203454	3.357285
amind	2.106802	.7185245	2.18	0.029	1.079745	4.110795
mexamer	.8682453	.1416187	-0.87	0.386	.6306723	1.195312
white	1.391168	.1015783	4.52	0.000	1.205668	1.605208
other	2.012288	.4504589	3.12	0.002	1.297613	3.120578
female	.9397502	.0499158	-1.17	0.242	.8468372	1.042857
g2earn10000	1.024964	.0075866	3.33	0.001	1.010202	1.039942
g1age	1.006623	.0041152	1.61	0.106	.9985901	1.014721
g2age	1.012027	.0046979	2.58	0.010	1.002861	1.021277
g2numbro	1.02946	.0168516	1.77	0.076	.9969558	1.063024
/cut1	-.2197333	.2851794			-.7786746	.339208
/cut2	1.663156	.2857951			1.103008	2.223305
/cut3	2.15882	.2864267			1.597434	2.720206
/cut4	2.882052	.274971			2.318568	3.445537
/cut5	3.415402	.2884828			2.849987	3.980818

SAS output — Odds Ratio Estimates:

Effect	Point Estimate	95% Wald Confidence Limits	
g1yrschl	0.976	0.907	1.050
sqg1yrschl	1.006	1.002	1.009
g2numsis4	0.991	0.784	1.252
g2numsis56	0.773	0.593	1.007
g2numsis7p	2.010	1.237	3.268
amind	2.108	1.036	4.287
mexamer	0.868	0.632	1.193
white	1.391	1.208	1.603
other	2.012	1.301	3.110
female	0.940	0.847	1.043
g2earn10000	1.025	1.010	1.040
g1age	1.007	0.999	1.015
g2age	1.012	1.003	1.021
g2numbro	1.029	0.997	1.063

■ Display B.17.12 Predicted Values for Ordered Logit Model

Syntax

```
data predo10;
set predround;
g2earn10000=0;
run;

proc logistic descending data=GSSch17;
Model g1mileso=g1yrsch1 sqg1yrsch1 g2numsis4
g2numsis56 g2numsis7pamind mexamer
white other female g2earn10000
g1age g2age g2numbro;
Score data=predo10 out=predo10s;

proc means data=predo10s;
var p_1 p_8 p_30 p_123 p_350 p_1500;
run;
```

```
margins, predict(outcome(1)) at(g2earn10000=0 g1yrsch1=11 sqg1yrsch1=121   ///
g2numsis4=0 g2numsis56=0 g2numsis7p=0                                      ///
amind=0 mexamer=0 white=1 other=0 female=1                                 ///
g1age=60 g2age=34 g2numbro=1)                                              ///

margins, predict(outcome(8)) noatlegend at(g2earn10000=0 g2numsis56=0      ///
sqg1yrsch1=121 g2numsis4=0 g2numsis56=0                                    ///
g2numsis7p=0 amind=0 mexamer=0 white=1                                     ///
other=0 female=1 g1age=60 g2age=34 g2numbro=1)                             ///

margins, predict(outcome(30)) noatlegend at(g2earn10000=0 g2numsis56=0     ///
sqg1yrsch1=121 g2numsis4=0 g2numsis56=0                                    ///
g2numsis7p=0 amind=0 mexamer=0 white=1                                     ///
other=0 female=1 g1age=60 g2age=34 g2numbro=1)                             ///

margins, predict(outcome(123)) noatlegend at(g2earn10000=0 g1yrsch1=11     ///
sqg1yrsch1=121 g2numsis4=0 g2numsis56=0                                    ///
g2numsis7p=0 amind=0 mexamer=0 white=1                                     ///
other=0 female=1 g1age=60 g2age=34 g2numbro=1)                             ///

margins, predict(outcome(350)) noatlegend at(g2earn10000=0 g1yrsch1=11     ///
sqg1yrsch1=121 g2numsis4=0 g2numsis56=0                                    ///
g2numsis7p=0 amind=0 mexamer=0 white=1                                     ///
other=0 female=1 g1age=60 g2age=34 g2numbro=1)                             ///

margins, predict(outcome(1500)) noatlegend at(g2earn10000=0 g1yrsch1=11    ///
sqg1yrsch1=121 g2numsis4=0 g2numsis56=0                                    ///
g2numsis7p=0 amind=0 mexamer=0 white=1                                     ///
other=0 female=1 g1age=60 g2age=34 g2numbro=1)                             ///
```

Results

Variable	N	Mean	Std Dev	Minimum	Maximum
P_1	1	0.1467200	.	0.1467200	0.1467200
P_8	1	0.3838203	.	0.3838203	0.3838203
P_30	1	0.1192160	.	0.1192160	0.1192160
P_123	1	0.1429307	.	0.1429307	0.1429307
P_350	1	0.0742976	.	0.0742976	0.0742976
P_1500	1	0.1330155	.	0.1330155	0.1330155

```
Expression :  Pr(g1mileso=1), predict(outcome(1))
at         :  g1yrsch1    =     11
              sqg1yrsch1  =    121
              g2numsis4   =      0
              g2numsis56  =      0
              g2numsis7p  =      0
              amind       =      0
              mexamer     =      0
              white       =      1
              other       =      0
              female      =      1
              g2earn10000 =      0
              g1age       =     60
              g2age       =     34
              g2numbro    =      1
```

	Margin	Delta-method Std. Err.	z	P>|z|	[95% Conf. Interval]
_cons	.146713	.0064259	22.83	0.000	.1341184 .1593075

(continued)

■ Display B.17.12 Predicted Values for Ordered Logit Model in Stata, using Stata's *margins* command (continued)

	Margin	Delta-method Std. Err.	z	P>|z|	[95% Conf. Interval]	
_cons	.383817	.0079131	48.50	0.000	.3683075	.3993264

	Margin	Delta-method Std. Err.	z	P>|z|	[95% Conf. Interval]	
_cons	.119219	.004826	26.60	0.000	.1104333	.1280046

	Margin	Delta-method Std. Err.	z	P>|z|	[95% Conf. Interval]	
_cons	.142933	.0050775	28.15	0.000	.1329813	.1528848

	Margin	Delta-method Std. Err.	z	P>|z|	[95% Conf. Interval]	
_cons	.0742982	.0037516	19.80	0.000	.0669453	.0816512

	Margin	Delta-method Std. Err.	z	P>|z|	[95% Conf. Interval]	
_cons	.1330198	.0058624	22.69	0.000	.1215297	.1445099

Results

APPENDIX B

Display B.17.13 Discrete Change and Marginal Effects from Stata's *prchange* Command Following *ologit*

Syntax

```
ologit g1mileso g1yrschl sqg1yrschl g2numsis4 g2numsis56 g2numsis7p ///
    amind mexamer white other female g2earn10000 g1age g2age g2numbro
prchange, fromto
```

Results

```
ologit: Changes in Probabilities for g1mileso

g2earn10000
            Avg|Chg|           1          8          30         123         350        1500
from:x=min         0   .13734224  .37399274   .12071273   .14770807   .07809997   .14214423
  to:x=max         0   .01521856  .07698562    .0507031    .1128539   .11364435   .63059449
dif:min->max  .17466487  -.12212368 -.29700712  -.07000963  -.03485417   .03554437   .48845026
from:x-1/2         0   .13000371  .36548737   .12169646   .15149018   .08127239    .1500499
  to:x+1/2         0    .1272023  .36208797     .122017   .15291911   .08251391   .15322179
dif:-+1/2   .00205429  -.00276348  -.0033994   .00032053   .00142893   .00124152   .00317189
from:x-1/2sd       0   .13388607  .37007949   .12119869    .1494612   .07957193   .14577772
to:x+1/2sd         0    .1235231   .3573816   .12239979    .154813   .08422579   .15767185
dif:-+sd/2  .00770143  -.01036297 -.01274133    .0012011   .00535518   .00465386    .0189414
MargEfct    .00205432  -.00276346  -.0033995   .00032055   .00142897   .00124155   .00317188

...
                   1          8          30         123         350        1500
Pr(y|x)     .12861565  .3637937   .12186114   .15220778   .08189271   .15162903
```

	g1yrschl	g2earn10000	sqg1yrschl	g1age
x=	11.4006	3.07057	138.617	60.0875
sd_x=	2.94021	62.2587		11.3023

	g2numsis4	g2numsis56	g2numsis7p	amind	mexamer	white	other
x=	.044773	.03655	.009868	.004569	.030336	.809942	.012975
sd_x=	.206825	.187671	.098858	.067444	.171527	.392383	.113177

	female	g2age	g2numbro
x=	.602887	34.2939	1.4333
sd_x=	.489344	10.0098	1.56628

Display B.17.14 Survey Logit Model in SAS and Stata

	SAS	Stata
Syntax		
Results		

SAS

Syntax

```
proc surveylogistic rate="c:\nsfh_distance\SAS\rate";
   model g1milesD45(descending)=
mexamer white other female g2earn10000 g2age
g2numbro g2numsis4 g2numsis5p
g1yrschl sqg1yrschl g1age;
   domain DistanceSample;
   cluster PSU;
   strata StratumC;
   weight adjweight;
run;
```

Results

Analysis of Maximum Likelihood Estimates

Parameter	Estimate	Standard Error	Wald Chi-Square	Pr > ChiSq
Intercept	-2.0693	0.2865	52.1505	<.0001
mexamer	-0.3224	0.2242	2.0673	0.1505
white	0.4058	0.0824	24.2762	<.0001
other	0.7444	0.2250	10.9475	0.0009
female	0.0150	0.0638	0.0557	0.8135
g2earn10000	0.0352	0.00832	17.8675	<.0001
g2age	0.00439	0.00584	0.5664	0.4517
g2numbro	0.0528	0.0186	8.0767	0.0045
g2numsis4	0.0219	0.1401	0.0243	0.8760
g2numsis5p	-0.0457	0.1475	0.0961	0.7566
g1yrschl	-0.0814	0.0433	3.5393	0.0599
sqg1yrschl	0.00840	0.00187	20.2596	<.0001
g1age	0.0131	0.00473	7.7253	0.0054

Stata

Syntax

```
svyset PSU [pw=adjweight], strata(Stratum) singleunit(certainty)

svy, subpop(DistanceSample):logit g1milesD45
     mexamer white other female g2earn10000  g2age       ///
     g2numbro g2numsis4 g2numsis5p                        ///
     g1yrschl sqg1yrschl g1age                            ///
```

Results

```
Survey: Logistic regression

Number of strata   =    68      Number of obs       =      6477
Number of PSUs     =   100      Population size     = 7057.8878
                                Subpop. no. of obs  =      5472
                                Subpop. size        =      5472
                                Design df           =        32
                                F(  12,    21)      =     28.10
                                Prob > F            =    0.0000
```

		Linearized		
g1milesD45	Coef.	Std. Err.	t	P>|t|
mexamer	-.3224212	.224031	-1.44	0.160
white	.4058414	.0822931	4.93	0.000
other	.7443781	.2247678	3.31	0.002
female	.0150475	.0637168	0.24	0.815
g2earn10000	.0351546	.008309	4.23	0.000
g2age	.004394	.0058332	0.75	0.457
g2numbro	.0528165	.0185674	2.84	0.008
g2numsis4	.0218593	.1399651	0.16	0.877
g2numsis5p	-.0457153	.1473679	-0.31	0.758
g1yrschl	-.0813964	.0432261	-1.88	0.069
sqg1yrschl	.0084002	.0018645	4.51	0.000
g1age	.0131431	.0047243	2.78	0.009
_cons	-2.069253	.2862737	-7.23	0.000

Note: strata with single sampling unit treated as certainty units.

APPENDIX B

APPENDIX B

■ Display B.17.15 Survey Multinomial Logit Model in SAS and Stata

	SAS	Stata

Syntax	`proc surveylogistic rate="c:\nsfh_distance\SAS\rate";`
	`model g1milesN(descending)=`
	`mexamer white other female g2earn10000 g2age`
	`g2numbro g2numsis4 g2numsis5p`
	`g1lyrsch1 sqg1lyrsch1 g1age`
	`/ link=glogit;`
	`domain DistanceSample;`
	`cluster PSU;`
	`strata StratumC;`
	`weight adjweight;`
	`run;`
		`svyset PSU [pw=adjweight], strata(Stratum) singleunit(certainty)`
		
		`svy, subpop(DistanceSample):mlogit g1milesN`
		`    mexamer white other female g2earn10000   g2age`
		`    g2numbro g2numsis4 g2numsis5p`
		`    g1lyrsch1 sqg1lyrsch1 g1age`
		`    , baseout(23)`

Stata output:

```
Survey: Multinomial logistic regression

Number of strata    =    68    Number of obs        =      6477
Number of PSUs      =   100    Population size      = 7057.8878
                                Subpop. no. of obs   =      5472
                                Subpop. size         =      5472
                                Design df            =        32
                                F( 24,    9)         =      9.87
                                Prob > F             =    0.0006

                          Linearized
g1milesN       Coef.      Std. Err.     t     P>|t|

273
mexamer     -.5305576    .2200159   -2.41    0.022
white        .5260773    .0962487    5.47    0.000
other        .6910349    .2488438    2.78    0.009
female       .1126779    .0778045    1.45    0.157
g2earn10000  .0419577    .0090143    4.65    0.000
g2age        .000911     .0071719    0.13    0.900
g2numbro    -.0386724    .0241638    1.60    0.119
g2numsis4    .0476672    .1689108    0.28    0.780
g2numsis5p  -.1015227    .2643425   -0.38    0.703
g1lyrsch1   -.0788982    .0535493   -1.47    0.150
sqg1lyrsch1  .0074262    .0023713    3.13    0.004
g1age        .0135059    .0057012    2.37    0.024
_cons       -2.555869    .3355047   -7.62    0.000
```

SAS output — Results:

Analysis of Maximum Likelihood Estimates

Parameter	1milesN	Estimate	Standard Error	Wald Chi-Square	Pr > ChiSq
Intercept	1500	-3.0487	0.4723	41.6745	<.0001
Intercept	273	-2.5559	0.3362	57.7844	<.0001
mexamer	1500	-0.1041	0.2660	0.1532	0.6955
mexamer	273	-0.5303	0.2205	5.7829	0.0162
white	1500	0.2519	0.1231	4.1886	0.0407
white	273	0.5261	0.0965	29.7458	<.0001
other	1500	0.8066	0.2718	8.8091	0.0030
other	273	0.6910	0.2494	7.6782	0.0056
female	1500	-0.1210	0.0586	4.2604	0.0390
female	273	0.1127	0.0780	2.0883	0.1484
g2earn10000	1500	0.0254	0.00868	8.5625	0.0034
g2earn10000	273	0.0420	0.00903	21.5713	<.0001
g2age	1500	0.00918	0.00710	1.6726	0.1959
g2age	273	0.000911	0.00719	0.0161	0.8991
g2numbro	1500	0.0712	0.0187	14.4395	0.0001
g2numbro	273	0.0387	0.0242	2.5503	0.1103

(continued)

Display B.17.15 Survey Multinomial Logit Model in SAS and Stata (continued)

SAS

Results

Analysis of Maximum Likelihood Estimates

Parameter	1milesN	Estimate	Standard Error	Wald Chi-Square	Pr > ChiSq
g2numsis4	1500	-0.0119	0.1670	0.0050	0.9434
g2numsis4	273	0.0477	0.1693	0.0793	0.7783
g2numsis5p	1500	0.0242	0.1469	0.0272	0.8690
g2numsis5p	273	-0.1015	0.2649	0.1469	0.7016
g1yrschl	1500	-0.0821	0.0584	1.9737	0.1601
g1yrschl	273	-0.0789	0.0537	2.1615	0.1415
sqg1yrschl	1500	0.00960	0.00256	14.0754	0.0002
sqg1yrschl	273	0.00743	0.00238	9.7659	0.0018
g1age	1500	0.0127	0.00627	4.0975	0.0429
g1age	273	0.0135	0.00571	5.5877	0.0181

Stata

1500				
mexamer	-.1040932	.2653711	-0.39	0.697
white	.2518502	.1227902	2.05	0.049
other	.8066186	.2711819	2.97	0.006
female	-.1209701	.0584801	-2.07	0.047
g2earn10000	.0253915	.0086587	2.93	0.006
g2age	.0091841	.0070859	1.30	0.204
g2numbro	.0711998	.0186965	3.81	0.001
g2numsis4	-.0118528	.1666086	-0.07	0.944
g2numsis5p	.0242315	.1465736	0.17	0.870
g1yrschl	-.0821007	.0583122	-1.41	0.169
sqg1yrschl	-.0096044	.0025544	3.76	0.001
g1age	.0126973	.006259	2.03	0.051
_cons	-3.048697	.4712327	-6.47	0.000

(g1milesN==23 is the base outcome)
Note: strata with single sampling unit treated as certainty units.

▪ Display B.17.16 Survey Ordered Logit Model in SAS and Stata

	SAS	Stata

Syntax	`proc surveylogistic rate="c:\nsfh_distance\SAS\rate";`
	`    model g1milesN(descending)=`
	`    mexamer white other female g2earn10000 g2age`
	`    g2numbro g2numsis4 g2numsis5p`
	`    g1yrschl sqg1yrschl g1age;`
	`    domain DistanceSample;`
	`    cluster PSU;`
	`    strata StratumC;`
	`    weight adjweight;`
	`run;`
		`svyset PSU [pw=adjweight], strata(Stratum) singleunit(certainty)`
		
		`svy, subpop(DistanceSample):ologit g1milesN`
		`    mexamer white other female g2earn10000  g2age`
		`    g2numbro g2numsis4 g2numsis5p`
		`    g1yrschl sqg1yrschl g1age`

Results — SAS

Analysis of Maximum Likelihood Estimates

Parameter		Estimate	Standard Error	Wald Chi-Square	Pr > ChiSq
Intercept	1500	-3.3067	0.3055	117.1592	<.0001
Intercept	273	-2.0355	0.2981	46.6319	<.0001
mexamer		-0.2964	0.2262	1.7180	0.1899
white		0.3373	0.0851	15.7024	<.0001
other		0.7447	0.2174	11.7347	0.0006
female		-0.0436	0.0541	0.6493	0.4203
g2earn10000		0.0220	0.00558	15.5197	<.0001
g2age		0.00543	0.00532	1.0409	0.3076
g2numbro		0.0536	0.0161	11.0148	0.0009
g2numsis4		-0.00030	0.1311	0.0000	0.9982
g2numsis5p		-0.0347	0.1152	0.0907	0.7633
g1yrschl		-0.0622	0.0415	2.2446	0.1341
sqg1yrschl		0.00751	0.00177	18.0602	<.0001
g1age		0.0126	0.00442	8.1116	0.0044

Results — Stata

Survey: Ordered logistic regression

Number of strata = 68	Number of obs	= 6477
Number of PSUs = 100	Population size	= 7057.8878
	Subpop. no. of obs	= 5472
	Subpop. size	= 5472
	Design df	= 32
	F(12, 21)	= 31.18
	Prob > F	= 0.0000

g1milesN	Coef.	Linearized Std. Err.	t	P>|t|
mexamer	-.2965085	.238726	-1.26	0.216
white	.3373229	.0874555	3.86	0.001
other	.7447525	.2242296	3.32	0.002
female	-.0436139	.0542011	-0.80	0.427
g2earn10000	.0219998	.0053928	4.08	0.000
g2age	.0054316	.0052988	1.03	0.313
g2numbro	.0535913	.0161219	3.32	0.002
g2numsis4	-.0003039	.1292971	-0.00	0.998
g2numsis5p	-.0346895	.1178956	-0.29	0.770
g1yrschl	-.0621706	.0429441	-1.45	0.157
sqg1yrschl	.0075049	.0018181	4.13	0.000
g1age	.0125799	.0044132	2.85	0.008
/cut1	2.035629	.312149	6.52	0.000
/cut2	3.306811	.3190155	10.37	0.000

Note: strata with single sampling unit treated as certainty units.

SCREENSHOTS OF DATA SET DOCUMENTATION

The following are screenshots from data set archives and documentation files.

Each is numbered to refer to this appendix letter (C), the chapter number where it is referenced and its order of reference in the chapter. For example, Display C.2.1 would be the first screenshot referred to in Chapter Two.

Note that because many of these screenshots were taken from active web sites they may not exactly match what you see if you visit the current web site.

APPENDIX C

▪ Display C.2.1 Browsing the ICPSR Data holding

Study Search Results - Windows Internet Explorer

http://www.icpsr.umich.edu/icpsrweb/ICPSR/studies/classifications/ICPSR.XVIII/4.ssortBj=10&pg/mg_rows=25

File   Edit   View   Favorites   Tools   Help

x Convert ▾ Select

Favorites | Suggested Sites ▾ Web Slice Gallery ▾

Study Search Results

Log In / Create Account

ICPSR | INTER-UNIVERSITY CONSORTIUM FOR POLITICAL AND SOCIAL RESEARCH

Home | Find & Analyze Data | About ICPSR | Deposit Data & Findings | Digital Curation | Membership | Partners & Projects | Teaching & Learning | Help

Find & Analyze Data

Find ICPSR Data
Bibliography of Data Related Literature
Variables Database
Analyze Data Online
Thematic Collections
Restricted Data
Publication-Related Archive

Study Search Results

If you weren't looking for datasets, you can also perform your query against our citations database or database of variables/questions. You may also wish to look over our searching tips, or utilize our subject thesaurus to refine your search.

Query:

160 results found

Results per page: 25 ▾

Sort by: Most Downloaded ▾

1 - 25 ▶ ▶|

Study No.	Study Title/Investigator	No. of Downloads
21600	National Longitudinal Study of Adolescent Health (Add Health), 1994-2008 Harris, Kathleen Mullan; Udry, J. Richard	892
22626	India Human Development Survey (IHDS), 2005 Desai, Sonalde; Vanneman, Reeve; National Council of Applied Economic Research, New Delhi	238
4549	The 500 Family Study [1998-2000: United States] Schneider, Barbara; Waite, Linda J	200
20520	Children of Immigrants Longitudinal Study (CILS), 1991-2006 Portes, Alejandro; Rumbaut, Rubén G.	175
4701	Welfare, Children, and Families: A Three-City Study Angel, Ronald; Burton, Linda; Chase-Lansdale, P. Lindsay; et al.	131
26149	American Time Use Survey (ATUS), 2008	81

Filter Results

Filter by Subject
adolescents (70)
neighborhoods (57)
birth control (50)
family planning (46)
child development (45)
view all

Filter by Geography
United States (112)
Chicago (48)
Illinois (47)
Global (24)
Asia (6)
view all

Filter by Time Period
from [   ] to [   ] Go
Enter year only, formatted as YYYY.

Filter by Author
Brooks-Gunn, Jeanne (44)
Earls, Felton J. (44)
Raudenbush, Stephen W. (44)
Sampson, Robert J. (44)
Harris, Kathleen Mullan (19)
view all

Search for Data   Search Web site

[Search]

Internet | Protected Mode: On

■ Display C.2.2 Searching the ICPSR Variables Database

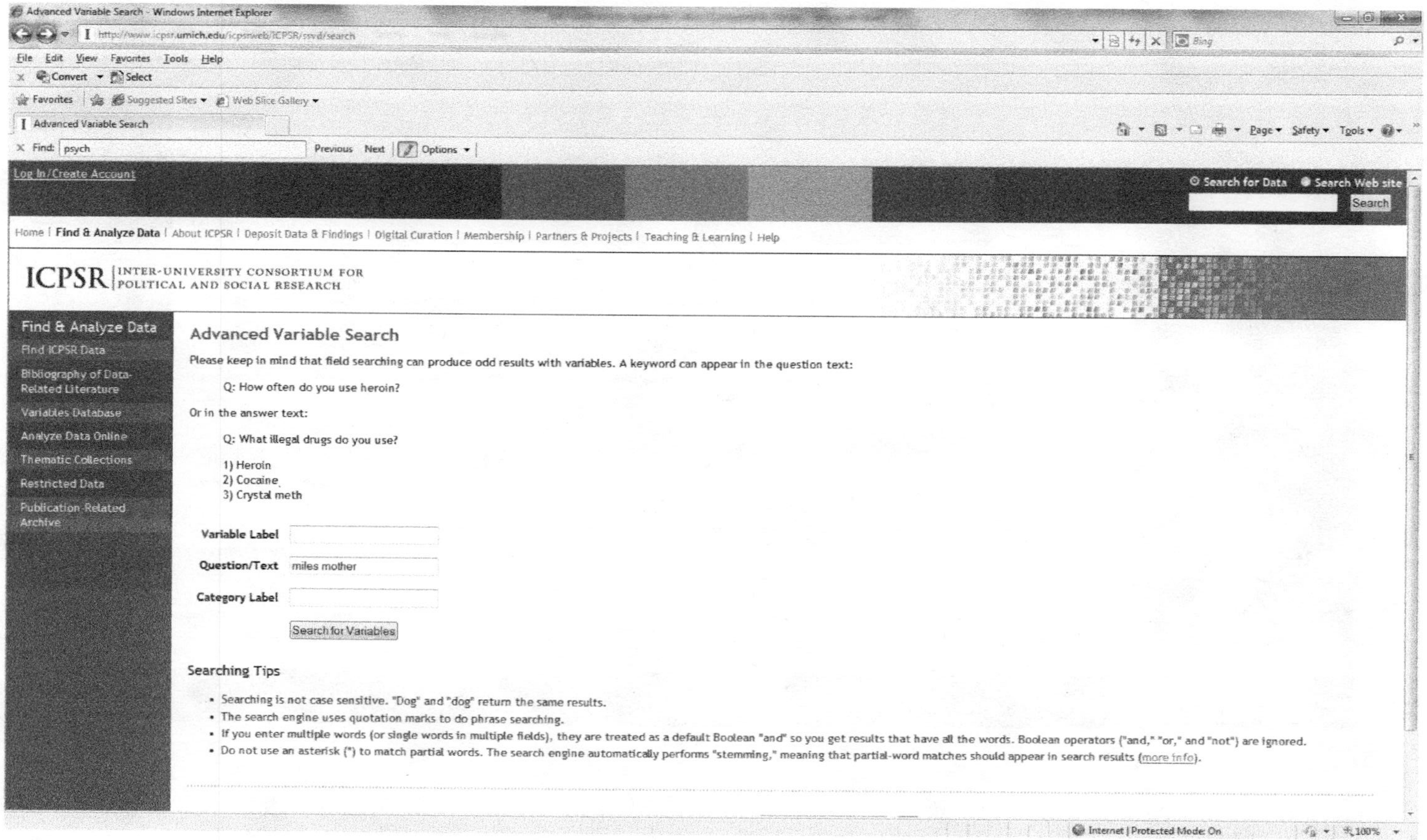

▪ Display C.2.3 Searching the ICPSR Bibliography

■ Display C.3.1 The BADGIR Utility

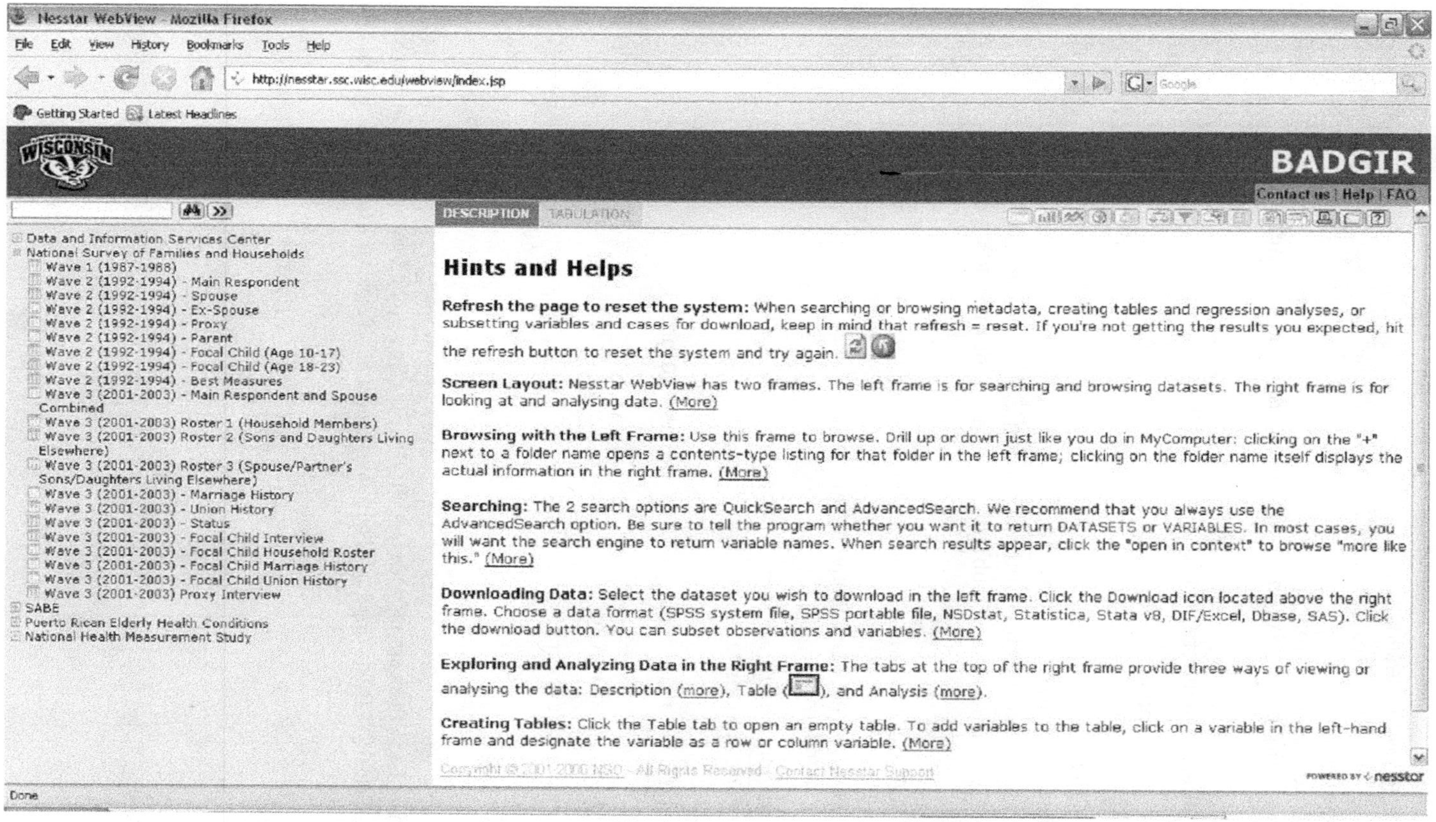

Nesstar WebView - Mozilla Firefox

File   Edit   View   History   Bookmarks   Tools   Help

http://nesstar.ssc.wisc.edu/webview/index.jsp   ▼   G ▼ Google

Getting Started   Latest Headlines

WISCONSIN

Data and Information Services Center
National Survey of Families and Households
  Wave 1 (1987-1988)
  Wave 2 (1992-1994) - Main Respondent
  Wave 2 (1992-1994) - Spouse
  Wave 2 (1992-1994) - Ex-Spouse
  Wave 2 (1992-1994) - Proxy
  Wave 2 (1992-1994) - Parent
  Wave 2 (1992-1994) - Focal Child (Age 10-17)
  Wave 2 (1992-1994) - Focal Child (Age 18-23)
  Wave 2 (1992-1994) - Best Measures
  Wave 3 (2001-2003) - Main Respondent and Spouse Combined
  Wave 3 (2001-2003) Roster 1 (Household Members)
  Wave 3 (2001-2003) Roster 2 (Sons and Daughters Living Elsewhere)
  Wave 3 (2001-2003) Roster 3 (Spouse/Partner's Sons/Daughters Living Elsewhere)
  Wave 3 (2001-2003) - Marriage History
  Wave 3 (2001-2003) - Union History
  Wave 3 (2001-2003) - Status
  Wave 3 (2001-2003) - Focal Child Interview
  Wave 3 (2001-2003) - Focal Child Household Roster
  Wave 3 (2001-2003) - Focal Child Marriage History
  Wave 3 (2001-2003) - Focal Child Union History
  Wave 3 (2001-2003) Proxy Interview
SABE
Puerto Rican Elderly: Health Conditions
National Health Measurement Study

BADGIR

Contact us | Help | FAQ

DESCRIPTION   TABULATION

Hints and Helps

Refresh the page to reset the system: When searching or browsing metadata, creating tables and regression analyses, or subsetting variables and cases for download, keep in mind that refresh = reset. If you're not getting the results you expected, hit the refresh button to reset the system and try again.

Screen Layout: Nesstar WebView has two frames. The left frame is for searching and browsing datasets. The right frame is for looking at and analysing data. (More)

Browsing with the Left Frame: Use this frame to browse. Drill up or down just like you do in MyComputer: clicking on the "+" next to a folder name opens a contents-type listing for that folder in the left frame; clicking on the folder name itself displays the actual information in the right frame. (More)

Searching: The 2 search options are QuickSearch and AdvancedSearch. We recommend that you always use the AdvancedSearch option. Be sure to tell the program whether you want it to return DATASETS or VARIABLES. In most cases, you will want the search engine to return variable names. When search results appear, click the "open in context" to browse "more like this." (More)

Downloading Data: Select the dataset you wish to download in the left frame. Click the Download icon located above the right frame. Choose a data format (SPSS system file, SPSS portable file, NSDstat, Statistica, Stata v8, DIF/Excel, Dbase, SAS). Click the download button. You can subset observations and variables. (More)

Exploring and Analyzing Data in the Right Frame: The tabs at the top of the right frame provide three ways of viewing or analysing the data: Description (more), Table ( ), and Analysis (more).

Creating Tables: Click the Table tab to open an empty table. To add variables to the table, click on a variable in the left-hand frame and designate the variable as a row or column variable. (More)

powered by ✓ nesstar

Done

■ Display C.3.2 Identification of Relevant Variables in NSFH Content Outline

VIII. OUTLINE OF THE CONTENT OF THE
NATIONAL SURVEY OF FAMILIES AND HOUSEHOLDS

INTERVIEW WITH PRIMARY RESPONDENT

Household Composition
    A. Household composition
       1. Household composition – age, sex, marital status

Social and Economic Characteristics
    A. Social background
       1. Race
       2. Religious preference and activity
       3. Recent residential movement
       4. Parent's occupation and education
       5. Family's receipt of public assistance during R's youth

SELF-ADMINISTERED QUESTIONNAIRE: PRIMARY RESPONDENT

SE-13 Parents, Relatives, and General Attitudes
    (all respondents)

    A. Information about mother
       1. Current age or age at death
       2. Health
       3. Quality of relationship with mother (Global)
       4. Current residence
       5. Contact with mother

    D. Brothers and sisters
       1. Number
       2. Quality of relationship

Source: Sweet, James, Larry Bumpass and Vaughn Call. 1988. The Design and Content of the National Survey of Families and Households. NSFH Working Paper No. 1. Available at *http://www.ssc.wisc.edu/cde/nsfhwp/nsfh1.pdf*

■ **Display C.3.3 Questionnaires and Skip Maps**

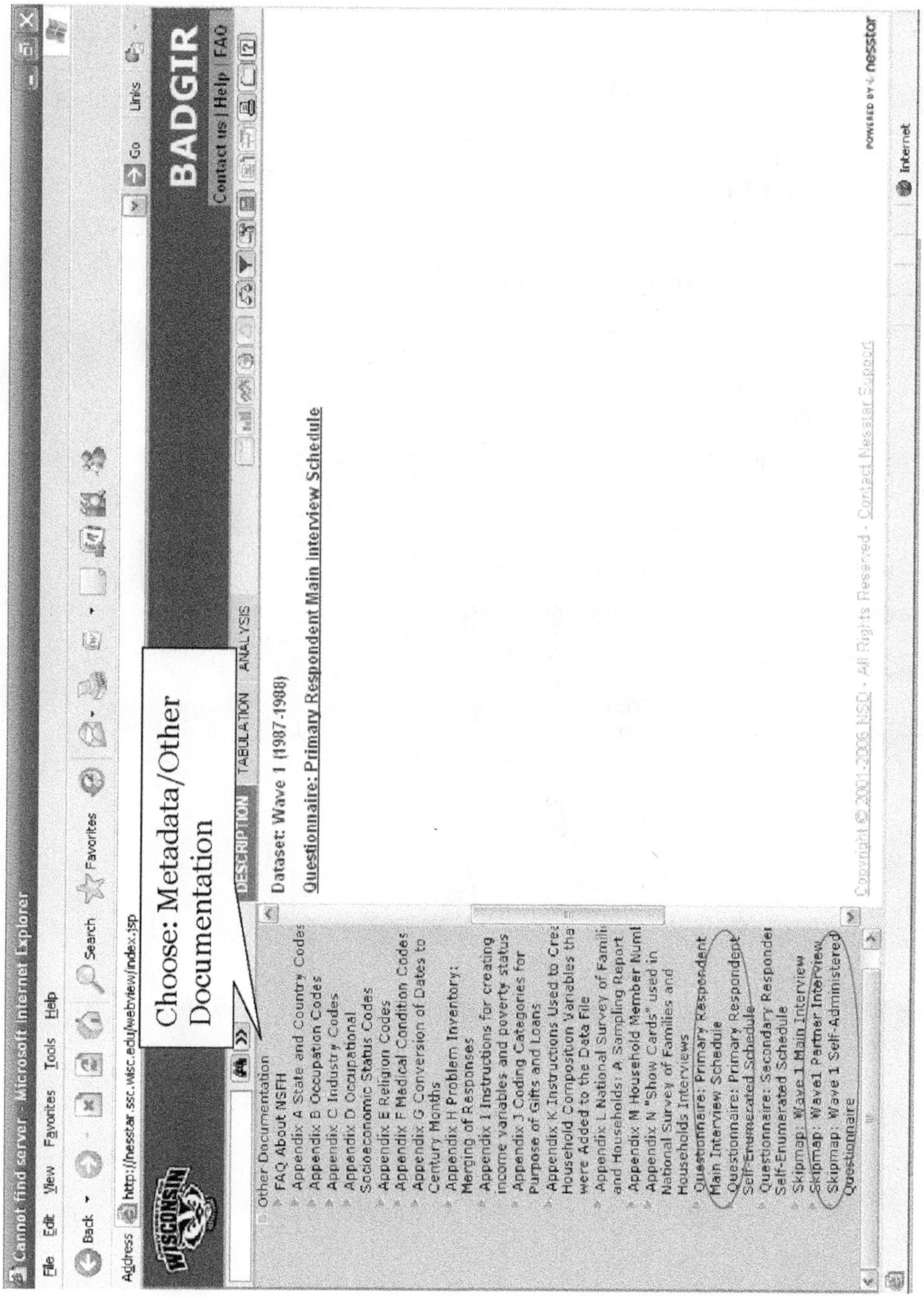

▨ **Display C.3.4 Example Skip Map: Mother's Age and Distance**

```
SE - 13 PARENTS, SIBS, AND ATTITUDES
* Includes: All Respondents
* SE Questionnaire pages 57-64
* Main Interview instructions on page 157
```

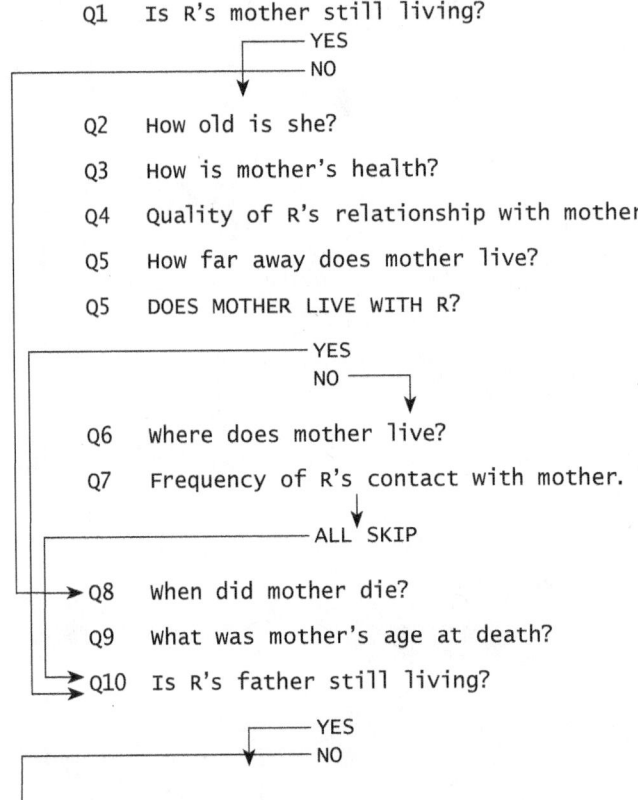

Q1   Is R's mother still living?
— YES
— NO

Q2   How old is she?

Q3   How is mother's health?

Q4   Quality of R's relationship with mother

Q5   How far away does mother live?

Q5   DOES MOTHER LIVE WITH R?
— YES
NO —

Q6   Where does mother live?

Q7   Frequency of R's contact with mother.
— ALL SKIP

Q8   When did mother die?

Q9   What was mother's age at death?

Q10 Is R's father still living?
— YES
— NO

Source: Self-Enumerated Questionnaire Skip Map. Available at *ftp://elaine.ssc.wisc.edu/pub/nsfh/T1se.pdf*

■ Display C.3.5 Example Questionnaire: Mother's Age and Distance

1. Is your mother: (circle one)

   1 Still living   OR   2 Deceased
   :   :

2. How old is she?   8. In what year did she die?

   _____ Years old   _____
                                         (year)

3. How would you describe your   9. What was her age when
   mother's health?   she died?

   1 Very poor   _____ Years old

   2 Poor

   3 Fair   — (GO TO THE NEXT PAGE)   —

   4 Good

   5 Excellent   —   —

4. How would you describe your relationship with your mother?

                    1   2   3   4   5   6   7
      VERY POOR :____ ____ ____ ____ ____ ____ ____: EXCELLENT

5. About how far away does she live?   (IF YOUR MOTHER LIVES HERE WITH
                                        YOU, GO TO THE NEXT PAGE.)

   _____ Miles IF YOU DO NOT   CITY _____
              KNOW, WRITE IN HER: STATE _____

6. Does she live in:

   1 Her own home or apartment

   2 With a son or daughter

   3 In a nursing home

   4 Someplace else: (please specify) _____
                     —

7. During the past   ABOUT   SEVERAL   1–3   ABOUT   SEVERAL
   12 months,   NOT AT   ONCE   TIMES A   TIMES A   ONCE   TIMES A
   about how often ALL   A YEAR   YEAR   MONTH   A WEEK   WEEK
   did you:

a. See your mother   1   2   3   4   5   6

Source: Primary Respondent Self-Enumerated Schedule. Available at *ftp://elaine.ssc.wisc.edu/pub/nsfh/i1se.001*

Display C.3.6 Example Codebook: Mother Living or Deceased

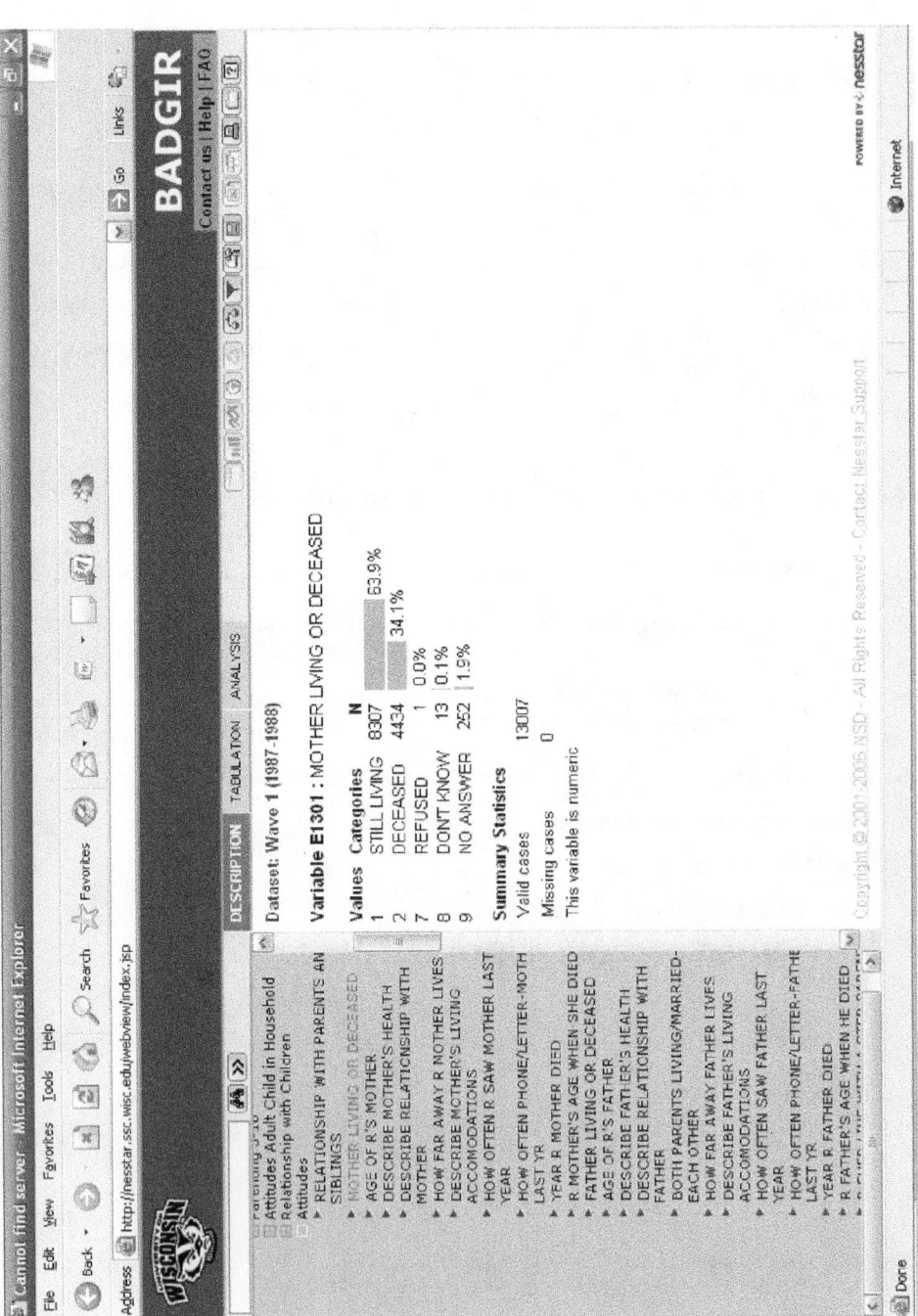

■ **Display C.3.7 Example Codebook: Mother's Age**

APPENDIX C

■ Display C.3.8 Example Codebook: Mother's Distance

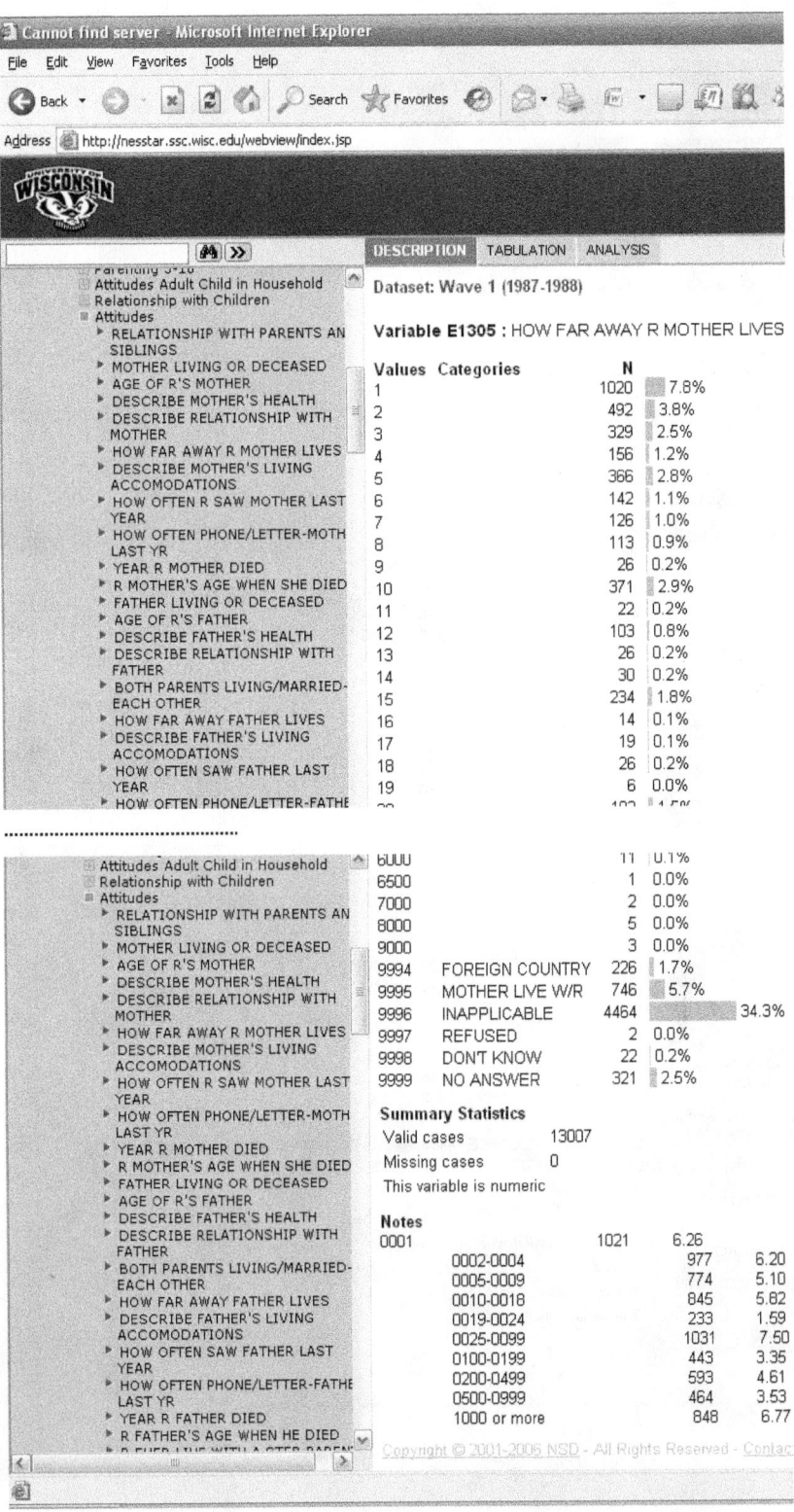

■ Display C.10 BADGIR Codebook Screenshots for M2DP01 and M484

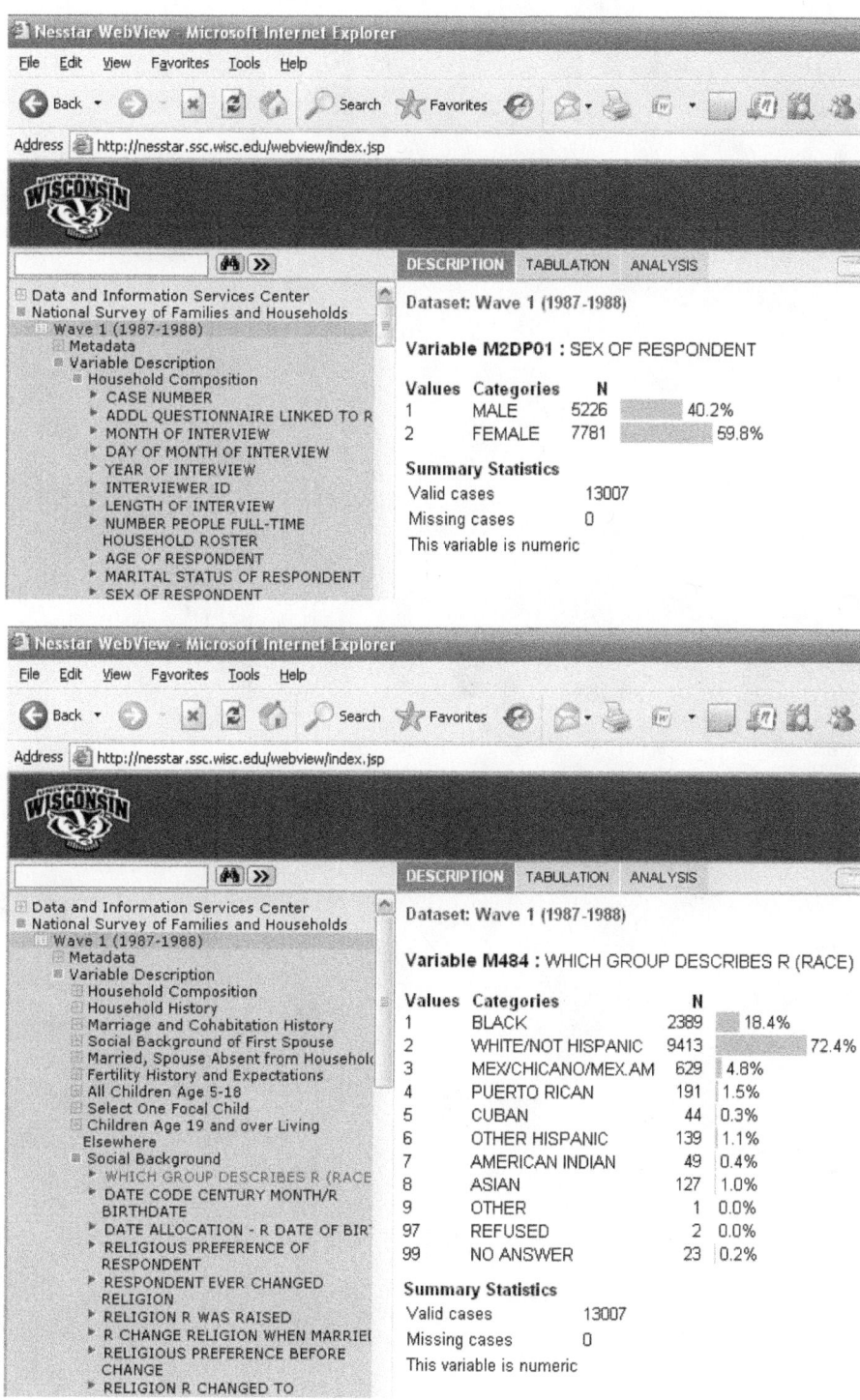

ACCESSING THE NATIONAL SURVEY OF FAMILIES AND HOUSEHOLDS RAW DATA FILE

The archives we covered in Chapter 2 make data available over the Internet, so they are readily accessible. But, not all data are available in the same formats. Thus, the steps you will need to follow to download the data and read them into SAS and Stata will vary from archive to archive. Most archives make data available for download already formatted to be read directly into at least one statistical package. But, some will require you to translate the raw data from plain text format using a batch program. In most cases, archives provide a template batch program to accomplish this task which you will need to modify slightly. In this Appendix, we walk through the process of downloading the NSFH data. Appendix E provides notes about accessing the NHIS data set used in the Chapter Exercises. If you locate your own data, for the course exercises or for a project or thesis, you may need to follow a somewhat different process.

Downloading the Data in Stata Format

If you did not already, you want to begin by preparing a new project folder called *c:\nsfh_ distance* on your hard drive to store the raw data files. Within this folder, create two subfolders, called *SAS* and *Stata*, where you will store each version of the downloaded raw data and the relevant batch programs and output.

Next, go to the BADGIR web site to access the data. Display D.1 shows the BADGIR screen for downloading the data. Clicking on the listed file called *d1all004* provides general information about the data file. Circled in green are the filename, *d1all004.NSDstat*, and number of observations (13,007) and variables (4,355). The *Download* icon is circled in black. When you click on this icon, you will be prompted to login or register. The registration screen requires you to affirm appropriate use of the data, including that you will not try to identify respondents, and that you will appropriately cite the data and notify the Center for Demography of Health and Aging at the University of Wisconsin and contact your local IRB office if you plan to use data for research purposes. (The latter is not needed if you only download the data to complete course exercises. But, if you decide to write a research paper based on the data, then you should contact your local IRB regarding their policy on existing public use data sets and share your work with the Center for Demography of Health and Aging at the University of Wisconsin.)

BADGIR allows the data to be downloaded in numerous formats, as shown in Display D.2. This includes three versions of Stata (Versions 6, 7, and 8) and one SAS format. Similar to word processing software, Stata's formats often change with new releases to accommodate new features. They are "backward compatible" but not "forward compatible," meaning that data saved in older formats can be read with a newer release of Stata, but newer formats cannot be read by older releases of Stata. Stata 11 can read any of the earlier formats available from BADGIR, so we will select the most recent (version 8) for downloading. For SAS, the note circled in dashed black on Display D.1 tells us that BADGIR will produce SAS statements to read the plain text data (rather than a *.sas7bdat* file directly in SAS format). We will discuss below how to make three small modifications to the downloaded batch SAS batch program in order to convert the raw data file from plain text to SAS format.

The Stata Version 8 file is downloaded from BADGIR as a compressed file, with a *.zip* extension. When you double-click on this *.zip* file, your computer should associate the extension with a utility that will reveal its contents (a *.dta* Stata data file and a file that ends with *.missRecode*).

You should extract or copy these files to your Stata project folder (*c:\nsfh_distance\Stata*), and see something like the following:

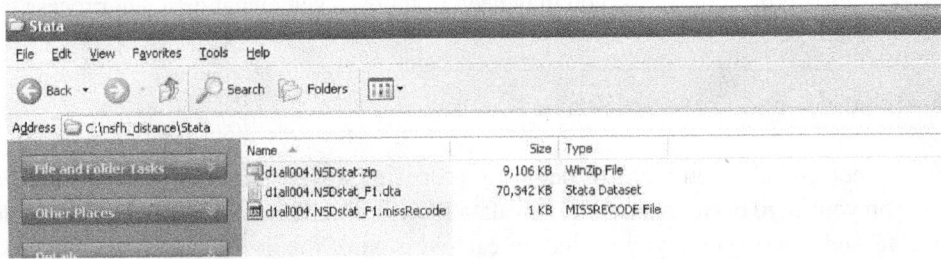

Notice that the Stata Data Set is much larger than the *.zip* file (size of over 70,000 versus 9,000 kbyte), which is why the compressed version is provided for downloading. The *.missRecode* file can be ignored. (Notice that the *.missRecode* extension is not meaningful to your computer— it does not know what software to use to open the file. In fact, it is a plain text file containing a single sentence: "Recoding of missing values exported to Stata.")

By default, Stata accesses only a certain amount of computer resources. On our computer, Stata allocates 10 MB for the data when we double click a *.dta* file, enough to open a moderately sized data set. Above, we saw that our data file was over 70,000 kbyte (70 Mb). Our data set is thus too large for the defaults. The number of variables also exceeds the limit of 2,047 for Stata/IC. Because of this, we read just a few variables and subset of cases from the data file in our example batch programs (in Displays B.4.4 and B.4.7).

If your computer has Stata/SE or Stata/MP you can open the full *d1all004.NSDstat_F1.dta* data set. But, first you need to tell Stata to allocate more of the computer's memory. We know we need more than 70 Mb for our data file, perhaps 100 Mb. The command to tell Stata to do this is `set memory 100m`. If we put this single line into a plain text file called "*profile.do*", then Stata will allocate this much memory every time we double-click on our NSFH Stata data set *d1all004. NSDstat_F1.dta*. Note that this *profile.do* file should be stored in the same directory as the *.dta* file. An alternative approach is to permanently allocate more memory to Stata on your computer with the command "`set memory 100m, permanently`." This is a good alternative if you have Stata installed on your personal computer.

Creating the SAS Raw Data File using StatTransfer

Especially since BADGIR does not provide the data file directly in SAS format, one easy way to obtain the SAS format is to use file conversion software to translate the data from Stata format to SAS format. StatTransfer and DBMS/Copy are widely used for this purpose (Hilbe 1996), although DBMS/Copy has been discontinued and does not directly read the latest versions of Stata. If you have access to such file conversion software, they offer a straightforward interface to select the type and location of the file to convert (in this case, the Stata Version 8 file *c:\nsfh_distance\Stata\d1all004.NSDstat_F1.dta*) and the file to create (in this case, a SAS Version 9 file for Windows to be stored in *c:\nsfh_distance\SAS\d1all004_NSDstat_F1. sas7bdat*). Notice that we renamed the file slightly to make it easier to read in SAS (changing the first . to _) and match the name in our examples in Display B.4.4 and B.4.7.

Creating the SAS Raw Data File with the BADGIR Utility

Let's now go back to BADGIR and download the plain text raw data and batch program to read it into SAS format. You will need to use this option if you do not have access to file conversion software like StatTransfer.

After choosing SAS format in BADGIR (see again Display D.2), we download a new compressed *.zip* file, save it to the SAS folder in our project folder (*C:\nsfh_distance\SAS*), and uncompress its contents to the same location. As expected, the compressed file contains the plain text ASCII raw data (with *.txt* extension) and the SAS batch program (with *.sas* extension).

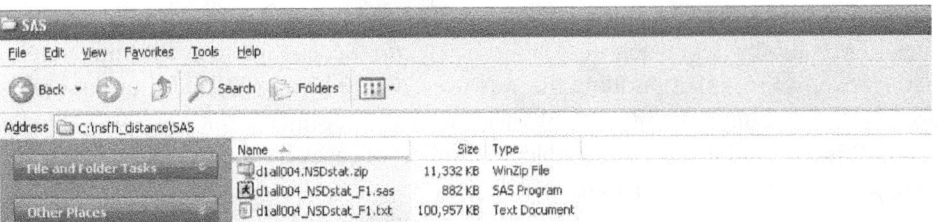

We now need to open the *.sas* file in the enhanced editor window in SAS (launch SAS and choose File/Open after clicking in the enhanced editor window). The SAS batch program contains over 36,000 lines of code, and almost certainly looks overwhelmingly complicated to you. But, someone else invested the time to write and proof these 36,000 lines of syntax! All we need to do is to make a few simple changes so that the software knows where to find the *.txt* file and save the files on our computer.

Display D.3 shows the batch program, with the enhanced editor window in SAS maximized to show more lines of text. The first two lines, circled in green, are two of the three places where we need to make changes to the file. The remainder of the batch program is all prewritten, and should be left untouched (for example, the remaining visible lines provide value labels for two of the file's variables).

First and Second Change

We need to first replace the empty quotes in the first two lines with our project folder's location, as follows:

```
LIBNAME LIBRARY ' ';
LIBNAME OUT ' ';
```

to

```
LIBNAME LIBRARY 'c:\nsfh_distance\SAS';
LIBNAME OUT 'c:\nsfh_distance\SAS';
```

This batch program illustrates the advantage of the SAS *libname*, discussed in Chapter 4. Although *libnames* can seem abstract to students, especially when first learning SAS, they provide an easy way to tailor a batch program to run on various computers. All we need to do is substitute between the quotes the location of the project folder on our computer.

Third Change

The third change we need to make is embedded in the middle of the long batch program. We can use SAS's search utility to find it (see Display D.4 for the code we are searching). Select *Edit/*

Find from the menus or type *Ctrl-F*. Type the word "INFILE" in the search box. You should make the following change, adding the path to our project folder so that SAS knows where to find the downloaded plain text (*.txt*) raw data file.

```
INFILE 'dlall004_NSDstat_F1.txt' LRECL = 7946;
```

to

```
INFILE 'c:\nsfh_distance\SAS\dlall004_NSDstat_F1.txt' LRECL = 7946;
```

Now, you need to save these changes to the batch program. We strongly encourage you to save the file with a new name. We chose the name *dlall004_NSDstat_F1R.sas* for the new name, adding *R* to the end of the original filename to indicate *Revised*. By only slightly changing the filename, it is easy to connect it to the original (and we left the original file intact, in case we receive any errors messages when we run the batch program).

You are now ready to try running the batch program (e.g., click the icon of the little running person circled in black in Display D.4). The results, shown in Display D.5, report that the raw data file was appropriately read from our project folder. And, the correct number of cases is listed (13,007). If you don't see this message, scroll up in the Log Window to look for error messages, which will be in red or can be located by searching for the word ERROR in the Log Window. Check that you don't have typos in the path and filenames that you added to the batch program, and that you did not accidentally delete one of the quotes or other portions of the text (compare the spots where you made changes to the original file).

After the batch program runs successfully, you should see two new files in your project folder: (a) the data file *dlall004_nsdstat_f1.sas7bdat*, and (b) a file called *formats.sas7bcat* which stores the labels for the variables.

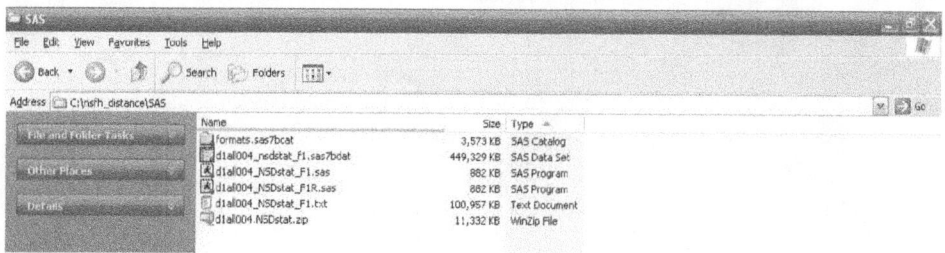

We included the following line at the beginning of our batch programs (see again Display B.4.4 and B.4.7) so that SAS will be able to locate the *formats.sas7bcat* file and associate the correct value and variable labels to the variables: `LIBNAME LIBRARY 'c:\nsfh_distance\SAS';` Although we will not focus on the formats in this book, this statement is needed for your batch program to run properly if you created the SAS raw data file by running the BADGIR SAS batch program. Otherwise, you will receive an error message.

▪ Display D.1 Notes on NSFH Wave 1 Data Set in BADGIR

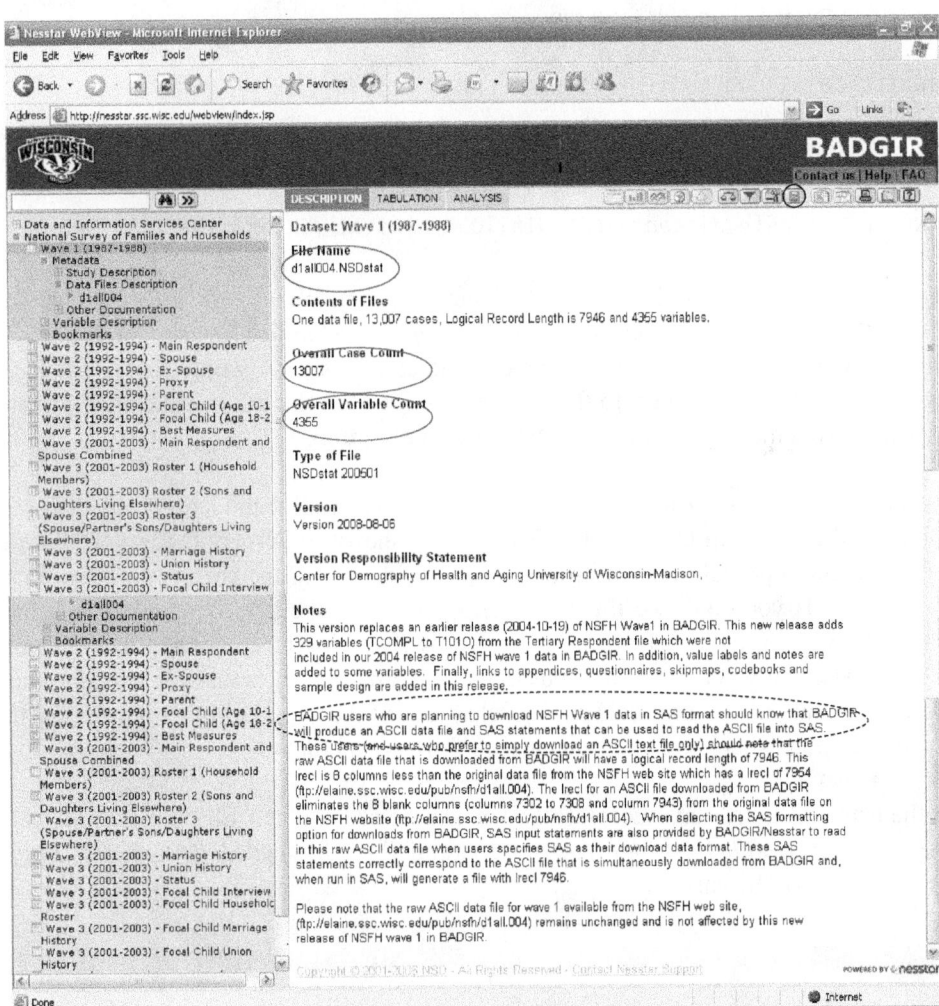

■ Display D.2 BADGIR Download Screen for NSFH Wave 1 Data Set

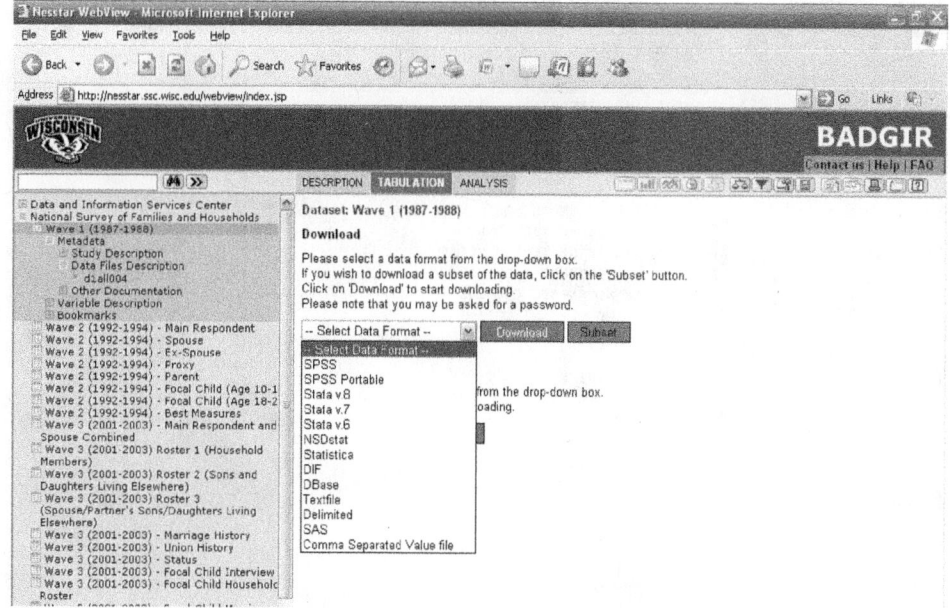

■ Display D.3 SAS Editor Window: Updating LIBNAMES

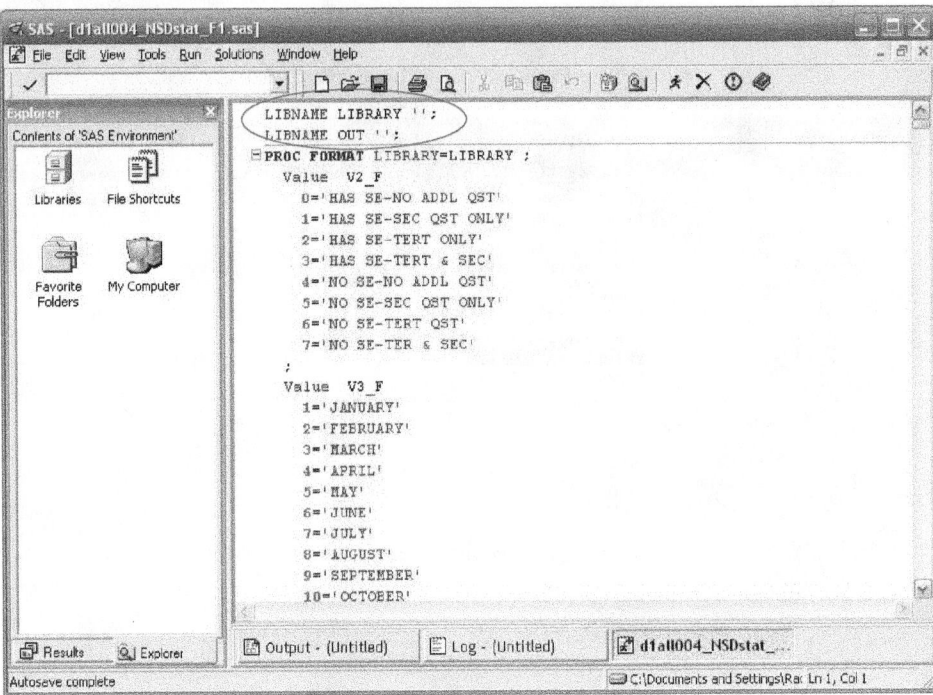

■ Display D.4 SAS Editor Window: Updating Raw Data File Location

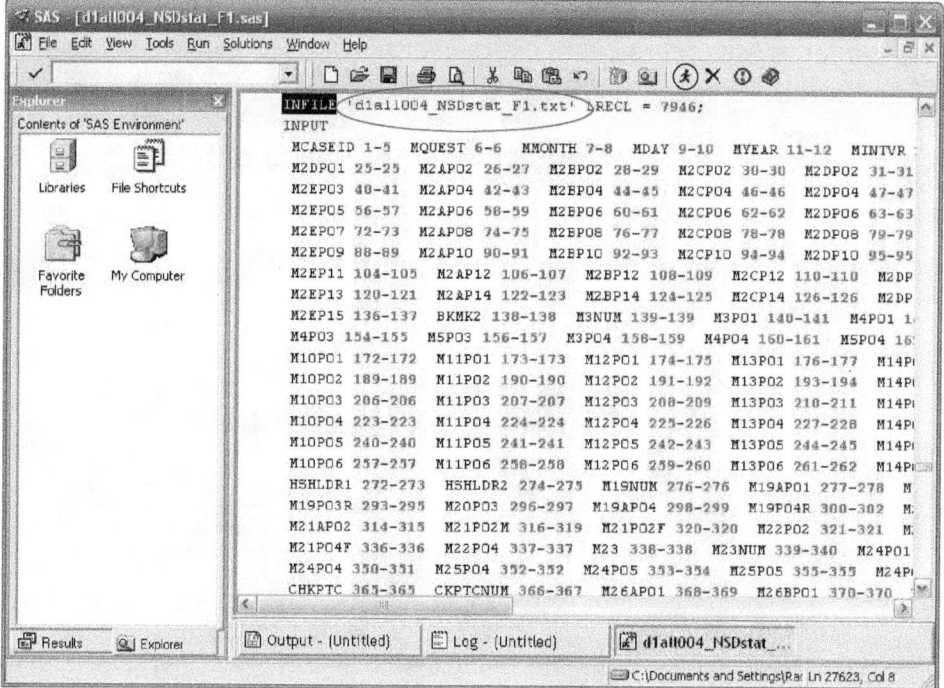

■ **Display D.8 Log window after submitting SAS batch program to read NSFH Wave 1 Data**

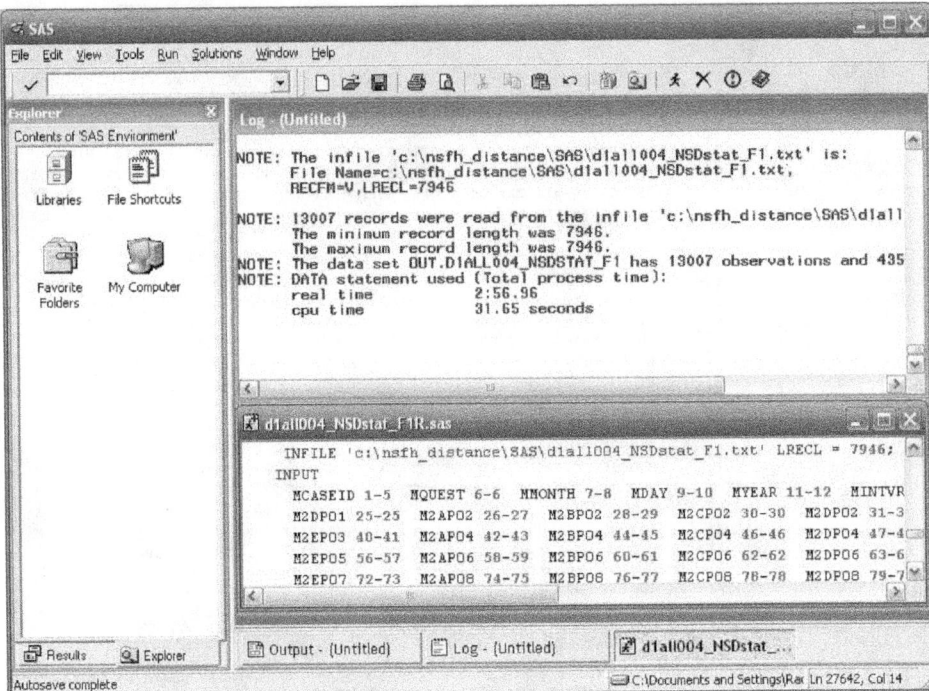

Appendix E

ACCESSING THE NHIS DATA

The NHIS 2009 data can be downloaded from ICPSR directly in SAS and Stata format.

For the Chapter Exercises, we will use only one of the NHIS 2009 data sets: the Sample Adult level data. This is the 4th data set in the full ICPSR collection of NHIS 2009 data sets.

You can download the data in various ways from the ICPSR web site (Persistent URL: *http://dx.doi.org/10.3886/ICPSR28721*). We recommend one of two ways.

1. If you have a high-speed internet connection and ample space on your computer (and if you want to explore the data sets beyond the Sample Adult data file in the NHIS 2009), you can choose to "Download all files" from the main NHIS 2009 web page in the ICPSR archive (Persistent URL: *http://dx.doi.org/10.3886/ICPSR28721*). Once you agree to the Terms of Use a compressed *.zip* file with all of the NHIS 2009 data sets will download to your computer. Upon extracting the files from the compressed *.zip* folder, you will have a folder *NHIS_28721* which contains all of the data and documentation for the NHIS 2009. The Sample Adult files are found within the *DS0004* subfolder. The file *28721-0004-Data.stc* is a SAS transport data file. The file *28721-0004-Data.dta* is a Stata data file. The main *NHIS_28721* folder and the *DS0004* subfolders also contain documentation files that you will need as you work with the data.

2. If you have a relatively slow internet connection and/or limited space on your computer (and you do not want to explore the data sets other than the Sample Adult data file in the NHIS 2009), you can choose "Download select files" from the main NHIS 2009 web page in the ICPSR archive (Persistent URL: *http://dx.doi.org/10.3886/ICPSR28721*). You will then be taken to a page where you can select different data sets (e.g., Household Level, Family Level, Person Level, Sample Adult Level) of different types (e.g., SAS, SPSS, Stata). For the Chapter Exercises, you will want to go to this page twice, one time selecting the "Sample Adult Level" file in SAS format and another time selecting the "Sample Adult Level" file in Stata format. Each time you do so, you will be asked to agree to the Terms of Use and then a compressed *.zip* file with the Sample Adult data file of each format (SAS and Stata) will download to your computer. Upon extracting the files from each compressed *.zip* folder, you will have a new folder *NHIS_28721* which contains all of

the data and documentation for the NHIS 2009. The Sample Adult files will be found within the *DS0004* subfolder. Extracted from the SAS compressed *.zip* folder that you downloaded will be the file *28721-0004-Data.stc* in the *DS0004* subfolder; this is a SAS transport data file. Extracted from the Stata compressed *.zip* folder that you downloaded will be the file *28721-0004-Data.dta*, a Stata data file. The main *NHIS_28721* folder and the *DS0004* subfolders also contain documentation files that you will need as you work with the data.

Regardless of the approach you take to download the SAS and Stata data files from ICPSR, you will ultimately have a SAS transport file *28721-0004-Data.stc* and a Stata data file *28721-0004-Data.dta*. We copied these files to a SAS and Stata working folder for our chapter exercises: *c:\nhis2009d4\SAS* and *c:\nhis2009d4\Stata*. After doing so, we can use the Stata data file directly in Stata with the procedures introduced in the book (e.g., `use c:\nhis2009d4\Stata\28721-0004-Data.dta`.) The SAS transport file *28721-0004-Data.stc* is the format SAS uses to allow a data file to be read from many different versions of SAS and many different operating systems. We used the following syntax to import the data file and formats file in the SAS format that we can then use with the syntax introduced in the book.

```
libname import "C:\nhis2009d4\sas\";
proc cimport
  file="C:\nhis2009d4\SAS\28721-0004-Data.stc"
  library=import;
run;
```

Once you execute this syntax, you will see two new files in the *c:\nhis2009d4\sas* working directory: (1) the SAS data file *da28721p4.sas7bdat* and (2) the SAS formats file *formats.sas7bcat*. These files can be used with the syntax introduced in the book, for example:

```
libname library "C:\nhis2009d4\sas\";
data nhis2009d4;
  set "C:\nhis2009d4\SAS\da28721p4.sas7bdat";
run;
```

where the `libname library "C:\nhis2009d4\sas\";` command is needed to tell SAS where to find the formats that go along with the *da28721p4.sas7bdat* data file.

As noted above, the main *NHIS_28721* folder and the *DS0004* subfolders also contain documentation files that you will need as you work with the data. Of particular importance for working with the Sample Adult data file are the five *.pdf* files found in the subfolder *ICPSR_28721/DS0004*. (Note that these five files will be in the *ICPSR_28721/DS0004* folder regardless of whether you download all of the NHIS 2009 data files together or whether you just selected the Sample Adult files in SAS and Stata formats).

1) The files *28721-0004-Questionnaire-English.pdf* and *28721-0004-Questionnaire-Spanish.pdf* contain the actual questions asked of respondents, either in English or in Spanish. This file contains useful information about values used to designate various responses, values used to code missing values, and skip patterns.

2) The file *28721-0004-Record_layout.pdf* repeats some of the information found in the questionnaire files, but also includes information about recoding variables and creation of new variables; these recoded variables and created variables are contained within the data downloaded from ICPSR.

3) The file *28721-0004-Frequencies.pdf* contains the number of cases that fall in various categories of valid responses and missing data codes for each variable.

4) The file *28721-0004-Documentation-varsum.pdf* contains a list of each variable found in the data file (the location and length information would be used if reading the data from ASCII format).

Appendix F

USING SAS AND STATA'S ONLINE DOCUMENTATION

In Chapter 18, we provide a number of ideas and references for learning more about SAS and Stata. But, here we provide basic information about using the online documentation for each.

In Stata, typing help <command name> in the command line, and hitting return, will open a window with information about the purpose and syntax rules for the command. We provide a portion of Stata's help file for the use command in Display F.1 as an example. (Note that clicking on the word varlist (which will be blue on your screen) in the help window for help use would open another window that gives help about varlist defining it as "a list of variable names with blanks between.")

In Display F.1, we circled in black the aspects of the command that we used in Chapter 4, but you can see that there is more that you might want or need to know related to this command if you continue programming with Stata.

You can also get help about a particular command, or browse the help files, by choosing Help from the menus. The first portion of Help/Contents, for example, provides information about the basic structure of Stata's commands. Browsing this section may be helpful to you, now or (if it still feels too overwhelming at this stage) when we get to the end of the book.

Stata's manuals are available in .pdf format and can be accessed through the help screens. For example, we circled in green in Display F.1 a link to the manual entry for the use command. SAS's complete set of documentation is also available electronically from its Help menu. This can make it hard to find a simple description of a command in SAS online files. But, it means that once you find what you need, you will have a wealth of information at your fingertips. We show an example in Display F.2 of entering the word "freq" into the SAS help Index. We can use the other tabs to Search for keywords. And, we can browse the Contents for help as well (most of the commands we use in this book are found in Base SAS and SAS/STAT).

APPENDIX F

■ **Display F.1 Example Stata Help Page for** use

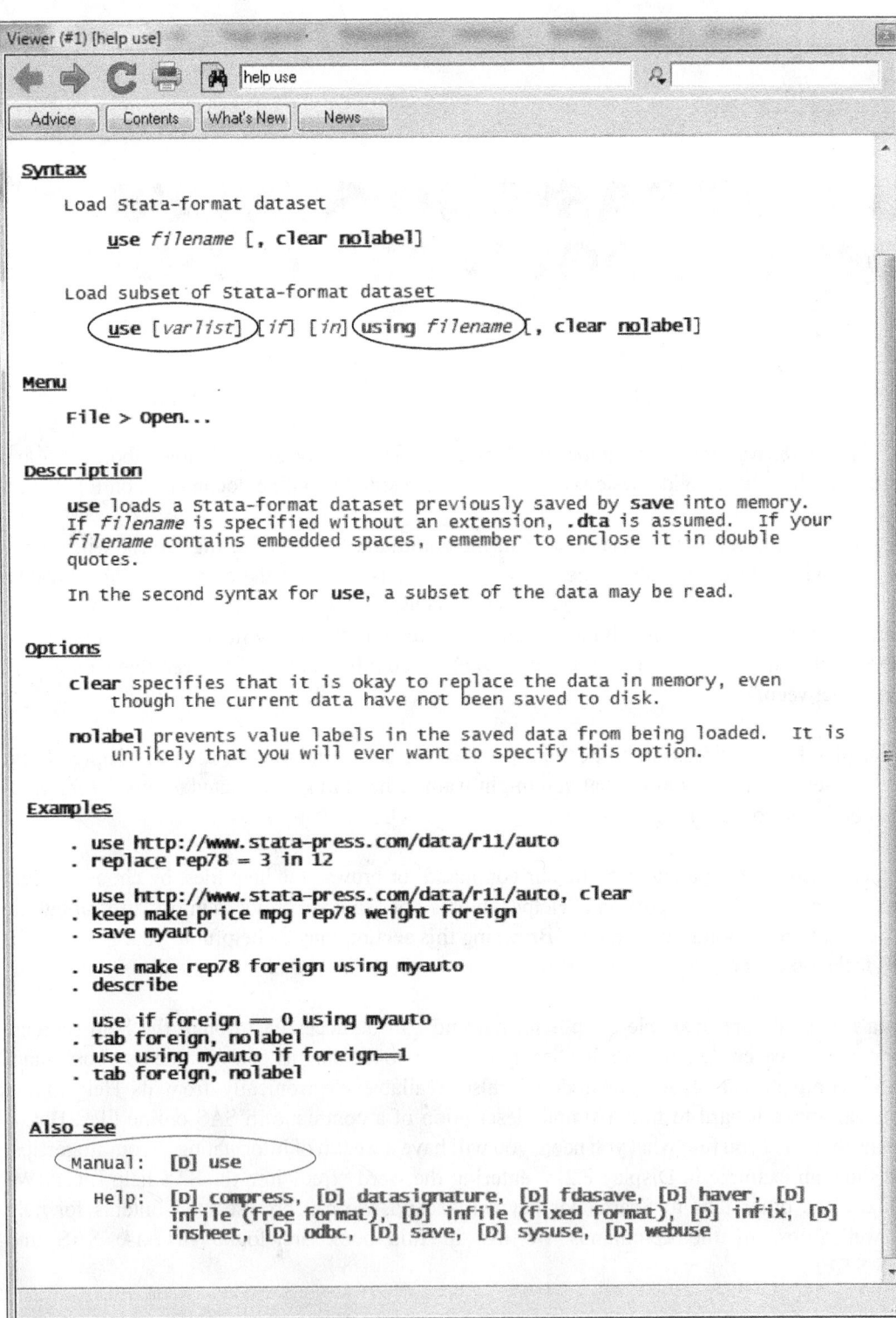

■ Display F.2 Example SAS Help Page for PROC FREQ

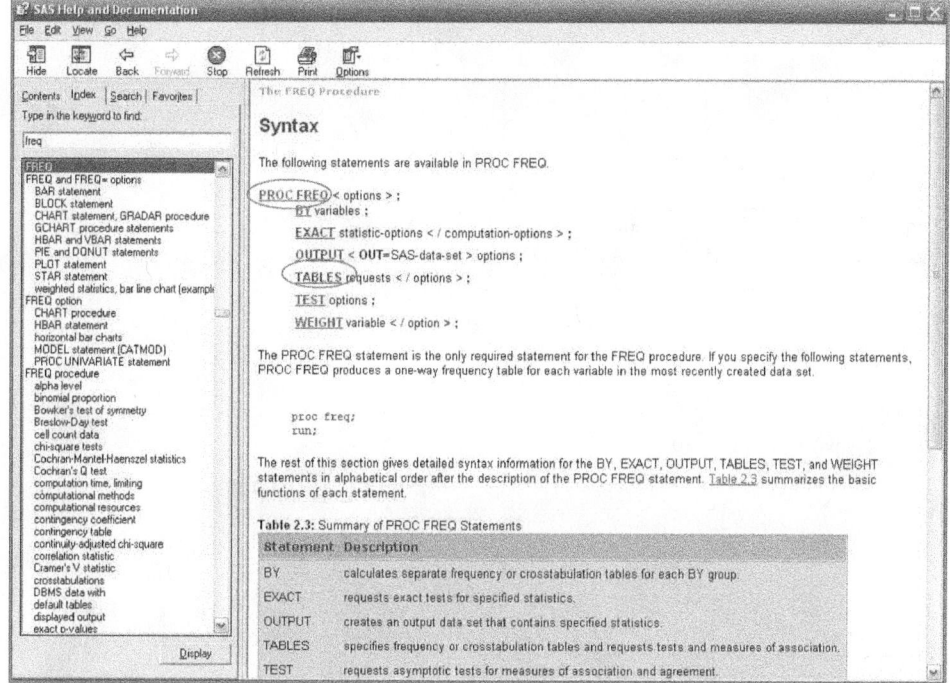

Appendix G

EXAMPLE OF HAND-CALCULATING THE INTERCEPT, SLOPE, AND CONDITIONAL STANDARD DEVIATION USING STYLIZED SAMPLE

	hrchores	numkid	$Y_i - \bar{Y}$	$X_i - \bar{X}$	$\Sigma(X_i - \bar{X})(Y_i - \bar{Y})$	$\Sigma(X_i - \bar{X})^2$	$\hat{Y}_i$	$Y_i - \hat{Y}_i$	$\Sigma(Y_i - \hat{Y}_i)^2$
1	21	0	−15.04	−2	30.08	4	23.78	−2.78	7.7284
2	28	0	−8.04	−2	16.08	4	23.78	4.22	17.8084
3	25	0	−11.04	−2	22.08	4	23.78	1.22	1.4884
4	21	0	−15.04	−2	30.08	4	23.78	−2.78	7.7284
5	32	0	−4.04	−2	8.08	4	23.78	8.22	67.5684
6	19	0	−17.04	−2	34.08	4	23.78	−4.78	22.8484
7	22	0	−14.04	−2	28.08	4	23.78	−1.78	3.1684
8	18	0	−18.04	−2	36.08	4	23.78	−5.78	33.4084
9	21	0	−15.04	−2	30.08	4	23.78	−2.78	7.7284
10	22	0	−14.04	−2	28.08	4	23.78	−1.78	3.1684
11	24	1	−12.04	−1	12.04	1	29.91	−5.91	34.9281
12	35	1	−1.04	−1	1.04	1	29.91	5.09	25.9081
13	25	1	−11.04	−1	11.04	1	29.91	−4.91	24.1081
14	41	1	4.96	−1	−4.96	1	29.91	11.09	122.9881
15	40	1	3.96	−1	−3.96	1	29.91	10.09	101.8081
16	34	1	−2.04	−1	2.04	1	29.91	4.09	16.7281
17	38	1	1.96	−1	−1.96	1	29.91	8.09	65.4481
18	25	1	−11.04	−1	11.04	1	29.91	−4.91	24.1081

APPENDIX G

	hrchores	numkid	$Y_i - \bar{Y}$	$X_i - \bar{X}$	$\Sigma(X_i - \bar{X})(Y_i - \bar{Y})$	$\Sigma(X_i - \bar{X})^2$	$\hat{Y}_i$	$Y_i - \hat{Y}_i$	$\Sigma(Y_i - \hat{Y}_i)^2$
19	26	1	−10.04	−1	10.04	1	29.91	−3.91	15.2881
20	27	1	−9.04	−1	9.04	1	29.91	−2.91	8.4681
21	32	2	−4.04	0	0	0	36.04	−4.04	16.3216
22	37	2	0.96	0	0	0	36.04	0.96	0.9216
23	47	2	10.96	0	0	0	36.04	10.96	120.1216
24	29	2	−7.04	0	0	0	36.04	−7.04	49.5616
25	34	2	−2.04	0	0	0	36.04	−2.04	4.1616
26	33	2	−3.04	0	0	0	36.04	−3.04	9.2416
27	33	2	−3.04	0	0	0	36.04	−3.04	9.2416
28	33	2	−3.04	0	0	0	36.04	−3.04	9.2416
29	37	2	0.96	0	0	0	36.04	0.96	0.9216
30	37	2	0.96	0	0	0	36.04	0.96	0.9216
31	44	3	7.96	1	7.96	1	42.17	1.83	3.3489
32	45	3	8.96	1	8.96	1	42.17	2.83	8.0089
33	38	3	1.96	1	1.96	1	42.17	−4.17	17.3889
34	50	3	13.96	1	13.96	1	42.17	7.83	61.3089
35	53	3	16.96	1	16.96	1	42.17	10.83	117.2889
36	36	3	−0.04	1	−0.04	1	42.17	−6.17	38.0689
37	50	3	13.96	1	13.96	1	42.17	7.83	61.3089
38	40	3	3.96	1	3.96	1	42.17	−2.17	4.7089
39	34	3	−2.04	1	−2.04	1	42.17	−8.17	66.7489
40	36	3	−0.04	1	−0.04	1	42.17	−6.17	38.0689
41	41	4	4.96	2	9.92	4	48.3	−7.3	53.29
42	48	4	11.96	2	23.92	4	48.3	−0.3	0.09
43	44	4	7.96	2	15.92	4	48.3	−4.3	18.49
44	53	4	16.96	2	33.92	4	48.3	4.7	22.09
45	53	4	16.96	2	33.92	4	48.3	4.7	22.09
46	40	4	3.96	2	7.92	4	48.3	−8.3	68.89
47	45	4	8.96	2	17.92	4	48.3	−3.3	10.89
48	52	4	15.96	2	31.92	4	48.3	3.7	13.69
49	44	4	7.96	2	15.92	4	48.3	−4.3	18.49
50	60	4	23.96	2	47.92	4	48.3	11.7	136.89

Average:	36.04	2		Sum:	613	100		0	1614.23
				Slope	6.13				
				Intercept	23.78				
				RMSE	5.799119904				

Appendix H

USING EXCEL TO CALCULATE AND GRAPH PREDICTED VALUES

The following Appendices show how to calculate and plot predicted values in Excel. The examples are primarily drawn from Chapter 11 (interaction models), but the concepts can be extended to plotting regression results from additive models. We also demonstrate their use with the nonlinear models from Chapters 12, 16, and 17.

The Appendices are organized with this appendix letter (H) followed by the chapter number and the order in which they are discussed in the chapter.

Illustrations within each Appendix are referred to as displays, and are similarly given this appendix letter (H) followed by the chapter number and the order in which they are discussed in the Appendix.

■ Appendix H.11.1 Basic Steps of Creating Graphs in Excel

We will use the following basic steps across all of the interaction models examined in Chapter 11:

Step 1.   Copy the variable names and coefficient estimates from the results to Excel.
Step 2.   Make a cross-tabulation of the variables from the interaction, listing the values we would like to use in predictions.
Step 3.   If needed, choose values for the other variables in the model.
Step 4.   Write a formula for the prediction equation, using the copied coefficient estimates and selected values of the predictor variables.
Step 5.   Insert a chart (bar chart for interactions of two dummy variables, or line graph for interactions involving one or more interval variables).
Step 6.   Edit the chart as desired.

Steps 1–4

Begin by opening Microsoft Excel. Excel will open with three worksheets (Sheet 1, Sheet 2, and Sheet 3) and the cursor in the top left cell (Column A, Row 1). We recommend that you save the worksheet in your project folder using a name that signals the purpose and contents of the file (e.g., *c:\hrchores\fem_marr.xlsx*). And, rename the first worksheet (e.g., to *PredictedValues*).[1]

For Step 1, it is easiest to cut-and-paste the results using an editor that will allow for selection of a rectangle. This is possible, for example, in the SAS output and editor windows, in Microsoft Word, or in some third-party text editors, such as TextPad or UltraEdit. In SAS and Microsoft Word, press the *Alt-* key before beginning the selection.[2] Start at the top left of the rectangle, and end at the bottom right corner. Display H.11.1 shows the difference between a regular selection and rectangle selection. You can then copy and paste this rectangle into Excel. Click on a cell in Excel and paste, and the values will be placed in a column of four separate cells. We clicked on cell B3 before pasting so we can also cut-and-paste the variable names into Column A (similarly select the rectangle containing the column of names in SAS) and add some labels. See Display H.11.2.

For Step 2, we next type in the levels of the predictors for which we would like to make predictions. In this case, the values are just 0 and 1 on each of our dummy variables. We can place these values anywhere within the worksheet. We put them slightly below our coefficient estimates, with labels so that we can refer to one set of predictions as the levels of the *married* variable and the other as the levels of the *female* variable (see top panel of Display H.11.3). Step 3 is not needed for this model, because we have no other variables in the model. In Appendix H.11.3, we will see how to choose values for other variables.

At Step 4, we type the prediction equation in Excel, referencing the cells that contain coefficient estimates and levels of the predictors. To do this, we click in the cell representing unmarried, males (cell C12 in our worksheet) and then we click in the formula bar (circled in green in

Display H.11.3). Any equation can be typed in the formula bar after an equals sign, and Excel will calculate the result for you (e.g., Type "=2+2" in the formula bar, being sure to begin with the equals sign. When you hit enter, you should see the result 4).

Excel makes it easy to make calculations based on values contained in various cells of a worksheet. If we type the equals sign into the formula bar, and then click on any cell, Excel will enter a reference for that cell. For example, if we type the equals sign in the formula bar and then click on cell B3, the formula bar will contain =B3. We can use operators (+ for addition and * for multiplication) and click on the relevant cells to create our prediction equation. The result is shown in the bottom of Display H.11.3. Notice that Excel uses colors for the cell references to help us prove that our equation is correct. (The full colors are not shown in this book, but will be visible on your computer screen.)

We reproduce the equation here to make clear its relationship to Equation 11.1.

$$=B3+B4*C11+B5*B12+B6*C11*B12$$

The equation takes the four coefficient estimates, from cells B3 to B6, and sums them after multiplying by the relevant value of the predictor variables. Specifically, the equation begins with Cell B3 which contains the intercept (22.31). Next, it adds the product of Cell B4 (which contains the coefficient estimate for the first dummy, *married*, of −2.60) and Cell C11 (which contains a value of the first dummy, *married*, in this case 0). Next, it adds the product of Cell B5 (which contains the coefficient estimate for the second dummy, *female*, of 10.20) and Cell B12 (which contains a value of the second dummy, *female*, in this case 0). Finally, it adds the product of Cell B6 (which contains the coefficient estimate for the product term, *fem_marr*, of 6.64) and Cells C11 and B12 (which contain the values of the two dummy variables).

After you hit enter, Excel will calculate the results of the equation. Because we referenced the value of 0 for *married* and 0 for *female* for our first prediction, the result should be the predicted value for unmarried males. The result calculated by Excel of 22.31 matches our hand calculation from Table 11.8.

We could similarly type and click to create the equation for each of the three remaining cells. But, a great functionality of Excel is the ability to copy an equation so that it can be recalculated with different values. Normally, Excel uses *relative* cell references to do this. Display H.11.4 shows what happens when we click on cell C12, type Ctrl-C for copy and then click on cell D12 and type Ctrl-P for paste. Because the new cell is one position to the right of the old cell, all of the references in the equation have shifted one position to the right. This is what we desire for the value of *marry* but not for the rest of the values.

In Excel, we can use an *absolute* rather than a relative reference by placing a dollar sign ($) in front of any column letter or row number. The bottom panel of Display H.11.4 reproduces Excel help on absolute references and the top right panel shows how we used this approach to refer to the estimates for the coefficients by placing a $ before their column letters and row numbers. We also made the references to the predictor values partially absolute by placing a $ before the row number for the *married* reference and before the column letter for the *female* reference. Now, when we copy the formula to Cell D12 and click on it to see the cells boxed in color, the references look correct (see top/right screenshot in Display H.11.4). Finally, we copied and pasted the equation across all four cells and verified that Excel calculated all of the same predicted values as we calculated by hand in Table 11.8 (see top of Display H.11.5).

Steps 5–6

We are now ready for Step 5, inserting a chart. Excel provides numerous chart styles, but we will use a simple bar chart. To do so, we first highlight the box of Cells from B11 at the top left to D13 at the bottom right (see again top panel of Display H.11.5). Then, we choose the `Insert` tab and click on `Column` and choose a 2-D Clustered Column from the top left (see green circles at top of Display H.11.5). This creates a basic bar chart (see bottom panel of Display H.11.5).

Finally, at Step 6, we can use the Chart Tools, shown in the toolbars in the bottom panel of Display H.11.5 to improve the look of the chart. For example, we clicked on Move Chart Location (circled with a black dotted line in Display H.11.5) to switch the chart to its own worksheet tab. We clicked on Layout tab (circled in green in Display H.11.5) to add titles to the chart and axes. We clicked on the gray chart style (circled in black in Display H.11.5) to change the fill of the bars to grayscale from color. We clicked on the Home tab (circled in black in Display H.11.5) to increase the font size. Finally, we clicked on Select Data (circled with a green dotted line in Display H.11.5) to label the series. Display H.11.6 shows how clicking on Select Data opens several boxes which allow us to select the words rather than values to label the legend series and horizontal axis.

■ Display H.11.1 Using Alt-Key to Select a Rectangle in SAS

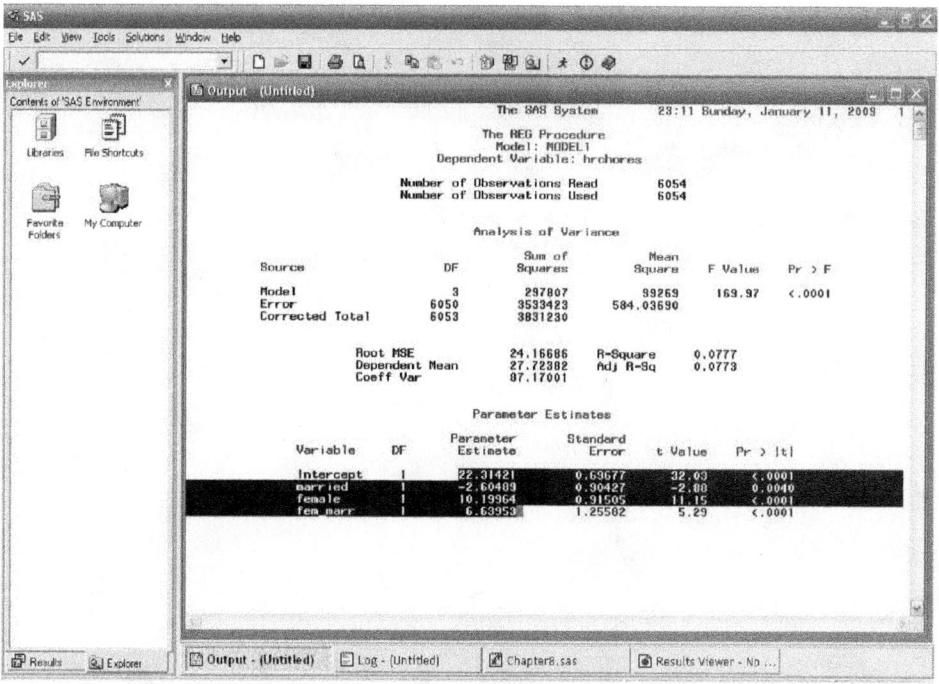

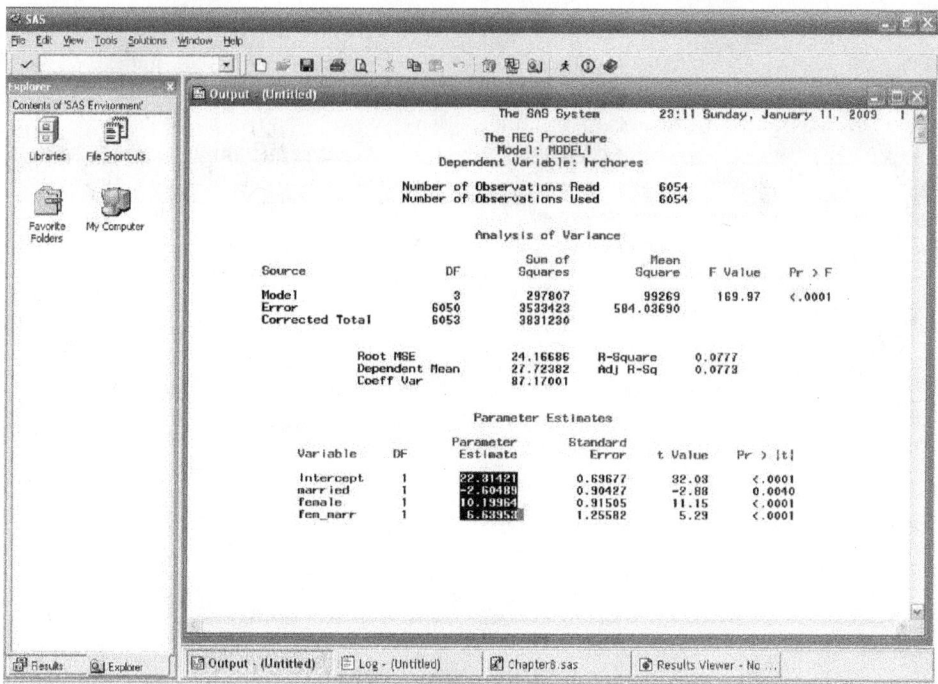

■ Display H.11.2 Pasting Coefficients into Excel

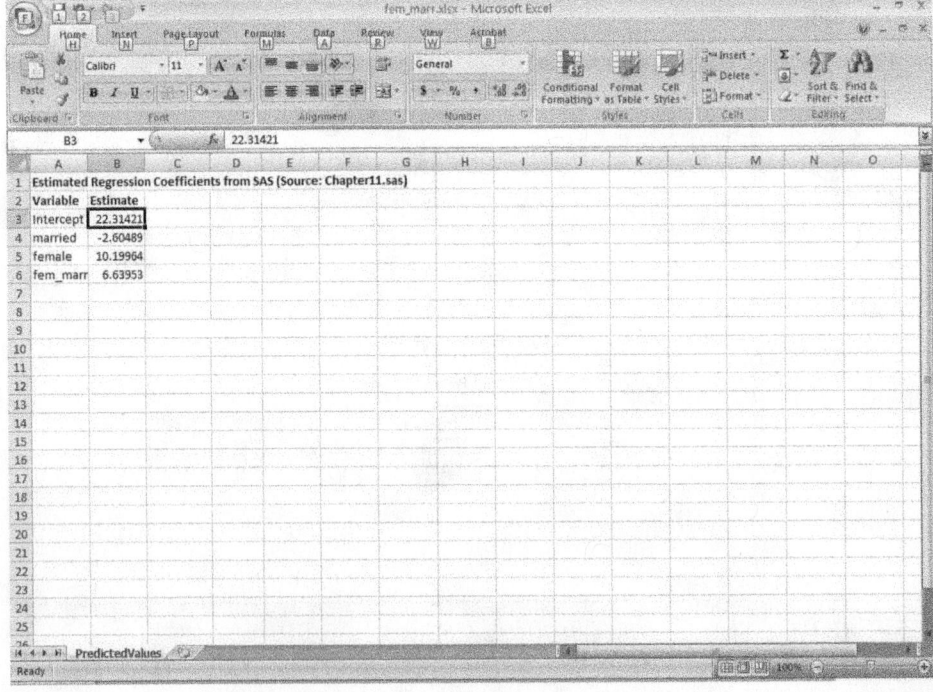

Display H.11.3 Adding Levels of Predictors and Prediction Equation

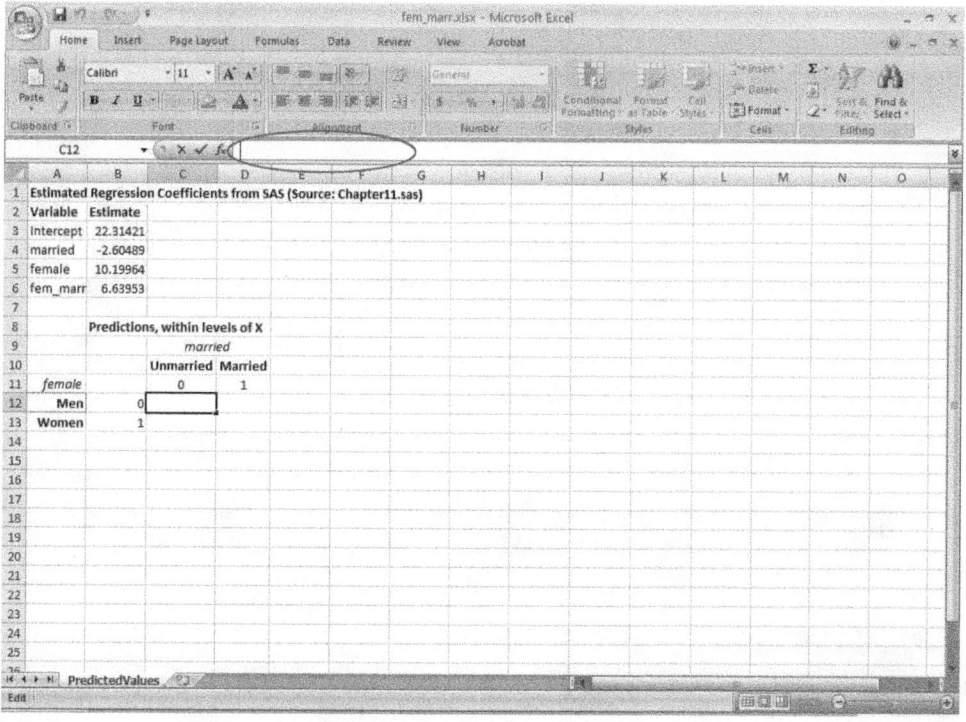

▪ Display H.11.4 Using Fixed References

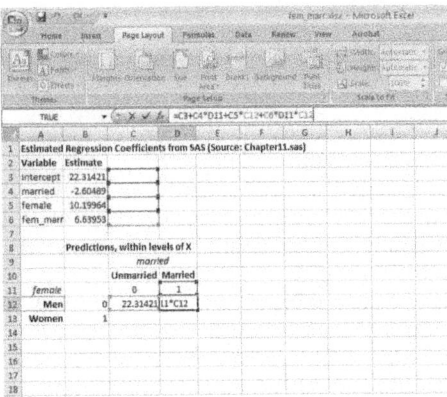

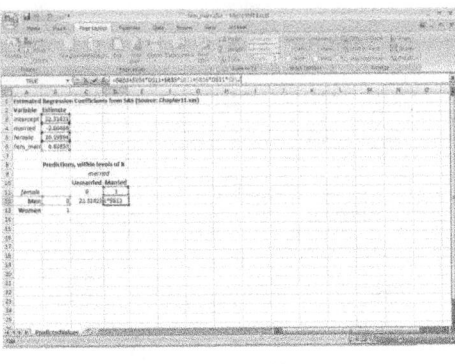

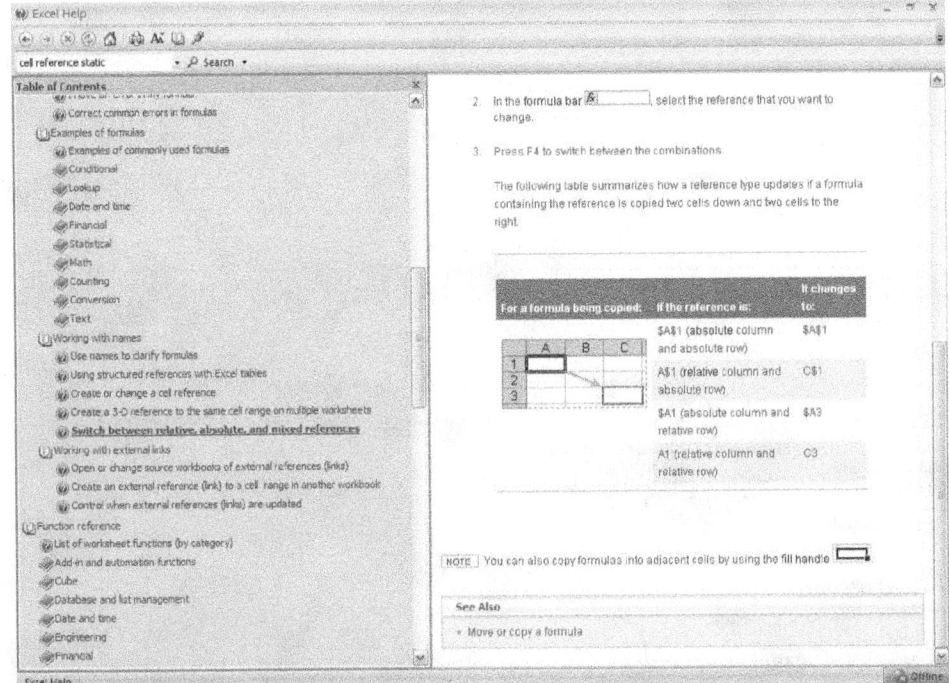

APPENDIX H: USING EXCEL TO CALCULATE AND GRAPH PREDICTED VALUES ■ ■ ■ H9

■ Display H.11.5 Inserting a Chart

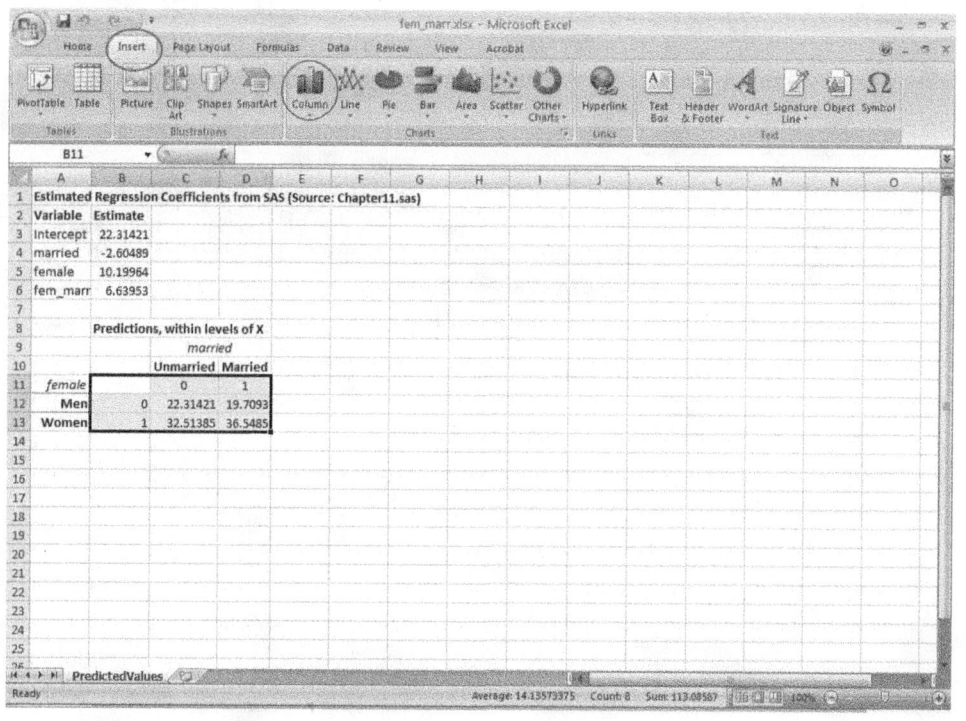

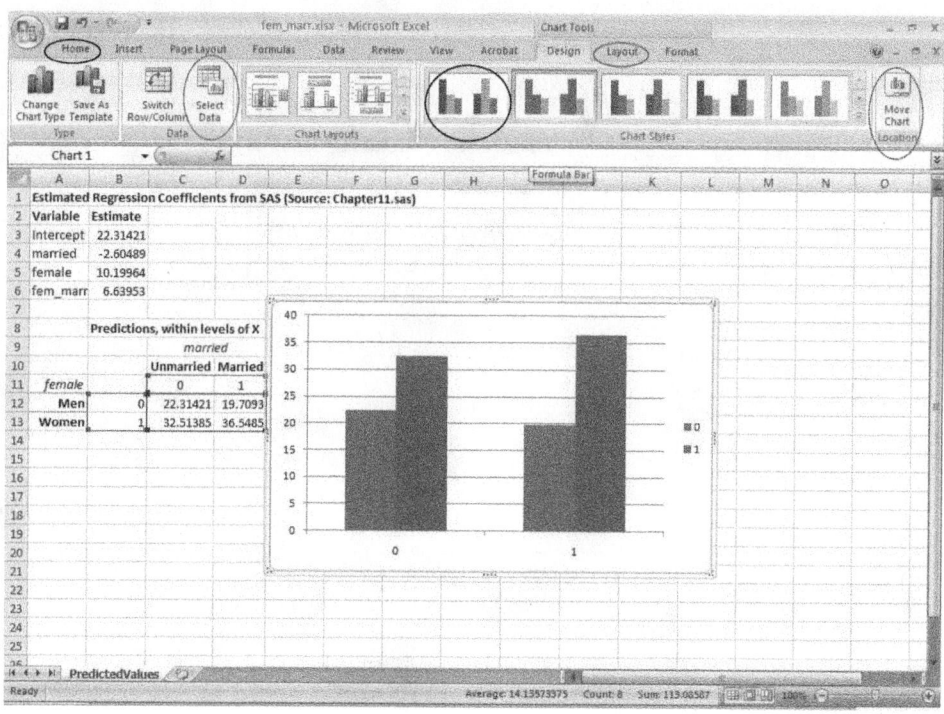

APPENDIX H

■ **Display H.11.6 Labeling Series**

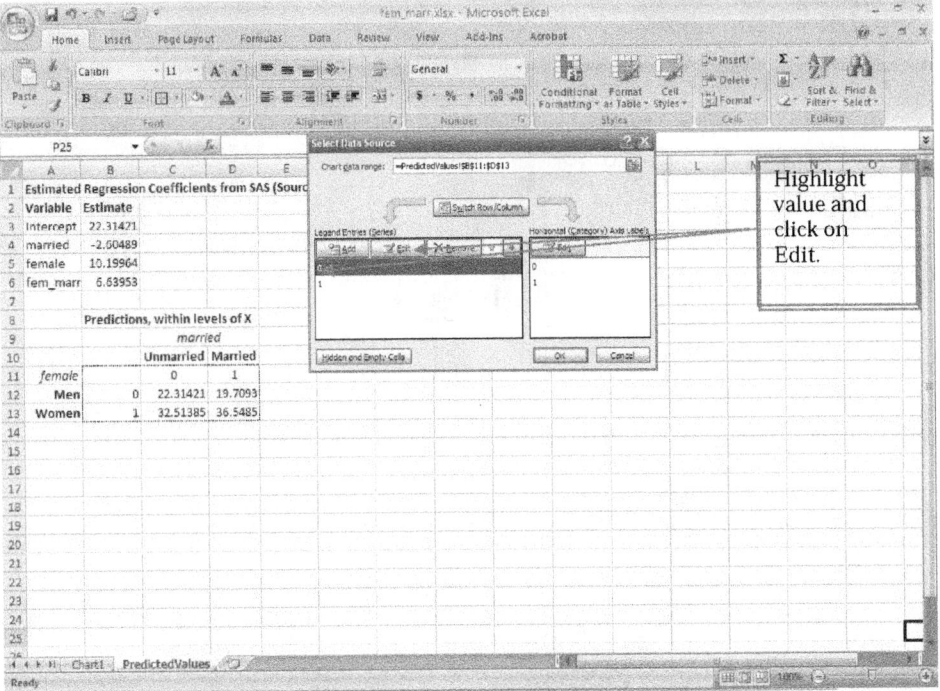

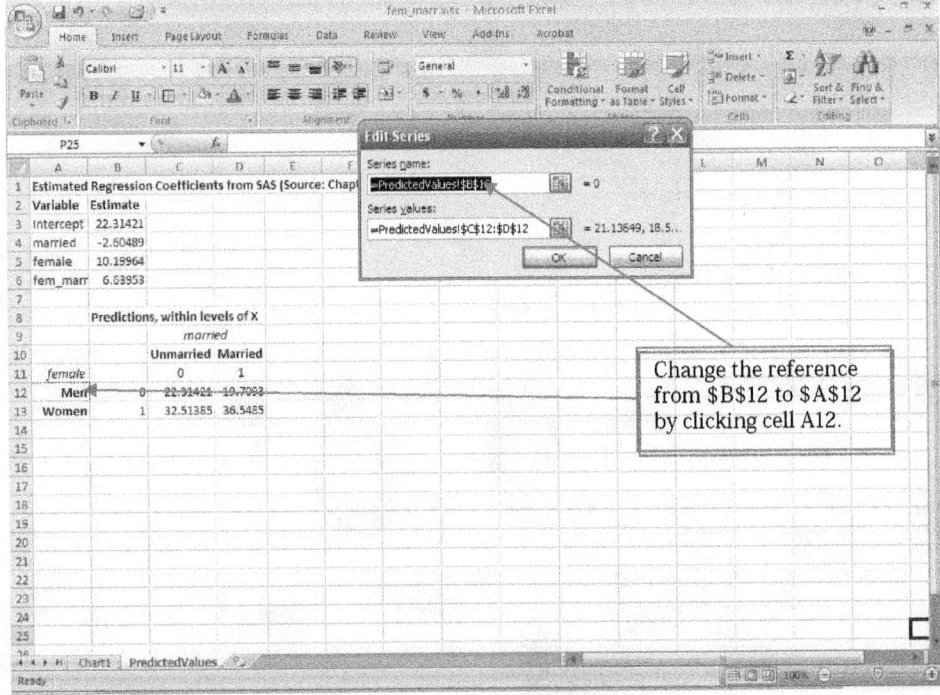

■ Appendix H.11.2 Graphing a Dummy by Interval Interaction and Calculating Conditional Effects (in Unstandardized, Semistandardized, and Standardized Form)

We can follow the basic steps introduced in Appendix H.11.1 to create a graph of a dummy by interval variable. The two main differences are that (a) we will provide more than two values for the interval variable for calculating predictions and (b) we will choose a Line chart from the Insert menu.

Display H.11.7 shows the values from the regression coefficients from Display B.11.6 cut-and-paste into Excel. Note that the *Predictions, within levels of X* are calculated similarly as in Appendix H.11.1, except that we now use five levels of the interval *hrwork* variable. The chart is also created similarly to the chart shown in Appendix H.11.1, except that we began by selecting a Line chart from the menus.

Display H.11.8 shows how we can use the formula bar to calculate differences between predicted values, both in their raw units and relative to the standard deviation of the outcome.

Display H.11.9 shows how we can also calculate the conditional effects of *hrwork* based on the coefficients, and use the standard deviation of the predictor (*hrwork*) and outcome (*hrchores*) to completely standardize these conditional effects.

■ **Display H.11.7 Presenting Results of a Dummy by Interval Variable Interaction in Excel**

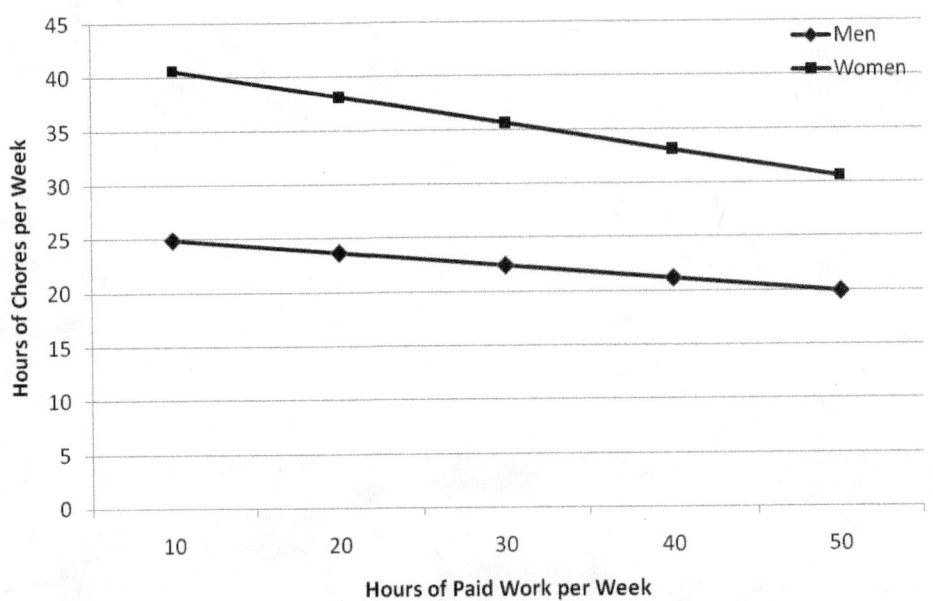

**Predicted Values for Hours of Chores
with Interaction between Hours of Paid Work and Gender**

Display H.11.8 Calculating Differences in Predictions and Effect Size in Excel

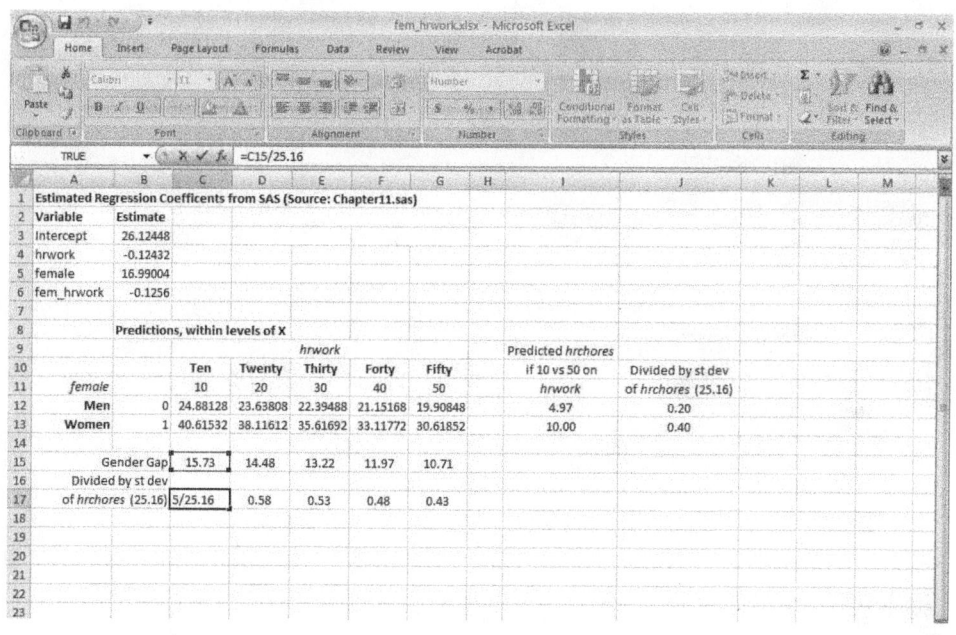

▪ Display H.11.9 Calculating Standardized Effect of Interval Variable in Excel

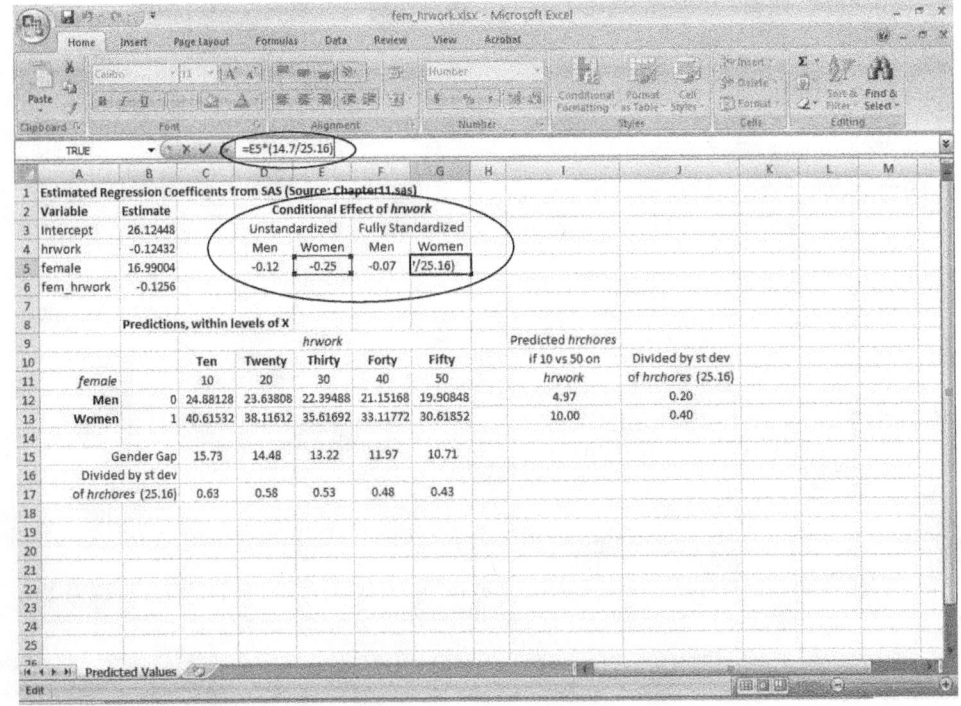

■ Appendix H.11.3 Graphing Results from a Fully Interacted Model

We will recalculate the results from Figure 11.2, which plotted the interaction between gender and hours of paid work, using the fully interacted model to illustrate how to make predictions with additional variables in the model, beyond those in the interaction.

Display H.11.10 shows the means for the predictor variables in the subsample included in the fully interacted model. Display H.11.11 shows where we added these mean values to our Excel spreadsheet and updated our equation.

The complete equation for cell C21 is now:

=\$B\$3+\$B\$5*C\$19+\$B\$9*\$B21+\$B\$11*C\$19*\$B21

+\$B\$4*\$I\$4+\$B\$6*\$I\$6+\$B\$7*\$I\$7+\$B\$8*\$I\$8

+\$B\$10*\$B21*\$I\$4+\$B\$12*\$B21*\$I\$6+\$B\$13*\$B21*\$I\$7+\$B\$14*\$B21*\$I\$8

For example \$B\$4*\$I\$4 multiplies the coefficient estimate for marital status (−3.18486) by the mean value of marital status (0.5297251); and, \$B\$10*\$B21*\$I\$4 multiplies the coefficient estimate for the interaction of gender and marital status (4.48267) by gender (0 or 1, depending on the row) and the mean value of marital status (0.5297251).

Clearly, these equations become lengthy with numerous variables in the model, and in Chapter 12 we illustrate how to ask SAS and Stata to calculate predicted values (see also Long and Freese 2006 for their excellent *spost* utilities for calculating and graphing predicted values in Stata).

APPENDIX H

■ Display H.11.10 Means of *married, hrwork, numkid, aframer,* and *mexamer*

Regression Model								
	proc means; var married hrwork numkid aframer mexamer; run;							

SAS

Variable	N	Mean	Std Dev	Minimum	Maximum
married	5820	0.5297251	0.4991585	0	1.0000000
hrwork	5820	38.9218213	14.7683344	0	93.0000000
numkid	5820	0.8159794	1.0449523	0	4.0000000
aframer	5820	0.1713058	0.3768084	0	1.0000000
mexamer	5820	0.0398625	0.1956530	0	1.0000000

Select Results

Stata

summarize married hrwork numkid aframer mexamer

variable	Obs	Mean	Std. Dev.	Min	Max
married	5820	.5297251	.4991585	0	1
hrwork	5820	38.92182	14.76833	0	93
numkid	5820	.8159794	1.044952	0	4
aframer	5820	.1713058	.3768084	0	1
mexamer	5820	.0398625	.1956530	0	1

■ Display H.11.11 Predicted Values from Fully Interacted Model, Illustrating Interaction between Hours of Paid Work and Gender

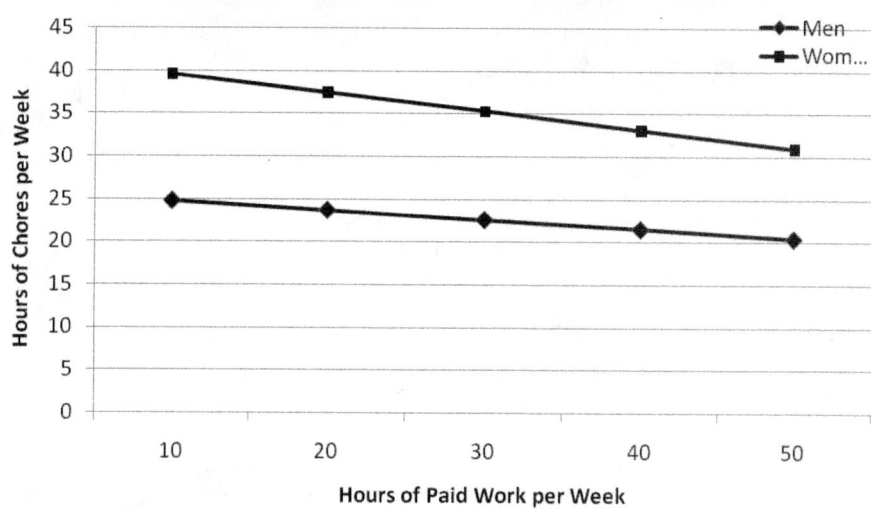

The formula bar shows: `$B21*$I$6+$B$13*$B21*$I$7+$B$14*$B21*$I$8`

Estimated Regression Coefficients from SAS (Source: Chapter11.sas)

Variable	Estimate
Intercept	25.18235
married	-3.18486
hrwork	-0.10947
numkid	1.44579
aframer	6.04183
mexamer	5.76834
female	9.50929
fem_marr	4.48267
fem_hrwork	-0.10563
fem_numkid	4.79426
fem_aframer	-1.97854
fem_mexamer	8.495

Conditional Effect of hrwork

Unstandardized		Fully Standardized	
Men	Women	Men	Women
-0.11	-0.22	-0.06	-0.13

Mean

0.5297251
38.92182
0.8159794
0.1713058
0.0398625

Predictions, within levels of X

		Ten	Twenty	Thirty	Forty	Fifty
	hrwork					
female		10	20	30	40	50
Men	0	24.84523	23.75053	22.65583	21.56113	20.46643
Women	1	B21*$I$8	37.43351	35.28251	33.13151	30.98051
Gender Gap		14.74	13.68	12.63	11.57	10.51
Divided by st dev of hrchores (25.16)		0.59	0.54	0.50	0.46	0.42

Predicted hrchores

if 10 vs 50 on hrwork	Divided by st dev of hrchores (25.16)
4.38	0.17
8.60	0.34

Sheet tabs: Chart1 | Predicted Values

Predicted Values for Hours of Chores with Interaction between Hours of Paid Work and Gender

Legend: ◆ Men   ■ Wom...

Y-axis: Hours of Chores per Week (0 to 45)

X-axis: Hours of Paid Work per Week (10, 20, 30, 40, 50)

▧ Appendix H.11.4 Graphing Results from an Interaction between Two Interval Variables

Display H.11.12 shows how we extend the procedures used for dummy by dummy and dummy by interval interactions for an interaction between two interval variables.

We first cut-and-pasted the coefficient estimates from the model shown in Display B.11.15 into Excel. We then added the multiple levels of number of children and copied the formula for calculating predictions across the cells.

We also added calculations of the unstandardized, semistandardized (divided by the standard deviation of the outcome), and completely standardized (multiplied by the standard deviation of the predictor and divided by the standard deviation of the outcome) coefficients.

We plotted the results as a Line chart, modifying the default layout to increase readability (including deleting the lines for families with one and with three children, to reduce the amount of information and make it easier to compare the steepness of lines for the middle number of children, two, and the extremes, none and four).

▪ Display H.11.12 Presenting Interaction between Two Interval Variables in Excel

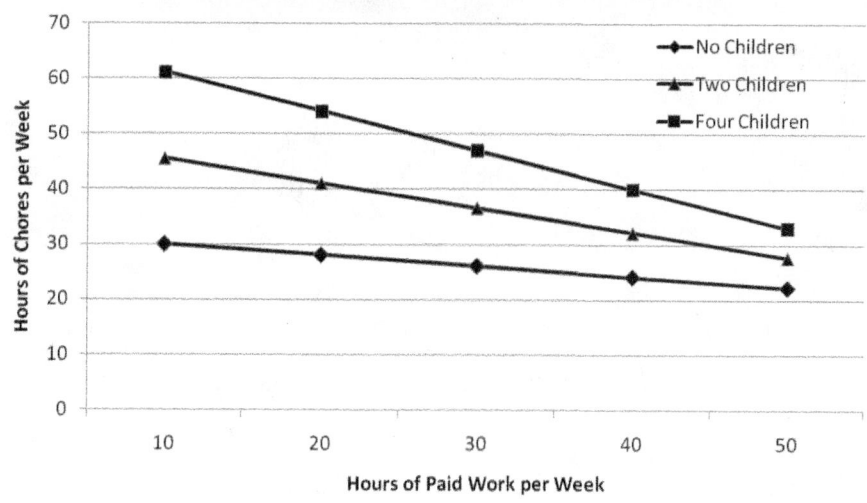

Excel spreadsheet: numkid_hrwork.xlsx — Microsoft Excel

Formula bar: `=$B$3+$B$4*$B12+$B$5*C$11+$B$6*$B12*C$11`

	A	B	C	D	E	F	G	H	I	J	K	L
1	Estimated Regression Coefficents from SAS (Source: Chapter11.sas)											
2	Variable	Estimate										
3	Intercept	31.89119										
4	numkid	9.06985										
5	hrwork	-0.19367										
6	numk_hrw	-0.12751										
7												
8	Predictions, within levels of X											
9					hrwork				10 Hour Increase in hrwork			
10		numkid	Ten	Twenty	Thirty	Forty	Fifty			Partially	Completely	
11			10	20	30	40	50		Unstandardized	Standardized	Standardized	
12		0	2*C$11	28.01779	26.08109	24.14439	22.20769		-1.94	-0.08	-0.11	
13		1	37.74924	34.53744	31.32564	28.11384	24.90204		-3.21	-0.13	-0.19	
14		2	45.54399	41.05709	36.57019	32.08329	27.59639		-4.49	-0.18	-0.26	
15		3	53.33874	47.57674	41.81474	36.05274	30.29074		-5.76	-0.23	-0.34	
16		4	61.13349	54.09639	47.05929	40.02219	32.98509		-7.04	-0.28	-0.41	
17												
18	Unstandardized		7.79	6.52	5.24	3.97	2.69					
19	Semi-Standardized		0.31	0.26	0.21	0.16	0.11					
20	Completely Standardized		0.25	0.21	0.17	0.13	0.09					

Sheet tabs: Chart1, Predicted Values

Predicted Values for Hours of Chores with Interaction between Hours of Paid Work and Gender

Line chart. Y-axis: Hours of Chores per Week (0 to 70). X-axis: Hours of Paid Work per Week (10 to 50). Legend: No Children (diamond), Two Children (triangle), Four Children (square).

■ Appendix H.12 Graphing Results for Nonlinear Relationships

This appendix illustrates how Excel can be used to calculate and graph predicted values from various models that capture nonlinear relationships between the predictor and outcome variables.

Display H.12.1 shows predictions from the six alternative models for relating mother's years of schooling to the distance she lives from her adult child discussed in Chapter 12: the lin-lin, lin-log, lin-sq, log-lin, log-log, and log-sq models.

Display H.12.2 shows predictions from a flexible dummy variable model which relates numbers of sisters to distance using seven dummy variables.

Display H.12.3 shows results similar to Display H.12.2, but collapses to three dummy variables.

■ Display H.12.1 Nonlinear Models for Distance Predicted by Mother's Years of Schooling

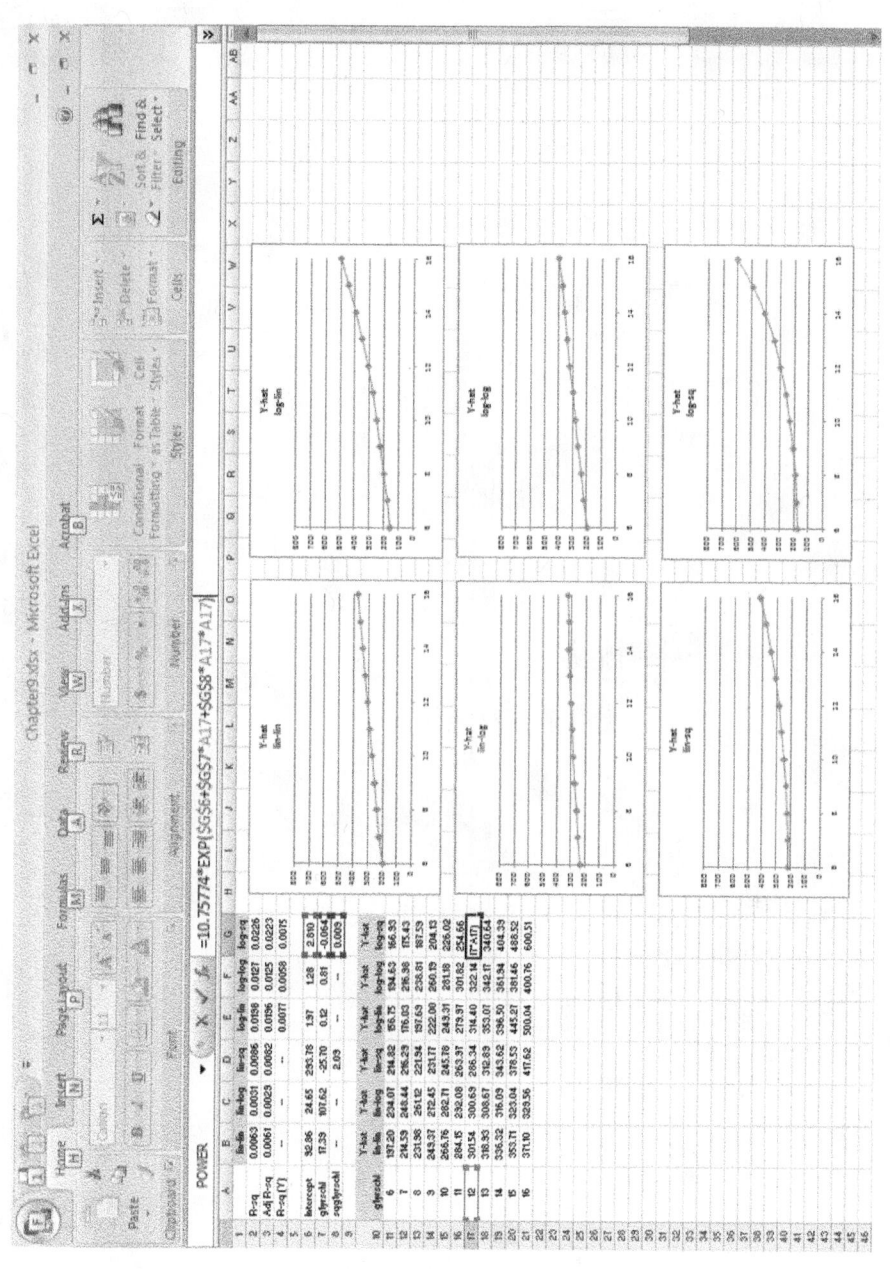

■ Display H.12.2 Predicted Values and Graph of Dummy Variable Specification for Number of Sisters

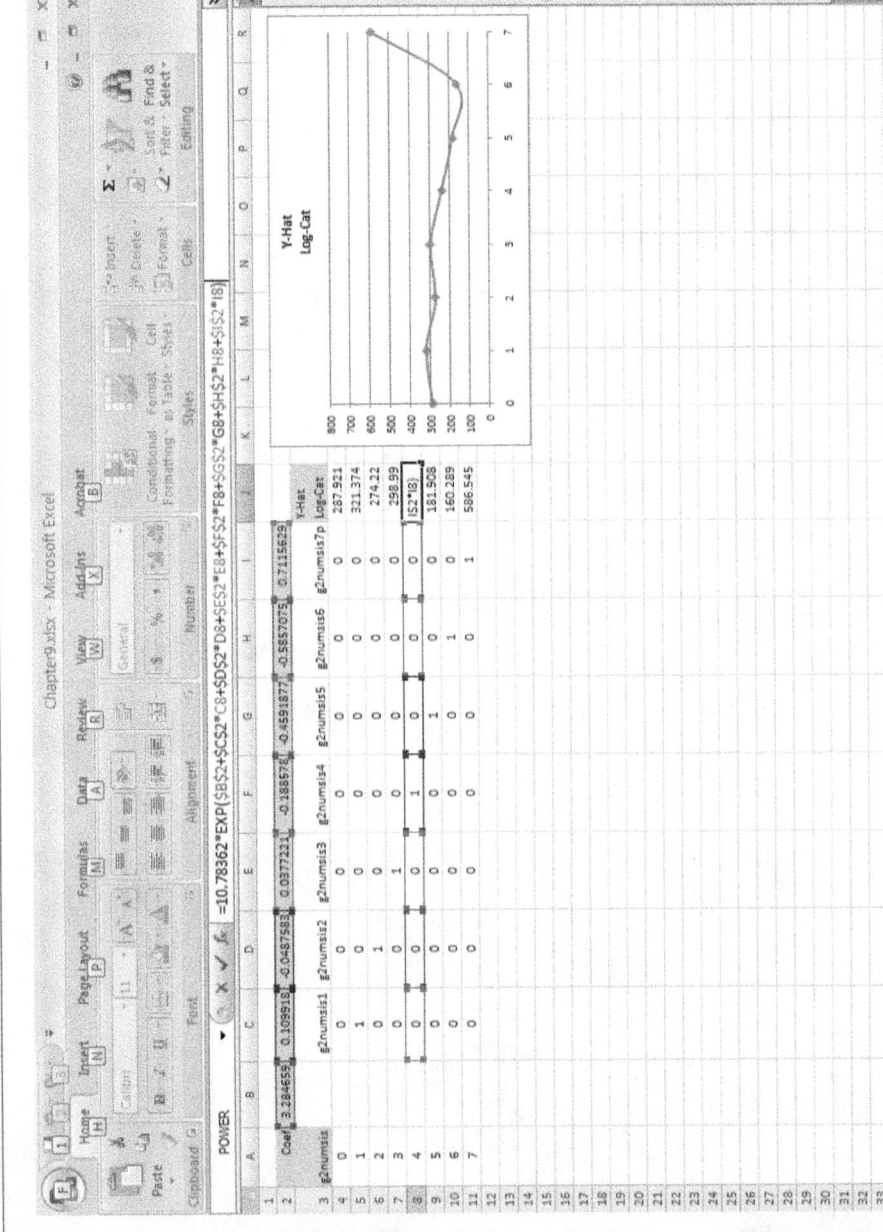

■ Display H.12.3 Predicted Values and Graph of Dummy Variable Specification for Number of Sisters, Collapsed Model

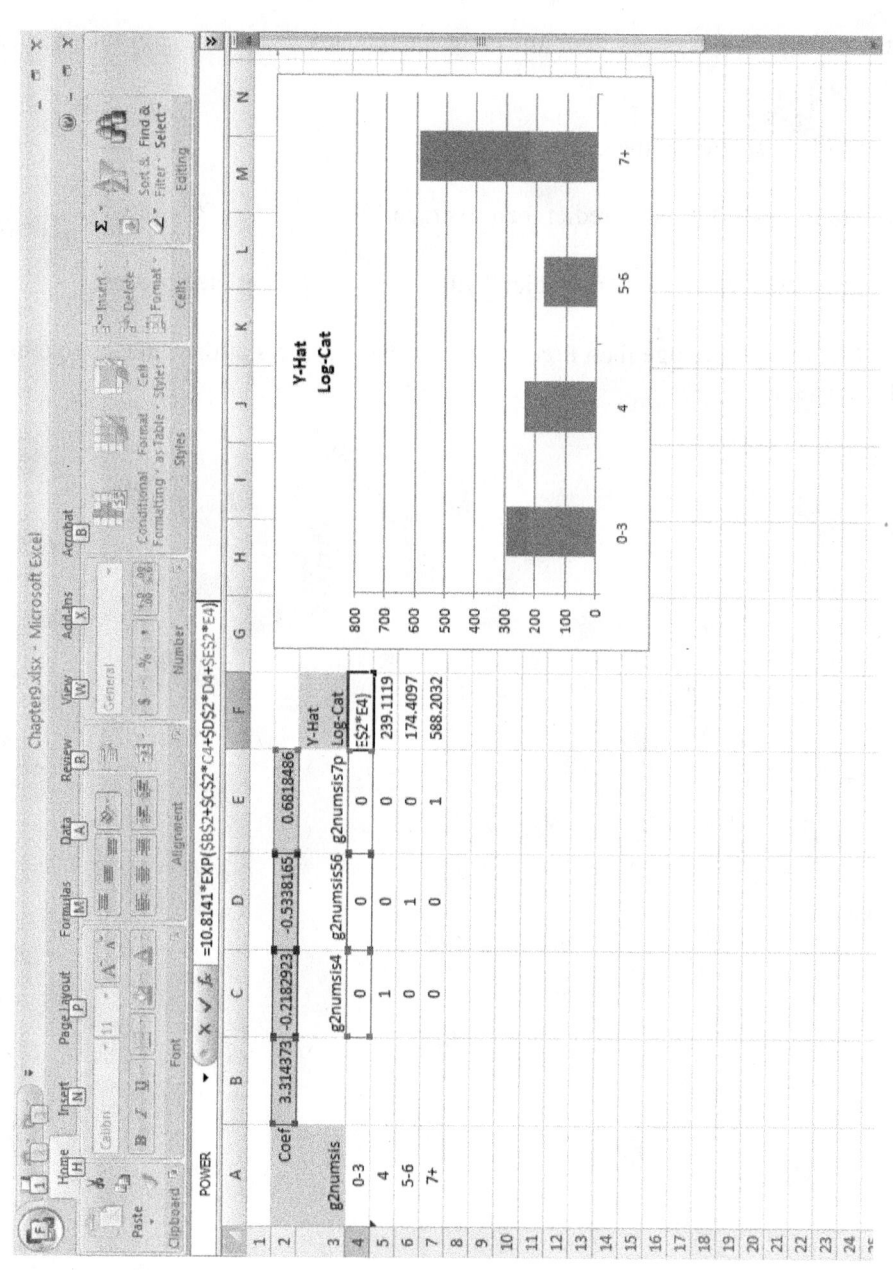

■ Appendix H.16 Graphing Results for Logit Models

This Appendix illustrates how Excel can be used to graph predicted probabilities from a logit model.

The four different displays use four different approaches to holding constant the predictor variables:

Display H.16.1 uses "Predict then Average."

Display H.16.2 uses "Modified Predict then Average."

Display H.16.3 uses "Average then Predict" with other variables at their means.

Display H.16.4 uses "Average then Predict" with other variables at their means rounded to the nearest valid value.

■ Display H.16.1 Graph of "Predict then Average" Values

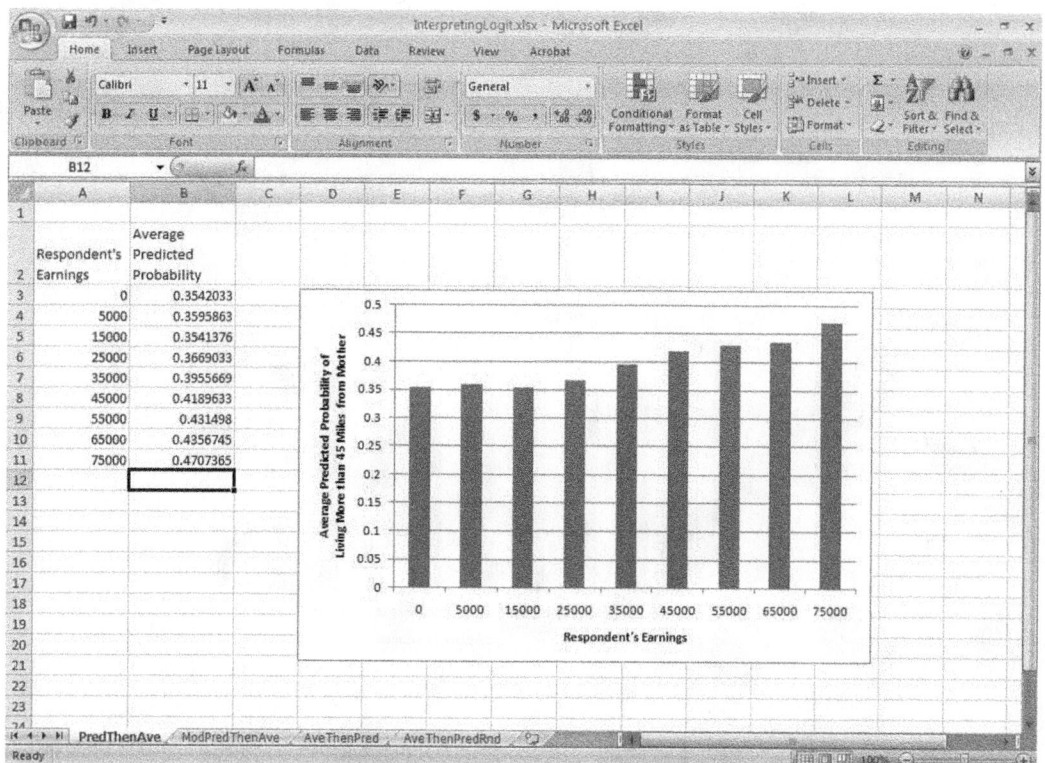

■ **Display H.16.2 Graph of "Modified Predict then Average" Values**

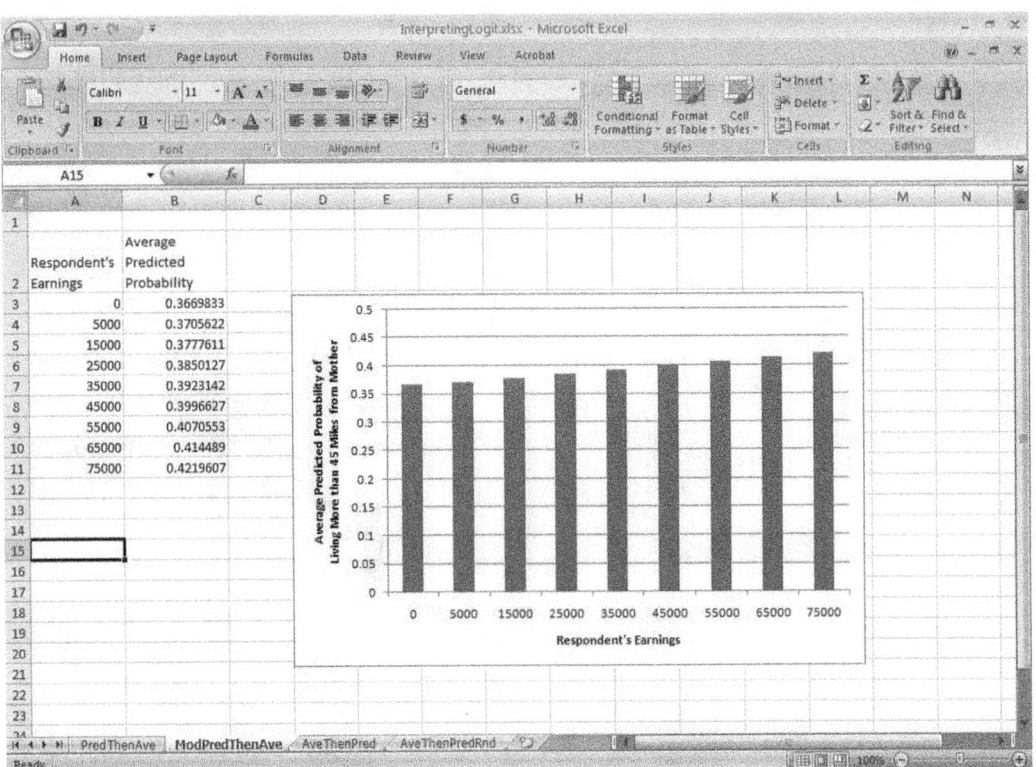

■ **Display H.16.3 Graph of "Average then Predict" Values with Values Other then Earnings Held Constant at their Means**

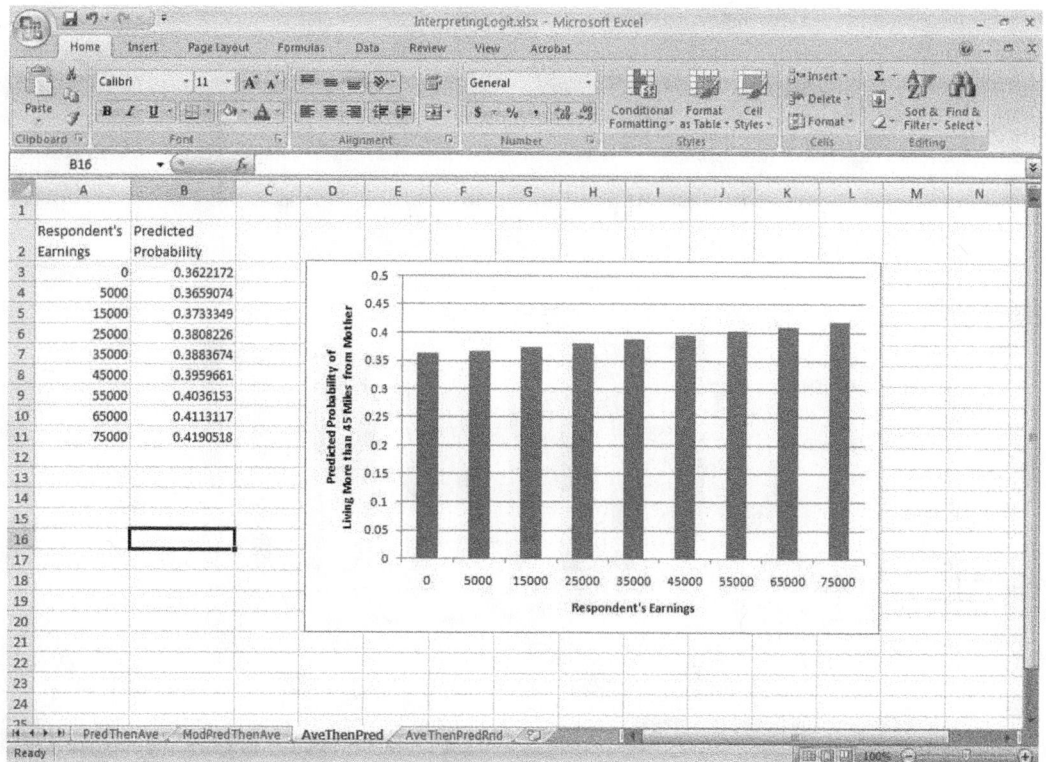

▪ Display H.16.4 Graph of "Average then Predict" Values with Values Other then Earnings Rounded to the Nearest Valid Value

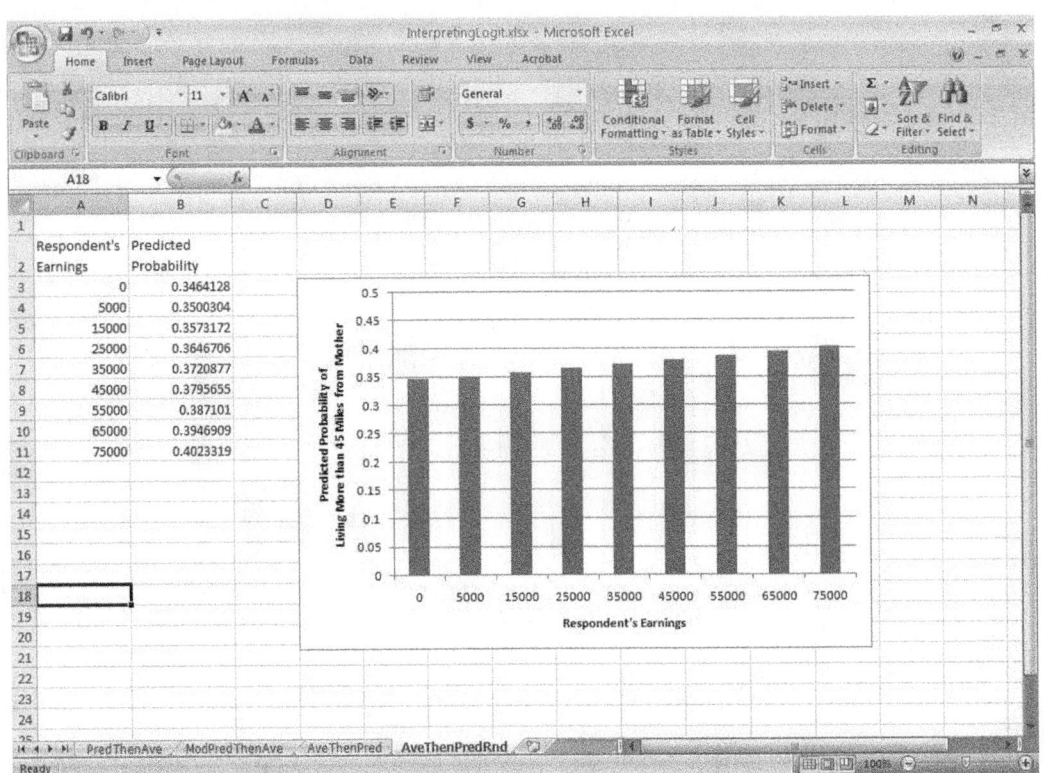

■ Appendix H.17 Graphing Results and Calculating Discrete Change for Multinomial Logit and Ordered Logit Models

This Appendix illustrates how Excel can be used to graph predicted probabilities and to calculate discrete change for multinomial logit and ordered logit models.

The two different displays show results for each type of model:

Display H.17.1 shows the multinomial logit results.

Display H.17.2 shows the ordered logit results.

■ Display H.17.1 Plot of Predicted Probabilities and Calculation of Discrete Change for Multinomial Logit Model

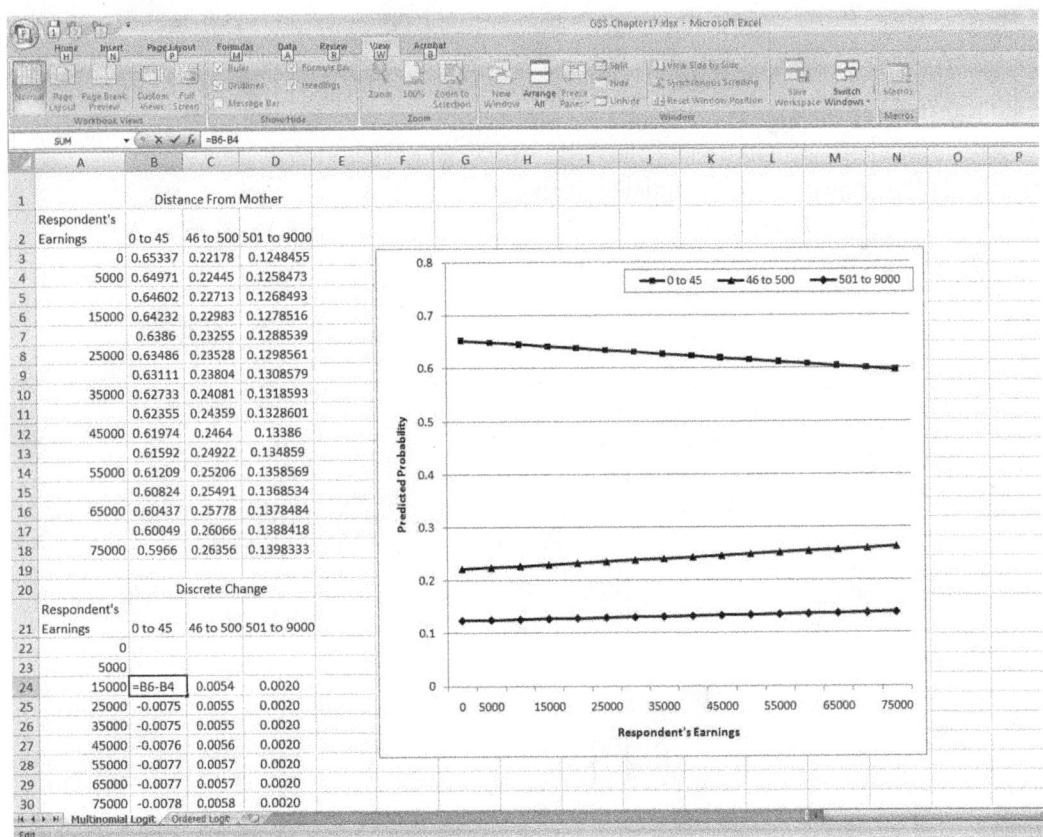

Display H.17.2 Plot of Predicted Probabilities and Calculation of Discrete Change for Ordered Logit Model

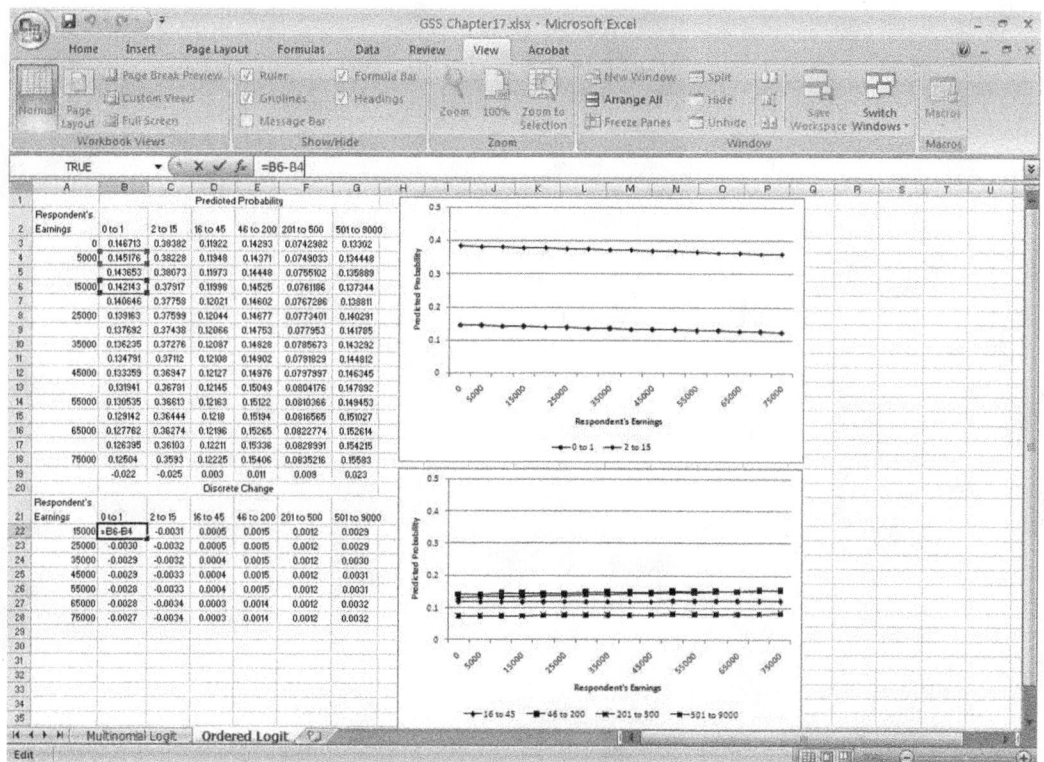

USING HAYES-CAI SAS MACRO FOR HETEROSKEDASTICITY-CONSISTENT STANDARD ERRORS

This Appendix provides instructions for using the SAS macro written by Hayes and Cai (2007) to estimate heteroskedasticity-consistent standard errors in releases of SAS prior to 9.2.

The SAS macro, called *hcreg.sas* should be saved to your computer from the link on their web site: *http://www.comm.ohio-state.edu/ahayes/SPSS%20programs/HCSEp.htm.* (Do not try to type the SAS syntax in or cut-and-paste!)

To use the macro, you must first execute its syntax. This can be done readily with the `%include` command in SAS. When we place a filename after this command, SAS executes the code in that file.

We downloaded the macros and saved them in our *c:\nsfh_distance\SAS* folder so that our command reads:

```
%include "c:\nsfh_distance\sas\hcreg.sas";
```

The syntax for using the new command created by the macro is:

```
%HCREG(data = <filename>, dv = <depvar>, iv = <variable list>);
```

where *filename* is the name of a SAS data file, *dv* is the dependent variable, and *iv* is a list of variables separated by spaces. By default, the HC3 heteroskedasticity-consistent standard errors are calculated.

For our model regressing distance on mother's years of schooling we would use:

```
%HCREG(data = miles, dv = g1miles, iv = g1yrschl);
```

The filename should be a one-word name, so we use the temporary data set called *miles*.

NOTES

Chapter 1
* Terms in color in the text are defined in the glossary/index.

Chapter 2
1   These summary files and public use microdata files for the census are also available through the ICPSR archive.

2   Students can check if their university is a member and allows direct data access at: *www.icpsr.umich.edu/icpsrweb/ICPSR/administration/institutions*. Students at universities that do not allow direct data access should contact their organizational representative to get access.

3   These resources should be available through your local library. See *http://www.annualreviews.org/* and *wokinfo.com*.

Chapter 3
1   It also is possible to use Stata's `cmdlog` command to capture the commands you type interactively for later editing.

2   The self-administered questionnaire, in Display C.3.4, does not allow respondents to circle *don't know* or *refused*; thus it is sensible that most are recorded as *no answer*. The few recorded as *don't know* or *refused* may have written something on the questionnaire that allowed this coding or may have been among the small subset of respondents who were administered the survey via telephone.

3   The number coded as *inapplicable* is larger than the number who reported the mother to be deceased (4,434 in Display C.3.6) but smaller than the number who also did not provide a valid response to the first question (266 = 1 + 13 + 252 in Display C.3.6). With paper and pencil administration, especially in these self-administered questionnaires, skip errors are possible. These could be further explored after the raw data are downloaded.

4   As we will discuss when recoding this variable, most distances among continental US locations should be at most 5,000 miles, suggesting some respondents with larger values may have reported an incorrect value or may have provided a value for mothers living outside the USA. Such errors are especially likely in paper-and-pencil administrations.

5   Multiple imputation is increasingly used by researchers to deal with missing data but beyond the scope of this textbook (see Allison 2001 for an accessible treatment). We focus on appropriately coding missing values as '.' missing. The data coded with '.' missings could be later re-analyzed with multiple imputation, if desired.

6   The NSFH data set also includes 52 replicate half-sample indicators which can be used to calculate what are known as balanced repeated replications for estimating standard errors. This approach is sometimes required, when surveys do not report the PSUs and strata due to confidentiality concerns. We will not discuss this approach in detail because the NSFH (and National Health Interview Survey which is used in the Chapter Exercises) includes identifiers of the PSUs and strata (for more information on this approach, see Campbell and Berbaum 2010; Heeringa 2010; Lehtonen and Pahkinen 1994).

7   As examples of complexities you might deal with in an actual paper based on the NHIS, we point out that a small number of Sample Adults had responses provided by a proxy individual and the NHIS imputed missing values on race-ethnicity (see ICPSR 2010).

Chapter 4

1   Stata also has drop and keep commands that allow for excluding variables and cases from the data file with an if qualifier. However, when reading large data sets like the NSFH into Stata it is helpful to read only a portion of the cases on the use command because of memory limitations.

2   The symbols 1:1 represent a "one-to-one" match of the one record for each *MCASEID* in each data file. Stata's syntax can also be used to represent other types of matches, such as "one-to-many" and "many-to-one" and "many-to-many," when one or both files have more than one record associated with an identifier that is used for merging. A "many-to-one" merge might be needed, for example, if a database of information about households within neighborhoods (many records in each neighborhood, reflecting the various households) was merged with a database of information about neighborhoods (one record per neighborhood) using the neighborhood identifier.

3   There are many additional data management techniques in both SAS and Stata, including additional ways to read *ascii* data files and to merge data files. We overview opportunities for learning about these, and other techniques not covered in the book, in Chapter 18.

4   Another method is explicitly to change the "end of command" delimiter to the same symbol—a semicolon—used by SAS. Programmers who switch frequently back and forth between SAS and Stata sometimes like this approach. To do so, we type #delimit ; After this, Stata treats all words from a command name to the semicolon as part of one command. The command #delimit cr can be issued after the long line to switch back to using the end of the line delimiter (*cr* stands for carriage return which is the code that marks the end of the line to the computer, although not visible to us in most text editors or word processors).

5   You may want to think about and discuss with your instructor and classmates other ways you could recode these values of 96 and/or other ways the survey might have probed these cases to identify whether some respondents who reported 96 could be re-coded to a valid value.

Chapter 5

1   You may also have heard of ratio variables in conjunction with the other three types. We do not discuss ratio variables because they are rare in the social sciences.

2   The field of psychometrics has developed various models to convert the simple sums based on such ordinal response categories to interval values (see for example de Ayala 2009; Embretson and Reise 2000; Frank and Kim 2004).

3   Based on the text, the variables "Wife at least two years older" and "Husband at least five years older" appear to actually be two categories of a three category construct, with wife one year older to four years younger than the husband as the third category.

4   Unlike Teachman, Gee and colleagues show percentages in both levels of some two-category variables, like gender and marital status; but, they don't for others like mental disorder and employment status, where the percentage in the other level must be deduced; for example, $100 - 64.1 = 35.9\%$ of study participants are not employed.

5 Spreadsheet software like Excel can be used to easily present frequency and percentage distributions of nominal variables with graphs. In Appendix H we discuss how to use Excel to make similar graphs, based on regression results. We also discuss in this chapter how to use SAS and Stata's powerful graphics commands to request box plots and histograms. Both can also create many other types of graphs (Heath 2008; Mitchell 2008; Rodriguez 2009).

6 The median, and some other percentiles, can also be obtained from other commands in both SAS and Stata (such as in the default `proc univariate` in SAS and by adding the `detail` option to the `summarize` command in Stata). We focus on the presented commands because they each provide concise output focused on the percentiles.

7 If your SAS license does not include SAS Graph, you will not be able to use the `proc sgplot` command. Display A.5.1 shows how you may use the `plots` option in the `proc univariate` command to request basic graphs in SAS.

8 We can of course request the exact values of the quartiles with the `proc means` statement in SAS and the `centile` command in Stata. Doing so reveals that the median is in fact exactly 60, the 1st quartile is 52 and the 3rd quartile is 68. Thus, the interquartile range is more precisely $68 - 52 = 16$ and $1.5 * 16 = 24$. Thus, more precisely, the upper whisker extends to the largest value not exceeding $68 + 24 = 92$; and, the lower whisker extends to the smallest value not less than $52 - 24 = 28$.

9 SAS plans to add bin width control to the **proc sgplot** command in a future release (SAS Technical Support, personal communication, September 13, 2010).

10 Notice that in this equation we did not explicitly show the lower and upper limits of the sum. When we do this, it is implicit that the sum is over all cases (i.e., $\Sigma(Y_i - \bar{Y}) = 0$ implies $\Sigma_{i=1}^{n} (Y_i - \bar{Y}) = 0$.

11 This example also illustrates the greater stability of the median, in the sense that the year-to-year differences are more similar for the median than the mean (from 1994 to 1996 and 1996 to 1998, the median changes by $55,010 - 41,000 = 14,010$ and $41,000 - 24,400 = 16,600$ respectively whereas the mean changes by $102,620 - 96,017 = 6,603$ and $96,017 - 71,451 = 24,566$ respectively).

12 Notice that we included the keywords in SAS for the four statistics shown in the default output (n mean std min max) as well as the median p50, to show comparable output as in the Stata summarize and centile output. We could also have just listed the mean and median keywords in SAS to show only those two values.

13 To simplify the presentation, we show the formula without reference to strata and PSUs, although the formula can also be written to explicitly show the summation over these units.

14 As discussed in Section 5.7, we may sometimes want to delete cases in this way (or otherwise address item-level missing data) so that all of our analyses are based on the same sample size. But, for this example, we want to match the sample sizes shown in Display B.5.11 so that we can compare "apples to apples" when evaluating the unweighted to the weighted means.

Chapter 6

1 As discussed in Chapter 5, the mean is larger than the median in a skewed distribution; and, for the skewed distribution we might not view the mean as good a representation of the typical value of the distribution.

2 The skewed distribution in Figure 6.1b is based on the Poisson distribution. We will not cover the Poisson distribution in this book, although the methods we discuss in Part 4 can draw on this distribution to appropriately model count outcome variables (see Long 1997).

3 We could use SAS and Stata to determine these values using commands similar to those shown in Display A.6.

4 Such tables can often be found "in the back of the book" in basic statistics texts (e.g., Agresti and Finlay 2009; Daniel 2009; Larsen and Marx 2006; Moore 2010; Nachmias and Leon-Guerrero, 2009;

Wackerly, Mendenhall, and Scheaffer 2008). They are also available online (e.g., *http://www.socr. ucla.edu/Applets.dir/T-table.html*).

5   An exception is the test for equal variances in two groups which we will consider in Chapter 7 (Gallagher 2006). We will show how to calculate a two-tailed *p*-value for that test in Chapter 7.

Chapter 7

1   The exception is the last row, where they show the median of couples' income. In their footnote to the table, they mention that they do so due to the skewness of this variable. Although not covered in this text because they are not commonly reported in all subfields of the social science literature, tests of differences in medians and other tests that are specific to ordinal variables are available (Agresti 2010; Sprent and Smeeton 2001). Indeed, the authors of Literature Excerpt 7.1 do not report a statistical test for median couples' income.

2   Recall that a matrix is an array of numbers organized into rows and columns.

3   We can request this probability in SAS and Stata (as shown in Chapter 6) as `di 2*Ftail(5,8,1.6374)` and `pf=2*(1-probf(1.6374,5,8))`, respectively.

4   For the t-test assuming unequal variances, we can calculate the p-value using `di 2*(ttail(8.97,abs(–1.20)))` and `pt=(1-probt(abs(–1.20),8.97))*2;`

5   For the t-test assuming equal variances we can calculate the p-value using `2*(ttail(13,abs(–1.26)))` and `pt=(1-probt(abs(–1.26),13))*2;`

6   As we shall see in Chapter 9 and 10, these sums of squared deviations are related to each other as follows: $\sum_{i=1}^{n} (Y_i - \overline{Y})^2 = \sum_{i=1}^{n} (\overline{Y}_i - \overline{Y}_g)^2 + \sum_{i=1}^{n} (\overline{Y}_g - \overline{Y})^2$.

7   This *p*-value can be calculated using `di Ftail(1, 13, 1.60)` in Stata and `pf=(1-probf(1.60, 1, 13))` in SAS.

8   Recall from Box 7.4 that we restricted the analytic sample to respondents who had five or fewer brothers and five or fewer sisters in order to simplify the output.

9   The degrees of freedom in this case represents the number of cell values that we can assign freely (within the constraints of the total sample size and the row and column margins). In our example, we have r = 3 and c = 2, thus we can set $(r - 1) * (c - 1) = (3 - 1) * (2 - 1) = 2 * 1 = 2$ cells freely. For example, sticking with our row margins, once we assign two values we can figure out the rest through subtraction. For example, if we assign $n_{11} = 5$ and $n_{32} = 2$, then we can figure out the remaining cells. We illustrate this below, using A, B, C and D in the unknown cells, for convenience.

5	A	13
C	B	13
D	2	14
17	23	40

Since there are only two columns in our example, the cells A and D can readily be solved for by subtraction from the row margins. A = 13 − 5 = 8. D = 14 − 2 = 12. With those two results, we can now figure out C and B. B = 23 − (8 + 2) = 13. C = 17 − (5 + 12) = 0.

10   Additional tests are available for cases in which this criterion is not met (see Agresti 2007, 2010; Libetrau 1983; Reynold 1984).

11   The *p*-value can be calculated in Stata with `di chi2tail(2,0.1585)` and in SAS with `pc=(1-probchi(0.1585,2));`.

12   The SAS output lists several additional measures of association. Again, see Agresti (2007, 2010), Hildebrand, Laing, and Rosenthal (1977), Libetrau (1983), and Reynolds (1984) for good introductions to such other measures of association for categorical variables.

13 The *p*-value can be calculated with di 2*(ttail(13,abs(1.99))) in Stata and pt=(1-probt(abs(1.99)),13))*2; in SAS.

14 The lack of significance for a correlation of this size reflects the small size of our hypothetical example. The relationship between the *t*-value and the sample size, given the correlation, is clear in Equation 7.12. In fact, in our case, the correlation of 0.4836 would become significant at the .05 alpha level when the sample size is increased by just two cases, to 17.

15 To assure that the weights sum to the sample size, this adjustment must be implemented carefully when calculating subgroup means and when some analytic variables have missing data. We created three versions of the adjusted weights: (1) *adjweight1* is the original weight divided by the mean of the weights for the cases not missing *g1miles* within each subgroup of number of sisters, to be used when calculating subgroup means of *g1miles* within levels of *g2numsis*, (2) *adjweight2* is the original weight divided by the mean of the weights of cases not missing *g2numsis* and *g2numbro* for use in the cross-tabulation of number of brothers and sisters, and (3) *adjweight3* is the original weight divided by the mean of the weights of cases not missing *g1age* and *g2age* for use in the correlation of mothers' and respondents' ages. Of the results we show in this chapter, taking care that the weights sum to the sample size has the greatest importance in SAS's calculation of the observed frequencies in the cross-tabulation. In an application, the process of carefully creating the relative weights might be simplified by first "listwise" deleting cases missing on any of the variables used in the analysis (although subgroup analyses would need to be treated with care and other approaches to missing data are becoming popular, but beyond the scope of this book; see Allison 2001).

Chapter 8

1 That is, first substitute $\hat{Y}_i$ for $\hat{\beta}_0 + \hat{\beta}_1 X_i$ in Equation 8.3 (i.e., $Y_i = \hat{Y}_i + \hat{e}_i$). Then, subtract $\hat{Y}_i$ from both sides ($Y_i - \hat{Y}_i = \hat{e}_i$).

2 For illustrative purposes, we first trimmed about 1 percent of cases with the most extreme values of hours (over 140 hours per work). Then, after regressing hours of chores on number of children, we kept a random set of 10 cases within each level of number of children whose residuals fell within half a standard deviation of the fitted line. We also omitted about 30 cases who reported more than four children in the household.

3 Recall that the empirical rule tells us that in a normal distribution about 95 percent of the values lie within two standard deviations of the mean, about 68 percent fall within one standard deviation of the mean, and nearly 100 percent fall within three standard deviations of the mean.

4 This can be seen, for example, by solving Equation 8.6 for $\bar{Y}$. Adding $\hat{\beta}_1 \bar{X}$ to both sides results in $\hat{\beta}_0 + \hat{\beta}_1 \bar{X} = \bar{Y}$.

5 As we saw in Chapter 5, $s_y = \sqrt{\Sigma(Y_i - \bar{Y})^2/(n-1)}$. In this sample $s_y = \sqrt{5371.92/(50-1)} = 10.47$ (the numerator is calculated by squaring the values in the third column and then summing the results). Note that because we drew cases with small residuals to create the stylized sample, the difference between the conditional and unconditional standard deviations is larger in this set of 50 cases than in the full NSFH sample.

6 Recall that the central limit theorem states that the sum of identically distributed random variables approaches a normal distribution as the sample size increases. This convergence to the normal distribution happens even if the original variables are not normally distributed, although larger sample sizes are required as the original variables' distributions deviate more from the normal.

7 Stata's commands can be abbreviated to the first three letters (e.g., reg for regress). We use the full command because the full commands are usually easier for students to understand as they start to learn the Stata syntax.

8 The abbreviation _cons in Stata stands for *constant*. The intercept is sometimes referred to as the constant because its value is included in the predicted value for every case (i.e., it is a "constant") in contrast to the slope whose contribution varies depending on the level of X.

9   SAS and Stata differ in rounding the values. This is especially important in our case with *g2earn*, because of the small size of the coefficient estimate. In this case, Stata leaves more significant digits on the estimate, where significant digits are values that contribute to the meaning of the value (ignoring leading and trailing zeros). As we discuss below, it is possible to rescale a variable before estimating the model to eliminate the leading decimals and assure the presentation of more significant digits in the output. It is also important to take care when rounding coefficient estimates for the prediction equation and presenting results in papers: presenting fewer digits is easier to read but keeping more digits will reduce rounding error in calculations. We can always read the *t*-value off the output, and we will see in later chapters how to ask SAS and Stata to make predictions for us (thus reducing rounding errors).

10   The DF column in SAS does not list the degrees of freedom for the *t*-test. We will learn in Chapter 6 how these DF correspond to related *F*-tests. Also note that the computer calculates the *t*-value based on the stored values of the coefficient and standard error. The coefficient estimate and its standard error, listed in the output, have been rounded to a smaller number of digits. Thus, a *t*-value hand calculated based on the listed coefficient estimate and standard error differs slightly from the computer's calculation of the *t*-value. To minimize rounding error in values reported in a manuscript, it is preferable to use the statistic as calculated by the statistical software.

11   To fully examine the latter idea, we might want to measure the child's educational attainment and occupation in addition to earnings. And, ideally, we might measure professional networks and personal jobseeking strategies.

12   To minimize rounding error, we used in our calculation the most significant digits available across the packages (from Stata for the point estimate and from SAS for the standard error).

13   Based on Equation 8.1, we should also subtract the mean value to calculate a standardized variable. For example, $newY_i = (1/s_Y)(Y_i - \bar{Y})$. But, subtracting a constant, like the mean, will not affect the estimate of the slope.

14   This result is explicit in SAS's correlation output, which lists the same correlation value above and below the diagonal (see again Display B.8.7).

15   In the full NSFH sample, the completely standardized coefficient estimate is smaller, 0.25, just above Cohen's cutoff for a small effect, but still larger than the effect for *g1miles* and *g2earn* in our distance example.

16   A careful reader may ask the question: Couldn't the regression analysis take into account the different associations between outcome and predictor within the two groups? This is exactly one of the strategies used in the model-based approach, and we will learn how to allow for such differences across groups in associations between outcome and predictor in Chapter 11. If we were able to use this alternative model-based approach to account for all of the bias due to oversampling, then we would not need to apply the sampling weights and, usually, our standard errors will be smaller (the estimates more efficient). The problem (as we will discuss in Chapter 13) is that when we use the model-based approach it is difficult to be sure that we have accounted fully for all of the bias due to oversampling, especially in complicated models with multiple predictors and complex sampling designs with multiple types of oversampling (DuMouchel and Duncan 1983; Gelman 2007; Kailsbeek and Heiss 2000; Korn and Graubard 1991; Little 2004).

17   In advance of the study, survey statisticians balance the benefits of clustering (reduced interviewing costs because sample members live close to one another) with the costs of clustering (increased standard errors because of the potential similarity of sample members who live close to one another). Depending on the anticipated similarity on key variables of sample members within clusters, a complex sampling design that uses clustering will usually need to have a larger total sample size than would a simple random sampling design without using clustering (Kalsbeek and Heiss 2000; Kish 1965).

Chapter 9

1 We might also use the indicator variable approach considered in Chapter 10 and Chapter 12 to distinguish various levels of educational attainment. This approach would be especially important if we thought that the effect of one more year of high school differed from the effect of one more year of college.

2 We excluded cases missing any of the variables used for the miles examples in this chapter, thus the sample size in Display B.9.1 is slightly smaller than the sample size in Chapter 8 ($n = 5,475$). The standard deviations are thus slightly different than those used in Chapter 8.

3 As in Chapter 8, we might want to instead semistandardize the coefficient for earnings rescaled to $10,000 units. Then, we would have $10,000 * 0.001022/645.0074 = 0.016$. Thus, a $10,000 increase in earnings is associated with the adult living about 0.016 of a standard deviation further from the mother.

4 The abbreviations are used differently in different subfields. For example, SSE is sometimes used to abbreviate Explained Sum of Squares which we use instead here for Sum of Squared Errors. In the SAS output, TSS is listed as "Corrected Total," SSE is the "Error Sum of Squares," and MSS is the "Model Sum of Squares."

5 Although some researchers use the overall F-test in a fashion similar to the Bonferroni-type adjustment (i.e., not examining individual coefficients unless the model F is significant), having a nonsignificant F-test when individual t-statistics are significant is unusual in well-specified models. The more common importance of the model F-test is in identifying multicollinearity. As we'll see in Chapter 14, a hallmark of multicollinearity is the nonintuitive situation in which the model F-test is significant while none of the individual t-tests for the slopes is significant.

6 That is: $(n - 1) - (n - 2) = n - 1 - n + 2 = (n - n) + (2 - 1) = 1$

7 SAS and Stata round the t-value to two decimals. If you instead calculate the t-value directly using the listed coefficient and standard error, you can match the F-value more exactly. $6.383609 /0.435193 = 14.668455$ and $14.668455 * 14.668455 = 215.16$.

8 That is: $(3,116 - 1) - (3,116 - 3) = 3,116 - 1 - 3,116 + 3 = 3 - 1 = 2$.

9 For the numerator, $(3,116 - 2) - (3,116 - 3) = 3,116 - 2 - 3,116 + 3 = 1$

10 Notice that Stata's sum of squares tables in Display B.9.1 and Display B.9.8 list the residual and total sum of squares in scientific notation because of their large size. We can read the values directly from SAS's output, or we can calculate them more precisely in the Stata output by multiplying the MS column value in the residual row (e.g., 412,112.921 in Display B.9.1) by the residual degrees of freedom (e.g., 5,472 in Display B.9.1) although this introduces some rounding error. We will also see later in the text how to ask SAS and Stata to calculate the F-value directly for us, to avoid rounding error.

11 That is: $(5,475 - 3) - (5,475 - 7) = 5,475 - 3 - 5,475 + 7 = 4$.

12 We will later learn how to use these `test` commands to test other null hypotheses, such as that the coefficients for two variables are equivalent.

13 It is useful to remember that a Pearson correlation between two variables can be squared to determine how much variation the variables share. It is also instructive to note that a correlation of .50 reflects just 25 percent shared variation. It is not until the correlation exceeds .70 that the two variables share 50 percent variation ($.7 * .7 = .49$).

14 The R-squared for this stylized sample is larger than the R-squared found in Display B.9.4 for the full NSFH sample of n = 3,116 ($r = 0.0646$) because we chose the stylized sample of 50 to include observations that fell relatively close to the regression line.

15 In fact, an effect size measure for multiple regression is based on R-squared (Cohen 1992).

16 Presentation of confidence intervals for coefficients has become the norm in some fields, such as public health. In Chapter 10, we present an example of the presentation of confidence intervals. As noted earlier, presenting confidence intervals is useful because they make explicit that the population coefficient is estimated with uncertainty.

Chapter 10

1   In general, there are usually multiple ways to perform data management tasks, such as data creation. One person's code may be simpler than another's for a particular task, but as long as both accomplish the objective, both are fine. As a student, it is important to use the approach that you find easiest to understand initially. Then, you can move on to more compact syntax. As a student and scientist, it is also important that your code is easy for you to proof and for others to understand. Sometimes longer, less elegant, syntax can be easier to check for errors or to be understood by others (or by you a few months down the road). At times, SAS or Stata will also have an approach to a specific task not offered in the other package. For example, in Stata, it is possible to create dummy variables using the tabulate command combined with a generate option. For example, "tabulate M484 if M484<97, gen(M484)" creates dummy variables for each category of the original variable, assigning missing values to '.' missing. Similarly, xi i.M484 does the same, although missing values must be dealt with separately and the smallest variable is used as reference by default (the command char M484[omit] 2 can be used to instead exclude the second category).

2   SAS has syntax that allows us to type the *if* qualifier just once, referred to as if-then-do. Statements that follow the do are executed only for cases that meet the expression, until a closing end statement. For example, we could define our dummies as follows:

```
if M484<97 then do;
  aframer=(M484=1);
  white= (M484=2);
  mexamer=(M484=3);
  amind= (M484=7);
  other= ((M484>=4 & M484<=6) | M484=8 | M484=9);
end;
```

3   The result in Equation 10.3 will be clear to some students, recognizing that the two β_0 terms in the equation $(\beta_0 + \beta_1) - (\beta_0)$ cancel out, because one is positive and one is negative. To show why this is so, we can rewrite the equation as follows:

$$(\beta_0 + \beta_1) - (\beta_0) = \beta_0 + \beta_1 - \beta_0 = \beta_0 - \beta_0 + \beta_1 = \beta_1$$

Using the distributive property of multiplication, we first multiply through to remove the parentheses, then collect terms (put the two β_0 terms side by side), and then subtract one β_0 from the other. To put this another way, the β_0 term is common to both expected values, so when we subtract one expected value from the other, we are left with the term that is not common to both: β_1.

4   More specifically, the OLS results are analogous to the *t*-test assuming equal variance on the outcome across the groups. This is analogous to the homoskedasticity assumption in OLS regression. We will discuss in Chapter 14 how to test this assumption and, if needed, attempt to make the data better conform to this assumption in OLS.

5   Like the analogy of the two-sample *t*-test to a regression with a single dummy variable, Analysis of Variance (ANOVA) and Analysis of Covariance (ANCOVA) conduct hypothesis tests that parallel those of regression models with sets of dummies and interval-level controls. Whereas interpretation of regression models focuses on the coefficients for individual variables, ANOVA and ANCOVA

focus on partitioning the variance, often for sets of variables at a time. The sums of squares decomposition that we discussed in Chapter 9 is fundamental to ANOVA.

6 As noted, other strategies for coding the categories allow for different interpretations. See Endnote 10.1.

7 What if we were interested in a contrast between an included group and all other groups combined? Then, we could include just one dummy variable to indicate that group, and exclude the rest. For example, if we were interested in contrasting whites versus all other groups combined, then we would estimate the model: $Y_i = \beta_0 + \beta_3 D_{3i} + \varepsilon_i$. By grouping American Indians and Mexican Americans with African Americans as a single reference category, this model implies that the means for these omitted groups do not differ. This could be tested by estimating the initial model: $Y_i = \beta_0 + \beta_1 D_{1i} + \beta_2 D_{2i} + \beta_3 D_{3i} + \varepsilon_i$. If the coefficient estimates for the dummy variables D_1 and D_2 were insignificant, we would have empirical evidence that the means for these groups do not differ from the reference group (African Americans), which could be used to justify re-estimating the model with both D_1 and D_2 excluded. Researchers sometimes use this approach to simplify the presentation of their results, referring to it as "collapsing together" categories. Sometimes the approach is used to collapse together categories with small sample sizes, although ideally the approach is supported by conceptual reasons or prior empirical results suggesting that the other groups would not differ from one another (i.e., if the sample sizes of the subgroups are small, then the standard errors will be relatively large, and it will be difficult to reject the null hypothesis that the means for the subgroups are equivalent).

8 This rationale implies a directional hypothesis (whites less than American Indians; whites less than Mexican Americans). Although we will use two-tailed tests throughout this chapter, as we discussed in Chapter 8, if you have strong *à priori* rationale for a directional hypothesis, and your results are consistent with your hypothesis, then you can calculate the one-tailed p-values by dividing the p-values reported by SAS and Stata in half.

9 We speculated in the text that the other groups might live closer to their mothers than would whites, implying a one-sided test. In the bottom panel of Display B.10.7, the coefficient estimates for Mexican Americans and African Americans are negative, consistent with the hypothesis that they live closer to their mothers than do whites. Thus, to calculate the one-sided p-value, we would divide the listed p-value in half (0.197/2 = 0.0985 for *mexamer* and 0.022/2 = 0.011 for *aframer*). In contrast, the coefficient estimate for American Indians is positive, inconsistent with our hypothesis. Thus, to calculate the one-sided p-value for *amind* we should subtract half the listed p-value from one ([1−(.433/2)] = .7835). Doing so does not change any of our conclusions with a 5 percent alpha level, although the difference between Mexican Americans and whites is now a trend or marginally significant (just below the cutoff often used for marginal significance of $\alpha = 0.10$).

10 In each row, we simplified the algebra for the difference, by first multiplying the −1 through the parentheses using the distributive property of multiplication (e.g., $-(\beta_0 + \beta_2)$ becomes $-\beta_0 - \beta_2$). And, the positively and negatively signed β_0 terms cancel out.

11 We might have used theory and prior research to hypothesize in advance that women would live closer to their mothers than men. If so, then our coefficient estimate would be consistent with our hypothesis, and thus, to calculate the one-sided p-value, we would divide the p-value listed by SAS and Stata in half. For *female*, the two-sided p-value in Display B.10.12 is 0.072. Thus, the one-sided p-value would be 0.072/2 = 0.036.

12 If we had hypothesized in advance that African Americans would live closer to their mothers than other groups, then the positive coefficient estimates in Display B.10.12 would be consistent with our hypotheses and we would divided SAS and Stata's two-sided p-values in half (making the contrasts with *amind* and *white* marginally significant, since 0.150/2 = 0.075 and 0.164/2 = 0.082). We also know from the test commands in Display B.10.9 that the other contrasts, among the included groups, are not significant (even for one-sided hypotheses). Had any been significant, a common way to indicate such contrasts would be to put superscript letters on pairs of categories that do (or do not)

have coefficient estimates that differ significantly from each other. Literature Excerpt 10.2 provides an example of using such subscripts.

13 As we will discuss in Chapter 11, it is possible to make the intercept meaningful by altering what a zero on the predictor variable represents, a technique often referred to as *centering* the predictor.

14 The authors' inclusion of only the coefficient estimates and *p*-values conserves space, and space is always a premium in journals; however, we will recommend providing standard-errors in tables (because the standard errors can help us to identify problems with our models, which we will discuss in Chapter 14).

15 These outcome variables could also be treated as ordinal. For example, each value of educational expectations is linked to an explicit level of education, and whether the differences between those levels are equal is not known (e.g., is moving from not finishing high school to graduating from high school equivalent to moving from completing a few years of college to graduating from a four-year college?). In Chapter 17, we will introduce models specifically designed for this kind of ordinal outcome.

16 The authors do not tell us whether these are one-tailed or two-tailed *p*-values, although most likely they are two-tailed. Although some of the authors' arguments suggest directional alternative hypotheses, they have generally laid out two mechanisms (family resources and family instability) with somewhat different predictions.

17 The authors also related the family types to the child's likelihood of having graduated high school and enrolled in college by Wave 2. Importantly, these models also reveal that children in cohabiting families are less likely than one or more other groups to graduate from high school and to enroll in college. These strengthen the findings we discuss in the text of this chapter because they are based on the child's own report, rather than the mother's reports. The maternal reports could be picking up effects of family type on mother's perceptions of the child, rather than actual child effects.

18 That is, $(0.58/10) * (2/2) = 1.16/20$. Similarly, $(0.37/10) * (2/2) = 0.74/20$ and $(0.80/10) * (2/2) = 1.60/20$.

19 That is, $(0.08/10) * (10/10) = 0.80/100$. And, $(1.36/10) > (1/10)$.

Chapter 11

1 All of the Excel spreadsheets from this chapter are on the textbook web site *http://www.routledge. com/cw/gordon/*.

2 Because of our focus on gender differences, it is useful to have in mind that the NSFH asked respondents to report the time they spent on household tasks in nine different categories, covering stereotypically male and female chores. The items, from Self-Enumerated Questionnaire #1, are: (1) Preparing meals, (2) Washing dishes and cleaning up after meals, (3) Cleaning house, (4) Outdoor and other household maintenance tasks (lawn and yard work, household repair, painting, etc.), (5) Shopping for groceries and other household goods, (6) Washing, ironing, mending, (7) Paying bills and keeping financial records, (8) Automobile maintenance and repair, and (9) Driving other household members to work, school, or other activities.

3 We do not code cohabiting partners in this example, although it would be possible to do so in the NSFH. Indeed, when we have done so, we found that women who are cohabiting have statistically equivalent average hours of chores as single women.

4 It is also possible to respecify the model using dummies for the four cells in the cross-tabulation of the two dummies. We can think of the four cells as a four-category variable capturing joint characteristics across the two dummy variables. We will need to create new dummy indicators for three of the cells, and allow one cell to be the reference category. For example, we might specify:

$$Y_i = \beta_0^+ + \beta_1^+ D_{1i}^+ + \beta_2^+ D_{2i}^+ + \beta_3^+ D_{3i}^+ + \varepsilon_i$$

where D_{1i}^+ indicates being married and male, D_{2i}^+ indicates being unmarried and female, and D_{3i}^+ indicates being married and female. The reference group is unmarried males. The results will be equivalent to the results for including two dummies and their product, although the interpretation will differ. Each coefficient now captures the difference in means between the group with each pair of characteristics, and the reference category. To test whether the effect of one variable differs depending on the level of the other variable would require tests of equality of coefficients. For the effect of being married to be the same within gender we would test whether $(\beta_3^+ - \beta_2^+) = \beta_1^+$. For the effect of being female to be the same within marital status we would test whether $(\beta_3^+ - \beta_1^+) = \beta_2^+$. These two equations are equivalent. Both test whether $\beta_3^+ = \beta_1^+ + \beta_2^+$. This tests whether the sum of the effect of having just one of the characteristics (married but not female, D_{1i}^+; female but not married, D_{2i}^+) relative to neither characteristic (the reference category of not married and not female) equals the effect of having both characteristics simultaneously (being married and female, D_{3i}^+), relative to neither characteristic (the reference category of not married and not female). Because we typically want to first test this equality constraint, it is more common in the social sciences to use the product term approach than to use the explicit coding for the joint characteristics across the categorical variables.

5 In a real world project, rather than being simple means, the predicted values would take advantage of multiple regression and be adjusted for other variables in the model. We show how to make such predictions, with controls, in Display H.11.11.

6 These are about the 10th and 90th percentiles for women. For men, the 10th and 90th percentiles are about 30 and 60, although at least 5 percent of men work 15 or fewer hours per week

7 As we have emphasized previously, SAS and Stata conduct a two-sided test by default. In this case, the sign of the product term is negative, but its absolute value of 2.87 is greater than the cutoff of 1.96. Above, we laid out a directional hypothesis, expecting that the sign on *hrwork* would be negative for both genders, but of larger magnitude (more negative) for women than men. The sign on *hrwork* and on the product term *fem_hrwork* are both negative, and thus consistent with these directional hypotheses. Thus, to conduct a one-sided hypothesis test, we would divide the *p*-values in half (doing so has little practical effect in our case, however, because the *p*-values are both less than 0.001).

8 It is preferable to have SAS and Stata make the calculations that will be presented in a manuscript, to avoid rounding error (and other human error). We could also use the full estimates in Display B.11.6 in our hand calculation (rather than rounding them to two significant digits as we did in Equation 11.3). This would give $- 0.1243169 - 0.1256042 = -.2499211$.

9 Again, it is preferable to have SAS and Stata make the calculations that will be presented in a manuscript, to avoid rounding error (and other human error). If we need to make hand calculations to present in a paper, we could also use the full estimates in Display B.11.6 (rather than rounding them to two significant digits as we did in Equation 11.3). For 10 hours of paid work, this would give $16.99004 - 10 * 0.1256042 = 15.73$.

10 The standard deviation of *hrwork* is similar within gender, at 14.08 for men and 14.17 for women.

11 Clearly, for a publication, we would introduce additional variables to the model. For example, our rationale for marital status and number of children may extend also to the number and/or characteristics of other adults in the household.

12 We present just the `lincom` results for simplicity, now that we have fully examined all three approaches. We could also use the other approaches of recentering each variable and re-estimating the regression, using the `test` command, or requesting the variance–covariance matrix of coefficients.

13 The footnote on the front page which notes that some of the data for the study (e.g., percentage of Evangelical Protestants in a county) came from the American Religion Data Archive (now the Association of Religion Data Archives; *http://www.thearda.com/*), an important resource for students interested in religion. The authors combine these data with other sources, primarily the 2000 US Census.

14 The authors do not report how fully sex segregation and percentage women in the labor force vary and covary across counties. If the empirical distribution of sex segregation does not vary completely, from zero to one, within one or more of the conditions (45 percent, 55 percent and 65 percent in the labor force), then the predictions would be out of range. It is always important to check the univariate range and bivariate distribution of predictors when specifying and interpreting interactions. If these are constrained, using larger existing data sources may be more appropriate for testing a substantive interaction. For example, family and neighborhood income tend to be highly correlated, especially in localized studies. Large national samples may be better suited to testing interactions between these variables.

Chapter 12

1 Other bases for the logs are of course possible, but in our regression models we will always use the natural log.

2 Each of the data sets is available publicly, most of them through ICPSR. Cornwell, Laumann, and Schumm (2008) use the National Social Life and Health Aging Project (*http://www.norc.org/Research/Projects/Pages/national-social-life-health-and-aging-project.aspx*). Willson (2003) uses the Mature Women cohort of the National Longitudinal Surveys of Labor Market Experience (*http://www.bls.gov/nls/*). Pritchett and Summers (1996) data come from the Penn World Tables (*http://pwt.econ.upenn.edu/php_site/pwt_index.php*) and the World Bank (*http://www.worldbank.org/*; see the paper for additional notes about their use of these data). Glauber (2007) uses the National Longitudinal Survey of Youth (NLSY 1979; *http://www.bls.gov/nls/*).

3 This formula is derived by taking the derivative of Equation 12.1, setting the result equal to zero, and solving for X; that is, $\beta_1 + 2\beta_2 X = 0$ leads to $X = -\beta_1/2\beta_2$.

4 This formula is the derivative of Equation 12.1.

5 Recall that the exponential is often referred to as the anti-log and $\exp[\ln(X)] = X$.

6 Generally, $b^{(m+n)} = b^m b^n$. For exponentials, $e^{(m+n)} = e^m e^n$ or equivalently $\exp(m+n) = \exp(m)\exp(n)$.

7 In our simple model, we do not include the adult's own education. Because of intergenerational correlations in educational attainment, the basic association between mothers' education and distance may be picking up some effects of the adult's education.

8 An alternative hypothesis, we will see some evidence for below, is that larger families may be more family oriented and may stay close together.

9 As we noted above, the linear model is nested in the quadratic model. Thus, they can be compared with the general linear F-test. There is only one restriction in the null hypothesis for this test, and the square of the t-value for the quadratic term is equivalent to the F-value for this general linear F-test.

10 Six and 16 are the 5th and 95th percentiles for *glyrschl* and thus contain most of the observations (the full range of *glyrschl* is 0 to 17).

11 In the chapter table, we round the values to at least three significant digits to make it readable. This introduces some rounding error. In practice, you can use Excel, SAS, or Stata to make calculations, but this table emphasizes the accounting of the transformations.

Chapter 13

1 This is difficult to understand fully based on the information provided in the articles, although the direction of effect of education is opposite of the authors' expectations, and differs from the bivariate associations shown in their Table 2. And, the coefficient on missing income is significant in the multiple regression but not bivariate associations.

2 This outcome is really ordinal, rather than interval. In the roadmap in Chapter 18, we discuss alternative models designed explicitly for ordinal outcomes.

Chapter 14

1 Although scholars (including the original developer of DFFIT) have tried to change the name (Welsch 1986), it is commonly used (sometimes as DFITS rather than DFFITS).

2 Although DFFITS is sometimes presented in absolute value in the formula, so that it only takes on positive values, both SAS and Stata calculate DFFITS with the sign indicated. Thus, the absolute value should be taken before comparing with the approximate cutoff.

3 As discussed in Chapter 5, Stata graphs can be easily saved using the command graph export. For example, we could type graph export box_g1miles.wmf to export the graph created by graph box g1miles.

4 These graphs can also be saved with the graph export command in Stata. The jitter option can improve readability for large data sets (we used the option, jitter(17) for the graphs shown in Figure 14.3).

5 Recall that ods stands for output delivery system and we also use an ods command to save the output to a rich text file.

6 Because the DFBETAS are specific to individual predictors, we also created separate dummy indicators of whether a case was extreme on the overall measures (hat diagonal, studentized residual, Cook's distance, and DFFITS) and whether a case was extreme on the DFB for mother's years of schooling (either the linear *DFB_glyrschl* or quadratic *DFB_sqglyrschl* terms) and whether a case was extreme on the DFB for any of the number of sisters' dummies (*DFB_g2numsis4, DFB_g2numsis56, or DFB_g2numsis7p*). Results were similar, so we focus on a measure that combines these three.

7 This can be done directly in Stata, since the diagnostic variables are added to the original data set. In SAS, the diagnostics must be merged into the original data file using the following command: data influence3; merge miles influence2; run; where *influence2* is the datafile we created in Display B.14.1. Note that this adds a new data step to our batch program. The SAS system refers to the most recently created data file by default. This has been fine in earlier batch programs, because we had only one data step in the batch program. But, when we have multiple data steps in a batch program, we can use the data= option on procedures to refer to the desired data set (e.g., proc reg data=miles; or proc reg data=influence3;).

8 The predictions for mother's years of schooling were made by substituting in the indicated value and holding the rest of the variables constant at their means. The resulting predicted value in log Y units was converted to natural units by taking the exponential and calculating the adjustment factor, using the process shown in Chapter 12. The predicted values for number of sisters were similarly calculated by substituting in the relevant pattern of zeros and ones on the dummies and holding the remaining variables constant at their means, and then converting the predicted log Y value to Y units.

9 We rewrote these formulas using the conventions introduced in Chapter 13 for calculating direct and indirect effects, using 1 for the outcome, 2 for the first predictor, and 3 for the second predictor.

10 For example, suppose the correlation taken to six digits, rather than rounded to four digits, is 0.990556. Then,

$$VIF = \frac{1}{(1 - 0.990556)} = 105.89$$

11 Many courses in psychometric approaches are available. Check your local universities as well as resources like summer courses at the University of Michigan (*http://www.icpsr.umich.edu/sumprog/*) and the University of Kansas (*http://www.quant.ku.edu/StatsCamps/overview.html*) and likely at your local university.

Chapter 15

1 It is possible to use other estimation techniques within the generalized linear model framework (see Dobson 1990) and to use maximum likelihood estimation outside of the generalized linear model framework (see Eliason 1993).

2 The constant π should not be confused with the parameter for the probability, which we will examine in Chapters 16 and 17.

3 Recall again that based on the empirical rule we expect about 68% of values to fall within one standard deviation above and below the mean, 95% within two standard deviations of the mean, and nearly all (99.7%) within three standard deviations of the mean.

4 We use this notation because it emphasizes the fact that we are using the same function in both cases, but shifting which value we take as unknown. In the first case, we take particular values of the parameters and calculate the density for different values of Y. In the second case, we take particular values of Y (those in the data we have in hand) and calculated the density for different values of the parameters.

5 Recall $\ln(q_1 * q_2) = \ln(q_1 q_2) = \ln(q_1) + \ln(q_2)$

6 With other models, not covered in Chapters 16 and 17, the program may "fail to converge" meaning that a maximum could not be identified based on the programmed rules. In these cases, alternative rules might be needed to achieve convergence (different starting points, different algorithms for how far and what direction to move, different convergence criteria).

7 Maximum likelihood estimates require large sample size. Although there is no hard-and-fast rule for what is large enough, generally several hundred cases are needed (the more complicated the model, such as with more predictor variables and more interactions among them, the more cases needed). Thus, using large publicly available data sets to obtain a larger sample size is a particularly useful strategy for your research if your outcome variable is better suited for the models discussed in Chapters 16 and 17 than for OLS.

8 If you calculate a negative value based on the formula, you likely reversed the log-likelihoods for the full and reduced models.

9 Fox 2008 provides an excellent treatment of the generalized linear model that is more advanced and covers more models than this text, but is still quite accessible.

10 Nelder and Wedderburn (1972) actually used Y on the left hand side, but more recent treatments use η.

11 The scale parameter, circled in black in Stata, estimates the conditional variance. In SAS, the square root of this value is reported in the parameter estimates table ($\sqrt{403351.9} \approx 634.9999$). This value is close to the Root MSE of 635.1 reported in the OLS output in Display B.8.1. The slight difference is not just rounding error. Indeed, the calculation of the OLS and maximum likelihood estimates of the conditional variance differ slightly, although the difference will be small in large samples. The maximum likelihood estimator of the conditional variance is $\hat{\sigma}^2 = \frac{\sum \hat{\varepsilon}_i^2}{n}$ whereas the OLS estimator was $\hat{\sigma}^2 = \frac{\sum \hat{\varepsilon}_i^2}{n-k}$.

12 Because we estimated a linear regression model using the identity link we can assess the substantive significance of earnings using the same techniques that we learned in Part 3 (e.g., our re-scaling techniques and calculation of predicted values). As we will see in Chapters 16 and 17, for models that use other links, we will need to learn new techniques for interpretation.

Chapter 16

1 The association will also be fairly linear if the range of probabilities is quite small, even in the curvilinear portions below 0.20 and above 0.80.

2 We can ask SAS and Stata to calculate probits for us. In Stata the syntax is `display invnorm(0.40)` to show the Z-value associated with a probability of 0.40. The result of this command is $-.2533471$. In SAS the syntax for the same result is `data _null_; z=probit(.40); put "z-value for p:" z 5.3; run;`

3 Of course, in social science applications, we expect the probability of success to vary across observations. In logit and probit models we will include predictor variables and focus on conditional probabilities, allowing cases with different X values to have different conditional probabilities.

4 For example, imagine we had four people, Mary, John, Felicia, and Juan. The six pairs we could form from these four people are: Mary-John, Mary-Felicia, Mary-Juan, John-Felicia, John-Juan and Felicia-Juan.

5 Recall that the logit is also actually based on the logistic cumulative distribution function.

6 We can ask SAS or Stata to look up the number for us. In Stata, the command is `display normal(0.52)` to look up the cumulative probability associated with a Z-value of 0.52. To get the same result in SAS, we type `data _null_; pz=probnorm(abs(0.52)); put "p-value for z:" pz 5.3; run;`

7 You may also seen these equations written as: $Maximum\ Likelihood\ R^2 = 1 - \left[\dfrac{L(M_{intercept\ only})}{L(M_{full})}\right]^{2/n}$ and

$Cragg\ \&\ Uhler's\ R^2 = \dfrac{1 - \left[\dfrac{L(M_{reduced})}{L(M_{full})}\right]^{2/n}}{1 - [L(M_{reduced})]^{2/n}}$. These equations are equivalent to those shown in the body

of the text and produce the same results, although those shown in the main text are easier to compute based on the log-likelihoods shown in statistical output.

8 Burnham and Anderson (2002) suggest an alternative formula when the sample size is small relative to the number of parameters. Specifically, if $\dfrac{n}{k+1} < 40$ then the adjusted formula is: $-2lnL(M_{full}) + 2k$
$* \left(\dfrac{n}{n-k}\right)$. This formula converges to the unadjusted formula as the sample size increases.

9 In fact, the `spost` commands do not work following the `glm` command.

10 The basic process of writing new commands in Stata is straightforward (although the time it takes to write and proof these commands may be substantial, depending on the complexity of the task the command aims to achieve). The programs that contain the syntax for the commands are saved in files with an *.ado* extension, similar to *.do* files. These *.ado* files are stored on your computer. If you are working in a computer lab where your files are only available during your session, you can store the *.ado* files in your project directory. Or, your instructor may be able to ask the lab technicians to install the *.ado* files so they are available to all lab users.

11 The textbook web site includes an Excel file called Chapter16.xlsx which can be used to calculate the values not available in SAS.

12 The Excel file on the textbook web site called Chapter16.xlsx also shows how to calculate these values.

13 Specifying `pprob=0.50` asks SAS to classify predicted probabilities as successes if they are at or above 0.50. This is the most commonly used cutoff and matches the default in Stata.

14 The Excel file Chapter 16.xlsx on the textbook web site shows how to calculate the values not available in the SAS output.

15 In SAS, the standardized Pearson residuals are available from `proc genmod`.

16 Stata refers to the first two as the "average response" versus "response at average" (p. 964–965).

17 The option p is not required since the predicted probability is the default prediction following the logit command.

18 In our dataset, the 5th percentile of earnings is 0 and the 95th percentile is about \$83,000.

19 Long and Freese (2005) also provide various commands for making predictions in their spost suite of commands.

20 Either a single equals sign or double equals sign may be used with the at() option.

21 This file will be in your SAS work library, and it is instructive to open it to verify the means and to see that there is just one case in this data file (since we requested the overall sample means for each variable). Even though this is a small data file, it is exactly what we want to use as input for the score command.

22 Note that the proc means output lists a '.' for the standard deviation since there is only one case in each data file; this is expected since we created a data file with the unconditional means.

23 Of course, although these rounded means are more acceptable because they reflect values that could possibly be observed on the control variables, it may still be the case that no sample person is observed to have this set of characteristics. But, they represent the "average person" in the sample in our thought experiment.

24 The Z-value and p-value listed in Stata are identical when the logit coefficients and the odds ratios are reported. This Z-value is the ratio of the unexponentiated coefficient to its standard error. The ratio of the odds ratio to its standard error does not equal the Z-value. The standard error of the odds ratio is calculated as the standard error of the (unexponentiated) coefficient times the odds ratio (the exponential of the coefficient).

25 In calculus terminology, the marginal effect is the partial derivative of the function relating the predictor and outcome with respect to the variable of interest.

26 We created this table in Excel. Cutting and pasting the coefficients and means from our SAS or Stata output makes it easier to make these calculations.

27 These calculations are available in the Excel file Chapter 16.xlsx available on the textbook web site.

28 The Excel file Chapter 16.xlsx on the textbook web site provides examples of making these calculations, which can be used with the SAS results.

Chapter 17

1 As in the case with a dummy predictor variable, we will see that which outcome category we choose as reference is arbitrary, that we can recover additional contrasts between outcome categories from a single estimation of the model, and that there strategies that can be used to simplify presentation of these additional contrasts.

2 Because they do not specify what level they held their other variables constant at when making these predictions, we will assume the average level was used for the covariates (i.e., the "average then predict" method introduced in Chapter 16).

3 This value is not strictly the log of the odds, since the odds is defined as the ratio of a probability to its complement (i.e., the ratio of a probability of success to the probability of failure). The ratio of two probabilities that may not sum to one is referred to as a relative risk in biostatistics, although it is defined as the ratio of the probability of an event for a treatment group relative to the probability of an event for a comparison group, which is also different from our ratio of outcome probabilities (Daniel 2009). We will see below that Stata refers to the ratio of probabilities in multinomial logit models as relative risks.

4 This can be shown using the property of logs that $\ln\left(\frac{a}{b}\right) = \ln(a) - \ln(b)$. We begin with:

$$\ln\left(\frac{\pi_1}{\pi_3}\right) - \ln\left(\frac{\pi_2}{\pi_3}\right) - \ln\left(\frac{\pi_1}{\pi_2}\right) = 0$$

Then using $\ln\left(\dfrac{a}{b}\right) = \ln(a) - \ln(b)$ we rewrite as follows:

$$(\ln \pi_1 - \ln \pi_3) - (\ln \pi_2 - \ln \pi_3) - (\ln \pi_1 - \ln \pi_2) = 0$$

Multiplying through we have:

$$\ln \pi_1 - \ln \pi_3 - \ln \pi_2 + \ln \pi_3 - \ln \pi_1 + \ln \pi_2 = 0$$

Rearranging terms we see the cancellation:

$$(\ln \pi_1 - \ln \pi_1) + (\ln \pi_2 - \ln \pi_2) + (\ln \pi_3 - \ln \pi_3) = 0$$

5 In fact, an intuitive extension of the dichotomous model would be to iteratively keep only the sample members with two of the outcome categories (for example, keep just parents who use center child care or family day care providers) and then estimate a dichotomous logit based on those two categories (for example, define center child care as the success coded one and family day care as the failure coded zero in a binary logit model). This process could be repeated for each pair of outcome categories. Although similar, the results of this approach will not exactly equal the results from a multinomial logit model because the multinomial model imposes the constraint shown in Equation 17.2 and because simultaneous estimation of all equations is more efficient (Long 1997).

6 Note that we did this implicitly in the binary logit model. In that case, there were two outcome categories ($C=2$) and we used the outcome category coded zero as the reference outcome category.

7 Again the *Spost* listcoef commands written by Long and Freese (2006) provide a convenient way to list the contrasts between included outcome categories for all predictor variables if you are using Stata.

8 In general, the number of pairs can be calculated by the first part of the binomial formula with $s = 2$ and $N = C$. That is, the number of pairs that we can form from C categories is: $\dfrac{C!}{2!(C-2)!}$. So, for example, when $C = 3$, the number of pairs is $\dfrac{3!}{2!(3-2)!} = \dfrac{3 \times 2 \times 1}{2 \times 1 \times 1} = 3$. And, when $C = 6$, the number of pairs is $\dfrac{6!}{2!(6-2)!} = \dfrac{6 \times 5 \times 4 \times 3 \times 2 \times 1}{2 \times 1 \times 4 \times 3 \times 2 \times 1} = 10$

9 Again, if you are using Stata, the Long and Freese (2006) *Spost* commands, such as listcoef and mlogplot, can simplify this process, although in our experience digesting the volume of output when there are many outcome categories and numerous predictors can still be overwhelming, especially if you have not laid out in advance a strong conceptual rationale for how the various predictors are expected to associated with the contrasts between each pair of outcomes.

10 Again, if you are using Stata, using the listcoef command will let you easily show the coefficients for all contrasts after a single estimation of the model.

11 Had we reversed the two coefficients for *g2earn10000* the result would have been the same, but opposite in sign (i.e., $0.0272 - 0.0351 = -.0079$).

12 Stata's hausman command can also be used to test the assumption, although implementing it is somewhat more complex.

13 Stata follows the practice of referring to the exponential of coefficients from a multinomial logit model as relative risk ratios (Stata 2009b, see also Daniel 2009).

14 As noted above, additional *Spost* commands (Long and Freese 2006) are available to facilitate calculation of predicted probabilities, for example prvalue is similar to margins (providing a particular predicted probability with a confidence interval), prtab makes it easy to generate predicted probabilities for tables, and prgen makes it easy to generating predicted probabilities for figures.

15 In SAS, we "set" in the data step the *predround* data set that was created in Chapter 16.

16 Different approaches may also lead to different signs on the predictor variables' coefficients, although the approaches we will examine, which are used by SAS and Stata, do not.

17 If you work with a practical example in which it makes sense to re-categorize your outcome variable you will want to balance several concerns in choosing the categories, including: (1) the conceptual rationale for each category (do the cutoffs make substantive sense?), (2) the sample size in each category (even if a category makes substantive sense, there may be too few members of your sample in that category to define it) and (3) the empirical results (in a multinomial logit model, we discussed how to test whether two categories can be combined).

18 We will examine this six-category outcome estimated for the multinomial logit model in the "Putting It All Together" section. As we discuss, there are some ways to handle the large volume of results. For example, you might focus on and present in a paper just the contrasts between adjacent categories, if you examine an ordinal outcome with a multinomial model. And, graphs can help you work through the full set of results (see Long 1997 for numerous strategies for accomplishing these goals and Long and Freese 2006 for Stata commands to make these strategies easier to implement).

19 Note that, consistent with the violation of the proportional odds assumption for this variable, this odds ratio is closer to the result for the odds ratio for far ("1500") versus close ("23") of 1.028 than for far ("1500") versus mid-range ("273") of $\frac{1}{1.007928} = 0.992134$ than for mid-range ("273") versus close ("23") of 1.036 that we saw in Display B.17.5 for the multinomial logit model.

20 The results seem to suggest that the smallest two and the fourth and fifth categories might be combined. We used Stata's mlogtest command after estimating the multinomial logit model for our six-category outcome. The results show that there is evidence for collapsing together the two adjacent pairs among the three largest categories (46 to 200 with 200 to 201; 201 to 500 with 501 to 9000) but not the third (46 to 200 with 501 to 9000). On the other hand, there is not empirical evidence for collapsing the two smallest categories (within one mile and 2 to 15 miles).

21 We examined the other contrasts between the remaining pairs of outcome categories using the listcoef command from the *Spost* suite of Stata commands (Long and Freese 2006). For the six-category outcome, only two significant contrasts are not shown in Table 17.5 (for number of brothers in the contrast of the category "2–15 Miles" with the category ">500 Miles" and for five or more sisters in the contrast of the category "46–200 Miles" with the category ">500 Miles"). Two significant contrasts are also not shown in the table for the three-category outcome (for female in the contrast of the category "46–500 Miles" with the category ">500 Miles" and for five or more sisters in the contrast of the category "46–500 Miles" with the category ">500 Miles").

22 Other researchers might make different decisions for how to address this small, heterogeneous category. For example, another strategy would be to exclude the 96 cases in this "other" racial-ethnic category completely from all models, and base the results on the 5,376 cases who are of African American, Mexican American or white race-ethnicity. Whatever decision we make, our decision should be clear in the Methods section of our paper and/or in our table notes. For example, in the note to Table 17.5 we indicate that the "other" category is included in the models but not presented in the table.

23 Because both respondents' and mothers' ages are significant in Column 6, but with opposite signs, we examined how the coefficient for each variable changed when the other was excluded from the model. Indeed, the respondents' ages and mothers' ages are the most highly correlated predictors, with a simple correlation of 0.85, indicating that they share considerable variation. However, the results in Column 6 appear to reflect a complex suppressing relationship. With mothers' ages excluded, respondents' ages is still positive in sign but closer to zero and no longer statistically significant. Likewise, with respondents' ages excluded, mothers' ages are still negative in sign but closer to zero and no longer statistically significant.

24 As noted in Table 17.5, our earnings variables was rescaled so that one more reflected $10,000 more in annual earnings, which is why we use a $10,000 increment to examine discrete change in Table 17.8.

25 One option to address this compression if we wanted to present these results for the "close" ideal type would be to reduce the maximum value of the Y-axis. However, we would want to be careful if we presented multiple graphs with different minimum and maximum values on the Y-axis, since reducing the range shown in the axis will make results appear bigger to the eye (Few 2004, 2009; Tufte 2001).

Chapter 18

1 It is not entirely clear from the text, however, whether the coefficients in the table for the *Child characteristics* are from the reduced model (without *Risk factors and child–mother interaction* controlled) or the full model (with *Risk factors and child–mother interaction* controlled). The author's text suggests that they are from the reduced model (p. 215). With only one set of coefficients and standard errors presented for each outcome, we also cannot see how one set of coefficients and standard errors change when the other set of variables are controlled.

2 In fact, Li-Grining reports this partially standardized result for gender in the text (p. 215). The text also clarifies that the variable, labeled *Gender*, is coded a "1" for boys and "0" for girls (pp. 213, 215).

3 Note that the exact *t*-values that Vaisey reports are important in his case because his sample size has just 50 observations.

Appendix H

1 To rename the worksheet, right click on the tab named "Sheet 1" and choose "Rename." To delete the other two worksheets, right click on their tabs, and choose delete.

2 If you replicate your models in both SAS and Stata, you can always select a rectangle directly in the SAS windows. If you only use Stata and open the results .log in Microsoft Office, we recommend switching the Font to *Courier New* style of *9 point* size. Doing so will make it easier to view the results on the screen, without wrapping. A powerful text editor, like TextPad (*www.textpad.com*) or UltraEdit (*www.ultraedit.com*), is worth the investment if you regularly use Stata.

BIBLIOGRAPHY

Acock, Alan C. 2005. "SAS, Stata, SPSS: A Comparison." *Journal of Marriage and the Family* 67: 1093–5.

Acock, Alan. 2008. *A Gentle Introduction to Stata*. College Station, TX: Stata Press.

Agresti, Alan. 2002. *Categorical Data Analysis* (2nd Edition). New York: Wiley.

Agresti, Alan. 2007. *An Introduction to Categorical Data Analysis* (2nd Edition). Hoboken: Wiley.

Agresti, Alan. 2010. *Analysis of Ordinal Categorical Data (2nd Edition)*. New York: Wiley.

Agresti, Alan and Barbara Finlay. 2009. *Statistical Methods for the Social Sciences,* (4th Edition). Pearson.

Akaike, Hirotugu (1974). "A New Look at the Statistical Model Identification." *IEEE Transactions on Automatic Control*, 19(6): 716–723.

Allison, Paul D. 1999. "Comparing Logit and Probit Coefficients Across Groups." *Sociological Methods and Research*, 28: 186–208.

Allison, Paul D. 2001. *Missing Data*. Thousand Oaks: Sage.

Allison, Paul D. 2005. *Fixed Effects Regression Methods for Longitudinal Data Using SAS*. Cary, NC: SAS Institute.

Allison, Paul D. 2009. *Statistical Horizons*. Available at *http://www.statisticalhorizons.com/*.

American Psychological Association. 2009. *Publication Manual of the American Psychological Association*. Washington DC: Author.

American Sociological Association. 2007. *American Sociological Association Style Guide*. Washington DC: Author.

Andrich, David. 1988. *Rasch Models for Measurement*. Thousand Oaks: Sage.

Baisden, Katherine L. and Paul Hu. 2006. "The Enigma of Survey Data Analysis: Comparison of SAS Survey Procedures and SUDAAN Procedures." Proceedings of the Thirty-first Annual SAS® Users Group International Conference. Cary, NC: SAS Institute Inc.

Baker, Frank B. and Seock-Ho Kim. (Eds.). 2004. *Item Response Theory: Parameter Estimation Techniques* (2nd Edition). New York: Dekker.

Bakker, Arthur and Gravemeijer, Koeno P.E. 2006. "The Historical Phenomenology of Mean and Median." *Educational Studies in Mathematics*, 62: 149–168.

Baron, Reuben M. and David A. Kenny. 1986. "The Moderator–Mediator Variable Distinction In Social Psychological Research: Conceptual, Strategic, and Statistical Considerations." *Journal of Personality and Social Psychology*, 51(6): 1173–82.

Batanero, Carmen, LilianaMabel Tauber, and Victoria Sánchez. 2004. "Students' Reasoning about the Normal Distribution" Chapter 11 (257–258) in D. Ben-Zvi and J. Garfield (Eds.). *The Challenge of Developing Statistical Literacy, Reasoning and Thinking*. Dordrecht, Netherlands: Kluwer.

Belsey, David A., Edwin Kuh, and Roy E. Welsch. 1980. *Regression Diagnostics: Identifying Influential Data and Sources of Collinearity*. New York: Wiley.

Berk, Richard A. 2004. *Regression Analysis: A Constructive Critique*. Thousand Oaks: Sage.

Bickel, Robert. 2007. *Multilevel Analysis for Applied Research: It's Just Regression!* New York: Guilford.

Black, Dan A. and Jeffrey A. Smith. 2002. "How Robust is the Evidence on the Effects of College Quality? Evidence from Matching." *Journal of Econometrics*, 121: 99–124.

Bland, J. Martin and Douglas G. Altman. 1995. "Multiple Significance Tests: The Bonferroni Method." *British Medical Journal*, 310: 170.

Blossfeld, Hans-Peter and Götz Rohwer. 2002. *Techniques of Event History Modeling* (2nd Edition). New York: Lawrence Erlbaum Associates.

Bollen, Ken A. 1989. *Structural Equation Models with Latent Variables*. New York: Wiley.

Botman, SL, Moore, TF, Moriarity, CL, and Parsons, VL. 2000. "Design and estimation for the National Health Interview Survey, 1995–2004." National Center for Health Statistics. Available at *http://www. ncbi.nlm.nin.gov/pubmed/11707926*

Box, G.E.P. and D.R. Cox. 1964. "An Analysis of Transformations." *Journal of the Royal Statistical Society, Series B*, 26: 211–52.

Brant, R. 1990. "Assessing Proportionality in the Proportional Odds Model for Ordinal Logistic Regression." *Biometrics*, 46: 1171–1178.

Brumbaugh, Stacey M., Laura A. Sanchez, Steven L. Nock, and James D. Wright. 2008. "Attitudes Toward Gay Marriage in States Undergoing Marriage Law Transformation." *Journal of Marriage and Family*, 70: 345–59.

Burnham, Kenneth P. and David R. Anderson. 2002. *Model Selection and Multimodel Inference: A Practical Information-Theoretic Approach,* (2nd Edition). New York: Springer.

Bushway, Shawn, Brian D. Johnson, and Lee Ann Slocum. 2007. "Is the Magic Still There? The Use of the Heckman Two-Stage Correction for Selection Bias in Criminology." *Journal of Quantitative Criminology*, 23: 151–78.

Campbell, Richard T. and Michael L. Berbaum. 2010. "Analysis of Data from Complex Surveys." Chapter Eight (221–262) in Peter V. Marsden and James D. Wright (Eds.). *Handbook of Survey Research,* (2nd Edition). London: Emerald Group Publishing.

Caudill, Steven B. 2000. "Pooling Choices or Categories in Multinomial Logit Models." *Statistical Papers*, 41: 353–358.

Centers for Disease Control and Prevention. 2010. *National Survey of Family Growth*. Available at *http:// www.cdc.gov/nchs/nsfg.htm*.

Center for Multicultural Mental Health Research. 2010. *National Latino and Asian American Study*. Available at *http://www.multiculturalmentalhealth.org/nlaas.asp*.

Chance, Beth, Robert delMas, and Joan Garfield. 2004. "Reasoning about Sampling Distributions." Chapter 13 (295–323) in D. Ben-Zvi and J. Garfield (Eds.). *The Challenge of Developing Statistical Literacy, Reasoning and Thinking*. Dordrecht, Netherlands: Kluwer.

Chatterjee, Samprit and Ali S. Hadi. 1986. "Influential Observations, High Leverage Points, and Outliers in Linear Regression." *Statistical Science*, 1(3): 379–93.

Chatterjee, Sangit and Mustafa Yilmaz. 1992. "A Review of Regression Diagnostics for Behavioral Research." *Applied Psychological Measurement*, 16: 209–27.

Cheng, Simon and J. Scott Long. 2000. "XPost: Excel Workbooks for the Post-estimation Interpretation of Regression Models for Categorical Dependent Variables." Available at *http://www.indiana.edu/~jslsoc/files_research/xpost/xpost.pdf*.

Cheng, Simon and J. Scott Long. 2007. "Testing for IIA in the Multinomial Logit Model." *Sociological Methods & Research*, 35: 583–600.

Chow, Gregory C. 1960. "Tests of Equality between Sets of Coefficients in Two Linear Regressions." *Econometrica*, 28(3): 591–605.

Clark, William A.V. and Suzanne Davies Withers. 2007. "Family Migration and Mobility Sequences in the United States: Spatial Mobility in the Context of the Life Course." *Demographic Research*, 17: 591–622.

Cohen, Jacob. 1969. *Statistical Power Analysis for the Behavioral Sciences*. New York: Academic Press.

Cohen, Jacob. 1992. "A Power Primer." *Psychological Bulletin*, 112(1): 155–9.

Collins, Linda M., and Stephanie T. Lanza. 2010. *Latent Class and Latent Transition Analysis: With Applications in the Social, Behavioral, and Health sciences*. New York: Wiley.

Cook, Andrew, & Daponte, Beth. 2008. "A Demographic Analysis of the Rise in the Prevalence of the US Population Overweight and/or Obese." *Population Research and Policy Review*, 27(4): 403–426.

Cooney, Teresa M. and Peter Uhlenberg. 1992. "Support from Parents Over the Life Course: The Adult Child's Perspective." *Social Forces*, 71: 63–84.

Cornwell, Benjamin, Edward O. Laumann, and L. Philip Schumm. 2008. "The Social Connectedness of Older Adults: A National Profile." *American Sociological Review*, 73: 185–203.

Cutler, David M., Glaeser, Edward L., and Shapiro, Jesse M. 2003. "Why Have Americans Become More Obese?" *The Journal of Economic Perspectives*, 17(3): 93–118.

Daniel, Wayne W. 2009. *Biostatistics: A Foundation for Analysis in the Health Sciences*. New York: Wiley.

Davis, Brennan and Christopher Carpenter. (2009). "Proximity of Fast-Food Restaurants to Schools and Adolescent Obesity." *American Journal of Public Health*, 99: 505–510.

Davis, Shannon N. and Lisa D. Pearce. 2007. "Adolescents' Work-family Gender Ideologies and Educational Expectations." *Sociological Perspectives*, 50: 249–271.

De Ayala, R.J. 2009. *The Theory and Practice of Item Response Theory*. New York: Guilford.

de Leeuw, Jan and Richard Berk. 2004. *Introduction to the Series, Advanced Quantitative Techniques in the Social Sciences*. Thousand Oaks: Sage.

Decker, Sandra L. 2005. "Medicare and the Health of Women with Breast Cancer." *The Journal of Human Resources*, 40: 948–968.

Delwiche, Lora and Susan Slaughter. 2003. *The Little SAS Book: A Primer*, (3rd Edition). SAS Press.

Dobson, Annette J, 1990. *An Introduction to Generalized Linear Models*. London: Chapman and Hall.

Dooley, David and Joann Prause. 2005. "Birth Weight and Mothers' Adverse Employment Change." *Journal of Health and Social Behavior*, 46: 141–55.

Downs, George W. and David M. Rocke. 1979. "Interpreting Heteroscedasticity." *American Journal of Political Science*, 23(4): 816–28.

DuMouchel, William H. and Greg J. Duncan. 1983. "Using Sampling Weights in Multiple Regression Analyses of Stratified Samples." *Journal of the American Statistical Association*, 78: 535–543.

Duncan, Greg J., Chantelle J. Dowsett, Amy Claessens, Katherine Magnuson, Aletha C. Huston, Pamela Klebanov, Linda S. Pagani, Leon Feinstein, Mimi Engel, Jeanne Brooks-Gunn, Holly Sexton, Kathryn Duckworth, and Crista Japel. 2007. "School Readiness and Later Achievement." *Developmental Psychology*, 43: 1428–46.

Eliason, Scott R. 1993. *Maximum Likelihood Estimation: Logic and Practice*. Newbury Park, CA: Sage.

Embretson, Susan E. and Steven P. Reise. 2000. *Item Response Theory For Psychologists*. Mahwah, NJ: Erlbaum.

Fairweather, James S. 2005. "Beyond the Rhetoric: Trends in the Relative Value of Teaching and Research in Faculty Salaries." *Journal of Higher Education*, 76: 401–22.

Few, Stephen. 2004. *Show Me The Numbers: Designing Tables and Graphs to Enlighten*. Oakland, CA: Analytics Press.

Few, Stephen. 2009. *Now You See It: Simple Visualization Techniques For Quantitative Analysis*. Oakland, CA: Analytics Press.

Fox, John. 1991. *Regression Diagnostics*. Newbury Park: Sage.

Fox, John. 2008. *Applied Regression Analysis and Generalized Linear Models,* (2nd Edition). Thousand Oaks: Sage.

Fox, John. 2010. Appendices to *Applied Regression Analysis and Generalized Linear Models,* (2nd Edition). Available from *http://socserv.socsci.mcmaster.ca/jfox/Books/Applied-Regression-2E/Appendices.pdf*

Fox, John and Robert Andersen. 2006. "Effect Displays for Multinomial and Proportional-odds Logit Models." *Sociological Methodology*, 36: 225–255.

Freese, Jeremy. 2007. "Replication Standards for Quantitative Social Science: Why Not Sociology?" *Sociological Methods and Research*, 36: 153–72.

Gallagher, James. 2006. "The *F*-test for Comparing Two Normal Variances: Correct and Incorrect Calculation of the two-Sided *p*-value?" *Teaching Statistics*, 28: 58–60.

Gee, Gilbert C., Ro, Annie, Gavin, Amelia, and David T. Takeuchi. 2008. "Disentangling the Effects of Racial and Weight Discrimination on Body Mass Index and Obesity Among Asian Americans." *American Journal of Public Health*, 98: 493–500.

Gelman, Andrew. 2007. "Struggles with Survey Weighting and Regression Modeling." *Statistical Science*, 22: 153–164.

Ghilagaber, Gebrenegus. 2004. "Another Look at Chow's Test for the Equality of Two Heteroscedastic Regression Models." *Quality and Quantity*, 38: 81–93.

Giordano, Peggy C., Monica A. Longmore, and Wendy D. Manning. 2006. "Gender and the Meanings of Adolescent Romantic Relationships: A Focus on Boys." *American Sociological Review*, 71: 260–87.

Glauber, Rebecca. 2007. "Marriage and the Motherhood Wage Penalty among African Americans, Hispanics, and Whites." *Journal of Marriage and Family*, 69: 951–61.

Goesling, Brian. 2007. "The Rising Significance of Education for Health?" *Social Forces*, 85: 1621–1644

Greene, William H. 2008. *Econometric Analysis*. Saddle River, NJ: Pearson-Prentice Hall.

Grossbard-Shechtman, Shoshana. 1993. *On the Economics of Marriage: A Theory of Marriage, Labor, and Divorce*. Boulder: Westview Press.

Gujarati, Damodar N. 1970a. "Use of Dummy Variables in Testing for Equality between Sets of Coefficients in Two Linear Regressions: A Note." *American Statistician*, 24(1): 50–2.

Gujarati, Damodar N. 1970b. "Use of Dummy Variables in Testing for Equality between Sets of Coefficients in Two Linear Regressions: A Generalization." *American Statistician*, 24(5): 18–22.

Gujarati, Damodar N. 2003. *Basic Econometrics*. Boston: McGraw-Hill.

Harrington, Donna. 2008. *Confirmatory Factor Analysis*. Oxford: Oxford University Press.

Hayes, Andrew F. and Li Cai. 2007. "Using Heteroskedasticity-Consistent Standard Error Estimates in OLS Regression: An Introduction and Software Implementation." *Behavior Research Methods*, 39: 709–22. See *http://www.comm.ohio-state.edu/ahayes/SPSS%20programs/HCSEp.htm* for downloadable macros.

Heath, D. 2008. *Effective Graphics Made Simple Using SAS/GRAPH SG Procedures*. Available at *http://www2.sas.com/proceedings/forum2008/255–2008.pdf*.

Heckman, James J. 1979. "Sample Selection Bias as a Specification Error." *Econometrica*, 47: 153–61.

Heeringa, Steven G., West, Brady T., and Berglund, Patricia A. 2010. *Applied Survey Data Analysis*. Boca Raton, FL: CRC Press.

Hilbe, Joseph. 1996. "Windows File Conversion Software." *The American Statistician*, 50: 268–70.

Hoaglin, David C., Frederick Mosteller, and John W. Tukey. 2000. *Understanding Robust and Exploratory Data Analysis*. New York: Wiley.

Hoaglin, David C. and Peter J. Kempthorne. 1986. "Comment." *Statistical Science*, 1(3): 408–12.

Hoffman, John P. 2004. *Generalized Linear Models: An Applied Approach*. Boston: Pearson.

Hosmer, David W., Scott Taber, and Stanley Lemeshow. 1991. "The Importance of Assessing the Fit of Logistic Regression Models: A Case Study." *American Journal of Public Health*, 81: 1630–1635.

House, James S., James M. LaRocco, and John R.P. French, Jr. 1982. "Response to Schaefer." *Journal of Health and Social Behavior*, 23: 98–101.

Huberty, Carl J. 2002. "A History of Effect Size Indices." *Educational and Psychological Measurement*, 62: 227–40.

Huffman, Matt L. 1999. "Who's in Charge? Organizational Influences on Women's Representation in Managerial Positions." *Social Science Quarterly*, 80: 738–56.

Iacobucci, Dawn. 2008. *Mediation Analysis*. Thousand Oaks: Sage.

ICPSR. 2009. *Summer Program in Quantitative Methods of Social Research*. Available at *www.icpsr.umich.edu/sumprog*.

ICPSR. 2010. *National Health Interview Survey, 2009: User's Guide*. Ann Arbor, MI: ICPSR.

Imbens, Guido W. and Jeffrey M. Wooldridge. 2009. "Recent Developments in the Econometrics of Program Evaluation." *Journal of Economic Literature*, 47: 5–86.

Iverson, Cheryl, Stacy Christiansen, Annette Flanagin, et al. 2007. *AMA Manual of Style: A Guide for Authors and Editors,* (10th Edition). New York: Oxford University Press.

Jaccard, James and Robert Turrisi. 2003. *Interaction Effects in Multiple Regression*. Thousand Oaks: Sage.

Jann, Ben 2007. "Making Regression Tables Simplified." *The Stata Journal*, 7(2): 227–44.

Jarrell, Stephen B. and T.D. Stanley. 2004. "Declining Bias and Gender Wage Discrimination? A Meta-Regression Analysis." *Journal of Human Resources*, 39: 828–38.

Jayakody, Rukmalie and Ariel Kalil. 2002. "Social Fathering in Low-Income, African American Families with Preschool Children." *Journal of Marriage and Family*, 64: 504–516.

Kalleberg, Arne L., David Knoke, and Peter V. Marsden. 2001. "National Organizations Survey (NOS), 1996–1997." Available at *www.icpsr.org.*

Kalleberg, Arne L., David Knoke, Peter V. Marsden, and Joe L. Spaeth. 1994. "National Organizations Survey (NOS), 1991." Available at *www.icpsr.org.*

Kalsbeek, W. and G. Heiss. 2000. "Building Bridges Between Populations and Samples in Epidemiological Studies." *Annual Review of Public Health*, 21: 147–169.

Kalton, Graham. 1983. *Introduction to Survey Sampling*. Newbury Park: Sage.

Kish, Leslie. 1965. *Survey Sampling*. New York: John Wiley.

Kolenikov, Stanislav. 2001. "Review of Stata 7." *Journal of Applied Econometrics*, 16: 637–46.

Korn, Edward L. and Barry I. Graubard. 1991. "Epidemiological Studies Utilizing Surveys: Accounting for the Sampling Design." *American Journal of Public Health*, 81: 1166–1173.

Korn, Edward L. and Barry I. Graubard. 1995. "Examples of Differing Weighted and Unweighted Estimates from a Sample Survey." *The American Statistician*, 49: 291–5.

Kraemer, Helena Chmura and Sue Thiemann. 1987. *How Many Subjects: Statistical Power Analysis in Research*. Newbury Park: Sage.

Kumiko, Imai, Gregg, Edward W., Chen, Yiling J., Zhang, Ping, de Rekeneire, Nathalie, & Williamson, David F. 2008. "The Association of BMI with Functional Status and Self-Rated Health in U.S. Adults." *Obesity*, 16(2): 402–408.

Kutner, Michael H., Christopher J. Nachtsheim, and John Neter. 2004. *Applied Linear Regression Models*, (4th Edition). New York: McGraw-Hill.

LaRocco, James M., James S. House, and John R. P. French Jr. 1980. "Social Support, Occupational Stress, and Health." *Journal of Health and Social Behavior*, 21: 202–18.

Larsen, Richard J. and Morris L. Marx. 2006. *An Introduction to Mathematical Statistics and Its Applications* (4th Edition). Upper Saddle River, NJ: Pearson.

Lawton, Leora, Merril Silverstein, and Vern Bengtson. 1994. "Affection, Social Contact, and Geographic Distance Between Adult Children and Their Parents." *Journal of Marriage and Family*, 56: 57–68.

Lee, Eun Sul and Forthofer, Ronald N. 2006. *Analyzing Complex Survey Data* (2nd Edition). Thousand Oaks: Sage.

Lehtonen, Risto and Pahkinen, Erkki J. 1994. *Practical Methods for Design and Analysis of Complex Surveys*, (Revised Edition). New York: John Wiley & Sons.

Lemeshow, Stanley and David W. Hosmer. 1982. "A Review of Goodness-of-Fit Statistics for Use in the Development of Logistic Regression Models." *American Journal of Epidemiology*, 115: 92–106.

Liao, Tim Futing. 1994. *Interpreting Probability Models: Logit, Probit and Other Generalized Linear Models*. Thousand Oaks: Sage.

Li-Grining, Christine P. 2007. "Effortful Control among Low-Income Preschoolers in Three Cities: Stability, Change, and Individual Differences." *Developmental Psychology*, 43(1): 208–21.

Little, Roderick J. 2004. "To Model or Not to Model? Competing Modes of Inference for Finite Population Sampling." *Journal of the American Statistical Association*, 99: 546–556.

Long, J. Scott. 1983. *Confirmatory Factor Analysis: A Preface to LISREL*. Thousand Oaks: Sage.

Long, J. Scott. 1997. *Regression Models for Categorical and Limited Dependent Variables*. Thousand Oaks: Sage.

Long, J. Scott. 2007. "SPost: Postestimation analysis with Stata." Downloaded May 30 2008 from *www. indiana.edu/~jslsoc/spost.htm*.

Long, J. Scott. 2009. "Group Comparisons in Logit and Probit Using Predicted Probabilities." Available at *http://www.indiana.edu/~jslsoc/research_groupdif.htm*.

Long, J. Scott. 2009. *The Workflow of Data Analysis Using Stata: Principles and Practice For Effective Data Management and Analysis*. College Station, TX: Stata Press.

Long, J. Scott and Jeremy Freese. 2006. *Regression Models for Categorical Dependent Variables Using Stata* (2nd Edition). College Station, TX: Stata Press.

Long, J. Scott and Laurie H. Ervin. 2000. "Using Heteroscedasticity Consistent Standard Errors in the Linear Regression Model." *The American Statistician*, 54: 217–24.

Lyons, Christopher J. 2007. "Community (Dis)Organization and Racially Motivated Crime." *American Journal of Sociology*, 113(3): 815–63.

MacKinnon, David. 2008. *Introduction to Statistical Mediation Analysis*. New York: Erlbaum.

Maddala, G.S. 1983. *Limited-Dependent and Qualitative Variables in Econometrics*. New York: Cambridge University Press.

Magdol, Lynn and Diane R. Bessel. 2003. "Social Capital, Social Currency, and Portable Assets: The Impact of Residential Mobility on Exchanges of Social Support." *Personal Relationships*, 10: 149–69.

Magidson, J., & Vermunt, J.K. (2002). "Latent Class Models for Clustering: A Comparison with K-means." *Canadian Journal of Marketing Research*, 20: 37–44.

Marsden, Peter V., Arne L. Kalleberg, and Cynthia R. Cook. 1993. "Gender Differences in Organizational Commitment: Influences of Work Positions and Family Roles." *Work and Occupations*, 20: 368–90.

Martin, Jack K., Bernice A. Pescosolido, Sigrun Olafsdottir, and Jane D. McLeod. (2007). "The Construction of Fear: Americans' Preferences for Social Distance from Children and Adolescents with Mental Health Problems." *Journal of Health and Social Behavior*, 48: 50–67.

Mather, Mark. 2009. "Children in Immigrant Families Chart a New Path." *Population Bulletin*, 1–15.

McCartney, Kathleen and Robert Rosenthal. 2000. "Effect Size, Practical Importance, and Social Policy for Children." *Child Development*, 71: 173–80.

McCullagh, Peter and John Ashworth Nelder. 1983. *Generalized Linear Models*. London: Chapman and Hall.

McGrath, Donald M. & Lisa A. Keister. 2008. "The Effect of Temporary Employment on Asset Accumulation Processes." *Work and Occupations*, 35: 196–222.

McVeigh, Rory and Julianna M. Sobolewski. 2007. "Red Counties, Blue Counties, and Occupational Segregation by Sex and Race." *American Journal of Sociology*, 113: 446–506.

Michielin, Francesca and Clara H. Mulder. 2007. "Geographical Distances between Adult Children and Their Parents in the Netherlands." *Demographic Research*, 17: 655–78.

Mitchell, Michael N. 2008. *A Visual Guide to Stata Graphics*. College Station, TX: Stata Press.

Moore, David S. 2010. *The Basic Practice of Statistics,* (5th Edition). New York: Freeman.

Morales, Leo S., Peter Guitierrez, and Jose J. Escarce. 2005. "Demographic and Socioeconomic Factors Associated with Blood Lead Levels among American Children and Adolescents in the United States." *Public Health Reports*, 120(4): 448–54.

Mueser, Peter R., Kenneth Troske, and Alexey Gorislavsky 2007. "Using State Administrative Data to Measure Program Performance." *Review of Economics and Statistics*, 89(4): 761–83.

Mulder, Clara H. 2007. "The Family Context and Residential Choice: A Challenge for New Research." *Population, Space and Place*, 13: 265–78.

Murphy, Padraic. 2008. "An Overview of Primary Sampling Units (PSUs) in Multi-Stage Samples for Demographic Surveys." Paper presented at the Joint Statistical Meetings of the American Statistical Association. Available at *http://www.amstat.org/sections/srms/proceedings/y2008/Files/301835.pdf.*

Muthén, L.K., & Muthén, B.O. (1998–2007). *Mplus User's Guide*. Los Angeles: Muthén & Muthén.

Nachmias, Chava Frankfort and Anna Leon-Guerrero. 2009. *Social Statistics for a Diverse Society,* (5th Edition). Newbury Park, CA: Pine Forge Press.

National Institutes of Health. 2003. Final NIH Statement on Sharing Research Data. Available at *http://grants.nih.gov/grants/guide/notice-files/NOT-OD-03–032.html.*

National Institutes of Health. 2007. NIH Data Sharing Policy. Available at *http://grants.nih.gov/grants/policy/data_sharing/.*

National Survey of Families and Households. 1990b. *National Survey of Families and Households: A Sampling Report (Appendix L)*. Available at *ftp://elaine.ssc.wisc.edu/pub/nsfh/c1app_1.001.*

National Survey of Families and Households. n.d. Available at *ftp://elaine.ssc.wisc.edu/pub/nsfh/sudaan.dat* and *ftp://elaine.ssc.wisc.edu/pub/nsfh/sudaan.doc.*

Nelder, J.A. 1975. "Announcement by the Working Party on Statistical Computing: GLIM (Generalized Linear Interactive Modeling Program)." *Applied Statistics*, 24: 259–261.

Nelder, J.A. and R.W.M. Wedderburn. 1972. "Generalized Linear Models." *Journal of the Royal Statistical Society A*, 135, 370–384.

NSFH. 1990a. *National Survey of Families and Households: Main Questionnaire, Codebook*. Available at *ftp://elaine.ssc.wisc.edu/pub/nsfh/c1all.001.*

O'Brien, Robert M. 2007. "A Caution Regarding Rules of Thumb for Variance Inflation Factors." *Quality and Quantity*, 41: 673–90.

Ostini, Remo and Michael L. Nering. 2006. *Polytomous Item Response Theory Models*. Thousand Oaks: Sage.

Peterson, Bercedis and Frank E. Harrell. 1990. "Partial Proportional Odds Models for Ordinal Response Variables." *Applied Statistics*, 39: 205–217.

Pinquart, Martin. 2003. "Loneliness in Married, Widowed, Divorced, and Never-Married Older Adults." *Journal of Social and Personal Relationships*, 20: 31–53.

Pregibon, Daryl 1981. "Logistic Regression Diagnostics." *Annals of Statistics*, 9: 704–724.

Primary Respondent Self-Enumerated Schedule. Available at *ftp://elaine.ssc.wisc.edu/pub/nsfh/i1sc.001.*

Pritchett, Lant and Lawrence H. Summers. 1996. "Wealthier is Healthier." *Journal of Human Resources*, 31: 841–68.

Rabe-Hesketh, Sophia and Anders Skrondal. 2005. *Multilevel and Longitudinal Modeling Using Stata*. College Station, TX: Stata Press.

Raftery, Adrian E. 1995. "Bayesian Model Selection in Social Research." *Sociological Methodology*, 25: 111–63.

Raley, R. Kelly, Michelle L. Frisco and Elizabeth Wildsmith. 2005. "Maternal Cohabitation and Educational Success." *Sociology of Education*, 78: 155.

Raudenbush, Stephen W. and Anthony S. Bryk. 2002. *Hierarchical Linear Models: Applications and Data Analysis Methods* (2nd edition). Thousand Oaks: Sage.

Reading, Chris and Shaughnessy, J. Michael. 2004. "Reasoning about Variation." In *The Challenge of Developing Statistical Literacy, Reasoning, and Thinking*. Springer.

Reiter, Jerome P., Elaine L. Zanutto, and Larry W. Hunter. 2005. "Analytical Modeling in Complex Surveys of Work Practices." *Industrial and Labor Relations Review*, 59: 82–100.

Reskin, Barbara and Debra Bran McBrier. 2000. "Why Not Ascription? Organizations' Employment of Male and Female Managers." *American Sociological Review*, 65: 210–33.

Roan, Carol L. and R. Kelly Raley. 1996. "Intergenerational Coresident and Contact: A Longitudinal Analysis of Adult Children's Response to their Mother's Widowhood." *Journal of Marriage and the Family*, 58(3): 708–17.

Rodriguez, Robert N. 2009. *Getting Started with ODS Statistical Graphics in SAS 9.2*. Available at *http://support.sas.com/rnd/app/papers/intodsgraph.pdf*.

Rogerson, Peter A., Richard H. Weng, and Ge Lin. 1993. "The Spatial Separation of Parents and Their Adult Children." *Annals of the Association of American Geographers*, 83: 656–71.

Sampson, Robert J. and John H. Laub. 1995. *Crime in the Making: Pathways and Turning Points Through Life*. Boston: Harvard University Press.

Sanders, Seth, Smith, Jeffrey, & Zhang, Ye. 2007. "Teenage Childbearing and Maternal School Outcomes: Evidence from Matching." Working Paper, University of Maryland and Maryland Population Research Center, College Park, Maryland. Available at *http://client.norc.org/jole/soleweb/826.pdf*.

SAS Institute Inc. 2008a. *SAS®/STAT 9.2 User's Guide: The SurveyMeans Procedure*. Cary, NC: SAS Institute Inc.

SAS Institute Inc. 2008b. *SAS/STAT 9.2 User's Guide*. Cary, NC: SAS Institute Inc.

SAS Institute Inc. 2009. *Courses and Schedules*. Available at *http://support.sas.com/training/us/*.

SAS Institute Inc. 2009a. *Base SAS® 9.2 Procedures Guide*. Cary, NC: SAS Institute Inc.

SAS Institute Inc. 2010. *Usage Note 41516: Using the TEST statement in PROC LOGISTIC to test hypotheses in LINK=GLOGIT models*. Available at: *http://support.sas.com/kb/41/516.html*.

Sastry, Jaya and Catherine E. Ross. 1998. "Asian Ethnicity and Sense of Personal Control." *Social Psychology Quarterly*, 61(2): 110.

Schaefer, Catherine. 1982. "Shoring Up the 'Buffer' of Social Support." *Journal of Health and Social Behavior*, 23: 96–8.

Schochet, Peter Z. 2008. *Technical Methods Report: Guidelines for Multiple Testing in Impact Evaluations*. Washington, DC: National Center for Education Evaluation and Regional Assistance, Institute of Education Sciences, US Department of Education.

Schwarz, Gideon E. 1978. "Estimating the Dimension of a Model." *Annals of Statistics*, 6(2): 461–464.

Scientific Software International. 2009. *LISREL 8.8*. Available at *www.ssicentral.com*.

Seidman, David. 1976. "On Choosing Between Linear and Log-Linear Models" *The Journal of Politics*, 38: 461–6.

Self-Enumerated Questionnaire Skip Map. Available at *ftp://elaine.ssc.wisc.edu/pub/nsfh/T1se.pdf*.

Shaffer, Juliet Popper. 1995. "Multiple Hypothesis Testing." *Annual Review of Psychology*, 46: 561–84.

Sharkey, Patrick, 2008. "The Intergenerational Transmission of Context." *American Journal of Sociology*, 113: 931–69.

Singleton, Royce. 1989. "On Teaching Sampling: A Classroom Demonstration of Concepts, Principles, and Techniques." *Teaching Sociology*, 17: 351–355.

Smith, Tom W., Arne L. Kalleberg, Peter V. Marsden. 2005. "National Organizations Survey (NOS), 2002." Available at *www.icpsr.org*.

Sribney, Bill. 2005. "How Can I Estimate Correlations and Their Level of Significance With Survey Data?" Available at *http://www.stata.com/support/faqs/stat/survey.html*.

Sribney, Bill. 2009. "Why Doesn't Summarize Accept Pweights? What Does Summarize Calculate When You Use Aweights?" Available at *http://www.stata.com/support/faqs/stat/supweight.html*.

StataCorp. 2009a. *Which Stata is Right for Me?* Available at *www.stata.com/products/whichstata.html*.

StataCorp. 2009b. *Stata Survey Data Reference Manual: Release 11*. College Station, TX: StataCorp LP.

StataCorp. 2009c. *Training*. Available at *www.stata.com/training/*.

StataCorp. 2009d. *Stata Base Reference Manual: Release 11*. College Station, TX: StataCorp LP.

Stavig, Gordon R. 1977. "The Semistandardized Regression Coefficient." *Multivariate Behavioral Research*, 12: 255–8.

Stevens, S. S. 1946. "On the Theory of Scales of Measurement." *Science* 103: 677–680.

Stigler, Stephen M. 1986. *The History of Statistics: The Measurement of Uncertainty Before 1900*. Cambridge, MA: Harvard University Press.

Stolzenberg, Ross M. and Daniel A. Relles. 1997. "Tools for Intuition about Sample Selection Bias and Its Correction." *American Sociological Review*, 62(3): 494–507.

Suits, Daniel B. 1957. "Use of Dummy Variables in Regression Equations." *Journal of the American Statistical Association*, 52(280): 548–51.

Sweet, James, Larry Bumpass, and Vaughn Call. 1988. *The Design and Content of the National Survey of Families and Households (NSFH Working Paper No. 1)*. Madison, WI: Center for Demography and Ecology, University of Wisconsin Madison. Available at *http://www.ssc.wisc.edu/cde/nsfhwp/nsfh1.pdf*.

Teachman, Jay. 2008. "Complex Life Course Patterns and the Risk of Divorce in Second Marriages." *Journal of Marriage and Family*, 70: 294–305.

Tufte, Edward R. 2001. *The Visual Display of Quantitative Information*. Cheshire, CT: Graphics Press.

Tukey, John W. 1977. *Exploratory Data Analysis*. Reading, MA: Addison-Wesley.

UCLA Academic Technology Services, Statistical Consulting Group. n.d. *Stata Programs for Teaching*. Available from *http://www.ats.ucla.edu/stat/stata/ado/teach/* (accessed June 15, 2010).

UCLA Statistical Computing Group. 2009. *Overview of the Statistical Consulting Group*. Available at *www.ats.ucla.edu/stat/overview.htm*.

University of Kansas. 2009. *KU Summer Institute in Statistics*. Available at *http://quant.ku.edu/StatsCamps/overview.html*.

U.S. Bureau of Labor Statistics. 2008. *Consumer Price Index for All Urban Consumers (CPI-U)*. Available at *ftp://ftp.bls.gov/pub/special.requests/cpi/cpiai.txt*

U.S. Bureau of Labor Statistics. 2010. *National Longitudinal Surveys*. Available at *http://www.bls.gov/nls/nlsy79.htm*.

U.S. Census Bureau. 2010a. *T1. Population Estimates, by Region*. Available from American FactFinder at http://factfinder.census.gov/.

U.S. Census Bureau. 2010b. *American Community Survey*. Available at *http://www.census.gov/acs*.

U.S. Department of Justice. 2007. *Hate Crime by Jurisdiction*. Available at *www2.fbi.gov/ucr/hc2007/ jurisdiction.htm*.

Vaisey, Stephen. 2007. "Structure, Culture, and Community: The Search for Belonging in 50 Urban Communes." *American Sociological Review*, 72: 851–73.

Vavra, Janet K. 2002. "Preservation: Maintaining Information for the Future." ICPSR Bulletin, XXII(3): 1–8.

Velleman, Paul F. & Wilkinson, Leland. 1993. "Nominal, Ordinal, Interval, and Ratio Typologies Are Misleading." *American Statistician*, 47: 65–72.

Wackerly, Dennis, William Mendenhall, and Richard L. Scheaffer. 2008. *Mathematical Statistics with Applications*. Florence, KY: Cengage Learning.

Weakliem, David. 2004. "Introduction to the Special Issue on Model Selection." *Sociological Methods and Research*, 33: 167–87.

Webster's Revised Unabridged Dictionary. 2008. Dummy. Retrieved June 02, 2008, from Dictionary.com website: Available at *http://dictionary.reference.com/browse/dummy*.

Webster's Revised Unabridged Dictionary. 2009. Mediate. Retrieved June 02, 2009, from Dictionary.com website: Available at *http://dictionary.reference.com/browse/mediate*.

Webster's Revised Unabridged Dictionary. 2009. Moderate. Retrieved June 2, 2009, from Dictionary.com website: Available at *http://dictionary.reference.com/browse/moderate*.

Welsch, Roy E. 1986. "Comment." *Statistical Science*, 1(3): 403–5.

West, Candace and Don. H. Zimmerman. 1987. "Doing Gender." *Gender and Society*, 1(2): 125–51.

Wheaton, Blair. 1985. "Models for the Stress-Buffering Functions of Coping Resources." *Journal of Health and Social Behavior*, 26: 352–64.

Williams, Richard. 2006. "Generalized Ordered Logit/Partial Proportional Odds Models for Ordinal Dependent Variables." *The Stata Journal* 6(1): 58–82.

Williamson, Elizabeth, Ruth, Morley, Alan Lucas, and James Carpenter. 2011. "Propensity Scores: From Naïve Enthusiasm to Intuitive Understanding." *Statistical Methods in Medical Research*, 20: 1–21.

Wills, Hugh. 1987. "A Note on Specification Tests for the Multinomial Logit Model." *Journal of Econometrics*, 34: 263–274.

Willson, Andrea E. 2003. "Race and Women's Income Trajectories: Employment, Marriage, and Income Security over the Life Course." *Social Problems*, 50: 87–110.

Wolf, Douglas A., Vicki Freedman, and Beth J. Soldo. 1997. "The Division of Family Labor: Care for Elderly Parents." *The Journals of Gerontology*, Series B, 52B: 102–9.

Wooldridge, Jeffrey. 2002. *Econometric Analysis of Cross Section and Panel Data*. Cambridge, MA: MIT Press.

Wooldridge, Jeffrey M. 2009. *Introductory Econometrics: A Modern Approach* (4th Edition). Mason, OH: South-Western.

Wright, Sewall. 1921. "Correlation and Causation." *Journal of Agricultural Research*, 20: 557–85.

Wu, Zheng. 2005. "Generalized Linear Models in Family Studies." *Journal of Marriage and Family*, 67: 1029–1047

Wybraniec, John and Janet Wilmoth. 1999. "Teaching Students Inferential Statistics: A 'Tail' of Three Distributions." *Teaching Sociology*, 27: 74–80.

Yamaguchi, Kazuo. 1991. *Event History Analysis*. Newbury Park: Sage.

GLOSSARY/INDEX

Negative Binomial: Regression model appropriate for a count outcome (e.g., number of hospital visits, number of symptoms, number of arrests); differs from the Poisson model in that the conditional variance can be larger or smaller than the mean, 523, 678

Nested: One model can be produced by placing constraints on the coefficients of another model (in the applications of this book, typically one model contains a subset of the variables in another model), 309–10, 399, 443, 449–50, 538, 539

Nominal categories, 677

Nominal Variable: Variable whose values classify groups with no intrinsic order, 97–103, 105–7, 337–8, 349–62

  frequency distribution, 105–6

  literature excerpt, 107

  mode, 107

Non-directional Alternative Hypothesis: The alternative hypothesis states that the population parameter is not equal to the hypothesized value, 169–70

Non-response Adjustments: Using weights to adjust for the fact that some selected members of the population did not participate in the survey, 36, 59, 60

Nonlinear relationships, 433–56

  choosing among models, 449–50

  dummy variables, 448, 454–6

  literature excerpts on, 437–42

  logarithmic transformation, 443

  possible shapes of, 434–7

  quadratic form, 442–3

Nonsystematic Component: The error term (the difference between the observed value of the outcome and the value predicted based on the intercept, slope, and observed value on the predictor(s)), 246

Normal distribution, 154–5, 165, 524(box), 525

  hypothetical examples, 156

Normality assumption, 259

NSFH: National Survey of Families and Households; data set used for chapter examples throughout this book, 29, 36, 49, 50–60, 68–76, 84–6, 98, 106, 110–11, 117, 120, 122–3, 127–8, 131, 132–5, 209–12, 213–14, 218, 222, 227, 472, 624–33, 643–7

Null Hypothesis: The converse of the alternative hypothesis (sometimes reflecting the status quo), 168–79, 219–22, 225, 227, 260, 263, 270, 281, 286, 394, 411(box), 455, 537–41, 583, 626, 627, 630, 643, 661(box)

Numerator Degrees of Freedom: Degrees of freedom associated with the numerator in a formula to calculate an F-value. In OLS regression, the numerator degrees of freedom equals the number of constraints in the null hypothesis, 184

Observational Data: Data in which people were not assigned experimentally to treatment and control groups, such as population surveys or program records, 6

  confounders in, 464–7

Odds: Ratio of probability of success to probability of failure, 150, 564–5, 594–7, 601–2, 603, 617–23, 630–1, 633–5, 640–1, 643–5, 650–2, 664

Omitted category *see* **Reference Category**